NCLEX®-RN

Wilda Rinehart, Diann Sloan, Clara Hurd

P9-AZX-947

NCLEX®-RN Exam Prep

Copyright ℗ 2011 by Pearson Education, Inc.

ISBN-13: 978-0-7897-4527-9
ISBN-10: 0-7897-4527-5

Library of Congress Cataloging-in-Publication Data
Rinehart, Wilda.
 NCLEX-RN exam prep / Wilda Rinehart, Diann Sloan, Clara Hurd.
     p. ; cm.
 Includes bibliographical references and index.
 ISBN-13: 978-0-7897-4527-9 (pbk. w/cd)
 ISBN-10: 0-7897-4527-5 (pbk. w/cd)
1. National Council Licensure Examination for Registered Nurses--Study guides 2. Nursing--Examinations, questions, etc. I. Sloan, Diann. II. Hurd, Clara. III. Title.
 [DNLM: 1. Nursing--Examination Questions. WY 18.2 R579na 2011]
RT55.R564 2011
610.73076--dc22

                       2010025765

Printed in the United States on America

Third Printing: May 2011

Trademarks

Warning and Disclaimer

Bulk Sales

Que Publishing offers excellent discounts on this book when ordered in quantity for bulk purchases or special sales. For more information, please contact

U.S. Corporate and Government Sales
1-800-382-3419
corpsales@pearsontechgroup.com

For sales outside of the U.S., please contact

International Sales
international@pearsoned.com

PUBLISHER
Paul Boger

ASSOCIATE PUBLISHER
David Dusthimer

ACQUISITIONS EDITOR
Betsy Brown

SENIOR DEVELOPMENT EDITOR
Christopher Cleveland

MANAGING EDITOR
Sandra Schroeder

PROJECT EDITOR
Mandie Frank

COPY EDITOR
Megan Wade

INDEXER
Angela Martin

PROOFREADER
Leslie Joseph

TECHNICAL EDITORS
Jamie Burns
Maura Cappiello
Jacqueline Ruckel
MaryEllen Schwarzbek

PUBLISHING COORDINATOR
Vanessa Evans

DESIGNER
Gary Adair

PAGE LAYOUT
Bronkella Publishing

Rinehart and Associates

Prepare With the Best
Rinehart and Associates

For Nursing Students and Nursing Graduates- "Rinehart and Associates "NCLEX® Review Seminars", a three or four day seminar that provides a **complete, comprehensive review of nursing theory and practice with emphasis of the "NEW" NCLEX® test plan.**

We will come to your school and conduct a mini-review for you:

"Pharmacology Made Easy", a mini workshop for students reviewing commonly prescribed drugs as well as **hints** for remembering drug categories and nursing implications.

"Testing for Nursing School and NCLEX® Success", a mini workshop for nursing students to enhance success in nursing school and beyond.

"Fluid and Electrolytes- A Practical Approach", a mini workshop to increase the student's knowledge of Fluid and Electrolytes and Acid Base Disorders.

Pass the Licensure Exam the First Time

For more information on these and other workshops call:
662-728-4622
662-416-3340

Visit our web site at www.nclexreview.net
e-mail wrinehar@tsixroads.com or visit www.nclexreview.net
NCLEX is a registered trademark of the National Council of State Boards of Nursing

Contents at a Glance

Table of Contents

About the Authors

Wilda Rinehart received an associate's degree in nursing from Northeast Mississippi Community College in Booneville, Mississippi. After working as a staff nurse and charge nurse, she became a public health nurse and served in that capacity for a number of years. In 1975, she received her nurse practitioner certification in the area of obstetrics-gynecology from the University of Mississippi Medical Center in Jackson, Mississippi. In 1979, she completed her bachelor of science degree in nursing from Mississippi University for Women. In 1980, she completed her master of science degree in nursing from the same university and accepted a faculty position at Northeast Mississippi Community College, where she taught medical-surgical nursing and maternal-newborn nursing. In 1982, she founded Rinehart and Associates Nursing Consultants. For the past 28 years, she and her associates have worked with nursing graduates and schools of nursing to help graduates pass the National Council Licensure Exam for Nursing. She has also worked as a curriculum consultant with faculty to improve test construction. Ms. Rinehart has served as a convention speaker throughout the southeastern United States and as a reviewer of medical-surgical and obstetric texts. She has coauthored materials used in seminars presented by Rinehart and Associates Nursing Review. As the president of Rinehart and Associates, she serves as the coordinator of a company dedicated to improving the quality of health through nursing education.

Dr. Diann Sloan received an associate's degree in nursing from Northeast Mississippi Community College, a bachelor of science degree in nursing from the University of Mississippi, and a master of science degree in nursing from Mississippi University for Women. In addition to her nursing degrees, she holds a master of science in counseling psychology from Georgia State University and a doctor of philosophy in counselor education, with minors in both psychology and educational psychology, from Mississippi State University. She has completed additional graduate studies in healthcare administration at Western New England College and the University of Mississippi. Dr. Sloan has taught pediatric nursing, psychiatric mental health nursing, and medical surgical nursing in both associate degree and baccalaureate nursing programs. As a member of Rinehart and Associates Nursing Review, Dr. Sloan has conducted test construction workshops for faculty and nursing review seminars for both registered and practical nurse graduates. She has coauthored materials used in the item-writing workshops for nursing faculty and Rinehart and Associates Nursing Review. She is a member of Sigma Theta Tau nursing honor society.

Clara Hurd received an associate's degree in nursing from Northeast Mississippi Community College in Booneville, Mississippi (1975). Her experiences in nursing are clinically based, having served as a staff nurse in medical-surgical nursing. She has worked as an oncology, intensive care, orthopedic, neurological, and pediatric nurse. She received her bachelor of science degree in nursing from the University of North Alabama in Florence, Alabama, and her master of science degree in nursing from the Mississippi University for Women in Columbus, Mississippi. Ms. Hurd is a certified nurse educator. She currently serves as a nurse educator consultant and an independent contractor and has taught in both associate degree and baccalaureate degree nursing programs. She was a faculty member of Mississippi University for Women; Austin Peay State University in Clarksville, Tennessee; Tennessee State University in Nashville; and Northeast Mississippi Community College. Ms. Hurd joined Rinehart and Associates in 1993. She has worked with students in preparing for the National Council Licensure Exam and with faculty as a consultant in writing test items. Ms. Hurd has also been a presenter at nursing conventions on various topics, including item-writing for nursing faculty. Her primary professional goal is to prepare the student and graduate for excellence in the delivery of healthcare.

About the Contributing Authors

Rosemary Marecle, MSN, BSN, RN. Ms. Marecle received an associate degree in nursing from Northeast Mississippi Community College, a bachelor of science degree in nursing from the University of Alabama (Huntsville), and a master of science degree in nursing from the University of Mississippi. She is a professor of nursing at Mississippi University for Women in Columbus, Mississippi.

Robin Phillips, MSN, BSN, RN. Ms. Phillips received an associate degree in nursing from Northeast Mississippi Community College, a bachelor of science degree in nursing from Mississippi University for Women, and a master of science in nursing Education from Alcorn State University,(Natchez). She is an instructor in medical surgical nursing at Itawamba Community College.

About the Technical Editors

Jamie C. Burns, RN, JD, MPH, has extensive experience in the practice of health law with emphasis on the discipline of radiology. Ms. Burns was one of the original founders of National Imaging Associates, Inc. (NIA), a radiology benefit management company acquired by Magellan Health Services, Inc .(MGLN) in January 2006. At NIA, she held the position of chief legal and compliance officer. She now has a private consulting practice for specialty utilization and care management clients faced with compliance, quality, and accreditation matters.

Maura Cappiello received her bachelor's degree from Boston College and her master's degree in healthcare administration from Seton Hall University. She is also a certified case manager and has worked as a staff RN in the NICU and the pediatric home care environment. Currently, she works as the director for staff development for Alere, a case management company.

Jacqueline Ruckel graduated from Boston College with a bachelor's degree in nursing. She obtained her master's in nursing from the University of California, San Francisco. She worked for six years as a preoperative nurse practitioner in anesthesia at both University of California San Francisco and the San Francisco Veterans Affairs (VA) medical center. She is currently working at the San Francisco VA as a nurse practitioner in cardiology.

MaryEllen Schwarzbek graduated from Boston College with a BSN and from New York University with a master's degree in nursing education. She is also certified in oncology nursing. She has worked as a staff RN in medical/surgical and general pediatrics and currently works as a clinical nurse specialist in the genitourinary department of the Memorial Sloan Kettering Cancer Center. She also as an employee wellness educator at Morristown Memorial Hospital.

Dedication

We would like to thank our families for tolerating our late nights and long hours. Also, thanks to Gene Sloan for his help without pay. Special thanks to all the graduates who have attended Rinehart and Associates Review Seminars. Thanks for allowing us to be a part of your success.

We are also delighted that Jessica Rinehart Wentz, RN; Whitney Hurd, RN; and Brad Sloan, RN, chose nursing as their profession above so many other professions.

Acknowledgments

Our special thanks to our editors, support staff, and nurse reviewers for helping us to organize our thoughts and experiences into a text for students and practicing professionals. You made the task before us challenging and enjoyable.

We Want to Hear from You!

As the reader of this book, *you* are our most important critic and commentator. We value your opinion and want to know what we're doing right, what we could do better, what areas you'd like to see us publish in, and any other words of wisdom you're willing to pass our way.

As an associate publisher for Pearson, I welcome your comments. You can email or write me directly to let me know what you did or didn't like about this book—as well as what we can do to make our books better.

Please note that I cannot help you with technical problems related to the topic of this book. We do have a User Services group, however, where I will forward specific technical questions related to the book.

When you write, please be sure to include this book's title and author as well as your name, email address, and phone number. I will carefully review your comments and share them with the author and editors who worked on the book.

Email: feedback@pearsoncertification.com

Mail: David Dusthimer
           Associate Publisher
           Pearson
           800 East 96th Street
           Indianapolis, IN 46240 USA

Reader Services

Visit our website and register this book at www.pearsonitcertification.com/register for convenient access to any updates, downloads, or errata that might be available for this book.

Introduction

Since the first day of your nursing program, you have accumulated stacks of notes and materials that you were asked to learn. There is no way that you can study all of those materials. For this reason, we have developed a concise text that will help you organize your knowledge. This book will help you to prepare for the NCLEX RN using tried-and-true techniques used by the experts. This Introduction discusses the changes that have occurred in the NCLEX exam. You will learn about the future of the exam and how you can be a successful candidate. Whether you are taking the exam for the first time or have taken the exam several times, this book is designed for you.

The *Exam Prep* books help you to understand and appreciate the subject material that you need to know to pass nursing school and the exam. This book includes an in-depth discussion of all topics covered on the NCLEX. We take you on a self-guided tour of all of the areas covered on the NCLEX test plan and give you tips for passing. This book also contains practical tips for your nursing practice. You will find a user-friendly "Fast Facts" quick reference sheet containing lab values, normal fetal heart tones, and much more. Study tips, exam prep tips, case studies, math review, and test banks will help you practice those difficult pharmacology questions and help you manage the questions and alternative items that you will encounter on the exam. This book also includes chapters on the cultural aspects of nursing care and legalities. Each chapter concludes with a series of practice questions to help reinforce your understanding of the topics within the chapter and to help you prepare for the exam.

The nurse is a valued member of the healthcare team. The National Council of State Boards of Nursing (NCSBN) is responsible for allocating the number and type of questions that the nurse must take as well as the percentage of questions in each category. The differences between the test questions for a PN and RN are often subtle. Some examples of these differences are

  ▶ **Client care responsibility:** Because the RN is ultimately responsible for the coordination and management of client care as well as delegation of duties, RN candidates will get more questions on these topics whereas PN candidates will be tested on their knowledge and application of how to care for clients.

  ▶ **Intravenous therapy and medication:** The RN is responsible for initiating IVs and giving medication, but the PN is expected to be able to monitor IV lines and medication and know how to recognize problems and the steps to take to correct them.

▶ **Blood administration:** The RN is primarily responsible for initiating a blood transfusion, but the PN is expected to know the signs of a transfusion reaction and the action to be taken if such a reaction occurs.

▶ **Central line care:** The RN is primarily responsible for central line care, but the PN is expected to know how to care for the central line site and be aware of signs of an air emboli.

Each chapter in the *Exam Prep* is extremely useful to the nurse seeking licensure as a practical nurse or registered nurse.

Organization

This book is organized by body systems. This method uses a format that most students find helpful for learning material quickly and easily.

▶ Each chapter begins with an outline of topics—this is a list of subtopics covered in the chapter.

▶ Each chapter has helpful notes, tips, and cautions that will help you study for the exam.

▶ Each chapter includes an in-depth discussion of the topics in that unit.

▶ Each chapter includes pharmacological agents used in the care of the client.

▶ Each chapter includes diagnostic studies used to determine client needs.

▶ Each chapter ends with a case study. This allows the student to use critical-thinking skills in the treatment of the client.

Instructional Features

This book provides multiple ways to learn and reinforce the exam material. Following are some of the helpful methods:

▶ **Study strategies:** Study strategies are discussed in a chapter called "Study and Exam Preparation Tips."

▶ **Key terms:** A list of key terms that the student must know appears as a glossary.

▶ **Notes, tips, and cautions:** Notes, tips, and cautions contain various kinds of useful or practical information such as tips on nursing practice.

▶ **Apply Your Knowledge:** Questions covering the material in that particular chapter are included at the end of each chapter. There are three test banks of 166 items and an additional test bank of management and pharmacology questions. You will also find a CD of test questions to help you practice the NCLEX format. These help you to determine what you need to study further and what you already know.

▸ **Suggested Readings and Resources:** At the end of each chapter, this section directs you to additional resources for study. This book is also designed to be a tool used by nursing students and nurses in practice.

Extensive Practice Test Options

This book provides you with many opportunities to assess your knowledge and practice for the exam. The test options are as follows:

▸ **Exam questions:** Each chapter ends with a series of questions relevant to the chapter material.

▸ **Case studies:** Each chapter includes a case study in which you can practice applying all the information to a real-life scenario.

▸ **Practice exams:** This book includes three complete practice exams that reflect the type of questions you will see on the NCLEX exam. Use them to practice and to help you determine your strengths and weaknesses so that you can return to your weakest areas for further study.

▸ **CD exam:** The exam engine included on the CD includes questions from the book as well as additional questions for your review. Be sure to use the study mode first and then try the exam mode. The CD allows you to repeat the exam as often as you need, so don't hesitate to try again and again if you need to.

Final Review

The final review section of the book provides you with two valuable tools for preparing for the exam:

▸ **Fast Facts:** This is a condensed version of the information contained in the book and is an extremely useful tool for last-minute review.

▸ **Exam questions:** Three complete practice exams are included in this book plus more on the CD-ROM. All questions are written in the style and format used on the actual exam. Use these exams to prepare for the real exam until you are comfortable with your level of knowledge.

Other Valuable Tools

This book also includes several other valuable tools for preparing for the NCLEX exam:

▸ Appendix A, "Things You Forgot," contains a list of information commonly used by nurses.

▸ Appendix B, "Need to Know More?" includes a list of websites and organizations that are helpful resources for the nurse in practice.

- ▶ Appendix C, "Calculations," provides you with a quick-and-easy guide to medication administration.

- ▶ Appendix D, "Most-Prescribed Medications in the United States," is a list of commonly prescribed drugs with the generic and brand names and common nursing implications for use.

- ▶ Appendix E, "Alphabetical Listing of Nursing Boards in the United States and Protectorates," is a useful list for nurses.

- ▶ An index provides a complete source of the location of specific information.

About the NCLEX Exam

The Computer Adaptive Test (CAT) provides a means for individualized testing of each candidate seeking licensure as a professional nurse. Selecting from a large test bank, the computer chooses questions based on the candidate's ability and competence as demonstrated on the prior question.

For the RN exam, the minimum number of questions is 75 with a maximum of 265. The average candidate's exam comprises 160 items. You must answer the question that appears on the screen before another question is given, and you cannot skip questions or return to a previous question. It is imperative that you read each question carefully before you select a response. We suggest that you cover the answers with your nondominant hand and read the stem before looking at the answers. RN candidates are allowed six hours to take the exam.

The NCLEX consists of questions from the cognitive levels of knowledge, comprehension, application, and analysis. The majority of questions are written at the application and analysis levels. Questions incorporate the five stages of the nursing process:

- ▶ Assessment

- ▶ Analysis

- ▶ Planning

- ▶ Implementation

- ▶ Evaluation

There are also questions from the four categories of client needs (noted in bold in Table I.1). Client needs are divided into subcategories (noted in italics in Table I.1) that define the content within each of the four major categories tested on the NCLEX. Table I.1 outlines the categories and subcategories of client needs.

TABLE I.1   NCLEX RN Exam Categories and Subcategories

Client Needs	Percentage of Items from Each Category/Subcategory
Safe, Effective Care Environment	
Management of Care	16%–22%
Safety and Infection Control	8%–14%
Health Promotion and Maintenance	6%–12%
Psychosocial Integrity	6%–12%
Physiological Integrity	
Basic Care and Comfort	6%–12%
Pharmacological and Parenteral Therapies	13%–19%
Reduction of Risk Potential	10%–16%
Physiological Adaptation	11%–17%

The percentage of questions allotted to each category is determined by the National Council and depends on the results of a survey the council sends out every three years to new graduates. Based on the activity statements, the percentages change accordingly. It is safe to say that as the patient population changes, these categories will also change. This book reflects those changes particularly as they relate to the need for nurses in management roles, cultural diversity, and client criticality.

Computerized adaptive testing offers the candidate several advantages over the former paper-and-pencil exam. The test questions are stored in a large test bank and classified by test plan areas and level of difficulty. Depending on the answer given by the candidate, the computer presents another question that is either more difficult or less difficult. This allows the computer to determine the candidate's knowledge of the subject matter more precisely.

The pass/fail decision is not based on how many questions the candidate answers correctly, but on the difficulty of the questions answered correctly. Even though candidates might answer different questions and different numbers of questions, the test plan remains the same. All NCLEX examinations conform to this test plan. Each time you answer a question correctly, the next question gets harder until you miss a question; then an easier question is given until you answer correctly. This way the computer concludes whether a candidate has met the passing standard. If you are clearly above the passing standard at the minimum number of questions, the computer stops asking questions. If you are clearly below the passing standard, the computer stops asking questions. If your ability estimate is close to the passing standard, the computer continues to ask questions until either the maximum number of questions is asked or time expires. Should time expire, the last 60 questions are reviewed. To pass, the candidate must remain above the passing standard on the last 60 items.

The CAT exam offers another advantage. The candidate can schedule the exam at a time that is convenient and usually receives test results in 7days or sooner. The candidate can retake the exam after 45 days in most states. We suggest that you review this text and others, and, if needed, take a review seminar prior to taking the NCLEX. Allow at least one week to study and prepare for the exam. Remember: You want to take the exam only one time. You should visit the National Council's website at www.ncsbn.org for information regarding how to schedule your test. We suggest that you read the application process thoroughly to learn how you can register to take the exam.

Advice for Preparing for the Exam

Judicious use of this book, either alone or with a review seminar such as the one provided by Rinehart and Associates, will help you achieve your goal of becoming licensed to practice nursing. We suggest that you find a location where you can concentrate on the material each day. A minimum of two hours per day for at least two weeks is suggested. This book provides you with tips, notes, and sample questions. These questions will acquaint you with the types of questions you will see during the exam. The mock exam is formulated with those difficult management and delegation questions that you can score to determine your readiness to test. Pay particular attention to the notes, tips, and warnings throughout the book as well as the "Fast Facts" chapter. Using these elements will help you gain knowledge and reduce your stress as you prepare to take the test.

Advice for Test Day

From our years of experience in nursing and teaching, we have this advice for you:

- ▶ **Remember to know where you are going:** Be sure that you know the exact location of the exam. It is easy to get caught in traffic, and if you are late, you forfeit the exam time and your money. You will have to reschedule your exam and pay again.

- ▶ **Have your authorization number and forms of ID with you:** If you forget to take your identification, you will have to reschedule and will forfeit your testing time. Remember you will be photographed and fingerprinted prior to entering the testing site, so do not let this upset you.

- ▶ **Eat a high-protein meal prior to the exam:** You want good food for thought prior to taking the exam. Studies have shown that a meal high in vitamins such as B9 help us think more clearly during stressful times.

- ▶ **Take your time during the test:** Remember, you do not have to complete all the questions.

- ▶ **If you need to take a break, get up and walk around:** The clock will continue to tick, so don't take too much time.

- ▶ **Dress in layers:** The testing site might be cold or warm.

Hints for Using This Book

Each *Exam Prep* book follows a regular structure, along with cues about important or useful information. Here's the structure of a typical chapter:

- ▶ **Outline of topics:** Lists the topic headings within the chapter.

- ▶ **Headings and subheadings:** These are the main chapter topics and ancillary subtopics, designating the core content for study within the chapter.

- ▶ **Case studies:** This allows the student to use critical thinking skills in a specific client situation. The answers and complete explanations for the case study are included.

- ▶ **Key Concepts:** This section of the chapter includes the following three components for you to review and study to ensure your understanding of the chapter topics:

  - ▶ **Key Terms:** A list of the key terms from the chapter that you should be able to define.

  - ▶ **Diagnostics:** When appropriate, this section lists diagnostics used in the care of the client with a condition covered within the chapter.

  - ▶ **Pharmacological agents used in the care of the client with disorders found in the chapter:** This information is found in a table form and includes the generic name and brand name of the drug by category, the action of the drug, the potential side effects, and the nursing implications and care of the client taking that category of drugs.

- ▶ **Apply Your Knowledge:** Exam questions about the chapter content with answers and explanations are included in each chapter.

- ▶ **Suggested Reading and Resources:** Each chapter concludes with a supplementary resource list (including books, websites, and journals) relevant to the chapter content.

We suggest that you study from the front of the book and proceed in a logical sequence. When you have completed the case study and questions at the end of each chapter, you might feel the need to research using the resource list.

Contact the Author

We are interested in your study and success, and want you to pass on the first attempt. If after reviewing with this text, you would like to contact us, you can do so at Rinehart and Associates, PO Box 124, Booneville, MS 38829 or visit our website at www.nclexreview.net. You can contact us by phone at (662) 728-4622.

Remember, knowing the material is important, but being able to apply that knowledge is a must. When you understand the material, passing the NCLEX exam will be easy.

Good luck!

Study and Exam Preparation Tips

There are many ways to approach studying for the NCLEX exam. The following tips have been found useful in helping the candidate study more quickly and retain more information.

Study Tips

Although individuals vary in the ways they learn, some basic principles apply to everyone. Adopt a study strategy that takes advantage of these principles:

- ▶ Learn the detailed information first.

- ▶ After you master the small details, look at the big picture.

- ▶ Devote at least one to two hours per day to studying the information.

- ▶ Don't try to pull out all your notes from nursing school. Focus on this book and the suggested resources.

- ▶ Learn from your mistakes. If you miss a question, look at the answer explanation carefully and look up information you don't understand.

- ▶ Talk out loud if you like. Others might think you're odd, but hearing the material spoken could help you to concentrate and remember.

- ▶ Study with a friend. If your study group focuses on success, it will help you to concentrate. But if they do not, don't waste your time with an ineffective group.

- ▶ Attend a live review like that offered by Rinehart and Associates. Participating in a live review where the instructors are dedicated to helping you succeed is immeasurable in value.

- ▶ When you feel ready to take the test, schedule a time. Don't put off taking the test too long because you might start to forget what you have learned.

As you can see by looking at the outline of this book, we organized the material in a logical sequence. Follow the outline and focus on learning the details as well as the big picture. Memorizing is not fun, but it is necessary when dealing with things such as laboratory values, conversion factors, and nutrition. First look at the details and then master the major concepts. Understanding "why" helps you to remember, so be sure you master the concept before you move on to the next topic.

Research has shown that attempting to assimilate both overall and detailed types of information at the same time can interfere with the overall learning process. For best performance on the exam, separate your study time into learning the details and then the big picture.

Exam Prep Tips

After learning the materials, you might want to use a number of testing tips:

- ▶ Read the questions carefully.

- ▶ Look for keywords.

- ▶ Watch for specific details.

- ▶ Eliminate options that are clearly wrong or incorrect.

- ▶ Look for similar options.

- ▶ Look for opposite answers.

- ▶ Use common sense.

These strategies provide you with additional skills, but do not consider them a substitute for good study habits or adequate knowledge of the content. Most questions that appear as test items above the pass point require the candidate to pull together information from a variety of sources. If you have thorough knowledge of the content, use good testing skills, and can apply your knowledge, you will pass the exam. Remember that testing skills, like any other skill, improve with practice.

Before discussing each strategy for successful test-taking, you should be familiar with the following terms:

- ▶ **Test item:** This is the entire question.

- ▶ **Stems:** Within a test item, these are the portions that ask a question or propose a problem.

- ▶ **Options:** These are the potential answers.

- ▶ **Alternative item:** These are the items that require the candidate to use a diagram, list in order of priority, check all that apply, calculate math or intake and output, or fill in blanks.

The candidate might be asked to read a graph or to put on earphones and listen to heart or breath sounds. He might also be asked to view a video and make an interpretation of the information given. You will want to practice listening to rales, rhonchi, and wheezing to review for the audio portion of the exam.

Read the Question Carefully

Reading ability and careful reading of exam questions often affect exam scores. Before selecting an answer, ask the following questions:

1. What is the question asking?

2. Does the question include keywords?

3. Is there relevant information in the stem?

4. How would I ask this question (in my own words)?

5. How would I answer this question (in my own words)?

After answering these questions, see whether there is an option similar to your answer. Is this option the best or most complete answer to the question?

Look for Keywords

Keywords in the stem should alert you to use care in choosing an answer. Avoid selecting answers that include keywords such as *always*, *never*, *all*, *every*, *only*, *must*, *no*, *except*, and *none*. Answers that contain these keywords are seldom correct because they limit and qualify potentially correct answers.

Watch for Specific Details

Careful reading of details in the stem can provide important clues to the correct option. For example, if the item seeks information on a short-term goal, look for something accomplishable within the hospital stay; if the item seeks information on a long-term goal, look for something accomplishable in the home or community.

Eliminate Options That Are Clearly Wrong or Incorrect

By systematically eliminating distracters that are clearly incorrect, you increase the probability of selecting the correct option. With the elimination of each distracter, you increase the probability of selecting the correct option by 25%.

Look for Similar Options

If a test item contains two or more options that could feasibly be correct or are similar in meaning, look for an umbrella term or phrase that encompasses the other correct options. The following list gives you hints about how to read the question and its options to identify the correct answer accurately:

▸ **Look at the parts of the options:** If an answer contains two or more parts, you can reduce the number of possible correct answers by identifying one part as incorrect.

▸ **Identify specific determiners:** Look for the same or similar words in the stem and in the options. The word in the stem that clues you to a similar word in the option or that limits potential options is a *specific determiner*. The option with a specific determiner is often the correct answer.

▶ **Identify words in the option that are closely associated with, but not identical to, words in the stem:** The option that contains words closely associated with words appearing in the stem is often the correct answer.

▶ **Be alert for grammatical inconsistencies:** The correct option must be consistent with the form of the question. If the item demands a response in the singular, an option in the plural would be incorrect, so look for an option in the singular.

▶ **Use relevant information from an earlier question:** Test writers often provide information that you can use in subsequent questions. For example, the test might ask several questions on the topic of diabetes mellitus. Write information that you remember about this topic on the paper or slate provided in the testing area. That information can help you later in the test when you encounter a similar question.

▶ **Look for the answer that differs from the other options:** This testing strategy is called *odd answer out*. An example of this type of question follows:

The nurse is attempting to evaluate the client's knowledge of diabetes. Which statement made by the client indicates a need for further teaching?

    A. The client states that he will check his blood glucose levels before meals.

    B. The client selects a 10-ounce steak from his menu.

    C. The client demonstrates how he will give himself insulin.

    D. The client verbalizes understanding of ways to improve circulation.

Answer B is correct. Answers A, C, and D all indicate knowledge of diabetes. Answer B indicates that the client lacks understanding because the portion size for steak is 3 ounces.

Look for Opposite Answers

When you see opposites, one of these options is usually correct. Here is an example of this testing strategy:

A client with hemophilia is admitted with bleeding. Which action by the nurse indicates an understanding of hemophilia?

  A. The nurse applies heat to the joints.

  B. The nurse applies ice to the joints.

  C. The nurse offers to perform passive range of motion.

  D. The nurse elevates the extremity.

Answer B is correct. Hemophilia is a genetically obtained disorder in which there is an absence of clotting factor. Applying heat vasodilates and causes increased bleeding. This answer is the opposite of the correct choice, which is answer B. Answer C is incorrect because range of motion should not be performed during bleeding episodes; doing so potentiates further bleeding. Perform range of motion after controlling the bleeding. In answer D, elevating the extremity is good, but it will not stop active bleeding.

CAUTION

Remember that when dealing with the legality questions on the NCLEX exam, the nurse should assign the most critical client to the registered nurse and the most stable to the nursing assistant. If skilled nursing care is required, assign the stable client to the licensed practical nurse and self-assign the most critical client. In this situation, the term *self-assign* indicates the client that you would take care of yourself.

Finally, follow common sense practice when studying. Study when you are alert, reduce or eliminate distractions, take breaks when you are tired, and focus on the goal. Remember, you want to take the NCLEX exam only one time.

CHAPTER ONE

Pharmacology

For a number of years, I have searched for a way to help students understand and apply knowledge of pharmacology to nursing practice. The graduate nurse is frequently responsible for instructing the client and the client's family regarding the safe administration of medications. The study of pharmacology is constantly changing as new drugs are constantly being approved for public use by the Food and Drug Administration (FDA). The recent test plan approved by the National Council Licensure Exam devotes 13%–19% of the Physiological Integrity section to pharmacology. This chapter contains useful information to help you look at the classification and generic name of drugs. If you can remember the drug classification, frequently you can understand why the drug was ordered.

Three Areas of Pharmacology

It is important to note that the study of pharmacology includes three areas:

▶ **Pharmacokinetics:** This is the study of how drugs are absorbed, distributed, metabolized, and excreted by the body. Elderly clients and clients with renal or liver disease frequently have difficulty metabolizing and excreting medications. These clients can develop drug toxicity more easily than those with no renal or liver impairment.

▶ **Pharmacodynamics:** This is the study of how drugs are used by the body. For example, pharmacodynamics of oral hypoglycemics explain how the blood glucose is reduced by stimulating the pancreatic beta cells to produce more insulin, by also making insulin receptor sites more sensitive to insulin, and by increasing the number of insulin receptor cells. These drugs are effective only if the client's pancreas is producing some insulin.

▶ **Pharmacotherapeutics:** This is the study of how the client responds to the drug. A client might experience side effects such as gastrointestinal symptoms to a number of medications, including antibiotics. Side effects might cause discomfort but are usually not severe enough to warrant discontinuation of the medication. Demerol (meperidine HCl) is a narcotic analgesic that can cause nausea and vomiting. To prevent these side effects, the physician frequently orders an antiemetic called Phenergan (promethazine) to be given with Demerol. These drugs have a synergistic effect that provides pain relief while preventing the discomfort of side effects.

Adverse effects of medications result in symptoms so severe that it is necessary to reduce the dosage or discontinue the medication completely. Antituberculars and anticonvulsants are two categories of medications that can have adverse effects on the liver. The nurse should carefully assess the client's liver function studies as well as assess for signs of jaundice that indicate drug-related hepatitis, in which case the medication will be discontinued.

How Nurses Work with Pharmacology

Nurses are expected to utilize their knowledge of pharmacology to:

- ▸ Recognize common uses, side effects, and adverse effects of the client's medication
- ▸ Challenge medication errors
- ▸ Meet the client's learning needs

Generally, the medication the nurse is expected to administer depends on the area of practice and the assigned client. The following medication classifications are commonly prescribed for adult clients within a medical/surgical setting:

- ▸ **Anti-infectives:** Used for the treatment of infections. Common side effects include GI upset.

- ▸ **Antihypertensives:** Lower blood pressure and increase blood flow to the myocardium. Common side effects include orthostatic hypotension. Other side effects are specific to types of antihypertensive prescribed.

- ▸ **Antidiarrheals:** Decrease gastric motility and reduce water content in the intestinal tract. Side effects include bloating and gas.

- ▸ **Diuretics:** Decrease water and sodium absorption from the loop of Henle (loop diuretics) or inhibit antidiuretic hormone (potassium-sparing diuretics). Side effects of non–potassium-sparing diuretics include hypokalemia.

- ▸ **Antacids:** Reduce hydrochloric acid in the stomach. A common side effect of calcium- and aluminum-based antacids is constipation. Magnesium-based antacids frequently cause diarrhea.

- ▸ **Antipyretics:** Reduce fever.

- ▸ **Antihistamines:** Block the release of histamine in allergic reactions. Common side effects of antihistamines are dry mouth, drowsiness, and sedation.

- ▸ **Bronchodilators:** Dilate large air passages and are commonly prescribed for clients with asthma and chronic obstructive lung disease. A common side effect of these is tachycardia.

- ▸ **Laxatives:** Promote the passage of stool. Types of laxatives include stool softeners, cathartics, fiber, lubricants, and stimulants.

- **Anticoagulants:** Prevent clot formation by decreasing vitamin K levels and blocking the clotting chain or by preventing platelet aggregation.

- **Antianemics:** Increase factors necessary for red blood cell production. Examples of antianemics include B12, iron, and Epogen (erythropoetin).

- **Narcotics/analgesics:** Relieve moderate to severe pain. Medications in this category include opioids (morphine and codeine), synthetic opioids (meperidine), and NSAIDs (ketorolac).

- **Anticonvulsants:** Used for the management of seizure disorder and the treatment of bipolar disorder. Medications used as anticonvulsants include phenobarbital, phenytoin (Dilantin), and lorazepam (Ativan).

- **Anticholinergics:** Cause the mucous membranes to become dry; therefore, oral secretions are decreased. Anticholinergics such as atropine are often administered preoperatively.

- **Mydriatics:** Dilate the pupils. Mydriatics are used in the treatment of clients with cataracts.

- **Miotics:** Constrict the pupil. Miotics such as pilocarpine HCl are used in the treatment of clients with glaucoma.

Time-released Drugs

The following abbreviations indicate to the nurse that the drug is time-released. These preparations should not be crushed or opened:

- **Dur** = Duration

- **SR** = Sustained release

- **CR** = Continuous release

- **SA** = Sustained action

- **Contin** = Continuous action

- **LA** = Long acting

Enteric-coated tablets and caplets are those coated with a thick shell that prevents the medication from being absorbed in the upper GI tract, allowing the medication to be absorbed more slowly. *Spansules* are capsules containing time-released beads that are released slowly. The nurse should not alter the preparation of these types of medications. The physician should be notified to obtain an alternative preparation if the client is unable to swallow a time-released preparation.

Administering Medications

When preparing to administer medications, the nurse must identify the client by reviewing the physician's order. She must also administer the medication by the right route. Many medications are supplied in various preparations. The physician orders the method of administration. The choice of medication administration is dependent on several factors, including the desired blood level, the client's ability to swallow, and the disease or disorder being treated.

The Seven Rights of Administering Medication

The nurse is expected to use the seven rights when administering medications to the client. These include five rights of drug administration, plus two from the Patient's Bill of Rights.

The Patient's Bill of Rights was enacted to protect the client's well-being, both mentally and physically. The client has the right to refuse treatment, which can include medications. The nurse must document any treatment provided to the client. Documentation of care given must be made promptly to prevent forgetting any details and to ensure that another nurse does not duplicate medication administration.

The seven rights of medication administration are

- ▶ **Right client:** Identification of the client must be done by asking the client to state his name and checking the identification band.

- ▶ **Right route:** The physician orders the prescribed route of administration.

- ▶ **Right drug:** Checking both the generic and trade names with the physician's order ensures that the right drug is administered. If the client's diagnosis does not match the drug category, the nurse should further investigate the ordered medication.

- ▶ **Right amount:** The nurse is expected to know common dosages for both adults and children.

- ▶ **Right time:** The nurse can administer the medication either 30 minutes before the assigned time or 30 minutes after.

- ▶ **Right documentation (from the Patient's Bill of Rights and legality issues in nursing):** This right is different from the others in that it must be done to prevent duplicating drug administration.

- ▶ **Right to refuse treatment (from the Patient's Bill of Rights):** The client has the right to refuse medication or treatment.

Understanding and Identifying the Various Drugs

It is important to know that drugs generally have several names. The following list explains these different names for you:

▶ **Chemical name:** This is often a number or letter designation that tells you the chemical makeup of the drug. This name is of little value to the nurse in practice.

▶ **Generic name:** This is the name given by the company that developed the drug, and it remains the same even after the patent is released and other companies are allowed to market the medication.

▶ **Trade name:** This is the name given to the drug by the originating company. After the drug has been released to the market for approximately four years, a trade-named medication can be released by an alternative company. The trade name will be different, while the generic name will remain the same

It is much safer for the nurse to remember the *generic name* rather than the trade name because the trade name will probably change.

EXAM ALERT

On the NCLEX exam, both the generic and trade names of medications might be included for clarification. The generic name will be given.

Approximately 80% of the time generic drugs in the same category have common syllables. If you can identify the commonality within the generic names, you can more easily learn the needed information for the NCLEX. The sections that follow look at some commonly given categories of drugs and help you to recognize the commonalities in the names. As you will see, each drug has a common part in its name, which will help you to quickly identify a particular drug by the common part of the name for that drug category.

Angiotensin-Converting Enzyme Inhibitors

This category of drugs is utilized to treat both primary and secondary hypertension. These drugs work by inhibiting conversion of angiotensin I to angiotensin II. Notice that all the generic names include the syllable *pril*. When you see these letters, you will know that they are angiotensin-converting enzyme (ACE) inhibitors. Table 1.1 highlights these in more depth.

TABLE 1.1   Angiotensin-Converting Enzyme Inhibitors

Action/Use	Drug Name*
Antihypertensives	Benazepril (Lotensin)
	Lisinopril (Zestril)
	Captopril (Capoten)
	Enalapril (Vasotec)
	Fosinopril (Monopril)
	Moexipril (Univas)
	Quinapril (Acupril)
	Ramipril (Altace)

*The generic name is listed first with the trade name in parentheses.

When working with angiotensin-converting enzyme inhibitors, it is important to know the potential side effects. The following list details the possible side effects/adverse reactions with this drug category:

▸ Hypotension

▸ Hacking cough

▸ Nausea/vomiting

▸ Rashes

▸ Angioedema

The following items are nursing considerations to know when working with ACE inhibitors:

▸ Monitor the vital signs frequently.

▸ Monitor the white blood cell count.

▸ Monitor the potassium and creatinine levels.

▸ Monitor the electrolyte levels.

Beta Adrenergic Blockers

Beta adrenergic blockers are drugs that help lower blood pressure, pulse rate, and cardiac output. They are also used to treat migraine headaches and other vascular headaches. Certain preparations of the beta blockers are used to treat glaucoma and prevent myocardial infarctions. These drugs act by blocking the sympathetic vasomotor response.

Notice the syllable *olol*. When you see these letters, you will know that these drugs are beta blockers. Table 1.2 highlights these beta blockers in more detail.

TABLE 1.2   Beta Adrenergic Blockers

Action/Use	Drug Name*
Act by blocking sympathetic vasomotor response	Acebutolol (Monitan, Rhotral, Sectral)
	Atenolol (Tenormin, Apo-Atenol, Nova-Atenol)
	Carvedilol (Coreg)
	Esmolol (Brevibloc)
	Propanolol (Inderal)
	Toprol-XL (Metoprolol)

*The generic name is listed first with the trade name in parentheses.

The potential side effects/adverse reactions of beta adrenergic blockers are listed here:

▶ Orthostatic hypotension

▶ Bradycardia

▶ Nausea/vomiting

▶ Diarrhea

▶ May mask hypoglycemic symptoms

The following list gives you some nursing interventions for working with clients using beta adrenergic blockers:

▶ Monitor the client's blood pressure, heart rate, and rhythm.

▶ Monitor the client for signs of edema. The nurse should assess lung sounds for rales and rhonchi.

▶ Monitor the client for changes in lab values (protein, BUN, creatinine) that indicate nephrotic syndrome.

▶ Teach the client to:

    ▶ Rise slowly

    ▶ Report bradycardia, dizziness, confusion, depression, or fever

    ▶ Taper off the medication

Anti-Infectives (Aminoglycosides)

Anti-infective drugs include bactericidals and bacteriostatics. They interfere with the protein synthesis of the bacteria, causing the bacteria to die. They are active against most aerobic gram-negative bacteria and against some gram-positive organisms.

Notice that these end in *cin*, and many of them end in *mycin*. So, when you see either of these syllables, you know these are anti-infectives. Table 1.3 explains the various anti-infectives.

TABLE 1.3 Anti-Infective Drugs

Action/Use	Drug Name*
Interfere with the protein synthesis of the bacteria, causing the bacteria to die	Gentamicin (Garamycin, Alcomicin, Genoptic)
	Kanamycin (Kantrex)
	Neomycin (Mycifradin)
	Streptomycin (Streptomycin)
	Tobramycin (Tobrex, Nebcin)
	Amikacin (Amikin)

*The generic name is listed first with the trade name in parentheses.

The following list highlights some possible side effects/adverse reactions from the use of anti-infectives (aminoglycosides):

▸ Ototoxicity

▸ Nephrotoxicity

▸ Seizures

▸ Blood dyscrasias

▸ Hypotension

▸ Rash

The following are nursing interventions you need to be aware of when working with clients using anti-infectives (aminoglycosides):

▸ Obtain a history of allergies.

▸ Monitor intake and output.

▸ Monitor vital signs during intravenous infusion.

▸ Maintain a patent IV site.

▸ Monitor for therapeutic levels.

▸ Monitor for signs of nephrotoxicity.

▸ Monitor for signs of ototoxicity.

▸ Teach the client to report any changes in urinary elimination.

▸ Monitor peak and trough levels.

TIP

Tests on peak and trough levels are done to obtain a blood level and determine the dosage needed for the client. They should be done 30–60 minutes after the third or fourth IV dose or 60 minutes after the third or fourth IM dose. Trough levels should be drawn 5 minutes before the next dose if possible. The client should be taught to report any change in renal function or in hearing because this category can be toxic to the kidneys and the auditory nerve.

CAUTION

These drugs are frequently used to treat super-infections such as methicillin-resistant staphylococcus aureus (MRSA). Clients with MRSA can exhibit the following symptoms: fever, malaise, redness, pain, swelling, perineal itching, diarrhea, stomatitis, and cough.

Benzodiazepines (Anticonvulsants/Antianxiety)

These drugs are used for their antianxiety or anticonvulsant effects.

Notice that all these contain the syllable *pam*, *pate*, or *lam*. Table 1.4 gives you a breakdown of these drug types.

TIP

Not all the benzodiazepines contain *pam*; some of them contain *pate* and *lam*, as in *aprazolam* (Xanax). However, they all contain *azo* or *aze*.

TABLE 1.4   Benzodiazepines (Anticonvulsants/Sedative/Antianxiety) Drugs

Action/Use	Drug Name*
Sedative-hypnotic; also used as anticonvulsants; have antianxiety effects	Clonazepam (Klonopin)
	Diazepam (Valium)
	Chlordiazepoxide (Librium)
	Lorazepam (Ativan)
	Flurazepam (Dalmane)

*The generic name is listed first with the trade name in parentheses.

The following list gives you some possible side effects and adverse reactions from the use of this classification of drugs:

- Drowsiness
- Lethargy
- Ataxia
- Depression
- Restlessness
- Slurred speech
- Bradycardia
- Hypotension
- Diplopia
- Nystagmus
- Nausea/vomiting

▶ Constipation

▶ Incontinence

▶ Urinary retention

▶ Respiratory depression

▶ Rash

▶ Urticaria

The following are some nursing interventions to know when working with the client taking benzodiazepines:

▶ Monitor respirations.

▶ Monitor liver function.

▶ Monitor kidney function.

▶ Monitor bone marrow function.

▶ Monitor for signs of chemical abuse.

Phenothiazines (Antipsychotic/Antiemetic)

These drugs are used as antiemetics or neuroleptics. These drugs are also used to treat psychosis in those clients with schizophrenia. Some phenothiazines, such as Phenergan (promethazine) and Compazine (prochlorperzine), are used to treat nausea and vomiting.

CAUTION

Because they are irritating to the tissue, Z-track method should be used when administering phenothiazines by intramuscular injection. If the client is allergic to one of the phenothiazines, she probably is allergic to all of them. If the client experiences an allergic reaction or extrapyramidal effects, a more severe reaction, she should be given Benadryl (diphenhydramine hydrochloride) or Congentin (benztropine mesylate).

Notice that all these contain the syllable *zine* (see Table 1.5).

TABLE 1.5   Phenothiazines (Antipsychotic/Antiemetic) Drugs

Action/Use	Drug Name*
Used as antiemetics or major tranquilizers	Chlopromazine (Thorazine)
	Prochlorperazine (Compazine)
	Trifluoperazine (Stelazine)
	Promethazine (Phenergan)
	Hydroxyzine (Vistaril)
	Fluphenazine (Prolixin)

*The generic name is listed first with the trade name in parentheses.

The following list gives you some possible side effects and adverse reactions from the use of phenothiazines:

▶ Extrapyramidal effects

▶ Drowsiness

▶ Sedation

▶ Orthostatic hypotension

▶ Dry mouth

▶ Agranulocytosis

▶ Photosensitivity

▶ Neuroleptic malignant syndrome

The following are some nursing interventions to know when working with a client taking phenothiazines:

▶ Protect the medication from light.

▶ Do not mix the liquid forms of Prolixin (Fluphenazine HCL) with any beverage containing caffeine, tannates, or pectin due to physical incompatibility.

▶ Monitor liver enzymes.

▶ Monitor renal function.

▶ Protect the client from overexposure to the sun.

Glucocorticoids

These drugs are used in the treatment of conditions requiring suppression of the immune system or to decrease inflammatory response. They are also used in Addison's disease, chronic obstructive pulmonary disease (COPD), and immune disorders. These drugs have anti-inflammatory, anti-allergenic, and anti-stress effects. They are used for replacement therapy for adrenal insufficiency (Addison's disease); as immunosuppressive drugs in post-transplant clients; and to reduce cerebral edema associated with head trauma, neurosurgery, and brain tumors.

Notice that all these contain *sone* or *cort* (see Table 1.6).

TABLE 1.6   Glucocorticoid Drugs

Action/Use	Drug Name*
Used to decrease the inflammatory response to allergies and inflammatory diseases or to decrease the possibility of organ transplant rejection	Prednisolone (Delta-Cortef, Prednisol, Prednisolone)
	Prednisone (Apo-Prednisone, Deltasone, Meticorten, Orasone, Panasol-S)
	Betamethasone (Celestone, Selestoject, Betnesol)
	Dexamethasone (Decadron, Deronil, Dexon, Mymethasone, Dalalone)
	Cortisone (Cortone)
	Hydrocortisone (Cortef, Hydrocortone Phosphate, Cortifoam)
	Methylprednisolone (Solu-cortef, Depo-Medrol, Depopred, Medrol, Rep-Pred)
	Triamcinolone (Amcort, Aristocort, Atolone, Kenalog, Triamolone)

*The generic name is listed first with the trade name in parentheses.

The following list gives you some possible side effects and adverse reactions from the use of this drug type:

- ▶ Acne
- ▶ Poor wound healing
- ▶ Leukocytosis
- ▶ Ecchymosis
- ▶ Bruising
- ▶ Petechiae
- ▶ Depression
- ▶ Flushing
- ▶ Sweating
- ▶ Mood changes (depression), insomnia, hypomania
- ▶ Hypertension
- ▶ Osteoporosis
- ▶ Diarrhea
- ▶ Hemorrhage

CAUTION

These drugs can cause Cushing's syndrome. Signs of Cushing's syndrome include moon faces, edema, elevated blood glucose levels, purple straie, weight gain, buffalo hump, and hirsutism.

The following are nursing interventions used when working with a client taking gluco-corticoids:

- ▶ Monitor glucose levels.

- ▶ Weigh the client daily.

- ▶ Monitor blood pressure.

- ▶ Monitor for signs of infection.

Antivirals

These drugs are used for their antiviral properties. They inhibit viral growth by inhibiting an enzyme within the virus. Herpetic lesions respond to these drugs. Clients with acquired immune deficiency syndrome (AIDS) are often treated with this category of drugs either alone or in combination with other antiviral drugs. These drugs are also used to treat herpetic lesions (HSV-1, HSV-2), varicella infections (chickenpox), herpes zoster (shingles), herpes simplex (fever blisters), encephalitis, cytomegalovirus (CMV), and respiratory syncytial virus (RSV).

Notice that all these drug names contain *vir*. Table 1.7 lists some of these drug types.

TABLE 1.7   Antiviral Drugs

Action/Use	Drug Name*
Used for their antiviral effects	Acyclovir (Zovirax)
	Ritonavir (Norvir)
	Saquinovir (Invirase, Fortovase)
	Indinavir (Crixivan)
	Abacavir (Ziagen)
	Cidofovir (Vistide)
	Ganciclovir (Cytovene, Vitrasert)

*The generic name is listed first with the trade name in parentheses.

The following list gives some side effects and adverse effects that are usually associated with this drug category:

- ▶ Nausea

- ▶ Vomiting

- ▶ Diarrhea

- ▶ Oliguria

- ▶ Proteinuria

- ▶ Vaginitis

- ▶ Central nervous side effects (these are less common):

> ▸ Tremors

> ▸ Confusion

> ▸ Seizures

> ▸ Severe, sudden anemia

The following nursing interventions are used when working a client taking antivirals:

> ▸ Tell the client to report a rash because this can indicate an allergic reaction.

> ▸ Watch for signs of infection.

> ▸ Monitor the creatinine level frequently.

> ▸ Monitor liver profile.

> ▸ Monitor bowel pattern before and during treatment.

Cholesterol-Lowering Agents

This drug type is used to help the client lower cholesterol and triglyceride levels and to decrease the potential for cardiovascular disease. Notice that all these contain the syllable *vastatin*. It should be noted that many advertisements call these "statin" drugs. These drugs should not be confused with the statin drugs used for their antifungal effects. These can include nystatin (trade name Mycostatin or Nilstat). Table 1.8 lists some of the cholesterol-lowering agents.

TABLE 1.8 Cholesterol-Lowering Drugs

Action/Use	Drug Name*
Used to lower cholesterol	Atorvastatin (Lipitor)
	Fluvastatin (Lescol)
	Lovastatin (Mevacor)
	Pravastatin (Pravachol)
	Simvastatin (Zocar)
	Rosuvastatin (Crestor)

*The generic name is listed first with the trade name in parentheses.

CAUTION

This category should not be taken with grapefruit juice and should be taken at night. The client should have regular liver studies to determine the presence of liver disease.

Here is a list of side effects and adverse reactions that could occur with the use of cholesterol-lowering agents:

▶ Rash

▶ Alopecia

▶ Dyspepsia

▶ Liver dysfunction

▶ Muscle weakness (myalgia)

▶ Headache

CAUTION

Rhabdomyolysis, a muscle-wasting syndrome, has been linked with the use of cholesterol-lowering agents. The client should be instructed to report cola-colored urine and unexplained muscle soreness and weakness to the physician because these can be signs of rhabdomyolysis.

The following nursing interventions are used when working with a client taking cholesterol-lowering agents:

▶ Include a diet low in cholesterol and fat in therapy.

▶ Monitor cholesterol levels.

▶ Monitor liver profile.

▶ Monitor renal function.

▶ Monitor for muscle pain and weakness.

Angiotensin Receptor Blockers

These drugs block vasoconstrictor- and aldosterone-secreting angiotensin II. They are used to treat primary or secondary hypertension and are an excellent choice for clients who complain of the coughing associated with ACE inhibitors. Notice that all these contain *sartan*. Table 1.9 lists some of these drugs.

TABLE 1.9 Angiotensin Receptor Blocker Drugs

Action/Use	Drug Name*
Used to lower blood pressure and increase cardiac output	Valsartan (Diovan)
	Candesartan (Altacand)
	Losartan (Cozaar)
	Telmisartan (Micardis)

*The generic name is listed first with the trade name in parentheses.

The following list gives some side effects and adverse effects that accompany the use of angiotensin receptor blockers:

- ▸ Dizziness
- ▸ Insomnia
- ▸ Depression
- ▸ Diarrhea
- ▸ Nausea/vomiting
- ▸ Impotence
- ▸ Muscle cramps
- ▸ Neutropenia
- ▸ Cough

The following nursing interventions are used when working with a client taking angiotensin receptor blocker agents:

- ▸ Monitor blood pressure.
- ▸ Monitor BUN.
- ▸ Monitor creatinine.
- ▸ Monitor electrolytes.
- ▸ Tell the client to check edema in feet and legs daily.
- ▸ Monitor hydration status.

Histamine 2 Antagonists

These drugs are used in the treatment of gastroesophageal reflux disease (GERD), acid reflux, and gastric ulcers. They inhibit histamine 2 (H2) release in the gastric parietal cells, therefore inhibiting gastric acids.

Notice that all these contain the syllable *tidine* (see Table 1.10).

TABLE 1.10   Histamine 2 Antagonist Drugs

Action/Use	Drug Name*
Block histamine 2 receptor sites, decreasing acid production; used to treat gastric ulcers and GERD	Cimetidine (Tagamet)
	Famotidine (Pepcid)
	Nizatidine (Axid)
	Rantidine (Zantac)

*The generic name is listed first with the trade name in parentheses.

The following list gives some side effects and adverse effects associated with histamine 2 antagonists:

▶ Confusion

▶ Bradycardia/tachycardia

▶ Diarrhea

▶ Psychosis

▶ Seizures

▶ Agranulocytosis

▶ Rash

▶ Alopecia

▶ Gynecomastia

▶ Galactorrhea

Following are some nursing interventions when working with a client taking H2 antagonists:

▶ Monitor the blood urea nitrogen levels.

▶ Administer the medication with meals.

▶ If the client is taking the medication with antacids, make sure he takes antacids one hour before or after taking these drugs.

▶ Cimetidine can be prescribed in one large dose at bedtime.

▶ Sucralfate decreases the effects of histamine 2 receptor blockers.

Proton Pump Inhibitors

These drugs suppress gastric secretion by inhibiting the hydrogen/potassium ATPase enzyme system. They are used in the treatment of gastric ulcers, indigestion, and GERD.

Notice that all these drugs contain the syllable *prazole* and should be given prior to meals. Table 1.11 highlights proton pump inhibitor drugs.

TABLE 1.11 Proton Pump Inhibitors

Action/Use	Drug Name*
Used in the treatment of GERD, gastric ulcers, and esophagitis	Esomeprazole (Nexium)
	Lansoprazole (Prevacid)
	Pantoprazole (Protonix)
	Rabeprazole (AciPhex)

*The generic name is listed first with the trade name in parentheses.

The following list gives some side effects and adverse effects associated with proton pump inhibitors:

▶ Headache

▶ Insomnia

▶ Diarrhea

▶ Flatulence

▶ Rash

▶ Hyperglycemia

Some nursing interventions to use when working with a client taking proton pump inhibitors are as follows:

▶ Do not crush pantoprazole (Protonix). Use a filter when administering IV pantoprazole.

▶ Advise the client to take proton pum inhibitors before meals for best absorption.

▶ Monitor liver function.

Anticoagulants

These drugs are used in the treatment of thrombolytic disease. These drugs are used to treat pulmonary emboli, myocardial infarction, and deep-vein thrombosis; after coronary artery bypass surgery; and for other conditions requiring anticoagulation.

Notice that all these drugs contain the syllable *parin* and are heparin derivatives. The client should have a PTT check to evaluate the bleeding time when giving heparin. The antidote for heparin is protamine sulfate. Table 1.12 lists some common anticoagulants.

TABLE 1.12 Anticoagulant Drugs

Action/Use	Drug Name*
Used to treat clotting disorders and to thin the blood	Heparin sodium (Hepalean)
	Enoxaparin sodium (Lovenox)
	Dalteparin sodium (Fragmin)

*The generic name is listed first with the trade name in parentheses.

The following list gives side effects and adverse effects of heparin derivatives:

▶ Fever

▶ Diarrhea

▶ Stomatitis

▶ Bleeding

- Hematuria

- Dermatitis

- Alopecia

- Pruritus

Nursing interventions to use in caring for a client taking an anticoagulant (heparin derivative) include the following:

- Blood studies (hematocrit and occult blood in stool) should be checked every three months.

- Monitor PTT often for heparin (therapeutic levels are 1.5–2.0 times the control). There is no specific bleeding time done for enoxaparin (Lovenox); however, the platelet levels should be checked for thrombocytopenia.

- Monitor platelet count.

- Monitor for signs of bleeding.

- Monitor for signs of infection.

More Drug Identification Helpers

These are some of the commonly given medications that allow you to utilize the testing technique of commonalities. Looking at these similarities will help you manage the knowledge needed to pass the NCLEX and better care for your clients.

Here are some other clues that can help you in identifying drug types:

- **Caine** = anesthetics (Lidocaine)

- **Mab** = monoclonal antibodies (Palivazumab)

- **Ceph or cef** = cephalosporins (Cefatazime)

- **Cillin** = penicillins (Ampicillin)

- **Cycline** = tetracycline (Tetracycline)

- **Stigmine** = cholinergics (Phyostigmine)

- **Phylline** = bronchodilators (Aminophylline)

- **Cal** = calciums (Calcimar)

- **Done** = opioids (Methodone)

CAUTION

Do not give tetracycline to pregnant women or small children. It stains the child's teeth dark and stunts the growth of small children.

Herbals

Herbals are not considered by some to be medications. They are not regulated by the FDA and can be obtained without a prescription. They do, however, have medicinal properties. Herbals are included on the NCLEX in the category of pharmacology. The list that follows includes some common herbals used by clients as well as some associated nursing precautions:

▶ **Feverfew:** This is used to prevent and treat migraines, arthritis, and fever. This herbal should not be taken with Coumadin, aspirin, NSAIDs, thrombolytics, or antiplatelet medications because it will prolong the bleeding time.

▶ **Ginseng:** This is used as an anti-inflammatory. It has estrogen effects, enhances the immune system, and improves mental and physical abilities. This herbal decreases the effects of anticoagulants and NSAIDs. It also should not be taken by clients taking corticosteroids because the combination of these two can result in extremely high levels of corticosteroids. High doses cause liver problems. A client with hypertension and bipolar disorder should be cautioned regarding the use of ginseng because this herbal can interfere with medications used to treat these disorders.

▶ **Ginkgo:** This improves memory and can be used to treat depression. It also improves peripheral circulation. Ginkgo should not be taken with MAO inhibitors, anticoagulants, or antiplatelets. It increases the bleeding time in clients taking NSAIDs, cephalosporins, and valproic acid. Clients with seizure disorders should not take ginkgo because it can exacerbate seizure activity.

▶ **Echinacea:** This is used to treat colds, fevers, and urinary tract infections. This herbal can interfere with immunosuppressive agents, methotrexate, and ketoconizole.

▶ **Kava-kava:** This herb is used to treat insomnia and mild muscle aches and pains. It increases the effects of central nervous system (CNS) suppressants and decreases the effects of levodopa. It can also increase the effect of MAOIs and cause liver damage.

▶ **St. John's Wort:** This is used to treat mild to moderate depression. This herbal increases adverse CNS effects when used with alcohol or antidepressant medications.

▶ **Ma Huang:** This is used to treat asthma and hay fever, for weight loss, and to increase energy levels. It increases the effect of MAOIs, sympathomimetics, theophylline, and cardiac glycosides.

Drug Schedules

It is important for the nurse to be aware of the drug schedules because several questions might be asked on the NCLEX exam regarding safety. The list that follows characterizes the various drug schedules:

▶ **Schedule I:** Research use only (for example, LSD). These drugs are not medically safe to take and have a high potential for abuse.

▶ **Schedule II:** Requires a written prescription for each refill. No telephone renewals are allowed (for example, narcotics, stimulants, and barbiturates).

▶ **Schedule III:** Requires a new prescription after six months or five refills; it can be a telephone order (for example, codeine, steroids, and antidepressants).

▶ **Schedule IV:** Requires a new prescription after six months (for example, benzodiazepines).

▶ **Schedule V:** Dispensed as any other prescription or without prescription if state law allows (for example, antidiarrheals and antitussives).

Pregnancy Categories for Drugs

These drug categories might also be included on the NCLEX exam. It is important for the nurse to know which categories the pregnant client should avoid:

▶ **Category A:** No risk to fetus.

▶ **Category B:** Insufficient data to use in pregnancy.

▶ **Category C:** Benefits of medication could outweigh the risks.

▶ **Category D:** Risk to fetus exist, but the benefits of the medication could outweigh the probable risks.

▶ **Category X:** Avoid use in pregnancy or in those who may become pregnant. Potential risks to the fetus outweigh the potential benefits.

Key Concepts

The study of pharmacology is often difficult for the nurse to understand. This chapter provided information in a simple to understand format. The NCLEX exam includes questions on this topic under the category of physiologic integrity. The nurse should use the key terms and information found in this chapter to answer pharmacololgy questions.

Key Terms

- ▶ Adverse reactions
- ▶ Agonist
- ▶ Allergic response
- ▶ Antagonists
- ▶ Buccal
- ▶ Contraindications
- ▶ Enteral administration
- ▶ Enteric coating
- ▶ FDA
- ▶ Intradermal
- ▶ Intramuscular
- ▶ Nursing implication
- ▶ Oral
- ▶ Peak drug level
- ▶ Pharmacodynamics
- ▶ Pharmacokinetics
- ▶ Pharmacotherapeutics
- ▶ Side effects
- ▶ Spansules
- ▶ Subcutaneous
- ▶ Synergistic
- ▶ Toxicity
- ▶ Trough drug level

The nurse is responsible for the administration of pharmacological agents. Examples of these skills are

▶ Drug calculations

▶ Administering oral medication

▶ Administering parenteral medication

▶ Administering suppositories

▶ Interpreting normal lab values

Apply Your Knowledge

This chapter includes much needed information to help the nurse apply knowledge of pharmacology. The nurse preparing for the licensure exam should commit to memory the both the generic and trade names when appropriate.

1. Which instruction should be given to the client taking alendronate sodium (Fosamax)?

    A. Take the medication before arising

    B. Force fluids while taking this medication

    C. Remain upright for 30 minutes after taking this medication

    D. Take the medication in conjunction with estrogen

2. The client is discharged from the unit with a prescription for Evista (raloxifene HCl). Which of the following is a side effect of this medication?

    A. Leg cramps

    B. Hot flashes

    C. Urinary frequency

    D. Cold extremities

3. An elderly diabetic who has been maintained on metformin (Glucophage) is scheduled for a cardiac catheterization. Which instruction should be given to the client?

    A. Take the medication as ordered prior to the exam

    B. Limit the amount of protein in the diet prior to the exam

    C. Discontinue the medication prior to the exam

    D. Take the medication with only water prior to the exam

4. The client's mother contacts the clinic regarding medication administration stating, "My daughter can't swallow this capsule. It's too large." Investigation reveals that the medication is a capsule marked *SR*. The nurse should instruct the mother to:

   A. Open the capsule and mix the medication with ice cream

   B. Crush the medication and administer it with 8 oz. of liquid

   C. Call the pharmacist and request an alternative preparation of the medication

   D. Stop the medication and inform the physician at the follow-up visit

5. A 5-year-old is being treated for an acute attack of asthma using racemic epinephrine (epinephrine hydrochloride) nebulizer stat. Which finding indicates an adverse effect of this medication?

   A. Excitability

   B. Tremors

   C. Heart rate 150

   D. Nausea

6. The client is being treated with intravenous Vancomycin for MRSA when the nurse notes redness of the client's neck and chest. Place in ordered sequence the actions to be taken by the nurse:

   A. Call the doctor

   B. Stop the IV infusion of Vancomycin

   C. Administer Benadryl as ordered

   D. Take the vital signs

7. A client with leukemia is receiving oral prednisolone (Prednisone). An expected side effect of the prolonged use of prednisoline is which of the following?

   A. Weight loss

   B. Decreased appetite

   C. Hirsutism

   D. Integumentary bronzing

8. Which laboratory result would concern the nurse caring for a client who is receiving furosemide (Lasix)?

   A. Potassium level of 2.5

   B. Sodium level of 140

   C. Glucose level of 110

   D. Calcium level of 8

9. Which instruction should be given to a client taking Lugol's solution prior to a thyroidectomy?

    A. Take at bedtime

    B. Take the medication with juice

    C. Report changes in appetite

    D. Avoid sunshine while taking the medication

10. A client is admitted to the recovery room following an exploratory laparotomy. Which medication should be kept nearby?

    A. Nitroprusside (Nipride)

    B. Naloxone hydrochloride (Narcan)

    C. Flumazenil (Romazicon)

    D. Diphenhydramine (Benadryl)

11. A client with renal failure has an order for erythropoietin (Epogen) to be given subcutaneously. The nurse should teach the client to report which of the following?

    A. Severe headache

    B. Slight nausea

    C. Decreased urination

    D. Itching

Answer Rationales

1. Answer C is correct. Alendronate sodium is a drug used to treat osteoporosis. Let's use testing strategies for this question. Look at answers A and C; these are opposites. When you are in the bed, you are lying down. The drug should not be given while lying down, nor should it be taken with medication or with estrogen. In answer C, you are upright. This drug causes gastric reflux, so you should remain upright and take it with only water. Notice the clue in the name of the drug: *fosa*, as in fossils. All the drugs in this category contain the syllable *dronate*.

2. Answer B is correct. This drug is in the same category as the chemotherapeutic agent tamoxifene (Novaldex) used for breast cancer. In the case of Evista, this drug is used to treat osteoporosis. Notice that the *E* stands for estrogen. This drug has an agonist effect, so it binds with estrogen and can cause hot flashes. This drug does not cause leg cramps, urinary frequency, or cold extremities, so answers A, C, and D are incorrect.

3. Answer C is correct. Glucophage can cause renal problems. The dye used in cardiac catheterizations is also detrimental to the kidneys. The client may be placed on sliding scale insulin for 48 hours after the dye procedure or until renal function returns. Note the syllable *phage*, as seen in the syllable *phagia*, which means eating. Also note that answers A and C are opposites. Answer A is incorrect because the medication should be withheld; answer B is incorrect because limiting the amount of protein in the diet prior to the exam has no correlation to the medication. Taking the medication with water is not necessary, so answer D is incorrect.

4. Answer C is correct. *SR* means sustained release. These medications cannot be altered. In answers A and B, crushing or opening the capsule is not allowed. In answer D, the doctor should be notified immediately.

5. Answer C is correct. Adverse effects of epinephrine include hypertension and tachycardia. Answers A, B, and D are expected side effects of racemic epinephrine.

6. The correct order is B, D, A, C.

7. Answer C is correct. Notice that the testing strategy "odd item out" can be used in this question. Answers A, B, and D are symptoms of Addison's disease. Answer C is the answer that is different from the rest. Hirsutism, or facial hair, is a side effect of cortisone therapy.

8. Answer A is correct. Furosemide (Lasix) is a loop diuretic. Note that most of the loop diuretics end in *ide*. In answers B, C, and D, the findings are all within normal limits.

9. Answer B is correct. Lugol's solution is a soluble solution of potassium iodine and should be given with juice because it is bitter to taste. In answer A the medication can be taken at another time, so it is incorrect. Reporting changes in appetite is unnecessary, so answer C is incorrect. Answer D is incorrect because it is also unnecessary.

10. Answer B is correct. During the postoperative period, narcotics are given. Narcan is the antidote to narcotics, so answer B is correct. Nipride is utilized to lower blood pressure, so answer A is incorrect. Romazicon is the antidote for the benzo-diazepines, so answer C is incorrect. Benadryl is an antihistamine, so answer D is incorrect.

11. Answer A is correct. Severe headache can indicate impending seizure activity. Slight nausea is expected when beginning the therapy, so answer B is incorrect. A client with renal failure already has itching and decreased urination, so answers C and D are incorrect.

CHAPTER TWO

Fluid and Electrolyte and Acid/Base Balance

Cells maintain a balance, or *homeostasis*, by transference of fluid and electrolytes in and out of the cell. This fluid constantly bathes the cell. Although fluid and electrolyte balance and acid/base balance are separate entities, they directly relate to one another. For example, dehydration results in a decrease in the pH or *metabolic acidosis*, whereas overhydration results in an increase in the pH or *metabolic alkalosis*. To understand how this happens, let's review the basics of fluid movement across the cell membrane.

Water and small particles constantly move in and out of the semipermeable membrane in the cell through active transport and o*smosis*. This process transports nutrients, hormones, proteins, and other molecules into the cell. It also aids in the movement of waste products out of the cell for excretion from the body. Along with other functions, fluid also assists with body temperature regulation. When the client has an infection resulting in an elevated temperature, he tends to perspire. This loss of body fluid can lead to dehydration. Dehydration occurs when there is more fluid output than fluid intake.

Other body fluids exist in the form of pericardial fluid, pleural fluid, and spinal fluid. These fluids are compartmentalized into two types:

▶ **Intracellular fluid (fluid that is within the cell):** Two-thirds of the body's fluid is intracellular.

▶ **Extracellular fluid (fluid that is outside the cell):** One-third of the body's fluid is extracellular. These fluids are divided between the intravascular and interstitial spaces.

> **NOTE**
>
> Intravasular fluid (fluid that is within the vascular space) is composed of blood products, water, and electrolytes.
>
> Interstitial fluid (fluid that is within the interstitial space) is fluid found in organs or tissues.

Total Body Water Calculation

The distribution of body fluid is dependent on age and muscle mass. Total body water in an adult equals approximately 60% of total body weight in kilograms. Infants and the elderly have a higher percentage of body fluid averaging 70%–80%. Fatty tissue contains less water than muscle. For that reason, the elderly and infants lose fluid more quickly than adults and become dehydrated at a more rapid rate, as noted in Figure 2.1.

Total body water (TBW) = Extracellular space + Intracellular fluid space (ICF = 2/3 TBW)

Interstitial fluid space + Intravascular fluid space

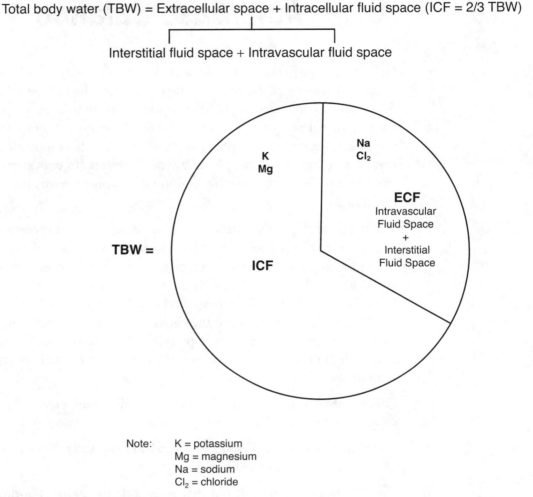

TBW =

K
Mg

Na
Cl₂

ECF
Intravascular
Fluid Space
+
Interstitial
Fluid Space

ICF

Note: K = potassium
         Mg = magnesium
         Na = sodium
         Cl₂ = chloride

FIGURE 2.1 Total body water calculations.

Diffusion is the process whereby molecules move from an area of higher concentration to an area of lower concentration. Diffusion is affected by the amount and type of molecular particles. These molecular particles are removed from body fluid as they pass through semipermeable membranes in a process known as *filtration*.

Molecular particles can also pass from an area of lower concentration to one of higher concentration by a process known as *active transport*. Diffusion and active transport allow positively charged particles, called *cations*, and negatively charged particles, called *anions*, to pass in and out of the cell. These particles are also known as *electrolytes* because they are positively or negatively charged. As cations and anions concentrate, they result in changes in the pH. Some examples of anions are bicarb (HCO_3-), chloride ($Cl-$), proteins, phosphates, and sulfates. Examples of cations are sodium ($Na+$), potassium ($K+$), magnesium ($Mg++$), and calcium ($Ca++$).

Positive and negatively charged particles are either acidic or alkaline in nature. An *acid* is a substance that releases a hydrogen ($H+$) ion when dissolved in water, and a base is a substance that binds with a hydrogen ion when released in water. Therefore, when there is a decrease in bicarbonate hydrogen ions (HCO_3-) or an accumulation of carbonic acid, *acidosis* exists; when there is an increase in bicarbonate hydrogen ions (HCO_3-) or a loss of carbonic acid, *alkalosis* exists.

This chapter discusses how these factors affect acid/base balance (pH) and the regulation of fluid and electrolytes. You will also discover the disease processes that contribute to these alterations.

The sections that follow cover the alteration in acid/base balance as it affects electrolytes and pH.

Management of the Client with Imbalances in Fluid and Electrolytes

All body fluid compartments contain water and solutes or electrolytes. The concentration of electrolytes depends on the fluid volume and the body's ability to regulate the *fluid:solvent ratio*. The electrolytes are as follows:

- ▶ Sodium (Na+)
- ▶ Potassium (K+)
- ▶ Chloride (Cl–)
- ▶ Calcium (Ca+)
- ▶ Magnesium (Mg+)
- ▶ Phosphorus (P–)
- ▶ Hydrogen (H+)
- ▶ Bicarbonate (HCO_3-)

The major intracellular electrolytes are potassium and magnesium. The major extracellular electrolytes are sodium and chloride. The majority of these electrolytes come from our food and fluid intake. Other sources that can affect electrolytes are medications, blood administration, hyperalimentation, and intravenous fluids.

Types of Intravenous Fluids

Intravenous fluid replacement changes the serum by adding electrolytes and/or fluid. There are several indications for the use of intravenous fluid replacement. When the client is unable to maintain a state of fluid and electrolytes within normal limits, the physician might need to institute fluid and electrolyte replacement. Some of the reasons that the physician might choose to use intravenous fluid replacement are surgery, trauma, gastrointestinal loss of fluid, nothing-by-mouth status, burn injuries, and bleeding. Intravenous fluids are categorized by their composition. Types of IV fluids include isotonic, hypotonic, hypertonic, and colloid. Table 2.1 discusses the type of solution, uses for these solutions, and some examples of each.

TABLE 2.1   Intravenous Fluid Solutions

Type of Solution	Uses for These Solutions	Examples
Isotonic solutions: same osmolality as the plasma.	Used to treat isotonic dehydration, burns, mild acidosis, diarrhea	0.9 sodium chloride (normal saline) Lactated Ringer's solution
Hypotonic solutions: more dilute than the plasma; contains more water than particles.	Used to treat the client with edema and kidney disease	5% dextrose and water (D5W) 0.45 sodium chloride (1/2 normal saline) 0.33 sodium chloride
*Hypertonic solutions: higher concentration of particles in solution compared to the plasma.	Used to balance the concentration of fluid and particles across fluid compartments	3% sodium chloride Protein solutions **Hyperalimentation solution 10% dextrose, 50% dextrose, 70% dextrose
Colloid solutions: contain solutes of a higher molecular weight than the serum. These include proteins and are hypertonic. They pull water from the interstitial space.	Used to mobilize third-space fluid; correct hypotension; replenish protein loss during multisystem organ failure, glomerulonephritis, renal failure, or liver disease	Plasmanate Dextran Hespan Salt-poor albumin

*Hypertonic solutions are used only to treat severe hyponatremia and negative nitrogen balance. Hyperalmentation can lead to hyperglycemia, so the client must be monitored for hyperglycemia and might need to have insulin added to the solution or given subcutaneously during the therapy.

**If the infusion is completed and there is no additional hyperalimentation on hand, the nurse should hang a bag of dextrose to prevent a hypoglycemic reaction.

How the Body Regulates Electrolytes

The body's electrolytes are regulated by

- ▶ **The kidneys:** The kidneys regulate several electrolytes either directly or indirectly. In the kidneys, the glomeruli filter the small particles and water but retain the large particles. Therefore, the waste as well as potassium and sodium are filtered out as needed and the protein—a large particle—is retained.

- ▶ **The endocrine system:** The endocrine system helps by stimulation of an antidiuretic hormone that helps keep sodium and potassium within a normal range.

- ▶ **The gastrointestinal system:** The gastrointestinal system helps by regulating gastric juices in the stomach and across the small bowel.

- ▶ **The vascular system:** The heart transports electrolytes in the blood.

Table 2.2 shows the values from several laboratory tests used to evaluate fluid and electrolytes.

TABLE 2.2   Fluid and Electrolytes Values

Test	Normal Values
Serum sodium	135–145 mEq/L
Serum potassium	3.5–5.5 mEq/L
Total serum calcium	8.5–10.5 mg/dl or 3.5–4.5 mEq/L
Serum magnesium	1.3–2.1 mEq/L

TABLE 2.2 *Continued*

Test	Normal Values
Serum phosphorus	2.5–4.5 mg/dl
Serum chloride	95–108 mEq/L
Carbon dioxide content	35–45 mEq/L
Serum osmolality	280–295 mOsm/kg
Blood urea nitrogen (BUN)	7–22 mg/dl
Serum creatinine	.6–1.35 mg/dl
Hematocrit	Male: 44–52% Females: 39–47%
Serum glucose	70–110 mg/dl
Serum albumin	3.5–5.5 g/dl
Urinary pH	4.5–8.0 mOsm/L

mEq/L (milliequivalents/liter)

mg/dl (milligram/deciliter)

mOsm/kg (milliosmoles/kilogram)

g/dl (gram/liter)

mOsm/L (milliosmoles/liter)

NOTE

Lab values vary by age and gender, and some laboratory books might have different reference values.

If there is an alteration in electrolytes, the client experiences a state of disequilibrium. The following sections discuss alterations in electrolytes.

Potassium

Potassium is the most abundant cation in the body. If damage occurs to the cell, potassium leaves the cell. This can result in hyperkalemia or hypokalemia, depending on renal function. Table 2.3 details the causes, symptoms, and treatments of hypokalemia and hyperkalemia.

TABLE 2.3   Hypokalemia and Hyperkalemia: Causes, Symptoms, and Treatments

Condition	Causes	Symptoms	Treatment
Hypokalemia	Medications such as diuretics, steroids, and digoxin	Weak pulse, lethargy, confusion, nausea, vomiting, decreased specific gravity of the urine, EKG changes such as depressed S-T segment, inverted T waves	Assess vital signs. Diet (foods high in potassium such as melons, bananas, dried fruits, and baked potatoes with the peel). IV KCl on an IV pump or IV controller. Potassium supplements with juice. Switch to potassium-sparing diuretics. Evaluate the client's intake and output. Check Mg, Cl, and protein when replacing K.

(continues)

TABLE 2.3 *Continued*

Condition	Causes	Symptoms	Treatment
Hyperkalemia	Use of salt substitutes, Addison's disease, renal failure, potassium-sparing diuretics	Muscle twitching, cramps, diarrhea, muscle weakness, paresthesia, slow pulse rate, EKG changes (tall T waves, wide QRS complexes, or prolonged P-R intervals)	Assess vital signs. Dialysis. Measure the intake and output. Calcium gluconate might be given to decrease antagonistic effects of hyperkalemia on the heart. EKG evaluation. Glucose/insulin. Na Bicarb. Polystyrene sulfonate (Kayexalate) PO or enema. Because Kayexalate is constipating, sorbitol is given to induce diarrhea. Monitor lab values. Monitor digitalis levels. Sodium (sodium and chloride go together).

CAUTION

The nurse should assess renal function prior to administering potassium. She should also administer oral liquid potassium with juice because potassium is bitter to taste. If administering with juice, remember that the more acidic juices such as orange or tomato juice are excellent choices because they mask the taste and the ascorbic acid in the juice helps with absorption of the potassium. If the nurse is administering a potassium IV, always infuse using a controller because hyperkalemia can result in cardiac arrhythmias and death (see Figures 2.2 and 2.3). Because potassium can burn the vein and cause discomfort for the client, the nurse should dilute the medication and be sure that the IV is patent.

Sodium

Sodium is the major extracellular fluid cation. The major source of sodium is dietary with a minimum sodium requirement for adults of 2 grams per day. Most adults consume more than the necessary amount. Sodium along with potassium facilitates impulse transmission in nerves and muscle fibers. Table 2.4 details the causes, symptoms, and treatments of hyponatremia (a lower-than-normal sodium level) and hypernatremia (a higher-than-normal sodium level).

TABLE 2.4 **Hyponatremia and Hypernatremia: Causes, Symptoms, and Treatments**

Condition	Causes	Symptoms	Treatment
Hyponatremia	Diuretics, wound drainage (particularly GI wounds), renal disease, hyperglycemia, congestive heart failure	Rapid pulse, generalized muscle weakness, lethargy, decreased sensorium, headache, polyuria, decreased specific gravity, dry skin and mucous membranes, anorexia, oliguria	Assess vital signs, replace Na (diet, measure IV therapy), intake and output, foods high in sodium, check complete blood count (will see increased hematocrit), check specific gravity
Hypernatremia	Renal failure, corticosteroids, Cushing's disease, excessive ingestion of sodium, fever	Decreased myocardial control, diminished cardiac output, agitation and confusion, dry and flaky skin	Assess vital signs, correct water balance, administer diuretics, measure intake and output, dialysis, treat fever, decrease sodium intake

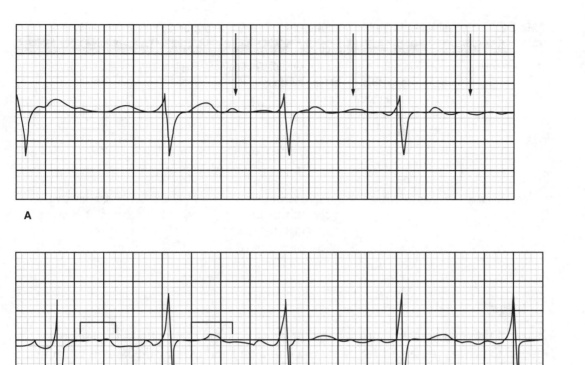

A

B

FIGURE 2.2 A: Presence of U waves (hypokalemia); B: Fusion of T and U waves with hypokalemia.

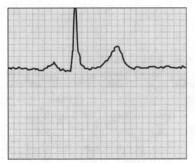

FIGURE 2.3 Hyperkalemia and the presence of peaked T waves.

Chloride

Chloride is taken in through the diet, especially from foods rich in salt. It is found in combination with sodium in the blood as sodium chloride (NaCl) and is found in the stomach as a hydrogen chloride ion. The function of chloride is to assist sodium with maintaining serum osmolarity. Chloride is regulated primarily by the kidneys and the gastrointestinal system. Table 2.5 details the causes, symptoms, and treatments of hypochloremia (a lower-than-normal chloride level) and hyperchloremia (a higher-than-normal chloride level).

TABLE 2.5 Hypochloremia and Hyperchloremia: Causes, Symptoms, and Treatments

Condition	Causes	Symptoms	Treatment
Hypochloremia	Excessive loss in vomitus, nasogastric suction, sodium deficits, losses through the renal system, excessive water within the body due to overinfusion of hypotonic solutions	Accompany loss of sodium, but are nonspecific to chloride.	Replace sodium and chloride, monitor for signs of acidosis
Hyperchloremia	Increased salt intake	No specific symptoms are associated with hyperchloremia, but symptoms usually accompany an excess of sodium.	Monitor electrolytes, monitor intake and output, decrease intake of salt

Calcium

Most of the total body calcium is found in bone. Calcium not found in the bone is bound to plasma protein. Most of the calcium found and used by the body is taken in through the diet with a recommended daily calcium intake of 800mg. For calcium to be used, vitamin D must be present. Several systems help in the regulation of calcium. The gastrointestinal system absorbs calcium, and the renal system filters calcium in the glomerulus and absorbs it in the tubules. Calcitonin (a thyroid hormone) helps to regulate calcium by moving it from plasma to bone. The parathyroid gland responds to low plasma levels by releasing parathyroid hormone. Table 2.6 details the causes, symptoms, and treatments of hypocalcemia (a lower-than-normal calcium level) and hypercalcemia (a higher-than-normal of calcium).

TABLE 2.6 Hypocalcemia and Hypercalcemia: Causes, Symptoms, and Treatments

Condition	Causes	Symptoms	Treatment
Hypocalcemia	Lactose intolerance, celiac disease, Crohn's disease, end-stage renal disease, immobility, acute pancreatitis, thyroidectomy	Increased heart rate, prolonged S-T and Q-T intervals, anxiety, psychosis, hyperactive deep tendon reflexes, positive Trousseau's sign, positive Chvostek's sign, thin hair, dental caries (see Figure 2.4 and Figure 2.5 for diagrams of Trousseau's sign and Chvostek's sign), prolonged Q-T intervals if calcium levels drop below 5.4 mg/dl (see Figure 2.6), osteoporosis, fatigue, dull skin	Assess vital signs, administer calcium supplements, administer vitamin D replacement, check EKG, seizure precautions, place tracheostomy set at bedside in case client experiences laryngeal spasms, monitor for metabolic acidosis
Hypercalcemia	Excessive intake of calcium and vitamin D, thiazide diuretics, hyperparathyroidism, glucocorticoids	Decreased clotting, tachycardia, shortened Q-T intervals (see Figure 2.7), hypertension, disorientation, muscle weakness, increased urinary output and renal calculi, hypotonic bowel sounds	Assess vital signs, advise client to decrease intake of calcium and vitamin D, maintain hydration, monitor for renal calculi, watch for digitalis intoxication, monitor for metabolic alkalosis

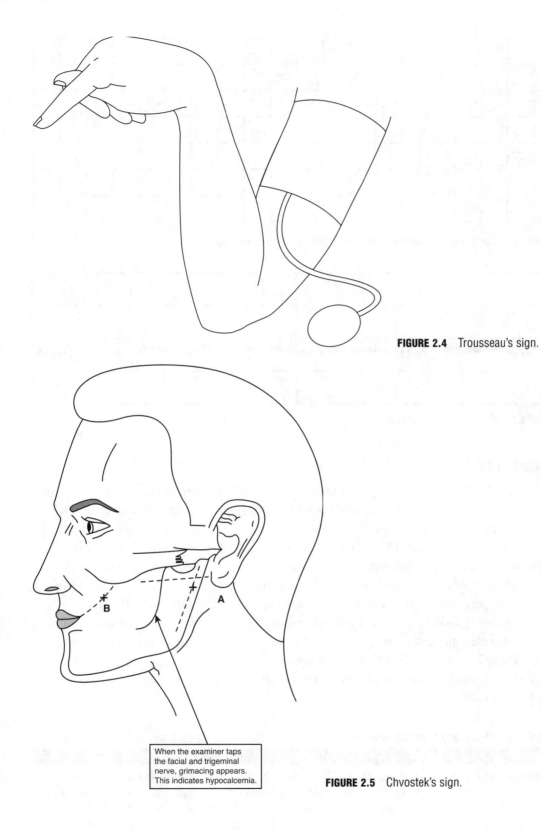

FIGURE 2.4 Trousseau's sign.

When the examiner taps the facial and trigeminal nerve, grimacing appears. This indicates hypocalcemia.

FIGURE 2.5 Chvostek's sign.

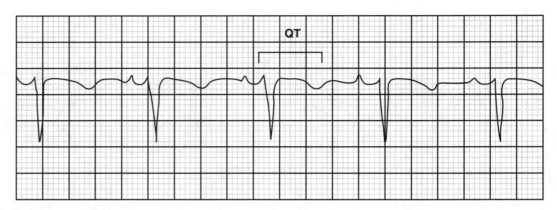

FIGURE 2.6 Prolonged Q-T intervals if calcium levels drop below 5.4 mg/dl.

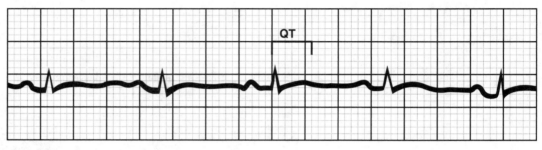

FIGURE 2.7 Shortened Q-T intervals.

Phosphorus

Phosphorus is the major anion in the intracellular fluid. Its concentration inside the cell is approximately 100 mEq/L. Normal sources of phosphorus intake include almost all foods, especially dairy products. When the phosphorus level is elevated, the calcium level is low, and vice versa. Phosphorus acts as the critical component of the phosphate buffer system that aids renal regulation of acids and bases. Phosphorus is also a major factor in bone and teeth development; cell integrity; and the function of red blood cells, muscles, and the neurologic system. It is also a component of DNA and RNA. Phosphorus is reabsorbed in the proximal end of the renal tubule along with sodium. The parathyroid gland secretes parathyroid hormone in response to serum calcium levels. Table 2.7 details the causes, symptoms, and treatments of hypophospatemia (a lower-than-normal phosphorus level) and hyperphospatemia (a higher-than-normal phosphorus level).

TABLE 2.7   Hypophospatemia and Hyperphospatemia: Causes, Symptoms, and Treatments

Condition	Causes	Symptoms	Treatment
Hypophosphatemia	Malnutrition, use of aluminum or magnesium antacids, hyperglycemia	Cardiomyopathy, shallow respirations, decreased deep tendon reflexes, irritability	Assess vital signs, eat a diet high in phosphorus, administer phospho soda, be alert for muscle weakness, perform neurological assess, monitor EKG, check calcium levels

TABLE 2.7 *Continued*

Condition	Causes	Symptoms	Treatment
Hyperphosphatemia	Decreased renal function, increased intake of phosphorus, hypoparathyroidism	Muscle spasms, positive Chvostek's and Tousseau's signs, elevated serum phosphorus levels, and hypocalcemia	Administer phosphate-binding medications such as aluminum hydroxide, administer calcium supplements along with phosphate binders, hemodialysis, instruct the client to decrease foods and medications containing phosphorus

Magnesium

Magnesium is taken in through the diet and eliminated through the kidneys and gastrointestinal system. It exerts effects on the myoneural junction affecting neuromuscular irritability. Magnesium assists with cardiac and skeletal muscle cells and contributes to vasodilation. Magnesium also activates intracellular enzymes in carbohydrate and protein synthesis. Table 2.8 details the causes, symptoms, and treatments of hypomagnesemia (lower-than-normal magnesium level) and hypermagnesemia (higher-than-normal magnesium level).

TABLE 2.8 **Hypomagnesemia and Hypermagnesemia: Causes, Symptoms, and Treatments**

Condition	Causes	Symptoms	Treatment
Hypomagnesemia	Malnutrition, diarrhea, celiac disease, Crohn's disease, foods containing citrate, alcoholism	Dysrhythmias, increased blood pressure, positive Trousseau's sign, positive Chvostek's sign, hyperreflexia, confusion	PO, IV, IM magnesium. (If IV magnesium is administered, always infuse with an IV controller.) Check renal function prior to administration of Mg (insert a Foley catheter for hourly intake and output). Oliguria indicates toxicity to magnesium. Tell the client to expect flushing, sweating, and headache. Monitor magnesium levels and vital signs hourly (decreased respiration is a sign of toxicity to magnesium). Monitor deep tendon reflexes (absence of deep tendon reflexes indicates toxicity to magnesium).
Hypermagnesemia	Increased intake of magnesium, renal failure	Bradycardia, hypotension, drowsiness, lethargy, diminished deep tendon reflexes, respiratory depression	Calcium gluconate. Ventilator support. Dialysis. Monitor hourly intake and output and hourly vital signs. Check DTRs (the absence of patella reflex is the first sign of toxicity). Check LOC. Do not assign the nursing assistant to monitor vital signs or intake and output with this client.

How the Body Regulates pH

Many organs are involved in maintaining homeostasis. They are

- Lungs
- Heart
- Pituitary
- Adrenal
- Kidneys
- Blood vessels
- Parathyroids

The body maintains its pH by keeping the ratio of HCO_3 (bicarb) to $H2CO_3$ (carbonic acid) at a proportion of 20:1. HCO_3, or bicarbonate, is a base, whereas carbonic acid is acidic. This relationship constantly changes and is compensated for by the kidneys and lungs. The normal pH is 7.35–7.45, with the ideal pH being 7.40. If the carbonic acid concentration increases, acidosis occurs and the client's pH falls below 7.40. A pH below 7.35 is considered uncompensated acidosis. If the HCO_3 concentration increases, alkalosis occurs and the client's pH rises above 7.40. A pH above 7.45 is considered uncompensated alkalosis. Figure 2.8 illustrates that alkali and acid balance in the body.

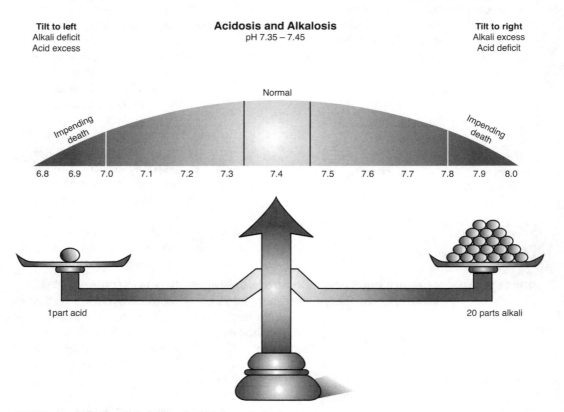

FIGURE 2.8 Indicates that alkali and acid balance in the body.

Although several systems assist with the regulation of pH, there are primarily two buffer systems of the body:

▶ **Kidneys:** By retaining or excreting $NaHCO_3$ (sodium bicarb) or by excreting acidic urine or alkaline urine. They also help by reabsorbing $NaHCO_3$– and secreting free H+ ions.

▶ **Lungs:** By retaining carbonic acid in the form of CO_2 (carbon dioxide) or by rapid respirations excreting CO_2.

When there is a problem with the capability of either the lungs or the kidneys to compensate, an alteration in this balance results.

Metabolic Acidosis

Metabolic acidosis results from a primary gain of carbonic acid or a loss of bicarbonate HCO_3 with a pH below 7.40.

Causes of Metabolic Acidosis

The following is a list of some causes of metabolic acidosis:

▶ **Certain disease states:** Disease states that create excessive metabolism of fats in the absence of usable carbohydrates, leading to the accumulation of ketoacids.

▶ **Diabetes mellitus:** Lack of usable insulin, leading to hyperglycemia and ketoacidosis.

▶ **Anorexia:** Leads to cell starvation.

▶ **Lactic acidosis:** Due to muscle and cell trauma, such as myocardial infarction.

▶ **Renal failure:** Leading to waste accumulation in the body and elevated levels of creatinine, BUN, uric acid, and ammonia. All these substances are acidic.

▶ **Diarrhea:** With a loss of HCO_3. This loss of HCO_3 and fluid leads to dehydration. When the client is dehydrated, acidosis is likely.

▶ **Excessive ingestion:** Ingestion of aspirin or other acids.

▶ **Overuse of diuretics:** Particularly non–potassium-sparing diuretics.

▶ **Overwhelming systemic infections:** Also called *sepsis*. Overwhelming infections lead to cell death and nitrogenous waste accumulation.

▶ **Terminal stages of Addison's disease:** Adrenal insufficiency results in a loss of sodium and water. This leads to a decrease in blood pressure and hypovolemic shock.

Symptoms of Metabolic Acidosis

The following list highlights symptoms of metabolic acidosis that a nurse needs to be aware of for both the NCLEX and for on-the-job observations:

▸ **Neurological:** Headache, lethargy, drowsiness, loss of consciousness, coma, death

▸ **Gastrointestinal:** Anorexia, nausea, vomiting, diarrhea, fruity breath

▸ **Respiratory:** Hyperventilation (due to stimulation of the hypothalamus)

▸ **Renal:** Polyuria and increased acid in the urine

▸ **Lab values:** Decreased pH, decreased $PaCO_2$, decreased serum CO_2, often increased potassium

Management of the Client with Metabolic Acidosis

Metabolic acidosis is rarely present without an underlying disease process. Treatment involves early diagnosis and treatment of the causative factors:

▸ **Monitor the potassium level (K+) and treat accordingly:** Because potassium (K+) is an intracellular cation, changes in potassium levels commonly occur with metabolic acidosis. The symptoms of hyperkalemia are malaise, generalized weakness, muscle irritability, flaccid paralysis, nausea, and diarrhea. If the potassium is excreted through the kidneys, hypokalemia can result. The symptoms of hypokalemia are diminished reflexes, weak pulse, depressed U waves on the ECG exam, shallow respirations, shortness of breath, and vomiting.

> **CAUTION**
>
> If administering potassium, always check renal function prior to administration. The kidney assists in regulating potassium. If the client has renal disease, life-threatening hyperkalemia can result. Because potassium is bitter to taste, it should be administered with juice. Ascorbic acid also helps with absorption of the potassium. If administering an IV, always control infusion by using an IV pump or controller. An infusion that is too rapid can result in cardiac arrythymias. If giving an IV, dilute the potassium with IV fluids to prevent hyperkalemia and burning of the vein.

▸ **Treat diabetes:** Treat with insulin for hyperglycemia; treat with glucose for hypoglycemic.

▸ **Treat hypovolemia:** Treat with a volume expander and blood transfusions, and treat shock.

▸ **Treat renal failure:** Treatment includes dialysis or transplant. The diet for renal failure clients should control protein, sodium, and fluid. Supplemental with calories and carbohydrates is suggested.

▸ **Treat lactic acidosis:** Treatment includes oxygen and $NaHCO_3$.

▸ **Treat Addison's disease:** Treatment includes cortisone preparations, a high-sodium diet, and fluids for shock.

Nursing care of the client with metabolic acidosis includes frequent monitoring of vital signs and attention to the quality of pulses, intake and output, and oral hygiene. Clients with vomiting should be positioned on their side, with a nasogastric tube to Levin suction. Those with diabetes should be taught the importance of frequent finger sticks and urine checks for hyperglycemia.

Respiratory Acidosis

Respiratory acidosis occurs when there is a decrease in the rate of ventilation to the amount of carbonic acid production. Hypoventilation leads to CO_2 accumulation and a pH value less than 7.35. Loss of the lungs as a buffer system causes the kidneys to compensate. In chronic respiratory acidosis, the kidneys attempt to compensate by retaining HCO_3.

Causes of Respiratory Acidosis

The following list highlights causes of respiratory acidosis you need to know. All these involve accumulation of carbonic acid (CO_2) and/or a lack of oxygenation:

▶ Oversedation or anesthesia.

▶ Head injury (particularly those affecting the respiratory center). This type of head injury leads to an increase in intracranial pressure and suppression of the respirations.

▶ Paralysis of the respiratory muscles (for example, Guillian-Barrè, myasthenia gravis, or spinal cord injury).

▶ Upper airway obstruction.

▶ Acute lung conditions (such as pulmonary emboli, pulmonary edema, pneumonia, or atelectasis).

▶ Chronic obstructive lung disease.

▶ Prolonged overbreathing of CO_2.

CAUTION

When the client has been given general anesthesia followed by narcotic administration, there is a risk of narcotic overdose. The nurse should keep naloxone hydrochloride (Narcan) available as the antidote for narcotic overdose. Flumazenil (Romazicon) is the antidote for the client who is admitted with an overdose of benzodiazepines such as diazepam (Valium).

Symptoms of Respiratory Acidosis

The following list gives the symptoms of respiratory acidosis you need to know:

▶ **Neurological:** Dull sensorium, restlessness, apprehension, hypersomnolence, coma

▶ **Respiratory:** Initially increased respiratory rate, perspiration, increased heart rate; later, slow respirations and periods of apnea or *Cheyne-Stokes respirations* (breathing marked by periods of apnea lasting 10–60 seconds followed gradually by hyperventilation) with resulting cyanosis

---

NOTE

Cyanosis is a late sign of hypoxia. Early signs are tachycardia and tachypnea.

Caring for the Client with Respiratory Acidosis

Care of the client with respiratory acidosis includes attention to signs of respiratory distress, maintaining a patent airway, encouraging fluids to thin secretions, and chest physiotherapy.

NOTE

Percussion, vibration, and drainage should be done on arising, before meals, and prior to bedtime. Mouth care should be offered after percussion, vibration, and drainage. Cupped hands should be used to prevent trauma to the skin and bruising.

Asthma and cystic fibrosis are common disorders that result in spasms of the airway and accumulation of mucous. These disorders are discussed at length in Chapter 16, "Care of the Pediatric Client." Because these illnesses are common in childhood, the nurse should be aware of the use of play therapy. Effective toys for children with asthma or cystic fibrosis are toys such as horns, pinwheels, and whistles. These toys prolong the expiratory phase of respirations and help with CO_2 exhalation. The best sport is swimming.

Metabolic Alkalosis

Metabolic alkalosis results from a primary gain in HCO_3 or a loss of acid that results in a pH level above 7.45.

Causes of Metabolic Alkalosis

The following list highlights causes of metabolic alkalosis that you need to be aware of:

▶ Vomiting or nasogastric suction that might lead to loss of hydrochloric acid

▶ Fistulas high in the gastrointestinal tract that might lead to a loss of hydrochloric acid

▶ Steroid therapy or Cushing's syndrome (hypersecretion of cortisol) that might lead to sodium, hydrogen (H+) ions, and fluid retention

▶ Ingestion or retention of a base (for example, calcium antacids or $NaHCO_3$)

Symptoms of Metabolic Alkalosis

Symptoms of metabolic alkalosis include

- **Neurological:** Fidgeting and twitching tremors related to hypokalemia or hyperkalemia

- **Respiratory:** Slow, shallow respirations in an attempt to retain CO_2

- **Cardiac:** Atrial tachycardia and depressed T waves related to hypokalemia

- **Gastrointestinal:** Nausea, vomiting, and diarrhea, causing loss of hydrochloric acid

- **Lab changes:** pH levels above 7.45, normal or increased CO_2, increased $NaHCO_3$

Caring for the Client with Metabolic Alkalosis

The following items are necessary care items a nurse should know for treating clients with metabolic alkalosis:

- Administering potassium replacements

- Observing for dysrhythmias

- Observing intake and output

- Assessing for neurological changes

Respiratory Alkalosis

Respiratory alkalosis relates primarily to the excessive blowing off of CO_2 through hyperventilation. Causes of respiratory alkalosis include

- Hypoxia

- Anxiety

- High altitudes

Symptoms of Respiratory Alkalosis

The following list details symptoms of respiratory alkalosis that you will need to know as a nurse and for the exam:

- **Neurological:** Numbness and tingling of hands and feet, tetany, seizures, and fainting

- **Respiratory:** Deep, rapid respirations

- **Psychological:** Anxiety, fear, and hysteria

- **Lab changes:** Increased pH, decreased $PaCO_2$, decreased K levels, and normal or decreased CO_2 levels

To correct respiratory alkalosis, the nurse must determine the cause for hyperventilation. Some causes for hyperventilation are stress and high altitudes. Treatments include

▶ Stress reduction

▶ Sedation

▶ Breathing in a paper bag to facilitate retaining CO_2 or using a re-breathing bag

▶ Decreasing the tidal volume and rate of ventilator settings

EXAM ALERT

Use the following acronym to help you with respiratory and metabolic questions on the exam:

ROME: Respiratory Opposite, Metabolic Equal

This means in respiratory disorders, the pH is opposite to the CO_2 and HCO_3; in metabolic disorders, the pH is equal to or moves in the same direction as the CO_2 and HCO_3. Here's an explanation:

▶ **Respiratory acidosis:** pH down, CO_2 up, HCO_3 up

▶ **Metabolic acidosis:** pH down, CO2 down, HCO3 down

▶ **Respiratory alkalosis:** pH up, CO2 down, HCO3 down

▶ **Metabolic alkalosis:** pH up, CO_2 up, HCO_3 up

It is important for you to understand the normal blood gas values as they relate to respiratory alkalosis and acidosis. Table 2.9 will help you to determine whether the client is in respiratory or metabolic acidosis or alkalosis.

TABLE 2.9   Determining Respiratory/Metabolic Acidosis/Alkalosis

Blood Gas Values	Acidosis	Alkalosis
pH	pH less than 7.35 (n. 7.35–7.45)	pH less than 7.35 (n. 7.35–7.45)
PaCO2 abnormal with a normal HCO3 indicates that the disorder is respiratory	PaCO2 greater than 45 is respiratory (n. 35–45 mm Hg)	PaCO2 less than 35 mm Hg is respiratory
An abnormal HCO3 with a normal PaCO2 indicates a metabolic disorder	HCO3 less than 22 mEq/L is metabolic (n. 22–26 mEq/L)	HCO3 greater than 26 mEq/L is metabolic

Case Study

A 78-year-old client with chronic obstructive pulmonary disease is admitted to the unit with acute respiratory distress. You are the nurse assigned to his care.

1. What would you expect the client's ABGs to be?

2. What part does the client's chronic pulmonary condition play in the treatment of her symptoms?

3. Which action should the nurse take to decrease the client's respiratory distress?

4. What would you expect the pH, CO_2, and HCO_3 to reveal?

(continues)

(continued)

Answers to Case Study

1. The nurse would expect the client with COPD and respiratory distress to have an alteration in blood gases. He would expect to see an elevation in CO_2 levels due to the fact that the client cannot blow off excess CO_2. This elevation in CO_2 levels will lead to acidosis. The nurse expects this acidosis to be respiratory because the underlying problem is with the lungs. The nurse would also expect the HCO_3 level to elevate if the kidneys are functioning and able to assist with compensation.

2. The nurse would see changes in the client's ability to compensate to changes in pH because her lungs are not functioning adequately. The nurse is expected to know that oxygen should be administered at no more than 3 liters per nasal cannula. To prevent hypoxia, ventilator support might also be required if the client is unable to breath at an adequate rate and depth. Bronchodilators and expectorants will most likely be ordered. The nurse should monitor the client for signs of toxicity to the bronchodilator. If the client is experiencing an underlying infection, antibiotics will be ordered. Sputum specimens will be ordered to assess the origin of any infection that might be present.

3. The nurse should talk calmly to the client and provide sedatives as ordered while remaining aware that narcotics and sedatives can suppress respiration. Maintenance of the ventilator requires extensive knowledge of the machine. The nurse must be aware of the alarm systems of these machines. Those are discussed in Chapter 5, "Care of the Client with Respiratory Disorders."

4. The nurse would expect the pH to be less than 7.35 if the client is in uncompensated acidosis, the HCO_3 to be elevated if the kidneys are compensating, and the CO_2 to be elevated because the client is having difficulty exhaling CO_2.

Key Concepts

The study of acid-base balance and electrolyte regulation are often difficult concepts for the nurse to understand. This chapter provided information in a simple to understand format. The NCLEX includes questions on this topic under the categories of physiologic integrity, safe effective care, and pharmacology. The nurse should use the key terms, diagnostic, and pharmacological agents to answer these questions.

Key Terms

- Acidosis
- Active transport
- Alkalosis
- Anions
- Cations
- Diffusion
- Electrolytes
- Filtration
- Osmosis
- pH

Diagnostic Tests

Many diagnostic exams are used to determine fluid and electrolyte and acid base balance. While reviewing these diagnostic exams, the exam reviewer should be alert for information that would be an important part of nursing care for these clients:

- Serum levels for electrolytes
- Serum pH levels
- Chest x-ray
- Urinary lab values
- Sweat analysis

Pharmacological Agents Used in the Treatment of Clients with Alterations in Fluids and Electrolytes

An integral part of care to clients with fluid and electrolyte disorders is pharmacological intervention. The nursing exam reviewer needs to focus on the drugs in Table 2.10. Included in this table are the most common side and adverse effects of drugs that are

used to treat imbalances in fluid-electrolytes and acid- base balance and pertinent
nursing care.

**TABLE 2.10   Pharmacologic Agents Used in the Treatment of Clients with Alterations in Fluid
and Electrolytes**

Name	Action	Side Effects	Nursing Care
Aluminum hydroxide (Amphoget)	Neutralizes gastric acids	Constipation, decreased phosphorus	Liquid forms are more effective than tablet. Tablets should be chewed and followed with 1/2 glass of water.
Calcium carbonate (Tums)	Rapid onset, elevates gastric pH to reduce pepsin activity	Constipation, hypercalcemia	Liquid forms are more effective than tablet. Tablets should be chewed and followed with 1/2 glass of water.
Magaldrate (Riopan)	Neutralizes gastric acid, low in sodium	Increases magnesium levels, might lead to diarrhea	Monitor the client's magnesium level during treatment.
Sodium bicarbonate	Systemic and local alkalizer	Might lead to acid rebound and alkalosis	Monitor pH of blood.
$MgSO_4$	Used to treat hypomagnesemia	Hot flashes, diarrhea	Insert Foley catheter. If given IV, obtain an IV controller. If given IV and titrate dosage, obtain hourly intake and output. Observe for toxicity (oliguria, hypotension, absence of knee jerk reflex, and decreased respiration).
Potassium chloride	Used to treat hypokalemia	Bitter to taste, irritating to the vein, may lead to cardiac arrhythmias and muscle spasms	Irritating to the vein if given IV. Never give IV push, and always obtain an IV controller for infusion. If given orally, give with fruit juice that is acidic in nature. Make sure that renal function is present.
Calcium gluconate	Used to treat magnesium toxicity and hypocalcemia	Can lead to hypercalcemia and constipation	Watch for signs of calcium renal calculi.

Apply Your Knowledge

This chapter includes much needed information to help the nurse apply knowledge of
fluid and electrolyte regulation and acid base balance to the NCLEX exam. The nurse
preparing for the licensure exam should commit to memory the normal laboratory
values, and be able to apply this knowledge to assist the client with meeting client needs.

Exam Questions

1. The client is admitted complaining of nausea and vomiting for the past three days. The doctor has ordered D51/2NS with potassium added. Which action by the nurse is most appropriate?

    A. Obtain an IV controller

    B. Check the client's vital signs hourly

    C. Check the sodium level

    D. Obtain an 18-gauge cathlon to begin the infusion

2. The client is admitted to the unit with third-degree burns to his chest and neck. The nurse should be vigilant to assess which of the following?

    A. Circulation

    B. Airway

    C. Urinary output

    D. Pain

3. The client with hypoparathyroidismhas a lack of parathyroid hormone. This client will most likely have a serum calcium level of which of the following?

    A. 3.5 mg/dl

    B. 10.9 mg/dl

    C. 14.7 mg/dl

    D. 18.5 mg/dl

4. The client is admitted with a pH of 7.30, $PaCO_2$ of 48mm Hg, and a HCO_3 of 30. The nurse assesses these findings as which of the following?

    A. Metabolic acidosis

    B. Metabolic alkalosis

    C. Respiratory acidosis

    D. Respiratory alkalosis

5. The client is admitted following a motor vehicle accident. Extensive internal bleeding is suspected. The serum pH is 7.0, the $PaCO_2$ is 32 mm/Hg and the HCO_3 is 20 mEq/dl. The nurse should assess the laboratory finding as which of the following?

   A. Metabolic acidosis

   B. Metabolic alkalosis

   C. Respiratory acidosis

   D. Respiratory alkalosis

6. Which of the following equipment should be obtained to safely administer magnesium sulfate?

   A. An internal fetal heart monitor

   B. An IV rate controller

   C. A blood administration set

   D. A wall suction device

7. Which medication can potentiate a fluid volume deficit?

   A. Insulin

   B. Inderal (propanolol)

   C. Lasix (furosemide)

   D. Valium (diazepam)

8. The client is admitted to the unit with anorexia nervosa. The nurse is aware that this client might show signs of which of the following?

   A. Metabolic alkalosis

   B. Metabolic acidosis

   C. Respiratory alkalosis

   D. Respiratory acidosis

9. The client is admitted with a blood glucose level of 545 mg/dl. Which action by the nurse indicates that the nurse is aware of the client's needs?

   A. The nurse prepares an IV of D10W.

   B. The nurse prepares to administer insulin IV.

   C. The nurse obtains NPH insulin for administration.

   D. The nurse inserts a Foley catheter.

10. The function of the lungs in acid-base balance is to perform which of the following?

   A. Control HCO_3 levels

   B. Retain or blow off CO_2

   C. Regulate potassium levels

   D. Maintain sodium levels

Answers to Exam Questions

1. Answer A is correct. If potassium is added to IV fluids, a controller is required because a too-rapid infusion of potassium can lead to cardiac arrhythmias. Answer B is incorrect only because there is no data to indicate that hourly vital signs should be obtained. Answer C is incorrect because the client has an order for D51/2NS, which is the same in saline as the client's normal sodium level. Answer D is incorrect because an 18-gauge cathlon is not required. The nurse can use any size cathlon for this infusion.

2. Answer B is correct. Because the client has burns to the chest, it is likely that he has airway difficulty. The nurse should also assess the client for smoke inhalation. Answer A is incorrect because there is no data to indicate that circulation is the priority, although this is also important. Answer C is incorrect because there is no data to indicate an alteration in renal function. Answer D is incorrect because pain, although important, is not life-threatening.

3. Answer A is correct. The normal calcium level is 8.5–10.5 mg/dl. Answers B, C, and D are incorrect because all of these findings are elevated.

4. Answer C is correct. When assessing arterial blood gases, the nurse should look at the pH. In this case, the pH is low. After assessing the pH, the nurse should look at the $PaCO_2$. In this case the $PaCO_2$ is elevated. Finally, look at the HCO_3. In this question, the HCO_3 is elevated. Answers A, B, and D are incorrect findings because they are not consistent with the lab values given in the question.

5. Answer A is correct. The client with internal bleeding will most likely have metabolic acidosis. The laboratory findings reflect this suspicion. The pH is down, the $PaCO_2$ is down, and the HCO_3 is down. Answers B, C, and D are incorrect because they are not consistent with the lab values given in the question.

6. Answer B is correct. An IV rate controller must be obtained in order to safely administer magnesium sulfate. If magnesium sulfate is administered too quickly, toxicity can result, leading to respiratory arrest. Answer A is incorrect because there is no need to insert an internal fetal monitor. If magnesium sulfate is administered to the pregnant client, an external fetal monitor is sufficient. Answer C is incorrect because a standard IV administration set is used. Answer D is incorrect because there is no specific need for wall suction to be available with the administration of magnesium sulfate.

7. Answer C is correct. Lasix is a non–potassium-sparing diuretic. This drug can potentiate fluid volume deficit. Answer A is incorrect because insulin will force fluid back into the cell and will not increase fluid volume deficit. Answer B is incorrect because Inderal (propanolol) is a beta blocker used for the treatment of hypertension and cardiac disease. Inderal does not potentiate diuresis. Answer D is incorrect because Valium (diazepam) is a phenathiazine used as an anti-anxiety medication. This drug does not potentiate fluid volume deficit.

8. Answer B is correct. The client with anorexia nervosa is in a state of negative nitrogen balance. She is likely experiencing metabolic acidosis. Answer A is incorrect because metabolic alkalosis is reflected as an increase in HCO_3. Clients with anorexia will show a deficit in HCO_3. Answers C and D are incorrect because anorexia nervosa clients have a metabolic disorder, not a respiratory disorder.

9. Answer B is correct. The client with a blood glucose of 545 mg/dl is in metabolic acidosis. An IV with insulin will be ordered. Answer A is incorrect because D10W will increase the glucose level and potentiate the client's condition. Answer C is incorrect because regular insulin will be ordered, not NPH, which is long-acting. Answer D is incorrect because although a Foley catheter might be ordered, it is not necessary for the improvement of the client's condition.

10. Answer B is correct. The lungs assist in the control of acid-base balance by regulating the amount of CO_2 that is retained or exhaled. The lungs are not in control of HCO_3, potassium, or sodium; therefore, Answers A, C, and D are incorrect.

Suggested Reading and Resources

- Hogan, Mary Ann, and Daryle Wane. *Fluid, Electrolytes, and Acid-Base Balance*. Upper Saddle River, NJ: Pearson, 2003.

- Paradiso, Catherine. *Lippincott's Review Series, Fluid and Electrolytes and Acid Base Balance*. Philadelphia: Lippincott, Prentice Hall, 1988.

- Rinehart, Sloan, Hurd, *Exam Cram NCLEX-RN*. Indianapolis: Que Publishing, 2005.

CHAPTER THREE

Care of the Client with Cardiovascular Disorders

The cardiovascular system comprises the heart and blood vessels and is responsible for the transport of oxygen and nutrients to the organ systems of the body. The heart is a cone-shaped organ made up of four chambers. The right atrium receives blood from the venous system by way of the superior and inferior vena cavae. Most of the venous blood flows through the tricuspid valve and into the right ventricle during the filling phase of cardiac contraction. The blood then moves to the lungs where carbon dioxide is released and oxygen is taken on. The left side of the heart then pumps the oxygenated blood to the body. During systole, the pressure exerted on the ventricle closes the mitral valve to prevent blood from flowing backward into the left atrium and opens the aortic valve to assist the ventricle to pump adequate oxygenated blood out of the heart into the aorta and to the body. Arteries and veins are types of blood vessels. *Arteries* transport oxygenated blood, and *veins* transport deoxygenated blood. Figure 3.1 provides an illustration of the anatomy of the heart for reference throughout the chapter.

In this chapter, you will discover diseases that affect the cardiovascular system, treatment of these diseases, and their effects on the client's general health status.

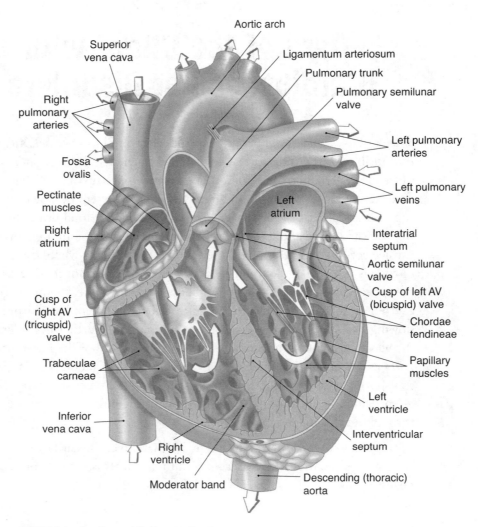

FIGURE 3.1 Anatomy of the human heart.

Hypertension

Blood pressure is the force of blood exerted on the vessel walls. *Systolic* pressure is the pressure during the contraction phase of the heart and is the top number of a blood pressure reading. *Diastolic* pressure is the pressure during the relaxation phase or filling phase of the heart and is the bottom number of a blood pressure reading. Factors that alter peripheral resistance, heart rate, and stroke volume affect the blood pressure. *Hypertension* is defined as a systolic blood pressure greater than or equal to 140 over 90 mm Hg. If the client has diabetes or kidney disease, a systolic blood pressure greater than 130 mm Hg systolic and a diastolic blood pressure of 80 mm Hg or higher is considered hypertension and should be treated. The autonomic nervous system and circulating blood volume control blood pressure. Blood pressure also directly relates to circulating hormones such as antidiuretic hormones.

Hypertension is classified as either primary or secondary. *Primary* or *essential* hypertension develops without apparent cause; *secondary* hypertension develops as the result of another illness or condition. Some examples of diseases that result in secondary hypertension are diabetes, peripheral vascular disease, renal disease, preeclampsia, coarctation of the aorta, adrenal tumors such as pheochromocytomas, brain tumors, encephalitis, and primary aldosteronism. This and other chapters of the book discuss these diseases. Obesity and smoking also affect blood pressure. Appropriate treatment of the contributing illness improves the symptoms associated with secondary hypertension.

Malignant hypertension is an extremely elevated blood pressure that often results in a cerebral vascular accident or a myocardial infarction. Secondary hypertension occurs when another disease process causes the blood pressure to elevate above normal limits. Many medications can lead to secondary hypertension. Some examples of medications that can lead to hypertension are NSAIDs (nonstreroidal anti-inflammatory drugs), cocaine, amphetamines, bronchodilators, and estrogen preparations. The client might complain of a headache, blurred vision, and dyspnea. If renal function is impaired, the client will exhibit signs of uremia. A systolic blood pressure greater than 200 mm Hg and a diastolic blood pressure greater than 150 mm Hg is life-threatening. To prevent further deterioration of the client's condition, medical personnel must implement prompt intervention.

Diagnosing the Client with Hypertension

The accuracy of a BP reading depends on the correct selection of cuff size. The bladder of the blood pressure cuff size should be sufficient to encircle the arm or thigh. According to the American Heart Association, the bladder width should be approximately 40% of the circumference or 20% wider than the diameter of the midpoint of the extremity. A too-small blood pressure cuff yields a false high reading, whereas a too-large blood pressure cuff yields a false low reading. For accuracy, the arm being used to check the blood pressure should be held at the level of the heart. The blood pressure should be taken on at least two occasions sitting, standing, and in a supine position. Diagnosis of hypertension involves conducting a comprehensive history of illness and stressors in the client's life and medications taken by the client. Laboratory studies must be completed to determine any underlying illness that might be present. Some laboratory studies indicate the presence of protein in the urine. Others studies measure serum creatinine levels, blood urea nitrogen, serum corticoids, and 17-ketosteroids in the urine. The presence of serum corticoids and 17-ketosteroids in the urine is diagnostic of Cushing's disease or increased function of the adrenal glands. A radiography study, such as an intravenous pyelography (IVP), can confirm renal disease. X-rays and computer tomography (CT) scans to determine the presence of tumors might also be ordered. An electrocardiogram (ECG) is valuable in determining the extent of cardiovascular involvement. Ultrasounds of the kidneys or the presence of adrenal tumors can also assist the physician with making a diagnosis of secondary hypertension.

Managing the Client with Hypertension

Management of hypertension includes a program of stress reduction, diet, smoking cessation, and exercise. A diet low in sodium is suggested. If the client's cholesterol level is elevated, a low-fat, low-cholesterol diet is ordered The National Cholesterol Education Program recommends screening guidelines based on

► Total serum cholesterol and high-density lipoprotein (HDL) levels in persons that do not show signs of cardiac or peripheral vascular disease

► Total serum cholesterol and HDL levels in clients with risk factors for heart disease

A desirable high-density lipoprotein level is above 40 mg/dL, and a desirable low-density lipoprotein (LDL) level is below 100 mg/dL. A triglyceride level of 150 mg/dl is considered normal. A triglyceride level of 200 mg/dL or higher indicates that the client is at risk for cardiovascular disease. Scientists recently found that homocysteine, a sulfur-containing amino acid derived from dietary protein, plays a part in the development of heart disease. A serum homocysteine level greater than 15 μmol/L is considered a risk factor.

Current studies show consumption of folic acid can help to lower homocysteine levels. Monounsaturated fats found in canola oil, olive oil, and nuts are high in polyunsaturated oils. These oils are recommended for individuals at risk for coronary disease. Eggs are saturated fats and should be limited by clients with risk for heart disease. The client is taught to avoid palm oil and coconut oil. If a change in diet does not lower the client's cholesterol level, the doctor might prescribe hyperlipidemic medications such as simvastatin (Zocor), gemfibrozil (Lopid), or ezetimibe (Zetia).

If diet, weight control, and exercise are unsuccessful in controlling the client's hypertension, the healthcare provider might need to treat the client with a diuretic and/or an antihypertensive medication. There are three types of diuretics. Thiazide diuretics such as hydrochlorothiazide (HCTZ) and Furosemide (Lasix), a loop diuretic, do not spare potassium. The nurse should assess the client taking non–potassium-sparing diuretics for signs of hypokalemia. Potassium-sparing diuretics work by inhibiting the creation of antidiuretic hormone, thereby decreasing the amount of sodium ions. Diuretics are usually prescribed to be taken in the morning on a one-time-daily regime. Taking the diuretic in the morning allows the client to sleep comfortably during the night rather than experiencing nocturia (night-time voiding).

If diuretics alone are unsuccessful in lowering the blood pressure, the physician might need to add an antihypertensive medication. Beta-adrenergic blocking agents lower blood pressure by blocking the beta receptors. Bradycardia (a heart rate of less than 60 beats per minute) and congestive heart failure are possible complications of this type of medication. The client should be taught to check his pulse rate daily and report bradycardia to the physician. Clients with a history of asthma taking beta-adrenergic agents should be watched for complications such as bronchospasms. Side effects include fatigue, weakness, sexual dysfunction, and depression. These drugs might be prescribed in combination with a diuretic.

Calcium channel blockers such as verapamil hydrochloride (Calan) lower the blood pressure by interfering with calcium ions. This reduction in calcium ions results in vasodilation.

Angiotensin-converting enzyme (ACE) inhibitors are also used alone or in combination with a diuretic. ACE inhibitors work by inhibiting angiotensin I to angiotensin II, a very potent vasoconstrictor. An example of an ACE inhibitor is lisinopril (Zestril). When the client starts taking an ACE inhibitor, he should be taught to remain in bed for three to four hours because it can cause initial postural hypotension in some clients. One of the most common side effects of ACE inhibitors is a chronic cough. If the client experiences chronic coughing, he should report it to the healthcare provider. Angioedema, a condition marked by the development of edematous and itching areas of the skin or mucous membranes and visceral edema, are signs of a reaction to the medication. If the client experiences signs of angioedema, the healthcare provider should be notified immediately.

Angiotensin II receptor antagonists block the binding of angiotensin II while allowing angiotensin-converting enzymes to function normally. This allows vasodilation to occur. An example of an angiotensin II receptor antagonist is losartan (Cozaar). They are an excellent choice for clients who experience a hacking cough when taking ACE inhibitors.

Central alpha adrenergic receptor blockers act on the central nervous system and prevent reuptake of norepinephrine. This results in vasodilation. Two examples of central apha agonists are clonidine (Catapres) and methyldopa (Aldomet). Male clients sometimes experience impotence when taking methyldopa (Aldomet). Anemia and liver dysfunction are possible complications of this category of medication.

Vasodilators such as Nitrobid and Nitropress relax and dilate smooth muscles, thereby causing a decrease in peripheral vascular resistance. Alpha-adrenergic receptor agonists dilate arterioles and veins, therefore lowering the blood pressure quickly. An example of this category of drugs is prazosin (Minipress). Most clients with essential hypertension require maintenance with medication and diet for the rest of their lives.

Coronary Artery Disease

Coronary artery disease (CAD) affects the arteries. When narrowing of the *coronary arteries* (the large arteries that supply the myocardium with blood) occurs, the result is *ischemia*. Narrowing of the coronary arteries is usually due to atherosclerosis.

Atherosclerosis and Arteriosclerosis

Though atherosclerosis and arteriosclerosis are related problems, they are not the same. *Atherosclerosis* is a *type* of arteriosclerosis involving cholesterol deposits and triglyceride deposits. Atherosclerosis is the overgrowth of smooth muscle cells. Narrowing of the blood vessels is the result of an overgrowth of intimal smooth muscle cells. This narrowing causes decreased blood flow to the heart and major organs. *Arteriosclerosis* is the thickening and hardening of the arterial walls.

Symptoms of arteriosclerosis and atherosclerosis include intermittent claudication, decreased circulation to the extremities, changes in skin color and coolness of the extremities, headaches, dizziness, and loss of memory. Factors that contribute to arteriosclerosis and atherosclerosis are age, obesity, cigarette smoking, diabetes, and familial predisposition. Treatment of systemic signs of arteriosclerosis involves weight control with a diet low in fats and cholesterol. Stress reduction and smoking cessation also help to decrease the client's risk factors.

Conduction System of the Heart

The normal conduction system of the heart is composed of the sinoatrial (SA) node located at the junction of the right atrium and the superior vena cava. The SA node is the main pacer of the heart rate. This area contains the pacing cells that initiate the contraction of the heart. The atrioventricular (AV) node is located in the interventricular septum. The AV node receives the impulse and transmits it to the bundle of His, which extends down through the ventricular septum and merges with the Purkinje fibers in the lower portion of the ventricles. Figure 3.2 shows an anatomical drawing of the conduction system of the human heart.

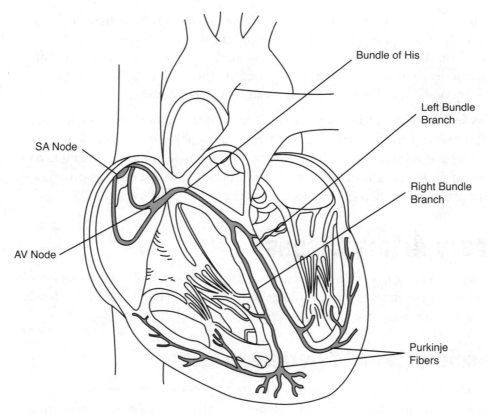

FIGURE 3.2 Electrical system of the heart.

Heart Block

Heart block can occur as the result of structural changes in the conduction system (such as myocardial infarctions, coronary artery disease, tumors, and infections of the heart) or toxic effects of drugs (such as digitalis).

First-degree AV block occurs when the SA node continues to function normally but transmission of the impulse is slowed. Because of the conduction dysfunction and ventricular depolarization, the heart beats regularly but the P-R interval is slowed. These clients are usually asymptomatic, and all impulses eventually reach the ventricles.

Second-degree heart block is a block in which some impulses reach the ventricles but others do not.

In third-degree heart block or *complete heart block*, none of the sinus impulses reach the ventricle. This results in erratic heart rates in which the sinus node and the atrioventricular nodes beat independently. The result of this type of heart block can be hypotension, seizures, cerebral ischemia, or cardiac arrest. A heart block is detected by assessing an electrocardiogram.

Toxicity to Medications

Toxicity to medications such calcium chanel blockers, betablockers, or digitalis can be associated with heart block. Clients taking betablockers or digoxin (Digitalis) should be taught to check their pulse rate and to return to their physician for regular evaluations of their digitalis levels. Judicious monitoring of the digoxin (Digitalis) blood levels is an important factor in the care of the client. The therapeutic level for digoxin (Digitalis) is 0.9–1.2 ng/mL. If the client's blood level of digoxin (Digitalis) exceeds 2.0 ng/mL, the client is considered toxic. Clients with digoxin toxicity often complain of nausea, vomiting, and seeing halos around lights. A resting pulse rate of less than 60 bpm in an adult client, less than 80 bpm in a child, and less than 100 bpm in a neonatal client should alert the nurse to the possibility of toxicity. Treatment for digitalis toxicity includes checking the potassium level because hypokalemia can contribute to digitalis toxicity. The physician often will order potassium be given IV or orally and that the digitalis be held until serum levels return to normal. Another medication, such as Isuprel or atropine, is frequently ordered to increase the heart rate. A high-fiber diet will also be ordered because constipation contributes to digitalis toxicity.

Malfunction of the Conduction System

Because a malfunction of the conduction system of the heart is the most common cause of heart block, a pacing mechanism is frequently implanted to facilitate conduction. Pacemakers can be permanent or temporary and categorized as demand or set. A *demand* pacemaker initiates an impulse if the client's heart rate falls below the prescribed beats per minute. A *set* pacemaker overrides the heart's own conduction system and delivers an impulse at the rate set by the physician. Pacemakers can be combined with an internal defibrillation device. Figure 3.3 shows a graph that depicts a pacemaker spike with a normal ECG.

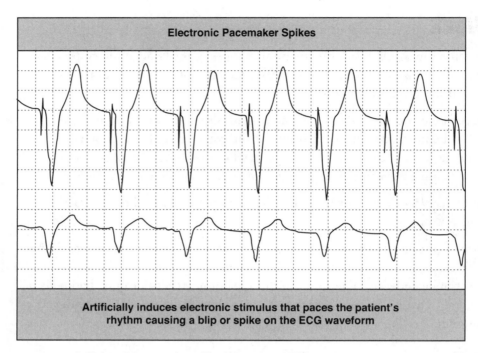

Electronic Pacemaker Spikes

Artificially induces electronic stimulus that paces the patient's rhythm causing a blip or spike on the ECG waveform

FIGURE 3.3 Indicates the pacemaker spike with a normal ECG.

Cardiac Monitoring

An ECG provides a tracing of the heart's electrical currents. Electrodes attach to the client's chest with adhesive pads and then attach to cables (*leads*) connected to the electrocardiograph machine. Leads are made up of positive and negative electrodes. The relationship between the positive and negative electrodes is responsible for the deflections seen on the ECG machine. Figure 3.4 shows the correct placement of electrodes.

The most commonly used ECG consists of 12 leads. Six leads are placed on the chest wall (V1–V6). These 6 leads provide a picture of the heart's electrical activity from a variety of positions on the chest wall. The chest leads are placed on the horizontal axis of the chest. The limb leads are attached to the arms and legs. The client should be taught to remain as still as possible during ECG assessment and should be positioned in a semireclined position. For continuous ECG monitoring, the use of limb leads is not recommended because limb movement causes an inaccurate reading.

Continuous ECG readings are most commonly done using the modified chest lead (MCL) system, which incorporates only three leads. If only three leads are used the white electrode is placed just below the mid-clavicle area on the client's right side, the black lead is placed below the mid-clavicle area on the client's left side and the positive (red) is placed at the mid-clavicular region on the client's left side. If the six lead system is used the client is monitored using the V1 position located at the fourth intercostals position at the right sternal border. V2 is placed at the fourth intercostals space at the left sternal border. V3 is located midway between V2 and V4. V5 is located at the fifth intercostals space at the anterior axillary line. V6 is located at the fifth intercostals space at the midaxillary line. The ground electrode can be placed anywhere but is usually placed under the right clavicle. For accuracy of chest lead placement, the client's chest hair should be clipped with scissors rather than shaved because shaving can abrade the skin.

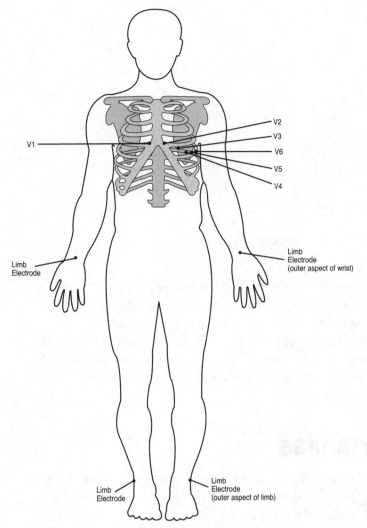

FIGURE 3.4 Twelve-lead ECG electrode placement.

Reading an Electrocardiogram

Figure 3.5 shows a normal ECG reading. The P wave represents atrial depolarization. *P-R interval* is the time required for the atria to depolarize and the impulse to travel through the conduction system to the Purkinje fibers. It is measured from the beginning of the P wave to the end of the P-R segment. The *QRS complex* represents the contraction phase of the heart and is measured from the beginning of the Q wave or R wave to the end of the S wave. The *T wave* represents repolarization of the heart.

After you look at the ECG reading for the presence of the P wave, QRS complex, and T wave, you will want to start your evaluation of the heart rate. Measure the rate by counting the number of P-P intervals or R-R intervals on a 6-second ECG strip. Timing should begin with the P wave or the QRS complex and end 30 large blocks later. The heart rate can be determined by looking at a 6-second strip, counting the cardiac cycles and the number of QRS complexes, and multiplying by 10. This method provides an accurate rate analysis of whether the rate is regular or irregular.

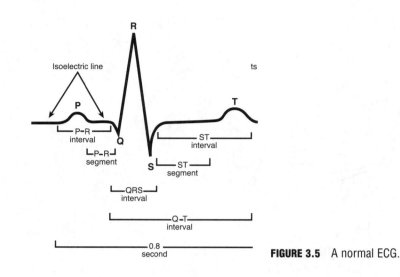

FIGURE 3.5 A normal ECG.

A normal rhythm is one that originates in the SA node, is regular, has a rate of 60–100 beats per minute (bpm), has a P wave that is consistent, and is followed by a QRS complex. ECG tracing paper measures electrical impulses in duration of time. Each large block on the paper is 5 mm or 0.20 seconds and contains 25 small blocks. Each small block on the paper is 1 mm or 0.04 seconds. The normal ECG rhythm has a P-R interval of 0.12–0.20 seconds and has a QRS complex with a duration of 0.04–0.12 seconds.

Cardiac Dysrhythmias

Cardiac dysrhythmias occur when the heart loses its regular pacing capability. They are classified according to their origins. These abnormal rhythms can be lethal or of no danger to the client's well-being. *Tachydysrhythmias* are characterized by a heart rate greater than 100 bpm. If the client has coronary artery disease, blood flow to the heart might be decreased. *Bradydysrhythmias* are characterized by a heart rate less than 60 beats per minute. Dizziness and syncopy are often the only symptoms the client notices. The client might tolerate this slow rate, or bradydysrhythmias might cause the blood pressure to be subnormal, leading to shock or ischemia. Another alteration in the normal beat the client might experience is bigeminy, a condition in which arrhythmias occur in pairs. The pairs can be junctional, atrial, or ventricular beats. A *junctional* beat is one originating at the AV and bundle of HIS. An *atrial* dysrhythmia originates in the atria of the heart, while a *ventricular* dysrhythmia originates in the ventricle of the heart.

See Table 3.1 for characteristics and treatment of atrial dysrthymias.

TABLE 3.1   Supraventricular Rhythm Characteristics

Supraventricular Rhythms	Explanation of ECG	Treatment
Normal sinus rhythm	Rhythm is regular, rate between 60 and 100 bpm	None.
Sinus tachycardia	Rhythm is regular, rate between 101 and 150 bpm	Metoporolol or atenolol.

TABLE 3.1 *Continued*

Supraventricular Rhythms	Explanation of ECG	Treatment
Sinus bradycardia	Rhythm is regular, rate below 60 bpm	Symptomatically; pacemaker insertion or atropine might be used.
Premature atrial contractions (PAC)	Rhythm is irregular, rate is variable	Usually none.
Paroxysmal supraventricular tachycardia (PSVT)	Rhythm is regular, rate between 150 and 250 bpm	Symptomatically, vagal stimulation, valsalva maneuvers (baring down as if to defecate), carotid massage, oxygen therapy, verapamil (Calan), procainamide HCL (Pronestyl), or other medications to slow the heart rate.
Atrial flutter	Rhythm usually regular, rate as high as 240 bpm with the ventricular rate dependent on the amount of AV block. Atrial flutter rates are typically slower than Afib. Aflutter typically stays </= 150, where Afib ventricular rates are higher.	Synchronized cardioversion with medications to slow the ventricular rate. Carduac ablation is a procedure performed either during an electrophysiology study or in the surgery in which the source of an arrhythmia is mapped, localized, and then destroyed. Ablation is accomplished by applying radio frequency (RF) energy, applying electrical energy, or freezing the area responsible for the arrhythmia. This creates a small scar that is electrically inactive and thus incapable of generating heart arrhythmias. Cardioversion can be used for both atrial flutter and atrial fibrillation if the patient is symptomatic.
Atrial fibrillation	Rhythm irregular, rate too rapid to count, ventricular rate between 100 and 180 bpm Atrial flutter rates are typically slower than Afib. Aflutter typically stays </= 150, where Afib ventricular rates are higher.	Synchronized cardioversion with medication to slow the ventricular rate. Cardioversion is used for both if patients are symptomatic. This is an important concept because two million+ people live with Afib.

Unlike tachydysrhythmias and bradydysrhythmias, which usually originate in the atria, ventricular dysrhythmias are life-threatening and their impulses originate in the ventricles.

Ventricular Tachycardia

Ventricular rhythms are those originating in the ventricle. These rhythms can result in decreased oxygen perfusion to the body and possible death. See Table 3.2 for the characteristics and treatment of ventricular rhythms.

TABLE 3.2   Ventricular Rhythm Characteristics

Ventricular Rhythms	Explanation of ECG	Treatment
Premature ventricular contractions (PVC)	Rhythm irregular, rhythm originates in the ventricle with a compensatory pause after the complex	Instruct the client to avoid stimulants; medications to slow rate are used if PVCs persist. Examples of drugs used are lidocaine, quinidine, propanolol, phennytoin, and others.
Ventricular tachycardia (See later in this chapter.)	Rhythm regular, rate 150–250 bpm, no P wave, bizarre wide QRS complex	Medications such as lidocaine, procainamide, amiodarone, and others are used to slow the rate. Streptokinase can be used because clot formation is a risk. Defibrillation if the client loses consciousness.
Ventricular fibrillation (See the section "Ventricular Fibrillation" that follows.)	Rhythm irregular, rate too rapid to count, bizarre complex with no identifiable PQRS complex	Defibrillation immediately to prevent standstill.
Heart blocks Example: Third-degree AV block (complete)	Rhythm regular, rate 60–100 bpm atrial, 15–60 bpm ventricular	Pacemaker insertion.

Because ventricular tachycardia is lethal, the item writers for NCLEX might ask the student to identify an ECG rhythm. It should be noted that ventricular tachycardia is a rapid irregular rhythm with the absence of a P wave. The rate can be 250 bpm, and the SA node continues to discharge independently of the ventricle. Ventricular tachycardia is often associated with valvular heart disease, heart failure, hypomagnesium, hypotension, and ventricular aneurysms. Figure 3.6 shows an ECG reading indicative of ventricular tachycardia.

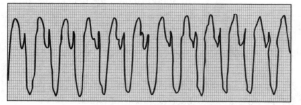

FIGURE 3.6   Evidence of ventricular tachycardia.

Ventricular Fibrillation

Ventricular fibrillation (V-fib) s the primary mechanism associated with sudden cardiac arrest. This disorganized chaotic rhythm results in a lack of pumping activity of the heart. Without effective pumping, no oxygen is sent to the brain and other vital organs. If this condition is not corrected quickly, the client's heart stops beating and asystole is seen on the ECG. The client quickly becomes faint, loses consciousness, and becomes pulseless. Hypotension, or a lack of blood pressure, and abnormal heart sounds are present. Figure 3.7 shows a diagram of the chaotic rhythms typical with V-fib.

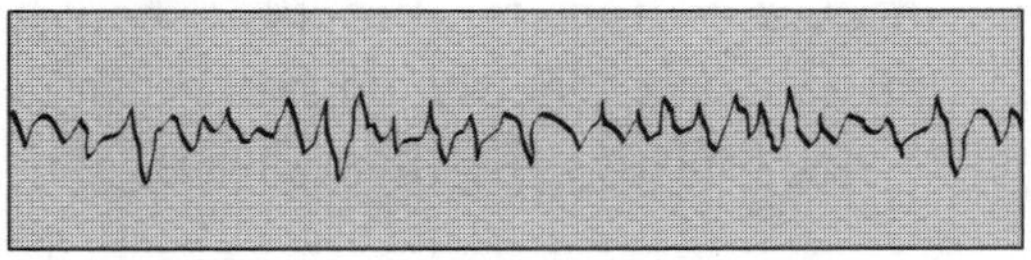

Ventricular Fibrillation
(V Fib)

"sawtooth"

FIGURE 3.7 Ventricular fibrillation diagram.

Treatment of ventricular fibrillation is done with a defibrillator set at approximately 200 joules. Three quick, successive shocks are delivered, with the third at 360 joules. If a defibrillator is not readily available, a precordial thump can be delivered. If cardiac arrest occurs, the nurse should initiate cardiopulmonary resuscitation (CPR) and be ready to administer first-line drugs such as epinephrine or vasopressin (Pitressin).

Internal Pacemaker/Internal Cardiac Defibrillators

An internally implanted pacemaker and cardioverter/defibrillator are used to treat ventricular fibrillation, heart block, and other dysrhythmias. These devices are usually implanted on the client's left side and are connected to the myocardium with electrical leads. If the client experiences fibrillation or ventricular tachycardia, the defibrillator delivers a shock to the heart and corrects the pattern. The internal defibrillator also records dysrhythmias the client has experienced so that the physician is aware of her condition. A client with an internal cardiac defibrillator or permanent pacemaker should be taught to

- ▶ Avoid elevating her left arm above her head for approximately two weeks or until the doctor instructs otherwise.

- ▶ Wear a medic alert stating that a pacemaker/internal defibrillator is implanted. Identification will alert the healthcare worker so that alterations in care can be made.

- ▶ Take pulse for one full minute and report the rate to the physician.

- ▶ Avoid applying pressure over the pacemaker. Pressure on the defibrillator or pacemaker can interfere with the electrical leads.

- ▶ Inform her dentist of the presence of a pacemaker because electrical devices are often used in dentistry.

- ▶ Avoid having a magnetic resonance imaging (MRI) test. Magnetic resonance interferes with the electrical impulse of the implant.

- ▶ Avoid close contact with electrical appliances, electrical or gasoline engines, transmitter towers, antitheft devices, metal detectors, and welding equipment because they can interfere with conduction.

- ▶ Be careful when using microwaves. Microwaves are generally safe for use, but the client should be taught to stand approximately five feet away from the device while cooking.

- ▶ Report fever, redness, swelling, or soreness at the implantation site.

- ▶ If beeping tones are heard coming from the internal defibrillator, the client should immediately move away from any electromagnetic source. She should stand clear from other people because shock can affect anyone touching the client during defibrillation.

- ▶ Report dizziness, fainting, weakness, blackouts, or a rapid pulse rate. The client will most likely be told not to drive a car for approximately three months after the internal defibrillator is inserted to evaluate any dysrhythmias.

- ▶ Report persistent hiccupping because this can indicate a misfiring of the pacemaker/internal defibrillator.

NOTE

Because a dye is used to identify the correct placement of the leads, the client should be questioned regarding allergies to shell fish or iodine and advised to force fluids after the procedure and report any difficulty voiding. (See the section "Cardiac Catheterization" for detailed instructions.)

Cardiopulmonary Resuscitation

The American Heart Association (AHA) releases new guidelines for professionals and the public periodically, so the graduate nurse should review the changes for updates.

NOTE

Refer to the AHA website (http://www.americanheart.org/) for current updates.

Angina Pectoris

Angina pectoris is defined as chest pain caused by disruption of the balance and demand for oxygen by the heart. This disruption results in a lack of oxygen to the myocardium.

Several risk factors predispose the client to cardiac ischemia. These include

- ▶ Hypertension

- ▶ Hyperlipidemia

- ▶ Smoking

- ▶ Obesity

- ▶ Familial history

- ▶ Diabetes

- ▶ Anemia

- ▶ Stress

The nurse caring for the client with angina pectoris assesses the type and location of chest pain. The pain is usually located in the substernal to retrosternal area and radiates down the left arm and to the jaw or shoulder. The onset is usually precipitated by a large meal, exertion, stress, anxiety, smoking, alcohol, or drugs, and it might occur immediately when the client awakens. The client's skin is usually warm and dry, but it might be cool and clammy. He might complain of nausea and vomiting and gripping chest pain.

Women, the elderly, and diabetics frequently do not complain of the typical chest pain associated with angina but might complain of fatigue and shortness of breath. An ECG often reveals S-T segment depressions and T wave inversion; there might be S-T depressions. If the client has Prinzmetal's angina, there might be an elevation in the S-T segment.

Treatment involves the application of oxygen and the administration of nitroglycerine sublingually, topically, or intravenously. The client should be taught to take one nitroglycerine tablet sublingually every five minutes, not to exceed three tablets. If the first tablet does not relieve the pain, a second can be taken. If the pain is still not relieved after taking three tablets, the client should go directly to the hospital or call an ambulance. The client should be taught to replenish his supply of nitroglycerine every six months and protect the pills from light by leaving them in the brown bottle. It is important for the client to understand that light decreases the effectiveness of nitroglycerine. Nitroglycerine patches and creams should be applied to dry skin. The site should be relatively free of hair. Most resources suggest that the hair should be clipped and not shaved because shaving might abrade the skin and cause irritation. Nurses should always wear gloves when applying nitroglycerine creams or patches to prevent application of the medication to themselves. Intravenous nitroglycerine must be administered with an infusion rate controller.

Myocardial Infarction

When there is a disruption in blood supply to the myocardium, the client is considered to have had a *myocardial infarction (MI)*. Factors contributing to diminished blood flow to the heart include arteriosclerosis, emboli, thrombus, shock, and hemorrhage. If circulation is not quickly restored to the heart, the muscle becomes necrotic. Hypoxia from ischemia can lead to vasodilation. Acidosis associated with electrolyte imbalances often occurs, and the client can slip into cardiogenic shock. The most common site for an MI is the left ventricle. Only 10% of clients report the classic symptoms of a myocardial infarction. Women often fail to report chest pain and, if they do, they might tell the nurse that the pain is beneath the shoulder or in the back. Clients with diabetes have fewer pain receptors and might report little or no pain.

The most commonly reported signs and symptoms associated with MI include

▶ Substernal pain or pain over the precordium for a duration greater than 15 minutes

- Pain that is described as heavy, vise-like, and radiating down the left arm
- Pain that begins spontaneously and is not relieved by nitroglycerin or rest
- Pain that radiates to the jaw and neck
- Pain that is accompanied by shortness of breath, pallor, diaphoresis, dizziness, nausea, and vomiting
- Increased heart rate, decreased blood pressure, increased temperature, and increased respiratory rate

Diagnosis of Myocardial Infarction

The diagnosis of a myocardial infarction is made by looking at both the ECG and the cardiac profile that consist of the cardiac enzymes. The following are the most commonly used diagnostic tools for determining the type and severity of MI:

- Electrocardiogram
- Serum enzymes and isoenzymes

Other tests that are useful in providing a complete picture of the client's condition are white blood cell count (WBC), sedimentations rate, and blood urea nitrogen (BUN).

The best serum enzymes used to diagnose myocardial infarction are creatine kinase (CKMB), troponin T and 1, CRP, and LDH. The enzyme CKMB is released when there is damage to the myocardium and elevates quickly. The troponin T and 1 are specific to striated muscle and are often used to determine the severity of the attack. Troponin T and 1 can remain elevated for as long as two weeks following the MI. C-reactive protein (CRP) levels are used with the CKMB to determine whether the client has had an acute MI and the severity of the infarction. Lactic dehydrogenase (LDH) is a nonspecific enzyme that is elevated with any muscle trauma.

Management of a Client with Myocardial Infarction

Management of a client with myocardial infarction includes monitoring of blood pressure, oxygen levels, and pulmonary artery wedge pressures. Because the blood pressure can fall rapidly, medication such as dopamine is prescribed. Other medications are ordered to relieve pain and to vasodilate the coronary vessels—for example, morphine sulfate IV is ordered for pain. Thrombolytics, such as streptokinase, will most likely be ordered. Early diagnosis and treatment significantly improve the client's prognosis.

A client suffering an MI can present with dysrhythmias. Ventricular dysrhythmias, such as ventricular tachycardia or fibrillation, can lead to cardiac stand-still and death if not treated quickly.

A client with an MI should be given small, frequent meals. The diet should be low in sodium, fat, and cholesterol. Adequate amounts of fluid and fiber are encouraged to

prevent constipation. Stool softeners are often ordered to prevent straining during defecation. Post-MI teaching should stress the importance of a regular program of exercise,
stress reduction, regular bowel elimination, and cessation of smoking. Because caffeine
causes vasoconstriction, caffeine intake should be limited. The client can resume sexual
activity in six weeks or when he is able to climb a flight of stairs without experiencing
chest pain. Medications such as sildenafil (Viagra) can lead to uncontrolled hypotension
if taken within 24 hours of taking a nitrite. For this reason, the client should be taught
to consult the cardiologist if taking Viagra. Clients should be taught not to perform the
Valsalva maneuver or bend at the waist to retrieve items from the floor. Placing items in
top drawers helps to prevent increased intrathoracic pressure. The client will probably
be discharged on an anticoagulant such as aspirin, clopidogrel (Plavix), enoxaparin
(Lovenox), or sodium warfarin (Coumadin).

NOTE

Anticoagulants such as heparin are used to decrease the potential for clotting. The nurse should check the
partial thromboplastin time (PTT). The normal control level in the most common laboratory ranges is
approximately 30–60 seconds, however these values vary. Some text record levels are as low as 24
seconds. The graduate should refer to his or her laboratory. The therapeutic bleeding time should be from
one and a half to two times the control. The medication should be injected in the abdomen 2" from the
umbilicus using a tuberculin syringe. Do not aspirate or massage. The antidote for heparin derivatives is
protamine sulfate. Anticoagulants should be stopped at least 24 hours prior to surgery and are usually
restarted 12–24 hours following surgery.

If Coumadin (sodium warfarin) is ordered, the nurse should check the prothrombin time (PT). The control
level for a prothrombin time is 10–12 seconds. The therapeutic level for Coumadin should be from one
and a half to two times the control. The antidote for Coumadin is vitamin K. The international normalizing
ratio (INR) is usually done for oral anticoagulants. The therapeutic range is 2–3. If the level exceeds 7,
watch for spontaneous bleeding.

Exercise Electrocardiography

An exercise electrocardiography test, also known as a stress test or an exercise tolerance
test, helps to determine the function of the heart during exercise. The client is
instructed to eat a light meal and refrain from smoking or consuming caffeine the
morning of the test. Prior to the test, the cardiologist assesses the heart using an ECG
tracing and blood pressure monitor. The client then walks on a treadmill or bicycles at a
steadily progressing rate of speed of 1–10 miles per hour and can also be adjusted from
flat to inclined. She is asked to report any shortness of breath or chest pain.
Abnormalities can then be assessed. The client continues the test until

▶ A rapid heart rate is reached and maintained.

▶ Signs or symptoms of chest pain; fatigue; or extreme dyspnea, hypotension, or
ventricular dyshythmias appear on the ECG.

▶ S-T segment depressions are noted on the ECG.

The client remains in the unit for approximately 2 hours after the test to ensure that
there are no signs of hypotension or cardiac dyshythmias. Due to mobility problems,
some clients are not able to walk on the treadmill or ride the bicycle. Cardiac stimulants

are then used to induce stress. An example of medications used is dobutamine (Dobutrex).

A Cardiolite scan is a scan that is done in conjunction with a treadmill test and ECG to evaluate the blood flow though the coronary arteries. Cardiolite is injected intravenously to stress the heart. Persantine, a vasodilator, is used for non-stress studies. Persantine is injected to increase blood flow to the coronary vessels while scans are done to determine blockages.

Echocardiography

Echocardiography is a noninvasive test used to determine the size of the ventricle, the functionality of the valves, and the size of the heart. There is no special preparation for the echocardiography, and this test takes only 30–60 minutes.

A transesophageal echocardiography is a more invasive method of assessing the structures of the heart. A transducer is placed into the esophagus or stomach to examine the posterior cardiac structures. This test requires that the client be NPO after midnight the day of the procedure and the throat be anesthetized to prevent stimulation of the gag reflex. Following the procedure, the client is checked for return of the gag reflex prior to offering food.

> **NOTE**
>
> The gag reflex is stimulated by placing a tongue blade on the back of the throat. Absence of the gag reflex increases the chances of aspirating liquids.

Cardiac Catheterization

Cardiac catheterization is used to detect blockages associated with myocardial infarction and dysrhythmias. Cardiac catheterization, as with any other dye procedure, requires a signed consent. This procedure can also accompany percutaneous transluminal coronary angioplasty. Prior to and following this procedure, the nurse should

- Assess for allergy to iodine or shellfish.

- Maintain the client on bed rest for approximately 8 hours after the test with the leg straight.

- Maintain pressure on the access site after the procedure for at least five minutes or until no signs of bleeding are noted. Many cardiologists use a device called an Angio-Seal to prevent bleeding at the insertion site. The device creates a mechanical seal, anchoring a collagen sponge to the site. The sponge absorbs in 60–90 days.

- Use pressure dressing and/or ice packs to control bleeding after the test.

- Check distal pulses after the procedure because diminished pulses can indicate a hematoma at the catheter insertion site and should be reported immediately.

- Force fluids to clear dye from the body after the test.

Percutaneous Transluminal Coronary Angioplasty and Stent Placement

A percutaneous transluminal coronary angioplasty (PTCA) is a less invasive procedure than coronary artery bypass surgery. Many clients are relieved of chest pain following this procedure. Clients with noncalcified lesions, such as plaque, benefit most from a PTCA and recover relatively quickly.

During the procedure, the physician inserts a catheter while visualizing the coronary vessels. A balloon is used to push plaque into the wall of the vessel. A stent might be placed in the artery following the balloon procedure. A *stent* is a mesh tube usually made of stainless steel. This tube is inserted following an angioplasty to prevent restenosis.

When angiography indicates that the vessel is 50% or more open, the procedure is complete. An IV of heparin is administered in a continuous infusion. Nitroglycerin or sublingual nifedipine is often given to prevent spasms of the myocardium.

Coronary Artery Bypass Graft

When the client does not respond to medical management of a coronary artery occlusion and is experiencing chest pain, the physician might perform coronary artery bypass graft (CABG) surgery. The decision to perform a CABG is based on the results of the cardiac catheterization. If the client has the following symptoms, a CABG might be performed:

▶ Angina with greater than 50% blockage of the left anterior descending artery

▶ Unstable angina with two vessels severely blocked or three vessels moderately blocked

▶ Ischemia of the myocardium

▶ Has had an acute MI

▶ Has ischemia following an angiography or PTCA

During a coronary artery bypass, a sternal incision is performed and a donor vessel is removed. A common vessel used to bypass a blockage in the coronary arteries is the saphenous vein located in the back of the leg. Other vessels, such as the mammary artery and the radial artery, can also be used to bypass the blockage. When the client is asleep, the team of surgeons goes to work harvesting the donor vessel while another team prepares to place the client on the cardiopulmonary bypass machine. The cardiopulmonary bypass machine is often used to provide oxygen to the lungs and body during the time that the heart is stopped. Blood that is heparinized and oxygenated passes through the machine and back into the client by way of the ascending aortic vessel or the femoral artery. While the client is on the bypass machine, the core body temperature is lowered to approximately 85° F. The rationale for lowering the body temperature is that the body's oxygen needs are lowered when the body is cooled. A potassium solution is used to bathe the heart and help prevent dysrhythmias. After the heart is stopped, the surgeon anastomoses the donor vessel to bypass the blockage. When the procedure is finished, the client is warmed and transported to the intensive care unit.

The family should be instructed that the client will return to the intensive care unit with several tubes and monitors. The client will have mediastinal tubes to drain fluid from the chest cavity. The client might also have chest tubes if reinflation of the lungs was necessary. If the client bleeds and the blood is not drained from the mediastinal area, fluid accumulates around the heart and cardiac tamponade results. If this occurs, the myocardium becomes compressed and the accumulated fluid prevents the filling of the ventricles and decreases cardiac output.

During surgery, a Swan-Ganz catheter for monitoring central venous pressure—pulmonary artery wedge pressure—is inserted in the pulmonary artery. A radial arterial blood pressure monitor is inserted to measure vital changes in the client's blood pressure. An ECG monitor and oxygen saturation monitor are also used. Other tubes used to assess and stabilize the client are a nasogastric tube to decompress the stomach, an endotracheal tube to assist in ventilation, and a Foley catheter to measure hourly urinary output.

Some clients experience depression or recurrent nightmares following coronary artery bypass graft surgery. The family should be made aware that this is a common problem and that this problem might take several months to resolve. It is important to tell both the family and the patient to notify the surgeon if these experiences occur.

Cardiac rehabilitation is recommended and includes a plan of exercise, diet, and weight reduction. The client should be taught regarding the need to stop smoking and to moderate alcohol consumption. Drugs used to treat sexual dysfunction, such as Viagra, should not be used within 24 hours of taking nitrites such as nitroglycerine.

Congestive Heart Failure

Congestive heart failure occurs when the heart loses its ability to meet the body's need for oxygen. There are some terms that you will want to be familiar with when reviewing the concept of congestive heart failure. One of these is *cardiac output*, which is the amount of blood that is pumped in one minute. If you multiply the stroke volume by the heart rate, you can determine the cardiac output. The ejection fraction is the stroke volume divided by the end-diastolic blood volume. A healthy heart has an ejection fraction of about 50%–70%.

Another term that is helpful to understand when discussing congestive heart failure is *preload*, which is the amount of stretch needed to force blood out of the ventricle at the end of diastole. Finally, *afterload* should be understood because it is the amount of force needed to eject the blood volume. If the heart is overstretched for an extended period of time, it loses its ability to recoil. Eventually, the heart fails and congestive heart failure occurs.

The nurse must monitor for signs of fluid retention. Left-sided congestive heart failure occurs when fluid backs into the lungs and is indicated by rales and blood-tinged sputum. Distended neck veins are also an indication, as well as the client's report of needing to sleep on two or more pillows to breathe. Right-sided congestive heart failure occurs when the blood backs into the periphery causing peripheral edema, fatigue, and asites.

The diagnosis of congestive heart failure is made by the evaluation of the signs and symptoms as well as looking at the client's cardiac function. This can be done by evaluation of the blood pressure, ECG, central venous pressure monitoring (CVP), pulmonary artery wedge pressure monitoring (PAWP), echocardiogram, atrial natriuretic peptide (ANP), and brain natriaretic peptide (BNP). The normal BNP is less than 100; a poor prognosis is determined if the levels exceed 400–500. Electrolyte evaluation is also helpful in determining the clinical picture. See Table 3.3 for other diagnostic tools used to determine congestive heart failure.

TABLE 3.3 Diagnostic Tools for Determining Congestive Heart Failure

Diagnostic tools Used to Diagnose Congestive Heart Failure	Prepation for Exam	Normals
Electrolytes	Usual NPO.	Sodium: 135–145 mEq/L Potassium: 3.5–5.5 mEq/L Chloride: 95–105 mEq/L Magnesium: 1.5–2.5 mEq/L Calcium: 8.5–10.5 mg/dl
ANP BNP	NPO for ANP.	Insignificant amounts present in normal individuals Less than 100
Urinalysis	None.	Check for creatinine:.6–1.35 mg/dL
Liver function	None.	BUN, ALT, AST, serum bilirubin (see the "Fast Facts" element later in the book)
Arterial blood gases	None.	
Chest x-ray	None.	
ECG	None.	
echocardiogram	None.	
Cardiac CTA (computer tomography angiography)	Preparation is the same as other CAT scans (allergies to dyes, renal function studies done prior to test, force fluids after the exam). (See Chapter 13, "Care of the Client with Neoplastic Disorders.")	To determine size and shape of heart as well as blockages

Treatment includes diuretics, inotropes, and a diet low in sodium. Other drugs might be prescribed to decrease preload and afterload. IV nitroprusside, milrinone (Primacor), or nitroglycerine nesiritide (natrecor) are often used to improve cardiac contractility. Other medications used to support cardiac function are angiotensin receptor blockers (ARBs), angiotensin-converting enzyme (ACE) inhibitors, and beta blockers. These drugs increase the force of cardiac contractions. Morphine is often given to control pain as well as to treat preload.

If the client's condition deteriorates despite the use of cardiac drugs, an intra-aortic balloon pump (IABP) might be inserted. The IABP is inserted into the aorta. A balloon is inflated during diastole and deflates just before systole, reducing the afterload. This procedure improves perfusion to the heart, brain, and lungs and decreases perfusion to the kidneys and lower extremities.

With use of the IABP, perfusion to the lower extremities and the kidneys could be impeded during inflation of the pump, so assessment of pulses distal to the pump insertion site and assessment of urinary output is essential.

Other management of CHF includes monitoring O_2 saturation, pulmonary artery wedge pressure (PAWP) with an attempt to maintain PAWP between 15 and 20 mm/hg. Central venous pressure (CVP) monitoring and frequent checking of vital signs are essential nursing care for the client with CHF.

Cardiogenic Shock

There are three types of shock: cardiogenic shock, hypovolemic shock, and vasogenic or neurogenic shock. *Cardiogenic shock* occurs when the heart fails to pump enough blood to perfuse the tissues adequately. This type of shock might be due to a myocardial infarction, congestive heart failure, pericarditis, cardiac tamponade (fluid around the heart that constricts the heart muscle), severe vascular disease, or rupture of an abdominal aortic aneurysm. Hypovolemic shock occurs when there is insufficient blood flow to maintain blood pressure. This results in decreased oxygenation to vital organs. Vasogenic or neurogenic shock occurs when there is trauma to the brain or spinal cord. This results in shock secondary to the nervous systems inability to maintain vasoconstriction. Chapter 10, "Care of the Client with Neurological Disorders," discussses this type of shock in detail. In cardiogenic shock, there is necrosis of more than 40% of the left ventricle. Most of the clients experiencing cardiogenic shock complain of chest pain. Other symptoms include

- ► Hypotension
- ► Tachycardia
- ► Tachypnea
- ► Frothy, pink-tinged sputum
- ► Restlessness
- ► Orthopnea
- ► Oliguria

The mortality rate of cardiogenic shock is extremely high if it is not detected early. Treatment includes oxygen therapy. The physician will order a pain reliever such as morphine sulfate. Diuretics, nitroglycerin, and other medications to reduce the preload are also parts of the treatment. In extreme situations, an intra-aortic balloon pump might be used to decrease the workload of the heart.

Aneurysms

An *aneurysm* is a ballooning of an artery, as illustrated in Figure 3.8. The greatest risk for these clients is rupture and hemorrhage. Aneurysms can occur in any artery in the body and might be the result of congenital malformations, arteriosclerosis, or secondary to hypertension. There are several types of aneurysms:

▸ **Fusiform:** Affects the entire circumference of the artery

▸ **Saccular:** An outpouching affecting only one portion of the artery

▸ **Dissecting:** Bleeding into the wall of the vessel

The client with an abdominal aortic aneurysm will frequently complain of feeling "my heart beating in my abdomen" or low back pain. Any such complaint should be further evaluated. On auscultation of the abdomen, a bruit could be heard. Diagnosis can be made by ultrasound, computer tomography, arteriogram, or abdominal x-rays. If the aneurysm is found to be 5 centimeters or more, surgery might be scheduled. During surgery, the aorta is clamped above and below and a donor vessel is anastamosed in place. When the client returns from surgery, pulses distal to the site should be assessed. Because the blood supply is stopped to the kidneys and lower extremities during surgery the nurse should monitor the client's renal function and pedal pulses. Endovascular stents are now being used to relieve pressure on the aneurysm and reinforce the weakened vessel. The stents are threaded through an incision in the femoral artery. Postoperative care is much the same as that of the client who has undergone a cardiac catheterization.

CAUTION

Do not palpate the mass because pressure on the weakened vessel can lead to rupture and hemorrhage.

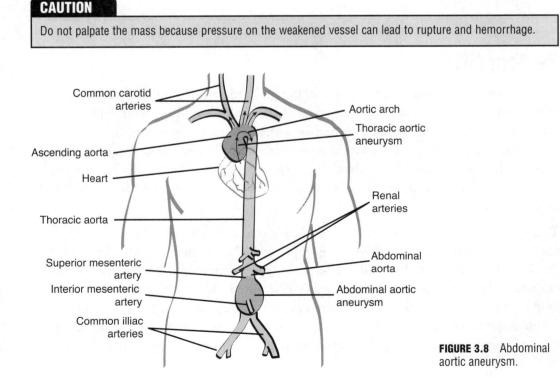

FIGURE 3.8 Abdominal aortic aneurysm.

Inflammatory Diseases of the Heart

Inflammatory and infectious diseases of the heart often are a result of systemic infections that affect the heart. Inflammation and infection might involve the endocardium, pericardium, valves, or the entire heart.

Infective Endocarditis

Infective endocarditis, also known as *bacterial endocarditis*, is usually the result of a bacterial infections or collagen diseases. Endocarditis can also be related to cancer metastasis. As a result, the heart is damaged and signs of cardiac decompensation results. The client commonly complains of shortness of breath, fatigue, and chest pain. On assessment, the nurse might note distended neck veins, a friction rub, or a cardiac murmur.

Treatment involves treating the underlying cause with antibiotics, anti-inflammatory drugs, and oxygen therapy. Bed rest is recommended until symptoms subside. If the valve is severely damaged by infection, a valve replacement might have to be performed. Replacement valves are xenograft (bovine [cow] or porcine [pig]), cadaver, or mechanical. If the client elects to have a mechanical valve replacement, he will have to take anticoagulants for life. Following surgery, the nurse must be alert for signs of complications. These include decreased cardiac output or heart failure, infection, and bleeding. The physician often will prescribe digoxin, anticoagulants, cortisone, and antibiotics postoperatively.

> **NOTE**
> A porcine valve will probably be rejected by a client who is Jewish. A bovine valve will probably be rejected by a client who is Hindu.

Pericarditis

Pericarditis is an inflammatory condition of the pericardium, which is the membrane sac around the heart. Symptoms include chest pain, difficulty breathing, fever, and orthopnea. Clients with chronic constrictive pericarditis show signs of right-sided congestive heart failure. During auscultation, the nurse will likely note a pericardial friction rub. Laboratory findings might show an elevated white cell count. ECG changes consist of an S-T segment and T wave elevation. The echocardiogram often shows pericardial effusion.

Treatment includes use of nonsteroidal anti-inflammatory drugs to relieve pain. The nurse should monitor the client for signs of pericardial effusion and cardiac tamponade that include jugular vein distention, *paradoxical pulses* (systolic blood pressure higher on expiration than on inspiration), decreased cardiac output, and muffled heart sounds. If fluid accumulates in an amount that causes cardiac constriction, the physician might decide to perform a pericardiocentesis to relieve the pressure around the heart. Using an echocardiogram or fluoroscopic monitor, the physician inserts a large-bore needle into the pericardial sac. After the procedure, the nurse should monitor the client's vital signs and heart sounds. In severe cases, the pericardium might be removed.

> **NOTE**
>
> If the client has a history of pericarditis or endocarditis and is scheduled for dental work or surgery, he will be placed on prophylactic antibiotics to prevent exacerbation of his condition.

Peripheral Vascular Disease

The term *peripheral vascular disease (PVD)* refers to a group of diseases affecting both arteries and veins. Peripheral arterial disease, the most common type of PVD, often results in amputations, kidney disease, and ulcerations of the extremities.

Signs of PVD include a decrease in pulse rate and strength, coldness of the extremity, intermittent claudication (burning and leg cramps on ambulation), and swelling of the extremity.

Treatment is aimed at restoring blood flow to the extremity. Treatment includes a sympathectomy to sever the sympathetic ganglia as a last resort, thereby resulting in vasodilation, vasodilating drugs, or femoropopliteal bypass graft. Stents can also be used to maintain an open vessel. If circulation to the extremity is not restored, an amputation might be required.

Femoral Popliteal Bypass Graft

When blood flow to the lower legs is interrupted, the physician might elect to perform to bypass the blockage in the vessel. Grafts can be made of synthetic materials such as polytetrafluoroethylene, Gore-Tex, and Dacron. Donor vessels can also be used.

Preoperatively, the nurse should assess renal function and the extremity for pulses, swelling, color, and temperature. If a Doppler is used to obtain pulses, it should be documented. Dye studies might also be ordered prior to the surgical procedure to determine the extent of the disease. The nurse should assess the client's potential complications associated with dye procedures such as allergies to iodine.

During the graft procedure, the doctor removes the donor vessel and bypasses the block vessel. Following the procedure, the nurse should monitor for signs of graft rejection. These include redness at the site and signs of decreased oxygenation to the extremity. Other nursing care includes

- ► Assessing color, temperature, and pulses
- ► Assessing for pain and administering medication as ordered
- ► Monitoring blood pressure
- ► Instructing the client to keep the affected extremity straight and not to cross her legs at the knee
- ► Assessing the incision site

At discharge, the client should be taught to avoid sitting at a 90° angle or crossing her legs and to take anticoagulants and vasodilating drugs as ordered. She should also be taught to report signs of decreased oxygenation to the extremity. If graft occlusion does occur, a thrombectomy, tissue plasminogen activator, or revision of the graft might be required.

Varicose Veins/Thrombophlebitis

Varicose veins occur when the valves that serve to push blood back to the heart become weak and collapse. This allows blood to pool in the vein. The stagnant blood often clots and occlusion of the vessel occurs. If a clot breaks loose, it can travel to the heart or lungs resulting in a pulmonary emboli.

Thrombophlebitis occurs when a vein becomes inflamed and a clot forms. Most thrombophlebitis occurs in the lower extremities, with the saphenous vein being the most commonly affected vein. *Homan's sign* is an assessment tool used for many years by healthcare workers to detect deep vein thrombi. It is considered positive if the client complains of pain on dorsiflexion of the foot. Homan's sign should not be performed routinely because it can cause a clot to be dislodged and lead to a pulmonary emboli. If a diagnosis of thrombophlebitis is made, the client should be placed on bed rest with warm, moist compresses to the leg. An anticoagulant such as enoxaparin, heparin, or sodium warfarin is ordered, and the client is monitored for complications such as cellulitis. If cellulitis is present, antibiotics are ordered.

Antithrombolitic stockings or compression devices are ordered to prevent venous stasis. When antithrombolitic stockings are applied, the client should be in bed for a minimum of 30 minutes prior to applying the stockings. The circumference and length of the extremity should be measured to prevent rolling down of the stocking and a tourniquet effect.

Raynaud's Phenomenon

Raynaud's phenomenon occurs when there are vascular vasospasms brought on by exposure to cold. Raynaud's is more common in women and has been linked to decreasing estrogen levels. The most commonly affected areas are the hands, nose, and ears. Management includes preventing exposure, stopping smoking, and using vasodilators. The client should be encouraged to wear mittens when outside in cold weather.

Buerger's Disease

Buerger's disease (thromboangiitis obliterans) results when spasms of the arteries and veins occur primarily in the lower extremities. These spasms result in blood clot formations and eventually destruction of the vessels. Symptoms associated with Buerger's disease include pallor of the extremities progressing to cyanosis, pain, and paresthesia. As time progresses, trophic changes occur in the extremities. Management of the client with Buerger's disease involves the use of Buerger-Allen exercises, vasodilators, and oxygenation. The client should be encouraged to stop smoking.

Case Study

A 77-year-old male reports to the doctor with complaints of shortness of breath. On examination, the doctor finds crackles in the base of the lungs, a blood pressure of 190/96, slight tachycardia, and a gain of 10 pounds since the client's last check-up. The doctor has prescribed medications to control congestive heart failure. Total cholesterol is 240 mg/dL, sodium is 160 mEq/L, and potassium is 3.6 mEq/L.

1. Are the client's symptoms consistent with right-sided or left-sided congestive heart failure?

2. What medications should the nurse expect the doctor to prescribe?

3. How does the client's blood pressure affect the client's cardiac function?

4. What is the correlation between the weight gain and the congestive heart failure?

5. If the client's congestive heart failure is not treated effectively, what will be the result?

6. What dietary management should be implemented for this client?

Answers to Case Study

1. The client's symptoms are consistent with both right-sided and left-sided congestive heart failure. In left-sided congestive heart failure, fluid backs up into the lungs. In right-sided congestive heart failure, fluid backs up into the extremities. This client has weight gain, shortness of breath, and crackles heard on auscultation.

2. Treatment of congestive heart failure is threefold. The diet should be low in sodium. Medications include diuretics such as furosemide (Lasix), milrinone (Primacor), or nesiritide (Natrecor) to increase cardiac output and pain management with morphine.

3. The client's blood pressure is elevated. The peripheral resistance increases the workload on the heart. This further compromises the cardiac condition and leads to worsening congestive heart failure.

4. The weight gain is a sign of right-sided congestive heart failure.

5. If the client's congestive heart failure is not treated, the client's lungs will fill with fluid. Fluid in the lungs prevents oxygenation to the heart and brain. The heart failure will worsen and lead to death.

6. The dietary management is low sodium, low fat, and low cholesterol.

Key Concepts

This chapter discussed the most common types of cardiovascular problems. The key concepts will help the nursing graduate on the NCLEX by focusing on the most commonly used key terms, diagnostic exams, and pharmacological agents used to treat these problems. This section is covered on the NCLEX in the area of physiological integrity.

Key Terms

- ▶ Aneurysms
- ▶ Angina pectoris
- ▶ Angioplasty
- ▶ Atherosclerosis
- ▶ Blood pressure
- ▶ Buerger's disease
- ▶ Cardiac catheterization
- ▶ Cardiac tamponade
- ▶ Cardiopulmonary resuscitation
- ▶ Cholesterol
- ▶ Conduction system of the heart
- ▶ Congestive heart failure
- ▶ Coronary artery bypass graft
- ▶ Defibrillation
- ▶ Diastole
- ▶ Electrocardiogram
- ▶ Heart block
- ▶ Hypertension
- ▶ Implantable cardioverter
- ▶ Myocardial infarction
- ▶ Pacemaker
- ▶ Raynaud's phenomenon
- ▶ Systole
- ▶ Thrombophlebitis

▸ Varicose veins

▸ Ventricular fibrillation

▸ Ventricular tachycardia

Diagnostics

The exam reviewer should be knowledgeable of the preparation and care of clients receiving exams to diagnose cardiovascular problems. While reviewing these diagnostic exams, the exam reviewer should be alert for information that would be an important part of nursing care for these clients. The pertinent labs and exams are as follows:

▸ Cardiac catheterization

▸ Cardiac CTA

▸ Cardiac profile

▸ Central venous pressure monitoring

▸ Chest x-ray

▸ Clotting studies

▸ Complete blood count

▸ Doppler studies

▸ Dye studies for cardiac functions

▸ Echocardiogram

▸ Electrophysiologic studies

▸ Exercise Tolerance Test

▸ Fluoroscopy

▸ MRI

▸ Oxygen saturation levels

▸ Serum cholesterol and triglycerides

▸ Serum electrolytes

▸ Thallium scans

▸ Ultrasonography

▸ Vital signs

Pharmacological Agents Used in the Treatment of Clients with Cardiovascular Disorders

An integral part of care to clients with cardiovascular disorders is pharmacological intervention. These medications provide an improvement or cure of the clients' cardiac problems. Table 3.4 lists examples of drugs used to treat cardiovascular disorders, but it is not inclusive of all the medications used to treat disorders of the cardiovascular system. Please refer to your pharmacology text for further information.

The nursing exam reviewer needs to focus on the drugs in Table 3.4. Included in this table are the most common side and adverse effects and pertinent nursing care.

TABLE 3.4   Pharmacologic Agents Used in the Treatment of Clients with Cardiovascular Disorders

Drug	Action	Side Effect	Nursing Care
Thiazide diuretics; examples of this category of drugs are chlorothiazide (Diuril) and hydrochlorothiazide (Esidrix, HCTZ)	This category of drugs increases excretion of water and sodium by inhibiting resorption in the early distal tubule. They are used for hypertension, edema in congestive heart failure, and intraocular pressure in glaucoma.	Electrolyte imbalances; dehydration; can lead to increases in urea and gout.	Check potassium levels and teach the client to increase his consumption of potassium-rich foods. Care should be taken when administering diuretics to the elderly. The client should be taught to take the medication in the morning to prevent nocturia.
Loop diuretics; an example of this type of drug is furosemide (Lasix)	Loop diuretcs inhibit resorption of sodium and chloride in the loop of Henle.	Same.	Same.
Osmotic diuretics; examples of this type of drug are mannitol (Mannitol, Osmitrol, Resectisol), Urea	Osmotic diuretics increase the osmotic pressure of glomerular filtrate, thereby decreasing absorption of sodium.	Same.	Same.
Potassium-sparing diuretics; examples of this type of drug are spironolactone (Aldactone), amiloride, (Midamore), and triamterene (Dyrenium)	Acts on the distal tubule to inhibit reabsorption of sodium and chloride and increase potassium retention. This drug is used for hypertension and for Cushing's disease. It can be used in some CHF patients.	Can cause nausea and vomiting; lead to electrolyte imbalances such as hyperkalemia and hyponatremia; and lead to liver and blood dyscrasias. Gynecomastia is important to note.	Because this drug category is potassium sparing, there is no need to increase potassium in the diet. Teach the client to take the drug with food to decrease gastrointestinal upset. Teach the client to avoid prolonged exposure to the sunlight because photosensitivity can occur.

TABLE 3.4 *Continued*

Drug	Action	Side Effect	Nursing Care
Beta-adrenergic blockers;examples of this category of drugs are propanolol (Inderal), metopolol (Lopressor), and nadolol (Corgard)	Used to treat hypertension, ventricular dysrhythmias, and angina pectoris. Nonselective blockers produce a fall in blood pressure with reflex tachycardia or bradycaria through a mixture of B-blocking effects. Selective B-blockers compete for stimulation of B-receptors in cardiac smooth muscles.	Orthostatic hypotension; bradycardia; diarrhea; nausea; and vomiting.	Teach the client to rise slowly. It should be used with caution in the elderly. It can lead to congestive heart failure so the client should be taught to report signs of edema. It should be used with caution in a client with diabetes, pregnancy, or asthma. It can lead to CHF if given in a client with acute failure.
Calcium channel blockers;examples of this type of drug are nifedipine (Procardia, Adalat), verapamil (Calan, Isoptin), and amilodipine (Norvasc)	This category of drugs is used to treat hypertension and dysrhythmias, unstable angina, and stable angina. They produce calcium ion influx across the cell membrane in cardiac and vascular smooth muscle. They dilate coronary arteries, slow the SA and AV nodes, and dilate peripheral arteries.	The most common side effects are dysthythmias and edema. The client might experience a headache, fatigue, drowsiness, or facial flushing. These drugs should not be used in clients with second- and third-degree heart block, or cardiogenic shock because they can worsen symptoms. Caution should be taken when treating the client with congestive heart failure with this category of drugs.	Teach the client to check his pulse and to report signs of edema such as shortness of breath and swelling of the feet or ankles.
Angiotensin-converting enzyme inhibitors; examples of this type of drug are captopril (Capoten) and lisinopril (Zestril)	This type of drug acts by selectively suppressing rennin-angiotensin I to angiotensin II. They dilate the arteries and veins.	The most common side effect is hypotension. These drugs can cause a cough and angioedema. The nurse should check creatinine levels and electrolytes to ensure that the client is not experiencing hyperkalemia.	The client should be taught to remain at rest for approximately 30 minutes after taking the first dose to prevent orthostatic hypotension. The client should be taught to report signs of renal failure.

(continues)

TABLE 3.4 *Continued*

Drug	Action	Side Effect	Nursing Care
Central alpha agonists (also known as central acting adrenergics); examples of this type of drug are clinidine hcl (Catapress) and methylodopa (Aldomet)	This type of drug acts by inhibiting the sympathetic vasomotor center in the central nervous system. These drugs are used to treat hypertension.	Can lead to hypotension and bradycardia and reduce cardiac output. Assess blood studies such as neutrophils, platelets, and renal function. Can cause dry mouth and allergic reactions such as rash, fever, and pruritis, urticaria.	Aldomet can cause impotence and turn the urine dark brown when it is exposed to sunlight. Also can cause photosensitivity. Administer this category of drugs prior to meals.
Vasodilators; an examples of this type of drug are hydralazine (Apresoline), nitroglyerine (Tridil), and nitroprusside (Nipride)	This type of drug is used to treat hypertension and congestive heart failure.	Can lead to nasal congestion, muscle cramps, cardiac palpitations, headaches, dizziness, nausea, vomiting, anorexia, diarrhea, or constipation. Can cause a rash or pruritus and lead to bone marrow suppression. This drug category is contraindicated in a client with coronary artery disease and concomitant rheumatic fever.	Teach the client to take with food to decrease gastrointestinal upset. Notify the healthcare provider if the client experiences fever, severe fatigue, or muscle or joint pain. Teach the client to rise slowly to prevent orthostatic hypotension and notify the healthcare provider if the client is pregnant. Nitroglyerine should be protected from light.
Alpha-receptor blockers; an example of this type of drug is doxazosin (Cardura)	Causes pheripheral blood vessels to dilate, lowers peripheral resistance, and reduces blood pressure. Also used to increase urinary outflow in a client with prostate disease.	Can lead to dizziness, headaches, drowsiness, vertigo, and weakness. This type of drug can also cause nausea, vomiting, and abdominal pain. If the client is allergic to quinazolines, there might be a cross-allergic reaction. Use with caution in a pregnant client.	Take the first dose at bedtime to prevent ortostatic hypotention.

TABLE 3.4 *Continued*

Drug	Action	Side Effect	Nursing Care
Angiotensin receptor blockers; examples of this type of drugs are valsartan (Diovan), losartan (Cozaar), candesartan (Atacand), and telmisartan (Micardis)	Blocks the vasoconstrictor and aldosterone-sereting effects of angiotensin II and blocks the binding of angiotensin II to the AT1 receptor found in tissue. Used to treat hypertension.	Can lead to dizziness, insomnia, anxiety, diarrhea, dyspepsia, anorexia, and vomiting. Can cause myalgia. Can cause a cough, but this is less common in this category of drugs than in the ACE drugs. Increases digoxin levels. The nurse should check the creatinine levels for renal function. Should be used cautiously with NSAIDs.	Teach the client to notify the health care provider if the he develops mouth sores, fever, or edema.
Antidyshythmics; examples of this type of drug are quinidine sulfate (Quinadine), procainamide hydrochloride (Pronestyl), lidocaine (Xylocaine), amiodarone hydrochloride (Cordarone), atropine sulfate, magnesium sulfate, and digoxin (Lanoxin)	These drugs are used to treat atrial fibrillation, premature atrial tachycardia, ventricular tachycardia, and atrial flutter.	Can cause headaches, dizziness, confusion, psychosis, tinnitus, blurred vision, hearing loss, and disturbed color vision. Nausea, vomiting, diarrhea, and anorexia have been reported. Bone marrow suppression can occur. Quinidine can interact with other drugs such as digoxin (Digitalis) and anticoagulants such as sodium warfarin (Coumadin). Quinidine can prolong Q-T intervals. This drug can also cause Torsades de pointes (a very rapid ventricular tachycardia characterized by a gradually changing QRS complex). Lidocaine should be administered in a glass bottle with an infusion pump. Amiodarone HCL (Cordarone) can lead to pulmonary fibrosis. Atropine can lead to tachycardia, and magnesium sulfate can lead to hypermagnesemia. Digoxin can lead to bradycardia.	Monitor heart rate and rhythm. Teach the client taking anti- dyshythmics to report hearing difficulty, tell the doctor if she could be pregnant, and report visual disturbances and renal disease. The client taking digoxin should be taught to take her pulse for one full minute prior to taking the medication. If the pulse rate is below 60 in the adult, 80 in the child, or 100 in the neonate, the dose should be held and the healthcare provider notified. Signs of toxicity to digoxin are bradycardia, halos around lights, and nausea. The therapeutic level of digoxin is .5-2 ng/ml.

(continues)

TABLE 3.4 *Continued*

Drug	Action	Side Effect	Nursing Care
Anticoagulants; examples of anticoagulants are warfarin sodium (Coumadin), heparin, and enoxaparin (Lovenox)	Used to treat clients with thrombosis, warfarin sodium decreases vitamin K absorption thereby prolonging the bleeding time. Heparin and the derivatives of heparin prolong the bleeding time by interfering with the clotting chain.	Hemorrhage, agranulocytosis, leucopenia, eosinophilia, and thrombocytopenia. These drugs interact with salicylates (aspirin), steroids, and NSAIDs. Blood studies such as partial prothrombin time (PTT) and protime (PT) should be done periodically during the course of treatment. The client should report a rash, a fever, or urticaria. The antidote for coumadin is vitamin K, and the antidote for heparin is protamine sulfate.	Teach the client to report to the dentist that he is taking an anticoagulant prior to any dental work. Watch for bleeding during flossing, tooth brushing, shaving, and so on. Teach the client the correct method of taking the drug. Heparin and heparin derivatives should be given in the abdomen approximately two inches from umbilicus. The client should not aspirate after the injection or massage the area. Teach the client regarding signs of prolonged bleeding times. If the client is taking coumadin, he should be taught to limit the intake of dark green leafy foods such as turnip greens. Other example of foods to limit are cabbage, rhubarb, and cauliflower because these foods contain high amounts of vitamin K. The client should report to the doctor the intake of herbals, vitamin E, or green tea because these substances prolong bleeding times. Note: enoxaparin (Lovenox) doses are based on weight and renal function.
Thrombolytics; examples of thrombolytics are streptokinase (Streptase), t-PA (Tissue Plasminogen Activator), and abbokinase (Urokinase)	These drugs are used to destroy a clot. They are used to treat coronary thrombus, acute ischemia associated with a hemorrhagic cerebro vascular accident, or deep vein thrombus.	Clients with a history of streptococcal infections might not respond to treatment with streptokinase because antibodies are present. The nurse should check the bleeding times.	Instruct the client to report signs of bleeding. A drug history should check for previous use of streptokinase because many physicians do not recommend that this drug be repeated only every two years. (This might be a life-long restriction.) Also, check for recent stroke history.

Apply Your Knowledge

The nurse reviewing for the licensure exam must be able to apple knowledge to meet client needs. Utilization of information found in this chapter will help the graduate to answer questions found on the NCLEX.

Exam Questions

1. A client with hypertension has an order for furosemide. Which lab finding should be reported to the physician?

    A. Phosphorus 2.5 mEq/L

    B. Potassium 1.8 mEq/L

    C. Calcium 9.4 mg/dl

    D. Magnesium 2.4 mEq/L

2. A client is admitted with a diagnosis of heart block. The nurse is aware that the pacemaker of the heart is the:

    A. AV node

    B. Purkinje fibers

    C. SA node

    D. Bundle of His

3. A client is being treated with nitroprusside (Nitropress). The nurse is aware that this medication:

    A. Should be protected from light

    B. Is a non–potassium-sparing diuretic

    C. Causes vasoconstriction

    D. Decreases circulation to the extremities

4. A client being treated with lisinopril (Zestril) develops a hacking cough. The nurse should tell the client to:

    A. Take half the dose to control the problem

    B. Take cough medication to control the problem

    C. Stop the medication

    D. Report the problem to the doctor

5. An elderly client taking digitalis develops constipation. The nurse is aware that constipation in a client taking digitalis might:

    A. Develop an elevated digitalis level

    B. Have a decrease in the digitalis levels

    C. Have alterations in sodium levels

    D. Develop tachycardia

6. The client is suspected of having had a myocardium infarction. Which diagnostic finding is most significant?

    A. LDH

    B. Troponin

    C. Creatinine

    D. AST

7. A client with an internally implanted defibrillator should be taught to:

    A. Avoid driving a car

    B. Avoid eating food cooked in a microwave

    C. Refrain from using a cellular phone

    D. Report swelling at the site

8. A client is scheduled for a cardiac catheterization. Following the procedure, the nurse should:

    A. Assess for allergy to iodine

    B. Check pulses proximal to the site

    C. Assess the urinary output

    D. Check to ensure that the client has a consent form signed

9. A client with Buerger's disease complains of pain in the lower extremities. The nurse is aware that Buerger's disease is also called:

    A. Pheochromocytoma

    B. Intermittent claudication

    C. Kawasaki disease

    D. Thromboangiitis obliterans

10. A client with an abdominal aneurysm frequently complains of:

    A. A headache

    B. Shortness of breath only during sleep

    C. Lower back pain

    D. Difficulty voiding

Answers to Exam Questions

1. Answer B is correct. The client taking furosemide is at risk for developing hypokalemia (decreased potassium) because this drug is a non–potassium-sparing diuretic. A potassium level of 1.8 is extremely low and might result in cardiac dysrhythmias. Answers A, C, and D are incorrect because the levels noted in the question are within normal levels.

2. Answer C is correct. The pacemaker of the heart is the SA node. The impulse moves from the SA node to the AV node on to the right and left bundle branches and finally to the Purkinje fibers. This makes answers A, B, and D incorrect.

3. Answer A is correct. Nitroglycerine preparations should be protected from light because light decreases the effectiveness of this category of medication. Answer B is incorrect because Nitropress is not a diuretic. Answer C is incorrect because Nitropress is a vasodilator, not a vasoconstrictor. Answer D is incorrect because nitroglycerine does not decrease circulation to the extremities.

4. Answer D is correct. A hacking cough is a common side effect and should be reported to the doctor. The client should not be told to half the dose because this can result in an elevated blood pressure, so answer A is incorrect. Answer B is incorrect because taking a cough medication will mask the symptom of a possible allergic reaction. Answer C is incorrect because, although the client stops taking the medication, this answer states that the client can report the finding to the doctor at the time of the scheduled visit. She should report this finding immediately.

5. Answer A is correct. The client taking digitalis should avoid constipation because constipation can lead to digitalis toxicity. Answer B is incorrect because constipation will not lead to a decrease in the digitalis levels. Answer C is incorrect because constipation does not result in alterations in the sodium level. Answer D is incorrect because digitalis toxicity will result in brachycardia, not tachycardia.

6. Answer B is correct. The best diagnostic tool for confirming that the client has experienced a myocardial infarction is the troponin level. Another lab value associated with a myocardial infarction is the CKMB. Answer A is incorrect because the LDH is also elevated in clients with muscle trauma not associated with an MI. Answer C is incorrect because the creatinine level indicates renal function. Answer D is incorrect because the AST level is elevated with gallbladder and liver disease as well as muscle inflammation.

7. Answer D is correct. The client with an implantable defibrillator should report redness, pain, and swelling at the site of the implant. Answers A, B, and C are incorrect because the client can drive a car, eat food cooked in a microwave, and use a cellular phone. The client probably will be told to wait three months to drive a car. He should put his food in the microwave and step five feet away from the microwave during cooking. A cellular phone can be used but should be held in the right hand.

8. Answer C is correct. The dye used in the procedure can cause a decrease in renal function. The client's renal function should be assessed and changes reported to the doctor immediately. Answer A is incorrect because the client's allergies should be checked prior to the procedure, not after the procedure. The femoral artery is commonly used as the site for a catheterization. Answer B is incorrect because the pulses should be checked distal to the site. Answer D is incorrect because the permit should be signed prior to the procedure.

9. Answer D is correct. The other name for Buerger's disease is thromboangiitis obliterans. Answer A is incorrect because pheochromocytoma is an adrenal tumor. Answer B is incorrect because intermittent claudication is pain in an extremity when walking. Answer C is incorrect because Kawasaki disease is an acute vasculitis that can result in an aneurysm in the thoracic area.

10. Answer C is correct. Clients with abdominal aortic aneurysms often complain of nausea, lower back pain, and feeling their heart beat in the abdomen. Answer A is incorrect because a headache is a symptom of a cerebral aneurysm. Answer B is incorrect because, although the client with an abdominal aneurysm might have shortness of breath, this symptom is not particular to during sleep. Answer D is incorrect because difficulty voiding is not associated with an abdominal aneurysm.

Suggested Reading and Resources

▶ Deglin, Judith H., and April H. Vallerand. *Davis Drug Guide for Nurses*. Philadelphia: F. A. Davis, 2009.

▶ Ignatavicius, D., and Workman, S. *Medical Surgical Nursing: Critical Thinking for Collaborative Care.* 5th ed. Philadelphia: Elsevier, 2007.

▶ Rinehart, Wilda, Diann Sloan, and Clara Hurd. *NCLEX Exam Cram*. Indianapolis: Que Publishing, 2005.

▶ *Taber's Cyclopedic Medical Dictionary*. Philadelphia: F. A. Davis, 2005.

▶ Vanetzian, Eleanor V. *Critical Thinking: An Interactive Tool for Learning Medical-Surgical Nursing*. Philadelphia: F.A. Davis, 2005.

CHAPTER FOUR

Care of the Client with Endocrine Disorders

The endocrine system comprises glands distributed throughout the body and is responsible for secretion and regulation of hormones. The endocrine system is made up of the following glands:

▶ Pituitary gland

▶ Adrenal glands

▶ Thyroid gland

▶ Pancreas

▶ Parathyroid glands

▶ Ovaries, testes

Figure 4.1 shows a diagram of the endocrine system.

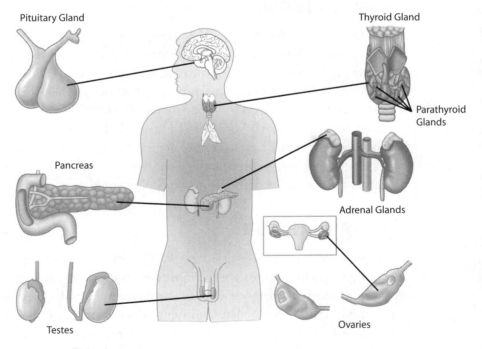

FIGURE 4.1   Endocrine system.

Problems with the endocrine system occur when there is too little production or excess production of hormones. The onset of endocrine disorders can appear suddenly and be life-threatening, or can appear gradually.

Pituitary Gland

The pituitary gland is located in the center of the skull at the base of the brain in an area called the *sella turcica*. The anterior lobe, or *adenohypophysis*, secretes hormones that stimulate the thyroid gland, adrenal cortex, and the gonads. Growth hormone and prolactin are produced by the anterior pituitary gland. The posterior pituitary produces vasopressin or antidiuretic hormone and oxytocin. The neurohypophysis, the posterior portion of the pituitary gland, stores hormones produced by the hypothalamus. The hypothalamus shares a circulatory system with the anterior pituitary gland. This system of nerve fibers connects the hypothalamus to the posterior pituitary and controls how the central nervous system and endocrine system regulate homeostasis of the body. Other functions of the pituitary gland include development of the gonads, regulation of heart rate and rhythm, and assisting other glands in the endocrine system to secrete their hormones.

The diagnosis of pituitary disorders is done by evaluating various hormone levels. Computer tomography (CT) scans, x-rays, and magnetic resonance imaging (MRI) can also identify tumors. Alterations in pituitary function are often reflected as a decrease in pituitary hormone or an increase in pituitary hormone. The sections that follow discuss these problems in greater detail.

Hypopituitarism

Hypopituitarism is a disorder in which there is a deficiency of one or more of the hormones produced in the anterior pituitary. Deficiencies in thyroid-stimulating hormone (TSH) and adrenocorticotropic hormone (ACTH) often result in hypotension and can be life-threatening. Other problems that occur when there is a lack of pituitary function are failure to develop secondary sex characteristics associated with a lack of gonadotropins, luteinizing hormone (LH), and follicle-stimulating hormone (FSH). A lack of these hormones is not life-threatening but can alter body image and prevent the client from being able to reproduce. Management of hypopituitarism consists of early diagnosis and treatment with hormone supplementation.

Hyperpituitarism

Hyperpituitarism is a state that occurs with anterior pituitary tumors or hyperplasia of the pituitary gland. Tumors are the most common reason for hyperpituitarism. Women with prolactinomas usually experience anovulation, irregular menses, reduction in sex drive, and lactation. Other signs and symptoms of pituitary tumors include headache, visual disturbances, and altered levels of consciousness. Gigantism (increased levels of growth hormone in the child) or acromegaly (increased levels of growth hormone in the adult) can also result from hyperpituitarism.

Management depends on the type and location of the tumor. Many clients respond well to medical management with bromocriptine mesylate (Parlodel) or cabergoline (Dostinex). These drugs should be given with food to decrease gastrointestinal disturbance. Pregnant clients should not be prescribed Parlodel.

Surgical removal of the tumor can be accomplished by a transsphenoidal approach. This type of surgery is performed by passing an instrument through the sphenoid sinus (see Figure 4.2). Clients return from surgery with nose packing in place. Postoperatively the client should be taught to avoid coughing, sneezing, nose blowing, and bending. Soft toothbrushes should be used for several weeks following surgery. Any discharge from the nose should be checked for glucose because cerebrospinal leakage can occur.

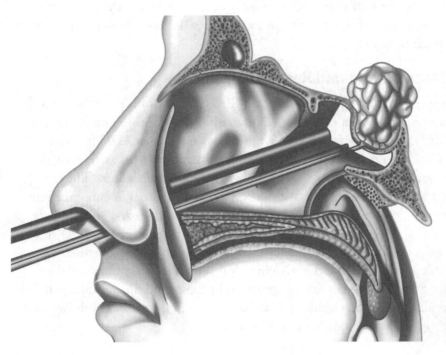

FIGURE 4.2
Transsphenoidal surgery for the removal of pituitary tumors.

X-ray therapy is sometimes used to shrink the tumor. *Radiotherapy*, a stereotactic radiation, is generally preferred over external beam radiation because a higher dose of radiation can be delivered to the tumor with less radiation to normal brain structures. Damage to pituitary structures of the brain can occur with this treatment, so the client must be assessed for signs of altered neurological function or brain infections such as meningitis.

Disorders of the Posterior Pituitary Gland

Two disorders of the posterior pituitary gland are diabetes insipidus and syndrome of inappropriate antidiuretic hormone (SIADH). These problems can be caused by a deficiency or excess of the hormone vasopressin (antidiuretic hormone).

Diabetes Insipidus

Diabetes insipidus is a result of either a decrease in antidiuretic hormone synthesis or an inability of the kidneys to respond to ADH. The lack of antidiuretic hormone will result in dehydration with resulting hypotension. The nurse should assess the client's urine for specific gravity. The normal specific gravity is 1.010–1.030. A client with diabetes insipidus will have a specific gravity of less than 1.010.

The diagnosis of diabetes insipidus is confirmed by a 24-hour urine screening for osmo-lality and a hypertonic saline test. This test is done by administering a normal water load to the client followed by an infusion of hypertonic saline and measuring the urinary output hourly. This test detects ADH release. A decrease in urinary output is a sign of ADH release. Treatment includes chlorpropamide (Diabinese) or clofibrate (Atromid-S) to increase the action of ADH, or if a severe deficiency in ADH exists, the client can be prescribed ADH in the form of vasopressin either nasally or parenterally. The client should be taught to alternate from one nostril to the other because this medication is irritating to the nasal passages.

Syndrome of Inappropriate Antidiuretic Hormone

Syndrome of inappropriate antidiuretic hormone (SIADH) is a disorder of the posterior pituitary gland where vasopressin (ADH) is secreted even when plasma osmolality is normal or low. SIADH, or Schwartz-Barter syndrome, occurs when ADH is secreted in the presence of a low plasma osmolality. This alteration results in increased levels of anti-diuretic hormone. High levels of ADH results in excretion of sodium. The inci-dence is unknown but might be related to cancers, viral and bacterial pneumonia, lung abscesses, tuberculosis, chronic obstructive pulmonary disease, mycoses, positive pres-sure ventilators, pneumothorax, brain tumors, head trauma, certain medications, and infectious diseases. Signs and symptoms include nausea, vomiting, muscle twitching, changes in level of consciousness, and low sodium levels with increased urine sodium. The treatment for SIADH includes fluid restrictions because fluid further dilutes the serum sodium levels, gradual replacement of sodium, and administration of demeclocy-cline (Declomycin) and intravenous hypertonic sodium.

Thyroid Disorders

The thyroid is located below the larynx and anterior to the trachea (see Figure 4.3). The thyroid gland produces two iodine-dependent hormones: thyroxine (T4) and triiodothy-ronine (T3). A third hormone known as thyrocalcitonin (calcitonin) is produced by the C cells of the thyroid gland in response to calcium levels. The C cell makes calcitonin that helps to regulate calcium levels in the blood. These hormones play a role in regu-lating the metabolic processes controlling the rate of growth, oxygen consumption, contractility of the heart, and calcium absorption.

Hypothyroidism

Hypothyroidism occurs when thyroid hormone production is inadequate. The thyroid gland often enlarges to compensate for a lack of thyroid hormone, resulting in a goiter. Another cause for development of a goiter is a lack of iodine in the diet. Other causes of primary hypothyroidism include genetic defects that prevent the metabolism of iodine. In the infant, this is known as *cretinism*. Other causes include eating a diet high in goitrogens, such as turnips, cabbage, spinach, and radishes, or taking the medications lithium, phenylbutazone, and para-aminosalicylic acid. Secondary hypothyroidism, known as *myxedema*, is the result of a lack of pituitary production of thyroid-stimulating hormone.

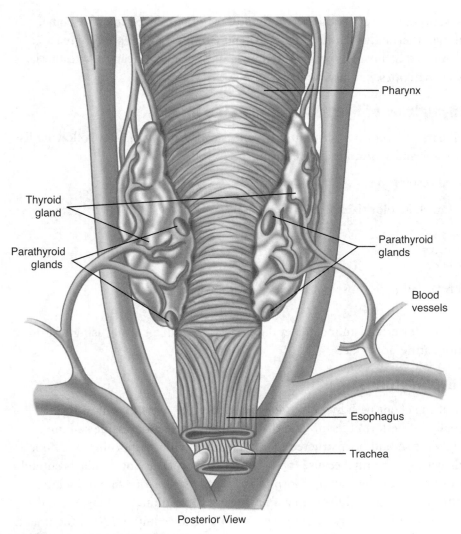

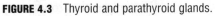

Posterior View

FIGURE 4.3 Thyroid and parathyroid glands.

Signs and symptoms of hypothyroidism in the adult are as follows:

- ▶ Fatigue and lethargy
- ▶ Decreased body temperature
- ▶ Decreased pulse rate
- ▶ Decreased blood pressure
- ▶ Weight gain
- ▶ Edema of hands and feet
- ▶ Hair loss
- ▶ Thickening of the skin

In severe cases, myxedema coma can occur. Symptoms of myxedema include coma, hypotension, hypothermia, respiratory failure, hyponatremia, and hypoglycemia. Myxedema coma can be brought on by withdrawal of thyroid medication, anesthesia, use of sedatives, narcotics, surgery, or hypothermia.

Signs and Symptoms of Hypothyroidism in the Infant

As mentioned earlier, hypothyroidism in an infant is called *cretinism*. The following list gives you the signs and symptoms of cretinism:

▸ Decreased respirations

▸ Changes in skin color (jaundice or cyanosis)

▸ Poor feeding

▸ Hoarse cry

▸ Mental retardation in those not detected or improperly treated

Diagnostic studies for cretinism include evaluation of T3 and T4 levels using test doses of thyroid-stimulating hormone.

Managing Hypothyroidism

Management of the client with hypothyroidism includes the replacement of thyroid hormone, usually in the form of synthetic thyroid hormone levothyroxine sodium (Synthroid). Clients should be instructed to take Synthroid in the morning one hour prior to meals with water only because food can alter absorption. Soy products should be limited because soy can also alter absorption. The client's history should include other drugs the client is taking. Prior to administering thyroid medications, the pulse rate should be evaluated. If the pulse rate is above 100 in the adult or 120 in the infant, the physician should be notified. The client requires a warm environment due to alteration in metabolic rate affecting temperature. Another problem associated with a slower metabolic rate is constipation. A high-fiber diet is recommended to prevent constipation. Treatment of myxedema coma includes treatment of hypotension, glucose regulation, and administration of corticosteroids.

Hyperthyroidism

Hyperthyroidism or thyrotoxicosis is caused by excessive thyroid hormone. Because the thyroid gland is responsible for metabolism, the client with hyperthyroidism often experiences increased heart rate, increased stoke volume, weight loss, and nervousness. The cause of hyperthyroidism is multifactorial. Some of these causes are autoimmune stimulation such as Graves' disease, hypersecretion of thyroid-stimulating hormone (TSH), thyroiditis, or neoplasms of the thyroid gland.

Graves' disease results from an increased production of thyroid hormone. The most common cause of hyperthyroidism is hyperplasia of the thyroid, commonly referred to as a *toxic diffuse goiter*.

Signs and symptoms of hyperthyroidism include

▶ Increased heart rate and pulse pressure

▶ Tremors or nervousness

▶ Moist skin and sweating

▶ Increased activity

▶ Insomnia

▶ Atrial fibrillation

▶ Increased appetite and weight loss

▶ Exophthalamus

A *thyroid storm* is an abrupt onset of symptoms of hyperthyroidism due to Graves' disease, inadequate treatment of hyperthyroidism, trauma, infection, surgery, pulmonary embolus, diabetic acidosis, emotional upset, or toxemia of pregnancy. Fever, tachycardia, hypertension, tremors, agitation, anxiety, and gastrointestinal upset occur. The treatment for a thyroid storm includes maintenance of a patent airway and medication to treat hypertensive crises. Propylthiouracil (PTU) and methimazole (Tapazole) are two antithyroid drugs used to treat thyroid storm. These drugs work by blocking the synthesis and secretion of thyroid hormone. Soluble solution of potassium iodine (SSKI) or *Lugol's solution* can be given to stop the release of thyroid hormone already in the gland. This drug can also be given prior to thyroid surgery to prevent a thyroid storm. The client should be taught to take the medication with a fruit juice high in ascorbic acid, such as orange or tomato juice, to increase the absorption of the medication and mask the taste. Taking the medication through a straw can also increase the palatability of the medication. Propranolol (Inderal) or other beta-blocking agents can be given to slow the heart rate and decrease the blood pressure. If fever is present, the client can be treated with a nonaspirin medication such as acetaminophen (Tylenol) or ibuprofen.

Diagnosis of hyperthyroidism involves the evaluation of T3 and T4 levels and a thyroid scan with or without contrast media. These thyroid function studies tell the physician whether the client has an adequate amount of circulating thyroid hormone. A thyroid scan can clarify the presence of an enlargement of tumor of the thyroid gland.

Management of the client with hyperthyroidism includes

▶ The use of antithyroid drugs (propylthiouracil or Tapazole)

▶ Radioactive iodine, which can be used to test and destroy portions of the gland

▶ Surgical removal of a portion of the gland

Prior to thyroid surgery, the client is given Lugol's solution (SSKI)—an iodine preparation—to decrease the vascularity of the gland. Postoperatively, the client should be carefully assessed for the following:

▶ Edema and swelling of the airway (the surgical incision is located at the base of the neck anterior to the trachea).

- ▶ Bleeding (check for bleeding behind the neck).

- ▶ Tetany, nervousness, and irritability (complications resulting from damage to the parathyroid). Calcium gluconate should be kept available to treat hypocalcemia.

Because the thyroid gland is located anterior to the trachea, any surgery in this area might result in swelling of the trachea. For that reason, it is imperative that the nurse be prepared for laryngeal swelling and occlusion of the airway. The nurse should keep a tracheostomy set at the bedside and call the doctor if the client has changes in her voice or signs of laryngeal stridor. The nurse should instruct the client to keep her head and neck as straight as possible. Vital signs should be monitored, and the client should be evaluated for signs of hypoparathyroidism. Those signs include tingling around the mouth. The nurse should check for hypocalcemia by checking Chvostek's sign. This is elicited when cranial nerves 7 and 5 are stimulated and result in facial grimacing when the cheek is tapped with the examiner's finger. Trousseau's sign is also an indication of hypocalcemia and is elicited by placing a blood pressure cuff on the arm and watching for carpopedal spasms. Refer to Figures 2.4 and 2.5 in Chapter 2, "Fluid and Electrolyte and Acid/Base Balance," for more information about Chvostek's sign and Trousseau's sign.

Parathyroid Disorders

The parathyroid glands are four small glands located on the thyroid gland (see Figure 4.3). The primary function of the parathyroid glands is the regulation of calcium and phosphorus metabolism. Diagnosis of parathyroid disorders is based on an evaluation of serum calcium and serum phosphorus levels and 24-hour urine levels of calcium and phosphorus. The normal serum calcium level is approximately 8.5–10.5 mg/dl; the normal phosphorus level is about 2.5–4.5 mEq/L. Radioimmunoassay exams are used to check serum parathormone. Potential disorders of these glands include hypoparathyroidism and hyperparathyroidism.

Hypoparathyroidism

Hypoparathyroidism is an inadequate production of parathormone and is most often related to the removal of the parathyroid glands during thyroid surgery. Parathyroid hormone (PTH) is responsible for the regulation of calcium and phosphorus levels in the blood. Calcium and phosphorus levels must be maintained within normal limits to have adequate nerve function. Bone density is also maintained by parathormone. Signs and symptoms of hypoparathyroidism include the following:

- ▶ Decreased blood calcium

- ▶ Increased blood phosphorus

- ▶ Neuromuscular hyperexcitability

- ▶ Carpopedal spasms (Trousseau's sign)

- ▸ Positive Chvostek's sign

- ▸ Urinary frequency

- ▸ Mood changes (depression)

- ▸ Dry, scaly skin and thin hair

- ▸ Cataracts

- ▸ Changes in teeth (cavities)

- ▸ Seizures

- ▸ Changes in EKG (prolonged Q-T intervals and inverted T waves)

TIP

Here's a way to remember that the facial nerve is cranial nerve 7: Place your hand on the cheek bone and move your finger out toward the ear and down the jaw line. You will note that you have formed the number seven.

Management of the client with hypoparathyroidism involves the administration of IV calcium gluconate and long-term use of calcium salts. If calcium gluconate is administered intravenously, the rate should be monitored carefully because rapid administration can result in cardiac arrhythmias. Phosphate binders such as calcium acetate (Phoslo) can be used to bind with phosphates. This will result in a rise in the calcium level. Vitamin D supplements can be given to increase the absorption of calcium preparations as well as calcium in the diet.

Hyperparathyroidism

Hyperparathyroidism is the direct opposite of hypoparathyroidism. In this disorder, you find an overproduction of parathormone. Signs and symptoms of hyperparathyroidism include

- ▸ Decreased blood phosphorus.

- ▸ Increased blood calcium.

- ▸ Muscle weakness.

- ▸ Osteoporosis.

- ▸ Bone pain and pathological fractures.

- ▸ Increased urinary output and renal calculi.

- ▸ Nausea and vomiting.

- ▸ Changes in EKG (shortened Q-T interval and signs of heart block). *Heart block* involves an alteration in the conduction system of the heart. In third- and fourth-degree heart block, there is an alteration in the heart's ability to transmit electrical impulses from the sinus node located in the right atria to the ventricle. This interference in the conduction system can cause a prolonged P-R interval and possibly deletion of atrial contractions.

Managing a client with hyperparathyroidism is accomplished by the removal of the parathyroid. Preoperative management involves the reduction of calcium levels. Postoperative management includes

- Assessment of the client for respiratory distress

- Maintaining suction, oxygen, and a tracheostomy set at bedside

- Checking for bleeding (1–5ml is normal)

- Checking the serum calcium and serum phosphorus levels

To prevent the need for lifelong treatment with calcium, the client might have a parathyroid transplant—implantation of one or more parathyroid glands to another part of the body. If this is not possible, a total parathyroidectomy might be performed. If this is the situation, or if inadequate production of parathormone is found, the client will require lifelong supplementation with calcium and vitamin D.

Diabetes Mellitus

There are two types of diabetes: type 1 and type 2. Type 1, also called *insulin-dependent diabetes mellitus (IDDM)* or *juvenile-onset diabetes*, is a condition where the islets of Langerhans in the pancreas do not produce needed insulin. Insulin is necessary for food to be metabolized. Antibodies have been found in the majority of clients with type 1 diabetes. These antibodies are proteins in the blood that are part of the client's immune system. It is believed that type 1 diabetes is in part genetically transmitted from parent to child. At stressful times in life, such as when infection is present, pregnancy or environmental toxins might trigger abnormal antibody responses that result in this autoimmune response. When this happens, the client's body stops producing insulin. Type 1 diabetes tends to occur in young, lean individuals, usually before 30 years of age; however, it can occur in older individuals. These individuals are referred to as *latent autoimmune diabetes in adults (LADA)*. Diabetes occurs in about 6% of Caucasians, 10% of African Americans, 20–50% of Native Americans, and 15% of Hispanics.

Type 2 diabetes was referred to as *non–insulin-dependent, adult-onset diabetes mellitus (ADDM)*. However, in recent years, more and more children have been diagnosed with ADDM. This trend can be attributed to obesity and sedentary lifestyle. In ADDM, the cells of the body, particularly fat and muscle cells, become resistant to insulin. This leads to increased insulin production with increased insulin resistance. Tests have also shown that this increased insulin resistance leads to a steady decline in beta cell production further worsening glucose control. This problem along with *gluconeogenesis*, a process in which the liver continues to produce glucose, leads to further hyperglycemia, metabolic acidosis, and deterioration of the client's health.

Signs and symptoms associated with diabetes mellitus include

▸ **Weight loss:** Insulin is required for carbohydrates to be converted into useable glucose; a lack of insulin results in a lack of glucose with cellular starvation.

▸ **Ketonuria:** The breakdown of fats leads to the production of ketones that causes characteristic fruity breath.

▸ **Polyphagia:** Cellular starvation causes the diabetic to increase food consumption.

▸ **Polyuria:** The kidneys attempt to regulate pH by increasing urinary output of ketones and glucose.

▸ **Polydipsia:** The loss of large amounts of fluid leads to metabolic acidosis and dehydration. To compensate for the fluid loss, the client drinks large amounts of water.

▸ **Delayed wound healing:** Increased blood sugar contributes to poor wound healing.

▸ **Elevated blood glucose:** Normal is 70–110 mg/dl. Uncorrected or improperly managed diabetes mellitus leads to coma and death.

Diagnosis of diabetes mellitus is made by checking blood glucose levels. Several diagnostic tests that can be performed to determine the presence and extent of diabetes are as follows:

▸ **Glucose tolerance test:** The glucose tolerance test is the most reliable diagnostic test for diabetes. Prior to the glucose tolerance test, the client should be instructed to eat a diet high in carbohydrates for three days and remain NPO after midnight the day of the test. The client should come to the office for a fasting blood glucose level, drink a solution high in glucose, and have the blood tested at one and two hours after drinking the glucose solution (glucola) for a test of glucose in the serum. A diagnosis of diabetes is made when the venous blood glucose is greater than 200 mg/dl two hours after the test.

▸ **Fasting blood glucose levels:** The normal fasting blood glucose is 70–110 mg/dl. A diagnosis of diabetes can be made if the fasting blood glucose level is above 140 mg/dl or above on two occasions. A blood glucose level of 800 mg/dl or more, especially if ketones are present, indicates a diagnosis of *hyperosmolar hyperglycemic nonketoic syndrome (HHNKS)*.

▸ **Two-hour post-prandial:** Blood testing for glucose two hours after a meal.

▸ **Dextrostix:** Blood testing for glucose.

▸ **Glycosylated hemoglobin assays (HbA1c):** The best indicator of the average blood glucose for approximately 90–120 days. A finding greater than 7% indicates non-compliance.

- **Glycosylated serum proteins and albumin levels:** Become elevated in the same way that HbA1c does. Because serum proteins and albumin turn over in 14 days, however, glycosylated serum albumin (GSA) can be used to indicate blood glucose control over a shorter time.

- **Urine checks for glucose:** Ketonuria occurs if blood glucose levels exceed 240 mg/dl.

- **Antibodies:** Checked to determine risk factors for the development of type 1 diabetes. Measurement of the cells' antibodies can also determine the rate of progression to diabetes.

Management of the client with diabetes mellitus includes the following:

- **Diet:** The diet should contain a proper balance of carbohydrates, fats, and proteins.

- **Exercise:** The client should follow a regular exercise program. He should not exercise if his blood glucose is above 240 mg/dl. He should wait until his blood glucose level returns to normal.

- **Medications:** Oral antidiabetic agents or insulin. Medications used to treat diabetes mellitus include sulfanylurea agents, alpha-glucosidase inhibitors, nonsulfanylurea agents, D-phenylalanine derivatives, and thiazolidinediones. Insulins are also used to treat clients with type 1 diabetes. Insulin can be administered subcutaneously, intravenously, or by insulin pump. An insulin pump administers a metered dose of insulin and can provide a bolus of insulin as needed. Byetta is an injectable medicine used to improve blood sugar control in adults with type 2 diabetes. This drug can be used with metformin (Glucophage) or other sulfonylureas.

> **NOTE**
>
> Regular insulin is the only insulin that can be administered intravenously. See the section "Pharmacological Agents Used to Treat Clients with Endocrine Disorders" for a discussion of the antidiabetic drugs.

Hyperglycemia

When there is lack of the hormone insulin, the glucose can't move from the outside of the cell to the inside of the cell where it can be used. It is very important that the nurse be aware of the signs of hyperglycemia to teach the client and family. Signs and symptoms of hyperglycemia are as follows:

- Headache

- Nausea/vomiting

- Coma

► Flushed, dry skin

► Glucose and acetone in urine

TIP

The following statements are a couple of helpful hints for dealing with diabetes mellitus clients:

- ► **Hot and dry; blood sugar high:** This means that if the diabetic's skin is hot and she is dehydrated, her blood glucose level is likely high.

- ► **Cold and clammy; need some candy:** This means that if the diabetic's skin is cold and clammy, her blood glucose level is low and she needs a glucose source.

Hypoglycemia

When there is a lack of glucose, cell starvation occurs. This results in hypoxemia and cell death. Signs and symptoms of hypoglycemia are as follows:

► Headache

► Irritability

► Disorientation

► Nausea/vomiting

► Diaphoresis

► Pallor

► Weakness

► Convulsions

CAUTION

If the client fails to eat her regular bedtime snack, he might experience Somogyi effect. This abrupt drop in the client's blood glucose level during the night is followed by a false elevation. The treatment of Somogyi effect is to teach the client to eat a bedtime snack consisting of a protein source, such as peanut butter and a glass of milk.

Managing Hyperglycemia and Hypoglycemia

Management of hypoglycemia includes giving glucose. Glucagon, a 50% glucose solution, is an injectable form of glucose given in emergency. Cake icing, orange juice, or a similar carbohydrate can be administered if the client is still conscious. The best bedtime snack is milk and a protein source, such as peanut butter and crackers. Fluid and electrolyte regulation is also a part of the treatment of both hyperglycemia and hypoglycemia.

Unchecked hyperglycemia leads to microangiopathic and macroangiopathic changes. These lead to retinopathies, nephropathy, renal failure, cardiovascular changes, and peripheral vascular problems.

Adrenal Gland

The adrenal gland is a vascular gland located at the top of the kidney. It comprises the cortex (outer portion) and the medulla (inner portion), as illustrated in Figure 4.4. The action of the adrenal gland consists of production of mineralocorticoids that help control the body's levels of minerals such as sodium and potassium. Glucocorticoids, androgens, and estrogens are made in the zona fasciculata and zona reticularis. The cortex produces the adrenal steroids and corticosteroids. The major mineralocorticoid produced in the cortex is aldosterone. As previously discussed, this mineralcorticoid helps to control reabsorption of sodium and potassium that the kidneys excrete. Other regulatory mechanisms controlled by the cortex are renin and adrenocorticotropic hormone (ACTH). The most prominent glucocorticoid secreted by the adrenal cortex is cortisol. This hormone helps to regulate the body's stress response, metabolism of food, emotional stability, and the immune response. Small amounts of androgens and estrogen are secreted by the adrenal cortex.

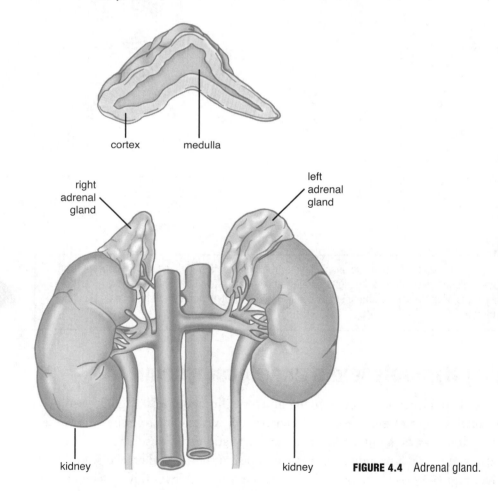

FIGURE 4.4 Adrenal gland.

The adrenal medulla is a sympathetic nerve ganglion that stimulates the sympathetic nervous system. This stimulation results in elevations in catecholamines such as norepi-nephrine and epinephrine. These chemicals help to control response to stress. The "fight or flight" response results in changes in pulse rate, blood pressure, and central nervous system response.

Adrenal Gland Disorders

Adrenal disorders result in many problems. Some of these include fatigue, weakness, suppression of the immune response, muscle and bone loss, and many others. This section covers some of the most common types of adrenal disorders along with their causes and treatments.

Primary Aldosteronism (Conn's Syndrome)

Conn's syndrome is a disease of the adrenal glands that involves an excessive production of aldosterone. The most common reasons for development of Conn's syndrome are a tumor of the adrenal gland or benign hyperplasia of the adrenal gland, but the syndrome can also be related to use of thiazide diuretics or high levels of angiotensin II caused by poor renal perfusion. Signs and symptoms of Conn's syndrome include an elevated serum sodium level, decreased potassium serum levels, and hypertension with a related headache. Positive Trousseau's and Chvostek's signs might be present. Diagnosis of Conn's is made by checking the serum levels for sodium and potassium and aldosterone levels. X-rays, CT scans, and an MRI confirm the presence of tumors. Treatment includes a low-sodium diet, potassium supplementation, and control of hypertension. Spironolactone (Aldactone)—a potassium-sparing diuretic—is prescribed to lower aldosterone levels and lower blood pressure. Surgical intervention is done when tumors are identified. Prognosis is good if the client is accurately diagnosed. If the client fails to receive an accurate diagnosis, the disease can lead to a stroke, heart attack, or renal disease.

Pheochromocytoma is a catecholamine-producing adrenal tumor that leads to a marked elevated blood pressure. Treatment includes treatment of malignant hypertension with drugs such as sodium nitroprusside (Nipride) or clonidine (Catapres). Removal of the tumor primarily corrects the hypertension. The client's blood pressure must be stabilized prior to surgery. This is usually done by administration of an alpha-adrenergic–blocking agent such as phenoxybenzamine hydrochloride (Dibenzyline).

Adrenocortical Insuffiency (Addison's Disease)

Addison's disease can occur as a result of long-term use of steroids or the rapid cessation of corticosteroids. It can also be caused by sepsis, surgical stress, or hemorrhage of the adrenal glands (Waterhouse-Friderichsen syndrome).

Signs and symptoms associated with Addison's disease include

▸ Weakness.

▸ Bronze-like pigmentation of the skin.

▸ Decreased glucose levels.

▸ Decreased blood pressure.

- Anorexia.

- Sparse axillary hair.

- Urinary frequency.

- Depression.

- Addisonian crises. The symptoms of Addisonian crises are severe hypotension, cyanosis, and shock. This constitutes an emergency situation. The nurse should call the doctor immediately to obtain orders for medications to treat shock.

Diagnosis of Addison's disease involves an evaluation of serum sodium and chloride levels. Evaluation of ketosteroids and 17-hydroxycorticoids is also done. Adrenal function is evaluated by administering adrenocorticoid-stimulating hormone (ACTH) and checking for changes in cortisol levels.

Management of the client with Addison's disease includes the use of intravenous cortisone and plasma expanders to achieve and maintain the blood pressure. When stable, the client can be given intramuscular cortisol in the form of dexamethasone (Decadron) or orally in the form of prednisolone (Prednisone). The client with Addison's disease requires lifelong maintenance with cortisone. The client should be instructed to take the medication exactly as prescribed and to avoid sudden cessation of the drug.

Adrenocortical Hypersecretion (Cushing's Disease)

The terms *Cushing's disease* and *Cushing's syndrome* are often used interchangeably although they are not the same. Cushing's syndrome or primary Cushing's syndrome can be caused by tumors of the adrenal cortex. Secondary Cushing's syndrome (Cushing's disease) often is caused by pituitary hypothalamus or adrenal cortex problems that result in an increased ACTH (adrenocorticotropic hormone). Long-term administration of glucocortidoids or *iatrogenic Cushing's syndrome* will also produce elevated levels of cortisole and symptoms associated with hypersecretion.

Diagnosis is made by checking serum cortisole, calcium, potassium, sodium, and glucose levels. Altered ACTH and 17 ketosteroid levels are also seen with Cushing's. A positive ACTH suppression test can be performed to check for changes in cortisole levels when ACTH is administrated.

Signs and symptoms associated with Cushing's disease include

- Pendulous abdomen

- Buffalo hump

- Moon faces

- Hirsutism (facial hair)

- Ruddy complexion (dark red)

- Increased BP

- Hyperglycemia

- Osteoporosis

- Decreased serum potassium and decreased serum chloride

- Increased 17-hydroxycorticoids

- Decreased eosinophils and decreased lymphocytes

Management of the client with Cushing's is accomplished by removing the cause—hyperplasia of the gland. Surgery can be required. A low-sodium diet, regulation of fluid and electrolytes, and administration of a potassium-sparing diuretic such as aldactone (Spironalactone) help to decrease the symptoms. Because elevated glucose levels are common in the client with Cushing's syndrome, the client often requires frequent checks of glucose levels and administration of insulin or oral antidiabetic medications.

Case Study

A 76-year-old male is admitted from home. His blood sugar on admission is 53mg/dl. He is awake and able to swallow.

1. List your interventions.

2. The client's blood sugar levels are normally below 180 but have been between 288 and 312 over the last 48 hours. He has injected his usual 7 a.m. dose of 15 U of NPH, his 7 p.m. dose of 10 U of NPH insulin, and an additional four to six units of regular insulin each time he has checked his capillary blood sugar levels. He performs a blood sugar test before each meal and at bedtime. The client denies increased caloric intake, alteration in amount or type of exercise, increased stress, or signs of illness.

   It is now 10:30 a.m., and when you test the blood sugar, you find that it is 55mg/dl.

   The client states that he is starting to feel a little "shaky." List your interventions.

3. The client is being treated for diabetic ketoacidosis. His capillary blood sugar level has just decreased to 249mg/dl. He is receiving continuous intravenous insulin at 10 U/hour that is piggy-backed to isotonic saline (0.9% sodium chloride). List your interventions.

4. You are the nurse assigned to oversee care of the client's diabetes since his admission for treatment of an infection. At 8:30 a.m., the nursing assistant reports that the client is feeling bad and is refusing morning care. His fever has increased to 102.8° F; his mouth and skin are dry; his urine output has been 250cc/hour since 6 a.m.; his respirations are deeper and 22/minute; and his current capillary blood glucose level reflects an increase to 308mg/dl. When notified, the physician orders 6 U of regular insulin to be given intramuscularly, additional diagnostic testing, and a new IV antibiotic. List your interventions.

Answers to Case Study

1. Administer a rapid-acting sugar, such as orange juice or hard candy.

   Check the blood sugar in 15 minutes; if no change, give another dose of simple sugar. After the blood sugar goes above 70, administer a longer-acting meal such as crackers and milk if a meal is not due to be served. Ask about storage, expiration dates, and use of old and new vials of insulin to determine potency.

(continues)

(continued)

Check his blood glucose machine for accuracy.

Check for signs of illness.

2. Treat the blood sugar problem with simple sugar and then a more complex meal.

    Because medications can alter blood glucose levels, ask about the consumption of medications that he normally has not taken.

    Evaluate injection sites for tissue damage that would hinder absorption

3. Call the doctor to get an IV changed to one containing dextrose to prevent hypoglycemia. The insulin rate can be changed also.

    Make continuous hourly assessments of signs of hypoglycemia or hyperglycemia and changes in the client's condition as his blood sugar continues to stabilize. Some clients who are accustomed to higher blood sugar levels might experience signs of hypoglycemia at a higher blood sugar level than someone whose blood sugar level is maintained at a more normal level.

4. The injection of insulin needs to be given stat. Intramuscular insulin will absorb more rapidly. Repeat the blood sugar every 15–30 minutes, and reassess the client for improvement or further signs of dehydration and acidosis. If cultures are ordered, specimens are collected before the new antibiotic is administered.

Key Concepts

This chapter discussed alterations in the endocrine system. The nursing student should use these key concepts to answer questions as they relate to the care of this client. Remembering the pathophysiology of the disease process, the treatment, and the laboratory values will help you to be able to answer questions in the physiologic integrity portion of the NCLEX exam.

Key Terms

- Acromegaly
- Adrenocortical hyperplasia
- Aldosterone
- Androgens
- Addison's
- Adrenal cortex
- Adrenalectomy
- Bromocriptine (Parlodel)
- Buffalo hump
- Corticosteroids
- Cortisol
- CT scan
- Cushing's disease
- Diabetes insipidus
- Dostinex (carbergoline)
- Estrogen
- FSH (follicle-stimulating hormone)
- Gigantism
- Gland
- Gonadotrophins
- Hirsutism
- Hormones
- Human growth hormone
- Hypopituitarism
- Hypothalamus

- ▸ Luteinizing hormone
- ▸ MRI (magnetic resonance imaging)
- ▸ Ovaries
- ▸ Parlodel (bromocriptine)
- ▸ Parathyroid gland
- ▸ Pituitary gland
- ▸ Prednisone
- ▸ Progesterone
- ▸ Prolactin
- ▸ Prolactinoma
- ▸ Thymus
- ▸ Thyroid gland
- ▸ Transsphenoidal hyposection

Diagnostics

The exam reviewer should be knowledgeable of the preparation and care of clients receiving exams to diagnose endocrine disorders. While reviewing these diagnostic exams, the exam reviewer should be alert for information that would be an important part of nursing care for these clients. The pertinent labs and exams are as follows:

- ▸ Laboratory test to determine hormone levels
- ▸ X-rays to detect tumors
- ▸ Computer tomography to detect tumors
- ▸ Magnetic imaging to detect tumors

Pharmacological Agents Used to Treat Clients with Endocrine Disorders

An integral part of care to clients with endocrine disorders is pharmacological intervention. These medications provide an improvement or cure of the clients' endocrine problems. The nursing exam reviewer needs to focus on the drugs in Table 4.1. Included in this table are the most common drugs used to treat endocrine disorders. These medications are not inclusive of all the agents used to treat endocrine disorders; therefore, you will want to keep a current pharmacology text handy for reference.

TABLE 4.1 Pharmacological Agents Used in the Treatment of Clients with Endocrine Disorders

Drug	Action	Side Effect	Nursing Care
Cortisone, hydro-cortisone, prenisone, and fludrocortisone (Florinet)	For replacement of a lack of cortisole or to suppress the immune response in a client suffering from allergic reaction, those with organ transplantation, or to suppress untoward effects of medications	Nausea and vomiting, weight gain, decreased immunity.	Instruct the client to take the medication with meals. Instruct the client to report the signs or symptoms of excessive drug therapy: signs of Cushing's syndrome.
Propylthiouracil (PTU, Propyl-Thracil)	Used to treat hyperthyroidism	Slow heart rate, fatigue, drowsiness headache, neuritis, nausea, vomiting, diarrhea, and myelosuppression.	Measured dosage should be spread over 24 hours to prevent hormone release from the thyroid.
Methimazole (Tapazole)	Antithyroid medication	Same as above.	Monitor vital signs, weigh the client weekly, observe for throat soreness, fever, headache, and skin ulcers.
Iodine product, strong iodine (Lugol's solution)	Used to decrease the potential for a thyroid storm, which is an abrupt release of thyroid hormone	Same as above.	Bitter to taste, give with fruit juice.
SSKI (saturated solution of potassium iodide)	Used to treat and prevent thyroid storm	Same as above plus: metallic taste, stomatitis, salivation, coryza, hyperthyroid adenoma, irregular heart rate, and mental confusion.	Signs of hypothyroidism might necessitate discontinuation.
Potassium iodide tablets, solution, and syrup	Used to treat iodide deficiency that can lead to a goiter	Same as above.	Take after meals to increase absorption.
Lithium carbonate (Lithobid, Carbolith, Lithizine)	Used to treat hyperthyroidism	Dizziness, lethargy, drowsiness, fatigue, slurred speech, psychomotor retardation, incontinence, EEG changes, arrhythmias, hypotension, impaired vision, thyroid enlargement, dry mouth, abdominal pain, pruitus, and thinning hair.	Observe for hypothyroidism. Instruct the client to drink 8–12 glassfuls of fluids per day. Instruct the client to maintain adequate sodium intake to prevent toxicity.
Propanolol (Inderal, Detensol)	A beta blocker used to treat hyperthyroidism	Bradycardia, edema, lethargy, and bone marrow suppression.	Monitor pulse rate, CBC, and for signs of congestive heart failure. Take with food to decrease GI upset.
Atenolol (Tenormin)	Same as above	Same as above.	Same as above.

(continues)

TABLE 4.1 *Continued*

Drug	Action	Side Effect	Nursing Care
Levothyroixine (Levo-T, Levothroid, Levoxyl, Levothyroixine Sodium, Synthyroid)	Used to treat hypothyroidism	Tachycardia, nausea, vomiting, diarrhea, and insomnia.	Check pulse rate routinely.
Bromocriptine (Alphagen, Parlodel)	Used to treat parkinsonism or for prolactinomas	Hypotension, nausea, vomiting, blurred vision, dry mouth, urticaria, and fatigue.	Watch for orthostatic hypotension. Should not be used by pregnant clients. Dizziness, headaches, abnormal vision, constipation, hot flashes, and parathesia. Check serum prolactin levels <20mcg/liter in women or <1 5 mg.
Carbergoline (Dostinex)	Used to treat prolactinomas; inhibits prolactin secretion	May cause headaches, depression, nervousness, and fatigue. Dysmenorrhea and facial flushing has also occurred.	Do not use with clients with liver disease.
Glimepride (Amaryl)	Used to treat hyperglycemia; works by increasing effects of client's own insulin	Hypoglycemia, watch for renal function.	Teach the client to watch for hypoglycemia, GI disturbance, allergic skin reactions, and photosensitivity. Take once daily before meals.
Glyburide (Micronase, Diabeta, glynase)	Same as above	Same as above, plus may cause gastrointestinal disturbance.	Watch for hypoglycemia. Take in divided doses.
Glipizide (Glucotrol, Glucotrol XL)	Same as above	Same as above.	Watch for hypoglycemia. Take before breakfast. Doses above 15mg should be divided. Glucotrol XL is long-acting, given one time per day.
Antidiabetic Medications— Meglitinides			
Repaglinide (Prandin)	Used to treat hyperglycemia	May lead to hypoglycemia.	Watch for hypoglycemia. If NPO, withhold medication.
Antidiabetic Medications — Biguanides			
Metformin (Glucophage)	Used to treat hyperglycemia; works by decreasing carbohydrate breakdown in the GI tract	Renal impairment, gastrointestinal upsepo, nausea, and vomiting.	Watch for hypoglycemia. Can cause GI disturbance, B-12 deficiencies, lactic acidosis, malaise, and respiratory distress. Contraindicated in renal disease clients, liver disease, and congestive heart failure. Clients going for radiographic studies should have glucophage withheld for 48 hours or until renal function returns.

TABLE 4.1 *Continued*

Drug	Action	Side Effect	Nursing Care
Antidiabetic Medications— Thiazolidinedione			
Rosiglitazone (Avandia)	Used to treat hyperglycemia; works by decreasing carbohydrate breakdown in the GI tract	Abdominal pain, nausea, vomiting, anorexia, and hypoglycemia.	Watch for hypoglycemia. Clients with liver or renal disease should not take this drug. Monitor liver enzymes. It might decrease effects of oral contraceptives. Watch for signs of congestive heart failure.
Alpha-glucosidase inhibitor—Acarbose (Precose)	Used to treat hyper-glycemia associated with diabetes	Flatulence, diarrhea, and abdominal discomfort.	Watch for hypoglycemia. Take with first bite of food. Contraindicated in clients with liver disease, inflamma-tory bowel disease, or renal disease.
Insulins			
Lispro (Humalog)	Onset five minutes, so have food available; peak 30–60 minutes; duration 2–4 hours; used to treat uncontrolled diabetes	Hypoglycemia	Watch for hypoglycemia.
Regular insulin	Onset 30–60 minutes; peak 2–4 hours; duration 6–8 hours	Hypoglycemia	Watch for hypoglycemia.
Intermediate-Acting Insulins			
NPH	Onset 1–2 hours; peak 6–12 hours; duration 18–24 hours	Hypoglycemia	Watch for hypoglycemia.
Humulin N	Same as above	Hypoglycemia	Watch for hypoglycemia.
Humulin L	Same as above	Hypoglycemia	Watch for hypoglycemia.
Long-Acting Insulins			
Ultra Lente	Onset 5–8 hours; peak 14–20 hours; duration 30–36 hours	Hypoglycemia	Watch for hypoglycemia.
Lantus	No peak; duration 24–36 hours	Hypoglycemia	Watch for hypoglycemia. Do not mix with other insulins. Usually given at night; however, the FDA has recently approved adminis-tration during the day.
Combination Insulins			
Humulin 70/30	Onset 30 minutes; peak 4–8 hours; durations 22–24 hours	Hypoglycemia	Watch for hypoglycemia.

(continues)

TABLE 4.1 *Continued*

Drug	Action	Side Effect	Nursing Care
Humulin 50/50	Onset 30 minutes; peak 4–8 hours; durations 22–24 hours	Hypoglycemia	Watch for hypoglycemia.
Exubera	An inhaled form of insulin recently released and approved by the FDA; delivers insulin directly into the lungs; rapid onset; duration several hours	Hypoglycemia	Watch for hypoglycemia.

> **NOTE**
>
> Sublingual insulin and insulin patches have been developed but are not at present widely used.

Apply Your Knowledge

The nurse reviewing for the licensure exam must be able to apple knowledge to meet client needs. Utilization of information found in this chapter will help the graduate to answer questions found on the NCLEX.

Exam Questions

1. The client is admitted to the hospital with a prolactinoma. Which symptom is not associated with a pituitary tumor?

   A. Amenorrhea

   B. Headache

   C. Blurred vision

   D. Weight loss

2. Which of the following is the drug commonly used to treat a prolactinoma?

   A. Gemcitabine (Gemzar)

   B. Gefitinib (Iressa)

   C. Cabergoline (Dostinex)

   D. Ganciclovir (Cytovene)

3. The client is admitted with Hashimoto's thyroiditis. The nurse is aware that he will exhibit signs of which of the following?

    A. Hyperthyroidism

    B. Hypothyroidism

    C. Hypoparathyroidism

    D. Hyperparathoidism

4. Management of hyperthyroidism might include a prescription for which of the following?

    A. Propylthiouracil (PTU)

    B. Fludrocortisone (Florinef)

    C. Levothyroxine (Synthroid)

    D. Glipizide (Glucotrol)

5. The client is admitted to the recovery room following a thyroidectomy. Which of the following actions by the nurse indicates understanding of care of the client with a thyroidectomy?

    A. The nurse offers extra blankets.

    B. The nurse places a tracheostomy tube at the bedside.

    C. The nurse insists that the client refrain from talking.

    D. The nurse administers pain medication every four hours.

6. The nurse is checking for hypoparathyroidism. To check for hypoparathyroidism, the nurse can check for the positive presence of which of the following signs?

    A. Kernig's

    B. Chadwick

    C. McBurney's

    D. Chvostek's

7. A client with Cushing's disease often complains of which of the following?

    A. Anorexia

    B. Difficulty swallowing

    C. Hirsutism

    D. Hot flashes

8. The most indicative test for diabetes mellitus is which of the following?

    A. Two hour post-prandial

    B. Dextrostix

    C. Glucose tolerance test

    D. Hemoglobin A-1C

9. The diabetic is being maintained on rosiglitazone (Avandia). Which lab test should be checked frequently?

    A. TSH levels (thyroid-stimulating hormone levels)

    B. AST levels (aspartate aminotransferase levels)

    C. HCG levels (human gonaditropin levels)

    D. LDH levels (lactic dehyrogenase levels)

10. The nurse is preparing to administer NPH insulin to the diabetic client. The nurse is aware that the onset of NPH insulin is which of the following?

    A. Five minutes

    B. Thirty minutes

    C. Ninety minutes

    D. Four hours

Answers to Exam Questions

1. Answer D is correct. Prolactinoma tumors are tumors arising from hyperplasia of the pituitary gland that are prolactin hormone–based. Amenorrhea and anovulation are associated with prolactinomas because the pituitary gland assists with stimulation of the ovaries and ovulation, so answer A is incorrect. Because the pituitary is located in the center of the skull, adjacent to the brain, answers B and C are associated with increased intracranial pressure. Answer D is incorrect because weight *gain* can occur, not weight *loss*.

2. Answer C is correct. Dostinex is used to shrink the prolactin based tumor. Answers A and B are antineoplastic drugs. Answer D is an antiviral medication.

3. Answer B is correct because in Hashimoto's thyroiditis, antibodies against thyroid hormone are produced, which leads to a decrease in thyroid hormone release. For this reason Answers A, C, and D are incorrect.

4. Answer A is correct. Propylthiouracil (PTU) is an antithyroid medication. Answer B is incorrect because this is a cortisone preparation. Answer C is incorrect because this drug is used for hypothyroidism. Answer D is incorrect because this drug is used to treat diabetes.

5. Answer B is correct. The thyroid is located anterior to the trachea; therefore, laryngeal stridor and airway obstruction is a risk following a thyroidectomy. Answer A is incorrect because this action is not necessary. The need for extra blankets is associated with hypothyroidism, but is not directly associated with thyroid surgery. Answer C is incorrect because the client can talk. Answer D is incorrect because pain medication should be offered as needed, not every four hours.

6. Answer D is correct. The test for Chvostek's sign is performed by tapping the facial nerve (C7) and the trigeminal nerve (C5) and observing for grimacing. Answer A is incorrect because Kernig's sign is nuchal (neck) rigidity associated with meningitis. Answer B is incorrect because Chadwick's sign is a bluish vagina associated with hormonal changes. Answer C is incorrect because McBurney's sign is rebound tenderness associated with appendicitis.

7. Answer C is correct. Hirsutism is facial hair. This is associated with hypersecretion of cortisol. Answers A, B, and D are not associated with Cushing's disease.

8. Answer C is correct. The most indicative test of diabetes is the glucose tolerance test. Answers A and B are used to detect an elevated blood glucose level, but are not the best to detect diabetes. Answer D is incorrect because this test detects compliance.

9. Answer B is correct. Liver enzymes such as AST should be assessed along with renal function (creatinine levels) and cardiac function. Answer A is not correct because this medication does not alter thyroid function. Answer C is not correct because HCG levels are not affected by rosiglitazone (Avandia). This hormone is associated with pregnancy. Answer D is incorrect because an elevated LDH is associated with muscle trauma. It is, however, elevated in a myocardial infarction.

10. Answer C is correct. NPH insulin onset is 90–120 minutes. Answer A is incorrect because Novalog insulin onset is 5–10 minutes. B is incorrect because regular insulin onset is 15–30 minutes. D is incorrect and is not associated with the onset of any insulin.

Suggested Reading and Resources

▶ American Diabetes Association: http://www.diabetes.org.

▶ Ignataricus, Donna D., and M. Linda Workman. *Medical-Surgical Nursing: Critical Thinking for Collaborative Care. 5th ed.* St. Louis: El Sevier, 2006.

▶ LeMone, Priscilla, and Karen Burke. *Medical-Surgical Nursing, Critical Thinking in Client Care. 4th ed.* Upper Saddle River, NJ: Prentice Hall, 2008.

▶ Smeltzer, Suzanne C., and Brenda G. Bure. *Testbook of Medical Surgical Nursing. 10th ed.* Philadelphia: Lippincott Williams and Wilkins, 2006.

CHAPTER FIVE

Care of the Client with Respiratory Disorders

According to the American Lung Association (2006), lung disease is the fourth leading cause of death in the United States. More than 35 million Americans live with chronic lung disease. Some of these diseases, such as asbestosis, are the result of occupational exposure and carry associated risks of lung cancer. Respiratory infections, particularly nosocomial pneumonia, are responsible for 11% of all hospital-acquired infections. This chapter covers common noninfectious disorders that contribute to chronic lung disease, occupational lung disorders, infectious diseases of the lower respiratory tract, acute respiratory disorders that threaten the client's life, and emerging pulmonary infections.

Noninfectious Disorders of the Lower Respiratory Tract

Noninfectious disorders of the lower respiratory tract affect the exchange of oxygen and carbon dioxide. The chronic and progressive nature of many of these disorders, such as emphysema, result in major changes in the person's lifestyle. Others, such as asbestosis and berylliosis, result from occupational exposure and increase the risk of lung cancer and premature death. Although many noninfectious disorders of the lower respiratory tract are preventable, other disorders—such as sarcoidosis—are not. This section reviews the chronic obstructive disorders, pulmonary hypertension, interstitial pulmonary disease, and occupational pulmonary disease.

Chronic Bronchitis

Chronic bronchitis refers to an inflammation of the bronchi and bronchioles. It is caused by a continuous exposure to infections or noninfectious irritants, such as tobacco smoke. Unlike emphysema, bronchitis is confined to the small and large airways rather than the alveoli. Thickening of the bronchial wall and the production of thick mucus blocks the smaller airways and narrows the larger ones. Chronic bronchitis can often be reversed with the removal of irritants; however, it is complicated by respiratory infections and can progress to right-sided heart failure, pulmonary hypertension, and in some instances to acute respiratory failure. Chronic bronchitis is most common in those age 40–55 years.

Symptoms associated with chronic bronchitis include the following:

- Shortness of breath
- Cough (which might be more common in the winter months)
- Increased sputum production
- Difficulty in eating (due to shortness of breath)
- Decreased weight
- Sleep difficulty (need to sleep sitting up to facilitate breathing)
- Auscultation of fine or coarse crackles and wheezes
- Prolonged expiration time

Treatment of chronic bronchitis includes the use of bronchodilators, steroids, antacids, and expectorants. Antibiotics are usually ordered if the client has an acute respiratory infection. Attention is given to correcting acid-base imbalances, meeting nutritional needs, providing frequent oral care, and providing oxygen at low settings (2–3 liters per minute).

Emphysema

Emphysema is a condition in which there is an irreversible overdistention of the alveoli that eventually results in destruction of the alveolar wall. Clients with emphysema are sometimes described using the terms *pink puffers* or *blue bloaters*. *Pink puffers* (those with involvement of the bronchiole, alveolar duct, alveoli) experience exertional dyspnea yet remain pink. *Blue bloaters* (those with involvement of the secondary lobule resulting in changes in O_2 perfusion) have problems with chronic hypoxia, cyanosis, pulmonary edema, and sometimes respiratory failure. The blue bloater, who is cyanotic even at rest, experiences increasing dyspnea and deepening cyanosis with exertion. Polycythemia predisposes the client with emphysema to the development of clots.

Physical assessment of the client with advanced emphysema reveals the following:

- Presence of a barrel chest
- Digital clubbing
- Rapid shallow respirations
- Prolonged expiratory phase with grunting respirations
- Muscle wasting
- Weight loss
- Peripheral cyanosis
- Violent coughing productive of thick sputum

Chest x-ray reveals flattening of the diaphragm. Arterial blood gases typically reveal increased CO_2 levels and decreased O_2 levels. Pulmonary studies reveal increased residual volume and decreased vital capacity. *Serum α_1-antitrypsin* levels are used to screen for deficiency of the enzyme, particularly in clients with a positive family history of obstructive airway disease, in those with early onset, women, and smokers who develop symptoms of COPD in their 40s. Normal adult *serum α_1 AT* levels range from 80 to 260mg/dL.

Many of the symptoms for the client with chronic bronchitis and emphysema are the same; therefore, the treatment of both conditions includes the use of bronchodilators, steroids, antacids, and expectorants. Antibiotics are usually ordered if the client has an acute respiratory infection. Prophylactic antibiotics might be prescribed for clients who experience four or more respiratory infections per year. Immunization against pneumococcal pneumonia and yearly influenza vaccination are recommended to reduce the risk of respiratory infections. Attention is given to correcting acid-base imbalances, meeting nutritional needs, providing frequent oral care, and providing oxygen at low settings (2–3 liters per minute). α_1-*antitrypsin* replacement therapy can be administered weekly by intravenous infusion for clients with emphysema due to genetic deficiency of the enzyme. Although expensive, the medication has been shown to reduce mortality rates.

Asthma

Asthma is the most common respiratory condition of childhood. *Intrinsic* (nonallergenic) asthma is precipitated by exposure to cold temperatures or infection. *Extrinsic* (allergenic or atopic) asthma is often associated with childhood eczema. Both asthma and eczema are triggered by allergies to certain foods or food additives. Introducing new foods to the infant one at a time helps decrease the development of these allergic responses. Easily digested, hypoallergenic foods and juices should be introduced first. These include rice cereal and apple juice.

Although asthma is the most common chronic disease of childhood, it can occur at any age. Many adults with asthma report having the disease in childhood.

Symptoms of asthma include expiratory wheeze; shortness of breath; and a dry, hacking cough, which eventually produces thick, white, tenacious sputum. In some instances, an attack might progress to status asthmaticus, leading to respiratory collapse and death.

Management of the client with asthma includes maintenance therapy with mast cell stabilizers and leukotriene modifiers. Treatment of acute asthmatic attacks includes the administration of oral or inhaled short-term and long-term B2 agonists and anti-inflammatories as well as supplemental oxygen. The nurse should instruct the client in the proper use of the inhaler (metered-dose and dry-powder) as detailed in the sidebar that follows. Methylxanthines, such as aminophylline, are rarely used for the treatment of asthma. These drugs, which can cause tachycardia and dysrhythmias, are administered as a last resort. Antibiotics are frequently ordered when a respiratory infection is present.

Client Teaching: Use of Metered-Dose and Dry-Powder

Inhaler:

1. Insert the metered-dose inhaler canister into the mouthpiece or spacer.

2. Remove the mouthpiece cap and shake the canister 3–5 seconds.

3. Exhale slowly and deeply.

4. Hold the canister upside down two fingers away from the mouth or use a spacer.

5. Inhale deeply for 3–5 seconds while pressing down on the canister.

6. Hold breath for 10 seconds, release pressure on the canister, remove mouthpiece from the mouth, and then exhale slowly.

7. Wait 60 seconds before repeating the procedure.

8. Rinse the mouth with water; rinse the inhaler mouthpiece and spacer and store them in a clean area.

Dry-Powder Inhaler:

1. Store the inhaler and medication in a dry area.

2. Remove the cap and hold the inhaler upright.

3. Load the inhaler according to the directions for use.

4. Hold the inhaler level with the mouthpiece end facing down.

5. Tilt your head back slightly; then breathe deeply and slowly.

6. Place the mouthpiece into your mouth; with the teeth over the mouth piece form a seal with the lips. Do not block the inhaler with your tongue.

7. Inhale rapidly and deeply for 2–3 seconds.

8. Remove the inhaler from your mouth and hold your breath for 10 seconds.

9. Exhale slowly through pursed lips. Do not exhale into the inhaler mouthpiece.

10. Rinse mouth with water and brush teeth after using the inhaler.

11. Store the inhaler in a clean, sealed plastic bag. Do not wash the inhaler unless directed by the manufacturer.

12. Clean the mouthpiece weekly using a dry cloth.

13. Notify the physician of the presence of a sore throat or sore mouth.

NOTE

For more detailed information on asthma, see the "Childhood Asthma" section in Chapter 16, "Care of the Pediatric Client."

> **CAUTION**
>
> When both antibiotics and aminophylline are administered intravenously, the nurse should check for compatibility. If only one IV site is used, the nurse should use the SAS procedure (saline, administer medication, saline) for administering medications. Administer IV doses using a controller.
>
> Clients receiving aminophylline should> be maintained on cardiorespiratory monitoring because aminophylline affects cardiac and respiratory rates as well as blood pressure. Because toxicity can occur rapidly, the nurse should monitor the client's aminophylline level. Symptoms of toxicity are nausea, vomiting, tachycardia, palpitations, hypotension. In extreme cases, the client could progress to shock, coma, and death.
>
> The therapeutic range for aminophylline is 10–20 mcg/mL.
>
> Refer to Table 5.1 at the end of the chapter for full details on the pharmacology agents administered for respiratory conditions.

Pleurisy

Pleurisy, (pleuritis) an inflammation of the pleural sac, can be associated with upper respiratory infection, pulmonary embolus, thoracotomy, chest trauma, or cancer. Symptoms include

- ► Sharp pain on inspiration
- ► Chills
- ► Fever
- ► Cough
- ► Dyspnea

Chest x-ray reveals the presence of air or fluid in the pleural sac. Management of the client with pleurisy includes the administration of analgesics, antitussives, antibiotics, and oxygen therapy. A thoracentesis is often necessary if there is pleural effusion. It is the nurse's responsibility to prepare the client for the procedure including positioning. The client can be positioned in one of the following ways:

- ► Sitting on the edge of the bed with her feet supported and with her head and arms resting on a padded over the bed table (see Figure 5.1)
- ► Sitting astride a chair with her arms and head resting on the back of the chair
- ► Lying on her unaffected side with her head of the bed elevated 30°–45° (for clients unable to sit upright)

Following the thoracentesis, the nurse should assess the client for complications, including bleeding, hypotension, and pneumothorax.

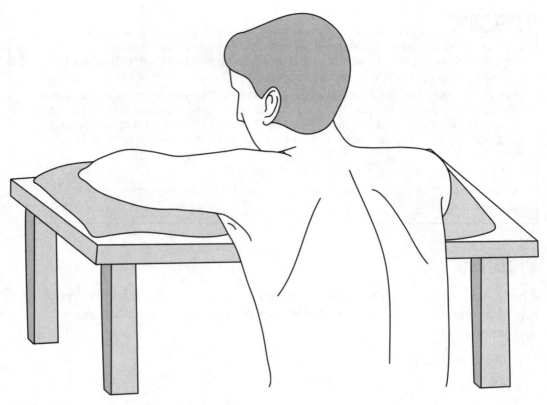

FIGURE 5.1 Client positioning for thoracentesis.

Pulmonary Hypertension

Pulmonary hypertension results when constriction of blood vessels increases vascular resistance in the lungs. Pulmonary hypertension is diagnosed by systolic pressures greater than 30 mm Hg in the pulmonary artery. In some instances, the condition occurs as a complication of other lung disorders. In the case of primary pulmonary hypertension (PPH), there is no lung disorder and the cause remains unknown. Pulmonary hypertension seems to occur in families and is more common in women 20–40 years of age.

The most common symptoms associated with pulmonary hypertension are chest pain, dyspnea and fatigue in an otherwise healthy adult. Eventually, the right side of the heart fails.

The diagnosis of pulmonary hypertension is made by a right-sided heart catheterization that reveals increased pressure in the pulmonary artery. Pulmonary function tests show decreased pulmonary volumes and decreased diffusion capacity. Abnormal ventilation perfusion scan and abnormal spiral CT help to confirm the diagnosis.

Medical treatment of pulmonary hypertension includes the use of anticoagulants, vasodilators, cardiotonics, calcium channel blockers, bronchodilators and diuretics. Daily doses of Coumadin (warfarin) are given to achieve an international normalized ratio

(INR) of 1.5–2.0. This elevated INR can prevent the common occurrence of thrombosis in situ. Cardizem (diltiazem) or other calcium channel blockers such as Procardia (nifedipine) are given to dilate blood vessels. Short-acting direct vasodilators can be used for clients who do not respond to calcium channel blockers. These short-acting direct vasodilators include intravenous Flolan (epoprostenol), intravenous Remodulin (treprostinol), and oral Tracleer (bosentan). The use of vasodilators is limited in the client with pulmonary hypertension because the medication can produce systemic hypotension. Instead, infusion of Adenocard (adenosine) into the pulmonary artery is recommended because it has a vasodilating effect that is specific to pulmonary circulation. Viagra (sildenafil) has been shown to cause preferential pulmonary vasodilation and is sometimes used to manage clients with primary and secondary pulmonary hypertension.

The cardiotonic drug Lanoxin (digoxin) and diuretics are indicated for the client with cardiac hypertrophy and cardiac failure. Bronchodilators improve hypoxemia and reduce pulmonary vascular resistance. Surgical management of pulmonary hypertension relies on whole lung transplant.

Interstitial Pulmonary Disease

Interstitial pulmonary disease, sometimes referred to as *fibrotic lung disease*, encompasses several lung disorders that share common characteristics. These characteristics include the following:

▶ Pathologic changes in the alveoli, blood vessels, and surrounding support tissue of the lungs instead of the airway

▶ Restriction in expansion and recoil rather than obstructive disease

▶ Thickening of lung tissue so that the lung becomes "stiff" or noncompliant with respirations

Sarcoidosis and idiopathic pulmonary fibrosis are two examples of interstitial pulmonary disease.

Sarcoidosis

Sarcoidosis is a multisystem disorder that is capable of producing granulomatous lesions in almost any organ or tissue. The disorder is believed to be a hypersensitive response to one or more agents such as bacteria, fungi, viruses, or chemicals.

Sites most commonly affected are the lungs, lymph nodes, spleen, liver, central nervous system, skin, eyes, and parotid glands. According to the American Lung Association (2006) more than 90% of clients with sarcoidosis have pulmonary involvement. In the lungs, granulomatous infiltration and fibrosis results in low lung compliance, impaired diffusing capacity, and decrease lung volume.

The disease is not gender specific; however, African Americans are affected 10 times more often than Caucasians with the onset occurring in the third and fourth decades of life.

The symptoms of sarcoidosis vary according to the system involved. Pulmonary symptoms include dyspnea, cough, hemoptysis, and congestion. Other symptoms include anorexia, fatigue, weight loss, and fever.

The diagnosis of sarcoidosis is made by chest x-ray and CT scan, which reveal disseminated miliary and nodular lesions in the lungs. Mediastinoscopy or transbronchial biopsy are performed to confirm the diagnosis. The presence of noncaseating granulomas is consistent with a diagnosis of sarcoidosis.

Some clients with sarcoidosis undergo remission without specific treatment. Others are treated with cytotoxic or immunosuppressive drugs. Commonly used medications include corticosteroids (prednisone), Plaquenil (chloroquine), Indocin (indomethacin), Imuran (azathioprine), and Rheumatrex (methotrexate).

Pulmonary Fibrosis

Pulmonary fibrosis or restrictive lung disease is most common in the older adult with a history of cigarette smoking or chronic exposure to respiratory irritants such as metal particles, wood fires, or organic chemicals. When the lungs are injured, an inflammatory process continues beyond the time of normal healing. Extensive fibrosis and scarring occur, leaving the alveoli damaged. Most persons with pulmonary fibrosis have progressive symptoms with few remissions. Even with proper treatment, most clients die within five years of diagnosis.

Early symptoms of pulmonary fibrosis include mild exertional dyspnea. As the disease progresses dyspnea and hypoxemia become more severe. Eventually the client continues to have hypoxemia even when high levels of oxygen are administered. The goal of treatment is to slow the disease process and to manage the client's dyspnea. Immunosuppressive drugs such as Cytoxan (cyclophosphamide) and Imuran (azathioprine) are used to reduce inflammation. Side effects of these drugs include immunosuppression, nausea, and hepatic damage. Lung transplantation is a curative therapy for pulmonary fibrosis.

Occupational Pulmonary Disease

Occupational pulmonary disease results when workers are exposed to organic and inorganic dusts or noxious fumes or aerosols. Factors affecting the development of occupational lung disease include the composition and concentration of the agent, the duration of exposure, and the individual's susceptibility to the irritant. Coexisting pulmonary irritants such as cigarette smoke increase the risk of certain types of lung cancer. Occupational pulmonary diseases include silicosis, pneumoconiosis (black lung), asbestosis, talcosis, and berylliosis.

The prevention of occupational pulmonary disease includes proper ventilation of the work environment and the use of protective gear, including face masks, hoods, and industrial respirators. Educational programs for smoking cessation improve overall health and help decrease the risk of occupational pulmonary disease. Workers exposed to asbestos and toxic dusts should be educated regarding health hazards to others from clothing and shoes. A copy of "right to know laws" should be available to all workers exposed to hazardous or toxic materials. Workers should be educated about hazardous or toxic substances they work with, effects of these substances on their health, and measures to protect themselves.

Silicosis

Silicosis is caused by the inhalation of silica dust, which produces nodular lesions throughout the lungs. These nodules eventually enlarge and coalesce, causing dense masses in the upper portions of the lungs. The lungs become unable to fully expand and secondary emphysema produces obstructive lung disease.

Silicosis affects 1–3 million workers in the United States. Persons employed as foundry workers and those employed in glass manufacturing, stone-cutting, and manufacturing of abrasives and pottery are at risk for silicosis. Finely ground silica found in soaps and polishes is particularly dangerous.

The client with acute silicosis complains of dyspnea, fever, cough, and weight loss. Those with chronic silicosis have symptoms of hypoxemia, restricted air flow, and right-sided heart failure.

There is no specific treatment for silicosis. Management usually includes the provision of supplemental oxygen as needed, bronchodilators, and diuretics for symptoms of right-sided heart failure.

Pneumoconiosis

Pneumoconiosis (*black lung*, *coal miner's lung*) results from inhalation of dusts that are a mixture of coal, kaolin, mica, and silica. When these particles are deposited in the alveoli and bronchioles, they are surrounded by macrophages that transport them to the terminal bronchioles. For a while, these deposits are removed by mucociliary action. However, in time, the clearance mechanism cannot remove the excessive dust load and macrophages and fibroplasts clog the bronchioles and alveoli, creating blackened dots on the lung. These blackened dots, known as *coal macules*, are the primary lesions of the disease. Enlarged and dilated bronchioles eventually produce localized emphysema.

Pneumoconiosis begins in the upper lobes of the lungs and with repeated exposure progresses to the lower lobes. Symptoms begin with a chronic productive cough similar to the cough of bronchitis. As the disease progresses, the client complains of shortness of breath and a cough productive of a black fluid. Later symptoms include those of right-sided heart failure.

Asbestosis

Asbestosis, the result of inhaling asbestos dust or fibers, produces diffuse pulmonary fibrosis that obliterates the alveoli. Federal laws restricting or eliminating the use of asbestos were passed when it was learned that asbestos posed a health hazard. Persons employed in asbestos mining and manufacturing, shipbuilding, and construction and demolition of buildings containing asbestos materials are at greatest risk. Examples of asbestos-containing materials include shingles, cement, vinyl asbestos tile, fireproof paints, filters, and brake linings.

Symptoms associated with asbestosis include progressive dyspnea, persistent dry cough, mild to moderate chest pain, anorexia, and weight loss. Pleural thickening and plaque formation reduce lung volume and oxygen and carbon dioxide exchange. The development of cor pulmonale and respiratory failure is common. Additional related diseases include asbestosis pleural effusion and malignant mesothelioma—a rare but fatal cancer of the pleura, peritoneum, or pericardium. The period of time between asbestos exposure and development of mesothelioma is long, ranging from 20 to 30 years. Depending on the person's health and time of diagnosis, the average survival time is 4–12 months.

Talcosis

Talcosis occurs after exposure to talc dust. Persons employed in the manufacture of paint, ceramics, cosmetics, roofing materials, and rubber goods are at greatest risk for the development of talcosis. The disease results in diffuse interstitial fibrosis that eventually results in restrictive lung disease. The symptoms are the same as those with other forms of restrictive lung disease.

Berylliosis

Berylliosis is more common in workers in industries in which metal is heated (steel mills or welding) or where metal is machined in such a way that a dust is created. There is a genetic component in some individuals that seems to increase susceptibility to the disease after exposure. Like talcosis, berylliosis produces interstitial fibrosis that results in restrictive lung disease.

Infectious Disorders of the Lower Respiratory Tract

Infectious disorders of the lower respiratory tract refers to diseases affecting the lungs. Pneumonia and pulmonary tuberculosis represent two major infectious disorders of the lower respiratory tract.

Pneumonia

Pneumonia is an inflammation of the parenchyma of the lungs caused by any number of organisms that include bacteria, viruses, and fungi. Community-acquired pneumonias include streptococcal pneumonia, *Haemophilus influenza*, Legionnaires' disease,

Mycoplasma pneumoniae, viral pneumonia, and chlamydial pneumonia. Hospital-acquired pneumonias include *Pseudomonas* pneumonia, staphylococcal pneumonia, *Klebsiella* pneumonia, *Pneumocystis carinii* pneumonia (PCP), and fungal pneumonia.

Presenting symptoms depend on the causative organism. The client with viral pneumonia tends to have milder symptoms, whereas the client with bacterial pneumonia might have chills and fever as high as 103°. Clients with cytomegalovirus, *Pneumocystis carinii*, or aspergillus will be acutely ill. General symptoms of pneumonia include

- ▶ Hypoxia
- ▶ Tachypnea
- ▶ Tachycardia
- ▶ Chest pain
- ▶ Malaise
- ▶ Fever
- ▶ Confusion (particularly in the elderly)

Care of the client with pneumonia depends on the causative organism. The management of bacterial pneumonias includes antibiotics, antitussives, antipyretics, and oxygen. Antibiotics that might be ordered include penicillin G, tetracycline, gentamicin , and erythromycin. Viral pneumonias do not respond to antimicrobial therapy but are treated with antiviral therapy. Fungal pneumonias are treated with antifungal therapy. Tables 5.2 and 5.3 at the end of the chapter provide examples of community- and hospital-acquired pneumonias as well as drugs used to treat them.

CAUTION

Some medications used in the treatment of pneumonia require special attention:

- ▶ Tetracycline should not be given to women who are pregnant or to small children because of the damage it can cause to developing teeth and bones.
- ▶ Garamycin (gentamicin), an aminoglycoside, is both ototoxic and nephrotoxic. It is important to monitor the client for signs of toxicity. Serum peak and trough levels are obtained according to hospital protocol. Peak levels for Garamycin are drawn 30 minutes after the third or fourth IV or IM dose. Trough levels for Garamycin are drawn 30 minutes before the third or fourth IV or IM dose. The therapeutic range for Garamycin is 4–10 mcg/mL.

Additional therapies for the client with pneumonia include providing for fluid and nutritional needs, obtaining frequent vital signs, and providing oral hygiene. Supplemental oxygen and chest percussion and drainage should be performed as ordered by the physician.

Oxygen Therapy

The goal of oxygen therapy is to provide adequate levels of oxygen to blood while decreasing the workload of the heart and lungs. As with other medications, a physician's order is required when administering oxygen, except in emergency situations when failure to do so would result in injury or death of the client.

Oxygen delivery systems are classified as low flow or high flow. Low-flow systems provide supplemental oxygen while the client continues to breathe some room air. Examples of low-flow systems are nasal cannula, simple mask, and rebreather masks. Nasal cannulas are capable of providing 1–6 liters of oxygen per minute. Masks are capable of providing 6–12 liters of oxygen per minute. Venturi and aerosol masks are examples of high-flow systems, which are capable of delivering 4–10 liters of oxygen per minute. Oxygen flow rates are prescribed by the physician according to the client's condition and oxygen requirements. Figure 5.2 illustrates a Venturi mask as well as nasal cannula.

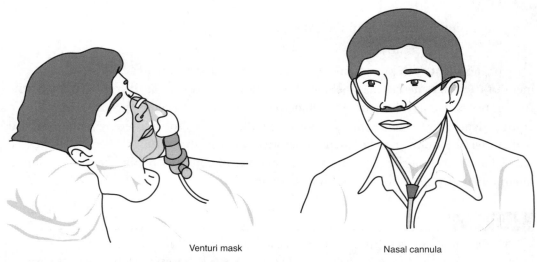

Venturi mask   Nasal cannula

FIGURE 5.2 Examples of oxygen delivery systems.

The nurse should observe the client's response to oxygen therapy as well as watching for signs of oxygen toxicity. Signs of oxygen toxicity include substernal discomfort, paresthesias, dyspnea, restlessness, fatigue, malaise, and progressive respiratory difficulty.

Chest Physiotherapy

Chest physiotherapy that includes percussion, vibration, and postural drainage is used to remove bronchial secretions and improve oxygenation. The nurse should assess the client for any conditions, such as recent thoracic surgery, that would contraindicate the use of chest physiotherapy.

Auscultation of the chest before and after the procedure is carried out to determine the effectiveness of treatment. A towel placed over the client's chest will make the client more comfortable during percussion. Using cupped hands, the nurse strikes the client's chest in a rhythmical fashion for 3–5 minutes for each lung segment. As the client exhales, manual vibration or tremor might be used to help loosen secretions. Figure 5.3 illustrates chest percussion and drainage.

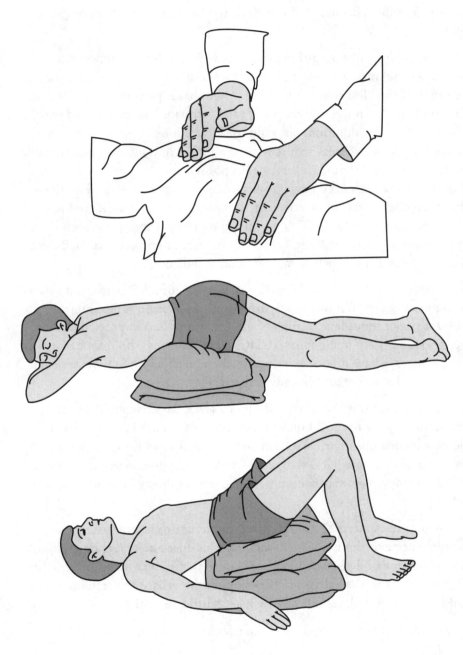

FIGURE 5.3
Chest percussion and postural drainage for sides (lower lobes) and back (upper lobes).

Tuberculosis

Tuberculosis (TB) is a highly contagious respiratory infection caused by the *mycobacterium tuberculosis*. The organism is transmitted by droplets from the respiratory tract. The incidence of TB has been steadily increasing in the United States and world wide for the past twenty years. Risk factors include living in overcrowded conditions, being immune compromised, and age. Duration of exposure affects transmission.

Symptoms of TB are varied. Some clients might have no symptoms; others might complain of fever (particularly in the afternoon), weight loss, anorexia, indigestion, cough that becomes productive, night sweats, shortness of breath, and changes in lung sounds. Sites most commonly affected by TB include the lungs, cervical lymph nodes, kidney, and spine.

Methods used for tuberculosis testing include the intradermal PPD (Mantoux) test and the multiple puncture (tine) test. The multiple puncture test is less accurate than the PPD test; therefore, it is used less often. The PPD (Mantoux) is performed by injecting 0.1 mL of PPD intradermally in the inner aspect of the forearm. The test is read within 48–72 hours with notation of induration, not redness. Indurations of 0 mm–4 mm are generally considered negative, whereas indurations of 5 mm–9 mm indicate questionable exposure. Indurations of 5 mm–9 mm are considered positive for those in close contact with a client with TB, those with HIV or who are immunocompromised, and in those who have an abnormal chest x-ray. Indurations of 10 mm–15 mm are considered positive for those born in a country where TB is prevalent; those who are intravenous drug users; residents of long-term care facilities, homeless shelters, or correctional facilities; and those with medical conditions such as malnutrition and diabetes.

Indurations greater than 15 mm are considered to be positive for all. Positive test results indicate exposure and infection, but not necessarily active disease. An induration of 5 mm is the cut-off for organ transplant recipients and other immunosuppressed clients treated with prednisone or TNF antagonists. (CDC, 2005) Persons who have had a positive skin test will always have a positive skin test, therefore they should be screened with a chest x-ray as needed to detect clinically active TB.

Positive skin tests can be measured accurately for up to seven days. Negative reactions can be measured accurately for only 72 hours. Factors that can cause false positive TB skin test include nontuberculous mycobacterium and inoculation with BCG vaccine. Factors that can cause false negative TB skin test include anergy (weakened immune system), recent TB infection, age, vaccination with live viruses, overwhelming TB, and poor testing technique.

TB is confirmed by positive sputum test. Automated radiometric culture systems (Bactec) yield results in one to three weeks. Blood tests that measure and compare the amount of interferon-gamma released by blood cells in response to antigens include the Quantiferon TB test and Quantiferon Gold. Two-step testing is used to establish a baseline skin test and for adults tested periodically such as healthcare workers:

▶ If the first TB skin test is read as positive, the client is considered infected.

▶ If the first TB skin test is read as negative, give second TB skin test one to three weeks later. If the second TB skin test is read as positive, the client is considered infected.

▶ If the second TB skin test is read as negative, the client is considered uninfected at the baseline.

Care of the client with TB includes the use of antimycobacterial drugs INH (isoniazid), Myambutol (ethambutol), Rifadin (rifampin), and streptomycin. Multiple drug therapy destroys organisms quickly and decreases the chance of developing drug-resistant organisms. Clients newly diagnosed with TB are typically treated with a regimen of four antituberulars: Rifadin(rifampin) and INH (isoniazid) are given throughout the course of treatment, and Tebrazid (pyrazinamide and Myambutol (ethambutol) are added for the first 2 months. The combination of medications reduces the treatment time to 6 months for most clients; however, clients with HIV infection are typically treated for 9 months.

Airborne precautions, which are used in the hospital setting, are not used if the client is convalescing home, however all household members need to be checked for infection. Sputum specimens are collected every 2–4 weeks. The client can return to work when he/she has three negative sputum specimens. Household contacts are generally treated with prophylactically with INH (isoniazid). Table 5.4, presented in the Key Concepts section later in the chapter, lists details about antitubercular drugs. Because of the length and intensity of treatment, the client should have the following lab studies performed before beginning therapy and on a regularly scheduled basis:

▸ Alanine transaminase (ALT)

▸ Aspartate transaminase (AST)

▸ Bilirubin

▸ Platelet count

▸ Serum creatinine

Adverse effects of ethambutol include changes in visual acuity and color vision; therefore, clients should have an eye exam before beginning therapy to detect any existing problems and should report visual changes to their physician. Adverse effects of streptomycin include ototoxicity, so audiometric testing should be performed before streptomycin therapy is begun to detect problems with hearing. Changes in hearing should also be reported to the physician.

Influenza

Influenza is an acute highly contagious viral infection that affects primarily the upper respiratory tract and is sometimes complicated by the development of pneumonia. Influenza is caused by one of three types of *Myxovirus influenzae*. Infection with one strain produces immunity to only that strain; therefore, annual immunization is needed to protect against the strain projected to be prevalent that year.

Symptoms of influenza include chills, laryngitis, sore throat, runny nose, muscle aches, headache, and fever greater than 102°. Complications associated with influenza include pneumonia, exacerbations of COPD (chronic obstructive pulmonary disease), and myositis. More serious complications include pericarditis and encephalitis. The elderly, children, and those with chronic illness are more likely to develop severe complications; therefore, it is recommended that these clients receive annual influenza immunization.

The vaccine is given in the fall, prior to the onset of annual outbreaks that occur in the winter months. The vaccine is produced in eggs, so it should not be given to anyone who is allergic to egg protein.

Treatment of influenza is aimed at controlling symptoms and preventing complications. Bed rest and increased fluid intake are important interventions during the acute phase. Decongestant nasal sprays, antitussives with codeine, and antipyretics help make the client more comfortable. Antibiotics are indicated if the client develops bacterial pneumonia. Clients with influenza as well as nonimmunized persons who have been exposed to influenza might receive chemoprophylaxis if an outbreak occurs. Antiviral medication such as Relenza (zanamivir) and Tamiflu (oseltamivir) are used in both the prevention and treatment of influenza A and B and can be used to reduce the duration and severity of symptoms.

Symmetrel (amantadine) or Flumadine (rimantadine) are also used to prevent or decrease symptoms of the flu.

Life-Threatening Pulmonary Disorders

Acute and chronic respiratory conditions can rapidly deteriorate into situations that require immediate intervention to save the client's life. Some of these conditions, such as flail chest, are related to traumatic injury of the chest. Others, such as pulmonary embolus and acute respiratory distress syndrome, are related to a variety of causes including fractures. In this section, we will discuss the most common life-threatening pulmonary disorders and the nursing care related to those clients.

Acute Respiratory Distress Syndrome

Acute respiratory distress syndrome, commonly known as *ARDS* or *noncardiogenic pulmonary edema*, occurs mostly in otherwise healthy persons. ARDS can be the result of intrinsic factors (such as anaphylaxis, sepsis, or pulmonary emboli) or extrinsic factors (such as aspiration or inhalation injury). ARDS can also occur as a complication from abdominal or thoracic surgery. The client with ARDS develops increased extravascular lung fluid that contains a high concentration of protein although the interstitial tissue remains relatively dry. ARDS can be diagnosed by a chest x-ray that reveals emphysematous changes and infiltrates that give the lungs a characteristic appearance described as *ground glass*. Assessment of the client with ARDS reveals:

- ▶ Hypoxia (decreased tissue oxygenation)
- ▶ Suprasternal and intercostal retractions
- ▶ Presence of crackles (rales) or rhonchi
- ▶ Diminished breath sounds
- ▶ Refractory hypoxemia (low levels of oxygen in the blood despite supplemental oxygen delivered at high concentrations)

Nursing care of the client with ARDS involves the following:

▸ Maintaining endotrachial intubation and mechanical ventilation with positive end expiratory pressure (PEEP) or continuous positive airway pressure (CPAP). The goal of ventilation is to maintain a PaO_2 greater than 60 mm Hg or O_2 saturation level greater than 90% at the lowest possible FiO_2 setting.

▸ Monitoring of arterial blood gases.

▸ Providing for nutritional needs either by tube feeding or hyperalimentation (clients with ARDS require 35–45 kcal/kg per day).

▸ Maintaining fluid volume to maintain adequate cardiac output and tissue perfusion.

▸ Monitoring of pulmonary artery wedge pressure (assesses fluid status and monitors for the development of pulmonary hypertension).

▸ Frequent change in position: placement in high Fowler's position. or use of specialized beds to minimize consolidation of infiltrates in large airways. Research has indicated that some clients with ARDS benefit from being placed in a prone position, however the nurse should carefully assess the client's respiratory effort before putting the client flat or in a head-down position.

▸ Preventing sepsis, pneumonia, and multisystem organ dysfunction.

▸ Use of low-molecular-weight heparin to prevent thrombophlebitis and possible pulmonary embolus or disseminated intravascular coagulation.

▸ Investigational therapies include the use of mediators (vitamins C and E, aspirin, interleukin, prostacyclin), nitric oxide, and surfactant replacement.

Nursing Care of the Client Requiring Mechanical Ventilation

The client with ARDS has severe problems with maintaining adequate gas exchange, therefore mechanical ventilation is usually required. Nursing care of the client requiring mechanical ventilation includes a general understanding of the type of ventilator and modes of control being used as well as interventions to support the client's physical and psychological well-being. This section begins with a review of mechanical ventilation followed by nursing interventions for the client who is ventilator dependent.

Indications for mechanical ventilation are as follows:

▸ $PaO_2 < 50$ mm Hg with $FiO_2 > 0.60$

▸ $PaO_2 > 50$ mm Hg but a pH < 7.25

▸ Respiratory rate > 35 breaths per minute

▸ Vital capacity < 2 times tidal volume

There are two basic types of ventilators:

- **Negative-pressure ventilators:** Work by changing pressures in the chest cavity rather than by forcing air directly into the lungs. Negative pressure ventilators such as the poncho or body wrap are used for clients with neuromuscular disease and chronic obstructive pulmonary disease. An artificial airway is not needed.

- **Positive-pressure ventilators:** Inflate the lungs by exerting positive pressure on the airway, which forces the alveoli to expand during inspiration. In most instances an endotracheal tube or tracheostomy is needed. Postive-pressure ventilators are classified according to the mechanism that ends inspiration and begins expiration. Positive-pressure ventilators are classified as pressure-cycled, time-cycled, flow-cycled, or volume-cycled. Key features of these as follows:

  - Pressure-cycled ventilators push air into the lungs until a preset airway pressure is obtained. Pressure-cycled ventilators are sometimes used for respiratory therapy or for the client just after surgery.

  - Volume-cycled ventilators push air into the lungs until a preset volume has been delivered. Tidal volume remains constant. Set pressure limits prevent excessive pressure from being exerted on the lungs.

  - Time-cycled ventilators push air into the lungs until a preset time has been reached. Tidal volume and pressure vary according to the client's needs.

  - Flow-cycled ventilators push air into the lungs until a preset flow rate is achieved during inspiration.

The controlling modes of ventilators are as follows:

- **Controlled:** The machine ventilates according to set tidal volume and respiratory rate. The client's spontaneous respiratory effort is blocked.

- **Assist controlled:** A preset volume of oxygen is delivered at a preset rate, but the client can trigger ventilations with negative inspiratory effort.

- **Synchronized intermittent mandatory:** A preset minimum number of respirations are delivered to the client, but the client can also take spontaneous breaths.

General guidelines for initial ventilator settings are as follows:

- Set the tidal volume required (10–15 mL/Kg).

- Adjust to the lowest concentration of O_2 to maintain a PaO_2 of 80–100 mm Hg.

- Set the mode according to doctor's order.

- For assist controlled mode, adjust sensitivity so that the client can trigger the ventilator with minimal effort.

- Record minute volume; measure PaO_2, $PaCO_2$, and pH every 20 minutes of continuous mechanical ventilation.

▶ Adjust settings according to the results of arterial blood gases to maintain normal levels or levels prescribed by doctor.

▶ If the client becomes confused or "fights" the ventilator unexpectedly, assess for hypoxemia and manually ventilate with resuscitation device and 100% oxygen.

Nursing Care of the Client Who Is Ventilator Dependent

Nursing interventions for the client who is ventilator dependent are as follows:

▶ Explain the purpose of the ventilator. Clients in ICU may become confused and need repeated explanations and reassurance.

▶ Assess vital signs and breath sounds every 30–60 minutes.

▶ Assess breathing pattern in relation to ventilation cycle to determine if the client is tolerating the ventilator.

▶ If an endotracheal tube is used, make sure that it is taped securely in place.

▶ Monitor pulse oximetry and arterial blood gases.

▶ Suction when needed, and observe the color and amount of respiratory secretions. Guidelines for performing endotracheal suctioning are given in the sidebar that follows.

▶ Provide the client with a means of communication such as Magic Slate or writing paper.

▶ Keep the call light within reach of the client.

Guidelines for Performing Endotracheal Suctioning:

1. Collect needed supplies (suction unit ; size 12–16 Fr sterile suction catheter; sterile normal saline; personal protective gear—goggles, mask, gown).

2. Explain procedure to client; provide a means of communication.

3. Set suction to setting of 80–120 mmHg.

4. Open sterile saline, leaving cap loosely in place.

In-Line Catheter:

1. Wearing exam glove, and attach the catheter to suction tubing.

2. Administer oxygen at 100% for three to four breaths.

3. Maintain sterility; insert the catheter through the plastic shield until resistance is met. Do not apply suction upon insertion of the catheter. Using a twirling motion, and apply suction while the catheter is being withdrawn.

4. Limit suctioning to no more than 10 seconds; provide supplemental oxygen and allow the client to rest 3–5 breaths; repeat the procedure if needed, but no more than 3 times.

5. Disconnect suction tubing from catheter; clear the tubing; turn off suction.

6. Remove and discard glove.

(continues)

(continued)

Catheter and Glove Kit:

1. Open kit containing suction catheter and glove. Remove saline cup and fill with sterile saline.

2. Don sterile gloves and attach the catheter to the suction tubing. Keeping the dominant hand sterile, and lubricate the catherter tip with the sterile saline.

3. With the nondominant hand, adjust the oxygen to 100% and administer 3 breaths.

4. With the nondominant hand, disconnect the ventilator tubing from the endotracheal tube. With the dominant hand (sterile), insert the suction catheter until resistance is felt. With the nondominant hand (nonsterile) applying suction, the dominant hand uses a twisting motion as catheter as the catheter is being withdrawn.

5. Limit suctioning to no more than 10 seconds; reconnect the ventilator and allow the client to rest 3–5 breaths; clear the suction catheter with sterile saline.

6. Repeat the procedure if needed, but no more than 3 times.

7. Reconnect the ventilator tubing to the endotracheal tube.

8. Clear the suction tubing; turn off suction; disconnect the catheter and discard with glove.

9. Observe the color, quantity, and consistency of sputum.

10. Assess the lung sounds and the client's tolerance of procedure.

11. Wash hands.

Pulmonary Embolus

Pulmonary embolus (PE) refers to the obstruction of the pulmonary artery or one of its branches by a clot, fat, or gaseous substance. Clots can originate anywhere in the body, but are most likely to migrate from a vein deep in the legs, pelvis, kidney, or arms. Fat embolus is associated with fractures of the long bones, particularly the femur. Air embolus, which is less common, can occur during the insertion or use of central lines. Amniotic embolus can be a complication of amniocentesis or abortion and is associated with a very high mortality rate Septic embolus can result from pelvic abscesses, damaged heart valves, osteomyelitis, infected intravenous catheters, or nonsterile injections of illegal drugs.

Pulmonary embolus affects approximately 500,000 people in the United States annually; therefore, prevention of PE should be a major concern for nurses. The following steps can significantly reduce the incidence of pulmonary embolus:

▸ Ambulate postoperative clients as soon as possible.

▸ Apply antiembolism and pneumatic compression stockings.

▸ Avoid pressure beneath the popliteal space.

▸ Check the status of peripheral circulation (do not perform Homans' sign because doing so might dislodge any clots that are present).

▸ Change the client's position every two hours.

▶ Check IV sites for signs of heat, redness, and swelling as well as blood return.

▶ Avoid massaging or compressing leg muscles.

▶ Teach client not to cross the legs.

▶ Encourage smoking cessation.

Common risk factors for the development of pulmonary embolus include immobilization, fractures, trauma, and history of clot formation. Situations, such as air travel that require prolonged sitting can also contribute to clot formation, particularly in those who are elderly or debilitated. Conditions associated with identified risk factors are smoking, pregnancy, estrogen therapy, use of oral contraceptives, cancer of the lung or prostate, obesity, thrombocytopenia, advanced age, atrial fibrillation, presence of artificial heart valves, sepsis, and congestive heart failure.

TIP

Remember the three Fs of fat emboli:

▶ Fat

▶ Femur

▶ Football player

Most fat emboli come from fractured femurs; most fractured femurs occur in young men 18–25, the age of most football players.

Symptoms of a pulmonary embolus depend on the size and location of the clot or undissolved matter. Symptoms generally include the following:

▶ Pleuritic chest pain

▶ Low-grade fever

▶ Tachypnea

▶ Dyspnea

▶ Hypoxemia

▶ Syncope

▶ Hemoptysis (due to pulmonary infarction)

▶ Tachycardia

▶ Transient changes in T wave and S-T segments

▶ Hypotension

▶ Sense of apprehension

▶ Petechiae over the chest and axilla (associated with development of DIC [disseminated intravascular coagulation])

▶ Distended neck veins (indicates right ventricular failure)

Diagnostic tests to confirm the presence of pulmonary embolus include chest x-ray, pulmonary angiography, ventilation-perfusion lung scan, and ECG to rule out myocardial infarction. Chest x-ray findings are often normal or can reveal pulmonary infiltration at the site of the embolus. Negative lung scan rules out the presence of pulmonary embolus. Pulmonary angiography, the most specific diagnostic test for ruling out pulmonary embolus, is used when results of the lung scan are inconclusive.

Management of the client with a pulmonary embolus includes

▸ Placing the client in an upright sitting position (high Fowler's position)

▸ Administering oxygen via mask

▸ Giving medication for chest pain

▸ Using thrombolytics (streptokinase, urokinase, tPA /anticoagulants [heparin, warfarin sodium])

Antibiotics are indicated for those with septic emboli. Surgical management using umbrella-type filters is indicated for those who cannot take anticoagulants as well as for client who have recurrent emboli while taking anticoagulants. Clients receiving anticoagulant therapy should be observed for signs of bleeding. The protime (PT), International normalized ratio (INR), and partial thromboplastin time (PTT) are three tests used to track the client's clotting time.

> **CAUTION**
>
> Streptokinase is made from beta strep; therefore, clients with a history of strep infections might respond poorly to anticoagulant therapy with streptokinase because they might have formed antibodies.
>
> Streptokinase is not clot specific; therefore, the client might develop a tendency to bleed from incision or injection sites.

Pneumothorax

Pneumothorax occurs when the pleural space is exposed to positive atmospheric pressure. Normally the pressure in the pleural cavity is negative or subamospheric. It is this negative pressure that keeps the lungs inflated. When either the parietal or visceral pleura is breached, air enters the pleural cavity and increases the intrathoracic pressure. This results in a collapse of a portion of the lung.

There are three classifications of pneumothorax:

▸ **Spontaneous pneumothorax:** A non–life-threatening condition that can result from the rupture of a bleb, or blister, on the surface of the visceral pleura or from chronic obstructive pulmonary disease. Blunt chest trauma and penetrating chest wounds are the main causes of traumatic and tension pneumothorax.

▸ **Traumatic pneumothorax:** Usually results from blunt trauma to the chest and is classified as either an *open* pneumothorax (outside air enters the pleural space) or a *closed* pneumothorax (air from the lung enters the pleural space). Both closed traumatic pneumothorax and tension pneumothorax are life-threatening emergencies that require early detection and treatment.

▶ **Tension pneumothorax:** Results from an air leak in the lung or chest wall that leads to collapse of the lung. Air enters the pleural space with each inspiration and does not exit during expiration. Air accumulation in the pleural space compresses blood vessels and decreases venous return. The result is reduced cardiac filling and decreased cardiac output. In addition to blunt chest trauma, tension pneumothorax can result from complications of mechanical ventilation with positive end expiratory pressure (PEEP) and insertion of central venous catheters.

Assessment of the client with a pneumothorax can reveal

▶ Reduced breath sounds on the affected side

▶ Hyperresonance on percussion of the chest

▶ Prominence of the affected side of the chest

▶ Tracheal deviation away from (closed pneumothorax) or toward (open pneumothorax) the affected side

▶ Tachypnea, respiratory distress, or cyanosis

▶ Pleuritic pain

▶ Subcutaneous emphysema in some cases

▶ Distended neck veins in some cases

Chest tubes are inserted after confirming the condition by chest x-ray. The initial treatment of tension pneumothorax is the insertion of a large bore needle at the second intercostal space, mid-clavicular line on the affected side followed by insertion of chest tubes connected to a water-sealed chest drainage system.

Hemothorax

Hemothorax, an accumulation of blood in the pleural space, can be caused by a number of conditions including blunt trauma, penetrating injury, thoracic surgery, and dissecting thoracic aneurysms. In the case of blunt trauma or penetrating injury pneumothorax may accompany hemothorax. The accumulation of blood in the pleural space exerts pressure on pulmonary structures. This causes the alveoli to collapse and decreases the surface area for gas exchange. Hypovolemia occurs as bleeding decreases the vascular volume. The severity of a hemothorax depends on the amount of blood loss. Massive hemothorax—blood loss greater than 1500 mL—can occur from trauma to the heart, great vessels, or intercostal arteries.

Assessment findings are dependent on the amount of blood loss. The client with a small hemothorax can be asymptomatic. Findings associated with a large hemothorax include

▶ Respiratory distress

▶ Diminished breath sounds

▶ Dull sound when the affected side is percussed

▶ Blood in the pleural space

Anterior and posterior chest tubes are inserted to remove blood. The physician may perform an open thoracotomy when the blood loss is excessive (from 1500 mL to 2000 mL) or persistent (200 mL per hour over a three hour period).

A key role of the nurse in caring for the client with a pneumothorax or hemothorax is assessing the chest drainage system and intervening appropriately if problems arise. Chest tubes are inserted for one of two reasons: to drain the chest cavity or to reinflate the lung. Chest drainage systems can be one-bottle, two-bottle, or three-bottle setups. Chest drainage systems using glass bottles have largely been replaced by lightweight disposable systems that use chambers rather than bottles as illustrated in Figure 5.4.

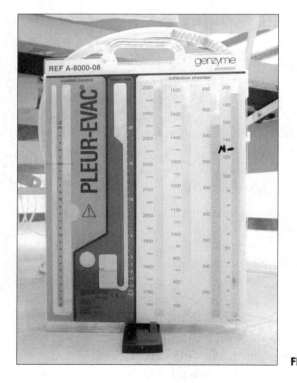

FIGURE 5.4 Chamber chest drainage system.

One-chamber set-ups do not allow for suction control and cannot handle large amounts of drainage. Two-chamber setups allow for suction and are capable of collecting large amounts of drainage. In the two-chamber setup, the first chamber collects the drainage, and the second chamber controls the amount of suction. In the traditional water seal or three-chamber setup, the first chamber collects the drainage, the second chamber acts as a water seal, and the third chamber controls the amount of suction. Refer to Figure 4.5 and the Points to Remember list that follows to help you review the management of a three-chamber water seal chest drainage system.

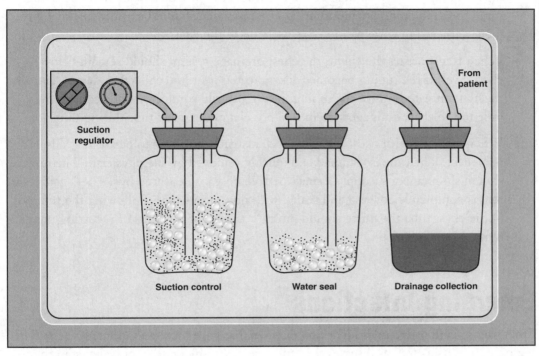

FIGURE 5.5 Three-Chamber chest drainage system.

The collection chamber acts as a reservoir for fluid that drains from the chest tube. A one-way valve in the water seal chamber prevents air from moving back into the chest when the client inhales. *Tidaling*, or an increase in water level, occurs with inspiration and returns to baseline with expiration. The suction control chamber regulates the amount of negative pressure applied to the chest cavity. The amount of suction applied is determined by the amount of water in the suction chamber. The amount of suction is generally set at 20 cm of water.

Points to remember for management of a three-chamber water seal chest drainage system include

- ▸ Monitor the color, amount, and consistency of the drainage.

- ▸ Note fluctuations in the water seal chamber. Fluctuations stop when the tubing is obstructed, when there is a dependent loop, or when the suction is not working properly.

- ▸ Assess the suction control chamber for bubbling. Constant bubbling in the water seal chamber can indicate an air leak. Assess the chest tube system for external air leaks. The physician should be notified at once if there is constant bubbling in the water seal chamber that is not related to an external air leak.

▶ Ensure that the drainage tube does not interfere with the client's movement. If the chest tube should become disconnected from the client, the nurse should cover the insertion site immediately with a petroleum gauze. (Petroleum gauze, sterile dressings, and tape should be kept at the client's bedside.) The client should be monitored for developing pneumothorax. The physician should be notified and equipment gathered in anticipation of reinsertion of the chest tube.

▶ When transporting the client, the chest drainage system should remain below chest level. If the tubing becomes disconnected from the collection device, cut off the contaminated tips of the tubing, insert a sterile connector, and reattach the tube to the chest drainage system. Do not clamp the chest tube during transport.

▶ When assisting with chest tube removal, instruct the client to perform a Valsalva maneuver. The tube is clamped and quickly removed by the physician. The nurse should simultaneously apply a small petroleum gauze covered by a 4"×4" gauze pad that is completely covered and sealed with nonporous tape. Following the removal of the chest tube the nurse should monitor the client for signs of recurring pneumothorax.

Emerging Infections

Emerging infections includes identified diseases that have increased in incidence within the past 20 years as well as diseases that are expected to increase in prevalence in the near future. Examples of emerging infections are West Nile virus, Legionnaires' disease, Lyme disease, hantavirus pulmonary syndrome, Ebola and Marburg viruses, and severe acute respiratory syndrome (SARS). Two emerging infections—SARS and Legionnaires' disease—will be covered in this section.

SARS

Severe acute respiratory syndrome is a pneumonia caused by a newly recognized coronavirus (CoV). The first human coronavirus, isolated in 1965, is responsible for about one-third of all colds. The virus is spread by droplets as well as contact with surface objects contaminated by droplets. Most cases of SARS have been in China, Taiwan, Singapore, Hong Kong, and Vietnam; however, limited cases have been identified in other areas. Symptoms include cough, shortness of breath or increased shortness of breath, and fever. Chest x-ray reveals the presence of pneumonia, which can develop into acute respiratory distress. Lab studies include immunofluorescent antibody testing (IgM and IgG), and reverse transcriptase polyermerase chain reaction to detect RNA on the SARS CoV. Care of the client with SARS includes isolation and quarantine. The client should be placed in a negative-pressure isolation room and caregivers should use airborne and contact precautions, including N95 masks and eye shields. Antibiotics and antiviral medications are ordered. The client is closely monitored for signs of acute respiratory distress. Figure 5.6 illustrates the symptoms indicative of SARS.

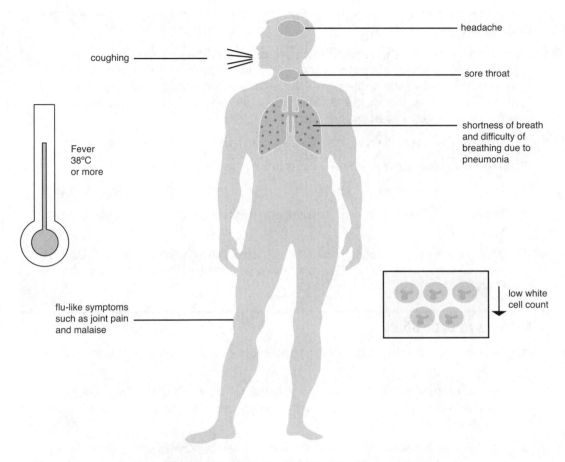

coughing

headache

sore throat

Fever
38°C
or more

shortness of breath
and difficulty of
breathing due to
pneumonia

low white
cell count

flu-like symptoms
such as joint pain
and malaise

Symptoms appear 3-7 days after exposure

FIGURE 5.6   Severe acute respiratory syndrome (SARS) symptoms.

Legionnaires' Disease

Legionnaires' disease is caused by *Legionella pneumophilia*, a gram negative bacteria
found in both natural and man-made water sources. The organism grows best in water
temperatures between 77° F and 107° F and is enhanced by water storage. Risk factors
include immunosuppression, advanced age, alcoholism, and pulmonary disease.
Legionnaires' primarily affects the lungs and other organs and produces symptoms that
include malaise, myalgia, headache, dry cough, chest pain, fever, diarrhea, and gastrointestinal complaints. Legionnaires' is diagnosed by routine culture, antibody titer, and
urinary antigen for *Legionella pneumophilia* serotype I. Management of the client with
Legionnaires' disease is the same as those used for clients with pneumonia. No special
isolation technique is used because there is no evidence of transmission between
humans. Antibiotic therapy includes the use of Zithromax (azithromycin), Biaxin (clarithromycin), Ilotycin (erythromycin), and Levaquin (levofloxacin). Zithromax
(azithromycin) is considered to be the drug of choice for the client with Legionnaires'
disease.

Case Study

Mr. Adams, a 65-year-old male, is admitted with a diagnosis of emphysema. The physician's orders include the following: oxygen 3 liters/min.; dextrose 5% in normal saline 1000 mL to infuse over eight hours; chest x-ray, routine CBC, and urinalysis; Claforan (cefotaxime) 750 mg IV every eight hours; Tussin (chlorpheniramine, hydrocodone, pseudoephedrine) 400 mg every four hours; aspirin grains ten every four hours as needed for temperature over 101°.

1. Which type of oxygen delivery system should be used to supply Mr. Adams's oxygen needs?

2. What physical changes would the nurse expect to find in the client with emphysema?

3. Discuss nutritional interventions needed for the client with chronic obstructive pulmonary disease.

4. Nursing care of Mr. Adams includes prevention of oxygen toxicity. List symptoms associated with oxygen toxicity.

5. The physician's order reads dextrose 5% in normal saline 1000 mL to infuse over eight hours. The IV setup delivers 12 drops per mL. The nurse should set the IV infusion rate at how many drops per minute?

Answers to Case Study

1. The oxygen delivery system best suited to the needs of the client with emphysema is the nasal cannula.

2. Physical changes in the client with emphysema include barrel chest, digital clubbing, prolonged respiratory phase and respiratory grunt, muscle wasting, weight loss, peripheral cyanosis, violent productive cough.

3. The client with chronic obstructive pulmonary disease should be provided with small, more frequent meals. The diet should be increased in calories with a greater percentage of the diet coming from fat calories because metabolism of fat produces less carbon dioxide than carbohydrates. Dry foods should be avoided because they increase coughing. Milk products should be avoided because they increase the thickness of secretions.

4. Symptoms of oxygen toxicity include substernal discomfort, paresthesias, dyspnea, restlessness, fatigue, malaise, and progressive respiratory distress.

5. The infusion should be set at 25 drops per minute.

Key Concepts

This chapter includes much needed information to help the nurse apply a knowledge of respiratory disorders to the NCLEX exam. The nurse preparing for the licensure exam should review normal laboratory values, common treatment modalities and pharmacological agents used in the care of the client with respiratory disorders.

Key Terms

▶ Acute respiratory failure

▶ Apnea

▶ Asthma

▶ Bronchitis

▶ Continuous positive airway pressure (CPAP)

▶ Cor pulmonale

▶ Cyanosis

▶ Dyspnea

▶ Emphysema

▶ Hemoptysis

▶ Hypoxemia

▶ Hypoxia

▶ Pleural effusion

▶ Pleurisy

▶ Pneumonia

▶ Pulmonary embolus

▶ Tachypnea

Diagnostic Tests

Many diagnostic exams are used to assess respiratory disorders. These clients would receive the usual routine exams: CBC, urinalysis, chest x-ray. The exam reviewer should be knowledgeable of the preparation and care of clients receiving pulmonary exams. While reviewing these diagnostic exams, the exam reviewer should be alert for information that would be an important part of nursing care for these clients:

▶ CBC

▶ Chest x-ray

▶ Pulmonary function tests

▶ Lung scan

▶ Bronchoscopy

Pharmacological Agents Used in the Care of the Client with Disorders of the Respiratory System

An integral part of care to clients with respiratory disorders is pharmacological intervention. These medications provide an improvement or cure of the client's respiratory problems. The nursing exam reviewer needs to focus on the drugs in Table 5.1 through Table 5.4. Included in these tables is information about the most common side and adverse effects as well as pertinent nursing care associated with these medications. These medications are not inclusive of all the agents used to treat respiratory disorders; therefore, you will want to keep a current pharmacology text handy for reference.

TABLE 5.1 Pharmacological Agents for Respiratory Conditions

Type	Name	Action	Side Effects	Nursing Care
Bronchodilators				
Methylxanthine	Theo-Dur (theophylline) Truphylline (aminophylline)	Relaxes bronchial smooth muscles	Palpitations; agitation; tachycardia; nausea; vomiting	Monitor for signs of toxicity. Therapeutic range 10–20 mcg/mL.
Cholinergic antagonists	Atrovent (ipratropium)	Relieve bronchospasm	Headache; nausea; dry mouth	Contraindicated in clients with soybean or peanut allergies.
Adrenergics	Epinephrine (adrenalin)	Stimulate alpha and beta receptors	Tremulousness; headache; tachycardia; vomiting	Teach client to read label of OTC meds.
Beta 2 agonists	Proventil (albuterol) Serevent (salmetrol)	Stimulate beta receptors in the lung, reduces airway resistance	Tremor; tachycardia; palpitations	Concurrent use with digoxin or beta blockers can affect drug level.
Corticosteroids				
Inhaled	Flovent (fluticasone) Vanceril (beclomethasone) Azmacort (triamcinolone)	Decreases inflammation and suppresses immune response	Hyperglycemia; Cushing's syndrome; increased BP; osteoporosis; muscle wasting; gastric upset	Give with meals. Monitor for signs of infection. Taper off medication.
Injectable/Oral	Decadron (dexamethasone) Solu-Cortef (hydrocortisone) Medrol (methyl-prednisolone)	Same as above	Same as above	Same as above.

TABLE 5.1 *Continued*

Type	Name	Action	Side Effects	Nursing Care
Mast cell stabilizers	Intal (cromolyn)	Inhibit release of histamine	Irritation of oral or mucous membranes	Monitor for drug interactions.
Leukotriene modifiers	Singulair (montelukast) Zyflo (zileuton) Accolate (zafirlukast)	Block inflammatory action	Headache; infection; elevated liver enzymes	Monitor for drug interactions. Client should avoid ASA and NSAIDs.
Antitussives	Codeine, dextromethorphan	Suppress cough reflex by direct effect on respiratory center	Nausea; vomiting; sedation	Take only as directed.
Expectorants	Ammonium chloride Guaifenesin K+ iodide	Loosen bronchial secretions	Nausea; drowsiness	Increase fluid intake.

TABLE 5.2 **Pharmacological Agents Used in the Treatment of Community Acquired Pneumonia**

Organism Responsible	Recommended Treatment	Action	Side Effects (Adverse Effects)	Nursing Care
Streptococcus pneumoniae	Penicillin, Claforan (cefotaxime), Rocephin (ceftriaxone), Levaquin (levofloxacin)	Bacteriacidal, effective against gram positive and gram negative organisms	Nausea; diarrhea; urticaria (pseudomembranous colitis; superimposed infections)	Assess for fluid imbalances. Diarrheal stools should be checked for the presence of blood, mucus, and white blood cells, which can indicate pseudomembranous colitis.
Haemophilus influenza	Omnipen (ampicillin), Zithromax (azithromycin), Biaxin (clarithromycin)	Bacteriostatic, effective against gram positive and gram negative organisms	Dizziness; headache; nausea; diarrhea; abdominal pain (superimposed infections)	Assess for signs of "ampicillin rash"—dull red nonallergic maculopapular rash and pruritis. Assess for signs laryngeal edema, which indicates anaphylactic reaction.
Legionella pneumophilia	Erythrocin (erythromycin), Levaquin (levofloxacin)	Bacteriacidal, effective against gram positive and gram negative organisms	Abdominal cramps; diarrhea; nausea; (psedomembranous colitis; superimposed infections)	Assess for fluid imbalances. Diarrheal stools should be checked for the presence of blood, mucus, and white blood cells, which can indicate pseudomembranous colitis.
Mycoplasma pneumoniae	Erythrocin (erythromycin), Acromycin (tetracycline) may be used with Rifadin (rifampin)	Bacteriacidal, effective against gram negative organisms	Abdominal cramps; diarrhea; nausea; (pseudomembranous colitis; superimposed infections)	Same as above.

(continues)

TABLE 5.2 *Continued*

Type	Name	Action	Side Effects	Nursing Care
Viruses (influenza A&B, CMV, and coronvirus)	Symmetrel (amantadine), Virazole (ribavirin aerosol)	Antivirals inhibit viral replication	Ataxia; drowsiness; blurred vision; dry mouth	Protect from falls. Offer fluids to prevent dry mouth.
C. pneumoniae (TWAR agent)	Acromycin (tetracycline), Erythrocin (erythromycin), Levaquin (levofloxacin)	Bacteriacidal, effective against gram positive and gram negative organisms	Abdominal cramps; diarrhea; nausea; (pseudo-membranous colitis; superim-posed infection)	Assess for fluid imbalances. Diarrheal stools should be checked for the presence of blood, mucus, and white blood cells which, can indi-cate pseudomembranous colitis.

TABLE 5.3 Pharmacological Agents Used in the Treatment of Hospital-Acquired Pneumonia

Organism Responsible	Recommended Treatment	Action	Side Effects (Adverse Effects)	Nursing Care
Pseudomonas aeruginosa	Amikin (amikacin), Kantrex (kanamycin), Garamycin (genta-micin), Geopen (carbenicillin)	Bacteriacidal; effective against gram-positive and gram-negative organisms	Abdominal cramps; diarrhea; nausea; (pseudo-membranous colitis; superim-posed infection; tinnitus; changes in urinary output)	Assess for fluid imbalances. Diarrheal stools should be checked for the presence of blood, mucus, and white blood cells; assess for signs of ototoxicity and nephrotoxicity.
Staphylococcus aureus	Unipen (nafcillin), Garamycin (gentamicin)	Same as above	Same as above	Same as above.
Klebsiella pneumoniae	Claforan (cefotaxime), Rocephin (ceftriaxone), Garamycin (genta-micin), Geopen (carbenicillin)	Same as above	Same as above	Same as above.
Pneumocystis carinii	Bactrim (trimetho-prim/sulfa metho-xazole), Pentam (pentamidine)	Bacteriacidal; effective against gram-positive and gram-negative organisms	Fatigue; headache; insomnia; vomiting; diarrhea; (anemia; nephrotoxicity; thrombocytopenia)	Pentamidine should be infused over 1–2 hours to decrease hypotension. Client should be observed for signs of renal impairment and hypoglycemia.
Aspergillus fumigatus	Fungizone (amphotericin B), Fungizone Nizoral (ketoconozole)	Kill or stop the growth of suscep-tible fungi by affecting cell membrane or interfere with protein synthesis within the cell	Headache; dizzi ness; nausea; diarrhea; myalgia; peripheral neuro-pathy (hepatoxi-city; nephrotoxicity)	Drug-to-drug interactions. Use caution when adminis-tering. Check vital signs frequently.

TABLE 5.4 Pharmacological Agents Used in the Treatment of Tuberculosis

Name	Action	Side Effects	Nursing Care
Isoniazid (INH) (first-line drug)	Interferes with cell wall	Deficiency of B6; peripheral neuritis; liver dysfunction	Observe for jaundice. Frequent hearing tests.
Ethambutol HCl (myambutol) (first-line drug)	Suppresses growth of mycobacterium	Optic neuritis; decreased acuity and color vision	Frequent visual tests.
Rifampin (first-line drug)	Same as above	N & V; HA; hepatitis; red discolorations of body fluids	Teach client to avoid alcohol. Teratogenic.
Fluoroquinolones (levoflaxacin, monofloxacin, gatifloxacin)	For strains resistant to RIF, INH, and EMB	N & V; drowsiness; photosensitivity; tendonitis; and tendon rupture	Teach client to avoid prolonged sun exposure, to increase fluid intake, and to report unexplained muscle tenderness
Streptomycin (second-line drug)	Inhibits protein synthesis and suppresses growth of mycobacterium	VIII cranial nerve damage; paresthesia of face, tongue, and hands; renal damage	Ask client to sit quietly 15–30 minutes after injection.
Kanamycin (second-line drug)	Same as above	Same as above	Observe for hematuria. Frequent hearing tests.
Pyrazinamide (first-line drug)	Unknown	Liver damage; gout	Teach client to increase fluid intake. Observe for jaundice.

NOTE

New drugs used in the treatment of tuberculosis are

▶ **Rifabutin:** Used for clients with HIV/AIDS
▶ **Rifapentin:** Used once weekly for HIV-negative adults with drug-susceptible noncavitary TB

Apply Your Knowledge

The study of respiratory disorders can often be difficult for the nurse to understand because of the complexity of many of the conditions. This chapter provided a review of common infections that affect the upper and lower respiratory tract as well as information on life-threatening conditions such as ARDS. Information was also provided regarding occupational lung disease. The following questions test your knowledge regarding the safe, effective care and management of the client with various respiratory disorders.

Exam Questions

1. The nurse is assessing a client admitted with injuries sustained in a motor vehicle accident. Which of the following injuries poses the greatest risk to the client?

    A. Fractures of the ribs

    B. Contusions of the lower legs

    C. Fractures of the humerus

    D. Lacerations of the face

2. Which one of the following findings is characteristic of a tension pneumothorax?

    A. Tracheal deviation toward the affected side

    B. Symmetry of the thorax and equal breath sounds

    C. Tracheal deviation toward the unaffected side

    D. Decreased heart rate and decreased respirations

3. The nurse is caring for a client with a closed chest drainage system. If the tubing becomes disconnected from the system, the nurse should:

    A. Instruct the client to perform the Valsalva maneuver

    B. Elevate the tubing above the client's chest level

    C. Decrease the amount of suction being applied

    D. Form a water seal and obtain a new connector

4. The physician has ordered Theo-Dur (theophylline) for a client with emphysema. An expected side effect associated with the medication is:

    A. Dry mouth

    B. Palpitations

    C. Hyperglycemia

    D. Anemia

5. Which condition would contraindicate the use of chest physiotherapy for a client with pneumonia?

    A. Recent abdominal cholecystectomy

    B. Diabetes mellitus

    C. Rheumatoid arthritis

    D. Emphysema

6. The nurse is interpreting the result of a client's TB skin test. Which one of the following factors is responsible for a false positive TB skin test?

    A. Vaccination with a live virus

    B. Weakened immune system

    C. Inoculation with BCG vaccine

    D. Poor testing technique

7. The physician has ordered Cytoxan (cyclophosphamide) for a client with pulmonary fibrosis. The nurse should instruct the client to:

    A. Walk 20 minutes a day to maintain muscle strength

    B. Expect a reddish discoloration of her urine

    C. Notify the doctor of a sore throat or fever

    D. Eat smaller, more frequent meals

8. The physician has received a limited supply of influenza vaccine. Which one of the following clients should receive priority in receiving the influenza immunization?

    A. An elementary school teacher

    B. A resident in a nursing home

    C. An office worker

    D. A local firefighter

9. The physician has ordered pyrazinamide for a client with tuberculosis. The nurse should tell the client to:

    A. Schedule frequent eye exams

    B. Expect red discoloration of his urine

    C. Increase his fluid intake

    D. Expect dizziness and ringing in his ears

10. The nurse is caring for a client with Legionnaires' disease. Which one of the following types of isolation should the nurse use when caring for the client?

    A. Droplet precautions

    B. Airborne precautions

    C. Contact precautions

    D. No isolation precautions are needed

Answers to Exam Questions

1. Answer A is correct. Fractures of the ribs can result in a closed pneumothorax, a life-threatening emergency, that requires early detection and treatment. Answers B, C, and D are incorrect because they do not pose a risk to the life of the client.

2. Answer C is correct. Assessment of the client with a tension pneumothorax reveals tracheal deviations towards the unaffected side. Answer A is incorrect because the deviation is toward the unaffected, not the affected side. Answer B is incorrect because the thorax is asymmetrical and breath sounds are absent on the affected side. Answer D is incorrect because the heart rate and respiratory rate are not decreased.

3. Answer D is correct. The nurse should form a water seal, remove the contaminated end, and insert a new sterile connector. The Valsalva maneuver is used when the chest tube is being removed therefore Answer A is incorrect. Answer B is incorrect because the chest drainage system is maintained below the client's chest level. Answer C is incorrect because the nurse cannot alter the amount of suction being applied without a doctor's order.

4. Answer B is correct. Side effects from bronchodilators such as theophylline include tremulousness, palpitations, and restlessness. Answers A, C, and D are incorrect because they are not expected side effects of bronchodilators.

5. Answer A is correct. Recent abdominal or thoracic surgery are contraindications for chest physiotherapy. Chest physiotherapy is not contraindicated for the client with diabetes mellitus, rheumatoid arthritis, or emphysema therefore answers B, C, and D are incorrect.

6. Answer C is correct. Inoculation with BCG vaccine will produce a false positive TB skin test. Vaccination with a live virus, weakened immune system, and poor testing technique are factors that can produce a false negative TB skin test, therefore Answers A, B, and D are incorrect.

7. Answer C is correct. Cytoxan is an immunosuppressive drug; therefore, the client should notify the doctor of symptoms associated with infection. Answers A and D are not associated with the use of Cytoxan; therefore, they are incorrect. The client taking Cytoxan can experience hemorrhagic cystitis due to inadequate fluid intake, but it is not an expected finding; therefore, answer B is incorrect.

8. Answer B is correct. Clients over age 65 and those with chronic conditions should receive priority in receiving influenza vaccine when supplies are limited. Answers A, C, and D are incorrect because they do not receive priority in receiving the immunization.

9. Answer C is correct. The use of pyrazinamide can result in gout-like symptoms; therefore, the client should increase his fluid intake. Answer A, B, and D are incorrect because they are associated with other antitubercular medications.

10. Answer D is correct. No isolation precautions are needed because there is no evidence of human to human transmission. Answers A, B, and C are incorrect because they are not indicated in the care of the client with Legionnaires' disease.

Suggested Reading and Resources

▶ Brunner, L., and D. Suddarth. *Textbook of Medical Surgical Nursing.* 12th ed. Philadelphia: Lippincott Williams & Wilkins, 2009.

▶ Ignatavicius, D., and S. Workman. *Medical Surgical Nursing: Critical Thinking for Collaborative Care.* 6th ed. Philadelphia: Elsevier, 2008.

▶ Lehne, R. *Pharmacology for Nursing Care.* 7th ed., Philadelphia: Elsevier, 2009.

▶ LeMone, P., and K. Burke. *Medical Surgical Nursing: Critical Thinking in Client Care.* 4th ed. Upper Saddle River, NJ: Pearson Prentice Hall, 2008.

▶ Lewis, S., M. Heitkemper, S. Dirksen, P. Obrien, and L. Bucher. *Medical Surgical Nursing: Assessment and Management of Clinical Problems.* 7th ed. Philadelphia: Elsevier, 2007.

▶ American Lung Association: www.lungusa.org.

▶ Centers for Disease Control and Prevention: www.cdc.gov.

▶ Health24: www.health24.com.

▶ The Pathology Guy: www.pathguy.com.

CHAPTER SIX

Care of the Client with Genitourinary Disorders

Disorders of the genitourinary system include diseases and disorders that affect the urinary bladder, ureters, and kidneys as well as disorders of the prostate and testes. The nurse should be particularly sensitive to the client's emotional needs because many genitourinary disorders affect both the client's physical and emotional well-being, as well as her sexuality. The nurse should provide clients with a list of the various support groups who offer services to those with genitourinary disorders. Some of these resources can be found in the Suggested Reading and Resources section. This chapter reviews the most common renal and genitourinary disorders, including the treatment of acute and chronic renal failure. For reference, Figure 6.1 provides a diagram of the genitourinary system as well as a detailed look at the kidney.

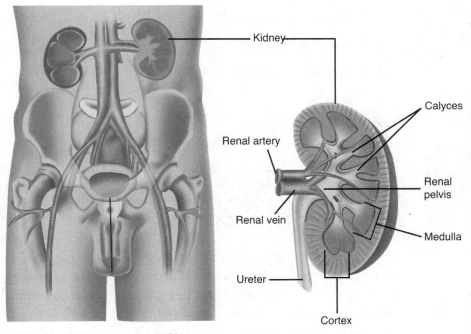

FIGURE 6.1 Genitourinary system/kidney.

Renal Disorders

Renal disorders refer to conditions that affect functioning of the kidneys. The kidneys play a key role in the elimination of waste products in the urine, in maintaining fluid and electrolyte balance, and in regulating acid-base balance. Other functions of the kidneys include the production of *erythropoietin*, a hormone responsible for the formation of red blood cells. Renal disorders can be the result of infection, inflammation, obstruction, malformation, cancer, drugs, and toxins.

Acute Glomerulonephritis

Acute glomerulonephritis (AGN) often results from an infection of the skin or respiratory tract with Group A beta-hemolytic *Streptococcus* or gram-negative bacteria. Other causes include systemic disorders such as scleroderma and systemic lupus erythematosus. Symptoms of acute glomerulonephritis include

- Edema of the face (periorbital) and hands
- Oliguria (urinary output of less than 400 mL per day)
- Smoky-, rusty-, or cola-colored urine
- Elevated blood pressure
- Nausea and vomiting
- Generalized weakness
- Headache
- Anorexia

NOTE

Elderly clients with AGN have less noticeable symptoms. Proteinuria, malaise, nausea, and arthralgia are more likely to occur while hypertension and edema occur less often.

The diagnosis of acute glomerulonephritis is based on the client's symptoms and the results of blood and urine tests. Early morning urine specimens are preferred because the urine is more acidic and formed elements are more evident early in the day. The urinalysis typically reveals hematuria and proteinuria, while blood studies typically reveal elevated serum creatinine and blood urea nitrogen levels and decreased serum albumin levels. Antistreptolysin-O titers are increased after infections with Group A beta-hemolytic Streptococcus. Additional studies include collection of a 24-hour urine sampling for creatinine clearance and percutaneous renal biopsy.

Procedure for Collecting a 24-Hour Urine Sampling

1. Obtain a special collection bottle from the lab.

2. Explain the procedure to the client.

3. Label the collection bottle with the client's name

4. Ask the client to void and discard the first specimen.

5. Place a sign on the client's door and collection bottle stating the time at which the collection began.

6. Place each voiding in the labeled *collection bottle*. Failure to save any voiding requires that the test be stopped, a new collection bottle obtained, and the collection to begin again

7. Keep the collection bottle in a specimen refrigerator or container of ice in the bathroom. Specimens collected in settings other than the hospital should also be placed on ice or refrigerated.

8. Ask the client to obtain a voided specimen in the last 15 minutes of the urine collection period.

Care of the client with acute glomerulonephritis is aimed at promoting renal function and preventing complications. Appropriate anti-infectives such as penicillin, Erythromycin, and Zithromax (azithromycin) are usually prescribed if the condition is due to an infection. Other medications include diuretics and antihypertensives to control edema, circulatory congestion, and hypertension. A strict record of the client's output is used as a guide for fluid replacement. The usual fluid allowance is equal to the client's urinary output for 24 hours plus 500 mL–600 mL for insensible fluid loss. Dietary restrictions depend on the stage and severity of the disease. Protein is restricted when renal insufficiency is present and when blood urea nitrogen levels are elevated. The suggested amount of protein on a low-protein diet is 0.6 g/Kg/day. Sodium is restricted to 2–4 gm per day(no salt added to foods) when the client has hypertension, edema, and signs of heart failure. Foods with substantial amounts of potassium, such as bananas, as well as dried fruits, are restricted during periods of oliguria.

Chronic Glomerulonephritis

Chronic glomerulonephritis (CGN), or *chronic nephritic syndrome*, can be the result of acute glomerulonephritis or a milder antigen-antibody reaction. In many instances, the exact cause remains unknown because the kidneys become atrophied and tissue is not available for biopsy. The kidneys deteriorate and failure develops over a period of 20–30 years or longer.

Signs and symptoms of chronic glomerulonephritis vary from person to person. Mild proteinuria, hematuria, hypertension, and occasional edema are common manifestations. Later complaints are associated with anemia, peripheral neuropathy, and gout. As the kidneys fail, the client develops uremia. Signs and symptoms associated with uremia include slurred speech, ataxia, tremors, pruritus, and skin eruptions.

Diagnostic assessment of the client with CGN includes blood work, urinalysis, computerized tomography, and sometimes percutaneous renal biopsy.

If a renal biopsy is performed, the client should be positioned on her abdomen. Following the procedure, the client is instructed to remain in bed for several hours. Because the kidneys are very vascular organs, the nurse should maintain pressure on the biopsy site for at least 10 minutes and the client should be observed for signs of internal bleeding. Signs of internal bleeding include abdominal pain, decreased blood pressure, increased pulse rate, and decreased urine output. Other signs of internal abdominal bleeding are included in Chapter 18, "Emergency Care." Renal biopsy also carries with it the risk of infection; therefore, the client should be carefully monitored for elevations in temperature and changes in urine output

Renal biopsy is rarely performed in clients in the later stages of renal failure because the kidneys are too small to obtain suitable tissue samples.

Blood work reveals elevations in serum creatinine and blood urea nitrogen. Serum creatinine levels, which depend on the client's muscle mass, are usually greater than 6 mg/dL. Blood urea nitrogen (BUN) levels vary according to the client's dietary intake of protein. Serum electrolyte levels are usually abnormal due to decreased renal function and the development of oliguria. Changes associated with oliguria include hyperkalemia and hyperphosphatemia. Sodium retention is common; however, dilution of the plasma with excess fluid leads to normal or low serum sodium levels. Serum calcium levels are usually normal or slightly below normal.

Urinalysis of the client with CGN reveals the presence of protein, red blood cells, and casts, which suggests chronic renal disease. Dilute specific gravity reflects the loss of renal ability to concentrate waste products. The 24-hour urine sampling reveals a decreased creatinine clearance.

Care of the client with CGN is focused on slowing the disease process and preventing complications. Medications include diuretics and antihypertensives. Erythropoietic therapies are ordered to treat chronic anemia; Kayexalate (sodium polystyrene sulfonate) is used to treat symptoms of hyperkalemia. Dietary interventions include the restriction of protein and sodium. Eventually, renal failure is managed by peritoneal dialysis, hemodialysis, or renal transplant.

Goodpasture's Syndrome

Goodpasture's syndrome is a rare autoimmune disorder characterized by the formation of antibodies in the glomerular basement membrane. These antibodies can also bind to the alveolar basement membrane with resulting alveolar damage and pulmonary hemorrhage. Renal manifestations include hematuria, proteinuria, and edema. Rapid progression can lead to renal failure. Damage to the alveolar membrane can lead to mild or life-threatening pulmonary hemorrhage. Early signs of pulmonary involvement include cough, shortness of breath, and hemoptysis. Management of the client with Goodpasture's syndrome includes the use of corticosteroids, immunosuppressive drugs, and plasmapheresis.

Nephrotic Syndrome

A number of conditions, including glomerulonephritis, systemic illness, or allergic response, can cause nephrotic syndrome. Signs and symptoms associated with nephrotic syndrome include pallor, anorexia, and generalized edema. Lab findings reveal severe proteinuria, hypoalbuminemia, and hyperlipidemia. If serum protein levels remain low the client might have elevated triglycerides. The care of the client with nephrotic syndrome is geared toward decreasing symptoms and preserving renal function.

Nursing care of the client with nephrotic syndrome includes

▶ Providing bed rest with frequent changes in position.

▶ Preventing chaffing and skin breakdown by keeping the skin clean and dry.

▶ Providing scrotal support for male clients with scrotal edema will increase comfort.

▶ Recording daily weights to detect increased or decreased edema.

▶ Monitoring vital signs to detect infection or complications.

▶ Observing for signs of infection.

▶ Maintaining a record of strict intake and output.

▶ Providing a moderate-protein (0.8 gm/Kg/day), low-sodium , low-saturated-fat diet. High biologic proteins (dairy products, eggs, meat) should be provided. Dietary changes are dependent on the client's glomerular filtration rate.

▶ Administering prescribed medications.

▶ Administering ACE inhibitors to decrease proteinuria.

▶ Administering cholesterol-lowering agents to treat hyperlipidemia

▶ Administering Heparin to lower proteinuria, decrease coagulability, decrease risk of renal and pulmonary embolus, and reduce renal insufficiency.

▶ Administering Diuretics to control edema and hypertension.

▶ Administering corticosteroids or immunosuppressive medications to improve immunologic processes.

Additional nursing interventions for the client with nephrotic syndrome focus on teaching the client about medication, diet, and signs of exacerbation. Some clients with exacerbations of nephrotic syndrome are treated at home, therefore it is important that the client learns the importance of taking medications as directed and adhering to prescribed dietary restrictions. Information on angiotensin-converting enzyme inhibitors, anticoagulants, and antilipidemics can be found in Chapter 2, "Fluid and Electrolyte and Acid/Base Balance." Information on immunosuppressives can be found in Chapter 4, "Care of the Client with Endocrine Disorders," and Chapter 12, "Care of the Client with Immunologic Disorders."

Polycystic Kidney Disease

Fluid-filled cysts in the epithelial cells of the nephrons characterize polycystic kidney disease (PKD), one of the most commonly occurring congenital disorders (see Figure 6.2). The disorder can be inherited as an autosomal-dominant trait or less commonly as an autosomal-recessive trait. In the recessive form, nearly all the nephrons are involved at birth; therefore, most affected infants die within the first two months of life. Affected infants have changes in physical appearance that include epicanthal folds, pointed nose, small chin, and low-set ears. Unlike the infant, adults with polycystic kidney disease have a normal appearance.

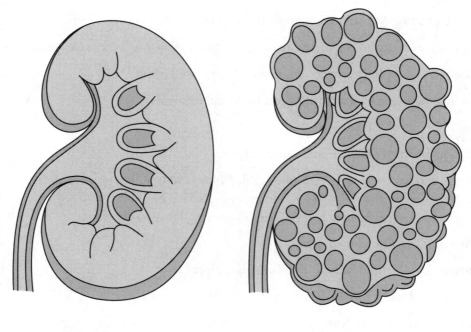

Normal Kidney   **Polycystic Kidney**

FIGURE 6.2   Polycystic kidney disease.

Most adults with an autosomal-dominant trait are diagnosed between the ages of 30 and 50. Cysts located in the nephrons, which might be small at first, become progressively larger and more widely distributed. The kidneys enlarge two to three times the normal size, displacing abdominal organs. Eventually the membrane of the glomeruli and renal tubules become damaged. The cysts are prone to infection, rupture, and bleeding. About one-half of clients with polycystic kidney disease develop kidney failure by age 50.

Cysts can occur in tissues other than the kidneys, including the liver, cerebral blood vessels, and cardiac blood vessels. Rupture of "berry aneurysms" can lead to subarachnoid hemorrhage and death. Signs and symptoms of polycystic kidney disease include

▶ Protruding, distended abdomen

▶ Flank pain

- ▶ Bright red- or cola-colored urine (cystic rupture)

- ▶ Dysuria, nocturia

- ▶ Cloudy or foul-smelling urine (infection)

- ▶ Anorexia, nausea, vomiting

- ▶ Edema

- ▶ Hypertension

- ▶ Visual disturbances (aneurysms)

Diagnostic studies used for the client with polycystic kidney disease include renal sonography, CT scan, and MRI. Other studies include blood work and urinalysis. As kidney function declines, the serum creatinine and blood urea nitrogen increase. Urinalysis reveals proteinuria and hematuria and 24-hour urine testing reveals a decreased creatinine clearance. Urine testing for culture and sensitivity are indicated when signs of infection are present.

Management of the client with polycystic kidney disease focuses on pain management, treatment of urinary tract infection, and management of hypertension. Dietary intervention might include the provision of a low-sodium, low-protein diet. Polycystic kidney disease eventually progresses to end stage renal failure that is managed by dialysis or renal transplant.

Hydronephrosis/Hydroureteronephrosis

Hydronephrosis and hydroureteronephrosis are the result of obstructions in urinary flow. *Hydronephrosis*, or urine accumulation in the renal pelvis, causes the kidney to enlarge. Over time, sometimes in only a few hours, blood vessels and renal tubules can become extensively damaged. Obstructions lower in the urinary tract caused by urine accumulation result in *hydroureteronephrosis*. Hydroureteronephrosis is most likely to occur from obstruction at the ureteropelvic junction, the ureterovessicular junction, or the pelvic brim. Urethral strictures or very low obstructions cause bladder distention.

Disorders associated with hydronephrosis and hydroureteronephrosis include tumors, stones, trauma, retroperitoneal fibrosis, and congenital structural defects. The most common causes of obstruction are prostatic hypertrophy and renal calculi.

The client with hydronephrosis or hydroureter complains of pain in the abdomen or flank. Urinary tract infections are common and produce chills, fever, and malaise. Increased serum creatinine and BUN levels are evident in the client with renal damage. Further diagnostic studies include IV angiography, renal sonography, and CT scan.

Management of the client with hydronephrosis or hydroureteronephrosis is aimed at relieving the obstruction and preserving renal function. Temporary management can be achieved by internal stent placement, or placement of percutaneous nephrostomy or ureterostomy tubes. In the instance of blood clots or kidney stones, symptoms will resolve without surgical treatment Surgical correction of obstructions and dilation of urethral strictures provide permanent solutions. Other interventions are aimed at treating infection and correcting acid-base and fluid imbalances.

> **NOTE**
>
> Percutaneous nephrostomy or ureterostomy tubes should not be clamped or irrigated. If the client has bilateral nephrostomy or ureterostomy tubes, the nurse should record the urinary output from each tube.

Pyelonephritis

Pyelonephritis, a bacterial infection in the kidney or renal pelvis, can be classified as either acute or chronic. Acute pyelonephritis is the result of active infection with microorganisms that ascend from the lower urinary tract or from blood-borne infection. Infection results in abscesses in the capsule, cortex, or medulla of the kidney. Areas of fibrosis and scar tissue develop as the inflammation subsides. Organisms from the urinary tract commonly responsible for acute pyelonephritis include *Escherichia coli, Enterococcus faecalis, Proteus mirabilis, Klebsiella,* and *Pseudomonas aeruginosa.* Blood-borne organisms include *Staphylococcus aureus* and *Salmonella.* Pyelonephritis is more common in women than in men. Signs and symptoms of acute pyelonephritis include low-grade fever, chills, hematuria, abdominal discomfort, pain in the back and flank, nausea, vomiting, tachycardia, and tachypnea.

Chronic pyelonephritis is generally due to malformations, urinary obstruction, or vesicoureteral reflux. Childhood vesicoureteral reflux is responsible for the renal scarring typically seen in the adult with chronic pyelonephritis. Others with chronic pyelonephritis include those with a history of spinal cord injury, bladder tumor, renal calculi, and prostatic hypertrophy. Symptoms associated with chronic pyelonephritis are less dramatic than those with acute pyelonephritis, but include increased blood pressure and nocturia. The client with chronic pyelonephritis is unable to conserve sodium and tends to develop hyperkalemia and acidosis.

Factors contributing to pyelonephritis are urinary catheterization, chronic formation of renal calculi, diabetes mellitus, and overuse of non-steroidal anti-inflammatory drugs (NSAIDs), bladder infection, and benign prostatic hypertrophy. To a lesser degree, pyelonephritis can result from an autoimmune reaction.

Diagnostic measures for the client with pyelonephritis include urinalysis; urine culture and sensitivity; cystourethrogram; x-ray of the kidney, ureter, and bladder (KUB); and intravenous pyelography (IVP).

Interventions for clients with pyelonephritis are aimed at treating infection and making the client more comfortable. Dietary changes and fluid restrictions are sometimes indicated. Surgical interventions include ureteral reimplantation, pyelolithotomy, and nephrectomy (as a last resort).

Acute and Chronic Renal Failure

Acute renal failure (ARF) is the abrupt deterioration of renal function that results in marked reduction of urinary output. The causes of acute renal failure are classified as follows:

▶ **Prerenal:** Prerenal ARF is often related to conditions that affect blood flow to the kidneys. Causes include cardiovascular disorders, hypovolemia, septic shock, anaphylactic shock, and obstruction of the renal artery.

▶ **Intrarenal:** Intrarenal or intrinsic ARF results from the actual destruction of the renal parenchyma. Nephrotoxic chemicals and ischemic injury damage the renal tubules, making them less functional. Chemicals capable of damaging the renal tubules include antibiotics (aminoglycosides and sulfonamides) diuretics, nonsteroidal anti-inflammatories, and contrast media. Ischemic injury of the renal tubules occurs when the mean arterial blood flow is reduced. Ischemic injuries that can result in intrarenal failure include cardiac arrest and hypovolemic shock.

▶ **Postrenal:** Postrenal ARF is caused by obstruction to urinary outflow. Kinking of catheter tubing, urinary infections, renal calculi, and prostatic enlargement are examples of obstructions that can lead to postrenal ARF.

Signs and symptoms associated with acute renal failure depend on whether the client is in the oliguric or diuretic stage of failure. In the oliguric stage, the client shows symptoms of fluid overload. These symptoms include hypertension, tachycardia, and peripheral edema. Auscultation of the lungs reveals the presence of respiratory crackles. Lab results reveal hyperkalemia, hypernatremia, and hypercholesterolemia, as well as alterations in phosphorus and magnesium levels. In the diuretic stage, the client appears dehydrated with dry skin and mucous membranes, poor tissue turgor, hypotension, and flattened neck veins.

The final stage of acute renal failure, the recovery stage, is characterized by the gradual return of normal urine output and removal of metabolic wastes. The condition should resolve in two to four weeks, although some clients might have some degree of renal impairment for three months or longer. In some instances, the damage is sufficient to result in chronic renal failure.

Diagnostic measures used for the client with acute renal failure include urinalysis, CBC, serum electrolytes, arterial blood gases, MRI, and renal biopsy.

Management of the client with acute renal failure depends on the cause as well as the symptoms and stage of failure. When the client is in the oliguric or anuric stage, diuretics such as Lasix (furosemide) are ordered to promote urinary output. Fluid restriction and a diet low in sodium and protein are ordered to decrease fluid retention and the accumulation of nitrogen wastes. In the diuretic stage, fluid volume replacement based on the client's output is ordered. A diet sufficient in sodium to maintain fluid balance is needed for the client with hyponatremia. Potassium restrictions are based on lab results. The overall diet should be high in carbohydrates and limited in protein.

Other interventions include the use of water-soluble vitamin supplements, Kayexalate (sodium polystyrene sulfonate) to lower potassium levels, and Epogen (epoetin) to reverse anemia. In some instances, peritoneal or hemodialysis is needed. Clients in acute renal failure who are unable to tolerate hemodialysis and rapid fluid removal can be treated using continuous renal replacement therapy (CRRT).

Chronic Renal Failure

Chronic renal failure (CRF) is a progressive irreversible loss of renal function. The disorder is characterized according to how much renal function (glomerular filtration rate [GFR]) remains. GFR is the amount of filtrate produced by the kidney each minute. The normal GFR is 125 mL per minute. Chronic renal failure is divided into the following four stages:

- **Reduced renal reserve:** GFR 35%–50% of normal

- **Renal insufficiency:** GFR 25%–35% of normal

- **Renal failure:** GFR 20%–25% of normal

- **End stage renal failure:** GFR 15%–20% of normal or less

Like acute renal failure, there are many causes of CRF. Causes include hereditary disorders, connective tissue disorders, inflammatory conditions, vascular disease, metabolic disorders, obstructive disease, infections, and nephrotoxic agents. Regardless of the cause, clients with CRF experience physiologic changes related to the kidneys' inability to excrete waste products and to regulate blood pressure, acid-base balance, and RBC production.

Symptoms of CRF vary according to the stage of renal compromise. Common symptoms include decreased urinary output, weight gain, anemia, anorexia, nausea, joint pain, decreased alertness, and changes in sensation in the hands and feet. Assessment of the client with CRF reveals an elevated blood pressure, rapid irregular heart rate, and dry fragile skin that bruises easily. The client might complain of intense itching, and the nurse might note the presence of uremic frost on the skin as well as the odor of urine on the skin and breath.

Diagnostic measures include CBC, urinalysis, serum electrolytes, ABGs, BUN, serum creatinine, and 24-hour urine collection. The client with CRF will have an elevated BUN and serum creatinine level with decreased urine creatinine level. Serum electrolytes and ABGs typically reveal metabolic acidosis, hypocalcemia, hyperkalemia, and hyperphosphatemia.

Complications associated with CRF include uremia, congestive heart failure, hypertension, electrolyte imbalances, anemia, pathologic fractures, and sexual dysfunction. Mental status changes range from mild to loss of consciousness and seizures.

Dietary interventions and medications ordered for the client with CRF are the same as those for the client with acute failure. Although dietary interventions and medications prolong renal function, care of the client with CRF ultimately centers on renal replacement therapy in the form of dialysis or renal transplantation.

Peritoneal Dialysis

Peritoneal dialysis is a procedure that replaces the work of the kidneys by using the lining of the peritoneal cavity to remove waste, water and chemicals from the body. It is often the preferred method of certain clients with ESRF. These clients include those who are hemodynamically unstable, those who cannot tolerate anticoagulant therapy, and those who prefer flexibility in their schedule. Peritoneal dialysis cannot be performed if the client has abdominal adhesions because insufficient surface area of peritoneal lining does not permit adequate dialyzing exchange.

Peritoneal dialysis is accomplished by the surgical placement of a flexible catheter that remains in the peritoneal cavity. Immediately after insertion, the catheter is irrigated with heparinized dialysate to remove blood and fibrin from the catheter. A waiting period of 1–2 weeks is preferred before beginning a schedule of peritoneal dialysis. After warming to body temperature, the dialysate is instilled in a sterile process and allowed to remain in the peritoneal cavity where osmotic pressure allows the dialysate to remove metabolic wastes. There are two basic types of peritoneal dialysis: automated peritoneal dialysis (cycler controls the fill, dwell, and drain phases) and continuous ambulatory peritoneal dialysis (manual fill four times a day). The type of peritoneal dialysis used depends on the client's ability and lifestyle. Installation and removal of the dialysate is done slowly to prevent disequilibrium syndrome. The client undergoing automated peritoneal dialysis usually has four or more exchanges at night with each exchange lasting 1–2 hours. The client undergoing continuous ambulatory peritoneal dialysis has a dwell time of 4–10 hours.

Complications associated with peritoneal dialysis include site infection and peritonitis. The client managed by peritoneal dialysis should be instructed to report the return of cloudy dialysate, abdominal pain, or fever because these indicate developing peritonitis. Other complications include abdominal pain, outflow problems, hernias, low back pain, bleeding, pulmonary complications, protein loss, carbohydrate and lipid abnormalities, encapsulating sclerosing peritonitis, and loss of ultrafiltration.

NOTE

The client managed with peritoneal dialysis will need an increased protein intake. Sources of protein include milk, eggs, meat, and nuts.

Figure 6.3 illustrates the client receiving peritoneal dialysis.

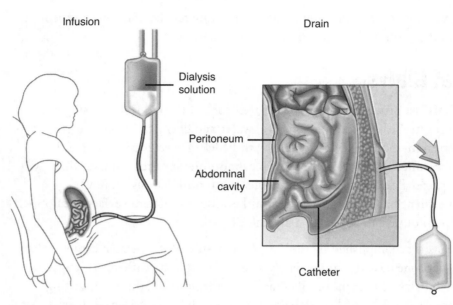

FIGURE 6.3 Peritoneal dialysis.

Hemodialysis

Hemodialysis refers to the removal of wastes, water, and chemicals by passing the blood through an artificial semi-permeable membrane.

Hemodialysis is accomplished through a surgical placement of a shunt, creation of an internal arteriovenous fistula, or using a temporary vascular access by which the client is connected to the hemodialysis unit. Blood pressure readings, fingersticks, and venopunctures are not obtained in the extremity with either a shunt or fistula. Long-acting antihypertensives, such as Capoten (captopril) are usually withheld if the client is scheduled for hemodialysis. Failure to withhold the medication can result in severe hypotension. Patency of the AV fistula is determined by the presence of a bruit. Complications of hemodialysis include hypotension, muscle cramps, blood loss, sepsis, hepatitis (HBV and HCV), and disequilibrium syndrome .

> **NOTE**
>
> Disequilibrium syndrome is caused by the rapid change in the components of extracellular fluid. Urea, sodium, and other solutes are removed from the blood more rapidly than from the cerebral spinal fluid and brain. A high osmotic gradient leads to the development of cerebral edema. Clinical manifestation of disequilibrium syndrome include confusion, nausea, vomiting, restlessness, headache, twitching, seizures, muscle cramps, and hypotension. The treatment of disequilibrium syndrome includes slowing or stopping dialysis and infusing hypertonic saline, albumin, or mannitol.

Continuous Renal Replacement Therapy

An alternative or adjunctive method for treating acute renal failure is the use of continuous renal replacement therapy (CRRT). CRRT can be used for clients who do not respond to dietary interventions and medications as well as those with cardiovascular instability. Types of CRRT include

▶ Continuous arteriovenous hemofiltration (CAVH)

▶ Continuous arteriovenous hemodialysis (CAVHD)

▶ Continous venovenous hemodialysis (CVVHD)

Although CRRT produces less hemodynamic instability, its use is contraindicated in clients with life-threatening manifestations of uremia, hyperkalemia, and pericarditis that require rapid treatment.

Figure 6.4 illustrates the mechanism by which blood leaves the body, passes through the dialysis machine and returns to the client. Figure 6.5 illustrates the client undergoing hemodialysis.

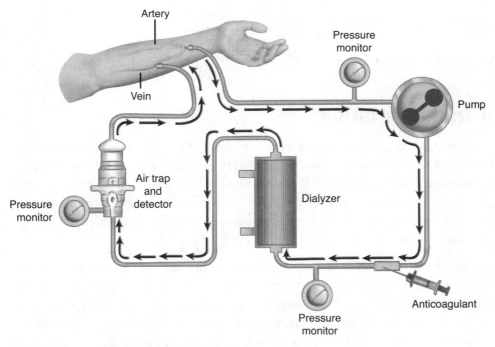

FIGURE 6.4 Hemodialysis mechanics.

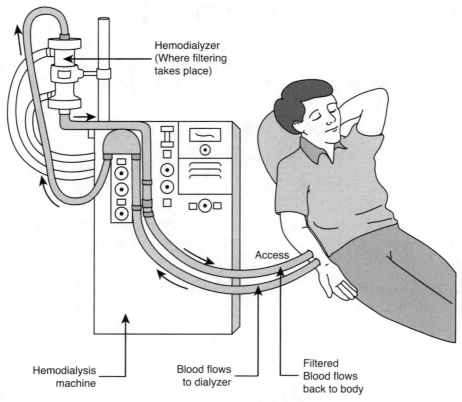

FIGURE 6.5 Client undergoing hemodialysis.

Renal Transplantation

Renal transplantation is a life-sustaining treatment for ESRD. Although renal transplantation is not considered a cure it improves the quality of life. Candidates for renal transplantation must be free of medical problems that would be made worse by the procedure and required post-transplant medication. Clients not suited for transplantation include those with advanced uncontrollable cardiac disease, metastatic cancer, chronic infection, and longstanding pulmonary disease.

Renal transplants are obtained from non–heart-beating donors or from living compatible donors. Prior to implantation, the client is carefully assessed for the presence of infection or conditions that would compromise transplant success. Following renal transplant, the client is placed on lifetime immunosuppressive therapy to prevent tissue rejection. Rejection of the transplanted organ might involve the following:

▶ **Hyperacute graft rejection:** Begins within 48 hours of transplantation. Those at greatest risk for hyperacute graft rejection are clients in whom the donated organ is of an ABO type different from their own, clients with a history of multiple blood transfusion, multiparous clients, and clients who have had a previous transplant. Hyperacute graft rejection, which involves the blood vessels, can become apparent within minutes or hours. Clinical manifestations of hyperacute graft rejection include increased temperature, increased blood pressure, and pain at the transplant site. The process cannot be stopped once it has begun and the rejected organ is removed as soon a hyperacute graft rejection is diagnosed.

▶ **Acute graft rejection:** Occurs one to three weeks after transplantation, and involves a cellular response that leads to death of the organ cells. Clinical manifestations of acute graft rejection vary with the client and the specific organ involved. Signs and symptoms of acute graft rejection include oliguria or anuria, increased temperature above 100° F, increased blood pressure, lethargy, fluid retention, increased serum creatinine, increased blood urea nitrogen, elevated potassium levels, and fluid retention. Treatment of acute graft rejection includes increasing doses of immunosuppressives. Episodes of acute graft rejection do not automatically mean that the client will lose the new organ.

▶ **Chronic graft rejection:** Happens due to chronic inflammation and scaring. Chronic rejection occurs gradually over a period of months to years. Clinical manifestations include increased blood urea nitrogen, increased serum creatinine levels, fluid retention, changes in serum electrolytes, and fatigue. The client with chronic rejection is treated with immunosuppressive drugs, including prednisone, Sandimmune (cyclosporine) and Neoral (cyclosporine), Prograf (tacrolimus), and CellCept (mycophenolate mofetil). Newer drugs include Target of Rapamycin (TOR) inhibitors, which are used in combination with cyclosporine for maintenance therapy. Rapamune (sirolimus) is an example of a TOR inhibitor.

Urinary Disorders

Disorders that affect the storage and elimination of urine are referred to as *urinary disorders*. Urinary disorders can result from infection or inflammation, as in the case of cystitis, or from inability to maintain bladder control.

Cystitis

Cystitis, inflammation of the urinary bladder, is generally considered to be an ascending infection caused by the entry of pathogens through the urethra. Cystitis is categorized as follows:

▶ **Infectious:** Infectious cystitis can be caused by a number of microorganisms. In most instances, however, it is the result of infections with *E. coli* or other organisms from the lower intestinal tract.

▶ **Noninfectious:** Exposure to chemical agents, such as cyclophosphamide and radiation can result in noninfectious cystitis.

▶ **Interstitial:** Interstitial cystitis has no known cause but results in chronic irritation of the bladder.

Although cystitis occurs in both sexes, women are more susceptible because of urethral shortness and proximity of the urethral opening to the anus. Other predisposing factors include urinary catheterization, surgery, decreased urination, spinal cord injury or disease, diabetes mellitus, and sexual activity (in women).

The normal aging process also increases the likelihood of cystitis for both sexes. Prostatic enlargement impedes normal urination, thereby increasing the risk of infection in men, whereas changes in the vaginal flora and lubrication contribute to cystitis in women.

Signs and symptoms associated with cystitis include dysuria, urinary urgency, and urinary frequency. The client experiences a sensation of incomplete emptying of the bladder so that the client voids more often than usual. Low-grade fever and complaints of lower abdominal or pelvic pain, foul-smelling urine, and hematuria are common.

Diagnostic tests for the client with cystitis include a CBC and clean catch urinalysis for culture and sensitivity as well as a Gram stain. A catheterized urine specimen is obtained if the client is unable to get a clean catch specimen. The urinalysis of a client with cystitis typically reveals the presence of WBCs and RBCs. The urine usually appears cloudy, although in some cases hematuria is present. The urinalysis for culture and sensitivity reveals bacterial counts greater than 10,000 per mL.

NOTE

Although the client with interstitial cystitis experiences the same symptoms of cystitis as the client with other forms, the urine is negative for bacteria.

Additional diagnostic tests for the client with recurrent cystitis include intravenous pyelogram, voiding cystourethrogram, retrograde pyelogram, and cystoscopy.

CAUTION

Contrast media containing iodine is used during intravenous pyelogram; therefore, the nurse should ask the client about allergies to shellfish or preparations containing iodine.

Interventions for the client with cystitis include medication, dietary changes, and comfort measures. Antibiotics such as Gantrisin (acetyl sulfasoxazole), Bactrim or Septra (trimethoprim-sulfamethoxazole), Cipro (ciprofloxacin hydrochloride), Floxin (ofloxacin) or Keflex (cephalexin) are ordered for clients with bacterial cystitis. Antibiotics are not indicated for those with noninfectious or interstitial cystitis. Additional medications include anti-inflammatories, antispasmodics, antihistamines, and tricyclics.

The client's diet should include all the food groups. Foods such as cranberries, plums, whole grains, meat, and cheese increase the acidity of the urine and help prevent the growth of bacteria. The client should restrict foods and beverages, such as peaches, apples, and carbonated beverages that increase the alkalinity of the urine.

The nurse should tell the client that the incidence of cystitis can be further reduced by increasing fluid intake, drinking cranberry juice, avoiding tub baths and bubble baths, wiping front to back after bowel movement, wearing cotton underwear, and avoiding tight-fitting clothing such as jeans.

Urinary Incontinence

Urinary incontinence refers to a loss of urinary control that is severe enough to cause problems with social functioning. Embarrassment and lack of understanding prevents many of those with urinary incontinence from seeking treatment.

There are five recognized forms of incontinence in adults. These forms include

▶ **Stress incontinence:** Inability to tighten the urethra sufficiently to prevent urination. Stress incontinence is characterized by the loss of small amounts of urine during sneezing, coughing, straining, jogging, or lifting.

▶ **Urge incontinence:** Inability to suppress signals from the bladder to the brain to prevent urination

▶ **Overflow incontinence:** Overdistention of the bladder to the point of absolute maximum capacity

▶ **Mixed incontinence:** Incontinence that combines features of stress, urge, and overflow incontinence

▶ **Functional incontinence:** Voiding at socially inappropriate times and places caused by the loss of cognitive function

Many factors contribute to urinary incontinence. These factors include having given birth, the use of certain medications, disease, depression, and lack of sufficient assistance needed for toileting.

Interventions aimed at maintaining urinary function depend on the type of incontinence. Nonsurgical interventions for the client with stress incontinence include muscle exercises (Kegel exercises) to strengthen the pelvic floor, weight reduction, and avoidance of alcohol and caffeine. Estrogen replacement therapy is often prescribed to relieve stress incontinence in postmenopausal women, and various surgical procedures are used to reposition the urethra and bladder.

Clients with urge incontinence are managed using drug therapy with antihistamines and anticholinergics. The client is told to avoid caffeine and alcohol and to space fluids at regular intervals throughout the day, limiting them in the evening.

Educational interventions for the client with urge incontinence include bladder training and habit training. Bladder training is dependent on the client's ability to override the urge to void. The schedule begins with the longest time that the client can comfortably resist the urge to void. For example, if the client can remain comfortable for half an hour without voiding, he is instructed to ignore the urge to void in less time. After the client is established in the initial schedule, the interval is gradually increased by 15–30 minutes until the client achieves bladder control. Habit training, or *scheduled toileting*, reduces incontinence in cognitively impaired clients. The client is assisted to the bathroom and asked to void every one to two hours.

Overflow incontinence can be caused by obstruction of the bladder outlet and results in increased urinary retention past the bladder's normal capacity. Interventions include bladder compression (Crede's method), intermittent self-catheterization, Foley catheter, and cholinergic medications to increase bladder pressure. Common surgical procedures include removal of the prostate and repair of genital prolapse.

Interventions for the client with functional or chronic incontinence focus on containment of urine and skin protection. Absorbent pads, urinary catheters, and condom catheters are commonly used for those with irreversible incontinence.

Urolithiasis

Urinary calculi, or kidney stones, can be the result of any of the following conditions: hyperparathyroidism, increased vitamin D intake, cancer, prolonged bed rest, or excessive secretion of uric acid. In most cases, the cause remains unknown. Kidney stones occur with greater frequency in those 30 to 50 years of age and in men more than women. Those with a history of two stones are more likely to have repeat stones. The majority of kidney stones are composed of calcium or magnesium in combination with phosphorus or oxalate. Stones vary in size; stones that are 0.5–1.0 mm in diameter are more likely to pass, whereas larger stones are removed using extracorporeal shock wave lithotripsy (ESWL) or surgery. Urinary tract obstruction is an emergency condition that requires immediate intervention to preserve renal function.

> **NOTE**
>
> Care of the client following ESWL includes frequent monitoring of vital signs as well as monitoring amount, color, and clarity of urine output. Urine might be bright red initially but bleeding should diminish within 48–72 hours.

Symptoms associated with a kidney stone depend on the location of the stone. Stones located in the kidney or uppermost ureter cause flank pain, whereas stones in the ureter or bladder cause abdominal pain. Severe pain, nausea and vomiting, dysuria, and hematuria are common. Diagnosis might be made through the use of ultrasound, CT, and MRI. Noncontrast helical CT has the highest sensitivity for locating urinary stones. Intravenous pyelogram is still used in some instances. Other lab studies include CBC and urine pH.

Nursing care of the client with kidney stones includes the following:

▶ Administering pain medication.

▶ Administering intravenous fluids.

▶ Straining the urine to detect passage of renal stones.

▶ Dietary management for the client with calcium phosphate stones focuses on increasing the acidity of the urine. Nutritional interventions include limiting the intake of foods high in animal protein to 5–7 servings per week. The client may benefit from limiting milk intake and by drinking cranberry juice Calcibind (cellulose sodium phosphate) can be given to lower calcium levels.

▶ Dietary management for the client with uric acid stones focuses on lowering uric acid levels and increasing the alkalinity of the urine. Nutritional interventions include limiting sources of purine. Foods high in purine include sardines, liver, herring, and sweetbreads. Foods moderate in purine include bacon, pork, ham, chicken. Zyloprim (allopurinol) can be given to lower uric acid levels.

▶ Dietary management for the client with oxylate stones focuses on limiting the intake of oxylate. Nutritional interventions include limiting foods such as spinach, strawberries, rhubarb, chocolate, tea, peanuts, and wheat bran. Liberal fluids should be given to keep the urine dilute.

Genitourinary Disorders

Genitourinary disorders are conditions that affect the genitals and the urinary system. Some of these disorders, such as prostatitis and epididymitis, can result from infection. Others, such as benign prostatic hypertrophy, can result from physiologic changes associated with aging. Figure 6.6 shows an image of the male genitourinary system.

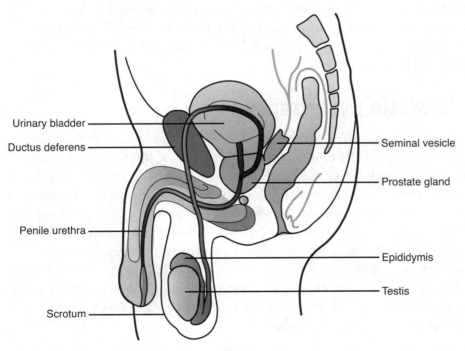

FIGURE 6.6 The male genitourinary system.

Prostatitis

Inflammation of the prostate can occur after a viral illness or infection with a sexually transmitted disease. In many instances, the cause is unknown.

Prostatitis is classified as either bacterial or nonbacterial. Bacterial prostatitis is usually associated with infection of the urethra or lower urinary tract. Common organisms responsible for bacterial prostatitis include *E. coli*, *Enterobacter*, *Proteus*, and Group D *streptococcus*. Although there is no identifiable organism, nonbacterial prostatitis can result in a chronic infection.

Signs and symptoms of prostatitis depend on whether the condition is acute or chronic. Symptoms associated with acute bacterial prostatitis include fever, chills, dysuria, urethral discharge, erectile dysfunction, and perineal pain that radiates to the sacral region. Examination of the prostate by the physician or nurse practitioner reveals a tender, firm, swollen prostate. Symptoms of chronic prostatitis are generally milder than those with acute infection.

The diagnosis is based on the client's symptoms and urine culture. Prostatic massage is not recommended because of the danger of bacteremia; however, this procedure might be performed by the physician to obtain prostatic fluid for culture. The presence of white blood cells with a negative culture confirms a diagnosis of nonbacterial prostatitis.

Management of the client with prostatitis depends on whether the infection is bacterial or nonbacterial. Bactrim (trimethoprim-sulfamethoxazole) and Cipro (ciprofloxacin hydrochloride) are examples of antibiotics used to treat prostatitis. Bed rest and sitz baths two to three times a day help relieve pain. The client should drink at least three liters of fluid a day unless otherwise instructed. When the acute infection is over, regular sexual intercourse or ejaculation is recommended to help drain prostatic secretions and lessen the likelihood of recurring infection.

Benign Prostatic Hypertrophy

Benign prostatic hypertrophy (BPH) is associated with injury and with aging. By age 50, at least half of all men have BPH to some degree. Symptoms of BPH include urinary frequency, nocturia, reduced force, and size of urinary stream. Nonsurgical management includes the use of medications. Proscar (finasteride) lowers the level of dihydrotestosterone (DHT), a major cause of prostate growth. Hytrin (terazosin), Cardura (doxazosin mesylate), and Flomax (tamsulosin) are alpha-blocking agents that constrict the prostate, reduce urethral pressure, and improve urine flow. Complementary therapies include herbal therapy with saw palmetto and lycopene. Caution should be advised when herbal remedies such as saw palmetto are used. Saw palmetto can falsely lower the PSA results and can mask signs of prostate cancer resulting in delayed diagnosis. Surgical interventions for benign prostatic hypertrophy include

- Transurethral resection of the prostate (TURP)
- Transurethral incision of the prostate (TUIP)
- Suprapubic resection

▶ Retropubic resection

▶ Perineal resection

Transurethral resection of the prostate (TURP) is the most common surgical intervention for BPH. There is no surgical incision because the approach is through a retroscope inserted through the urethra.

Postoperative care following a transurethral resection of the prostate (TURP) includes observing for bleeding. Postoperatively, the urine can be expected to be pink until the fourth day. Bright red bleeding with increased viscosity and many clots is indicative of arterial bleeding. In that case, the doctor should be notified immediately. Dark red bleeding with less viscosity and few clots is indicative of venous bleeding that can be controlled by placing traction on the catheter. The client's intake of fluid should be maintained at 2000–3000 mL per day to help keep the catheter free of clots. Antispasmodics such as B & O (belladonna and opium) suppositories, and Probanthine (propantheline) are used to prevent bladder spasms. The client should be monitored for signs of post-operative infection which include fever, dysuria, and cloudy urine. By the time of discharge, the client should be voiding 150–200 mL of clear yellow urine every three to four hours.

Discharge instructions include telling the client to increase fluid intake to 2,000–3,000 ml of water a day to decrease risk of bladder infections and to avoid alcohol, caffeinated beverages, and spicy foods. The nurse should encourage the client to perform Kegel's exercises to strengthen the pelvic muscles and help prevent incontinence. The client should avoid prolonged sitting and sexual activity for at least 10 days following surgery.

NOTE

Postoperative care of the client with a retropubic prostatectomy includes assessing the abdominal incision for signs of infection. Urine on the dressing should be reported to the physician because the bladder is not accessed in this type of procedure.

Postoperative care of the client with a suprapubic prostatectomy includes monitoring the output from the suprapubic and urethral catheters.

Postoperative care of the client with a perineal prostatectomy includes preventing infection. This is vital because the incision is near the anus. Avoid rectal temperatures and enemas.

Erectile Dysfunction

Erectile dysfunction (ED) or impotence occurs when the male is unable to achieve or maintain an erection for intercourse. The disorder can be classified as either organic or functional.

Organic ED involves a gradual deterioration of sexual function and is characterized by a decrease in firmness and frequency of erection. Causes of organic ED include

▶ Inflammation of the prostate, urethra, or seminal vessels

▶ Fractures of the pelvis

- ► Lumbosacral injuries

- ► Surgical procedures (prostatectomy)

- ► Medications (antihypertensives, psychotropics, and antidiabetics)

- ► Vascular diseases

- ► Endocrine disorders (diabetes and thyroid)

- ► Chronic neurological conditions

- ► Depression

- ► Alcohol and tobacco use

- ► Poor overall health

Functional ED has psychological origins. Males with functional ED report having normal nocturnal and morning erections. The presentation of symptoms is sudden and usually follows periods of high stress.

Assessment of the client with ED includes a complete medical exam with social and sexual history to determine whether the disorder is organic or functional. Serum testosterone and serum gonadatrophin testing might be ordered if the client complains of absent or low libido or if examination reveals small testes or diminished facial hair. Doppler or ultrasonograph are ordered to measure arterial and venous blood flow. Other diagnostic tests include nocturnal penile tumescence checks, which measure the number of nocturnal erections with each period of REM sleep.

There are a number of treatments for erectile dysfunction. These include vacuum devices, intracorporeal injections, intraurethral medications, penile implants, and anti-impotence drugs such as Viagra (sildenafil citrate) and Cialis (tadalafil). The following special instructions should be given to the client taking anti-impotence medications:

- ► One pill should be taken from 30 minutes to 4 hours before intercourse.

- ► Avoid taking the medication immediately after eating a meal (high-fat meals reduce the rate of absorption and decrease the peak serum levels).

- ► Avoid alcohol.

- ► Side effects can include headache, facial flushing, and diarrhea.

- ► Leg and back cramps, nausea, and vomiting could be experienced if more than one tablet is taken in 24 hours.

- ► Avoid taking the medication if you are already taking medication containing nitrates, such as nitroglycerin.

- ► Notify your physician if you experience erections lasting longer than 4 hours or if you experience priapism (erections lasting longer than 6 hours). Tissue damage and permanent loss of potency can occur if priapism is not treated immediately.

- ► Medication does not offer protection against sexually transmitted diseases.

- ► Notify the physician if you experience changes in vision or hearing

Epididymitis

The epididymis is a small oblong organ that rests on and beside the posterior surface of the prostate. Inflammation and infection of the epididymis, can result from infections of the prostate. Sexually transmitted infections with *Chlamydia trachomatis* or *Neisseria gonorrhea* are the most common cause in men under age 35, whereas bacterial infections account for most cases in men over the age of 35. Less common causes include prostatitis, urethritis, and chronic urinary tract infections.

Signs and symptoms associated with epididymitis include pain along the inguinal canal followed by swelling in the scrotal sac and groin. Additional symptoms include pyuria, bacteriuria, chills, and fever. If the client remains untreated, orchitis and sterility can result.

The diagnosis of epididymitis is based on the client's symptoms as well as the results of urinalysis, urine culture, and cultures for sexually transmitted infections. Bacteriuria, pyuria, and positive cultures for sexually transmitted infections are all associated with epididymitis. A positive *Prehn's sign*, or relief of pain when the scrotum is lifted, indicates inflammation of the epididymis. Additional diagnostic measures include ultrasound to rule out testicular torsion. Management of the client with epididymitis includes the use of antibiotics. If the infection is caused by chlamydia or gonorrhea, both the client and sexual partners are treated with antibiotic therapy. To prevent traction on the spermatic cord and to facilitate venous drainage, the client should be told to rest in bed with the scrotum supported on a small towel. Antipyretics and analgesics, as well as the intermittent use of cold compresses and warm sitz baths, can be used to decrease pain and swelling. The client should be instructed to avoid sexual activity for three to four weeks.

Priapism

Priapism refers to uncontrolled prolonged painful erections that are not related to sexual desire. Priapism can result from neural, vascular, or pharmacologic causes. Factors associated with priapism include

▶ Cancers that infiltrate the corporeal body

▶ Diabetes

▶ Sickle cell anemia

▶ Medication (antidepressants, antihypertensives, and anti-impotence medications)

▶ Trauma to the corpora cavernosa resulting in venous thrombosis

Priapism is a urological emergency because damage occurs to the tissue which can result in ischemia, thrombosis, and impaired erectile function. The goal of medical intervention is to improve venous drainage. Conservative measures include prostatic massage, sedation, and bed rest. Urinary catheterization is necessary if the client is unable to void. If conservative efforts fail, a local anesthetic is administered and blood is aspirated from the corpus cavernosum. If this is still insufficient, intra-cavernosal injections of phenylephrine are administered. The client should receive constant hemodynamic monitoring since the use of phenylephrine can result in severe hypertension as well as changes in heart rate and rhythm. If these measures fail shunts are inserted surgically. The condition should be resolved within 24 hours to prevent penile ischemia, gangrene, fibrosis, and impotence.

Case Study

Mr. Scott, a 65-year-old with a history of benign prostatic hypertrophy, is admitted for a transurethral prostatectomy. The following questions relate to the care of the client with benign prostatic hypertrophy and transurethral resection of the prostate (TURP):

1. What symptoms are typically reported by the client with benign prostatic hypertrophy?

2. Discuss nonsurgical management of the client with benign prostatic hypertrophy including complementary therapy.

3. List the advantages and disadvantages of a transurethral prostatectomy.

4. Why are continuous bladder irrigations with normal saline frequently ordered following TURP?

5. Postoperative care of the client with a TURP includes assessment of bleeding. Compare findings and interventions for the client with venous bleeding with those of the client with arterial bleeding.

6. The nurse is preparing to discharge Mr. Scott. What discharge instructions should be given regarding his care at home?

Answers to Case Study

1. Symptoms of benign prostatic hypertrophy include urinary frequency, nocturia, and reduced force and size of urinary stream.

2. Proscar (finasteride) lowers the levels of DHT, which is responsible for stimulating prostate growth. Alpha blockers such as Hytrin (terazosin), Cardura (doxazosin), and Flomax (tamsulosin) constrict the prostate, reduce pressure in the urethra, and improve urinary flow. Saw palmetto and lycopene are complementary therapies used for treating benign prostatic hypertrophy.

3. Advantages of TURP: No incision is needed, and hospitalization and convalescence is shorter than with other methods of prostate removal. Disadvantages of transurethral prostatectomy: Only chips or small pieces of the prostate are removed, so prostate tissue can grow back; recurring obstruction might require further surgical interventions.

4. Continuous bladder irrigations with normal saline help keep the catheter free of clots.

5. Dark red bleeding that is less viscous and containing few clots is typical of venous bleeding. Nursing interventions include maintaining traction on the urethral catheter by taping it to the thigh or abdomen. Bright red bleeding that is viscous and containing many clots is typical of arterial bleeding. The nurse should obtain vital signs, notify the physician, and prepare the client for return to surgery.

6. Discharge teaching should include the following instructions: drink 12–14 glasses of water daily; avoid alcohol and caffeine; avoid prolonged sitting; avoid straining at stool or lifting heavy objects; avoid sexual activity for at least 10 days; return for scheduled postoperative follow-up visit.

Key Concepts

The exam reviewer should be familiar with common key terms, diagnostic procedures, and pharmacological agents used in treating the client with genitourinary disorders. The NCLEX exam expects the nurse to be able to apply this information in providing safe effective care to clients.

Key Terms

- ▶ Anuria
- ▶ Arteriovenous graft
- ▶ Cystitis
- ▶ Dialysis
- ▶ Dysuria
- ▶ End stage renal failure
- ▶ Epididymitis
- ▶ Erectile dysfunction
- ▶ Fistula
- ▶ Glomerulonephritis
- ▶ Hematuria
- ▶ Nephrectomy
- ▶ Nephrotic syndrome
- ▶ Oliguria
- ▶ Polyarteritis nodosa
- ▶ Prostatitis
- ▶ Scleroderma
- ▶ Systemic lupus erythematosus

Diagnostics

Most of the diagnostic exams for genitourinary disorders similar to those used for clients with other disorders. These clients would receive the usual routine exams: CBC, urinalysis, ultrasound, and x-ray. In some instances, the anatomical part involved is examined directly through the use of specialized scopes. The exam reviewer should be knowledgeable of the preparation and care of clients receiving genitourinary exams. While reviewing these diagnostic exams, the exam reviewer should be alert for information that would be an important part of nursing care for these clients. Diagnostic measures used for the client with genitourinary disorders include the following:

- Routine urinalysis
- Urinalysis for culture and sensitivity
- Testosterone, calcium, and uric acid levels
- Complete blood count
- ASO titer, ESR
- Voiding cystourethrogram
- Intravenous pyelogram
- Cystourethroscopy
- Cystometrogram
- 24-hour urine
- Renal biopsy
- Ultrasound
- X-ray
- CAT scan
- MRI

Pharmacologic Agents for the Client with Genitourinary Disorders

An integral part of care to clients with genitourinary disorders is pharmacological intervention. These medications provide an improvement or cure of the clients' genitourinary problems. The nursing exam reviewer needs to focus on the drugs in Tables 6.1–6.3. These tables include information about the most common side and adverse effects as well as pertinent nursing care associated with these medications.

Pharmacologic agents used for the client with genitourinary disorders include anti-infectives, urinary analgesics, antispasmodics, and diuretics (see Table 6.1). Medications for the client with urinary incontinence include estrogen replacements, anticholinergics, and tricyclic antidepressants (see Table 6.2). Anti-impotence agents such as Viagra are used for the client with erectile dysfunction (see Table 6.3). Alpha blockers such as Flomax are used for the client with benign prostatic hypertrophy (see Table 6.4). These medications are not inclusive of all the agents used to treat renal and genitourinary disorders; therefore, you will need to keep a current pharmacology text handy for reference.

TABLE 6.1   Drugs Used to Treat Urinary Tract Infections

Type of Drug	Name	Action	Side Effects	Nursing Care
Anti-infectives	Keflex (cephalexin)	Inhibits bacterial synthesis of the cell wall.	Headache, nausea, vomiting, diarrhea, and rash	Assess for allergy to penicillin. Monitor liver and renal function, monitor for drug interactions. Watch IV site for extravasation.
	Gantrisin (acetyl sulfisoxazole)	Interferes with bacterial biosynthesis.	Headache, nausea, vomiting, stomatitis,diarrhea, rash, and photosensitivity	Administer on empty stomach. Increase fluids. Keep medication in a light-resistant container and check for allergy to sulfa.
	Bactrim (sulfamethazole and trimethoprim)	Same as above.	Same as above	Note the color and pH of urine. Administer with a full glass of water. Encourage fluids. Check for allergy to sulfa.
	Macrodantin (nitrofurantoin)	Inhibits bacterial enzymes.	Pruritus, rash, alopecia, nausea, and vomiting	Monitor liver and renal function. Administer with food or milk. Monitor glucose if diabetic.
	Cipro (ciprofloxacin)	Interferes with DNA in bacteria.	Headache, dizziness, fatigue, heartburn, tinnitus, and photosensitivity	Do not administer with Mg or Ca preparations. Tell the client to use sunscreen. Increase fluids to three liters per day.
	Amoxil (amoxicillin)	Interferes with cell wall replication.	Nausea, vomiting, diarrhea, anemia, and abdominal pain	Administer the medication on an empty stomach. Take medication with a full glass of water.
Potassium-sparing diuretics	Aldactone (spironolactone)	Potassium-sparing diuretics interfere with the reabsorption of sodium at the distal tubule.	Headache, confusion, drowsiness, anorexia, and nausea	Monitor electrolytes. Administer in the morning. Teach the client to avoid foods rich in potassium. Monitor weight and output.
	Dyrenium (triamterene)	Same as above.	Same as above	Same as above.
	Midamor (amiloride)	Same as above.	Cough, dyspepsia, impotence, paresthesia, and tremors	Same as above.
Thiazide diuretics	Diuril (chlorothiazide)	Thiazide diuretics increase the excretion of water and sodium by inhibiting reabsorption in the distal tubule.	Paresthesia, anxiety, depression, headache, and orthostatic hypotension	Administer in the morning. Monitor electrolytes. Monitor output and weight. Instruct the client to rise slowly from a sitting position.

(continues)

TABLE 6.1 *Continued*

Type of Drug	Name	Action	Side Effects	Nursing Care
Loop diuretics	Lasix (furosemide)	Loop diuretics inhibit reabsorption of sodium and chloride in the ascending loop of Henle.	Headache, fatigue, weakness, paresthesia, diarrhea, and dry mouth	Observe for signs of hypokalemia. Monitor hydration status. Monitor weight.
	Edecrin (ethacrynic acid)	Same as above.	Glycosuria, headache, fatigue, weakness, vertigo, blurred vision, and photosensitivity	Same as above. Monitor urine glucose.
Osmotic diuretics	Osmitrol (mannitol)	Osmotic diuretics increase osmotic pressure of glomerular filtrate.	Thirst, dizziness, headache, confusion, edema, and angina-like chest pain	Administer medication using IV filter over 30–60 minutes.

TABLE 6.2 **Drugs Used for Urinary Incontinence**

Type of Drug	Name	Action	Side Effects	Nursing Care
Estrogens	Premarin (conjugated estrogens)	Hormonal replacement for the treatment of stress incontinence caused by the thinning and weakening of vaginal, urethral, and pelvic floor muscles	Breast changes, headache, migraines, increased appetite, increased blood sugar, and increased weight. Adverse reactions include thrombo-phlebitis, stroke, and pulmonary emboli.	Monitor blood sugar and blood pressure. Monitor liver function. Administer with food or milk.
Analgesics and antispasmodics	Pyridium (phenazopyridine)	Anesthetic action on urinary tract mucosa	Headache, anorexia, and heartburn.	Administer with food. Tell the client the medication will turn his urine red or orange in color.
	Anaspas (hyoscyamine)	Inhibits the muscarinic action of acetylcholine	Confusion, headache, insomnia, and dry mouth.	Assess for constipation and urinary retention.
Anticholinergics/ Antispasmodics	Pro-Banthine (propantheline)	Inhibits muscarinic action of acetylcholine	Headache, insomnia, dizzi-ness, insomnia, anxiety, and rash.	Monitor heart rate and rhythm. Administer from 30 minutes to one hour before meals. Check for urinary retention.

TABLE 6.2 *Continued*

Type of Drug	Name	Action	Side Effects	Nursing Care
	Ditropan (oxybutynin)	Relaxes smooth muscle in the urinary tract	Dry mouth, hypotension, blurred vision, increased intra-ocular pressure, photophobia, and dizziness.	Offer hard candy and fluids. Evaluate for signs of glaucoma.
	Bentyl (dicyclomine hydrochloride)	Inhibits muscarinic action of acetylcholine	Headache, insomnia, dizziness, dry mouth tachycardia, and photosensitivity.	Administer between meals. Increase fluids and fiber in diet. Use sunscreen.
Tricyclic antidepressants	Tofranil (imipramine)	Blocks the reuptake of norepinephrine and serotonin at the nerve endings	Dizziness, hypotension, drowsiness, nausea, vomiting, hypotension, and photosensitivity.	Administer at bedtime. Monitor CBC and liver function. Monitor for urinary retention. Administer with food or milk. Tell client to avoid alcohol.
	Pamelor (nortriptyline)	Same as above	Same as above.	Same as above.
	Norpramin (desipramine)	Same as above	Same as above.	Same as above.

TABLE 6.3 Anti-Impotence Agents

Drug	Action	Side Effect	Nursing Care
Viagra (sildenafil)	Anti-impotence agents cause relaxation of the smooth muscle of the anticorpus cavernosum, which increases blood flow and produces an erection.	Headache, back pain, dizziness, blurred vision, increased sensitivity to light, and color-tinged vision with use of Viagra. Adverse effects include priapism and sudden cardio-vascular collapse.	Instruct the client to avoid use of anti-impotence medication with nitrates in any form because severe hypotension can result.
Cialis (tadalafil)	Same as above.	Same as above.	Same as above.
Levitra (vardenafil)	Same as above.	Same as above.	Same as above.

TABLE 6.4   Drugs Used to Treat Benign Prostatic Hypertrophy

Drug	Action	Side Effects	Nursing Care
Hytrin (terazosin)	Alpha–adrenergic antagonist relieves obstruction and increases flow of urine.	Orthostatic hypotension	Teach the client to change position slowly and to take and his record BP. Teach the client to talk with his doctor before taking OTC cold and allergy medications.
Cardura (doxazosin)	Same as above.	Same as above	Same as above.
Flomax (tamsulosin)	Same as above.	Same as above	Same as above.
Uroxatral (alfuzosin)	Same as above.	Same as above	Same as above.
Proscar (finasteride)	Anti-androgen Bbocks DHT and shrinks the prostate.	Decreased libido, impotence, and decreased volume of ejaculate	Crushed or broken tablets should not be handled by women who are or might become pregnant.
Avodart (dutasteride)	Same as above.	Same as above	Same as above.

Apply Your Knowledge

This chapter includes much needed information to help the nurse apply knowledge of genitourinary disorders to the NCLEX exam. The following questions test your knowledge regarding the safe, effective care and management of the client with various genitourinary disorders.

Exam Questions

1. The nurse is collecting a 24-hour urine sampling for creatinine clearance on a client hospitalized with acute glomerulonephritis. While making rounds, the nurse learns that the client discarded the 2 a.m. voiding. The nurse should:

   A. Continue the collection as ordered by the physician

   B. Discard the collected urine, obtain a new bottle, and begin the collection again

   C. Record the information in the client's chart and continue the collection

   D. Extend the collection time to replace the last voiding

2. A client with end stage renal failure has received a renal transplant. Which statement describes hyperacute graft rejection in the client with a renal transplant?

   A. Hyperacute graft rejection is due to chronic inflammation and scaring.

   B. Hyperacute graft rejection is a cellular response that occurs 1–3 weeks after transplantation.

   C. Hyperacute graft rejection is more likely in clients who have received multiple blood transfusions.

   D. Hyperacute graft rejection is managed by use of immunosuppressive medications.

3. The nurse is assessing an infant with polycystic kidney disease. Which structural anomaly is typical in the infant with polycystic kidney disease?

    A. Webbed neck

    B. High arched palate

    C. Scaphoid abdomen

    D. Low-set ears

4. Which meal selection is suitable for the client hospitalized with nephrotic syndrome?

    A. Tuna sandwich, pickle spear, potato chips, and iced tea

    B. Ham slice, tossed salad with dressing, gelatin, and coffee

    C. Tomato soup, crackers, peanut butter sandwich, and milk

    D. Hamburger steak, baked potato, lima beans, and milk

5. The physician has ordered fluid restrictions for a client with acute glomerulonephritis. The nurse knows that the client's oral intake will be limited to the amount of urinary output plus:

    A. 100 mL

    B. 300 mL

    C. 500 mL

    D. 700 mL

6. The nurse is preparing to administer Sandimmune (cyclosporine) oral solution. The nurse should avoid mixing the medication with:

    A. Chocolate milk

    B. Grapefruit juice

    C. Orange juice

    D. Milk

7. The physician has ordered several diagnostic measures for a client with suspected renal calculi. Which diagnostic measure has the highest sensitivity for detecting renal calculi?

    A. Magnetic resonance imaging

    B. Ultrasonography

    C. Noncontrast helical computerized tomography

    D. X-ray of the kidneys, ureter, and bladder

8. The nurse is teaching a client with recurrent cystitis regarding ways to decrease bladder infections. The nurse should tell the client to:

   A. Increase her intake of milk and dairy products.

   B. Avoid taking bubble baths

   C. Use underwear made from nylon

   D. Drink orange juice for breakfast

9. A client with hydroureteronephrosis has been scheduled for a nephrostomy. When caring for the client with a nephrostomy, the nurse should:

   A. Clamp the tubing for 15 minutes every hour

   B. Irrigate the tubing with normal saline to remove clots

   C. Avoid clamping or kinking the tubing

   D. Suspend the tubing above the level of the abdomen

10. Which medication is indicated for the client with hyperkalemia due to chronic glomerulonephritis?

    A. Kayexalate (sodium polystyrene sulfonate)

    B. K-Dur (potassium chloride)

    C. Cephulac (lactulose)

    D. PhosLo (calcium acetate)

Answers to Exam Questions

1. Answer B is correct. Failure to collect all urine voided in the 24-hour period invalidates specimen results; therefore, the nurse should obtain a new collection bottle, discard the collected urine, and begin the collection again. Answers A, C, and D are incorrect because they are improper ways of obtaining a 24-hour urine specimen.

2. Answer C is correct. Hyperacute graft rejection is more likely to occur in clients who receive a transplant from a donor with an ABO type different from their own, in those with a history of multiple blood transfusions, those with multiple pregnancies, or those with a previous transplant. Answers A and D are incorrect because they describe chronic graft rejection. Answer B describes acute graft rejection; therefore, it is incorrect.

3. Answer D is correct. Structural anomalies in the infant with polycystic kidney disease include low-set ears, pointed nose, and small chin. Answers A, B, and C are not associated with polycystic kidney disease; therefore, they are incorrect.

4. Answer D is correct. The client with nephrotic syndrome needs a diet with complete proteins and restricted sodium. Answers A, B, and C are incorrect because they contain high-sodium foods.

5. Answer C is correct. Fluid intake for the client with acute glomerulonephritis is limited to urinary output plus 500 mL to 600 mL. Answers A and B are incorrect because the intake is too limited. Answer D is incorrect because the intake is excessive.

6. Answer B is correct. Sandimmune oral solution should not be mixed with grapefruit juice. Answers A, C, and D are all suitable beverages for mixing with the medication; therefore, they are incorrect.

7. Answer C is correct. Noncontrast helical computerized tomography is the most sensitive means for diagnosing renal calculi. Magnetic resonance imaging, ultrasonography, and x-ray of the kidneys, ureters, and bladder are not as sensitive; therefore, answers A, B, and D are incorrect.

8. Answer B is correct. The nurse should tell the client to avoid tub baths as well as bubble baths. The client should be instructed to wear cotton underwear and to avoid tight-fitting clothing such as jeans. Answers A, C, and D do not decrease the incidence of cystitis; therefore, they are incorrect.

9. Answer C is correct. The nurse should avoid clamping or kinking the nephrostomy because urine would be retained in the kidney. Answer A is incorrect because the tubing should not be clamped. Answer B is incorrect because the tubing should not be irrigated because it would damage the renal tissue. Answer D is incorrect because suspending the tubing would cause urine to be retained in the kidney.

10. Answer A is correct. Kayexalate (sodium polystyrene sulfonate) is administered to lower potassium levels in the client with hyperkalemia. K-Dur is used for the client with hypokalemia; therefore, answer B is incorrect. Lactulose is used to lower ammonia levels in the client with liver disease; therefore, answer C is incorrect. PhosLo is used to lower phosphorus levels in the client with renal disease; therefore, Answer D is incorrect.

Suggested Reading and Resources

▶ Brunner, L., and D. Suddarth. *Textbook of Medical Surgical Nursing*. 12th ed. Philadelphia: Lippincott Williams & Wilkins, 2009.

▶ Ignatavicius, D., and S. Workman. *Medical Surgical Nursing: Critical Thinking for Collaborative Care*. 6th ed. Philadelphia: Elsevier, 2008.

▶ Lehne, R. *Pharmacology for Nursing Care*. 7th ed. Philadelphia: Elsevier, 2009

▶ LeMone, P., and K. Burke. *Medical Surgical Nursing: Critical Thinking in Client Care*. 4th ed. Upper Saddle River, NJ: Pearson Prentice Hall, 2008.

▶ Lewis, S., M. Heitkemper, S. Dirksen, P. Obrien and L. Bucher. *Medical Surgical Nursing: Assessment and Management of Clinical Problems.* 7th ed. Philadelphia: Elsevier, 2007.

▶ American Urological Association: www.urologyhealth.org.

▶ National Institute of Diabetes & Digestive & Kidney Diseases: www.niddk.nih.gov.

▶ National Kidney and Urologic Diseases Information Clearinghouse: www.kidney.niddk.nih.gov.

▶ National Kidney Foundation: www.kidney.org.

▶ Nephropathy Support Network: www.igansupport.org.

CHAPTER SEVEN

Care of the Client with Integumentary Disorders

The integumentary system comprises the skin, hair, and nails. Although we seldom think of the skin as an organ, it is the largest and one of the most complex organs of the body. Composed of three layers—epidermis, dermis, and subcutaneous tissue—the skin performs several vital functions, including

- ▶ Protection against infection
- ▶ Prevention of fluid and electrolyte imbalance
- ▶ Regulation of temperature
- ▶ Activation of vitamin D

The hair and nails are extensions of the keratin-producing epidermal layers of the skin.

Evaluation of the integumentary system reveals much about the client's overall state of health and well being. This chapter reviews some of the common infections affecting the integumentary system as well as immune disorders that affect the skin. We will also review traumatic injuries caused by prolonged pressure and burns.

Additional information on integumentary disorders such as skin cancer can be found in Chapter 12, "Care of the Client with Immunologic Disorders," and the integumentary disorders of dermatitis, scabies, pediculosis capitis, and tick borne illnesses can be found in Chapter 17, "Care of the Client with Psychiatric Disorers."

Common Infections of the Integumentary System

The integumentary system is vulnerable to a number of pathogens, including viruses, fungi (dermatophytes), and bacteria. This section discusses the most common skin disorder produced by each of these. Chapter 15, "Care of the Childbearing Client and the Neonatal Client," covers additional infections of the integumentary system.

Viral Infections

Viral infections occur when a virus enters the cell membrane and takes on the functions usually performed by healthy cells. Once this occurs, the virus is capable of assembling itself into a mature form that infects other cells.

Some viruses, such as herpes, have envelopes that enable them to adhere to cell membranes and avoid destruction by the host's immune system.

Herpes Simplex

Herpes simplex is the most common viral infection affecting adult skin. The herpes simplex virus (HSV) is classified either as HSV I (which produces cold sores) or HSV II (which produces genital herpes). The virus is spread through direct contact with an actively infected person and a susceptible host, or from one infected body part to another. For example, herpetic whitlow found at the fingertips is the result of touching an active lesion. After initial infection, the virus becomes dormant, residing in the nerve ganglia of the affected site. Recurrence of active lesions is triggered by physical or emotional stress.

Herpes simplex II, or genital herpes, is transmitted through sexual contact. In the initial episode, multiple painful vesicles erupt on the vulva, perineum, cervix, and perianal area three to five days after exposure to an infected partner. Use of condoms is recommended to prevent the transmission of herpes to non-infected persons.

Both spontaneous abortion in the first trimester and an increased risk of preterm labor are associated with active HSV II. Caesarean section is the preferred method of delivery if active lesions are present. Infected newborn can develop fever, hypothermia, jaundice, seizures, poor feeding, and vesicular skin eruptions.

Outbreaks of both HSV I and HSV II are characterized by tingling, itching, and pain at the site of the eruption. There is no cure for either form of herpes; however, Zovirax (acyclovir) is useful in relieving symptoms.

Infection with HSV is suggested by the characteristic appearance of clustered blisters on a red base. The diagnosis is confirmed by the use of viral culture and rapid assays. Nursing interventions include

- Teaching the client proper hand hygiene to avoid spreading the virus to other areas
- Teaching the client to get adequate rest and to avoid triggers such as prolonged exposure to sunlight and stress
- Teaching the client the symptoms associated with recurrent episodes

Herpes Zoster (Shingles)

Herpes zoster, or shingles, is a caused by reactivation of the varicella-zoster virus (VZV) in those who have had chickenpox. The virus remains dormant in the dorsal root ganglia of the spinal and sensory cranial nerves and is reactivated by disorders affecting the immune system. Conditions associated with shingles include AIDS, lymphoma, Hodgkin's lymphoma, and systemic lupus erythematosus.

The lesions of herpes zoster are similar in appearance to those of herpes simplex, but the pattern of distribution is different. Multiple lesions occur in a segmental area that is innervated by an infected nerve. Outbreaks occur most often in the thoracic region; however, the cervical, facial, lumbar, and sacral areas can also be affected. Symptoms of herpes zoster vary from mild irritation with itching to severe pain. In some instances, the client develops *post-herpetic neuralgia*, or pain that persists after the lesions have resolved.

A diagnosis of herpes zoster is based on the appearance and configuration of the vesicles. Patches of grouped vesicles appear in a band-like configuration along one side of the chest, neck, or head. The eruption of vesicles is usually preceded by pain and burning, which can radiate over the entire region supplied by the affected nerve. Other symptoms include itching and tenderness over the affected area.

Nursing interventions include monitoring the client for secondary complications which can include full thickness skin necrosis, Bell's palsy, and infection of the eyes. The client with herpes zoster can transmit chickenpox to those who have not had chickenpox as well as to those who are immune-suppressed; therefore, airborne and contact transmission-based precautions should be used when caring for the client with herpes zoster.

> **NOTE**
>
> The Centers for Disease Control and Prevention has published a guideline for preventing transmission of infectious diseases. You can download a copy of the CDC's guidelines from the website at http://www.cdc.gov/ncidod/dhqp/gl_isolation_references.html.

Treatment of the client with herpes zoster focuses on drying the lesions, relieving discomfort, and preventing secondary complications. Wet to dry dressings with Burow's solution are frequently ordered to dry the lesions. Antihistamines and analgesics are ordered to prevent itching and for mild pain relief. Narcotic preparations are ordered for those with more severe pain.

Valtrex (valacyclovir), an antiviral medication, is most effective for herpes zoster if it is given in the first 48 hours of the rash appearance.

Zostavax, a shingles vaccine, is available for adults age 60 and over. The vaccine has been shown to prevent shingles 60% of the time. Persons who are immune suppressed, who have an active infection, or who have a history of unusual or allergic reactions to vaccines should not take the vaccine. Clients receiving Zostavax can spread chickenpox; therefore, the client should avoid contact with others who have immune problems, with pregnant women who have not had chickenpox, as well as newborns born to women who have not had chickenpox.

Fungal Infections

Fungal infections are caused by a group of organisms known as *dermatophytes*. Dermatophytes live mainly in the soil, on animals, or humans. Infection occurs when the infective organism comes in contact with the impaired skin of a susceptible host. Although most fungal infections are transmitted by direct contact with infected humans or animals, some fungal infections, such as tinea capitis or tinea corporis, are transmitted by sharing personal items such as caps, clothing, and towels Tinea pedis, commonly known as athlete's foot, can be contracted from walking barefoot in showers or bath areas used by infected persons.

The appearance and location of lesions vary; however, most are described as circular patches with elevated borders and clear central areas. The lesions are singular or multiple, and itching is common.

Fungal infections are confirmed by a KOH (potassium hydroxide) test. Scales are scraped from the lesion, prepared with a solution of potassium hydroxide, and examined beneath the microscope for the presence of fungal hyphae. Additional tests include culture and skin biopsy.

Topical antifungal medications are used for the client with a dermatophyte infection. The medication is usually applied to the infected skin twice daily until the lesions have resolved. Therapy might continue for one to two weeks to prevent recurrence. Widespread or resistant fungal infections are treated with systemic antifungal medications such as Nizoral (ketoconazole).

Candidiasis infection is caused by *Candida albicans*, also known as moniliasis. The most common sites of infection are warm moist areas such as the groin area, oral mucosa, and submammary folds. Clients with depressed cell mediated immunity (HIV infection, chemotherapy, radiation, and organ transplantation) are at increased risk for candidiasis. Further discussion of candidiasis infection and treatment of the client with HIV can be found in Chapter 11, "Care of the Client with Disorders of the Immunological System."

Candidiasis infections of the skin are characterized by a diffuse papular red rash with pinpoint satellite lesions around the edges of affected skin. Management of cutaneous candidisis includes keeping the skin clean and dry. Mycostatin powder is effective in eradicating the infection.

Bacterial Infections

Cellulitis, an infection of the skin and subcutaneous tissue, can be caused by *Haemophilus influenzae*, *streptococcus*, or *staphylococcus* infections. Facial cellulitis in young children is associated with otitis media. Symptoms of cellulitis include redness, swelling, and firm infiltration of the affected tissue. Lymphangitis, or red streaks, might be noted coming from the affected area, and the involvement of regional lymph nodes can progress to abscess formation. Systemic effects of cellulitis include fever and malaise. Management of the client with cellulitis includes immobilization of the affected area, warm moist compresses to the area, and the administration of oral or parenteral antibiotics.

The diagnosis of bacterial infection is confirmed by cultures taken from the affected area and by elevations in the client's white blood cell (WBC) count. The cultures and complete blood count (CBC), which reflect changes in the white cell count, should be obtained before antibiotic therapy is begun.

Psoriasis

Psoriasis is a scaling disorder that affects the epidermal cells in the outer layers of the skin. Although the exact cause is unknown, psoriasis is believed to be due to an autoimmune reaction. The disease is characterized by exacerbations and remissions, and is greatly influenced by systemic factors such as illness, infection, hormonal changes, medication, and obesity. Some clients develop psoriatic arthritis, leading to degenerative changes similar to those seen in the client with rheumatoid arthritis. The two most common forms of psoriasis are as follows:

► **Psoriasis vulgaris:** Manifestations of psoriasis vulgaris include the presence of sharply defined thick red papules or plaques that are covered with silvery white scales. Bilateral lesions are usually present; that is, the same areas on both sides of the body are affected. The sites most commonly affected are the scalp, elbows, trunk, knees, sacrum, and outer surfaces of the extremities.

► **Exfoliative psoriasis:** Characterized by generalized erythema and scaling with no formed lesions. Because involvement is generalized, the client with exfoliative psoriasis can experience dehydration due to evaporative water loss.

The presence of the classic plaque, such as lesions, helps to confirm the diagnosis of psoriasis. There are no specific blood tests to diagnose the condition and biopsy of the skin is not helpful.

Management of the client with psoriasis includes topical therapies using steroids, tar preparations, anthralin paste, and ultraviolet light therapy. Newer topical therapies with Dovonex (calcipotriene; a vitamin D derivative) and Tazorac (tazarotene; a vitamin A derivative), are used to treat those with mild to moderate psoriasis.

Psoralen and ultraviolet light therapy are commonly performed on an outpatient basis. The client is instructed to take the psoralen two hours before exposure to the UVA light.

Psoralen causes strong photosensitivity; therefore, the client must wear dark glasses during treatment and for the remainder of the day after treatments. UVA treatments are limited to two to three times a week and not on consecutive days. The nurse should assess the client's skin for generalized redness, edema, and tenderness. Further UVA treatments are withheld until these subside.

Systemic therapy with cytotoxic agents (such as Folex [methotrexate]) and immunosuppressive drugs (such as Sandimmune [cyclosporine] and Imuran [azathioprine]) is indicated for clients with severe psoriasis that is resistant to topical therapy. Other systemic therapy includes the use of biologic response modifiers. Approved biologic response modifiers include Raptiva (efalizumab) given weekly by subcutaneous injection, and Amevive (alefacept) given for three months by weekly intramuscular injection.

Because of the appearance of the skin and the unpleasantness associated with many of the therapies, the client with psoriasis often has low self-esteem. It is especially important for the nurse to convey acceptance by providing emotional support. In this case, touch takes on added significance because it conveys a feeling of acceptance.

Pressure Ulcers

Pressure ulcers occur when the skin and underlying soft tissue are pressed between bony prominences and an external surface for extended periods. Although they can be found on any body surface, pressure ulcers are more likely to be found over the sacrum, hips, ankles, and scapula. Factors associated with pressure ulcer formation include limited mobility, excessive skin moisture, poor nutrition, increasing age, and skin damaged by mechanical forces such as friction and shearing. The Braden scale (see Table 7.1) is commonly used to predict the client's risk for developing pressure ulcers. Clients with total scores of 16 or less on the Braden scale have an increased risk for developing pressure ulcers.

TABLE 7.1 Braden Scale

Patient's Name ___ Evaluator's Name ___ Date of Assessment __ / __ / __

Category	1	2	3	4
Sensory perception Ability to respond meaningfully to pressure-related discomfort	**1. Completely limited**: Unresponsive (does not moan, flinch, or grasp) to painful stimuli, due to diminished level of consciousness or sedation, **OR** limited ability to feel pain over most of body surface.	**2. Very limited**: Responds only to painful stimuli. Cannot communicate discomfort except by moaning or restlessness, **OR** has a sensory impairment which limits the ability to feel pain or discomfort over 1/2 of body.	**3. Slightly limited**: Responds to verbal commands but cannot always communicate discomfort or need to be turned, **OR** has some sensory impairment which limits ability to feel pain or discomfort in 1 or 2 extremities.	**4. No impairment**: Responds to verbal commands. Has no sensory deficit which would limit ability to feel or voice pain or discomfort.
Moisture Degree to which skin is exposed to moisture	**1. Constantly moist**: Skin is kept moist almost constantly by perspiration, urine, etc. Dampness is detected every time patient is moved or turned.	**2. Moist**: Skin is often but not always moist. Linen must be changed at least once a day.	**3. Occasionally moist**: Skin is occasionally moist, requiring an extra linen change approximately once a day.	**4. Rarely moist**: Skin is usually dry; linen requires changing only at routine intervals.
Activity Degree of physical activity	**1. Bedfast**: Confined to bed.	**2. Chairfast**: Ability to walk severely limited or nonexistent. Cannot bear own weight and/or must be assisted into chair or wheel chair.	**3. Walks occasionally**: Walks occasionally during day but for very short distances, with or without assistance. Spends majority of each shift in bed or chair.	**4. Walks frequently**: Walks outside the room at least twice a day and inside room at least once every 2 hours during waking hours.
Mobility Ability to change and control body position	**1. Completely immobile**: Does not make even slight changes in body or extremity position without assistance.	**2. Very limited**: Makes occasional slight changes in body or extremity position but unable to make frequent or significant changes independently.	**3. Slightly limited**: Makes frequent though slight changes in body or extremity position independently.	**4. No limitations**: Makes major and frequent changes in position without assistance.
Nutrition Usual food intake pattern	**1. Very poor**: Never eats a complete meal. Rarely eats more than 1/3 of any food offered. Eats 2 servings or less of protein (meat or dairy products) per day. Takes fluids poorly. Does not take a liquid dietary supplement, **OR** is nothing per oral (NPO) and/or maintained on clear liquids or intravenous (IV) drip for more than 5 days.	**2. Probably inadequate**: Rarely eats a complete meal and generally eats only about 1/2 of any food offered. Protein intake includes only 3 servings of meat or dairy products per day. Occasionally will take a dietary supplement, **OR** receives less than optimum amount of liquid diet or tube feeding.	**3. Adequate**: Eats over half of most meals. Eats a total of 4 servings of protein (meat, dairy products) each day. Occasionally will refuse a meal, but will usually take a supplement if offered, **OR** is on a tube feeding or total parenteral nutrition (TPN) regimen, which probably meets most of nutritional needs.	**4. Excellent**: Eats most of every meal. Never refuses a meal. Usually eats a total of 4 or more servings of meat and dairy products. Occasionally eats between meals. Does not require supplementation.
Friction and shear	**1. Problem**: Requires moderate to maximum assistance in moving. Complete lifting without sliding against sheets is impossible. Frequently slides down in bed or chair, requiring frequent repositioning with maximum assistance. Spasticity, contractures, or agitation leads to almost constant friction.	**2. Potential problem**: Moves feebly or requires minimum assistance. During a move skin probably slides to some extent against sheets, chair, restraints, or other devices. Maintains relatively good position in chair or bed most of the time but occasionally slides down.	**3. No apparent problem**: Moves in bed and in chair independently and has sufficient muscle strength to lift up completely during move. Maintains good position in bed or chair at all times.	

Total Score: ___

Pressure ulcers are staged according to the degree of skin and tissue destruction.

▶ **Stage 1:** The skin is intact, is red, and fails to blanch with pressure. Changes in skin temperature, tissue consistency, and sensation are present. Developing pressure ulcers are characterized by persistent redness or bluish purple discoloration.

▶ **Stage 2:** The skin is no longer intact, with partial loss of the epidermis and dermis. Ulcers appear as abrasions, blisters, or shallow craters.

▶ **Stage 3:** Full thickness skin loss can lead to necrosis of the subcutaneous tissues. The damage extends to the underlying fascia. Deep crater-like ulcers and eschar might be present. Undermining or tunneling of the ulcer might be present.

▶ **Stage 4:** Full thickness skin loss, with extensive destruction and necrosis of the skin and underlying tissue. Damage can extend to muscle, bone, and supporting structures. Sinus tracts are caused by undermining, or separation of the skin layers at the margins.

The best treatment for pressure ulcers is prevention. Nursing interventions include proper positioning, nutritional support, and skin care as outlined in Table 7.2.

TABLE 7.2   Ulcer Prevention

Positioning	Nutrition	Skin Care
Apply foam, silica gel, or air pads to contact surfaces.	Ensure adequate intake of protein, vitamins, and minerals.	Clean the skin at routine intervals using a mild, heavily fatted soap.
If possible, avoid elevating the client's head over 30°.	Maintain adequate caloric intake.	Avoid using hot water or skin preparations that are drying.
Reposition the client at least every two hours while she is in bed; every hour while sitting.	Ensure fluid intake of 2,000–3,000 mL daily to provide optimal hydration.	Use minimal rubbing when cleaning soiled areas of the skin.
Keep the client's skin off plastic surfaces.	Provide nutritional supplements as needed to promote healing.	Pat the skin dry.
Use a lift sheet to avoid dragging or sliding the client on the bed surface.		Apply moisturizers while the skin is still damp.
Avoid placing the client in a side-lying position directly over the trochanter.		Apply absorbent pads under areas where moisture collects.
Keep the client"s heels off the surface of the bed.		Apply moisture barriers to areas affected by wound drainage or incontinence.
		Avoid massaging bony prominences, which can damage capillary beds.
		Increase environmental humidity.

A number of therapies are used for the client with pressure ulcers. These include wet to dry dressings, topical medications, electrical stimulation, and hyperbaric oxygen therapy.

Burns

Although the incidence of burn injury has declined, burns still account for more than one million injuries each year in the United States. According to the National Institute of General Medical Sciences (2005), about 45,000 persons require hospital care each year for treatment of their injuries. Those with burns greater than 25% total body surface area (TBSA) are at risk of dying from smoke inhalation and other complications associated with burns. Young children and the elderly are particularly vulnerable to local and systemic effects of burns because their skin is naturally thinner. Burns are the third leading cause of death in children under age 14 and are in the top 10 of causes of death for all age groups.

NOTE

For the latest information on burn injury statistics, visit the American Burn Association website at www.ameriburn.org.

Burns generally occur from one of four major sources:

- Thermal injuries (hot liquid, open flame)
- Electrical injuries (household current, lightning)
- Chemical injuries (alkaline or acid liquids or powders)
- Radiation injuries (sunburn, radiation treatment for cancer)

Most burns are thermal injuries that occur in the home. Cooking accidents from hot grease or stove fires result in a significant number of injuries, as do scalds from bathwater that is too hot.

CAUTION

To prevent burns, hot water heaters should be set no higher than 120° Fahrenheit.

Carbon monoxide, sulfur oxides, cyanide, chlorine, and other toxins are released from household contents during a fire. Inhalation of these gases damages the lower airway, resulting in the collapse of the alveoli and increasing the possibility of acute respiratory distress syndrome.

Burn Classifications

Before discussing caring for the client with burns, you must first understand how burns are classified. Treatment of the client with burns is dictated by whether the injury is classified as a minor burn, moderate burn, or major burn. These classifications are dependent on the degree of tissue involved and the total body surface area affected by the injury. Burns are further classified in terms of the depth of tissue destroyed or the thickness of the burn injury. The following list gives you an idea of the different degrees of burns, the symptoms experienced with the injury, and the expected time of healing:

▶ **Superficial partial thickness (first degree):** Tissue damage is confined to the epidermis and possibly a portion of the dermis. This is the type of injury produced by sunburn or a low-intensity flash. The skin appears red, but blanches with pressure. Blisters might or might not be present. The client usually complains of tingling, increased skin sensitivity, and pain that is relieved by the application of cool water or lotions containing aloe. The injury heals within a week. Although the skin peels, there is no scarring.

▶ **Deep partial thickness (second degree):** Tissue damage involves the epidermis, upper dermis, and portions of the deeper dermis. Deep partial thickness injury is common in scalds and flash flames. The area involved appears blistered with weeping and edema. The client experiences pain and increased skin sensitivity, which increases with exposure to air. The use of sterile sheets and overbed cradles minimizes contact with the air and makes the client more comfortable. Morphine sulfate or other opiate analgesics are given intravenously to control pain.

TIP

Pain medication is given intravenously to provide quick, optimal relief and to prevent overmedication as edema subsides and fluid shift is resolving.

Deep partial thickness injury generally heals in two to four weeks, although infection can delay healing. Infection can also take a deep partial thickness injury to a full thickness injury.

▶ **Full thickness (third degree):** Tissue damage involves the epidermis and entire dermis. The damage usually extends into subcutaneous tissue, including connective tissue, muscle, and bone. Full thickness burns result from prolonged exposure to hot liquids or open flame, electrical current, or exposure to chemical agents. Depending on the source of the injury, the affected area can appear dry, pale white, edematous, leathery, or charred. Destruction of nerve endings leaves the affected areas relatively pain-free. Complicating the care of the client with full thickness injury is the development of hypovolemic burn shock, hyperkalemia, and anemia. Electrical injuries, which appear as whitish areas at the points of entry and exit, can result in changes in heart rhythm or complete cardiac standstill.

TIP

The cardiac status of a client with electrical burns should be closely monitored for at least 24 hours following the injury to detect changes in electrical conduction of the heart.

Full thickness burns can damage muscles, leading to the development of myoglobinuria, in which case urinary output becomes burgundy in color. The client with myoglobinuria might require hemodialysis to prevent tubular necrosis and acute renal failure.

Burn Measurement with TBSA

A second means of classifying burns is based on the percentage of tissue injured. Three methods are used to determine the total body surface area injured in a burn:

▶ **The Rule of Nines:** The Rule of Nines assigns percentages of 9 to major body surfaces. The breakdown is as follows:

  ▶ Head = 9%

  ▶ Anterior trunk = 18%

  ▶ Posterior trunk = 18%

  ▶ Arms = 9% each

  ▶ Legs = 18% each

  ▶ Perineum = 1%

Figure 7.1 illustrates the Rule of Nines as well as the layers of skin.

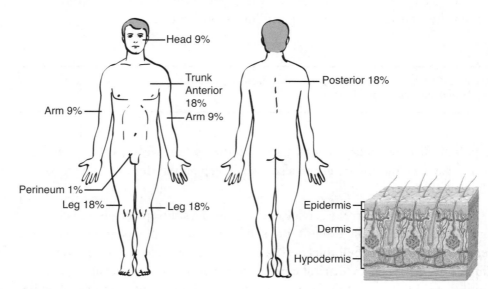

FIGURE 7.1   The Rule of Nines and layers of skin.

▶ **Lund and Browder method:** The Lund and Browder method of determining TBSA is more precise because it takes into account that anatomic parts, especially the head and legs, change with growth. Special charts divide the body into very small parts and provide for an estimate of the proportion of TBSA burned. The Lund and Browder method is used to estimate TBSA in children.

▶ **The palm method:** The percentage affected by scattered burns can best be calculated using the palm method. The size of the client's palm represents approximately 1% of the TBSA.

Minor burn injury involves a second-degree burn or less than 15% of TBSA in adults and less than 10% in children. Or it can involve a third-degree burn of less than 2% TBSA, but not involving areas requiring special care (face, eyes, ears, perineum, and joints of hands and feet). Minor burns do not include electrical burn injury, inhalation injury, those clients with concurrent illness or trauma, or age-related considerations.

Moderate burn injury involves second-degree burns of 15%–20% TBSA in adults, 10%–20% in children, or third-degree burns less than 10% TBSA that do not involve special care areas. Moderate burns, like minor burns, do not include electrical or inhalation injury, nor those with concurrent illness, trauma, or age-related considerations.

Major burn injury involves second-degree burns of greater than 25% TBSA in adults, 20% in children, or all third-degree burns greater than 10% TBSA. Major burns include all burns involving the structures of the head and face, hands, feet, and perineum as well as electrical and inhalation injury, concurrent illness, and trauma regardless of age.

TIP

It will be beneficial to review your nursing textbooks for local and systemic reactions to burns because these injuries affect all body systems and cardiovascular and renal function in particular.

Nursing Care for Burn Victims

Caring for a burned client represents a unique challenge to even the most experienced nursing staff because few injuries pose a greater threat to the client's physical and emotional well-being. There are three phases of burn injury, each requiring various levels of client care. The three phases are

▶ Emergent

▶ Intermediate

▶ Rehabilitative

Psychological Care of a Burn Patient

While interventions are focused on meeting the client's physiological needs during the emergent period, the nurse should keep in mind that the nature of the injury represents a time of extreme crisis for both the client and his family. Every effort should be made to provide emotional support by providing understandable explanations of procedures and making sure that the client is kept as comfortable as possible. When necessary, appropriate referrals should be made to clergy and other professionals. Interventions directed at stabilizing the client's condition as well as the type of emotional support will change as the client moves through the emergent, intermediate, and rehabilitative phases of injury.

The Emergent Phase

The emergent phase begins with the onset of burn injury and lasts until the completion of fluid resuscitation or a period of about the first 24 hours. During the emergent phase, the priority of client care involves maintaining an adequate airway and treating the client for burn shock. Emergency care of burns at the site of injury includes

- ▶ Extinguishing the burn source
- ▶ Soaking the burn with cool water to relieve pain and to limit local tissue edema
- ▶ Removing jewelry and non-adherent clothing
- ▶ Covering the wound with a sterile (or at least clean) dressing to minimize bacterial contamination
- ▶ Brushing off chemical contaminants, removing contaminated clothing, and flushing the area with running water

CAUTION

The eyes should be irrigated with water immediately if a chemical burn occurs. Follow-up care with an ophthalmologist is important because burns of the eyes can result in corneal ulceration and blindness.

Major Burns in the Emergent Phase

If the injury is determined to be a major burn injury, additional interventions will focus on assessment of:

- ▶ Airway
- ▶ Breathing
- ▶ Circulation

CAUTION

Important steps in treating a burn client include the following:

- ▶ **Treat airway and breathing**—Traces of carbon around the mouth or nose, blisters in the roof of the mouth, or the presence of respiratory stridor indicate the client has respiratory damage. Endotracheal intubation with assisted ventilation might be required to achieve adequate oxygenation.
- ▶ **Ensure proper circulation**—Compromised circulation is evident by a drop in normal blood pressure, slowed capillary refill, and decreased urinary output. These symptoms signal impending burn shock.

These interventions come next:

- ▶ Insertion of a large bore catheter for administering IV fluids
- ▶ Calculation of TBSA involved
- ▶ Calculation of fluid needs according to one of the fluid resuscitation formulas

CAUTION

It is important to remember that the actual burns might not be the biggest survival issue facing burn clients. Carbon monoxide from inhaled smoke can develop into a critical problem as well. Carbon monoxide combines with hemoglobin to form carboxyhemoglobin, which binds to available hemoglobin 200 times more readily than with oxygen. Carbon monoxide poisoning causes a vasodilating effect, causing the client to have a characteristic cherry red appearance. Interventions for carbon monoxide poisoning focus on early intubation and mechanical ventilation with 100% oxygen.

In the hours immediately following a major burn injury, loss of capillary permeability allows intravascular fluid to flood into the extracellular space. During the emergent or resuscitative phase, efforts are directed at preventing or reversing burn shock using fluid replacement formulas. Although there are a number of acceptable formulas for calculating fluid requirements, the Parkland formula and the Consensus formula are most often used.

The Parkland Formula

The Parkland formula provides a large volume of IV fluid in the first 24 hours to prevent deepening hypovolemic shock and further acidosis. After the first 24 hours, the amount of fluid infused should be titrated according to the urinary output, with the goal of maintaining the output between 30 mL and 50 mL per hour.

The following example steps you through a calculation of TBSA using the Rule of Nines and the fluid requirements using the Parkland formula:

Parkland formula:

> Ringer's Lactate 4 mL * kg body weight * % TBSA

A client receives full thickness burns of the arms, chest, back, and head at 0600 hours. The client weighs 180 pounds. Using the Parkland formula, how much fluid should the client receive by 1400?

Half of the amount is to be infused in the first 8 hours.

The remainder is to be infused over the next 16 hours.

With this information, what steps should you follow? The following steps will help you calculate this if you have difficulty:

1. Calculate the TBSA using the Rule of Nines:

   Arms (9% each arm) = 18% + chest (18%) + back (18%) + head (9%) = 63%

2. Convert the client's weight from pounds to kilograms:

   180 pounds ÷ 2.2 pounds (2.2 pounds = 1 kg) = 81.8 kg (round to 82 kg)

3. Calculate using the Parkland formula for fluid resuscitation:

   4 mL * 82 kg * 63 = 20,664 mL in 24 hours

According to the Parkland formula, half the calculated volume of lactated Ringer's solution is to infuse in the first eight hours; one fourth is to infuse in the second eight hours; and one fourth is to infuse in the remaining eight hours.

4. The injury occurred at 0600; the first eight hours will end at 1400. Therefore, the client should receive one half the total amount or 10,332 mL.

The Consensus Formula

Here's how you use the Consensus formula (for comparison with use of the Parkland formula):

Consensus formula:

Ringer's lactate or other balanced saline solution 2 ml–4 ml * kg body weight * % TBSA

Half of the amount is to be infused over the first eight hours.

The remainder of the amount is to be infused over the next 16 hours.

> **TIP**
>
> Fluid replacement formulas are calculated from the time of injury rather than from the time of arrival in the emergency room.

With this information, what steps should you follow? The steps given here will help you calculate this if you have difficulty:

1. Calculate the TBSA using the Rule of Nines:

   Arms (9% each arm) = 18% + chest (18%) + back (18%) + head (9%) = 63%

2. Convert the client's weight from pounds to kilograms:

   180 pounds ÷ 2.2 pounds (2.2 pounds = 1 kg) = 81.8 kg (rounded to 82 kg)

3. Calculate using the Consensus formula for fluid resuscitation:

   2 mL * 82 * 63 = 10,332 mL

   4 mL * 82 * 63 = 20,664 mL

   On the low end (2 mL), the amount to infuse over 24 hours would be 10,332 mL, with half to be infused in the first 8 hours and the remainder to be infused over the next 16 hours.

   On the high end (4 mL), the amount to infuse over 24 hours would be 20,664 mL, with half to be infused in the first 8 hours and the remainder to be infused over the next 16 hours.

Additional Interventions

These additional interventions are taken after assessment of airway and establishing IV access for fluid replacement. Airway treatment and maintaining fluid volume take priority over all the other interventions:

▶ Administering a tetanus booster

▶ Inserting a urinary catheter for determining hourly output

▶ Inserting a nasogastric tube attached to low suction to minimize aspiration

> **NOTE**
>
> Enteral feedings help meet the client's increased caloric needs and maintains the integrity of the intestinal mucosa, thereby minimizing systemic sepsis. Clients with major burn injury can require as much as 5,000 kilocalories a day. Enteral feedings are begun within 24–48 hours of the injury to offset hypermetabolism, improve nitrogen balance, decrease the risk of sepsis, and shorten the hospital stay.

▶ Elevating burned extremities to lessen edema formation

The Intermediate Phase

The intermediate phase of burn care begins about 48–72 hours following the burn injury. Changes in capillary permeability and a return of osmotic pressure bring about diuresis or increased urinary output. If renal and cardiac functions do not return to normal, the added fluid volume, which prevented hypovolemic shock, might now produce symptoms of congestive heart failure. Assessment of central venous pressure provides information regarding the client's fluid status.

> **NOTE**
>
> The normal central venous pressure (CVP) is 4–12 mm H_2O. Increased CVP indicates fluid volume overload; decreased CVP indicates fluid volume deficit.

Additional complications found during the intermediate phase include infections, the development of Curling's ulcers, paralytic ileus, anemia, disseminated intravascular coagulation, compartment syndrome, and acute respiratory failure.

> **CAUTION**
>
> Infections represent a major threat to the post-burn client. Bacterial infections (*Staphylococcus, Proteus, Pseudomonas, Escherichia coli,* and *Klebsiella*) are common due to optimal growth conditions posed by the burn wound; however, the primary source of infection appears to be the client's own intestinal tract. As a rule, systemic antibiotics are avoided unless an actual infection exists.

During the intermediate phase, attention is given to removing the eschar and other cellular debris from the burned area. *Debridement*, the process of removing eschar, can be done by placing the client in a tub or shower and gently washing the burned tissue away with mild soap and water or by the use of enzymatic substances that digest the burned tissue. Santyl (collagenase) is an important debriding agent for burn wounds. Enzymatic agents are discontinued after the eschar is removed and granulation tissue is evident.

> **CAUTION**
>
> Enzymatic debridement should not be used for burns greater than 10% TBSA, burns near the eyes, or burns involving muscle.

Following debridement, the wound is treated with a topical antibiotic and a dressing is applied (more on dressings is covered in the next section). Commonly used topical antibiotics include silver sulfadiazine (Silvadene); mafenide acetate (Sulfamylon); and silver nitrate, which can be used in an aqueous solution of 0.5% or Acticoat, a prepared dressing impregnated with silver nitrate. Silver nitrate has bacteriostatic properties that inhibit bacterial growth. The use of mafenide acetate, although painful, prevents *Pseudomonas* infections. Silvadene cools and soothes the burn wound, but does not prevent infection.

Dressings for Burns

Dressings for burns include standard wound dressings (sterile gauze) and biologic or biosynthetic dressings (grafts, amniotic membranes, cultured skin, and artificial skin).

The use of standard wound dressings makes the client more comfortable by preventing exposure of the wound to air. These dressings are usually applied every shift or once a day.

Biologic dressings are obtained from either human tissue (homograft or allograft) or animal tissue (heterograft or xenograft). These dressings, which are temporary, are used for clients with partial thickness or granulating full thickness injuries. The type of biologic dressing used depends on the type of wound and availability of the graft.

Homografts and allografts are taken from cadaver donors and obtained through a skin bank. These grafts are expensive and there is a risk of blood-borne infection. Heterografts and xenografts are taken from animal sources. The most common heterograft is pig skin (porcine) because of its compatibility with human skin.

> **CAUTION**
>
> Muslims and Orthodox Jews are two religious/ethnic groups who might be offended by the use of porcine grafts because the pig is considered an unclean animal. Christian groups such as Seventh Day Adventists might also reject the use of porcine grafts.

Amniotic membrane is used for full thickness burns because it adheres immediately to the wound. It is also an effective covering for partial thickness burns until reepithealization occurs. Amniotic membrane is low in cost, and its size allows for coverage of large wounds.

Cultured skin can be obtained by using a biopsy of epidermal cells taken from unburned portions of the client's body. The cells are grown in a laboratory and grafted to generate permanent skin. The process is long and costly, and extreme care is needed to prevent damage and loss of the graft.

Artificial skin (Integra) made of synthetic material and animal collagen becomes a part of the client's skin. The graft site is pliable, there is less hypertrophic scarring, and its use is helping to eliminate the need for compression dressings like the Jobst garment during the rehabilitative phase of care.

Permanent grafts include the autograft or skin transferred from an unburned area of the client's body to the burn wound. The client generally experiences more pain from the donor site than from the burn wound because the donor site has many pain receptors. The client should receive pain medication, and both the donor site and graft site should be carefully monitored for signs of infection.

The Rehabilitative Phase

The last phase in caring for a client with burn injury is the rehabilitative phase. Technically, this phase begins with closure of the burn and ends when the client has reached the optimal level of functioning. In actuality, it begins the day the client enters the hospital and can continue for a lifetime. In the emergent and intermediate phases, the focus is on establishing and maintaining physiological equilibrium. In the rehabilitative phase, the focus is on helping the client return to pre-injury life. If that is not possible, the focus is on helping the client adjust to the changes the injury has imposed.

Case Study

Mrs. Pratt, a 40-year-old woman, is diagnosed with psoriasis. According to the client's history, the condition has been in remission for several years but recently flared up with lesions appearing on the trunk and outer surfaces of her legs and arms. The following questions relate to the care of the client with psoriasis.

1. Describe the lesions observed in the client with psoriasis.

2. List systemic factors that can cause an exacerbation of psoriasis.

3. Identify the methods of treating the client with psoriasis.

4. List the long-term effects of ultraviolet light therapy.

5. Explain why clients with psoriasis need emotional support to deal with their illness.

(continues)

(continued)

Answers to Case Study

1. The skin of the client with psoriasis is described as having thick, reddened papules or plaques covered by silvery white scales. There is a sharp delineation between the lesions and surrounding normal skin. Lesions are less red and moist in the skin folds.

2. Systemic factors that can cause an exacerbation of psoriasis include illness or infection, hormonal changes, psychological stress, drugs, and obesity.

3. Topical steroids, ultraviolet light therapy, and systemic therapy with immunosuppressive medications are means of treating psoriasis.

4. Long-term effects of ultraviolet light therapy include premature aging of the skin, actinic keratosis, and increased risk of skin cancer.

5. The client with psoriasis often has low self-esteem because of the appearance of the skin lesions. People might tend to avoid touching the client for fear of contracting the disease. Topical medications including coal tar preparations look dirty and have an unpleasant odor, which further adds to the client's poor self-image.

Key Concepts

This chapter provided information regarding the care of clients with common skin infections as well as information on the care of clients with pressure ulcers and burns. The following questions test your knowledge regarding the safe, effective care and management of the client with various integumentary disorders. The nurse should use the key terms, diagnostics, and pharmacological agents sections to answer these questions.

Key Terms

- Allograft
- Autograft
- Biosynthetic graft
- Burn shock
- Consensus formula
- Contracture
- Debridement
- Donor site
- Emergent phase of burn injury
- Eschar
- Heterograft
- Homograft
- Intermediate phase of burn injury
- Jobst garment
- Lund and Browder method
- Palm method
- Parkland formula
- Rehabilitative phase of burn injury
- Rule of Nines
- Total body surface area (TBSA)

Diagnostic Tests

Many diagnostic exams are used to assess integumentary disorders. The exam reviewer should be knowledgeable of the preparation and care of clients receiving exams for the diagnosis of integumentary disorders. While reviewing these diagnostic exams, the exam reviewer should be alert for information that would be an important part of nursing care for these clients. Diagnostic measures used for the client with integumentary disorders include the following:

► CBC

► Erythrocyte sedimentation rate

► Viral culture

► Chest x-ray

Pharmacological Agents Used in the Care of the Client with Integumentary Disorders

An integral part of care to clients with integumentary disorders is pharmacological intervention. These medications provide an improvement or cure of the client's integumentary problems. These medications are not inclusive of all the agents used to treat integumentary disorders; therefore you will need to keep a current pharmacology text handy for reference. Table 7.3 and Table 7.4 focus on the medications used to treat psoriasis and fungal infections. Table 7.5 focuses on agents used to treat pressure ulcers. See Chapter 12, "Care of the Client with Immunonlogical Disorders," for more information on medications used to treat viral infections. See Chapter 5, "Care of the Client with Respiratory Disorders," for more information on medications used to treat bacterial infections and inflammation.

TABLE 7.3   Medications to Treat Psoriasis

Drug	Action	Side Effect	Nursing Care
Anthraforte (anthralin)	Coal tar preparation used to treat chronic psoriasis	Skin irritation; burning	Avoid contact with uninvolved skin. Observe for skin irritation.
Dovonex (calcipotriene)	Vitamin D derivative regulates skin cell division	Skin irritation	Apply only as directed.
Tazorac (tazrotene)	Vitamin A derivative used to treat those with minimal psoriasis	Skin irritation; can cause severe birth defects	Should not be used during pregnancy.
Folex (methotrexate)	Interferes with folic acid metabolism; immunosuppressive	Dizziness; headache; blurred vision; alopecia; can cause painful plaque erosion during treatment for psoriasis; liver toxicity	Monitor CBC and liver function. Monitor for dry nonproductive cough.
Psoralen	Increases sensitivity to ultraviolet light	Skin irritation; blister formation	Observe skin for redness, blisters, and edema.

TABLE 7.3 *Continued*

Drug	Action	Side Effect	Nursing Care
Imuran (azathioprine)	Purine antagonist, immunosuppressive	Pulmonary edema; anorexia; alopecia; arthralgia; anemia; hepatoxicity	Monitor CBC and liver function. Should not be used with echinacea or melatonin.
Raptiva (efalizumab)	Monoclonal antibody, used for chronic to severe plaque psoriasis	Nausea; arthralgia; chills; fever; thrombocytopenia	Contraindicated in those with active infection. Increased risk of adverse reaction from vaccines or immunizations.

TABLE 7.4 **Medications to Treat Fungal Infections***

Drug	Action	Side Effect	Nursing Care
Mycostatin (nystatin)	Affects synthesis of fungal cell wall; effective against all species of Candida	Burning; pruritus; redness; few toxic effects	Administration of vaginal tablets contraindicated in pregnancy. Avoid use of occlusive dressings over skin preparations. Hold oral preparations in the mouth several minutes before swallowing.
Mycelex, Lotrimin (clotrimazole)	Alters cell wall permeability	Burning; redness; pruritus; liver toxicity	Pregnancy category C. Observe for jaundice. Topical preparations should not be used in children under two years of age.
Tinactin (tolnaftate)	Fungicidal	Mild skin irritation	Dry skin thoroughly before applying. Should be used 2–3 weeks to clear infection.
Nizoral (ketoconazole)	Inhibits the synthesis of sterol in the fungal cell membrane	Nausea and vomiting; fever; headache; anemia; liver toxicity	Monitor for CBC and liver panel. May cause severe drug to drug interactions. Safe use in children has not been established.
Lamisil (terbinafine HCl)	Same as above	Nausea and vomiting; malaise; alopecia; adverse reactions include liver failure	Contraindicated in those with liver disease. Monitor CBC and liver panel.
Loprox (ciclopirox olamine)	Alters cell wall permeability	Skin irritation	Use only on nails and adjacent skin.

*Antifungal medications, also used in the treatment of *Candida albicans*, are available in any number of topical preparations including creams, ointments, and powders. Systemic preparations include oral solutions and tablets.

TABLE 7.5   Agents Used to Treat Pressure Ulcers

Ulcer Stage	Agent	Action
Stage I	Skin prep, Granulex	Toughens intact skin, increases blood supply
Stages I & II	DuoDerm (hydrocolloid dressing)	Prevents skin breakdown, prevents growth of anerobic organisms
Stages I & II	Tegaderm (transparent dressing)	Prevents moisture and bacterial growth
Stage III	Elase (proteolytic enzyme)	Debrides inflamed and infected areas
Stages III & IV	Wet to dry sterile saline gauze	Enhances healing
Stage IV	Wet to dry sterile saline gauze with vacuum-assisted closure	Reduces edema, increases blood supply and oxygenation, and decreases bacterial colonization

Apply Your Knowledge

This chapter includes much-needed information to help the nurse apply knowledge of integumentary disorders to the NCLEX exam. The nurse preparing for the licensure exam should be familiar with commonly ordered lab tests, including normal lab values, and medications, used to treat the client with skin disorders.

Exam Questions

1. The nurse is assessing a dark-skinned client for signs of jaundice. The nurse can best detect jaundice in the client by examining which of the following features?

    A. Hard palate

    B. Palms of the hands

    C. Sclera

    D. Soles of the feet

2. The physician has ordered an emollient cream for a client with dry skin. To facilitate rehydration of the skin, the nurse should do which of the following?

    A. Dry the skin thoroughly and apply the cream

    B. Use vigorous circular motion to apply the cream

    C. Apply the cream 2–3 minutes after the bath

    D. Use the cream only if flaking of the skin is noted

3. Friction and shear are mechanical forces that contribute to the development of pressure ulcers. Which of the following is an example of shear injury?

    A. Lying on a firm surface that does not distribute weight

    B. Resting in a semi-sitting position that allows gradual downward movement

    C. Rubbing or irritating the skin so that epithelial cells are removed

    D. Compression of blood vessels that leads to ischemia, inflammation, and tissue necrosis

4. The nurse is caring for a client with herpes zoster. Which medication is used to shorten the outbreak of herpes zoster?

   A. Amevive (alefacept)

   B. Folex (methotrexate)

   C. Famvir (famciclovir)

   D. Raptiva (efalizumab)

5. During the emergent phase of burn injury, primary interventions focus on correcting hypovolemic shock. The nurse is aware that hypovolemic shock after burn injury is the result of which of the following?

   A. Presence of serum albumin in the interstitial space

   B. Increased capillary permeability

   C. Erratic drainage of the lymphatic system

   D. Altered osmotic pressure in the blood vessels

6. A client with full thickness burn injury is scheduled for a skin graft. Which one of the following grafts is taken from an animal source?

   A. Autograft

   B. Isograft

   C. Allograft

   D. Xenograft

7. The nurse is caring for a client injured in a house fire. Which one of the following findings suggests carbon monoxide poisoning?

   A. Wheezing respirations

   B. "Cherry red" skin

   C. Gastric ulceration

   D. "Burgundy" colored urine

8. Which of the following conditions is associated with facial cellulitis in the young child?

   A. Diarrheal illness caused by salmonella

   B. Routine childhood immunization

   C. Eruption of primary teeth

   D. Otitis media

9. When caring for the client who is at risk for developing pressure ulcers, the nurse should avoid which one of the following?

   A. Cleansing the skin with a pH-balanced soap

   B. Lubricating the skin with a moisturizing cream

   C. Massaging reddened areas of the skin

   D. Using absorbent garments for incontinence

10. Which statement is true regarding fungal infections of the skin?

   A. Dermatophytes that cause fungal infections are spread only by human-to-human contact.

   B. Infection depends on inoculation and maintenance of the organism in the outer layers of the skin.

   C. Treatment of fungal infections continues only until lesions have disappeared.

   D. Systemic fungal infections are best treated with antibacterial medications.

Answers to Exam Questions

1. Answer A is correct. Jaundice in the dark-skinned client is best assessed by examining the hard palate. Answers B and D are incorrect because the palms and soles might take on a yellowish appearance if calluses are present. Answer C is incorrect because normal deposits of fat can produce a yellowish appearance of the sclera.

2. Answer C is correct. The application of an emollient cream to the skin two or three minutes after bathing helps seal in moisture. Answers A, B, and D are incorrect because they do not facilitate rehydration of the skin.

3. Answer B is correct. Shear or shearing forces occur whenever the skin is stationary while tissues below the skin are able to shift or move. Answers A and D are incorrect because they describe the physical force of pressure. Answer C refers to friction; therefore, it is incorrect.

4. Answer C is correct. Famvir (famciclovir), an antiviral medication, is used to shorten the outbreak of herpes zoster. Amevive, Folex, and Raptiva are used in the treatment of the client with psoriasis; therefore, answers A, B, and D are incorrect.

5. Answer B is correct. Hypovolemic shock is the result of increased capillary permeability that leads to third spacing or capillary leak syndrome. The loss of plasma fluids and proteins decreases blood volume and blood pressure. Answers A, C, and D do not relate to hypovolemic shock; therefore, they are incorrect.

6. Answer D is correct. Xenografts are taken from animal sources. Answers A, B, and C are incorrect because they originate from human donors.

7. Answer B is correct. The vasodilating action of carbon monoxide causes the client's skin to become "cherry red" in color. Answer A refers to inhalation injury, not carbon monoxide poisoning; therefore, it is incorrect. Answer C is incorrect because it refers to Curling's ulcer, which sometimes occurs as a result of major burn injury. Answer D is associated with myoglobinuria, not carbon monoxide poisoning; therefore, it is incorrect.

8. Answer D is correct. Facial cellulitis is associated with otitis media, a common ear infection in young children. Answers A, B, and C are not associated with the development of facial cellulitis; therefore, they are incorrect.

9. Answer C is correct. The nurse should avoid massaging reddened areas of the skin because it can result in damage to capillary beds and lead to tissue necrosis. Answers A, B, and D are appropriate interventions for the client at risk for pressure ulcers; therefore, they are incorrect.

10. Answer B is correct. Infection occurs when dermatophytes come in contact with a susceptible host that allows inoculation and maintenance in the outer layers of the skin. Answer A is incorrect because dermatophytes are spread by contact with contaminated soil, animals, or humans. Answer C is incorrect because therapy usually continues for one to two weeks after clearing in order to prevent recurrence. Answer D is incorrect because systemic fungal infections are treated with antifungal medications such as Nizoral (ketoconozole), not antibacterial medications.

Suggested Reading and Resources

▶ Brunner, L., and D. Suddarth. *Textbook of Medical Surgical Nursing.* 12th ed. Philadelphia: Lippincott Williams & Wilkins, 2009.

▶ Ignatavicius, D., and S. Workman. *Medical Surgical Nursing: Critical Thinking for Collaborative Care* 6th ed. Philadelphia: Elsevier, 2008.

▶ Lehne, R. *Pharmacology for Nursing Care.* 7th ed. Philadelphia: Elsevier, 2009

▶ LeMone, P., and K. Burke. *Medical Surgical Nursing: Critical Thinking in Client Care.* 4th ed. Upper Saddle River, NJ: Pearson Prentice Hall, 2008

▶ Lewis, S., M. Heitkemper, S. Dirksen, P. Obrien and L. Bucher. *Medical Surgical Nursing: Assessment and Management of Clinical Problems.* 7th ed. Philadelphia: Elsevier, 2007

▶ Burn Recovery Center: www.burn-recovery.org

▶ The Mayo Clinic: www.mayoclinic.com

▶ National Psoriasis Foundation: www.psoriasis.org

CHAPTER EIGHT

Care of the Client with Sensory Disorders

Most of us will agree that the abilities to see, hear, taste, perceive touch, and smell are pretty important. Without the ability to smell, food would have little, if any, taste. The sense of touch lets us know when we experience something pleasurable or are injured. But of all the senses, the abilities to see and hear are considered most important because they keep us most informed about the world around us. This chapter reviews problems affecting vision and hearing.

Disorders of the Eyes

Before discussing the various disorders of the eyes, it is important that you understand the anatomical structure of the eye. Figure 8.1 offers an illustration for reference.

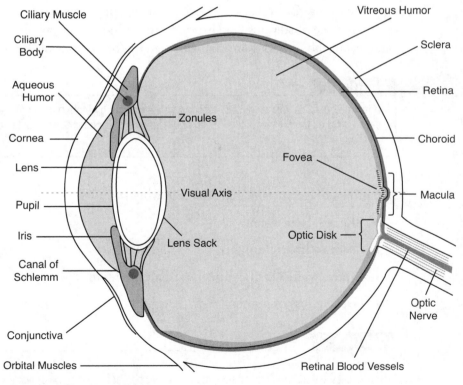

FIGURE 8.1 Structure of the eye.

Disorders of the eyes can be divided into the following categories:

- **Intraocular disorders:** These arise from within the eyeball. Examples include cataracts and glaucoma.

- **Retinal disorders:** These arise from the innermost layers of the eyeball. Examples include hypertensive retinopathy, diabetic retinopathy, and macular degeneration.

- **Refractive errors:** These affect the eye's ability to focus. Examples include myopia, hyperopia, presbyopia, and astigmatism.

- **Traumatic injuries:** These pose the risk of infection and loss of vision. Examples include hyphema, contusions, foreign bodies, lacerations, and penetrating injuries.

Intraocular Disorders

Intraocular disorders arise from within the eyeball. The primary intraocular disorders you need to understand include cataracts and glaucoma. The sections that follow discuss these two diseases in greater detail.

Cataracts

Cataracts, opacities in the lens of the eye, result in the distortion of images projected onto the retina. Cataracts are associated with aging, trauma, disease of the eye, prolonged use of steroids, and exposure to sunlight or ultraviolet light. Congenital cataracts of the newborn are characterized by the absence of the red reflex.

> **CAUTION**
>
> An infant should be able to visually follow a moving object by three months of age. If unable to do so, the infant's vision should be evaluated by an ophthalmologist. Congenital cataracts are found in 0.4%–0.5% of all newborns.

Symptoms of cataracts include the following:

- Blurred, hazy vision

- Glare from bright lights

- Yellow, white, or gray discoloration of the pupil

- Gradual loss of vision

> **CAUTION**
>
> Clients who are taking or have taken Flomax (tamsulosin) should talk with their doctor prior to surgery. During cataract surgery, a condition known as *intraoperative floppy iris syndrome* can occur if the client has taken Flomax.

Cataract surgery is generally performed in an outpatient surgery center. The client is given a sedative to lessen anxiety. Medications such as Diamox (acetazolamide) are given to reduce intraocular pressure. Mydriatic eye drops such as Neo-Synephrine (phenylephrine) are used in combination with cycloplegics such as Cyclogyl (cyclophenolate HCl) to paralyze the muscles of accommodation. After the client is in the operative area, an intravenous injection of Versed (midazolam) can be given to induce light anesthesia during administration of local anesthesia.

Removal of the affected lens is usually accomplished by an extracapsular cataract extraction (ECCE). The anterior portion of the lens is opened and removed along with the lens cortex and nucleus. The surgeon uses sound waves to break the affected lens into small pieces. These small pieces are then removed by suction. (This process is known as *phacoemulsion*.) The posterior lens capsule is left in place to provide support for the intraocular lens implant, a small plastic lens individually designed for the client. Although binocular vision and depth perception are immediately improved, most clients experience their best vision from four to six weeks after surgery. If an intraocular lens cannot be implanted, the client will be fitted with convex corrective glasses or contact lenses to correct vision.

Antibiotic drops and steroid ointments are instilled in the operative eye immediately after surgery. In most instances, the operative eye is left unpatched.

Postoperatively, the client is maintained in a semi-Fowler's position to reduce swelling and to prevent stress on the new lens implant. Clients are usually discharged within two to three hours following surgery. Before discharging the client, the nurse should instruct the client to do the following:

▶ Avoid activities that would increase intraocular pressure, such as bending from the waist, blowing the nose, wearing tight shirt collars, closing the eyes tightly, and placing the head in a dependent position.

▶ Report sharp, sudden pain in the operative eye. Pain early after surgery might indicate bleeding or increased intraocular pressure.

▶ Report signs of infection, which include yellow or green discharge. Creamy white or whitish dry, crusty drainage is normal following cataract surgery.

▶ Report changes in vision including decreasing vision, flashes of light, or visual floaters.

▶ Take a tub bath or shower facing away from the water.

▶ Administer eye medication as directed.

▶ Wear a protective shield when sleeping.

▶ Return for follow-up visits as directed.

Glaucoma

Glaucoma refers to a group of diseases that result in an increase in intraocular pressure. Glaucoma is the second leading cause of permanent blindness in the United States and the second leading cause of blindness in the world, according to the World Health Organization. Blindness from glaucoma is largely preventable with early detection and treatment. The three types of glaucoma and their characteristics are as follows:

- **Primary open-angle glaucoma (POAG):** This is the most common form of glaucoma. POAG affects both eyes, is usually asymptomatic, and is caused by a decrease in the outflow of aqueous humor. The intraocular pressure in those with POAG averages between 22 mm Hg and 32 mm Hg. Symptoms of POAG include the following:

  - Tired eyes

  - Diminished peripheral vision

  - Seeing halos around lights

  - Hardening of the eyeball

  - Increased intraocular pressure

- **Acute glaucoma:** This condition, sometimes called *narrow-angle glaucoma* or primary angle-closure glaucoma (PACG), is less common than primary open-angle glaucoma. Acute glaucoma is caused by a sudden reduction in the outflow of aqueous humor due to angle closure. Angle closure can result from the lens bulging forward (an age-related process) or from pupil dilation in the client with anatomically narrow angles. The condition can be precipitated by the use of mydriatics, emotional upset, or darkness. The onset of severe eye pain is sudden and without warning. Emergency treatment is necessary because rising intraocular pressure can exceed 30 mm Hg. Symptoms of acute glaucoma include the following:

  - Sudden, excruciating pain around the eyes

  - Headache or aching in the eyebrow

  - Nausea and vomiting

  - Cloudy vision

  - Pupil dilation

- **Secondary glaucoma:** This is caused by ocular conditions that narrow the canal of Schlemm or that alter eye structures that are involved in the production and circulation of aqueous humor. Secondary glaucoma is managed by treating the underlying ocular condition and by the use of anti-glaucoma medications.

NOTE

The normal intraocular pressure ranges from 10 to 21 mm Hg.

Management of a Client with Glaucoma

Conservative management of the client with POAG is aimed at reducing intraocular pressure with medications. Miotic eye drops such as Isopto Carpine (pilocarpine HCl) are instilled to constrict the pupil and increase the outflow of aqueous humor. Beta blockers such as Timoptic (timolol) and carbonic anhydrase inhibitors like Diamox (acetazolamide) decrease the production of aqueous humor, thereby lowering the intraocular pressure.

NOTE

Nursing Skill: Application of Eye Medications   Before instilling medication into the eyes, the lids and lashes should be cleaned using warm water. Only sterile ophthalmic preparations should be used. The nurse should avoid touching the eye with the applicator. Ointments should be applied from the inner to outer canthus of the eye. Eye drops should be dropped into the lower lid while the client is looking up. Gentle pressure should be placed over the tear duct, and the client should be instructed to refrain from tightly closing the eyelids.

Argon laser trabeculoplasty is an option when medications are not effective in reducing the intraocular pressure. A filtering procedure or trabeculectomy is indicated when medication and laser therapy are not successful. The success rate for trabeculectomy is between 75% and 85%. Surgical implantation of a small tube to shunt the aqueous humor away from the anterior chamber to an implanted reservoir is reserved for those in whom the filtering procedure failed.

Acute glaucoma or PACG is an ocular emergency that requires immediate intervention. Osmotics such as Osmitrol (mannitol) can be administered via IV to clients with acute glaucoma to rapidly reduce intraocular pressure and prevent permanent damage to the optic nerve. Laser peripheral iridotomy or iridectomy is necessary for long-term management and the prevention of future episodes.

Most surgical procedures for glaucoma are performed in outpatient surgery. Postoperatively, the client is placed in semi-Fowler's position and instructed to lie on the unaffected side, to avoid taking aspirin, and to report severe eye or brow pain. Changes in vital signs, a decrease in vision, and acute pain deep in the eye are symptoms of choroidal hemorrhage. These findings should be reported to the physician immediately.

CAUTION

Clients with known or suspected glaucoma should avoid over-the-counter medications that can increase intraocular pressure. Medications such as Visine cause vasoconstriction, which is followed by rebound vasodilation. Rebound vasodilation can raise pressures within the eye. Atropine is contraindicated in the client with glaucoma because it closes the canal of Schlemm and raises intraocular pressure.

Uveitis

Uveitis refers to inflammation of the iris, the ciliary body, and the choroid which together make up the uveal tract. Uveitis can occur in either the anterior or posterior portion of the eye.

Anterior uveitis affects the iris, ciliary body, or both. The cause is unknown; however, the condition can follow local or systemic infections, exposure to allergens, trauma, or systemic diseases such as rheumatoid arthritis or herpes zoster. Manifestations of anterior uveitis include periorbital aching, tearing, photophobia, visual blurring, pupillary changes (small, irregular, nonreactive pupils), and reddened "bloodshot" sclera.

Posterior uveitis includes inflammation of the retina, the choroid, or both. The condition occurs in clients with tuberculosis, syphilis, and toxoplasmosis. The onset of symptoms is slow and painless. The client has small, irregular, nonreactive pupils and visual impairment. Fundoscopic examination reveals grayish-yellow patches on the surface of the retina.

Management of the client with uveitis includes the use of topical cycloplegics, mydriatics, and steroids. Topical steroids are administered hourly to reduce inflammation and to prevent adhesion of the iris to the cornea and lens. Nonaspirin and nonopioid analgesics are given for pain and discomfort. Systemic antibiotics may be used. Additional comfort measures include cool or warm compresses for ocular pain. The use of sunglasses helps manage the client's photophobia.

Retinal Disorders

Retinal disorders involve disorders of the innermost layer of the eye. The most common retinal disorders are hypertensive retinopathy, diabetic retinopathy, and macular degeneration. Less common retinal disorders include retinitis pigmentosa and retinal detachment. The following sections cover these retinal disorders in greater detail.

Hypertensive Retinopathy

Hypertensive retinopathy occurs in the client with a long history of uncontrolled hypertension. Elevations in diastolic blood pressure create a copper wire appearance in the retinal arterioles. If the blood pressure remains elevated, arterioles become occluded by the formation of soft exudates known as *cotton wool spots*. Treatment focuses on control of systemic hypertension. Left untreated, hypertensive retinopathy can result in retinal detachment and loss of vision.

Diabetic Retinopathy

Diabetic retinopathy is the result of vascular changes associated with uncontrolled diabetes mellitus. Vascular changes are inherent in all diabetics; however, good control of blood sugar helps reduce the severity of the disease. The two types of diabetic retinopathy are as follows:

▶ **Background diabetic retinopathy:** This leads to the development of microaneurysms and intraretinal hemorrhages.

▶ **Proliferative diabetic retinopathy:** This leads to the development of new, fragile blood vessels that leak blood and protein into the surrounding tissue.

The treatment of diabetic retinopathy depends on the type and the degree of tissue involvement. Laser surgery can be used to seal microaneurysms and prevent bleeding.

Age Related Macular Degeneration

Age related macular degeneration affects the portion of the eye involved with central vision. The two types of age related macular degeneration are as follows:

▶ **Atrophic (dry):** This form is characterized by sclerosing of retinal capillaries with loss of rod and cone receptors, decreased central vision, and complaints of mild blurred vision. The condition progresses faster in smokers than nonsmokers. The risk for age related macular degeneration can be reduced by a diet rich in antioxidants; lutein; zeaxanthin; and carotenoids found in dark green, leafy vegetables.

▶ **Exudative (wet):** This form is characterized by a sudden decrease in vision due to serous detachment of the pigmented epithelium of the macula. Blisters composed of fluid and blood form underneath the macula, resulting in scar formation and decreasing vision.

Treatment of age-related macular degeneration is aimed at slowing the process. Laser therapy can be used to seal leaking blood vessels near the macula; however, this can cause retinal scarring and lead to blind spots. Newer procedures for treating wet age-related macular degeneration include photodynamic therapy using intravenous Visudyne (verteporfin), a dye, and cold laser to destroy the abnormal blood vessels; Macugen(pegaptamib) given intravenously to inhibit endothelial growth and slow vision loss; and Lucentis (ranibizumab), a biologic therapy injected monthly that blocks new vessel growth and leakiness. Persons at risk for age-related macular degeneration should supplement their diet with vitamins and minerals, particularly vitamin C, vitamin E, beta-carotene, and zinc.

Retinitis Pigmentosa

Retinitis pigmentosa is a condition that results in degeneration of retinal nerve cells. As these nerve cells die, the pigmented cells of the retina grow and move into the sensory areas of the retina, leading to further degeneration. Different forms of the disorder have been identified as being an autosomal dominant trait, an autosomal recessive trait, or an X-linked recessive trait.

Early symptoms include night blindness that frequently occurs in childhood. Visual acuity declines until the client is totally blind. Currently, no therapy-proven effective means exists to prevent or slow the progression of the disorder, although experimental treatments include a regimen of vitamin A and decreased exposure to bright light.

Retinal Detachment

Retinal detachment can result from a blow to the head, fluid accumulation in the subretinal space, or the aging process. Generally, the condition is pain-free; however, the client might complain of the following symptoms:

▶ Blurred vision

▶ Flashes of light

▶ Visual floaters

▶ A veil-like loss of vision

Management of Clients with Retinal Detachment

Conservative management usually involves placing the client with the area of detachment in a dependent position. The most common site for retinal detachment is the superior temporal area of the right eye. Sedatives and anxiolytics will make the client more comfortable. Spontaneous reattachment of the retina is rare, so surgical management is often required. The client with retinal detachment is usually referred to a retinal specialist for surgery.

Surgical management includes laser photocoagulation or cryotherapy that creates a scar to seal the retina to the choroid or by scleral buckling (see Figure 8.2) to shorten the sclera and improve contact between the retina and choroid. Intravitreal injection of gas (pneumatic retinopexy) might be used to close retinal breaks.

Before   After

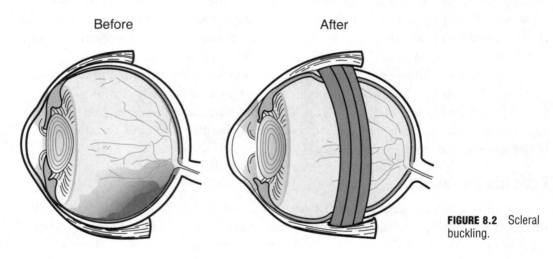

FIGURE 8.2 Scleral buckling.

Postop activity varies with the procedure used. If gas or oil has been instilled during the scleral buckling, the client is positioned on her abdomen with her head turned so that the operative eye faces upward. This position is maintained for several days or until the gas or oil is absorbed. An alternative is to allow the client to sit on the bedside and place her head on an overbed table. Bathroom privileges are allowed, but the client must keep her head bowed. The following discharge instructions should be given to the client with a scleral buckling:

▶ Report any sudden increase in pain or pain accompanied by nausea.

▶ Avoid reading, writing, and close work for the first postop week.

▶ Do not bend over so that the head is in a dependent position.

▶ Be careful not to bump the head.

Refractive Errors

Refractory errors refer to the capability of the eyes to focus images on the retina. Refractory errors are due to an abnormal length of the eyeball from front to back and the refractive power of the lens. Refractory errors include the following:

▶ **Myopia (nearsightedness):** Images focus in front of rather than on the retina; this is corrected by a concave lens.

▶ **Hyperopia (farsightedness):** Images focus behind rather than on the retina; this is corrected by a convex lens.

▶ **Presbyopia:** The crystalline lens loses elasticity and becomes unable to change shape to focus the eye for close work so that images fall behind the retina; this condition is age-related.

▶ **Astigmatism:** An uneven curvature of the cornea causes light rays to be refracted unequally so that a focus point on the retina is not achieved.

Nonsurgical management of refractory errors includes the use of eyeglasses and contact lenses. Surgical management includes the following:

▶ **Radial keratotomy (RK):** This treatment is used for mild to moderate myopia. Eight to sixteen cuts are made through 90% of the peripheral cornea. The incisions decrease the length of the eye by flattening the cornea. This allows the image to focus nearer the retina.

▶ **Photorefractive keratotomy (PRK):** This is used for the treatment of mild to moderate stable myopia and low astigmatism. An excimer laser is used to reshape the superficial cornea using powerful beams of ultraviolet light. One eye is treated at a time with a wait period of three months between surgeries. Complete healing can take up to six months.

▶ **Laser in-situ keratomileusis (LASIK):** This is used for the treatment of nearsightedness, farsightedness, and astigmatism. An excimer laser is used to reshape the deeper corneal layers. Both eyes are treated at the same time. Complete healing can take up to four weeks. LASIK is thought to be better than PRK because the outer layer of the cornea is not damaged, there is less pain, and the healing time is reduced.

▶ **Intacs corneal ring:** This is the newest vision enhancement for those with mild to moderate nearsightedness. The shape of the cornea is changed by using a polymeric ring on the outer edges of the cornea. The surgery does not involve the use of laser and is reversible Anesthetic eye drops are instilled to make the client more comfortable during the procedure. No needles or injections are required. The surgeon makes two tiny incisions through which the Intacs is inserted. The incisions are closed with a single stitch that is removed in a few days. The procedure usually takes 15–20 minutes for each eye.

Postoperative nursing care is minimal. Antibiotic and anti-inflammatory eye drops are prescribed to prevent infection and relieve local irritation. The client's vision should be sufficient to drive a car, 20/40 or better, on the first postoperative day. The vision should continue to improve over the next 6–12 months. Replacement rings can be inserted if the client's vision changes with aging.

Traumatic Injuries

Traumatic injuries to the eyes can occur from any activity. Traumatic injuries and their treatments include the following:

▶ **Hyphema:** Hemorrhage in the anterior chamber as the result of a blow to the eye. Treatment includes bed rest in semi-Fowler's position, no sudden eye movement for three to five days, cycloplegic eye drops, use of an eye patch and eye shield to protect the eye, and limited television viewing and reading.

▶ **Contusion:** Bruising of the eyeball and surrounding tissue. Treatment includes ice to the affected area and a thorough eye exam to rule out other eye injuries. Elevating the client's head 30°–45° will help to minimize edema and swelling.

▶ **Foreign bodies:** Objects that irritate or abrade the surface of the conjunctiva or cornea. Treatment includes transporting the client to the ER with both eyes covered by a cupped object, a visual assessment by a physician before treatment and instillation of fluorescein followed by irrigation with normal saline to remove foreign particles.

▶ **Lacerations and penetrating injuries:** Corneal lacerations are considered emergencies because ocular contents can prolapse through the laceration. Treatment can require the administration of IV antibiotics and surgery.

CAUTION

Objects protruding from the eye should never be removed by anyone except an ophthalmologist because greater damage can occur, including the displacement of ocular structures. Clients with penetrating eye injuries have the poorest prognosis for retaining vision.

Ocular Melanoma

Ocular melanoma, the most common form of malignant eye tumor, might or might not be readily apparent. Symptoms associated with ocular melanoma depend on the involved structures. The following structures might be affected:

▶ Macula, resulting in blurred vision

▶ Choroid, resulting in decreased visual acuity

▶ Canal of Schlemm, resulting in increased intraocular pressure

▸ Iris, resulting in changes in color of the iris

▸ Retina, resulting in retinal detachment

Treatment of ocular melanoma depends on the tumor size and growth rate. Tumors of the choroid are treated by enucleation and/or radiation. Following enucleation, a ball implant is inserted to provide a base for the socket prosthesis and to insure cosmetic results. An ocular prosthesis is fitted one month after surgery. Until the prosthesis is fitted, an antibiotic-steroid ointment is inserted into the cul-de-sac daily. Nursing care of the client with an ocular prosthesis includes the proper insertion and removal of the device.

Insertion of the ocular prosthesis includes the following steps:

1. Cover the chest with a cloth or towel.

2. Wash the hands and apply gloves.

3. Remove the prosthesis from its container and rinse it with tepid water.

4. Use the nondominant hand to lift the client's upper lid.

5. Place the prosthesis between the thumb and forefinger of the dominant hand (the notched end of the prosthesis should be closest to the client's nose).

6. Insert the prosthesis by slipping the top edge under the upper lid. Insertion should continue until most of the iris is covered by the upper lid. When insertion is complete, gently release the upper lid.

7. Gently retract the lower lid until the bottom edge of the prosthesis slips behind it.

Removal of the ocular prosthesis includes the following steps:

1. Assemble a container filled with saline.

2. Wash the hands and apply gloves.

3. Ask the client to sit up and to tilt the head slightly downward.

4. Placing the hand against the client's cheek (palm side up), pull the lower lid slightly down and to the side.

5. Allow the prosthesis to slide into the hand (pull slightly on the prosthesis if needed).

6. Place the prosthesis in the saline filled container and cover. The container should be labeled with the client's name.

A second method of treating ocular melanoma involves radiation therapy. Radiation is used to reduce the size and thickness of ocular melanomas. A round, flat, dime-sized disk containing radioactive material is sutured to the sclera over the site of the tumor. The length of time the disk remains in place depends on the size of the tumor and the amount of radiation ordered. Complications associated with radiation therapy include vascular changes, retinopathy, glaucoma, and necrosis of the sclera.

Disorders of the Ears

Most of what we know about our world is gained through vision; however, a well-functioning auditory system is also important. Disorders of the ears and hearing loss create problems with everyday living. Some conditions, such as Ménière's disease, interfere with balance and coordination. Other conditions, such as otosclerosis and age-related presbycusis, affect our ability to receive and give information accurately. The client with a significant hearing loss often becomes confused, mistrustful, and socially isolated from family and friends.

Before discussing the different disorders of the ears, it is important that you understand the anatomical structure of the ear. Figure 8.3 offers an illustration for reference.

Disorders of the ears can be divided into the following categories:

- ► Conditions affecting the external ear (otitis externa)
- ► Conditions affecting the middle ear (otitis media)
- ► Conditions affecting the inner ear (Ménière's, otosclerosis)
- ► Age-related hearing loss (presbycusis)
- ► Ear trauma

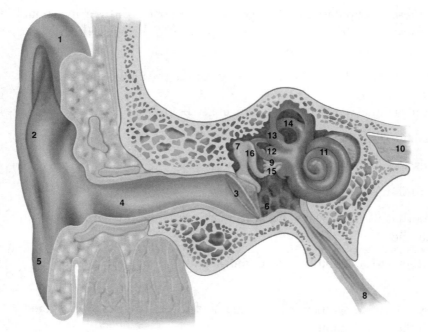

1. Helix
2. Antihelix
3. Tympanic membrane (eardrum)
4. External auditory meatus
5. Lobule
6. Middle ear
7. Round window
8. Eustachian tube
9. Stapes footplate covering oval

10. Cochlear and vestibular nerves
11. Cochlea
12. Lateral semicircular canal
13. Superior semicircular canal
14. Rear semicircular canal
15. Stapes
16. Incus
17. Malleus

FIGURE 8.3 Structures of the inner and outer ear.

Otitis Externa

Otitis externa is often referred to as *swimmer's ear* because it occurs more often in hot, humid environments. The condition can result from an allergic response or inflammation. Allergic external otitis media is often the result of contact with hair spray, cosmetics, earrings, earphones, and hearing aids. It can occur from infectious organisms, including bacteria or fungi. Most infections are due to pseudomonas aeruginosa, streptococcus, staphylococcus, and aspergillus. In rare cases, a virulent form of otitis externa develops, spreading the infection into the adjacent structures of the brain and causing meningitis, brain abscess, and damage to cranial nerves.

Clinical manifestations associated with otitis externa include pain, tenderness, cervical lymph node enlargement and discharge. The client might complain of hearing loss or a feeling of fullness in the affected ear. On examination, the ear canal is found to be red and edematous.

Nursing interventions in the treatment of the client with otitis externa are aimed at relieving pain, inflammation, and swelling. Topical antibiotics and steroids are usually ordered. Systemic antibiotics, either oral or intravenous, are used in severe cases. Additional interventions are aimed at teaching the client not to clean the external ear canal with cotton-tipped applicators because these can remove the protective layer of cerumen and to avoid letting water remain in the ear after swimming, shampooing, or showering. The risk of infection can be reduced by using antiseptic otic preparations, such as Swim Ear, after swimming.

Otitis Media

Otitis media is an infection of the middle ear that occurs more often in young children than adults because the Eustachian tube of the child is shorter and wider than that of the adult. *H. influenza* is the most common cause of acute otitis media. Signs and symptoms of acute otitis media include pain, malaise, fever, vomiting, and anorexia. Otoscopic examination reveals a red, bulging tympanic membrane.

Increased pressure can cause the tympanic membrane to rupture. Rupture of the tympanic membrane usually results in relief of pain and fever; however, repeated rupture can lead to scarring of the membrane with eventual loss of hearing.

Nursing interventions for the client with acute otitis media includes the administration of systemic antibiotics, analgesics for pain, and antihistamines and decongestants to decrease fluid in the middle ear. Antibiotic therapy, which is usually carried out at home, is continued for 7–10 days to ensure that the causative organism has been eliminated. If the tympanic membrane continues to bulge following antibiotic therapy, a small surgical incision is made in the tympanic membrane (myringotomy) and a polyethylene tube is inserted to allow continuous drainage of the middle ear.

> **Nursing Skill: Instillation of Ear Drops**
>
> Proper manipulation of the pinna is important when instilling ear drops. For a client under 3 years of age, the pinna should be gently displaced down and back. For a client over 3 years of age, the pinna should be gently displaced up and back. The nurse should instill the eardrops without inserting the dropper into the ear canal. After instilling the eardrops, the area anterior to the ear should be gently massaged to facilitate entry of the drops into the ear canal.

Mastoiditis

Mastoiditis refers to an infection of the mastoid air cells of the temporal bone. The condition most commonly results from untreated or inadequately treated otitis media. Tender enlarged post-auricular lymph nodes, low-grade fever, malaise, and anorexia are common characteristics of mastoiditis. In some instances, cellulitis develops on the skin and external scalp over the mastoid process. Facial cellulitis is commonly associated with otitis media in young children.

Nonsurgical management of mastoiditis includes the use of IV antibiotics; however, their use is limited because they do not penetrate bony structures of the mastoid process. If the infection does not respond with two to three days of therapy, or when other structures are involved, a simple or radical mastoidectomy or tympanoplasty is usually performed to remove infected material.

Nursing interventions for the client following a mastoidectomy include observing for complications which can include damage to the sixth and seventh cranial nerve. The nurse should notify the physician if there is any evidence of facial paralysis or abnormal deviation of the eye on the operative side. (You can find information on assessment of the cranial nerves in Chapter 11, " Care for the Client with Disorders of the Neurological System.")

Additional nursing interventions include teaching the client the following information:

▶ Take prescribed medications as directed

▶ Blow the nose gently, one side at a time, for one week after surgery; cough with an open mouth open for a few weeks after surgery

▶ Avoid straining, bending over, or lifting heavy objects (> 25 lbs.) for a few weeks after surgery

▶ Avoid getting water in the operative ear for two weeks after surgery

▶ Notify the physician if there is excessive ear pain or if there is excessive or purulent drainage from the operative ear

Ménière's Disease

Ménière's is a disease of the inner ear characterized by a triad of symptoms: vertigo, tinnitus, and a decreased ability to hear low tones. Symptoms can occur suddenly and last from several hours to several days. The exact cause of Ménière's is unknown, but it is associated with allergies as well as vascular and inflammatory responses that alter fluid balance.

Physical examination of the client with Ménière's disease is usually normal except for the evaluation of the auditory nerve. The Weber test (sounds from a tuning fork) can lateralize to the ear opposite the affected ear. Further assessment using an audiogram typically reveals a sensorineural hearing loss in the affected ear. The "Pike's Peak" pattern shows a sensorineural loss in the low frequencies. The hearing loss increases as the disease progresses.

Conservative management of the client with Ménière's disease includes the use of antihistamines, antiemetics, and diuretics to control edema of the labyrinth, and vasodilators to decrease vasospasm. Salt and fluid restrictions are recommended to decrease the amount of endolymphatic fluid produced. Cessation of smoking can also improve symptoms by helping to reduce vasoconstriction. Nicotinic acid has proven beneficial by producing a vasodilating effect.

Surgical management can involve one of the following: endolymphatic subarachnoid shunt, vestibular neurectomy, or labryinthectomy (last resort). Surgical management is controversial because hearing in the affected ear can be lost. Following surgery, the client will experience vertigo, nausea, and vomiting for several days. The nurse should tell the client to change positions slowly to avoid falls.

Acoustic Neuroma

Acoustic neuroma is a benign tumor involving the eighth cranial nerve. Growth of the tumor damages the structures of the cerebellum and could result in damage to hearing, facial movement, and sensation. Clinical manifestations include tinnitus, progressive sensorineural hearing loss, and vertigo. Nearby nerves are damaged as the tumor increases in size. Surgical removal is performed via a craniotomy. Although remaining hearing is lost, acoustic neuromas rarely recur following surgical removal. Chapter 11 covers care of the client following a craniotomy in greater detail.

Otosclerosis

Otosclerosis refers to the progressive hardening of the bony configuration known as the *stapes*, leaving them incapable of movement. Otosclerosis is the most common cause of conductive hearing loss. Symptoms of otosclerosis include tinnitus and conduction deafness.

Otoscopic examination of the client with otosclerosis usually reveals a normal tympanic membrane. Bone conduction (Weber test) is better than air conduction (Rinne test). The audiogram confirms a conduction loss, particularly in the low frequencies.

Management of otosclerosis involves a stapedectomy. The diseased stapes is removed; then the oval window is sealed and rejoined to the incus using a metal or plastic prosthesis. Nursing interventions for the client following a stapedectomy focus on client education. Key points included in the care of the client who has had a stapedectomy are as follows:

▶ Tell the client that hearing might decrease after surgery due to swelling and accumulation of fluid, but it should improve as blood and fluid are absorbed.

▶ Instruct the client to avoid activities that increase pressure within the ear (such as blowing the nose, extreme head movement, and air travel). Avoiding crowds will lessen the chance of getting upper respiratory infections with symptoms such as coughing and sneezing. If the client must cough or sneeze, she should do it with an open mouth.

▶ Tell the client to report pain and changes in taste or facial sensation because these can indicate cranial nerve damage.

▶ Instruct the client to avoid getting water in the ears for at least six weeks. Tub baths are better than showers.

▶ Instruct the client to take medications (antibiotics and antiemetics) as prescribed.

Presbycusis

Presbycusis associated with aging is a common cause of sensorineural hearing loss. This type of hearing loss is the result of damage to the ganglion cells of the cochlea and decreased blood supply to the inner ear. Deficiencies in vitamins B9 and B12 also have been found to play a role in the development of presbycusis. Sensorineural hearing loss is also related to the use of ototoxic drugs as well as exposure to loud noises. Like other disorders that affect hearing, sensorineural hearing loss is diagnosed using audiometric testing. Audiometric testing consists of pure-tone audiometry (sound stimulus is pure or musical) and speech audiometry (sound stimulus is spoken words). Three characteristics are important when evaluating hearing: frequency, pitch, and intensity. The measurement for measuring loudness is the decibel.

NOTE

Hearing loss of 50 decibels affects the client's ability to distinguish parts of speech. Presbycusis affects the ability to hear high-frequency, soft consonant sounds (t, s, th, ch, sh, b, f, p, and pa).

Ear Trauma

Injury to the tympanic membrane can result in pain, infection, and hearing loss. Most ear trauma is the result of jabbing injuries that damage the ear drum and inner ear or blows to the ear that result in extreme changes in pressure. Children frequently use the ears (and the nose) as hiding places for foreign bodies that become lodged, interfering with hearing and creating a source of infection. Foreign bodies in the ear or nose should receive the attention of a physician who will remove them and provide appropriate follow-up treatment.

Assisting Clients with Hearing Loss

Devices to assist the client with a hearing loss include hearing aids and cochlear implants. All hearing aids have a microphone, an amplifier, a speaker, an earpiece, and volume control. A variety of styles of hearing aids are available, and each style has advantages and disadvantages. These include

- In-canal style (appropriate for mild to moderate hearing loss). The use of completely in-canal aides might not be possible because of the shape of the ear canal or the severity of hearing loss.

- In-ear style (appropriate for mild to severe hearing loss)

- Behind-ear style (mild to profound hearing loss)

- Body style (appropriate for profound hearing loss).

If you are working with a client who is hearing impaired and he is not wearing a hearing aid, the following hints might prove helpful:

- Stand in front of the client when talking to him. Many hearing-impaired persons rely on lip reading and facial expression.

- Talk in a normal tone of voice. Raising your voice distorts the sound and can convey the wrong message.

- Keep the background noise to a minimum.

- Don't forget other means of communicating, such as writing, using pictures, and so on.

- Try to speak in lower tones. People who are hard of hearing can usually hear lower voices easier than those at a higher pitch. For example, the client can usually hear a male's voice easier than a female's voice.

A cochlear implant is sometimes the only means of restoring sound perception to the client with a sensorineural hearing loss (see Figure 8.4). The implant consists of a microphone, a speech processor, a transmitter and receiver/stimulator, and electrodes. The microphone picks up sounds that are then sent to the speech processor. The speech processor selects and processes useful sounds and sends these along to the transmitter and receiver/stimulator, where the signals are converted into electrical impulses. These impulses are then sent to electrodes for transmission to the brain. Magnets (magnetic resonance imaging or metal detectors), static electricity, heat, and water can damage the cochlear implant.

Culturally, deaf people tend to view deafness as a difference in human experience rather than a disability. These individuals have expressed concerns about preserving the use of sign language as a means of communication. As a result, they might oppose technological innovations such as a cochlear implants if the doctor insists that the client refrain from the use of sign language.

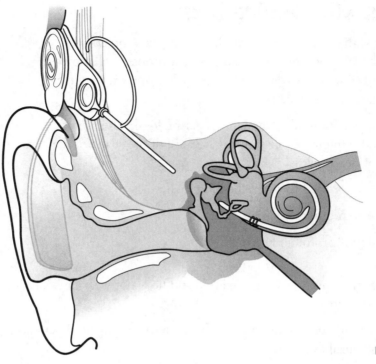

FIGURE 8.4 Cochlear implant.

Case Study

Mrs. Jackson, age 72, is scheduled for removal of a cataract from the left eye. The client states that she has always been a very active person and that she enjoys working in her flower garden where she grows prize-winning roses. Lately she has noticed that bright lights tend to blind her and she has limited her travel at night. The following questions relate to the client with cataracts.

1. List factors associated with the development of cataracts.

2. Discuss symptoms experienced by the client with cataracts.

3. Explain the process used for cataract removal.

4. What instructions are included in the client's discharge teaching following cataract removal?

Answers to Case Study

1. Factors associated with the development of cataracts include heavy sun exposure; trauma to the eyes; exposure to radioactive material or x-rays; systemic diseases such as diabetes and hypothyroidism; use of corticosteroids, chlorpromazine, or miotics; and intraocular disease.

2. The client with early cataracts frequently complains of blurred vision and decreased color perception. Without surgery, the client will develop diplopia, reduced visual acuity, presence of a whitish gray pupil, and blindness.

(continues)

(continued)

3. The most common form of cataract removal is extracapsular surgery. The front portion of the capsule is opened and removed. Sound waves are used to break up the cataractous lens, which is removed by suction. The replacement lens is seated and anchored by the posterior lens capsule. The intracapsular procedure, used less often, involves the removal of the lens and the entire capsule. The disadvantages of the intracapsular method are the increased risk of retinal detachment and loss of structural support for the intraocular lens implant.

4. Discharge instructions for the client following cataract removal include the following:

   ▶ Report pain (pain occurring early after surgery can indicate increased intraocular pressure or bleeding)

   ▶ Report increased redness, changes in visual acuity, tears, or photophobia

   ▶ Report yellow or green drainage (indicates infection)

   ▶ Wear a protective eye shield when sleeping

   ▶ Continue to use eye medications as directed by physician (instruct client in proper instillation of eye medications)

   ▶ Shampoo hair with head tilted back

   ▶ Shower facing away from shower or take tub baths

   ▶ Avoid driving and operating machinery until given permission by physician

Key Concepts

This chapter includes much-needed information to help the nurse apply knowledge of sensory disorders to the NCLEX exam. The nurse preparing for the licensure exam should be familiar with commonly ordered lab tests, including normal lab values, and medications, used to treat the client with sensory disorders.

Key Terms

- Aqueous humor
- Astigmatism
- Canal of Schlemm
- Cataract
- Conductive hearing loss
- Conjunctiva
- Cornea
- Decibel
- Glaucoma
- Hyperopia
- Intraocular pressure
- Legally blind
- Lens
- Macular degeneration
- Ménière's syndrome
- Mydriatic
- Myopia
- Miotic
- Otitis media
- Otosclerosis
- Ototoxic
- Presbycusis
- Presbyopia
- Retinal detachment
- Sensorineural hearing loss

Diagnostic Tests

Most of the diagnostic exams for disorders of the eyes and ears are directly related to the anatomical area needing visualization. The exam reviewer should be knowledgeable of the preparation and care of clients receiving exams for eye and ear disorders. While reviewing these diagnostic exams, the exam reviewer should be alert for information that would be an important part of nursing care for these clients.

Diagnostic measures used for the client with disorders of the eyes include the following:

- Snellen chart
- Ishihara polychromatic chart
- Amsler grid
- Tonometry

Diagnostic measures used for the client with disorders of the ears include the following:

- CBC
- MRI
- CAT scan
- Rinne
- Weber
- Audiometry

Pharmacological Agents Used in the Care of the Client with Disorders of the Eyes and Ears

Several drug categories are used in the care of the client with disorders of the ears. These drugs are frequently used to treat other conditions and are included in other chapters within the text. These drug categories include anti-infectives for those with ear infections and decongestants, steroids, and antihistamines for those with otitis media and other otic conditions.

A number of medications are used to treat eye disorders. Miotics, beta adrenergic blockers, and carbonic anhydrase inhibitors are examples of topical medications ordered for the client with glaucoma. Anti-infectives and topical steroids are used to treat inflammation and ocular infections. Table 8.1 lists examples of medications used to treat ocular disorders. Medications listed in Table 8.1 are not inclusive of all medications used to treat disorders of the eyes; therefore, you should have a current pharmacology text available for reference.

TABLE 8.1   Pharmacological Agents for Treating Eye Disorders

Name	Action	Side Effects	Nursing Care
Topical Anesthetics			
OcuCaine, Ak-Taine (proparacaine HCl) Pontocaine (tetracaine HCl, cocaine HCl)	Provides topical anesthesia for ophthalmic procedures	Slight increase in blood pressure and heart rate	Instruct client to avoid rubbing or touching the eye. Store in tightly closed bottle. Do not use if solution is discolored.
Topical Steroids			
OcuPred (prednisolone acetate) Dexotic (dexamethasone) Fluor-Op (liquifilm)	Reduces swelling and inflammation	May mask signs of infection, increased blood glucose	Shake medication vigorously before using. Monitor for corneal ulceration and signs of local infection.
Anti-Infectives			
Tobrex (tobramycin) Ilotycin (erythromycin) Ocuflox (ofloxacin)	Bactericidal, works by interfering with bacterial cytoplasmic membrane	Nausea, vomiting, potential for causing ototoxicity and nephrotoxic	Remove exudates from the eyes before administering medication. Tell client to use drops exactly as prescribed.
Alpha 2 Adrenergic Agonist			
Alphagan (brimonidine tartrate)	Reduces intraocular pressure	Can precipitate hypertensive crisis	Contraindicated in clients taking MAOIs. Wait 15 minutes before reinserting soft contact lenses.
Beta Adrenergic Blockers			
Betoptic (betaxolol) Ocupress (carteolol HCl) Timoptic (timolol)	Decreases the production of aqueous humor, which in turn reduces intraocular pressure	Headache, hypotension, dizziness, muscle weakness	Contraindicated in clients with chronic pulmonary disease. Monitor blood glucose. Use with systemic beta adrenergic blockers can affect heart rate and blood pressure.
Miotics (Direct Acting)			
Carboptic (carbachol) Isopto Carpine (pilocarpine)	Reduces intraocular pressure by constricting the pupil	Headache, conjunctival hyperemia	Contraindicated in clients with corneal abrasions. Tell the client not to increase the dosage or scheduling of the drug.
Miotics (Cholinesterase Inhibitors)			
Humorsol (demecarium bromide) Phospholine (echothiophate iodide)	Reduces intraocular pressure by constricting the pupil	Headache, conjunctival hyperemia	Advise client to have intraocular pressure checked more frequently.
Carbonic Anhydrase Inhibitors			
Trusopt (dorzolamide) Azopt (brinzolamide)	Decreases the production of aqueous humor, which in turn reduces intraocular pressure	Anorexia, tingling of face, hands, and feet	Do not use in clients who are sensitive to sulfonamides. Remove contact lenses prior to use, and do not reinsert for 15 minutes or clouding and discoloration of contact lens could occur.

Apply Your Knowledge

This chapter provided information regarding the care of clients with disorders of the eyes and ears. The following questions test your knowledge regarding the safe, effective care and management of the client with various sensory disorders. The nurse should use the key terms, diagnostics, and pharmacological agents sections to answer these questions.

Exam Questions

1. When ambulating the client who is blind, the nurse should:

    A. Walk one to two steps ahead with the client's hand on the nurse's elbow.

    B. Walk beside the client while holding her hand.

    C. Walk one to two steps behind with the nurse's hand on the client's elbow.

    D. Walk beside the client without touching her.

2. The nurse is assessing the client's pupils for size and symmetry. The normal pupil diameter is:

    A. 2–4 mm

    B. 3–5 mm

    C. 6–8 mm

    D. 7–9 mm

3. An elderly client tells the nurse that her ears have been "ringing" ever since the doctor started her on some new medication. Which of the client's medications is considered to be ototoxic?

    A. Amoxil (amoxicillin)

    B. K-Dur (potassium)

    C. B12 (cyanocobalamine)

    D. Tegretol (carbamazepine)

4. The nurse is caring for a client with Ménière's disease. Which nursing diagnosis should receive priority?

    A. Fear related to potential hearing loss

    B. Risk for injury related to loss of balance

    C. Activity intolerance related to perception of dizziness

    D. Anxiety related to loss of control

5. The physician has ordered fluorescein angiography for a client with diabetic retinopathy. The nurse should tell the client that:

    A. The procedure will take one to two hours.

    B. The client will be given oral medication to prepare for the test.

    C. The urine will be bright green until the dye is excreted.

    D. The client will need to limit fluid intake after the test.

6. Which statement indicates the client needs further teaching regarding care of his hearing aid?

    A. "I can soak the ear mold in mild soap and water to clean it."

    B. "I will need to keep an extra supply of batteries on hand."

    C. "I need to adjust the volume to the lowest setting that permits hearing."

    D. "I can use a toothpick to clean debris from the hole of the hearing aid."

7. Following a right stapedectomy the client complains of numbness and tingling in her right cheek. The nurse should report the client's complaints to the doctor because damage might have occurred to which cranial nerve?

    A. Third

    B. Fifth

    C. Seventh

    D. Ninth

8. A client scheduled for cataract removal asks the nurse when he can expect the best results from his eye surgery. The nurse knows that the client's best vision will not be present for:

    A. One to two weeks after surgery

    B. Four to six weeks after surgery

    C. Six months after surgery

    D. One year after surgery

9. The client with Ménière's disease might see an improvement in symptoms by:

    A. Taking supplements of B3

    B. Increasing sodium intake

    C. Eating a diet high in calcium

    D. Drinking additional fluids

10. Which recreational activity should be avoided by the client following cataract removal?

     A. Painting

     B. Watching television

     C. Golfing

     D. Attending the opera

Answers to Exam Questions

1. Answer A is correct. When ambulating the client who is blind, the nurse should allow the client to grasp his arm at the elbow. The nurse's arm should be kept close to the body so that the client can detect the nurse's direction or movement. Answers B, C, and D are improper ways of ambulating the client who is blind; therefore, they are incorrect.

2. Answer B is correct. The normal pupil diameter is between 3 and 5 mm in size. Answers A, C, and D are not normal pupil diameters; therefore, they are incorrect.

3. Answer D is correct. Tegretol (carbamazepine) is ototoxic. Answers A, B, and C do not pose a risk of ototoxicity; therefore, they are incorrect.

4. Answer B is correct. The client with Ménière's disease experiences a whirling sensation that could lead to falls. The nurse should give priority to the client's safety. Answers A, C, and D should be considered when planning for the client's care; however, they do not take priority over safety therefore they are incorrect choices.

5. Answer C is correct. Fluorescein will cause the client's urine to be bright green in color until the dye is excreted. Answer A is incorrect; the procedure takes only a few minutes because the vessels fill rapidly. Answer B is incorrect because the dye is injected intravenously. Answer D is incorrect because the client will need to drink additional fluids to help eliminate the dye.

6. Answer A is correct. The client should avoid excessive wetting of the ear mold; therefore, the client needs further teaching. Answers B, C, and D indicate that the client understands the nurse's teaching, so they are incorrect.

7. Answer C is correct. Damage to the seventh cranial nerve (facial nerve) might occur during a stapedectomy. Changes in facial sensation should be reported to the doctor. Stapedectomy complications do not include damage to the third, fifth, or ninth cranial nerves; therefore, answers A, B, and D are incorrect.

8. Answer B is correct. The final best vision will not be present until four to six weeks following cataract removal. Answer A is incorrect because sufficient healing has not taken place. Answers C and D are incorrect because the best vision is present four to six weeks after surgery.

9. Answer A is correct. Taking supplements of B3 (niacin) helps to improve the symptoms associated with Ménière's disease. Answer B is incorrect because the client needs to limit sodium intake. The client with Ménière's does not need additional sources of calcium; therefore, answer C is incorrect. Ménière's is not improved by increasing fluid intake; therefore, answer D is incorrect.

10. Answer D is correct. Golfing should be avoided by the client following cataract removal because it requires activity that increases intraocular pressure. Answers A, B, and C are incorrect because they do not increase intraocular pressure.

Suggested Reading and Resources

▶ Brunner, L., and D. Suddarth. *Textbook of Medical Surgical Nursing* 12th ed. Philadelphia: Lippincott Williams & Wilkins, 2009.

▶ Ignatavicius, D., and S. Workman. *Medical Surgical Nursing: Critical Thinking for Collaborative Care* 5th ed. Philadelphia: Mosby, 2008

▶ Lehne, R. *Pharmacology for Nursing Care* 7th ed. Philadelphia: Elsevier, 2009.

▶ LeMone, P., and K. Burke, K. in *Medical Surgical Nursing: Critical Thinking in Client Care* 4th ed. Upper Saddle River, New Jersey: Pearson Prentice Hall, 2008

▶ Lewis, S., M. Heitkemper, S. Dirksen, P. Obrien and L. Bucher. *Medical Surgical Nursing: Assessment and Management of Clinical Problems* 7th ed. Philadelphia: Elsevier, 2007

▶ "Adjustment to Blindness and Visual Impairment": www.whitsacre.info/vip.

▶ Disabled Online: Serving Special People with Special Needs: www.disabledonline.com/hearingimpairment.php.

▶ emedicine from WebMD: www.emedicine.com.

▶ National Institute on Deafness and Other Communication Disorders www.nidcd.nih.gov/health/hearing/coch.asp

▶ "Visual Impairment, Visual Disability and Legal Blindness": www.nlm.nih.gov/medlineplus/vsionimpairmentandblindness.html.

CHAPTER NINE

Care of the Client with Gastrointestinal Disorders

The gastrointestinal (GI) system begins with the mouth and ends with the anus. It is approximately 25 feet in length in the adult. The primary functions of the GI system are food digestion, extraction of nutrients, and waste elimination. Parts of the GI tract include

- ▶ Mouth
- ▶ Esophagus
- ▶ Stomach
- ▶ Small and large intestine
- ▶ Salivary glands
- ▶ Liver
- ▶ Gallbladder
- ▶ Pancreas

Please see Figure 9.1 for organs of the gastrointestinal system.

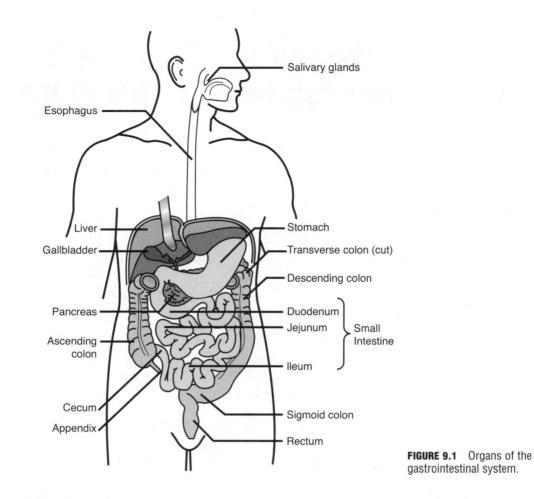

FIGURE 9.1 Organs of the gastrointestinal system.

Problems in the GI system can result in impaired function of the organs involved. Lack of nutrient absorption and waste elimination occurs with disorders in this system. Other problems, such as infection and cancer, can also occur. Conditions in the GI system can be both acute and chronic. Some disorders are presented as life-threatening emergencies.

Peptic Ulcer Disease

When a body's defense mechanisms fail to protect the stomach lining from acid and pepsin, an ulcer can develop. *Peptic ulcer disease* is a descriptive term used for ulcer disease of either the duodenal or gastric type. Several factors contribute to the development of an ulcer, including the following:

▸ Irritants that increase the secretion of hydrochloric acid; nonsteroidal anti-inflammatory drugs (NSAIDs), such as ibuprofen or Toradol; and steroids.

> **NOTE**
>
> Administer NSAIDs with food, milk, or antacids to reduce the likelihood of GI upset.

▸ Stress can cause hypersecretion of acid, which plays a part in ulcer development.

▸ *Helicobacter. pylori* (*H. pylori*) bacteria causes ulcers and can be transmitted from person to person.

▶ A family history of genetic predisposition to ulcers is a contributing factor.

Figure 9.2 shows the location of an ulcer or erosion associated with duodenal and gastric ulcers.

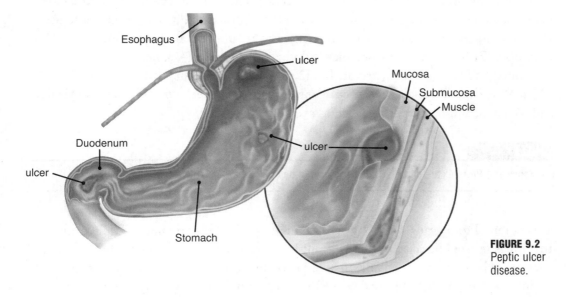

FIGURE 9.2
Peptic ulcer disease.

Types of Ulcers

An ulcer is referred to as *duodenal*, *gastric*, or *esophageal*, depending on its location in the gastrointestinal system. The two most common locations are the duodenum and gastric area; therefore, duodenal ulcers are erosions that occur on the mucosal lining of the duodenum, and when the erosion occurs in the gastric mucosa, the ulcer is classified as gastric.

The chart in Table 9.1 provides the clinical manifestations and characteristics of the two most common types of ulcers. Review the information in the chart focusing on the distinguishing characteristics with each type.

TABLE 9.1 Duodenal and Gastric Ulcer Characteristics

	Duodenal Ulcer	Gastric Ulcer
Age Group Affected	30—60 years old	Over 50
Pathophysiology	Hypersecretion of stomach acid	Normal or hyposecretion of stomach acid
Pain	Epigastric area 2–3 hours after meals; pain relieved by food	Mid-epigastric from one-half to one hour after meals; pain increased by food consumption
Vomiting	Uncommon	Common; produces some pain relief
Melena	Common	Uncommon

Diagnosis of Ulcers

The healthcare provider uses the client history of pain and discomforts to aid in the diagnosis. Other diagnostic tools utilized to differentiate the disorder are upper gastrointestinal x-ray, gastroscopy, and identification of *H. pylori* bacteria. This bacteria can be identified by a serologic test for antibodies, a C13 urea breath test, and stool exam.

Treatment of Ulcers

The treatment of ulcers follows two pathways. The first route is the conservative plan. This plan is followed most often because the dietary changes and pharmacological regimen is highly effective in treating the ulcers. Dietary modifications include avoiding highly seasoned or spicy foods, high-acid foods and drinks, high-fiber foods, caffeine, alcohol, smoking, and stress. Medications used to treat ulcers are proton pump inhibitors (PPIs), such as omeprazole (Prilosec), rabeprazole (Aciphex), pantoprazole (Protonix) and lansoprazole (Prevacid); H2 receptor antagonists, such as famotidine (Pepcid); Prostandin analogues, such as misoprostol (Cytotec); antacids, such as Maalox and Mylanta; and barrier drugs, such as sucralfate (Carafate).

> **NOTE**
>
> Aciphex and Protonix are enteric-coated and cannot be crushed for administration.

Ulcers found to be caused by *H. pylori* require a specific drug regimen. Triple drug therapy is utilized because no single agent has been shown to effectively eliminate the bacteria. The therapy is available in several combinations, but the most successful regimen is a bismuth compound or a PPI with a combination of two antibiotics, such as flagyl and tetracycline or clarithromycin and amoxicillin.

Nonsurgical management of GI bleeding can also be accomplished via an esophogastro-duodenoscopy (EGD). The gastroenterologist can stop the bleeding by using heat, epinephrine, laser, or clips directly at the site of the ulcer to suppress the bleeding and promote clot formation.

Gastrointestinal bleeding is a major complication of peptic ulcer disease. This complication requires astute nursing care to maintain homeostasis. Interventions must be performed to monitor and treat this complication. These interventions include the following:

▶ Assessment of nasogastric (NG) tube, stool, and emesis (might be exhibited as coffee ground) for blood

▶ Monitor vital signs for hypovolemic changes (low blood pressure, increased pulse)

▶ Assessment of hemoglobin and hematocrit levels for abnormalities

▶ Replacement of fluids as ordered by the physician

▶ Administration of blood products and medications as ordered

When clients with ulcers develop complications or cannot be managed conservatively, the second pathway of treatment is utilized. This alternative treatment plan is surgical intervention. Common procedures for ulcers include a gastrectomy, vagotomy, and pyloroplasty. After the surgical procedure, several nursing interventions should be included with the usual postoperative abdominal care, including the following:

▶ Assessing the NG tube for drainage (guidelines for insertion of an NG tube are given below)

CAUTION

In the first 12–24 hours, the nasogastric drainage should be small in amount, but might be bright red in appearance. After 24 hours, the drainage should turn darker in color and decrease further in amount.

Do not irrigate or reposition the NG tube after gastric surgery without a specific physician order from the surgeon.

▶ Monitor for symptoms of shock, such as a drop in BP, tachycardia, and decreased urinary output (less than 30 mL per hour)

▶ Assess for abdominal distention, which could indicate a paralytic ileus, perforation, or hemorrhage

Guidelines for Inserting a Large-bore NG Tube

1. Collect supplies:

   ▶ Single lumen gastric tube or salem sump tube (14–18 Fr). With the salem sump tube, the large lumen is used for suction while the small (blue) lumen is used as an air vent.

   ▶ Water-soluble lubricant.

   ▶ Tape.

   ▶ Glass of water with straw.

   ▶ 50 mL catheter tip syringe.

   ▶ Clean gloves.

   ▶ Suction tube and suction source.

   ▶ pH strips.

2. Explain the procedure.

3. Wash hands and don gloves.

4. Position the client at a 45° angle or higher with the head of the bed elevated.

5. Examine the nostrils, selecting the most patent nostril for tube insertion.

6. Measure the tube from the tip of the nose to the ear and then to the xiphoid process. Place a strip of tape at this measurement. Lubricate the tube.

7. With the patient's head slightly extended, insert the tube through the nostril to the back of the throat.

8. When the tube reaches the posterior pharynx, ask the client to sip water (if able) or dry swallow and to flex the head forward to facilitate passage into the esophagus.

   Listen for air exchange. If air sound is heard, the NG is progressing into the airway and the NG should be removed.

9. After tape mark is reached, determine placement by aspirating gastric content with the 50 mL syringe. The pH should be <5.0 for gastric secretions.

(continues)

(continued)

10. Tape the tube securely to the nose.

11. Plug the end of the tube or connect to suction.

12. Offer or perform oral/nasal care.

Dumping Syndrome

One common occurrence after gastric surgery for ulcers is *dumping syndrome*. This syndrome is caused due to the rapid emptying of food from the stomach into the jejunum. Clinical signs of dumping syndrome can appear similar to a heart attack and include the following:

▸ Dizziness

▸ Pallor

▸ Nausea and vomiting

▸ Palpitations

▸ Abdominal distention

The management of dumping syndrome can be accomplished by dietary modifications, which include the decrease of fluids with meals, low carbohydrate intake, small frequent meals, and resting in the recumbent position after meals. Medications prescribed to assist with this problem are pectin; somatostatin analogues, such as octreotide (Sandostatin); and antispasmotics, such as dicyclomine (Bentyl).

Irritable Bowel Syndrome

Irritable bowel syndrome (IBS) affects up to 15% of the Western population. In the United States, it is treated 2.5 times more often in women than men. IBS is characterized by irregular bowel patterns. It can be classified as IBS constipation, IBS diarrhea, or IBS mixed constipation and diarrhea. There is no known cause of the syndrome, but precipitating factors include stress, certain foods, anxiety, depression, gastroenteritis, and hormones.

Symptoms associated with IBS include

▸ Abdominal pain

▸ Excessive flatulence

▸ Bloating

▸ Feeling of incomplete evacuation

▸ Diarrhea

▸ Constipation

Diagnosis of IBS is made by ruling out other causes (for example, colorectal cancer, ulcer disease, or inflammatory bowel disease) and by a thorough history and physical exam. A sigmoidoscopy can reveal spastic contractions and pain with the procedure.

Treatment of IBS includes patient teaching, pharmacological agents, and complementary therapies. Dietary instructions are given to eliminate gas forming and specific triggering foods (grapes, apple juice, milk, and sugarless gums) from the diet. The patient is also taught to utilize stress reduction techniques. Pharmacological agents prescribed include anti-spasmodics such as dicyclomine (Bentyl) for abdominal pain and loperamide (Imodium) for diarrhea. Two pharmacological agents—tegaserod (Zelnorm) for constipation and alosetron (Lotrenox) for diarrhea—have been approved by the Food and Drug Administration for IBS treatment. Complementary therapies such as hypnosis and acupuncture are also utilized as forms of treatment.

Inflammatory Bowel Disorders

There are two major chronic inflammatory bowel diseases: Crohn's disease and ulcerative colitis. These diseases occur more often in women than men. The age group most often involved is 10–30 years. There is no known cause, but several factors have been found to be associated. These factors include triggering agents, such as pesticides, food additives, and radiation. A connection has also been shown to exist between clients with allergies, immune system deficits, and psychological and increased anxiety conditions. Both disorders are associated with periods of diarrhea and constipation. Clients with Crohn's disease and ulcerative colitis experience episodes without problems followed by exacerbations.

Crohn's Disease

Crohn's disease, also known as *regional enteritis*, is an inflammation in segments of the bowel resulting in swelling, thickening, and abscess formation. Because of these bowel changes, there is severe narrowing of the lumen of the bowel. Most symptoms of Crohn's disease occur as the result of the inflammatory process and include the following:

- Crampy abdominal pain
- Diarrhea
- Weight loss and malnutrition
- Anemia
- Ulcer formation

Ulcerative Colitis

The second form of inflammatory bowel disease is ulcerative colitis. In this disorder, the inflammation occurs in the colon and rectum. The inflammation usually begins at the rectum and proceeds upward. This disease can result in systemic involvement with fatalities. Symptoms are similar to Crohn's disease and include the following:

▸ Abdominal cramping

▸ Intermittent *tenesmus* (contracting spasms in which there is a desire to empty the bowels)

▸ Vomiting

▸ Weight loss

▸ Fever

▸ Bloody diarrhea

▸ Rectal bleeding

Management of the Client with Inflammatory Bowel Disease

The main focus in the care of these clients is to reduce the inflammation, which will result in management of diarrhea, pain, and prevention of complications. Treatment involves several methods. Nonsurgical care requires diet intervention and drug therapy. The client with Crohn's or ulcerative colitis with severe symptoms is kept NPO and/or an NG tube is inserted to allow the bowel to rest. If the client is malnourished, total parenteral nutrition (TPN) might be included in the treatment plan.

Tube-feeding formulas might be instituted. When the diet progresses to solids, high-fiber high-residue foods are usually restricted. Examples of high-fiber foods include fresh fruits and vegetables, whole grains, and nuts. Primary pharmacological therapy for ulcerative colitis include salicylate compounds such as sulfasalazine (Azulfidine), mesalamine (Asacol), and olsalzine (Dipentum) and steroids such as prednisone by mouth or Solu-Medrol intravenously if severely ill. Immunosuppressive agents such as cyclosporine (Gengraf) or methotrexate (Rheumatrex) are most effective for Crohn's but may be given for both types of IBD. Antidiarrheals (for example, Lomotil) might be given for symptomatic relief in Crohn's and ulcerative colitis. Two medications that are given mostly for Crohn's disease are infliximab (Remicade) and adalimumab (Humira). Classified as antirheumatic drugs, Remicade and Humira are given to clients with both types whose inflammatory bowel disease is not improving with other therapies.

Surgical management might be required in severe cases. If the client doesn't respond to treatment or develops a complication requiring it, surgery could be performed. Possible complications in clients with ulcerative colitis that make surgery necessary include perforation of the bowel, colon cancer, or hemorrhage. These surgeries might require a colectomy with an ileostomy, continent ileostomy, or ileoanal anastomosis with creation of a ileoanal reservoir or J pouch.

Postoperative care for clients after an ileostomy includes prevention of skin problems due to the liquid stool and high risk for irritation and excoriation of the skin around the stoma.

Intestinal obstruction and abscesses are complications requiring surgery, but are more common with Crohn's disease. A bowel resection is usually performed and can be done by minimally invasive surgery via a laparoscope.

Diverticular Disease

A person has diverticulosis when she has sac-like outpouchings (diverticulum) in the wall of the large intestine. Inflammation can occur when food and bacteria become trapped in these sacs. The main cause of diverticulosis is constipation, which increases intraluminal pressure and weakens the intestinal walls.

The disease is more prevalent in people over the age of 60. Diets high in seeds, nuts, and grains increase the risk because these ingredients can easily become trapped in the diverticula. Some signs of diverticulitis include bowel irregularities, pain and cramping in the left lower quadrant of the abdomen, fever, abdominal distention, and bouts of constipation.

Diagnosis of diverticular disease is usually made as a result of a barium enema and/or a colonoscopy. Many clients are diagnosed as the result of cancer screening colonoscopies.

Management of the Client with Diverticulitis

The treatment phase depends on the severity of the problem. The disease usually can be controlled without hospitalization by the use of diet and medications. The diet progresses from clear liquids to a high-fiber, low-fat, with increased fluids.

Medications used in treatment include antibiotics; analgesics, such as pentazocine (Talwin); antispasmotics; and fiber laxatives, such as Metamucil.

The management of diverticulitis changes to surgical when a complication such as perforation of the bowel, abscess formation, hemorrhage, or intestinal obstruction occurs. Depending on the degree of inflammation, infection, and so on, the surgical procedure might require performing a colostomy.

Hemorrhoids

Diseases that occur in the anorectal area are relatively common. Hemorrhoids occur when veins dilate in the anal area. The hemorrhoids are classified as *external* if located outside the anal sphincter and *internal* if above the anal sphincter. Anything that can increase the pressure in the anal area can cause hemorrhoids to develop. Pregnancy and constipation are common contributing factors. A client with hemorrhoids will usually complain of pain and itching in the anal area and blood with stools.

Management of hemorrhoids has one main goal—to relieve the symptoms. Some comfort measures that can be utilized include the following:

- Warm compresses
- Cold packs
- Sitz baths
- Astringent pads
- Rest
- Local pain-relieving ointments and suppositories

Other treatments involve the client increasing fluids and fiber in his diet, which softens the stools and prevents straining. If the client is suffering from advanced thrombosis of the vein, a surgical removal of the hemorrhoids (hemorrhoidectomy) might be required. Rubber band ligation and infrared photocoagulation are other forms of conservative surgical and nonsurgical treatment for nonthrombotic hemorrhoid conditions.

Appendicitis

The appendix is attached to the cecum and is located in the right lower abdomen. Infection of the appendix or appendicitis is common in teens and young adults and more common in males than females. Symptoms of appendicitis include the following:

- Pain starts with epigastric or periumbilical pain and localizes to the right lower quadrant of the abdomen. This area is known as *Mcburney's point* (see Figure 9.3).

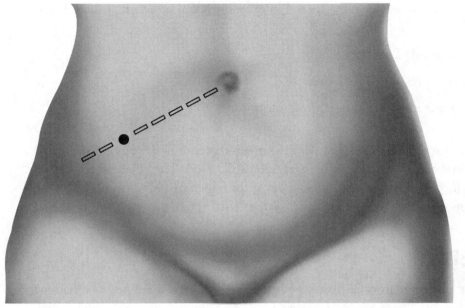

FIGURE 9.3
Mcburney's
point.

NOTE

Rebound tenderness can occur upon release of pressure in the epigastric or periumbilical area and indicates peritoneal inflammation.

A positive Rovsing's sign can also occur. This happens when the client experiences pain on the right lower quadrant of the abdomen when the examiner palpates the left lower quadrant.

CAUTION

If the appendix ruptures, the abdomen will be distended with unlocalized abdominal pain.

▶ Low-grade fever

▶ Nausea and/or vomiting

Diagnosis is made when evaluation of the cell blood count reveals an elevated white blood cell and neutrophil count (a left shift). A CT scan will also show right lower quadrant denseness with bowel distention.

Management of appendicitis is accomplished by surgical removal of the inflamed infected appendix.

CAUTION

Laxative and enemas are contraindicated and can cause perforation in clients with appendicitis.

If the client has an appendectomy, several interventions will be accomplished. Preop measures include the following:

- Administration of analgesics
- IV fluids to prevent dehydration
- Treating infection via antibiotic administration

Postoperative care will include some of the same interventions as pre-op. After the return of bowel function, the client is placed on solid food. The client is usually discharged the day of surgery or the next day if the appendix did not rupture and no complications occurred.

Peritonitis

Another acute inflammatory disorder is peritonitis. *Peritonitis* is defined as inflammation of the peritoneum. There are several common causes of peritonitis including appendicitis, perforated ulcer, and diverticulitis. The symptoms of peritonitis might be associated with the underlying cause. Some common signs are as follows:

- Pain that increases with movement
- Rebound tenderness
- Signs of paralytic ileus (abdominal distention, absent bowel signs)
- Rigidity of the abdomen and abdominal tenderness

Diagnosis of peritonitis is usually made by physical exam in combination with an elevated WBC, and decreased hemoglobin and hematocrit on the CBC laboratory exam. Abdominal x-rays show air and fluid with a distended bowel. CT scan shows evidence of abscess formation.

Management of peritonitis is directed at relieving symptoms, preventing complications, and eliminating the cause. Measures used to accomplish these goals include the following:

- Administration of pain and nausea medication.
- Placement of an NG tube to relieve abdominal distention.
- Oxygen administration due to fluid in the abdomen causing respiratory compromise.
- IV antibiotics to prevent and treat infection.
- Monitor IV fluid administration, which is given to replace fluid and electrolyte loss into the peritoneal cavity.
- Assess client's intake and output.
- Surgical intervention is performed to remove the cause of the peritonitis.

▶ Monitor for complications. The two most common complications are abscess formation and wound dehiscence or evisceration.

CAUTION

Pay attention. If the client states, "I feel like something burst open," assess the wound and report findings to the physician. Usually there will be reports of increased dressing changes or large amounts of serosanguinous drainage from the surgical wound before evisceration of the wound occurs.

NOTE

If dehiscence of the wound occurs, apply a non-adherent or moist saline dressing and notify the surgeon.

Intestinal Obstruction

Anything that interferes with the intestinal content (fluid, gas, gastric secretions) passing through the intestinal tract can cause a blockage or an intestinal obstruction. Obstructions are further classified as *mechanical* (due to pressure on the wall of the intestine; a tumor, for example) or *functional* (because of a lack of adequate muscle to propel contents through the intestinal tract; a client with muscular dystrophy, for example). The most frequent bowel obstructions occur in the small intestine, and the most common cause is adhesions. Large bowel obstructions usually happen in the sigmoid colon and account for approximately 10%–15% of intestinal obstructions. Other common causes of obstructions are hernias and carcinomas.

The signs of obstruction are caused by the pressure build-up in the intestines. Table 9.2 specifies some signs and symptoms of small bowel obstruction and large bowel obstructions. Review this table focusing on the signs that differentiate the two forms of obstructions.

TABLE 9.2   Bowel Obstruction Signs and Symptoms

Small Bowel Obstruction	Large Bowel Obstruction
Colicky abdominal pain	Pain usually in the lower abdomen
No passage of stool	No stool passage or stool passage that is thin and loose in character
Nausea and vomiting—may contain feces	Little vomiting; if so, it occurs late in the development of symptoms
Abdominal distention in the upper abdomen	Abdominal distention in the lower abdomen

Diagnosis of peritonitis is made by flat and upright abdominal x-rays that clearly show the distended bowels. Arterial blood gas evaluation could indicate metabolic alkalosis with small bowel obstruction or metabolic acidosis with large bowel obstructions. A CT scan might be ordered to assess the cause of the obstruction.

Management of the client with an intestinal obstruction includes both surgical and nonsurgical interventions. Important nursing measures to review for test preparation include the following:

▸ Monitor NG tube for patency.

▸ Measure the abdominal girth daily.

▸ Assess for nausea, emesis, and increasing abdominal distention.

▸ Monitor IV fluid replacement therapy.

▸ Assess serum electrolytes.

▸ Monitor fluid status by assessing urinary output, skin turgor, and mucous membranes.

▸ Monitor vital signs for abnormalities.

▸ Provide pain relief.

NOTE

Pain medications might be withheld initially to determine the client's problem.

▸ Surgical intervention is usually done via an exploratory laparotomy to determine and fix the cause of the obstruction.

Esophageal Disorders

The esophagus is the passageway for food from the mouth to the stomach. It has an opening that allows the food to travel through the diaphragm in the chest. Gastroesophageal reflux disease (GERD), Barrett's esophagus, and a hiatal hernia are diagnoses that are reflective of problems with the esophagus.

GERD

GERD is the most common gastrointestinal problem in the United States. That status makes this disorder a necessary review for test preparation. Normally GI content passes from the mouth through the esophagus to the stomach and the intestines. GERD occurs when there is a problem, usually with the lower esophageal sphincter, that allows contents to *reflux* (back up) into the esophagus. The signs and symptoms associated with GERD include the following:

▸ Heartburn (dyspepsia) defined as a burning sensation in the chest after meals, usually in the substernal area

▸ Regurgitation of food and/or fluids

> **CAUTION**
>
> Frequent regurgitation can cause an increased risk for aspiration. Monitor breath sounds for wheezing or crackles.

▶ Difficulty swallowing (dysphagia) or painful swallowing (odynophagia)

▶ Increase in saliva

▶ Belching (eructation)

▶ Flatulence

▶ Chest pain (clients might think they are having a heart attack)

▶ Sour taste in mouth upon awakening

▶ Coughing (due to irritation of airway by gastric secretions)

▶ Globus (a feeling that something is in the back of the throat)

Diagnosis is made by several methods. Some diagnostic exams might be done at a heart-burn or gastroenterology center. Those diagnostic tests include the following:

▶ pH monitoring gives the most accurate diagnosis. It is performed by insertion of an NG tube into the lower esophagus. The tube remains in place for 24 hours. The client keeps a log of activities while the NG tube is in place with a continuous recording of the reflux activity occurring. A pH of less than 4 above the LES can help diagnose GERD.

▶ An endoscopy exam via an EGD shows direct visualization of the esophagus.

▶ Barium swallow.

Management of Clients with GERD

The treatment of GERD includes conservative measures and surgical management. Conservative treatment is accomplished through diet, lifestyle modification, pharmacologic interventions, and endoscopy. Measures that are incorporated into the client's care include the following:

▶ **Diet recommendations:**

  ▶ Avoid foods that irritate the inflamed areas, such as chocolate, fats, spicy, and acidic foods

  ▶ Eliminate carbonated beverages, which increase the pressure in the stomach

  ▶ Serve frequent small meals

  ▶ Do not lie down for 2–3 hours after eating

  ▶ Avoid eating within 3 hours of bedtime

> ► **Lifestyle modifications:**
>
> > ► Avoid alcohol and smoking
> >
> > ► Use methods that decrease or prevent intra-abdominal pressure (reduce weight, don't strain, avoid bending over, don't wear tight clothes around the waist)
> >
> > ► Sleep with the head of the bed elevated on 4"–6" blocks
>
> ► **Pharmacologic treatments:**
>
> > ► Antacids (examples are Gaviscon and Mylanta)
> >
> > ► Histamine blockers to decrease acid (such as famotidine [Pepcid] and nizatidine [Axid])
> >
> > ► Proton pump inhibitors (for example, pantoprazole [Protonix] or esomeprazole [Nexium])
> >
> > ► Prokinetic drugs to increase gastric emptying (metoclopramide [Reglan] is an example)

NOTE

Side effects of Reglan you need to know are restlessness, anxiety, hallucinations, and insomnia.

> ► **Endoscopy procedures:**
>
> > ► Stretta, which works by inhibiting vagus nerve activity

NOTE

Care after this procedure includes monitoring for chest pain, a clear liquid diet for 24 hours, and a soft diet for the next two weeks.

Surgical management may also be required via a laparoscopic Nissen fundoplication (LNF). The open method procedure might be necessary if the client is not a candidate for the laparoscopic procedure. The laparoscopic repair procedure is performed by several small abdominal incisions. With either procedure, the surgeon wraps the fundus of the stomach around the esophagus to support the LES. Figure 9.4 demonstrates the repair procedure.

Postoperative care of clients after these procedures is a necessary component for you to review for a nursing exam. These interventions include the following:

► Prevent respiratory problems—Elevate the head of the bed, ambulate, use incentive spirometry, and perform cough and deep breathing exercises

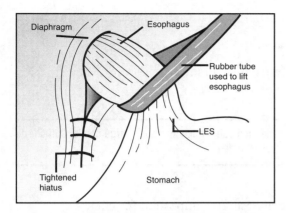

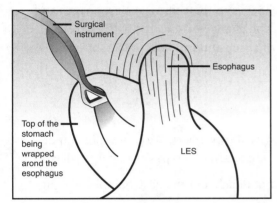

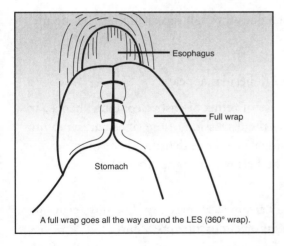

A full wrap goes all the way around the LES (360° wrap).

FIGURE 9.4 Nissen fundoplication.

CAUTION

Respiratory complications risks are higher in clients with the open method surgical procedure.

▶ Administer pain medication.

▶ Monitor NG tube with open method surgery.

▶ Diet progresses from clear liquids to frequent small meals.

> **NOTE**
>
> Due to the surgical procedure, the stomach size is smaller and cannot accommodate large meals. Caffeine and alcohol might need to be restricted or eliminated from the diet.

GERD is both a common and very treatable disease. It is important for clients to be treated. Long-term reflux of acid can cause changes to the cells in the esophagus and lead to a condition called *Barrett's esophagus*. The changes associated with Barrett's esophagus lead to malignant transformation of tissue and can be a precursor to esophageal cancer.

Hiatal Hernia

A person has a hiatal hernia when the esophagus allows a herniation or a portion of the stomach to protrude into the thoracic cavity. There are two types of hiatal hernias:

▶ *Sliding* or *rolling* hernia where the upper stomach and the gastroesophageal junction slide in and out of the chest cavity.

▶ *Paraesophageal* hernia where the stomach goes through the diaphragm beside the esophagus.

Figure 9.5 demonstrates how these two types of hernias appear.

Most of the signs of hiatal hernia occur because of reflux of gastric contents; hence, are the same as the symptoms of GERD (refer to the discussion of the signs and symptoms of GERD earlier in this chapter). One additional symptom that the client might exhibit is complaints of fullness in the neck due to the herniation of the stomach into the thorax.

The diagnosis of a hiatal hernia is made by a barium swallow x-ray. The physician might also diagnose the hernia via direct visualization by endoscopy procedure.

The management of clients with hiatal hernias are the same as for clients with GERD including the diet, lifestyle changes, education and surgical repair by Nissen procedure that have been discussed in the "Management of Clients with GERD" section.

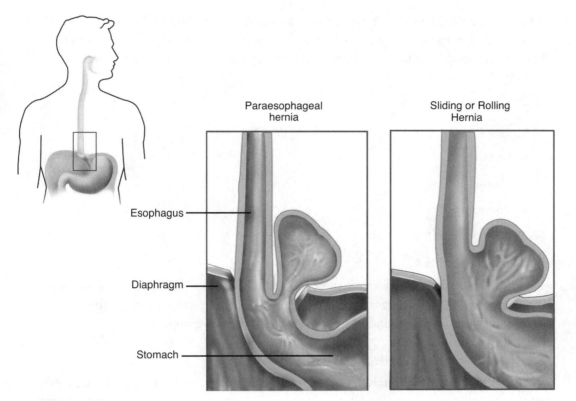

Esophagus

Diaphragm

Stomach

Paraesophageal
hernia

Sliding or Rolling
Hernia

FIGURE 9.5 Hiatial hernias.

Diseases Associated with the Liver

The liver is a large internal organ. Liver function is complex and any dysfunction of this organ affects all body systems. Liver disorders are common and can result from substances that destroy the liver, such as alcohol. These disorders can also result from a virus, such as hepatitis.

Hepatitis

Hepatitis is a viral infection that produces inflammation of the liver and can lead to destruction of liver cells. The six major types of hepatitis are known as *hepatitis A, B, C, D, E, and G*. Hepatitises A and E are similar in transmission: They have a fecal-oral route, but are not chronic. Hepatitises B, C, D, and G have similar characteristics in that they are transmitted by the same routes: parenteral, perinatal, or sexual.

Hepatitis A

Hepatitis A virus (HAV) is transmitted by the fecal-oral route. It can lead to an acute infection, but without the chronicity seen in other forms of the disease. Causes of hepatitis A include drinking contaminated water or eating fish from contaminated water. Outbreaks often occur in restaurants due to contamination by food handlers infected with HAV.

The symptoms of hepatitis A appear after an incubation period of 2–6 weeks. Hepatitis A is usually limited to 1–3 weeks of duration. People can have hepatitis A without knowing it because of the vagueness of the symptoms. Some symptoms that might be exhibited are as follows:

- Malaise
- Fever
- Jaundice
- Nausea
- Vomiting

Diagnosis of Hepatitis A

Diagnosing hepatitis A requires a stool specimen. This specimen can reveal the hepatitis A antigen for 7–10 days before the illness and 2–3 weeks after symptoms appear. Anti-HAV antibodies can be found in the serum after symptoms appear.

Prevention and Treatment of Hepatitis A

Treatment of hepatitis A includes many parameters. First, prevention of the transmission of hepatitis A is a key element. Obtaining the two-dose hepatitis vaccine (Havrix, Vaqta, and Avaxim) is highly recommended for the following groups: homosexuals; people traveling to unsanitary, hygiene-poor countries or locations; and healthcare workers. Hepatitis A vaccine can be administered to anyone over the age of 2.

The second dose of the vaccine should be given 6–12 months after the first dose. Protection begins a few weeks after the first dose and can last for up to 20 years. Administration of the immune globulin should be administered within 2 weeks of exposure to boost antibody protection and provide 6–8 weeks of passive immunity. The following two medications are important treatment options to remember for the exam:

- Hepatitis A vaccine (Havrix, Vaqta, Avaxim).
- Serum immune globulin (IG) for exposure to the disease.
- Twinrix (combination of Hepatitis A and Hepatitis B vaccines) can be administered for persons over 18 years of age.

TIP

Remember that hepatitis A has no long-term effects and is not chronic.

Hepatitis B

Hepatitis B virus (HBV) is transmitted through parenteral, perinatal, or sexual routes. People at the greatest risk of hepatitis B include the following:

- IV drug users

- Homosexual men

- Infants born to hepatitis B virus-infected mothers

- Healthcare workers

- Hemodialysis clients

Hepatitis B symptoms closely resemble hepatitis A's symptoms, but there is a much longer incubation period of 1–6 months. The following list gives you the symptoms of hepatitis B that you will need to know for the exam:

- Malaise

- Low-grade fever

- Rash

- Jaundice

- Arthritis

- Abdominal pain, especially in right upper quadrant

- Nausea and vomiting

Diagnosis of Hepatitis B

In diagnosing hepatitis B, HBsAg can appear in the blood of infected clients for 1–10 weeks after exposure to the hepatitis B virus and for 2–8 weeks before the onset of symptoms. Clients who have HBsAg persist in serum for 6 or more months after an acute infection are considered to be carriers. If a person becomes a carrier, they can be free of any symptoms of the illness while still infecting others.

Prevention and Treatment of Hepatitis B

When it comes to treating this problem, there are a lot of unknowns for hepatitis B—and for all other forms of hepatitis as well. However, treatments are available for hepatitis B, and the following lists the treatments you should be familiar with:

- **Hepatitis B vaccine (Engerix-B or Recombivax HB):** The hepatitis B vaccine is administered IM in three doses. The second and third doses are given at 1 month and 6 months, respectively, after the first dose. Doses are given in the deltoid muscle in adults.

- **Alpha interferon injections for chronic hepatitis B:** This medication can cause a flu-like reaction 3–6 hours after administration. Long-acting preparations (PEG-Intron, Pegasys) are given subcutaneously once weekly.

> ▸ **Hepatitis B immune globulin (HBIG):** This gives passive immunity to hepatitis B for people who have been exposed to the hepatitis B virus but have never received the hepatitis vaccine. The drug should preferably be administered within 24 hours of exposure to hepatitis B.

> **NOTE**
>
> The Centers for Disease Control recommends that the HBV vaccine be a part of routine child vaccination schedules.

> ▸ **Nucleoside analogs:** Lamivudine (Epivir), adefovir (Hepsera), entecavir (Baraclude), and telbivudine (Tyzeka) are a group of drugs that can be given orally. These drugs are administered for one year.

Hepatitis C

Hepatitis C virus (HCV) is transmitted through the same routes as hepatitis B (parenteral, perinatal, or sexual). Most transmission of hepatitis C is blood to blood; sexual and perinatal transmissions are rare. Examples of populations at high risk for hepatitis C are as follows:

- ▸ People who share IV needles (most common mode of transmission)
- ▸ Healthcare workers (needle sticks)
- ▸ People who obtain tattoos by unsanitary means

Cases of viral hepatitis not classified as A, B, or D are given the classification of hepatitis C. The age group with the highest incidence of hepatitis C is 40–59 years of age. Hepatitis B and C are similar, but a chronic carrier state exists more often with hepatitis C. More people with hepatitis C progress to chronic liver disease, including cirrhosis and liver cancer, than any other type of hepatitis.

> **NOTE**
>
> Symptoms of hepatitis C are similar to those of hepatitis B. Some say the symptoms are mild and variable. The reason so many people are predicted to have hepatitis C is because of the lack of symptoms and vagueness. Consequently, those infected often do not seek assistance. A great deal of people with hepatitis C are carriers of the disease but do not know they have it.

Diagnosis of Hepatitis C

Diagnosis of hepatitis C is confirmed by the presence of anti-HCV in serum. Another diagnostic tool utilized for any clients with chronic hepatitis is a liver biopsy. A liver biopsy can confirm the diagnosis, and evaluate the liver for changes, deterioration, or improvement.

Treatment of Hepatitis C

The combination therapy used to treat hepatitis C (interferon and ribavirin) has been shown to produce positive results. Some clients experience complete remission as a result of the drug regimen. These drugs are also used for relapses in the client's condition. The following are important to keep in mind for the exam:

▸ No vaccine is available for hepatitis C.

▸ Medications for treating hepatitis C include a combination of alpha interferon and ribavirin (Rebetol, Copegus).

EXAM ALERT

Women taking the drug should avoid becoming pregnant. Men with female partners should inform them of the need to avoid pregnancy.

Hepatitis D

Hepatitis D virus (HDV) is a delta hepatitis that requires the HBV surface antigen for replication. Only people with hepatitis B are at risk for hepatitis D. The virus is common among IV drug users, hemodialysis clients, and clients who have received multiple blood transfusions. Symptoms are similar to hepatitis B, except the incubation period is 3–20 weeks. These clients are also more likely to develop chronic active hepatitis and cirrhosis.

Diagnosis of Hepatitis D

Hepatitis D is diagnosed by a laboratory test. The presence of anti-delta antibodies in the presence of HBsAg will be revealed in the serum test results.

Treatment of Hepatitis D

Treatment of hepatitis D includes alpha interferon.

Hepatitis E

Hepatitis E (HEV) is transmitted by the fecal-oral route. Drinking of contaminated water is the most common route of transmission. Like hepatitis A, it is not a chronic condition and has been found to develop mostly in persons living in underdeveloped countries. Many outbreaks have occurred in areas where flooding and heavy rains have occurred.

Symptoms are similar to hepatitis A, and the incubation period for this hepatitis is 15–64 days.

Diagnosis of Hepatitis E

Diagnosis is made by the presence of anti-HEV in serum. This test is available only in research laboratories.

Prevention/Treatment of Hepatitis E

There is currently no known treatment for hepatitis E. Prevention is accomplished by practicing good hygiene and hand-washing techniques. Treatment with immune globulin after exposure has not been shown to be effective.

Hepatitis G

Hepatitis G virus (HGV) is one of the latest to be identified. It is spread parenterally and sexually. It can also be transmitted by blood transfusions. There is no known treatment at this time.

Prodromal Stage and Icteric Stage

Regardless of the type of hepatitis, clients experience symptoms associated with two stages:

▶ **The prodromal stage:** The prodromal stage of the hepatitis episode is the period of time when the client is exhibiting vague symptoms. This is the period when the patient's bile is not being excreted as it should (signified by dark urine and colored stools) and is collecting in the blood stream. Prodromal stage symptoms last from a few days to two weeks and include the following:

   ▶ Fatigue

   ▶ Malaise

   ▶ Anorexia

   ▶ Nausea

   ▶ Vomiting

   ▶ Fever

   ▶ Dark urine

   ▶ Clay-colored stools

▶ **The icteric stage:** Icteric stage symptoms occur 5–10 days after the prodromal stage begins and include the following:

   ▶ Jaundice

   ▶ Pruritus

   ▶ Tenderness in the right upper quadrant of the abdomen

   ▶ Hepatomegaly

   ▶ Elevated liver enzymes

Treatment for Clients with Hepatitis

Specific treatment for each type of hepatitis have been discussed. There are several general management techniques than are utilized for any client with a hepatitis of any type, which include the following:

- ▶ Bed rest for those with prodromal or icteric symptoms

- ▶ Small and frequent high carbohydrate, increased calorie meals

- ▶ Increased fluid intake (3000 mL/day)

- ▶ Avoidance of drugs detoxified by the liver

- ▶ Cool baths and soothing lotions to treat pruritus

- ▶ Medications used for treating forms of hepatitis, including steroids and immuno-suppressives

- ▶ Anti-inflammatory medications, such as Motrin and Advil. The healthcare provider should practice standard precaution control measures while providing care for these clients.

> **NOTE**
>
> Not all cases of hepatitis are reported. Hepatitis A is widespread with approximately 25,000 occurring in the United States annually. Hepatitis C causes much concern because it can lead to cirrhosis and liver cancer. Due to the number of clients with hepatitis C, the need for liver transplants is increasing, as is the number of deaths from liver disease.

Cirrhosis

Cirrhosis is the scarring or fibrosis of the liver, which results in the distortion of the liver structure and vessels. The most common causes of cirrhosis are alcoholism and hepatitis.

The nodules that develop from cirrhosis can block the flow of blood in the liver. This process eventually shrinks the liver and can lead to complications that can be severe and life-threatening. One of the major complications is portal hypertension. When this occurs, pressure increases resulting in obstruction of blood flow and causes the blood to find a channel around the high-pressure areas. Several complications can occur due to the portal hypertension, the first of which is *ascites* (fluid accumulation in the peritoneal cavity). The development of ascites is worsened by albumin and the liver's decreased capability to synthesize this protein. Treatment of ascites is generally conservative and includes the following:

- ▶ Dietary reduction of sodium

- ▶ Diuretic administration (spironolactone [Aldactone] and/or furosemide [Lasix])

- ▶ Paracentesis to remove the fluid from the peritoneal cavity.

Important nursing responsibilities for clients undergoing a paracentesis are listed in the box that follows.

Nursing Interventions for Paracentesis Procedure:

1. Have the patient void to empty the bladder prior to the procedure (prevents accidental puncture of the bladder).

2. Assist the patient to a high Fowler's or sitting position.

3. Monitor the patient's vital signs before, during, and after the procedure.

4. Assess the amount of fluid removed and send a specimen to the laboratory as directed.

5. Monitor for symptoms of hypovolemia.

6. Monitor the site of paracentesis for bleeding, drainage, and signs of infection.

The second complication due to the portal hypertension is heptorenal syndrome. This disorder is defined as functional renal failure. There is no actual kidney damage. Liver transplantation is the recommended treatment. Another life-threatening complication associated with portal hypertension is bleeding esophageal varices. The backup of blood from the liver gets into esophageal and gastric vessels, which become distended and bleed. This bleeding can be manifested by the vomiting of blood and/or rectal bleeding. Bleeding varices results in hypovolemia, shock, and death. This complication is an emergency, requiring immediate interventions that can be both nonsurgical and surgical therapies and include the following:

▶ Pharmocological agents vasopressin (Pitressin), propranolol (Inderal), and octreotide (Somastatin) to constrict the arterial bed and decrease portal hypertension.

▶ Balloon tamponade via insertion of a Sengstaken-Blakemore tube (shown in Figure 9.6) to put direct pressure on the bleeding sites.

CAUTION

Rupture of the balloon can cause airway obstruction and aspiration of GI secretions. Asphyxiation can also occur if the tube is pulled into the oropharynx area.

▶ Endoscopic procedures involve the use of sclerotherapy by direct injection of the varices with a sclerosing agent or use of rubber bands to perform banding ligation to cause sclerosing of the area.

▶ Transjugular intrahepatic portosystemic shunting (TIPS) involves the use of a threading technique to advance a cannula into the portal vein and the use of a stent.

▶ Surgical treatments include shunting or bypass by using a portal systemic shunt, ligation of the varices, or esophageal transection or devascularization.

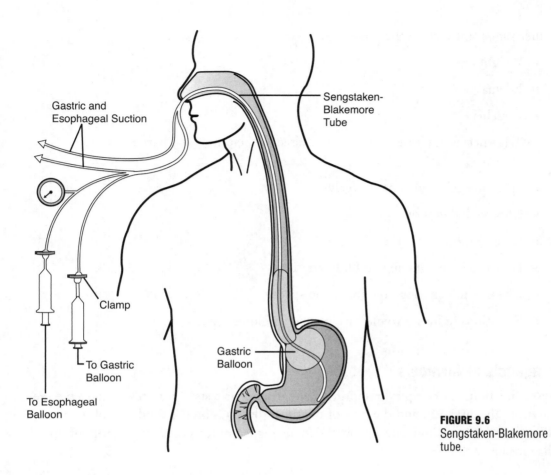

Gastric and
Esophageal Suction

Sengstaken-
Blakemore
Tube

Clamp

To Gastric
Balloon

To Esophageal
Balloon

Gastric
Balloon

FIGURE 9.6
Sengstaken-Blakemore
tube.

Other complications of cirrhosis of the liver include the following:

▶ Coagulation abnormality

▶ Jaundice

▶ Peritonitis

Another complication not related to portal hypertension is hepatic encephalopathy or hepatic coma. Occurring in later stages of cirrhosis, it is thought to result from toxic substances not being broken down by the liver to be eliminated. This results in accumulation of the waste in the client's blood and elevated serum ammonia levels. Signs of encephalopathy include restlessness, agitation, mental changes, asterixis (flapping tremors of the hands when arms are outstretched), and fetor hepaticus (a musty, sweet odor of a patients' breath).

Early indications of cirrhosis may be non-specific and include the following:

▶ Malaise

▶ Weight changes

▶ Abdominal pain and tenderness

▶ Dry skin and itching

Other symptoms include the following:

▶ Weight loss

▶ Edema

▶ Petechiae

▶ Telangiectasias (vessel lesions that are red in the center and have extended branches)

▶ Splenomegaly and hepatomegaly

▶ Chronic indigestion

▶ Constipation or diarrhea

▶ Deficiencies of vitamins A, D, E, and K

▶ Changes in behavior, cognition, and speech

▶ Elevations in liver enzymes, BUN, and ammonia levels

Diagnosis of Cirrhosis

Liver functions are complex, requiring many diagnostic tests. These tests determine the extent of the cirrhosis, and the type of treatment depends on the condition of the liver. The test reviewer will need to know the following list of tests or exams important in diagnosing cirrhosis:

▶ Laboratory tests (liver enzymes—elevated AST, ALT, LDH, prothrombin time-prolonged, and increased ammonia levels)

▶ Upper gastrointestinal x-ray

▶ CT scan

▶ Liver ultrasound

▶ Esophogastroduodenoscopy (EGD)

▶ Liver biopsy

CAUTION

Frequent assessments for bleeding are necessary in clients who have had a liver biopsy performed. Coagulation tests are usually done prior to the procedure for safety reasons. After the procedure, clients lie on their right side on a sandbag or a rolled towel to provide pressure to the area to prevent bleeding.

Treatment of Cirrhosis

The treatment regimen for clients with cirrhosis is based on the symptoms the client is exhibiting. For example, if the client is retaining fluids, diuretics are prescribed. Diet interventions include a diet to promote healing of liver tissue. The client would need increased calories, increased proteins, and low-sodium food sources.

> **NOTE**
>
> If the client has advanced liver disease or portal-systemic encephalopathy(PSE), protein sources are restricted due to the liver's inability to convert protein to urea for excretion.

Medications prescribed for clients with cirrhosis include antacids for gastric distress that could lead to bleeding, diuretics for fluid and ascites, and cathartics and enemas (lactulose [Cephulac]) to correct the pH in the bowel and rid the body of ammonia. Other treatments the candidate should know for the exam include the following:

- Teach the client to avoid alcohol and medications detoxified by the liver
- Heme-test all stools and vomitus
- Record weight
- Intake and output
- Measure abdominal girth daily
- Use small needles for injections and maintain pressure for five minutes after injections due to bleeding tendencies

Acute Pancreatitis

Pancreatitis is an acute inflammation of the pancreas associated with auto digestion. The disease can be life-threatening. Enzymes secreted by the pancreas (lipase, amylase, trypsin, and so on) destroy the tissue of the pancreas. Consistent alcohol intake for 5–10 years is the common causative factor in middle-aged men with pancreatitis. Women are most often affected after gallbladder inflammation or problems in the biliary tract. The following list highlights some of the causes of pancreatitis:

- Biliary disease
- Alcoholism
- Bacterial or viral infections
- Blunt abdominal trauma
- Peptic ulcer disease
- Ischemic vascular disease
- Surgery on or near the pancreas
- Long-term use of steroids, thiazide diuretics, oral contraceptives, sulfonamides, or opiates
- Familial, inherited pancreatitis
- Endoscopic retrograde cholangiopancreatography (ERCP) procedure

The symptoms of pancreatitis vary by the degree of involvement. One of the prominent symptoms correlating with this disorder is pain. The pain is usually in the epigastric area and can radiate to the back. Other symptoms of pancreatitis include the following:

▶ Nausea and vomiting

▶ Abdominal distention

▶ Positive Cullen's and Turner's signs

NOTE

Cullen's sign is recognized as periumbilical bluish discoloration of the skin. When the ecchymosis is noted on the flank area it is called Turner's sign. These signs may indicate intraperitoneal hemorrhage.

▶ Palpable abdominal mass

▶ Steatorrhea

Diagnosis of Pancreatitis

A diagnosis of acute pancreatitis is made by the clinical picture of the client and diagnostic tests. The major laboratory tests to diagnose this disorder are serum amylase and lipase. These tests will show an elevation with pancreatitis. More laboratory tests—for example, elevated white blood cell counts, decreased calcium and magnesium, and elevated glucose levels—might also be done to determine a diagnosis.

NOTE

Amylase levels elevate in 12–24 hours after inflammation and stay elevated for 3–4 days. Lipase levels are more specific for pancreatitis and remain elevated for up to 2 weeks.

Hypocalcemia and hypomagnesia indicate that fat necrosis has occurred.

Other exams, x-rays, and endoscopic procedures affiliated with the diagnosis of pancreatitis that you should know are as follows:

▶ CT scan

▶ MRI

▶ ERCP

Treatment of Pancreatitis

The treatment modalities for the client with pancreatitis focus on relieving the client's symptoms and preventing or treating complications. The client is kept NPO, in the acute episode, with administration of IV fluids to inhibit stimulation and secretion of pancreatic enzymes. A nasogastric tube is usually inserted to decrease abdominal distention, prevent vomiting, and prevent hydrochloric acid from entering the duodenum. Other forms of therapy utilized to treat these clients include the following:

▶ Observe for signs of bleeding. To prevent excessive bleeding, use small-gauge needles for IM, IV, or subcutaneous injections and maintain pressure for five minutes after any injections have been given.

▶ Medications, including the following:

  ▶ Analgesics for pain which may be given by the PCA method.

  ▶ Ranitidine (Zantac)

  ▶ Calcitonin (Calcimar)

  ▶ Viokase

  ▶ Vitamins A, D, E, and K

  ▶ Antibiotics

  ▶ Insulin

▶ After oral feedings begin, the diet should be low-fat and low-protein and the client should avoid caffeine and alcohol.

▶ ABGs to detect early respiratory complications.

▶ ERCP if gallstones need to be removed, along with a sphincterotomy.

▶ Monitor vital signs.

Surgical intervention is required if gallstones are present and cannot be removed by ERCP or if complications such as pseudocysts and abscesses have formed. Clients requiring drainage of cysts or abscesses could have external drains post operatively. Nursing postoperative interventions include the following:

▶ Monitoring drainage tubes for amount, character, and patency

▶ Meticulous skin care and dressing changes

▶ Working with an enterostomy nurse for promotion and maintenance of skin integrity

Cholecystitis/Cholelithiasis

Cholecystitis is inflammation of the gallbladder. Cholelithiasis occurs when gallstones are formed due to bile that is usually stored in the gallbladder hardening into stone-like material. Precipitates of cholesterol, bilirubin, and calcium produce gallstones.

Causes of gallbladder disease include a familial tendency for the development of this disease, but it can also be due to dietary habits. It is also associated with certain drugs, such as cholesterol-lowering agents. People with diabetes, hemolytic blood disorders, and Crohn's disease have a higher risk of development.

> **TIP**
>
> An easy way to remember who usually develops gallstones is to remember these four Fs of gallbladder disease:
>
> ► Female (sex)
> ► Forty (usual age)
> ► Fat (usually obese)
> ► Fertile (usually have children)

Symptoms of Cholecystitis and Cholelithiasis

The symptoms that occur with cholecystitis and cholethiasis are usually associated with pain. The client might also exhibit jaundice of the skin, sclerae, and upper palate. With cholelithiasis, the stones might block the flow of bile from the gallbladder. Symptoms the nurse might observe include the following:

► Abdominal pain in right upper quadrant, especially after a fatty meal or a large volume meal. The pain can radiate to the right shoulder.

► Abdominal distention.

► Dyspepsia.

► Eructation.

► Flatulence.

► Fever.

► Clay-colored stools.

► Dark urine.

► Nausea and vomiting.

► Palpable mass in the abdomen.

► Steatorrhea.

Diagnosis of Cholecystitis/Cholelithiasis

The client's health assessment, pain location, and history assist in diagnosis. There is no specific laboratory test, but the CBC might reveal an elevated WBC, and liver and pancreatic enzymes might be elevated if the liver and pancreas are involved. Other X-ray exams that may be performed are as follows:

► Abdominal x-ray

► Gallbladder ultrasound (the most frequently ordered test for diagnosis)

- Cholecystography (rarely done) using contrast media (Telepaque, Cholografin, or Oragrafin):

    - The client is held NPO for 10–12 hours before x-ray.

    - A laxative or cleansing enema is ordered the evening prior to x-ray.

- Hepatobiliary scan.

- ERCP (used in clients who have an allergy to contrast media).

Treatment of Cholecystitis

Interventions for gallbladder inflammation and stones are supportive. Clients with cholecystitis might be treated conservatively or surgically. Conservative treatment is directed toward the relief of inflammation of the gallbladder and eliminating pain. This goal is accomplished by placing the client NPO with IV fluids and NG suction. Anticholinergics may be given to help with the spasm of smooth muscles.

Antibiotics are administered intravenously, especially if the client's WBC count is elevated. When the client has improved, diet intake is reinstituted with a gradual introduction of low-fat liquids and a high-protein, high-carbohydrate diet. Foods allowed and foods to avoid for clients recovering from a gallbladder attack are as follows:

- **Foods allowed:** Skim milk, cooked fruits, rice, tapioca, lean meats, mashed potatoes, non–gas-forming vegetables, bread, coffee, and tea

- **Foods to avoid:** Eggs, cream, pork, fried foods, cheese, rich dressings, gas-forming vegetables, and alcohol

Treatment of Cholethiasis

General treatments of cholethiasis include PO medication, lithotripsy procedures, and surgery. Small stones and radiolucent cholesterol stones can be treated with ursodeoxycholic acid (UDCA) or chenodeoxycholic acid (CDCA). These drugs are bile acids that can be used to dissolve the gallstones. It can take up to two years for the medication to work and is usually reserved for older clients who are not good surgical candidates. Approximately one-half of people who take these drugs have a recurrence of the stones after the medication is stopped.

Another form of treatment that can be used for clients with gallstones is extracorpeal shock wave lithotripsy (ESWL). A patient must have normal gallbladder function, mild symptomology, and small stones to meet the criteria for ESWL. In this procedure, the client is placed in certain positions as repeated shockwaves are directed at gallstones to cause them to fragment. After the stones are broken into small pieces, they can then pass through the common bile duct easily, be retrieved by endoscopy, or be dissolved by the bile acid drugs mentioned previously. This procedure is done on an outpatient basis, and the client resumes a regular routine within 48 hours.

The final and most common type of treatment for gallstones is surgery. The surgeries that can be performed are laparoscopic and abdominal cholecystectomy. Laparoscopic surgery is a minimally invasive surgery and accounts for more than half of all cholecystectomies.

When this surgical procedure is used, a small incision or puncture wound is made through the abdominal wall. Other puncture wounds allow for the introduction of surgical instruments to remove the gallbladder and stones.

Laparoscopic surgery is usually performed as same-day surgery in an ambulatory care facility. Its advantages are less postoperative pain, decreased likelihood of paralytic ileus, and quicker resumption of preoperative activity. After the surgery, the patient's diet consist of clear liquids on the day of the procedure and light meals for a few more days after the procedure.

The second type of procedure is the abdominal cholecystectomy. This procedure is reserved for those with large stones or with extensive involvement of the duct system. The surgical procedure involves ligation of the cystic duct and artery and removal of the gallbladder. Insertion of a Penrose drain allows the drainage of serosanguinous fluid and bile into an absorbent dressing. If the common bile duct was manipulated, a T-tube is usually inserted in the duct to keep it open until swelling diminishes. The T-tube can remain in place for up to six weeks. The diet of clients who have undergone abdominal cholecystectomies is advanced from clear liquids to solid foods. The client usually returns to his usual routine or work in four to six weeks.

Clostridium Difficile

Clostridium difficile (C. difficile) is a serious bacterial infection that is a common cause of antibiotic associated diarrhea. The bacteria is highly associated with being in a healthcare setting. The risk of getting the spore forming bacillus increases with

- Exposure to antibiotics
- Lengthy stays in a healthcare setting
- The patient being immunosuppressed
- The patient being elderly
- Postoperative gastrointestinal surgery or manipulation

Symptoms associated with C. difficile include the following:

- Mild to severe watery diarrhea
- Elevated temperature

▶ Abdominal pain or cramping

▶ Anorexia

Common laboratory test used to diagnose this include a stool culture for the presence of C. difficile. Stool culture results are available after 48–96 hours of the performance of the test. Antigen C. difficile testing consists of a rapid detection test that can provide results in one hour or less, but it needs to be performed with toxin testing to verify a diagnosis.

Management of a patient with C. difficile is accomplished via pharmacological treatment with antibiotics. Metrodnidazole (Flagyl) is prescribed initially. If Flagyl is not effective, vancomycin (Vancocin) is usually ordered. Symptoms might end without treatment when a patient's antibiotics are discontinued. The nurse should be alert for progression of the disease that can lead to associated C. difficile complications, including:

▶ Pseudomembranous colitis

▶ Perforation of the colon

▶ Sepsis

An important part of nursing care for these patients includes infection control measures. The disease is usually transmitted by healthcare personnel who have touched a contaminated surface or item. Any object contaminated with the feces can serve as a reservoir for the spores. The spores can remain on inanimate objects for several days. Preventive measures include

▶ Placing patients with C. difficile in private rooms

▶ Using contact precautions for patients with known or suspected C. difficile (gown and gloves for care, dedicated room equipment)

▶ Strict handwashing with alcohol-based hand rub or soap and water

▶ Teaching family members infection-control measures

Food-Borne Illnesses

Food-borne illnesses commonly cause gastrointestinal problems in clients in the United States. These illnesses result when a person receives an infectious organism with the intake of food. You need to be prepared to answer questions relating directly to these diagnoses. Table 9.3 discusses the most common types of illnesses and accentuates the major points of these disorders.

TABLE 9.3 Food-Borne Illnesses

Illness	Source of Infection	Symptoms	Treatment	Preventative Measures
Botulism (incubation time is 18–36 hours)	Improperly canned fruits and vegetables; it's less common in meats and fish.	Nausea, vomiting, diarrhea, weakness, dysphagia, dysarthria, paralysis, and respiratory failure.	NPO, IV fluid replacement, trivalent botulism antitoxin, and respiratory support	Home-canning containers should be boiled for at least 20 minutes.
E. Coli (incubation time varies with specific strain)	Undercooked beef and shellfish; food and water contaminated with fecal material.	Vomiting, diarrhea, abdominal cramping, fever. Some cases have proven fatal due to rapid fluid loss and organ failure.	IV fluid replacement and antibiotic administration	Thoroughly cook meat.
Salmonella (incubation time is 8–24 hours)	Contaminated food and drinks, raw eggs.	Fever, nausea, vomiting, cramping, abdominal pain, diarrhea.	NPO, IV fluid replacement	Good hand-washing.
Staphylococcal (incubation time is 2–4 hours)	Meat, dairy products, human carriers.	Abrupt vomiting, abdominal cramping, diarrhea, weakness.	Replacement of lost fluid volume and electrolytes	Properly prepare and store food.

Case Study

A 44-year-old is admitted with pain in the epigastric region of the abdomen. The probable diagnosis is pancreatitis. As the primary nurse for this client, evaluate the following scenarios:

1. What laboratory tests and x-rays will you expect the physician to order to confirm your client's pancreatitis diagnosis?

2. The treatment regimen includes prescriptions to start an IV of NS @ 150 mL/hr; insert an NG tube to low wall suction; keep the client NPO; Demerol 100 mg every 4 hours as needed for pain; consult the pharmacy for total parenteral nutrition (TPN). Discuss the purpose of each of the preceding physician prescriptions.

3. Within 24 hours, a diagnosis of pancreatitis is confirmed. You are documenting a nursing care plan for this client. Which priority nursing diagnoses will you include in the plan of care?

4. What are some important assessments you will make on this client while he is in your care?

Answers to Case Study

1. The nurse caring for a client with pancreatitis would expect an order for a serum lipase and serum and urine amylase. These values increase because pancreatic enzymes are released into the blood stream with the auto digestion of the pancreas. Serum amylase levels will return to normal in 48–72 hours and serum lipase levels remain up for 1–2 weeks. A CBC might reveal a decrease in hemoglobin and hematocrit levels and an increase in white blood cell count. A serum calcium, magnesium, and glucose would also be ordered, revealing hypocalcemia, hypomagnesium, and hyperglycemia. X-ray studies that the nurse would anticipate include abdominal and chest x-rays, CT scan, and ultrasound. These x-rays demonstrate cysts and abscesses in the pancreas and rule out other causes of the client's symptoms.

(continues)

(continued)

2. These physician prescriptions are common for clients with pancreatitis. IV fluids are ordered to administer medications and replace fluids and electrolytes. Insertion of an NG tube and NPO status serve several functions: they prevent nausea and vomiting, relieve pain, allow the intestines and pancreas to rest, decrease pancreatic secretion of enzymes, and promote ventilation by relieving distention. TPN is ordered because the client is not permitted food and fluids and the nutritional status must be maintained. The nurse should monitor laboratory exams and weigh the client daily to assess the efficiency of the TPN treatment. Demerol is given for pain to provide comfort for the client.

3. The major nursing diagnoses for a client with pancreatitis will focus on his immediate problems, as well as prevention of common complications that can develop from the pancreatitis. These include the following:

   ▶ Ineffective breathing pattern related to pain, pancreas proximity to the diaphragm, and possible pleural effusion

   ▶ Acute pain related to inflammation of the pancreas

   ▶ Imbalance in nutrition related to inability to ingest needed nutrients, increased caloric body demands, and anorexia

4. The nurse must be astute when caring for clients with this diagnosis because complications commonly occur. The nurse will assess for pain, its location and intensity, precipitating factors, and relieving methods. Alcohol intake is often associated with a pancreatitis diagnosis, so the nurse questions the client about alcohol intake. The nurse will also monitor for associated nausea and vomiting, constipation, and steatorrhea. Assessment of the abdomen is done for the presence or absence of bowel sounds, areas of pain and tenderness, and distention and rigidity. The nurse assesses for breath sounds, as well as respiratory pattern, chest movement, and skin color, for any indications of respiratory distress. Along with the physiological assessments, the nurse must also be aware of the psychosocial needs by monitoring for emotional stability and effective coping methods.

Key Concepts

This chapter includes much-needed information to help the nurse apply knowledge of gastrointestinal disorders to the NCLEX exam. The nurse preparing for the licensure exam should be familiar with commonly ordered lab tests, including normal lab values, and medications used to treat the client with gastrointestinal disorders.

Key Terms

- Alopecia
- Anorexia
- Ascites
- Asphyxiation
- Asterixis
- Cullen's sign
- Dyspepsia
- Dysphagia
- Eructation
- Evisceration
- Extrapyramidal
- Fetor hepaticus
- Flatulence
- Hememesis
- Hepatic coma
- Hepatomegaly
- Intermittent tenesmus
- Jaundice
- Malaise
- Melena
- Neutropenia
- Odynophagia
- Polyarthralgia
- Rovsing's sign

- Splenomegaly
- Steatorrhea
- Tardive dyskinesia
- Thrombocytopenia
- Turner's sign

Diagnostic Tests

Most of the diagnostic exams for the gastrointestinal system are directly related to the anatomical area needing visualization. These clients would receive the usual routine exams: CBC, urinalysis, chest-xray. The exam reviewer should be knowledgeable of the preparation and care of clients receiving gastrointestinal exams. While reviewing these diagnostic exams, the exam reviewer should be alert for information that would be an important part of nursing care for these clients:

- Barium enema
- Barium swallow
- Colonoscopy and sigmoidoscopy
- CT scan
- Endoscopic exams
- ERCP
- Gallbladder and abdominal ultrasound
- Gastric analysis and biopsy
- *H. pylori*
- Liver biopsy
- pH monitoring

Pharmacological Agents Used in the Care of the Client with Disorders of the Gastrointestinal System

An integral part of care to clients with gastrointestinal disorders is pharmacological intervention. These medications provide an improvement or cure of the client's GI problems. The nursing exam reviewer needs to focus on the drugs in Table 9.4. Included in this table are the most common side and adverse effects and pertinent nursing care. These medications are not inclusive of all the agents used to treat gastrointestinal disorders; therefore, you should keep a current pharmacology text handy for reference.

TABLE 9.4   Pharmacological Agents Used in the Care of the Client with Disorders of the Gastrointestinal System

Name/Classification	Action	Side Effects	Nursing Care
Pantoprazole (Protonix)/ proton pump inhibitor	Decreases gastric acid	Headache, abdominal pain, diarrhea, flatulence, increased blood sugar.	Assess for melena and hememesis; IV doses should be administered through a filter over a 15-minute period.
Famotidine (Pepcid)/H2 antagonist	Management of hypersecretion	Confusion, dizziness, headache, altered taste, diarrhea, decreased sperm count, anemia, neutropenia, thrombocytopenia.	IV administration over at least 2 minutes after diluting to 2 mL with NaCl. Assess for blood in stool and emesis. Assess for confusion, especially in the elderly. Instruct the client to avoid alcohol and drugs containing aspirin or NSAIDs.
Misoprostol (Cytotec)/ prostaglandin	Antisecretion of gastric acid and increases protective mucus	Headache, abdominal pain, dyspepsia, flatulence, menstrual disorders.	Causes spontaneous abortion. Assess for blood in stool and emesis.
Esomeprazole (Nexium)/ proton pump inhibitor	Decreases acid	Same as Protonix.	Increase risk of bleeding with warfarin. Do not crush or chew pellets; capsule can be emptied, mixed with apple-sauce, and swallowed imme-diately if the patient has dysphagia. Assess for melena and hememsesis.
Magnesium hydroxide/ aluminum hydroxide (Maalox, Mylanta), (Gaviscon) antacids	Neutralizes gastric acid, decreases gas bubbles	Constipation, diarrhea, magnesium salts cause increased serum magnesium levels. Aluminum salts cause decrease in serum phosphorus.	Destroys coating of enteric-coated drugs resulting in altered absorption of these drugs.
Mesalamine (Asacol); olsalazine/ GI anti-inflammatory (Dipentum)	Decreases inflammation in the colon	Headache, dizziness, malaise, weakness, nausea and vomiting, flatulence. Olsalazine can cause blood dyscrasias and drug-induced hepatitis. Mesalamine only can cause pancreatitis, hair loss, runny nose, and pharyngitis.	Be alert for allergy to sulfa drugs. The client needs to drink 6–8 glasses of fluids per day to prevent crystalluria and kidney stones.

TABLE 9.4 *Continued*

Name/Classification	Action	Side Effects	Nursing Care
Infliximab (Remicade)/ antirheumatic, GI anti-inflammatory	Anti-inflammation in joints and the colon	Fatigue, headache, upper respiratory infection, abdominal pain, nausea and vomiting, dysuria, acne, alopecia, rash, fever, infusion reactions.	Assess for IV infusion reaction: fever, chills, rash, polyarthralgia, and itching. Reaction can occur 2 hours after administration. Reaction can occur even if the first dose didn't cause a reaction.
Metoclopramide (Reglan)/antiemetic	Hastens gastric emptying	Drowsiness, extrapyramidal reactions, restlessness, arrhythmias, hyper- or hypotension, constipation, diarrhea.	Give slowly IV over a 2-minute duration. Monitor the client for tardive dyskinesia, and extrapyramidal side effects.
Midazolam (Versed)/ sedative, hypnotic	Produces central nervous system depression	Agitation, drowsiness, apnea, laryngospasm, respiratory depression, hiccups, arrhythmias.	Assess for side effects, especially respiratory depression. Have resuscitative equipment and reversal drug flumazenil (Romazicon) available.

CAUTION

Versed administration is usually limited to a registered nurse with sedation training.

Propofol (Diprivan)/ general anesthetic	Short-acting hypnotic	Dizziness, headache, apnea, bradycardia, hypotension, respiratory depression.	Assess respiratory status continually during therapy. Aseptic technique is required when handling the drug due to rapid bacterial growth in the solution.

CAUTION

This is usually administered by a certified registered nurse anesthetist. It can be used in the intensive care unit on mechanically ventilated patients by a registered nurse.

Apply Your Knowledge

This chapter provided information regarding the care of clients with gastrointestinal disorders. The following questions test your knowledge regarding the safe, effective care and management of the client with various GI disorders. The nurse should use the key terms, diagnostics, chapter content, and pharmacological agents sections to assist in answering these questions.

Exam Questions

1. A client presents to the clinic complaining of heartburn and difficulty swallowing. A tentative diagnosis of GERD is made by the healthcare provider. What other symptom would the nurse expect the client to exhibit?

   A. Globus

   B. Dryness of the mouth

   C. Vomiting

   D. Blood in the stool

2. The nurse is performing discharge teaching to a client diagnosed with GERD. Which statement by the client indicates a need for further instruction?

   A. "I should limit food intake to three large meals per day."

   B. "I need to remain upright for one to two hours after meals."

   C. "Since I am overweight, I need to follow a weight reduction diet."

   D. "I should avoid wearing tight-fitting clothes."

3. A client has returned from an open surgical procedure for a hiatal hernia repair. Which nursing intervention is a priority?

   A. Providing pain medication as needed

   B. Assisting with and monitoring incentive spirometry

   C. Assessing for bladder distention every four hours

   D. Lowering the head of the bed to prevent hypovolemia

4. A client is complaining of epigastric pain after eating. The physician suspects peptic ulcer disease (PUD) and orders a urea breath test for *H. pylori*. Which would the nurse include in the teaching plan for test preparation?

   A. Clear liquids the day before the test

   B. Nothing by mouth the night before the test

   C. High-fat meal two hours before the test

   D. Asking the client to bring a sputum sample with her for analysis

5. The nurse is caring for a client with cholecystitis. Which clinical manifestation would the nurse expect the client to exhibit?

   A. Hiccups

   B. Dysphagia

   C. Fever

   D. Bradycardia

6. The nurse in the emergency room observes a physician examining a client with possible appendicitis. The physician presses downward on the right lower quadrant of the abdomen and asks the client to instruct him when he feels pain (application of pressure or pressure release). What is the physician assessing for?

   A. Rebound tenderness

   B. Rovsing's sign

   C. Turner's sign

   D. Ascites

7. The nurse is caring for a client admitted with a diagnosis of pancreatitis. Which laboratory value is the most reliable indicator of acute pancreatitis?

   A. Hemoglobin of 12.0 g/dL

   B. White blood cell count of 14,000

   C. Amylase of 460

   D. Potassium of 3.1 mEq/L

8. A client who has long-term cholethiasis is being assessed for fat-soluble vitamin deficiencies. Which clinical manifestation would correlate with a deficiency in these vitamins?

   A. Numbness on the side of the face

   B. Yellow sclera

   C. Bleeding gums

   D. Constipation

9. A client is admitted with cirrhosis of the liver and fluid in the peritoneal cavity. The physician instructs the nurse to prepare the client for a paracentesis. Which intervention would be included in preparation?

   A. Placing the client in the prone position

   B. Starting an IV with an 18-gauge needle

   C. Obtaining a lipid profile

   D. Assessing that the client empties the bladder

10. The nurse has instructed a client with diverticulosis in a high-fiber diet. Which menu selection indicates understanding of the diet?

   A. Sliced turkey on white bread

   B. Beef broth

   C. Spinach salad

   D. Froot Loops cereal with milk

Answers to Exam Questions

1. Answer A is correct. Globus, or a feeling that something is in the back of the throat, is a clinical manifestation of GERD and should be expected. Answers B, C, and D are not usually associated with GERD, so they are incorrect.

2. Answer A is correct. Clients with GERD should eat four to six small meals per day to prevent reflux rather than three large meals. Answers B, C, and D are recommendations for health promotion tactics to control reflux. Other aspects include no snacking in the evening; no food two to three hours before bedtime; elevating the head of the bed at night; avoiding heavy lifting and straining; and limiting fatty, spicy foods, coffee, chocolate, alcohol, and colas.

3. Answer B is correct. Prevention of any respiratory complications is the primary focus of nursing interventions after an open procedure to repair a hiatal hernia. Incentive spirometry promotes deep breathing and lung expansion. Answers A and C are both important nursing interventions, but do not directly relate to the respiratory system, so they are incorrect. Answer D has no data in the stem to support the action, making it incorrect. The client would need the HOB to be elevated to lower the diaphragm and facilitate lung expansion.

4. Answer B is correct. The only preparation for *H. pylori* urea breath test is NPO after midnight. In this test, the client drinks a carbon-enriched urea liquid and then CO_2 is measured for *H. pylori*. Answers A, C, and D are not part of the preparation for an *H. pylori* urea breath test, so they are incorrect options.

5. Answer C is correct. Other clinical manifestations include pain, nausea, vomiting, rebound tenderness upon palpation, flatulence, and indigestion. Answers A, B, and D are not associated with cholecystitis, so they are incorrect.

6. Answer A is correct. Rebound tenderness indicates peritoneal irritation. The client experiences increased pain when the examiner releases pressure in a positive result of this assessment technique. Answers B and C are exhibited by other assessment measures, so they are incorrect. Answer D is a condition of excessive peritoneal fluid in the abdominal cavity associated with liver disorders.

7. Answer C is correct. Amylase and lipase are reliable tests used for pancreatitis diagnosis. The answers in A, B, and D are not directly related to the pancreas and not diagnostic, so they are incorrect.

8. Answer C is correct. The fat-soluble vitamins are A, D, E, and K. A deficiency in vitamin K results in ineffective prothrombin, which can cause bleeding and bruising. The answers in A and D have no relationship to gallstones, so they are incorrect. Answer B occurs with blockage and backup of bile, so it is incorrect.

9. Answer D is correct. The bladder should be empty for a paracentesis procedure to prevent incidental puncturing. Answer A is incorrect because the client sits upright for the procedure and prone places the client on the abdomen. Answer B and C are not necessary interventions for a paracentesis, so they are incorrect.

10. Answer C is correct. Spinach has a larger amount of fiber than any of the other choices listed. The answers in A, B, and D have minimal fiber content, so they are incorrect.

Suggested Reading and Resources

▶ Brunner, L., and D. Suddarth. *Textbook of Medical Surgical Nursing*. 10th ed. Philadelphia: Lippincott Williams & Wilkins, 2009.

▶ Deglin, Judith H., and April H. Vallerand. *Davis Drug Guide for Nurses*. Philadelphia: F. A. Davis, 2009.

▶ Ignatavicius, D., and S. Workman. *Medical Surgical Nursing: Critical Thinking for Collaborative Care*. 6th ed. Philadelphia: Elsevier, 2007.

▶ Lewis, S., M. Heitkemper, S. Dirksen, P. O'Brien, and L. Bucher. *Medical Surgical Nursing: Assessment and Management of Clinical Problems*. 7th ed. Philadelphia: Elsevier, 2007.

▶ Rinehart, Sloan, Hurd, *NCLEX-RN Exam Cram*. Indianapolis: Que Publishing, 2007.

▶ Smith, F., D. Duell, and B. Martin, *Clinical Nursing Skills Basic to Advanced Skills*. 7th ed. Upper Saddle River, NJ: Pearson Prentice Hall, 2008.

▶ Centers for Disease Control and Prevention: www.cdc.gov

CHAPTER TEN

Care of the Client with Hematological Disorders

The hematologic system consists of blood, blood cells, and blood forming organs. Because the circulation of blood provides oxygen and nutrients to all body systems, a functioning hematological system is essential to health and well-being. A disorder in the system might result from a lack of function, a reduction in production, or an increase in the destruction of blood cells. This chapter reviews common disorders affecting the blood.

Anemia

When anemia occurs, people have a decrease in the number of red blood cells or a decrease in the capability of these red blood cells to carry oxygen. Anemia is not a disease but is a symptom of other disorders, such as thalassemia and iron deficiency anemia. The causes of anemia are as follows:

- ▶ Increased red blood cell destruction
- ▶ Blood loss
- ▶ Poor dietary iron intake
- ▶ Poor absorption
- ▶ Parasites

The symptoms of anemia are as follows:

- ▶ Fatigue
- ▶ Pallor (skin might be waxy)
- ▶ Tachypnea
- ▶ Cardiac changes (heart murmur, cardiomegaly)
- ▶ Dyspnea
- ▶ Headaches
- ▶ Dizziness
- ▶ Depression
- ▶ Growth retardation
- ▶ Late sexual maturation

> **CAUTION**
>
> Children with persistent anemia might experience frequent bouts of otitis media and upper respiratory infections.

Pernicious Anemia

The intrinsic factor is missing in pernicious anemia, resulting in an inability to absorb vitamin B12. Pernicious anemia is common in the elderly and clients who have had a gastric resection. It can also occur from poor dietary intake of foods containing B12, especially in vegetarian diets or those lacking dairy products. Symptoms of pernicious anemia include

- Pallor
- Jaundice
- Smooth, beefy red tongue (glossitis)
- Fatigue
- Weight loss
- Paresthesia
- Diarrhea
- Problems with proprioception (sense of position in space)

The treatment for pernicious anemia is the administration of injections of cyanocobalamin (vitamin B12). The injections are given weekly until adequate levels are reached, and then monthly for maintenance. The nurse should be aware of the following points when giving this drug:

- Do not mix in a syringe with other medications.
- Administer IM or deep subcutaneously.

Aplastic Anemia

Aplastic anemia is a rare disorder that occurs when there is depression of the blood-forming elements of the bone marrow. The cells are replaced with fat. Symptoms associated with aplastic anemia include

- Decreased erythrocytes
- Leukopenia
- Thrombocytopenia

Aplastic anemia can be either primary (congenital) or secondary (acquired). Approximately half of all acquired cases are from unknown causes. Several factors can contribute to the development of aplastic anemia and can include

- Drug toxicity, especially chemotherapeutic agents and the antibiotic chloramphenicol
- Multiple blood transfusions
- Radiation exposure
- Autoimmune states
- Sickle cell syndrome
- Leukemia
- HIV
- Hepatitis B

Treatment of acquired aplastic anemia is accomplished by first identifying that something is preventing the bone marrow from carrying out its basic function. The focus of treatment is on the identification and removal of the offending agent. The client might also receive immunosuppressive therapies, including

- Antilymphocyte globulin (ALG) or antithymocyte globulin (ATG)
- Androgens
- Cyclosporine (Sandimmune)
- Methylprednisolone

Because of the possible fatal course that can develop from this disease, a bone marrow transplantation is also a treatment for consideration early in the disease.

Sickle Cell Anemia

Sickle cell anemia is the most common genetic disease found in the United States. It is more common in the African-American population. This disorder is inherited as autosomal recessive. A disease inherited in this manner is characterized by each parent having the sickle cell trait, resulting in a 25% chance of producing offspring with sickle cell anemia with each pregnancy.

A client with sickle cell anemia has red blood cells that have an abnormal crescent shape, as illustrated in Figure 10.1. Because they cannot flow easily through tiny capillary beds, they can become clumped, cause obstruction, and become an impairment in tissue perfusion. Red blood cells containing Hgb S are prone to sickling when exposed to decreased oxygen in the blood. After they become sickled, they are more fragile, rigid, and rapidly destroyed.

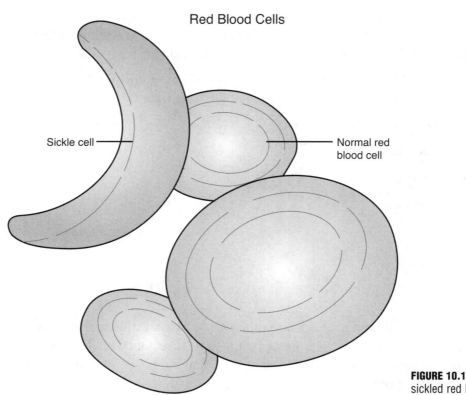

FIGURE 10.1 Normal and sickled red blood cells.

The most common forms of this disease in the United States are

▶ **Sickle cell anemia:** Homozygous form (Hgb S). This is the most severe form; there is no cure.

▶ **Sickle cell-C disease:** Heterozygous (Hgb S and Hgb C).

▶ **S thalassemia disease:** A combination of sickle cell trait and B+–thalassemia trait (patients can still produce normal hemoglobin).

Some clients might have *sickle cell trait*. When this occurs a child inherits normal hemoglobin from one parent and hemoglobin S(the abnormal hemoglobin) from the other. The same defect exists as in sickle cell anemia, but only portions of the hemoglobin are Hgb S. The majority of the blood is Hgb A(normal hemoglobin). These clients might not exhibit symptoms. If these clients are exposed to low oxygen levels, symptomology and severe anemia can occur. Non-painful gross hematuria is the major complication that might occur with sickle cell trait.

The defect in sickle cell anemia can result in an obstruction in blood flow due to sickling or increased destruction of red blood cells (RBCs). Clinical manifestations of the disease are related to these defects and include

▶ Splenomegaly

▶ Hepatomegaly

▶ Hematuria

- Dilute urine

- Enuresis

- Skeletal deformities

- Headaches

- Aphasia

- Seizures

- Stroke

- Cardiomegaly

- Anorexia

- Exercise intolerance

- Hemosiderosis

- Gallstones

- Leg ulcers

- Growth retardation

Several crises or exacerbations happen with sickle cell anemia. Table 10.1 outlines the types of crises associated with sickle cell anemia. The basic pathophysiology for most of the crises involves circulatory compromise in the micro circulation caused by the sickled cells. You should study this table, differentiating the types and placing primary focus on the most common type of crisis: vaso-occlusive.

TABLE 10.1 Sickle Cell Anemia Crises

Type of Crisis	Description	Associated Symptoms Include
Vaso-occlusive	Usually appears after the age of five. Sickling of cells results in obstruction of blood vessels, leading to a lack of oxygen to the area, which causes localized hypoxia and necrosis. It's usually not life-threatening. Hand-foot syndrome can be a result of this crisis. It is a skeletal problem that occurs in children six months to two years of age. Swelling is found in the hands and feet but usually resolves itself in two weeks.	Severe pain: Bone, abdominal, muscular, or thoracic. Jaundice, dark urine, priapism, fever, leukocytosis, lethargy, fatigue, sleepiness.
Sequestration	Occurs between the age of two months and five years. There is massive pooling of RBCs in the liver and spleen.	Lethargy, pale skin, hypovolemia (tachycardia, decrease in urinary output, and so on).

(continues)

TABLE 10.1 *Continued*

Type of Crisis	Description	Associated Symptoms Include
Aplastic	Results from bone marrow depression, is associated with viral infections (especially human parvovirus), and leads to RBC lysis and severe anemia.	Lethargy, pale skin, shortness of breath, altered mental status.
Hyperhemolytic	Rare; the result of certain drugs or infections. RBC destruction occurs.	Abdominal distention, jaundice, dark urine, reticulocytosis. If reticulocytosis occurs, it suggests some other associated problem (for example, a deficiency in glucose-6 phosphate dehydrogenase [G6PD]).
Stroke	Sickled cells block major blood vessels in the brain leading to an infarction.	Neurological impairments (see Chapter 11, "Care of the Client with Neurological Disorders," for clinical manifestations of a stroke).
Chest Syndrome	Similar to pneumonia; due to sickling in lung blood vessels.	Chest pain, fever, cough, anemia.
Overwhelming Infection	Especially streptococcus pneumonia, Haemophilus influenzae. It is due to a defect in spleen function. Alert: This is the number one cause of death in children under the age of five!	Symptoms of infection and septicemia (high fever, tachycardia, tachypnea, and so on).

*Sickle cell crises might be preceded by a recent infection or stressor, dehydration, strenuous activity, or high altitudes.

> **NOTE**
>
> The vaso-occlusive crisis is the primary crisis type that causes the client to have pain.

The treatment for sickle cell anemia is twofold. The goals are to prevent sickling and treat sickle cell crises. This is accomplished by several measures, including

- Decrease energy needs by the use of bedrest during exacerbations or crises.

- Provide frequent rest periods during everyday activities.

- Provide hydration.

- Avoid contact sports due to splenomegaly.

- Replace missing electrolytes.

- Administer prescribed antibiotics.

- Provide vaccination with HIB, pneumococcal, and meningococcal immunizations.

- Administer oxygen as prescribed.

- Administer ordered short-term blood transfusions:

  - Packed RBC in aplastic crises, hyperhemolytic, splenic sequestration, chest syndrome, and stroke.

▶ Blood is also given before major surgery to prevent anoxia and to suppress sickle cell formation.

CAUTION

When multiple transfusions are given, reduce iron overload and hemosiderosis with subcutaneous chelating injections of deferoxamine (Desferal).

▶ A splenectomy might be performed for splenic sequestration.

▶ Manage pain; apply heat to painful areas, if appropriate.

▶ Teach the client to seek medical attention with signs of infection.

▶ Teach the client to avoid high altitudes.

▶ Assess vital signs.

▶ Monitor intake and output.

▶ Pharmacological interventions include

  ▶ Pain medication including morphine sulfate, patient-controlled analgesia, oxycodone, Tylenol with codeine, and NSAIDs

  ▶ Hydroxurea (Droxia)

▶ Provide genetic counseling, including the following information:

  ▶ Sickle cell anemia is an autosomal-recessive disorder.

  ▶ There is a 25% chance of passing the disease to a child.

  ▶ If a child acquires one gene, the child is also a carrier.

TIP

An easy way to remember general nursing care for clients with sickle cell anemia is to remember the following:

  ▶ H—Heat
  ▶ H—Hydration
  ▶ O—Oxygen
  ▶ P—Pain relief

Iron Deficiency Anemia

There is a simple lack of iron in this disorder. It is the most prevalent nutritional disorder in the United States. The cause could be the result of poor dietary intake of iron sources. Age and financial status have an influence in this disorder with 25% of children 6–24 months of age in the low socioeconomic population having a diagnosis of anemia. Adolescents are at risk due to rapid growth needs and inadequate nutritional eating practices. Premature and multiple birth babies have reduced fetal iron supplies, making them at risk of iron deficiency anemia. Other causes are associated factors include

- People on vegetarian diets
- Maternal iron deficiency
- Malabsorptive disorders
- Diarrhea
- Hemorrhage
- Parasite infestations
- B12 and folic acid deficiency

The symptoms of iron deficiency anemia are the same as general anemia. There are a few symptoms for severe, prolonged anemia that are different (included here):

- Brittle nails
- Cheilosis (ulcers in the corner of the mouth)
- Sore tongue
- Koilonchyia (concave or spoon-shaped fingernails)
- Pica (craving to eat unusual substances such as clay or starch)

The management of iron deficiency anemia is conservative. The cause of the anemia is explored. The healthcare provider will focus on determining the source of the blood loss. A stool specimen for occult blood and endoscopic exam might be ordered to rule out these common GI sources of bleeding. A thorough menstrual history is obtained from female patients with anemia to determine whether blood loss might be the source of the anemia.

The treatment for iron deficiency anemia includes treating the underlying cause of the anemia, medications for iron replacement, client education, and administration of blood transfusions in severe cases of depletion. The drugs used during therapy include ferrous sulfate (Feosol) and iron dextran injection (Imferon).

> **TIP**
>
> *IM* iron is called IMferon.

The examinee should remember the following teaching and administration points when giving iron:

- Administer iron preparations with orange juice to enhance absorption.
- If giving an iron elixir, it should be administered through a straw to prevent staining the teeth.

▶ When administering iron IM, it should be given through the IM Z track method.

▶ Instruct the patient that her stools might be dark green or black when taking iron preparations.

▶ When administering IM or IV, monitor closely for anaphylaxis.

▶ Client education should focus on drug administration and side effects. The client should be instructed to increase dietary iron intake (good sources of iron include egg yolk; green, leafy vegetables; iron-fortified cereals; peanut butter; raisins; molasses; beans; oatmeal; dried fruit; and organ meats).

Thalassemia

Thalassemia is an autosomal-recessive group of hereditary blood disorders that is found mostly in the African-Americans, Asian, and the Middle East populations. The most common forms are

▶ **Heterozygous**

  ▶ Thalassemia minor or thalassemia trait (mild microcytic anemia occurs)

  ▶ Thalassemia intermedia (splenomegaly and severe anemia are manifested)

▶ **Homozygous**

  ▶ Thalassemia major or Cooley's anemia (severely anemic), where patients cannot live without blood transfusions.

  ▶ The client's red blood cells are destroyed prematurely.

The signs and symptoms associated with thalassemia are frequently associated with anemia and include

▶ Pallor

▶ Loss of weight

▶ Hepatosplenomegaly

▶ Severe anemia

▶ Folic acid deficiency

▶ Osteoporosis and associated fractures

▶ Heart murmurs

▶ Darkening of skin

▶ Headache

▶ Epistaxis

▶ Gout

▸ Bone pain

▸ Hemosiderosis (excess iron in body tissues)

▸ Hemochromatosis (excess iron storage resulting in cell damage)

The treatment of thalassemia revolves around maintenance of adequate hemoglobin that will allow oxygenation of tissues and prevention and treatment of complications. The following objectives will be accomplished by the nurse:

▸ Administering ordered blood transfusion

▸ Monitoring for excess hemosiderosis and hepatitis

▸ Observing for signs and symptoms of infection

▸ Administering ordered folic acid

▸ Teaching to prevent fractures: no contact sports, slippery rugs, and so on

▸ Implementing iron chelation treatment with deferoxamine (Desferal)

▸ Supporting the patient and family during bone marrow transplantation

Polycythemia Vera

The polycythemia vera disorder is characterized by thicker than normal blood. With polycythemia vera, there is an increase in the client's hemoglobin to levels of 18 g/dL, RBC of 6 million/mm, or hematocrit at 55% or greater and increased platelets.

The clinical manifestations that are assessed in clients with polycythemia vera relate to the increased viscosity of the blood. The following list describes some of the symptoms that are associated with polycythemia vera:

▸ Enlarged spleen

▸ Ruddy or flushed (plethoric) complexion

▸ Angina

▸ Thrombophlebitis

▸ Dizziness

▸ Tinnitus

▸ Fatigue

▸ Paresthesia

▸ Dyspnea

▸ Pruritus

▸ Burning sensation in fingers and toes (erythromelalgia)

If polycythemia vera is not treated, few patients will live longer than two years. Treatments revolve around reducing the thickness of the client's blood and providing an easier flow of blood through the blood vessel. This is accomplished by

- Repeated phlebotomies (2–5 times per week)

- Increasing hydration (3 liters of fluid a day)

- Promoting venous return through

    - Elevation of legs when sitting

    - Use of support hose

- Pharmacological interventions, including the following:

    - Anticoagulant therapy

    - Allopurinol for increased uric acid levels

    - Persantine for ischemic symptoms

    - Hydroxurea (Droxia)

    - Low-dose aspirin

    - Agrylin

> **CAUTION**
>
> With polycythemia, the client is at risk for cerebrovascular accident (CVA), myocardial infarction (MI), and bleeding due to dysfunctional platelets.

Hemophilia

In hemophilia, there is a deficiency of one of the factors necessary for blood coagulation. An abnormal clotting pattern occurs, resulting in an ineffective clot. Hemophilia is inherited as a sex-linked disorder. It is an x-linked recessive disorder. The mother passes this disorder to her male children. When a female inherits the gene from her father, she has a 50% chance of transmitting it to her son. Approximately 40% of patients with hemophilia have no hereditary genetic links. Clients lacking factor VIII have hemophilia A (Classic hemophilia); clients lacking factor IX have hemophilia B (Christmas disease). The discussion that follows focuses on Factor VIII deficiencies because they are the most common (75% of cases).

There are varying degrees of severity associated with hemophilia that relate to the amount of Factor VIII activity. Severe hemophilia occurs when there is 1% of Factor VIII activity. This client can have spontaneous bleeding without trauma. Moderate hemophilia happens with 1%–5% of Factor VIII activity and bleedings occurs with trauma. The last degree of severity is the mild form that occurs with 5%–50% of Factor

VIII active. Clients with mild hemophilia bleed with severe trauma or when surgery is performed. Signs or symptoms of hemophilia include

- Bleeding and bruising easily.

- Prolonged bleeding from any orifice or anywhere in the body.

- Hemorrhaging from minor cuts or with teeth eruption.

- Joint hemorrhages or hemarthrosis. Early signs are stiffness, tingling or aching in the joint, and inability to move the joint. Other symptoms are warmth, redness, swelling, and pain.

- Post-operative hemorrhaging.

- Epistaxis.

- Hematuria.

- Internal bleeding. Spinal cord hematomas can lead to paralysis.

- Intracranial bleeding.

CAUTION

Intracranial bleeding is the major cause of death in clients with hemophilia.

The primary goals of treatment for clients with hemophilia are to promote adequate blood clotting and to prevent and treat complications or problems associated with the disease. Nursing measures for goal accomplishment include the following:

- Administration of prescribed Factor VIII concentrate (monoclonal) and recombinant Factor VIII concentrate (sold as a drug, not a drug product); factor replacement might be administered prophylactically

CAUTION

Cryoprecipitates are no longer used for treatment of hemophilia because HIV and hepatitis cannot be removed.

- **Control localized bleeding**

    - Topical coagulants

    - Institute R-I-C-E (rest, ice, compression, elevation) treatment

- Manage pain (ibuprofen is used with caution due to its platelet inhibition properties)

- No rectal temperatures

- Administer blood transfusion as ordered

▶ Administer prescribed desmopressin acetate (DDAVP) for mild hemophilia (increases Factor VIII by releasing factors from storage sites)

▶ Consult with physical therapy after bleeding under control for muscle and joint strengthening; no passive range of motion due to possibility of rebleed

▶ **Teach family injury prevention**

    ▶ Medic-Alert bracelet

    ▶ Padding of furniture corners, if toddler

    ▶ Avoid contact sports (suggest swimming or golf)

    ▶ Signs and symptoms of hemarthrosis

    ▶ Use of soft toothbrush and regular dental visits

    ▶ Avoid aspirin

    ▶ Genetic counseling

Transfusion Therapy

When clients lack blood or blood components, it might be necessary for these components to be replaced. Possible causes of the need for a transfusion include trauma, red blood cell destruction disorders, and bone marrow depression. Table 10.2 lists some types of blood components with their use, pertinent responsibilities, and information about the specific component. You should recognize the nursing care required with this aspect of care.

TABLE 10.2 Blood Components

Blood Product	Use	Nursing Implications
Whole blood	Trauma, clients who need RBCs and fluid volume, clients with Hgb >6 g/dLor >6–10 g/dL if symptomatic.	Transfuse as soon as possible (usually within 30 minutes from laboratory). Infuse with normal saline only. Volume of 450–500 mL Complete transfusion in four hours. Alert: Never add drugs to blood.
Packed red blood cells (PRBCs)	Loss of blood due to surgery or trauma. Usually given for Hgb less than 6 g/dL; 6–10 g/dL if symptomatic. Used in anemic clients who don't need the volume of whole blood.	Most commonly given blood product. Transfuse as soon as possible (usually within 30 minutes from laboratory). Infuse with normal saline only. Volume 200–250 mL. May transfuse in 2 hours in patients without fluid volume excess risks, but it must be completed in four hours. Alert: Never add drugs to blood.
Platelets	Clients with platelet counts less than 20,000 or less than 80,000 if active bleeding present.	Filter can be used for administration. Volume of 300 mL. Infuse in 15–30 minute time span.

(continues)

TABLE 10.2 *Continued*

Blood Product	Use	Nursing Implications
Fresh frozen plasma (FFP)	Clotting factor deficiency, liver disease, disseminated intravascular coagulation (DIC), clients with prothrombin time (PT) or partial thromboplastin times (PTT) greater than 1.5 times normal.	Benefits only if fresh frozen. Infuse over 20–30 minutes. Volume of 200 mL. Use blood filter for infusion.
White blood cells (WBCs); rarely given	Clients with low WBC counts or sepsis related to neutropenia.	Infuse over one hour. Volume of 400–430 mL. Note: If client has amphotericin B ordered, the drug needs to be separated from this transfusion by a 4–6 hour time span.
Factor VIII or IX	Hemophilia A or B, Von Willebrand's disease, hypofibrinogenemia.	Volume is 10–20 mL/unit. Infuse over 20–30 minutes.

NOTE

If a client is receiving blood components, assess the chart for a physician order, identify the patient by armband numbers, blood bag label, attached tag, requisition slip, and blood expiration date. Each identification should be checked by two registered nurses with documented signatures of the assessment by both.

It is imperative that the nurse follow safety precautions of hospital outlined policies for transfusing blood. Pertinent nursing responsibilities for transfusions include

- ▶ Recording vital signs before starting the transfusion and, per policy, during and post-transfusion.

- ▶ If a client has a temperature above 100° F, the nurse should consult the healthcare provider prior to proceeding with the transfusion.

- ▶ Starting the transfusion slowly. Administer the blood at 3–5 mL/ min for the first 15 minutes. The nurse should stay with the patient during this time period.

CAUTION

Severe reactions occur during the first 50 mL of blood transfused. Stay with the patient for the initial 15–30 minutes of the infusion.

- ▶ Assessing for transfusion reaction (see Table 10.3 for additional information).

- ▶ Administering any prescribed pretransfusion medications (Tylenol and/or Benadryl).

- ▶ Infusing blood at prescribed rate depending on the type or component (refer to Table 10.2).

- ▶ If patient is receiving multiple transfusions, the tubing set should be discontinued within 4 hours to decrease the risk of bacterial contamination.

Transfusion Reactions

Table 10.3 outlines types of reactions associated with blood transfusions. Study the symptoms extensively and expect to see items related to reactions on your nursing exams.

TABLE 10.3   Blood Transfusion Reactions

Type of Reaction	Symptoms	Treatment
Hemolytic (due to blood type or Rh incompatibility)	Headache, chest pain, anxiety, lower back pain, hypotension, tachycardia, tachypnea, hemoglobinemia, bronchospasm, vascular collapse	Stop blood transfusion. Send tubing and blood to laboratory. Maintain blood volume and renal perfusion.
Febrile reaction	Chills, tachycardia, fever, hypotension	Antipyretic administration; pretreat with future transfusions or give washed RBCs.
Allergic reaction (patient usually has a history of allergies)	Urticaria, itching, respiratory distress, anaphylaxis	Pretreat with antihistamine.
Bacterial reaction due to contaminated blood (not a common occurrence)	Tachycardia, hypotension, fever, chills, shock	Same treatment as septic shock.
Circulatory overload (more likely in elderly, children, and clients with multiple transfusions of whole blood)	Symptoms of congestive heart failure: hypertension, bounding pulse, distended neck veins	Monitor intake and output. Infuse blood slowly. Administer ordered diuretics.

Case Study

Joey is a 5-year-old boy admitted to the pediatric unit with a diagnosis of sickle cell anemia. He is in pain, and his parents reported that he had been running a temperature for three days due to bronchitis. The doctor diagnoses vaso-occlusive crisis. Joey's temperature is 101.8°, F and you assess edema of the right knee.

1. What events could have triggered this crisis? Give a description of vaso-occlusive crisis, as well as signs and symptoms associated with the disorder.

2. Name three priority nursing diagnosis on admission of the child.

3. Which plans do you expect to be included in the physician's prescription?

4. This is Joey's first admission with this diagnosis. Name five teaching plans you will use to educate Joey's parents prior to discharge.

(continues)

(continued)

Answers to Case Study

1. Triggers of a crisis include low oxygen levels, stress, infection, and dehydration. A probable cause of Joey's crisis is the infection and fever noted in the client history.

   Vaso-occlusive crisis occurs when sickling cells cause occlusion of vessels, decreasing the amount of oxygen to the localized site causing pain and necrosis. Signs and symptoms include fever, pain, and tissue engorgement.

2. Priority nursing diagnoses include

   - Risk for injury

   - Infection

   - Pain

   - Impaired tissue perfusion

3. The nurse would expect plans to include

   - Hydration implementation PO or IV

   - Oxygen orders and/or blood products to improve tissue perfusion and prevent further sickling

   - Pain medication around the clock

   - A heating pad to involved areas to improve comfort

4. Education needs are related to the disease process and include

   - Preventing crisis (adequate hydration, avoiding altitudes and low oxygen levels, avoiding stress)

   - Signs to observe that indicate a crisis episode

   - Signs and symptoms of infection

   - Resumption of age-appropriate activities that are no contact; for example, swimming

   - Explanation of the disease process and genetic factors

   - Explanation of the healthcare regimen prescribed by the physician

Key Concepts

This chapter discussed the most common types of hematological disorders. The key concepts will help the nursing graduate on the NCLEX exam by focusing on the most commonly used key terms, diagnostic exams, and pharmacological agents used to treat these disorders. This section is covered on the NCLEX exam in the area of physiological integrity.

Key Terms

- Dyspnea
- Enuresis
- Fatigue
- Hemarthrosis
- Hemolysis
- Jaundice
- Leukopenia
- Otitis media
- Pallor
- Paresthesia
- Priapism
- Pruritus
- Sequestration
- Tachypnea
- Thrombocytopenia
- Tinnitus
- Upper respiratory infections

Diagnostic Tests for Review

The diagnostic tests for a client with hematological disorders are the same as any other routine hospitalization of a client (CBC, urinalysis, and chest x-ray). Specific tests, such as the Schilling test for B12 deficiency, and sickledex and Hgb electrophoresis, are used to diagnose sickle cell anemia and thalassemia. Review these tests prior to taking an exam for a better understanding of the disease process:

- Schilling test
- CBC with differential
- Hemoglobin electrophoresis

Pharmacological Agents Used in Hematological Disorders

A client with a hematological disorder will receive a number of medications to stimulate red blood cell production and replace needed vitamins or nutrients. Analgesics are also a requirement for the pain associated with some diseases. You'll need to review the drugs listed in Table 10.4 prior to an exam for knowledge of their effects, side effects, adverse reactions, and nursing implications. These medications are not inclusive of all the agents used to treat gastrointestinal disorders; therefore, you will want to keep a current pharmacology text handy for reference.

TABLE 10.4 Hematological Pharmacological Agents

Name	Action	Side Effects Include	Pertinent Nursing Implications
Vitamin B12 (cyanocobalamin)	Necessary for metabolic processes and required for RBC formation. Prevents B12 deficiency and treats pernicious anemia.	Diarrhea, itching, rash, hypokalemia, anaphylaxis, pain at IM site.	Available IM, subcutaneously, intranasal (useful by this route only if need is due to a nutritional deficiency). Teach foods high in vitamin B12: meats, seafood, egg yolk, and fermented cheese. PO can be administered with meals or mixed with fruit juice. Intranasal (use within an hour of hot food or liquid). Instruct of lifelong need after gastrectomy.
Ferrous sulfate (Femiron, Feostat) Imferon Tip: IM iron is Imferon	An essential mineral found in hemoglobin. Prevents and treats iron deficiency.	IM and IV: dizziness, seizures, tachycardia, hypotension. IM: skin staining, arthralgia, myalgia, anaphylaxis. PO: constipation, dark stools, diarrhea, pain in epigastric region, staining of teeth with liquid preparations.	Assess for signs of anaphylaxis (rash, itching, laryngeal edema with wheezing). Monitor Hgb and Hct levels. Monitor for overdose: stomach pain, fever, nausea and vomiting, bluish lips and fingernails, seizures, and tachycardia. Avoid antacids, coffee, tea, dairy products, or whole grain breads when on PO iron. Dilute liquid iron in water or fruit juice. Administer with a straw or place drops at back of throat. Give iron with citrus fruit or juice to enhance absorption (can also be taken with vitamin C pill).
Hydroxyurea (Droxia)	Reduces painful crises in sickle cell anemia. An anticancer agent.	Anorexia, nausea, vomiting, constipation, hepatitis, alopecia, rashes, pruritus, leukopenia, anemia, thrombocytopenia.	Monitor laboratory values for signs of leukopenia, anemia, and thrombocytopenia in the client. Assess for side and adverse effects.

Apply Your Knowledge

This chapter provided information regarding the care of clients with hematological disorders. The following questions test your knowledge regarding the safe, effective care and management of these clients. The nurse should also refer to the key terms, diagnostics, and pharmacological agents sections to assist in answering these questions.

Exam Questions

1. The nurse can best promote hydration in a 4-year-old with sickle cell anemia by which of the following?

    A. Telling the child how important it is to drink fluids

    B. Forcing fluids of bottled water every two hours

    C. Providing soup on the lunch and dinner meals

    D. Offering flavored ice pops or iced Slurpees

2. The nurse administering a blood transfusion suspects a reaction has occurred. Which signs and symptoms would the nurse expect with an allergic reaction to blood?

    A. Fever and chills

    B. Hypotension and tachycardia

    C. Rash and hives

    D. Decreased urinary output and hypertension

3. The nurse is caring for an adult with hemophilia. Which clinical manifestation causes the nurse the most concern?

    A. Hemarthrosis of the elbow

    B. Bruise of the ankle

    C. Oozing of blood at the IV site

    D. Unilateral numbness and lack of movement of arm

4. A client with iron deficiency anemia has been noncompliant with iron medications. He is admitted requiring a blood transfusion due to severe anemia. The nurse starts the transfusion at 1300 and realizes it must be completed by:

    A. 1400

    B. 1500

    C. 1600

    D. 1700

5. Which should the nurse observe for as a complication of Factor VIII administration?

    A. Fluid volume excess

    B. Sepsis

    C. Blood transfusion reaction

    D. Thrombus formation

6. Which of the following is not a named sickle cell anemia crisis?

    A. Aplastic

    B. Vaso-occlusive

    C. Splenic sequestration

    D. Erythropoiesis

7. A client receiving a blood transfusion exhibits lower back pain, fever, and dyspnea. What is the nurse's initial action?

    A. Stop the blood transfusion and keep the vein open with normal saline

    B. Administer epinephrine per unit protocol

    C. Notify the physician

    D. Obtain a set of vital signs

8. A client has been admitted with sickle cell anemia in crisis. Which physician prescription would the nurse anticipate?

    A. Restrict fluids 200mL/shift

    B. Ice to painful joints

    C. Start O_2 at 3 L/min

    D. Ambulate in hall every two hours

9. A child is in the hospital with a diagnosis of thalassemia major. Multiple blood transfusions have been ordered along with a chelating agent. The father asks the nurse, "Why does my son get this drug every time he gets blood?" What does the nurse explain as the purpose of chelating drugs?

    A. Stabilize clots in the vascular system

    B. Decrease the chance of a blood reaction

    C. Eliminate iron excess

    D. Boost oxygen delivery to the cells

10. Which does the nurse recognize as the most accurate in diagnosing sickle cell anemia?

    A. Sickledex

    B. Hemoglobin electrophoresis

    C. Partial thromboplastin time

    D. Complete blood count

Answers to Exam Questions

1. Answer D is correct. A child will likely accept the fluids in this answer better than the others listed. The child is too young to understand the statement in answer A, so it is inappropriate. Answers B and C are good sources of fluids but would not be best or acceptable for a 3-year-old, so they are incorrect.

2. Answer C is correct. Other symptoms include respiratory distress and anaphylaxis. Answer A describes febrile nonhemolytic reaction, so it is incorrect. Answer B occurs with hemolytic reaction and answer D is not associated with a blood transfusion reaction, so they are incorrect.

3. Answer D is correct. The neurological symptoms could mean an intracranial bleed has occurred. The answers in A, B, and C are reasons for concern, but they are not the priority, so they are incorrect.

4. Answer D is correct. Blood must be finished within four hours of the start time. Answers in A, B, and C are before the four-hour time limit, so they are incorrect.

5. Answer C is correct. Factor VIII is a blood product, so the nurse would monitor for a transfusion reaction. Answer A is unlikely due to the small volume of fluid administered, so it is wrong. Answers B and D are not immediate concerns for this short-term infusion, so they are incorrect.

6. Answer D is correct. Erythropoiesis is the formation of RBCs not related to sickle cell crisis. The answers in A, B, and C are types of sickle cell anemia crises, so they are incorrect.

7. Answer A is correct. The nurse would first ensure that the patient doesn't get any more of the wrong blood due to displaying symptoms of a hemolytic blood reaction. Answers B, C, and D are proper actions with a blood transfusion reaction, but none is the initial action, so they are incorrect.

8. Answer C is correct. It is not unusual for patients to receive oxygen to prevent additional sickling of cells. The answers in A and B are incorrect because these are contraindicated in sickle cell anemia. Answer D is not recommended for patients in sickle cell crisis, so it is incorrect.

9. Answer C is correct. A chelating agent such as deferoxamine (Desferal) is given to eliminate excess iron. The answers in A, B, and D are not the action of chelating agents, so they are incorrect.

10. Answer B is correct. Hemoglobin electrophoresis is the test that verifies the diagnosis of sickle cell and is the most accurate because it separates the different hemoglobins. Answer A is a screening tool that lacks the accuracy of electrophoresis, so it is incorrect. The answers in C and D are not directly related to sickle cell, so they are incorrect.

Suggested Reading and Resources

▸ Brunner, L., and D. Suddarth. *Textbook of Medical Surgical Nursing*. 10th ed. Philadelphia: Lippincott Williams & Wilkins, 2009.

▸ Deglin, Judith H., and April H. Vallerand. *Davis Drug Guide for Nurses*. Philadelphia: F. A. Davis, 2009.

▸ Hogan, M. *Child Health Nursing Reviews and Rationales*. 2nd ed. NJ: Prentice Hall, 2007.

▸ Horkenberry, M., and D. Wilson. *Wong's Nursing Care of Infants and Children*. 8th ed. St. Louis: Mosby, 2007.

▸ Ignatavicius, D., and S. Workman. *Medical Surgical Nursing: Critical Thinking for Collaborative Care*. 6th ed. Philadelphia: Elsevier, 2007.

▸ Lewis, S., M. Heitkemper, S. Dirksen, P. O'Brien, and L. Bucher. *Medical Surgical Nursing: Assessment and Management of Clinical Problems*. 7th ed. Philadelphia: Elsevier, 2007.

▸ Rinehart, Sloan, Hurd,. *NCLEX Exam Prep*. Indianapolis: Pearson Que Publishing, 2007.

▸ Smith, F., D. Duell, and B. Martin. *Clinical Nursing Skills Basic to Advanced Skills*. 7th ed. Upper Saddle River, NJ: Pearson Prentice Hall, 2008.

CHAPTER ELEVEN

Care of the Client with Disorders of the Neurological System

Neurological assessment and function is an integral part of many aspects of nursing. Disorders in the neurological system can be due to several causes such as direct injuries to the brain and spinal cord because of trauma or deficiencies in neurotransmitters. Figure 11.1 shows a picture of the brain and spinal cord. These disorders can be acute and life-threatening or chronic with gradual progression. The nurse reviewer must be knowledgeable of the implications of neurological disorders, as well as essential assessment and monitoring techniques.

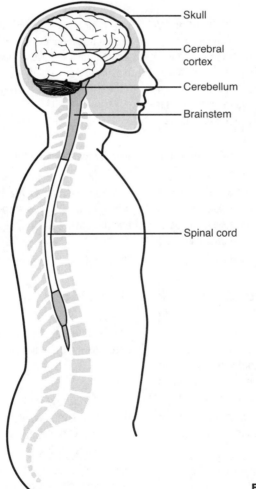

Skull

Cerebral cortex

Cerebellum

Brainstem

Spinal cord

FIGURE 11.1 Brain and spinal cord.

Neurological Assessment

The client assessment is a major component of nursing care. Early recognition of a deficit in neurological status can mean a more favorable outcome in the client's condition. The information in the sections that follow offers insight into three forms of assessment techniques—cranial nerve assessment, Glasgow coma scale, and intracranial pressure monitors—that can be used to identify deficits in a client.

Cranial Nerve Assessment

Table 11.1 highlights the 12 cranial nerves, their names, their functions, and the assessment methods.

TABLE 11.1 Assessment of Cranial Nerves

Cranial Nerve	Function	Assessment Method
1 Olfactory	Smell	Identify common odors.
2 Optic	Visual acuity	Snellen chart (central vision) and peripheral vision check.
3 Oculomotor; 4 Trochlear; 6 Abducens	Cranial nerves III, IV, and VI regulate eye movement, accommodation, and the elevation of the eyelids. IV is responsible for inferior and medial eye movement. VI is responsible for lateral eye movement.	Check for pupil constriction; check for accommodation and convergence as the object is brought near the eyes; check for strength of lid closure.
5 Trigeminal	Facial sensation; corneal reflex; mastication.	Identify the location of the stimulus; check jaw strength.
7 Facial	Movement of facial muscles; facial expression; tear formation; salivation; taste sensation in anterior tongue.	Check for symmetry of facial expressions; muscle strength. Identify sweet, sour, and salty taste on anterior area of the tongue.
8 Acoustic (Vestibulocochlear)	Hearing and equilibrium.	Use Weber and Rinne test for hearing loss.
9 Glossopharyngeal	Taste sensation in post third of the tongue.	Identify sweet, sour, and salty tastes on posterior area of the tongue.
10 Vagus	Pharyngeal contraction; symmetrical movement of vocal cords and soft palate; movement and secretion of thoracic and abdominal viscera.	Ask client to say "Ah"; uvula should rise midline; check ability to swallow.
11 Spinal Accessory	Movement of trapezius and sternocleidomastoid muscles.	Have client shrug shoulders against resistance. Neck strength is checked by having the client turn his head against resistance.
12 Hypoglossal	Tongue movement	Have client stick out tongue, observe for deviations or tremors, check strength of tongue movement as it presses against tongue blade.

Figure 11.2 presents a visual method for you to review the cranial nerves. Study this picture to assist you with remembering cranial nerve information.

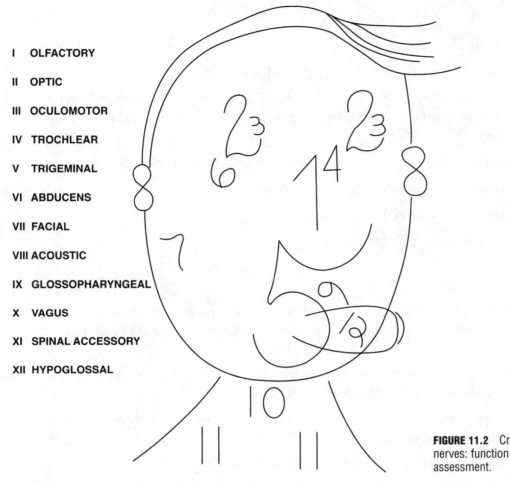

I   OLFACTORY

II OPTIC

III OCULOMOTOR

IV TROCHLEAR

V   TRIGEMINAL

VI ABDUCENS

VII FACIAL

VIII ACOUSTIC

IX GLOSSOPHARYNGEAL

X   VAGUS

XI SPINAL ACCESSORY

XII HYPOGLOSSAL

FIGURE 11.2 Cranial nerves: function and assessment.

Glasgow Coma Scale

The Glasgow coma scale assesses neurologic status based on the client's motor, verbal, and eye-opening responses. Lower responses indicate central nervous system impairment, whereas higher responses indicate central nervous system functioning. The scale is universal, which makes it a popular screening tool. The nurse reviewer should be aware of the following information for the nursing exam:

Eye Opening:

▶ Spontaneous opening = 4

▶ To speech = 3 (Do not confuse with an awaking of a sleeping person; if so, score 4, not 3.)

▶ To pain = 2 (Put pressure on the patient's fingernail bed; if no response, try supra-orbital and sternal pressure/rub.)

▶ No response = 1

Best Motor Response:

▶ Obeys verbal command = 6 (The patient does simple things as asked.)

▶ Localizes pain = 5 (Purposeful movements toward changing painful stimuli; for example, hand crosses midline and gets above clavicle when supraorbital pressure applied.)

▶ Withdraws = 4 (Pulls part of body away when pinched; normal flexion.)

▶ Abnormal flexion = 3 (Decorticate response)

▶ Extends = 2 (Decerebrate response)

▶ No response = 1

Verbal Response:

▶ Oriented = 5 (Patient responds coherently and appropriately to questions such as the patient's name and age, where they are and why, the year, the month, and so on.)

▶ Confused conversation = 4 (The patient responds to questions coherently, but there is some disorientation and confusion.)

▶ Inappropriate words = 3 (Random or exclamatory articulated speech, but no conversational exchange.)

▶ Incomprehensible words = 2 (Moaning but no words.)

▶ No response = 1 (An *E* would need to be recorded if an endotracheal tube is in place and a *T* if patient had a tracheostomy tube in place.)

Total points = 3 (lowest possible score) to 15 (fully awake). A score less than or equal to 8 indicates a severe coma; a score of between 9 and 12, inclusive, indicates a moderate coma; a score of greater than or equal to 13 indicates a minor coma.

Intracranial Pressure Monitors

The third assessment tool is the most invasive and accurate of the ones mentioned. An intracranial pressure (ICP) monitor is inserted by the physician. This is a sensing device inside the skull that is attached to a transducer. This device gives an electronic recording of intracranial pressure. The normal ICP reading is 10-20 mm Hg. The monitoring device can also be used to drain cerebrospinal fluid.

Monitors are also available to assess oxygen saturations in brain tissue. The LICOX PMO measures oxygen and temperature via a single probe monitoring system. This device is contraindicated in clients with coagulopathy disorders. Another device utilized is the jugular venous bulb oximeter. The catheter is placed in the internal jugular vein with the tip placed at the base of the brain. Blood leaving the brain is measured with an oxygen normality range of 50%–75%.

An ICP reading is necessary to calculate a client's cerebral perfusion pressure (CPP). The CPP is the pressure needed to provide adequate blood flow to the brain, and it is calculated by subtracting the ICP reading from the mean arterial pressure (MAP). A CPP above 70 is needed to have adequate brain viability. It is important for you to have the knowledge required for clients with ICP monitors in place to prevent complications and institute safe nursing care. The nurse should

- Assess for complications or problems with the ICP monitor:
  - Infection at site
  - Cerebrospinal fluid (CSF) leak
  - Loose connections
  - Meningitis
  - Microhemorrhages
  - Edema
- Interpret and report abnormal results to the physician
- Utilize sterile technique when handling the equipment
- Balance and recalibrate the monitor as prescribed or policy dictates
- Keep dressing over catheter site dry and change the dressing as prescribed

Brain Injuries

Brain injuries occur when a force is applied to the brain, causing damage. The age group at greatest risk is 15–44. An injury of this type can cause extreme emotional adjustments and disability.

Injuries can be classified as open or closed, coup or contrecoup, and acceleration or deceleration.

An open head injury occurs when there is a penetration of the dura, allowing exposure to the environment. Several fractures can occur with an open injury:

- Linear-simple clean break
- Depressed-inward bone depression to at least the skull thickness
- Comminuted-fragmented bone into the brain tissue

A basilar skull fracture is a fracture at the base of the skull.

> **CAUTION**
>
> Instruct the client with a basilar fracture to avoid coughing or blowing the nose.

These fractures can be severe. The trademarks of basilar skull fractures are the specific symptoms, which include

- ▶ CSF leakage from the ear (otorrhea) or the nose (rhinorrhea)

> **TIP**
>
> Indicators of CSF are the halo sign (a blood stain that develops a yellowish circle around it) or drainage that tests positive for glucose.

- ▶ Battle's sign—Ecchymosis at the mastoid area
- ▶ Raccoon eyes—Ecchymosis around the eyes

Figure 11.3 shows the symptoms of basilar skull fractures.

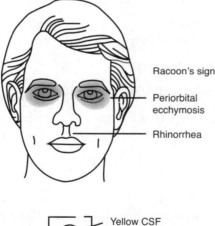

A

- Racoon's sign
- Periorbital ecchymosis
- Rhinorrhea

C

- Yellow CSF
- Red blood

Halo sign

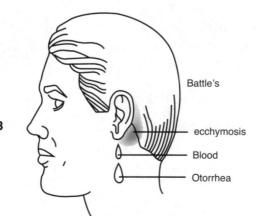

B

- Battle's
- ecchymosis
- Blood
- Otorrhea

FIGURE 11.3 Basilar skull fracture symptoms.

CAUTION

There is an increased risk of infection and cerebrospinal fluid leakage with a basilar skull fracture.

Treatment of skull fractures depends on the extent of the injury caused by the fracture. Patients with nondepressed or depressed skull fractures without contamination or deformities usually require only observation. Penetrating fractures usually require surgery with debridement, cleansing, and antibiotic administration.

When a person has a closed head injury, the dura is not torn and the skull remains intact. The extent of damage depends on the mechanism of injury. The injury can occur directly under the site of impact (*coup*) or can damage an area opposite the site of impact (*contrecoup*). Figure 11.4 shows illustrations of coup and contrecoup injuries. Another important factor is whether the injury was an acceleration injury caused from the impact or force putting the head in motion or a deceleration injury caused when the head stops on impact with an object.

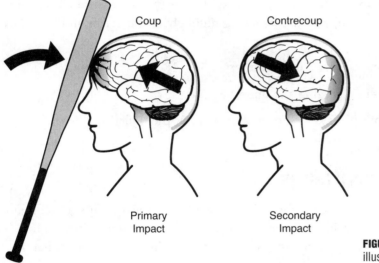

Coup   Contrecoup

Primary Impact   Secondary Impact

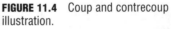

FIGURE 11.4 Coup and contrecoup illustration.

Types of closed head injuries include mild concussions, diffuse axonal injuries (DAI), contusions, and hemorrhages. When a person has a concussion, loss of consciousness is brief. The client usually recovers without interventions. Some clients can develop post-concussion syndrome. This is characterized by headache, irritability, fatigue, and depression.

The second type of closed head injury is a DAI. A DAI usually occurs with high-speed injuries (for example, motor vehicle accidents). There is damage to the axons in the white matter of the brain. If a client has a severe DAI, she is usually comatose on admission.

When a contusion occurs, the brain is bruised. Contusions are usually due to coup or contrecoup injuries. Symptoms can be focal or generalized depending on the amount of bruising.

The last type of closed head injuries is a hemorrhage. This can happen due to the primary impact or because of damages to the blood vessels or skull fractures. There are three types of hemorrhages: epidural, subdural, and intracerebral. The information that follows discusses these.

Epidural Hematomas

The first type of hematoma is the epidural. It usually develops from an arterial bleed, which makes it more acute. An epidural hematoma occurs when there is a collection of blood between the skull and dura. The symptoms indicating an epidural hematoma involve a pattern of consciousness, a lucid interval, followed by the client being critical and then comatose.

Subdural Hematoma

The second type of hematoma is a subdural hematoma. It is usually venous in origin and occurs when a collection of blood is between the dura and above the arachnoid space. Subdural hematomas are subdivided into three classifications that are identified by their time of development after the injury. The following highlights these terms and how they are identified:

▸ **Acute:** Occurs within the first 2 days of injury

▸ **Subacute:** Occurs 2–14 days after the injury

▸ **Chronic:** Occurs from 14 days to several months after the injury

Intracerebral Hematomas

The third type of hematoma is intracerebral. This type of hematoma occurs in the brain tissue itself. It can be due to tearing of arteries and veins within the brain tissue. The frontal and temporal lobes of the brain are common sites for this type of hematoma to occur.

Treatment of Hematomas

Clients with hematomas are treated depending on the amount of space occupied by the hematoma. If the client has increased intracranial pressure, measures included in the following section on increased ICP are used. Surgical interventions include insertion of burr holes and a craniotomy to evacuate the hematoma.

Increased Intracranial Pressure

Increased intracranial pressure can result from any alteration that increases tissue or fluid volume within the cranium. See Figure 11.5 for contents of the skull.

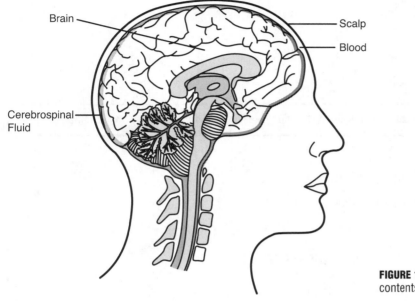

FIGURE 11.5 The skull and its contents.

The skull is rigid with no flexibility; therefore, there is no room for any additional fluid or blood or a space-occupying lesion. Some causes of increased ICP are as follows:

▸ Accumulation of cerebral spinal fluid in the ventricles

▸ Brain tumors

▸ Central nervous system infections

▸ Cerebral edema

▸ Intracranial bleeding

The client with increased ICP exhibits specific signs and symptoms that you need to be able to recognize and report to the physician for early intervention. These clinical manifestations include:

▸ Blurred vision

▸ Changes in cognition

▸ Changes in the level of consciousness

  ▸ **Early:** Lethargy, disorientation, confusion

  ▸ **Late:** Nonresponsiveness, responsive to painful stimulus, coma

---

TIP

Changes in the level of consciousness can be the first indication of a neurological problem.

- ▶ Cheyne-Stokes respiration
- ▶ Coma
- ▶ Decerebrate posture

NOTE

Decerebrate posture indicates brain stem dysfunction (see Figure 11.6).

- ▶ Decorticate posture (see Figure 11.6)
- ▶ Decreased motor responsiveness
- ▶ Diplopia
- ▶ Doll's eye phenomena (see Figure 11.7)
- ▶ Headache
- ▶ Papilledema (edema of the optic disc)
- ▶ Personality and behavior changes
- ▶ Projectile vomiting
- ▶ Pupil changes
- ▶ Seizures
- ▶ Vital signs changes (also called *Cushing's triad/response*):
    - ▶ Increased BP with a widening pulse pressure
    - ▶ Decreased pulse rate
    - ▶ Decreased respirations

TIP

Note that these vital sign changes are actually the opposite of shock—if you know one, you know the other and vice versa.

It is important for the nurse reviewer to be aware of the differences of symptoms that can occur in infants. The following focuses on the clinical manifestations of increased ICP you need to know for the infant:

- ▶ Bulging fontanels
- ▶ A high-pitched cry
- ▶ Irritability
- ▶ Restlessness

Figure 11.6 illustrates decorticate and decerebrate posturing, which indicates midbrain and brain stem dysfunction.

Figure 11.7 illustrates Doll's eye phenomena. Doll's eye absence indicates brain stem dysfunction.

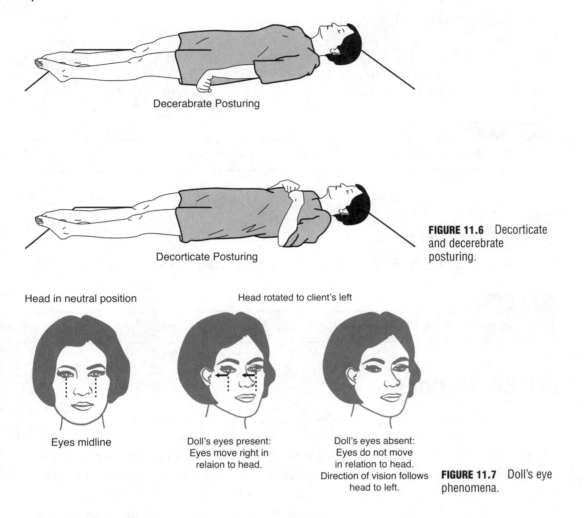

Decerabrate Posturing

Decorticate Posturing

FIGURE 11.6 Decorticate and decerebrate posturing.

Head in neutral position   Head rotated to client's left

Eyes midline

Doll's eyes present:
Eyes move right in
relaion to head.

Doll's eyes absent:
Eyes do not move
in relation to head.
Direction of vision follows
head to left.

FIGURE 11.7 Doll's eye phenomena.

Treatment of increased ICP is directed toward paths that will both prevent further increases in intracranial pressure and help in the recognition of it so that early intervention is possible. The following interventions are important for you to know for the exam:

▶ Keep the head of the bed elevated 30°

▶ Keep the client well oxygenated

▶ Perform frequent neurological assessment

▶ Restrict intake and assess output to prevent overhydration

▶ Prevent seizures by administering anticonvulsants when due for blood level maintenance

▶ Treat nausea and vomiting

▶ Maintain the client in chemical restraint or paralysis for control of restlessness and agitation

▶ Maintain hypocapnia (PCO_2 35–38 mm Hg),as prescribed, to prevent vasodilation of cerebral blood vessels and decrease ICP

▶ Use pharmacological interventions, including

    ▶ Steroids

    ▶ Mannitol (Osmitrol) (an osmotic diuretic; you should observe for signs of congestive heart failure due to a possible alteration of cardiac enzymes)

NOTE

IV administration requires the use of a filter to eliminate microscopic crystals.

▶ Anticonvulsants

▶ Loop diuretics

▶ Avoid narcotics or medications that depress respiration

CAUTION

Pain medications can mask symptoms, which can make assessments inaccurate.

Brain Tumors

A brain tumor can be either primary (originating within the brain) or secondary (spreading to the brain from other cancers, such as breast, lung, pancreas, and so on). Brain tumors occur most often in persons 50–70 years old. Brain tumors that grow (even though there is no malignancy) can cause death due to increasing intracranial pressure. There are several different kinds of brain tumors. These tumors are grouped into specific classes. Table 11.2 identifies some of the tumors with characteristics associated with each type.

TABLE 11.2   Brain Tumor Categories

Type of Tumor	Characteristics
Glioma Brain Tumors:	
Astrocytomas Glioblastomas Oligodendrocytomas Medulloblastomas Ependymomas	Most common types of brain tumors. It is difficult to remove all of an astrocytoma tumor due to infiltration qualities.
Developing Tumors (Angiomas)	Composed of abnormal blood vessels. Most develop in cerebellum. There is a high risk of brain attack with these tumors.

TABLE 11.2 *Continued*

Type of Tumor	Characteristics
Tumors That Arise from Support Structures:	
Meningiomas	Slow-growing tumor that is usually benign and encapsulated.
Acoustic neuromas	Tumors of the eighth cranial nerve. Usually arise in auditory meatus. Tumor might be large before diagnosis.
Pituitary adenomas	Can cause pressure on the optic nerves, hypothalamus, or third ventricle.

The clinical manifestations of brain tumors are highly associated with the type of brain tumor. For example, pituitary tumors cause symptoms associated with hormone secretion, ACTH secretion causes Cushing's symptoms, excessive prolactin produces amenorrhea in females. Generalized clinical manifestations of brain tumors include

▸ Symptoms of increased intracranial pressure (refer to the "Increased Intracranial Pressure" section earlier in this chapter). Specifics for brain tumors are early morning headache, vomiting not associated with food intake, and *papilledema*.

▸ Seizures.

▸ Mental status changes.

▸ Hemiparesis.

▸ Visual changes.

Treatment of Brain Tumors

The modalities of treatment for brain tumors are similar to treatment of other cancers. Three-fold management can be done via radiation, surgery, and/or pharmacological interventions. Both external beam and brachytherapy radiation techniques can be used and combined with a surgical intervention. Surgical removal of the tumor has two primary goals. The first goal is to relieve the symptoms, and the second goal is to remove all of the tumor without causing an increase in neurological deficits. Table 11.3 lists the types of surgical techniques that might be performed.

TABLE 11.3 **Surgical Techniques for Brain Tumor Removal**

Type of Surgical Procedure	Description
Craniotomy	Used for most tumor removals.
Transphenoidal microsurgical	Used for pituitary adenomas (see Figure 11.8).
Stereotactics	Uses a three-dimensional frame and imaging studies to locate the tumor so that laser or radiation is more precise.
Insertion of implantable chemotherapy	Biodegradable anhydrous wafers containing chemotherapy drugs, these are implanted into the tumor during surgery.
Gamma knife	Used for deep inaccessible tumors. With the assistance of stereotactics, radiation is delivered to a precise location without the use of surgical incision.

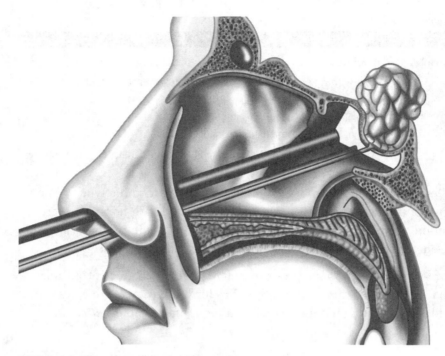

FIGURE 11.8 Transphenoidal surgical procedure.

Care of the Client with Intracranial Surgery (Craniotomy)

A craniotomy might be performed on any client with a neurological disorder. The focus of care is early detection and prevention of any complications. If a client has a craniotomy, postoperative care is of particular importance. The following postoperative craniotomy interventions are important for you to know:

- ▶ Monitor vital signs and neurological assessments.

- ▶ Monitor cardiac rhythm.

- ▶ Perform passive range of motion exercises on the client.

- ▶ Assist the client to turn, cough, and deep breathe every two to three hours.

CAUTION
Be careful with coughing exercises because they can increase intracranial pressure.

- ▶ Use cold application for periorbital edema and bruising.

- ▶ Prevent deep vein thrombosis by compression stocking application.

- ▶ Position the client after surgery depending on which area of the brain was involved in the surgical procedure. Postoperatively, the client is positioned as follows:

▶ **Supratentorial surgery (anterior and middle fossa):** Elevate the head of the bed 30°.

▶ **Infratentorial surgery (posterior fossa):** Flat on either side. Use this position for one to two days after surgery.

If bone flap has been removed, keep the client off of the operative side.

▶ Maintain the head in the neutral position and avoid hip or neck flexion.

▶ Assess head dressing and drainage from wound suction devices.

> **NOTE**
> Excessive drainage from wound is more than 50 mL in eight hours.

▶ Monitor ABGs and laboratory values.

▶ Assess urinary output. (Note: Excessive urinary output could indicate the complication of diabetes insipidus.)

▶ Use the following pharmacological interventions:

  ▶ Anticonvulsants

  ▶ Steroids

  ▶ Histamine blockers and/or proton pump inhibitors

  ▶ Prophylactic antibiotics

▶ Assess for complications.

Complications of brain surgery are sometimes unavoidable. For example, cerebral edema is expected due to the inflammatory process and can lead to an increase in intracranial pressure. The nurse reviewer should be aware of the complications that can occur with a craniotomy:

▶ Increased intracranial pressure.

▶ Hydrocephalus due to blockage of CSF drainage from the inflammatory process.

  ▶ **Signs and symptoms:** Increased intracranial pressure symptoms.

  ▶ **Treatment of hydrocephalus:** Ventriculostomy. Long-term treatment requires shunt placement to drain CSF to another body site—ventriculoperitoneal, lumbar peritoneal, or ventriculoatrial.

▶ Respiratory complications, such as pneumonia.

▶ Wound infection.

▶ Meningitis.

▶ Brain herniation occurs when untreated increases in ICP cause cerebral tissue to move to a more compliant area. A lethal complication of herniation occurs when the cerebellum herniates through the tentorium and puts pressure on the brain stem. Figure 11.9 illustrates the various areas of herniation that can occur.

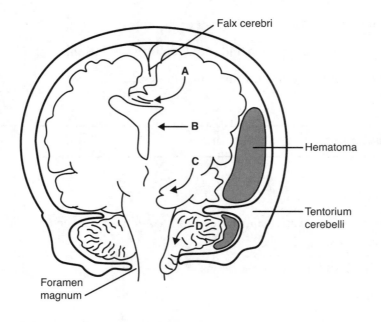

A: Cingulate herniation occurs when the cingulate gyrus is compressed under the falx cerbri
B: Central herniation occurs when a centrally located lesion compresses central and midbrain structures
C: Lateral herniation occurs when a lesion at the side of the brain compresses the uncus or hippocampal cyrus
D: Infratentional herniation occurs when the cerebellar tonsils are forced downward, compressing the medulla and top of the spinal cord

FIGURE 11.9 Herniation of the brain.

▶ Fluid and electrolyte imbalances: Syndrome of inappropriate antidiuretic hormone (SIADH).

    ▶ Clinical manifestations of SIADH:

        ▶ Decreased urinary output < 20 mL/hr

        ▶ Hyponatremia

        ▶ Muscle weakness

        ▶ Changes in level of consciousness-headaches, irritability, and hostility

        ▶ Tachycardia

        ▶ Seizures

    ▶ Treatment of SIADH:

        ▶ Fluid restriction

        ▶ Sodium replacement IV (3% saline infusion)

▶ Neurological assessments

▶ Pharmaceutical agents: diuretics, lithium carbonate, demeclocycline (Declomycin)

▶ Monitor intake and output

▶ Weigh daily

> **TIP**
>
> A loss of 2 pounds indicates 1 liter of fluid loss.

Clients with pituitary tumors have a distinct surgical approach (transphenoidal). The information that follows provides information on the special care of clients who have this surgery. Specific needs must be met or assessed both pre- and postoperative transphenoidal surgery. Those needs include the following:

Preoperative Care

▶ Assess endocrine tests

▶ Perform fundoscopic exam to assess the effects on the optic nerve

▶ Monitor for sinus infection (surgical procedure is contraindicated if infection present)

▶ Teach deep breathing exercises to be done post operatively

▶ Teach the client to avoid the following after surgery (due to risk of causing a cerebrospinal fluid leak):

　▶ Coughing

　▶ Sucking through a straw

　▶ Blowing the nose

　▶ Sneezing

Postoperative Care

▶ Administer ordered antimicrobials, corticosteroids, and pain medications

▶ Assess visual acuity

> **CAUTION**
>
> Visual problems could indicate a large hematoma has developed.

▶ Monitor vital signs and perform neurological checks

▶ Elevate the head of the bed 30° for at least two weeks postoperatively

▶ Monitor intake and output

▶ Assess urine specific gravity

▶ Check nasal packing for blood or CSF (packing is usually removed in three to four days)

▶ Provide comfort and hygiene

  ▶ Oral care every four hours

  ▶ Instruct patient not to brush the teeth until incision above the teeth heals

  ▶ Provide warm saline rinses

  ▶ Cool mist humidifier at bedside

Cerebrovascular Accident/Stroke

Strokes or "brain attacks" are the third leading cause of death and the leading cause of disability in the United States. Risk factors for a stroke include hypertension, long-term hypercoagability, diabetes, illicit drug use (usually cocaine), and obesity (especially in the abdominal area).

NOTE

Phenylpropanolamine (found in appetite suppressants and cough and cold remedies) has been identified as a risk factor, especially in women.

Ischemic and hemorrhagic strokes are the two major types of strokes. Although similar, these two types of strokes have important differences.

Ischemic Stroke

Table 11.4 outlines the ischemic stroke, its causes, its pathophysiology, its clinical manifestations, and its treatments. You should review this table for your exams expecting parts of this information to be tested.

TABLE 11.4   Ischemic Stroke

Causes	Pathophysiology	Clinical manifestations	Non surgical Treatment	Surgical Treatment
Small penetrating artery thrombosis Large artery thrombosis (the most common cause) Atherosclerosis Cardiogenic embolus-atrial fibrillation Other causes: Cocaine use, coagulaiton disorders, migraines	Disruption of the blood flow in the brain occurs. The area surrounding the infarct (called the penumbra) can be salvaged from damage with the use of drugs if given early enough.	Numbness or weakness usually on one side of the body, hemiparesis, hemiplegia, paresthesia, Dizziness and loss of balance and coordination, Sudden headache, Visual perceptual changes—homonymous, hemianopsia, Aphasia—receptive or expressive, apraxia, mental status changes, dysarthria (difficulty forming words), dysphagia (difficulty swallowing	Thrombolytics t-PA (within three hours) Warfarin (Coumadin) to get INR @ 2.5 level Platelet-inhibiting medications, Ticlopidine (Ticlid), aspirin, clopidogrel (Plavix), Heparin Monitor and treat increased ICP Monitor neurological status Monitor vital signs. Maintain BP less than 180/100	Carotid endarterectomy Transluminal angioplasty

The main surgical treatment for ischemic strokes is a carotid endarterectomy. This procedure is probably the most performed vascular procedure in the United States and requires further discussion. When this is done, atherosclerotic plague is removed from the carotid artery. It is usually done for clients with mild strokes or transient ischemic attacks (TIA) to prevent a cerebrovascular accident. Criteria for selection includes patients with 70%–99% blockage who has had a mild stroke or TIA or a patient with 50%–69% stenosis who has other risk factors. After the surgical procedure is done, you must employ nursing interventions that will recognize and prevent complications. These include

▸ **Maintain adequate BP:** Hypotension is avoided because it can cause ischemia and thrombosis. Hypertension can cause a cerebral hemorrhage, edema, hemorrhage of the site, and damage to the surgical reconstructive site.

▸ **Monitor for complications:**

  ▸ **Hematoma at the incision site:** Assess for swelling, complaints of pressure in the neck, dyspnea.

> ▶ **Hypertension or hypotension:** Check BP frequently and report abnormalities to neurosurgeon for treatment; assess for new neurological deficits.

> ▶ **Hyperfusion syndrome:** Capillary bed injury, edema, and hemorrhage. Assess for headache on one side of the head that improves when the client sits upright or stands.

> ▶ **Intracerebral hemorrhage:** Monitor neurological status and report any changes or new deficits immediately.

> ▶ **Thrombus at site of endarterectomy:** Assess for new neurological deficits or increased deficits.

> ▶ **Cranial nerve dysfunction:** Assess cranial nerves, especially cranial nerves VI, X, XI, and XII (refer to cranial nerve assessment discussion earlier in this chapter).

Another procedure, transluminal angioplasty, is performed by inserting a balloon through a stenosed artery to open it. Intravascular stent placement via this procedure is now a less invasive, more popular option to the carotid endarterectomy.

Hemorrhagic Stroke

Hemorrhagic strokes lead to blood in the brain. Causes of a hemorrhagic stroke include

> ▶ Ruptured cerebral aneurysm (A cerebral aneurysm occurs when the wall of a cerebral artery dilates). Most occur in arteries of the circle of willis (see Figure 11.10).

> ▶ Uncontrolled hypertension.

> ▶ Ruptured arteriovenous malformation (AVM). An AVM is an embryonic development of abnormal arteries that are tangled without a capillary bed.

The pathophysiology that occurs with a hemorrhagic stroke is related to the loss of blood vessel integrity. An aneurysm or AVM enlarges and presses on cranial nerves or brain tissue resulting in rupture. This causes an influx of blood that increases ICP, injures or kills brain tissue, decreases cerebral perfusion, and increases the risk of vasospasm in the cerebral artery.

Clinical manifestations of a hemorrhagic type of stroke can be the same as an ischemic stroke (see Table 11.4) with additional symptoms of tinnitus.

NOTE

A sudden severe headache is classic with AVM and cerebral aneurysm rupture. The patient might state, "This is the worst headache I've ever had."

Diagnosis is made by a CT scan or an MRI. These x-ray exams also assist to differentiate whether the stroke is hemorrhagic or ischemic in origin. A lumbar puncture might also be performed to detect a cerebral bleed (revealed as blood in the CSF).

The Circle of Willis

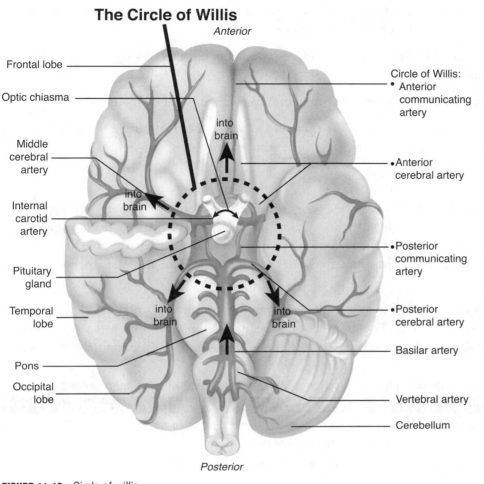

FIGURE 11.10 Circle of willis.

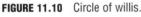

> **CAUTION**
>
> Lumbar punctures are contraindicated with increased intracranial pressure because the procedure can cause herniation of the brain.
>
> Anticoagulants are contraindicated in clients with hemorrhagic strokes.

The treatment plans used for clients with hemorrhagic strokes focus on preventing complications, allowing the brain to recover from the bleed, and preventing a rebleed. Plans and interventions utilized for care of the client with a hemorrhagic stroke include

- Assess for neurological status changes
- Provide bed rest and sedation
- Administer pain medication (such as, codeine and Tylenol)
- Administer oxygen to maintain adequate cerebral perfusion
- Assess for and treat seizures

▶ Monitor for vasospasm (occurs after a cerebral aneurysm rupture and results in narrowing of the cerebral blood vessel)

▶ Prevent and treat vasospasm-administer calcium channel blocker (Nimodipine [Nimotop])

▶ Administer anti-hypertensive medications (such as labetalol [Normodyne])

▶ If a ruptured aneurysm is the cause of the stroke the client might be placed on aneurysm precautions, these include visitor restrictions, dim lighting, no caffeine, and bedrest.

The nurse reviewer must also be aware of the need to monitor for complications of a hemorrhagic stroke such as, hydrocephalus and rebleeding. Most clients are managed non-surgically, but if the clients' condition deteriorates, surgery may be required. A craniotomy might be performed to repair an AVM or cerebral aneurysm, or to remove a blood clot.

Clients who have had strokes usually have common impairments requiring special nursing considerations. The information presented in the Table 11.5 will assist you in gaining the necessary knowledge to answer questions about these common impairments.

TABLE 11.5 Common Impairments after a Stroke with General Nursing Interventions

Impairment	Nursing Interventions
Communication difficulties	Ask simple questions that require a yes or no answer.
	Speak in a normal voice tone.
	Start and maintain a daily routine or schedule.
	Be patient and give the client proper time to respond.
	Do not force the client to communicate, especially if he becomes frustrated.
	Provide a quiet environment in which to communicate (no TV, radio, and so on).
Dysphagia	Keep client at 90° at feeding.
	Teach the client to keep the head flexed forward when preparing to swallow.
	Teach the client to sit up 30 minutes after meals.
	Place food on unaffected side of the client's mouth.
	Check the client's mouth for food pocketing after eating.
	Assess for gag reflex prior to feeding the client.
	Avoid thin liquids. A commercial thickening agent can be used.
	Avoid milk because it increases mucus thickness and increases the amount of saliva.
Unilateral Neglect	Arrange the client's personal items on his unaffected side.
	Teach the client to scan left to right to visualize the area.
	When trying to get the client's attention, touch the unaffected side.
	Position the client's bed so visitors and staff approach his unaffected side.
	Progress the client to reintegrate the whole body by gradually moving items to his affected side as he learns to compensate.

Seizures

Seizures are episodes of abnormal motor, sensory, or autonomic activity that result from the excessive discharge of electrical impulses from cerebral neurons. All seizures affect the level of consciousness; however, the degree is dependent on the type of seizure. Most seizures occur without a cause. Any abnormality in the central nervous system (CNS) can cause seizure activity.

> **NOTE**
> When a person has recurring unprovoked seizures, she is said to have epilepsy.

The significant causes of a seizure you need to know for a nursing exam are as follows:

- ▶ Abrupt withdrawal of drugs or alcohol
- ▶ Brain tumors
- ▶ Central nervous system infections
- ▶ Head injuries
- ▶ High fevers
- ▶ Hypertension
- ▶ Hypoglycemia or other electrolyte abnormalities
- ▶ Cerebrovascular disease (especially in the elderly)

Types of Seizures

There are two main categories for classifying seizure: the generalized seizure and the partial, or focal, seizure. The following sections describe these two seizure categories in more detail.

Generalized Seizures

With this type of seizure, the whole brain is involved in the seizure activity. Within this category, two types of seizures are identified. The first type is the tonic-clonic, or grand mal, seizure; the second is the absence, or petit mal, seizure.

Tonic-Clonic Seizures

Tonic-clonic seizures can last for up to five minutes. The following highlights the signs and symptoms of tonic-clonic seizures you need to know:

- ▶ Aura preictally (period prior to seizure activity)
- ▶ Brief episodes of apnea
- ▶ Chewing of the tongue

- ▶ Incontinence

- ▶ Loss of consciousness

- ▶ Loss of motor function

- ▶ Tonic (muscle tension) and clonic (alternating muscle contraction and relaxation) movements

> **NOTE**
>
> An aura can be any type of sensory sensation, such as a smell or flashing lights, that signals to the client that the seizure is about to occur. Children usually do not have an aura.

There is a risk for injury for any client involved in this type of seizure activity. You must become familiar with nursing care required for the general safety and physiological care of the client before and after the seizure. You also need to know the importance of accurately documenting the seizure because this will assist the physician with the diagnosis. You should gain knowledge of the following aspects of care and expect to see them on your exam:

- ▶ Assess the client's behavior and surroundings prior to the seizure.

- ▶ Loosen his clothing.

- ▶ Maintain a patent airway (oxygen, suction).

- ▶ Note any loss of consciousness, aura, or incontinence.

- ▶ Provide client safety (place padding under the client's head and move objects out of reach of the client to prevent self-injury).

- ▶ Time and document the seizure activity (body part movements, where seizure begins and ends, and so on).

- ▶ Turn the client on his side.

- ▶ If the client is in bed, remove the pillow and raise the side rails.

- ▶ An oral airway can be inserted if the client has an aura and time permits.

Don't

- ▶ Put anything in the client's mouth after a seizure has begun.

- ▶ Restrain the client.

After the seizure (postictal period), the client will be lethargic, tired, and confused. The nursing care after a tonic/clonic seizure includes

- ▶ Allow the client to sleep.

- ▶ Keep the client side-lying to decrease the risk of aspiration.

▶ Orient the client to the environment.

▶ Assess neurological status and vital signs.

Table 11.6 describes other generalized seizures that can occur. These are mostly variations of the tonic/clonic seizure.

TABLE 11.6 Tonic/Clonic Seizure Variations and Other Generalized Seizures

Type Seizure	Characteristics	Duration of Activity
Tonic	Sudden muscle tone increase.	30 seconds to several minutes
	Loss of consciousness.	
	No autonomic signs.	
Clonic	Muscles relax and contract.	Several minutes
Myoclonic	Jerking or stiffness of extremities—one or all.	Seconds
Akinetic	Loss of muscle tone with the seizure.	Seconds
	Confusion after the seizure.	
	Might cause a fall, resulting in injury.	

Absence Seizures

The second type of generalized seizure is absence, or petit mal, seizure. This type is more common in children and might improve by adolescence. There is little or no loss of consciousness and it can be mistaken for daydreaming due to the client's blank stares during the seizure activity.

Partial Seizures

The second category of seizures is called *partial*, or *focal*, seizures. These seizure types affect one cerebral hemisphere. Mostly found in adults, these seizures respond unfavorably to medical regimens. Focal seizures are further divided into two classifications. The first type is the simple partial seizure and the second is the complex partial seizure.

Simple Partial

With a simple partial seizure, the client's finger, arm, or hand might shake, autonomic symptoms (for example, flushing or heart rate changes), or special sensory symptoms might occur. The client often has an aura but does not lose consciousness.

Complex Partial

The second type of focal seizure is the complex partial. One of the major differentiating factors is that these clients do lose consciousness, whereas in simple partial they do not. The seizure can last for up to three minutes. Some characteristics you need to know for the exam include

▶ Automaticisms (behaviors that the person is not aware of, such as hand movements, lip smacking, repeated swallowing, and picking at clothes) might occur.

▶ These seizures are common in adults.

▶ The client usually has amnesia of episode.

Treatment of Seizure Clients

The treatment of clients with seizures concentrates on stopping the seizure activity. This goal is most often accomplished by the use of anticonvulsant medications. Another method of treatment involves the insertion of a vagal nerve stimulator (VNS). In this procedure, an electrode is placed on the vagal nerve and gives intermittent stimulation to the nerve, preventing seizures. The VNS is used most often for simple or complex partial type seizures. If a client with a VNS has an aura, self-activation can occur via a magnet. Side effects of the VNS are hoarseness and throat discomfort. Clients who continue to have seizures with treatment might require surgical removal of the section of the brain causing the seizure; however, this is a last resort. The area to be removed must not perform any major brain function. An anterior temporal lobe resection (where most partial seizures arise) is both safe and effective.

Status Epilepticus

A person in status epilepticus has a continuation of tonic clonic seizures without a normal recovery period. The client does not regain consciousness between attacks, despite medical intervention. Any one seizure that lasts longer than 5 minutes or repeated seizures longer than 30 minutes are classified as *status epilepticus*. This disorder is life-threatening if not corrected. Possible causes of status epilepticus include sudden noncompliance of anticonvulsant medications, head trauma, and alcohol withdrawal.

Clients experiencing status epilepticus are treated as a neurological emergency. Maintenance of the airway is a priority. Interventions important for the nurse candidate to know are administration of oxygen, initiation of IV access, and establishment and maintenance of a patent airway (intubation by an anesthetist or a physician might be required). Medications must be given to stop the seizure, as well as drugs to prevent another seizure. If the seizure activity continues despite efforts, general anesthesia might be required. The drugs you need to know for this disorder are as follows:

▶ IV diazepam (Valium) or lorazepam (Ativan) to stop the seizure activity. The dosage can be repeated 10 minutes after the initial administration.

▶ Valium and Ativan are followed by phenobarbital and diphenyldantion (Dilantin) or fosphenytoin (Cerebyx).

Parkinson's Disease

Parkinson's is classified as a degenerative neurological disorder. In its most common forms, symptoms develop in a person in his 50s, but can develop as early as age 30. Parkinson's is more common in men. Although there is no specific cause identified, several factors are associated with this disease, including the following:

▸ Head trauma

▸ Long-term antipsychotic medications

▸ Genetics

▸ Atherosclerosis

The clinical manifestations develop slowly, and eventually the disease might cause the client to become disabled. Classic symptoms that are distinguishing for Parkinson's disease are slow, abnormal movements (bradykinesia); resting slow tremors; and rigidity. Other signs and symptoms include the following:

▸ Hypokinesia

▸ Micrographia

▸ Dysphonia

▸ Dysphagia

▸ Autonomic symptoms (excessive sweating, urinary retention, and so on)

▸ Dementia

▸ Stooped posture

The management of Parkinson's disease is usually accomplished by pharmaceutical interventions, including levodopa-carbidopa (Sinemet), benztropine mesylate (Cogentin), amantidine hydrochloride (Symmetrel), ropinirole hydrochloride (Requip), pramipexole (Mirapex), MAO inhibitors (for example, selegiline [Eldepryl]), CONT inhibitors (for example, entacapone [Comtess]), antidepressants (for example, Elavil or Prozac), and antihistamines (for example, Benadryl) for mild anti-cholinergic effects.

Clients who are disabled due to the symptoms associated with Parkinson's disease or those who cannot tolerate the Levodopa due to dyskinesia response from long-term use might require surgery. There are several surgical techniques utilized, including

▸ **Stereotactic:** A thalamotomy or pallidotomy is done to break the nerve pathways by use of an electrical stimulator.

▸ **Brain stimulator:** Similar to a pacemaker. Brain implants are done via an electrode placed in the thalamus that is connected to a generator inserted under the subcutaneous tissue below the clavicle or in the abdomen. This procedure serves as a means to block nerve pathways and relieve the symptoms.

General nursing interventions for clients with Parkinson's disease involve measures that focus care on maintaining function and mobility, independence, and nutritional stability. These goals can be accomplished by the following interventions

▸ Encouraging exercises to maintain joint mobility. Clients should use a wide-based gait.

- Teaching the client to follow a high-fiber diet to help with constipation.

- Decrease the risk of aspiration by teaching clients to avoid thin liquids and sit up for meals.

- Monitor the client's intake and output.

- Obtain daily weights.

- Consult speech therapy.

Meningitis

The meninges are the coverings of the brain and spinal cord. When a patient has a meningitis diagnosis, their meninges have become infected or inflamed. Meningitis is more common in children due to frequent upper respiratory infections. There are two major categories of meningitis:

- **Aseptic:** Due to viruses or secondary to another disorder (for example, lymphoma, leukemia).

- **Bacterial:** Caused by previous infection with *Neisseria meningitides* (occurs more often in densely populated areas such as college campuses or military communities), *Stretococcus pneumoniae*, or *Hemophilus influenzae*.

Most clinical manifestations are associated with the irritation of the meninges and include

- Severe headache and fever (earliest symptoms)

- Nuchal rigidity

- Positive Kernig's sign (see Figure 11.11)

- Positive Brudsinski's sign (see Figure 11.12)

- Rash (purpuric lesions on face and extremities) is usually associated with Neisseria meningitides (meningococcal)

- Photophobia

- Exaggerated deep tendon reflexes (DTR)

- Opisthotonos

- Level of consciousness changes

- Signs of increased intracranial pressure

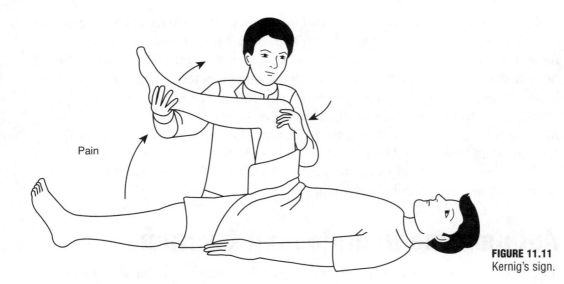

FIGURE 11.11
Kernig's sign.

Pain

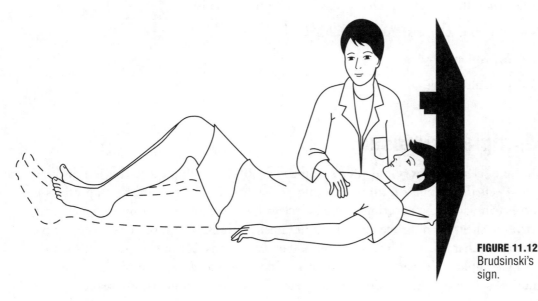

FIGURE 11.12
Brudsinski's
sign.

Meningitis is treated by the use of pharmacological agents. It is imperative that proper antibiotics be administered early in the course of the disease for a positive outcome. These antibiotics include

▸ Piperacillin/tazobactam (Zosyn).

▸ Ampicillin (Omnipen).

▸ Ceftriazone (Rocephin).

▸ Cefotaxime sodium (Claforan).

▸ Vancomycin (Vancocin) with rifampin (Rifadin) for resistant strains of bacteria.

▸ Other medications such as dexamethasone (Decadron) or phenytoin (Dilantin) might also be administered.

Nursing measures should also be instituted to assess the client's status. Neurological and vital signs should be monitored frequently. The client is placed on seizure precautions because a seizure can occur from the disease or extreme temperature elevations. Droplet precautions are done until the client has been on antibiotics for 24 hours. People who have been in contact with meningoccal meningitis should be treated with rifampin (Rifadin) in combination with ciprofloxacin (Cipro) or ceftriaxone (Rocephin). Meningitis is a severe illness that might require the client to be admitted to critical care for support and treatment. It is very important for the nurse to educate the general public to the importance of vaccination against *Hemophilus influenzae* and *Streptococcus pneumoniae* for children and at-risk adults.

Autoimmune Neurological Disorders

The following discussion gives information about three neurological diseases that can occur when the body's immune system is abnormal or fails:

▶ Multiple sclerosis

▶ Myasthenia gravis

▶ Guillain-Barré

Multiple Sclerosis

Multiple sclerosis most often affects women age 20–40. Multiple sclerosis is a disorder that affects the myelin sheath or covering of the nerves. The myelin sheath protects the nerves (similar to the covering over an electrical wire). The nerves can become damaged when the sheath is destroyed, resulting in impaired transmission of impulses. Multiple sclerosis is characterized by remissions and exacerbations. It can change from a patient having complete recovery between exacerbations to a *secondary progressive* form of multiple sclerosis, wherein there are no remissions, but continuous progression occurs. Another type, known as *primary progressive*, exhibits continuous advancement of symptoms and decline in the patient's condition, which produces disability. Clinical manifestations of multiple sclerosis include the following:

▶ Weakness

▶ Loss of balance

▶ Pain

▶ Visual changes (blurring of vision, double vision, scotoma, fatigue, spasticity, numbness, cognitive changes)

Treatment of multiple sclerosis revolves around three primary goals: stop or delay progression, control the symptoms, and decrease the frequency of and treat exacerbations. There is no cure for multiple sclerosis. Many of the primary treatments are focused on the use of medications and the immune response. Pharmacological interventions include

- ▶ Interferon beta-1a (Avonex, Rebif).

- ▶ Interferon beta-1b (Betaseron).

- ▶ Glatiramer acetate (Copaxone).

- ▶ Mitoxantrone (Novantrone).

- ▶ NSAIDs (for example, Motrin) can be given for the flu-like symptoms associated with the medications.

- ▶ Corticosteroids for immune response suppression.

- ▶ Tizanidine (Zanaflex) and/or baclofen (Lioresal) for spasticity.

- ▶ Other treatments or nursing measures:

  - ▶ Exercises—muscle stretching, swimming—for spasticity

  - ▶ Frequent rest periods for fatigue

  - ▶ Prevent skin impairments—encourage mobility, assess for loss of skin integrity, turn every two hours if bedridden

  - ▶ Be aware of risk for aspiration

  - ▶ Diplopia is treated by patching one eye

  - ▶ Try to keep patient independent

  - ▶ Monitor for secondary complications such as constipation, urinary tract infections, decubitus ulcers, contractures, pneumonia, depression

Myasthenia Gravis

The second type of autoimmune neurological disorder is myasthenia gravis. It is characterized by muscle weakness. The underlying factor is a lack of acetylcholine, weakness, and a loss of facial expression due to weakness in these muscles.

CAUTION

Weakness in the larynx area can lead to aspiration and choking. Intercostal weakness provides a risk for respiratory failure.

The treatment of myasthenia gravis is primarily achieved by the use of medications. These medications increase the acetylcholine which relieves the symptoms or suppresses the immune system. Management of myasthenia gravis includes

- ▶ **Pharmacological agents**

  - ▶ Pyridostigmine bromide (Mestinon)

  - ▶ Neostigmine bromide (Prostigmin)

> ▸ Corticosteroids (for example, Prednisone)
>
> ▸ Cyclophosphamide (Cytoxan)
>
> ▸ Azathioprine (Imuran)
>
> ▸ Plasmapheresis and IV immune globulin—Reduces antibodies in the bloodstream

▸ **Surgical intervention**—Thymectomy (removal of the thymus gland)

TIP

The priority for postop thymectomy is respiratory function.

▸ Monitor for complications of myasthenia gravis:

> ▸ **Myasthenic crisis:** Severe muscle weakness leads to respiratory function compromise.
>
> ▸ **Causes:** Can occur after infection, surgery, medication change, hot temperatures.
>
> ▸ **Treatment:** Neostigmine (Prostigmin) IM or IV, plasmapheresis, IVIG, endotracheal intubation, and ventilator.
>
> ▸ **Cholinergic crisis:** Patient has too much anticholinergic drugs. Symptoms are same as myasthenia. Edrophonium (Tensilon) is used to differentiate. The treatment is to stop medications and administer ordered atropine sulfate (anticholinergic drug antidote).

NOTE

The Tensilon test can also be used to diagnose myasthenia gravis. Muscle contractility improves and increases in people with myasthenia gravis after an IV injection of Tensilon. If muscle weakness does not improve or the weakness increases, Atropine (a cholinergic antagonist) must be available to administer during the diagnostic exam.

▸ **Nursing interventions:**

> ▸ Patient teaching, especially on medications.

CAUTION

Drugs must be given on time. Loss of medication in the bloodstream can make muscle weakness so severe that the patient is too weak to take the drugs.

> ▸ Teach the client to take frequent rest periods.
>
> ▸ Teach methods to help with dysphagia (soft foods, pureed diet, and so on).

▸ **Specific interventions during crisis:**

- ▸ Respiratory function takes priority

- ▸ Suction and postural drainage

- ▸ Monitor laboratory work

- ▸ Intake and output

- ▸ Weights daily

- ▸ Avoid medications that cause respiratory depression, e.g. sedatives

Guillain-Barré

The last type of neurological autoimmune disorder is called Guillain-Barrè. Guillain-Barrè is a rapidly ascending progressive paralysis or weakness. It can also be descending, but this progression is uncommon. Guillain-Barrè is an acute inflammatory process. Respiratory complications are the usual cause of death. Although the exact cause is unknown, it has been shown to be related to a para-infection or post-infection immune response. It frequently develops one to three weeks following an upper respiratory or gastrointestinal infection. It has also been linked to clients with a history of a recent immunization or allergy, surgery, acute illness, or trauma. The most distinguishing diagnostic criteria is cerebrospinal fluid that reveals an increased protein with little or no increase in cell count levels. A client with Guillain-Barrè displays the following symptoms:

- ▸ Diminished or absent tendon reflexes

- ▸ Low-grade fever

- ▸ Muscle weakness that gradually moves up the arms, trunk, and face

> **CAUTION**
>
> The muscle weakness could eventually lead to respiratory compromise.

- ▸ Numbness, pain, and tingling in the lower extremities

- ▸ Autonomic dysfunction—instability of the cardiovascular system-hypertension, hypotension, tachycardia, bradycardia

The treatment phase for Guillian-Barrè is directed toward performing in-depth assessments and paying particular attention to the need for assisted ventilation. Emotional support and adequate nutrition are also used. You also need to be aware of other treatment modalities, including medications such as immunoglobulin (must use filter to deliver IV) and plasmapheresis. Plasmapheresis is used to remove circulating antibodies and speed the healing process. Other important aspects of care are to monitor the client for cardiac arrhythmias and manage any pain.

Degenerative Neurological Disorders

Several neurological disorders have similar pathophysiological features: There is a deficit in a neurotransmitter or an impairment of nerve conduction. Table 11.7 discusses these disorders, giving you an overview of each condition. As you study this table, keep in mind that the medications for treatment in several of the disorders are used to replace the deficiencies that can occur with the disease. You should study and learn this table and expect some of this information to be on the exam.

TABLE 11.7   Degenerative Neurological Disorders

	Alzheimer's	Amyotrophic Lateral Sclerosis (Lou Gehrig's Disease)	Huntington's Disease
Typical Age of Onset	30–65	40–70	30–50
Predisposition in Men or Women	Males and females equally	More men than women	Males and females equally
Possible Causes	None known; risk factors: Down syndrome, familial, genetics, older age	Unknown. Theories: autoimmune disease, overexcitation of nerves by glutamate, and free radical damage.	Genetic
Pathophysiology or area affected	Neuro-fibrillary tangles, decreased acetylcholine	Atrophic changes to muscle cells	Premature death of cells in basal ganglia that are involved in movement control. Loss of cortex cells also occurs (associated with thinking, memory, and judgment).
Symptoms	Forgetfulness and memory loss, depression, unable to recognize familiar faces, places and objects, disorientation. Sundowning, which is agitation and disorientation in the afternoon and evening	Depends on cells affected. Fatigue, muscle weakness that is progressive, twitching of the face, loss of coordination, spasticity, increased deep tendon reflexes, voice changes, dysphagia, dystonia.	Symptoms include emotional instability, chorea, uncontrollable body movements, difficulty chewing, dysphagia, loss of bowel and bladder control, mental deterioration
Pharmacalogic Treatment	Tacrine hydrochloride (Cognex) Donepezil (Aricept) Rivastigmine (Exelon) Galantamine hydrobromide (Reminyl) Memantine (Namenda)	Riluzole (Rilutek) Baclofen (Lioresal) Dantrolene sodium (Dantrium)	Thiothixene hydrochloride (Navane) Haloperidol decanoate (Haldol) Reserpine (Serpalen)
Nursing Treatment and Care	Promote maintenance of independence and patient functioning Ensure safety Provide structure Promote adequate nutrition	Rehabilitative services Promote adequate nutrition: enteral feedings Mechanical ventilation, reduce risk of aspiration	Explain genetic component (autosomal-dominant disorder) Manage symptoms Need increased calories due to choreic movements.

Cranial Nerve Disorders

Two types of cranial nerve disorders are discussed in the sections that follow:

- ▶ Trigeminal neuralgia (tic douloureux)
- ▶ Bell's palsy

These disorders result in pain or loss of motor or sensory function.

Trigeminal Neuralgia

Trigeminal neuralgia involves cranial nerve V. It occurs more often in women than men and is more common in the middle-aged population. There is chronic pressure or irritation on the trigeminal nerve. The main clinical manifestation is unilateral facial pain and contraction. Triggers of the pain include washing the face, brushing the teeth, and chewing.

Conservative treatment involves the use of medication therapy with antiseizure drugs, such as carbamazepine (Tegretol) and gabapentin (Neurontin). Local anesthetics can be used to block the nerve and control the pain. More invasive interventions are required if pain is not relieved by these measures.

Four types of surgical procedures are utilized:

- ▶ Glycol Rhizotomy
- ▶ Microvascular decompression of the trigeminal nerve
- ▶ Percutaneous radiofrequency rhizotomy
- ▶ Gamma knife radiosurgery.

Nursing measures in caring for clients with this disorder include

- ▶ Ice packs to the jaw after percutaneous radio frequency procedure.
- ▶ Instruct the client to chew on the unoperative side until sensation returns.
- ▶ Instruct the client to practice meticulous oral hygiene
- ▶ Assess for pain and administer medication to relieve it.
- ▶ Protect the eyes with artificial tears, eye shield.
- ▶ Instruct the client to use an electric razor to shave.

Bell's Palsy

The second type of cranial nerve disorder is Bell's palsy. This disorder is displayed by paresis without a cause (for example, stroke). The cranial nerve affected is VII. It is common in the age group of 20–60, and facial weakness and disfigurement of the face occur. There is unilateral inflammation of the cranial nerve with compression due to the edema. Necrosis of the nerve can occur. Symptoms associated with this disorder include

▸ One-sided facial pain and distortion

▸ Dystonia

▸ Loss of or excessive tearing

Management of a client with Bell's palsy include the use of heat to the area and pharmacological therapy with corticosteroids and antivirals (such as acyclovir (Zovirax). Nursing measures in the care of the client include

▸ Methylcellulose (artificial tears) instillation and eye protective shields

▸ Teaching of facial exercises

▸ Teaching the client to use dark sunglasses

▸ Teaching the client to chew on her unaffected side

Spinal Cord Injuries

Spinal cord injuries occur most often in young men between the ages of 16 and 30. Most cord injuries occur at the 5th, 6th, or 7th cervical, or at the 12th thoracic or the 1st lumbar. These areas are weaker due to the range of mobility needed. Cervical injuries above the C 4 level result in the loss of respiratory muscle function.

A spinal cord injury is classified as *complete* (no function below the level of injury) or *incomplete* (partial function remains). These injuries can occur from diseases—for example, tumors causing compression and damage—but the most frequent causes are trauma and falls. Clients with spinal cord injuries display the following characteristics:

▸ Acute respiratory failure

▸ Compromised respiratory function

▸ Loss of bowel and bladder tone

▸ Loss of sweating and vasomotor tone

▸ Marked reduction in BP due to loss of peripheral vascular resistance

▸ Sensory and motor paralysis below the level of injury

NOTE

Acute respiratory failure is the primary cause of death in high-level cord injuries.

Treatment of Spinal Cord Injuries

Treatment of spinal cord injuries follows the path of stabilization, monitoring and assessing, and preventing further damage. The following measures are important aspects of care:

- Use the Glasgow coma scale to assess the level of consciousness.

- Stabilize respiratory and cardiovascular system.

- Transport the client on a spinal board to prevent further damage.

- Administer Dextran to increase capillary blood flow in the spinal cord and help with hypotension. Dopamine (Intropin) might also be given to keep a systolic of at least 90.

- Corticosteroids to decrease or control spinal cord edema.

- Surgical reduction and alignment might be necessary. The procedures used include a surgical decompression laminectomy or spinal fusion with Harrington rod placement.

- The client with a cervical fracture might be placed in traction (after a reduction procedure or initially if the client is too unstable for surgery) with the use of skeletal tongs (see Figure 14.6 in Chapter 14, "Care of the Client with Musculoskeletal and Connective Tissue Disorders," for a picture of tong traction). Three types of tongs are

  - Crutchfield

  - Gardner-Wells

  - Vinke

CAUTION

Clients in tong traction must be moved carefully and as a unit (log roll). You will need a physician's instruction for turning.

A *halo vest* is another type of alignment immobilization device that provides immobilization of the bone with ambulation allowed. These clients, as well as clients with tongs, require pin care per hospital protocol with H_2O_2 or normal saline and/or possibly an antibiotic cream. Clients with thoracic and lumbar injuries may require a body cast or brace with bedrest.

NOTE

You must ensure that the vest is not causing pressure. Assess skin often. There should be enough space between the vest and skin for a finger to fit comfortably.

Dantrolene (Dantrium) and baclofen (Lioresal) can be given for spasticity. Long-term severe spasticity might require intrathecal baclofen via insertion of a pump.

Potential Complications with SCI Clients

Because of the damage to the spinal cord and autonomic nervous system, clients with SCIs can develop two main complications. The first complication is spinal shock, which occurs because of the sudden failure in the communication of the upper and lower neurons. Spinal shock can last for three to six weeks. Clients exhibit the following symptoms:

- ▶ Decreased heart rate
- ▶ Flaccid paralysis
- ▶ No perspiration below the level of the lesion
- ▶ Low blood pressure
- ▶ No reflex activity below the level of the lesion

Another complication from this syndrome is autonomic hyperreflexia or dysreflexia. Most often seen in injuries higher than T6, this disorder usually occurs after the spinal shock has resolved. This is a neurological emergency. You need to be familiar with clinical manifestations, which include the following:

- ▶ Bradycardia
- ▶ Headache
- ▶ Hypertension
- ▶ Nasal congestion
- ▶ Piloerection
- ▶ Profuse sweating
- ▶ Flushing above the level of the lesion
- ▶ Cold, dry, and pale skin below the level of the lesion

The treatment plan for autonomic dysreflexia focuses on removing the trigger or cause and lowering the blood pressure. The immediate interventions you will need to know are as follows:

- ▶ Remove the triggering stimuli. A full bladder is the most common cause.
- ▶ Elevate the head.
- ▶ Empty the bladder or check the Foley catheter tubing for kinks.
- ▶ Monitor blood pressure and administer ordered antihypertensive medications.
- ▶ Check for impaction after the episode has resolved.

> **NOTE**
>
> If inserting a Foley or checking for an impaction, use anesthetic ointment on the catheter tip or gloved finger.

Other complications associated with a spinal cord injuries are mainly associated with immobility and include the following:

▶ Clotting risks such as deep vein thrombosis (DVT) and emboli

▶ Impaired skin integrity—pressure ulcers

▶ Contractures

▶ incontinence

Intervertebral Disk Disease

Back pains are usually related to disk disease. These disorders have great social and economic impact. A *herniated* disk refers to the prolapse of the nucleus pulposus and protrusion of the invertebral disk into the spinal column, allowing pressure to be placed on spinal nerves. The herniated disk can occur anywhere in the spinal column, but most often occur at either the cervical or lumbar area. Most herniated lumbar disks are located at the fourth or fifth lumbar disk or at the fifth lumbar and first sacral disks and at the C5–6 and C6–7 interspaces for cervical disks herniations.

Symptoms of a herniated disk depend on the location of the herniation and generally include muscle spasms, pain, and stiffness in the back and neck. Clinical manifestations of lumbar disk herniation also include a positive straight leg test and sciatica pain with radiation of the pain into one hip and into the leg.

Table 11.8 offers management and treatment options for clients with cervical disk and lumbar disk. You should review the table recognizing the differences in care required for the cervical disk herniation compared to lumbar disk herniations.

TABLE 11.8 Herniated Disk Management and Treatment

	Lumbar Disk	**Cervical Disk**
Nonsurgical Treatment	Bedrest in the Williams position (semi-Fowler's with moderate hip and knee flexion). Massage. Hot, moist heat. Medications: NSAIDs (such as Toradol), analgesics (such as Vicodin), muscle relaxants (such as Skelaxin), steroids.	Bedrest Cervical collar Cervical traction (see Figure 14.7 in Chapter 14) Medications: Same as with lumbar

(continues)

TABLE 11.8 *Continued*

	Lumbar Disk	Cervical Disk
Surgical Treatment	Involves the removal of the herniated disk. It can be done with a spinal fusion, which involves the use of bone grafted from the iliac crest or from a bone bank to stabilize the area. The procedure is called a lumbar laminectomy. Two microsurgical techniques—the microdiscectomy and percutaneous discectomy—result in less blood loss, less pain, and shorter hospital stays. Another procedure, intradiscal electrothermal therapy (IDET), uses high temperatures of heat to seal the disk wall resulting in decreased bulging of the disk.	Endoscopic microdiscectomy (shorter hospital stay with less trauma) Cervical discectomy; may be performed anterior or posterior
Postoperative Care	Monitor for complications: arachnoiditis, adhesions of spinal nerves, and failed disk syndrome—pain that returns after surgery. Inspect wound for bleeding. Monitor neurological motor and sensory function. Assess for urinary retention.	Monitor for complications: anterior approach injuries—carotid or vertebral damage. Laryngeal nerve damage. Posterior approach—spinal cord damage. Both types: Assess operative site for serosanguinous drainage (might indicate a CSF leak) or assess for a hematoma. Note for both types: Remember that if the patient had a fusion done with a bone graft from the same patient, she will have two sites to assess. Perform neurological checks for motor and sensory function and report changes. Alert for both types: A large hematoma could cause damage to spinal cord and paralysis. Alert for both types: Pay attention! If client has sudden return of pain, it could mean that spine is unstable. Notify the doctor. Inspect skin under the cervical collar (usually worn for six weeks postoperative) for irritation.
Patient Teaching	Turn by using the log roll method to keep spine aligned; avoid sitting; avoid driving or riding in a car in a sitting position; avoid heavy work for two or three months.	Avoid sitting or standing for more than 30 minutes; avoid twisting, flexing, extending or rotating the neck; avoid sleeping on abdomen; keep the head in a neutral position; no high heel shoes.

Diabetes Insipidus

Diabetes insipidus is an endocrine disorder that occurs due to a deficit in secretion of the antidiuretic hormone (ADH) or vasopressin. It is a dysfunction occurring in the posterior pituitary gland. Disorders associated with the development of diabetes insipidus include head trauma, brain tumors, brain surgery, stroke, CNS infections, and medications that might interfere with ADH (such as lithium carbonate, Dilantin, or alcohol).

Just remember that ADH causes the body to retain fluids; therefore, a lack of ADH would cause the body to lose large amounts of fluids. The clinical manifestations of diabetes insipidus are associated with fluid loss. The two major symptoms are polydipsia (patient might crave cold ice water) and polyuria. Other symptoms include the following:

- Nocturia
- Weight loss
- Dehydration—poor skin turgor and dry mucous membranes
- Weakness
- Dilute excessive urine output (5– 20 liters per day) with a specific gravity of 1.001– 1.005

The treatment of diabetes insipidus includes measures that will replace the ADH, prevent complications that can occur from fluid loss, and correct the cause. These goals are accomplished by the use of pharmacological agents and astute assessment and nursing care, including

- Administration of prescribed medications
    - Desmopressin (DDAVP)—most commonly given

NOTE

The common route of administration for DDAVP is intranasal, but it can also be given orally or parenterally.

- Assess for dehydration
- Monitor electrolyte levels
- Accurate intake and output
- Administer prescribed fluids

Case Study

1. Mr. Tye is a 50-year-old male who is admitted after reporting numbness and weakness in his left arm. The doctor orders a CT scan in the emergency room to affirm the stroke type. Why is it important to get this test done right away?

2. The CT scan showed an ischemic stroke. Symptoms on Mr. Tye started two hours ago. How long do you have to administer t-PA after stroke symptoms occur? Explain what t-PA is and how is it administered?

3. Mr. Tye experiences an additional stroke and exhibits aphasia. Describe communication techniques for a patient with aphasia?

4. Mr. Tye is preparing for discharge and rehabilitation. Describe five products you could suggest to help the patient with enhanced self-care and maintenance of optimal functioning.

Answers to Case Study

1. It is important to find out which type of stroke the patient has had to determine treatment. One treatment of ischemic strokes is the administration of anticoagulation drugs. This drug would be contraindicated in clients with a hemorrhagic stroke and would make the hemorrhage more pronounced.

2. t-PA must be administered within three hours of a stroke; therefore, time is of the essence. Tissue plasminogen activator (t-PA) is produced by DNA technology. It is used to disintegrate clots. Recommended dose is 100 mg (60 mg in the first hour, followed by additional increments over the second and third hour). Most common complication is internal bleeding. It is given as an IV.

3. The nurse should implement the following when communicating with the aphasia patient:

   ▶ Speak in normal tone; don't talk loudly

   ▶ Use gestures, pictures, and objects to help with explanations

   ▶ Help the patient communicate by naming an object when the patient handles the object

   ▶ Turn off the TV, close the door, and so on to decrease any background noise before attempting to communicate

   ▶ Limit conversation to short simple sentences

   ▶ Use the same language and gestures each time for continuity

   ▶ Face the client and use eye contact when speaking

4. There are several available products that can be used by anyone to maintain safety, self-care, and functioning, including

   ▶ Mats that won't skid for under plate

   ▶ Handheld shower heads for bathing

   ▶ Shower and tub seats

   ▶ Grab bars in the shower

   ▶ Wide grip utensils or Velcro wrap handles

   ▶ Transfer boards and belts for mobility

   ▶ Velcro closures on clothing and shoes

Key Concepts

This chapter includes much-needed information to help the nurse apply knowledge of neurological disorders to the NCLEX exam. The nurse preparing for the licensure exam should be familiar with commonly ordered lab tests, including normal lab values, and medications used to treat the client with neurological disorders.

Key Terms

- ▶ Acetylcholine
- ▶ Apnea
- ▶ Apraxia
- ▶ Arachnoidtitis
- ▶ Areflexia
- ▶ Aura
- ▶ Automaticism
- ▶ Burr holes
- ▶ Cheyne-Stokes respirations
- ▶ Chorea
- ▶ Craniotomy
- ▶ Decerebrate posture
- ▶ Decorticate posture
- ▶ Diplopia
- ▶ Doll's eye phenomena
- ▶ Dysphasia
- ▶ Dyskinesia
- ▶ Exacerbation
- ▶ Expressive aphasia
- ▶ Fundoscopic
- ▶ Hemiplegia
- ▶ Hemiparesis
- ▶ Hydrocephalus
- ▶ Hypokinesia
- ▶ Hypocapnia
- ▶ Log roll
- ▶ Micrographia

- Nuchal

- Opisthotono

- Paresthesia

- Piloerection

- Plasmapheresis

- Postictal

- Ptosis

- Pulse pressure

- Receptive aphasia

- Rinne test

- Sciatica

- Scotoma

- Spasticity

- Tinnitus

Diagnostics

A part of the neurological assessment includes diagnostic exams. Routine laboratory work, such as the CBC, chest x-ray, and urinalysis will also be done. Blood cultures are also required to identify the causative agent in CNS infections. Clients with head injuries and spinal cord injuries need skull x-rays, CT scans, and MRIs to identify defects. When reviewing the diagnostic exams that follow, remember which tests are commonly done for a specific disorder. For example, the electroencephalogram is used for epilepsy and seizure activity:

- Cerebral arteriogram

- CT scan

- Electroencephalogram

- Lumbar puncture

- Magnetic resonance angiography (MRA)

- Magnetic resonance imaging (MRI)

- Positron emission tomography (PET)

- Skull x-rays

- Transcranial Doppler ultrasound

Pharmacological Agents Used in the Care of Clients with Neurological Disorders

Pharmacological interventions are used in most types of neurological problems. Some drug classifications are used in several disorders. For example, anticonvulsants are used in clients with epilepsy, but also in head injuries and brain tumors. While reviewing the drugs in Tables 11.9 through 11.13, you should recognize the most common ones, such as anticonvulsants, and realize that these drugs have a higher probability of being tested. Continue to look for the commonality in side effects of the drugs you are reviewing and focus on nursing considerations and adverse drug effects. These medications are not inclusive of all the agents used to treat neurological disorders; therefore, you will want to keep a current pharmacology text handy for reference.

TABLE 11.9 Antiparkinsonian Medications

Name	Action	Side Effects Include	Pertinent Nursing Implications
Levodopa (Laradopa; Dopar) Note: The most effective drug	Changes to dopamine in the basal ganglia.	GI irritation, psychiatric disturbances, orthostatic hypotension, cardiac irregularities, blurred vision.	Use with caution in clients with liver, respiratory, endocrine, peptic ulcer disease, and cardiovascular disease. B6 reverses effect of the medication. May darken client's urine.
Carbidopa- levodopa (Sinemet)	Provides the same action of Laradopa, but at lower doses.	Same as above.	Same as above.
Amantidine (Symmetrel)	Works in the central nervous system (CNS) to potentiate action of dopamine.	Restlessness, mental and emotional changes, leukopenia, hypotension.	Tolerated well, but less effective than levodopa. Assess vital signs, especially blood pressure. Monitor laboratory values and report abnormals to the healthcare provider.
Trihexyphenidyl (Artane)	Relieves tremor and rigidity by blocking muscarinic receptors at cholinergic CNS synapses.	Dry mouth, constipation, blurred vision, mental dullness, urinary retention. Symptoms increase with sudden withdrawal.	Administer after meals. Avoid rapid cessation of medication. Monitor for psychosis, increased blood sugar, and signs of glaucoma.
Benzatropine mesylate (Cogentin)	Same as above.	Same as above.	Same as above.
Ropinirole (Requip)	Stimulates dopamine receptors.	Dizziness, syncope, drowsiness, hallucinations, increased dyskinesia, sleep attacks, constipation, orthostatic hypotension, increased sweating.	Monitor for unexpected drowsiness or fall asleep episodes. No driving or operation of machinery until response to medication is known.

(continues)

TABLE 11.9 *Continued*

Name	Action	Side Effects Include	Pertinent Nursing Implications
Pramipexole (Mirapex)	Used to treat tremors, stiffness, and slow movements.	Hallucinations (especially in elderly), weakness, amnesia, drowsiness, dizziness, confusion, dyspepsia, leg cramps, urinary frequency.	Same as above.
Selagiline (Eldepryl)	Same as Requip. Used as adjunct to levodopa or in place of it if tolerance has developed. Inhibits MAO.	Insomnia, vivid dreams, dry mouth, confusion, dizziness.	Do not use with Demerol or opiods, SSRIs, antidepressants, or tricyclic antidepressants. Can cause severe reaction with those drugs. Alert: Assess for MAO-induced high BP, headache, chest pain, nausea and vomiting, photosensitivity, and pupil dilation.

> **NOTE**
>
> Other antiparkinson's drugs include COMT inhibitors, which increase the effects of levodopa. Entacapone (Comptan) is used in a combination with levodopa and carbidopa. Stalevo is a combination of levodopa, carbidopa, and entacapone.

TABLE 11.10 **Anticonvulsants (Antiepileptics)**

Name	Action	Side Effects Include	Pertinent Nursing Implications
Carbamazepine (Tegretol)	Limits seizures by increasing or decreasing movement of sodium across the cell membrane.	Dizziness, dry mouth, blurred vision, GI upset, drowsiness, agranulocytosis, glycosuria.	Watch for signs of infection, give with food, CBC (monitor platelet and reticulocyte count weekly for three months; then monthly). Monitor for electrolyte imbalance, especially hyponatremia.
Clonazepam (Klonopin)	Acts on limbic system, thalamus, and hypothalamus.	Leukopenia, rash, dysuria, drowsiness, confusion, nystagmus.	Use with caution in those with liver disease, chronic respiratory disorders, or narrow angle glaucoma. Do not discontinue abruptly—may cause status epilepticus.
Valproate sodium (Depakene)	Increases brain levels of aminobutyric acid.	Thrombocytopenia, increased bleeding time, depression, psychosis, GI upset, hepatitis.	Give with food or milk; obtain liver panel, platelet count, and protime before beginning medication and every month afterward.

TABLE 11.10 *Continued*

Name	Action	Side Effects Include	Pertinent Nursing Implications
Diazepam (Valium)	Decreases stimulation of CNS at the limbic and subcortical levels.	Drowsiness, lethargy, GI upset, nystagmus.	Avoid alcohol and CNS depressants, monitor CBC and liver function. Parenteral administration— do not mix with other drugs or fluids. IV administration; monitor respirations every 5–15 minutes. Do not mix with other IV fluids.
Gabapentin (Neurontin)	Used as adjunct to other drugs in the treatment of partial seizures. Action is unknown.	Drowsiness, ataxia, tremors, nystagmus, dizziness.	Warn client to avoid driving or other tasks that require alertness until drug effects are known.
Phenytoin (Dilantin)	Limits seizure propagation by inhibiting ion transport.	Nystagmus, gum hyperplasis, rashes, aplastic anemia, agranulocytosis.	Watch for signs of infection, CBC every six months. Therapeutic range is 10–20 mcg/mL. Rapid IV administration causes cardiovascular arrest. No more than 50 mg/min IV. Do not infuse IV with dextrose—will precipitate. Give IV with normal saline only. Monitor for folate deficiency.
Lamotrigine (Lamictal)	Same as Neurontin.	Dizziness, visual disturbances, headache, rash, GI upset.	Same as neurontin. Drug might increase sensitivity to light.
Levetiracetam (Keppra)	Appears to inhibit burst firing in the synapse of brain. Adjunct therapy for partial-onset seizures.	Somnolence, ataxia, headache vertigo, personality changes.	Alert: When used with Neurontin, increases its risk of toxic levels. Monitor CBC, renal, and liver function tests; instruct to rise slowly from sitting or lying position. Should use reliable birth control when taking this drug.
Zonisamide (Zonegran)	Adjunctive therapy. Appears to inhibit sodium channels.	Same as Keppra with the addition of difficulty in concentrating.	Teach to increase fluid intake; monitor for hyponatremia; monitor for kidney stones; caution about driving or operating machinery until effects are known. Instruct to rise slowly from sitting or lying position. Alert: Use with sulfonamides can cause a fatal reaction.

(continues)

TABLE 11.10 *Continued*

Name	Action	Side Effects Include	Pertinent Nursing Implications
Fosphenytoin (Cerebyx)	Same as Dilantin.	Same as Dilantin.	Developed to reduce problems associated with IV administration of Dilantin. Monitor vital signs and cardiac rhythm when giving a loading dose. Can be administered with dextrose solution IV.

NOTE

Other anticonvulsants include ethosuximide (Zarontin) for absence seizures and felbamate (Felbatol) for partial seizures.

TABLE 11.11   Alzheimer's Disease Drugs

Name	Action	Side Effects Include	Pertinent Nursing Implications
Tacrine hydrochloride (Cognex)	A cholinesterase inhibitor, increasing acetylcholine levels.	Mild GI upset.	Has high incidence of adverse effects; decreasing frequency in prescribing. Not to be used in clients with decreased liver function.
Donepezil (Aricept)	Same as above.	Mild GI upset, agitation with initial treatment—decreases with use.	Take with food to decrease or eliminate GI upset. Cholinergic crisis occurs with overdose—treat with atropine sulfate IV.
Galantamine hydrobromide (Reminyl)	Same as above.	Same as Donepezil.	Instruct to take drug on time and not miss a dose. If drug is abruptly discontinued, will have to restart as initially begun and client will lose all effects.
Rivastigmine (Exelon)	Same as above.	Same as above.	Same as Aricept
Memantine (Namenda)	Attaches to nervous system receptors called n-methyl-d- aspartate (NMDA) to control glutamate levels.	Headache, dizziness, confusion, and constipation.	Gradual dosing should be done for best and safest effects.

TABLE 11.12   Multiple Sclerosis Medications

Name	Action	Side Effects Include	Pertinent Nursing Implications
Metaxalone (Skelaxin)	Skeletal muscle relaxation.	Dizziness, nervousness, nausea, urinary retention.	Instruct in safety of use due to side effects. No alcohol use when taking this drug. No driving or operation of machinery until effects of drug are known.
Dantrolene (Dantrium)	Also used for malignant hyperthermia. Acts on skeletal muscle, relaxing by calcium release in muscle cells.	Drowsiness, muscle weakness, confusion, dizziness, headache, insomnia, tearing, vision changes, GI bleeding, myalgia. GI upset.	Might have to discontinue due to consistent diarrhea; can cause choking and dysphagia. Use sunscreen and clothing to block the sun for photosensitivity.
Tizanidine (Zanaflex)	Reduces spasticity at motor neuron level.	Weakness, drowsiness, dizziness, blurred vision, dyspepsia, urinary frequency, myasthenia, fever, paresthesis.	Monitor for orthostatic hypotension and sedation. Client might have increased risk for falls.
Baclofen (Lioresal)	Decrease spasticity by inhibiting spinal reflex.	Dizziness, drowsiness, fatigue, nasal congestion, depression, tinnitus, ataxia.	Can be given intrathecal (IT). Alert: IT test doses can have life threatening effects—respiratory. Have resuscitation equipment available.
Rebif Interferon beta-1a (Avonex) Interferon beta-1b (Betaseron)	Regulates immunity and an antiviral.	Flu-like symptoms (malaise, aches, chills, fever, and so on), GI upset, chest pain, palpitations, depression, weakness, confusion, alopecia, photosensitivity.	Monitor for depression, monitor CBC, and blood chemistry test, especially liver function. Teach injection administration. Should wear sunscreen and protective clothing when going outside.

NOTE

Other drugs for multiple sclerosis include mitoxantrone (Novantrone)-an anti tumor antibiotic that is also given in prostate cancer and glatiramer acetate (Copaxone).

TABLE 11.13   Medications to Diagnose and Treat Myasthenia Gravis

Name	Action	Side Effects Include	Pertinent Nursing Implications
Endrophonium (Tensilon)	Anticholinesterase short acting	GI symptoms, muscle twitching, weakness, hypotension, toxic effects, cholinergic crisis	Used as a diagnostic agent and in emergency treatment (differentiates disease from cholinergic crisis). Antidote is Atropine and should be available during diagnostic test.
Neostigmine methysulfate (Prostigmine)	Blocks the breakdown of acetylcholine at the myoneural junction	Same as above	Give the smallest dose that provides relief of symptoms; monitor vital signs; note CNS irritability.
Pyridostigmine bromide (Mestinon)	Same as above	Same as above	Same as above. Give before meals.

Apply Your Knowledge

This chapter provided information regarding the care of clients with neurological disorders. The following questions test your knowledge regarding the safe, effective care and management of the client with various neurological disorders. The nurse should use the key terms, diagnostics, chapter content, and pharmacological agents sections to assist in answering these questions.

Exam Questions

1. The nurse realizes that most partial seizures arise from which area of the brain?

    A. Frontal lobe

    B. Occipital lobe

    C. Temporal lobe

    D. Parietal lobe

2. A client is on the neurological unit after a sports injury resulting in a thoracic fracture. The nurse's assessment reveals an intact halo device, flushing of the face and upper chest area, goose bumps, and a stuffy nose. What additional assessment would be most important at this time?

    A. Breath sounds

    B. Deep tendon reflexes

    C. Blood pressure

    D. Bowel sounds

3. The nurse assessing the laboratory values of a client with possible Guillain-Barrè recognizes which value as the most distinguishing feature of the disease?

   A. CSF protein elevation with a normal cell count

   B. WBC count of 2800 mm

   C. Abnormal liver function test

   D. Abnormal electromyographic (EMG) studies

4. Which item is necessary for a client who has a halo device in place after cervical fracture reduction surgery?

   A. Ambu bag

   B. IV controller

   C. Bit drill

   D. Torque screwdriver

5. A college student is recovering from Guillain-Barré. The student asks the nurse, "Will having this disease affect my ability to learn and function mentally?" Which response is appropriate?

   A. "Guillain-Barrè does not affect cognitive function."

   B. "Don't worry about school at this time."

   C. "I will ask your doctor for you."

   D. "You should get in touch with your school because you will not be able to handle the stress of trying to learn."

6. The nurse is making rounds on a client who is in cervical tongs. Assessment reveals detachment of one of the pins. Which nursing action is most appropriate?

   A. Call for help immediately and stabilize the clients' head in the neutral position.

   B. Go to the nursing station and call the neurosurgeon immediately.

   C. Lower the head of the bed and add more weight to the traction.

   D. Turn the client to the left side, raising the knee gatch on the bed.

7. A client post craniotomy has been diagnosed with SIADH. Which symptoms would the nurse expect the client to exhibit?

   A. Polydipsia and bradycardia

   B. Euphoria and polyuria

   C. Muscle weakness and irritability

   D. Ringing in the ears and blurred vision

8. A client with meningitis has been admitted from a small community hospital after no improvement from previous treatment. Which medication will the nurse be prepared to administer?

    A. Vancomycin (Vancocin) IV

    B. Ampicillin (Omnipen) PO

    C. Ceftriazone (Rocephin) IM

    D. Cefotaxime sodium (Claforan)

9. A client with multiple sclerosis has been prescribed the drug baclofen (Lioresal). What is the action of this drug?

    A. Reduces spasticity

    B. Skeletal muscle relaxation

    C. Immune suppression

    D. Prevents viral infections

10. Parkinson's disease has been diagnosed in a client exhibiting tremors. Which of the following is lacking in this disorder?

    A. Celestone

    B. Dopamine

    C. Serotonin

    D. Anti-diuretic hormone

11. A client has an ICP monitor in place. The nurse recognizes which as an abnormal level of ICP reading?

    A. 10

    B. 15

    C. 20

    D. 25

12. The nurse is observing the physician in assessment of a client with suspected meningitis. The doctor is seen raising the thigh upon the body to see whether pain occurs in the hamstring muscle. What is the doctor checking for?

    A. Kernig's sign

    B. Brown-Sequard's syndrome

    C. Brudsinski's sign

    D. Doll's eye reflex

Answers to Exam Questions

1. Answer C is correct. Partial seizures usually originate in the temporal lobe, making Answers A, B, and D incorrect because partial seizures do not usually occur in the other lobes.

2. Answer C is correct. The patient is exhibiting symptoms of autonomic dysreflexia. The hypertension can be severe and requires treatment; therefore, this assessment is essential. The assessments in Answers A, B, and D might all be done, but C is the priority, so the others are incorrect.

3. Answer A is correct. This is the most definitive diagnostic result. The client would experience and elevated white blood cell count, which makes Answer B incorrect. Answers C and D can occur with many diagnoses, so they are not specific for Guillain-Barrè and are incorrect.

4. Answer D is correct. This equipment is necessary in case the pins become loose. The family should also be instructed in this before discharge for home care. The answers in A, B, and C are not necessary are appropriate due to a halo vest application.

5. Answer A is correct. Cognitive function is not affected by Guillain-Barrè. The answers in B, C, and D offer no reply to the stated question and are inappropriate communication techniques, so they are incorrect.

6. Answer A is correct. The priority concern is patient safety and prevention of damage to the spinal cord. Answers B, C, and D are not appropriate actions by the nurse, so they are incorrect.

7. Answer C is correct. Other symptoms of SIADH include loss of thirst, tachycardia, hostility, and decreased urinary output. This makes Answers A and B incorrect. The answer in D is not associated with SIADH, so it is incorrect.

8. Answer A is correct. Vancomycin IV would be the antibiotic of choice for resistant strands of meningitis. The client would need the medication to work quickly, making Answers B and C incorrect. Answer D is an antibiotic used for meningitis, but would not be the one of choice for resistant strains of meningitis, so it is wrong.

9. Answer A is correct. The drug Baclofen (Lioresal) might also improve bowel and bladder function. Answers B, C, And D do not refer to the drug Lioresal, so they are incorrect.

10. Answer B is correct. The neurotransmitter dopamine is missing in clients with Parkinson's disease. Most of the treatment involves replacement of this drug. Answer A is a steroid. Answer C is a neurotransmitter not missing in Parkinson's disease, and Answer D is secreted by the pituitary gland not related to the stated diagnosis; therefore Answers A, C, and D are incorrect.

11. Answer D is correct. The normal ICP reading is 10–20. 25 would be increased and abnormal. Answers A, B, and C are all within the normal range, so they are incorrect.

12. Answer A is correct. A positive result would be indicated by pain in the hamstring when the actions in the stem are done. Answers B and D do not relate to meningitis. Brudsinski's sign, Answer C, is elicited by attempting to flex the patients' head causing severe pain if positive, so this is incorrect. Both Kernig's and Brudsinski's signs are indications of meningeal irritation found in meningitis.

Suggested Reading and Resources

▶ Brunner, L., and D. Suddarth. *Textbook of Medical Surgical Nursing* 10th ed. Philadelphia: Lippincott Williams & Wilkins, 2009.

▶ Deglin, Judith H., and April H. Vallerand. *Davis Drug Guide for Nurses*. Philadelphia: F. A. Davis, 2009.

▶ Lemone, P., and K. Burke. *Medical-Surgical Nursing Critical Thinking in Client Care* 4th ed. Upper Saddle River, NJ: Pearson Prentice Hall, 2008.

▶ Lewis, S., M. Heitkemper, S. Dirksen, P. O'Brien, and L. Bucher. *Medical Surgical Nursing: Assessment and Management of Clinical Problems* 7th ed. Philadelphia: Elsevier, 2007.

▶ Rinehart, Sloan, Hurd. *Exam Cram NCLEX-RN*. Indianapolis: Que Publishing, 2007.

▶ Rinehart, Sloan, Hurd. *NCLEX Exam PREP*. Indianapolis: Pearson Education. Vue Publishers, 2007.

▶ Smith, F., D. Duell, B. Martin. *Clinical Nursing Skills Basic to Advanced Skills* 7th ed. Upper Saddle River, NJ: Pearson Prentice Hall, 2008.

▶ Centers for Disease Control and Prevention: www.cdc.gov

12

Care of the Client with Immunologic Disorders

A number of body systems serve to protect the body against pathogens. These include the skin, mucous membrane, cilia in the lungs, saliva, hydrochloric acid in the stomach, flushing action of urinary flow in the renal system, and lower pH in the reproductive system. When there is a threat to the normal cellular function, the immune system responds. Hypersensitivity is an exaggerated immune response by an otherwise normal immune system that is caused by exposure to medications, pet dander, foods, or other allergens. When exposure occurs, the body responds with bronchial spasms, wheezing, rhinorrhea, and urticaria. Treatment of allergies includes the use of antihistamines such as diphenhydramine (Benadryl), cetirizine hcl (Zyrtec), Loratidine (Claritin), steroid preparations, and others. Immunoglobulin titers and skin testing can be done to determine the degree of response and the allergen responsible for the reaction.

There are other types of reactions. The Gell and Coombs Classification of Hypersensitivity Reactions is a method of classifying allergic response into four types of reactions:

▶ **Type I:** An allergic response, it can be immediate or a cumulative response. Examples of Type I are allergies to pet dander.

▶ **Type II:** Cytotoxic and cytolytic response, in which the production of autoantibodies results in the client's cells and tissues being destroyed. Examples of this type of response include Goodpasture's syndrome.

▶ **Type III:** Antigen-antibody complexes. Examples of this type of reaction include systemic lupus erythematosus and rheumatoid arthritis. See Chapter 14, "Care of the Client with Musculoskeletal and Connective Tissue Disorders," for a discussion of lupus erythematosus and rheumatoid arthritis.

▶ **Type IV:** Delayed hypersensitivity reaction, which involves T-lymphocytes. Examples of this type are graft rejection, reaction to plant proteins such as poison ivy, and exposure to tubercle bacilli.

See other chapters that are specific to these disorders for treatment.

Immunodeficiency Syndrome

Immunodeficiency syndrome occurs when there is a failure of the body's ability to fight infection. This syndrome can be a result of either a genetic disorder or infection with a retrovirus.

The client with immune disorders often presents to the doctor with signs of multisystem involvement. The cause is usually unknown and the infections are difficult to control. Iatrogenic causes of immunodeficiency might be secondary to other diseases, such as cancers, or could relate to treatments that suppress the normal function of the immune system, such as chemotherapy or radiation. Nurses dealing with clients who are immune suppressed must be aware of the dangers associated with disease transmission. Utilization of negative pressure rooms, isolation, handwashing, and sterile techniques help to prevent disease transmission. Room arrangement to avoid placing immune suppressed clients near clients with active infection, coughing, vomiting, or diarrhea are also necessary. When visiting several clients, the nurse should visit the immune suppressed client before visiting the client with infections.

Human Immunodeficiency Virus (HIV) leads to depletion of the CD4+ (T4) helper cells. This depletion causes an inability to fight off opportunistic infections. Infected CD4+ (T4) helper cells are targeted by Human Immunodeficiency Virus CD8+ killer cells. Acquired immune deficiency syndrome (AIDS) is caused by the HIV virus. AIDS was first identified in the 1980s and is believed to derive from infections found in the green monkey of Africa. It is thought that for some reason the virus mutated and became a virus that affects human beings. There are two types of HIV:

- ▶ **Type 1 (HIV-1):** Found in Western Europe and Asia
- ▶ **Type 2 (HIV-2):** Found in West Africa

HIV results in an abnormal cell that cannot fight infection. That abnormal cell duplicates, producing more of the virus. The result is a decrease in the helper cells and an increase in the suppressor cells.

Transmission occurs through sexual contact or parenteral or perinatal exposure to the retrovirus. Sexual contamination occurs when there is exposure of the mucous membranes to infected semen or vaginal secretions. Parenteral contamination occurs when needles or equipment is contaminated from infected blood or when the client receives contaminated blood products. Perinatal exposure occurs when the placenta is contaminated from contact with maternal blood and body fluids during birth or through breast milk from an infected mother.

Because the client is immune-suppressed, she is at risk for opportunistic infections. Some examples of opportunistic infections include the following:

- ▶ Candidiasis (If the client has persistent yeast infections, either vaginal or oral, that have been treated and are not responsive to treatment, the nurse should suspect that the client might be HIV positive.)

▶ Histoplasmosis (a fungal infection transmitted by bird feces)

▶ Pneumocystis carinii (caused by the protozoa jiroveci)

▶ Toxoplasmosis (transmitted by cat feces)

▶ Encephalopathies

▶ Kaposi sarcoma

▶ Salmonella septicemia (transmitted through uncooked eggs or egg-laying animals)

▶ Herpes (transmitted by contact with lesions or blood)

▶ Mycobacterium (transmitted by droplets from the respiratory system)

▶ Wasting syndrome of HIV

▶ Cytomegalovirus (transmitted by blood and body fluids)

▶ Crytococcosses (transmitted by inhaling the fungus into the lungs)

▶ Cryptosporidiosis (transmitted by contact with the parasite in the intestines)

Diagnoses

Diagnosis of immunological disorders is made by examination of the blood or body fluids. Testing includes antibody tests to measure the client's antibody response to the presence of HIV. These tests are the Enzyme-Linked Immunosorbent Assay (ELISA) test and the Western Blot Analysis test. Initially the client is checked using the ELISA test. If this test is positive on two occasions, the Western Blot Analysis test is performed. The Western Blot Analysis test is considered to be the most diagnostic test. This laboratory test identifies HIV antibodies. The indirect immunofluorescence assay (IFA) is also used to confirm the diagnosis. The advantage of the IFA is that it is easily performed and gives a faster response. Another test is the radioimmunoprecipitation assay (RIPA), which detects the HIV protein rather than antibodies.

An oral mucosal transudate (OMT) test is an alternative to the standard blood test. A treated pad is placed in the client's mouth and gently rubbed between the cheek and gum. The pad collects an oral fluid called *oral mucosal transudate*. This reveals whether the client has HIV antibodies present. The urine HIV antibody test uses the urine E1A (ELISA) and urine Western Blot technique to detect HIV antibodies. The Home Access and the Oracle test are quick tests for antigens.

The progression of the disease can be tracked by monitoring several tests, including

▶ **p24 levels:** This test tracks the amount of viral core protein (p24 antigen). The person with HIV who is asymptomatic will present with a low p24 level, whereas the person with advanced AIDS will have an elevated p24 level.

▶ **Viral load:** A client with a viral load of less than 400 is considered relatively free of circulating virus.

▶ **Lymphocytes counts:** This test is part of complete blood count. Clients with AIDS are often leukopenic (a WBC below 3500 cells/mm³) and usually lymphopenic (less than 1500 lymphocytes/mm³).

▶ **CD4/CD8 counts:** The percentage and number of CD4+ (T4) and CD8+ (T8) count indicates the amount of suppressor cells as they compare to the helper cells. People with AIDS have a lower than normal number of CD4+ cells. The normal ratio of CD8+ cells is approximately 2:1. (The first letters indicate the number of helper cells [CD4], and the second letters indicate the number of suppressor cells [CD8].) The normal ratio is to have twice as many helper cells as suppressor cells, but in the client with HIV, the number of suppressor cells is twice as many as helper cells.

▶ **Viral culture:** This test measures the amount of reverse transcriptase (RT) activity over 28 days. The more RT, the more active the virus.

After making the initial diagnosis of HIV, the physician makes a determination of the clinical status of the client. The Centers for Disease Control (CDC) and Prevention has classified HIV infection by the CD4 count and the opportunistic diseases that the client has experienced. Table 12.1 describes the CDC's clinical categories.

TABLE 12.1   CDC Classification of HIV Infection

Classification	Description
Clinical Category A (Asymptomatic)	A1: CD4 + T-cell count greater than or equal to 500 cubic mm/liter
	A2: CD4 + T-cell count of 200–499 cubic mm/liter
	A3: CD4 + T-cell less than 200 cubic mm/liter
	Confirmed HIV; persistent lymphadenopathy; acute (primary) HIV infection with accompanying illness or history of acute infection
Clinical Category B (Symptomatic)	B1: CD4 + T-cell count greater than or equal to 500 cubic mm/liter
	B2: CD4 + T-cell count 200–499 cubic mm/liter
	B3: CD4 + T-cell count less than 200 cubic mm/liter
	All the signs found in clinical category A, plus the client might have bacillary angiomatosis; oral leukoplakia; candidiasis; cervical carcinoma; diarrhea for one month or more; herpes zoster; idiopathic thrombocytopenic purpura; listeriosis; pulmonary mycobacterium tuberculosis; nocardiosis, pelvic inflammatory disease; peripheral neuropathy
Clinical Category C (Symptomatic)	C1: CD4 + T-cell count greater than or equal to 500 cubic mm/liter
	C2: CD4 + T-cell count of 200–499 cubic mm/liter
	C3: CD4 + T-cell count less than 200 cubic mm/liter
	All the signs found in clinical categories A and B, plus the client might have candidiasis of bronchi; cervical cancer; coccidioidomycosis; cryptococcoses; cryptosporidiosis; cytomegalovirus; retinitis; encephalopathy; herpes; histoplasmosis; Kaposi's sarcoma; mycobacterium; Pneumocystis carinii pneumonia; Salmonella septicemia; toxoplasmosis of the brain; wasting syndrome of HIV

HIV Prevention

The focus of prevention of the transmission of the HIV is education. The client should be taught the modes of transmission and the risk involved when the client has unprotected sexual contact or shares needles and parenteral drug equipment. Latex or nonlatex condoms with a water-soluble lubricant containing spermicide should be used during intercourse. Oral dams or condoms should be used during oral sex. Lambskin condoms are less effective in the prevention of transmission of the virus. Because transmission can occur during intercourse, the risk of introducing the virus during an attempt to conceive is present. Infection by artificial insemination using processed semen from an HIV-infected partner is being studied; however, results at present are inconclusive.

Healthcare workers and those who care for clients with AIDS should take precautions to prevent contamination with blood and body fluids. Standard precautions, including wearing gloves, masks, and/or gowns, should be taken when blood and body fluids are present. A hypochlorite solution of 1 part bleach to 10 parts water has proven to destroy the AIDS virus. The hypochlorite solution should be mixed each day, and the seal should be tight on the container to prevent loss of the bleach by evaporation. The sections that follow describe standard precautions and treatment for exposure.

Standard Precautions

▶ Gloves should be worn when there is a chance of contact with blood and body fluids, when handling other potentially infected material, and when performing vascular access procedures.

> **NOTE**
>
> Body fluids likely to transmit blood-borne disease include blood, semen, vaginal/cervical secretions, tissues, cerebral spinal fluid, amniotic fluid, synovial fluid, pleural fluid, peritoneal fluid, pericardial fluid, and breast milk.
>
> Body fluids not likely to transmit blood-borne disease unless blood is visible include feces, nasal secretions, sputum, vomitus, sweat, tears, urine, and saliva (with the exception of during oral surgery or dentistry).

▶ Gloves should be changed after each client contact and between contact procedures with the same client.

▶ Masks and protective eyewear should be used when there is a likelihood of splashes or when body fluids might become airborne.

▶ Gloves and aprons should be worn during procedures in which there is a likelihood of splashes of blood or body fluids.

▶ Handwashing should be done immediately after contact with body fluids or other potentially infected material and as soon as gloves are removed.

▶ Needles and sharps should be disposed in a sharps container—no recapping, bending, or breaking of needles.

▶ Mouth-to-mouth resuscitation should be performed using a mouthpiece or another ventilation device.

Airborne Transmission–Based Precautions (Second Tier of CDC Guidelines for Infection Control)

Infections caused by organisms remain suspended in the air for prolonged periods of time. Examples of infections that can be transmitted by airborne means include tuberculosis, measles (rubeola), chicken pox (varicella), and disseminated zoster (shingles). Nursing precautions for managing the client with an infection that can be spread by airborne means include

▶ Placing the client in a private room with negative airflow (and with the door remaining closed)

▶ Equipping persons entering the room with a HEPA mask or an N-95 mask

▶ Lighting the room with ultraviolet light

▶ Transporting the client only when essential

▶ Fitting the client with a surgical mask when being transported

Infections are spread in several different ways. The sections that follow explain these methods of transmission and how the nurse can help to prevent the spread of germs.

Droplet Transmission–Based Precautions (Second Tier of CDC Guidelines for Infection Control)

Droplet transmission–based infections are those caused by organisms suspended in droplets that may travel three feet but are not suspended in the air for long periods of time. Examples of droplet transmission–based infections include influenza, mumps, pertussis, rubella, diphtheria, pneumonia, scarlet fever, streptococcal pharyngitis, and meningitis caused by *N. meningitidis* or *H. influenza B*.

Nursing precautions for managing the client with a droplet transmission–based infection include

▶ Placing the client in a private room or cohort with a client who has the same illness. The door may remain open.

▶ Placing clients no closer than three feet from one another.

▶ Making sure caregivers wear a mask for face-to-face contact.

Contact Transmission–Based Precautions (Second Tier of CDC Guidelines for Infection Control)

Contact transmission–based infections are those caused by organisms spread by direct contact. Examples of contact transmission-based infections include RSV, scabies, and colonization with MRSA and VRE.

Nursing precautions for managing the client with a contact transmission–based infection include

▸ The client should be placed in a private room or cohort with a client who has the same condition.

▸ Caregiver should glove when entering room.

▸ Gowns should be worn to prevent contact with clients.

▸ Hands should be washed with antimicrobial soap before leaving the client's room.

▸ Equipment used by the client should remain in the room and should be disinfected before being used by anyone else.

▸ Client should be transported only for essential procedures; during transport, precautions should be taken to prevent disease transmission.

Treatments After Occupational Exposure

If the healthcare worker is contaminated with blood or body fluid, the CDC recommends treatment dependent on the type and source of contamination. The nurse should notify the office of employee health and safety in his hospital to report exposure.

Management of the Client with HIV

Clients with AIDS are treated with several categories of drugs. Highly active antiretroviral therapy (HAART), formerly known as the AIDS "cocktail," consists of treatment with multiple drugs. Examples of drugs used in this type of therapy include the following:

▸ **Nucleoside analog reverse transcriptase inhibitors:** Inhibit reverse transcriptase. Examples include nevirapine (Viramune), delavirdine (Rescriptor), efavirenz (Sustiva), zidovudine (AZT), and lamivudine (3TC). AZT is used during pregnancy to decrease maternal-fetal transmission. After delivery, the infant will probably be given AZT for approximately the first six weeks of life.

▸ **Protease inhibitors:** Block the HIV protease enzyme and prevent viral replication and the release of viral particles. Examples include indinavir (Crixivan), ritonariv (Norvir), saquinavir (Invirase), nelfinavir (Viracept), amprenavir (Agenerase), lopinavir (ABT- 378r, Kaletra), and TMC-114 darunavir (Prezista).

> ▶ **Ribonucleotide reductase inhibitors:** As a new use for cytotoxic therapies, they interfere with DNA synthesis and stop viral replication. Examples include hydroxyurea (Hydrea).

> ▶ **Entry inhibitors:** This group of drugs is newly released and has been shown to reduce the viral load significantly. Fusion drugs inhibit the HIV from entering target cells by binding protein in the virus. When the virus is bound to the drug, the virus cannot adhere to the cell membrane. Examples include Enfuvirtide (Fuzeon).

Opportunistic diseases are also treated specifically dependent on the pathogen responsible for the infection. Some examples of these opportunistic illnesses and their treatment include the following:

▶ **Protozoal infections:**

> ▶ Pneumocystis carinii pneumonia: TMP/SMX (Bactrim).

> ▶ Toxoplasmosis encephalitis: Pyrimethamine and sulfadiazine.

> ▶ Cryptosporidiosis: Metronidazole (Flagyl), antidiarrheal (Lomotil).

▶ **Fungal infections:**

> ▶ Candidiasis: Fluconazole (Diflucan), ketoconazole (Nizoral).

> ▶ Cryptococcosis: Fluconazole (Diflucan).

> ▶ Histoplasmosis: Ketoconazole (Nizoral).

> ▶ Unresolved vaginal yeast infections for a year or more might indicate presence of HIV.

▶ **Bacterial infections:**

> ▶ Mycobacterium avium: Intracellular complex (MAC), ciprofloxacin (Cipro), clofazimine (Lamprine).

> ▶ Tuberculosis: Pyrazinamide (Tebrazid), isoniazid (Lanzid).

▶ **Viral infections:**

> ▶ Cytomegalovirus (CMV): Ganciclovir (Cytovene).

> ▶ Herpes simplex virus (HSV): Acyclovir (Zovirax).

> ▶ Varicella: zoster virus (VZV): Acyclovir (Zovirax).

The client should be cautioned regarding the use of herbals such as echinacea because they decrease the effectiveness of antiviral medications.

Comfort measures include pain management and nonsteroidal anti-inflammatory medications for myalgia and inflammation. Antidepressants such as amitriptyline (Elavil) are used to treat depression associated with the disease and the prognosis. Anticonvulsants such as phenytoin (Dilantin) might be ordered to treat seizure disorders associated with neuropathies.

Diet therapy should include education regarding the need to increase calories, protein, vitamins, and minerals. The client should be educated in the risk of eating contaminated foods. The client should be instructed to wash and/or cook food to destroy bacteria. Eating from a salad bar, eating foods grown in or on the ground, and eating cultured foods such as yogurt and cottage cheese should be discouraged. The client should avoid drinking standing water or liquids because bacteria begins to grow in standing water after 20 minutes. The cap should be kept on the bottle, and liquids should be stored in the refrigerator or cooler to minimize bacterial growth. Vitamin supplementation and total parenteral nutrition (TPN) might be ordered for clients with severe nutritional deficits.

Other treatment for the client with AIDS includes mouth care, skin care, oxygen therapy, emotional support, chemotherapy for cancers associated with AIDS, and seizure precautions. The prognosis depends on the progression of the illness. Since the discovery of the HIV virus, the development of a vaccine to prevent HIV infection has been the focus of research. Vaccines that stimulate the immune system are also being developed, but at present none are available.

Case Study

Jeff is a 30-year-old male hospitalized with *Pneumocystis carinii* pneumonia. Several months ago, he was diagnosed with HIV and has since progressed to Category C AIDS.

1. What are the diagnostic tests for HIV?

2. What is the treatment for *Pneumocystis carinii* pneumonia?

3. Give some examples of disease experienced by the client with Category C AIDS.

4. List four nursing diagnoses for the client with AIDS.

5. Discuss Jeff's prognosis.

Answers to Case Study

1. The diagnostic test for HIV are the ELISA test, the Western Blot, the immunofluorescence assay (IFA), and the radioimmunoprecipitation assay (RIPA). Other tests for progression of the disease are the viral load, T-cell counts, and complete blood cell count. The diagnosis of *Pneumocystis carinii* pneumonia is made by a culture of sputum and a chest x-ray.

2. The treatment for *Pneumoncystis carinii* pneumonia includes use of TMP-SMZ (Bactrim). IV pentamidine can be used to treat the infection or as a prophylactic to prevent the infection. The combination of oral trimethoprim (Proloprim, Trimpex) and dapsone (Avlosulfon, DDS) has been used to treat Pneumoncystis pneumonia. Other medications used are clindamycin (Cleosin HCl), oral primaquine, trimetrexate, hydroxynaphthoquinone, and atovaquone (Mepron). Some patients with PCP benefit from treatment with systemic corticosteroid therapy.

(continues)

(continued)

3. Examples of diseases experienced by the client with Category C AIDS include candidiasis of the bronchi, cervical carcinoma, coccidioidomycosis, cryptococcoses, cryptosporidiosis, retinitis, encephalopathy,herpes, histoplasmosis, Kaposi's sarcoma, mycobacterium, *Pneumocystis carinii* pneumonia, *Salmonella* septicemia, toxoplamosis of the brain, and wasting syndrome of HIV, plus others experienced by the client with clinical categories A and B.

4. Four nursing diagnoses for the client with AIDS are as follows:

   ▶ Risk for infection related to immunodeficiency

   ▶ Diarrhea related to enteric pathogens or HIV infection

   ▶ Altered nutrition, less than body requirement, related to decreased oral intake

   ▶ Ineffective airway clearance related to *Pneumocystis carinii* pneumonia, increased bronchial secretions, and inability to cough effectively

5. The prognosis for Jeff depends on his response to treatment. Each time the client has Pneumocystis pneumonia, scarring of the lung occurs. There is also a risk for abscess formation in the lungs.

Key Concepts

This chapter discussed immunologic disorders. The nursing student should use these key concepts to answer questions as they relate to the care of this client. Remembering the pathophysiology of the disease process, the treatment, and the laboratory values will help you to be able to answer questions in the physiologic integrity portion of the NCLEX exam.

Key Terms

- AIDS
- Clinical categories
- ELISA
- HAART (Highly Active Antiretroviral Therapy)
- Helper T4 lymphocyte
- Kaposi's sarcoma
- Nucleoside analog reverse transcriptase inhibitors
- Opportunistic infection
- *Pneumocystis carinii* pneumonia (PCP)
- Polymerase chain (PCR)
- Protease inhibitor
- Retrovirus
- Ribonucleotide reductase inhibitors
- Standard precautions
- Viral culture
- Viral load
- Wasting syndrome
- Western Blot assay

Diagnostic Tests

The exam reviewer should be knowledgeable of the preparation and care of clients receiving exams to diagnose immunologic disorders. While reviewing these diagnostic exams, the exam reviewer should be alert for information that would be an important part of nursing care for these clients. The pertinent labs and exams are as follows:

- Human Leukocyte Antigen (HLA)
- Anti-DNA antibody testing

- ▶ Erythrocyte Sedimentation Rate (ESR)
- ▶ Serum complement levels
- ▶ ELISA
- ▶ Western Blot assay
- ▶ Oral mucosal transudate test
- ▶ Urine HIV antibody test
- ▶ Rapid HIV antibody test
- ▶ Home testing kits
- ▶ Viral Load
- ▶ Viral culture
- ▶ CD4/CD8 counts + T cell count
- ▶ Lymphocyte counts (WBC)
- ▶ P24 antigen assay
- ▶ Quantitative RNA assay: polymerase chain reaction
- ▶ Biopsies for cancers
- ▶ Pap smears for cervical cancer
- ▶ Urinalysis
- ▶ Chest x-rays
- ▶ Sputum of lung secretions
- ▶ Cultures and cell smears for other opportunistic diseases

Pharmacological Agents Used in the Care of the Client with Immunologic Disorders

An integral part of care to clients with immunologic disorders is pharmacological intervention. These medications provide an improvement of the clients' endocrine problems. The nursing exam reviewer needs to focus on the drugs in Table 12.2. Included in this table are the most common drugs used to treat immunologic disorders. These medications are not inclusive of all the agents used to treat HIV and immune disorders; therefore, you will want to keep a current pharmacology text handy for reference.

TABLE 12.2   Pharmacological Agents Used in the Treatment of Clients with Immunologic Disorders

Drug Name	Action	Side Effects	Nursing Care
Nucleoside Analog Reverse Transcriptase Inhibitors	These drugs are used to treat viral infections such as cytomegalovirus, herpes simplex virus (HSV), and varicella-zoster. They inhibit reverse transcriptase.		
Zidovudine (Retrovir, AZT) *Combivir is a combination drug containing AZT and 3TC.		Drug crosses the blood-brain barrier, causing dizziness.	Assess for dizziness; check CBC, liver, and renal function; can cause bone marrow suppression.
Didanosine (ddI, Videx)		Could lead to peripheral neuropathies; food decreases absorption of the drug. Might suppress bone marrow.	Administer on an empty stomach; monitor hearing and vision as well as neuro-logical function. Can increase effects of allopurinol (Zyloprim), magnesium sulfate, aluminum antacids. Can cause GI symptoms, pancreatitis, stomatitis. Rash, myalgia, hypertension, palpitations, ear pain and photophobia.
Zalcitabine (ddC, HIVID)		Same as above plus avoid alcohol.	Same as above, plus assess liver function.
Lamivudine (Epivir, 3TC)		Same as above; plus can lead to pancreatitis.	Same as above, plus avoid fatty foods.
Stavudine (d4T, Zerit)		Same as above.	Same as above.
Abavir (Ziagen)		Flu-like symptoms might indicate hypersensitivity to the drug. Stop drug and inform doctor immediately.	Same as above, plus assess for flu-like symptoms.
Non-Nucleoside Analog Reverse Transcriptase Inhibitors	These drugs inhibit synthesis of the enzyme reverse transcriptase.		
Nevirapine (Viramune)		May cause headaches and arthralgia.	Do not give with antacids because they decrease the effectiveness of the drug.
Efavirenz (Sustiva)	Drug crosses blood-brain barrier.	Drug can lead to head-aches and vivid dreams.	Same as above.
Delavirdine (Rescriptor)		Could cause headaches and hives.	Keep in cool location because heat deteriorates medication.

(continues)

TABLE 12.2 *Continued*

Drug Name	Action	Side Effects	Nursing Care
Protease Inhibitors	These drugs work to block the HIV protease enzyme and to prevent viral replication and release of viral particles.		
Saquinavir (Invirase)		Take with a high-fat, high-calorie meal for maximum effect.	Teach the client to avoid the sun because the medication could cause sun sensitivity.
Indinavir (Crixivan)			Administer on an empty stomach. Teach the client that taking on an empty stomach increases absorption. Could cause hepatotoxicity.
Ritonavir (Norvir)		Drug could cause diarrhea and increased blood glucose levels.	Administer with food. Monitor blood glucose levels.
Nelfinavir (Viracept)		Same as above.	Same as above.
Amprenavir (Agenerase)		Same as above.	Same as above.
Lopinavir (Kaletra, ABT-378/r)		Same as above.	Same as above; do not give to clients with allergies to sulfonamides.
Ribonucleotide Reductase Inhibitors	These drugs interfere with DNA synthesis and help to stop viral replication.		
Hydroxyurea (Hydrea)		Monitor CBC because drug could suppress bone marrow function.	Teach the client to report extreme fatigue.
Entry Inhibitors	Prevents the virus from fusing with the inside of a cell.		
Enfuvirtide (Fuzeon, T-20)		Local reactions at the injection site. GI upset and diarrhea.	Monitor the injection site for nodules, errythema, and purities at the injection site.
Drugs Used to Treat Pneumocystis Carinii Pneumonia (PCP)			
Trimethoprim/ sulfamethoxazole (Apo-Sulfatrim, Bactrim, Cotrim, Septra), metronidazole (Flagyl)		Could lead to nausea, vomiting, hyponatremia, rashes, fever, leucopenia, thrombocytopenia, and liver problems. Taking Flagyl with alcohol causes extreme nausea.	Should be given either prophylactically to prevent PCP or to treat. Do not take Flagyl with alcohol.

TABLE 12.2 *Continued*

Drug Name	Action	Side Effects	Nursing Care
Pentamidine isethionate (Pentacarinate, Pentam)	This drug is given prophylactically for clients with a CD4+ count less than 200 and those with PCP.		Usually given IV, IM, or may be given in an aerosol preparation. Should be given with a bronchodilator to prevent bronchospasms.
Narcotics/Analgesics Examples: morphine sulfate, meperidine (Demerol), hydrocodone (Lortab)	These drugs are used to treat myalgia and pain associated with AIDS.		Monitor for respiratory depression and oversedation.
Anticonvulsants Examples: phenytoin (Dilantin), fosphenytoin (Cerebyx), phenobarbital	These drugs are used to treat seizure disorders related to neurological effects of AIDS.		Monitor CBC; monitor for respiratory depression; oversedation. Dilantin could lead to gingival hypertrophy. (See Chapter 11, "Care of the Client with Neurological Disorders.")
Drugs Used to Treat Fungal Infections Fluconazole (Diflucan) for cryptococcosis Ketoconazole (Nizoral) for histoplasmosis Nystatin (Monistat) for vaginal yeast infections * Unresolved vaginal yeast infections may indicate infections with HIV.		These drugs can cause nausea and vomiting.	Monitor CBC.
Drugs Used to Treat Tuberculosis Pyrazinamide (Tebrazid), isoniazid (Laniazid)		See Chapter 5, "Care of the Client with Respiratory Disorders."	

Apply Your Knowledge

This chapter includes much needed information to help the nurse apply knowledge of immunologic disorders to the NCLEX exam. The following questions test your knowledge regarding the safe, effective care and management of the client with immunologic disorders.

Exam Questions

1. The client is seen in the clinic requesting screening for HIV. Which of the following is a screening test for HIV?

   A. Viral load

   B. Viral culture

   C. ELISA

   D. CD4/CD8 count

2. The nurse has just taken a report and is preparing for the day's activities. Which client with AIDS should be seen first?

   A. The client with Kaposi's sarcoma

   B. The client with oral leukoplakia

   C. The client with vaginal candidiasis

   D. The client with *Pneumocystis carinii* pneumonia

3. The client with AIDS has a CD4 +T-cell count of 175 cu.mm/liter. The nurse is aware that:

   A. He is relatively free of HIV.

   B. He is at risk for opportunistic infections.

   C. He is likely to be asymptomatic.

   D. He is in remission with his disease.

4. Which medication is usually prescribed for the pregnant client with AIDS to prevent transmission of the virus from mother to infant?

   A. Acyclovir (Zovirax)

   B. Sulfamethaxazole (Bactrim)

   C. Zidovudine (AZT)

   D. Fluconazole (Diflucan)

5. The pregnant client with AIDS asks whether she should try to breast feed her baby after delivery. Which response is most appropriate?

   A. You can breast feed after the third day post-partum.

   B. Breast milk can cause cross contamination, leading to HIV infection in the infant.

   C. There is no risk with breast-feeding your infant when you have HIV infection.

   D. What did your doctor tell you about breast-feeding?

6. Which statement, if made by a client with AIDS, indicates understanding of the illness?

    A. I need to eat yogurt every day to provide needed calcium for my bones.

    B. I should peel and cook fruits before eating them.

    C. I can enjoy foods from the salad bar at my local restaurant.

    D. I might have to floss my teeth more often to prevent gum disease.

7. The client has been prescribed metronidazole (Flagyl) for *Pneumocystis carinii* pneumonia and candida. Which instruction should be given to the client taking Flagyl?

    A. Take the medication with water only.

    B. Arise slowly after taking the medication.

    C. Abstain from drinking alcohol while taking the medication.

    D. Remain supine for 30 minutes after taking the medication.

8. The client has a viral load of 1500 copies per mL. The nurse recognizes that this finding indicates the client is:

    A. At risk for opportunistic infections

    B. Relatively free of HIV infection

    C. In remission with his HIV infection

    D. Within the normal limits for viral load results

9. The nurse should use which solution to destroy HIV?

    A. Mild soap and water

    B. A hypochlorite solution

    C. Water only

    D. Bath oil

10. The client infected with HIV might be prescribed several medications to control replication of the AIDS virus. The combination of drug therapy is known by the abbreviation:

    A. ELISA

    B. RIPA

    C. IFA

    D. HAART

Answers to Exam Questions

1. Answer C is correct. Answers A, B, and D are incorrect because these tests are used to track the progression of the illness, not to screen for the presence of HIV. Answer C is correct because the ELISA test is done on two occasions; if they are positive, a Western Blot assay is done to confirm the diagnosis.

2. Answer D is correct. Answer A is incorrect because Kaposi's sarcoma is a cancer of the connective tissue. The multifocal lesions are purplish in color and somewhat painful; however, there is no indication that this client is unstable. Answer B is incorrect because oral leukoplakia is a precancerous lesion that is not life-threatening. Answer C is incorrect because vaginal candidiasis or yeast is also not life threatening. Answer D is correct because *Pneumocystis carinii* pneumonia often causes airway closure and alterations in oxygen perfusion.

3. Answer B is correct. The client with a CD4 +T-cell count of less than 200 is at risk for opportunistic diseases so B is correct. Answers A, C, and D are incorrect statements.

4. Answer C is correct. The pregnant client with AIDS is treated with zivovudine (AZT) during pregnancy, and the infant is treated after delivery. Acyclovir, sulfamethazole, and fluconazole are not used to prevent transmission of the virus from mother to baby, so Answers A, B, and D are incorrect.

5. Answer B is correct. Breast-feeding your infant when you are HIV positive is contraindicated. Answer A is incorrect because it does not matter whether the mother breast-feeds immediately after delivery or waits to begin breast-feeding for three days. The breast milk is still likely to be contaminated. Answer C is incorrect because there is a risk with breast-feeding. Answer D is incorrect because this answer does not help the client to make an informed decision regarding breast-feeding with HIV.

6. Answer B is correct. Fruits should be washed thoroughly and peeled before eating because they often contain bacteria. Answer A is incorrect because yogurt contains live cultured bacteria and can lead to opportunistic infections. Answer C is incorrect because the client should avoid eating from the salad bar; bacteria grows in foods that are not kept refrigerated. In addition, foods grown in or on the ground should be avoided. Answer D is incorrect because flossing the teeth might cause bleeding and infection. Use of soft toothbrushes and frequent dental check-ups help to prevent oral disease.

7. Answer C is correct. Alcohol taken with Flagyl can cause extreme nausea; therefore, it should not be consumed by this client. Answer A is incorrect because Flagyl can be taken with juice or other liquids. Answers B and D are incorrect because Flagyl is not affected by position.

8. Answer A is correct. A viral load greater than 400 copies/mL indicates the client is at risk for development of opportunistic infections. Answers B, C, and D are incorrect because they are untrue statements.

9. Answer B is correct. A hypochlorite solution is 1 part bleach to 10 parts water. This solution has been found to effectively kill the virus that causes AIDS. Answer A is incorrect because hot water and strong soaps should be used, but these are not the most effective solution for killing HIV. Answers C and D are incorrect because water only and bath oil have not been shown to kill the virus that causes AIDS.

10. Answer D is correct. HAART stands for *Highly Active Retroviral Therapy*. This therapy combines two or three different categories of drugs to combat HIV. Answer A is incorrect because ELISA stands for *Enzyme Linked Immunosuppressant Assay*. Answer B is incorrect because RIPA stands for *Radiommunoprecipitation Assay*, a screening test. Answer C is incorrect because IFA stands for *Immunofluoruescence Assay*, another screening test.

Suggested Reading and Resources

▸ British Guidelines: BHIVA, "Guidelines for the Management of HIV Infection in Pregnant Women and the Prevention of Mother-to-child Transmission of HIV," March 2005.

▸ Brunner, L., and D. Suddarth. *Textbook of Medical Surgical Nursing*. 10th ed. Philadelphia: Lippincott Williams & Wilkins, 2006.

▸ Ignatavicius, D., and S. Workman. *Medical Surgical Nursing: Critical Thinking for Collaborative Care*. 5th ed. Philadelphia: Mosby, 2006.

▸ U.S. Guidelines: Public Health Service Task Force, "Recommendations for Use of Antiretroviral Drugs in Pregnant HIV-1-Infected Women for Maternal Health and Interventions to Reduce Perinatal HIV-1 Transmission in the United States," February 2005.

▸ The Body. The Complete HIV/AIDS Resource: http://bbs.thebody.com.

▸ Safety and Toxicity of Individual Antiretroviral Agents in Pregnancy, 24 February 2005: http://aidsinfo.nih.gov/.

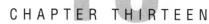

CHAPTER THIRTEEN

Care of the Client with Neoplastic Disorders

Cancer occurs when an overproliferation of abnormal cells harms the host by growing into a body system or by robbing the body of nutrients. Cancer happens more often in men than women and ranks second to cardiovascular disease as the leading cause of death in the United States. African-Americans who have cancer usually have a lower five-year survival rate than whites.

The cancer cells that develop have invasive qualities that allow them to access the lymph nodes and blood vessels. This quality gives the cancer cells the capability to travel. An increased risk of spreading of cancer cells occurs with certain types of cancer. For example, breast cancer affects an area with extensive lymphatics, providing easier access. *Metastasis* refers to the spread of cancer from a primary site to a secondary site.

NOTE

Common sites of metastasis are to the bone and brain (breast cancer) and to the liver and brain (lung cancer).

American Cancer Society's Seven Warning Signs of Cancer

Malignant, or cancer, cells are initiated by alterations in cell growth patterns. The warnings offered by the American Cancer Society alert the public to occurrences that could indicate a problem. The following are the seven warnings you should know:

EXAM ALERT

Remember the acronym CAUTION as a mnemonic to help you recall the seven warnings of cancer:

- ▶ **C**hange in bowel or bladder habits
- ▶ **A** sore that does not heal
- ▶ **U**nusual bleeding or discharge
- ▶ **T**hickening or lump in breast or elsewhere
- ▶ **I**ndigestion or difficulty in swallowing
- ▶ **O**bvious change in wart or mole
- ▶ **N**agging cough or hoarseness

The Four Major Categories of Cancer

The types of cancers are classified according to the tissue from which they originate. The following list identifies the major cancer groups:

▶ **Carcinoma:** Cancer arising from epithelial tissue (for example, basal cell carcinoma)

▶ **Sarcoma:** Cancer arising from connective tissue, muscle, or bone (for example, osteosarcoma)

▶ **Lymphoma:** Cancer arising from lymphoid tissue (for example, Burkitt's lymphoma)

▶ **Leukemia:** Cancer of the blood-forming cells in the bone marrow (for example, acute lymphocytic leukemia)

Risk Factors for Specific Cancers

Some environmental and intrinsic factors are associated with an increased incidence of certain cancers. Included here are risk factors associated with specific cancers. You should study these in preparation for an exam focusing on the type of cancer and specific factors associated with that cancer:

▶ **Bladder:** Risk factors include smoking and environmental carcinogens such as dyes, paint, rubber, ink, and leather.

▶ **Breast:** Risk factors include a family history in first-degree relatives, the birth of the first child after age 30, abnormality in genes BRCA-1 and BRCA-2, menarche before age 12 and menopause after age 55, obesity, the use of birth control pills and hormonal replacement, alcohol intake, and a diet high in fat.

▶ **Cervical:** Risk factors include early sexual activity, early childbearing, multiple partners, human papillomavirus (HPV) or human immunodeficiency virus (HIV) infection, smoking, use of DES by the mother during pregnancy, and chronic cervical infections.

NOTE

The American Cancer Society recommends routine HPV vaccination with the vaccine Gardasil for females 11–12 years of age. It is also recommended that females ages 13–18 be administered the vaccine to catch up missed vaccines or complete the series. The vaccine can be started as early as age 9. Three injections are given over a six-month period. Caution should be used in administering to people with yeast or latex allergies. Gardasil protects four HPV types responsible for 70% of all cervical cancer and 90% of genital warts.

▸ **Colon:** Risk factors include family history, polyps, chronic inflammatory bowel disease, alcohol use, smoking, and a diet high in fat and protein and low in fiber.

▸ **Esophagus:** Risk factors include use of tobacco, use of alcohol, and chronic irritation.

▸ **Larynx:** Risk factors include use of tobacco, nutritional deficiencies (riboflavin), chronic laryngitis, use of alcohol, and exposure to carcinogens.

▸ **Leukemia:** Risk factors include exposure to ionizing radiation, use of chemicals and drugs (for example, anticoagulants), genetics, people with Down syndrome, and people who are immunosuppressed.

▸ **Hodgkin's lymphoma:** Risk factors include exposure to chemical agents, and viral infections.

▸ **Liver:** Risk factors include cirrhosis, hepatitis B, exposure to certain toxins, smoking, and alcohol use.

▸ **Lung:** Risk factors include smoking and secondhand smoke, air pollution, occupational exposure to radon, vitamin A deficiency, and heredity.

▸ **Multiple myeloma:** Risk factors include chemical and radiation exposure.

▸ **Ovarian:** Risk factors include a diet high in fat; alcohol use; a history of cancer of the breast, endometrium, or colon or a family history of ovarian or breast cancer; anovulation; nulliparity; and infertility.

▸ **Non-Hodgkin's lymphoma:** Risk factors include viral infections; exposure to chemicals and/or ionizing radiation; autoimmune disorders.

▸ **Pancreas:** Risk factors include a diet high in fat, smoking, exposure to industrial chemicals, diabetes mellitus, and chronic pancreatitis.

▸ **Prostate:** Risk factors include race (African-Americans), first degree relatives, high-fat diet, and age (55 and older).

TIP

Prostate-specific antigen (PSA) is a laboratory test used to monitor response to treatment and to detect recurrence and progression of prostate cancer.

▸ **Renal:** Risk factors include tobacco use, exposure to industrial chemicals, obesity, high blood pressure, and dialysis.

▸ **Skin:** Risk factors include exposure to sun, exposure to various chemicals (arsenic and coal tar), scarring or chronic irritation of the skin, and ancestry (highest incidence in those of Celtic ancestry with red or blond hair, fair skin, and blue eyes).

> **TIP**
>
> Remember the alphabet A-B-C-D when assessing skin lesions. If the answer is yes to any questions listed here, it could indicate a possible malignant lesion:
>
> ▶ **A**—Is the lesion **A**symmetrical in shape?
> ▶ **B**—Are the **B**orders of the lesion irregular?
> ▶ **C**—Are there different **C**olors within the lesion?
> ▶ **D**—Is the **D**iameter of the lesion more than 5mm?

▶ **Stomach:** Risk factors include a diet high in smoked foods and lacking in fruits and vegetables, gastric ulcers, *Helicobacter pylori* bacteria, heredity, pernicious anemia, and chronic gastritis.

▶ **Testes:** Risk factors include infections, genetic or endocrine factors, and cryptorchidism.

Cancer Prevention

An early diagnosis can mean a better cure rate for a patient with cancer. Certain cancers can even be prevented by interventions. The nurse can make a substantial impact through the use of education in preventive teaching and early detection techniques. One way the incidence of cancer can be decreased is by a change in eating habits. For example, the risk of colon cancer is decreased by avoiding fatty, fried foods and increasing the intake of fruits, vegetables, and whole grains. Another way to decrease colon cancer incidence is by staying away from carcinogens such as smoking, alcohol, excessive sun exposure, and toxins. The nurse should also encourage the use of cancer screening, such as the prostate-specific antigen test, for males 50 or older; digital rectal exams for prostate cancer: Papanicolaou (Pap) test for cervical cancer beginning three years after vaginal intercourse or for any female over 21; and colonoscopy (every 10 years beginning at age 50) and occult blood test for colon cancer.

It is important for the nurse reviewer to know the importance of patient education when studying for an exam. A part of the early detection process relies on the patient to perform regular exams to find any growths or abnormalities. The following gives information about the best time to perform these exams and the current recommendations by the American Cancer Society:

▶ Males should be instructed to perform a self-examination of the testes monthly while taking a shower.

▶ Pre-menopausal females should be instructed to perform self-exams of their breasts monthly, one week after menses. Post-menopausal women should select a date for performing the exam and perform consistently on that date.

▶ A baseline mammogram should be done at age 40 and yearly after age 40.

▶ Clients should avoid the use of deodorant or body powder prior to the mammogram because these can produce areas that appear as calcifications.

> **TIP**
>
> Malignant breast masses appear most often in the upper outer quadrant of the breast.

> **TIP**
>
> The most definitive diagnosis of any type cancer is made based on a biopsy rather than a lab test or x-ray exam.

Major Types of Cancer

Cancer is a priority healthcare issue. It ranks as the second-leading causes of death in the United States. There are several types of cancer. The American Cancer Society lists the four most prevalent new cancers as colon, lung, breast, and prostate. Initial in-depth discussion will follow on these four major types of cancer.

Colorectal Cancer

Tumors that develop in the colorectal area are common. Most cancers occur in the proximal sections of the large intestine (rectum, sigmoid, and descending) with approximately 22% in the cecum and ascending colon and 11% in the transverse colon. This cancer affects men and women equally and tends to increase in risk with increasing age. The number of deaths from colorectal cancer decreased in recent years due to improved screening devices.

The symptoms associated with colorectal cancer are associated with the area of the colon affected. These symptoms include

- Abdominal cramping or pain
- Constipation or diarrhea
- Melena
- Rectal pain
- Tenesmus
- Change in bowel habits

> **TIP**
>
> A change in bowel habits is the most common symptom of colorectal cancer.

- Low hemoglobin and hematocrit levels
- Anorexia
- Palpable mass in right lower quadrant
- Weight loss
- Fatigue

The diagnosis of colorectal cancer is made mainly by physical exam and x-rays. A digital rectal exam can identify the presence of fecal occult blood. Barium enemas are usually performed with the use of air and barium (double contrast). Proctosigmoidoscopy can be done for a partial view. A colonoscopy gives a more complete view of the colorectal area and is the definitive diagnostic tool. Blood tests include the CBC, which will reveal anemia, and the CEA, which might be elevated.

The treatment regimen for clients with colorectal cancer is selected based on the determined extent of the cancer. Dukes' classification may be used to stage the cancer. This system identifies the depth of invasion and distant metastasis by the use of classes A, B, C, and D, where A indicates the least invasion and D shows evidence of advanced metastasis to lung, bone, and liver.

Typical treatment involves chemotherapy with 5-fluorouracil (FU), oxaliplatin (Eloxatin), leucovorin (Wellcovorin), and/or levamisole (Ergamisol). Radiation might be done before and after surgery. Clients with cancer in the rectal area may receive 5-FU and radiation to the pelvis. Radiation can also be palliative if extensive cancer is present. A very important part of curative treatment is surgery. Surgical resection gives primary control and can include several types of procedures, including

▶ Segmental resection with anastomosis removes the tumor, as well as the bowel, blood vessels, and lymph nodes next to the tumor (see Figure 13.1).

SURGERY FOR BOWEL CANCER: COLECTOMY

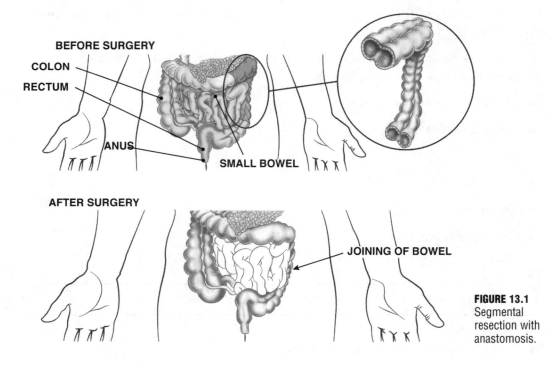

FIGURE 13.1 Segmental resection with anastomosis.

▶ Abdominoperineal resection with permanent colostomy removes the tumor, some of the sigmoid, the rectum, and the anal sphincter (see Figure 13.2).

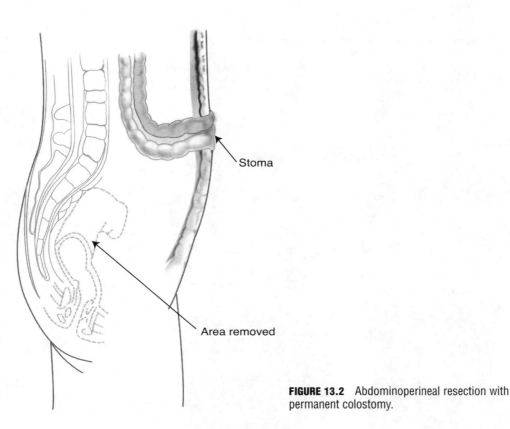

Stoma

Area removed

FIGURE 13.2 Abdominoperineal resection with permanent colostomy.

▶ Temporary colostomy with segmental resection and anastomosis with later reanastomosis.

▶ Permanent colostomy or ileostomy if the tumor mass is not resectable or is obstructing.

▶ J pouch construction, in which a temporary loop ileostomy is performed to divert the stool to the J pouch (see Figure 13.3).

Prior to the surgery, the nurse must provide psychological as well as physiological interventions for the client. These include

▶ Teaching the client to eat a diet high in calories, protein, and carbohydrates and low in residue

▶ Monitoring intake and output

▶ Assessing for obstruction or perforation (increasing distention, loss of bowel sounds, pain in or rigidity of abdomen)

▶ Monitoring for hypovolemia (tachycardia and low blood pressure)

▶ Cleansing the bowel via ordered laxatives, enemas, and administration of antibiotics to reduce the bacteria in the intestines (sulfonamides, or neomycin [mycifradin])

▶ Assessing for anxiety and teach relaxation techniques

▶ Planning a visit from enterostomal nurse, if appropriate

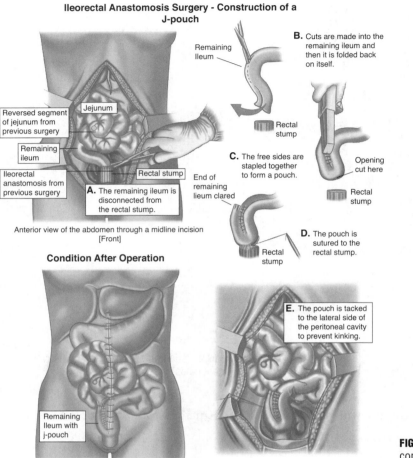

Ileorectal Anastomosis Surgery - Construction of a J-pouch

Reversed segment of jejunum from previous surgery
Jejunum
Remaining ileum
Ileorectal anastomosis from previous surgery
Rectal stump
A. The remaining ileum is disconnected from the rectal stump.

Anterior view of the abdomen through a midline incision [Front]

Remaining Ileum
B. Cuts are made into the remaining ileum and then it is folded back on itself.
Rectal stump

Opening cut here
Rectal stump

End of remaining lleum clared
C. The free sides are stapled together to form a pouch.

Rectal stump
D. The pouch is sutured to the rectal stump.

E. The pouch is tacked to the lateral side of the peritoneal cavity to prevent kinking.

Condition After Operation

Remaining lleum with j-pouch

FIGURE 13.3 J pouch construction.

Postoperative nursing interventions focus on prevention and assessment for problems, and providing comfort. These include

▶ Monitor for and provide pain relief

▶ Abdominal assessment (bowel sounds, abdominal girth)

▶ Monitor for complications (anastomosis site leakage [abdominal distention and rigidity], elevated temperature, and shock symptoms), prolapse or retraction of the stoma, perforation of the intestine, skin irritation, respiratory compromise

NOTE

Pulmonary complications are common, especially if the client is more than 50 years of age.

▶ Administer ordered antibiotics and IV fluids

▶ Monitor vital signs

▶ Turn, cough, and deep breathe every two hours

▶ Early ambulation

▶ Assess for melena (might indicate hemorrhage)

▶ Assess condition of stoma

Lung Cancer

In the United States, lung cancer causes more deaths in men and women than any other type of cancer. It is the leading cause of cancer-related deaths in the world. Lung cancer in men has remained constant, but the rate of lung cancer in women has increased. In most clients diagnosed with lung cancer, the cancer has already spread to lymph nodes or other sites before a diagnosis is obtained. Table 13.1 lists the types of lung cancer with their characteristics and frequency of occurrence. You should study this table, noting specifics associated with each particular type.

TABLE 13.1   Lung Cancer Types

Cancer Type	Characteristics	Frequency of Occurrence
Non-Small Cell (70%–75% of Tumors)		
Squamous cell	Grows and spreads rapidly	30%
Large cell	Slow-growing	10%–16%
Adenocarcinoma	Slow-growing	31%–34%
Small Cell (Arises in Major Bronchi)		
	Fast-growing, highly malignant, widespread metastasis can occur	20%–25%

The clinical manifestations of lung cancer are not always apparent. Symptoms depend on the tumor size, where it is located, and whether the cancer has spread. These signs and symptoms include

▶ Cough

▶ Wheezing

▶ Shortness of breath

▶ Chest pain and tightness

▶ Hoarseness

▶ Dysphagia

▶ Edema of head and neck

▶ Weakness, anorexia, and weight loss

▶ Blood-tinged sputum

The diagnosis of lung cancer is made by both the presence of the preceding signs and symptoms, history of smoking, and diagnostic exams. Radiologic exams utilized are a chest x-ray, CT scan, and esophageal ultrasound. A bronchoscopy with washings and biopsies are helpful to confirm diagnosis. The physician will also require tests to determine whether metastasis has occurred: position emission tomography (PET), liver scan, MRI, bone scan, and mediastinoscopy (to retrieve mediastinal lymph nodes for analysis).

The physician's treatment regimen will depend on the amount of tumor involvement. Surgical removal is usually preferred for non–small-cell carcinomas. Surgical procedures are either lobectomies or pneumonectomies. The client will be assessed prior to surgery for pulmonary sufficiency via pulmonary function tests (PFT) and ABGs to assess her ability to tolerate lung removal. Radiation therapy might be done to

▶ Control symptoms, if inoperable

▶ Make the tumor an operable size

▶ Relieve pressure on vital structures

Several types of chemotherapy are used, depending on the stage of the cancer cells. The drugs used include

▶ Alkylating agents (ifosfamide)

▶ Platinum analogues (cisplatin)

▶ Taxanes (paclitaxel)

▶ Vinca alkaloids (vinblastine)

▶ Doxorubicin (Adriamycin)

▶ Erlotinig (Tarceva)

Other therapies that might be utilized involve the use of laser energy (bronchospopic laser and photodynamic therapy), airway stents for obstruction, and cryotherapy (freezing of the tumor cells). The general nursing interventions for clients with lung cancer accentuate monitoring for post-surgical, radiation, and chemotherapy complications, which include

▶ Pericarditis

▶ Myelitis

▶ Cor pulmonale

▶ Pulmonary fibrosis with radiation pneumonia

▶ Respiratory failure

The nurse would also provide the usual respiratory nursing interventions (turn, cough, and deep breathing; oxygen; bronchodilator drugs; and energy conservation techniques). Post-surgical positioning is important and depends on the type of surgery performed. Please use Table 13.2 as a guide for post-operative lung surgery positioning. For more discussion of interventions, please refer to Chapter 5, "Care of the Client with Respiratory Disorders."

TABLE 13.2   Post-operative Lung Surgery Positions

Surgical Procedure	Desired Post-operative Position
Pneumonectomy	Supine, operative side
Resected segment of lung	Supine, non-operative side
Lobectomy	Supine, opposite side

Prostate Cancer

Cancer of the prostate is the most common invasive cancer for men in America. Almost all prostate cancers are adenocarcinomas. These types of cancers occur more frequently in African-American men. Prostate cancer is one of the slowest-growing cancers and usually spreads to the bones of the pelvis, sacrum, and lumbar spine. Organ metastasis to the lungs, liver, and kidneys occurs late in the course of the disease.

The signs and symptoms associated with prostate cancer are rare early in the disease process. Urinary symptoms can occur with obstruction causing urine frequency, retention, and a decrease in urinary flow. Other symptoms include

▶ Hematuria

▶ Pain during ejaculation

▶ Anemia

▶ Weight loss

▶ Pain in the back and hips if metastasis has occurred

Early diagnosis of prostate cancer means a more positive outcome; therefore, detection techniques are recommended. Digital rectal exams (DRE) should begin at age 40. Confirmation of diagnosis is made by a biopsy of the prostate. A prostate-specific antigen blood test is done as a screening device but is more accurate as a measurement of response to prostate cancer treatment. An increased PSA (more than 4 ng/mL) combined with a hard nodular prostate on DRE is highly suspicious. Other diagnostic tests include

▶ Transrectal ultrasound (TRUS) where a probe is placed in the rectal area with a biopsy possible through the probe

▶ Bone scans and CT scans (for metastasis)

▶ Renal function tests

▶ Prostatic acid phosphatase (PAP) because elevated blood levels might indicate prostate cancer

As with many cancers, the treatment plan for clients with prostate cancer depends on the stage of disease, the age of the client, and the related symptoms the client exhibits. The major management of the disease is accomplished by surgery, radiation, and/or hormone administration.

A radical prostatectomy is the standard procedure for men in early stages of the disease and gives a high cure rate. When this procedure is done, the entire prostate gland is removed along with seminal vesicles and part of the bladder neck. Side effects include urinary incontinence and impotence. Clients who have a nerve-sparing prostatectomy have a chance of erection recovery. There is a lack of ejaculation (due to seminal vesicle and transection of the vas deferens). A transurethral resection of the prostate (TURP) is done in men with advanced disease and helps with the symptoms caused by obstruction. The problem with impotence is rare after a TURP, but clients might experience retrograde ejaculation. Important nursing interventions after prostate surgery include the following (Additional discussion available in Chapter 6, "Care of the Client with Genitourinary Disorders."):

▶ Assessment for hemorrhage via a three-way Foley system.

CAUTION

Bright red viscous bleeding with numerous clots is arterial bleeding.

▶ Administer pain medication and anti-spasmodics.

▶ Avoid rectal trauma to reduce the chance of hemorrhage:

  ▶ Administer stool softeners

  ▶ Give a low residue diet

  ▶ Avoid use of enemas or rectal tubes

  ▶ Avoid rectal temperatures

▶ Accurate intake and output is necessary to assure patency of the catheter and irrigation system.

▶ Monitor for signs and symptoms of infection (elevated temperature; chills; and symptoms of urinary tract infection, such as dysuria and frequency).

▶ Monitor for complications:

  ▶ Hemorrhage

  ▶ Obstructed catheter

  ▶ Distended bladder

  ▶ Infection

  ▶ Urinary incontinence

  ▶ Erectile dysfunction

▶ Allow time for clients to discuss an understanding of sexual dysfunction.

Radiation treatment by external beams is used as an alternative curative treatment, as an adjunct to surgery to radiate the lymph nodes and cancer cells, and for palliative care.

Low-dose radiation seeds injected into the prostate gland can provide direct radiation (see Figure 13.4).

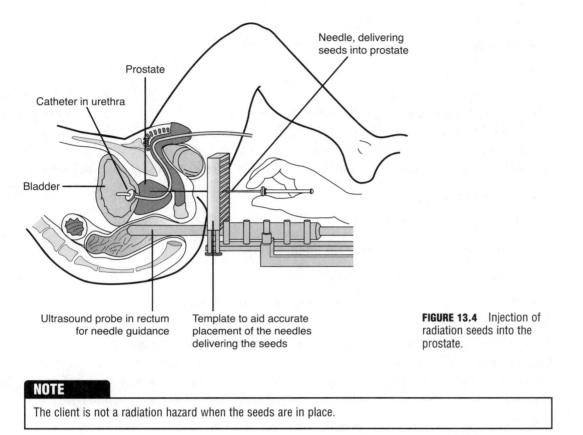

Prostate

Needle, delivering seeds into prostate

Catheter in urethra

Bladder

Ultrasound probe in rectum for needle guidance

Template to aid accurate placement of the needles delivering the seeds

FIGURE 13.4 Injection of radiation seeds into the prostate.

NOTE

The client is not a radiation hazard when the seeds are in place.

Chemotherapy might be used, but it has little effectiveness as a main treatment agent. Drugs used include docetaxel (Taxotere) with prednisone and estramustine (Emcyt). Prostate cancer is a hormone-dependent tumor and can be managed by depriving the cancer of androgen. Measures utilized to accomplish this deprivation are

▶ Testicular removal (bilateral orchiectomy)

▶ Administration of estrogen or gonadotropin-releasing hormones, such asleuprolide (Lupron), magestrol (Megace), medroxyprogesterone (Depo-Provera), abarelix (Plenaxis), flutamide (Eulexin), goserelin (Zoladex), bicalutamide (Casodex), and diethystilbestrol (DES)

Breast Cancer

Breast cancer is the most common invasive cancer in women. It is a major healthcare problem in the United States. Breast cancer has a lifetime risk that one in eight women will develop the disease. Because of these statistics and predictions, much has been done to prevent the development in high-risk women. This is being done by chemopreventive medications, such as tamoxifen citrate (Nolvadex) and raloxifene (Evista) and by the use of surgery (prophylactic mastectomies). There is also evidence that certain factors can protect women from developing breast cancer. These include

▶ Exercise

▶ Breastfeeding

▶ Pregnancy before age 30

The signs and symptoms of breast cancer are mainly associated with a mass in the early stages. This fact accentuates the importance of self breast exams (SBE) and mammographies. Malignant breast masses are usually in the upper outer quadrant of the breast. The noticeable symptoms that occur are usually in later stages of the disease and include

▶ Marked breast pain

▶ Dimpling in the breast

▶ Sudden development of nipple retraction

▶ Ulcerative lesions or discharge

▶ Peau d'orange (skin edema with orange peel appearance)

X-ray mammography can detect the tumor before it is palpable. An ultrasound of the breast can be used to verify the mammogram results. Diagnosis of breast cancer is made by biopsy of the lesion. After the biopsy, certain tests are done to assist with staging of the cancer. These tests include chest x-ray, bone scan, liver function tests, and MRI.

The client's treatment plan and prognosis are based on the client's cancer stage. The staging classification system utilized is the TNM.

NOTE

The TNM classification system is a commonly used cancer staging system that allows a description of the severity of the cancer based on *T* (the description of the extent of the tumor), *N* (the spread to lymph nodes), and *M* (the spread beyond the area to other parts of the body).

The patient might be treated with surgery, radiation, and/or chemotherapy. The goal of the surgical procedure is cancer control. Several types of surgery might be performed. They range from a breast-conserving procedure, such as a lumpectomy (removal of the lump along with varying degrees of tissue), to a radical mastectomy wherein the following are removed:

▶ Breast tissue

▶ Minor and major pectoral muscle

▶ Axillary lymph nodes

During the breast surgery, lymphatic mapping and sentinel node biopsies are usually performed. With this technique, a dye is injected into the lesion prior to surgery.

During the surgery, the surgeon uses a device that identifies the sentinel or primary drainage node. One to four nodes are usually excised. These nodes are removed and examined by the laboratory. If the removed nodes are negative, the other nodes are left intact. If the removed nodes are positive for cancer, all the nodes are removed. Clients with four or more nodes containing cancer cells have the greatest risk of the cancer reoccuring. This procedure helps to prevent negative aspects of node excision, such as decreased mobility of the limb, numbness, and lymphedema. If radiation is used as treatment, it is usually external beam and is done after the client has recuperated from surgery (usually six weeks). Chemotherapy is done along with surgery to kill the tumor and prevent metastasis. The agents used are given in combination with varying intervals and include

- Cyclophosphamide (Cytoxan)
- Methotrexate (Trexall)
- 5-Fluorouracil (5-FU)
- Doxorubicin (Adriamycin)
- Paclitaxel (Taxol)
- Vinorelbine (Navelbine)

If the biopsy of the tumor indicates that it is hormonal dependent (ER-positive), the client might have surgery, such as an oophorectomy, to suppress hormone secretion. The client could be treated with drugs. These drugs include tamoxifen, anastrazole (Arimidex), and trastuzumab (Herceptin). A monoclonal antibody could also be given to slow tumor growth and stimulate immunity.

Clients undergoing breast surgery require astute nursing care that focuses on physiological as well as psychological aspects. Nursing interventions focus on postoperative care, including

- Assess for and treat pain
    - Pain medication administration
    - Elevate involved extremity on a pillow
- Assess drainage sites for blood and incision sites for hematoma
- Promote positive body image
    - Allow client to discuss emotions
    - Provide privacy during dressing changes, but allow client to view incision
- Assist with ambulation (support the non-operative side)
- Patient teaching points:
    - Teach exercise regimen to increase muscle strength, prevent contractures, and restore full range of motion. Exercises should be done three times a day for four to six weeks

▸ Teach anyone with axillary lymph node dissection to never let the arm be dependent and to allow no blood pressure, venipuncture, or injury to the involved arm.

▸ Assess for complications, such as lymphedema

> **NOTE**
> It is normal for the patient to have post-surgical transient edema. This is not lymphedema.

Patient Instructions for Pulley Exercises

Pulley exercises help with forward motion of the shoulder. Hang a rope or cord over the top of an open door. Grasp an end in each hand. Gently pull the higher hand down and raise the lower arm in a see-sawing motion. Gradually increase stretch each time (see Figure 13.5).

FIGURE 13.5 Pulley exercise.

Patient Instructions for Hand Wall-Climbing Exercises

Hand wall-climbing exercises help with forward shoulder motion. Stand close to and facing a wall, with the feet a shoulder width apart. Place hands flat against the wall, close to the level of the shoulder, and gradually raise hands higher up the wall. See Figure 13.6.

FIGURE 13.6 Hand wall-climbing exercise.

Patient Instructions for Arm Circle Exercises

Rest the unaffected arm on a firm surface and bend forward at the waist. Allow the affected arm to hang loosely from the shoulder and swing backward and forward, from side to side, and then in small circles. The goal is to increase the size of the circle (see Figure 13.7).

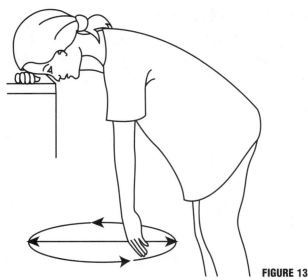

FIGURE 13.7 Arm circle exercise.

Complications from Breast Surgery

Table 13.3 lists the common complications that can develop from breast surgery. You should study this table, noting the complications and nursing actions necessary when reviewing for a test.

TABLE 13.3 Treatment and Intervention for Complications from Breast Surgery

Complication	Treatment/Interventions
Lymphedema	▶ Notify the physician
	▶ Elevate the arm above the elbow
	▶ Hand pump exercises
	▶ Might require referral to physical therapist for elastic sleeve or exercises
Hematoma as evidenced by excessive swelling at site and increased drainage output	▶ Notify the surgeon
	▶ Ace wrap at site
	▶ Ice packs
	▶ Possible surgical intervention
Infection	▶ Monitor vital signs
	▶ Oral or IV antibiotics
	▶ Cultures of drainage

Other Major Cancers

Table 13.4 lists other cancers that occur, their frequency, and other information necessary for you to review prior to an oncological nursing exam. Please refer to the "Risk Factors for Specific Cancers" section if necessary for other pertinent information.

TABLE 13.4   Other Major Cancer Types

Cancer Type	Clinical Manifestations	Diagnostics	Treatment	Other Pertinent Information
Skin cancer Squamous cell— rapid invasion with metastasis Basal cell carcinoma— metastasis rare. Melanoma— rapid invasion and metastasis; high mortality	Please refer to the A, B, C, D, evaluation listed in the "Risk Factors for Specific Cancers" section. Common sites of melanomas are the skin of the back, legs, between toes, feet, face, scalp, and the back of the hands.	Diagnosis is made by assessment of the lesion and the excision results from pathology.	Pharmacological interventions: 5-FU cream, interferon, as well as systemic chemotherapy. Surgery: "Freezing" cryosurgery with liquid nitrogen; excision. Radiation: For clients with deep tumors and that are not surgical candidates.	Major cause of skin cancer is excessive sun exposure.
Esophageal cancer	Dysphagia, feeling of mass in throat, Odynophagia, Foul breath, Hiccups, Vomiting, Anorexia and weight loss, Change in bowel habits.	Barium swallow, EGD with biopsy, CT scan, EUS, and mediastinoscopy to detect spread.	Pharmacological interventions: Chemotherapy with 5-FU and cisplatin. Surgery: Esophagectomy, endoscopy to provide esophageal dilatation. Radiation: Photodynamic therapy.	The nurse collaborates with speech pathology and dieticians to assure adequate nutrition and swallowing ability. Alert: Post surgery, the NG tube should not be manipulated. If surgery is performed through the thorax, the airway is a priority.
Bladder cancer	Painless, intermittent hematuria (major sign), dysuria, frequency, and urgency.	Cystoscopy with biopsy, CT scan, MRI.	Pharmacological interventions: Multi-agent chemotherapy (methotrexate [Folex]), 5-fluorouracil (5-FU), vinblastine, doxorubicin (Adriamycin), cisplatin (Platinol). Intravesical chemotherapy with bacillus Calmette Guérin (BCG). Note: BCG is a vaccine against tuberculosis. It is also used for bladder and colorectal cancer as an immunotherapy agent. Surgery: Partial or total cystectomy with urinary diversions (ileal conduit, continent pouch, uterosigmoidoscopy).	
Renal cancer (kidney adenocarcinoma)	Triad of symptoms: flank pain, gross blood in urine (a late but common sign), weakness, anemia.	Laboratory: Urinalysis, hemoglobin and hematocrit (decreased), calcium (increased), ESR (elevated), elevated hormone levels (adreno- corticotropic, human chorionic gonadotropin [HCG], cortisol, renin, and parathyroid). X-rays; MRI, CT scan, and ultrasound show a renal mass. Direct view via a cystoscopy.	Pharmacological intervention: Biological response modifiers (BRM)— interleukin 2. Surgery: The preferred usual treatment is a nephrectomy with or without radiation. A renal artery embolization and MRI assisted radio frequency ablation might also be performed.	

(continues)

TABLE 13.4 *Continued*

Cancer Type	Clinical Manifestations	Diagnostics	Treatment	Other Pertinent Information
Gastric/stomach cancer	Heartburn, abdominal pain, epigastric or back pain, weight loss, vomiting, weakness and fatigue, anemia, anorexia, constipation.	Laboratory: Anemia, liver function test are abnormal with metastasis. CEA elevation in late disease. X-ray: Upper gastrointestinal, CT scan. Endoscopy: EGD, EUS.	Pharmacological intervention: 5-FU, doxo-rubicin, Mitomycin-C, cisplatin, etoposide. Surgery: Subtotal or total gastrectomy. Radiation therapy might also be done. Radiation used with metastasis causes tumor infarction.	See Chapter 9, "Care of the Client with Gastrointestinal Disorders," for further discussion on nursing care after gastrectomy.
Pancreatic cancer	Jaundice (clay stools, dark urine): May be initial symptom due to gall-bladder or liver involvement. Pain, ascites, fatigue, anorexia, weight loss, glucose intolerance, enlarged spleen.	Laboratory: Elevated CEA, amylase, lipase, and bilirubin (depending on involvement). Tumor markers: CA 19-9, CA 242, CA 72-4, HCG beta. X-ray: CT scan, MRI, ERCP (most definitive diagnostic tool).	Pharmacological intervention: 5-FU, cisplatin, mitomycin. Surgery: Whipple procedure. Endoscopy: Biliary stents can be inserted to relieve obstruction. Radiation: Usually external beam radiation. Radioactive iodine seeds might be implanted. Intraoperative radiation therapy might be used.	
Ovarian cancer	Vague symptoms, ascites, dyspepsia, flatulence, abdominal mass, increasing abdominal girth.	Laboratory: CA 125 (a ovarian antibody). Not useful as diag-nostic tool because benign problems can also cause elevation. X-ray: Ultrasound, CT scan, IVP, UGI.	Pharmacological intervention: cisplatin, carboplatin, paclitaxel. Surgery: Exploratory laparotomy to diagnose and stage, or total abdominal hysterectomy and bilateral tube and ovary removal to diagnose, stage, treat, and remove tumor. Radiation: Done with chemotherapy or alone for invasive cancer.	
Cervical cancer (most are squamous cell carcinomas)	Most symptoms occur with invasion. Painless vaginal bleeding, flank pain, leg pain or swelling, weight loss, pelvic pain, painful urination, blood in urine, melena.	Pap smear, colposcopy, endocervical curettage.	Pharmacological intervention: Usually has a poor response; paclitaxel, carboplatin, hydroxyurea. Surgery: Depending on extent—conization, hysterectomy, pelvic exenteration. Treatments: LEEP (loop electrosurgical excision procedure); laser therapy; cryotherapy. Radiation: External followed by intracavity.	Instruct clients who have had endocervical curettage procedures that they can bleed for two weeks post procedure.

TABLE 13.4 *Continued*

Cancer Type	Clinical Manifestations	Diagnostics	Treatment	Other Pertinent Information
Leukemia (unregulated WBC proliferation in bone marrow)	Frequent infections/colds, decreased platelet functions evidenced by nosebleeds, hematuria, bruising, and so on, weight loss, fatigue, anorexia, headache, bone pain or swelling.	Laboratory: Decreased hemoglobin and hematocrit; abnormal WBC (usually very high); abnormal clotting time. Alert: The higher the WBC count, the poorer the prognosis. Bone marrow aspiration and biopsy is the definitive diagnostic tool.	Pharmacological intervention: Done in three phases: Induction phase—cytosine, arabinoside for seven days, and daunorubicin the first three of the seven days. Consolidation phase—same drugs on different days. Maintenance phase—different drugs depending on type of leukemia being treated; mercaptopurine, methotrexate and/or all trans retinoic acid (ATRA) for acute lymphocytic leukemia. Note: ATRA is a vitamin A derivative that boosts the immune system. Adverse/side effects include fever, dyspnea, chest pain, pleural and pericardial effusion. Other medications: antibiotics and antibacterials (for example, aminoglycosides [Gentamicin, Tobramycin, vancomycin], antifungals [amphotericin B, Nizoral], and antivirals [ganciclovir]). Bone marrow (stem cell) transplantation: Please see the section on bone marrow transplants later in this chapter for further discussion.	Bleeding and infection are major causes of death from leukemia.
Multiple myeloma	Fatigue, easy bruising, bone pain and fractures (classic symptoms), anemia.	Laboratory: Urinalysis (presence of Bence-Jones proteins), increased protein in serum protein electrophoresis, and hypercalcemia. Bone marrow biopsy confirms diagnosis.	Pharmacological intervention: Chemotherapy is the standard treatment— melphalan, vincristine, cyclophosphamide combined with Decadron, doxorubicin, thalidomide (Thalomid). Clients with no improvement after treatment might be treated with bortezomib (Velcade). Biphosphanates are also prescribed. Bone marrow transplantation.	

(continues)

TABLE 13.4 *Continued*

Cancer Type	Clinical Manifestations	Diagnostics	Treatment	Other Pertinent Information
Hodgkin's lymphoma	Fever, malaise, night sweats, coughing, dysphagia, dyspnea, swollen cervical lymph nodes, fatigue, pruritis, pain in cervical lymph nodes when drinking (especially alcohol), weight loss.	Laboratory: Biopsy of nodes reveals Reed-Sternberg cells. Staging of Hodgkin's disease: 1—Single node, single site. 2—More than one node, localized to a single organ on the same side of the diaphragm. 3—Both sides of the diaphragm have lymph node involvement. 4—Diffuse involvement with disease disseminated in organs and tissues.	Pharmacological intervention: Chemotherapy with radiation if extensive stage involvement. Surgery: A splenectomy might be performed to prevent pooling of blood. Radiation: Used alone if client is in stage 1 or 2.	
Non-Hodgkin's lymphoma (lymphoid tumors without presence of Reed- Sternberg cells)	Enlarged lymph nodes (might be the only symptom)— axillary, inguinal, femoral.	Biopsy with cells without Reed-Sternberg cells. Staging done as with Hodgkin's lymphoma.	Pharmacological intervention: multi- or single chemotherapy (Fludarabine) use, Rituximab (Rituxan). Radiation: Radiation therapy may be used.	

General Interventions for Clients with Cancer

Treatments for cancer patients are focused on curing the cancer, prolonging survival time, or improving the quality of the patient's life. Clients with cancer usually die within weeks without treatment. The therapies included here can involve one treatment or a combination of all three:

▶ **Surgery:** This procedure is done to remove the tumor or the diseased tissue for a cure. Surgery can also be used for diagnosis, as a preventive measure, as a palliative treatment, or for reconstruction. The care of the patient with surgery would be as for any patient postoperatively with a focus on the body part involved or removed.

▶ **Radiation:** This is performed to shrink the tumor.

▶ **Chemotherapy:** This is undertaken to destroy cancer cells by interfering with mitosis or by destroying the cell wall. Biologic response modifiers might be given along with the chemotherapy to boost the client's immune system and destroy abnormal malignant cells.

Radiation

Radiation therapy is used to destroy cancer cells without major destruction of the normal cells. The nurse reviewer should examine all aspects of nursing care dealing with radiation. This section focuses on the different types of radiation, side effects, and related nursing care.

The cells exposed to radiation either die or are prevented from rapidly dividing. Radiation can be delivered by gamma, beta, or alpha rays. Gamma rays are the most common type used for cancer treatment and can produce deep tissue penetration. Gamma rays can cause severe damage to tissues. Beta and alpha rays don't penetrate as well as gamma rays and require either a long or repeated exposure to cause damage to tissue.

Radiation is usually given in small doses over a specific period to decrease damage to normal cells. There are two types of radiation delivery systems:

▶ **Teletherapy:** An external (distant) radiation source. In this form, the client does not pose any radiation exposure hazards. The radiologist might mark the client's body to ensure the proper position for each treatment.

CAUTION

Radiation markings on the skin should not be removed during hygienic care.

▶ **Brachytherapy**: A direct (close) form of therapy. With this form of therapy, there is continuous direct contact with the tumor or malignant cells. Clients emit radiation during the time the radiation is in place, posing exposure hazards.

These brachytherapy radiations can be sealed or unsealed. *Sealed* radiation emits radiation to tumor tissues and can be implanted (as seeds) and remain in place permanently (such as seeds used in prostate and breast cancer). With sealed radiation, excreta is not contaminated; therefore, no special nursing care is required to dispose of body waste. *Unsealed* radiation can be given orally, intravenously, or injected in a body cavity. These unsealed forms of radiation are not confined to one body part, so the client's waste would be contaminated and requires special care for disposal (such as radioactive iodine for thyroid cancer).

The side effects and nursing care required for clients receiving radiation therapy depend on the specific area receiving the radiation. For example, uterine cancer radiation could cause damage to the colon and a client who has had radiation to the throat area could experience esophageal damage. Table 13.5 includes general radiation side effects and associated nursing care for clients who have received external radiation. The exam reviewer should be familiar with this information for testing purposes.

TABLE 13.5   Radiation Side Effects and Nursing Care

Side Effects of Radiation	Nursing Care of Clients Receiving External Radiation
Fatigue	Encourage rest periods during the day. Space activities.
Altered taste and anorexia	Avoid spicy foods. Assess for food likes and dislikes. Provide foods that are palliative and pleasing to the eye.
Tissue fibrosis and scarring (can occur years after treatment)	Teach the client that these complications can occur. The nurse should also teach the client to be alert for any symptoms of problems near the radiation site.
Dry skin	Avoid soaps, alcohol skin preparations, and hot baths. Use moisturizers.

CAUTION

Clients who have received external radiation should avoid sun exposure to any radiated areas during treatment and up to 12 months after treatment.

It is important to discuss another form of radiation provided to clients with cervical cancer. This radiation is a form of brachytherapy that involves the use of a sealed radiation source implanted inside the patient. In this case, the radiation is to the patient's cervix inserted through the vagina.

NOTE

While the implant is in place, the client emits radiation but her body fluids are not radioactive.

Care of the client with radiation therapy implants requires that the nurse pay attention to time, distance, and shielding when caring for these clients. The nurse should

▸ Limit the amount of time spent in contact with the client

▸ Maximize the distance by standing to the side of the bed and refraining from close contact

▸ Shield himself by using a lead-lined apron during patient contact

This type of radiation therapy is temporary. It is a contraindication for a nurse that is pregnant to care for these clients. Visitors should be limited to a 30-minute-per-day time span and instructions given to stay six feet from the radiation source. While the implant is in place, the nursing interventions focus on prevention of dislodgement. Accomplishment of this outcome is helped by instituting nursing measures, to include

▸ Bed rest

▸ Low-residue diet (to decrease bowel contents)

▸ Foley catheter (to prevent collection of urine in the bladder)

Chemotherapy

Chemotherapy has detrimental effects on the development of both normal and malignant cells. Chemotherapeutic agents include

▸ **Alkylating agents, antimitotics, and antimetabolites:** Interfere with cell metabolism and growth

▸ **Antitumor antibiotics:** Interfere with the cell wall

▸ **Hormones:** Suppress hormonal-dependent tumors; examples include progesterone for ovarian cancer and estrogen for prostate or testicular cancer

▸ **Cytoprotectants and colony-stimulating factors:** Used mostly to prevent problems caused by chemotherapy or other cancer treatments

▸ **Topoisomerase inhibitors:** Breaks DNA and kills the cells

▸ **Biological response modifiers:** Charges the immune system

There are commonalities in the side effects of chemotherapeutic agents. You should become familiar with these side effects in preparation for the exam. Table 13.6 highlights the common side effects and some measures to relieve them.

TABLE 13.6 Common Side Effects Associated with Chemotherapeutic Agents

Side Effect	Treatment
Anorexia, nausea, and vomiting	Prophylactic antiemetics; small, frequent meals that are palatable and nourishing; avoidance of foods that are too hot or too spicy; a diet of soft bland foods.
Alopecia	Teach the client that hair loss will be immediate but not permanent; help the client select a wig before treatment begins. Cut long hair before therapy, and avoid excessive combing of hair. Note that the regrowth of hair is usually different from the hair that was lost.
Bone marrow and platelet depression	Observe for petechiae and ecchymosis; use small gauge needles; apply pressure over injection and venipuncture sites for at least 10 minutes; avoid dental work; no aspirin; no enemas—use stool softeners to prevent straining; clients should avoid anal sex; use electric razors only. Teach the client to avoid crowds, practice proper hand hygiene, and not eat foods grown in or on the ground without cooking and peeling them first.
Mucosal membrane ulcerations	Rinse mouth with a solution of one-half strength peroxide and normal saline; xylocaine viscous (place on a cotton-tip applicator and apply to lesions); oral hygiene with a soft toothbrush.
Sterility	Sperm bank or egg deposits prior to chemotherapy administration.

Total Parenteral Nutrition

Clients with cancer often have inadequate nutrition due to the side effects of nausea, vomiting, and anorexia. These clients frequently require supplemental nutrition by the use of total parenteral nutrition (TPN).

NOTE

A central line is required for TPN administration.

Problems Associated with TPN

With TPN, the fluid is delivered directly into the venous system. This fluid has a high level of osmolarity, which can cause a fluid shift as well as electrolyte imbalances. The high dextrose content puts the client at risk for hyperglycemia and infection. Hyperglycemia is usually treated by sliding scale insulin coverage. Clients with infections due to TPN are treated with antibiotics and removal of the central line catheter with culture of the tip upon removal.

Dressing Changes for TPN

Because of the danger of infection, these clients are at a higher risk of developing sepsis. The following list gives the recommendations for a dressing change on the central line of a client receiving TPN:

▶ Sterile technique is utilized.

▶ Recommended dressing is either a gauze dressing taped on all four sides or a transparent dressing.

Nursing Implementations

General nursing care for a client with TPN includes the following measures:

- Blood should not be drawn from the TPN port, but it can be drawn from the venous port.

- Avoid air entrance into the central line. If air embolism occurs, the nurse should clamp the catheter, place the client in left Trendelenberg position, call the doctor, and administer ordered oxygen.

- TPN must be tapered to be discontinued.

> **NOTE**
>
> If the TPN is not immediately available and the infusion is empty, the nurse should give D10W until the solution is obtained.

- Any loose or soiled dressing should be changed immediately.

- Solution should be prepared under laminar flow hood.

- Monitor blood glucose levels and serum electrolytes.

- Monitor weight.

- Provide an accurate intake and output.

- TPN requires a pump or other type of controller delivery system for administration.

Chemotherapy and TPN require special care in methods of administration to prevent extravasation of the tissue by the damaging agents. Table 13.7 provides guidelines for the various types of IV administration catheters that might be used when administering chemotherapy and TPN to clients. The implantation of devices for chemotherapy administration has become common for patients with cancer; therefore, skill review for this procedure is also included in this section.

TABLE 13.7 IV Administration Catheter Guidelines

Type of Catheter	Use	Nursing Interventions
Peripherally inserted central venous catheter (PICC)	Short-term IV therapy, blood administration, blood drawing, IV piggyback drug administration, continuous drug administration	▸ No BP or blood to be drawn in the arm with the PICC line in place. ▸ Observe for complications—catheter occlusion, phlebitis. ▸ In suspected infection, culture tip of catheter on removal as ordered. ▸ Perform sterile dressing changes per institutional protocol.
Implanted infusion ports (see skills guidelines that follows)	Same as PICC, but can be used for long-term IV therapy	▸ Huber needle must be used to access the port to prevent causing damage to the septum of the port. ▸ Regular flushing is required. ▸ Assess for complications such as clotting, migration of the catheter, infection, bleeding, and air embolism.

> **TIP**
>
> When flushing IV lines, remember the acronym SASH:
>
> - ▶ **S**aline
> - ▶ **A**dminister the drug
> - ▶ **S**aline
> - ▶ **H**eparinize

Guidelines for accessing a venous access port are as follows:

1. Draw up 10 mL of normal saline in a 10 mL syringe and 5 mL dilute heparin into a 10 mL syringe.

2. Apply clean gloves.

3. Palpate for and locate the port by placing the forefinger and thumb of your dominant hand and feel for the septum with your other hand.

4. Clean the skin with antimicrobial (30 seconds) and allow to air dry.

5. Connect 10 mL normal saline into the extension tubing of the Huber needle and prime the needle and tubing (keep the syringe connected).

6. Remove and dispose of clean gloves.

7. Follow hospital policy—apply mask, wash hands, and apply sterile gloves.

8. Stabilize the part by using thumb and index finger or middle finger and index finger.

9. Insert needle into port at a 90° angle until resistance is met (hits metal).

10. Check placement of needle-aspirate for blood. If no blood, reposition the client and try again.

11. If correct placement, inject saline. Assess for infiltration into subcutaneous tissue. Close the clamp of the extension tubing.

12. Instill heparin flush solution.

13. Tape the site and apply transparent sterile dressing.

Neoplastic-Associated Disorders and Emergencies

Cancer clients are at risk for complications that are associated with the tumor as well as the treatment regimen prescribed. Some of the complications are not specific to the cancer. One complication in this category is sepsis-associated disseminated intravascular coagulation (DIC). When a person experiences sepsis, organisms invade his bloodstream. Cancer clients are prime candidates for this invasion because most are immune-suppressed and have low white blood cell counts. DIC can occur in any client with a severe illness and trauma. DIC, which is a blood-clotting abnormality, occurs in cancer clients due to sepsis either by release of clotting factors from the cancer cells or because of the many blood transfusions these patients receive. DIC is characterized by extensive clotting followed by bleeding from many orifices. It is a life-threatening condition. Treatment of sepsis-associated DIC is antibiotics for the sepsis, chemotherapy and radiation for the tumor, thrombolytics, blood transfusions, and anti-fibrinolytics (for example, Amicar). Table 13.8 addresses some other complications that occur with neoplastic disease. You should review these complications and be able to recognize the associated signs and symptoms and treatments involved for neoplastic exams.

TABLE 13.8   Complications of Neoplastic Disorders: Manifestations and Treatment

Complication	Clinical Manifestations	Treatment
Spinal cord compression	Paresthesia, paralysis, weakness, back pain, bowel and bladder dysfunction or weakness	Steroids to decrease edema, chemotherapy and radiation to reduce the tumor, surgery or radiation treatments to decreasepressure, braces to support spinal column and reduce pressure.
Hypercalcemia (usually due to cancer spread to the bone)	Increased urinary output, polydipsia, muscle weakness, hyporeflexia, dysrhythmias, calcium levels above 12mg/dL	Fluid administration, drugs to decrease calcium levels (calcitonin, mithramycin), loop diruretics, biphosphonates (for example, Zometa, Aredia), dialysis in severe cases.
Superior vena cava syndrome (obstruction of the superior vena cava by growth of the tumor), Usually associated with lung cancer	Edema of face and eyes, cough and dyspnea, nosebleeds, mental status changes, seizures	High-dose radiation to the mediastinum; stent placement; medications include thrombolytics, steroids, diuretics, and chemotherapy.
Tumor lysis syndrome (associated with tumor treatment— chemotherapy/ radiation). Rapid destruction of cancer cells causes release of cell contents into the blood stream faster than they can be eliminated, especially potassium and purines.	Fatigue, mental changes, tetany, seizures, high blood pressure, dysrhythmias, hyperuricemia, hyperphosphatemia, hyperkalemia, decreased calcium	Hydration via IV fluids. Medications include diuretics to increase urine flow, allopurinol and rasburicase (Elitek) to decrease purines. Dialysis might be necessary.

Bone Marrow and Peripheral Stem Cell Transplantation

Bone marrow transplantation involves the destruction of the client's bone marrow (this is accomplished by high-dose chemotherapy administration and whole body irradiation). The client then receives a stem cell or bone marrow transplant infusion. Sources of stem cells include bone marrow, peripheral circulating blood, and umbilical cord.

Transplantation of bone marrow can be used to treat the following:

▶ Aplastic anemia

▶ Thalassemia

▶ Sickle cell anemia

▶ Immunodeficiency disorders

▶ Certain cancers, such as acute leukemia, chronic myelogenous leukemia, Hodgkin's lymphoma, non-Hodgkin's lymphoma, and testicular cancer

Types of Transplants

The types of bone marrow transplants are based on the source of the donor cells. The three types of transplants available are

▶ **Autologous transplant**: Involves the harvesting, cryopreservation, and reinfusion of the client's own marrow to correct bone marrow hypoplasia resulting from chemotherapeutic drugs.

▶ **Allogenic transplant**: Involves the transplantation of bone marrow from a compatible donor. It has the following requirements:

    ▶ The prospective donor must be tissue- and blood-typed.

    ▶ The donor should be of the same racial and genetic type to be successful.

▶ **Syngeneic transplant:** Involves the transplantation of bone marrow from an identical twin; this type is rare.

Nursing Care After Transplantation

Until the new bone marrow *takes*, or *engrafts*, the client has no immunity or normal bone marrow function. When there is a reduction in leukocytes, erythrocytes and platelets, the client is experiencing bone marrow suppression. The exam reviewer must recognize the major risk of bleeding and infection in these clients. Interventions after a transplant focus on the assessment and prevention of complications of the transplant, including failure to engraft, graft versus host disease, and veno-occlusive disease. The nurse institutes measures to reduce the risk of bleeding and infection, as well treats these disorders if they occur. The nurse should

▶ Provide a private room for the client

▶ Ensure that there are no sick visitors

▶ Avoid invasive procedures (for example, Foleys and so on)

▶ Make sure that there are no fresh flowers or plants in the room

▶ Place the client on a low-bacteria diet that includes no raw vegetables, no pepper, no paprika, and only well-done meats

▸ Use sterile technique when performing care

▸ Assess for signs of complications or rejection of transplant, including jaundice, pain in right upper quadrant, weight gain, and hepatomegaly

▸ Monitor for bleeding

▸ Administer ordered blood transfusion

▸ Administer ordered platelets

▸ Institute bleeding precautions, including

  ▸ Avoid IM injections.

  ▸ Avoid venipunctures.

  ▸ Avoid flossing of teeth.

  ▸ Avoid bending at the waist.

  ▸ Avoid contact sports.

  ▸ Refer to the row on bone marrow and platelet depression in Table 13.6 for other bleeding precautions.

▸ Monitor for infection

CAUTION

A temperature elevation of .5° F could be significant in these clients.

▸ Pharmacological interventions include

  ▸ Steroids

  ▸ Immunosuppressants

▸ Colony-stimulating factors as ordered

Neoplastic Disorder Case Study

The nurse is caring for multiple patients with cancer on the oncology unit:

Client #1 is a transfer from the intensive care unit on the previous shift. He is three days post-surgical laryngectomy for cancer of the larynx. He has a tracheostomy and is receiving a tube feeding at 60 mL/hr.

Client #2 is a patient with small cell lung cancer with metastasis to the bone with a WBC count of 17,000 μL.

Client #3 has just arrived after an ultrasound biopsy of her right breast revealed a malignancy. She is being admitted for evaluation and possible right mastectomy.

Client #4 has colon cancer with a colon resection three months ago, followed by chemotherapy. The client has just been admitted for further treatment and has a WBC count of 1600.

(continues)

(continued)

1. Which client should the nurse assess first? Why?

2. Client #4 has a WBC count of 1600 μL. What does this indicate?

3. Client #2's vital signs assessment reveals a temperature of 102.4° F, pulse rate of 100, respirations 18, and blood pressure of 126/70. The physician orders vancomycin 1 g IVPB in 250 mL of NS over 60 minutes. The IV set delivers 15 gtt/mL. You would set the IV drop rate at how many drops per minute to deliver the medication in the prescribed time period?

4. Client #2 has small cell lung cancer. What are some characteristics of this type of cancer?

5. In a client with bone metastasis, as in client #2, what laboratory values would you expect the client to exhibit?

Answers to Case Study

1. The client that is the most in danger is client #1. A client with a laryngectomy and tracheostomy has an ineffective airway risk and should receive the priority assessment.

2. The client is neutropenic and at risk for infection. The client should also be placed on neutropenic precautions to reduce the risk for infection. These include no sick visitors, a private room, avoid invasive procedures, and a low-bacteria diet.

3. The drip rate should be set at 63 drops per minute.

   gtts/min = 15 gtt/1 ml ∞ 250/60 min = 250/4 = 63

4. Small cell lung cancer is fast-growing and metastasis has usually developed before the cancer is diagnosed. It accounts for 20%–25% of all lung cancers and is the most aggressive. It is, however, more responsive to chemotherapy and radiation. The median survival from diagnosis is 8– 16 weeks.

5. Clients with bone metastasis usually show elevations in calcium levels which can cause cardiac dysrhythmias. Symptoms of hypercalcemia include lethargy, weakness, loss of appetite, nausea and vomiting, flaccid muscles, and heart block. Alkaline phosphatase values are also elevated because of abnormal osteoblast activity.

Key Concepts

This chapter includes much-needed information to help the nurse apply knowledge of neoplastic disorders to the NCLEX exam. The nurse preparing for the licensure exam should be familiar with commonly ordered lab tests, including normal lab values, and medications used to treat the client with neoplastic disorders.

Key Terms

▶ Angioedema

▶ Anovulation

▶ Asthenia

▶ Colposcopy

▶ Cryptorchidism

▶ Dysphagia

▶ Dyspnea

▶ Electropharesis

▶ Emaciated

▶ Failure to engraft

▶ Graft versus host disease

▶ Hand pump exercises

▶ Hyperthermia

▶ Lymphedema

▶ Malaise

▶ Neuritis

▶ Neutropenia

▶ Nulliparity

▶ Oliguria

▶ Oophorectomy

▶ Palliative

▶ Paresthesis

▶ Polydipsia

▶ Polyphagia

▶ Postcoital

▶ Proliferation

- ▶ Pruritis
- ▶ Sepsis
- ▶ Skin desquamation
- ▶ SIADH
- ▶ Somnolence
- ▶ Splenectomy
- ▶ Tetany
- ▶ Urticaria
- ▶ Veno-occlusive disease
- ▶ Vesiculation
- ▶ Whipple procedure

Diagnostic Tests

Cancer clients require extensive diagnostic exams to determine the primary site of the cancer or tumor, as well as whether metastasis has occurred.

The tests are also important in determining the treatment options: radiation, chemotherapy, and/or surgery. Laboratory exams such as carcinogenic embryonic acid (CEA) and prostate-specific antigen (PSA) are important in determining the disease and its progression. Routine laboratory exams such as chest x-rays, urinalysis, and cell blood counts (CBCs) with differentials also need to be reviewed.

Particularly important when caring for the cancer client receiving chemotherapy is the CBC. This test monitors for the side effects and bone marrow depression that can result from antineoplastic drugs. These diagnostic tests include

- ▶ Biopsy
- ▶ Bone marrow aspiration
- ▶ Bone scan
- ▶ Bronchoscopy
- ▶ CBC
- ▶ CEA
- ▶ CT scan
- ▶ Magnetic resonance imagery (MRI)
- ▶ Mammogram
- ▶ Mediastinoscopy
- ▶ PET scan

► PSA

► Radioactive scan

It is important to discuss the specific requirements and safety hazard for clients who are to receive an MRI. MRIs function by the use of a powerful magnet. Clients with metal in their body cannot take the exam. No metal can be in the room of the client receiving an MRI; therefore, tubings for equipment must be lengthened to accommodate the client on oxygen or other life support equipment. The candidate for the exam must consider the factors in the following list to determine whether an MRI would be contraindicated or whether special accommodations would need to be made for a client who is scheduled for an MRI:

► Pregnancy of client

► Client weight greater than 260 pounds (open MRI would be required due to client size)

► Clients with pacemakers or electronic implants

► Clients who have metal fragments, metal clamps, or aneurysm clips

► The ability of the client to communicate clearly

► Use of life support equipment

► Ability of the client to lie still in a supine position for 30 minutes

► Use of oxygen by the client

► Clients receiving an IV infusion

Pharmacologic Agents Used in the Care of the Client with Specific Neoplastic Disorders

The nurse reviewer studying for an NCLEX type exam needs to be familiar with agents' side effects, adverse effects, and specific nursing care interventions. Although most nurses who administer chemotherapeutic drugs have extensive training, these drugs can be tested on an NCLEX type exam, and the nursing reviewer is expected to have knowledge of the drugs. The nurse must be aware of the impact of these drugs on the client's quality of life and recognize that some of these drugs have life-threatening, adverse effects. Nurses who administer chemotherapy must also keep in mind the importance of self-protection from the drug agents by wearing appropriate equipment when coming in contact with the agents. The reviewer should also keep in mind that a lot of these drugs are vesicants and priority should be given to ensure that the intravenous route is not compromised during the infusion of IV chemotherapeutic agents. These medications are not inclusive of all the agents used to treat oncological disorders; therefore, you will want to keep a current pharmacology text handy for reference.

Table 13.9 gives you common chemotherapeutic medications, the side/adverse effects, and the pertinent nursing care interventions. The most common side effects (and interventions required to treat them) of most of the agents are intentionally not included in this table because these have been addressed in Table 13.6.

TABLE 13.9   Pharmacological Agents Used in the Care of Clients with Neoplastic Disorders

Type of Chemotherapeutic Agent	Action of the Drug	Side/Adverse Effects	Pertinent Nursing Care or Interventions
Alkylating agents:	Cross-linking of DNA, inhibiting division of cells.		
Cyclophosphamide (Cytoxan)		Pulmonary and myocardial fibrosis, hemorrhagic cystitis, symptom of inappropriate diuretic hormone (SIADH).	Assess cardiac and respiratory status, force fluids, use with mesna to prevent hemorrhagic cystitis (assess for hematuria).
Chlorambucil (Leukeran)		Secondary malignancy, hepatoxicity, Stevens- Johnson syndrome, angioneurotic edema, rash.	Monitor for side effects. Assess laboratory values for suppression of bone marrow and liver function.
Altretamine (Hexalen)		Seizures, malaise, weakness, nephrotoxicity, hepatotoxicity, hypocalcemia, hypokalemia, hypomagnesemia, peripheral neuropathy, pruritus, and skin rash.	Monitor for signs of anaphylaxis: facial edema, wheezing, dizziness, fainting, tachycardia. Observe for side effects. Monitor laboratory test for myelosuppression and liver function.
Ifosfamide (IFEX)		Toxicity to the central nervous system (CNS), cardiotoxicity, renal toxic, hemorrhagic cystitis.	Monitor for toxicity associated problems: somnolence, confusion, cranial nerve dysfunction, chest pain, shortness of breath, arrhythmias, oliguria, lethargy, edema.
Busulfan (Myleran)		Seizures, confusion, weakness, nosebleed, liver veno-occlusive disease, pulmonary fibrosis, chest pain, hypotension, arrhythmias, arthralgia, back pain, hepatomegaly.	Monitor for side effects. Drug may be discontinued if symptoms of pulmonary fibrosis occur—fever, cough, shortness of breath.
Mechlorethamine (Nitrogen mustard)		Hyperuricemia.	Monitor for symptoms of gout. Encourage fluids. Assess liver function tests and CBC. Use immediately after mixing; avoid vapors; avoid skin contact (if contact occurs, flush immediately); ensure proper IV placement before administration.
Antimetabolites	Impairs cell division.		
5-FU fluorouracil (Adrucil, Efudex, Fluiroplex)		Nail loss, phototoxic, diarrhea, dermatitis.	Client should use sunscreen and protective clothing to prevent phototoxic reaction.

TABLE 13.9 *Continued*

Type of Chemotherapeutic Agent	Action of the Drug	Side/Adverse Effects	Pertinent Nursing Care or Interventions
Cytarabine (Cytosar-U, Ara-C)		Corneal toxicity, hemorrhagic conjunctivitis, pulmonary edema, hepatotoxic, cytarabine syndrome.	Monitor for cytarabine syndrome: fever, muscle aches, bone pain, chest pain, rash, conjunctivitis. Treat with steroids or pre-medicate with corticosterooids.
6-mercaptopurine (Purinethol)		Hepatoxicity, tumor lysis syndrome, urate nephropathy, nephrolithiasis.	Drug given with allopurinol to increase drug potency (inhibits uric acid production from cell destruction).
Anti-Tumor Antibiotics	Inhibits DNA, RNA synthesis.		
Bleomycin (Blenoxane)		Mental changes, hypotension, pain at the tumor site, anaphylactic reaction.	Monitor for anaphylactic reaction: fever, chills, low blood pressure, wheezing.
Dactinomycin (Cosmegen)		Hepatotoxicity, anaphylaxis, pneumonitis, chelitis, hypocalcemia, myalgias, and skin pigmentation abnormality.	Monitor for liver function, assess respiratory status for signs of pneumonia.
Daunorubicin (cerubidine)		Rhinitis, abnormal vision, cardiotoxicity, hepatotoxicity.	Assess for congestive heart failure, arrhythmias. Note: Red urine is a side effect of this drug, but is not significant.
Mitomycin (Mutamycin, Mitomycin-C)		Edema, pulmonary toxicity.	Monitor for pulmonary toxicity: cough, hemoptysis, bronchospasm. Alert: Pulmonary toxicity is a life threatening condition.
Mylotarg		Headache, hypoxia, dyspnea, hypotension or hypertension, mucositis, hepatoxicity, rash, hyperglycemia, low potassium, chills, fever, tumor lysis syndrome.	Assess laboratory for increased blood sugars, decreased potassium, and abnormal liver function tests. Monitor for side effects.
Topisomerase Inhibitors	Kills rapidly replicating cells.		
Etoposide (VP16, Vepesid)		Fatigue, headache, vertigo, drowsiness, pulmonary edema, congestive heart failure, myocardial infarction, hypotension, peripheral neuropathy, fever.	Monitor for anaphylaxis: fever, chills, bronchospasm, rash, low blood pressure, tachycardia.
Irinotecan (Camptosar)		Same as above. Hepatotoxic, nephrotoxic, muscle cramps.	Given with 5-FU and leucovorin. Alert: Diarrhea can occur and it could be severe and life-threatening.
Topotecan (Hycamtin)		Headache, fatigue, weakness, dyspnea, abdominal pain, diarrhea, anorexia, arthralgia.	Monitor for side effects.

(continues)

TABLE 13.9   *Continued*

Type of Chemotherapeutic Agent	Action of the Drug	Side/Adverse Effects	Pertinent Nursing Care or Interventions
Antimitotics	Prevents cell division.		
Docetaxel (Taxotere)		Fatigue, weakness, ascites, cardiac tamponade, pulmonary edema, pericardial effusion, myalgia, neurological deficits.	Monitor for anaphylactic reaction: bronchospasm, hypotension, erythema. Measure abdominal girth to assess for ascites.
Paclitaxel (Taxol)		Abnormal ECG, malaise, weakness, bradycardia, hypotension, abnormal liver function tests, rash, alopecia, itching, arthralgia, myalgia, peripheral neuropathy, anaphylaxic reaction, Stevens-Johnson syndrome, toxic epidermal necrolysis.	Monitor for anaphylactic reaction: dyspnea, hypotension, chest pain. Assess liver function test results. Monitor for symptoms of Stevens-Johnson syndrome—skin vesicles, erosions, and crusts. Monitor for toxic epidermal necrolysis—epidermal peeling.
Vincristine (Oncovin)		Mental status changes, diplopia, bronchospasm, abdominal cramps, ileus development, nocturia, syndrome of inappropriate anti- diuretic hormone (SIADH), and peripheral neuropathy.	Monitor neurological status and report abnormalities to the healthcare provider. Monitor intake and output for decreased urinary output associated with SIADH. Assess for gout symptoms (pain, erythema, swelling in joints, especially the great toe). Alert: Bronchospasm can be life threatening.
Vinblastine (Velblane)		Mental depression, neurotoxic weakness, bronchospasm, gonadal suppression, dermatitis, vesiculation, SIADH, hyperuremicia, neuritis, paresthesia, peripheral neuropathy.	Same as above with Vincristine.
Cytoprotectants			
Amifostine (Ethyol)	Reduces renal toxicity from cisplatin. Prevents severe xerostomia post radiation to the head and neck.	Dizziness, somnolence, nausea and vomiting, flushing, decrease in calcium, anaphylaxis, Stevens-Johnson syndrome, toxic epidermis necrolysis, toxoderma, erythema multiforme, exfoliative dermatitis.	Monitor for side/adverse effects. Monitor laboratory values for hypocalcemia.

TABLE 13.9 *Continued*

Type of Chemotherapeutic Agent	Action of the Drug	Side/Adverse Effects	Pertinent Nursing Care or Interventions
Dexrazoxane (Zinecard)	Reduces cardio-toxic effects of Doxorubicin administration.	Hyperactivity, restlessness, depression, dizziness, palpitations, tachycardia. High blood pressure, anorexia, metallic taste, impotence, increased libido, urticaria.	Note: Medication should be administered 30 minutes before Doxorubicin dose. Instruct client to avoid caffeine in the diet. Monitor for side effects.
Mesna (Mesenex, Uromitexan)	Antidote ifosfamide.	Dizziness, drowsiness, headache, unpleasant taste, flushing, flu-like symptoms.	Inform client of unpleasant taste prior to administration. Monitor for side effects.
Pamidronate (Aredia)	Reverses malignancy associated hypercalcemia.	Fatigue, conjunctivitis, blurred vision, rhinitis, arrhythmias, tachycardia, abdominal pain, hypocalcemia, hypokalemia, hypomagnesia, hypophostemia, hypothyroidism, muscle stiffness, bone pain, osteonecrosis of the jaw.	Instruct of visual side effects and related machine operation disability. Monitor for fluid and electrolyte depletions and hypothyroidism. For further discussion, refer to Chapter 2, "Fluid and Electrolyte and Acid/Base Balance," and Chapter 4, "Care of the Client with Endocrine Disorders."
Biological Response Modifiers, Mono-clonal Antibodies, and Targeted Cancer Therapy	Boost immune system, gives targeted therapy directly to tumor.		
Rituximab (Rituxan)		Headache, bronchospasm, cough, dyspnea, arrhythmias, hypotension, peripheral edema, abdominal pain, altered taste, dyspepsia, flushing, urticaria, hyperglycemia, hypocalcemia, arthralgia, back pain, tumor lysis syndrome, anaphylaxis, angioedema.	Monitor for severe reaction: hypotension, angioedema, hypoxia, bronchospasm.
Trastuzumab (Herceptin)		Dizziness, headache, insomnia, weakness, depression, dyspnea, cough, pharyngitis, cardio-toxicity, rash, edema, back pain, arthralgia, bone pain, neuropathy.	Assess for hypersensitivity reaction: chills, fever, infection, and pain. Monitor for allergic reaction and flu-like symptoms. Monitor for cardiotoxicity and pulmonary hypersensitivity reactions.
Cetuximab (Erbitux)		Malaise, depression, headache, insomnia, conjunctivitis, renal failure, nail disorder, pruritis, skin desquamation.	Check for infusion reactions: airway obstruction symptoms—stridor, bronchospasm. Monitor for dematologic toxicity: acneform rash, skin drying, and skin fissures.

(continues)

TABLE 13.9 *Continued*

Type of Chemotherapeutic Agent	Action of the Drug	Side/Adverse Effects	Pertinent Nursing Care or Interventions
Imatinib (Gleevec)		Ascites, pleural effusion, pulmonary edema, CHF, anasarca, pericardial effusion, GI bleed, hemorrhage of CNS.	Monitor CBC and liver function tests. Monitor for serious adverse effects listed.
Colony-Stimulating Factors			
Pegfilgrastim (Neulasta)	Activates neutrophils, prevents infection.	ARD, ruptured spleen, anaphylaxis, musculoskeletal and bone pain, splenomegaly, onset of sickle cell crisis in clients with sickle cell, flank pain, abdominal pain, headache, hypotension, leukocytosis, hyperuricemia.	Assess for bone pain. Monitor for symptoms of ARD— fever, lung infiltration, respiratory distress. Absorbs well with subcutaneous injection.
Sargramostim (Leukine, Prokine)	Accelerates bone marrow recovery. Stimulates macrophages and granulocytes.	Pleural and pericardial effusion, capillary leak syndrome, arrhythmias, anaphylaxis, respiratory distress, fever, asthenia, headache, chills, diarrhea, myalgias, bone pain, rash, pruritis, edema, dyspnea, hypotension, tachycardia, syncope, and dizziness.	Monitor for side effects as listed, especially capillary leak syndrome (edema of feet or lower legs, sudden increase in weight, dyspnea). Assess for reaction at first dose (flushing, hypotension, syncope, weakness).
Epoetin (Epogen, Procrit)	Erythropoiesis stimulant (increasing RBCs)	High blood pressure, CHF, blood clots, myocardial infarction, seizures, headache, tachycardia, fever, arthalgia, dyspnea, swelling, rash, fatigue, congestion and cough, asthenia, paresthesia.	Monitor for side effects, assess vital signs. Note: Anti-hypertensive medications might be required.
Filgrastin (Neupogen)	Same as Neulasta above.	Leukocytosis, injection site reaction, bone pain.	Monitor for side effects. Assess CBC results.
Darbepoetin alfa (Aranesp)	Stimulates RBC production.	Fatigue, headache, cough dyspnea, arrhythmias, CHF, clotting problems, edema, high blood pressure, hypotension, abdominal pain, myalgia, arthralgia, fever allergic reaction.	Monitor for side effects. Teach patient to report any chest pain or heart beat irregularities, numbness, blurred vision, or symptoms of clots.
Oprelvekin (Neumega)	Stimulates platelets.	Pulmonary edema, exfoliative dermatitis, ocular bleeding, papilledema, atrial arrhythmias, stroke, pulmonary edema, capillary leak syndrome, edema, dyspnea, tachycardia, palpitations, asthenia.	Monitor for common and severe side effects. Inform client to report any chest pain, unrelieved irregular heartbeat, blurred vision, or neurological deficits.

TABLE 13.9 *Continued*

Type of Chemotherapeutic Agent	Action of the Drug	Side/Adverse Effects	Pertinent Nursing Care or Interventions
Other Agents Used in Neoplastic Disorders			
Hydroxyurea (Hydrea)	Antimetabolite.	Drowsiness, constipation, hepatitis, dysuria, renal tubular dysfunction, pruritus, rash, hyperuricemia, chills, fever, malaise.	Observe for rash. Instruct that might cause drowsiness and not to operate machinery or drive.
Leucovorin (Wellcovorin)	Antidote for methotrexate.	Allergic reaction: rash, urticaria, wheezing. thrombocytosis.	Observe for allergic reaction.
Thalidomide (Thalomid)	An immuno-suppressant.	Dizziness, drowsiness, bradycardia, edema, orthostatic hypotension, thromboemboli, constipation, rash, photosensitivity, peripheral neuropathy, birth defects, increase in HIV viral load.	Monitor for side effects. Assess for hypersensitivity reaction-rash, tachycardia, and hypotension.
Tamoxifen Citrate (Tamofen, Novaldex)	Anti-estrogen, anti-neoplastic.	Confusion, depression, headache, weakness, blurred vision, pulmonary emboli, stroke, vaginal bleeding, uterine malignancy, hypercalcemia, hot flashes, bone pain (might indicate drug is effective; pain will decrease over time).	Teach to report edema. Bone pain might require analgesia.
Interferons	Immune response modifier.	Neuropsychiatric disorders, confusion, dizziness, depression, trouble thinking, blurred vision, clotting problems, pancreatitis, taste disorder, peripheral neropathy, cardiomyopathy, arrhythmias, hypertension, autoimmune disorders, flu-like symptoms, rash, arthralgia.	Assess for psychological problems (suicidal ideation, aggressive behavior). Monitor for infection, clotting problems, and other side effects.
All trans-retinoic acid (ATRA), retinol	Immune booster.	Fever, dysphea, chest pain, pleural and pericardinal effusions.	Observe for adverse effects.
Interleukins	Cytokine.	Apnea, respiratory failure, pulmonary edema, arrhythmias, high blood pressure, exfoliative dermatitis, coagulation disorders, hypotension, tachycardia, ascites, hepatomegaly, proteinuria, renal failure, capillary leak syndrome, myocardial infarction, stroke.	Monitor for side effects. Alert: Cardiac arrest could occur.

Apply Your Knowledge

This chapter provided information regarding the care of clients with neoplastic disorders. The following questions test your knowledge regarding the safe, effective care and management of the client with various neoplastic disorders. Use the key terms, diagnostics, chapter content, and pharmacological agents sections to assist in answering these questions.

Exam Questions

1. The nurse is caring for a 24-year-old who is three months pregnant. The client has just been informed that she has breast cancer. The nurse assesses signs of increased anxiety. Which statement by the nurse is most appropriate?

    A. "Do you have any questions?"

    B. "You seem to be upset. Tell me about your feelings."

    C. "There is no need to be worried. The baby will be fine."

    D. "I'm going to call the chaplain to visit."

2. A client with lung cancer is six hours post-surgical lobectomy procedure. The nurse assesses 260 mL bloody chest tube drainage for the past hour. What is the most appropriate initial action?

    A. Elevate the head of the bed.

    B. Increase the IV fluid rate.

    C. Assess the wound dressing for drainage.

    D. Notify the doctor of the assessment finding.

3. The nurse assesses a respiratory rate of 10 on a client with cancer who has just received a hydromorphone hydrochloride (Dilaudid) injection. Which drug should the nurse be prepared to administer?

    A. Naloxone (Narcan)

    B. Flumazenil (Romazicon)

    C. Benztropine (Cogentin)

    D. Meperidine (Demerol)

4. The nurse is performing discharge teaching on a client with lung cancer who is to receive external radiation treatment to the chest area. Which statement by the client indicates a need for further teaching?

   A. "I can wash the area gently with mild soap and water."

   B. "I should expose the area radiated to the sun three times a day."

   C. "I should wear soft clothing over the area."

   D. "I should dry the area with patting motions rather than rubbing it."

5. The nurse is in the room of a client who is neutropenic. Which action by the nursing assistant, observed by the nurse, would indicate a need for action?

   A. Placing a Foley bag in the bed with the client when turning her

   B. Raising the head of the bed prior to feeding the client

   C. Adding pillows to the client's back area for support after turning and repositioning

   D. Providing mouth care to a client who is NPO

6. A client with cervical cancer has a sealed implant in place. Which would be included in the nursing plan for this client?

   A. Admit to a semi-private room.

   B. Visitors are limited to four hours per day.

   C. No pregnant women or children younger than 16 can visit.

   D. Excreta requires special precautions.

7. The nurse is assessing the laboratory values of a client with cancer who is awaiting discharge. The values reveal a platelet count of 10,000 μL. Which action is appropriate to add to the client's discharge plan?

   A. Suggest an order for Plavix be added to the prescriptions.

   B. Encourage participation in contact sports.

   C. Teach the client to eat a low-bacteria diet—no raw fruits or vegetables.

   D. Instruct the client to use an electric razor for shaving to avoid injury.

8. A client with bone metastasis has a calcium level of 20.8 mg/dL. The nurse should be alert for which symptom correlating with the level?

   A. Hyperactivity

   B. Oliguria

   C. ECG changes

   D. Polyphagia

9. The nurse is caring for a client with cancer who is neutropenic. Which plan would be inappropriate?

   A. Notify the doctor of any temperature over 100° F.

   B. Use sterile technique when performing invasive procedures.

   C. Avoid any spicy foods.

   D. Avoid client exposure to anyone who is ill.

10. Which is a correct guideline for performance of self breast exams (SBE) in a 22-year-old female client?

    A. Perform the SBE monthly one week after the menstrual cycle.

    B. SBE should be done two weeks after the menstrual cycle.

    C. Perform the SBE on the same day of the month. It doesn't matter which day.

    D. The breast exam should be performed when the breasts are tender and/or swollen.

11. A client who has a diagnosis of possible prostate cancer is being discharged after a transrectal ultrasound with biopsy of the prostate. The nurse should instruct the client to report which symptom indicating a common complication of this procedure?

    A. Headache

    B. Leg pain

    C. Dysuria

    D. Constipation

12. The nurse is admitting a client with advanced prostate cancer and a history of myocardial infarction and pulmonary emboli. Which would the nurse expect to be prescribed for this client?

    A. Leuprolide acetate (Lupron)

    B. Flutamide (Euflex)

    C. Diethylstilbestrol (DES)

    D. Goserelin acetate (Zoladex)

13. The nurse is giving instructions to a client who is to obtain a fecal occult blood test (FOBT). The client should be instructed to avoid which food for two days prior to giving the stool specimen?

    A. Peas

    B. Broccoli

    C. Corn

    D. Beets

14. The nurse is caring for a client with lung cancer. The nurse recognizes which type of lung cancer as fast-growing with spread usually occurring before a diagnosis is made?

    A. Small cell

    B. Non-small cell

    C. Epidermoid carcinoma

    D. Adenocarcinoma

15. The nurse is providing care for a client with possible pancreatic cancer. Which test is the most definitive diagnostic exam for this type of cancer?

    A. Serum amylase

    B. Pancreatic ultrasonography

    C. CT scan

    D. ERCP with cytologies

Answers to Exam Questions

1. Answer B is correct. The nurse should encourage the client to discuss her feelings. Answer A restricts conversation, so it is incorrect. The answers in C and D options either provide false reassurance or offer no help, so they are wrong.

2. Answer D is correct. The nurse should report excessive drainage from the chest tube to the physician as a priority action. Answers B and C may also be performed, but Answer D is the initial action, which makes them incorrect. Assessments revealing hypovolemia would lead to a lowering of the head, rather than head elevation, making Answer A incorrect.

3. Answer A is correct. Narcan is the reversal drug for narcotics. The drugs in Answers B, C, and D would not be used to reverse Dilaudid effects, so they are incorrect.

   Remember: **nar**cotic-**nar**can

4. Answer B is correct. The radiated area should not be exposed to sunlight or heat. Answers A, C, and D are all appropriate measures to be used with external radiation, so they are incorrect.

5. Answer A is correct. Allowing urine to back flow into the bladder is improper handling technique and increases the risk of infection. The actions in Answers B, C, and D are appropriate actions, so they are incorrect.

6. Answer C is correct. This is a safe recommendation. It is also recommended that pregnant nurses not care for these clients. A private room is necessary for these clients, visitors are limited to 30 minutes in a 24-hour period, and there are no special precautions for the excreta of a client with a sealed implant in place. These facts make the options in Answers A, B, and D incorrect.

7. Answer D is correct. The client's platelet count is low, which increases the risk for bleeding and injury. Electric razors provide safety and prevent cuts. Answer A would be incorrect because it is an anti-platelet medication and increases the risk of bleeding. A low-bacteria diet is related to a decreased white blood cell count to decrease the chance of infection, so Answer C is incorrect. The client should avoid contact sports, making Answer B incorrect.

8. Answer C is correct. A 20.8 mg/dL level is hypercalcemia. A symptom of hypercalcemia is changes in the ECG. Other symptoms include fatigue, increased urine output, and loss of appetite; therefore, Answers A, B, and D are incorrect.

9. Answer C is correct. This option is not related to a client with neutropenia (low neutrophils) who is at increased risk for infections. Answers A, B, and D are all important interventions to prevent an infection for immunosuppressed clients, so they are incorrect.

10. Answer A is correct. This is the recommendation for premenopausal women. Answers B and D are not recommended times for SBE, so they are incorrect. Answer C is the recommendation for post-menopausal women or women with menopause induced by surgery (for example, by hysterectomy), so it is incorrect.

11. Answer C is correct. Possible complications of TRUS include hematuria, infection, and/or perineal pain. Dysuria could indicate infection. Answers A, B, and D are not related symptoms of complications, so they are incorrect.

12. Answer D is correct. Zoladex is a drug that can be given for palliative therapy if estrogen is contraindicated, for example, due to this client's history. Answers A, B, and C are associated with estrogen and would be contraindicated with this client, so they are incorrect.

13. Answer D is correct. Certain foods and medications can cause a false positive test result of a FOBT. Clients should avoid aspirin, vitamin C, horseradish, beets, and meat for two days prior to giving the stool specimen. The foods in Answers A, B, and C do not have to be avoided prior to the test, so they are incorrect options.

14. Answer A is correct. Small cell lung cancer is characterized as fast-growing with early metastasis, mostly associated with cigarette smoking. The type of lung cancers in Answers B, C, and D lack these characteristics, so they are incorrect.

15. Answer D is correct. ERCP with aspirates provides visualization and evidence of malignant cells. The tests in Answers A, B, and C serve to assist in diagnosis of pancreatic cancer but are not as definitive as the ERCP.

Suggested Reading and Resources

▶ Brunner, L., and D. Suddarth. *Textbook of Medical Surgical Nursing*. 10th ed. Philadelphia: Lippincott Williams & Wilkins, 2009.

▶ Deglin, Judith H., and April H. Vallerand. *Davis Drug Guide for Nurses*. Philadelphia: F. A. Davis, 2009.

▶ Ignatavicius, D., and S. Workman. *Medical Surgical Nursing: Critical Thinking for Collaborative Care*. 6th ed. Philadelphia: Elsevier, 2007.

▶ Kee, J. *Laboratory and Diagnostic Tests with Nursing Implications*. New York: Prentice Hall, 2010.

▶ Lemone, P,. and K. Burke. *Medical-Surgical Nursing Critical Thinking in Client Care*. 4th ed. Upper Saddle River, NJ: Pearson Prentice Hall, 2008.

▶ Lewis, S., M. Heitkemper, S. Dirksen, P. O'Brien, and L. Bucher. *Medical Surgical Nursing: Assessment and Management of Clinical Problems*. 7th ed. Philadelphia: Elsevier, 2007.

▶ Olsen, J., D. Giangrasso, P. Dillon. *Medical Dosage Calculations*. 9th ed. Upper Saddle River, NJ: Prentice Hall, 2008.

▶ Rinehart, Sloan, Hurd, *Exam Cram NCLEX-RN*. Indianapolis,: Que Publishing, 2007.

▶ Smith, F., D. Duell, B. Martin. *Clinical Nursing Skills Basic to Advanced Skills*. 7th ed. Upper Saddle River, NJ: Pearson Prentice Hall, 2008.

▶ American Cancer Society: www.cancer.org

▶ Centers for Disease Control and Prevention: www.cdc.gov

▶ Epocrates: www.epocrates.com

CHAPTER FOURTEEN

Care of the Client with Musculoskeletal and Connective Tissue Disorders

The musculoskeletal system includes muscles, bones, and joints, as illustrated in Figure 14.1. It is a large body system. Injury to the musculoskeletal system is one of the primary reasons for disability in the United States. Advancing age and weakened bones due to osteoporosis are major risk factors for fractures. Musculoskeletal trauma can be minor requiring short term care or major with long term or permanent disabilities. Connective tissue disorders, such as rheumatoid arthritis and lupus, not only affect the joints, but have systemic effects. Nurses should be knowledgeable of the treatment and interventions necessary to provide care for clients with deficits in the musculoskeletal system and those with connective tissue disorders.

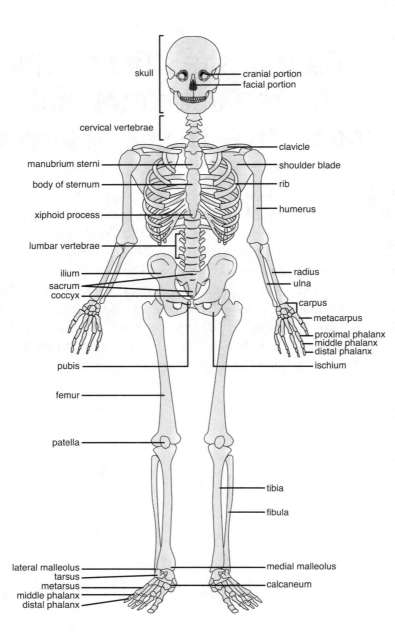

FIGURE 14.1 Bones of the human skeleton.

Fractures

A fracture is defined as simply a break in the continuity of the bone. Four major categories of bone fractures are classified according to the amount of tissue damage:

▶ **Simple or closed:** With this type of fracture, there is no break in the skin.

▶ **Compound or open:** The skin surface is broken with these fractures..

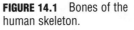

CAUTION

There is more danger of infection and osteomyelitis with compound fractures.

▶ **Comminuted:** This type of fracture causes damage to soft tissue nerves and blood vessels.

▶ **Green stick:** This type of fracture occurs more often in children. The break occurs through only part of the bone with a green stick fracture.

Figure 14.2 demonstrates bones with fractures described.

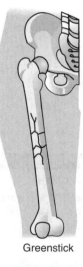

Greenstick

Simple

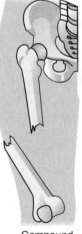

Compound

Comminuted

FIGURE 14.2 Types of fractures.

A fifth type of fracture is the pathological fracture. These fractures occur without major injury or trauma. The bones on these clients have been weakened by diseases such as osteoporosis, osteogenesis imperfecta, or metastatic cancer.

The exam reviewer must be aware of the need for early intervention in the care of clients with fractures. Symptoms indicating a fracture include the following:

▶ Coolness and blanching distal to the break

▶ Crepitation

▶ Disalignment

▶ Shortness of the affected limb

▶ Swelling

▶ Pain

▶ Inability to use the limb

Major Fracture Sites

The treatments of certain fractures are different depending on the location of the break. Table 14.1 lists the common sites of fractures with treatment measures specific to the sites.

TABLE 14.1   Common Fracture Sites and Treatment

Site of Fracture	Treatment
Mandibular	Fixed occlusion for 6–10 weeks. Insertion of permanent titanium plates. Use of resorbable plates and screws. Inner maxillary fixation (bones realigned and wired with bite closed). Nursing care: Oral care with irrigating device, liquid diet. Alert: Wire cutters must be accessible at all times due to the risk for aspiration if vomiting occurs.
Clavicle	Self-healing. Immobilize with splint or fix with surgery of open reduction and internal fixation (ORIF).
Elbow or olecranon	Reduction with a posterior splint or cast. Healing takes two months or more. ORIF.
Femur	Skeletal traction. ORIF or external fixation. Healing takes six months or more.
Tibia or fibula	Closed reduction with long leg cast for two to two and a half months. ORIF.
Pelvic	Ischial rami or iliac crest fractures: Bedrest on a firm mattress. Takes two months or more to heal. Acetabulum fractures: ORIF or external fixation device. Nonweight-bearing for three months.
Colles's (wrist) fracture	Closed reduction. Cast application.

NOTE

Adverse Effects   Alert: With pelvic fractures, assess for internal damage to major organs and blood vessels in this area. Assess for hematuria, melena, rigid abdomen, and signs of hypovolemia (for example, low BP or tachycardia).

General Treatment for Fractures

Treatment of fractures focuses on measures to limit movement, control pain, decrease edema, prevent complications, and promote healing. The following highlights the care you must know for taking the exam:

▶ Splinting above and below the affected area. Air splints are used if available.

▶ Elevating the affected extremity.

- Removing any jewelry from the extremity.

- Covering open fractures wounds with a sterile dressing due to the possibility of contamination.

- Administering medication, such as

    - Antibiotics for open fractures susceptible to gas-growing clostridium

    - Antithrombotics

    - Heparin (Hepalgan)

    - Enoxaparin (Lovenox)

    - Narcotics and muscle relaxers for pain

- Using traction to maintain bone alignment.

Traction

It is important to explore a little more on the traction treatment. Traction utilizes a pulling force to maintain proper alignment of the bone so that healing can occur. It can also reduce the fracture and decrease muscle spasms, which decreases pain. The following information outlines the types of traction and your role in the care of traction necessary for effectively taking the exam:

- **Manual traction:** Maintained by the caregiver's hand.

- **Skin traction:** Maintained by using straps or wraps applied to the skin—for example, Buck's traction (see Figure 14.3) and Bryant's traction (see Figure 14.4). Buck's traction is often used for fractured hips. The weight is no more than 5– 10 pounds to prevent damage to the skin.

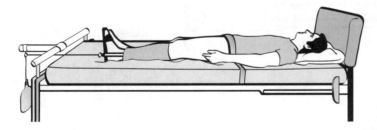

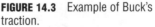

FIGURE 14.3 Example of Buck's traction.

- **Skeletal traction:** Maintained by using pins or wires inserted into the bone. Examples are 90–90 (see Figure 14.5), Crutchfield tong traction (see Figure 14.6), and halo vest traction (see Figure 14.7). These tractions (usually 15– 30 pounds) aid in realignment of the bone. Crutchfield tong traction and Halo vest traction are used for clients with cervical fractures of the spine.

CAUTION

With the use of skeletal traction, these weights should not be removed unless it is an emergency situation because removal of the weight can defeat the purpose of the traction and injure the client.

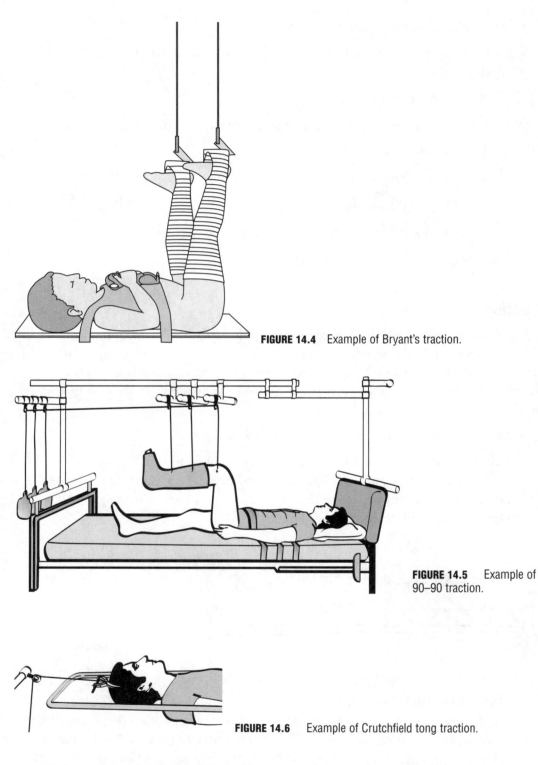

FIGURE 14.4 Example of Bryant's traction.

FIGURE 14.5 Example of 90–90 traction.

FIGURE 14.6 Example of Crutchfield tong traction.

▶ **Balanced suspension traction:** Uses more than one force of pull to establish alignment (see Figure 14.8).

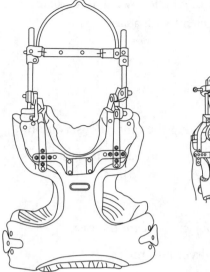 

FIGURE 14.7   Example of halo vest traction.

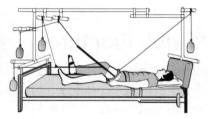

FIGURE 14.8   Example of balance suspension with Thomas ring splint and Pearson attachment.

Here are some points to remember in maintaining traction:

▶ Weights must hang free.

▶ Linens should not lie on ropes.

▶ Ropes should remain within the pulley.

▶ Assess circulation, pulses, and movement of extremity.

▶ Maintain proper body alignment.

▶ Skeletal traction requires specific assessment for signs of inflammation or infection at the entry site of the pins or screws. Pin care with cleansing might be done at the site, depending on the facility.

▶ Countertraction is usually provided by the clients' weight.

▶ Assess for complications of immobility (pneumonia, deep vein thrombosis [DVT], pressure ulcers, and so on).

Casts

Related to traction is the use of casts for fracture healing. Casts are rigid devices used to keep a specific body part immobile. They allow the bone fragments to stay in place and heal. Casts can be made of nonplaster or plaster. Plaster casts require from one to three days to dry, while fiberglass casts dry in one hour or less. The following accentuates what you need to know about the management of the client with a cast:

▶ Allow the cast to dry from the inside out.

▶ Handle a wet cast with the palms of your hands.

▶ Place the extremity on a plastic-lined pillow.

▶ Note any drainage on the cast by circling it and noting the time of observation.

▶ Evaluate any areas that feel hot (this might mean the client has an underlying infection).

▶ Petal the rough edges of the cast.

▶ Instruct the client not to scratch or place small objects beneath the cast.

▶ Relieve itching by blowing cool air from a blow dryer into the cast.

▶ Assess circulation, pulses, and movement of extremity.

Common Complications Associated with Fractures

Both casts and traction are utilized to promote the healing of the bone after a fracture. The nurse needs to be alert to problems that can occur that will impede healing. The discussion that follows addresses some common complications that can occur after a fracture. Major complications such as shock, pulmonary and fat embolism, and deep vein thrombosis were discussed in Chapter 3, "Care of the Client with Cardiovascular Disorders," and Chapter 5, "Care of the Client with Respiratory Disorders."

Compartment Syndrome

A complication that can occur after a fracture is compartment syndrome. This is a serious condition resulting from pressure within different compartments (these separate the blood vessels, muscles, and nerves) that cause decreased circulation to the area—usually the leg and forearm. This disorder can lead to irreversible motor weakness, infection, and amputation of the limb.

A major element in compartment syndrome is prevention. The exam reviewer must be able to recognize the clinical manifestations of compartment syndrome, which include the following:

▶ Cyanosis

▶ Numbness

▶ Pain (especially pain that is unrelieved by medication)

▶ Pallor

▶ Paresis/paralysis

▶ Swelling

▶ Tingling

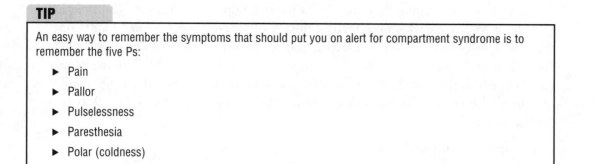

TIP

An easy way to remember the symptoms that should put you on alert for compartment syndrome is to remember the five Ps:

- ▶ Pain
- ▶ Pallor
- ▶ Pulselessness
- ▶ Paresthesia
- ▶ Polar (coldness)

Treatment of compartment syndrome requires a means to relieve the pressure. Two types of treatments can be used to accomplish this goal:

- ▶ **Bivalve treatment:** Bivalve treatment means cutting the cast on each side. It is done if the cast is too tight, causing pressure and restricting blood flow.

- ▶ **Fasciotomy:** If symptoms persist, the client might require the second type of treatment—a surgical procedure called a fasciotomy. This is done by the surgeon making an incision through the skin and subcutaneous tissue into the fascia to relieve the pressure and improve circulation.

Osteomyelitis

Another complication that can occur with fractures is osteomyelitis. Osteomyelitis occurs when an infection has invaded the bone area. Clients at risk for osteomyelitis include the malnourished, the elderly, the overweight, and people who have a chronic illness (such as cardiovascular disease). The symptoms that can occur with osteomyelitis are as follows:

- ▶ Fever

- ▶ Malaise

- ▶ Swelling in the infected area

- ▶ Tenderness in the infected area

- ▶ Purulent drainage in the infected area

- ▶ Pain in the infected area

- ▶ Tachycardia

Preventive measures are important. Prophylactic antibiotics and sterile technique during and after surgery are essential in prevention of this disorder.

CAUTION

It is recommended that clients who have undergone a joint replacement usually receive antibiotics prior to dental or other invasive procedures (such as a gastroscopy).

The treatment of osteomyelitis can involve several modalities. One course of treatment includes medications, which can include the use of long-term (4– 6 weeks) antibiotic therapy. The specific antibiotics used depend on the wound and blood culture results. Ciprofloxacin (Cipro) twice daily is a common oral therapy regimen. Pain medication is also prescribed. Surgical debridement of the wound might also speed the elimination of infection in the bone. The following contains nursing interventions you need to know for the exam:

- Immobilize the body part
- Administer pain medication
- Perform neurovascular assessment
- Perform sterile dressing changes
- Teach the client how to use IV access devices for at-home antibiotic administration
- Provide a diet high in protein and vitamin C

Delayed Union or Healing

Most fractures take months to heal. An adequate blood supply to the area and the client's physical condition and proper nutrition affect bone healing. Sometimes healing doesn't occur as it should and nonunion or delayed union of the bone is evidenced. Clinical manifestations include client complaints of continued discomforts and the fracture site having abnormal movement.

The management of this condition includes surgical internal fixation, use of bone grafts, and electrical bone stimulation. An electrical bone stimulator uses an electrical current to increase mineral deposits, promoting healing of the bone. Nursing care required to review for clients with bone grafts include:

- Assessing for infection at bone graft donor and recipient sites
- Nonweight-bearing and immobilization of graft site
- Teaching the client about wound care and signs of infection

Nursing care required to review for clients with bone stimulators include

- Immobilization of site
- Weight-bearing restrictions
- Correct use of stimulator device

> **NOTE**
>
> Bone stimulators can not be used in upper extremities if the client has a pacemaker.

Osteoporosis

Osteoporosis is a disease wherein bone demineralizes, resulting in bone density reduction. The wrist, hip, and vertebral column are most often affected. The density of bones decreases rapidly in postmenopausal women due to decreases in estrogen. It has been determined that almost one-half of women over age 65 have osteoporosis. The following highlights the risk factors associated with osteoporosis:

▸ Age (there's a greater incidence over age 60)

▸ Low body weight

▸ Race (it occurs more in Asian and Caucasian women)

▸ Sedentary lifestyle

▸ Low dietary calcium intake

▸ Smoking

▸ Alcohol consumption

▸ Decreased estrogen levels

▸ Excess caffeine intake

▸ Early menopause

▸ Family history of osteoporosis

▸ Prolonged steroid use

▸ Comorbidities of endocrine disorders (thyroid problems, diabetes, Cushing's Syndrome)

Clinical manifestations of osteoporosis include

▸ Back pain

▸ Constipation

▸ Decrease in height

▸ Dowager's hump (humped back)

▸ Fractures

Treatment of osteoporosis involves direct involvement of the client. To increase the muscles, exercises including walking, swimming, and water aerobics are recommended. The client should be taught to eat foods high in calcium, vitamin D, fiber, and protein. Foods high in calcium include molasses, apricots, breads, cereal, milk, dairy products (especially yogurt), spinach, sardines, beans, carrots, asparagus, and collard greens. In addition, the client should be taught to avoid alcohol and caffeine.

> **NOTE**
>
> Excess caffeine can cause the excretion of calcium in the urine.

Another important aspect of teaching clients with osteoporosis involves safety measures—for example, avoiding the use of throw rugs and teaching the client to avoid falls.

Medications have been developed that are efficient in combating and preventing the disease, and some general medications are given for pain relief:

- Biphosphonates (examples are Fosamax, Boniva, and Didronel)
- Salmon calcitonin (Calcimar)
- Calcium supplements
- Estrogen for postmenopausal women
- Muscle relaxers
- NSAIDs
- Selective estrogen receptor modules or SERMs (for example, Evista)

Osteoarthritis

Osteoarthritis is a nonsystemic, noninflammatory progressive disorder of movable joints. The primary pathophysiological changes are associated with increasing age and/or trauma. Osteoarthritis is the most common arthritic condition. Predisposing factors for the development of osteoarthritis include the following:

- Aging
- Obesity
- Genetics
- Joint injuries
- History of occupations requiring excessive joint movement and stress (for example, professional athletes and dancers)

Clinical manifestations of osteoarthritis usually occur between the fifth and sixth decades of life. These symptoms include

- Pain and stiffness, especially in the morning
- Immobility of the joint or limb due to the pain and joint changes
- Enlarged and/or nodular joints
- Crepitation
- Deformities

▸ Heberden's nodes (effects distal interphalangeal joints) (see Figure 14.9)

▸ Bouchard's nodes (effects proximal interphalangeal joints) (see Figure 14.9)

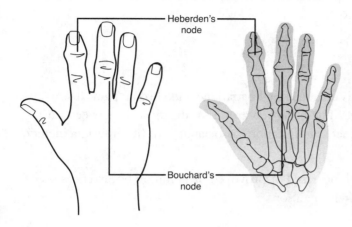

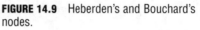

FIGURE 14.9 Heberden's and Bouchard's nodes.

Diagnosis of Osteoarthritis

Diagnosis is made by physical assessment, client history, and laboratory tests. These tests might reveal a slight elevation in the erythrocyte sedimentation rate (ESR) if inflammation is present in the synovial fluid. X-rays might be done to identify degeneration of the joint.

Treatment of the Client with Osteoarthritis

Interventions used to treat osteoarthritis revolve around two main goals: providing client comfort and maintaining function and mobility. Measures used to accomplish these goals include the use of pharmacological agents. These drugs are usually given orally, applied topically, or injected by the healthcare provider (HCP) directly into the joint area. Some drugs used in treatment are acetaminophen (Tylenol), meloxicam (Mobic), cortisone (taken orally or injected into the joint by the HCP), muscle relaxers (Skelaxin), and arthritic rubs (such as Aspercreme and capsaicin cream [Zostrix]). Another treatment is viscosupplementation with hyaluronic acid (HA) injections (examples are Nuflexxa and Hyalgan). These are administered as injections directly into the affected area. These injections can provide relief for up to a year. Other measures of treatment other than drugs include the following:

▸ Application of heat or application of heat packs and paraffin dips by physical therapy

▸ Losing or controlling weight, which reduces stress on the joints involved

▸ Use of a transcutaneous electrical nerve stimulator (TENS) unit for pain control

▸ Guided imagery, touch, and massage for pain control

Surgical intervention might be required if the patient loses function of the joint or pain relief cannot be given. Total joint replacement is the surgical procedure performed. (See the "Musculoskeletal Surgical Procedures" section later in this chapter for information about nursing care for these clients.)

Fibromyalgia

Fibromyalgia is a syndrome that is characterized by fatigue and chronic pain. It usually affects women of childbearing age. The usual age group for diagnosis is between the ages of 30 and 50 years old. Clinical manifestations associated with fibromyalgia include the following:

▶ Pain that is intermittent and increased or provoked by common occurrences such as stress or changes in weather conditions

▶ Fatigue

▶ Insomnia

The characteristics of this disease are vague. This sometimes causes frustration in clients who are frequently misdiagnosed. There is no known cause of the disorder, but it has been shown to be related to the flu, lupus, arthritis, and medications.

The treatment for fibromyalgia focuses on the client's symptoms and includes the following:

▶ Medications:

  ▶ Antidepressive agents (for example, amtriptyline [Elavil])

  ▶ NSAIDs (ibuprofen)

  ▶ Skeletal muscle relaxants (cyclobenzaprine [Flexeril])

  ▶ Fibromyalgia treatment with pregabalin (Lyrica)

  ▶ Short-term sleep aids (for example, Zolpidem [Ambien])

▶ Physical therapy

▶ Exercise; swimming and water exercises are frequently recommended

Ankylosing Spondylitis

Ankylosing spondylitis is also known as Marie-Strümpell disease and rheumatoid spondylitis. This disorder affects white males under the age of 40 more frequently than any other group. The most common area affected is the spine. The cause of this disorder has been shown to be associated with the HLA B27 antigen. Clinical manifestations associated with this disorder include the following:

- Arthralgia or achy joints
- Malaise
- Fatigue
- Weight loss

The treatment of ankylosing spondylitis is the same as treatment for osteoarthritis. The drugs used to treat this disorder also include the disease-modifying antirheumatic drugs (DMARDs) group and infliximab (Remicade).

Gout

Gout is the formation of uric acid deposits in the joints, particularly the joint of the great toe. It is an arthritic condition resulting from the body's inability to metabolize purine foods. This characteristic is thought to have a genetic component. In this condition, too much uric acid is secreted, or the kidneys are unable to get rid of the uric acid as they should, or a combination of both. The buildup of uric acid, the end product of purines, causes inflammation in the joints involved. Certain precipitators have been found to cause an attack: fad starvation diets, stress, and illness.

Symptoms of gout include painful joints and tophi (growths of urate crystals) that occur most often on the outer ear of the client with gout. When urate builds up in the joints, inflammation results causing symptoms which include the following:

- Painful joints.

NOTE

Clients with gout experience an attack with podagra (pain and inflammation in the great toe). This is the most common initial clinical manifestation of gout.

- Tophi usually on the outer ear, hands, and great toe. These usually develop after several attacks of gouty arthritis.
- Kidney stones and renal abnormalities.

Early attacks usually resolve themselves within a 10-day period without treatment, but most clients cannot tolerate the pain. When a treatment regimen is instituted, it follows two distinct paths: diet with weight maintenance or reduction, or drugs. Diet is the path directed toward decreasing purine in the diet. The following foods are low in purine and should be increased in the diet:

- Cheese
- Eggs
- Fats

- ▶ Gelatin
- ▶ Milk
- ▶ Most vegetables
- ▶ Nuts
- ▶ Sugar
- ▶ Increased fluids
- ▶ Citrus juices
- ▶ Cherries

The client should limit alcohol and avoid high-purine foods such as these:

- ▶ Dried beans
- ▶ Fish, especially sardines
- ▶ Liver
- ▶ Lobster
- ▶ Oatmeal
- ▶ Oysters
- ▶ Peas
- ▶ Asparagus
- ▶ Poultry
- ▶ Spinach

The second path of treatment for clients with gout is drugs, which are the primary element in the care of this client. Colchicine (Colsalide) and an NSAID, such as ibuprofen (Motrin), is prescribed for an acute episode of gout. Allopurinol (Zyloprim) is used for chronic gout both to reduce the production of uric acid and to promote the excretion of it. Probenecid (Benemid) might be given to help with the excretion of uric acid. Losartan (Cozaar) is an effective treatment for elderly clients who have high blood pressure and gout.

Rheumatoid Arthritis

Rheumatoid arthritis (RA) is a connective tissue disorder believed to be due to a C-reactive protein immune response. The pathophysiological effects target the synovial joints. Rheumatoid arthritis is characterized by inflammation of the tissue, eventually causing increased thickness of the tissue inside the joint and destruction of the joint. It can also cause joint deformities. The usual onset of the disease is between 30 and 50 years of age, and it affects women three times more often than men. There is an increase in a human leukocyte antigen (HLA)-DR4 in white clients who have rheumatoid arthritis. RA is a systemic disease, and a client with RA exhibits many symptoms. The following highlights the most common symptoms you need to be familiar with for the exam:

- Subcutaneous nodules (usually on the ulnar surface of the arm)

- Warmth, tenderness, and swelling in the affected joints

- Weakness

- Stiffness (especially in early morning hours)

- Loss of appetite

- Weight loss

- Pleurisy

- Pneumonia

- Pericarditis

- Iritis of the eyes

- Sjögren's syndrome (dryness of the eyes, mouth, and vagina)

Diagnosis is made by the history of the clinical course of the disease, as well as elevations in the following laboratory tests:

- C-reactive protein

- Rheumatoid factor

- Sedimentation rate

- Antinuclear antibody (ANA)

X-rays, such as a CT scan, or an MRI might be done to assess for joint deterioration. An arthrocentesis can assist with the diagnosis by the identification of inflammatory cells and immune complexes in the aspirated synovial fluid. Other diagnostic exams are done to identify body system involvement. Examples are pulmonary function tests (PFT) for lung involvement and echocardiograms for cardiac assessment.

The treatment plan for RA involves the use of a combination of drugs, exercise, and pain relief measures such as heat and ice. If the interventions are not effective in providing mobility and pain relief, surgery might be required to replace the joint. The following highlights medications, comfort measures, and joint mobility interventions you need to know when testing on the topic of rheumatoid arthritis:

- Medications (refer to Table 13.2 for further discussion), including

  - Antiarthritics (for example, etanercept [Enbrel], infliximab [Remicade], and adalimumab [Humira])

  - Antibiotic therapy (for example, minocycline [Minocin])

> ▸ Cytotoxic agents (for example, methotrexate [Rheumatrex])

> ▸ DMARDs

> ▸ Hydroxychloroquine (Plaquenil)

> ▸ Gold salts—usually reserved for clients who can't tolerate anything else

> ▸ NSAIDs

> ▸ Salicylates

▸ Sulfasalazine (Azulfidine)

NOTE

NSAIDs and salicylates are usually given with misoprostol (Cytotec) to prevent gastrointestinal complications or discomfort.

> ▸ Steroids

> ▸ Immune modulators, such as leflunomide (Arava)

▸ Application of heat and ice to the affected joints. This can be done at home or by a physical therapy department.

▸ A regular exercise program to maintain joint mobility. Isometric exercises of the gluteal, quadriceps, and abdominal muscles while sitting helps to maintain muscle strength and trunk stability.

▸ Lightweight splints can be used to rest the inflamed joints.

▸ Plasmapheresis might be prescribed in severe cases.

▸ Proper nutrition. Fish oil tablets can be utilized to decrease inflammation.

CAUTION

Fish oil is contraindicated in clients taking anticoagulants.

Lupus Erythematosus

There are two types of lupus erythematosus:

▸ **Systemic lupus erythematosus (SLE):** Affects the skin and various body systems, including the kidneys.

▸ **Discoid lupus erythematosus (DLE):** A much milder form, it affects the skin only.

SLE is the most frequently diagnosed form of lupus. The disease, which is characterized by remissions and exacerbations, is more common in women between the ages of 15 and

40. It is also more prevalent in African-American women than men. There is a genetic link to the disease including genes from HLA complex HLA-DR3.

SLE is a chronic progressive inflammatory disorder of connective tissue that frequently results in organ failure. Although the exact cause is unknown, SLE is believed to be an autoimmune disorder because the client produces abnormal antibodies. The production of these antibodies creates immune complexes in the serum and organ tissue that cause inflammation and damage. Chronic inflammation eventually leads to a vasculitis that robs the organ of its blood supply.

Because SLE affects so many organ systems, the symptoms vary during exacerbations or flare-ups. These systems and symptoms include

▶ **Integumentary:** Presence of dry, scaly "butterfly" rash on the face and upper body that are especially prominent when the client is exposed to sunlight or ultraviolet light; alopecia; and "coinlike" lesions in the client with DLE.

▶ **Musculoskeletal:** Polyarthritis similar to rheumatoid arthritis but with less severe deformities affects mostly small joints, myositis and muscle atrophy caused by invasion of the muscle by immune complexes, and Raynaud's phenomenon.

▶ **Cardiovascular:** Pericarditis and myocardial ischemia.

▶ **Neurological:** Paresis, migraines, cranial nerve involvement, and peripheral neuropathies.

▶ **Gastrointestinal:** Abdominal pain due to mesenteric arteritis, pancreatitis due to inflammation of the pancreatic artery, chronic ulcers, and an enlarged spleen.

▶ **Respiratory:** Pleural effusion and pneumonia.

▶ **Renal:** Renal impairment that can eventually result in renal failure and death. Stages of renal impairment include

  ▶ Minimal lupus nephritis characterized by slightly irregular glomeruli and the presence of immunoglobulins and serum complexes visible to electron microscope

  ▶ Focal or mild lupus nephritis characterized by glomerular changes and immune complexes associated with early renal impairment

  ▶ Diffuse or severe lupus nephritis characterized by involvement of over half the glomeruli and renal failure

Nursing care of the client with SLE focuses on providing physical and emotional support. The client should be told to use mild soap and to avoid harsh perfumed substances, which can dry the skin. Cosmetics should contain sun protection and moisturizers. The client should be taught to avoid prolonged exposure to sunlight and ultraviolet light and to use a sunscreen with an SPF of at least 30. The client should avoid hair treatments such as permanents and coloring.

The nurse should carefully assess the client for symptoms associated with exacerbations of SLE. Fever, fatigue, anorexia, and weight loss are reported to the doctor because they might indicate that the client is no longer in remission. Fever is a classic finding in those clients with exacerbations. Additional assessments include checks of muscle mass and strength, changes in neurological function, changes in vital signs, and changes in urinary output such as hematuria and fluid retention.

Pharmacological management of the client with lupus erythematosus depends on the type and the presenting symptoms. Topical cortisone preparations are used to treat the rash associated with both DLE and SLE. Immunosuppressive medications including cyclophosphamide (Cytoxan) and prednisone are used to achieve and maintain remission. NSAIDs and hydroxychloroquine (Plaquenil) might also be administered. Plasmapheresis, renal transplant, and allogenic stem cell transplant are used to treat those clients who respond poorly to drug therapy.

A key element in providing care for those with lupus lies in providing emotional support. The client lives not only with a chronic, unpredictable illness, but also with changes in appearance brought on by the disorder or its treatment. Clients with DLE and SLE are often embarrassed by their appearance because the disfiguring rash cannot be completely hidden by makeup. Steroid therapy, which is essential to treatment, produces changes that result in Cushing's syndrome. Clients with SLE are often socially isolated due to the need to avoid social gatherings with crowds and outdoor activity. Added emotional support can be provided by referring the client to the Lupus Foundation.

Musculoskeletal Surgical Procedures

A client who has a dysfunction of the musculoskeletal system might have to undergo a surgical procedure. Surgery might be performed to relieve pain, provide stability, and improve function of the joint. The discussion that follows focuses on the care necessary for clients who have had a break in a hip, have had a joint disability or damage, or require an amputation because of disease or trauma.

Fractured Hip and Hip Replacement

Fracture of the hip is most common in white, elderly females. A fractured hip can contribute to death in the elderly because it predisposes them to infection and respiratory complications. The most definitive symptoms associated with a fractured hip are disalignment and shortening of the affected leg. The client also cannot move the leg without pain and complains of pain in the hip and groin on the affected side. Diagnosis is made by a hip x-ray that confirms the break.

CAUTION

Because infection can result in failure of a prosthesis, total joint replacement surgery is contraindicated on a patient with infection anywhere in his body.

The treatment option for a hip fracture in the trochanteric area is to repair it by the use of internal fixation devices (open reduction internal fixation [ORIF]). Fractures of the femoral neck with disrupted blood supply require prosthetic joint placement. The preoperative care of a hip fracture includes the use of Buck's traction (see Figure 14.3) to immobilize the hip, resulting in a reduction of muscle spasms and pain. Medications are also administered to relieve pain, relax the muscle, and prevent complications.

After the surgery, the nurse needs to become familiar with assessments and specific nursing measures. The following highlights the care required after hip surgery:

▶ Assess for bleeding and shock.

▶ Monitor for deep vein thrombosis and embolisms.

▶ Encourage the use of incentive spirometry.

▶ Assess the client and the surgical site for signs of infection (fever, redness, drainage, edema, and so on).

▶ Ambulate the client early, with no weight-bearing on the affected leg.

▶ Have the client sit in a recliner and not in straight chairs. The affected leg should be bent no more than 45°.

▶ When in bed, the client should be turned to the unaffected side or both sides depending on hospital policy.

▶ Teach the client to have no more than 90° hip flexion for 4– 6 weeks postoperatively with total hip replacements.

▶ Total hip replacement clients must keep their legs in abduction. An abduction pillow can be utilized for disoriented, noncompliant clients or clients who have trouble remembering to remain in the abduction position. These clients also need elevated toilet seats, can't cross their legs, and can't twist or reach behind.

▶ Administer anticoagulants as ordered to prevent complications.

▶ Blood transfusions may be necessary. Assess for hemoglobin and hematocrit results. Autologous (clients receiving their own blood) transfusions are frequently performed.

▶ Monitor output from any existing drains.

▶ Collaborate with physical therapy on mobility treatments and exercises.

Total Knee Replacement

Total knee replacements are performed for clients who have severe joint pain that makes them immobile. It is also considered when people have arthritic destruction of the articular cartilages or deformity of the knee and in clients who are not able to walk or those who have limited motion due to knee instability.

The goal of the surgery is twofold:

► Restore full flexion and extension

► Provide adequate strength and stability of the knee for most functional activities

Postoperative efforts for the client after total knee replacement are directed toward preventing complications and restoring mobility. You should consider the nursing care requirements for this client when studying for the exam. Along with the usual medication administration (pain medication, antithrombotics, and antibiotics), these clients need specific limb care and physical therapy. The following includes the specific care of the postoperative knee replacement, use of the continuous passive motion (CPM) machine, and physical therapy regimen that are important to know for the exam:

► Keep the knee in extension to prevent contractures. Usually the knee will be placed in a splint or an immobilizer after the pressure dressing is removed.

► Maintain the patella in alignment with the toes.

► Use two persons for transfer until the client regains muscle strength.

► Support the affected leg during a transfer.

► Follow a set protocol for movement, ambulation, and weight-bearing. Dislocation is not of concern as with hip replacements.

Clients are usually placed on a CPM machine in the recovery room. This device is applied early to increase circulation, to prevent scar tissue from forming, and to increase the range of motion of the knee joint. Flexion of the knee is an important aspect of care because if it is not achieved, another surgery might be required.

NOTE

CPM control machines are usually placed at the foot of the bed, beyond the reach of the client.

Physical therapy for total knee replacement is invaluable in providing supervision of the exercises for strength and range of motion.

Clients with total knee replacements are usually discharged within three to four days with a plan for continued exercises. An initial appointment is needed with the physical therapy department within 48–72 hours of discharge. The client usually starts with use of a walker (crutches if a younger client) and then advances to a cane. After one month, if the client can walk without a severe limp, no assistive devices are necessary.

Amputations

An amputation occurs when a part of the body, usually an extremity, is removed. Causes for amputations include trauma, infection and possible sepsis, peripheral vascular disease, and accidents.

> **NOTE**
>
> Peripheral vascular disease is the most common cause for amputation.

Amputations are done to relieve pain or improve the client's quality of life. They can also be required to save the patient's life.

Interventions Post–Amputation Surgery

The exam reviewer needs to be aware of the nursing care required for amputation clients. Specific problems that might occur with the client after an amputation include pain, contractures, hemorrhage, and infection.

You need to be aware of the therapeutic measures to use with phantom limb pain that commonly occurs in amputation. One way to deal with phantom limb pain is to treat it as any other pain would be treated. The nurse should not respond to pain complaints by reminding the client that the limb is missing. A Transcutaneous Electrical Nerve Stimulator (TENS) unit might be used to relieve the pain. Other pharmacological measures for pain relief are prescribed depending on the type of pain the client describes and include

- ▶ Intravenous Calcimar
- ▶ Beta blockers such as propranolol (Inderal)
- ▶ Anticonvulsants (Neurontin)
- ▶ Antispasmodics (Bentyl)

Other nursing measures you need to focus attention on are assessments. Hemorrhage and infection are possible complications, so you must monitor for these. The client will arrive after surgery with a compression bandage. It is also important that mobility be restored; this can be fostered by collaborating with physical therapy and encouraging the use of a prosthetic limb. Additional nursing measures that focus on mobility and prevention of complications are as follows:

- ▶ Exercises (a trapeze bar is used to move in bed).
- ▶ A firm mattress is needed to make movement easier.

Prevent contractures by using the following nursing interventions:

- ▶ Placing the client in a prone position for 30 minutes three to four times a day
- ▶ Using a sandbag to the knee
- ▶ Ensuring that the residual limb stays flat on the bed
- ▶ Having the client avoid sitting in a chair for over 1 hour

NOTE

The residual limb might be elevated for the first 24 hours after surgery to reduce swelling and pain.

Wrapping the stump can be effective in shrinking the limb, reducing the swelling, help with shaping for a prosthesis, and keeping the dressing in place. The stump is wrapped using the figure-eight technique to prevent impeding blood flow.

The exam reviewer must also be aware of the psychological aspects of the loss of a limb. A disturbance in body image occurs with an amputation. The nurse should expect the client to go through the grief process.

Assistive Devices for Ambulation

Clients with musculoskeletal disorders often need devices to assist them with mobility. The following sections discuss how to measure and fit for three of these devices: crutches, canes, and walkers. This information will assist you in answering questions on an exam that refer to these topics.

Crutches

Crutches are prescribed for clients who need partial weight-bearing or nonweight-bearing assistance and are the most common assistive devices. A person who is to use crutches needs to have balance, upper body strength, and an adequate cardiovascular system. The procedure used to fit the client for crutches follows: With the crutch tip extended 6 inches diagonally in front of the foot, two to three finger widths should be allowed between the axilla and the top of the crutch to prevent nerve damage.

Five types of crutch-walking gaits exist, with the use depending on the amount of weight-bearing allowed:

▶ **Two-point gait:** This permits limited weight-bearing bilaterally. The right leg and left crutch move simultaneously; the left leg and right crutch move simultaneously.

▶ **Three-point gait:** Nonweight-bearing or partial weight-bearing is allowed on the affected leg. Both crutches and the affected leg move in unison. Body weight is supported on the unaffected leg. This is the most common gait for musculoskeletal injuries.

▶ **Four-point gait:** This permits weight-bearing on both legs. The crutches and feet move alternately. The left crutch and right foot move, and then the right crutch and left foot.

▶ **Swing through:** No weight-bearing is permitted on the affected legs. Both crutches move forward and both legs swing through between the crutches. The weight is borne by the crutches.

▶ **Stairs:** This is for climbing stairs. The client leads with the unaffected leg, and the crutches and affected leg move together. For descending stairs, the client leads with the crutches and affected leg.

TIP

Go up the stairs with the good leg first, and go down the stairs with the bad leg first.

Canes

Canes are the least stable of ambulation devices and should not be used for non weight-bearing or partial weight-bearing activities. The cane does, however, give a client greater balance and support and is recommended when this is needed. The top of the cane should be at the greater trochanter area. The cane goes on the unaffected side with no more than 30° elbow flexion. There are three types of canes: the four-foot adjustable (quad or hemi), the adjustable, and the offset adjustable. Here's how you adjust the cane for proper fit:

▸ To determine the proper length of the cane, the client should be standing or lying supine.

▸ The client's arm should lie straight along the side with the cane handgrip level with the greater trochanter.

▸ The cane should be placed parallel to the femur and tibia with the tip of the cane on the floor or at the bottom of the shoe heel.

Walkers

Indications for walker use include the need for balance, stability, and decreased weight-bearing, and are most commonly used for older clients. Walkers provide anterior and lateral stability with a wide base of support. Proper walker adjustment allows for 20°–30° elbow flexion. The three types of walkers are the standard, the folding, and the rolling walker. The following highlights the instructions that the exam taker should be aware of for the use of a walker.

The instructions for using walkers for partial weight-bearing or nonweight-bearing are as follows:

1. Advance the walker an arm's length.

2. Place all four legs on the floor.

3. Advance the affected leg.

4. Push the body weight through the arms.

5. Advance the unaffected leg.

The instructions for using walkers for balance and stability are as follows:

1. Advance the walker an arm's length.

2. Set all four legs on the floor.

3. Take two complete steps into the walker.

CAUTION

For safety reasons, a gait belt is necessary when initiating cane and walker use.

Case Study

Tom is a 35-year-old who is admitted with a fractured femur following a motor vehicle accident. He is alert and oriented to time, place, and person. Vital signs are temperature, 99° Fahrenheit; pulse, 86 and regular; respirations, 22; blood pressure, 136/72. Oxygen saturation is 100% with lungs clear in all lobes on auscultation.

1. What are further essential assessments you will make as the nurse assigned to this client?

2. The physician visits and orders that Tom be placed in skeletal traction. What relevant assessments would be documented for Tom associated with his skeletal pin traction?

3. Two days after Tom's admission, he suddenly becomes confused and disoriented with obvious shortness of breath. Tom has a confirmed diagnosis of a fat embolus. What is the priority data you will collect to report to the physician?

4. List four priority nursing diagnosis.

5. Tom's condition deteriorates and laboratory results are available for you to assess. Results reveal the following:

CBC	Chemistry Profile	Arterial Blood Gases (ABGs)
Hgb 13.6 g/dL	Potassium 3.9 mEq/L	pH 7.23
Hct 42%	Chloride 102 mEq/L	pCO_2 63
WBC 8,000/mm	Glucose 100 mg/dL	HCO_3 23 mEq/L
Platelets 250,000		pO_2 50
		O_2 saturation 84

Based on the preceding laboratory results, you anticipate that the physician's priority order will be:

Answers to Case Study

1. The client after a motor vehicle accident might have other injuries, so the nurse would assess all body systems. Before assessment begins, place the client supine. Inspect the site of the fracture for bone deformity. Inspect the client's ability to move. If a grating sound is heard on movement, this is called crepitation. The rapid swelling that occurs with fractures may cause compromise to the neurovascular system, so the nurse would assess:

   ► Skin color and temperature

   ► Sensation

   ► Pain: character and frequency

   ► Distal pulses

   ► For immediate capillary refill

(continues)

(continued)

2. The nurse would assess the pin sites for inflammation or infection (redness, odor, edema, drainage). If the client has clear drainage from the pin sites, this is no reason for concern. The nurse should ensure that the ropes of the traction are within the pulleys, weights are hanging freely, and that the client has the proper amount of weight (usually 15–30 pounds). In addition, neurovascular assessments (as in answer 1) should be completed.

3. Fat embolisms usually occur with fractures of long bones, such as a fractured femur. The clinical manifestations that the nurse should assess for include the following:

   ▶ Mental status changes

   ▶ Respiratory distress

   ▶ Increased heart rate and respiratory rate

   ▶ Fever

   ▶ Petechiae-type rash that can be exhibited on the neck, upper arm, chest, and abdomen

TIP

The petechiae type rash is a hallmark symptom of fat embolism.

4. Priority nursing diagnosis include

   ▶ Impaired gas exchange related to imbalance in ventilation-perfusion

   ▶ Alteration in tissue perfusion related to blockage causing inability of oxygen to be transported to tissues

   ▶ Risk for acute pain related to lack of oxygenation

   ▶ Anxiety related to hypoxia and life threatening condition

5. The ABG results are the priority in this scenario. The client is severely hypoxemic as evidenced by the low pO_2 and low O_2 saturation. He is also suffering from uncompensated respiratory acidosis as evidenced by a low pH and high pCO_2. Because Tom is unable to maintain oxygenation and ventilation on his own, a mechanical ventilator is necessary and would be anticipated by the nurse.

Key Concepts

This chapter includes much needed information to help the nurse apply knowledge of musculoskeletal and connective tissue disorders to the NCLEX exam. The nurse preparing for the licensure exam should review normal laboratory values, common treatment modalities, and pharmacological agents used in the care of the client with musculoskeletal and connective tissue disorders.

Key Terms

- ▶ Abduction
- ▶ Arthralgia
- ▶ Bone density
- ▶ Clostridium
- ▶ Contractures
- ▶ Crepitation
- ▶ Demineralize
- ▶ Dowager's hump
- ▶ Fasciotomy
- ▶ Gait belt
- ▶ Isometric exercises
- ▶ Paresis
- ▶ Pathological fractures
- ▶ Purine
- ▶ Sedentary
- ▶ TENS unit

Diagnostics

The diagnostic exams that are used for the musculoskeletal system are associated with the body part involved. Fractures are easily diagnosed by an x-ray of the area. As with all diseases or disorders, the usual exams are the CBC, urinalysis, and chest x-ray. Direct visualization is obtained by the use of scopic devices—for example, arthroscopes are typically used with knees. For clients with bone weaknesses, density testing is done to measure the degree of the problem. While reviewing the diagnostic exams that follow, you should be alert for the abnormalities that correlate with specific musculoskeletal diseases, such as the elevation levels of rheumatoid factor in rheumatoid arthritis:

- Arthrography
- Arthroscopy
- Bone biopsy
- Bone density testing
- Bone scan
- CT scan
- Electromyography
- Gallium or thallium scan
- Laboratory tests, including rheumatoid factor, antinuclear antibody titer, and erythrocyte sedimentation rate (ESR)
- MRI
- Muscle biopsy
- Ultrasound

Pharmacologic Agents Used in Musculoskeletal and Connective Tissue Disorders

Medications are invaluable as a method of treatment for musculoskeletal disorders. These medications are important in preventing some of the common complications that can occur with immobility. Commonly used medications include antithrombotics and antimicrobials. The uric acid inhibitors function well in curing the disease of gouty arthritis, and the disease-modifying antirheumatic drug (DMARD) classification has helped with osteoporosis. You need to focus on the drug classifications in this table, which are included in the first column. You also need to think about the commonalities of side effects in drug classifications. Table 14.2 includes common medication side and adverse effects and pertinent nursing care associated with the drugs. When studying the drugs, make a note of which drug would be used in which musculoskeletal disorder. These medications are not inclusive of all the agents used to treat musculoskeletal disorders; therefore, you will want to keep a current pharmacology text for reference.

TABLE 14.2   Musculoskeletal Pharmacological Agents

Name/Classification	Action	Side Effects	Nursing Care
Alendronate (Fosamax) Etidronate (Didronel) Risedronate (Actonel) Ibandronate (Boniva) Classification: Biphosphanates Raloxifene (Evista) Classification: Selective estrogen receptor modulators (SERM)	Inhibits bone resorption Evista mimics estrogen producing estrogenlike effects of decreased bone resorption and decreased bone turnover	Esophageal ulcers, dyspepsia, dysphagia, acid regurgitation, headache, eye pain, and inflammation. Didronel also can cause bone pain, diarrhea, nausea and a metallic taste if given IV. Actonel can cause weakness and chest pain. Evista side effects include hot flashes and leg pain.	Client must take biphosphonates upon arising with 6–8 ounces of water and wait 30 minutes (60 minutes with Boniva) before having anything else by mouth. Client should be taught to remain upright for 30 minutes after the dose. Monitor clients on Didronel for hypocalcemia and hypercalcemia. Clients who are taking Evista need adequate vitamin D and calcium, and should also be taught to discontinue the Evista three days prior to long periods of immobility. Clients who are taking Evista also have an increased risk of thromboembolism.
Ketorolac (Toradol) Aspirin Ibuprofen (Advil, Motrin) Meloxicam (Mobic) Naproxen (Naprosyn) Indomethacin (Indocin)	Anti-inflammatory	GI upset and delayed clotting are side effects of all. Aspirin can cause tinnitus. Ibuprofen can elevate the blood pressure and cause renal damage. Toradol also causes drowsiness, euphoria, and headache. Mobic can produce anemia, leucopenia, and thrombocytopenia. Indocin can produce bone marrow depression.	Administer these drugs with food to help with the GI upset and watch the client for bleeding. Clients who are prescribed Toradol should have it IV or IM before starting the PO medication and the drug should not be given for longer than five days. Monitor clients taking ibuprofen for renal and hepatic function. Clients taking Mobic who have asthma should be watched carefully for a reaction due to the increased risk in these clients. Mobic also requires that the client remain upright for 30 minutes after the dose. Monitor CBC results on clients taking Mobic and Indocin.

TABLE 14.2 *Continued*

Name/Classification	Action	Side Effects	Nursing Care
Allopurinol (Zyloprim) Colchicine given for acute attacks of gout Classification: Anti-gout	Zyloprim decreases uric acid. Colchicine decreases the response to urate crystals.	GI distress, aplastic anemia, agranulocytosis. Zyloprim can also cause a headache.	Monitor the client for GI upset. Administer with food. The client taking colchicine should force fluids of 6–8 glasses/day. Monitor clients taking Zyloprim for renal and hepatic function and assess the CBC.
Calcitonin (salmon) Given IM, SQ, and intranasal Classification: Hormone	Decreases serum calcium, reducing the rate of bone turnover post-menopause	Headache, facial flushing. Alert: Swelling and tingling in the hands can indicate an anaphylactic reaction.	Perform a test for sensitivity prior to administering full dose. Inspect dose site after administration for redness, swelling, or pain. Assess for signs of hypercalcemia. The client should expect flushing and warmth after the injection.
Etanercept (Enbrel) Classification: DMARD	Anti-inflammation	GI distress, decreased taste, skin rash or itching, bone marrow depression, proteinuria.	Slow-acting drug. Teach clients that onset may take two to three months. Administer with NSAIDs. Assess for GI distress. Monitor CBC and urinalysis every two to four weeks.
Hydroxy- chloroquine (Plaquenil) Classification: DMARD	Anti-inflammation	Seizures, personality changes, retinopathy, and visual disturbances, tinnitus, ototoxic, hypotension, GI upset, agranulocytosis, aplastic anemia, leucopenia, thrombocytopenia.	Assess deep tendon reflexes for abnormalities. Monitor laboratory values for abnormalities on CBC. Requires an eye exam before and every three to six months during therapy to assess for retinal damage. Treatment may require six months of dosage to see improvement.
Infliximab (Remicade) Classification: DMARD	Anti-inflammation	GI distress. Fatigue, headache, bronchitis, dysuria, paresthesia.	Assess for a reaction (fever, chills, rash). Administration IV with polyethylene tubing and a filter. If client experiences severe rash, hypotension, and difficulty breathing during infusion, a hypersensitivity reaction is occurring and the drug might have to be discontinued.

(continues)

TABLE 14.2 *Continued*

Name/Classification	Action	Side Effects	Nursing Care
Methotrexate (Rheumatrex) Classification: DMARD	Anti-inflammation *Methotrexate is the gold standard for rheumatoid arthritis treatment.	GI upset (anorexia, nausea and vomiting, stomatitis). Hepatoxic, alopecia, photosensitivity, rash, aplastic anemia, leucopenia, thrombocytopenia.	Assess for bone marrow suppression, GI ulcerations. Monitor for side effects, CBC, liver enzymes, creatinine for kidney effects. Advise patient of contraceptive measures because of teratogenicity.
Leflunomide (Arava) Classification: DMARD	Anti-inflammation	Flu-like syndrome, dizziness, weakness, headache, GI upset. Alopecia, rash, arthralgia.	Monitor liver function tests. Advise of teratogenic effects of the drug. Requires loading dose followed by daily administration.
Adalimumab (Humira) Classification: DMARD	Anti-inflammation	Headache, high blood pressure, GI distress, rash, back pain.	Assess for an infection— clients with an infection cannot receive the drug. Monitor for signs of an anaphylactic reaction (difficulty breathing, facial edema, and rash).
Cyclosporine (Neoral) Classification: DMARD	Depresses the immune system	Confusion, tremors, seizures. Liver and kidney toxic, gingival hyperplasia. GI upset.	Administered by slow dose titration upward until a positive response or toxicity signs occur. Assess for bleeding gums and fluid retention. Monitor liver and kidney function tests.
Cyclophosphamide (Cytoxan) Classification: Alkylating agent	Depresses the immune system	Pulmonary and myocardial fibrosis, syndrome of inappropriate antidiuretic hormone (SIADH), hematuria (causes hemorrhagic cystitis), alopecia, leucopenia, thrombocytopenia, hyperuricemia.	Force fluids. Bone marrow suppression should be assessed for. Monitor laboratory values (CBC, liver function, and kidney function tests).
Pennicillamine (Cuprimine) Classification: DMARD	Anti-inflammation	Blurred vision, eye pain, wheezing, shortness of breath, GI upset, proteinuria, arthralgia. Aplastic anemia, eosinophilia, leucopenia, elevated or decreased thrombocytes.	Observe for side effects. Ensure that client has adequate kidney function prior to administration. Monitor laboratory values for side effects.

Apply Your Knowledge

The study of musculoskeletal and connective tissue disorders can often be difficult for the nurse to understand because of the complexity of many of the conditions. The following questions test your knowledge regarding the safe, effective care and management of the client with various musculoskeletal and connective tissue disorders. Use the key terms, diagnostics, chapter content, and pharmacological agents sections to assist in answering these questions.

Exam Questions

1. A client with cancer is being evaluated for metastasis to the bone. Which laboratory value would correlate with the suspected metastasis?

   A. Serum phosphorus of 3.0 mg/dL

   B. Alkaline phosphatase of 70 units/L

   C. Serum calcium 16.0 mg/dL

   D. Aldolase 3.5 units/dL

2. The nurse is assessing a client who is complaining of numbness in her hands and wrists from carpal tunnel syndrome. Which test is measured by placing a blood pressure cuff on the upper arm and inflating to the systolic pressure?

   A. Phalen's maneuver

   B. Tinel's sign

   C. Chevotsky's sign

   D. Turner's sign

3. The nurse is assessing traction of a client with a fracture who is in skeletal traction. Assessment reveals a loosened pin on the bone. Which action is appropriate?

   A. Notify the physician

   B. Remove the weight to release the pressure on the pin

   C. Reposition the client to the supine position

   D. Try to remove the pin for examination

4. A client has a fractured tibia from a football injury. A cast was applied to the leg. Assessment reveals complaints of pain unrelieved by pain medication, restricted toe movements, edema, and slow capillary refill. What is the nurse's best action?

   A. Elevate the extremity on a pillow

   B. Administer pain medication

   C. Notify the physician of the assessment findings

   D. Perform a neurovascular reassessment

5. The nurse is performing discharge teaching on a client with rheumatoid arthritis who has been prescribed hydroxychloroquine (Plaquenil). Which statement by the client indicates that he understood the instructions given?

   A. "I should report any blurred vision or headache."

   B. "I have to take folic acid with this drug."

   C. "I should expect results in six months."

   D. "I should take this medication on an empty stomach."

6. The nurse has been notified to assist in a disaster. Which plan would be included in the emergency care of a fracture?

   A. Turn the clients to the left side

   B. Immobilize the extremity by splinting above and below the fractured site

   C. Provide manual traction of the fracture site

   D. Reinsert any protruding bones and apply a sterile dressing

7. The nurse is caring for a client admitted with a pelvic fracture. Which assessment receives priority status?

   A. Bowel sound auscultation

   B. Pupillary response to light

   C. Assessing for hematuria

   D. Cranial nerve 8 assessment

8. The nurse is assisting a student nurse to wrap a stump. The nurse instructs the student to use the figure-eight technique. The nurse realizes that the main reason this technique is utilized is to prevent what problem?

   A. Constriction of blood flow

   B. Immobilization of the joint

   C. Formation of a decubitus ulcer

   D. Oozing of blood from the wound

9. A client is admitted with a mandibular fracture that has been realigned by wiring. Which piece of equipment is essential at the bedside?

   A. Waterpik

   B. Wire cutter

   C. Humidifier

   D. Oral rinse

10. The nurse is caring for a client with hepatitis C who also has osteoporosis. Which medication would the nurse expect to be excluded from the healthcare provider's plans?

    A. Risedronate (Actonel)

    B. Alendronate (Fosamax)

    C. Ibandronate (Boniva)

    D. Raloxifene (Evista)

Answers to Exam Questions

1. Answer C is correct. Serum calcium levels rise with metastatic cancer of the bone. Normal calcium is 9.0 mg/dL–10.5 mg/dL. Answers A and D are incorrect because these are within normal limits and not related to bone metastasis. Normal phosphorus level is 3.0–4.5 mg/dL and normal aldolase level is 3.0–8.2 units/dL. Alkaline phosphatase is elevated in bone metastasis and Answer B is within the normal of 30–120 units/L, so it is incorrect.

2. Answer B is correct. This test is measured as described and can result in pain and a tingling sensation if the client has carpal tunnel syndrome (CTS). Answer A is incorrect because it is a test in which the client is asked to place the back of the hands together and flex the wrist at the same time causing pain. Answers C and D are exams not related to CTS, so they are incorrect.

3. Answer A is correct. The nurse should notify the physician so that the pin can be repaired. Answers B and D are actions that can have negative results on the bone healing process, so they are incorrect. Answer C will not help, so it is wrong.

4. Answer C is correct. The physician must be notified because the client is at risk for compartment syndrome. The healthcare provider might order that the cast be bivalved, or a fasciotomy might be required. Answers A, B, and D will not take the action necessary to prevent the complication of compartment syndrome.

5. Answer A is correct. Clients on Plaquenil should have eye exams every 6–12 months because it can cause retinal damage. Answers B and C are inaccurate statements for the drug Plaquenil, so they are incorrect. Answer D is incorrect because the medication should be taken with food or a snack.

6. Answer B is correct. The nurse should splint the extremity, cover the area, and do a neurovascular assessment. Answer A is incorrect because the client should be in the supine position. Answer C is not recommended, so it is incorrect. Answer D is detrimental and increases the risk of infection, so it is incorrect.

7. Answer C is correct. The pelvis is close to major organs and the nurse needs to assess for damage to associated organs. The bladder could have been damaged and hematuria assessment would be a priority. Answers A, B, and D are important assessments, but are not the priority, so they are incorrect.

8. Answer A is correct. Wrapping an elastic bandage on a stump using the circular technique can cause the wrap to act as a tourniquet and restrict blood flow, so a figure eight technique is utilized to prevent this from occurring. Answers B, C, and D are not the primary reasons for use of the figure eight technique, so they are incorrect.

9. Answer B is correct. Wire cutters must be at the bedside at all times to decrease the risk of aspiration with vomiting. Answers A and D are usually used in the care of clients with a fractured mandible, but are not as essential as the wire cutters, so they are incorrect. The answer in C is not a usual piece of equipment for clients with fractured mandibles, so it is incorrect.

10. Answer D is correct. Evista should not be given to clients with liver disease because it can make the condition worse. Answers A, B, and C are not contraindicated in liver disease clients, so they are incorrect.

Suggested Reading and Resources

▶ Bartz, Barbara, Candice Kumagai, and L. Lacharity. *Prioritization, Delegation & Assignment*. St. Louis: Mosby Elsevier, 2006.

▶ Brunner, L., and D. Suddarth. *Textbook of Medical Surgical Nursing* 10th ed. Philadelphia: Lippincott Williams & Wilkins, 2009.

▶ Deglin, Judith H., and April H. Vallerand. *Davis Drug Guide for Nurses*. Philadelphia: F. A. Davis, 2009.

▶ Ignatavicius, D., and S. Workman. *Medical Surgical Nursing: Critical Thinking for Collaborative Care* 6th ed. Philadelphia: Elsevier, 2007.

▶ Kee, J. *Laboratory and Diagnostic Tests with Nursing Implications*. New York: Prentice Hall, 2010.

▶ Lemone, P., and K. Burke. *Medical-Surgical Nursing Critical Thinking in Client Care* 4th edition. Upper Saddle River, NJ: Pearson Prentice Hall, 2008.

▶ Lewis, S., M. Heitkemper, S. Dirksen, P. O'Brien, and L. Bucher. *Medical Surgical Nursing: Assessment and Management of Clinical Problems* 7th ed. Philadelphia: Elsevier, 2007.

▶ Rinehart, Sloan, Hurd, *Exam Cram NCLEX-RN*. Indianapolis: Que Publishing, 2007.

▶ Smith, F., D. Duell, B. Martin. *Clinical Nursing Skills Basic to Advanced Skills* 7th ed. Upper Saddle River, NJ: Pearson Prentice Hall, 2008.

▶ www.NOF.org

CHAPTER FIFTEEN

Care of the Childbearing Client and the Neonatal Client

Pregnancy is a special time in a woman's life. Considered a normal state of health, most cultures believe that the woman is well. This belief might cause the client to refuse to visit the doctor. Studies have shown that good prenatal care can reduce the incidence of infant mortality and improve pregnancy outcome. This chapter focuses on the health needs of the obstetric client and the newborn infant. This chapter also covers methods of birth control, prenatal care, and diseases affecting women. After reviewing this chapter, the nurse should be able to answer commonly asked questions and provide teaching for the client and family.

Prenatal Care

Early prenatal care provides the nurse the opportunity to teach the client and family members. A systematic physical exam and health history provide the healthcare provider with the information needed to treat and prevent fetal anomalies. Using Naegele's rule the examiner can determine the estimated date of delivery. This is done by counting from the first day of the woman's last menstrual period plus one year. The nurse should then subtract three months and add seven days to that date. McDonald's method can also be used to determine gestational age. This is done by measuring the fundal height in centimeters. Screening tests should be performed during the prenatal visit to detect diseases that affect the mother and fetus. It has been found that the earlier the pregnant client begins to visit the doctor, the better the outcome for the infant and mother. In this section, you will discover the signs of pregnancy, prenatal topics, and information that might be tested on the NCLEX exam.

Signs of Pregnancy

Signs of pregnancy include the following:

▶ **Presumptive signs:** These are subjective and can be associated with some other gynecological alteration. Presumptive signs of pregnancy are those signs and symptoms that lead the client to believe she is pregnant, which include

  ▶ Amenorrhea

  ▶ Breast sensitivity

  ▶ Chadwick's sign

  - ► Fatigue

  - ► Fingernail changes

  - ► Urinary frequency

  - ► Weight gain

  - ► Quickening

  - ► Nausea and vomiting (morning sickness)

► **Probable signs:** Can be documented and are more conclusive; however, these signs can also be associated with conditions other than pregnancy. Even though the client believes she is pregnant, more tests should be done to conclude that a pregnancy exists. The probable signs of pregnancy are

  - ► **Ballottement:** Ballottement is noted when there is easy flexion of the uterus when the examiners finger pushes sharply against the uterus and detects the presence or position of the fetus by return impact.

  - ► **Chadwick's sign:** Chadwick's sign is the bluish discoloration of the vagina and cervix. This finding is also present immediately prior to menstruation.

  - ► **Goodell's sign:** Goodell's sign is softening of the vaginal portion of the cervix.

  - ► **Hegar's sign:** Hegar's sign is softening of the portion of the cervix between the uterus and vaginal portion of the cervix.

  - ► Positive pregnancy test.

  - ► McDonald's sign indicated by uterine enlargement.

  - ► Mask of pregnancy, which is a rash that appears on the face due to hormonal influences.

  - ► Positive pregnancy test, which measures Human Chorionic Gonadotropin in blood or urine.

► **Positive signs:** Only three physical findings establish the diagnosis of pregnancy, and these are known as positive signs of pregnancy. These signs are

  - ► Fetal heart tones

  - ► Leopold's maneuver, which is fetal outline noted on palpation of the abdomen

  - ► Ultrasound of the fetal outline

Prenatal Diet and Weight Maintenance

The best assurance for a healthy outcome for both the mother and the infant is good nutrition. If the mother is malnourished prior to the pregnancy she should be encouraged to eat a well balance diet adequate in vitamins and minerals. A weight gain of approximately 25–35 pounds is allowable, and weight reduction during pregnancy is discouraged. Prior to pregnancy, the client should be encouraged to increase the intake of foods high in vitamins such as B9 (folic acid). The ingestion of multivitamins with folic acid has been linked to a reduction of neural tube defects such as spina bifida and myelomeningocele. Some cultures do not encourage the use of vitamins with iron because pregnancy is considered a hot time and iron is considered a hot medication. This belief has been shown to increase the number of spinal defects in that population. Prenatal diagnostic studies, such as alpha-fetoprotein screening, can be performed to detect neural tube defects.

> **NOTE**
> Vaginal ultrasounds require that the bladder be empty.

Some of the tests that can be performed on the amniotic fluid are

- Lecithin/sphingomyelin (L/S) ratios, which detects lung maturity
- Estriol levels, which indicate fetal distress
- Creatinine levels, which indicate renal function

Teratogenic effects of drugs and disease can also be detected by checking the amniotic fluid. Some examples of teratogenic agents are as follows:

- **Accutane:** Used for cystic acne. This drug is made from vitamin A and is extremely teratogenic. The client should have liver studies and a pregnancy test done prior to beginning the medication and during the course of the treatment.
- **Alcohol:** Causes dependence in the fetus and fetal-alcohol syndrome.
- **Cytomegalovirus:** Causes multiple fetal anomalies.
- **Herpes:** Causes multiple fetal anomalies. If a herpetic lesion is noted on the perineum or in the vagina, the doctor will most likely plan for a Cesarean section. Antivirals such as Acyclovir can be given to prevent active herpes during the last month of pregnancy.
- **LSD:** Causes dependence in the fetus and multiple fetal anomalies.
- **Rubella virus:** A live virus. Vaccines for rubella should not be given during pregnancy. The nurse should be sure to ask the client when her last menstrual period was prior to giving the vaccine.
- **Syphilis:** Sexually transmitted disease that can cause multiple fetal anomalies.
- **Tetracycline:** Stains the teeth of the baby and can affect the growth of bones.
- **Toxoplasmosis:** Transmitted by cat feces. The mother should be instructed not to empty the litter box or work in dirt without gloves during pregnancy due to the risk of contracting toxoplasmosis.

> **NOTE**
>
> TORCHS is a syndrome that includes toxoplasmosis, rubella, cytomegalovirus, herpes, and syphilis.

Measuring Fetal Heart Tones

The fetal heart tone should be checked frequently to measure the viability and status of circulating blood to the fetus. This noninvasive technique can be obtained through the use of a fetoscope or tocomonitor.

Fetal heart tones can be heard with a fetoscope at approximately 18–20 weeks and with a Doppler ultrasound at approximately 12 weeks. Fetal heart tones can also be detected as early as 8 weeks using vaginal ultrasound. The normal range of fetal heart tones is 110–160 beats per minute. Fewer than 110 beats per minute is considered *bradycardia*, and greater than 160 beats per minute is considered *tachycardia*.

Measuring Fundal Height

The fundal height is measured from the top of the symphysis pubis to the top of the fundus in centimeters. The formula for estimating the gestational age based on the fundal height is outlined here:

Measurement in centimeters from the top of the symphysis pubis in centimeters multiplied by 8. The number is then divided by 7. The number obtained is the weeks gestation. For example:

20 centimeters * 8 = 160, divided by 7 = 22 weeks and approximately 8 days.

Prelabor Testing

Several tests can be performed to predict possible complications to the fetus and mother:

▶ **Alpha fetoprotein (AFP):** Performed to screen for neural tube defects. Alpha-fetoprotein levels can be done between 16 and 20 weeks gestation. Alpha-fetoprotein levels are considered a screening tool and are not diagnostic for neural tube defects. This level can be tested by obtaining a blood sample from the mother. Alpha-fetoprotein is a glucoprotein produced by the fetal yolk sac, gastrointestinal tract, and liver. This protein passes through the placenta to the maternal circulation and is excreted through fetal circulation and into the mother's circulation. Normal ranges for each week of pregnancy are measured. When abnormal levels are detected, an amniocentesis should be performed.

▶ **Ultrasound:** If the client is having an ultrasound early in the pregnancy, she should be instructed to drink large amounts of fluids to fill the bladde and not to void until after the exam. An ultrasound can assist in the determination of the gastrointestinal and renal functions of the fetus because the amount of amniotic fluid is directly affected by the ability of the fetus to swallow and urinate.

▶ **Amniocentesis:** This can be done as early as 16 weeks, which allows adequate time for amniotic fluid to accumulate. An ultrasound exam of the uterus is performed prior to the amniocentesis to locate the placenta and the pockets of amniotic fluid. If the client is less than 20 weeks gestation, the bladder should remain full during the procedure. The full bladder pushes the uterus up in the abdominal cavity, making it easier to obtain a sample of amniotic fluid. After the client is past 20 weeks gestation, the client should be instructed to void prior to the amniocentesis. A sample of amniotic fluid is then removed using a large-bore needle. Because there is an increased incidence of miscarriages, the client is instructed to remain in the clinic for approximately two hours and to report any bleeding. The sample of amniotic fluid can be used to determine chromosomal abnormalities, gender, lung maturity (L/S ratio), fetal well-being (estriol levels), and other information that is vital to the planning for a safe outcome.

▶ **Chorionic villus (CVS) sampling:** A collection of tissue from the fetal side of the placenta is obtained. This test is usually performed late in the first trimester between weeks 10 and 12 and can be used to determine fetal genetic abnormalities and chromosomal defects, but not neural tube defects.

▶ **Biophysical profile:** Acquired via ultrasound, it is used to determine lung function, body movement, heart rate, and the amount of amniotic fluid present.

▶ **Glucose tolerance test:** A screening test to determine gestational diabetes. At approximately 24 weeks gestation, the client is asked to come to the office for a non-fasting oral glucose screening. One hour after consuming glucose, a blood glucose level is obtained. If the level is greater than 130 mg/dl, the client is asked to return for a fasting glucose tolerance test. During this test, the client is instructed to remain NPO for 8 hours prior to the test. When the client arrives in the clinic, a fasting blood glucose is drawn. The client is then asked to drink a 100-gram oral glucose preparation. Blood glucose levels are drawn four at a time. If two of the four blood glucose tests are abnormal, the client is considered to be gestational diabetic.

▶ **Lecithen to sphingomyelin (L/S) Ratio:** Used to determine lung maturnity. The ratio of lecithin to sphingomyelin should be 2:1 if the lungs are mature.

▶ **Phosphatidylglycerol (PG):** This test performed by sampling the amniotic fluid indicates lung maturity. Phosphatidyl glycerol usually becomes detectable in amniotic fluid at about 35 or 36 weeks gestation. The presence of phosphatidyl glycerol in the amniotic fluid generally indicates there is minimal risk for neonatal respiratory distress.

▶ **Triple-screening:** The triple-screening test is done between 15 and 20 weeks gestation. This test checks for neural tube defects (alpha-fetoprotein); human chorionic gonadotropin (HCG); and unconjugated estriol, which indicates fetal well-being.

▶ **Nonstress test:** This test is done frequently during the third trimester to determine fetal response to cyclical periods of rest and activity. A fetal monitor is applied for approximately 90 minutes. During this time, the client is instructed to press the response button each time the baby moves. Normal fetal response is an increase in fetal heart rate of 15 beats per minute. This finding indicates the likelihood of a positive fetal outcome.

▶ **Contraction stress test:** Though not performed routinely, a contraction stress test is used in high-risk clients to determine fetal response to contractions. The length of time for an contraction stress test is generally 90–120 minutes. Contractions are stimulated by beginning an infusion of oxytocin (Pitocin). Ten units of oxytocin (Pitocin) are diluted in 1000 mL of IV fluid, begun at 3 milliunits per minute, and increased every 15 minutes until three contractions in 10 minutes are observed. If fetal bradycardia (fetal heart tone [FHT] is less than 110 bpm) or tachycardia (FHT is greater than 160 bpm) is observed or if the blood pressure of the mother rises above normal, the test is considered abnormal. An abnormal reading can indicate that labor might not be advisable. After the exam, the oxytocin (Pitocin) is discontinued.

▶ **Fetal Fibronectin (fFN) test:** This test is used in clients with preterm labor to determine the likelihood that the client can continue the pregnancy for at least two more weeks. The presence of Fetal Fibronectin (fFN) in cervico-vaginal secretions indicates that the fetus is at risk for preterm delivery.

Other tests that are often done during pregnancy are CBC, urinalysis, blood type and Rh factor, platelet counts, and liver function studies.

NOTE

If the physician decides to induce labor, the Pitocin used in a contraction stress test can be continued with prostaglandin gel.

CAUTION

Pitocin should always be infused using a pump or controller because rapid infusion can lead to hypertonic uterine contractions, premature placental separation, and uterine rupture.

Intrapartal Care

Labor is defined as both the process by which the fetus is expelled from the uterus and the time period immediately after. Five factors influence the labor process:

▶ **Passageway:** The birth canal, which consists of the uterus, bony pelvis, and vagina.

▶ **Passenger:** The baby. This consideration during the intrapartal period involves evaluation and management of distress.

▶ **Powers:** The mother's body's power to expel the fetus; it consists of the uterine contractions.

▶ **Position:** The position of the fetus in utero. This factor can affect the ability of the cervix to dilate and efface. For example, a breech position requires a longer labor.

▶ **Psychological response:** The psychological response of the mother makes a difference in the labor experience. If the mother is prepared and in control, the labor process is much more likely to proceed smoothly.

The intrapartal period is divided into stages and phases of labor, as covered in the following sections.

Stages of Labor

The stages of labor describe the process of dilation and descent of the baby. The four stages of labor are as follows:

▶ **Stage 1:** 0–10 centimeters dilation of the cervix

  The first stage of labor is divided into three phases of labor:

  ▶ **Phase 1:** Early labor or prodromal (0–3 cm dilation)

  ▶ **Phase 2:** Active labor (4–7 cm dilation)

  ▶ **Phase 3:** Transition (8–10 cm dilation)

▶ **Stage 2:** From complete dilation to delivery of the baby

▶ **Stage 3:** From delivery of the baby to delivery of the placenta

▶ **Stage 4:** From delivery of the placenta until completion of the recovery period

Important Terms You Should Know

Several terms associated with labor and delivery are listed here. You should know these for the exam:

▶ **Presentation:** The part of the fetus that engages and presents first at delivery. Cephalic presentation, or head presentation, is the most common type of presentation; however, breech presentation (buttocks or feet first) account for many cesarean births.

▶ **Position:** The relationship of the presenting part to the mother's pelvis. For example, left occiput anterior (LOA) means that the back of the baby's head is anterior to the pelvis and tilted to the left side. Right occiput anterior (ROA) means that the back of the baby's head is anterior and tilted to the right side; occiput anterior (OA) means that the back of the baby's head is directly to the front of the mother's pelvis.

- ▶ **Fetal lie:** The relationship of the fetus to the long axis of the mother. This can be determined by performing Leopold's maneuvers. Leopold's maneuver is a technique performed by the healthcare provider by palpating the maternal abdomen to determine where the fetal back, legs, head, and so on are located. This technique is a noninvasive way of estimating the fetal lie and whether the baby is engaged or in the true pelvis.

- ▶ **Dystocia:** This term is associated with an abnormal progression of labor. Dystocia is frequently related to malpresentation or malposition of the fetus or hypotonic uterine contractions.

- ▶ **Effacement:** This is the thinning of the cervix.

- ▶ **Dilation:** This is the opening of the cervix.

- ▶ **Precipitate delivery:** This term is associated with a rapid and uncontrolled labor and delivery. The client with precipitate delivery is at risk for uterine rupture, vaginal lacerations, amniotic emboli, and postpartal hemorrhage. Fetal complications include hypoxia and intracranial hemorrhage.

- ▶ **Station:** This refers to the biparietal diameter or the widest part of the fetal head as it relates to the maternal ischial spines (0 station is at the ischial spines). If the fetus is in a non-vertex presentation station refers to to the fetal body as it relates to the ischial spines.

Complications Associated with Pregnancy

Pregnancy brings about changes in the cardiovascular status of the client as well as other possible complications. This section discusses these changes and the nursing care needed to insure a safe outcome for the mother and infant.

Cardiac Disease During Pregnancy

During pregnancy, the client's fluid volume triples. The increase in fluid volume causes the heart to work harder. If, however, there is damage to the heart, cardiac failure ensues. The most stressful times on the circulatory system during pregnancy are the last trimester, labor, and the immediate postpartum period.

Cardiac disease affects 0.5%–3% of pregnant clients. The New York Heart Association's functional classifications for the pregnant client are as follows:

- ▶ **Class I:** Asymptomatic at normal activity

- ▶ **Class II:** Symptomatic with moderate activity

- ▶ **Class III:** Symptomatic with activities of daily living

- ▶ **Class IV:** Symptomatic at rest

During the prenatal period, the nurse should assess the blood pressure, heart sounds, and respiratory status. Several signs might indicate the presence of cardiac disease, including the following:

- Fatigue
- Difficulty breathing
- Coarse breath sounds
- Cardiac palpitations
- Swelling of the face, feet, legs, and fingers
- Rapid, irregular, weak pulse
- Orthopnea
- Cyanosis of the lips and nail beds

If the nurse notes any of these signs, she should report them to the physician. Further testing for cardiac decompensation using electrocardiography, echocardiograms, cardiac catheterization, and others might be indicated.

Some of the cardiac diseases affecting pregnant clients include valvular disease, congestive heart failure, cardiomyopathy, and myocardial infarction. These disorders can also be associated with abnormal clotting. Use of heparin to prevent and treat clots is often considered. The nurse should be aware that warfarin sodium (Coumadin) is contraindicated in pregnancy because it crosses the placental barrier and can cause bleeding in the fetus.

The goal of treatment is to decrease the workload on the heart and prevent damage to the myocardium. The workload of the heart can be reduced through stress control, a diet low in cholesterol and sodium, and prompt treatment of infections. Prophylactic use of antibiotics for invasive procedures such as dental work or cesarean section is a consideration because endocarditis or pericarditis would further compromise cardiac function. Sodium intake should be monitored because hypernatremia will lead to fluid retention. Furosemide (Lasix) is used to treat fluid retention. Because Lasix is not potassium sparing, the client should be monitored for hypokalemia. Hyponatremia and hypokalemia should also be treated promptly because they can lead to irregular cardiac rhythms.

Other cardiac diseases affecting pregnancy include rheumatic heart disease, infective endocarditis, mitral valve prolapse, and Marfan's syndrome. *Marfan's syndrome* is an autosomal-dominant disorder characterized by weakness of connective tissue. About 90% of these individuals have mitral valve prolapse and 25% have aortic insufficiency. Management includes rest, cardiotonic medications, and oxygen support.

Antepartum Precautions for Cardiac Disease

Pregnant clients with Class I heart disease though generally asymptomatic should be protected against cardiac decompensation. Vaccines against pneumonia and influenza are recommended. If the client is a Class III or IV, she might be asked to rest on her left side for much of the day. Resting on the left side helps to increase the blood supply to the kidneys.

Multivitamins with iron and a diet high in protein will be prescribed to prevent anemia. Stool softeners to prevent constipation are recommended because the Valsalva maneuver (straining with defecation) is contraindicated.

If anticoagulant therapy is required, heparin or a heparin derivative such as enoxaparin (Lovenox) is used. Oral anticoagulants such as sodium warfarin (Coumadin) are contraindicated because they cross the placental barrier and can lead to bleeding in the mother and fetus. Spontaneous abortions and preterm labor are more prevalent in clients with cardiac disease. In addition, intrauterine growth retardation (IUGR) related to a decrease in oxygen to the fetus is more common.

Intrapartum Precautions for Cardiac Disease

Labor is a particularly stressful time for the cardiac client. Class III or IV will probably be scheduled for a cesarean section, although some texts suggest that surgery should be avoided because of the stress of anesthesia and recovery. If the client elects to have a vaginal delivery, epidural or pudendal anesthesia is recommended. Prophylactic antibiotics will be prescribed to prevent infections. Oxygen and positioning on the side improves oxygenation to the client's heart and to the fetus. Oxytocin (Pitocin) is not recommended for augmentation of labor. Syntocinon, a synthetic oxytocin, can be used for induction of labor because it does not seem to cause the extreme vasoconstriction associated with oxytocin.

Postpartum Precautions for Cardiac Disease

During the postpartum period, the client should be placed in a quiet, private room to encourage rest. Positioning on the left side is recommended because better renal perfusion and excretion of fluid is achieved when the client lies on her side. Urinary output should be closely monitored because oliguria and edema can indicate renal compromise and congestive heart failure. If congestive heart failure is a problem, the client will be treated with furosemide (Lasix) and cardiotonic drugs. Stool softeners and laxatives, along with a diet high in fiber, help to prevent constipation. Breast feeding is not recommended for Class III or IV clients because it can cause fluid retention.

Hypertrophic cardiomyopathy (HCM) is a structural abnormality in which the heart wall and septum hypertrophy leaving small chambers. Symptoms can be vague until the ventricle is extremely small. The client might complain of exertional dyspnea, syncope, and extreme fatigue. Ventricular arrhythmias and an S_3 gallop might be present on auscultation.

Idiopathic peripartum cardiomyopathy is heart failure occurring during pregnancy without any previous history of heart disease. Symptoms include dyspnea, edema, and tachyarrhythmia. The prognosis is good if the heart returns to normal size and function by six months postpartum. If the heart does not return to normal size and shape, the prognosis for complete recovery decreases and a heart transplant might be necessary.

Clients with Class II, III, or IV heart disease should be taught regarding the dangers of subsequent pregnancies. Birth control can be accomplished through use of barrier methods such as diaphragms or condoms. Oral contraceptives are not recommended because they increase the risk for thrombus formation and might cause elevations in blood pressure. Intrauterine devices are not recommended because of the increased risk for infection.

Diabetes in Pregnancy

Clients with diabetes and their infants are at risk for complications during pregnancy. Infants of diabetic mothers tend to be large for gestational age. Because glucose crosses the placenta, whereas insulin does not, these infants tend to gain weight. At birth they appear pudgy, ruddy, and lethargic. The high glucose environment impedes lung development and, although they are large for gestational age, they are often premature. Complications of maternal diabetes to the infant include

- Patent ductus arteriosus

- Polyhydramnios

- Premature delivery

- Respiratory distress syndrome

Complications of maternal diabetes to the mother include

- Hypertension

- Renal disease

- Vascular compromise

- Ketoacidosis

- Seizure activity related to hypoglycemia

Fluctuations in maternal blood sugar can result in fetal brain damage or sudden fetal death due to ketosis. Clients with diabetes should be taught to check their blood glucose levels frequently during the day. Levels over 120 mg/dL should be reported to the doctor.

The best diagnostic test for diabetes is a glucose tolerance test, which should be performed early in the pregnancy. Infants born to diabetic mothers might be delivered by cesarean section due to their large sizes (macrosomia). They should be assessed immediately after delivery for hypoglycemia by performing a dextrostix. A finding of 40 mg/dl or lower indicates hypoglycemia in the infant. The blood is usually obtained by performing a heel stick. The infant should be stuck on the lateral aspect of the heel. Blood tests should be performed to detect hypocalcemia, hypokalemia, and acidosis.

Preeclampsia

Preeclampsia is an abnormality found only in pregnancy. The diagnostic criteria are an elevated blood pressure above 140/90, facial edema, and proteinuria. Preeclampsia is more common in primagravidas and in women less than 16 years of age or over age 35. Clients with preeclampsia tend to have infants that are small in birth weight for gestational age. These infants can also suffer from respiratory distress syndrome and congenital heart defects such as patent ductus arteriosus. Clients with mild preeclampsia are treated with bed rest and a low-sodium diet. Severe preeclampsia is diagnosed when

- ▶ The blood pressure is equal to or greater than 160/110 on two occasions at least six hours apart with the woman on bed rest.

- ▶ Proteinuria is found to be greater than or equal to 5 grams in a 24-hour urine specimen.

- ▶ Oliguria equal to or less than 400 mL in 24 hours is found.

- ▶ Cerebral or visual disturbances are reported.

- ▶ The client complains of epigastric pain.

- ▶ Pulmonary edema or cyanosis is reported.

- ▶ HELLP syndrome is diagnosed.

> **NOTE**
>
> HELLP syndrome is hemolysis, elevated liver enzymes, and low platelets. This syndrome results in an enlarged liver and associated bleeding. If it's not treated, the client can die as a result of bleeding. The treatment for this problem is early delivery of the fetus.

Management of severe preeclampsia consists of:

- ▶ Complete bed rest on the client's left side is recommended.

- ▶ Monitor sodium and potassium levels (a diet moderate in sodium is recommended).

> **NOTE**
>
> A low-sodium diet is no longer recommended because a low sodium level in the fetus can adversely affect fetal outcomes.

- ▶ Magnesium sulfate. A level of 4.8–9.6 mg/dl is recommended. The nurse should assess for possible toxicity. The signs of magnesium toxicity include

  - ▶ Absence of the knee-jerk (patella) reflex. Deep tendon reflexes (DTRs) should be monitored.

  - ▶ Oliguria. A Foley catheter should be inserted to monitor hourly urinary output.

- ▶ Respirations less than 12 per minute, which can indicate impending respiratory arrest.

- ▶ Other signs of magnesium toxicity are visual disturbances, facial flushing, GI upset, intestinal obstruction, and hypercalcemia. Because magnesium is excreted by the kidneys, the client should be monitored for signs of renal impairment.

If the nurse notes signs of toxicity, he should stop the infusion of magnesium sulfate and prepare to administer calcium gluconate. Safe administration requires the use of an IV pump or a controller. Common side effects of $MgSO_4$ are drowsiness and hot flashes. Magnesium levels should be checked approximately every six hours and the results reported to the doctor.

> **NOTE**
>
> The treatment for magnesium sulfate toxicity is calcium gluconate. This medication should be kept at the bedside along with an airway and a tracheotomy Set.

> **NOTE**
>
> Fetal hypotonia and central nervous system depression can result from the use of magnesium sulfate.

Every effort should be made to prevent seizures. A quiet, dark environment must be maintained and visitors should be restricted. The client should be assessed for signs of toxicity, which include hyporeflexia, oliguria, and decreased respirations.

Antihypertensive medications are also frequently used to control the client's blood pressure during pregnancy. Beta blocker, angio-receptor blockers, and others categories might be ordered. Angiotensin converting enzyme inhibitors (ACE) are not generally recommended during pregnancy.

Ectopic Pregnancy

An *ectopic* pregnancy is defined as any pregnancy that occurs outside the body of the uterus. The most frequent site of implantation is the fallopian tube. Often the client does not know that she is pregnant, but she might have amenorrhea or experience some scanty vaginal bleeding. Tests for pregnancy are frequently positive. The diagnosis of an ectopic pregnancy can be made by ultrasound studies. Treatment includes laparoscopic surgery to evacuate the zygote. If the fallopian tube ruptures, bleeding and peritonitis can result. Scarring in the fallopian passage can result in an inability of the ovum to travel through the tube, resulting in sterility in the affected tube.

Hydatidiform Mole

A hydatidiform mole is a type of gestational trophoblastic neoplasms. There are two types: complete molar pregnancy and partial molar pregnancy. Hydatidiform mole occurs in one of every 1,200 pregnancies. The most common type is the complete or classic type where fertilization of an egg whose nucleus has been lost. The mole resembles a bunch of white grapes. This results in a rapid proliferation of hydropic (fluid-filled) vesicles. These vesicles grow rapidly, causing the uterus to enlarge quickly. Usually the mole contains no fetus, placenta, amniotic fluid, or membrane. The rapid proliferation of these vesicles associated with the hydatiform mole can be associated with chorionic carcinoma. In the early stages, the signs and symptoms are the same as those of a normal pregnancy. Around the end of the first trimester, the client may experience vaginal bleeding. The bleeding might be dark brown or bright red. Most clients experiencing a hydatidiform mole have a rapidly growing uterus that is much larger than that normal for dates. Abdominal cramping is often present.

Diagnosis is made by ultrasound exam, and treatment involves evacuation of the hydatidiform mole using a dilation and curettage. The client should be instructed not to become pregnant for at least a year following a hydatidiform mole because a rising human chorionic gonadatropin (HCG) level can contribute to development of choriocarcinoma.

Incompetent Cervix

An incompetent cervix is characterized by a painless dilation of the cervix. The result of this dilation is a spontaneous abortion. The cause is unknown, but might be associated with traumatic birth, dilation and curettage, or ingestion of diethylstilbestrol by the woman's mother during pregnancy. Other factors are a congenitally short cervix and uterine abnormalities. Diagnosis is usually made after the woman experiences more than one miscarriage.

Management includes closure of the cervix until the fetus is a near term or when the fetus is viable outside the uterus. There are several surgical procedures used to achieve closure of the cervix. *McDonald cerclage*, (commonly done between weeks 10 and 14 of pregnancy) is a procedure where a band of homologous fascia is placed beneath the mucosa to constrict the internal os (opening of the cervix). The suture is left in place until near term when it is clipped and labor is allowed. Another procedure is Shirodkar's, which involves the use of a suture that remains in place permanently. Births are accomplished by cesarean section.

Types of Abortions

Several types of abortions can be experienced by the client:

▶ **Elective abortion:** Evacuation of the fetus. There are several types of elective abortions, but all of them require early diagnosis of the pregnancy.

▶ **Threatened:** Produces spotting. The treatment is bed rest. If bleeding or cramping continues, the client should contact the physician immediately because the doctor might order tocolytic medications such as magnesium sulfate, Brethine, or Yutopar.

▶ **Inevitable:** If there are no fetal heart tones and parts of the fetus are passed, the client is said to be experiencing an inevitable abortion. This type of abortion produces bleeding and passage of fetal parts. The treatment is a dilation and curettage (D & C).

▶ **Incomplete:** In an incomplete abortion, fetal demise exists, but part of the conception is not passed. The treatment is a dilation and evacuation (D & E).

▶ **Complete:** In a complete abortion, all parts of the conception are passed. There is no treatment.

▶ **Septic:** A septic abortion includes the presence of infection. The treatment is administering antibiotics.

▶ **Missed:** In a missed abortion, there is fetal demise but no expulsion of the fetus. The treatment is an induction of labor or a surgical removal of the fetus.

Complications of all types of abortion include bleeding and infection. The client should be taught to report to the doctor any bleeding, lethargy, or elevated temperature.

Placenta Previa

In *placenta previa*, the placenta is implanted at the lower uterine segment. Placenta previa is described as complete or partial. In complete (or total) placenta previa, the placenta is located over the cervix. In partial or marginal placenta previa, the edge of the placenta approaches the internal os. When the cervix begins to open, the client experiences painless bleeding. Diagnosis is made by ultrasound exam. If the client presents to the clinic or hospital with a placenta previa, the nurse should immediately contact the physician who will instruct her to prepare the client for a cesarean section. Because the bleeding is maternal, the client might exhibit signs of hypotension and shock. The mother can die from shock, whereas the infant can die from a lack of oxygen perfusion through the placenta. The nurse should refrain from performing a vaginal exam to check for cervical dilation if gross bright, red bleeding is present.

Abruptio Placenta

Abruptio placenta, or premature separation of the placenta, is detachment of the placenta from the wall of the uterus prior to the third stage of labor. The separation is graded by the degree of separation and the location of the separation. Diagnosis is made by ultrasound, but frequently is suspected when the fetus experiences variable decelerations. Pain and a rigid abdomen are associated with abruptio placenta. The degree of separation can be partial or complete. Like placenta previa, the bleeding is maternal; therefore, the client will show signs of shock. The infant will die from a lack of oxygen. Management involves early diagnosis and fluid replacement. Vital signs should be monitored frequently. Oxygen administered by face mask helps to improve perfusion of oxygen to mother and baby. Whole blood and Ringer's lactate are infused to insure a urinary output of at least 30 mL per hour. A cesarean section might be performed if bleeding is extensive or if the fetus is showing signs of lack of oxygen perfusion. Both placenta previa and abruptio placenta can be medical emergencies that result in the death of both mother and fetus.

Complications Associated with Labor and Delivery

Premature labor is defined as one that occurs prior to 37 weeks gestation. Early detection of preterm labor is key to the prevention of preterm delivery. The determination of prematurity is done by assessing the client's expected date of delivery. This is frequently done by using Naegele's rule. To calculate Naegele's rule, the nurse should subtract three months from the first day of the last menstrual period and add seven days. Because many women experience irregular menses, it is often difficult to determine the exact due date, so other tests can be done. An ultrasound can be done to determine the size of the fetus and an amniocentesis can be done to determine lung maturity, renal function, and estriol levels. Obtaining a sample by amniocentesis requires that the client have an ultrasonography prior to the test. This provides a picture of the location of the placenta and the pockets of amniotic fluid.

In approximately half of the cases, the reason for preterm births cannot be determined. One-third of the cases are due to premature rupture of the membranes (PROM). Other causes include multiple gestation pregnancies (twins, triplets, and so on), polyhydramnios, incompetent cervix, premature separation of the placenta, and maternal infections such as chlamydia.

The woman should promptly report abdominal cramping or vaginal bleeding to the physician. The diagnosis of labor is made by both vaginal exam and fetal monitoring for the presence of contractions. If uterine contractions persist, the client will be placed on bed rest and told not to have sexual intercourse until the physician determines it is safe to do so. Resting on the left side helps to relieve pressure on the vena cava and increases oxygen perfusion to the fetus. If labor is not stopped by bed rest, the doctor might order a tocolytic drug. The drugs commonly used are terbutaline (Brethine), and magnesium sulfate (Slow Mag).

Terbutaline (Brethine) is another beta-adrenergic agent that is commonly used as a bronchodilator and has been found to decrease uterine contractions. Terbutaline (Brethine) can be given by a subcutaneous injection or orally. Nursing assessment for women using a terbutline pump include assessment to evaluate the presence of tachycardia, weight gain, and congestive heart failure. Terbutaline can cause elevations in blood glucose levels; therefore, frequent monitoring for hyperglycemia should be done.

Magnesium sulfate, a drug used to treat preeclampsia, has also been found to decrease uterine contractions. Many physicians prefer magnesium sulfate over Brethine because it is less stressful on the heart. A loading dose of four grams is usually administered over 20 minutes and maintained at 2 grams per hour. A Foley catheter with hourly intake and output monitoring should be part of the nursing care plan. Magnesium levels should be checked every six hours to monitor for toxicity. Signs of toxicity include absence of the knee-jerk reflex, oliguria, and decreased respirations. The normal magnesium level is 1.4–2.5 meq/dL and the therapeutic range for client receiving magnesium therapy is 4.0–9.6 meq/L. If the client becomes toxic while taking magnesium sulfate, the nurse should contact the doctor, who will order calcium gluconate, the antidote for magnesium sulfate. Magnesium is usually given intravenously by pump or controller until contractions are under control. If labor progresses and the infant is delivered prematurely, the infant can have signs of hypermagnesium. These signs include decreased muscle tone, drowsiness, and hypercalcemia. When the client is discharged, she might be required to continue magnesium sulfate orally.

Respiratory distress and bronchopulmonary dysplasia are common in preterm infants. If the preterm labor cannot be stopped, the doctor might order betamethasone (Decadron) to speed lung maturity. The injection should be administered intramuscularly to the mother at least 24–48 hours prior to delivery and no longer than seven days before birth to optimize the effects of the drugs.

Fetal Malpresentation

Fetal malpresentation can result in injury to the fetus and a long and painful labor. The most common type of presentation and the one that provides the best outcome is the vertex or head presentation. When the fetus presents in any of the following presentations, the risk of a poor outcome increases:

▶ **Brow presentation:** Fetal forehead presents first.

▶ **Face presentation:** May result in bruising and swelling to the face.

▶ **Breech presentation:** There are three types of breech presentation. With a breech presentation, there is increased risk for the need for a cesarean delivery. The three types of breech presentation are

  ▶ Frank breech, in which the sacrum presents first with the legs extended.

  ▶ Complete breech involves the sacrum with the knees flexed.

  ▶ Footling breech is the presentation of one or both legs first.

Post-term Labor and Birth

Post-term birth is defined as a delivery occurring beyond 42 weeks gestations or 294 days from the first day of the last menstrual period. The risk to both mother and fetus with post-term delivery are primarily due to the size of the baby and dysfunctional labor. Risk factors also increase with the use of forceps and suction delivery. Vaginal lacerations and retained placenta increase the incidence of bleeding. Birth trauma and shoulder dystocia are other risk factors associated with post-term deliveries. With aging of placenta often comes the risk of poor placental perfusion. Many physicians prefer to induce labor if spontaneous labor does not occur.

Precipitate Delivery

Precipitate delivery is generally a labor and delivery that are two to four hours in length. This rapid dilation of the cervix and descent of the baby through the birth canal increases the danger of hypoxia in the post-delivery period. Oxygen supplementation, suctioning, and preventing heat loss through conduction, convection, radiation, and evaporation is part of the nursing care.

Cord Prolapse

Umbilical cord prolapse occurs when the umbilical cord is expelled with rupture of the membranes. Factors that contribute to the occurrence of a prolapsed umbilical cord are breech presentation, premature birth, multiple gestation pregnancies, and polyhydramnios. If pressure is exerted on the cord by the presenting fetal part, fetal hypoxia results. Manual pressure on the head or presenting part might be required to relieve pressure on the presenting umbilical cord. Treatments include placing the client in Trendelenburg or knee-chest position, rapid IV infusion of normal saline or lactated Ringer's solution, and oxygen administration. Vital signs and fetal heart tones are evaluated, and the client is readied for a cesarean section. If the cord remains outside the uterus, drying will occur, causing a loss of oxygen-carrying capacity. Treatment with sterile saline soaks is recommended until a cesarean section can be performed.

Cesarean Birth

There are several situations that contribute to the need for a cesarean birth. Some examples are

- ▶ Fetal malpresentation.

- ▶ Fetal distress.

- ▶ Cephalopelvic disproportion. The definition of cephalopelvic disproportion is when the fetus-presenting part is too large for the maternal pelvis

- ▶ Maternal hypertension/HELLP. This is an acronym for hemolysis, elevated liver enzymes, and low platelets.

- ▶ Maternal diabetes.

- ▶ Active genital herpes.

- ▶ Previous cesarean sections and fear of uterine rupture. A vaginal birth after a cesarean section delivery (VBAC) can be attempted if there is minimal scarring of the uterus.

- ▶ Prolapsed umbilical cord.

- ▶ Hemorrhage due to abruptio placenta.

- ▶ Placenta previa.

Risk factors associated with cesarean section deliveries are much like other major surgery risks. The nurse assigned to care for the client who has had a cesarean delivery should assess the client for signs of infection, hemorrhage, urinary problems, thrombophlebitis, and other post-surgical complications. Because a cesarean section delivery is often done when the fetus is too large to pass through the birth canal, hemorrhage is a risk. Post-partal management with oxytocin (Pitocin) helps to decrease the potential for hemorrhage.

Prior to surgery, the client's blood is tested to detect anemia and bleeding times. Surgical, blood transfusions, and anesthesia permits must be obtained prior to surgery. An abdominal shave is usually ordered and a Foley catheter is inserted to monitor urinary output.

Following surgery dressing changes using sterile technique will be ordered. Antibiotics might be ordered prophylactically to treat any infection present. Pain management with narcotics or other analgesics will be ordered. Ambulation will be encouraged to help to promote blood flow to the extremities and help to decrease the likelihood of thrombus formation. The client should be instructed to refrain from lifting anything heavier than her baby or driving for approximately two weeks. Deep breathing, coughing, and the use of an incentive spirometer help to prevent lung complications. The client should be monitored for return of bowel sounds and the first bowel movement. Maintaining fluid and electrolytes with oral and intravenous fluid ensures hydration.

Assisted Birth

Use of forceps or vacuum extraction helps to shorten the second stage of labor. Forceps, an instrument applied to the presenting part, assist in the movement of the fetus to the perineum. Vacuum extraction is thought by some physicians to be safer. A cup is placed on the presenting part and, through suction applied to the infant, the physician pulls the fetus to the perineum where it can be delivered. A caput succedaneum, edema of the head that crosses the suture line, is often a result of vacuum extraction, but this method is otherwise believed to be harmless.

Fetal Monitoring

Fetal monitoring can be done continuously by using an external tocodynamometer monitor. *External monitoring* is a noninvasive procedure that allows the nurse to observe the fetal heart tones and uterine contractions. Internal fetal monitoring is recommended if fetal heart tones and contractions cannot be evaluated externally. The duration of a contraction is evaluated by measuring from the beginning of a contraction to the end of the same contraction. The frequency of a contraction is evaluated by measuring from the beginning of one contraction to the beginning of the next contraction or from the peak of one contraction to the peak of the next.

Bradycardia is a deceleration of fetal heart tones. Decelerations are associated with fetal hypoxia. The three types of decelerations are as follows:

▶ **Early decelerations:** Transitory drops in the fetal heart rate caused by head compression. If the client is complete and pushing and the baby is in a cephalic presentation, this finding is relatively benign. An early deceleration mirrors the contraction in depth and length. If there is a rapid return to the baseline fetal heart rate and the fetal heart rate is within normal range, no treatment is necessary. Figure 15.1 shows graphs of early decelerations.

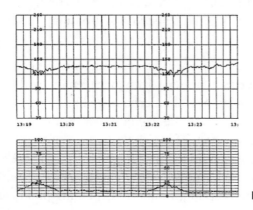

FIGURE 15.1   Early decelerations.

Note the drop in the fetal heart tones prior to the peak of the contraction. If good variability and return to normal baseline fetal heart tones, no treatment is necessary.

▶ **Variable deceleration:** V-shaped transitory decreases in the fetal heart tones that occur anytime during the contraction. They can also occur when no contractions are present. Variable decelerations are caused by cord compression (see Figure 15.2). Possible causes of variable decelerations are cord compression, prolapsed cord, and a cord that is entangled or around the baby's neck (nuchal cord). Because hypoxia can result from the cord being compressed, intervention is required. Treatment includes Trendelenburg position; oxygen administration; IV fluids; amnioinfusion with warm, sterile normal saline or lactated ringers; and notification of the physician. If fetal distress continues, the client should be prepared for a C-section.

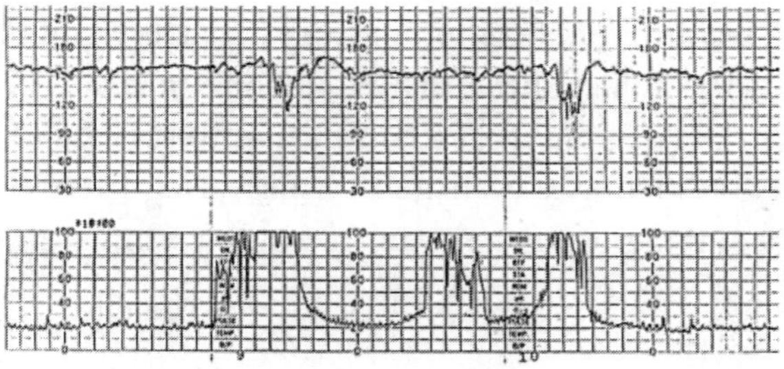

FIGURE 15.2   Variable decelerations.

Note the drop in the fetal heart tones that are V-shaped and do not correlate to the contractions. These decelerations are caused by cord compression. The treatment is to turn the client to the side, turn off Pitocin, and apply oxygen. Contact the doctor if these continue after treatment.

▶ **Late decelerations**—Drops in the fetal heart tones late in the contraction are caused by utero-placental insufficiency. These decelerations are U-shaped and mirror the contractions. Late decelerations are ominous because they result in fetal hypoxia. Treatments for these decelerations include discontinuing Pitocin, applying oxygen, and changing the mother's position. The recommended position is left side–lying. If late decelerations continue despite interventions, the physician should be notified to expedite delivery. Figure 15.3 shows graphs of late decelerations.

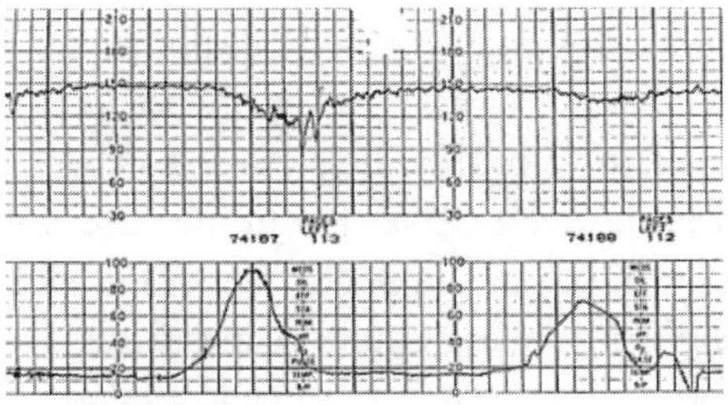

FIGURE 15.3   Late decelerations.

Pharmacologic Management of Labor

Several methods are used to relieve the pain of labor, including

▶ **Sedatives:** Examples include barbiturates, narcotics, and agonist-antagonist compounds. Butorphanol (Stadol) and nalbuphine (Nubain) are two agonist medications commonly used in labor. These drugs provide pain relief with little suppression of fetal heart tones. To decrease the amount of medication crossing the placental barrier, the medication should slowly be administered via IV push during a contraction. Ataractics such as promethazine (Phenergan) can also be used to relieve pain and prevent nausea associated with labor.

▶ **Nerve blocks:** Several types of nerve blocks are useful in labor. The following six items are examples of nerve blocks:

 ▶ **Local infiltration:** This uses xylocaine for an episiotomy.

 ▶ **Pudendal block:** Useful for the second stage of labor, episiotomy, and birth, this blocks nerve impulses to the perineum, cervix, and vagina.

 ▶ **Subarachnoid (spinal) anesthesia:** This is injected through the third, fourth, or fifth lumbar interspace into the subarachnoid space. It is useful in relieving uterine pain. Because complete anesthesia is achieved, the client should be observed for hypotension and bradycardia. She will probably be unable to assist with pushing during the third stage of labor.

> **NOTE**
>
> Leakage of spinal fluid can result in a headache. The client should be maintained supine following delivery for eight hours, and fluids should be encouraged. If a spinal headache occurs following spinal anesthesia, the doctor might perform a blood patch. A blood patch is done by injecting maternal blood into the space where spinal fluid is being lost. This allows for quicker replenishing of spinal fluid and restoration of equilibrium.

▶ **Epidural block:** This is useful for uterine labor pain. This type of anesthesia is commonly used in laboring clients because it does not suppress fetal heart tones and does not result in complete anesthesia. This type of anesthesia is also preferable because there is no entry to the dura and less likelihood of spinal fluid leakage. The client that has an epidural block is able to assist with pushing, but is relatively free of pain. Maternal hypotension is a complication. Two thousand milliliters of IV fluid should be given immediately prior to an epidural or spinal anesthesia to prevent hypotension. This increase in the amount of circulating volume helps prevent the associated hypotension. If hypotension occurs, the nurse should increase the IV infusion, apply oxygen, and reposition the client on her left side. Platelet counts should be monitored. Obstetric clients having epidural anesthesia often complain of shivering; explain to the client that this is expected and provide extra blankets.

▶ **Spinal/epidural narcotics:** Narcotics can be administered into the spinal or epidural space. Fentanyl or morphine is commonly used. Side effects include nausea, itching, urinary retention, and respiratory distress.

▶ **General anesthesia:** This is rarely used for the laboring client and is reserved for cesarean section deliveries.

Postpartum Care

To reduce bleeding and improve uterine tone, the nurse should massage the fundus often. Oxytocin (Pitocin) is often used to augment uterine contractions after the placenta delivers. *Lochia rubra*, or bright red bleeding, occurs after delivery and lasts approximately three days. *Lochia serosa*, or blood and serous fluid, is usually noted on the third or fourth postpartum day. *Lochia alba*, or the white or clear discharge, can last several weeks following delivery. Allowing breast feeding immediately after delivery is encouraged because it stimulates oxytocin release and uterine contractions.

An episiotomy is often performed to prevent laceration of the vagina and perineum. Assessment for REEDA (redness, edema, ecchymosis, discharge, and approximation of the wound) should be performed by the nurse to ensure healing.

Applying ice packs to the perineum for the first 12– 24 hours helps to decrease pain and swelling of the perineum. After the first 24 hours, heat packs or sitz baths help to relieve pain and increase healing. Urinary retention often increases postpartal bleeding and is a problem during the early postpartal period, especially in clients who have epidural or spinal anesthesia for relief of labor pain. If the nurse notes that the fundus is deviated to the side, the bladder is probably distended. Encourage the client to void, or insert a French or Foley catheter to empty the bladder and enhance uterine contractions.

Breast feeding is suggested by some physicians because breast milk provides added immunity to infectious diseases and helps to decrease the incidence of allergies. Colostrum is the first liquid to come into the breast on approximately the third post-partal day. When teaching the mother regarding breast feeding, tell the mother to clean the breast with water one time per day. Alcohol and soaps can cause drying and breast irritation. A support bra is suggested and breast-feeding pads can prevent leakage of milk and soiling. Heat is suggested to help bring in breast milk and ice is suggested if the mother decides not to breast feed. Breast binders are also helpful in preventing engorgement. Infants should produce six or more wet diapers if they are getting adequate fluid with feedings.

TIP

A good way to remember nursing assessment need during the postpartal period is BUBBLEDE: (**B**reast, **U**terus, **B**ladder, **B**owels, **L**ochia, **E**pisiotomy, **D**eep vein thrombus, **E**motional status).

Newborn Care

After cutting the umbilical cord, the physician hands the infant to the nurse. The nurse should dry the infant and suction the mouth first and then the nose. Stimulation of the infant to cry helps to increase oxygen to the lungs and brain. The nurse might be asked to assess the infant using an Activity, Pulse, Grimace, Appearance, Respiration (APGAR) score. This survey is done at one and five minutes.

Table 15.1 outlines APGAR scoring.

TABLE 15.1   APGAR Scoring

Characteristic Score	0	1	2
Activity (muscle tone)	Limp	Some flexion	Active
Pulse (heart rate)	Absent	Slow / less than100 bpm	Over 100 bpm
Grimace (reflex irritability)	None	Grimace	Cry
Appearance (color)	Cyanotic	Acrocyanosis	Pink
Respiration	Absent	Weak	Strong

The infant should be dried immediately and the head covered to prevent cold stress. Identifying banding should be placed on each of the infant's ankles and the nurse might perform a rapid head to toe assessment including auscultation of the heart and lungs. In some facilities, footprinting is done to further identify the infant. Allowing breast feeding in the delivery room is often encouraged to increase bonding and promote uterine contractions. Some cultures do not believe that colostrum is good for the baby, so the nurse should investigate cultural preferences prior to implementing breast feeding. Cord blood to check for conjugated and unconjugated bilirubin should be sent to the lab to determine the presence of Rh factor. If the infant is found to be Rh positive and the mother is Rh negative, exchange transfusions might be required as well as administration of RhoGAM within 72 hours of birth. If the client experiences a miscarriage RhoGam is also administered to prevent antibody formation to the Rh factor.

On admission to the nursery, the nurse should check the infant's vital signs including a temperature. After the first passage of stool, a rectal temperature can be checked; however, until that time, the temperature should be checked axillary because an imperforate anus might be present. For this reason, most hospitals refrain from performing rectal temperatures. After the baby is taken to the nursery, the baby is weighed and measured for head circumference and length and placed in a radiate warmer. Blood glucose levels might be checked to determine hypoglycemia. The normal blood glucose in the neonate is 40–60 mg/dL. This test is done by sticking the lateral aspect of the infant's heel. If the blood glucose is found to be extremely low, dextrose might be given either orally or by IV catheter. Bilirubin levels are done to determine the need for phototherapy. A complete blood count is checked to determine anemia and infections. The normal hemoglobin in the newborn is 14–20 gm per 100 mL.

Antibiotic drops or ointment such as erythromycin is placed in the eyes to prevent opthalmia neonatorum caused by contamination during childbirth. Administration of Vitamin K (AquaMEPHYTON) is given to the infant to prevent bleeding. Vitamin K is produced in the gastrointestinal tract starting soon after microorganisms are introduced. Until approximately eight days, infants do not have vitamin K in their intestines and tend to bleed. Another medication commonly given to the newborn while in the nursery is the HBIG (HBV [Hepatitis B Virus] Immune Globulin) vaccine. Prior to discharge, the baby is checked for phenylketonuria, thyroid functions, and lactose intolerance. Genetic anomalies might also be tested to determine chromosomal aberrations.

Terms Associated with the Normal Newborn

The following terms are associated with normal newborns. You should be familiar with these terms for the exam:

- **Acrocyanosis:** This is a bluish discoloration of the hands and feet of the newborn.

- **APGAR scoring:** This permits a rapid assessment of the need for resuscitation based on five signs. This survey is done at one and five minutes. Table 15.1 demonstrates the measures for APGAR scoring.

- **Ballard score:** This survey is used to determine neuromuscular and physical characteristics of the newborn. The higher the score, the more mature the newborn is. The finding is then plotted on a graft along with weight, length, and head circumference.

- **Brazelton Scale (Neonatal Behavioral Assessment Scale):** This scale can be done on infants up to two months and, it measures 28 behaviors and 18 reflex items. These behaviors are then plotted on a graph.

- **Caput succedaneum:** This is an edema that crosses the suture line on the baby's scalp.

- **Cephalohematoma:** This is blood that does not cross the suture line on the baby's scalp.

- **Hyperbilirubinemia:** An elevation in the infant's bilirubin level caused by an immature liver. Although the baby will become jaundiced, no treatment is necessary. The mother should be taught to place the baby in the sunshine to help with breakdown of the bilirubin.

- **Milia:** These are tiny, white bumps that occur across the newborn's nose.

- **Mongolian spots:** These are darkened discolorations that occur on the sacral area of dark-skinned infants.

Rh Incompatibility

Problems with hemolysis occur if the mother is Rh negative and the fetus is Rh positive. Maternal and fetal blood do not mix in utero until the third stage of labor, when the placenta separates from the wall of the uterus. At that time, a fetal-maternal transfusion can occur. This mixing of incompatible blood types causes isoimmunization and a transfusion reaction.

Usually no problems are seen in the first pregnancy. If, however, the mother becomes pregnant with another Rh-positive fetus, her body will react as if the fetus were a foreign object and destroy the baby's red blood cells. This destruction is known as *erythroblastosis fetalis*.

To prevent isoimmunization, the mother should be given RhoGAM during pregnancy as early as 20 weeks or postpartally within the first 48–72 hours. *Kernictertus* is the condition that results when unconjugated bilirubin crosses the blood-brain barrier. This often results in conditions such as cerebral palsy. Infants with pathologic jaundice should be assessed for alertness, presence of a high-pitched cry, hydrops fetalis, seizure activity, and a decreased sucking reflex. Treatment for pathological jaundice involves exchange transfusion either in utero or immediately after delivery.

Physiologic jaundice is a benign condition resulting from an immature liver. As the amount of conjugated bilirubin builds in the baby's blood, the infant becomes jaundice. This jaundice does not become evident until 48–72 hours and, although it does cause the infant to be irritable, it does not cause brain damage. Treatment of physiological jaundice includes placing the baby under a bili light. The bili lights should be placed 12–30 inches from the infant to prevent burning of the infant and skin irritation. Clothing should be removed and the eyes and genitals covered to prevent damage to fragile tissue. Feedings and fluids should be increased to promote defecation and urination. The infant should be turned often and vital signs should be monitored frequently. When the baby is ready for discharge, the mother should be instructed to place the baby's crib in the sunlight.

Women's Health Issues

It is important for the nurse to be aware of the most common types of illnesses effecting women. This section includes the most common issues effecting women and the treatment of each.

Pelvic Inflammatory Disease

Pelvic inflammatory disease (PID) is an infection or inflammation of the fallopian tubes, uterus, ovaries, and other surrounding tissues. There are several causes of pelvic inflammatory disease. Some of these include sexually transmitted diseases such as gonorrhea. Pelvic inflammatory disease can be acute or chronic. Subjective signs include abdominal cramping, nausea, and malaise. If untreated adhesions, sterility and peritonitis can result. The treatment for underlying infections includes use of antibiotics and medications for pain. Surgical intervention is sometimes used to open blockages in the tube.

Menopause

Menopause refers to the ending of menses. During the postmenopausal period, changes occur in the reproductive system and other organs. When estrogen levels decline, the uterus becomes smaller, the vagina and labia atrophy, and vaginal tissue becomes thinner. Irritation of tissue can lead to infection and pain. Use of estrogen replacements either systemically or in the form of a vaginal cream help to treat senile vaginitis and promote comfort. Other symptoms of menopause include hot flashes, depression, and decreased libido. Oral estrogen and progesterone combination drugs help to treat symptoms and prevent osteoporosis. These drugs, however, have been associated with coronary artery disease and breast and uterine cancer. Clients should be informed of the risk and benefits of these drugs. Other drugs used to treat postmenopausal symptoms of hot flashes include herbal preparations. Osteoporosis can be prevented and treated with calcium supplementation in combination with vitamin D. Drugs such as alendronate (Fosamax), risedronate (Atonel), raloxifene (Evista), and calcitonin (Miacalcin) help to replace and prevent bone loss. Weight-bearing exercises such as walking should be encouraged to promote bone calcification and prevent bone loss.

Maternal Infections

Infections during pregnancy are responsible for significant mortality and morbidity. Sexually transmitted infections are detrimental to the mother and fetus and should be treated promptly. Some vaginal infections such as candida, a fungal infection, are treated with antifungal drugs. Other infections affecting women include those spread by intercourse as outlined in Table 15.2.

TABLE 15.2   Sexually Transmitted Infections

Disease	Symptoms	Diagnosis	Treatment
Syphilis (caused by the spirochete Treponema pallidum)	Primary stage: Chancre, regional lymph node enlargement that disappears within six weeks. Secondary stage: Malaise, low-grade fever, sore throat, headache, muscle aches, generalized rash, and pustules that disappear in 4–12 weeks. Tertiary stage: Benign lesions of skin and mucosa and heart and central nervous system involvement.	VDRL, RPR, FTA-ABS (fluorescent treponemal antibody absorption test; it's most sensitive to all stages).	Penicillin or other antibiotics.
Gonorrhea (caused by gram-negative bacteria Neisseria gonorrhea; onset occurs 3–10 days after exposure)	Males: Dysuria and yellowish-green discharge. Females: Dysuria, vaginal discharge, no symptoms in many; late in course of the illness, pelvic inflammatory disease can occur.	Culture of discharge.	Penicillin, tetracycline, Rocephin 125 mg IM in a single dose with Vibramycin 100 mg twice daily for one week.
Chlamydia trachomatis (caused by a bacteria; onset occurs in 1–3 weeks)	Males: Urethritis, dysuria, frequent urination, discharge. Females: Frequent urination and mucopurulent cervicitis.	Gram stain of the discharge.	Vibramycin 100 mg twice daily. Azithromycin one gram and treat the client and partner.
Genital herpes (HSV2) (caused by a virus; incubation period is 2–4 weeks)	Local symptoms are caused by blisters, which erupt and leave shallow ulcers that disappear after 2–6 weeks. Systemic symptoms include fever, malaise, anorexia, painful inguinal lymph nodes, and dysuria. HSV harbors in one or more of the nerve ganglia. Physical and emotional stress trigger recurrent episodes. (If there is an active lesion during labor, a cesarean section is performed because direct contact can lead to transmission of the virus to the infant.)	Direct visualization of lesions and a viral culture.	Antiviral medications such as acyclovir.

(continues)

TABLE 15.2 *Continued*

Disease	Symptoms	Diagnosis	Treatment
Condylomata acuminate (caused by human papilloma virus [HPV] that is transmitted by skin-to-skin contact; the presence of HPV has been linked to vaginal and cervical cancers)	A dry wart located on the vulva, cervix, rectum, or vagina.	Visualization, biopsy, and Pap smear.	Antiviral medications, Podophyllin 20% in tincture of benzoin (Podophyllin is not recommended for pregnant clients because this drug can cause birth defects) or Antineoplastics such as 5-FU have been used successfully. Imiquinod cream (Aldara0, trichloro aceticacid (TCA) can be used during pregnancy. Cryotheraphy. Recently, the FDA has approved Gardasil (Human papilloma virus vaccine), a vaccine for the prevention of types 6, 11, and 18 HPV. This vaccine is recommended for girls ages 9–26. The medication is given by injection in three doses, The first at a time suggested by the client's physician, the second two months later, and the third six months after the first dose.
Human immuno-deficiency virus/ acquired immuno-deficiency syndrome (acquired primarily through blood and other body fluids)	Seroconversion to HIV occurs in approximately 10 weeks. Many opportunistic illness can affect the client, including parasitic infections (enterocolitis), bacterial (tuberculosis), viral infections (cytomegalovirus), fungal infections (candidiasis), and malignancies (Kaposi's sarcoma).	ELISA; western blot; viral T-cell count. A T-cell count of less than 200 indicates that the client is at risk for opportunistic diseases. Load/burden; a viral load of less than 400 copies/mL indicates the client is relatively free of circulating virus. A white blood cell count less than 3,200 requires evaluation. Presence of opportunistic infections.	Antiviral medications: Nucleoside analog transcriptase inhibitors (AZT, primarily Zidovudine, is given to the pregnant client and the infant after delivery). Non-nucleoside reverse transcriptase inhibitors. Protease inhibitors. Highly active antiretroviral therapy (HAART), previously known as an AIDS cocktail, is a combination of these medications given in conjunction with other medications used to treat anemia and infections. Bactrim is used to treat Pneumocystis carinii pneumonia (PCP). Blood and body fluids should be cleaned up with a hypochlorite solution (1 part bleach and 10 parts water).

NOTE

Clients with herpes can breast feed if there is no lesion on the breast. Clients with HIV cannot breast feed because of the risk of transmission of the HIV infection to the infant.

Methods of Contraception

Contraception is the voluntary prevention of pregnancy. This can be accomplished using several methods as outlined in Table 15.3.

TABLE 15.3   Contraception Methods

Method Name	Description	Effectiveness
Coitus interruptus	Withdrawal of the penis from the vagina before ejaculation.	Not very effective and should be discouraged. It does not prevent STDs.
Abstinence	Voluntarily refraining from sexual intercourse.	Very reliable if the client abstains from sexual intercourse and there is no presence of ejaculatory fluid.
Rhythm method	The client is instructed to refrain from intercourse during ovulation.	Very reliable if the client has adequate knowledge of ovulation. Ovulation usually occurs 12–18 days after the first day of the menstrual cycle. The client's temperature decreases and then sharply rises at the time of ovulation.
Cervical mucus method	The cervical mucus method is also called the Billings Method and the Creighton Model. This method helps the client determine whether ovulation has occurred. If the mucus is slippery, the client should abstain from sexual intercourse until ovulation is past.	Adequate amounts of thin cervical mucus is required for the sperm to have motility. This method of birth control is less effective than many others because it requires the client to make a judgment of the consistency of the mucus.
Barrier methods	Condom/Diaphragm: One concern with the use of a diaphragm is the occurrence of Toxic Shock Syndrome, a potentially life-threatening problem caused by bacterial invasion of the uterus. To prevent the occurrence of this problem, the woman should be taught to clean the diaphragm after each use and remove it after eight hours. She should not use the diaphragm during menses. Signs of TSS include hypotension, fever, dizziness, and a rash. Treatment includes antibiotics. Condoms are the only method of birth control that is also helpful in preventing sexually transmitted infections. Latex condoms are recommended.	Very reliable. Latex condoms also help decrease the incidence of STDs. The condom should be removed from the vagina while the penis is still erect. Diaphragms should be resized if the client gains or loses 10 pounds, has abdominal surgery, or has a baby. The diaphragm is used in conjunction with spermicidal gel or cream and should be left in for 6–8 hours after intercourse. The client should not douche after intercourse.
Hormonal methods	Birth control pills.	Very reliable if taken consistently. If the client misses a pill, she should be instructed to take it as soon as she remembers. If she misses more than two, another method of contraception such as a condom should be used until the end of the cycle. If antibiotics are taken, oral contraceptives might be ineffective.
Intrauterine device (IUD)	Several types exist. These prevent implantation, not fertilization.	Very reliable. They should not be used in clients with a history of PID, diabetes, or bleeding disorders.

(continues)

TABLE 15.3 *Continued*

Method Name	Description	Effectiveness
Sterilization (tubal ligation and vasectomy)	Tubal fulguration in females is the destruction of a portion of the fallopian tube by an electric current. A vasectomy is cutting the vasa deferentia to prevent the passage of sperm.	Very reliable.

Case Study

A 35-year-old primigravida who is 34 weeks gestation is admitted with a blood pressure of 190/98. She has been experiencing abdominal pain and nausea for the last two days. On further examination, she is found to have a BUN of 30 and a platelet count of 75,000.

1. What other laboratory test would the nurse expect the doctor to order?

2. What interventions should the nurse take to facilitate lowering of the blood pressure and promoting comfort?

3. What medication will the doctor order to lower the blood pressure?

4. During the administration of magnesium sulfate, what nursing interventions will be instituted to ensure safe administration of this drug?

5. The client is diagnosed with HELLP syndrome. What does this acronym stand for?

6. The doctor decides to perform a cesarean section delivery. What preparation is necessary for a cesarean section delivery of a premature infant?

7. What postpartum problems should the nurse anticipate?

Answers to Case Study

1. The nurse should expect the doctor to order a complete blood count, other liver enzymes, and urinary studies to check for creatinine and protein.

2. Bed rest will be ordered and the client should be instructed to rest on her side, preferably on the left side to promote renal perfusion. The room should be dark and visitors should be limited. Keeping the room quiet and dark promotes rest and assist in lowering the blood pressure.

3. Magnesium sulfate is the drug of choice for the client with preeclampsia.

4. During magnesium sulfate administration, the nurse would anticipate and order a Foley catheter insertion with hourly intake and output monitoring. The medication should be administered through an intravenous controller to be sure that the correct amount of medication is administered. Magnesium levels should be checked every six to eight hours to check for a therapeutic level (4.0–9.6 meq/L) and signs of toxicity should be evaluated. The signs of toxicity are absence of the knee jerk reflexes, oliguria, and respirations of less than 12 per minute.

5. HELLP stands for hemolysis, elevated liver enzymes, and low platelets.

(continues)

(continued)

6. To prepare the client for a cesarean section, delivery the nurse should anticipate an order for the Foley catheter to be continued. Intravenous fluids will be ordered to assure hydration. The client should be instructed to remain NPO until after the surgery. A preoperative medication to begin sedation will most likely be ordered and an abdominal prep and shave will be done. Permits for blood administration and surgical intervention must be signed and psychological interventions will help the client to cope with the pregnancy termination. Because this infant will be born premature, there are risks, requiring the need to alert the neonatal intensive care unit and calling the neonatologist.

7. Because the client's platelet count is low, bleeding is a concern. Blood and platelet transfusions might be ordered. Continued monitoring of blood pressures and other vital signs must be done and precautions taken to prevent seizures. Magnesium sulfate will most likely be continued and the client should be checked for magnesium levels. Calcium gluconate, the antidote for magnesium sulfate, and a tracheostomy set should be kept at the bedside.

Key Concepts

This chapter includes much-needed information to help the nurse apply knowledge of the childbearing and neonatal client to the NCLEX exam. The nurse preparing for the licensure exam should be familiar with commonly ordered lab tests, including normal lab values, and medications, used to treat the childbearing and neonatal client.

Key Terms

▶ Abortion

▶ Alpha-fetoprotein

▶ Amenorrhea

▶ Caput succedaneum

▶ Cervix

▶ Cesarean section

▶ Chadwick's sign

▶ Colostrum

▶ Condylomata acuminate

▶ Contraception

▶ Decelerations

▶ Disseminated intravascular coagulation

▶ Dystocia

▶ Ectopic pregnancy

▶ Epidural anesthesia

▶ Estriol

▶ Fetal monitoring

▶ Fundus

▶ Goodell's sign

▶ Gravida

▶ Hegar's sign

▶ HELLP

▶ Herpes

▶ Human papillomavirus (HPV)

▶ Hydatidiform mole

▶ Hyperbilirubinemia

- Isoimmunization

- Leopold's maneuvers

- Linea nigra

- McDonald cerclage

- Multigravida

- Naegele's rule

- Oligohydramnios

- Oxytocin

- Papanicolaou smear

- Para

- Pica

- Polyhydramnios

- Preeclampsia

- Premature rupture of membranes

- Preterm labor

- Prostaglandin

- Pulmonary surfactants

- Rubella

- Sexually transmitted infections

- TORCH

- Toxic Shock Syndrome

- Toxoplasmosis

- Ultrasonography

Diagnostic Tests

The following are diagnostic tests you should review before taking the NCLEX exam.
These tests are performed to determine potential problems in the obstetric client and
the fetus:

- 24-hour urine to determine renal disease

- Alpha fetoprotein to determine neural tube defects

- CBC to indicate anemia or infections

- Creatinine to determine renal disease

- ► Estriol levels to determine fetal well-being

- ► Ferning test/nitrozine testing to confirm amniotic fluid

- ► Glucose tolerance test to determine whether an elevated blood glucose and possibly diabetes exists

- ► L/S ratio to determine lung maturity

- ► Pap smear to detect cervical cancer

- ► Ultrasound/amniocentesis to determine fetal anomalies

- ► Urinalysis to detect kidney infections

Pharmacological Agents Used in the Care of the Obstetric Client

An integral part of care to obstetric clients is pharmacological intervention. The nursing exam reviewer needs to focus on the drugs in Table 15.4. Included in this table are the most common side and adverse effects and pertinent nursing care.

TABLE 15.4 Pharmacological Agents Used in the Care of the Obstetric Client

Name	Action	Nursing Care	Side Effects
Clomiphene citrate (Clomid)	Used to treat infertility. Causes ovulation and sustained function of the corpus luteum.	Client should be taught of the possibility of multiple gestation pregnancies. Clients experiencing blurring of vision should be reported to the doctor. Visual disturbance usually resolves within a few days of discontinuation of the medication.	Flushing of the skin. Hot flashes, midcycle abdominal pain, mittelschmerz (pain on ovulation).
Dinoprostone (Prostin E2)	Used to promote labor induction. A uterine and gastrointestinal circular smooth muscle stimulant. When used during pregnancy, it increases the amplitude and frequency of uterine contractions and induces cervical softening and dilation. Dinoprostone is used to evacuate uterine content after fetal death.	If given in gel intracervically, the hips should be elevated for at least 30 minutes to prevent loss of the gel.	Nausea, vomiting, diarrhea. Can also cause an elevated temperature. Temperatures above 100.6° should be treated. Aspirin does not inhibit drug induced hyper-pyrexia. Sponge baths and NSAIDs such as acetamino-phen (Tylenol) might be given.

TABLE 15.4 *Continued*

Name	Action	Nursing Care	Side Effects
Ergonovine maleate (Methergonovine, Ergotrate, Methergine) Hemabate	Directly stimulates uterine contractions as well as other smooth muscles.	Used to treat postpartal hemorrhage not controlled by oxytocin (Pitocin).	Headache, hypertension, nausea, vomiting. Other side effects include dizziness, dyspnea, tinnitus, and palpitations. This drug should not be given in preeclampsia or cardiac disease. Can cause suppression of lactation.
Oxytocin (Pitocin, Syntocinon)	Used to treat and prevent postpartal bleeding and to induce labor.	If given intravenously this drug must be given via an intravenously infusion controller.	Overdosing can cause hypertonic contractions and uterine rupture. Pain is usually increased with labor where oxytocin is used.
Magnesium Sulfate (MgSO4)	Used to treat pre-eclampsia of pregnancy.	Blood pressures and magnesium levels should be checked; should be given by intravenous controller; monitor for signs of toxicity that include absence of the knee jerk reflex, oliguria, and decreased respirations. The therapeutic range is 4.0–9.6 meq/L. keep calcium gluconate and a tracheostomy set at the bedside. A Foley catheter with hourly intake and output should be done.	Hot flashes, drowsiness, nausea, vomiting, and diarrhea can occur.

Apply Your Knowledge

This chapter provided information regarding the care of childbearing and neonatal clients. The following questions test your knowledge regarding the safe, effective care and management of these clients. The nurse should use the key terms, diagnostics, and pharmacological agents sections to answer these questions.

Exam Questions

1. Which of the following obstetric clients should the nurse see first?

    A. The client who is 40 weeks gestation having contractions every 5 minutes lasting 50 seconds

    B. The client who is 32 weeks gestation with terbutaline (Brethine) intravenously

    C. The one-day postpartum client who has changed two peri-pads in the last six hours

    D. The diabetic obstetric client with a blood glucose level of 90 mg/dL

2. The client visits the prenatal clinic stating she believes she is pregnant. A pregnancy test is done to detect elevated levels of:

    A. Prolactin

    B. Human chorionic gonadotropin

    C. Lecithin-sphingomyelin

    D. Estriol

3. Which instruction should be given to the client being discharged after evacuation of a hydatidiform mole?

    A. Return to the clinic in six weeks for a urinalysis

    B. Avoid exercise for at least six weeks

    C. Do not become pregnant for at least twelve months

    D. Return to the clinic in six months for liver enzyme studies

4. The pregnant client with AIDS is diagnosed with cytomegalovirus. The nurse is aware that the client probably contracted cytomegalovirus from:

    A. Blood or body fluid exposure to the virus

    B. Emptying her cat's litter box

    C. Contaminated food or water

    D. Pigeon feces

5. The client being treated for preeclampsia has an infusion of magnesium sulfate. The magnesium level is checked and found to be 6.3 meq/L. Which action by the nurse is most appropriate?

    A. Stop the magnesium sulfate and administer calcium gluconate

    B. Continue the magnesium sulfate as ordered

    C. Contact the doctor immediately

    D. Prepare for an emergency delivery

6. The pregnant client is admitted to the emergency room with a prolapsed umbilical cord. Which action is most appropriate?

    A. Cover the cord with dry, sterile gauze

    B. Place the client in high Fowler's position

    C. Push up on the presenting part with an examining finger

    D. Begin an IV of normal saline at keep-open rate

7. Which test is most diagnostic for syphilis?

    A. Culture

    B. VDRL

    C. RPR

    D. FTA-ABS

8. The client is diagnosed with genital herpes. Which medication is used to treat genital herpes?

    A. Acyclovir (Zovirax)

    B. Podophyllin

    C. AZT (Retrovir)

    D. Isoniazid (Lanzid)

9. The client with premature labor is being treated with terbutaline (Brethine). Which assessment should be done prior to beginning Brethine?

    A. Creatinine

    B. Cortisol levels

    C. Blood glucose

    D. Liver profile

10. Which finding would require intervention in the client receiving oxytocin (Pitocin) for augmentation of labor?

    A. Contractions every 5–6 minutes lasting 60 seconds

    B. Variability of 6–8 beats per minute

    C. Drops in fetal heart tones after contractions lasting 90 seconds with hesitant return to baseline

    D. Drops in fetal heart tones prior to the contractions during pushing

Answers to Exam Questions

1. Answer B is correct. The client who is 32 weeks gestation receiving Brethrine is unstable and requires further nursing assessment. Answer A is incorrect because the client who is 40 weeks gestation having contractions every five minutes lasting 50 seconds is normal. Answer C is incorrect because changing two peripads in the last six hours is normal; therefore, it is not highest priority. Answer D is incorrect because a blood glucose of 90 mg/dL is within normal limits.

2. Answer B is correct. HCG levels elevate rapidly and can be detected as early two days after the missed period. Answer A is incorrect because prolactin is elevated with a prolactinoma, a type of pituitary tumor. Answer C is incorrect because lecithin/sphingomyelin (L/S ratio) is indicative of lung maturity. Answer D is incorrect because estriol levels indicate fetal well-being.

3. Answer C is correct. The client that has experienced a hydatidiform mole should avoid becoming pregnant again for one year because chorionic carcinoma is associated with a hydatidiform mole. If the client does become pregnant and there are cells for chorionic carcinoma, the hormonal stimulation can cause rapid cell proliferation and growth of the cancer. Answer A is incorrect because a urinalysis in six weeks is not necessary. Answer B is incorrect because exercise is not contraindicated after a hydatidiform mole. Answer D is incorrect because checking liver enzymes in six months is not necessary after a hydatidiform mole.

4. Answer A is correct. Cytomegalovirus virus is transmitted predominantly by blood or body fluid exposure to the virus. Answer B is incorrect, toxoplasmosis is transmitted through contaminated cat feces. Answer C is incorrect because contaminated food or water can cause many illnesses; for example, *E. coli*, *listeria*, *Clostridium difficile*, and many others. Answer D is incorrect because histoplasmosis is transmitted by bird feces.

5. Answer B is correct. The therapeutic range for magnesium sulfate is 4.0–9.6 meq/L; therefore, with a magnesium level of 6.3meq/L, the nurse should continue the infusion. Answers A, C, and D indicate that the nurse believes the level to be toxic. This is an incorrect conclusion, making these answers incorrect.

6. Answer C is correct. The nurse should push on the presenting part to relieve pressure on the cord and facilitate blood flow through the cord. Answer A is incorrect because the sterile gauze should be moist, not dry. Answer B is incorrect because the client should be placed in Trendelenburg position, not high Fowler's position. Answer D is incorrect because the IV fluid should be rapid, not keep-open rate, to increase hydration and blood flow to the fetus.

7. Answer D is correct. The fluorescent treponemal antibody test (FTA-ABS) is most diagnostic for syphilis. Answer A is incorrect because a culture of the discharge is used to diagnose gonorrhea, not syphilis. Answers B and C are incorrect because they are screening tests and are not as diagnostic as the FTA-ABS is.

8. Answer A is correct. Acyclovir is used to treat genital herpes. Answer B is incorrect because Podophyllin is used to treat condyloma acuminata (venereal warts). Answer C is incorrect because AZT (Retrovir) is used prevent HIV transmission from mother to baby. Answer D is incorrect because isoniazid is used to treat tuberculosis, not herpes.

9. Answer C is correct. Terbutaline (Brethine) is a bronchodilator that can also relax smooth muscles. Brethine can cause elevations in blood glucose levels so the client should have blood glucose levels checked prior to beginning treatment with Brethine. Answers A, B, and D are not laboratory studies that are required prior to beginning Brethine.

10. Answer C is correct. This describes a late deceleration. These decelerations are caused by uteroplacental insufficiency and require intervention by the nurse. The treatment is STOP (**S**top Pitocin if infusing; **T**urn the client to her side; begin **O**xygen therapy; **P**repare for delivery). Increasing IV fluids helps to increase blood to the uterus. Answer A is within normal limits. Answer B is also within normal limits. Answer D is incorrect because a drop in fetal heart tones prior to the contraction describes an early deceleration caused by head compression. This is expected during pushing.

Suggested Reading and Resources

▸ McKinney, Emily Stone, Susan Rowen James, Sharon Smith Murray, and Jean Weiler Ashwill. *Maternal-Child Nursing* 2nd ed. Philadelphia: Saunders, 2005.

▸ Rinehart, Sloan, Hurd. *NCLEX-RN Exam Cram*. Indianapolis: Que Publishing, 2005.

CHAPTER SIXTEEN

Care of the Pediatric Client

There are few areas in nursing more challenging or more rewarding than working with children and their families. Most nurses who work with pediatric clients will jokingly tell you that one of the first things that attracted them to the specialty was the brightly painted walls with images of Charlie Brown, Linus, and Snoopy or the fact that they get to wear uniforms imprinted with the likeness of our favorite cartoon characters. No other unit transports patients to surgery or x-ray in a bright red wagon pulled by the staff or provides much-needed R&R in the unit play room. But taking care of a sick child involves more than reading a bedtime story or making a balloon from a surgical glove. The pediatric nurse combines the knowledge of disease process with an understanding of how illness and injury affect normal growth and development and uses the best of his /her communication skills to help parents cope with illness and injury. This chapter reviews principles of normal growth and development and some of the most common disorders affecting children as well as life-threatening conditions, including childhood cancer. Conditions of the endocrine system, which require lifetime therapy, are included in Chapter 4, "Care of the Client with Endocrine Disorders."

Growth and Development

Growth and development refers to the numerous changes that take place over a lifetime. For the nurse, growth and development represents a guide for assessing and providing care to children from birth through adolescence. Key elements include physical growth, development of gross motor and fine motor skills, and socialization through play. Although there are individual differences in growth and development, Tables 16.1–16.4 provide useful information regarding overall developmental changes.

Infant (28 Days to 1 Year)

The infancy stage is marked by rapid changes in growth and development. In fact, there is no other time in life when changes occur so quickly and dramatically. Body weight triples and length increases by 50% in the first year of life (Aren't we glad that doesn't continue!). Infant reflexes are replaced with fine motor and gross motor skills. These skills occur in an orderly fashion in a head-to-toe and center-to-peripheral sequence, which is referred to as cephalocaudal–proximodistal development. Table 16.1 summarizes infant development elements that are important for you to know for the exam.

TABLE 16.1   Key Elements in the Development of Infants

Type of Development	Characteristics
Physical growth and development	Weight: The birth weight (average is 7–9 pounds) doubles by approximately six months of age and triples by one year of age.
	Length: The length at birth (average is 19–21 inches) increases by one inch per month during the first six months of life. By one year of age, the birth length has increased by 50%.
	Head circumference: The head circumference at birth (13–14 inches) increases to an average of 17 inches by six months and 18 inches at one year of age. The posterior fontanel closes by approximately 2 months of age; the anterior fontanel closes by approximately 18 months of age. As the brain matures, the infant's reflexes (Moro, tonic neck, Babinski, stepping, and rooting) are replaced by purposeful movements that influence motor development.
	Chest circumference: The lateral diameter becomes greater than the anteroposterior diameter. By one year of age, the circumferences of the head and the chest are approximately the same.
Development of gross motor and fine motor skills	1–3 months: The infant can lift the head, grasp and hold objects for a brief period of time, and roll from side to back. The eyes become more coordinated, and the infant can focus on objects.
	3–6 months: The infant gains head control, rolls from abdomen to back, sits with support, and can move her hand to her mouth. The lower central incisors erupt and, by 6 months of age, new foods are added to the infant's diet, including crackers, melba toast, rice cereal, vegetables, fruits, meat, and egg yolk.
	9 months: The infant can sit without support, transfer objects from hand to hand, bang cubes together, play patty-cake, creep on hands and knees, and pull herself to a standing position. Upper lateral incisors begin to appear.
	12 months: The infant cruises well, can walk with one hand being held, begins to take her first steps alone, can sit down from a standing position unassisted, can turn pages in a book, and recognizes familiar pictures like animals (likes to make animal sounds). The use of a pincer grasp allows placement and retrieval of small objects. The 1-year-old has from six to eight deciduous teeth.
Socialization	1–3 months: The infant smiles, recognizes the primary caregiver, and vocalizes by cooing.
	3–6 months: The infant now socializes by imitating sounds and laughing aloud.
	9 months: The infant now reaches for familiar people, can say "mama" and "dada," and responds to simple verbal requests.
	12 months: The infant shows affection (blows kisses on request), explores away from parents, and seeks a security blanket or favorite toy when upset. The infant plays alone (solitary play) and enjoys mobiles, busy boxes, soft cuddle toys, and soft picture books.

Toddler (1–3 Years)

By the end of the first year of life, the infant has acquired the skills necessary for mobility. Sitting up and pulling to a standing position give rise to the more advanced gross motor skills of walking, running, and climbing. These skills, along with advancing fine motor development, allow the child to explore his environment as he tries to find out how things work. In the midst of toddlerdom is the stage known as *the terrible twos*, in which the most often-heard word from both parent and child is *no*. Every day is a new adventure for the toddler and getting into things is a way of life. Parenting the toddler involves allowing exploration but setting limits, overcoming the struggles of toilet training, and (in some cases) managing sibling rivalry. Table 16.2 highlights important developmental elements for toddlers.

TABLE 16.2   Key Elements in the Development of Toddlers

Type of Development	Characteristics
Physical growth and development	Weight: On average, the birth weight quadruples by the time the toddler is age 2 1/2 years. Weight gain slows to an average of 4–6 pounds per year.
	Height: The toddler is approximately one-half his adult height by the age of 2 1/2 years.
	Head circumference: The anterior fontanel closes. The head circumference is about 19 inches by 15 months of age and about 20 inches by 2 years of age. Brain growth increases to 90% of the adult size.
	Chest circumference: The chest circumference is greater than the head circumference, giving the toddler a more adult appearance.
Development of gross motor and fine motor skills	12–18 months: The toddler can kick a ball forward, walk up steps, build a tower of two or four cubes, use a spoon, drink from a cup, push and pull toys, remove clothes, and scribble with crayons or pencils.
	19–24 months: The toddler can run, jump in place, throw a ball overhand, kick a ball forward without falling, walk up and down steps with two feet on each step, build a tower of from four or six cubes, copy a vertical line, wash and dry his hands, gains bowel control, and helps dress himself.
	2–3 years: The toddler can balance on one foot, jump with both feet, take a few steps on tiptoe, ride a tricycle, build a tower of eight cubes, and copy vertical and horizontal lines. Day time bladder control has been achieved. The toddler at this age can give his first and last name and name a friend and one color.
Socialization	12–18 months: At this age, the toddler imitates housework, points to at least one named body part (nose, eyes, and so on), and has a vocabulary of 10 words.
	19–24 months: At this age, the toddler has understandable speech, can combine three or four words, has a vocabulary of 300 words, and can name pictures.
	2–3 years: At this age the toddler has a vocabulary of 900 words. The toddler plays beside another child with little or no interaction in a fashion known as parallel play. Toddlers enjoy nesting toys, picture books, push-pull toys, riding toys, pounding boards, sand, soap bubbles, talking toys, balls, dolls, and dress-up clothes.

Preschooler (3–5 Years)

If toddlers are best known for the terrible twos, the preschooler should be known as a delightful paradox. He loves secrets and yet he will share all the family secrets with a total stranger. He can recite the sweetest of prayers and yet swear like a sailor. He can be brutally honest and yet invent the tallest of tales. He explores his world; imitates the adults in it; and yet lives in the fantasy world of adventure figures, becoming them from time to time. No one has more fun than the preschooler, who will run with total aban-donment through the largest, muddiest puddle of water. Many of his baby features have given way to those of the older child. The potbelly of the toddler disappears and is replaced by a thinner, more athletic preschooler's body. Unfortunately, the potbelly will reappear when you least want it—and you can count on the preschooler to point it out to you in case you didn't notice. Although physical growth slows a bit, cognitive and language development continue at a rapid rate, preparing the child for a major life event: entering school. Table 16.3 summarizes important elements that are key to the development of preschoolers.

TABLE 16.3 Key Elements in the Development of Preschoolers

Type of Development	Characteristics
Physical growth and development	Weight: The average weight gain is about 5 pounds per year so that the 3-year-old weighs about 37 pounds, the 4-year-old about 42 pounds, and the 5-year-old about 47 pounds.
	Height: The average increase in height is about 2–3 inches per year, which is mostly due to an elongation of the legs rather than the trunk. The average 3-year-old is 37 inches tall, the average 4-year-old is 40 inches tall, and the average 5-year-old is 43 inches tall.
	Head and chest circumference: Unlike the squatty, potbellied appearance of the toddler, the physical proportions of the preschooler are more like that of the adult. The preschooler is usually slender and agile and takes great pride in showing off for others.
Development of gross motor and fine motor skills	3 years: The 3-year-old can pedal a tricycle, jump in place, broad jump, balance on one foot, walk up and down steps using alternating feet, build a tower of 9 or 10 cubes, copy a circle, put facial features on a circle, and feed and dress himself.
	4 years: The 4-year-old can balance on one foot for five seconds, walk heel to toe, catch a ball, throw a ball overhand, skip and hop on one foot, use scissors, lace shoes, copy a square, and add three parts to a stick figure.
	5 years: The 5-year-old can skip and hop on alternate feet, throw and catch a ball, jump rope, jump from a height of 12 inches, balance on alternate feet with eyes closed, tie shoelaces, use scissors, begin to print a few letters or numbers, copy a diamond and triangle, and draw a stick figure with seven to nine parts.
Socialization	3 years: The 3-year-old has a vocabulary of about 900 words and can use complete sentences of 3–4 words, asks many questions, and begins to sing songs.
	4 years: The 4-year-old understands time in relation to daily events, prizes inde-pendence, takes pride in her accomplishments, enjoys entertaining others, shares family secrets with outsiders, and commonly has an imaginary friend. Four-year-olds use sentences and have a vocabulary of 1,500 words. Egocentrism, or the inability to envision situations from perspectives other than their own, is a key feature of this age group.
	5 years: The 5-year-old has a vocabulary of approximately 2,100 words and can use sentences with 6–8 words. He asks the meaning of words and has many questions. At this age, the child can name the days of the week and the months of the year. The preschooler enjoys associative play, group play with similar or identical activities but without organization or rules. Preschoolers enjoy wading pools, tricycles, wagons, dolls, books with pictures, musical toys, finger paints, and toys that imitate objects used by adults.

School Age (6–12 Years)

School age begins with the child's entrance into the school environment, which has a profound effect on the child's development and relationship to the outside world. The freedom of expression enjoyed by the preschooler is less tolerated in the classroom, and the child learns to conform to social expectations. Associative play gives way to cooperative play in which following the rules is a must with little or no tolerance for those who do not. It is a time of leaders and followers as well as the emergence of in-crowds and out-crowds. Children with special learning needs, the overweight, those with physical limitations, and the poor often find themselves in the out-crowd, making the school years a time of loneliness and frustration. In some instances, this has later given way to school violence with tragic results. Parents and teachers can help by making children more sensitive to the needs of others and by providing opportunities for all children to achieve their potential. Table 16.4 highlights development milestones for the school-age child.

TABLE 16.4   Key Elements in the Development of School-Age Children

Type of Development	Characteristics
Physical growth and development	Weight: During the period known as school age, the child gains an average of 6–8 pounds a year, reaching an average of 85–90 pounds by age 12 years.
	Height: Between the ages of 6 and 12, children grow an average of 2 inches per year. By age 12, the child should be approximately 5 feet tall.
	Head and waist circumference: Head and waist circumference decrease in relation to standing height. Leg length increases, and the child takes on a more mature appearance. Permanent tooth eruption is complete by 12 years of age.
Development of gross motor and fine motor skills	6–8 years: The child has boundless energy, which is motor channeled into activities such as swimming, skating, biking, dancing, and sports. Fine motor skills become more developed as dexterity becomes more refined. Among the skills acquired during the early school years the ability to read, tell time, and use simple math are important.
	9–12 years: The child uses tools and equipment well, follows direction, is enthusiastic at work and at play, and looks for ways to earn money.
Socialization	6–8 years: During these years interest in group activities heighten and the child wants to be with peers. Participation in group activities such as scouting begin.
	9–12 years: The older school-age child loves secrets and might help organize secret clubs. The school-age child participates in cooperative play or activities that are organized with rules. Play activity is mostly with same-sex groups, but with some mix in the later years. The school-age child enjoys board games, video games, music, and sporting activities that are shared with others.

Adolescence (12–18 Years)

Adolescence is a time of rapid growth with the peak growth spurt spanning 24–36 months. Secondary sex characteristics appear, with physical and sexual maturity occurring in late adolescence. Next to the first year of life, adolescence is the second most rapid period of physical growth.

By the onset of menarche, girls have achieved approximately 95% of their mature height. Growth in height generally ceases by age 17 in girls and age 18–20 in boys. Boys generally gain more in height and weight than girls. In early adolescence (12–15 years), the teen is usually uncoordinated with awkward movements due to the increasing length of the legs and the size of the feet. In later adolescence (16–18 years), the teen has increased coordination with more graceful movement. This no doubt accounts for the perfecting of athletic ability in high school and college.

The teen years represent a time of developmental crisis for the adolescent as well as the parents. The adolescent is usually on an emotional roller coaster, with highs and lows and periods of sociability and isolation. The desire for increased independence and changing roles within the family often leads to parent-child conflicts. Peer relationships are all-important and friendships can replace the influence parents have had during the childhood years. Adolescents enjoy music, sports, video games, and activities where there are others of the same age.

TIP

You should review nursing textbooks for Erikson's Theory of Psychosocial Development, Kohlberg's Theory of Moral Development, and Piaget's Theory of Cognitive Development as they relate to normal growth and development.

Caring for the Child with Respiratory Disorders

These disorders include infections of the upper airway and lower airway and as well as infections of the ears. Three points should be made about respiratory disorders in children:

▶ Respiratory disorders are more common, and often more serious, in infants and children than adults. Some infections, such as otitis media, occur with greater frequency because of anatomical differences.

▶ Although all children are at risk, certain children are more vulnerable to respiratory disorders. This includes premature and low birth weight infants and children with AIDS.

▶ Children with respiratory disorders are more likely than adults to develop gastrointestinal symptoms such as vomiting and diarrhea, which increase the risk of dehydration and acidosis.

This section focuses on the care of children with the most common pediatric respiratory disorders.

Upper Airway Infections

Respiratory infections are generally classified according to the involvement of structures in the upper or lower airway. Upper airway infections include those disorders that affect the nose and pharynx. Common upper respiratory infections include tonsillitis, acute otitis media, and the croup syndromes.

Tonsillitis

Tonsillitis often accompanies pharyngitis and is a major cause of illness in young children. The tissue referred to as *tonsils* is actually made up of several pairs of lymphoid tissue:

- The adenoids
- The lingual tonsils
- The palatine tonsils
- The pharyngeal tonsils

Symptoms of tonsillitis include

- Sore throat
- Swollen glands in the jaw and neck
- Difficulty swallowing and breathing
- Enlargement of the tonsils
- Inability to smell and taste
- Mouth breathing
- Snoring

The condition can be viral or bacterial in origin. Viral infections are usually self-limited, and management is aimed at relieving the symptoms of soreness and dryness of the throat.

Tonsillitis is usually caused by a virus; therefore, management focuses on the relief of symptoms. However, if the infection is caused by Group A beta hemolytic streptococcus, antibiotic therapy is ordered. A *tonsillectomy*—surgical removal of the palatine tonsils—is indicated if tonsillar enlargement interferes with eating or breathing, if there are frequent bouts of tonsillitis (5–7 during a 12 month period),if there is a recurrent history of frequent streptococcal infection, or if there is a history of peritonsillar abscesses. An *adenoidectomy*—surgical removal of the adenoids—is recommended if enlarged adenoids block breathing. In most cases, the tonsils are not removed before 3 years of age because of the possible complications associated with blood loss in very young children and the possibility of the regrowth of lymphoid tissue.

Preoperative nursing care includes obtaining a detailed history (including a history of unusual bleeding), assessing for signs of upper respiratory infection, and noting whether any teeth are loose. Routine vital signs are obtained to serve as a baseline for postoperative comparison, and a bleeding and clotting time are requested.

Postoperatively, the child should be closely observed for continual swallowing, which is an indication of bleeding. An ice collar can be applied to the throat to increase comfort, and analgesics can be given intravenously or rectally for the first 24 hours to decrease pain and promote rest. Use of a cool mist humidifier helps to soothe the child's irritated throat. When the child is awake and responsive, ice chips and cool, clear liquids are given. Popsicles should be offered to the child with a tonsillectomy because they are soothing to the sore throat and provide a source of liquid and sugar. Citrus foods, hot foods, and foods with rough textures should be avoided as well as foods that are red, orange, or brown in color. At discharge, the parents should be instructed to keep the child out of crowds for 1–2 weeks because the child is more susceptible to infections and to report any signs of new bleeding, which is most likely 7–10 days after surgery. The doctor should be notified immediately if bleeding occurs after discharge.

> **TIP**
>
> Food or beverages that are red, orange, or brown in color should be avoided following a tonsillectomy since these may be mistaken for fresh or old blood in emesis.
>
> Milk products should be avoided following a tonsillectomy because milk thickens oral secretions and may cause the child to further irritate the area by attempting to clear his throat.

Infectious Mononucleosis

Infectious mononucleosis is an acute self-limiting infection that is most common among persons under 25 years of age. The principal cause is the herpes-like Epstein-Barr virus. The virus is transmitted by direct contact with oral secretions. Characteristic symptoms include malaise, sore throat, fever, generalized enlargement of the lymph nodes, enlarged liver, and enlarged spleen. In some instances, a discrete macular skin rash is present.

The diagnosis of infectious mononucleosis is based on clinical manifestations and laboratory findings. The Monospot, a quick inexpensive means of diagnosis, is frequently ordered with a CBC and strep test. Other tests include peripheral blood smears and heterophil antibody test. Peripheral blood smears that reveal an increase in the number of atypical white cells and a heterophil antibody test titer of 1:160 help confirm the diagnosis. Clients with a positive Monospot test, increased number of WBCs, reactive lymphocytes, and symptoms suggestive of mononucleosis are diagnosed with the disease.

The only treatment for mononucleosis is aimed at relieving the symptoms. Comfort measures include bedrest, analgesics, gargles, and medicated troches. Rare complications include pneumonitis, myocarditis, hemolytic anemia, and rupture of the spleen.

Acute Otitis Media

Acute otitis media (AOM) is one of the most common respiratory diseases in childhood. The incidence is highest in children 6 months to 3 years of age. Otitis media is more prevalent in the young child because the eustachian tube is straighter, shorter, and wider than in older children or adults. The shorter eustachian tube allows bacteria and viruses to find their way into the middle ear more easily. Normal adenoidal enlargement in children can interfere with opening of the eustachian tubes and increase the incidence of infection. Other factors that contribute to AOM in infants and young children are immaturity of the immune system, passive smoking, attendance at day care, and supine positioning with bottle feeding. In AOM, the child develops a high fever (103°–104°F), anorexia, vomiting, and pain. Assessment of the tympanic membrane reveals redness and bulging of the eardrum due to the presence of fluid in the middle ear. The infant or young child might be seen rubbing or pulling at the affected ear or rolling her head from side to side. Increasing pressure can rupture the eardrum. If rupture occurs, pain and fever subside and purulent fluid may be noted in the ear canal.

The organism responsible for AOM is usually *H. influenza*, although other organisms (such as *S. pneumoniae* and *M. catarrhalis*) can also produce an acute infection. Treatment of AOM involves the use of antibiotics, including oral amoxicillin, sulfonamides, erythromycin, or cephalosporins. Antipyretics such as ibuprofen or acetaminophen can be given to reduce fever and pain.

> **TIP**
>
> Oral antibiotic suspensions are usually administered for 7–10 days. It is important that parents comply by giving the medication for the full course of treatment. Single-dose injections of an appropriate antibiotic can be used if the child has poor absorption of the drug, the child refuses to take the medication, or the parents fail to comply with oral therapy.

Complications of AOM include mastoiditis, meningitis, and hearing loss. Hearing evaluation is recommended for a child who has bilateral OM for a total of 3 months. Children with AOM should be seen after antibiotic therapy to check for any residual infection and to identify potential complications.

> **NOTE**
>
> More information on otitis media, including myringotomy and insertion of PE tubes, is included in Chapter 8, "Care of the Client with Sensory Disorders."

Croup Syndromes

Croup syndromes affect the larynx, trachea, and bronchi. Laryngeal involvement dominates the clinical symptoms because of the severe effects on voice quality and breathing. Croup syndromes, which produce difficulty with inspiration, are usually described according to the area affected. These include epiglottitis, laryngitis, laryngotracheobronchitis, and tracheitis. Croup syndromes are treated with a high humidity environment.

Acute Epiglottitis

This is an upper airway infection that primarily affects children 2–5 years of age, but it can also occur at any age from infancy to adulthood. Epiglottitis requires immediate attention since the condition may progress rapidly and can result in total airway obstruction. The primary cause of acute epiglottitis is *H. influenza*.

> **TIP**
>
> The 4 Ds of Epiglottitis: Drooling, Dysphagia, Dysphonia, and Distressed Inspirations.

> **NOTE**
>
> The American Academy of Pediatrics recommends that all children receive the *H. influenza* B conjugate vaccine beginning at 2 months of age as part of the routine childhood immunization series. This recommendation can account for the decline in the incidence of epiglottitis.

The child with epiglottitis is much sicker than symptoms suggest. Typically, the child goes to bed with no symptoms but awakens complaining of a sore throat and pain on swallowing. Additional symptoms include drooling, muffled phonation, inspiratory stridor, and sitting in a tripod position. Upon examination, the physician notes the appearance of a cherry-red epiglottis.

> **CAUTION**
>
> Remember that only the physician should assess the child's throat because visualization can precipitate immediate airway obstruction. A tracheostomy set should be readily available because emergency intervention might be necessary to support respiratory efforts.

Endotracheal intubation or tracheostomy is usually performed if the child has *H. influenza* epiglottitis. These procedures, as well as initiation of intravenous fluids and antibiotics, are usually carried out in the operating room. Even if intubation and assisted ventilation are unnecessary, the child should be maintained in an intensive care area for continual observation for at least 24 hours. Dramatic improvement occurs in 24 hours with antibiotic therapy, and the epiglottis is almost normal within 2–3 days.

Laryngotracheobronchitis

This is the most common form of croup in hospitalized children and is a viral infection of the upper airway. It is most common in children between 3 months and 8 years of age. Unlike acute spasmodic croup, which appears suddenly at night, the onset of laryngotracheobronchitis (LTB) begins with an upper respiratory infection and low-grade fever. The child is restless and irritable, with noticeable hoarseness and a brassy cough.

The goal of care is to maintain the airway and ensure adequate oxygenation. The child with mild croup is often managed at home and treated symptomatically. The symptoms of hoarseness, cough, and inspiratory stridor can be relieved by providing high humidity with cool mist. The child should be offered fluids frequently to maintain adequate hydration.

> **CAUTION**
>
> Immediate medical attention should be sought if the child develops labored respirations, continuous stridor, or intercostal retractions or refuses to take oral fluids.

If the respiratory condition worsens, treatment includes withholding oral intake and administering IV fluids until the respiratory condition improves. Other measures include cool mist vaporizers, supplemental oxygen, and the administration of antibiotics to treat coexisting infections and steroids to reduce bronchial swelling. Beta-agonists and beta-adrenergics (albuterol, racemic epinephrine) aerosols are administered via face mask. These agents decrease bronchial secretions and mucosal edema.

Acute Spasmodic Laryngitis

Acute spasmodic laryngitis (spasmodic croup) is sometimes referred to as "twilight croup" because it is characterized by paroxysmal attacks of croup that occur at night. Children ages 1–3 years are most often affected, inflammation is mild or absent, and there is uneventful recovery. The child typically awakens with a "barking" cough, hoarseness, noisy respirations, and restlessness. There is no fever and the attack usually subsides in a few hours. Management of mild attacks includes the use of either cool mist or warm mist vaporizers. Management of those with moderate to severe attacks includes hospitalization and the administration of nebulized medications such as racemic epinephrine or albuterol and steroids.

Bacterial Tracheitis

Bacterial tracheitis occurs in children from one month to six years of age. The disorder, which has features of both croup and epiglottitis, is most often caused by Staphylococcus aureus, although group A ß-hemolytic streptococci and *H. influenzae* have been implicated. The condition frequently follows a recent viral upper respiratory infection. Symptoms associated with bacterial tracheitis include stridor, a high-pitched sound with breathing, increased breathing difficulty, high fever, and some instances respiratory arrest. Tracheitis requires hospitalization and almost always an endotracheal tube to maintain an open airway.

Lower Airway Infections

Lower airway infections involve the bronchi, bronchioles, and alveoli. Composed of smooth muscle, these areas are often referred to as the reactive portion of the airway because of the ability of constrict. Bronchitis and bronchiolitis are examples of lower airway infections.

Bronchitis

Bronchitis, an inflammation of the large airways, is often associated with an upper respiratory infection. The most common causes of bronchitis are viruses, although *M. pneumoniae* is a common cause in children over age six. Symptoms include a dry, hacking, nonproductive, night-time cough. The illness is usually self-limiting, but requires symptomatic treatment. Treatment modalities include analgesics, antipyretics, and increased humidity. Cough suppressants are useful in promoting rest and sleep.

Bronchiolitis

This is a lower airway infection that occurs most often in infants and children under 2 years of age and causes difficulty with expiration. The respiratory synctial virus (RSV) accounts for most cases of bronchiolitis; however, the condition is also caused by adenoviruses, parainfluenza viruses, and *M. pneumoniae*. Outbreaks occur most commonly in the winter and spring months

Symptoms of bronchiolitis include low grade fever, dyspnea, nonproductive cough, wheezing, nasal flaring, intercostal and sternal retractions, expiratory grunting, and emphysema. Enzyme-linked immunoabsorbent assay (ELISA) or direct fluorescent assay can be performed on nasal wash specimens to identify the causative virus.

NOTE

Infants who test positive for RSV are isolated or roomed together with other infected infants. Contact and droplet precautions should be used when caring for infants with RSV. Healthcare workers should practice good handwashing and sanitation of surfaces. RSV can live on nonporous surfaces for several hours. Infection with RSV does not confer immunity.

Management of the client with bronchiolitis depends on the age and presenting symptoms. Older children with bronchiolitis can be treated at home, but infants are more likely to need hospitalization. Treatment is aimed at maintaining the respiratory status, decreasing the chance of aspiration, treating the infection, and maintaining acid-base balance. Nursing care includes careful assessment of the vital signs and respiratory status as well as attention to intake and output. Oral fluids might be withheld until respiratory function improves. Additional measures include the use of cool mist vaporizers with or without supplemental oxygen. Respiratory therapy with ribavirin (Virazole) is ordered for those with bronhiolitis caused by respiratory synctial virus.

CAUTION

To be effective, ribavirin should be administered within 3 days of the infection. Healthcare workers who are pregnant should avoid direct care of the client receiving aerosolized ribavirin (Virazole) because the medication can cause birth defects or death of the fetus. Surgical masks do not provide adequate filtration of the Virazole particles.

> **NOTE**
>
> The American Academy of Pediatrics recommends that high-risk infants receive five monthly injections of palivizumab (Synagis) beginning in early November to prevent RSV infection. High-risk infants include infants born before 32 weeks gestation, infants and children under 24 months of age with chronic lung disease due to prematurity, infants under 24 months of age with complicated congenital heart disease, and immunocompromised infants and children. Intravenous RSV immune globulin, once recommended, is no longer marketed in the United States.

Long-Term Respiratory Disorders

Long-term respiratory disorders affect respiratory function over extended periods of time. These disorders range from milder conditions such as seasonal allergic rhinitis or hay fever to more severe conditions such as asthma and cystic fibrosis. Long-term respiratory disorders such as cystic fibrosis can lead to chronic obstructive lung disease.

Childhood Asthma

Asthma is the most common chronic disease of childhood. The disorder can occur at any age; however, the majority of children with asthma have symptoms before 4 or 5 years of age. The National Asthma Education and Prevention Program developed a classification of asthma based on symptoms of disease severity. Table 16.5 describes these classifications.

TABLE 16.5   Asthma Classifications

Classification	Symptoms	Nighttime	Lung Function	Medications
Mild Intermittent Asthma	< 2 times a week; brief exacerbations, intensity varies	Nighttime symptoms < 2 times a month	Asymptomatic, normal peak expiratory flow (PEF) between exacerbations	No daily meds needed
Mild Persistent Asthma	> 2 times a week, < 1 day a time, exacerbations affect activity	Nighttime symptoms > 2 times a month	PEF/forced expiratory volume (FEV) > 80% predicted value	Low-dose inhaled corticosteroid, Cromolyn nebulizer, Leukotriene receptor antagonist
Moderate Persistent Asthma	Daily symptoms, use of inhaled short-acting beta agonists. Exacerbations > 2 times a week, lasting for days, and affecting activity.	Nighttime symptoms > 1 time a week	PEF/FEV from >60% to <80% of predicted value	Low-dose inhaled corticosteroid and long-acting B2 agonist; medium-dose inhaled cortiocosteroid; low-dose inhaled corticosteroid and Leukotriene receptor antagonist or theophylline
Severe Persistent Asthma	Continual symptoms, frequent exacerbations, limited activity	Nighttime symptoms frequent	PEF/FEV in one second < 60% of expected value	High-dose inhaled corticosteroid and long-acting inhaled B2 agonist. Oral corticosteroids if needed

Factors affecting the development of asthma include heredity, gender (boys are affected more often than girls, until adolescence), and passive smoking. Symptoms are triggered by things in the environment. Triggers that tend to precipitate or aggravate asthmatic exacerbations are allergens (mold, pollen, animal dander), respiratory irritants (dust), exercise, changes in weather or temperature changes, particularly cold air, respiratory infections, foods and food additives, and certain medications including NSAIDs. It is unlikely that asthma results from one single cause or trigger; rather, it appears that asthma results from a complex interaction among inflammatory cells, mediators, and cells and tissues present in the airway. Inflammation and edema of the mucus membranes and accumulation of thick, sticky secretions produces the characteristic "wheeze" and dyspnea associated with asthma. Additional information regarding the management of asthma in included in Chapter 5, "Care of the Client with Respiratory Disorders."

CAUTION

Status asthmaticus refers to unrelenting respiratory distress and bronchospasm in the child with asthma despite pharmacologic and supportive interventions. Without appropriate care, the child with status asthmaticus can develop respiratory failure. Emergency interventions may include endotracheal intubation and assisted ventilation.

Cystic Fibrosis (Mucoviscidosis)

This is most often inherited as an autosomal recessive gene. The mutated gene responsible for cystic fibrosis is located on the long arm of chromosome 7. The disease affects the exocrine system, causing the production of thick, sticky mucous that block the ducts and produces abnormalities in the lungs, pancreas, and sweat glands. Involvement of the pancreas places the client at risk for diabetes mellitus. Although cystic fibrosis affects these systems, the prognosis depends on the degree of lung involvement.

Symptoms of cystic fibrosis include meconium ileus, frequent upper respiratory infections, malabsorption, failure to gain weight, and heat prostration. Additional health problems include reoccurring nasal polyps and rectal prolapse. Reproductive capability is reduced for both sexes.

Cystic fibrosis is usually diagnosed in infancy or early childhood; however, the triple screen can detect the disease at 15–20 weeks gestation. Newborn screening using dried blood samples for immunoreactive trypsinogen is mandatory in some states with follow-up genetic testing of the infant's DNA to confirm positive results. An additional means of diagnosing cystic fibrosis is made by pilocarpine iontophoresis, more commonly known as the "sweat test," which reveals elevated sodium and chloride levels (chloride levels greater than 60 mEq/L are diagnostic for CF). The absence of pancreatic enzymes results in malabsorption and steatorrhea or undigested fat in stools. Stool analysis requires a 72-hour sample with accurate food intake recorded during that time. Chest x-ray typically reveals emphysematous changes in lungs.

The treatment of infants and children with cystic fibrosis includes the use of antibiotics to prevent or treat respiratory infections. Intermittent inhalation therapy (repeating cycles of 28 days on, 28 days off) with Tobramycin, an aminoglycoside, improves pulmonary function by suppressing chronic infection with *P. aeruginosa*. The use of aerosol therapy with dornase alpha (Pulmozyme) improves pulmonary function by decreasing the viscosity of sputum, making it easier to remove. Dornase alpha is well tolerated by most. Common side effects of the medication include hoarseness, sore throat, and laryngitis. To remain effective, the medication—which is costly (approximately $12,000 annually plus $2,000 for the inhaler)—must be given every day for life. Aerosolized bronchodilators are administered before chest physiotherapy to open large and small airways. Chest physiotherapy (percussion, vibration, and drainage) is usually performed twice a day for all lung segments.

NOTE

Transmission-based precautions: Children with cystic fibrosis should be placed in a private room to reduce the spread of infectious organisms *P. aeruginosa* and *B. cepacia*. Caregivers should use standard precautions when caring for children with cystic fibrosis.

NOTE

Individuals with cystic fibrosis who are infected with *B. cepacia* are no longer permitted to attend events and camps sponsored by the Cystic Fibrosis Foundation. This restriction is aimed at reducing the health risk in those with cystic fibrosis who are not yet infected with the organism. *B. cepacia* infection can cause serious respiratory illness and rapid decline in lung function. More information on *B. cepacia* can be found at the Cystic Fibrosis Foundation: website www.cff.org.

Additional nursing interventions focus on the client's nutritional needs. Pancreatic enzymes (Cotazyme, Pancrease, Viokase) are given to improve absorption and promote weight gain. Pancreatic enzymes are usually enteric-coated microspheres. The medication should be taken with meals and with snacks. The client's diet should be high in calories (120%–150% RDA of calories), high in carbohydrates, high in protein (200% RDA of protein), and moderate in fat. Extra salt is allowed, and the diet is supplemented with water-soluble preparations of vitamins A, D, E, and K. Deficiencies in vitamins A and E are common in those with cystic fibrosis.

TIP

Pancreatic enzyme replacement is based on the client's age and the consistency of the stools. These enzymes, which are given with each meal and snack, are best tolerated when given in applesauce because it disguises the taste.

Caring for the Child with Gastrointestinal Disorders

Gastrointestinal (GI) disorders include infections, malformations, and structural changes that affect the digestion and absorption of nutrients. When we think of the GI tract, and we seldom do unless there is a problem, we typically think only of its role in digestion and elimination. However, the GI tract plays a key role in maintaining fluid and electrolyte balance through its interaction with the kidneys and lungs. Gastrointestinal disorders are considered to be more severe in the infant and young child because of the danger of dehydration and metabolic acidosis.

Disorders of Motility

Disorders of motility refer to conditions caused by alterations in the frequency, consistency, or ease of passing stools. Some disorders of motility such as gastroenteritis are the result of infection. Others such as Hirschsprung's Disease are the result of anatomical alterations.

Gastroenteritis

Gastroenteritis, or acute vomiting and diarrhea, can be caused by an infection with rotavirus, salmonella, or another organism, or it can accompany another illness such as an upper respiratory or urinary tract infection. Additional causes include ingestion of sorbitol or fructose in juices. Regardless of the cause, acute gastroenteritis is a more severe illness in infants and very young children because they develop dehydration more quickly than adults. Untreated, the condition can quickly progress to a life-threatening situation.

Treatment focuses on determining the cause of the illness, assessing for signs of fluid and electrolyte imbalance, ensuring adequate hydration, and reintroducing adequate diet. Stool and urine cultures are ordered in addition to the routine lab studies.

Oral rehydration is indicated for mild to moderate dehydration. Solutions such as Pedialyte and Infalyte might temporarily replace or supplement regular formula or breastfeeding. Intravenous fluids such as Ringer's lactate with electrolytes are initiated for infants and children with severe dehydration and signs of hypovolemia. After symptoms have subsided, the child can resume a pre-illness diet. Many parents and healthcare providers continue to provide a BRAT diet (bananas, rice, applesauce, and tea or toast), although some research suggests that such a diet is not nutritionally sound and includes foods that actually contribute to increased stools.

> **CAUTION**
>
> Potassium replacement should be instituted only after assessing for the presence of urinary output. A child should produce 1–2 mL of urine/kg/hr.

Hirschsprung's Disease (Congenital Aganglionic Megacolon)

This anomaly refers to the congenital absence of ganglion cells in the distal colon that results in decreased peristalsis and an accumulation of intestinal contents. Although it accounts for about 25% of all cases of neonatal bowel obstruction, it might not be diagnosed until later in infancy or childhood. Hirschsprung's disease is more common in males and is frequently associated with other congenital anomalies such as congenital heart defects or chromosomal abnormalities such as Down syndrome. The symptoms of Hirschsprung's disease depend on the amount of bowel involved, the occurrence of complications, and the age at time of diagnosis.

Symptoms in the newborn include failure to pass meconium within the first 24–48 hours, refusal to feed, bile-stained vomitus, passage of flat, ribbon-like stools, abdominal distention, and intestinal obstruction. During infancy, symptoms include the failure to gain weight, constipation, abdominal distention, and episodes of vomiting. In childhood, the symptoms become chronic and include poor appetite; poor growth; abdominal distention; infrequent passage of foul smelling, ribbon-like stools; and palpable fecal masses.

The diagnosis of Hirschsprung's disease is made using a barium enema, rectal biopsy, and *anorectal manometry* (a procedure that records the pressure response of the internal anal sphincter). In the case of Hirschsprung's disease, the internal sphincter fails to relax.

In some cases, a child with Hirschsprung's disease can be managed with dietary modifications such as increasing fluid and fiber intake. Management also includes the administration of occasional enemas using isotonic or normal saline solutions. These solutions can be purchased without a prescription or can be prepared by adding one level measuring teaspoon of noniodized salt to one pint of tap water.

CAUTION

The use of tap water enemas, concentrated salt solutions, soap solutions, or phosphate preparations is discouraged because frequent use of nonisotonic solution can lead to water intoxication and the dilution of serum electrolytes.

Most children with Hirschsprung's disease require surgical correction. The child's fluid and electrolyte is stabilized, and a temporary colostomy is performed to relieve the obstruction and allow the bowel to return to normal. Following the initial surgery, a complete corrective surgery is performed. Several surgeries are used; however, one of the most common includes a pull-through procedure in which the end of the normal bowel is pulled through the muscular sleeve of the rectum. The temporary colostomy is closed at the same time. Postoperative nursing care includes assessing the client for abdominal distention and for the return of bowel sounds and the passage of stool. The abdominal wound is assessed and cared for the same as any abdominal wound.

Gastroesophageal Reflux

Gastroesophageal reflux (GER) is the passive regurgitation of gastric contents into the esophagus because of an incompetent esophageal sphincter. Additional signs and symptoms include increased appetite with poor weight gain, hemetest positive emesis, anemia, irritability, gagging or choking with feeding, and recurrent pneumonia related to microaspiration. Complications associated with GER include aspiration pneumonia and esophagitis due to irritation of the esophageal lining from stomach acids. Those at highest risk for developing GER are preterm infants, infants with bronchopulmonary dysplasia, and those with tracheoesophageal fistulas or esophageal repairs.

Upper GI studies, endoscopy, and scintigraphy help to establish the diagnosis. Management of the child with gastroesophageal reflux is much like that of the adult with GER. (Refer to Chapter 9, "Care of the Client with Gastrointestinal Disorders.") Conservative management of infants with GER includes offering small frequent feedings with rice-thickened formula, frequent burping, and placing the infant in prone position to help minimize the amount of reflux. The American Academy of Pediatrics recommends placing the infant supine or side-lying for sleep to minimize the risk of SIDS (sudden infant death syndrome); however, infants with GER are exempt.

Pharmacological management includes the use of antacids, histamine blockers, and proton pump inhibitors to reduce acid present in gastric contents and to help prevent esophagitis. Metoclopramide (Reglan) increases pressure in the lower esophageal sphincter and improves gastric emptying and esophageal peristalsis.

Surgical management is reserved for infants and children who continue to have reflux. Although there are several antireflux procedures, Nissen fundoplication is the most commonly performed procedure. Postoperatively, the child might develop dumping syndrome or small bowel obstruction.

Structural Defects

Structural defects can occur in any portion of the gastrointestinal tract from the mouth to the anus. Most of these defects are the result of the failure of normal development during a crucial period of embryonic life. These defects which can involve atresia, malposition, non-closure, or any number of variations, are apparent at birth or shortly thereafter.

Cleft Lip and Cleft Palate

Cleft lip and cleft palate are craniofacial deformities that involve the lip, hard palate, or soft palate. These can occur as separate malformations or they can occur together. Surgical repair of a cleft lip is generally performed between 1 and 3 months of age, whereas cleft palate repairs are performed between 12 and 18 months of age of age, depending on whether the defect involves the hard palate or soft palate. At this age, the child is usually weaned and speech has not yet developed.

> **CAUTION**
>
> Lip repair is performed earlier than palate repair to facilitate feeding and promote parental-infant bonding. The nurse should assess the amount and quality of parental interaction with the infant because the bonding process can be negatively affected by the infant's appearance.

Preoperatively the nurse should teach the parents to feed the infant using a Breck feeder or flanged nipple. The infant should be fed slowly to prevent aspiration and should be burped more frequently to prevent gastric distention. The infant's weight should be closely monitored.

> **CAUTION**
>
> Postoperatively the nurse should give priority to assessing the respiratory status of the infant. Surgical correction of the soft tissue of the mouth and palate can result in airway obstruction.

Additional postoperative care includes feeding the infant using a Breck feeder to prevent stress on the suture line caused by sucking. The mouth and suture line are cleansed of formula residue using sterile water. The suture line of the lip is cleaned using half-strength hydrogen peroxide. The suture line is reinforced with a Logan bar, which lessens stress on the suture line caused by crying. Elbow restraints prevent the infant placing his hands near his face or mouth.

> **NOTE**
>
> A multidisciplinary team is involved in the care of the infant with cleft lip/cleft palate. This team can include the physician, nurse, orthodontist, speech therapist, otolaryngologist, and social worker.

Esophageal Atresia or Tracheoesophageal Fistula

Esophageal atresia (EA) is a failure of the esophagus to develop a continuous passage, and *tracheoesophageal fistula* (TEF) is an abnormal opening between the trachea and esophagus. These can occur alone or in combination. Symptoms of EA and TEF include

- The presence of maternal polyhydramnios (excessive amniotic fluid)
- Excessive mucus and drooling in the newborn
- Coughing, choking, and cyanosis with the first feeding
- An x-ray of the esophagus that confirms the presence of a blind pouch at each end, widely separated with no connection (EA) or the presence of an abnormal connection between the trachea and esophagus (TEF)

> **TIP**
>
> The 3 Cs of Tracheoesophageal Atresia are
> - Coughing
> - Choking
> - Cyanosis

Prior to surgical correction, intravenous fluids are started and the infant is positioned to facilitate drainage of secretions. Frequent suctioning of secretions from the mouth and pharynx decreases the likelihood of aspiration. A double-lumen catheter placed in the esophageal pouch is attached to intermittent low suction. Keeping the infant's head in an upright position makes it easier to remove collected secretions.

The surgical correction of esophageal atresia can be performed in one operation or staged in one or two operations. Surgical correction of TEF involves a thoracotomy, a division and ligation of the TEF, and an end-to end anastomosis. The head of the bed should remain elevated 35°–45°postoperatively. If the repair is to be done in stages, a gastrostomy tube is inserted to permit tube feedings. Prior to feeding, the gastrostomy tube is elevated and secured above the level of the infant's stomach. This allows gastric contents to pass into the duodenum and lessens the likelihood of aspiration. Gastrostomy feedings are continued until the esophageal anastomosis is healed. Oral feedings are begun about one week postoperatively and are started with sterile water followed by small, frequent feedings of formula.

Esophageal atresia and tracheoesophageal fistula are associated with several other anomalies, including congenital heart disease, anorectal malformations, and genitourinary anomalies. The prognosis depends on the preoperative weight, associated congenital anomalies, and prompt diagnosis. Long term problems include the development of strictures, anastomotic leaks, and esophageal dysmotility. Premature and low birth weight infants as well as those with severe respiratory complications have poorer prognoses.

Obstructive Disorders

Obstructive disorders of the gastrointestinal system refer to conditions in which the passage of nutrients and secretions is impeded by constrictions, occlusions, or impaired gastric motility. These disorders may be either congenital or acquired.

Hypertrophic Pyloric Stenosis

This problem involves a narrowing of the sphincter at the outlet of the stomach, and it occurs most often in white, full-term firstborn males. This narrowing causes a partial obstruction. At birth the infant feeds normally, but within 2 to 3 weeks develops projectile vomiting after feeding. A palpable olive-shaped mass is found in the right upper quadrant of the abdomen. X-ray confirms the presences of hypertrophy and an elongation of the pylorus. The disorder is corrected surgically by a procedure known as a *pyloromyotomy* or *Fredet-Ramstedt procedure*. Feedings are usually begun 4–6 hours after surgery with small frequent feedings of glucose, water, or electrolyte solution. If clear fluids are retained, formula feedings or breast milk in small increments are started about 24 hours after surgery. The amount of formula or breast milk and the intervals between feedings are increased until a full feeding schedule is reinstituted about 48 hours after surgery. The infant should be fed in an upright position and burped frequently. Following feedings, the infant should be positioned on the right side. The prognosis following surgery is excellent.

Intussusception

This problem involves an invagination or telescoping of one portion of the bowel into another resulting in total obstruction. The most common site for intussusception is the ileocecal valve or the point where the large and small intestines join. Signs and symptoms associated with intussusception include colicky abdominal pain, vomiting, drawing the knees to the abdomen, abdominal distention, palpable sausage shaped mass in the abdomen and the passage of "currant jelly" stools by an otherwise healthy child. Diagnosis and conservative management includes the use of air enemas. Barium enemas, once used to diagnose the disorder, are no longer used because of the danger of causing barium peritonitis. If conservative measures fail, surgical intervention is required to restore normal bowel function.

Imperforate Anus

This deformity includes a number of malformations in which there is no obvious anal opening or where an abnormal opening exists between the anus and the perineum or genitourinary system. Surgical repair depends on the extent of the malformation. The imperforate anal membrane is removed, followed by dilation. More extensive surgery is required for the infant with perineal defects. Postoperative nursing care is directed toward healing the operative site and preventing complications. Nursing interventions can include administering IV fluids and antibiotics, providing stoma care, and providing pain management.

> **CAUTION**
>
> Passage of meconium does not always indicate anal patency—particularly in females—because a fistula might be present, allowing evacuation of the meconium. In males, meconium might pass through a fistula in the midline. This can appear as ribbonlike meconium at the base of the scrotum or near the base of the penis.

Biliary Atresia

This problem causes fibrosis of the intrahepatic and extrahepatic bile ducts and gradually results in liver failure. Most affected infants are full term and appear healthy at birth. Jaundice, dark urine, clay-colored stools, and hepatomegaly occur early in the disease. Later symptoms are associated with the development of cirrhosis and splenomegaly.

Treatment of biliary atresia includes surgical procedures that allow drainage of the bile (hepatic portoenterostomy or Kasai procedure), and orthotopic liver transplantation, now considered to be the definitive therapy for biliary atresia.

> **CAUTION**
>
> Jaundice that exists longer than 2 weeks accompanied by elevations in direct (conjugated) bilirubin point to the possibility of biliary atresia.

Inflammatory and Parasitic Disorders

The intestinal tract is the site of a number of inflammatory disorders. Some inflammatory conditions such as Meckel's diverticulum, are the result of congenital malformation, while others such as ulcerative colitis and Crohn's disease involve an autoimmune reaction. Parasitic disorders are also capable of creating an inflammatory response within the bowel. This section reviews nursing interventions for pediatric clients with Meckel's diverticulum and enterobiasis. Information regarding care of clients with Crohn's disease and ulcerative colitis can be found in Chapter 9, "Care of the Client with Gastrointestinal Disorders."

Meckel's Diverticulum

Meckel's diverticulum is the most common congenital malformation of the gastrointestinal tract. The disorder, which occurs in approximately 2% of the population, is caused by the presence of a fibrous band that connects the small intestine to the umbilicus. The diverticulum, which is most often 3–6 centimeters in length, can be found in a variety of shapes and sizes. Most of those affected do not develop symptoms. Others exhibit symptoms caused by iron deficiency anemia, bleeding, obstruction, and inflammation. Obstruction occurs most often in affected adults, whereas children with Meckel's are more likely to develop volvulus and intussusception. Radiographic scintigraphy (Meckel's scan) is used to confirm the diagnosis. The standard treatment is surgical removal because the disorder can result in hemorrhage and bowel obstruction. Postoperative care includes the administration of IV fluids, nasogastric suction, and observation for complications.

Enterobiasis (Pinworms)

Pinworms occur when the eggs of the nematode *Enterobiasis vermicularis* are ingested or inhaled. The movement of the pinworms on the skin and mucous membranes produces intense perianal itching. Other symptoms include general irritability, poor sleep, restlessness, and bed wetting. The most common means of diagnosing infection with pinworms is the "tape test." To perform the tape test, a loop of transparent tape is placed sticky side out around the end of a tongue depressor. The tape is pressed firmly against the child's perianal area. Specimens are collected in the early morning before the child awakens and before the child has a stool or bathes.

The drug of choice for treating the child with pinworms and the family is mebendazole (Vermox) which is safe, effective, and convenient. The drug is repeated in two weeks to prevent reinfestation. Clothing and bed linens should be washed in hot water and the house should be thoroughly vacuumed to remove any remaining eggs. The child's fingernails should be kept short to prevent scratching, and the family should observe good hand washing after toileting and before eating.

TIP

Vermox is a single chewable tablet. Another medication used to treat enterobiasis is pyrantel (Pin-X, Pin-Rid) which is also taken in 2 doses 2 weeks apart. It is important to note that even if only one child in the household is infected, all individuals living in the house are treated since pinworms are easily spread to others in the household.

Malabsorptive/Metabolic Syndromes

Malabsorptive syndromes are characterized by chronic diarrhea and failure to absorbed needed nutrients and fluids. Malabsorption can be caused by a lack of enzymes needed for digestion as in the case of cystic fibrosis or by absorptive defects as in the case of celiac disease. Metabolic syndromes such as phenylketonuria (PKU) and galactosemia prevent the child from metabolizing protein and galactose which can result in physical abnormalities and mental retardation.

Celiac (Gluten-Induced Enteropathy, Celiac Sprue)

This condition is a malabsorptive disorder of the proximal small intestine caused by an intolerance to gluten. Gluten is found in the grain of wheat, oats, barley, and rye. Digestive problems most often appear between the ages of 1 and 5 years when the child begins to ingest various foods containing gluten. Symptoms vary but generally include malabsorption, steatorrhea, abdominal distention, and muscle wasting (particularly in the buttocks and extremities). Diagnosis is based on jejunal biopsy, which reveals changes in the intestinal mucosa. The treatment of celiac involves the replacement of gluten-containing grains with corn, rice, and millet as well as avoiding hidden sources of gluten. Hydrolyzed vegetable protein, a common ingredient in many commercially prepared foods, contains gluten and can cause an exacerbation of symptoms. Associated problems include deficiencies in iron, folic acid, and fat-soluble vitamins that are treated with vitamin and mineral supplements.

> **NOTE**
>
> Strict adherence to dietary restrictions can help minimize the development of small intestine lymphoma, one of the most serious complications of celiac.

Phenylketonuria

Phenylketonuria (PKU) is a genetic disorder in which the child is unable to metabolize phenylalanine into tyrosine. Tyrosine is essential to the formation of melanin (responsible for hair, skin, and eye color) and the hormones epinephrine and thyroxine. Accumulation of phenylalanine affects the normal development of the brain and central nervous system. Without early detection and treatment, the child with PKU develops irreversible brain damage.

Clinical manifestations of PKU include irritability, frequent vomiting, failure to thrive, and seizures. Older children with PKU have bizarre behaviors such as head banging, screaming, arm biting, and other psychotic behaviors.

The most commonly used screening test for PKU is the Guthrie blood test. All newborns are screened for PKU before discharge or within the first week of life because early detection and treatment are necessary to prevent mental retardation.

> **CAUTION**
>
> The Guthrie test is obtained from a heel stick. Remember to stick the newborn on the side of the heel to avoid nerve damage. The test is most reliable if the infant has ingested a source of protein. If the specimen is obtained before the infant is 24 hours old, a subsequent sample should be obtained before the infant is 2 weeks old.
>
> Normal blood phenylalanine level is about 1 mg/dl. In PKU, levels can range from 6 to 80 mg/dl.

The treatment for PKU consists of instituting a low-phenylalanine diet that is begun as soon as possible after diagnosis and maintained through adulthood. The goal is to maintain the blood level of phenylalanine between 2 and 10 mg/dl. Specially prepared formulas include Lofenalac and Pro-Phree Total. Partial breast feeding can be allowed if phenylalanine levels are closely monitored. Solid foods such as cereal, fruits, and vegetables are added according to the recommended schedule. Most high-protein foods are either eliminated or restricted to small amounts. Artificial sweeteners containing aspartame should be avoided because they are converted to phenylalanine.

Galactosemia

Galactosemia is an autosomal recessive disorder in which one of the three enzymes necessary to covert galactose to glucose is missing. The infant with galactosemia appears normal at birth, but within a few days of ingesting a formula containing lactose, the infant begins to vomit and lose weight. Additional symptoms arise from accumulations of galactose, which target the major organs.

> **TIP**
>
> Autosomal recessive disorders mean that if two carriers have a baby the likelihood of the baby having the disorder is 25%.

Damage done to the liver and spleen results in jaundice, cirrhosis, and portal hypertension. Infections with E. coli are common in untreated infants. Cataracts—opacities in the lens of the eyes—are usually evident by 1–2 months of age. Lethargy and hypotonia associated with brain damage are evident soon afterward. Galactosemia can ultimately result in mental retardation and possibly death; therefore, it is imperative that treatment begin as soon as possible.

Newborn screening for galactosemia is required in most states. Diagnosis is based on history, physical exam, and increased levels of serum galactose. The treatment of galactosemia is aimed at eliminating all milk- and lactose-containing foods, including breast milk. Instead, the infant is fed a soy-protein formula.

> **CAUTION**
>
> Medications that contain lactose should also be avoided.

Ingestion of Hazardous Substances

Injuries and death related to accidental poisoning have declined over the past three decades. This is largely due to the Poison Prevention Packaging Act of 1970, which requires that potentially hazardous drugs and household products be sold in child-resistant containers. However, poisoning remains a significant health concern for children under 6 years of age. Common sources of household poisoning are plants, cosmetics, and perfumes, cleaning products, and petroleum distillates. Over-the-counter medications such as cough and cold remedies, laxatives, and dietary supplements are also frequently ingested by children.

> **CAUTION**
>
> A physician or Poison Control Center should be consulted before administering any antidote.

Salicylate Overdose

Salicylate, or aspirin overdose, results in an acid-base imbalance. Symptoms include nausea, vomiting, dehydration, tinnitus, hyperpnea, hyperpyrexia, bleeding, convulsions, and coma. Treatment is aimed at removal through emesis, lavage, or the use of activated charcoal. Additional measures include sodium bicarbonate infusion to correct metabolic acidosis, vitamin K to control bleeding, and diazepam to control seizures. Hemodialysis might be needed in the most severe cases.

Acetaminophen Overdose

Acetaminophen overdose results in severe and sometimes fatal damage to the liver. Initial drug levels are drawn 4 hours after the drug is ingested, but treatment should begin before the lab results are obtained. Acetaminophen overdose is treated with IV acetylcysteine. Plasma levels of 300 mcg/mL occurring 4 hours after ingestion or 50 mcg/mL occurring 12 hours after ingestion are associated with hepatotoxicity. In spite of treatment, there can be continuing hepatic damage that makes liver transplantation a necessity.

Lead Poisoning (Plumbism)

Lead poisoning or plumbism results in irreversible damage to the brain. Sources of lead include lead-based paint, lead crystal, ceramic wares, dyes, playground equipment, stained glass, and collectible toys. Lead poisoning affects the hematopoietic, renal, and neurological systems. With low-dose exposure, the child might experience symptoms of impulsivity, hyperactivity, and distractibility. With higher-dose exposure, the child can experience mental retardation, paralysis, blindness, convulsions, and death.

Lead enters the body through one of the following routes: ingestion, inhalation, or prenatally. Primary sources of lead poisoning include pica, paint chips or dust from sources of lead-based paint or lead pipes or soil contaminated with leaded gasoline. Houses constructed before 1950 are more likely to have leaded paint. Lead-based paints were officially banned for use in 1978. Examples of cultural practices that expose the child to lead are outlined here:

- ▶ Azarca (Mexico) treatment to prevent digestive problems, an orange powder, it is mixed with oil, milk, or sugar; may be given as a tea, or included in tortilla dough

- ▶ Payloohah (Southeast Asia) treatment for rash or fever

- ▶ Surma (India) black powder applied to the inner lower eyelid as a cosmetic

- ▶ Ayurvedis (Tibet) rolled into small balls, used to improve slow development

Chelation therapy, usually administered by deep intramuscular injection, is used to remove lead from the circulating blood. Commonly used chelation agents include calcium disodium edetate (EDTA), calcium disodium versenate (Versenate), British anti-Lewisite (BAL/Dimercaprol), and succimer (Chemet). Versenate can be given intravenously. Chemet can be given orally.

> **CAUTION**
>
> BAL/Dimercaprol is given only deep IM. It should not be used in those with glucose 6-phosphate dehydrogenase deficiency (G6PD) or those with peanut allergy. The medication is prepared in a peanut oil solution.

Nursing care includes the administration of chelating medication, which is often painful. Procaine, a local anesthetic, is injected along with EDTA to lessen the pain of injection. The nurse should rotate injection sites to prevent the formation of painful fibrotic areas. If renal function is adequate, Versenate can be given intravenously; otherwise, it is given by deep intramuscular injection. The nurse should assess the client receiving Versenate for signs of cerebral edema and provide seizure precautions. Cerebral edema is treated with intravenous Osmitrol (mannitol) or Decadron (dexamethasone). The side effects of heavy metal antidotes include malaise, paresthesia, nausea, and vomiting. Additional nursing interventions include obtaining a detailed history to identify sources of lead contamination in order to prevent re-exposure.

Iron Overdose

Iron overdose is usually the result of ingesting vitamins or iron-containing medications intended for adults. Initial symptoms of iron poisoning include vomiting of blood and blood in the stools. If the condition is left untreated, the victim becomes restless, hypotensive, tachypneic, and cyanotic. Hepatic injury, coma, and death can occur within 48–96 hours after ingestion. The treatment of iron poisoning includes emesis or gastric lavage. In cases of severe intoxication, chelation therapy with deferoxamine (Desferal) is necessary.

Ingestion of Hydrocarbons and Corrosives

Hydrocarbons such as gasoline and paint thinner produce rapid symptoms when taken internally. Clinical symptoms include gagging, choking, nausea and vomiting, lethargy, and respiratory symptoms. Pulmonary involvement leads to tachypnea, grunting respirations, retractions, and cyanosis. In some instances, the child develops chemical pneumonia. The victim is treated symptomatically. Inducing vomiting is generally contraindicated because of the danger of aspiration. Gastric emptying and gastric decontamination are questionable practices because of the increased risk of aspiration. If gastric emptying or decontamination is used, a cuffed ET tube is inserted prior to gastric lavage. Oxygen, hydration, and antibiotics are used for those with chemical pneumonia.

Corrosives are strong acids or alkalis that are contained in most household cleansers such as drain cleaners, oven cleaners, bleach, and dishwasher detergents. Liquid corrosives generally cause more damage than granular corrosives. Clinical symptoms of corrosive ingestion include burning of the throat and mouth, swelling of the mucus membranes, drooling, agitation, and shock. Inducing vomiting is contraindicated in the treatment of corrosive ingestion because it re-damages the mucosa. The victim should be given water or milk to dilute the poison.

CAUTION

No attempt should be made to neutralize the corrosive because this will result in a thermal burn as well as a chemical burn.

Management of a child with corrosive ingestion includes maintaining a patent airway, administering analgesics, and withholding oral intake. Esophageal strictures that result from the injury might require repeated dilations and surgery.

Caring for the Child with Cardiovascular Disorders

Cardiovascular disorders are classified as congenital heart defects and acquired heart disorders. *Congenital heart defects* involve structural defects in the anatomy of the heart and blood vessels that are apparent at birth or shortly thereafter. These affect the function of the heart and are evident in the development of congestive heart failure and hypoxemia. *Acquired heart disorders* refers to disease processes that affect the structure and function of the heart. Acquired heart disease can be the result of bacterial infection, autoimmune response, environmental factors, or heredity.

This section focuses on three of the most common congenital heart defects: coarctation of the aorta, septal defects, and Tetralogy of Fallot. Three acquired heart diseases—rheumatic fever, subacute bacterial endocarditis, and Kawasaki disease—are also reviewed in this chapter. Medications used in the treatment of cardiovascular disease are included in Chapter 3, "Care of the Client with Cardiovascular Disorders."

Congenital Heart Defects

Heart defects are the major cause of death during the first year of life, with the exception of those infants who die from prematurity. In most cases, the cause of congenital heart defects (CHD) remains unknown. However, certain maternal risk factors have been identified:

- Alcoholism
- Maternal age over 40
- Rubella during pregnancy
- Type 1 diabetes

CHD is more likely to be diagnosed when the infant is several weeks old rather than at the time of birth.

NOTE

The rapid heart rate of the newborn, the instability of the circulatory system, and the fact that many newborns have a benign murmur present for the first few days of life often delay diagnosis. It is more likely that a congenital heart defect will be diagnosed when the infant is several weeks old. Normal heart rate in the newborn is 100–150 beats per minute.

Symptoms of CHD in the infant and child depend on the type and severity of the defect but include

- Cyanosis with feeding
- Dyspnea
- Failure to gain weight
- Fatigue
- Respiratory congestion

Complications of CHD include delayed growth and development, polycythemia, clot formation, and congestive heart failure.

CAUTION

Early signs of congestive heart failure include tachycardia while sleeping, profuse sweating (especially on the scalp), fatigue, irritability, respiratory distress, and weight gain.

Congenital heart defects are classified as obstructive defects (coarctation of the aorta), defects with increased pulmonary blood flow (septal defects), defects with decreased pulmonary blood flow (Tetralogy of Fallot), and mixed defects (transposition of the great vessels).

TIP

At this point, you might want to review heart structure and normal circulation in a nursing textbook as well in an anatomy and physiology textbook. It is difficult to understand the abnormal if you don't know the normal.

As you probably realize, the content area of congenital heart defects is quite large, so we'll focus on one or two examples of each of the general classifications that are most common.

Obstructive Defects

Obstructive defects exist when blood that is leaving the heart meets an area that is narrowed or stenosed. This results in altered blood flow before the narrowed site (increased pressure) as well as after (decreased pressure). Coarctation is an example of an obstructive heart defect.

Coarctation refers to a narrowing within the aorta that alters blood flow to the extremities as illustrated in Figure 16.1. Coarctation can occur anywhere in the aorta from above the aortic valve to the abdominal aorta. The location of the coarctation and the presence or absence of associated cardiac anomalies influence the clinical presentation. Associated cardiac anomalies include ventricular septal defect, patent ductus arteriosus, and bicuspid aortic valve.

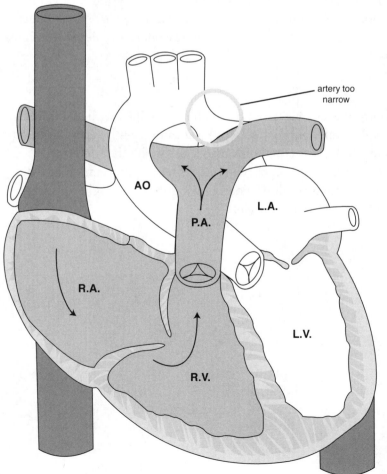

FIGURE 16.1 Coarctation of the aorta.

Clinical manifestations of coarctation of the aorta (COA) include elevated blood pressure and bounding pulses in the upper extremities and diminished blood pressure and weak or absent pulses in the lower extremities. Infants who develop congestive heart failure require hospitalization for stabilization of the blood pressure and treatment of acidosis. Older children with COA might complain of dizziness; headache; fainting; and nosebleed, which can indicate that the blood pressure is higher than usual. The average blood pressure for the newborn is 73/50; for the 1-year-old, it is 90/56.

Correction of COA involves resection of the coarcted portion with an end-to-end anastomosis of the aorta or by enlargement of the narrowed portion using either a prosthetic graft or a graft taken from the left subclavian artery. The defect is outside the heart and pericardium, so cardiopulmonary bypass is unnecessary.

Residual hypertension following surgery seems to be related to the age of the child at the time of repair, so elective surgery should be performed within the first 2 years of life. The prognosis is good, with less than 5% mortality in children with no other defects.

Defects with Increased Pulmonary Bloodflow

Openings that occur within the inner walls or septum of the heart or abnormal connections between the great arteries allow blood to flow from the left side of the heart to the right side of the heart. The resulting increase in blood volume on the right side of the heart means an increase in pulmonary blood flow and a decrease in systemic blood flow. Defects that increase pulmonary blood flow include ventricular and atrial septal defects and patent ductus arteriosus. The client with this type of heart defect typically has signs of congestive heart failure.

Ventricular Septal Defect

Ventricular septal defect (VSD) is characterized by an abnormal opening between the right and left ventricles, as illustrated in Figure 16.2. VSD can vary in size and location. The majority are membranous. VSD is commonly associated with other defects including pulmonary stenosis, transposition of the great vessels, or coarctation of the aorta. Left-to-right shunts occur as a result of blood flowing from the higher-pressure left ventricle to the lower-pressure right ventricle.

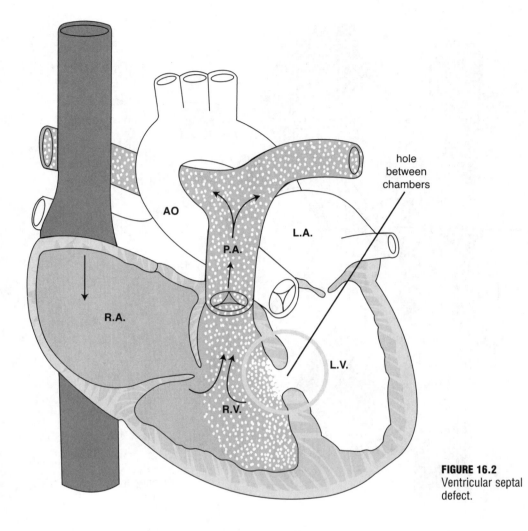

FIGURE 16.2
Ventricular septal defect.

Symptoms associated with VSD include a characteristic murmur and signs of congestive heart failure. Surgical treatments for those with VSD include pulmonary artery banding, which decreases pulmonary blood flow, and purse string suturing or patching the opening. The prognosis depends on the size of the defect and other associated cardiac defects.

Atrial Septal Defect

Atrial septal defect (ASD) is characterized by an abnormal opening between the right and left atria, as illustrated in Figure 16.3. As with VSD, atrial septal defect can vary in size and location. Openings in the lower end of the septum might be associated with mitral valve deformities, whereas openings near the junction of the superior vena cava and right atrium might be associated with partial anomalous pulmonary venous connection. Abnormal communication between the right and left atria allows blood to flow from the left atria where pressures are greater to the right atria where pressures are lower.

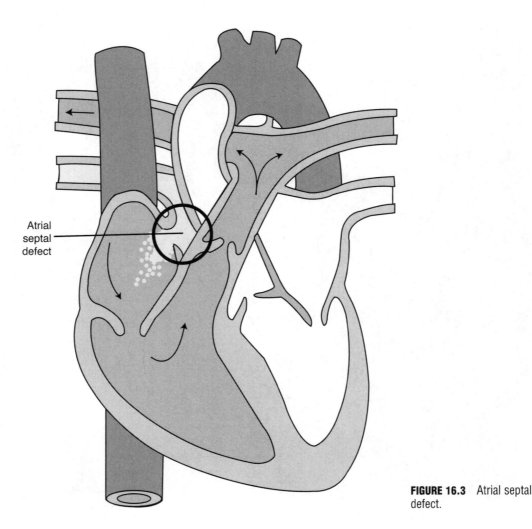

Atrial
septal
defect

FIGURE 16.3 Atrial septal
defect.

Clients with ASD might be asymptomatic. Others develop a characteristic murmur and symptoms of congestive heart. Those with ASD have an increased risk of atrial dysrhythmias, pulmonary vascular obstructive disease, and emboli. Surgical treatment is similar to that of the client with VSD. The prognosis is excellent, with an operative mortality of less than 1%.

Defects with Decreased Pulmonary Blood Flow

Obstruction of blood flow and anatomical defects such as VSD or ASD result in defects with decreased pulmonary blood flow. Because blood has a difficult time in leaving the heart, pressures in the right side of the heart exceed pressures in the left side of the heart. This allows deoxygenated blood to shunt right to left and enter into the systemic circulation. Clients with these type of defects are typically hypoxemic and cyanotic. Two of the more common defects resulting from decreased pulmonary blood flow are Tetralogy of Fallot (TOF) and tricuspid atresia.

As the name implies, Tetralogy of Fallot (TOF) involves four separate defects. These defects include pulmonic stenosis, ventricular septal defect, overriding aorta, and right ventricular hypertrophy, as illustrated in Figure 16.4.

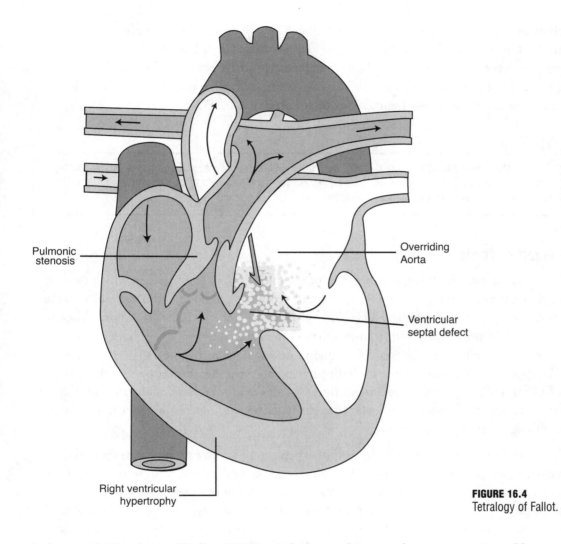

Pulmonic stenosis

Overriding Aorta

Ventricular septal defect

Right ventricular hypertrophy

FIGURE 16.4
Tetralogy of Fallot.

Infants with Tetralogy of Fallot (TOF) might have a history of acute cyanosis and heart murmur at birth that worsens over the first year of life. Acute episodes of cyanosis and anoxia, referred to as *blue spells* or *tet attacks*, occur during crying or feeding because the infant's oxygen demands are greater than the blood supply. Children with TOF have noticeable cyanosis, increased respiratory rate, gasping respirations, clubbing of the fingers, and growth retardation. Arterial blood gases reveal metabolic acidosis. When oxygenation is compromised, a child with TOF assumes a squatting position which decreases blood flow to the extremities. Children with TOF are at risk for developing emboli, seizures, loss of consciousness, or sudden death following an anoxic episode.

CAUTION

Nursing care for the infant or child with a hypoxic or "tet" attack involves placing the child in knee chest position, providing supplemental oxygen, and medicating with morphine sulfate to reduce spasms and slow respirations.

Surgical treatment is palliative shunt (Blalock-Taussig procedure) to increase blood flow to the lungs thereby providing for better oxygenation. Complete elective repair, involving correction of each of the four defects, is usually performed in the first year of life. Surgical repair requires the child to be placed on cardiopulmonary bypass. The operative mortality is less than 5% for total correction of TOF.

> **TIP**
>
> A wonderful movie depicting the pioneering work of Drs. Blalock, Taussig, and Thomas is *Something the Lord Made* (2004). The work done on "blue babies" began the whole field of cardiovascular surgery. This movie should be seen by any student interested in this area of nursing.

Mixed Defects

The term *mixed defects* refers to a group of complex cardiac anomalies in which the client's survival depends on a mixing of blood from the pulmonary and systemic circulations. Symptoms vary but usually include some degree of cyanosis and signs of congestive heart failure. Those with transposition of the great arteries (TGA) have severe cyanosis in the first few days of life and later develop congestive heart failure. Others, like those with truncus arteriosus, have severe congestive heart failure in the first weeks of life and mild cyanosis. Assessment findings generally reveal an infant who is small for her age, who feeds poorly, and who tires easily. Later findings reveal polycythemia and clubbing of the fingers and toes.

Transposition of the great arteries results when the pulmonary artery exits from the left ventricle and the aorta exits from the right ventricle, as illustrated in Figure 16.5. This creates two separate circulations with no communication between systemic and pulmonary blood flow. Signs and symptoms depend on the type and size of associated defects. Those with minimal communication between systemic and pulmonary blood flow are severely cyanotic from the time of birth, whereas those with large septal defects or patent ductus arteriosus are less cyanotic. Heart sounds vary according to the type of defect.

Management of the infant with TGA is aimed at providing intracardiac mixing. Intravenous prostaglandin E may be initiated temporarily to increase the mixing of systemic and pulmonary blood flow. Cardiac catheterization with a balloon atrial septostomy (Rashkind procedure) increases mixing and maintains cardiac output for a longer period of time. Surgical correction involves an arterial switch procedure. Potential complications of arterial switch include narrowing at the anastomosis sites and coronary artery insufficiency.

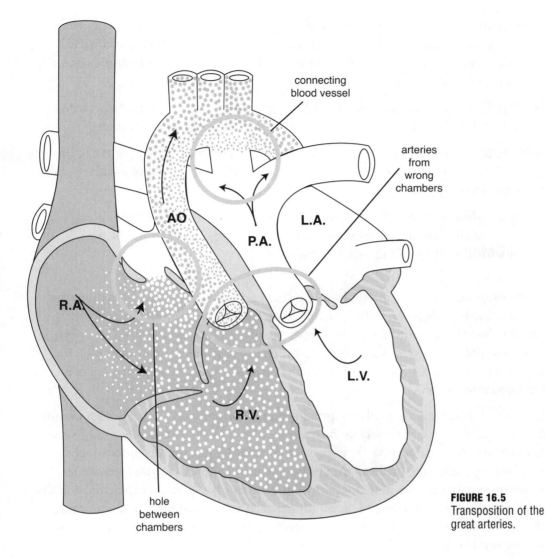

FIGURE 16.5
Transposition of the great arteries.

Acquired Heart Disease

Acquired heart disease refers to disease processes that occur after birth and can be found in those with a normal heart and cardiovascular system. Examples of acquired heart disease are rheumatic fever, subacute bacterial endocarditis, and Kawasaki's disease.

Rheumatic Fever

Rheumatic fever is an autoimmune response to Group A *beta hemolytic streptococcal* infection. The disease, which is self-limiting, affects the skin, joints, brain, serous surfaces, and heart. The most serious complication of rheumatic fever is damage to the valves of the heart, and the valve most often affected is the mitral valve.

The major clinical manifestations of rheumatic fever are the result of inflammation and the appearance of hemorrhagic lesions (Aschoff bodies) that are found in all the affected tissues. The symptoms associated with each of the major manifestations are

▶ **Carditis (heart):** Includes the presence of an apical systolic murmur, aortic regurgitation, tachycardia, cardiomegaly, complaints of chest pain, and development of mitral stenosis.

▶ **Polymigratory arthritis (joints):** Includes the presence of red, swollen, painful joints, particularly the larger joints (knees, elbows, hips, shoulders, and wrists). The symptoms move from one joint to another and are most common during the acute phase of illness.

▶ **Erythema marginatum (skin):** Includes the presence of a distinct red macular rash with a clear center found on the trunk and on proximal extremities.

▶ **Subcutaneous nodules (serous surfaces):** Includes the presence of small, painless swellings located over the bony prominences of the feet, hands, elbows, vertebrae, scalp, and scapulae.

▶ **Syndenham's chorea (brain):** Includes the presence of aimless, jerking movements of the extremities; involuntary facial grimacing; speech disturbances; emotional lability; and muscle weakness.

In addition to the major manifestations, the client with rheumatic fever has minor manifestations that include fever, arthralgia, an elevated erythrocyte sedimentation rate, and a positive C-reactive protein. Supporting evidence of a preceding Group A *beta hemolytic streptococcal* infection includes a positive throat culture and a positive antistreptolysin-O (ASLO) titer. An ASLO titer of 333 Todd units indicates that the child has had a recent streptococcal infection.

The goals of treatment are eradicating the hemolytic streptococcal infection, preventing permanent cardiac damage, making the child more comfortable, and preventing recurrences of Group A *beta hemolytic streptococcal* infection. Nursing interventions include administering prescribed medications (such as penicillin, salicylates, and steroids), promoting rest and proper nutrition, providing emotional support for the child and the family, and teaching regarding the need for periodic follow-up with the physician. In addition, the nurse plays a key role in emphasizing the need for good dental hygiene and regular dental visits.

Bacterial Endocarditis

Bacterial endocarditis refers to an infection of the valves and inner lining of the heart. The condition most often follows an episode of bacteremia in those with acquired heart disease or a congenital anomaly of the great vessels. Common portals of infection are the oral cavity (dental work), urinary tract (catheterization), heart (cardiac surgery using synthetic valves, patches, or conduits), and blood stream (prolonged use of peripheral catheters or central lines). Microorganisms growing on the endocardium produce vegetative growths that invade adjacent tissues such as heart valves. These lesions are capable of producing emboli or clots that travel to the spleen, kidneys, central nervous system, lung, skin, and mucous membranes.

Symptoms of bacterial endocarditis include low-grade intermittent fever, malaise, headache, arthralgia, and weight loss. Additional clinical manifestations are associated with emboli formation. These manifestations include splinter hemorrhages (black lines beneath the nails), Osler nodes (red, painful intradermal nodes on the pads of the fingers), Janeway spots (painless, hemorrhagic areas on the palms and soles), and petechiae on the oral mucosa.

Diagnosis is based on the client's history, clinical manifestations, ECG findings (prolonged P-R interval), and changes in blood work (elevated erythrocyte sedimentation rate and leukocytosis). Vegetation and myocardial abscesses can be found on two-dimensional echocardiography.

A key element in the management of bacterial endocarditis is prevention. The client and family should be taught the importance of excellent dental care and the use of prophylactic antibiotic therapy before dental procedures are done. A number of medications are used for the prevention of bacterial endocarditis including amoxicillin (Amoxil), clindamycin (Cleocin), and azithromycin (Zithromax). Management of the client with bacterial endocarditis includes the use of high dose intravenous antibiotics for two to eight weeks.

Kawasaki's Disease (Mucocutaneous Lymph Node Syndrome)

Kawasaki's disease is an acute systemic vasculitis. The exact cause remains unknown, although it appears to be a problem with the immune system. The disease mainly affects male children under 5 years of age, with the peak incidence occurring in toddlers. The disease is best known for the damage done to the heart; however, it involves all the small- and medium-size blood vessels. The most common sequela of Kawasaki's disease (KD) is the dilation of coronary arteries, which results in aneurysm formation. Infants under 1 year of age and those over 5 years of age appear to be at the greatest risk for developing coronary problems. KD is one of the major causes of acquired heart disease in children in the United States.

The child with KD develops a high fever that lasts 5 or more days and fails to respond to antipyretics or antibiotics. Other symptoms include redness of the bulbar conjunctiva, inflammation of the pharynx and oral mucosa, red cracked lips, "strawberry tongue," and swelling of the cervical lymph nodes. One of the most notable symptoms is desquamation that begins at the fingertips and toes and gradually spreads, leaving the soles and palms red and swollen. Swelling is also noted in the weight-bearing joints. Additional findings include increased platelet counts and increased coagulation.

NOTE

Most cases of KD are reported in the winter and early spring. There is also an increased incidence in children who are exposed to recently cleaned carpet, which suggests there is perhaps an immune response.

There is no specific test for KD. The diagnosis is based on the presence of symptoms and supporting lab work that reveals a decreased number of RBC, an increased number of immature WBC, and an increased erythrocyte sedimentation rate. Medical management includes the use of IV immunoglobulin (2 g/kg given in a single infusion) and aspirin.

The nursing care of the child with KD focuses on relieving symptoms, providing emotional support, administering medications, and educating the family. The nurse should carefully monitor the vital signs and assess for signs of cardiac complications, which include congestive heart failure and myocardial infarction.

TIP

Signs of myocardial infarction in the infant or young child include abdominal pain, vomiting, restlessness, inconsolable crying, pallor, and shock. Signs of congestive heart failure include respiratory distress, tachycardia, and decreased urinary output.

Nursing interventions during the acute phase focus on the relief of symptoms. Inflammation of the skin and mucous membranes accounts for much of the child's discomfort during the acute phase. The nurse can help minimize discomfort by applying soothing, unscented lotions to the skin. Mouth care with a soft-bristled toothbrush is followed by the application of lubricating ointment to the lips. Acetaminophen can be given for fever and to relieve joint pain. The child should be placed in a quiet environment to promote rest.

The administration of intravenous gamma globulin requires that the nurse carefully assess vital signs and observe for signs of an allergic reaction, which include chills, fever, dyspnea, and flank pain.

CAUTION

The nurse must ensure patency of the IV line before administering gamma globulin because extravasation can result in tissue damage.

The child with KD might be discharged on high doses of aspirin for an extended period of time. The nurse should teach parents the side effects and symptoms of aspirin toxicity, including tinnitus, dizziness, headache, and confusion. Low-dose aspirin can be continued indefinitely if the child has coronary abnormalities. A child with coronary abnormalities should avoid contact sports.

CAUTION

The nurse should instruct the parents to discontinue the aspirin and notify the physician if the child is exposed to influenza or chickenpox.

Caring for the Child with Genitourinary Disorders

Genitourinary disorders that affect children include congenital anomalies, infections, and obstructive disorders. Because conditions such as pyelonephritis and renal calculi affect adults as well as children, these conditions and others are discussed in Chapter 6, "Care of the Client with Genitourinary Disorders." In this section, we will review the care of the child with obstructive uropathy and those with the external defects of hypospadias and epispadias/exstrophy of the bladder.

Obstructive Uropathy

Obstructive uropathy refers to structural or functional abnormalities of the urinary tract that result in diminished outflow of urine. Obstructions, which can occur anywhere along the urinary tract from the kidney to the urethral meatus, can result in pain, infection, sepsis, and loss of renal function. Urinary obstructions are particularly critical in the neonate and the very young children because increased vascular resistance and immaturity of the kidneys can lead to scarring and irreversible damage. In cases where only one kidney is affected, the unaffected kidney might compensate for the loss.

Symptoms associated with obstructive uropathy depend on the age of the child and the location of the obstruction. The child with congenital urethral obstruction could be asymptomatic or might present with urinary infections and an abdominal mass. Obstruction of the renal pelvis, the ureter, or ureteropelvic junction typically produces renal colic, whereas obstructions in the bladder result in poor urinary stream and incomplete emptying of the bladder.

Radionuclide scans and ultrasonography are preferred diagnostic measures because they expose the child to less radiation and there is no risk of an adverse reaction to contrast media. Additional diagnostic measures include imaging studies that show the severity of the obstruction.

Management of a child with obstructive uropathy depends on the location and severity. In some instances, such as obstruction in the posterior ureteral valve, aggressive intervention is needed to prevent damage to the entire urinary system. A transient or permanent urinary diversion is sometimes needed to prevent irreparable damage. Nursing interventions for the child with obstructive uropathy are similar to those of the adult client. These interventions are covered in Chapter 6.

External Defects (Hypospadias, Epispadias, Exstrophy of the Bladder)

External defects of the genitalia are particularly upsetting to parents because the nature of these defects affects both the ability to control elimination and future sexual ability. In some instances, the defect is easily repaired. In others, the defect is so severe that additional testing is needed to determine the sex of the newborn before correction takes place.

Hypospadias is a condition in which the urethra opens on the ventral or underside of the penile shaft. The condition varies in severity. In mild cases, the urethral opening is just below the tip of the penis. In the most severe cases, the urethral opening is located on the perineum between the scrotal halves. Chordee, or a fibrous band, is usually found with the more severe forms. Surgical correction is performed between 6 and 18 months of age before the child develops a body image or castration anxiety. The goal of correction is to enable the child to void standing, to improve the physical appearance, and to preserve a sexually adequate organ.

The choice of surgical procedure is affected by the severity of the defect and the presence of associated anomalies. A urinary stint can be used to allow optimal healing and to maintain the position of the newly formed urethra. Nursing interventions are aimed at providing sedation and pain control, caring for the operative site, preventing infection, and teaching parents regarding home care, which can include care for an indwelling catheter or stint. Parents should be told to avoid placing the infant in a tub until the stint is removed to prevent infection. Play activities that could result in trauma, such as straddle toys and sandbox, should be avoided until healing is complete.

> **CAUTION**
>
> Circumcision should not be performed on the newborn with hypospadias because the foreskin will be used in reconstruction.

Epispadias/Exstrophy of the Bladder

Epispadias refers to a defect in the urinary system characterized by a failure in urethral canalization. *Exstropy of the bladder* refers to a severe defect characterized by external bladder, splaying of the urethra, and failure of tubular formation often times with separation of the pelvic bone. Both defects are congenital anomalies that range in the degree of severity. In mild defects (glandular epispadias), the urethral opening is located on the topside or dorsal surface of the penis. In severe defects (cloacal extrophy), multiple organ systems are affected. Fortunately, the more severe defects are rare.

The repair of epispadias and exstrophy of the bladder requires multistage correction. Because the bladder is open to the outside, it is usually closed during the first two days of life. Additional procedures include correction of pelvic separation and repair of inguinal or umbilical hernias. The final phase of correction is the repair of the epispadias which includes formation of the urethral canal.

Management goals for the infant with epispadias/exstrophy of the bladder includes preserving renal function, attaining urinary control, preventing urinary tract infection, and preserving optimum external genitalia with urinary continence and sexual function.

> **CAUTION**
>
> Prior to surgery, the exposed bladder is covered with a clear plastic protective wrap or film dressing. The dressing should not contain an adhesive because this would damage the bladder mucosa. No petroleum jelly should be applied because this also damages the bladder mucosa.

> **TIP**
>
> The collection of urine prior to surgical repair is performed by holding the infant prone over a basin and allowing the urine to drip into the container or by using a medicine dropper or syringe to aspirate the urine directly from the bladder.

Caring for the Child with Neoplastic Disorders

Childhood cancer is a leading cause of death in children under 15 years of age. Although survival has increased for most types of cancer, few diagnoses present a greater challenge for the nurse as she cares for the child and his family. Refer to Chapter 13, "Care of the Client with Neoplastic Disorders," for a detailed review of cancer, treatment modalities, and nursing care. This section briefly reviews the key points of the following childhood cancers: leukemia, Wilms' tumor, retinoblastoma, neuroblastoma, osteosarcoma, Ewing's sarcoma, and rhabdomyosarcoma.

Leukemia

Leukemia, a cancer of the blood-forming elements of the bone marrow, is the most common form of childhood cancer. Pathological changes are related to the rapid proliferation of immature white blood cells, and symptoms include anemia, fatigue, lethargy, fever, joint and bone pain, pallor, petechiae, enlargement of the spleen, liver, and kidneys, and infections that do not respond to antibiotics Acute lymphoid leukemia, the most common form, is more prevalent in males 1–5 years of age.

Treatment involves a combination of cytotoxic drugs and possible bone marrow transplantation. Nursing interventions include preparing the child and family for diagnostic procedures, administering chemotherapy and pharmacologic agents including analgesics to control pain, observing for signs of infection, ensuring appropriate nutrition and hydrationand providing continuous emotional support. Additional interventions include strict adherence to handwashing to prevent infection and observance for signs of bleeding related to low platelet counts. Additional information about leukemia and its treatment can be found in Chapter 13.

Wilms' Tumor (Nephroblastoma)

This is the most common type of renal cancer. Parents usually find the tumor while diapering or bathing the infant. The tumor, which is confined to one side, is characteristically firm and nontender. The tumor is also usually encapsulated, so it is responsive to chemotherapy. Survival rates for Wilms' tumor are the highest of all childhood cancers.

CAUTION

The nurse should post a DO NOT PALPATE THE ABDOMEN sign on the bed of the child suspected of having Wilms' tumor to prevent examination trauma to the tumor site.

Retinoblastoma

Retinoblastoma is a cancer that arises from the retina. It is the most common intraocular malignancy of childhood. Most children with retinoblastoma are diagnosed between the ages of 1 and 2 years. Clinical manifestations include the presence of a "whitish glow" in the pupil (cat's eye reflex), strabismus, red, painful eye, orbital cellulitis, unilateral mydriasis. Other manifestations include changes in the color of the iris, hyphema, and blindness. Diagnosis is made by indirect ophthalmoscopy. Treatment depends on the stage of the tumor. Unilateral tumors staged as 1, 2, or 3 are treated with irradiation. Treatment of advanced tumors includes enucleation and chemotherapy. An ocular prosthesis is usually inserted within three weeks following surgery. Refer to Chapter 8, "Care of the Client with Sensory Disorders," for a more complete discussion of the client with ocular cancer and ocular prosthesis.

Neuroblastoma

Neuroblastoma refers to tumors that originate from the neural crest cells. These cells normally give rise to the sympathetic nervous system and the adrenal medulla. The primary site is the abdomen, although tumors can be located in the head, neck, chest, and pelvis. Clinical manifestations depend on the location and stage of the tumor. The most common finding is the presence of a firm, nontender, irregular mass in the abdomen that crosses the midline.

Additional symptoms include hypertension, tachycardia, flushing, and diuresis associated with increased catecholamine production. The location of primary tumors in other sites can result in neurological impairment, respiratory obstruction, and paralysis. Signs of distant metastasis include supraorbital ecchymosis and bone pain.

Diagnostic tests include CT scan, bone scan, and skeletal survey. Lab tests include urinary VMA (vanillylmandelic acid), HVA (homovanillic acid), dopamine, and norepinephrine levels. VMA and HVA are byproducts of adrenal hormones, and their levels are elevated in the urine of affected children. Increased amounts of ferritin, neurospecific enolase, and ganglioside are typical in those with neuroblastoma. Amplification of a specific gene (N-myc gene) and chromosomal abnormalities are generally associated with a poor prognosis.

The treatment of neuroblastoma depends on the stage. Surgical removal is the preferred treatment of choice for stage I and stage II tumors. Stage III and stage IV tumors are treated with radiotherapy and chemotherapy. Drugs used in the treatment of neuroblastoma include vincristine, doxorubicin, cyclophosphamide, and cisplatin. Refer to Chapter 12 for a listing of drugs used in the treatment of neuroblastoma.

Osteosarcoma and Ewing's Sarcoma

Sarcomas are rare types of cancer that develop in the supporting structures of the body. Sarcomas fall into two main types: bone and soft tissue sarcomas. *Osteosarcoma* and

Ewing's sarcoma are malignant bone tumors. Osteosarcoma is most frequently found near the epiphyseal plates of the long bones. The peak incidence of osteosarcoma is in males 10– 25 years of age. Treatment includes the use of antineoplastic drugs; high doses of methotrexate, doxorubicin, actinomycin, and cisplatin.

Ewing's sarcoma affects flat bones, ribs, and skull as well as the shaft of the femur, tibia, and humerus. The peak incidence is in males 4– 25 years of age. The treatment of Ewing's sarcoma includes surgery, radiation, and chemotherapy. Chemotherapeutic agents used in the treatment of Ewing's sarcoma include vincristine, dactinomycin, and cyclophosphamide.

Rhabdomyosarcoma

Rhabdomyosarcoma is a malignant neoplasm of striated or skeletal muscle. These tumors occur in many sites; however, the most common sites are the head and neck, especially the eye orbit, bladder, and testes. Initial signs and symptoms depend on the site of the tumor and the degree of compression on surrounding organs.

Clinical manifestations of the orbit include unilateral proptosis, conjunctival ecchymosis, and strabismus. Symptoms associated with tumors affecting the nasopharynx and paranasal sinuses include nasal stuffiness, nasal obstruction, local pain and swelling, sinusitis, and epistaxis. Involvement of the middle ear results in symptoms of chronic serous otitis media. Large tumors can produce facial nerve palsy.

Tumors of the retroperitoneal areas are generally "silent"; that is, they produce few if any symptoms unless they are large, invasive, and widely metastatic. Symptoms associated with retroperitoneal tumors are abdominal mass, pain, and intestinal or genitourinary obstruction.

Diagnostic measures include CT, MRI, bone surveys, and lumbar puncture. Treatment of rhabdomyosarcoma depends on tumor staging. Generally a multimodal approach consisting of surgery, radiation, and chemotherapy is used.

Surviving Childhood Cancer

Each year approximately 12,400 children ranging in age from birth to 19 years are diagnosed with some form of cancer. Medical advances in early diagnosis and more effective treatments have dramatically improved cancer survival rates among the young. Those who survive are at an increased risk for post-treatment health problems. These health problems include cognitive disabilities, growth retardation, hormonal dysfunction, sterility, and secondary cancers. For a more complete discussion of the health problems encountered by childhood cancer survivors visit the website of Candlelighters Childhood Cancer Foundation at www.candlelighters.org.

Caring for the Child with Cerebral Disorders

Cerebral disorders affecting children include epilepsy, tumors, head trauma, intracranial infections, and Reye syndrome. Several of these disorders, their treatment, and nursing care are discussed in Chapter 11, "Care of the Client with Neurological Disorders." In this section, we will review the care of the child with intracranial infections and Reye's syndrome because they specifically relate to the pediatric client.

Intracranial Infections (Encephalitis and Bacterial Meningitis)

Encephalitis is an inflammatory process affecting the central nervous system. The condition is caused by a variety of organisms, including bacteria and viruses. It may also be a post-infection following a viral illness. In childhood, the majority of cases of encephalitis are associated with communicable illness such as measles and varicella. In the case of West Nile encephalitis, the vector reservoir is the mosquito. Most cases occur in the summer and subside in the fall.

Symptoms of encephalitis vary from mild manifestations, which look like aseptic meningitis, to fulminating encephalitis, which reflects severe and sometimes fatal involvement of the central nervous system. Symptoms can include malaise, fever, headache, nausea and vomiting, ataxia, tremors, stupor, seizures, spasticity, coma, and death.

The diagnosis of encephalitis is based on clinical manifestations, CT scan, and routine lab work. Management and nursing interventions include providing adequate nutrition and hydration, monitoring for signs of increasing intracranial pressure, monitoring vital signs, and administering prescribed medications. The prognosis depends on the child's age, general health, type of organism, and effectiveness of treatment.

Bacterial meningitis refers to an acute inflammation of the meninges and the cerebrospinal fluid. Bacterial meningitis is caused by a variety of bacteria; however, infections caused by *Haemophilus influenza b*, *S. pneumoniae*, *Neisseria meningitides* account for 95% of the cases in children over two months of age. Leading causes of bacterial meningitis in the neonatal period are group *B streptococci*, *E. coli*, and *Listeria monocytogenes*. The occurrence of meningitis varies with the season, with *H. influenza* infections occurring more often in the autumn and early winter, whereas *pneumococcal* and *meningococcal* infections occur more commonly in the winter and early spring.

> **CAUTION**
>
> Meningococcal meningitis occurs in epidemics and is the only form readily transmitted by droplets from the nasopharynx. Caregivers should use droplet precautions when caring for a client with meningococcal menintitis.
>
> The incidence of bacterial meningitis has declined since the use of conjugate vaccines against *H. influenza b*. It is hoped that the use of the pneumococcal conjugate vaccine will result in a decline in bacterial meningitis caused by *S. pneumoniae*.

Clinical manifestations of acute bacterial meningitis depend on the causative organism and the age of the child. Table 16.6 compares the symptoms of meningitis in the neonate and premature infant, infants and young children, and children and adolescents.

TABLE 16.6   Meningitis Symptoms by Age

Neonate/Premature Infant	Infants/Young Children (3 months to 2 years)	Children and Adolescents
Symptoms are vague and nonspecific, but include refusal of feedings, poor sucking ability, vomiting, diarrhea, poor muscle tone, poor cry, hypothermia or fever, apnea, irritability, bulging fontanels.	Symptoms include fever, poor feeding, vomiting, irritability, restlessness, seizures, high-pitched cry, bulging fontanels, nuchal rigidity, positive Brudzinski's and Kernig's signs.	Symptoms include fever, chills, headache, vomiting, altered sensorium, seizure, irritability, photophobia, vomiting, diarrhea, nuchal rigidity, positive Brudzinski's and Kernig's signs. Petechiae and purpura occur in half of the clients with meningococcal infection.

Complications associated with bacterial meningitis include obstructive hydrocephalus, subdural effusion, meningococcemia, and Waterhouse-Friderichsen syndrome. This syndrome is characterized by overwhelming septic shock, disseminated intravascular coagulation, massive hemorrhage of the adrenal glands, and purpura. These clients require prompt emergency treatment with placement in the intensive care unit. The mortality rate for those with Waterhouse-Friderichsen is as high as 90%.

Other acute complications include SIADH, cerebral edema, and inflammation of the cranial nerves that can result in visual impairment, hearing loss, and nerve palsies. Long-term complications include cerebral palsy, seizure disorder, and mental handicaps.

Diagnostic measures used for the child with bacterial meningitis include CBC, urinalysis, and lumbar puncture for cell count, Gram stain, culture and sensitivity, protein, and glucose. Nursing care of the child with bacterial meningitis includes maintaining appropriate isolation techniques, administrating antimicrobial medication, observing for signs of increasing intracranial pressure, ensuring adequate nutrition and hydration, and observing for complications. Additional aspects of care are discussed in Chapter 11.

NOTE

Broad spectrum antimicrobials are not initiated until results of cultures are obtained. Isolation is maintained for at least 24 hours after initiation of antimicrobial therapy.

Reye's Syndrome

Reye's syndrome (RS), which most commonly affects children between 4 and 16 years of age, is a toxic encephalopathy characterized by cerebral edema and fatty infiltration of the liver. The cause of Reye's syndrome is unclear; however, in most instances, it follows a common viral illness such as influenza or varicella.

> **CAUTION**
>
> There is an association between the use of aspirin and other salicylates in the treatment of children with viral illnesses such as chickenpox and influenza and the development of Reye's syndrome. Aspirin and medications containing "hidden" salicylates (for example, Pepto-Bismol) should not be given to children with viral illnesses.

Symptoms of Reye's syndrome typically appear 3–5 days after the onset of chickenpox, but can occur any time from 1 to 14 days after a viral infection. Symptoms begin with profuse vomiting and varying degrees of neurological impairment including deterioration of consciousness. If left untreated, the condition deteriorates and the child can develop seizures, coma, and respiratory arrest.

The definitive diagnosis for Reye's syndrome is established by liver biopsy, which reveals the presence of fatty infiltration. The prognosis depends on early recognition and aggressive therapy. Interventions are aimed at controlling intracranial pressure, preventing cerebral edema, and monitoring for impaired coagulation.

Caring for the Child with Integumentary Disorders

The skin and hair are common sites of infection in the pediatric client. Some of these disorders such as eczema are associated with childhood conditions like asthma. Others, such as scabies and pediculosis capitis, are the result of infestation with parasites. While these conditions are uncomfortable, they do not threaten the general health of the client as do the tick borne illnesses of Lyme disease and Rocky Mountain spotted fever. This section reviews each of these disorders. Other integumentary disorders, including burns, are discussed in Chapter 7, "Care of the Client with Integumentary Disorders."

Eczema (Atopic Dermatitis)

Eczema, a skin condition often associated with allergies, usually begins in infancy or early childhood. There are three forms of eczema, which are based on the age of onset and the distribution of skin lesions as defined in Table 16.7.

TABLE 16.7 Eczema Characteristics

Infantile Eczema	Childhood Eczema	Adolescent/Adult Eczema
Appearance of lesions: erythematous vesicles or papules that weep; crusting and scaling lesions that are often symmetrical; infant frequently has a history of food allergies.	Appearance of lesions: symmetric clusters of erythematous or flesh-colored papules; scaling patches; dry, hyperpigmented lichenification.	Appearance of lesions: symmetric clusters of erythematous or flesh-colored papules; dry, thick lesions; scaling patches; dry hyperpigmented lichenification.

Additional symptoms include itching, swollen lymph nodes, increased palmer creases, dark circles beneath the eyes ("allergic" shiners), and increased susceptibility to skin infections.

Management of the client with eczema is aimed at hydrating the skin, controlling pruritus, preventing flare-ups, and preventing secondary skin infections. Bathing should be done using tepid water with a mild, nonperfumed soap. An emollient lotion such as Aquaphor or Eucerin is applied immediately while the skin is still damp. Soft cotton pajamas or one-piece sleep outfits that prevent scratching of exposed skin should be worn. Nails should be kept short and socks and mittens applied to prevent rubbing or scratching the lesions. Parents should be taught to avoid conditions that increase pruritus. These conditions include furry stuffed animals, perfumed soaps and fabric softeners, perfumed diaper wipes, woolen clothes and blankets, rough fabrics, and hot temperatures. Exposure to articles containing latex should also be avoided.

Pharmacological agents used in the treatment of eczema include antihistamines (to control itching), topical steroids (to control flare-ups), and anti-infectives (for secondary infections). Additional therapies include the use of topical immunosuppressives, interferons, and essential fatty acids. Elidel (1% topical pimecrolimus) has been proven to be effective in treating eczema in children two years of age and older.

Scabies

Scabies refers to a contagious skin disease caused by mite infestation. Scabies is transmitted by close contact with persons who are infested. Although scabies is associated with poor hygiene and crowded living conditions, the mite can be carried by pets. Transmission among school children is common.

Signs and symptoms associated with scabies include visible white ridges between the fingers, on the palms and inner aspects of the wrists, and intense itching that becomes worse at night. Sores on the body can become infected with bacteria, making antibiotic therapy necessary. Hypersensitive reactions result in excoriated papules and crusted lesions on the elbows, lower abdomen, buttocks, and axillary folds.

Scabies is confirmed by scraping the lesion and examining the specimen under a microscope for the presence of mites and eggs. Scabicides such as Elimite (permethrin 5% cream) are recommended for the treatment of scabies. Medications containing lindane (Kwell), which are more toxic and less effective, are not recommended in the treatment of infants and children with scabies. The nurse should instruct the parents regarding the proper use of the medication as well as the care of clothes and personal items to eliminate the mites.

Pediculosis Capitis (Head Lice)

Pediculosis capitis is an infection of the scalp caused by a common parasite, *Pediculosis humanus capitis*. The adult female louse deposits her eggs at night along the hair shaft close to the skin. The only signs associated with lice infestation are intense itching (especially in the occipital area of the scalp, behind the ears, and along the nape of the neck) and the presence of nits or egg cases that attach to the hair shaft.

TIP

Nits are differentiated from dandruff by their attachment to the hair shaft. The nurse should wear gloves when examining the hair of the child with lice.

Therapeutic management of the child with lice consists of the application of a pediculi-cide such as Nix (permethrin 1% cream rinse) or RID (pyrethrin/piperonyl butoxide), which kills adult lice and nits. These products, which are safer than products containing lindane, can be purchased without a prescription. Manual removal of nits is done using a nit comb or flea comb. Complete combing of the entire head should be performed each day until all the nits are removed.

To prevent the spread and reoccurrence of lice, the nurse should caution children against sharing personal items such as combs, hair ornaments, caps, scarves, and other items used on or near the head.

Lyme Disease

Lyme disease is transmitted by a spirochete (*Borrelia burgdorferi*) from an infected tick. Hosts include sheep, cattle, deer, and mice. The incidence is highest in the spring to late fall. The most characteristic finding is an expanding skin lesion 4–20 days after the bite. The skin lesion can appear anywhere on the body. The skin lesion begins as a red macule or papule and expands to form an annular or circular erythema with a "bull's eye" appearance. Weeks or months later, abnormalities can occur in the heart, joints, or nervous system. Serologic tests show a rise in antibodies against the spirochete. Management includes the use of intramuscular or oral antibiotics (tetracyclines or peni-cillins), attention to skin care, and assessment of CNS status.

> **TIP**
>
> Tetracyclines should not be administered during pregnancy or to children between ages 4 months and 8 years because it can result in yellow or brown discoloration of the teeth. When taken after the fourth month of gestation, tetracyclines can cause staining of the deciduous teeth; discoloration of the permanent teeth occurs when tetracyclines are taken between the ages of 4 months to 8 years. Tetracycline has also been shown to negatively affect fetal bone development resulting in skeletal retardation.

Rocky Mountain Spotted Fever

Rocky Mountain spotted fever is transmitted by a rickettsia (*Rickettsia rickettsii*), and it is the most commonly reported ricketsial illness in the United States. Sometimes referred to as *tick-borne fever*, it originates from a tick bite, from skin contamination by crushing an infected tick against the skin, or by the conjunctiva becoming contaminated by infected secretions. The most common hosts are the wood tick and dog tick. The inci-dence is highest in the months of April, May, and June.

Symptoms appear several days after the bite and include severe headache, photophobia, malaise, anorexia, fever, and muscle and joint pains. Extreme restlessness, insomnia, hyperparesthesia, changes in mental status, and enlargement and tenderness of the spleen are common. The most distinguishing symptom is the development of rose-colored macules on the wrists, ankles, soles, and palms, which spread over the body. The rash becomes darker in hue and takes on a dusky appearance with the development of petechiae, purpura, and skin hemorrhages. Damage to the endothelial and smooth muscle cells result in changes in capillary permeability, setting up generalized vasculitis with hemorrhage and thrombus formation. At the extreme peripheral vasculature (ear lobes, fingers, toes, and scrotum), vascular collapse can result in necrosis.

Management includes the use of antibiotics (tetracycline or chloramphenicol) early in the illness. If treatment is not instituted early in the illness, the disease progresses rapidly to circulatory collapse and death. Nursing care includes careful monitoring of renal function, attention to blood work (CBC), and general comfort measures. Figure 16.6 shows the signs and symptoms associated with Rocky Mountain spotted fever.

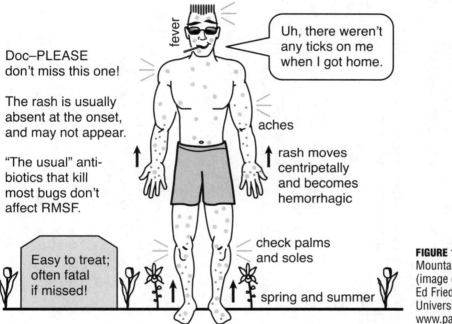

FIGURE 16.6 Rocky Mountain spotted fever (image courtesy of Dr. Ed Friedlander, University of Kansas; www.pathguy.com).

Caring for the Child with Communicable Disease

Illness and death from common childhood communicable diseases have dramatically declined since the advent of immunizations. Despite this, infectious diseases do occur; therefore, the nurse should be familiar with the manifestations of common communicable diseases in childhood, their modes of transmission, and appropriate nursing interventions. Table 16.8 reviews some of the more common communicable diseases of childhood.

For the most up to date immunization schedules, visit the American Academy of Family Physicians (www.aafp.org) or the Centers for Disease Control and Prevention (www.cdc.gov). For a listing of transmission-based precautions, visit the Centers for Disease Control and Prevention (www.cdc.gov).

TABLE 16.8   Communicable Diseases of Childhood

Communicable Disease	Mode of Transmission	Incubation Period	Communicable Period	Presenting Symptoms	Treatment
Measles (rubeola) Etiology: Viral	Respiratory secretions, blood, urine, direct contact with droplets	10–20 days	4 days before to 5 days after the rash appears	Fever, cough, coryza, malaise, conjunctivitis, Koplik's spots, erythematous maculopapular rash over face and body; rash becomes brownish in appearance after 3–4 days	Bedrest, vitamin A supplements, soft foods, increase fluids, dim light. Airborne precautions. Antibiotics might be given to high-risk children to prevent secondary complications.
Mumps Etiology: Parmyxovirus	Droplets from saliva of infected persons	14–21 days	Immediately before and after swelling occurs	Fever, headache, malaise, enlarged painful parotid glands	Bedrest, fluids, analgesics, soft foods. Droplet precautions. To prevent orchitis, tight-fitting, soft underpants should be worn for support.
German Measles (rubella) Etiology: Rubella virus	Droplets from nasopharyngeal secretions, feces, and urine	14–21 days	7 days before to about 5 days after the rash appears	Low-grade fever, headache, malaise, anorexia, cough, sore throat, pinkish red maculopapular rash that begins on face and spreads downward over the trunk and legs; rash disappears within 3 days	Antipyretics and analgesics Droplet precautions. Congenital Rubella-Contact precautions for 1 year as well as droplet precautions. Caution: A child with rubella should be isolated from pregnant women.
Chickenpox (varicella) Etiology: Varicella zoster virus	Airborne droplets, direct contact, contaminated objects	2–3 weeks	1 day before the eruption of lesions to the time when all lesions are crusted	Eruptions of papules, vesicles, and crusts more prominent on the trunk, pruritus	Antivirals and antihistamines. High-risk infants and children can be given VZIG after exposure. Airborne precautions. Contact precautions with lesions. Caution: The use of aspirin is contraindicated in a child with varicella.
Whooping Cough (pertussis) Etiology: Bordetella pertussis	Direct contact with droplets or articles contaminated with droplets	3–21 days	Greatest during catarrhal stage before onset of paroxysms or cough; may extend for 4 weeks after paroxysms begin	Catarrhal stage: Symptoms of URI, dry hacking cough. Paroxysmal stage: short, rapid cough, followed by high-pitched crowing sound; flushed cheeks. Vomiting or cyanosis can occur after the attack.	Bedrest, small frequent fluids, placement in high humidity, observe for signs of airway obstruction. Droplet precautions.
Diphtheria Etiology: Cornybacterium diphtheriae	Direct contact with respiratory secretions	Varies, generally 2–5 days	Usually 2–4 weeks	Sero-sanguinous nasal discharge, sore throat, low grade fever, white or gray membrane in the throat	Antibiotics, bedrest, observe for respiratory obstruction Diptheria antitoxin IV. Droplet precautions Caution: Assess client for allergies to horse serum before administering antitoxin.
Roseola Etiology: HHV 6 (Human herpes virus type 6)	Unknown	5–15 days	Unknown	Persistent high fever for 3–4 days, discrete rose pink macular or maculopapular rash appearing on the trunk and spreading to the neck, face, and extremities. The rash appears 2–3 days after the onset of fever and lasts 1–2 days.	Nonspecific, antipyretics. Standard precautions.
Fifth's Disease Etiology: HPV B 19 (Human antiparavirus B 19)	Respiratory secretions or blood from infected persons	4–14 days, may be as long as 20 days	Uncertain; usually 1 week before the onset of symptoms	Three stages: Stage 1: "slapped" cheek erythema Stage 2: maculopapular red spots symmetrically distributed on arms and legs Stage 3: rash subsides but reappears if the skin is irritated	Antipyretics, analgesics, antiparavirus inflammatories, isolation if hospitalized. Airborne and standard precautions.

Caring for the Child with Musculoskeletal Disorders

These disorders involve alterations in bones, joints, muscles, or cartilaginous tissues. Musculoskeletal disorders, like fractures, are the result of trauma (refer to Chapter 14, "Care of the Client with Musculoskeletal and Connective Tissue Disorders"). Disorders such as congenital hip dysplasia and clubfoot involve prenatal or genetic factors. Other musculoskeletal disorders include scoliosis, Legg-Calvé-Perthes Disease, and muscular dystrophy. Juvenile rheumatoid arthritis (juvenile idiopathic arthritis), a chronic inflammatory disease, produces symptoms similar to those seen in the adult with rheumatoid arthritis.

Congenital Clubfoot

Also known as *talipes equinovarus*, this problem is a structural deformity in which the foot is turned inward, causing the child to walk on the outer border of the foot. Congenital clubfoot can be classified as *positional* (due to intrauterine crowding), *teratologic* (associated with other congenital anomalies), or *true* clubfoot (due to a bony abnormality). The affected foot is usually smaller and shorter than the unaffected foot. If the defect is unilateral, the affected limb is smaller with atrophy of the calf muscle.

Treatment begins in the nursery or shortly after birth with the application of casts. The cast is changed and the affected limb is manipulated weekly for the first 8–12 weeks until maximum correction is achieved. If the deformity has not been corrected with casting, the child might be placed in a splint or reverse shoe so that the foot turns outward rather than inward. If the deformity is not corrected with either of these methods, surgical intervention may be implemented. Surgical correction involves pin fixation and the release of tight joints and tendons followed by casting for 2–3 months. After the cast is removed, a varus-prevention brace is worn.

Developmental Hip Dysplasia

Developmental hip dysplasia (DHD) most commonly involves subluxation or incomplete dislocation of the hip. The disorder can affect one or both hips; if only one hip is involved, it is most often the left hip. Although the cause is unknown, certain factors such as gender, family history, intrauterine position, method of delivery, and postnatal positioning affect the risk of DHD. Females are affected more often than males, and there is an increased incidence if one of the parents or a sibling had the disorder. DHD is more common in the infant with frank breech presentation and delivery by Cesarean section.

NOTE

DHD is found more often in groups that use cradle boards or papoose boards for carrying the infant (such as Native Americans) than those groups that carry the infant on the back or on the hips (such as Asians).

Symptoms of DHD in the infant 2–3 months of age include laxity in the hip joint and the presence of the *Ortolani click*—the audible sound that is made when the affected hip is abducted. Other signs include shortening of the affected limb (Allis' sign), asymmetrical thigh and gluteal folds, and limited abduction of the affected side. Symptoms of DHD in the older child include delays in walking, the presence of extra gluteal folds, and a positive Trendelenburg sign when weight bearing. If both hips are affected, the child develops a waddling gait and lordosis.

Early diagnosis and correction of DHD are important because correction becomes more difficult as the child ages. Correction in the infant less than 6 months of age involves the use of a Pavlik harness. This device allows movement but prevents hip extension or adduction and is worn continuously for about 3–6 months. Other nursing interventions include triple diapering to keep the leg abducted. Failure to diagnose the condition before the child begins to stand results in apparent contractures of the hip adductor and flexor muscles. Correction at this point involves traction, open or closed reduction, and the application of a hip spica cast. Because of non-compliance with treatment, casts are usually used as the treatment of last resort.

CAUTION

The infant is growing rapidly, so the straps of the Pavlik harness should be checked every 1–2 weeks for needed adjustments because vascular or nerve damage can occur with improper positioning.

Osteogenesis Imperfecta

Osteogenesis imperfecta, the most common form of osteoporosis in childhood, is due to a malfunction in the body's production of the protein collagen. There are four different types of the disorder with each having varying degrees of severity.

Children with Type 1 osteogenesis imperfecta (the most common type) typically have variable fractures with normal or near normal stature. The incidence of fractures decreases after puberty. Additional findings include the presence of blue sclera, weakened tooth dentin, joint laxity, and hearing loss that becomes apparent in adolescence.

Type 2 osteogeneis imperfecta is characterized by extensive involvement of the ribs and skeleton. Babies with Type 2 osteogenesis imperfecta frequently die in utero or early infancy due to multiple fractures and underdevelopment of the lungs.

Type 3 osteogenesis imperfecta is identified in the newborn period and is associated with the presence of numerous fractures, blue sclera, bone fragility, and kyphoscoliosis. Most children with Type 3 osteogenesis imperfecta die in childhood from cardiorespiratory failure.

Type 4 osteogenesis imperfecta is characterized by fractures without other symptoms of the disorder. The child might have bowing of the legs and other structural deformities; however, the incidence of fractures decreases with puberty.

Treatment of the child with osteogenesis imperfecta focuses on providing physical care and emotional support for the child and parents. Parents might be suspected of physically abusing their child because of the frequent treatment of fractures. These suspicions can interfere with providing needed care to the child and his family.

Because the cure for OI has not been found, treatment of the disease relies on managing the symptoms, preventing complications, and developing and maintaining bone mass and muscle strength. Conservative treatments are aimed at treating the fracture, preventing contractures and deformities, preventing osteoporosis, and preserving lower extremity joints needed for weight-bearing. (See Chapter 14 for additional information on the treatment of fractures.) Physical therapy and activities to strengthen muscles and improve bone density are included in the client's plan of care. Water exercises are well suited to the child with osteogenesis imperfecta because they provide light passive resistance for strengthening bones and muscles.

Newer interventions with biphosphates such as alendronate (Fosamax), molecular therapies, and bone marrow transplant have shown promise in treating the child with osteogenesis imperfecta.

Legg-Calvé-Perthes Disease (Coxa Plana)

This disease is a self-limiting disorder in which there is an aseptic necrosis of the head of the femur. Although the exact cause is unknown, it occurs most often in males 4–8 years of age.

Symptoms include soreness, aching, stiffness, and the appearance of a limp on the affected side. Pain and joint dysfunction are most evident on arising or at the end of the day.

The goal of treatment is to keep the head of the femur within the acetabulum and to prevent microfractures of the epiphysis. Initial measures include bedrest and nonweight-bearing activity. An abduction brace, leg casts, or leather harness sling can be used to prevent weight-bearing. Conservative therapy is continued for 2–4 years. Although the condition is self-limiting, the ultimate outcome depends on early recognition and effective treatment.

Scoliosis

Scoliosis refers to a lateral curvature of the spine with rotation of the vertebrae. It is the most common spinal deformity and is associated with physiological alterations in the spine, chest, and pelvis. There are two classifications of scoliosis: functional (curvature straigtens with side bending) and structural (curvature does not straighten with side bending). Idiopathic scoliosis is more prevalent in adolescent females, and there is some evidence that it might be genetically transmitted as an autosomal dominant trait. Routine scoliosis screening is often a part of the adolescent physical exam especially for those 10– 13 years of age.

> **NOTE**
>
> The Adams position is used to screen for scoliosis. With the examiner standing behind, the child is asked to bend from the waist while allowing the arms to hang freely. When viewed from behind, the child with scoliosis is noted to have a primary and compensatory curvature of the spine. Additional findings include shoulder, hip, and waist asymmetry and prominence of the shoulder blade.

Conservative treatment includes the use of either the Milwaukee brace or Boston brace and exercise. Surgical correction consists of realignment and straightening the spine with internal fixation. Two surgical methods that can be used are Harrington rods and Luque wires. The Cotrel-Dubousset approach uses both Harrington rods and Luque wires. The caregiver should use logrolling technique when turning the client with Harrington rods.

Postoperative nursing care includes assessment of vital signs, medication administration for pain, assessment of operative site, and providing emotional support to the client and family. Additional nursing interventions are directed at helping the child deal with changes in body image.

Juvenile Rheumatoid Arthritis (Juvenile Idiopathic Arthritis)

Juvenile rheumatoid arthritis (JRA), sometimes referred to as *juvenile idiopathic arthritis*, is a group of chronic inflammatory diseases that affect the joints and other tissues. Girls are affected more often than boys, with the peak age of onset between ages 1 and 3 years and again between ages 8 and 10 years.

Clinical manifestations of the disorder are similar to those of the adult with rheumatoid arthritis. Symptoms include swelling and loss of motion in affected joints. The joints are swollen, warm to the touch, but seldom red. Stiffness or "gelling" in the joints is worse in the morning or after a period of inactivity. Features that distinguish JRA from rheumatoid arthritis are the age of onset, negative rheumatoid factor, and a tendency for the arthritis to become inactive with age.

There is no definitive test for diagnosing JRA. The diagnosis is based on clinical criteria including the age at onset, the number of joints affected, and the elimination of other illnesses.

Just as there is no definitive test for JRA, there is no cure. Interventions are aimed at controlling pain, preserving range of motion in the joints, minimizing inflammation and formation of deformities, and promoting normal growth and development in a child with chronic illness. Pharmacologic agents used in the treatment of JRA include nonsteroidal antiinflammatory drugs (NSAIDs), slower acting antirheumatic drugs (SAARDs), cytotoxic agents, and steroids. Biologic response modifiers are usually not used in the treatment of JRA. (See Chapter 14 for information regarding medications and other therapies used in the treatment of rheumatoid arthritis.)

Caring for the Child with Neuromuscular Disorders

Neuromuscular disorders can result from a number of factors including prematurity, congenital anomalies, or hereditary conditions. In this section, we will review three disorders affecting the newborn and young child: cerebral palsy, neural tube defects, and muscular dystrophies. Disorders such as Guillain-Barré, which affect the adolescent and adult, are discussed in Chapter 10.

Cerebral Palsy

Cerebral palsy (CP) includes several different types, all of which involve motor deficits, as summarized in Table 16.9.

TABLE 16.9   Types of Cerebral Palsy

Type	Area of Injury	Clinical Manifestation
Spastic	Cerebral cortex or pyramidal tract	Persistent hypertonia
Dyskinetic	Extrapyramidal, basal ganglia	Voluntary muscle impairment
Ataxic	Cerebellum	Abnormal voluntary movement involving balance
Mixed	Multiple areas	No dominant motor pattern

Causes of cerebral palsy include prematurity, birth trauma, hypoxia, and pathological jaundice. Care of the child with CP includes several treatment modalities. Exercises to improve tongue control are essential for speech therapy and to improve feeding. The use of suckers, straws, and pinwheels improve tongue movement and help to decrease the extrusion reflex. Orthopedic interventions include braces, splints, and positioning devices. These devices are used to promote range of motion, provide skeletal alignment and stability, and prevent contractures. Surgical interventions might be needed to improve function by balancing muscle power and stabilizing joints. Pharmacological interventions include the use of anticonvulsants to control seizures and skeletal muscle relaxants to control spasticity. Injections of botulinum toxin into specific muscles is a relatively new treatment for controlling spastic movements. The prognosis for the child with cerebral palsy depends on level of involvement. Most children with CP have visual and auditory problems that require special aids. Those with hemiplegia or ataxia show improvement as they age and are eventually able to ambulate. Others might require ongoing assistance with mobility and activities of daily living. Most children and adults with CP are cared for in the home, although those with more severe deficits may be cared for in long-term care facilities.

Neural Tube Defects

Central nervous system (CNS), or neural tube defects, make up the largest group of congenital anomalies. The incidence of neural tube defects is drastically reduced by supplementing the mother's diet with folic acid prior to conception. Avoiding extremes of temperature during early fetal development likewise reduces the risk of neural tube defects.

CAUTION

The pregnant client should avoid external heat exposure, such as hot tubs and saunas, electric blankets, and so on because these have been identified as factors that increase the risk of neural tube defects.

Spina Bifida

This disorder is marked by a failure of the bony spine to close. It is the most common defect of the central nervous system. There are two types of spina bifida: spina bifida occulta and spina bifida cystica. Of these two types, spina bifida cystica, an external sac-like protrusion, causes the greatest CNS damage.

The major forms of spina bifida cystica are *meningocele* (the defect contains the meninges and spinal fluid) and *myelomeningocele* (the defect contains the meninges, nerve tissue, and spinal fluid). Unlike the child with a meningocele, who usually has no neurological deficit, the child with a myelomeningocele often has serious neurological deficit.

In most instances, myelomeningocele occurs in the lumbar or lumbosacral area. Regardless of where the defect is located, higher and larger defects result in more neurological damage.

The major preoperative goal is to prevent infection. The defect, which is usually enclosed in a thin membrane, should be protected from trauma as well as contamination with urine and stool, which can cause infection. Any stool or urine near the sac is gently removed using sterile saline, and the sac is examined for signs of leakage.

> **CAUTION**
>
> During the preoperative period, the nurse should give priority to preventing injury to or drying of the sac. The sac should be covered with a sterile, nonadherent dressing moistened with sterile normal saline. Dressings are changed every 2–4 hours. The newborn should be placed prone with the hips slightly flexed and elevated (low Trendelenburg) to prevent stretching of involved nerves.

Surgical correction usually takes place within the first 24–72 hours of life to prevent local infection and trauma to the exposed tissues. Several neurosurgical and reconstructive procedures are used for skin closure. Postoperative nursing interventions include elevating the head of the bed, measuring the head circumference each shift, monitoring the intake and output, providing meticulous skin care, and providing range of motion exercises. Parents should be taught how to empty the bladder using the Crede method as well as proper techniques for performing a straight catheterization. Complications of myelomeningocele include the development of hydrocephalus, urinary tract infection, meningitis, pressure sores, and contractures.

Symptoms of meningitis in the infant include a high-pitched cry, temperature instability, poor feeding, and bulging fontanels. Symptoms of meningitis in the child include fever, projectile vomiting, headache, and visual disturbances

Muscular Dystrophies

Muscular dystrophies refer to a group of inherited degenerative diseases that affect the cells of specific muscle groups resulting in muscle atrophy and weakness. The most common type, Duchenne muscular dystrophy, is inherited as a sex-linked disorder; weak, hypertrophied leg muscles; and the use of Gower's maneuver (see Figure 16.7) to stand erect. Children with Duchenne muscular dystrophy lose the ability to walk by 9–12 years of age.

> **NOTE**
>
> With Gower's maneuver, the child places his hands on his knees and moves his hands up his legs until he's standing erect.

The goal of treatment is aimed at maintaining mobility and independence for as long as possible. Nursing interventions include dietary teaching to prevent obesity and complications associated with limited mobility, coordinating healthcare services provided by physical therapy, and providing emotional support to the child and family.

1.

2.

3.

FIGURE 16.7 Gower's maneuver.

Caring for the Abused and Neglected Child

One of the most difficult clients for the pediatric nurse to care for is the child who is the victim of abuse or neglect. It is hard to imagine how anyone could endanger the safety and life of a child, yet neglect and abuse do occur. The nurse must learn to cope with personal feelings of anger and frustration in order to provide the best of care to the child and his family.

In some> instances, the signs of abuse are obvious. Such is the case of certain types of burns, fractures, and head injury. Other signs of abuse include a history of old injuries, apathy or withdrawal in the child, inappropriate reaction to injury, wariness of physical contact. In other cases, such as Munchausen's (abuse by proxy) and shaken baby syndrome, the abuse is more subtle. The priority of the nurse is to prevent further injury and to remove the child from the abusive situation. Some inherited conditions (osteogenesis imperfecta) or cultural practices (coining) give the appearance of abuse when they are not. Table 16.10 outlines the common characteristics in the child, the parents, and the environment where abuse occurs. Specific care of many abuse injuries (burns, fractures, and head trauma) are covered in other sections of the text.

TABLE 16.10 Characteristics of Child Abuse

Common Characteristics of the Abused Child	Common Characteristics of the Abusive Parent	Common Characteristics in the Abusive Environment
Difficult temperament (ADHD, conduct disorder)	History of being abused	Chaotic household
Illegitimate	Difficulty controlling aggressive impulses	Parental separation, divorce, foster home placement
Unwanted	Free expression of violence	Unemployment
Mental or physical handicap	Socially isolated	Poor housing
Preterm birth	Low self-esteem; inadequate knowledge of childrearing	Frequent relocation, alcohol and drug use, poor interpersonal boundaries

Nursing interventions for the child who is abused include a thorough physical examination and detailed history of how the injury occurred. Documentation should be stated objectively with as much of the history recorded verbatim if possible. The nurse might encounter a number of responses from the child and parent. In some instances, the child might be very passive, accepting painful treatments with little or no sign of emotion. In others, the child might be intolerant of separations from the parent. Providing a consistent caregiver will help the child adjust to separations from the parent while in the hospital.

NOTE

The child must be protected from further injury. Suspected child abuse is reported to local authorities. Referrals are assigned to a caseworker with child protective services.

Case Study

Jason Utley, age 4, and his younger brother, Justin, live with their parents in a modest, two-story Victorian home. Lately Jason's mother has noticed that both children are pale, irritable, and more easily distracted than usual. Because their symptoms have not improved, the mother scheduled a visit with the pediatrician. Lab studies reveal that both boys are iron deficient and that they have elevated serum lead levels. The following questions relate to the care of the child with lead poisoning.

1. Discuss factors that might have contributed to lead poisoning in Jason and his brother.

2. Explain why lead poisoning occurs with greater frequency in children than adults.

3. Laboratory results revealed anemia in both children. Describe the relationship between lead poisoning and anemia.

4. Discuss the physiological effects of severe lead poisoning.

5. Describe chelation therapy as used for lead poisoning.

(continues)

(continued)

Answers to Case Study

1. The major cause of lead poisoning in children in the United States is exposure to lead-based paint, which was widely used in homes such as Jason's. These homes were built between 1900 and 1950. Lead-based paint continued to be used until 1978, when lead in household paint was banned. Other means of lead exposure include pica, playing in lead-containing soil, and inhalation of dust created by paint deterioration.

2. Lead poisoning occurs more frequently in children than adults because young children absorb about 50% of the lead they are exposed to, whereas adults absorb only about 10%. The normal hand-to-mouth behavior of children combined with the presence of lead dust provides sufficient exposure for poisoning to result.

3. Children with iron deficiency absorb iron more readily than those with sufficient iron stores. This might be due to the fact that lead attaches at the site where iron binds. Children with lead poisoning can have signs associated with anemia.

4. Most of the lead ultimately settles in the bones and teeth where it remains stored. The remaining portion can be found in the erythrocytes and in organs and tissues, including the brain and kidneys. Severe lead poisoning can result in anemia, damage to the cells of the proximal tubules, mental retardation, paralysis, convulsions, coma, and death. Because of the efforts to remove lead from the environment and more efficient treatments, children rarely die as a result of lead poisoning.

5. *Chelation therapy* refers to the use of medications to remove lead from the circulating blood and to some degree from organs and tissues. Chelating agents include British anti-Lewisite (BAL or dimercaprol), which is given deep IM; calcium disodium edetate (EDTA), which is given IV or IM; and succimer (Chemet), which is given orally. Chelation therapy is usually not instituted until the blood lead level is near 45 mg/dL or greater.

Key Concepts

This chapter includes much needed information to help the nurse apply knowledge of caring for the pediatric client to the NCLEX exam. The nurse preparing for the licensure exam should review normal laboratory values, common treatment modalities, and pharmacological agents used in the care of pediatric clients.

Key Terms

- ▶ Aganglionic
- ▶ Atresia
- ▶ Autosomal recessive disorder
- ▶ Congenital anomaly
- ▶ Craniofacial
- ▶ Dysplasia
- ▶ Enteropathy
- ▶ Extravasation
- ▶ Fistula
- ▶ Hyperpnea
- ▶ Hyperpyrexia
- ▶ Lordosis
- ▶ Meconium ileus
- ▶ Neural tube defect
- ▶ Palliative
- ▶ Polycythemia
- ▶ Respiratory synctial virus
- ▶ Sex-linked disorder
- ▶ Steatorrhea
- ▶ Stenosis
- ▶ Stridor

Diagnostics

The following are routine tests done on most all hospital admissions. Specific tests are ordered to confirm or rule out a particular illness. For example, an erythrocyte sedimentation rate and an antisteptolysin titer are ordered for the client with symptoms of rheumatic fever. Positive results on these tests indicate inflammation caused by a preceding infection with Group A *beta hemolytic streptococcus*. It is helpful if you have a text of laboratory and diagnostic tests with nursing implications as a reference while you review. The routine tests are as follows:

- ▶ CBC
- ▶ Urinalysis
- ▶ Chest x-ray

Pharmacological Agents Used in the Care of Pediatric Clients

The following drug classifications are most commonly ordered for the pediatric client. However, some situations require the nurse to know about drugs that are rarely given. You should have a pharmacology text with nursing implications available as you review. The following are the drug classifications commonly ordered for children:

- ▶ Anti-infectives
- ▶ Antiemetics
- ▶ Antipyretics
- ▶ Analgesics
- ▶ Antitussives
- ▶ Decongestants
- ▶ Expectorants
- ▶ Immunizations
- ▶ Vitamin supplements

Apply Your Knowledge

Caring for the pediatric client can often be challenging for the nurse because of the complexity of many of the conditions as well as the age and understanding of the pediatric client. The following questions test your knowledge regarding the safe, effective care and management of the pediatric client.

Exam Questions

1. The nurse is caring for a child with neutropenia. Which beverage is unsuitable for the client with a low neutrophil count?

   A. 2% milk

   B. Fresh squeezed lemonade

   C. Kool-aid

   D. Ginger ale

2. While caring for an 18-month-old with intussusception, the nurse notes the passage of a soft formed brown stool. The nurse should:

   A. Prepare the child for surgery

   B. Document the finding only

   C. Notify the physician

   D. Palpate the child's abdomen

3. The nurse is developing a teaching plan for the parents of an infant with Hirschsprung's disease. Part of the teaching plan should focus on:

   A. The correct way to perform postural drainage

   B. The preparation and use of isotonic enemas

   C. The collection of a specimen using the tape test

   D. The use of pinwheels and suckers to improve speech

4. The physician has ordered a sweat test for a child suspected of having cystic fibrosis. A positive sweat test is based on:

   A. Chloride level

   B. Potassium transport

   C. Serum sodium

   D. Calcium level

5. A 15-month-old is admitted with a diagnosis of bronchiolitis. Which medication is recognized as the only effective treatment for bronchiolitis?

   A. Ribavirin

   B. Respigam

   C. Sandimmune

   D. Synagis

6. The nurse is conducting a scoliosis screening clinic at the local school. The nurse knows that she is most likely to find scoliosis in:

   A. Adolescent males

   B. Preteen males

   C. Preteen females

   D. Adolescent females

7. The nurse is teaching the parents of a child with hemophilia regarding bleeding episodes. The nurse should emphasize that the greatest danger from bleeding is due to:

   A. Bleeding into the joints

   B. Cutaneous bleeding

   C. Bleeding into the oral cavity

   D. Intracranial bleeding

8. During a routine well-child check-up, the mother of a toddler asks when she should schedule her child's first dental visit. The nurse's response is based on the knowledge that most children have all their permanent teeth by age:

   A. 12 months

   B. 18 months

   C. 24 months

   D. 30 months

9. A child with a valvular defect is admitted with symptoms of infective bacterial endocarditis. Which finding is suggestive of embolization?

   A. Syndenham's chorea

   B. Polymigratory arthritis

   C. Splinter hemorrhages

   D. Erythema marginatum

10. Enterobiasis is more common in young children. A primary reason is that young children:

    A. Share hats and caps

    B. Wear training pants

    C. Engage in imitative play

    D. Have hand-to-mouth contact

Answers to Exam Questions

1. Answer B is correct. Clients with a low neutrophil count should adhere to a low bacteria diet. Fresh squeezed lemonade can be contaminated from bacteria on the lemon rind. Answers A, C, and D are suitable for the client with neutropenia therefore they are incorrect.

2. Answer C is correct. The passage of a soft formed brown stool is an indication that the intussusception is resolving. Answer A is incorrect because the condition is resolving without surgery. Answer B is incorrect because the physician should be notified in addition to documenting the finding. Answer D is incorrect because the nurse should not palpate the abdomen of a child recovering from intussusception.

3. Answer B is correct. The parents of a child with Hirschsprung's disease should be taught how to prepare and administer isotonic enemas. Answers A, C, and D are incorrect because they do not relate to the care of the child with Hirschsprung's disease.

4. Answer A is correct. A positive sweat test is reflected by elevations in the chloride level. Answers B, C, and D are not measured by the sweat test; therefore, they are incorrect.

5. Answer A is correct. The only effective treatment of bronchiolitis (respiratory synctial virus) is ribavirin. Answers B and D are incorrect because they are used prophylactically, not as a treatment for bronchiolitis. Sandimmune, an immuno-suppressive drug, is not used for treating bronchiolitis; therefore, Answer C is incorrect.

6. Answer D is correct. The most likely group to have scoliosis is adolescent girls. The groups in Answers A, B, and C are not as likely to have scoliosis; therefore, those answers are incorrect.

7. Answer D is correct. The greatest danger from bleeding in the child with hemo-philia is intracranial bleeding. The situations in Answers A, B, and C do not pose the greatest danger from bleeding; therefore, they are incorrect.

8. Answer D is correct. Most children have all their primary teeth by age 30 months. Answers A, B, and C are incorrect because tooth eruption is not complete.

9. Answer C is correct. Splinter hemorrhages, dark lines beneath the nails, are associated with embolization. Answers A, B, and D are associated with rheumatic fever, not infective bacterial endocarditis; therefore, they are incorrect.

10. Answer D is correct. Enterobiasis is most common in young children because of frequent hand-to-mouth contact. Answer A is incorrect because sharing hats and caps contributes to the spread of pediculosis capitis. Wearing training pants and playing with imitative toys is not associated with enterobiasis; therefore, Answers B and C are incorrect.

Suggested Reading and Resources

▶ Ball, J., and R. Bindler. *Pediatric Nursing: Caring for Children* 4th ed. Upper Saddle River, NJ: Pearson Prentice Hall, 2008.

▶ Hockenberry, M., and D. Wilson. *Wong's Essentials of Pediatric Nursing* 8th ed. St. Louis: Elsevier, 2009.

▶ www.aaai.org—American Academy of Allergy, Asthma, and Immunology

▶ www.aafp.org—The American Academy of Family Practice

▶ www.candlelighters.org—Candlelighters Childhood Cancer Foundation

▶ www.cdc.gov—Centers for Disease Control

▶ www.cff.org—Cystic Fibrosis Foundation

▶ www.lungusa.org—The American Lung Association

▶ www.pathguy.com—Dr. Ed Friedlander, pathologist

17

Care of the Client with Psychiatric Disorders

The past decade has been an exciting time for psychiatric nursing. Technological advances have given us the ability to study not only the physical structure of the brain, but also how chemical messengers (known as *neurotransmitters*) affect our mood and behavior. The depiction of the hopelessness of mental illness has been partly done away with by the release of movies and books that depict the challenges faced by those with mental illness. Finally, the discovery of newer and more effective drugs has made it possible for many of those with mental illness to lead more normal lives.

Although it is not possible to cover all the psychiatric disorders described in the Diagnostic and Statistical Manual of Mental Disorders (DSM-IV-TR), this chapter will review the most commonly diagnosed disorders: anxiety-related disorders, personality disorders, the psychotic disorders of schizophrenia and bipolar disorder, substance abuse, and the disorders most often seen in childhood and adolescence.

Alzheimer's disease and other degenerative neurological disorders are discussed in Chapter 11, "Caring for the Client with Neurological Disorders."

Anxiety-related Disorders

Anxiety-related disorders are sometimes referred to as *neurotic disorders* and include the following categories:

- ▶ Generalized anxiety disorder
- ▶ Post-traumatic stress disorder
- ▶ Dissociative identity disorder
- ▶ Somatoform disorder
- ▶ Panic disorder
- ▶ Phobic disorder
- ▶ Obsessive-compulsive disorder

Anxiety disorders are characterized by feelings of fear and apprehension accompanied by a sense of powerlessness. Anxiety-related disorders are listed on Axis I of the DSM-IV-TR.

Generalized Anxiety Disorder

Generalized anxiety disorder (GAD) is the most common form of anxiety disorder and frequently is accompanied by depression, somatization, and the development of phobias.

The client with GAD worries excessively over everything, and the stress this creates eventually affects every aspect of life. The client with GAD might try to gain a sense of control by retreating from anxiety-producing situations or by self-medication with drugs or alcohol.

Genetics and alterations in neurotransmitters seem to be the primary causes for GAD. Studies show a higher occurrence in those with an affected twin. Neurophysiology research suggests that alterations in serotonin, norepinephrine, and gamma-aminobutyric acid can account for some cases of generalized anxiety disorder.

Post-traumatic Stress Disorder

Post-traumatic stress disorder (PTSD) develops after exposure to a clearly identifiable threat. The nature of the threat is so extreme that it overwhelms the individual's usual means of coping.

PTSD is characterized according to the onset as either acute or delayed. *Acute PTSD* occurs within six months of the event, whereas *delayed PTSD* occurs six months or more after the event. Symptoms of PTSD include the following:

- Blunted emotions
- Feelings of detachment
- Flashbacks
- Moral guilt
- Numbing of responsiveness
- Survivor guilt

Additional symptoms include increased arousal, anxiety, restlessness, irritability, sleep disturbances, and problems with memory and concentration. Individuals with PTSD frequently have problems with depression and impulsive self-destructive behaviors, including suicide attempts and substance abuse.

PTSD is common in those who are survivors of combat, natural disasters, sexual assault, or catastrophic events.

CAUTION

Clients with PTSD who use cocaine or amphetamines are more vulnerable to paranoia and psychosis than those who do not use stimulants.

Dissociative Identity Disorder

Dissociative identity disorder (DID), formerly referred to as *multiple personality disorder*, is characterized by the existence of two or more identities or alter personalities that control the individual's behavior.

The traditional view of DID is that dissociation acts as a defense against an overwhelming sense of anxiety that is both painful and emotionally traumatic. The alter personality contains feelings associated with the trauma, which is often related to physical, emotional, or sexual abuse.

Each alter personality is different from the other, having its own name, ways of behaving, memories, emotional characteristics, and social relationships. Overwhelming psychological stress can cause the onset of a dissociative fugue. The major feature of a dissociative fugue is unexpected travel from home with the appearance of one of the alter personalities. The travel and behavior might seem normal to the casual observer who is unfamiliar with the client's history.

Somatoform Disorder

Somatoform disorder is characterized by the appearance of physical symptoms for which there is no apparent organic or physiological cause. The client with a somatoform disorder continuously seeks medical treatment for a physical complaint even though he has been told there is no evidence of physical illness. Somatoform disorders include the following:

- ▶ Conversion disorder
- ▶ Hypochondriasis
- ▶ Pain disorder
- ▶ Somatization disorder

Panic Disorder

Panic disorder is characterized by sudden attacks of intense fear or discomfort that peaks within 10–15 minutes. Clients with panic disorder might complain of not being able to breathe, of feeling they are having a heart attack, or that they are "going crazy." Panic attacks can occur during sleep or in anticipation of some event. In some instances, clients with panic disorder develop agoraphobia, or fear of having a panic attack in a place where they cannot escape. As a result, they restrict activities outside the safety of their home.

> **NOTE**
> Panic attacks can be brought on by ingestion of foods or beverages containing caffeine or sodium lactate.

Genetic and environmental factors appear to be involved in the development of panic disorder. Other findings suggest that there are alterations in the benzodiazepine receptor sites.

Phobic Disorders

Phobic disorders are expressed as intense, irrational fears of some object, situation, or activity. A person with a phobic disorder experiences anxiety when he comes in contact with the situation or feared object. Although the client recognizes that the fear is irrational, the phobia persists. According to the DSM-IV-TR, the three major categories of phobic disorders are as follows:

- Agoraphobia
- Social phobia
- Specific phobia

There are no clearly identifiable factors in the development of phobic disorders.

Obsessive-compulsive Disorder

Obsessive-compulsive disorder (OCD) is characterized by the presence of recurrent persistent thoughts, ideas, or impulses and the repetitive rituals that are carried out in response to the obsession. Persons with OCD know that their actions are ridiculous; still they must carry them out to avoid overwhelming anxiety. Unfortunately, this continual preoccupation interferes with normal relationships. The client with OCD is viewed by others as rigid, controlling, and lacking spontaneity.

There is some evidence that OCD, like other anxiety disorders, is related to genetic transmissions or alterations in the serotonin regulation.

Treatment of anxiety disorders depends on the diagnosis and severity of symptoms. Some disorders, such as panic disorder and obsessive-compulsive disorder, respond to treatment with antidepressant medication. Others, such as PTSD and phobic disorder, benefit from cognitive behavioral therapy and desensitization.

Nursing interventions in caring for the client with an anxiety disorder include

- Conveying an attitude of acceptance
- Creating an environment in which the client feels safe
- Helping the client become aware of situations that increase anxiety
- Helping the client to recognize symptoms of increasing anxiety
- Teaching the client techniques to interrupt responses to increasing anxiety
- Engaging the client in a variety of milieu activities to help reduce tension and anxiety

- ▸ Administering prescribed antianxiolytic or antidepressant medication
- ▸ Teaching cognitive behavioral methods for reducing anxiety

> **TIP**
> You should review your psychiatric nursing textbook for a discussion of the most commonly used defense mechanisms.

Personality Disorders

The second major category of reality-based disorders focuses on the client with faulty personality development.

Unlike clients with an anxiety disorder, who believe that everything is wrong with them, clients with personality disorders seldom seek treatment. They see nothing wrong with their behavior and therefore see no need to change. Personality disorders are listed on Axis II of the DSM-IV-TR.

> **NOTE**
> Disorders usually first diagnosed in infancy, childhood, and adolescence are listed on Axis I of the DSM-IV-TR.

Personality disorders refer to pervasive maladaptive patterns of behavior that are evident in the perceptions, communication, and thinking of an individual. The DSM-IV-TR divides personality disorders into three clusters according to the predominant behaviors:

- ▸ **Cluster A:** Includes odd, eccentric behavior
- ▸ **Cluster B:** Includes dramatic, erratic, emotional behavior
- ▸ **Cluster C:** Includes anxious, fearful behavior

Of these three clusters, those with dramatic, erratic behavior pose the greatest threat to others.

Each cluster contains from three to four identifiable personality disorders. The clusters and identified personality disorders of each are outlined in the following sections.

Cluster A

Cluster A disorders include paranoid, schizoid, and schizotypal personality disorders. Although these represent different personalities, they all involve behavior that is odd or eccentric in nature.

Paranoid Personality Disorder

Paranoid personality disorder is characterized by rigid, suspicious, and hypersensitive behavior. Persons with paranoid personality disorder spend a great deal of time and energy validating their suspicions. Unlike those with paranoid schizophrenia, the client with paranoid personality does not have fixed delusions or hallucinations. However, transient psychotic features can appear when the client experiences extreme stress, and the client might be hospitalized because of uncontrollable anger toward others.

Schizoid Personality Disorder

This disorder is characterized by shy, aloof, and withdrawn behavior. The client with schizoid personality disorder prefers solitary activities and is often described by others as a hermit. This client might be quite successful in situations where little interaction with others is required. Although the client with schizoid personality disorder is reality oriented, she often fantasizes or daydreams.

Schizotypal Personality Disorder

Like schizoid personality disorder, this disorder is found more often in relatives of those with schizophrenia. Their behaviors are similar to those of the client with schizoid personality—that is, they are shy, aloof, and withdrawn. However, clients with schizotypal personality disorder display a more bizarre way of thinking. They often appear similar to clients with schizophrenia but with less frequent and less severe psychotic symptoms. Because they are sensitive to the reactions of and possible rejection by others, clients with schizotypal and schizoid behavior avoid social situations.

Cluster B

This disorder set includes the histrionic, narcissistic, antisocial, and borderline personality disorders. Persons with these identified disorders tend to be overly dramatic, attention-seeking, and manipulative with little regard for others.

Histrionic Personality Disorder

This disorder is diagnosed most often in females. Sometimes referred to as *southern belle syndrome*, the picture of the histrionic female is one who is overly seductive, excitable, immature, and theatrical in her emotions. These behaviors are not genuine but are used to manipulate others. The client with histrionic personality disorder tends to form many shallow relationships that are always short lived.

Narcissistic Personality Disorder

This disorder is summarized by the expression "It's all about me." Characterized by self-absorption, persons with narcissistic personality have grandiose ideas about their wealth, power, and intelligence. They believe that they are superior to others and that, because they are superior, they are entitled to certain privileges and special treatment. Although they appear nonchalant or indifferent to the criticism of others, it is only a cover-up for deep feelings of resentment and rage. Clients with narcissistic personality tend to rationalize or blame others for their self-centered behavior.

Antisocial Personality Disorder

This is characterized by a pattern of disregard for the rights of others and a failure to learn from past mistakes. These clients frequently have a history of law violations, which usually begin before age 15. Common behaviors in early childhood include cruelty to animals and people, starting fires, running away from home, truancy, breaking and entering, and early substance abuse. Persons with antisocial personality disorder are often described as charming, smooth-talking, and extremely intelligent—characteristics that allow them to take advantage of others and escape prosecution when caught.

Persons with antisocial personality disorder do not feel remorse for wrongs committed and respond to confrontation by using the defense mechanisms of denial and rationalization.

Borderline Personality Disorder

Borderline personality disorder, the most commonly treated personality disorder, is seen most often in females who have been victims of sexual abuse. These clients have many of the same traits as those with histrionic, narcissistic, and antisocial personality disorder; thus, they have a difficult time identifying their feelings. Like many victims of sexual abuse, this client relies on dissociation as a means of coping with stress. This dissociation results in *splitting*, a very primitive defense mechanism that creates an inability to see oneself and others as having both good and bad qualities. Clients with borderline personality disorder tend to see themselves and others as all good or all bad. Feelings of abandonment and depression can escalate to the point of self-mutilation and suicidal behavior. These clients usually require hospitalization and treatment with anti-depressant medication as well as counseling for post-traumatic stress disorder.

Cluster C

Cluster C disorders include the avoidant, dependent, and obsessive-compulsive personality disorders, which are characterized by anxious, fearful behavior.

Avoidant Personality Disorder

Avoidant personality disorder is used to describe clients who are timid, withdrawn, and hypersensitive to criticism. Although they desire relationships and challenges, clients with this disorder feel socially inadequate, so they avoid situations in which they might be rejected. They tend to lack the self-confidence needed to speak up for what they want and so are seen as helpless.

Dependent Personality Disorder

Dependent personality disorder is characterized by an extreme need to be taken care of by someone else. This dependency on others leads to clinging behavior and fear of separation from the perceived caretaker. Clients with dependent personality disorder see themselves as inferior and incompetent, and they frequently become involved in abusive relationships. These abusive relationships are usually maintained because of a fear of being left alone.

Obsessive-Compulsive Personality Disorder

This disorder describes the individual who is a perfectionist, overly inhibited, and inflexible. Clients with obsessive-compulsive personality disorder are preoccupied with rules, trivial details, and procedures. They are cold and rigid with no expression of tenderness or warmth. They often set standards too high for themselves or others to make and, because they are fearful of making mistakes, tend to procrastinate. Clients with obsessive-compulsive personality disorder put off making decisions until all the facts are in; thus, they might do good work but not be very productive.

> **NOTE**
> Although they share some common traits, obsessive-compulsive anxiety disorder and obsessive-compulsive personality disorder are two different diagnoses.

Managing Clients with Personality Disorders

The management of the client with a personality disorder depends on the diagnosis. Pharmacological interventions are generally not appropriate for these clients. However, if there is a coexisting diagnosis such as depression or anxiety, medication will be ordered. The nurse caring for the client with a personality disorder should set limits on the client's behavior while at the same time conveying a sense of acceptance of the individual. Nursing interventions for the client with a personality disorder include

▶ Acting as a role model.

▶ Encouraging the client to talk about his feelings.

▶ Helping the client see that it is the behavior that is inappropriate, not the person.

▶ Helping the client discharge pent up energy by the use of large motor activity.

▶ Helping the client identify sources of anger.

▶ Helping the client express anger in an acceptable manner.

▶ Removing all dangerous objects from the environment.

▶ Securing a verbal contract, if the client shows signs of self-mutilation.

▶ Having sufficient staff available to show strength of staff, if coping is lost.

▶ Using a firm, reinforcing tone when communicating with the client when behavior is out of control. Do not attempt to coax or convince the client of what is "right" because he does not realize what is the "right thing" to do.

Many clients with personality disorders have disturbed personal boundaries; therefore, it is important to maintain a professional rather than a friendly relationship.

Psychotic Disorders

Psychotic disorders involve alterations in perceptions in reality. Common symptoms include hallucinations, delusions, and difficulty organizing thoughts. Psychotic symptoms are present in clients with schizophrenia, bipolar disorder, dementia, and drug intoxication or withdrawal. This section reviews two of the most common psychotic disorders: schizophrenia and bipolar disorder. Psychosis associated with drug use and withdrawal is covered later in the chapter.

Schizophrenia

This disorder is most often diagnosed in late adolescence or early adulthood, although symptoms might have been present at a much earlier age. The disorder equally affects both males and females; however, males seem to have an earlier onset of symptoms. Theories offered regarding the cause of schizophrenia include genetics, environmental factors, and biological alterations in the neurotransmitters serotonin and dopamine.

Clients with schizophrenia are best known for their odd appearance and behavior, which are sometimes summarized by the 4 A's. The 4 A's include

- **Affect:** Described as flat, blunted, or inappropriate

- **Autism:** Preoccupation with self and a retreat into fantasy

- **Association:** Loosely joined unrelated topics

- **Ambivalence:** Having simultaneous opposing feelings

The DSM-IV-TR classifies schizophrenia into subtypes based on the history and presenting symptoms:

- Catatonic

- Disorganized

- Paranoid

- Residual

- Undifferentiated

In addition to the subtypes, schizophrenia is classified as having either positive or negative symptoms. *Positive* symptoms of schizophrenia are those such as delusions and hallucinations; *negative* symptoms are those such as social withdrawal and failure to communicate with others. One of the main differences in the newer antipsychotic medications is that they work on both the negative as well as the positive symptoms of schizophrenia. The older medications worked primarily on clearing the hallucinations and delusions.

> **NOTE**
>
> You might want to refer to your nursing textbook for a more complete description of the subtypes and positive and negative symptoms associated with schizophrenia. Although there are overlapping symptoms, some have unique features. For instance, the client with catatonic schizophrenia exhibits waxy flexibility or stupor.

Nursing interventions in the care of the client with schizophrenia include

- ▶ Providing a quiet, supportive environment
- ▶ Establishing a trusting relationship
- ▶ Administering antipsychotic medication
- ▶ Assisting with the activities of daily living
- ▶ Attending to the client's physical needs, including nutrition and hydration

Instead of allowing the client to retreat to his room, the nurse should provide simple recreational activities such as painting.

> **NOTE**
>
> It is best to avoid challenging activities that can confuse and overwhelm the client.

The nurse shouldn't argue or try to change the client's delusional thinking; instead, redirecting the client to a reality-based subject will be more effective and less upsetting. In instances where the client is having hallucinations, the nurse should respond to the client's feelings and at the same time reinforce what is real. For example, the nurse should acknowledge the client's fear at hearing voices when no one is there, but then point out that the voices are not real and that the medication will soon help eliminate the voices.

The discovery of newer, more effective medications in the past decade has enabled many persons with schizophrenia to remain in their homes and communities for longer periods of time than the older medications did. These medications are often referred to as *atypical* or *novel antipsychotics*. Atypical antipsychotics, such as Risperdal (risperidone), can be given in smaller doses, produce fewer side effects, and help manage the negative symptoms of schizophrenia more effectively than the older antipsychotics such as Thorazine (chlorpromazine).

> **NOTE**
>
> The mainstay in the management of the client with schizophrenia is medication. Refer to the chapter on psychopharmacology in your psychiatric nursing textbook for more information on the typical and atypical antipsychotics.

One of the major reasons for non-compliance with prescribed anti-psychotic medication is the development of extrapyramidal side effects (EPSE). Extrapyramidal side effects:

▶ Akathisia (subjective feelings of restlessness, characterized by jitteriness, nervousness, frequent movement).

▶ Akinesia (absence of movement) or Bradykinesia (slow movement).

▶ Dystonias (abnormal postures caused by involuntary muscle spasms) Torticollis and oculogyric crisis are examples of dystonias.

▶ Tardive dyskinesia (tongue protrusion, lip smacking, teeth grinding).

NOTE

Unlike the EPSE of akathisia, akinesia, and dystonias, tardive dyskinesia is not caused by a dopamine-acetylcholine imbalance; therefore, anticholinergic medications do not improve tardive dyskinesia and might make the condition worse.

▶ Drug induced Parkinson's (mask-like faces, cogwheel rigidity, pill-rolling tremors).

▶ Neuroleptic malignant syndrome (muscle rigidity, tremors, impaired ventilations, muteness, altered consciousness and autonomic hyperactivity). The cardinal symptom is an increased body temperature. Although the temperature is likely to range between 101° F and 103° F, temperatures as high as 108° F have been reported.

CAUTION

Antipsychotic medication, particularly high-potency antipsychotics, such as Haldol (haloperidol) carry the risk of neuroleptic malignant syndrome, a potentially fatal adverse reaction. NMS is not related to toxic drug levels and may occur after only a few doses. The cardinal symptom of NMS is elevations in body temperature; therefore, the nurse should monitor the client's temperature carefully. Interventions for the client with NMS include discontinuing the antipsychotic medication and administering either Dantrium (dantrolene) or Parlodel (bromocriptine). Intubation and transfer to ICU may be needed in some instances.

The client's antipsychotic medication should not be resumed for at least two weeks after the resolution of NMS symptoms.

Schizophrenia is a chronic illness and, although the medications improve the client's quality of life, they do not cure the disease. The prognosis for the client with schizophrenia is based on the subtype, the severity of symptoms, and compliance with treatment.

Bipolar Disorders

This refers to a group of psychotic disorders that are evident in extreme changes in mood or affect. These disorders, like schizophrenia, are believed to be caused by alterations in serotonin, dopamine, and norepinephrine. Most clients with bipolar disorder have the type known as *bipolar I*, in which the client experiences periods of acute mania and major depression.

Acute Mania

Manic episodes are essential to a diagnosis of bipolar I disorder. During a manic episode, the client experiences profound changes in mood. These mood changes are described as elevated, expansive, or irritable. Additional symptoms associated with acute mania include

▸ Delusions of grandeur

▸ Flight of ideas

▸ Increased motor activity

▸ Increased risk taking and promiscuity

▸ Use of profanity

▸ Uncontrolled spending

▸ Failing to sleep or eat for long periods of time

When limitations are placed on the client's behavior, he typically reacts with sarcasm and belligerence.

Nursing interventions for clients with acute mania include providing a quiet, nonstimulating environment and protecting them from physical exhaustion. Most will have weight loss due to their excessive activity; therefore, nutritional needs can best be met by providing high-calorie, high-protein finger foods and snacks that can be eaten while moving. Nursing interventions also include the administering of medications to stabilize the mood. Medications commonly used as mood stabilizers include Lithobid (lithium), Depakote (divalproex sodium), and Tegretol (carbamazepine). Zyprexa (olanzapine), an atypical antipsychotic, has also been shown to be effective in treating clients with acute mania.

> **CAUTION**
>
> During the initiation of lithium therapy, lithium levels should be drawn twice weekly and then every two to three months during long-term therapy.
>
> The therapeutic range for a serum lithium level is 0.5–1.5 mEq /liter (therapeutic range for lithium may vary slightly). Lithium levels greater than 1.5 mEq/liter can lead to toxicity that can be fatal. Symptoms of lithium toxicity include muscle weakness, confusion, ataxia, seizures, cardio-respiratory changes, and multiple organ failure. A standard treatment for lithium toxicity is the administration of intravenous normal saline.

Major Depression

Major depression, the other side of bipolar I disorder, is characterized by a depressed mood lasting at least two weeks. Symptoms of major depression include feelings of worthlessness, diminished ability to concentrate, anorexia, sleep disturbances, and recurrent thoughts of death or suicide. A diagnosis of mental disorder or substance abuse is among the most significant risk factors for suicide.

CAUTION

The depressed client should be assessed for the presence of suicidal ideation and suicidal plan. Harmful objects should be removed from the client's environment, and the client should be placed on basic suicide precautions with constant observation by the nursing staff. The nurse must remember that the greatest risk for suicide exists when the client seems to be improving.

Nursing interventions for the client with major depression include providing a safe environment, meeting the client's physiological needs, reinforcing the client's sense of worth, assisting with electroconvulsive therapy, and administering antidepressant medications. Currently, the most frequently prescribed antidepressants are selective serotonin reuptake inhibitors (SSRIs). Less frequently prescribed medications include monoamine oxidase inhibitors (MAOIs) and tricyclic antidepressants (TCAs).

Electroconvulsive therapy (ECT) is sometimes used in conjunction with antidepressant medication to treat clients who are acutely suicidal, those with psychotic depression, and those with psychomotor retardation. ECT produces a tonic-clonic seizure through the application of electrical current applied to the brain. The exact mechanism by which ECT produces a therapeutic response is unknown, although it is believed to increase the circulating levels of several neurotransmitters including serotonin, dopamine, and norepinephrine.

The client scheduled for electroconvulsive therapy is premedicated with atropine sulfate or Robinul (glycopyrrolate) about 30 minutes prior to the procedure to decrease secretions and counteract the effects of vagal stimulation caused by the treatment. In the treatment room, the anesthesiologist administers a short-acting anesthetic such as Pentothal (thiopental sodium) and a muscle relaxant, usually Anectine (succinylcholine chloride) to prevent severe muscle contractions during the seizure. Anectine also paralyzes respiratory muscles therefore the client is oxygenated with pure oxygen before the treatment as well as immediately afterward. Nursing interventions for the client receiving ECT are the same as those used when caring for the client with tonic-clonic seizures. These are discussed in detail in Chapter 11, "Care of the Client with Neurological Disorders." The most common side effects associated with ECT are confusion and temporary memory loss.

CAUTION

The use of SSRIs with MAOIs, selective MAOIs, tryptophan, and St. John's wort (hypericum) is contraindicated. Serotonin syndrome, a potentially fatal condition, can occur as a result of drug interaction. Symptoms of serotonin reaction include confusion, hypomania, agitation, hyperthermia, hyperreflexia, tremors, rigidity, and gastrointestinal upset. The medication should be discontinued immediately. The physician will order medication to block the serotonin receptors, and artificial ventilation might be required. Most clients show improvement within 24 hours of discontinuing the SSRI.

> **NOTE**
>
> *Dysthymic disorder* refers to a chronic depressed mood that exists for at least two years in adults or at least one year in children. The symptoms associated with dysthymic disorder are generally milder than those with major depression.

Symptoms of depression in children and adolescents include frequent vague physical complaints, lack of social interaction, boredom, and sudden drop in school performance. Chronic illness, chaotic home life, family history of depressive illness, and academic difficulties (ADHD or learning disability) are associated with an increased incidence of childhood and adolescent depression.

Depression in the elderly is often misdiagnosed as a physical ailment or "just being old." Factors associated with depression in the elderly include loss of a spouse, loss of independence, loss of financial security, declining health, and imminence of death.

Substance Abuse

Substance abuse is defined as the excessive use of a drug that is different from societal norms. These drugs can be illegal, as in the case of heroin, or legal, as in the case of alcohol or prescription drugs. Symptoms of substance abuse include the following:

- ▶ Absenteeism
- ▶ Decline in school or work performance
- ▶ Frequent accidents
- ▶ Increased isolation
- ▶ Slurred speech
- ▶ Tremors

The primary substance abuse problem in the United States is alcohol addiction.

Alcoholism

Alcoholism is responsible for more than 100,000 deaths each year in the United States. Many of these deaths are the result of accidents. Premature death from cirrhosis, cardiovascular disease, esophageal varices, or cancer have also been linked to heavy alcohol consumption. It is important for the nurse to recognize the stages of alcohol withdrawal to keep the client safe. Symptoms of withdrawal usually begin about six to eight hours after the client's last drink, or when the amount consumed is less than usual. Four stages of alcohol withdrawal are generally recognized. The stages of withdrawal and the symptoms associated with each stage are as follows:

- ▶ **Stage 1 (6–8 hours after last use):** Symptoms include anxiety, anorexia, tremors, nausea and vomiting, depression, headache, increased blood pressure, tachycardia, and profuse sweating.

▶ **Stage 2 (8–12 hours after last use):** Symptoms include confusion, disorientation, hallucinations, hyperactivity, and gross tremors.

▶ **Stage 3 (12–48 hours after last use):** Symptoms include severe anxiety, increased blood pressure, profuse sweating, severe hallucinations, and tonic clonic seizures.

▶ **Stage 4 (3–5 days after last use):** Symptoms of delirium tremens include confusion, insomnia, agitation, hallucinations, and uncontrolled tachycardia. In spite of treatment, the client might die from cardiac complications.

NOTE

Although each stage has an expected timeframe and behaviors during the withdrawal, you should keep in mind that withdrawal is highly individual. The Addiction Research Foundation Chemical Institute Withdrawal Assessment-Alcohol (CIWA-Ar) is a useful instrument for quickly assessing the client's withdrawal status (see Figure 17.1).

Assessment of Alcohol Withdrawal

Patient: _____ Date: _____ Time: _____:_____

Pulse or heart rate, taken for one minute: _____ Blood pressure: ____/____

Nausea and vomiting. Ask "Do you feel sick to your stomach? Have you vomited?"
Observation:
0–No nausea and no vomiting
1–Mild nausea with no vomiting
2–
3–
4–Intermittent nausea with dry heaves
5–
6–
7–Constant nausea, frequent dry heaves, and vomiting
Tremor. Ask patient to extend arms and spread fingers apart.
Observation:
0–No tremor
1–Tremor not visible but can be felt, fingertip to fingertip
2–
3–
4–Moderate tremor with arms extended
5–
6–
7–Severe tremor, even with arms not extended
Paroxysmal sweats.
Observation:
0–No sweat visible
1–Barely perceptible sweating; palms moist
2–
3–
4–Beads of sweat obvious on forehead
5–
6–
7–Drenching sweats
Anxiety. Ask "Do you feel nervous?"
Observation:
0–No anxiety (at ease)
1–Mildly anxious
2–
3–
4–Moderately anxious or guarded, so anxiety is inferred
5–
6–
7–Equivalent to acute panic states as occur in severe delirium or acute schizophrenic reactions
Agitation.
Observation:
0–Normal activity
1–Somewhat more than normal activity
2–
3–
4–Moderately fidgety and restless
5–
6–
7–Paces back and forth during most of the interview or constantly thrashes about

Tactile disturbances. Ask "Do you have any itching, pins-and-needles sensations, burning, or numbness, or do you feel like bugs are crawling on or under skin?"
Observation:
0–None
1–Very mild itching, pins-and-needles, sensation, burning, or numbness
2–Mild itching, pins-and-needles sensation, burning, or numbness
3–Moderate itching, pins-and-needles sensation, burning or numbness
4–Moderately severe hallucinations
5–Severe hallucinations
6–Extremely severe hallucinations
7–Continuous hallucinations
Auditory disturbances. Ask "Are you more aware of sounds around you? Are they harsh? Do they frighten you? Are you hearing anything that is disturbing to you? Are you hearing things you know are not there?"
Observation:
0–Not present
1–Very mild harshness or ability to frighten
2–Mild harshness or ability to frighten
3–Moderate harshness or ability to frighten
4–Moderately severe hallucinations
5–Severe hallucinations
6–Extremely severe hallucinations
7–Continuous hallucinations
Visual disturbances. Ask "Does the light appear to be too bright? Is its color different? Does it hurt your eyes? Are you seeing anything that is disturbing to you? Are you seeing things you know are not there?"
Observation:
0–Not present
1–Very mild sensitivity
2–Mild sensitivity
3–Moderate sensitivity
4–Moderately severe hallucinations
5–Severe hallucinations
6–Extremely severe hallucinations
7–Continuous hallucinations
Headache, fullness in head. Ask "Does your head feel different? Does it feel like there is a band around your head?"
Do not rate for dizziness or lightheadedness; otherwise, rate severity.
0–Not present
1–Very mild
2–Mild
3–Moderate
4–Moderately severe
5–Severe
6–Very severe
7–Extremely severe
Orientation and clouding of sensorium. Ask "What day is this? Where are you? Who am I?"
Observation:
0–Orientated and can do serial additions
1–Cannot do serial additions or is uncertain about date
2–Date disorientation by no more than two calendar days
3–Date disorientation by more than two calendar days
4–Disoriented for place and/or person

Total score: _____ (maximum = 67): _____ Rater's initials _____

FIGURE 17.1 Clinical Institute Withdrawal Assessment for Alcohol (CIWA-Ar) scale.

Nursing interventions for the client with alcohol withdrawal include maintaining a safe environment, providing nutritional supplements, providing additional fluids to prevent dehydration, and administering pharmacological agents to prevent delirium tremens.

In some instances, aversion therapy might be used to help the client maintain sobriety. Antabuse (disulfiram) is capable of producing unpleasant and sometimes fatal reactions if the client comes in contact with alcohol. Aversive therapy is most effective for those clients who have a high level of internal motivation and who seek assistance through support groups such as Alcoholics Anonymous.

CAUTION

The nurse should teach the client taking Antabuse (disulfiram) to avoid alcohol or substances containing alcohol, including cough and cold preparations, mouthwash, colognes, or skin preparations containing isopropyl alcohol. Contact with alcohol in any form while taking Antabuse (disulfiram) can produce headache, nausea and vomiting, sweating, and hypotension. With blood alcohol levels of 125–150 mg /dL the client can experience a severe "disulfiram-alcohol" reaction which includes respiratory depression, tachycardia, chest pain, myocardial infarction, acute congestive heart failure, convulsions, and death. If Antabuse therapy is discontinued, the client should avoid sources of alcohol for at least 2 weeks to prevent a "disulfiram-alcohol" reaction.

The client should be instructed to carry a card noting participation in disulfiram therapy and health care professionals, including dentists should be made aware of the client's current treatment.

NOTE

Other medications used in the treatment of clients with alcoholism include the narcotic antagonist naltrexone (ReVia) and selective serotonin reuptake inhibitors. These agents appear to decrease the craving for alcohol in moderate drinkers.

Chemical Dependence

Other commonly abused substances include sedative-hypnotics, opiates, stimulants, hallucinogens, and cannabis. Tables 17.1–17.5 list the signs of use, signs of withdrawal, signs of overdose, and treatments for several of these substances.

Sedative-Hypnotics

Sedative-hypnotics are potent central nervous system depressants. This group, which includes barbiturates and benzodiazepines, is capable of producing both physiological and psychological dependence. Drugs in this category are regulated by the Controlled Substances Act. Table 17.1 highlights important signs and treatments related to clients abusing sedative-hypnotic drugs.

TABLE 17.1   Signs and Treatments Related to Sedative-Hypnotic Abuse

Signs of Use	Slurred speech, unsteady gait, drowsiness, decreased blood pressure, irritability, inability to concentrate
Signs of Withdrawal	Nausea and vomiting, tachycardia, diaphoresis, tremors, and seizures
Signs of Overdose	Cardiovascular and respiratory depression, seizures, shock, coma, death
Treatment of Overdose	Activated charcoal and gastric lavage, mechanical ventilation and dialysis as needed

CAUTION

Withdrawal from barbiturates should be done by slow taper to avoid the development of fatal seizures.

Opiates

This refers to a group of drugs used for their analgesic effects. These drugs include the natural opiates morphine and codeine as well as synthetic opiates such as meperidine and methadone. Opiates produce both physiological and psychological addiction. One of the most abused opiates, heroin, has no legal medical use. Others are regulated by the Controlled Substances Act. Table 17.2 highlights signs and treatments related to clients abusing opiates.

TABLE 17.2   Signs and Treatments Related to Opiate Abuse

Signs of Use	Constricted pupils, decreased respirations, decreased blood pressure, euphoria, impaired attention span, impaired judgment
Signs of Withdrawal	Anorexia, irritability, runny nose, nausea, bone pain, chills
Signs of Overdose	Dilated pupils, respiratory depression, seizures, coma, death
Treatment of Overdose	Narcan (a narcotic antagonist that reverses the central nervous system depression)

Stimulants

Stimulants excite various areas of the central nervous system. Some stimulants, such as the amphetamine and nonamphetamine groups, are used to treat attention deficit hyperactivity disorder and narcolepsy. Cocaine is used to control local bleeding and is an ingredient in some eye medications. Others, such as caffeine and alcohol, are widely accepted for social use. Stimulants are physiologically addicting; therefore, the more potent ones are regulated by the Controlled Substances Act. Table 17.3 highlights signs and treatments related to clients abusing stimulants.

TABLE 17.3   Signs and Treatments Related to Stimulant Abuse

Signs of Use	Euphoria, grandiosity, dilated pupils, tachycardia, elevated blood pressure, nausea and vomiting, paranoia, hallucinations, violent outbursts
Signs of Withdrawal	Agitation, disorientation, insomnia, depression, suicidal ideation
Signs of Overdose	Ataxia, hyperpyrexia, respiratory distress, seizures, cardiovascular collapse, coma, death
Treatment of Overdose	Provide respiratory and cardiac support, treatment of hyperpyrexia and seizures

Hallucinogens

Hallucinogens are capable of distorting perceptions of reality. Hallucinogens include those that occur naturally, such as mescaline and psilocybin, as well as those that are synthetically produced, such as LSD. There is no evidence of physiological dependence with hallucinogens; however, they can produce tolerance and psychological dependence. Table 17.4 highlights signs and treatments related to clients abusing hallucinogens.

TABLE 17.4   Signs and Treatments Related to Hallucinogens Abuse

Signs of Use	Dilated pupils, tachycardia, diaphoresis, irregular eye movement, grandiosity, hallucinations
Signs of Withdrawal	None known
Signs of Overdose	Psychosis, possible hypertensive crisis, hyperthermia, seizures
Treatment of Overdose	Provide a quiet environment and sedation for anxiety

Cannabis

Cannabis ranks as second among the drugs of abuse in the United States. Marijuana, which is composed of the dried leaves, stems, and flowers, is the most prevalent cannabis preparation. Hashish is derived from the flowering tops of the plant. Medical uses for marijuana include the management of glaucoma, treatment of the nausea that accompanies cancer therapy, and an appetite stimulant for clients with AIDS-related anorexia. Physical dependence and tolerance have been found in chronic users. Table 17.5 highlights signs and treatments related to clients abusing cannabis.

TABLE 17.5   Signs and Treatments Related to Cannabis Abuse

Signs of Use	Tachycardia, increased appetite, euphoria, slowed perception of time
Signs of Withdrawal	Irritability, restlessness, insomnia, tremors, sweating, gastrointestinal upset
Signs of Overdose	Fatigue, paranoia, psychosis
Treatment of Overdose	Treatment of presenting symptoms

Psychological Disorders of Childhood and Adolescence

These disorders refer to the emotional and behavioral alterations that become evident in the early years of life. This section, we review five of these disorders:

▶ Autistic disorder (and other pervasive developmental delay disorders)

▶ Conduct disorder

▶ Oppositional defiant disorder

▶ Attention deficit hyperactive disorder

▶ Eating disorders

Other emotional disorders, such as major depression and schizophrenia, were covered in previous sections of this chapter.

Autistic Disorder

Approximately 12%–16% of children have behavioral or developmental disorders. One of the most common sets of disorders is pervasive developmental delay, which includes autistic disorder, Asperger's syndrome, Rett's disorder, childhood disintegrative disorder, and pervasive developmental disorder not otherwise specified. The majority of cases of pervasive developmental delay are children with autistic disorder or simple autism. The number of children diagnosed with autism has increased sharply since 1985. The disorder is four times more common in males than females. Although symptoms often begin between 18 and 24 months, most children are diagnosed between the ages of 6 and 11 years. The cause of autism is not known, although there have been several theories including genetic transmission, immune responses, neuroanatomical changes, and alterations in the neurotransmitters dopamine and serotonin. There is a higher incidence in children with Down syndrome and phenylketonuria. To date, research has not indicated a relationship between the measles/mumps/rubella vaccine and the reported cases of the disorder.

Clinical manifestations commonly observed in the child with autism include impaired social interaction, impaired communication, problems adapting to new situations, and impaired attention span. The child with autism is often unable to converse normally and might fail to initiate conversations with others. Speech difficulties or delays in speech are common. Absence of babbling by one year of age, absence of two-word phrases by two years of age, and deterioration of previous language skills are common.

Autistic children are not able to relate to people or respond to social or emotional cues in a normal manner. Instead they engage in *stereotypy* or rigid, obsessive behaviors. These behaviors include head banging, twirling in circles, biting themselves, and flapping their hands or arms. Abnormal and exaggerated responses to sensory stimuli (touch, loud noise, or bright light) are common. Rituals when eating (eating only certain types or colors of food) or playing (playing with the same object over and over) is typical. Any attempts to change these rituals results in agitation and withdrawal.

Interventions for the child with autism include teaching and rewarding appropriate behaviors; encouraging positive, adaptive coping skills; and facilitating effective communication. Complementary therapies such as vitamin supplements and eliminating foods containing sugar, aspartame, milk products, and wheat have been advocated by some parents; however, there is limited evidence that these therapies are effective. Medications are not a part of the treatment of autism, but they can be used to treat associated behavioral disorders.

Conduct Disorder

Conduct disorder is characterized by persistent patterns of behavior in which the rights of others are violated. Early in life, some say by the age of 3, the child with conduct disorder is observed to be cruel and physically aggressive with people and animals. The child later develops antisocial behavior that includes destruction of property, truancy, and substance abuse. When confronted with their behavior, children with conduct disorder show a lack of guilt or remorse and frequently blame others for their acts. Conduct disorder gives way to an adult diagnosis of antisocial personality disorder. Some children with conduct disorder show improvement when treated with clonidine (Catapres).

Oppositional Defiant Disorder

Oppositional defiant disorder is characterized by persistent patterns of negativistic, hostile, and defiant behavior. Unlike a child with conduct disorder, a child with oppositional defiant disorder does not violate the rights of others. The behaviors of the child diagnosed with oppositional defiance are more likely to be argumentative, uncooperative, annoying, and spiteful.

Attention Deficit Hyperactive Disorder

Attention deficit hyperactive disorder (ADHD) is characterized by persistent patterns of hyperactivity, impulsivity, and inattention. The disorder, which is more common in boys, often goes unrecognized until the child enters school. The child with ADHD typically has problems following directions and lacks the attention necessary to complete assigned tasks. Theories as to the cause of ADHD include genetics, exposure to environmental lead, dietary influences, and alterations in dopamine and norepinephrine levels. Impairments in social, academic, and occupational functioning are common in those with ADHD.

The approach to the treatment of ADHD is threefold. Children with ADHD need counseling to help them develop positive self-esteem and gain the social skills necessary for making and keeping friends. These children also need educational interventions to help them succeed in school. Finally, children with ADHD can benefit from medication that helps control the symptoms of the disorder.

Eating Disorders

Eating disorders refer to the separate disorders of anorexia nervosa and bulimia nervosa. Both disorders, which are more common in females, have increased in incidence in the past three decades.

Anorexia Nervosa

Anorexia nervosa is defined as a morbid fear of obesity characterized by a preoccupation with food while refusing to eat. The client with anorexia nervosa sustains significant weight loss through strict dieting, excessive exercising, self-induced vomiting, and the abuse of laxatives and diuretics. The consequences of anorexia include atrophy of the cardiac muscle and cardiac dysrhythmias, deficiencies in estrogen leading to osteoporosis, and alterations in thyroid metabolism.

Anorexia nervosa is most common in adolescent females between the ages of 12 and 18. The cause of the disorder is believed to be a combination of biological, psychological, and social factors. Although psychological and social factors are cited most often, it is suggested that alterations in serotonin metabolism plays a significant role.

Bulimia Nervosa

Bulimia nervosa is characterized by the uncontrolled compulsive ingestion of enormous amounts of food in a short period of time. High-calorie, high-carbohydrate snacks that can be ingested quickly are preferred. The binging episode, which occurs in secret, is followed by feelings of guilt, which are relieved only by a period of purging. Although the client with anorexia does not see her behavior as abnormal, the client with bulimia nervosa is embarrassed by her disorder and spends a great deal of energy trying to conceal it. Clients with bulimia have difficulty expressing their feelings, are prone to be impulsive, and could become dependent on alcohol and drugs. Physical complications associated with bulimia nervosa include fluid and electrolyte imbalances, damage to the mucosa of the stomach and intestines, cardiac dysrhythmias, and dental caries.

Nursing interventions for the client with an eating disorder include stabilizing the client's physical condition. Complications from fluid and electrolyte imbalance and muscle wasting are often life-threatening, particularly in a client with anorexia. When the client's physical condition is stable, treatment modalities using behavior modification, individual therapy, and family therapy are begun. A detailed history of the client's dieting and patterns of binging and purging are essential to planning care. Although there are no specific medications to treat eating disorders, antidepressant medications (selective serotonin reuptake inhibitors) have been effective in treating some clients with eating disorders.

Case Study

Steve Pate, a 26-year-old with a history of paranoid schizophrenia, is brought to the local mental health clinic by his family. According to his brother, Steve's mental condition has deteriorated over the past two weeks. He is spending more time in his room and on several occasions has been heard arguing in a loud voice although there is no one in the room with him. He refuses to eat or to take his medication claiming that he is being poisoned because he "knows too much." He insists that he has been an agent with the CIA and that he has masterminded the overthrow of governments hostile to the United States. His family denies Steve's claims and report that his mental illness prevented him from finishing college or from being employed for any length of time. Steve is admitted for further evaluation and stabilization with antipsychotic medication. The following questions pertain to the client with paranoid schizophrenia.

1. Describe the four A's associated with a diagnosis of schizophrenia.

2. List the positive and negative symptoms common to those with schizophrenia.

3. Clients with schizophrenia frequently have hallucinations and delusional thinking. Explain the difference in hallucinations and delusions.

4. Describe the symptoms associated with neuroleptic malignant syndrome (NMS) and its treatment.

5. At home Steve had refused to eat or take his medication because he believed that he was being poisoned. What interventions should the nurse use when feeding or medicating the client with paranoid schizophrenia?

(continues)

(continued)

Answers to Case Study

1. According to Eugen Bluler, a Swiss psychologist, persons with schizophrenia typically exhibit the 4 A's: flat or blunted *Affect*, loose *Association*, *Ambivalence*, and *Autism*.

2. Positive symptoms of schizophrenia reflect an excess or distortion of normal function. Positive symptoms include hallucinations, delusions, and disorganized thinking and speech. Negative symptoms of schizophrenia reflect a diminished or loss of normal function. Negative symptoms of schizophrenia include flat affect, alogia, apathy, anhedonia, and social isolation.

3. *Hallucinations* are defined as false sensory perceptions. Auditory hallucinations or hearing voices although no one else is present is common in the client with a diagnosis of schizophrenia. Delusions are defined as firm fixed beliefs that are maintained despite evidence to the contrary. Persons with schizophrenia frequently have delusions of persecution, somatic delusions or religious delusions.

4. Symptoms of neuromalignant syndrome (NMS) are rare but can include: hyperthermia (temps as high as 107° F), spasms of the face, neck, and tongue, and respiratory distress. Treatment consists of discontinuing the antipsychotic medication and administering either Dantrium (dantrolene) or Parlodel (bromocriptine). The nurse should support the client's respiratory effort and be prepared to transfer the client to ICU if needed.

5. The nurse should provide Steve with food in sealed packages or food that has been unopened. Examples of foods and drinks that could be provided are boiled eggs, baked potato with the skin intact, sealed packages of cereal or crackers, unpeeled fruits, and unopened cartons of milk or juice. Medication should be provided in the sealed unit dose package for his inspection prior to opening.

Key Concepts

This chapter includes much needed information to help the nurse apply a knowledge of caring for the client with psychiatric disorders to the NCLEX exam. The nurse preparing for the licensure exam should review normal laboratory values, common treatment modalities and pharmacological agents used in the care of clients with psychiatric disorders.

Key Terms

- ▶ Anorexia nervosa
- ▶ Attention deficit hyperactive disorder
- ▶ Bipolar disorder
- ▶ Bulimia nervosa
- ▶ Conduct disorder
- ▶ Conversion
- ▶ Delusion
- ▶ DSM-IV-TR
- ▶ Dysthymic disorder
- ▶ Electroconvulsive therapy
- ▶ Extrapyramidal side effect
- ▶ Hallucination
- ▶ Hypertensive crisis
- ▶ Hypochondriasis
- ▶ Neuroleptic malignant syndrome
- ▶ Neurosis
- ▶ Neurotransmitter
- ▶ Pain disorder
- ▶ Personality disorder
- ▶ Psychosis
- ▶ Schizophrenia
- ▶ Somatization disorder

Diagnostics

The diagnostic tests for a client admitted with a psychiatric diagnosis include many of the tests used for clients with any hospital admission. Other tests are necessary for monitoring the client's response to certain medications. For example, a client on lithium therapy will continue to show signs of mania until a therapeutic level is reached. Some of the diagnostics requested for the client on a behavioral health unit include the following:

▶ CBC

▶ Complete metabolic panel

▶ Lithium level

▶ Urinalysis

Pharmacological Agents Used in the Care of the Client with Psychiatric Disorders

The client with a psychiatric diagnosis usually receives one or more of the psychotropic medications. Some conditions, such as ADHD, are treated with central nervous system stimulants or antidepressants. The categories of psychotropic medications commonly prescribed are

▶ Antipsychotics

▶ Antidepressants

▶ Mood stabilizers

▶ Anxiolytics

▶ Medications used to treat ADHD

These medications are not inclusive of all the agents used to treat psychiatric disorders; therefore, you will want to keep a current pharmacology text for reference. Side effects associated with psychotropic medications are too numerous for all of them to be listed in this section. Table 17.6 lists only the most commonly occurring side effects. Additional information about the medications can be found in a pharmacology text. The table also addresses the adverse effects associated with each class of psychotropic medication.

TABLE 17.6   Pharmacological Agents Used in the Care of the Client with Psychiatric Disorders

Drug	Action	Side Effect	Nursing Care
Antipsychotics		Drowsiness, orthostatic hypotension, dizziness, EPSE, dry mouth, weight gain, photosensitivity, decreased sweating, and changes in libido. Adverse effects associated with antipsychotic medication include seizures, neuroleptic malignant syndrome (rare), aplastic anemia, agranulocytosis, tardive dyskinesia, and dystonia.	
Chloropromazine HCl (Thorazine)	Blocks dopamine receptors	Sedation, dry mouth, Parkinsonian symptoms, weight gain, tardive dyskinesia, dystonia akathisia, photo-sensitivity, neuroleptic malignant syndrome (NMS).	Provide extra fluids and sugarless hard candy, protect from over exposure to sunlight, monitor the temperature and observe for signs of NMS (increased temperature, spasms of the face, neck, and tongue).
Haloperidol (Haldol)	Precise action unknown: blocks dopamine receptors	Sedation, orthostatic hypotension, weight gain, Parkinsonian symptoms.	Same as above.
Fluphenazine decanoate; fluphenazine HCl (Prolixin)	Blocks dopamine receptors	Extrapyramidal side effects that can include Parkinsonian symptoms, tardive dyskinesia, dystonia.	Protect medication from light. Do not mix the liquid form with any beverage containing caffeine, tannates, or pectin due to physical incompatibility.
Risperidone (Risperdal)	Combined antagonism of dopamine and serotoinin receptors	Headache, changes in appetite, changes in weight, orthostatic hypotension, dry eyes.	Monitor liver and renal profiles, protect client from overexposure to sunlight or artificial light.
Ziprasidone HCl (Geodon)	Exact mechanism unknown; combined antagonism of dopamine and serotonin receptors	Nausea, dry mouth, dizziness, rash, urticaria, orthostatic hypotension.	Tell client to rise slowly, Do not use in clients with a history of recent MI or cardiac irregularity.
Olanzapine (Zyprexa, Zyprexa, Zydis)	Combined antagonism of dopamine and serotonin receptors	Dysphagia, changes in weight, tachycardia, hypo/ hyperglycemia, arthritic symptoms, urinary retention.	Monitor liver and renal profiles, blood glucose level; monitor for ECG changes. Instruct the client to void before taking the drug to decrease urinary retention.

(continues)

TABLE 17.6 *Continued*

Drug	Action	Side Effect	Nursing Care
Quetiapine fumarate (Seroquel)	Exact mechanism unknown; might act as antagonist at dopamine D_2 and serotonin 5 HT_2 receptors	Rash, fever, weight gain, back pain, somnolence, orthostatic hypotension.	Use with caution in those with liver disease. ALT levels rise during initial therapy.
Aripiprazole (Abilify)	Exact mechanism unknown; partial agonist activity at D_2 and 5HT-1A and antagonist activity at 5HT-2A receptors	Nausea and vomiting, anorexia, bradycardia, arthralgia, rash, altered taste.	Monitor renal and liver function, monitor blood glucose level.
Antidepressants (Tricyclics)		Adverse effects associated with the use of tricyclic antidepressants include aplastic anemia, heart block, and sudden death.	
Amitriptyline HCl (Elavil)	Increases norepinephrine, serotonin, or both in the CNS by blocking their reuptake by presynaptic neurons	Tremors, excitation, nausea, rash, photosensitivity, headache, blurred vision, dry mouth, mydriasis, nocturia, changes in libido, changes in blood pressure.	Contraindicated in those with severe liver dysfunction, should not be used in clients recovering from MI. Do not use with MAOI. Monitor the CBC, renal and hepatic function tests. Might increase intraocular pressure. Client should not use with other drugs or with alcohol.
Doxepine HCl (Sinequan)	Same as above	Same as above.	Same as above.
Desipramine HCl (Norpramin)	Same as above	Same as above.	Same as above.
Amoxapine (Ascendin)	Same as above	Same as above.	Same as above.
Antidepressants (SSRI)		Adverse reactions associated with the use of SSRI include serotonin syndrome, cardiac failure, myocardial infarction, stroke, hepatotoxicity, nephrotoxicity, increased depression, and increased incidence of suicide. The safe use of SSRI in those under age 18 has not been established.	
Duloxetine HCl (Cymbalta)	Selective serotonin norepinephrine reuptake inhibitor	Nausea, dry mouth, constipation, decreased appetite, somnolence, increased sweating.	Might cause serotonin syndrome if used with another SSRI or MAOI.

(continues)

TABLE 17.6 *Continued*

Drug	Action	Side Effect	Nursing Care
Citalopram HCl (Celexa)	Same as above	Dry mouth, changes in heart rate, polyuria, rash, skin discoloration.	Monitor liver and renal panels; do not use with MAOI; avoid alcohol use while taking drug.
Escitalopram oxylate (Lexapro)	Same as above	Insomnia, dizziness, dry mouth, heartburn, myalgia, increased sweating.	Contraindicated in clients taking MAOI or Celexa (citalopram HCl); monitor ECG, electrolytes, liver and renal function.
Fluoxetine HCl (Prozac)	Same as above	Headache, dizziness, decreased ability to concentrate, nausea.	Same as above; avoid overexposure to sunlight.
Paroxetine HCl (Paxil)	Same as above	Blurred vision, confusion, postural hypotension, somnolence.	Same as above.
Sertraline HCl (Zoloft)	Same as above	Same as above.	Same as above.
Antidepressants (MAOI)		Adverse reactions associated with the use of MAOI include hypertensive crisis which can occur if the client ingests sources of tyramine or certain medications; and serotonin syndrome, which can result from the concurrent use of an MAOI and SSRI.	
Phenelzine (Nardil)	Inhibits reuptake of neurotransmitter monoamine oxidase	Headache, dry mouth, dizziness, blurred vision, postural hypotension, increased appetite, potential for hypertensive crisis.	Instruct the client to avoid foods containing tyramine (aged cheese, beer, red wine, liver, avocados, chocolate). Client should check the labels of OTC medications to determine safe use with MAOI.
Tranylcypromine (Parnate)	Same as above	Same as above.	Same as above.
Isocarboxazid (Marplan)	Same as above	Same as above.	Same as above.

TABLE 17.6 *Continued*

Drug	Action	Side Effect	Nursing Care
Mood Stabilizers			
Lithium carbonate (Eskalith, Lithobid)	Mechanism for anti-manic effect is unknown	Thirst, drowsiness, tremors, blurred vision, alopecia, glycosuria Adverse reactions associated with lithium include lithium toxicity. Signs of toxicity include muscle weakness, diarrhea, polyuria, fine tremors, confusion, persistent GI upset, excessive salivation, ataxia, seizures, ECG changes, respiratory complications, and multisystem organ failure. The management of lithium toxicity includes the use of intravenous sodium lactate, normal saline, aminophylline, urea, or mannitol.	Monitor for signs of toxicity. Signs of toxicity are closely related to serum lithium level. Instruct client to have adequate fluid and sodium intake to prevent toxicity.
Divalproex sodium (Depakote)	May increase levels of GABA	Dry mouth, nausea and vomiting, stomatitis, nystagmus, alopecia, dysuria.	Administer with food to decrease gastric upset; monitor CBC, bleeding time, and liver function tests.
Lamotrigine (Lamictal)	Exact mechanism unknown; used as a mood stabilizer for those with rapid-cycling bipolar II disorder	Dizziness, somnolence, confusion, nausea and vomiting, hot flashes, palpitations, polyuria, and anemia.	Monitor the client's CBC, renal, and liver function tests.
Anxiolytics (Benzodiazepines)		Adverse effects associated with the use of benzodiazepines include anemia, thrombocytopenia, hepatotoxicity, and nephrotoxicity. Benzodiazepines carry a high risk for dependence and abuse.	
Diazepam (Valium)	Enhances GABA-mediated presynaptic inhibition	Dizziness, sedation, hypotension, confusion, lethargy, lightheadedness.	Monitor CBC, renal, and liver function. Instruct client to avoid alcohol and other CNS depressants while taking the medication. Use with certain herbals (kavakava) could increase sedation.
Alprazolam (Xanax)	Potentiates effects of GABA	Same as above.	Same as above.

TABLE 17.6 *Continued*

Drug	Action	Side Effect	Nursing Care
Lorazepam (Ativan)	Stimulates GABA receptors in ascending reticular-activating system	Same as above.	Same as above.
Chlordiazepoxide (Librium)	Potentiates effects of GABA	Same as above.	Same as above.
Medications Used to Treat ADHD		Adverse effects associated with medications to treat ADHD include arrhythmias, development of tics, anorexia, and weight loss.	
Methylphenidate HCl (Ritalin)	Might act by blocking the reuptake mechanism of dopaminergic neurons	Nervousness, insomnia, anorexia, urticaria, leukopenia, tachycardia.	Contraindicated in those with severe depression, those with Tourette's syndrome; should not be used in children under the age of 6 years.
Amphetamine sulfate (Adderall)	Unknown; probably promotes release of stored norepinephrine from nerve terminals in the brain	Nervousness, insomnia, anorexia, tachycardia.	Use is contraindicated in children less than 3 years of age. The medication should not be taken with milk, juice, or antacids.
Atomoxetine HCl (Strattera)	Mechanism unknown; may be related to selective inhibition of presynaptic norepinephrine transport	Dizziness, sedation, dyspepsia, hypotension, flushing, anorexia.	Should not be taken by those using MAOI; should not be taken within two weeks after MAOI is discontinued. Strattera should not be taken with any other OTC medication, herbal, or dietary supplement without prior approval from the doctor.

Apply Your Knowledge

This chapter provided information regarding the care of clients with psychiatric disorders. The following questions test your knowledge regarding the safe, effective care and management of the client with various psychiatric disorders. The nurse should use the key terms, diagnostics, chapter content, and pharmacological agents sections to answer these questions.

Exam Questions

1. The physician has ordered Zoloft (sertraline) 50 mg daily for a client with depression. Which statement by the client indicates an understanding of the medication's side effects?

    A. "I need to avoid certain foods and drinks to prevent an increase in blood pressure."

    B. "I will schedule an appointment each month to have my blood level checked."

    C. "I will use hard candy or gum to keep my mouth from feeling too dry."

    D. "I will need to take my medicine before meals to improve its effect."

2. The nurse is preparing to discharge a client who is taking Nardil (phenelzine). The nurse should instruct the client to:

    A. Wear protective clothing and sunglasses when she is outside

    B. Avoid using dietary supplements and over the counter medications

    C. Make sure that she consumes adequate fluids each day

    D. Increase her intake of iron, including liver and lentils

3. A client with dysthymia has a nursing diagnosis of self-esteem disturbance related to feelings of worthlessness. Which goal reflects an increase in the client's self-esteem?

    A. The client identifies two personal behaviors that alienate others.

    B. The client attends and participates in morning goal-setting activities.

    C. The client eats in the cafeteria with other clients from the unit.

    D. The client identifies one or two positive self-attributes.

4. A client scheduled for electroconvulsive therapy asks the nurse how the therapy helps relieve her depression. The nurse's response is based on an understanding that ECT:

    A. Eliminates the neurotransmitter acetylcholine

    B. Increases the perception of external stimuli

    C. Decreases levels of cortisol from the adrenal cortex

    D. Produces a seizure that temporarily alters brain chemicals

5. When assessing the risk of suicide for a depressed client, the nurse knows that:

   A. People who talk about suicide are not likely to harm themselves.

   B. The availability of means is essential to even the simplest suicide plan.

   C. Clients who survive unsuccessful suicide attempts are not likely to try again.

   D. An overdose of pills is never as lethal as injury by firearms.

6. Which of the following findings is a factor in the development of lithium toxicity?

   A. Hyponatremia

   B. Hypercalcemia

   C. Hypocalcemia

   D. Hypernatremia

7. A client with depression and suicidal ideation is admitted to the behavioral health unit for observation. Which of the following interventions provides best for the client's safety?

   A. Day hall supervision

   B. Constant supervision

   C. Checks every 15 minutes

   D. One-on-one night supervision

8. The physician has ordered Paxil (paroxetine) for a client with generalized anxiety disorder. The nurse should instruct the client to avoid herbal preparations that contain:

   A. Hypericum

   B. Angelica

   C. Chamomile

   D. Echinacea

9. Clients with personality disorders rely on their ability to manipulate others. The nurse caring for a client with a personality disorder should:

   A. Allow the manipulation because it will allow the client a sense of control

   B. Appeal to the client's sense of reason to maintain a therapeutic milieu

   C. Realize that the client will not need to manipulate after a sense of trust is established

   D. Recognize that the client's anxiety will increase when manipulations are unsuccessful

10. The diagnoses of conduct disorder and antisocial personality are both characterized by:

    A. A lack of guilt or remorse for wrongdoing

    B. A lower than average level of intelligence

    C. Consistent parenting

    D. Close friendships among age-related peers

Answers to Exam Questions

1. Answer C is correct. Dry mouth is a common side effect of antidepressant medications. Using hard candy or gum helps to prevent mouth dryness. Answer A is incorrect because it refers to treatment with MAOI. Answer B is incorrect because it refers to treatment with lithium. Answer D is incorrect because taking the medication with food enhances the absorption rate of the medication.

2. Answer B is correct. Nardil, an MAOI, should not be used with dietary supplements or over the counter medications. Answer A refers to care of the client receiving antipsychotic medication; therefore, it is incorrect. Answer C refers to the client taking lithium; therefore, it is incorrect. Answer D is incorrect because liver is high in tyramine and should be avoided by the client taking Nardil.

3. Answer D is correct. An increase in the client's self-esteem is evidenced by the fact that he/she can recognize positive self attributes. Answers A, B, and C are incorrect because they do not reflect an increase in self-esteem.

4. Answer D is correct. Electroconvulsive therapy produces a tonic-clonic seizure that temporarily increases brain chemicals, serotonin, dopamine, and norepinephrine. Answers A, B, and C are not true statements; therefore, they are incorrect.

5. Answer B is correct. Even the simplest plan for suicide requires that the means be available. Answers A and C are not true statements; therefore, they are incorrect. Overdose by pills is sometimes as fatal as injury by firearms; therefore, Answer D is incorrect.

6. Answer A is correct. The client who is taking lithium needs an adequate intake of sodium and fluid to prevent the development of lithium toxicity. Answers B, C, and D are incorrect.

7. Answer B is correct. The client admitted with suicidal thoughts or suicidal gestures is best cared for by constant supervision. Answers A, C, and D do not provide for continual observations to ensure the client's safety; therefore, they are incorrect.

8. Answer A is correct. Clients taking antidepressant medication should avoid herbal preparations containing hypericum (St. John's wort) unless directed by the physician. Answers B, C, and D do not specifically apply to the client taking prescription antidepressants; therefore, they are incorrect. Note: The client taking any prescription medication should check with the physician before using herbals or dietary supplements.

9. Answer D is correct. The client with a personality disorder will experience increasing anxiety as manipulative behaviors fail. The staff should approach the client professionally, rather than friendly, and should set firm limits on the client's behavior; therefore, Answers A, B, and C are incorrect.

10. Answer A is correct. The child with conduct disorder and the adult with antisocial personality disorder are characterized by lack of guilt or remorse for wrongdoings. Answer B is incorrect because both can have a higher than average IQ. Answer C is incorrect because both have a history of parental neglect or inconsistent parenting. Answer D is incorrect because both lack close friendships.

Suggested Reading and Resources

▶ Ball, J., and R. Bindler. *Pediatric Nursing: Caring for Children*. 4th ed. Upper Saddle River, NJ: Pearson Prentice Hall, 2008.

▶ Kneisl, C., and E. Trigoboff. *Contemporary Psychiatric Mental Health Nursing*. 2nd ed. Upper Saddle River, NJ: Pearson Prentice Hall, 2009.

▶ Lehne, R. *Pharmacology for Nursing Care*. 7th ed. Philadelphia: Elsevier, 2009

▶ Townsend, Mary C. *Essentials of Psychiatric Mental Health Nursing*. 4th ed. Philadelphia: F. A. Davis Company, 2008.

18

Emergency Care

Nursing in the emergency department can be thought of as nursing in the fast lane. Unlike the routine of unit nursing, emergency nursing requires the nurse to respond to diverse conditions with much versatility. Many emergency situations confront the client and his family with fears of death or disability. Therefore, the ER nurse must assist with stabilizing the client's physical condition while providing emotional support to both the client and his family during a time of crisis. Faced with life and death on a daily basis, emergency nursing is not for everyone.

A primary principle in providing emergency care is *triage*, or the sorting of clients into one of three categories:

- ▶ Emergent
- ▶ Urgent
- ▶ Nonurgent

Using this system, the clients with the most life-threatening conditions are cared for first. This is different from the triage applied in disasters or in field situations where scarce resources are allocated to care for the greatest number.

In this chapter, you will review some of the most common conditions cared for in the emergency department. You will not spend time on the conditions covered in previous chapters; however, you might want to refer to those chapters after you complete this section. These conditions include burns (refer to Chapter 7, "Care of the Client with Integumentary Disorders"), fractures (refer to Chapter 14, "Care of the Client with Musculoskeletal and Connective Tissue Disorders"), ketoacidosis and insulin shock (refer to Chapter 4, "Care of the Client with Endocrine Disorders "), myocardial infarction (refer to Chapter 3, "Care of the Client with Cardiovascular Disorders"), and seizures and increased intracranial pressure (refer to Chapter 11, "Care of the Client with Disorders of the Neurological System"). Instead, you will focus on the ABCDs of emergency care and the treatment of trauma, poisonings, and poisonous bites. Finally, you will review the care of clients who are victims of radiation accidents as well as chemical agents and biological weapons.

The ABCDs of Emergency Care

Initial management of the client in the emergency department is based on the ABCD assessment:

▶ **Airway:** Airway obstruction, whether complete or partial, requires prompt intervention. In the case of complete obstruction, appropriate intervention is needed to prevent permanent brain damage or even death.

▶ **Breathing:** After the airway has been secured, the nurse assesses the client's breathing to determine whether the client's respiratory effort is sufficient or whether assisted ventilation and oxygen are needed.

▶ **Circulation:** Evaluation of the client's circulation and control of bleeding are next in the order of trauma assessment. Only relief of airway obstruction and care of sucking chest wounds take priority over the immediate control of bleeding.

▶ **Deficits:** With airway, breathing, and circulation under control, the nurse turns her attention to assessing for deficits. These include additional injuries such as fractures, burns, wounds, and neurological injuries.

Each of these areas is covered in greater detail in the sections that follow; they form the basis for trauma interventions.

Airway

The first consideration is to find out whether the airway is patent. Are there signs of partial obstruction or complete obstruction? Signs of partial obstruction include noisy breathing and coughing, and signs of complete obstruction include inability to breathe, inability to talk, inability to cough, and clutching the throat. Death from complete airway obstruction can result in as little as three to five minutes due to hypoxia.

Clients who need airway management include those with scores of less than 8 on the Glasgow coma scale (refer to Chapter 11 for detailed information on the Glasgow coma scale), those with maxiofacial injuries, those who have aspirated, and those with inhalation injuries from burns. You can find more information on inhalation injuries from burns can be found in Chapter 7.

Interventions are aimed at maintaining a patent airway. A client with partial obstruction of the airway should be encouraged to cough forcefully. In the event that the airway is completely obstructed, it can be opened using the head-tilt chin lift maneuver or the jaw-thrust maneuver.

After the airway is open, it will be maintained by an oropharyngeal or nasopharyngeal airway or an endotracheal tube.

NOTE

You might want to refer to nursing textbooks for guidelines for managing a foreign body airway obstruction and performing cardiopulmonary resuscitation.

> **CAUTION**
>
> Always provide cervical-spine immobilization before opening the airway of any client with undetermined or suspected neck injuries. The jaw–thrust maneuver should be used for a victim with suspected neck injury because it can be done without extending the neck.

Breathing

The next consideration is to find out whether the rate and depth of respirations are adequate. The normal respiratory rate for adults is 12–20 breaths per minute; for children it's 15–30 breaths per minute; and for infants it's 28–50 breaths per minute. Lung sounds should be clear and equal bilaterally.

Inadequate breathing in the adult is evident in slowed (fewer than 8 breaths per minute) or rapid (greater than 24 breaths per minute) respirations. Other signs of inadequate respirations are labored breathing, intercostal and suprasternal retractions, changes in lung sounds, asymmetry of the chest wall, and cyanosis.

Interventions for ineffective breathing patterns are aimed at providing relief of symptoms. These interventions include maintaining a patent airway and providing supplemental oxygen. High-concentration oxygen is used in any cardiac or respiratory arrest situation.

Circulation

Next you must find out whether circulation is adequate. Are there signs of bleeding? The nurse should assess the rate, rhythm, and strength of the pulse and obtain an admission blood pressure. If the radial pulse can be felt, the systolic blood pressure is usually above 80 mm Hg. The nurse should check for capillary refill. If capillary refill is adequate, the area being assessed returns to a normal color within 2–3 seconds after blanching. If the area remains white or blue, the area is not receiving adequate circulation.

Circulation is obviously affected by blood loss. With the client in a supine position, the nurse can assess for external bleeding by doing a blood sweep. This is carried out by running a gloved hand beneath the client from head to toe, pausing periodically to see whether the glove is bloody.

A major complication associated with abdominal trauma is internal bleeding. Assessment of the client for internal bleeding is covered in the section "Trauma," later in this chapter.

External bleeding can be controlled by applying direct pressure to the area, elevating or immobilizing the affected extremities, or applying direct pressure over arterial pressure points. In most cases, bleeding can be stopped by direct pressure over the artery, unless a major artery has been severed. Tourniquets or inflated blood pressure cuffs are applied to an extremity only if hemorrhage cannot be controlled by direct pressure. The tourniquet should be applied just proximal to the wound and only tight enough to control arterial blood loss. The tourniquet should be loosened periodically to prevent neurovascular damage. If there is no further arterial bleeding, the tourniquet should be removed and a pressure dressing applied.

Interventions for inadequate circulation and hypovolemic shock are aimed at restoring adequate circulation and maintaining the blood pressure within normal limits. Infusions of warmed lactated Ringer's solution are started in at least two veins using a large-bore catheter (14- or 16-gauge). IV access, using the upper and lower extremities, is necessary if there is bleeding from a major vessel in the chest or abdomen. Infusion of lactated Ringer's solution helps restore circulation and allows time for blood typing and screening. The restoration of circulating blood volume depends on blood replacement.

Additional interventions for a client with hypovolemic shock include the insertion of a central venous pressure (CVP) line, insertion of an indwelling urinary catheter, monitoring of arterial blood gases, monitoring of vital signs, maintaining normal body temperature, and treating acid-base disturbances. Lactic acidosis, a common side effect of hemorrhage and injury, is associated with poor cardiac function.

Resuscitative efforts continue until the client has a serum lactic acid lower than 2.5 mmol/L within 24 hours after the injury and there are no further signs of hemorrhage.

Deficits

Finally, you need to ascertain the client's mental status. Are there changes in the client's level of consciousness? Deficits in these areas can reflect neurological injury.

The nurse can test for deficits by assessing the client's responsiveness and orientation. These assessments can be done quickly. To test for responsiveness, the nurse notes the following key points, which are sometimes referred to as *AVPU*:

▶ **Alertness:** Is the client aware of his surroundings and circumstances? Does the client know his name? Is he able to state the year, month, and day? Does he know what happened and where he is?

▶ **Verbal stimuli:** Does the client respond to questions asked by the examiner? Can he state his name? Can he identify common objects? Can he respond to simple requests? If the client can respond appropriately to what he is asked, he is said to be alert and oriented.

▶ **Pain:** Is the client aware of painful stimuli? Can he identify where pain is located? Can he describe the pain? Can he assess the pain using a pain scale?

▶ **Unresponsiveness:** Does the client respond to any stimuli?

The nurse can test the client's orientation by checking the client's awareness of person, place, time, common objects, and event. Questions about his name; where he is; the day, month, and year; and what happened help establish that the client is oriented. If the client can answer all these questions and is alert, he is determined to be alert and fully oriented.

After checking for responsiveness and orientation, the nurse assesses the pupils for size, shape, equality, and reaction to light. Pupillary changes should be reported immediately because they indicate changes in neurological status.

Obtaining Client Information

After airway, breathing, circulation, and deficits have been assessed and stabilized, the nurse focuses on obtaining a history of the current condition as well as significant information regarding medications, allergies, and past medical history. The emergency room staff then focuses on the client's reason for seeking treatment.

Trauma

Trauma is defined as unintentional or intentional injury to the body, and it is the number-one cause of death in persons under 44 years of age. Most traumatic injuries are the result of motor vehicle accidents (MVAs). Areas affected most often in MVAs are the head, chest, and abdomen. Other traumatic injuries include suicides, homicides, and physical assaults.

After performing the ABCD interventions, the nurse assesses for signs of traumatic injury. Rapid trauma assessment, using a head-to-toe approach, can be done using the mnemonic DCAP—BTLS. The nurse assesses the client for the presence of the following conditions:

- ▶ Deformities
- ▶ Contusions
- ▶ Abrasions
- ▶ Punctures or penetrations
- ▶ Burns
- ▶ Tenderness
- ▶ Lacerations
- ▶ Swelling

Head Injuries

Head injuries account for more than one-third of the injuries sustained in MVAs. Other sources of head injury include falls and sports injuries. Head injuries are classified as follows:

- ▶ **Primary brain injuries (open or closed head trauma):** Examples of primary brain injuries are fractures and penetrating injury.

- ▶ **Secondary brain injuries (the result of the primary injury):** Examples of secondary brain injuries are increased intracranial pressure, hemorrhage, and loss of autoregulation.

Interventions focus on assessing and managing increased intracranial pressure, assessing the level of consciousness using the Glasgow coma scale, controlling seizures, and minimizing neurological deficits. Chapter 11 covers these points in greater detail.

> **NOTE**
>
> *Coup* and *contrecoup* injuries affect different portions of the brain. *Coup* (site of impact) injuries occur in the frontal area of the brain. *Contrecoup* injuries occur in the frontal and temporal areas of the brain.

> **CAUTION**
>
> The use of opiates is contraindicated for a client with a head injury because they cause central nervous system depression.

Chest Injuries

Chest injuries account for about one-fourth of the injuries sustained in MVAs. Trauma to the head and chest is drastically reduced by the proper use of seatbelts and air bags as well as child safety restraints. Chest injuries include pulmonary and cardiac contusions, pericardial tamponade, fractured ribs, flail chest, pneumothorax, hemothorax, and ruptured diaphragm. Interventions include maintaining adequate respirations, controlling hemorrhage, and treatment of the specific injury. For example, pneumothorax and hemothorax are treated with the insertion of chest tubes and closed chest drainage.

> **CAUTION**
>
> Flail chest should be suspected in clients with multiple rib fractures, scapular fractures, and pulmonary contusion. Unequal chest movement characterizes flail chest.

Abdominal Injuries

Abdominal injuries account for about one-fourth of the injuries sustained in MVAs. Abdominal injuries can be blunt injuries (such as from seatbelts) or penetrating injuries (such as from gunshots or stab wounds). Penetrating injuries can damage hollow structures, particularly the small bowel, or solid organs. The most frequently damaged solid organ is the liver.

The major cause of death from abdominal trauma is hemorrhage. An assessment for abdominal injury should include inspection of the anterior abdomen, flanks, back, genitalia, and rectum. In the case of intra-abdominal injury, blood tends to collect in these areas. Rectal and vaginal examination is performed to determine injuries that might have occurred to the pelvis, bladder, or intestines.

Assessment of abdominal injury begins with obtaining a history of the mechanism of injury. Was the injury penetrating, as in the case of a gunshot, or was it blunt, as in the case of a blow to the abdomen? The abdomen is then inspected for obvious signs of injury. Entrance and exit wounds are noted, as are bruises and characteristic markings such as those left by seatbelts. The examiner auscultates for the presence of bowel sounds and records findings for comparison with later assessments. Areas of progressive distention, involuntary guarding, and tenderness are noted. The nurse should assess the chest for signs of injury that might accompany abdominal trauma.

The incidence of complications from blunt abdominal trauma is greater than from penetrating injuries. This is especially true when there is blunt injury to the liver, kidneys, spleen, or blood vessels, which can result in massive blood loss that can go undetected for some time.

> **CAUTION**
>
> The nurse should be familiar with indications of intra-abdominal bleeding. Ecchymosis, or bruising, around the umbilicus (Cullen's sign) and ecchymosis on either flank (Turner's sign) indicate retroperitoneal bleeding into the abdominal wall.
>
> The nurse should be familiar with indications of damage to the spleen. With the client lying on the left side, the right flank is percussed. Resonance over the right flank (Ballance's sign) might be noted in a client with a ruptured spleen; pain in the right shoulder might indicate lacerations of the liver.

Additional indications of abdominal trauma include the absence of bowel sounds, progressive abdominal distention, abdominal pain and tenderness, and evisceration.

> **CAUTION**
>
> Exposed abdominal contents should be covered with a sterile normal saline-soaked gauze. The nurse should not try to return the abdominal contents to the abdominal cavity.

Interventions for the client with abdominal injuries include the insertion of two large-bore IV catheters for delivering fluid and blood replacement, cardiopulmonary monitoring, insertion of an indwelling urinary catheter, and insertion of a nasogastric tube.

> **CAUTION**
>
> You should not insert a nasogastric tube if there is a suspected skull fracture.
>
> The use of opiates for pain control is contraindicated because they can mask important signs and symptoms.

Documenting and Protecting Forensic Evidence

It is essential that the nurse provide accurate documentation and protection of forensic evidence when caring for trauma clients. When removing clothing, the nurse should avoid cutting through any tears, holes, blood stains, or dirt that might be used as evidence. Each piece of clothing should be labeled and placed in an individual paper bag before it is given to the police. The name of the receiving officer, the date, and the time should be documented in the client's chart. Valuables should be placed in the hospital safe or given to a family member with appropriate documentation.

If homicide is suspected, the body of the deceased will be examined by the medical examiner or coroner. All tubes and lines should remain in place. The client's hands should be covered with paper bags to protect evidence that might be on her hands or under her nails. Swabs will be used to obtain tissue samples from beneath the nails. The client's wounds and clothing will also be photographed.

Procedures for protecting forensic evidence are the same for physical and sexual assault.

> **NOTE**
>
> In cases of suspected sexual assault, the client is instructed not to shower, bathe, or change clothing. A rape trauma kit is used to collect forensic evidence. Swabs are used to obtain tissue specimens from the hands and fingernails. Specimens should be carefully labeled and protected as potential evidence. Photographs of wounds and clothing should include one with a reference ruler and one without a ruler.

Poisoning

Poisoning results from the ingestion, inhalation, or absorption of agents that cause chemical actions that injure the body. Emergency management of the client includes

▶ Removing or inactivating the poison

▶ Providing supportive care to maintain vital organ systems

▶ Administering specific antidotes

▶ Initiating treatment to facilitate the excretion of the absorbed poison

> **NOTE**
>
> The American Association of Poison Control Centers has a website at www.aapcc.org for further information.

> **CAUTION**
>
> Vomiting is never induced in a client who has ingested a corrosive or petroleum distillates.
> Psychiatric consultation should be obtained if the poisoning is determined to be a suicide attempt.

Management of clients with poisonings related to lead, iron, aspirin, and acetaminophen were covered in Chapter 16, "Care of the Pediatric Client." Chapter 11 covered treatment of clients with chemical injuries and those with carbon monoxide poisoning, and Chapter 9, "Care of the Client with Gastrointestinal Disorders," covered interventions for food poisoning. Chapter 17, "Care of the Client with Psychiatric Disorders," covered treatment of drug overdoses, such as narcotics and barbiturates. You might want to review those chapters for comparison with the overall management of poisoning.

Poisonous Stings and Bites

The poisons in stings and bites are produced mainly by hymenopterans (bees, yellow jackets, wasps, hornets, and fire ants) or by venomous snakes (pit vipers). Injected poisons result in clinical manifestations that range from generalized redness, itching, and anxiety to bronchospasm, shock, and death. Snake venom can affect multiple organ systems—especially the cardiovascular, respiratory, and neurological systems.

Management of a client with a sting includes removing the stinger and washing the area with soap and water. The client should be discouraged from scratching the affected area because scratching releases histamine. Oral antihistamines and analgesics lessen pain and itching.

In cases of anaphylaxis or severe allergic reaction, aqueous epinephrine is administered subcutaneously and the injection site is massaged to speed drug absorption. Additional interventions focus on maintaining the client's respiratory and cardiovascular function. Desensitization is recommended for clients with a history of significant local or systemic reactions to stings.

The management of venomous snake bites is a medical emergency. The client should be instructed to lie down. Constricting items such as rings are removed, and the affected area is immobilized below the level of the heart.

NOTE

If the snake is dead, it should be brought to the emergency room to help identify the species.

Interventions include determining the severity of poisonous effects; obtaining vital signs; measuring the circumference of the affected extremity; and obtaining laboratory specimens for complete blood count, urinalysis, and clotting studies. In cases of *envenomation*—the injection of venom—antivenin is administered. Antivenin is most effective when given within 12 hours of the snake bite.

CAUTION

Corticosteroids are contraindicated in the first 6–8 hours after the bite because they can interfere with the action of the antivenin.

A test dose of antivenin, using the skin test or eye test, should be done before administering the medication.

The most common cause of allergic reaction to antivenin is too-rapid infusion. Allergic reactions include feelings of facial fullness, itching, rash, and apprehension. These symptoms can be followed by tachycardia, dyspnea, hypotension, and shock. In case of allergic reaction, the antivenin should be discontinued immediately, followed by the intravenous administration of Benadryl (diphenhydramine).

Bioterrorism

The threat of bioterrorism has brought with it new concerns and challenges for emergency personnel. Acts of bioterrorism are carried out using biological and chemical agents that are capable of disabling or killing thousands of people in a relatively short period. The unique nature of biological and chemical weapons is extremely frightening. The substances can be liquid or dry; dispensed in food and water supplies; vaporized for inhalation; spread by direct contact; and spread by vectors, including animals, insects, and persons.

Two biological agents most likely to be used as weapons are anthrax and smallpox.

Chemical and Biological Agents

Chemical agents produce effects that are more apparent and occur more quickly than biological agents. Chemical agents are classified as nerve agents, blood agents, vesicants, and pulmonary agents. Some chemical agents, such as chlorine, phosgene, and cyanide, are widely used in industry; therefore, they are widely accessible. Table 18.1 provides information on the symptoms and treatment of various chemical and biological agents.

TABLE 18.1 Chemical and Biological Agents Symptoms and Treatments

Chemical Agent	Symptoms	Treatment
Nerve agents (Tabun; Sarin; Soman; VX)	Salivation; lacrimation; urination; defecation; gastric emptying; pinpoint pupils (everything looks dark); seizures.	Atropine. The initial dose is 2 mg. Additional doses are given until symptoms are resolved (will not reverse miosis). Pralidoxime Chloride: 1 gram IV over 20–30 minutes. Benzodiazepines are given for seizure control or to prevent seizures in severely intoxicated patients.
Cyanides (hydrogen cyanide; cyanogen chloride)	Nonspecific symptoms, including anxiety, hyperventilation, and respiratory distress. Cherry-red skin, although classic, is seldom seen. Lactic acidosis and increased concentration of venous oxygen.	A cyanide antidote kit is used. An amyl nitrite ampule is given, and first aid is used until an IV is established. Crush and place the ampule inside the mask of a BVM resuscitator (15 seconds of inhalation; then a 15-second break; repeat until IV is established). Sodium nitrite: 300 mg over 2–4 minutes. Sodium thoisulfate: 12.5 g over 5 minutes.
Vesicants (mustard; lewisite)	Redness and blisters; inhalation injury can result in respiratory distress; leukopenia; pancytopenia.	Topical antibiotics. Systemic analgesics. Fluid balance (do not overhydrate because it's not a thermal burn). Bronchodilators and steroids for pulmonary symptoms—only if lewisite is the poison—then British anti-lewisite (BAL) is the antidote.
Pulmonary intoxicants (chlorine; phosgene)	Delayed onset of noncardiogenic pulmonary edema.	Treat hypertension with fluid; no diuretics. Ventilate with PEEP. Use bronchodilators.
Riot control agents	Ear, nose, mouth, and eye irritation.	Irrigate. Treat bronchospasm with bronchodilators and steroids, as needed.

TABLE 18.1 *Continued*

Biological Agent	Symptoms	Treatment
Anthrax	I: 1–6d. FLS; a possibly widened mediastinum; gram stain (gram od) of blood and blood culture (late).	TBI: Treatment can be delayed 24 hours until cultures from incident site are available. PEP (only if instructed by government officials); ciprofloxacin or doxycycline po 8 weeks. In severe cases, ciprofloxacin, doxycycline, or penicillin IV is given. Care of the client with inhalation anthrax requires airborne and contact precautions.
Cholera	I: 4h–5d. Severe gastroenteritis with rice water diarrhea.	Oral rehydration with WHO solution or IV hydration. Tetracycline, doxycycline (dosage as below or 300 mg one time) po for three days. Ciprofloxacin or norfloxacin po for three days if it's a resistant strain.
Plague	I:2–3d. FLS; CXR: patchy infiltrates or consolidation; gram stain of lymph node aspirate, sputum, or CSP (gram negative, non–spore-forming rods).	Isolation. PEP: Doxycycline or cirpofloxacin for 7 days. Symptomatic: Gentamicin or doxycycline IV for 10–14 days. Meningitis: chloramphenicol.
Tularemia	I: 2–10d. FLS.	Gentamicin for 10–14 days.
Q fever	I: 10–40d. FLS.	Most cases are selflimited. Tetracycline or doxycycline. po for five to seven days.
Smallpox	I: 7–17d (average is 12). FLS. Later, an erythematous rash develops that progresses to pustular vesicles. Electron or light microscopy of pustular scrapings. PCR.	Isolation. PEP: Vaccinia vaccine scarification and vaccinia immune globulin IM. Care of the client with smallpox requires contact precautions.
Viral encephalitides	I: 1–6d. FLS. Immunoassay.	Supportive.
Viral hemorrhagic fevers	I: 4–21d. FLS. Easy bleeding and petechiae; enzyme immunoassay.	Isolation and supportive care. Some clients respond to ribavirin.
Botulism	I: 1–5d. Descending bulbar, muscular, and respiratory weakness.	Supportive. PEP: Toxoid. Symptomatic: anti--toxin.
Staphylococcus enterotoxin B	I: 3–12h. FLS.	Supportive.
Ricin	I: 18–24h. FLS, pulmonary edema, and severe respiratory distress.	Supportive.
T-2 mycotoxins	I: 2–4h. Skin, respiratory, and GI symptoms.	Supportive.

Abbreviation	Meaning	Dosages
CSF	Cerebro-spinal fluid	Chloramphenicol: 50–75 mg/kg/d, divided q 6 hrs.
CXR	Chest x-ray	Ciprofloxacin: po: 500 mg q 12 h; IV: 400 mg q 8–12 h.
d	Days	Doxycycline: po: 100 mg q 12 h; IV: 200 mg initially then 100 mg q 12h.
h	Hours	Erythromycin: po: 500 mg q 6 h.
FLS	Flu-like symptoms	Gentamicin: 3–5 mg/kg/d.
GLI	Gastrointestinal	Norfloxacin: po: 400 ml.

(continues)

TABLE 18.1 *Continued*

Abbreviation	Meaning	Dosages
I	Incubation period	Penicillin: IV: 2 million units q 2 h.
PCR	Polymerase chain reaction	Tetracycline: po: 500 mg q 6 h.
PEP	Post-exposure prophylaxis	Streptomycin: IM: 15 mg/kg/BID.
TBI	Threatened biologic incident	Vaccinia immune globulin: IM: 0.6 ml/kg.
WHO	World Health Organization	WHO solution: 3.5g NaCl, 2.5g NaHCO3, 1.5g KCl, and 20g glucose per liter of water.

Compiled by Richard N. Bradley, MD, Assistant Medical Director, Houston Fire Department, EMS Division. Permission to use the above charts granted by The Drop magazine, published by the Special Forces Association of Fort Bragg, North Carolina; Winter 2001 issue.

Nuclear Warfare

Another source of terrorist activity involves the threat of nuclear warfare. Radioactive material includes not only nuclear weapons, but also radioactive samples of plutonium and uranium as well as medical supplies such as those used in cancer treatments. Placement of this radioactive material in a public place could result in exposure to a large number of people.

The following list highlights three types of radiation injury that can occur:

▶ **External irradiation:** The client does not require special isolation or decontamination.

▶ **Contamination:** The client requires immediate medical management to prevent incorporation.

▶ **Incorporation:** The client requires immediate medical management because the cells, tissues, and susceptible organs (kidneys, bones, liver, and thyroid) have taken up the radioactive material.

Management of the client follows the hospital and countrywide guidelines for radiation disasters. These guidelines are very specific regarding decontamination and treatment of the injured. Staff is required to wear protective clothing, including two pairs of gloves, masks, caps, goggles, and booties. Dosimeter badges should be worn by all caregivers participating in the client's care.

Decontamination should take place outside the hospital whenever possible. Clothing should be removed, double-bagged, and placed in a plastic container outside the facility. In a case where decontamination is delayed until hospital arrival, the client should be assessed with the radiation survey meter to determine external contamination. The client is taken to an area away from the ER equipped with a shower, collection pool, tarp, and collection containers for clothing and personal items. Additional washings should continue until the client is free from contamination.

Internal contamination or incorporation requires the use of cathartics and gastric lavage with chelating agents. These agents bind with the radioactive substances, which are then excreted in the urine, feces, and vomitus. Samples are obtained to determine the effectiveness of internal decontamination.

Acute radiation syndrome (ARS) can occur after a radiation injury. The development of ARS is dependent on the dose of radiation rather than the source, and symptoms vary according to the body system. Effects on the hematopoietic system are evident in the decreased number of white blood cells, red blood cells, and platelets that make the client vulnerable to infection and bleeding. Neurological effects include headache, nausea, and vomiting. Radiation of the skin produces redness, desquamation, and (in some instances) necrosis.

Triage Categories for Disaster Victims

A final point should be made regarding the care of clients in disasters such as those posed by terrorist acts or nuclear accidents. In disasters, the rules of hospital triage no longer apply. Faced with hundreds and possibly thousands of casualties, caregivers must use the color-coding system developed by the North Atlantic Treaty Organization (NATO). Table 18.2 details the triage categories for disaster situations.

TABLE 18.2   NATO Triage Color Codings

Category	Color
Minimal—Injuries are minor and treatment can be delayed	Green
Immediate—Injuries are life-threatening but survivable with minimal care	Red
Delayed—Injuries are significant and require medical care	Yellow
Expectant—Injuries are extreme, and survival is unlikely	Black

Case Study

An F3 tornado ripped through a small farming community during the night, leaving dozens of people injured or missing. Within a short time, the emergency department of the local hospital is filled to capacity. A quick survey reveals a number of clients with fractures and lacerations as well as some with head, chest, and abdominal trauma. Triage is quickly done with the most severely injured transported to surgery or to nearby hospitals for treatment. The following situation refers to the care of clients admitted to the emergency department following a disaster.

1. Discuss the initial management of the client cared for in the emergency department.

2. Describe the findings the nurse can expect to see in the client with blunt abdominal trauma and intra-abdominal bleeding.

3. Explain why blunt abdominal trauma is a greater concern than a penetrating injury to the abdomen.

4. Discuss interventions for the client with head trauma.

5. Trauma to the chest can result in a number of injuries including fractured ribs and flail chest. What finding characterizes the condition known as flail chest?

(continues)

(continued)

Answers to Case Study

1. The initial management of the client in the emergency department is based on the ABCD assessment: airway, breathing, circulation, and deficits. Prompt attention is given to relieving airway obstruction. After the airway has been secured, breathing or respiratory effort is assessed to determine whether assisted ventilation or oxygen is needed. The next order of assessment is the evaluation of circulation and control of bleeding. With airway, breathing, and circulation under control, the nurse assesses the deficits. These include additional injuries such as fractures, burns, wounds, and neurological injuries.

2. Findings associated with blunt abdominal trauma include progressive distension, involuntary guarding, and tenderness. Signs of intra-abdominal bleeding include Cullen's sign (ecchymosis around the umbilicus) and Turner's sign (ecchymosis on either flank).

3. Blunt injuries to the abdomen can result in damage to the liver, kidneys, spleen, or blood vessels, which can result in massive blood loss. These injuries can go undetected for some time whereas penetrating injuries, which are more obvious, get immediate attention.

4. Interventions for the client with head trauma focus on assessing and managing increased intracranial pressure, assessing level of consciousness, controlling seizures, and minimizing neurological deficits.

5. Flail chest is characterized by unequal chest movement. Flail chest should be suspected in the client with multiple rib fractures, fractures of the scapula, and pulmonary contusions.

Key Concepts

This chapter discussed nursing in the emergency department. The nursing student should use these key concepts to answer questions as they relate to the care of this client. Remembering the pathophysiology of the disease process, the treatment, and the laboratory values will help you to be able to answer questions in the physiologic integrity portion of the NCLEX exam.

Key Terms

- Biological weapons
- Chemical agent
- Emergent
- Non-urgent
- Urgent

Diagnostics

Diagnostic tests carried out for clients in the ER are mostly the same as those used for hospitalized clients. In some instances, such as poisonings, more specific tests such as toxicology screens might be ordered. The nurse should be familiar with the tests and diagnostic procedures routinely performed in the ER. These tests include

- Bleeding tests (PT, PTT, INR)
- CBC
- Chest x-ray
- Complete metabolic panel
- CT scan
- Liver profile
- MRI
- Urinalysis

Pharmacological Agents Commonly Used in ER Treatment

Categories of medications administered in the ER are much the same as for clients admitted to medical surgical units. These categories include

- Analgesics
- Antiarrhytmics

- ► Antibiotics
- ► Anticonvulsants
- ► Antiemetics
- ► Antihistamines
- ► Anxiolytics
- ► Bronchodilators
- ► Cardiotonics
- ► Emetics
- ► Local anesthetics
- ► Vasoconstrictors

Consult the tables of pharmacological agents in previous chapters for more specific information.

Apply Your Knowledge

The nurse reviewing for the licensure exam must be able to apply knowledge to meet client needs. Utilization of information found in this chapter will help the graduate to answer questions found on the NCLEX.

Exam Questions

1. The nurse is triaging four clients injured in a train derailment. Which client should receive priority treatment?

    A. A 42-year-old with dyspnea and chest asymmetry

    B. A 17-year-old with a fractured arm

    C. A 4-year-old with facial lacerations

    D. A 30-year-old with blunt abdominal trauma

2. Direct pressure to a deep laceration on the client's lower leg has failed to stop the bleeding. The nurse's next action should be able to:

    A. Place a tourniquet proximal to the laceration

    B. Elevate the leg above the level of the heart

    C. Cover the laceration and apply an ice compress

    D. Apply pressure to the femoral artery

3. A pediatric client is admitted after ingesting a bottle of vitamins with iron. Emergency care would include treatment with:

   A. Acetylcysteine

   B. Deferoxamine

   C. Calcium disodium acetate

   D. British anti-lewisite

4. The nurse is preparing to administer Ringer's lactate to a client with hypovolemic shock. Which interventions is important in helping to stabilize the client's condition?

   A. Warming the intravenous fluids

   B. Determining whether the client can take oral fluids

   C. Checking for the strength of pedal pulses

   D. Obtaining the specific gravity of the urine

5. The emergency room staff is practicing for its annual disaster drill. According to disaster triage, which of the following four clients would be cared for last?

   A. A client with a pneumothorax

   B. A client with 70% TBSA full thickness burns

   C. A client with fractures of the tibia and fibula

   D. A client with smoke inhalation injuries

6. An unresponsive client is admitted to the emergency room with a history of diabetes mellitus. The client's skin is cold and clammy, and her blood pressure reading is 82/56. The first step in emergency treatment of the client's symptoms would be:

   A. Checking the client's blood sugar

   B. Administering intravenous dextrose

   C. Intubation and ventilator support

   D. Administering regular insulin

7. A client with a history of severe depression has been brought to the emergency room with an overdose of barbiturates. The nurse should pay careful attention to the client's:

   A. Urinary output

   B. Respirations

   C. Temperature

   D. Verbal responsiveness

8. A client is to receive antivenin following a snake bite. Before administering the antivenin, the nurse should give priority to:

    A. Administering a local anesthetic

    B. Checking for an allergic response

    C. Administering an anxiolytic

    D. Withholding fluids for 6–8 hours

9. The nurse is caring for a client following a radiation accident. The client is determined to have incorporation. The nurse knows that the client will:

    A. Not need any medical treatment for radiation exposure

    B. Have damage to the bones, kidneys, liver, and thyroid

    C. Experience only erythema and desquamation

    D. Not be radioactive because the radiation passes through the body

10. The emergency staff has undergone intensive training in the care of clients with suspected anthrax. The staff understands that the suggested drug for treating anthrax is:

    A. Ancef (cefazolin sodium)

    B. Cipro (ciprofloxacin)

    C. Kantrex (kanamycin)

    D. Garamycin (gentamicin)

Answers to Exam Questions

1. Answer A is correct. Following the ABCDs of basic emergency care, the client with dyspnea and asymmetrical chest should be cared for first because these symptoms are associated with flail chest. Answer D is incorrect because he should be cared for second because of the likelihood of organ damage and bleeding. Answer B is incorrect because he should be cared for after the client with abdominal trauma. Answer C is incorrect because he should receive care last because his injuries are less severe.

2. Answer B is correct. If bleeding does not subside with direct pressure, the nurse should elevate the extremity above the level of the heart. Answers A and D are done only if other measures are ineffective, so they are incorrect. Answer C would slow the bleeding, but will not stop it, so it's incorrect.

3. Answer B is correct. Deferoxamine is the antidote for iron poisoning. Answer A is the antidote for acetaminophen overdose, making it wrong. Answers C and D are antidotes for lead poisoning, so they are wrong.

4. Answer A is correct. Warming the intravenous fluid helps to prevent further stress on the vascular system. Thirst is a sign of hypovolemia; however, oral fluids alone will not meet the fluid needs of the client in hypovolemic shock, so answer B is incorrect. Answers C and D are wrong because they can be used for baseline information but will not help stabilize the client.

5. Answer B is correct. The client with 70% TBSA burns would be classified as an emergent client. In disaster triage, emergent clients, code black, are cared for last because they require the greatest expenditure of resources. Answers A and D are examples of immediate clients and are assigned as code red, so they are wrong answers. These clients are cared for first because they can survive with limited interventions. Answer C is wrong because it is an example of a delayed client, code yellow. These clients have significant injuries that require medical care.

6. Answer A is correct. The client has symptoms of insulin shock and the first step is to check the client's blood sugar. If indicated, the client should be treated with intravenous dextrose. Answer B is wrong because it is not the first step the nurse should take. Answer C is wrong because it does not apply to the client's symptoms. Answer D is wrong because it would be used for diabetic ketoacidosis, not insulin shock.

7. Answer B is correct. Barbiturate overdose results in central nervous system depression, which leads to respiratory failure. Answers A and C are important to the client's overall condition but are not specific to the question, so they are incorrect. The use of barbiturates results in slow, slurred speech, so answer D is expected, and therefore incorrect.

8. Answer B is correct. The nurse should perform the skin or eye test before administering antivenin. Answers A and D are unnecessary and therefore incorrect. Answer C would help calm the client but is not a priority before giving the antivenin, making it incorrect.

9. Answer B is correct. The client with incorporation radiation injuries requires immediate medical treatment. Most of the damage occurs to the bones, kidneys, liver, and thyroid. Answers A, C, and D refer to external irradiation, so they are wrong.

10. Answer B is correct. Cipro (ciprofloxacin) is the drug of choice for treating anthrax. Answers A, C, and D are not used to treat anthrax, so they are incorrect.

Suggested Reading and Resources

▶ *Brunner & Sudduth's Medical Surgical Nursing*. 12th ed. Philadelphia: Lippincott, Williams, & Wilkins, 2009.

▶ Ignatavicius, D., and M. Workman. *Medical Surgical Nursing:Critical Thinking for Collaborative Care*. 6th ed. St. Louis: Elsevier, 2008.

▶ Lehne, R. *Pharmacology for Nursing Care.* 7th ed. Philadelphia: Elsevier, 2009.

▶ LeMone, P., and K. Burke. in *Medical Surgical Nursing: Critical Thinking in Client Care.* 4th ed. Upper Saddle River, NJ: Pearson Prentice Hall, 2008.

▶ Lewis, S., M. Heitkemper, S. Dirksen, P. Obrien, and L. Bucher. *Medical Surgical Nursing: Assessment and Management of Clinical Problems.* 7th ed. Philadelphia: Elsevier, 2007.

CHAPTER NINETEEN

Legal Issues in Nursing Practice

Safe nursing practice requires knowledge of the practice and legal boundaries of the registered nurse, the licensed practical nurse, and the nursing assistant.

The state boards of nursing are responsible for ensuring that those licensed to practice nursing are safe practitioners and that they abide by approved standards of nursing practice. Practicing nurses, physicians, consumers, as well as an attorney and an executive officer appointed by the governor of the state, generally make up the state boards of nursing. In addition, the directors of nursing from nursing schools within the state make up some boards of nursing. The state boards of nursing also have the ability to suspend, restrict, and revoke the license of a nurse convicted of a felony or misdemeanor. In the case of alcohol and drug addiction, the state boards of nursing can require the nurse to enter a recovering nurse program under the direction of the board.

Nursing or Nurse Practice Acts define the authority of the board of nursing, define the boundaries of scope of nursing practice, state the requirements for licensure, identify the grounds for disciplinary action, and identify the titles and types of licensure. The purpose of the Nursing Practice Act is to protect the public from unsafe practitioners and to promote competence and quality in nursing practice.

No matter which state you have a license to practice in, the Nursing Practice Act of that state will bind you. Nursing Practice Acts vary from state to state, but they are all similar in many ways. Boards of nursing have authorization to take legal action against a nurse or a group of nurses found to be in violation of the state's nursing practice standards as set out by the legislature.

This chapter explores the laws that impact your nursing practice. It also defines and discusses issues affecting your nursing practice and some questions included on the NCLEX exam in relation to legal and ethical issues.

CAUTION

If asked to perform any activity or skill that is out of your scope of practice by a physician, a supervisor, an administrator, or any other person in direct authority over you, you have the right and the obligation to refuse. If asked to perform a skill that you learned in school but have never performed, ask for help. If asked to operate a type of equipment that you are unfamiliar with, ask for help. Remember that the law and the National Council of State Boards of Nursing expect you to ensure the safety of the client and you are responsible if harm comes to the client because of your care or lack of care.

Types of Laws

Several types of laws govern nursing practice: statutory/regulatory, civil, criminal, and common law. The nurse is responsible for abiding by each type of law.

Statutory Laws/Regulatory Laws

Statutory laws are those created by elected officials within the legislative body. An example of this type of law is the Nursing Practice Act. These laws and their implementing rules and regulations set forth which activities the nurse can perform. It is imperative that a newly licensed nurse be aware of these and abide by them in daily practice. Often, as a nurse, you might be asked to perform duties that you do not feel comfortable performing. Remember that if your nursing school did not teach you a task or skill, it probably is out of your scope of practice. Professional organizations, such as the National League for Nursing, American Association of Colleges of Nursing, and others, routinely review and approve nursing curriculums. So, you can be fairly certain that if you did not learn a task in school, it is within your rights to refuse to perform that task.

Civil Laws

Civil laws are laws passed to protect the civil and private rights of individuals and provide civil remedies as opposed to criminal laws. This type of law usually involves the violation of one's rights against another and ensures equal treatment for all clients without regard to race, social status, ability to pay for services, or country of origin. If a violation of civil law is found, federal or state funds can be withheld or suit can be brought against the doctor, the nurse, or the facility for which they work. Damages usually involve money and sanctions. If the nurse is found to have caused harm to the client because of a lack of care, further action can be filed.

Criminal Laws

A *felony* is a crime of a serious nature that is punishable by jail time and loss of the nurse's license. A *misdemeanor*, on the other hand, is a lesser crime that can result in imprisonment for less than one year or a fine. An example of a misdemeanor is the use of a controlled substance. A felony example is the possession of large quantities of drugs with the intent to sell them. Many other types of actions are also criminal, such as stealing from a client or abusing a client. These involve the police and the board of nursing taking action. Even if the nurse is not caring for clients at the time the crime is committed, the state board of nursing can take action against the nurse. Action taken by the board can include suspension or loss of the license to practice nursing.

Common Law

Common law is a non-statutory body of law that has evolved from court decisions and case law. Common law has provided the right to consent for services that need to be rendered when the client is unable to give consent herself or to provide for the right to refuse consent. The Patient's Bill of Rights describes these concepts, which are listed here:

As a client you have the right to

- ▶ Receive respectful treatment that will be helpful in the course of your recovery.

- ▶ Refuse a treatment or to end treatment without harassment by the healthcare community. This is often a problem because physicians want the client to survive. However, the client and family might be more concerned with death and dignity while dying. Hospice care can help during this time.

- ▶ A safe environment that is free from fear of physical, emotional, or sexual abuse or neglect. This includes cleanliness of the facility and the healthcare providers.

- ▶ Refuse electronic recording of your conversations with healthcare workers. You can also request that conversations be recorded.

- ▶ Have written information regarding any care that is being provided or that the physician proposes. You also have the right to a written statement of all fees and services and the cost of each. You also have the right to see the licensure, educational training, and experience of your healthcare provider. You can also ask to see to which professional organizations your healthcare providers belong and any limitations that have been placed on him by his regulatory organization.

- ▶ Report unethical or illegal behavior that you observe, and to ask questions about your care.

- ▶ Refuse to answer questions or to disclose any information you choose not to share.

- ▶ Confidentiality. You can take legal action if the healthcare worker does not abide by the Health Information Protection Privacy Act (HIPPA).

- ▶ Receive a second opinion from another healthcare worker, physician, counselor, or nurse practitioner.

- ▶ See your files and receive a photocopy of your chart.

- ▶ Request that the doctor, counselor, or nurse inform you of your progress or lack of progress during your treatment.

- ▶ Know who will know about you and be able to see your chart.

Code of Ethical Behavior in Nursing Practice

Ethics are the principles that guide nursing decisions and conduct as they pertain to what is right or wrong. They also involve moral behavior. The nurse is expected to behave in a way that maintains the integrity of the client and family. Situations often arise that require the nurse to make a judgment, and a dilemma results when the nurse's values differ from those of the client and family. The nurse must remember that clients have the right to make decisions for themselves without the expressed opinion of the nurse. In 2001, the American Nurses Association released the Code of Ethics for Nursing. This code discusses the obligation and duties of the nurse. The following list describes the Code of Ethics for Nursing:

▶ The nurse practices with compassion and respect for the dignity, worth, and uniqueness of the individual unrestricted by social or economic status, personal attributes, or the nature of the disease. For example, the nurse might not be comfortable caring for an alcoholic client but is ethically obligated to provide the best and most compassionate care possible.

▶ The nurse is committed to the client, whether the client is an individual, a family, or a community. The home health nurse might be asked to care not only for the client, but also the family and or the whole community. In some cultures, the family and community are included in decision making. The nurse must respect the client's wishes in this matter.

▶ The nurse is expected to serve as an advocate for the client. The nurse also is responsible for protecting the health, safety, and rights of the client.

▶ The nurse is responsible and accountable for delegating tasks consistent with optimal client care. The nurse is expected to be aware of the roles and responsibilities of other healthcare workers.

▶ The nurse is expected to preserve one's own integrity and safety, to maintain competence, and to continue personal and professional growth. This basically means that in states where continuing education units are required, the nurse will abide by these regulations to keep a current license.

▶ The nurse participates in activities that establish, maintain, and improve the conditions of the work environment. The nurse is responsible for promoting activities that foster ethical values in nursing.

▶ The nurse participates in the advancement of the profession through education, research, and development of nursing knowledge.

▶ The nurse collaborates with others in the health community to meet client needs.

▶ The nurse is responsible for maintaining the integrity of nursing and its practice and for shaping social policy through professional organizations.

Legal Theories That Affect Nursing Practice

Standards of care apply to the practice of nursing and all professions. Because legal action can be taken against the nurse for failure to follow the standard of care, it is important that the nurse be familiar with legal terminology. The following sections discuss several legal theories affecting nursing practice. These include negligence, malpractice, assault and battery, tort, and fraud. These are the most common causes of action brought against the nurse, so the sections that follow cover each in detail.

Negligence

First, *negligence* is defined as a lack of reasonable conduct and care. Negligence involves omitting an act expected of a person with knowledge or performing an act that a reasonable person would not perform. If the nurse fails to perform an act, such as putting the side rail up on a bed, and the client falls out of bed, resulting in injury, the nurse can be charged with negligence. It is reasonable for the client to expect the nurse to know that the side rail should be used to prevent injury. Other examples of negligence are the failure to administer medications ordered by the physician.

Malpractice

Malpractice is professional negligence, misconduct, or unreasonable lack of skill that results in injury or loss of professional services. A nurse can be accused of negligence and malpractice in the same context. If the nurse fails to take the vital signs, and the client's condition deteriorates and the client eventually dies, the nurse can be accused of both negligence and malpractice. Although malpractice is often thought of as more severe than negligence, both can result in harm to the client. Other examples of malpractice include medication errors, carelessness with application of heat and cold, and failure to assess symptoms such as shock and respiratory distress.

Witnessing Consent for Care

The nurse is responsible for witnessing informed consent. The nurse is not responsible for obtaining informed consent, even though the nurse might get the client to sign the form before surgery or blood administration. The legal responsibility for obtaining informed consent resides with the person providing the treatment. This individual is often the physician. The nurse documents and communicates information regarding client care to the doctor.

Tort

A *tort* is a legal wrong against a person or his property. If a psychiatric nurse is given the responsibility of searching the belongings of a client admitted to the unit and, during the search of the client's luggage, the clothes are torn and the property destroyed, the nurse can be alleged to have committed a tort. In this example, the tort was unintentional; however, a tort can be either intentional or unintentional. Other examples of a tort are assault, battery, or slander because they are wrongful acts carried out with the intent to do harm.

Assault and Battery

Assault is the unjustifiable threat or attempt to touch or injure another person. *Battery* is the actual touching of another without consent. An example is a nurse on the psychiatric unit who uses undue power to restrain a client during an altercation. In such a situation, the nurse can be charged with assault and battery.

Fraud

Fraud is the intent to mislead in any form. Examples of fraud are the recording of vital signs that were not taken and the recording of blood glucose levels that were not obtained.

Managing Client Care

A portion of the NCLEX exam, called *Safe Effective Care*, includes the management and delegation of client care. The nurse is responsible for delegating client assignments. Delegation is the handing over of a task to another person. The usual team of healthcare workers includes the registered nurses, the licensed practical nurses/licensed vocational nurses, and the nursing assistants (UAP; *unlicensed assistive personnel*). The National Council of State Boards of Nursing (NCSBN) and state boards of nursing are responsible for ensuring the safety of clients. They work with the American Hospital Association to formulate rules and regulations that govern the nursing practice of these workers. The nurse must utilize Maslow's Hierarchy of Needs when delegating care to others. The most critical clients should be assigned to the most educated and experienced nurse, whereas the most stable clients should be assigned to the care of the lesser-qualified personnel. The registered nurse coordinates the healthcare and makes assignments to other workers. When the client is admitted to the unit, the registered nurse should see the client first. A client being discharged home or to another unit must be seen by the registered nurse before discharge, as well.

The licensed practical nurse should be assigned to care for the client who needs skilled nursing care but is stable. Care of central venous infusions, blood transfusions, intravenous infusion of chemotherapy agents, and unstable clients are duties that should be assigned to the registered nurse. Administering medications orally or by injection, changing sterile dressing, and inserting nasogastric tubes are examples of duties that can be performed by the licensed practical nurse. The nursing assistant can perform activities of daily living, such as feeding and bathing the client. The nursing assistant can also be assigned to take the vital signs of the stable client. Your healthcare facility might have more strict or different policies, so be certain to know your hospital's policies. The following list provides examples of activities that can be performed by the registered nurse and activities that licensed practical nurses can perform:

▸ **Ambulating the client:** The nurse (RN/LPN) can measure the client for crutches, assist the client to ambulate using crutches, and teach him regarding the correct methods of ambulation with crutches. The nurse (RN/LPN) can ambulate the client, but the nursing assistant can only ambulate the stable client.

The nurse (RN/LPN) can measure the client for a walker, ambulate him with a walker, and teach him how to use the walker.

The nurse (RN/LPN) can measure the client for a cane, ambulate him with a cane, and teach him how to use the cane.

▶ **Applying heat and cold:** The nurse (RN/LPN) can apply heat lamps; heating pads; and warm, moist soaks. The nurse (RN/LPN) can also apply cold applications.

▶ **Applying restraints of all types:** The RN and the physician are the only two personnel who can place the client in seclusion on the psychiatric unit.

▶ **Bathing the client:** The nurse (RN/LPN/UAP) can bathe the client and assist the client with performing the activities of daily living.

▶ **Central venous pressure monitoring:** The nurse (RN/LPN) can check the central venous pressure and assist the doctor with inserting a central catheter. Even though both the RN and LPN have knowledge of the hemodynamics of the heart, the best nurse to assign to interpreting central venous pressures is the registered nurse.

▶ **Collecting specimens:** The nurse (RN/LPN) can collect specimens such as sputum, wound, urine, and stool.

▶ **Electrocardiogram interpretations:** The nurse (RN/LPN) can interpret the ECG monitor and should know the life-threatening arrhythmias and the management of each.

▶ **IV therapy:** The registered nurse can start, manage, and discontinue intravenous infusions. The licensed practical nurse can maintain, regulate, and discontinue IV infusions according to written protocol. The LPN is not authorized to start IV therapy unless the licensed vocational nurse (LVN) or LPN is certified to perform this task.

The RN can insert peripherally inserted central venous catheters (PICCs) with certification. The LPN, however, is not authorized to perform this skill.

The RN can hang and monitor blood transfusions. The LPN can take the vital signs of the client receiving the blood transfusion but should not be the primary nurse responsible for this client.

▶ **Medication administration:** The nurse (RN/LPN) can insert vaginal and rectal suppositories. The registered nurse can administer IV medications, an IV push, and IV piggyback medications. The LPN should not be assigned to this task unless he is IV certified. Intravenous push medications are not usually included in this certification. The nurse (RN/LPN) can administer oral medications, topical medications, intramuscular medications, intradermal medications, and subcutaneous medications.

▶ **Nasogastric tubes:** The nurse (RN/LPN) can insert nasogastric tubes for Levin suction or gavage feeding. The nurse (RN/LPN) can insert medications through nasogastric feeding tubes and percutaneous esophagoscopy gavage feeding tubes (PEG tubes). The RN and LPN can discontinue nasogastric tubes.

▶ **Tracheostomy care/endotracheal care:** The nurse (RN/LPN) can suction and provide ventilator support (the nurse is expected to know how to manage the client on the ventilator). The RN and LPN can clean the tracheostomy and provide oxygenation.

▶ **Traction:** The nurse (RN/LPN) can set up and maintain skin traction but cannot implement skeletal traction.

▶ **Teaching:** The RN is responsible for teaching the client prior to discharge. The LPN is part of the health team and supports the RN in the teaching plan.

▶ **Urinary catheters:** The nurse (RN/LPN) can insert Foley and French catheters. The RN and LPN can irrigate Foley catheters with a physician's order. Both can discontinue Foley and French catheters, as well.

▶ **Vital signs:** The nurse (RN/LPN) can perform the task of taking the vital signs and evaluating them. The nursing assistant can take the vital signs of the stable client.

▶ **Wound care (sterile):** The nurse (RN/LPN) can perform decubitus care, cast care, and sterile dressing changes.

NOTE

Nursing or Nurse Practice Acts vary from state to state. The nurse is responsible for knowing the laws in the state where he will practice. It is the responsibility of the nurse to contact the board of nursing to obtain a copy of the Nursing Practice Act. The state board of nursing has been authorized to take action against a nurse found guilty of failure to comply with rules and regulations set forth by the law. These examples are not a comprehensive list of all the skills registered nurses/licensed practical nurse can do.

CAUTION

Do not assign a nursing assistant to calculate hourly intake and output, take postoperative vital signs, or care for an unstable client. A registered nurse or licensed practical nurse should be assigned to these tasks.

The nurse must be aware of infection control and isolation needs. If the client has an infection, he should not be assigned to share a room with a client who is immune-suppressed or has had surgery. A pregnant client should not be assigned to share a room with a client with teratogenic infections or who is receiving medications that can be harmful to the fetus. A pregnant nurse should not be assigned to care for a client who has a radium implant or one who is receiving chemotherapy or other medication that can harm the baby.

Another responsibility of the registered nurse and the licensed practical nurse is to serve as a client advocate. He must ensure that referrals are made and that facility policies are maintained. The registered nurse helps with formulating the policies and often serves as the head nurse, supervisor, or director of nursing. Often the registered nurse is the one assigned to call social services, dietary, and other services, although the licensed practical nurse can assist with these responsibilities. As the charge nurse, the RN also might be called on to counsel co-workers and settle differences that arise among personnel.

Case Study

1. Amy, a recently licensed nurse, has been assigned to the critical care unit. On the third day of orientation, her preceptor tells her that she has been doing an excellent job and that she has decided to assign her six patients for the day. Amy feels unsure about this assignment. What should she do?

2. Amy is asked to perform a skill that she has never done. Which action would be best to ensure the safety of the client?

3. Amy's client asked for medication for a headache. After checking the chart, she finds that there is no order for pain medication. Amy decides to give two Tylenol (acetaminophen) for pain. What can Amy be charged with?

4. If harm comes to the client, what can Amy be charged with?

5. If Amy decides to chart medication that she did not give, with what can she be charged?

Answers to Case Study

1. Amy is a newly licensed nurse that has been on the unit for three days. Because she feels unsure of herself, she should explain this to the preceptor. If she is not comfortable with the tasks assigned to her, she should refuse the assignment and immediately contact the nurse in charge.

2. Amy should ask the preceptor to allow her to watch the skill performed and then perform the task herself with the preceptor watching. This action would allow her time and orientation to the task and ensure the safety of the client.

3. Amy can be charged with administering medication without an order by the state board of nursing.

4. Amy can be accused of malpractice if harm comes to the client.

5. Amy can be charged with fraud and falsifying documents.

Key Terms

- ▶ Assault
- ▶ Battery
- ▶ Civil laws
- ▶ Common laws
- ▶ Consent
- ▶ Criminal laws
- ▶ Ethics
- ▶ Felony
- ▶ Incident report
- ▶ Informed consent
- ▶ Intentional torts
- ▶ Invasion of privacy
- ▶ Licensure
- ▶ Malpractice
- ▶ Malpractice insurance
- ▶ Misdemeanor
- ▶ Negligence
- ▶ Nursing Practice Act
- ▶ Patient's Bill of Rights
- ▶ Regulatory laws
- ▶ Restraints
- ▶ Tort

Apply Your Knowledge

This chapter focuses on legalities within the nursing profession. Because a large portion of the NCLEX includes delegation of client care, the nurse must be aware of her/his scope of practice. Knowing which nurse to assign to a task is imperative to being able to answer these questions correctly on the exam.

Exam Questions

1. The nurse is making assignments for the day. Which client should be assigned to the pregnant nurse?

    A. The client receiving radium linear accelerator radiation therapy for cancer

    B. The client with a radium implant for vaginal cancer

    C. The client who has just been administered radioactive isotopes for cancer

    D. The client who returned from placement of iridium seeds for prostate cancer

2. The nurse is planning room assignments for the day. Which client should be assigned to the only private room?

    A. The client with Cushing's disease

    B. The client with diabetes

    C. The client with acromegaly

    D. The client with myxedema

3. The charge nurse witnesses the nursing assistant being abusive to a client in the nursing home facility. The nursing assistant can be charged with which of the following?

    A. Negligence

    B. Tort

    C. Assault

    D. Malpractice

4. Which assignment is outside the realm of nursing practice for the licensed practical nurse?

    A. Inserting a Foley catheter

    B. Discontinuing a nasogastric tube

    C. Obtaining a sputum specimen

    D. Starting a blood transfusion

5. The client returns to the unit from surgery with a blood pressure of 100/50, pulse 122, and respirations 30. Which action by the nurse should receive priority?

    A. Continue to monitor the vital signs

    B. Contact the physician

    C. Ask the client how he feels

    D. Ask the LPN to continue the postop care

6. Which nurse should be assigned to care for the client with preeclampsia?

  A. The RN with 2 weeks experience on postpartum

  B. The RN with 3 years experience in labor and delivery

  C. The RN with 10 years experience in surgery

  D. The RN with 1 year experience in the neonatal intensive care unit

7. Which information should be reported to the state board of nursing?

  A. The facility fails to provide literature in both Spanish and English.

  B. The narcotic count has been incorrect on the unit for the past three days.

  C. The client fails to receive an itemized account of his bills and services received during his hospital stay.

  D. The nursing assistant assigned to the client with hepatitis fails to feed the client and give him a bath.

8. The nurse is found to have charted blood glucose results without actually performing the procedure. After talking to the nurse, the charge nurse should do which of the following?

  A. Call the board of nursing

  B. File a formal reprimand and monitor the nurse

  C. Terminate the nurse

  D. Charge the nurse with a tort

9. The home health nurse is planning for the day's visits. Which client should be seen first?

  A. The 78-year-old who had a gastrectomy three weeks ago with a PEG tube

  B. The 5-month-old discharged one week ago with pneumonia who is being treated with amoxicillin liquid suspension

  C. The 50-year-old with MRSA being treated with vancomycin via a PICC line

  D. The 30-year-old with an exacerbation of multiple sclerosis being treated with cortisone via a centrally placed venous catheter

10. The emergency room is flooded with clients injured in a tornado. Which clients can be assigned to share a room in the emergency department during the disaster?

    A. A schizophrenic client having visual and auditory hallucinations and the client with ulcerative colitis

    B. The client who is six months pregnant with abdominal pain and the client with facial lacerations and a broken arm

    C. A child whose pupils are fixed and dilated and his parents and a client with a frontal head injury

    D. The client who arrives with a large puncture wound to the abdomen and the client with chest pain

Answers to Exam Questions

1. Answer A is correct. The pregnant nurse should not be assigned to any client with radioactivity present. The client receiving linear accelerator therapy travels to the radium department for therapy, and the radiation stays in the department. Thus, the client is not radioactive. The client in answer B poses a risk to the pregnant client, so answer B is incorrect. Answer C is incorrect because the client is radioactive in very small doses. For approximately 72 hours, the client should dispose of urine and feces in special containers and use plastic spoons and forks. The client in answer D is also radioactive in small amounts, especially upon return from the procedure, so answer D is incorrect.

2. Answer A is correct. The client with Cushing's disease has adrenocortical hypersecretion. This increase in the level of cortisone causes the client to be immune-suppressed. The client with diabetes poses no risk to other clients and is not immunosuppressed, so answer B is incorrect. The client in answer C has an increase in growth hormone and poses no risk to himself or others, so the answer is incorrect. The client in answer D has hyperthyroidism, or myxedema, and poses no risk to others or himself, so it is incorrect.

3. Answer C is correct. Assault is defined as striking or touching the client inappropriately. Negligence is failing to perform care for the client, so answer A is incorrect. A tort is a wrongful act committed on the client or his belongings, so answer B is incorrect. Malpractice is failing to perform an act that the nurse knows should be done or doing something wrong that causes harm to the client, so answer D is incorrect.

4. Answer D is correct. The LPN can be assigned to insert Foley and French urinary catheters, discontinue Levin and gavage gastric tubes, and obtain all types of specimens.

5. Answer B is correct. The vital signs are abnormal and should be reported immediately. Continuing to monitor the vital signs can result in deterioration of the client's condition, so answer A is incorrect. Asking the client how he feels would supply only subjective data, so answer C is incorrect. The LPN is not the best nurse to be assigned to this client because he is unstable, so answer D is incorrect.

6. Answer B is correct. The nurse in answer B has the most experience in knowing the possible complications involved with preeclampsia. The nurse in answer A is a new nurse to this unit, so the answer is incorrect. The nurse in answer C has no experience with the postpartal client, so the answer is incorrect. The nurse in answer D also has no experience with postpartal clients, so the answer is incorrect.

7. Answer B is correct. The Joint Commission on Accreditation of Hospitals will probably be interested in the problems in answers A and C, so they are incorrect. The failure of the nursing assistant to assist the client with hepatitis should be reported to the charge nurse. If the behavior continues, termination can result, but it doesn't need to be reported to the board, so answer D is incorrect.

8. Answer B is correct. The next action after discussing the problem with the nurse is to document the incident. If the behavior continues or if harm has resulted to the client, the nurse might be terminated and reported to the board of nursing, so answers A and C are incorrect. A tort is a wrongful act to the client or her belongings, so answer D is incorrect.

9. Answer D is correct. The client who should receive priority is the client with multiple sclerosis being treated with cortisone via the central line because this client is at highest risk for complications. The clients described in answers A and B are stable at the time of the assigned visit. They can be seen later. The client in C has methicillin-resistant staphylococcus aureus (MRSA). Vancomycin is the drug of choice and can be administered later, but it must be scheduled at specific times of the day to maintain a therapeutic level, so answer C is incorrect.

10. Answer B is correct. Out of all these clients, it is best to hold the pregnant client and the client with a broken arm and facial lacerations in the same room. The other clients need to be placed in separate rooms, so answers A, C, and D are incorrect.

Suggested Reading and Resources

▶ Tappen, Ruth M., Sally A. Weiss, and Diane K. Whitehead. *Essential Nursing Leadership and Management. 4th ed.* Philadelphia: F. A. Davis, 2006.

▶ National Council of State Boards of Nursing: http://www.ncsbn.org/

▶ State boards of nursing for respective states: http://www.allnursingschools.com/faqs/boards.php.

20

Cultural Practices Influencing Nursing Care

Cultural practices and beliefs are passed down from generation to generation. The United States has always been a melting pot of varying cultural groups. Today more than ever, nurses must be aware of traditional medicine practices and cultural beliefs that influence healthcare. Migration trends indicate that one in three Americans is an ethnic minority. Understanding your own views and those of the client, while avoiding stereotyping the client are an integral part of client care. The NCLEX exam has changed to reflect these differences in client populations. This chapter explores cultural differences including environmental, social, religious, communication, space, and time differences among varying populations. The chapter covers these differences as they affect healthcare practices and discusses how you as a nurse can utilize knowledge of these beliefs in nursing practice.

Cultural Assessment

The nurse must be able to assess the client for differences in beliefs and utilize the knowledge gained to plan care for the client. It is critical that you know about your client's beliefs and culture in order to effectively treat him and not engage in acts that might be considered offensive to him.

Understanding Client Beliefs

As you assess the cultural background and beliefs of your client, you should remember that beliefs can be considered beneficial, maladaptive, or neutral. An example of a *beneficial belief*, or one that is helpful to the nurse, in planning care for the client would be a Hispanic client who believes in the use of garlic with his antihypertensive medication to lower blood pressure. Because garlic has been linked to lowering cholesterol and triglyceride levels, this is beneficial. If, however, he refuses his blood pressure medication and uses only the garlic, this would be a *maladaptive* consideration. A *neutral* consideration is one that is neither helpful nor harmful to the client.

Folk medicine, used by many groups, involves the use of nonprofessional healthcare providers such as medicine men and midwives. These practitioners often use remedies that are not found in the local pharmacy. Herbs and potions are often used to treat fevers, pain, and upset stomach. The nurse should teach the client that, although not inherently harmful, some natural substances can interact with medications and ultimately either alter the effect of the medication or cause an adverse reaction.

Working with Clients Who Speak Different Languages

The nurse might not be able to speak the language of the client he is trying to help. For this reason, it is useful to be able to use other techniques to communicate during teaching sessions. The following are 10 tips to use if you do not speak the client's language:

1. Sit down next to the client. Regardless of language differences, the client will understand a calm, caring tone in your voice.

2. Respect the client's personal space and watch her body language for cues that you are getting too close or touching her inappropriately.

3. If a client is from a culture different from your own, don't treat her differently from other clients because she does not speak English. Do not talk to her as if she were deaf. Speaking loudly will not help her understand you.

4. Use an interpreter when one is available. Many hospitals have individuals employed in other areas of the hospital who can help with translation. Investigate these possibilities before the client arrives for the visit.

> **NOTE**
>
> Literature should be given to the client in her own language when available. Many hospitals and healthcare facilities provide interpreters when needed.

5. Explain medical and nursing terms simply and clearly. Ask the client to demonstrate when possible. Remember that demonstration is the best indicator that the client understands your teaching.

6. Involve the extended family when possible. In most cultures, family is an important part of the client's healthcare.

7. Be careful not to offend members of the family by asking them to perform duties that are not allowed or preferred in their culture. For example, in Hispanic culture, the father might not want to bathe his child. When you are unsure, always ask—and do not assume.

8. Be careful if you do not have a thorough knowledge of the language. Many words have an entirely different meaning when pronounced incorrectly.

9. Use the title Mr. or Mrs. unless you know the person well. Not using these titles is often seen as disrespectful.

10. Do not assume that the client is angry if she speaks more loudly. Do not assume that the client is disinterested if she does not make eye contact.

Healthcare of Hispanics/Latinos

The fastest-growing minority in the United States is the Hispanic/Latino population. Some Hispanic people believe that disease is caused by an imbalance in hot and cold. They also believe that health is maintained by preventing exposure to extreme temperatures. A "hot" disease is treated with a "cold" remedy. Some examples of "hot" conditions are diabetes, hypertension, pregnancy, and indigestion. These problems are treated with cold compresses and cold liquids. Some examples of "cold" conditions are menstrual cramps, colic, and pneumonia. These problems should be treated with hot liquids such as broths, hot tea, or hot coffee. Warm baths can also help relieve these conditions.

Food is an important part of socialization in the Hispanic/Latino population. Use of grains and spices is prevalent in food preparation. Cheese, eggs, milk, and lard are used to prepare many of their dishes. The nurse should be aware of these practices particularly when teaching the client about dietary modification for the client with hypertension and hypercholesterolemia.

Hispanics/Latinos use herbs to treat most illnesses and maintain health. Examples of the use of herbs are garlic to treat hypertension and cough; chamomile to treat nausea and anxiety; and a laxative tea combined with stomach massage to cure anorexia, stomach pains, and diarrhea. Peppermint is also used to treat dyspepsia. Manzanilla is another herb used as a tea to treat stomach and intestinal pain, and anise (a star-shaped seed) is used to treat nausea and colic and to increase breast milk.

A healer is often used to provide herbal remedies or to deliver babies. These *santero/santera* are well-respected in the community and should be considered part of the health team. Several differences that you should be aware of exist between the modern American healthcare provider and the traditional healer. Table 20.1 highlights some of these differences.

TABLE 20.1 Comparison of Hispanic/Latino Traditional Healers to Modern Medicine

Traditional Healers	Modern Medicine
Informal and know the entire family.	It's formal, and the visit is with the client and not the family unit.
Make house calls.	Doctor's visits occur only in the clinic and often only by appointment.
The male is considered the head of the household. Always discuss any decisions with the husband or father.	Information is released to the client only. Healthcare providers comply with laws in regard to confidentiality.
Bartering is used as payment and the cost is very low.	It's often very expensive.
Involves spirituality with healing.	Often the healthcare provider is a specialist who deals with only the system involved in the illness.
Most of the time, the healer is a part of the community where the client and family live.	The physician or nurse practitioner might be located many miles away.

Modified from *Spector RE: Cultural Diversity in Health and Illness, Sixth Edition,* Prentice Hall, 2003.

The "evil eye" (*mal de ojo*) is thought to cause fever, crying, and vomiting in the infant. It is believed to be brought on by a person with a strong eye who looks at the baby in an admiring manner. The treatment for the evil eye is to sweep the body with eggs, lemons, and bay leaves.

Susto, or fright sickness, is brought on by an emotional trauma. Any traumatic event can bring on a susto. The result is a fever, vomiting, or diarrhea. The treatment involves brushing the body with ruda, a rough object, for nine consecutive nights.

Bilis is a disease of the intestinal tract brought on by anger. If untreated, bilis can cause acute nervous tension and chronic illness.

Empacho is a disease that can affect children. It is caused by food particles being trapped in the intestine. To manage this illness, the client lies face down with his back bare. The healer pinches a piece of skin at the waist, listening for a snap as the skin is released. This is repeated several times to dislodge the material. Prayer should accompany these rituals. Many Puerto Rican parents believe that an amulet pinned to the baby's shirt will protect her from evil. *Jabon de la mano milagrosa* is a soap used by a miracle man to clean and protect a person from evil spirits. Many also believe that candles should be burned to ward off evil spirits. The nurse should consider the strong religious beliefs of many in the Hispanic culture. Often a priest is the spiritual advisor and should be notified in the case of birth, illness, or death.

Time Considerations

The Hispanic population often views time differently from Americans. Time is viewed in generalities, so the nurse must be aware that the client might view time as present, past, or future. This difference can also affect the teaching plan. If the nurse tells the client to take the medication two times per day, the client might not understand the need to take the medication every 12 hours.

Use of Nonverbal/Verbal Communication

Most Hispanics speak Spanish or a dialect of it as their primary language. They also might speak English. It is an untrue assumption that if the client does not speak English, he is less intelligent. Many drug companies now provide written material in both Spanish and English. The nurse should use a translator when needed and should allow time for the client to respond to teaching. Eye contact is often avoided out of respect. The nurse should not assume that the client is disinterested or bored if he avoids eye contact. A handshake is often used to communicate agreement or understanding. Intimate zones are reserved for family and close friends. A distance of approximately 1 1/2'–4' should be reserved for personal distance, and a distance of 4'–12' should be observed for social distance. The nurse should respect this spatial territory when providing healthcare.

Childbirth and Pain Response

It is very important for the nurse to be aware that the Hispanic client might not complain of pain. Watching the client's nonverbal cues will help to prevent complications. During labor, the woman might remain stoic. She will often not ask for pain medication until late in the labor process, if at all. Female relatives are often present for the birth of the infant.

Hispanic women might go into a 40-day period of rest after the birth of the infant. During this time the woman might be confined to the home with limited activity. An abdominal binder might be used to prevent air from entering the uterus and to promote healing. Filipino and Pacific Islanders might also perform this practice. Many in the Hispanic culture practice baptism of the infant by sprinkling. These clients do not believe that colostrum is good for the infant, so the nurse should consult with the mother and father before placing the baby to the breast in the delivery room. Modesty must be maintained during breast feeding.

Healthcare of Native Americans and Alaskan Natives

Native Americans are considered those whose ancestors inhabited North America and Alaska. There are 170 North American tribes, and Inuit are also included in this group. These groups identify themselves in families or tribes. In order to work effectively with this group, the nurse must form a working relationship with the tribe leader.

Native Americans believe in the need to be one with nature and hold in reverence animals such as the eagle, buffalo, and deer. This group, like the Hispanic population, uses medicine men. In Native American culture, this person is called a *shaman*. Native Americans believe that evil spirits and devils are responsible for illness, so masks are worn to hide from the devil. An amulet called a *thunderbird* is worn for good luck and protection. Navajo medicine men are often called on to use sand painting to diagnose ailments. Some Native Americans conduct sacred ceremonies that rely on having visions and using plants and objects that symbolize the individual or the illness that is being treated. Chanting, prayer, and dancing are also used to treat illness and drive off the evil spirits. Sweat lodges are used by some groups to help in the treatment of fever. Herbs, corn meal, and medicine bundles are used in the Indian population to treat most illness.

Although herbs are used, most Native Americans will take medications prescribed by the physician. Decisions regarding healthcare should be directed to the male members of the family.

Time Considerations

Most Native Americans and Inuit are relaxed in their view of time and view life in the present. An appointment time for a clinic visit might be ignored, or the client might arrive late. The nurse should consider this factor when making clinic appointments.

Use of Nonverbal/Verbal Communication

Many Native Americans and Inuit speak English as their primary language. However, some still speak the native language of their forefathers, especially when communicating with one another. The nurse might have difficulty understanding the native language because several dialects exist. The nurse might have problems understanding the client because he will probably speak in a low tone. These clients expect the listener to be very attentive during the discussion. The need for listening is compounded by the fact that eye contact often is considered disrespectful. To ensure adequate communication, the nurse should limit discussion to multiple parties at the same time and eliminate external noise when possible.

Childbirth and Pain Response

Native Americans tend to be very quiet. The nurse must be aware of nonverbal cues that indicate understanding of teaching. Some nonverbal clues are nodding positively or negatively or the client complying with the nurse's request. The client might be in a great deal of pain before the nurse realizes that she needs medication.

The family is extremely important to the well-being of the client during childbirth; the extended family typically attends the birth. Use of village women to assist with childbirth is also a part of their culture. Women might not complain of pain during the labor and birth. In Navajo culture, the umbilical cord is given to the family after the birth of the child to be buried near a tree so that the child will grow strong and wise.

Healthcare of Asian-Americans

Asian-Americans have come to the United States from more than 20 countries and speak more than 100 languages. Since 1965, their population in the United States has grown from 1 million to more than 10.9 million. The nurse dealing with this large minority must consider the variations in healthcare beliefs to promote the well-being of the client and family. The client who is Asian-American is respectful of those in authority. For this reason, he might not disagree with the nurse or doctor, though he does not hold the same thoughts or values. The client might nod in agreement rather than pointing out questions or concerns. This can lead to confusion and error in client treatment. Many in this group self medicate. This practice can lead to complications and prevent early diagnoses of disease. Asian medicine includes therapies such as acupuncture, acupressure, herbs, and dietary supplements. Clients might be reluctant to use herbs because they fear that Western doctors or nurses will disapprove of traditional remedies. Asian clients often believe in the yin (cold) and yang (hot) theory. They believe that illness is caused by a disruption in this environment. "Hot" foods include beef, chicken, eggs, fried foods, red foods, and foods served hot. "Cold" foods include pork, most vegetables, boiled foods, foods served cold, and white foods. Noodles and soft rice are considered neither cold nor hot. To maintain fluid balance, Chinese-Americans prefer hot tea to ice water.

Some Chinese believe that illness is a result of moral retribution by the gods, and rituals must be performed to satisfy the gods and restore balance. A poor combination of the stars with the birth order can also lead to disharmony.

Some Cambodians practice cupping, pinching, coining, or rubbing an ill person's skin to treat illnesses. Usually the forehead or abdomen is used, depending on the type and location of the illness. With the practice of *cupping*, a hot cup is placed on the skin. As it cools, the cup contracts and the skin is pulled into the cup, leaving a circular mark or blister on the skin. It is believed that this practice draws the evil spirit into the cup. *Pinching* is the practice of pinching the skin between the thumb and index finger to the point of producing a contusion on the chest, on the neck, on the back, at the base of the nose, or between the eyes. *Coining* is the rubbing of the skin with the side of a coin, causing bruising. The nurse should be careful not to assume child abuse if she witnesses this practice. However, teaching regarding the dangers to the infant should be included in the plan of care.

If the client is Hindu, Sikh, or Buddhist, he might have beliefs that affect medical treatment. Hinduism accepts modern medicine but believes that illness is caused by past sins. Because life and death are part of an unending cycle, efforts to prolong life are discouraged and CPR might be forbidden. Sikhism clients might accept healthcare but refuse certain aspects of treatment. Female clients often refuse examination by a male, and removing the undergarments might be very traumatic for the client.

Buddhist clients will probably refuse treatment on holy days. They believe that spirits invading the body cause illness and will ask for a priest in times of birth and death. They also believe the body should pass into eternity whole, which forbids organ donation and performance of an autopsy. When death is imminent, the priest is called. He will tie a thread around the neck or wrist to ensure that the person will pass into eternity in peace—the nurse should not remove this string. The priest will then pour water in the client's mouth and place the dying client on the floor. After death, the family washes the body before cremation. Some Buddhists might refuse to move the body because they believe that it takes time for the spirit to leave. In the Shinto religion, the body is wrapped in a white kimono and straw shoes are applied. Because reincarnation is a primary belief of this group, materials containing gelatin and insulin produced from beef are forbidden.

Time Considerations

Asian-Americans live in the present. Many of them believe in reincarnation and that, if they die, they go immediately to paradise. For this reason the nurse might encounter difficulty in teaching regarding preventive care.

Use of Nonverbal/Verbal Communication

For some Asian-Americans, direct eye contact is considered a sign of disrespect. The nurse should be aware of this difference in communication and should not consider a lack of eye contact as a sign of a lack of interest or difficulty hearing. The client might nod as a sign of compliance or understanding and respect. Shaking hands with a person of the opposite sex is considered forward and inappropriate.

Childbirth and Pain Response

Asian clients will probably be stoic and not complain of pain until it becomes unbearable. Childbirth is a time of celebration for the Asian-American family. The extended family is present and usually takes the infant after delivery, especially if the mother has had a Cesarean section. This allows the mother to rest and recover. This time is considered a "hot" time.

After the birth, the postpartum period is considered a "cold" time because the uterus is more open. The client might therefore refuse to shower or do peri-care in the traditional American manner; however, she might allow a heat lamp to be used to improve healing. The postpartal period is much longer in most Asian cultures: A length of 30–40 days is thought to provide time for healing. The family stays close during this time to provide emotional and physical support.

Most Chinese prefer to give birth side-lying because this position is thought to be less traumatic to the infant. Many in the Hindu religion believe that placing honey in the mouth of the infant ensures a sweet life. However, this practice is discouraged by healthcare providers in the United States because honey can carry botulism. Many in the Chinese culture believe that colostrum is not good for the baby. The mother is often given hot rice water to drink to restore the balance between the body and nature.

Healthcare of Arab-Americans

The term *Arab* is associated with people from a region of the Middle East extending from Northern Africa to the Arabian Gulf. The large majority of Arabs are members of the Islamic (Muslim) religion. Their cultural and religious beliefs direct most of their beliefs regarding healthcare. Prayer and fasting are a major part of the Muslim client's day. Nurses should be willing to accommodate the client's desire to pray, and the bed should be positioned facing toward Mecca. So, if the client is in the mainland United States, the bed should face southeast. A sick client who is unable to fully kneel and touch his head to the floor might be allowed by his religious leaders to sit up while praying. During Ramadan, Muslims must fast from sunrise to sunset. If the client has a life-threatening condition, accommodations can be made, but this fasting does pertain to IV therapy and most injections.

Cleanliness is very important to the Arab-American client. The left hand is used for toileting; therefore, the client will avoid using the left hand to eat or touch others. Food should be kept clean and free of odors. Because alcohol is forbidden, medications and liquids containing alcohol should be avoided.

Most Arab-Americans prefer to be treated by a healthcare worker of the same sex. When prescribing medications, pills and injections are preferred—suppositories should be avoided if possible.

In some countries, secluding women from men and restricting movement outside the home is practiced. Covering of women in public is practiced and harsh treatment of women is allowed.

The dying client must confess his sins to be taken to heaven. The body is washed and wrapped in a white cloth and the head is turned to the right shoulder. The body of the client who has died should be positioned facing east. A prayer called a *Kalima* is said.

Time Considerations

Arab-Americans live in the present, so many do not plan for retirement or save for future needs. Preventive medicine is a concept that is difficult for them to understand. This group, like many others, might be less aware of appointment times. Scheduling of office visits should allow for this cultural difference.

Use of Nonverbal/Verbal Communication

As with other cultures, nonverbal communication is used frequently in Arab cultures. Women are particularly prone to speaking softly and might not voice health concerns, especially to a male healthcare provider.

Childbirth and Pain Response

Response to pain differs with each individual. Some clients in this group will be stoic, but some might respond to pain by crying or moaning. It is generally believed that an injection of pain-killing medication works better than a pill. The nurse should assess changes in vital signs and other cues such as grimacing to be able to provide pain medication as needed. During childbirth, group prayer is used to strengthen the mother, and women assist the client during childbirth. At the time of birth, a prayer is said into the baby's ear. The mother is then secluded from the group for a period of time to allow for cleansing. Because blood is considered a pollutant, a ritual bath is performed before the woman can resume relations with her husband. In some African cultures, such as in Ghana and Sierra Leone, some women will not resume sexual relations with their husbands until after the baby is weaned.

Nursing Plan Dietary Considerations Across Cultures

Dietary considerations play a part in the nursing plan of care for all cultural populations. See Table 20.2 for information regarding variations in dietary management.

TABLE 20.2 Dietary Practices of Various Cultural Groups

Culture	Grains	Fruits	Vegetables	Meats	Milk
Hispanic	Prefer potatoes and corn.	Prefer most fruits.	Prefer spicy vegetables such as chili peppers, tomatoes, onions, beets, and cabbage.	Prefer eggs, pinto beans, and most meats (all are allowed).	Cheese is preferred, and milk is seldom consumed because lactose intolerance is common in this group.
Chinese	Consume starchy grains such as rice.	All fruits are eaten by this group.	Prefer Chinese vegetables such as water chestnuts and bean sprouts. These are used in cooking.	All meats are consumed.	They eat ice cream, but few other milk products.
Chinese (to include Buddhist)	All grains are allowed.	All fruits are allowed.	All vegetables are allowed.	Devout Buddhists restrict meats and do not eat beef.	Cheese and milk products are allowed.
Japanese	Prefer rice.	They do not consume most fruits.	All vegetables are consumed.	All meats are consumed.	There is a high incidence of lactose intolerance, and little milk is consumed.
Europeans (to include persons of the Jewish faith)	Most grains are allowed, but they must be prepared using Kosher standards. Leavened bread and cakes are forbidden during Passover.	All fruits are consumed.	All vegetables are consumed.	Pork is forbidden, as are fish without scales. All meats must be prepared according to Biblical ordinances, and blood is forbidden.	Milk products should not be eaten at the same meal that contains meat and meat products.
Arab-Americans (to include the Islamic religion)	All grains are allowed.	All fruits are allowed.	All vegetables are allowed.	Beef, pork, and some fowl are restricted; all meat must be slaughtered according to a ritual letting of blood.	Milk is allowed.

TIP

Do not assume that because a person is a member of a particular group that she will behave like others. The nurse must get to know the person.

Religious Beliefs and Refusal of Care Considerations

Various religious beliefs affect how the client is treated and can lead to a refusal of some traditional medicines. It is important for the nurse to understand these differences to assist the client with healthcare and teaching. Table 20.3 breaks down some religions, the treatments their practitioners might refuse, and how prayer plays a role in their medicinal views.

TABLE 20.3   Religious Beliefs Affecting Healthcare and Death

Religion	Treatment Considerations	Role of Prayer
Buddhism	Treatment is accepted, but beef and beef products are not allowed.	A priest is called for last rites to be performed.
Christian (Catholic)	They eat no meat on Fridays during Lent. They might want to attend mass during hospitalization on Friday, Saturday, or Sunday.	At the time of death, a priest is called for last rites.
Christian (Protestant)	All treatments are allowed to preserve life.	Practices vary in respect to death and burial.
Church of Jesus Christ of Latter-day Saints (Mormon)	Most treatments are allowed.	At the time of death, the religious leader is called for last rites. Burial is preferred to cremation.
Hindu	A priest is called for consultation prior to treatments. Believe in reincarnation, so the body should be preserved. Amputations of limbs or removal of diseased body parts might be refused.	Believe in prayers and rituals.
Judaism	Orthodox Jews interpret dietary laws stringently. There are three key characteristics of kosher food preparation: only designated animals can be eaten. Pork is not allowed, some animals must be ritualistically killed, dairy products and meats are not eaten at the same meal. Passover is a time of fasting. This practice can lead to dehydration in the elderly and sick. Matzoh, an unleavened bread, can result in constipation. The infant is circumcised on the eighth day of life.	At the time of death, the rabbi is called for last rites, the body is washed, and someone remains with the body until burial.
Jehovah's Witness	Might refuse blood transfusions and surgery or treatments.	Believe prayer will save.
Russian Orthodox Church	All treatments are allowed. Most followers observe fast days, and on Wednesdays and Fridays, most eat no meat. During Lent, all animal products (including dairy products) are forbidden.	At the time of death, the religious leader is called for last rites.
Sikhism	Treatment is accepted. After death, the client will receive the five Ks: kesh (uncut hair), kangna (wooden comb), kara (wrist band), kirpan (sword), and kach (shorts).	The priest is called to perform ritualistic last rites.

CAUTION

Be sure that you do not assume that a client understands your teaching. The best indicator of understanding is demonstration.

Case Study

1. Juanita is a recent immigrant from Mexico. She is admitted to the labor and delivery unit in active labor. Although she is very cooperative, she appears frightened and hesitant to follow instructions. Upon investigation, the nurse realizes that Juanita does not speak English. Which action by the nurse would help to calm Juanita and establish a therapeutic relationship?

2. Juanita's husband is present and speaks some English. During a brief discussion with Juanita's husband, the nurse finds that this is Juanita's third pregnancy. The nurse should realize that the husband should be included in signing permits because:

3. As Juanita's labor progresses, the nurse notices that she does not ask for pain medication. The nurse is aware that:

4. After delivery, the nurse asks Juanita whether she is planning to breast feed. When might Juanita initiate breast feeding?

5. After delivery, the nurse notices that Juanita does not get out of bed unless she is encouraged and does not actively help with the care of the infant. The nurse is aware that the reason for Juanita's actions might be:

Answers to Case Study

1. The first action by the nurse should be to assess the best method of communication. If the nurse does not speak Spanish, finding a translator that the client feels comfortable with would be an excellent beginning.

2. Juanita should sign her permits, but her husband should be included in the client's care because in many Hispanic families, the husband makes the decisions. If Juanita is unable to sign, her husband can sign the permit for her.

3. Some clients of Hispanic descent might not complain of pain. Ask the client if she would like to have pain medication and administer the medication as ordered.

4. Some clients of Hispanic decent do not believe that colostrum is good for the baby. The nurse should ask the client rather that assuming that she will want to breast feed in the delivery room.

5. Many clients of Hispanic decent practice a 40-day period of rest after delivery. The nurse should encourage Juanita to exercise to prevent emboli while respecting her cultural differences.

Key Terms

▶ Culture

▶ Ethnicity

▶ Heritage

▶ Religion

▶ Time orientation

▶ Tradition

▶ Value

Apply Your Knowledge

While studying for the NCLEX exam the nurse should be aware of cultural differences among ethnic groups. Key points in the chapter include respect for the client and the family and formulation of a therapeutic client-nurse relationship. The nurse must be aware that because the client believes differently from the nurse the client is not necessarily wrong. The NCLEX expects the nurse to be aware of the time and situation when she needs to perform duties for the client and when the nurse should allow the family or client to care for himself. This regard for the individual as it relates to culture is an integral part of the exam.

Exam Questions

1. The client is a practicing Hindu. Which food should be removed from the client's tray?

   A. Bread

   B. Cabbage

   C. Steak

   D. Apple

2. A Korean client is admitted to the postpartum unit following the delivery of a 9 lb. infant. Although the client does not refuse to shower, the nurse notices that she stands in the shower but does not allow the water to touch her. Which of the following should be the next action by the nurse?

   A. Ask the client why she refuses to shower.

   B. Call the doctor and report the client's refusal to shower.

   C. Tell the client that the nurse will obtain a heat lamp to assist in healing the perineum.

   D. Turn the shower so that the water sprays on the client.

3. An infant is admitted with a volvulus and scheduled for surgery. The parents are Jehovah's Witnesses and refuse to sign the permit. Which action by the nurse is most appropriate?

   A. Obtain a court order.

   B. Call the doctor.

   C. Tell them that the surgery is optional.

   D. Monitor the situation.

4. Which medication will most likely be refused by a Muslim client?

   A. Insulin

   B. Cough syrup

   C. NSAIDs

   D. Antacids

5. The condition of an Arab client who is terminally ill deteriorates and death seems imminent. If the client is hospitalized in the mainland United States, the nurse should position the bed facing which direction?

   A. Northeast

   B. Southeast

   C. West

   D. South

6. An 88-year-old female Jewish client is admitted to the hospital and diagnosed with diabetes. Which type of insulin is refused by this client?

   A. Beef

   B. Pork

   C. Synthetic

   D. Fish

7. The nurse observes that a Hispanic client and his family have been late for their appointment the last three times. Which of the following is the best explanation for this behavior?

   A. A lack of concern for the health of the client.

   B. An attempt to avoid talking to the nurse.

   C. The client probably forgot the appointment time.

   D. The client and family view time differently than does the nurse.

8. A 90-year-old client from Thailand is diagnosed with terminal cancer. The family seems unconcerned and, although they do not refuse treatment for the client, they do not assist with treatment. Which of the following is the nurse's likely assessment of this behavior?

   A. The family believes in the cycle of life and that death is a step into the next cycle.

   B. The family is in denial concerning the diagnosis and needs further teaching.

   C. The family is planning to get another opinion regarding the diagnosis.

   D. The family is not concerned with the treatment and care of the client.

9. The nurse is assisting a client from Iraq with her bath. The nurse notices that the client uses only her left hand to bathe her genital area. Which of the following is the correct assessment of this behavior?

   A. The client's dominant hand is her left one.

   B. The client is using her nondominant hand to more easily cleanse the perineum.

   C. The client believes that the right hand is reserved for eating and touching others and that the left hand is the dirty hand.

   D. The client has in some way injured her right hand, making it difficult to use it.

10. A Japanese client refuses to eat the ice cream or drink the milk on his tray. Which action by the nurse would indicate an understanding of the client's needs?

    A. She obtains yogurt for the client instead.

    B. She obtains an order for Lactaid dietary supplement.

    C. She removes the milk from the tray and says nothing to the client.

    D. She asks the client why he will not drink the milk.

Answers to Exam Questions

1. Answer C is correct. In the Hindu religion, beef is prohibited. All breads, vegetables, and fruits are allowed, so answers A, B, and D are incorrect.

2. Answer C is correct. Many in Asian cultures believe that the postpartal period is a "cold" time when the body is open. This is treated with heat, and a shower is thought to be a cold therapy that allows illness to enter the body. The nurse should comply with the client's wish not to shower at this time. A heat lamp might be accepted because it is a hot therapy and will assist with healing.

3. Answer B is correct. A volvulus is an emergency situation in which the bowel is twisted. Refusal of treatment can lead to death, so the next action to take is to call the doctor. It might require a court order to get a permit for the surgery or the court might comply with the parent's wishes, so answer A is incorrect. The surgery is not optional, so answer C is incorrect. Volvulus is an emergency situation and action must be taken if the child is to survive. Monitoring only waste precious time, so answer D is incorrect.

4. Answer B is correct. Most cough syrups contain alcohol, which is forbidden in the Islamic religion. Attempts should be made to obtain a cough suppressant that does not contain alcohol. The client will most likely take insulin, nonsteroidal anti-inflammatory drugs, and antacids, so answers A, C, and D are incorrect.

5. Answer B is correct. At the time of death, the Muslim client will wish to be positioned facing Mecca, which is to the southeast of the United States. Answers A, C, and D are therefore incorrect.

6. Answer B is correct. Pork is not allowed in the diet or medications of Jewish clients. Both synthetic and beef insulins are allowed, so answers A and C are incorrect. There is no such thing as fish insulin, so answer D is incorrect.

7. Answer D is correct. If the client misses an appointment or is late for the appointment, it is not necessarily true that the client is disinterested or forgot. Many in the Hispanic culture see time as a relative thing and live in the present.

8. Answer A is correct. Clients who practice the Hindu religion believe that death is part of the cycle of life. There is no data to support answers B, C, or D as an answer.

9. Answer C is correct. In the Islamic religion, the left hand is reserved for toileting. The right hand is considered clean and is used to eat and touch others. There is no data to support that the client is left handed or that the right hand might be injured, so answers A, B, and D are incorrect.

10. Answer B is correct. Many of Japanese descent are lactose intolerant—it is not that milk is not allowed in their culture. Yogurt also causes gas and bloating, so answer A is incorrect. Removing the items from the tray does not provide the needed calcium in the diet, so answer C is incorrect. It is inappropriate to ask "why" in most cultures, so answer D is incorrect.

Suggested Reading and Resources

▶ Brink, Pamela J. *Transcultural Nursing: A Book of Readings*. Englewood Cliff, NJ: Prentice Hall, 1976.

▶ Geiger, J. N., and and R. E. Davidhizar. *Transcultural Nursing: Assessment in Intervention*. St. Louis: Mosby, 1991.

▶ Potter, Patricia A., and Anne Griffin Perry. *Fundamentals of Nursing*. 6th ed., St. Louis: C. V. Mosby, 2005.

▶ Fernandez, Victor M., and Kathy M. Fernandez. *Transcultural Nursing: Basic Concepts and Case Studies*: http://www.culturaldiversity.org/2006.

Fast Facts

The NCLEX RN Exam Prep

This fast facts reference contains the distilled, key facts about the licensure exam. Review this information just before you enter the testing center, paying special attention to those areas where you feel you need the most review. You can transfer any of these facts from your head onto a blank sheet provided by the testing center. We also recommend reading the glossary as a last-minute cram tool before entering the test center. Good luck.

1. **Question minimum 75/maximum 265:** The maximum time allotted for the RN test is 6 hours. Don't get frustrated if you need to take the entire number of items or take the entire allotted time. Get up and move around and take breaks if you need a time-out.

2. **Take deep breaths and imagine yourself studying in your favorite location:** Take a small item with you that you have had with you during your study time.

3. **Read the question and all answers carefully:** Don't jump to conclusions too quickly.

4. **Look for keywords:** Avoid answers that include the word *always*, *never*, *all*, *every*, *only*, *must*, *no*, *except*, or *none*.

5. **Watch for specific details:** Avoid vague answers. Look for adjectives and adverbs.

6. **Eliminate answers that are clearly wrong or incorrect:** Eliminating any incorrect answer increases the probability of selecting the correct answer by 25%.

7. **Look for information given within the answers:** For example, the phrase *diabetic with acidosis* makes you think of normal pH.

8. **Look for the same or similar wording in the question and the answers.**

9. **Watch for grammatical inconsistencies:** Subjects and verbs should agree, meaning singular subject, singular verb or plural subject, plural verb. If the question is an incomplete sentence, the correct answer should complete the question in a grammatically correct manner.

10. **Don't read into questions:** Reading into the question can create errors in judgment. If the question asks for an immediate response or prioritization of action, choose the answer that is critical to the life and safety of the client.

11. **Make an educated guess:** If you're unsure after carefully reading the question and all the answers, choose the answer with the most information.

12. **Serum electrolytes:** It is important for you to remember these normal lab values because they might be included in questions throughout the test:

    ▸ **Sodium:** 135–145 mEq/L

    ▸ **Potassium:** 3.5–5.5 mEq/L

    ▸ **Calcium:** 8.5–10.5 mg/dL; 4.5–5.5 mEq/L

    ▸ **Chloride:** 95–105 mEq/L

    ▸ **Magnesium:** 1.5–2.5 mEq/L

    ▸ **Phosphorus:** 2.5–4.5 mEq/L

13. **Hematology values**

    ▸ **RBC:** 4.5–5.0 million/cu.mm

    ▸ **WBC:** 5,000–10,000/cu.mm

- **Platelets:** 200,000–400,000

- **HCT:** 12-14 gms women; 14-16 gms men

14. **ABG values**

- **HCO$_3$:** 24–26 mEq/L

- **CO$_2$:** 35–45 mEq/L

- **PaO$_2$:** 80%–100%

- **SaO$_2$:** > 95%

15. **Chemistry values**

- **Glucose:** 70–110 mg/dL

- **Specific gravity:** 1.010–1.030

- **BUN:** 7–22 mg/dL

- **Creatinine:** 0.6–1.35 mg/dL (< 2 in older adults)

- **LDH:** 100–190 U/L

- **CPK:** 21–232 U/L

- **Uric acid:** 3.5–7.5 mg/dL

- **Triglyceride:** <150 mg/dL

- **Total cholesterol:** 130–200 mg/dL

- **Bilirubin:** < 1.0 mg/dL

- **Protein:** 6.2–8.1 g/dL

- **Albumin:** 3.4–5.0 g/dL

16. **Therapeutic drug levels**

- **Digoxin:** 0.5–2.0 ng/mL

- **Lithium:** 0.8–1.5 mEq/L

- **Dilantin:** 10–20 mcg/dL

- **Theophylline:** 10–20 mcg/dL

17. **Vital signs**

- **HR:** 80–100 BPM

- **RR:** 12–20 RPM

- **BP:** 110–120 (systolic); 60–90 (diastolic)

- **Temperature:** 98.6° +/–1

18. **Maternity normals**

    ▸ **FHR:** 120–160 BPM

    ▸ **Variability:** 6–10 BPM

    ▸ **Contractions:** Normal frequency 2–5 minutes apart; normal duration < 90 sec.; intensity < 100 mm/hg

    ▸ **Amniotic fluid:** 500–1200 ml (nitrozine urine-litmus paper green/amniotic fluid-litmus paper blue)

    ▸ **Apgar scoring:** A = appearance, P = pulses, G = grimace, A = activity, R = reflexes (done at 1 and 5 minutes with a score of 0 for absent, 1 for decreased, and 2 for strongly)

    ▸ **AVA:** The umbilical cord has two arteries and one vein (arteries carry deoxygenated blood and the vein carries oxygenated blood)

19. **FAB9:** Folic acid = B9. B9 supplements decrease the incidence of neural tube defects; the client should begin taking B9 three months prior to becoming pregnant.

20. **Abnormalities in the obstetric client:** Decelerations are not normal findings on the fetal monitoring strip. These include

    ▸ **Early decelerations:** Begin prior to the peak of the contraction and end by the end of the contraction. They're caused by head compression. There is no need for intervention if the variability is within normal range, there is a rapid return to the baseline fetal heart rate, and the fetal heart rate is within normal range.

    ▸ **Variable decelerations:** Can occur any time during monitoring of the fetus and are V-shaped. They are caused by cord compress. The intervention is to change the mother's position, stop the pitocin infusion, apply oxygen, and increase IV fluids if accompanied by maternal hypotension. Contact the doctor if the problem does not resolve.

    ▸ **Late decelerations:** Occur after the peak of the contraction and mirror the contraction in length and intensity. These are caused by uteroplacental insufficiency. The intervention is to change the mother's position, stop the pitocin infusion, apply oxygen, and increase IV fluids if accompanied by maternal hypotension. Contact the doctor if the problem persists.

21. **TORCHS syndrome in the neonate:** This is a combination of diseases. TORCHS stands for toxoplasmosis, rubella, cytomegalovirus, herpes, and syphilis. (Nurses who are pregnant should not be assigned to care for the client with toxoplasmosis or cytomegalovirus.)

22. **STOP:** This is the treatment for maternal hypotension after an epidural anesthetic:

    1. Stop pitocin if infusing.

    2. Turn the client on the left side.

    3. Administer oxygen.

    4. Push IV fluids if hypovolemic.

23. **Anticoagulant treatment**

   ▸ **Coumadin (sodium warfarin) PT:** 10–12 sec. (control).

   ▸ **Antidote:** The antidote for coumadin toxicity is vitamin K.

   ▸ **Heparin/PTT:** 30–60 sec. (control) (values may vary).

   ▸ **Antidote:** The antidote for heparin toxicity is protamine sulfate.

   ▸ **Therapeutic level:** It is important to maintain the bleeding time slightly prolonged so that clotting will not occur; therefore, the bleeding time with medicine should be 1½–2 times the control. The control is the premedication bleeding time.

24. **Rule of Nines for burns**

   ▸ Head = 9%

   ▸ Chest = 18%

   ▸ Arms = 18% (9% each)

   ▸ Back = 18%

   ▸ Legs = 36% (18% each)

   ▸ Genitalia = 1%

25. **Arab-American cultural attributes:** Females avoid eye contact with males; touch is accepted by same-sex healthcare providers; most decisions are made by males; if they're Muslim of the Sunni branch, they'll refuse organ donation; most do not eat pork; they avoid icy drinks when sick or hot/cold drinks together; colostrum is considered harmful to the baby.

26. **Asian-American cultural attributes:** They avoid direct eye contact; feet are considered dirty (they should be touched last during assessment); men make the decisions; they usually refuse organ donation; they generally do not prefer cold drinks.

27. **Native-American cultural attributes:** They sustain eye contact; blood and organ donation is generally refused; they might refuse circumcision.

28. **Mexican-American cultural attributes:** They might avoid direct eye contact with authorities; they might refuse organ donation; most are very emotional during bereavement.

29. **Religions beliefs**

   ▸ **Jehovah's Witness:** No blood or blood products

   ▸ **Hindu:** No beef or items containing gelatin

   ▸ **Jewish:** No pork; diet is kosher

30. **Diets**

   ▸ **Renal failure diet:** High calorie, high carbohydrate, low protein, low potassium, low sodium, and fluid restricted to intake = output + 500 mL

> ► **Gout diet:** Low purine. Limit rich foods such as red meat, lobster, venison, chicken, and pork. Colchicine (think cold chicken) is used to treat acute episodes while allopurinol is used for maintenance therapy.

> ► **Heart healthy diet:** Low fat (less than 30% of calories should be from fat)

31. **Acid/base balance:** Normal = (acid) < 7.35–7.45 > (alkaline)

> ► ROME (respiratory opposite/metabolic equal) is a quick way of remembering that in respiratory acid/base disorders the pH is opposite to the other components. For example, in respiratory acidosis, the pH is below normal and the CO_2 is elevated, as is the HCO_3 (respiratory opposite). In metabolic disorders, the components of the lab values are the same. An example of this is metabolic acidosis. In metabolic acidosis, the pH is below normal and the CO_2 is decreased, as is the HCO_3. This is true in a compensated situation.

> ► pH down, CO_2 up, and HCO_3 up = respiratory acidosis

> ► pH down, CO_2 down, and HCO_3 down = metabolic acidosis

> ► pH up, CO_2 down, and HCO_3 down = respiratory alkalosis

> ► pH up, CO_2 up, and HCO_3 up = metabolic alkalosis

32. **Addison's versus Cushing's:** Addison's and Cushings are endocrine disorders of the adrenal glands that affect cortisol production.

> ► For Addison's, you add cortisone.

> ► With Cushing's, the client has too much cortisone.

33. **Treatment for spider bites/bleeding:** RICE (rest, ice, compression, and elevate extremity)

34. **Treatment for sickle cell vasoclussive crises is as follows:**

> ► HHOP (heat, hydration, oxygen, pain medications)

35. **Five Ps of fractures and compartment syndrome:** These are symptoms of fractures and compartment syndrome:

> ► Pain

> ► Pallor

> ► Pulselessness

> ► Paresthesia

> ► Polar (cold)

36. **Hip fractures:** Hip fractures commonly hemorrhage, whereas femur fractures are at risk for fat emboli.

37. **Profile of gallbladder disease:** Fair, fat, forty, female, and fertile.

38. **Management and delegation:**

> ▸ **Reserve IV therapy for the RN:** The RN should not delegate the administration of IV medication (push) to the LPN although the LPN may regulate IV rates, do IV site care, and discontinue IV line. Where nonskilled care is required, you can delegate the stable client to the nursing assistant. Choose the most critical client to assign to the RN, such as the client who has recently returned from surgery or who is being discharged. For room assignments, do not coassign the post-operative client with clients with vomiting, diarrhea, open wounds, or chest drainage. Remember airway first in choices that ask who would you see first. When performing triage, care for those clients with the most life threatening injuries. In the case of mass casualties, triage will focus on the care of clients who can be saved with the least expenditure of resources.

> ▸ **Legalities:** When it is necessary to place the emotionally disturbed client in seclusion, the RN or physician is responsible for ordering placement. The PN can monitor clients with IV therapy, catheters (can insert), and NG feeding tubes (can insert); apply restraints; and discontinue IVs, drains, and sutures.

39. **Types of drugs**

*The generic name is listed first with the trade name in parentheses:

> ▸ **Angiotensin-converting agents:** Benazepril (Lotensin), lisinopril (Zestril), captopril (Capoten), enalapril (Vasotec), fosinopril (Monopril), moexipril (Univas), quinapril (Acupril), ramipril (Altace)

> ▸ **Beta adrenergic blockers:** Acebutolol (Monitan, Rhotral, Sectral), atenolol (Tenormin, Apo-Atenol, Nova-Atenol), esmolol (Brevibloc), metaprolol (Alupent, Metaproterenol), propanolol (Inderal)

> ▸ **Anti-infective drugs:** Gentamicin (Garamycin, Alcomicin, Genoptic), kanamycin (Kantrex), neomycin (Mycifradin), streptomycin (Streptomycin), tobramycin (Tobrex, Nebcin), amikacin (Amikin)

> ▸ **Benzodiazepine drugs:** Clonazepam (Klonopin), diazepam (Valium), chlordiazepoxide (Librium), lorazepam (Ativan), flurazepam (Dalmane)

> ▸ **Phenothiazine drugs:** Chloromazine (Thorazine), prochlorperazine (Compazine), trifluoperazine (Stelazine), promethazine (Phenergan), hydroxyzine (Vistaril), fluphenazine (Prolixin)

> ▸ **Glucocorticoid drugs:** Prednisolone (Delta-Cortef, Prednisol, Prednisolone), prednisone (Apo-Prednisone, Deltasone, Meticorten, Orasone, Panasol-S), betamethasone (Celestone, Selestoject, Betnesol), dexamethasone (Decadron, Deronil, Dexon, Mymethasone, Dalalone), cortisone (Cortone), hydrocortisone (Cortef, Hydrocortone Phosphate, Cortifoam), methylprednisolone (Solucortef, Depo-Medrol, Depopred, Medrol, Rep-Pred), triamcinolone (Amcort, Aristocort, Atolone, Kenalog, Triamolone)

> ▸ **Protease inhibitor drugs:** Acyclovir (Zovirax), ritonavir (Norvir), saquinavir (Invirase, Fortovase), indinavir (Crixivan), abacavir (Ziagen), cidofovir (Vistide), ganciclovir (Cytovene, Vitrasert)

▶ **Cholesterol-lowering drugs:** Atorvastatin (Lipitor), fluvastatin (Lescol), lovastatin (Mevacor), pravastatin (Pravachol), simvastatin (Zocar), rosuvastatin (Crestor)

▶ **Angiotensin receptor blocker drugs:** Valsartan (Diovan), candesartan (Altacand), losartan (Cozaar), telmisartan (Micardis)

▶ **Cox 2 enzyme blocker drugs:** Celecoxib (Celebrex)

▶ **Histamine 2 antagonist drugs:** Cimetidine (Tagamet), famotidine (Pepcid), nizatidine (Axid), rantidine (Zantac)

▶ **Proton pump inhibitors:** Esomeprazole (Nexium), lansoprazole (Prevacid), pantoprazole (Protonix), rabeprazole (AciPhex)

▶ **Anticoagulant drugs:** Heparin sodium (Hepalean), enoxaparin sodium (Lovenox), dalteparin sodium (Fragmin)

40. **Drug schedules**

▶ **Schedule I:** Research use only (for example, LSD)

▶ **Schedule II:** Requires a written prescription

▶ **Schedule III:** Requires a new prescription after six months or five refills

▶ **Schedule IV:** Requires a new prescription after six months

▶ **Schedule V:** Dispensed as any other prescription or without prescription if state law allows

41. **Medication categories commonly used in medical/surgical setting**

▶ **Antacids:** Reduce hydrochloric acid in the stomach

▶ **Antianemics:** Increase red blood cell production

▶ **Anticholenergics:** Decrease oral secretions

▶ **Anticoagulants:** Prevent clot formation

▶ **Anticonvulsants:** Used for management of seizures/bipolar disorder

▶ **Antidiarrheals:** Decrease gastric motility and reduce water in bowel

▶ **Antihistamines:** Block the release of histamine

▶ **Antihypertensives:** Lower blood pressure and increase blood flow

▶ **Anti-infectives:** Used for the treatment of infections

▶ **Bronchodilators:** Dilate large air passages in asthma/lung disease

▶ **Diuretics:** Decrease water/sodium from the loop of Henle

▶ **Laxatives:** Promote the passage of stool

▶ **Miotics:** Constrict the pupils

▶ **Mydriatics:** Dilate the pupils

▶ **Narcotics/analgesics:** Relieve moderate to severe pain

Practice Exam I

This element consists of 166 questions that are representative of what you should expect on the actual exam. This exam should help you determine how prepared you are for the real exam and provide a good basis for what you still need to review. As you take this exam, treat it as you would the real exam: time yourself (about one minute per question is suggested) and answer each question carefully, marking the ones you want to go back and double-check. You will find the answers and their explanations in the "Practice Exam I Answers" element of the book.

The test items have been divided by chapter content. This format makes it easy for the student to review content by subject matter. After you take this exam, remember to load the CD-ROM and check out our exclusive ExamGear test engine, which is one of the best on the market.

Fluid and Electrolytes and Acid/Base Balance

1. The client is admitted with isotonic dehydration. The nurse would anticipate an order for which IV fluid?

    ◯ A. 5% dextrose and water

    ◯ B. 3% sodium chloride

    ◯ C. .9% sodium chloride

    ◯ D. .45% sodium chloride

2. The client with COPD is admitted with a serum carbon-dioxide content level of 42 mEq/L, oxygen saturation of 86%, and a blood glucose level of 190 mg/dl. The nurse is aware that the client's condition might require which of the following?

    ◯ A. An injection of NPH insulin

    ◯ B. Oxygen application with a venturi mask

    ◯ C. Renal dialysis using an arterio-venous shunt

    ◯ D. A prescription for a bronchodilator

3. The nurse is caring for a client admitted with a potassium level of 3.9 mEq/L, a blood glucose level of 98 mg/dL, a serum calcium level of 10.0 mg/dL, and a blood urea nitrogen level of 30 mg/dL. Which of these values should be reported to the physician immediately?

    ◯ A. The potassium level of 3.9 mEq/L

    ◯ B. The serum calcium level of 10.0 mg/dL

    ◯ C. The blood glucose level of 98 mg/dL

    ◯ D. The blood urea nitrogen level of 30 mg/dL

4. The ICU nurse is assessing several clients assigned to his care. Which client should receive priority of care?

    ◯ A. A 65-year-old client with emphysema with an oxygen saturation level of 82%

    ◯ B. A 45-year-old motor vehicle accident client with chest tubes and a CO_2 level of 48mE/L

    ◯ C. An 80-year-old diabetic with a blood glucose level of 430 mg/dl

    ◯ D. A 50-year-old client with cirrhosis of the liver and a blood urea nitrogen level of 35mg/dl

5. The client admitted with hypokalemia has an order for potassium to be administered orally. Prior to administering the potassium, the nurse should:

    ◯ A. Check the client's creatinine level

    ◯ B. Ask the doctor to order an ECG

    ◯ C. Insert a nasogastric tube

    ◯ D. Acquire milk to give the oral potassium

6. The nurse is preparing to administer potassium to the client with hypokalemia. The best liquid for the nurse to dilute the potassium in is:

    ◯ A. Cranberry juice

    ◯ B. Prune juice

    ◯ C. Tomato juice

    ◯ D. Chocolate milk

7. The client is admitted with a sodium level of 100 mEq/L. After checking the other laboratory values, the nurse should:

    ◯ A. Chart the finding

    ◯ B. Contact the doctor

    ◯ C. Teach the client about low-sodium meal options

    ◯ D. Check the client's deep tendon reflexes for hyperreflexia

8. The nurse is checking the client for a positive Trousseau's sign. Which finding indicates a positive Trousseau's sign?

    ◯ A. Facial grimacing

    ◯ B. Carpopedal spasms

    ◯ C. Nuchal rigidity

    ◯ D. Abdominal tenderness

9. The client with hypercholesterolemia asked about vitamins that can help to lower his cholesterol. Which vitamin has been shown to be helpful in lowering the client's cholesterol level?

    ◯ A. Cyanocobalamine

    ◯ B. Ascorbic acid

    ◯ C. Niacin

    ◯ D. Riboflavin

10. The client with hypoparathyroidism is admitted with a calcium level of 7.6 mg/dL. The nurse should anticipate an order for which of the following medications?

  ○ A. Furosemide (Lasix)

  ○ B. Levothyroxin (Synthroid)

  ○ C. PTH (Forteo)

  ○ D. Propanolol (inderal)

11. The client is admitted with a magnesium level of 10.0 mEq/L. Which sign indicates that the client has a toxic level of magnesium?

  ○ A. Hot flashes

  ○ B. Respirations of 10 per minute

  ○ C. Deep tendon reflexes of 2+

  ○ D. Urinary output of 40 mL per hour

12. Which staff member would be least appropriate to assign to the client receiving magnesium intravenously?

  ○ A. The nursing assistant

  ○ B. The licensed practical nurse

  ○ C. The graduate registered nurse

  ○ D. The surgical resident

13. Which of the following should be kept available when intravenous magnesium is ordered?

  ○ A. Protamine sulfate

  ○ B. Calcium gluconate

  ○ C. AquaMEPHYTON

  ○ D. Aminocaproic acid

14. The client is admitted with a pH of 7.48, a HCO_3 level of 34 mEq/L, and a CO_2 level of 48 mEq/L. The nurse is aware that these laboratory values reveal:

  ○ A. Metabolic acidosis

  ○ B. Metabolic alkalosis

  ○ C. Respiratory alkalosis

  ○ D. Respiratory acidosis

15. The client is admitted with chronic obstructive pulmonary disease. The client's laboratory values reveal a CO_2 level of 49 mEq/L. The HCO_3 level is 26 mEq/L, and the pH is 7.32. The nurse is aware that these laboratory values reveal:

   ○ A. Metabolic acidosis

   ○ B. Metabolic alkalosis

   ○ C. Respiratory alkalosis

   ○ D. Respiratory acidosis

16. While the client is taking Digoxin (digitalis), the nurse should check the client's laboratory values. Which laboratory value should be reported to the doctor?

   ○ A. Sodium level of 138 mEq/L

   ○ B. Chloride level of 98 mEq/L

   ○ C. Potassium level of 3.0 mEq/L

   ○ D. Magnesium level of 1.8 mEq/L

17. The client with renal disease has an order for a low-potassium diet. Which food is highest in potassium?

   ○ A. Marshmallows

   ○ B. Raisins

   ○ C. Cake

   ○ D. Mashed potatoes

18. The client with hypertension and renal disease is admitted to the clinic with a blood pressure of 190/100. The physician decides to order a beta blocker and a potassium-sparing diuretic. The nurse should anticipate an order for which diuretic?

   ○ A. Furosemide (Lasix)

   ○ B. Hydrochlorothiazide (HTCZ)

   ○ C. Spironolactone (Aldactone)

   ○ D. Torsemide (Demadex)

19. The client is admitted with Cushing's disease. The nurse is aware that clients with an adrenal disorder such as Cushing's disease will most likely exhibit signs of:

   ○ A. Hypercalcemia

   ○ B. Hyperkalemia

   ○ C. Hypernatremia

   ○ D. Hypermagnesemia

20. The client is admitted to the unit with diabetes insipidus. Which laboratory result supports this diagnosis?

  ○ A. Specific gravity of 1.000

  ○ B. Sodium of 140 mEq/L

  ○ C. Glucose of 110 mg/dL

  ○ D. Potassium of 3.8 mEq/dL

Care of the Client with Cardiovascular Disorders

21. The client is admitted to the intensive care area following a coronary artery bypass graft. The nurse caring for the client manages the fluid volume status by checking the central venous pressure and finds a reading of 4 mm Hg. Which action should the nurse take at this time?

  ○ A. Increase the rate of IV fluid using the protocol provided

  ○ B. Continue her care with no further action

  ○ C. Decrease the IV fluid using the protocol provided

  ○ D. Administer furosemide (Lasix) as ordered

22. The client with hypertension is being treated with diuretics and beta blockers for his hypertension. While taking beta blockers, the client should:

  ○ A. Refrain from operating heavy equipment such as a bulldozer

  ○ B. Check his pulse rate daily

  ○ C. Allow six weeks for the medication to reach its optimal level

  ○ D. Increase his intake of potassium-rich foods

23. The client has an order for furosemide (Lasix) to be taken every morning. Which food contains the most potassium?

  ○ A. One-half cup of mashed potatoes

  ○ B. One-fourth cup of sweet potatoes

  ○ C. One baked potato

  ○ D. One cup of french-fried potatoes

24. The client with hypercholesterolemia has an order to decrease the amount of cholesterol in his diet. Which cooking oil contains the most cholesterol?

   ○ A. Safflower

   ○ B. Sunflower

   ○ C. Palm

   ○ D. Canola

25. The client has been prescribed simvastatin (Zocor) for control of his hypercholesterolemia. When taking this medication, the client should be taught to:

   ○ A. Take the medication with grapefruit juice

   ○ B. Have his liver enzyme checked every six months

   ○ C. Take the medication in the morning for optimal absorption

   ○ D. Report any weakness or drowsiness to the physician

26. The client with hypertension has an order for lisinopril plus hydrochlorothiazide (HTCZ) (Zestorectic). Prior to his initial dose, the client should be taught to:

   ○ A. Check his pulse rate daily

   ○ B. Remain in bed for 3–4 hours after taking the initial dose

   ○ C. Expect a drop in his cholesterol level within six weeks

   ○ D. Increase his intake of folic-acid–rich food such as orange juice

27. Which of the following is an untoward effect of angiotensin-converting agents that should be reported to the doctor?

   ○ A. Postural dizziness

   ○ B. Occasional nausea

   ○ C. 1+ petal edema

   ○ D. Persistent hacking cough

28. The client with angina should be taught to take nitroglycerine sublingually with the onset of the first signs of chest pain. Which instructions should be included with your teaching plan?

   ○ A. Take one tablet every 10 minutes until the pain subsides.

   ○ B. If a burning sensation of the tongue occurs, stop the medication immediately.

   ○ C. Keep the medication in the brown bottle to preserve the strength of the medication.

   ○ D. Refill the supply of nitroglycerine every three months.

29. The client with a fourth-degree heart block has a permanent pacemaker implanted. Which activity should be avoided by the client with a pacemaker?

    ○ A. Using a cellular phone

    ○ B. Wearing a pager

    ○ C. Traveling by airplane

    ○ D. Having a magnetic resonance imaging test

30. Which breakfast selection would be best for the client taking digitalis (Lanoxin)?

    ○ A. Bran muffin, orange juice, and a cup of coffee

    ○ B. A bagel with jelly and a cup of coffee

    ○ C. Bacon and egg on toast and a cup of coffee

    ○ D. Ham-and-cheese biscuit and coffee

31. If the client becomes toxic to his digitalis, he will experience which of the following symptoms?

    ○ A. Tachycardia

    ○ B. Hypotension

    ○ C. Nausea and vomiting

    ○ D. Diarrhea

32. The nurse is performing an ECG tracing on the client with a history of cardiac disease. Where should the nurse apply the negative lead?

    ○ A. On the client's right chest at the second intercostal space

    ○ B. On the client's anterior right leg

    ○ C. On the client's left chest at the second intercostal space

    ○ D. On the client's left chest at the apex of the heart

33. The nurse is checking the pulse rate of a six-week-old patient with aortic stenosis who has an order for digitalis. The client's pulse rate is found to be 82 beats per minute. Which action is most appropriate?

    ○ A. Contact the physician prior to administering the medication

    ○ B. Administer the medication and recheck the pulse rate 30 minutes later

    ○ C. Administer the medication and document the pulse rate

    ○ D. Withhold the medication and document the finding

34. The client is admitted to the emergency room following a motor vehicle accident. An ECG reveals frequent premature ventricular contractions. Which medication is often used to treat premature ventricular contractions?

    ○ A. Amiodarone (Cordarone)

    ○ B. Atropine sulfate (Atropine)

    ○ C. Epinephrine bitartrate (Epinephryl)

    ○ D. Enoxaparin (Lovenox)

35. The client is admitted with ventricular fibrillation. The nurse should begin defibrillation by shocking at:

    ○ A. 360 Joules

    ○ B. 200 Joules

    ○ C. 400 Joules

    ○ D. 600 Joules

36. The nurse is caring for the client admitted with severe chest pain. After checking the vital signs, the nurse's next action should be to:

    ○ A. Prepare to administer oxygen by mask

    ○ B. Administer morphine

    ○ C. Prepare the defibrillator

    ○ D. Take a complete history

37. The client with arteriosclerosis is scheduled for a cardiac catheterization. Which of the following is the primary responsibility of the nurse prior to the procedure?

    ○ A. Explain the procedure to the client

    ○ B. Check the laboratory results for a prothrombin time

    ○ C. Take the client's vital signs

    ○ D. Obtain a permit for the examination

38. After the client's cardiac catheterization where the femoral artery is used as the access vessel, the nurse should:

    ○ A. Check for allergies to iodine

    ○ B. Tell the client to refrain from drinking liquids

    ○ C. Explain the need to flex and extend the leg

    ○ D. Check the pedal pulse in the operative leg

39. The client is admitted two weeks after the onset of chest pain. Which laboratory test is the most indicative for a myocardial infarction?

    ○ A. Creatine kinase (CK-MB)

    ○ B. Troponin level

    ○ C. Lactic acid dehydrogenase (LDH)

    ○ D. Blood urea nitrogen (BUN)

40. The client returns to the intensive care unit following a coronary artery bypass graft. The nurse notes that the client is suddenly experiencing shortness of breath with muffled heart sounds. The blood pressure is 90/40, and the pulse rate is 110 beats per minute. Which action is most appropriate initially?

    ○ A. Check the mediastinal tube for drainage

    ○ B. Recheck the vital signs

    ○ C. Administer pain medication

    ○ D. Decrease the intravenous flow rate

41. Which breakfast cereal choice is the best choice for the client recovering from a myocardial infarction?

    ○ A. Instant-cooking cereals

    ○ B. Puffed rice

    ○ C. Raisin Bran

    ○ D. Cocoa Puffs

42. The client with congestive heart failure has an order for milrinone (Primacor). If the doctor decides to check the BNP, the nurse should do which of the following?

    ○ A. Slow the rate of the Primacor infusion

    ○ B. Administer a diuretic prior to checking the BNP

    ○ C. Continue the Primacor as ordered

    ○ D. Stop the Primacor for two hours prior to the test

43. The client is discharged with a prescription for sodium warfarin (Coumadin). The nurse should instruct the client to:

    ○ A. Take the medication with water only

    ○ B. Eat green vegetables at least three times per week

    ○ C. Avoid constipation by increasing the amount of fiber in the diet

    ○ D. Administer the medication in the abdomen with a tuberculin syringe

44. A 55-year-old female is admitted to the emergency room complaining of indigestion and back and shoulder pain. She tells the nurse that she has taken several antacids for the past two days without relief of her symptoms. Which action would be most appropriate at this time?

   ○ A. Ask the client if she has a history of gastric ulcers

   ○ B. Allow the client to rest undisturbed

   ○ C. Take the client's vital signs and contact the physician

   ○ D. Obtain a history to rule out a hiatal hernia

45. The client is receiving Coumadin (warfarin sodium has a Protime level of 44 seconds). The nurse should anticipate an order for which of the following?

   ○ A. AquaMEPHYTON

   ○ B. Physostigmine

   ○ C. Ropivacaine

   ○ D. Methimazole

46. The client is admitted with a diagnosis of congestive heart failure. Which finding supports the diagnosis of left-sided congestive heart failure?

   ○ A. Pitting edema 3+

   ○ B. Ascites

   ○ C. Jugular vein distention

   ○ D. Fatigue

47. Which statement, if made by the client, would cause the nurse to suspect a sacular abdominal aortic aneurysm?

   ○ A. "I sometimes have indigestion when I lie down."

   ○ B. "I often have pulsating sensations in my abdomen."

   ○ C. "I feel fatigue and shortness of breath with minimal exertion."

   ○ D. "I have extreme pain radiating down my left arm."

48. The client returns from surgery following a coronary artery bypass graft with a mitral valve replacement. Which medication will be ordered for the client who has a metal valve replacement?

   ○ A. Chlorothiazide (Diuril)

   ○ B. Clonidine HCl (Catapres)

   ○ C. Sodium warfarin (Coumadin)

   ○ D. Propranolol (Inderal)

49. The client with peripheral vascular disease is diagnosed with intermittent claudication. Which action by the nurse would help the client to relieve symptoms of intermittent claudication?

  ○ A. Apply antithrombolytic stockings as ordered

  ○ B. Encourage the use of a heating pad to the effected leg

  ○ C. Massage the effected extremity

  ○ D. Encourage the client to ambulate

50. The client has a femoral popliteal bypass graft. Which instruction should be given to the client prior to discharge?

  ○ A. Rest in high Fowler's position

  ○ B. Avoiding crossing the legs at the ankles

  ○ C. Keep the procedural leg straight

  ○ D. Check the radial pulse rate daily

51. Which instruction should be given to the client being discharged after a myocardial infarction?

  ○ A. You can begin having intercourse when you can climb three flights of stairs without experiencing breathlessness.

  ○ B. You should take nitroglycerine at the first signs of chest pain.

  ○ C. You can take sildenafil (Viagra) for erectile dysfunction.

  ○ D. You should walk at least three miles every day to increase cardiac output.

52. The client is admitted with possible thrombophlebitis. Which action should be priority?

  ○ A. Ask the client to remain in bed

  ○ B. Assess using Homan's sign

  ○ C. Schedule the client for a Doppler study

  ○ D. Apply a moist heating pad to the extremity

53. The client with Raynaud's phenomena should be taught to:

  ○ A. Keep the feet elevated while resting

  ○ B. Wear mittens when she is out in the cold

  ○ C. Avoid caffeine intake

  ○ D. Drink warm liquids to loosen lung secretions

54. The client is being treated for Buerger's disease. Another name for Buerger's disease is:

    ○ A. Thrombophlebitis

    ○ B. Coronary thrombosis

    ○ C. Thromboangiitis obliterans

    ○ D. Arteritis

55. The nurse is preparing to monitor the client's central venous pressure. Which position would provide the most reliable measurement of the CVP?

    ○ A. Supine

    ○ B. High Fowler's

    ○ C. Left Sims'

    ○ D. Prone

Care of the Client with Endocrine Disorders

56. The client is admitted to the unit for treatment of a prolactinoma. Which symptom is associated with a prolactinoma?

    ○ A. Agranulocytosis

    ○ B. Anovulation

    ○ C. Polyuria

    ○ D. Bone pain

57. The client is seen in the clinic with a diagnosis of myxedema. Which food choice would be best for this client?

    ○ A. Turnip greens

    ○ B. Steak

    ○ C. Cheese

    ○ D. Milk

58. The client is scheduled for a transphenoidal hypophysectomy. During the immediate post-operative period, which nursing task should receive priority?

    ○ A. Checking the gag reflex

    ○ B. Assessing the urinary output

    ○ C. Checking nasal discharge for glucose

    ○ D. Checking for Homan's sign

59. The client with head trauma is admitted following a motor vehicle accident. The nurse notes 5000 ml of dilute urinary output within 3 hours of admission. Which finding would support a diagnosis of diabetes insipidus?

   ○ A. Decreased red blood cell count

   ○ B. Low specific gravity of urine

   ○ C. Increase blood urea nitrogen

   ○ D. Increased serum creatinine level

60. Which action by the nurse indicates that he is aware of the needs of the client with myxedema?

   ○ A. The nurse provides the client with a private room.

   ○ B. The nurse offers extra, warm blankets.

   ○ C. The nurse orders high-calorie foods for the client.

   ○ D. The nurse administers antihypertensive medications.

61. The client with myxedema is being treated with synthetic thyroid medication. Which instruction should be given to the client taking thyroid medication?

   ○ A. Take the medication with orange juice to increase medication's strength.

   ○ B. For best absorption, take the medication prior to bedtime.

   ○ C. Check your pulse rate prior to taking the medication.

   ○ D. Have your triglycerides checked every six months while taking the medication.

62. The client with Grave's disease is experiencing exopthalmos. Which action taken by the nurse indicates that the nurse is aware of the problems associated with sicca?

   ○ A. The nurse applies artificial tears to the client's lower conjuntiva.

   ○ B. The nurse offers a saliva substitute.

   ○ C. The nurse provides frequent mouth care.

   ○ D. The nurse instructs the client to avoid eating uncooked foods.

63. The client returns from surgery following a thyroidectomy. Which action by the nurse indicates understanding of the needs of the client that has a thyroidectomy?

   ○ A. The nurse checks the urinary output hourly.

   ○ B. The nurse places a tracheostomy set at the bedside.

   ○ C. The nurse offers pain medication every hour.

   ○ D. The nurse checks the abdominal dressing.

64. Which of the following laboratory results indicates hypoparathyroidism?

    ❍ A. Serum phosphorus level of 2.0 mEq/L

    ❍ B. Serum potassium of 3.0 mEq/L

    ❍ C. Serum magnesium level of 2.0 mEq/L

    ❍ D. Serum calcium level of .5 mEq/L

65. The nurse is assessing the client for Trousseau's sign. Which finding indicates a positive Trousseau sign?

    ❍ A. Tap cranial nerves 7 and cranial nerve 5 and check for grimacing of the face

    ❍ B. Place a blood pressure cuff on the arm and check for carpopedal spasms when the cuff is inflated

    ❍ C. Check the deep tendon reflexes by tapping the knee

    ❍ D. Monitor the client for nausea when cold water is used to irrigate the ear canal

66. The client returns to the unit following surgery for removal of a tumor of the parathyroid gland. Where should the nurse check for bleeding?

    ❍ A. Behind the neck

    ❍ B. Behind the ear

    ❍ C. On the abdomen

    ❍ D. In the groin

67. The client is seen in the clinic with complaint of fatigue, dry skin, and extreme thirst. Which test would best indicate the diagnosis of diabetes mellitus?

    ❍ A. Two-hour postprandial

    ❍ B. Dextrostix

    ❍ C. Glycosylated hemoglobin

    ❍ D. Glucose tolerance test

68. The client with diabetes presents to the emergency department with pupils dilated. Which action by the nurse indicates understanding of the client's presenting symptom?

    ❍ A. The nurse checks the client's Hgb A1C.

    ❍ B. The nurse begins an IV of normal saline.

    ❍ C. The nurse applies oxygen via mask at 3 liter/minute.

    ❍ D. The nurse gives the client 240 ml of apple juice.

69. Which action by the nurse indicates that she understands the necessary action to be taken if the client with diabetes has altered sensorium and skin that is cold and clammy?

    ○ A. The nurse administers regular insulin as ordered.

    ○ B. The nurse prepares to administer orange juice with sugar added.

    ○ C. The nurse maintains the intravenous infusion of normal saline.

    ○ D. The nurse inserts a Foley catheter to monitor urinary output.

70. The client is experiencing the Somogyi effect of his diabetes mellitus. Which action indicates that the nurse understands the Somogyi effect?

    ○ A. The nurse offers a bedtime snack.

    ○ B. The nurse administers insulin prior to bedtime.

    ○ C. The nurse checks the urine for glucose and ketones prior to meals.

    ○ D. The nurse offers an anti-emetic for nausea.

71. The client is experiencing dawn phenomena associated with diabetes mellitus. Which action by the nurse indicates knowledge of dawn phenomena?

    ○ A. The nurse offers peanut butter and crackers as a snack prior to bedtime.

    ○ B. The nurse wakes the client during the night to check her blood glucose level.

    ○ C. The nurse administers NPH insulin subcutaneously as ordered.

    ○ D. The nurse explains the need for frequent cortisole levels to be checked.

72. The client has an order for administration of 10 units of regular insulin to be given at 7:00 a.m. The nurse should offer a snack at:

    ○ A. 3:00 p.m.

    ○ B. 1:00 p.m.

    ○ C. 11:00 a.m.

    ○ D. 9:00 a.m.

73. The client is being treated with NPH insulin at 8:00 am. The nurse should offer a snack at:

    ○ A. 9:00 a.m.

    ○ B. 11:00 a.m.

    ○ C. 1:00 p.m.

    ○ D. 2:00 p.m.

74. The client scheduled for a pacemaker insertion has been taking metformin (Glucophage) for control of diabetes mellitus. Which instruction should the nurse give the client taking metformin?

    ○ A. Take the medication as ordered the morning of the procedure.

    ○ B. Let the doctor know if he is having burning when he urinates.

    ○ C. Use insulin the morning of the procedure to control his blood glucose levels.

    ○ D. Take half the dosage of the medication the morning of the procedure.

75. The client has been diagnosed with pheochromocytoma. Which finding supports a diagnosis of pheochromocytoma?

    ○ A. Malignant hypertension

    ○ B. Anorexia

    ○ C. Urinary frequency

    ○ D. Bronze pigmentation of the skin

76. Which action should receive priority if the client is experiencing Addisonian crises?

    ○ A. Judicious monitoring for hypotension and treatment of shock

    ○ B. Administration of an alpha-adrenergic blocker to treat extreme elevations in blood pressure

    ○ C. Treat the client by administering calcium carbonate to prevent osteoporosis

    ○ D. Explain to the client the need to continue treatment for adrenocortical hyposecretion

77. The client is admitted with Cushing's disease. Which symptoms support the diagnosis of Cushing's disease?

    ○ A. Hypoglycemia and weight loss

    ○ B. Increased lymphocytes and pale complexion

    ○ C. Osteoporosis and a pendulous abdomen

    ○ D. Decreased blood pressure and cyanosis

78. The client is taking rosiglitazone (Avandia) for control of his diabetes. Which laboratory result should be reported to the physician?

◯ A. Blood glucose of 110 mg/dL

◯ B. Creatinine level of 3.0 mg/dL

◯ C. Blood urea nitrogen level of 10 mg/dL

◯ D. White blood cell count of 8,000

79. The client is being treated with Lantus insulin. At 9:00 p.m., the client's blood glucose level is found to be 200 mg/dL. If the client has an order for Lantus insulin and sliding-scale insulin, the nurse should administer the two doses of insulin:

◯ A. Together in one syringe

◯ B. Separately in two syringes

◯ C. One hour apart in two syringes

◯ D. One hour apart in one syringe

80. A Jewish client is receiving insulin to control her diabetes. Which type of insulin would most likely be rejected by the Jewish client?

◯ A. Insulin of rDNA origin

◯ B. Insulin made from pork

◯ C. Insulin made from beef

◯ D. Insulin containing zinc

81. The client has a prescription for Strong Iodine (Lugol's solution). Which instruction should be given to the client taking Lugol's solution?

◯ A. Take the medication in the morning for best absorption.

◯ B. Check the medication with juice to mask the taste.

◯ C. Avoid abrupt changes in position to avoid postural hypotension.

◯ D. Allow two weeks for the drug to reach its optimal level.

82. The client with hyperthyroidism has a prescription for lithium carbonate (Lithobid). The client should be taught to take the medication:

◯ A. Two times per day

◯ B. With milk or meals

◯ C. With an antiemetic

◯ D. For the treatment of psychosis

83. The client is being treated with acarbose (Precose). Which laboratory results should be reported to the physician?

    ◯ A. White blood cell count of 5,000

    ◯ B. Blood urea nitrogen level of 26 mg/dL

    ◯ C. Creatinine level of 0.8 mg/dL

    ◯ D. Platelet count of 200,000

84. The nurse is preparing to administer cortisol (hydrocortisone) to the client with Addison's disease. Which action by the nurse indicates understanding of the correct administration of cortisol?

    ◯ A. The nurse checks the pulse rate prior to administering the medication.

    ◯ B. The nurse checks the urine specific gravity prior to giving the cortisol.

    ◯ C. The nurse gives the medication in the morning.

    ◯ D. The nurse monitors the red blood cell count while the client is receiving cortisol.

85. The client with Cushing's disease is admitted to the unit for treatment of his illness. Which medication is often used to treat Cushing's disease?

    ◯ A. Spironolactone (Aldactone)

    ◯ B. Nitroprusside (Nitropress)

    ◯ C. Dexamethasone (Decadron)

    ◯ D. Demeclocycline (Tetracycline)

86. The client is admitted with acromegaly. Which sign or symptom is associated with acromegaly?

    ◯ A. Rapid weight gain due to cortisol elevations

    ◯ B. Extreme height due to an increased growth hormone level

    ◯ C. A pendulous abdomen related to altered fat distribution

    ◯ D. A dowager hump secondary to osteoporosis

87. Which medication can be used to treat extreme hypoglycemia?

    ◯ A. Acarbose (Precose)

    ◯ B. Glyburide (Diabeta)

    ◯ C. Rosiglitazone (Avandia)

    ◯ D. Glucagon (GlucaGen)

88. The client with diabetes mellitus has a carbon dioxide level of 46 mEq/L. The nurse would expect to see which symptom is the client with a carbon dioxide level of 46 mEq/L?

   ○ A. Kussmaul breathing

   ○ B. Slow respirations

   ○ C. Eupnea

   ○ D. Absence of audible respirations

89. The client is admitted with hyperglycemic hyperosmolar nonketonic (HHNK) coma. Which action should the nurse take to treat the symptoms associated with HHNK?

   ○ A. Administer oxygen by nasal cannula

   ○ B. Provide adequate fluids

   ○ C. Offer a carbohydrate

   ○ D. Administer an oral antidiabetic medication

90. The client is admitted with SIADH. The nurse should prepare to administer a solution containing which of the following?

   ○ A. Magnesium

   ○ B. Phosphorus

   ○ C. Calcium

   ○ D. Sodium

Care of the Client with Immunological Disorders

91. A screen test for detection of human immunodeficiency virus (HIV) reveals a positive ELISA test. Which test will be used to confirm the diagnosis of HIV?

   ○ A. Radioimmunoprecipitation assay (RIPA) test

   ○ B. p24 levels

   ○ C. Lymphocyte count

   ○ D. Indirect immunofluorescence assay (IFA)

92. The client's viral load is 300 copies per mL. Evaluation of the test results indicate:

    ○ A. Rapid progression of the illness.

    ○ B. The client is relatively free of circulating virus.

    ○ C. The need for vigorous treatment of the virus.

    ○ D. The client is not capable of transmitting the illness to others.

93. The postpartal client asks the nurse whether she will be able to breastfeed her baby. Which instruction should the nurse give the client regarding breastfeeding if the client is positive for the human immunodeficiency virus?

    ○ A. You can breastfeed your baby after the first 48 hours because colostrum contains HIV.

    ○ B. Breast milk is allowed if you pump the milk and heat it before giving it to the baby.

    ○ C. Breastfeeding is permitted in the early stages of HIV syndrome.

    ○ D. Breastfeeding is not permitted because breast milk can be contaminated with the virus.

94. Which fruit is the best choice for the client that is immune-suppressed because he has HIV?

    ○ A. Strawberry

    ○ B. Grape

    ○ C. Banana

    ○ D. Apple

95. The nurse is teaching a group of clients regarding prevention of HIV transmission. The best method of birth control for the client with HIV is:

    ○ A. Oral contraceptives

    ○ B. Lamb's skin condoms

    ○ C. Intrauterine device

    ○ D. Latex condoms

96. Which activity is most likely to cause harm to the client with AIDS?

    ○ A. Petting a dog

    ○ B. Handling a turtle

    ○ C. Feeding wild birds

    ○ D. Feeding a cat

97. The nursing assistant is cleaning the floor where a urinary spill has occurred. Which action by the nursing assistant indicates understanding of standard precautions? The nursing assistant obtains a solution of:

    ○ A. Water

    ○ B. Soap

    ○ C. Bleach

    ○ D. Peroxide

98. The client with *Clostridium difficile* is admitted to the unit. To prevent the transmission of *Clostridium difficile* to the immune-suppressed client, the nurse should use:

    ○ A. Airborne precautions

    ○ B. Droplet precautions

    ○ C. Sputum precautions

    ○ D. Contact precautions

99. The client with AIDS is being treated with highly active retroviral therapy (HAART). The nurse is aware that HAART comprises:

    ○ A. Three categories of antiviral medications

    ○ B. Extremely high doses of nucleoside analog reverse transcriptase inhibitors for one week

    ○ C. Transfusions of stem cells for three consecutive days followed by a ribonucleotide reductase inhibitor

    ○ D. Four different protease inhibitors given one week apart

100. The client with acquired immune deficiency syndrome (AIDS) is being treated with metronidazole (Flagyl) for a protozoal infection. Which instruction should be given to the client taking metronidazole (Flagyl)?

    ○ A. Take the medication in the morning for optimal absorption.

    ○ B. Do not take this medication and also drink alcoholic beverages.

    ○ C. Allow six weeks for the medication to take effect.

    ○ D. Take the medication with an antacid to prevent nausea.

101. The client is admitted with *pneumocytis carinii* pneumonia. The nurse is aware that the physician will most likely order:

    ○ A. Zidovudine (Ritrovir)

    ○ B. Nivirapine (Viramune)

    ○ C. Efavirenz (Sustiva)

    ○ D. Sulfamethoxazole (Septra)

102. Which nursing intervention would be most beneficial in preparing the client psychologically for a diagnosis of HIV?

    ○ A. Include the family in the teaching.

    ○ B. Encourage the client to express his emotions.

    ○ C. Give a thorough explanation of the illness and prognosis.

    ○ D. Ask the client what he knows about acquired immune deficiency syndrome.

103. Which client problem relating to altered nutrition is a consequence of AIDS?

    ○ A. Increased appetite

    ○ B. Decreased protein absorption

    ○ C. Increase secretions of digestive juices

    ○ D. Decreased gastrointestinal absorption

104. The client with HIV is afraid of contracting toxoplasmosis. Which instruction should be given to the client to help decrease the chances of contracting toxoplasmosis?

    ○ A. The client should give his cat to a friend.

    ○ B. The client should not pet the cat.

    ○ C. The client should not pet kittens.

    ○ D. The client should not empty the cat's litter box.

105. Which sign is an early indicator of infection in the client that is immune suppressed?

    ○ A. A persistent sore throat

    ○ B. Elevated temperature

    ○ C. Elevated white blood cell count

    ○ D. Elevated creatinine levels

106. The client with AIDS develops Kaposi's sarcoma (KS). Which action by the nurse indicates understanding of Kaposi's sarcoma?

    ○ A. The nurse carries out percussion, vibration, and drainage every morning prior to breakfast.

    ○ B. The nurse provides mouth care after meals.

    ○ C. The nurse provides skin care and places the client on a floatation mattress.

    ○ D. The nurse does catheter care with the bath.

107. The client has a CD4 +T cell count of 500 cu.mm/liter. The correct assessment of this laboratory finding would be:

    ○ A. The CD4 +T cell count is extremely high; therefore, the client is at risk for opportunistic diseases.

    ○ B. The CD4 +T cell count is extremely low; therefore, the client is at risk for opportunistic disease.

    ○ C. The CD4 +T cell count is sufficiently high to indicate that the client will probably be asymptomatic.

    ○ D. The CD4 +T cell count is extremely low; therefore, the client is within the risk zone for opportunistic diseases.

108. The client who is pregnant asks the nurse how she can protect her baby from getting HIV from her blood. Which answer is correct?

    ○ A. There is no way to prevent the spread of the disease from mother to baby.

    ○ B. The doctor will prescribe an antibiotic to you during pregnancy to ensure that the disease is not spread to your infant.

    ○ C. An antiviral called zidovudine (AZT) will be prescribed to you during pregnancy and to the infant after birth to decrease the chances of the infant contracting the illness.

    ○ D. A drug called TMC-114 darunavir (Prezista) can be used to prevent the transmission of the illness across the placenta.

109. The client with AIDS is suffering from cytomegalovirus. Which sign is often associated with cytomegalovirus?

    ○ A. Multifocal lesions

    ○ B. Alterations in vision

    ○ C. Nausea and vomiting

    ○ D. Decreasing renal function

110. The client with genital herpes is seen in the clinic with an active lesion. The nurse should anticipate an order for:

    ○ A. Pyrazinamide (Tebrazid)

    ○ B. Isoniazid (Laniazid)

    ○ C. Ciprofloxacin (Cipro)

    ○ D. Acyclovir (Zovirax)

Care of the Childbearing Client and the Neonatal Client

111. The client is seen in the prenatal clinic. She tells the nurse that she has been trying to get pregnant for the past six months. Which vitamin will help to decrease the chances of neural tube defects in the baby?

  ○ A. B3

  ○ B. B2

  ○ C. B9

  ○ D. B1

112. The client who is 20 weeks gestation asks the nurse how much weight she should gain during her pregnancy. The nurse should tell the client that:

  ○ A. She should try not to gain more than 25 pounds during pregnancy.

  ○ B. She should gain about 36 pounds during pregnancy.

  ○ C. The client should gain 55 pounds during pregnancy.

  ○ D. The client should not gain more than 15 pounds.

113. The client has an Alpha Feta protein level drawn to check for a neural tube defect. The nurse should explain to the client that:

  ○ A. If the levels of Alpha Feta protein levels are abnormal, an amniocentesis will be ordered.

  ○ B. An Alpha Feta protein is a definitive test for neural tube defects.

  ○ C. The client will be asleep during the Alpha Feta protein test.

  ○ D. Alpha Feta protein levels can indicate lung disorders as well as neural tube defects.

114. The physician has ordered several medications for the client who is pregnant. The nurse is aware that the client should not take which of the following?

  ○ A. Propranolol (Inderal)

  ○ B. Penicillin (Amoxicillin)

  ○ C. Tetracycline (Achromycin)

  ○ D. Propafenone (Rythmol)

115. The client with gestational diabetes is scheduled for an ultrasound. Which finding would indicate possible hyperglycemia in the fetus?

  ○ A. Oligohydramnios

  ○ B. Meconium illeus

  ○ C. Esophageal atresia

  ○ D. Polyhydramnios

116. The doctor is performing an amniocentesis on the client at 17 weeks gestation to detect genetic anomalies. Which statement indicates the nurse understands the proper instructions for the client having an amniocentesis at 17 weeks gestation?

  ○ A. After the ultrasound exam, the client should empty the bladder.

  ○ B. After the ultrasound exam, the client should not void for the amniocentesis.

  ○ C. The ultrasound exam will be done at least eight hours prior to the amniocentesis.

  ○ D. The amniocentesis cannot be done prior to 20 weeks gestation.

117. The client is scheduled for a nonstress test to determine the status of fetal development. A positive nonstress test is considered:

  ○ A. Normal and there is no need for further evaluation

  ○ B. Abnormal, but there is no need for further evaluation

  ○ C. Abnormal with need for further evaluation

  ○ D. Normal with need for a repeat test in one week

118. The laboring client is experiencing contractions every 2–3 minutes lasting 90 seconds. The client's fetal heart rate is ranging from 130 to 140 beats per minute (BPM) with variability of 6p–10 beats per minute. Which action by the nurse is most appropriate?

  ○ A. Discontinue the IV fluid containing Pitocin (oxytocin)

  ○ B. Document the finding in the client's medical record

  ○ C. Contact the doctor at once and reposition the client

  ○ D. Insert an internal fetal scalp electrode monitor

119. The client is scheduled for an oxytocin challenge exam using 10 units of oxytocin (Pitocin) in 1000 mL of intravenous fluid. Which action by the nurse would ensure safe administration of oxytocin (Pitocin)?

○ A. The nurse inserts a Foley catheter.

○ B. The nurse checks the urinary output every hour.

○ C. The nurse obtains an intravenous infusion pump from central supply.

○ D. The nurse administers an anti-emetic prior to beginning the infusion.

120. The nurse is assessing the client in the first stage of labor. The fetal heart tones are checked using a fetoscope and found to be 105–115 per minute, the contractions by palpation are every three minutes, and the client is complaining of extreme pain in the lower abdomen. Which action should the nurse take at this time?

○ A. Document the finding

○ B. Assess the fetal monitor strip

○ C. Call the physician

○ D. Prepare for delivery

121. During the client's 30-week gestation, the doctor orders an immunization for rubella. Which action is most appropriate for the nurse to take?

○ A. Administer the injection in the hip

○ B. Withhold the injection and contact the physician

○ C. Ask the client whether she is allergic to shellfish

○ D. Have the client sign a permit prior to administering the immunization

122. The client is admitted at 39 weeks gestation for induction of labor. If the doctor uses prostaglandin gel the nurse should:

○ A. Administer Stadol (butorphanol) prior to the prostaglandin gel

○ B. Tell the client that the labor will be more painful

○ C. Elevate the client's hips for 30 minutes after the gel is inserted

○ D. Insert a Foley catheter prior to insertion of the gel

123. The client is receiving Pitocin (oxytocin) for augmentation of labor. Which finding would necessitate the need to discontinue the oxytocin?

   ○ A. The client's contractions are every three minutes, lasting 60 seconds.

   ○ B. The client complains of a desire to push with contractions.

   ○ C. The client's fetal heart tones are 110 beats per minute prior to contractions and 80 beats per minute at the end of the contraction for the last twenty minutes.

   ○ D. The client complains of nausea and vomiting with contractions.

124. The pregnant client is admitted to the emergency room with the umbilical cord protruding from the vagina. Which action should be taken first?

   ○ A. Place the client in Trendelenburg position

   ○ B. Call the physician to report the finding

   ○ C. Begin an IV of 5% dextrose

   ○ D. Cover the cord with sterile gauze

125. The client is admitted to the family planning clinic desiring oral contraceptive. Which finding in the client's history would need further investigation?

   ○ A. The client is HIV positive.

   ○ B. The client had pregnancy-induced hypertension.

   ○ C. The client is 18 years old.

   ○ D. The client is a gravida 5 para 4.

126. The pregnant client who has been a diabetic since age 10 requests a prescription for birth control pills. When teaching the client with diabetes concerning the use of birth control pills, the nurse should tell the client that they can cause which of the following?

   ○ A. Urinary tract infections

   ○ B. Elevated blood glucose levels

   ○ C. Prolonged clotting times

   ○ D. Altered oxygen needs

127. Vaginal examination in the laboring client reveals the anterior fontanel is toward the rectum. The nurse should chart that the baby is in which position?

   ○ A. Occipital posterior

   ○ B. Transverse

   ○ C. Occipital anterior

   ○ D. Breech

128. The client is found to be at +4 station. Which action is most appropriate for the nurse to take?

   ○ A. Prepare for delivery

   ○ B. Chart the finding

   ○ C. Administer pain medication

   ○ D. Increase the pitocin (oxytocin)

129. The client is admitted to the labor unit following spontaneous rupture of membranes. Upon assessment of the client's condition, the nurse notes the fetal heart tones are 160–170 beats per minutes. There is a dark green vaginal discharge, and the client's cervix is 50% effaced. The nurse's initial action should be to do which of the following?

   ○ A. Document the finding

   ○ B. Apply oxygen via mask

   ○ C. Insert a Foley catheter

   ○ D. Begin an IV of normal saline

130. The client with cardiac disease in pregnancy is admitted with shortness of breath and frothy sputum. Which action should the nurse take after completing her assessment?

   ○ A. Call the physician

   ○ B. Monitor the client's contractions

   ○ C. Elevate the head of the bed and reassess the respirations

   ○ D. Administer a diuretic

131. The client is admitted to the prenatal clinic. A history of cardiac disease exists. If the client is a class II cardiac client, the nurse should teach the client to:

   ○ A. Remain on strict bed rest during her pregnancy

   ○ B. Plan to have a therapeutic abortion

   ○ C. Avoid strenuous exercise

   ○ D. Use oxygen at night

132. While shopping at the local mall, the nurse observes a pregnant client choking on a piece of steak. Which action should be priority?

   ○ A. Perform abdominal thrust

   ○ B. Wait to see whether the client loses consciousness

   ○ C. Perform chest thrust

   ○ D. Do a finger sweep to clear the airway

133. The client with diabetes wants to become pregnant. Which instruction regarding control of diabetes in pregnancy should be priority?

    ◯ A. Teach the client to take her oral antidiabetic medications correctly

    ◯ B. Instruct the client to limit her weight gain to 18 pounds during pregnancy

    ◯ C. Tell the client that her blood glucose levels will be controlled with insulin

    ◯ D. Teach the client to check her urine for glucose and ketones

134. The nurse who is caring for the laboring client notes a decline of fetal heart tones from 136 to 90 beats per minute after the acme of the contractions. Which action is most appropriate at this time?

    ◯ A. Monitor the client's blood pressure

    ◯ B. Turn the client to her left side

    ◯ C. Assess the urinary output hourly

    ◯ D. Prepare the client for a cesarean section

135. The nurse is teaching the client regarding a scheduled glucose tolerance test. Which instruction should be priority?

    ◯ A. Eat a high-carbohydrate diet prior to the test.

    ◯ B. Do not eat after midnight the day of the test.

    ◯ C. Drink a glucose liquid prior to the first blood sample.

    ◯ D. Do not void prior to the exam.

136. The client is admitted with preeclampsia. Which finding requires that the nurse contact the physician immediately?

    ◯ A. The client's blood pressure is 140/90.

    ◯ B. The client has a 3 + pedal edema.

    ◯ C. The client's urine reveals 8 grams of protein in a 24-hour urine sample.

    ◯ D. The client's platelet count is 280,000.

137. The physician has ordered magnesium sulfate for the client with preeclampsia. Which action should be taken prior to beginning the magnesium sulfate?

    ◯ A. Insert a Foley catheter

    ◯ B. Check the deep tendon reflexes

    ◯ C. Administer a pain medication

    ◯ D. Darken the room

138. The client's magnesium level is checked every six hours during magnesium sulfate therapy. If the client's magnesium level is 9.0 mg/dL, the nurse should:

   ○ A. Obtain another magnesium level immediately

   ○ B. Chart the finding

   ○ C. Call the doctor

   ○ D. Administer calcium gluconate

139. The client is admitted to the emergency room with a tentative diagnose of ectopic pregnancy. The nurse should be least concerned with:

   ○ A. Controlling bleeding

   ○ B. Preventing infection

   ○ C. Preserving the pregnancy

   ○ D. Controlling pain

140. The 30-year-old client is diagnosed with a molar pregnancy. The nurse should tell the client:

   ○ A. To report any vaginal bleeding

   ○ B. To refrain from having intercourse for several months

   ○ C. To observe the baby's fetal movement

   ○ D. To avoid becoming pregnant again for at least one year

141. The client is admitted with fetal demise. A diagnosis of missed abortion requires that the fetus be evacuated by induction of labor. If the physician uses prostaglandin, the nurse should anticipate that the client will:

   ○ A. Complain of nausea

   ○ B. Become constipated

   ○ C. Need treatment with potassium supplementation

   ○ D. Require that a Foley catheter be inserted

142. The nurse has just received the shift report. Which client should the nurse see first?

   ○ A. The client with a hydatidiform mole

   ○ B. The client with placenta previa who is in labor

   ○ C. The client scheduled for a cesarean section

   ○ D. The client with mild preeclampsia

143. Which action is contraindicated in the client with placenta previa?

    ○ A. Ambulating the client to the bathroom

    ○ B. Performing a urinary catheterization

    ○ C. Applying a fetal monitor

    ○ D. Performing a vaginal exam for dilation

144. The client is admitted with premature labor. Which medication is least likely to be ordered for the client with diabetes?

    ○ A. Magnesium sulfate

    ○ B. Terbutaline (Brethine)

    ○ C. Magnesium gluconate

    ○ D. Meperidine (Demerol)

145. The physician has ordered Terbutaline (Brethine). To ensure correct administration of this medication, the nurse should obtain which of the following?

    ○ A. A 2-inch needle

    ○ B. An 18-gauge needle

    ○ C. A 1-inch needle

    ○ D. A 2.5-inch needle

146. The client is taking Ritodrine (Yutopar) for premature labor. Which finding needs to be reported to the physician?

    ○ A. Respiratory rate of 14 per minute

    ○ B. Blood pressure of 110/40

    ○ C. Pulse rate of 120 per minute

    ○ D. Temperature of 37° centigrade

147. The nurse is administering $MgSO_4$ to the client with preterm labor. If the client develops toxicity to the $MgSO_4$ the nurse should administer:

    ○ A. Protamine sulfate

    ○ B. Calcium gluconate

    ○ C. Atropine sulfate

    ○ D. AquaMEPHYTON (vitamin K)

148. The pregnant client is admitted with a deep vein thrombus in her left leg. The nurse should anticipate an order for which anticoagulant?

     ○ A. Sodium warfarin (Coumadin)

     ○ B. Ticlopidine (Ticlid)

     ○ C. Enoxaparin (Lovenox)

     ○ D. Warfarin (Warfilone)

149. The client comes to the emergency department with a prolapsed cord. Which nursing action should be a priority?

     ○ A. Cover the cord with a gauze

     ○ B. Reinsert the cord

     ○ C. Place the client in Trendelenburg position

     ○ D. Begin oxygen by nasal cannula

150. Which nurse would be best to care for the client with cesarean section delivery of a large for gestational baby?

     ○ A. A graduate associate degree nurse

     ○ B. A license practical nurse with 10 years experience in the post-partal unit

     ○ C. A registered nurse with 10 years experience in surgery

     ○ D. A registered nurse with 20 years experience in the orthopedic unit

151. The client is experiencing a decrease in the fetal heart tones beginning at the increment of the contraction and returning to baseline by the acme or end of each contraction. Between contractions the fetal heart tones are 130–140 beats per minute with good variability. Which action should be taken first?

     ○ A. Prepare for delivery

     ○ B. Perform a vaginal exam

     ○ C. Ask the client to push with each contraction

     ○ D. Call the doctor immediately

152. The client is experiencing a drop in the fetal heart rate. The decelerations are v-shaped and do not correlate to the contractions. The nurse is aware that this type of deceleration is which of the following?

  ○ A. Expected during the transition phase of labor

  ○ B. Ominous and requires intervention

  ○ C. Related to fetal head compression

  ○ D. Likely caused by uteroplacental insufficiency

153. The client has decided to use epidural anesthesia to control pain during labor. Prior to the epidural anesthesia, the nurse should:

  ○ A. Offer liquids by mouth

  ○ B. Insert a Foley catheter

  ○ C. Offer pain medications

  ○ D. Bolus the client with 2000 mL of intravenous fluids

154. The nurse is assessing the client two hours after delivery of a 9 lb. infant. Which problem should receive priority?

  ○ A. Redness and edema of the perineum

  ○ B. Extreme thirst and complaints of pain in the perineium

  ○ C. Uterus displacement to the left side of the abdomen

  ○ D. Breast tenderness and dripping of colostrum from the nipples

155. The newborn is admitted to the nursery. Which finding requires further evaluation?

  ○ A. The infant's Apgar score is 8 at one minute and 10 at five minutes.

  ○ B. The infant's identification band is applied to the infant's left wrist.

  ○ C. The infant's feet are slightly blue.

  ○ D. The infant's heart rate is 110 beats per minute.

156. The charge nurse is observing a new graduate performing all the following skills. Which observation requires further instruction?

  ○ A. The graduate nurse holds the baby cradled in her arms during feeding.

  ○ B. The graduate nurse obtains blood for a dextrose stick by pricking the tip of the heel.

  ○ C. The graduate places a drape over the scale prior to weighing the baby.

  ○ D. The graduate measures the infant using a paper tape measure.

157. While assessing the newborn, the nurse notes edema that crosses the cranial suture line. The nurse is aware that edema that crosses the infant's cranial suture line is:

　　○ A. A dangerous finding that should be reported immediately

　　○ B. A common occurrence following a vaginal delivery

　　○ C. A cephalohematoma that should be monitored

　　○ D. A subdural hematoma that will require surgical correction

158. The nurse notes dark spots on the African-American infant's back and buttocks. Which action should the nurse take after making this assessment?

　　○ A. Call the supervisor

　　○ B. Call the doctor

　　○ C. Document the finding

　　○ D. Ask the parents what caused the spots

159. The obstetric client with blood type AB– is being evaluated in the prenatal clinic. The nurse should be concerned with this finding because:

　　○ A. The infant can suffer from kernicterus.

　　○ B. The mother will probably have hypertension.

　　○ C. The infant will need to be delivered by cesarean section.

　　○ D. The mother will need to have an exchange transfusion.

160. The Rh negative mother is admitted to the post-partal unit. If the infant is found to be Rh positive, the nurse should prepare to administer which of the following?

　　○ A. Rh(D) immune globulin

　　○ B. Ribavirin (Rebetol)

　　○ C. Repaglinide (Prandin)

　　○ D. Raloxifene (Evista)

161. The nurse is teaching a mother how to care for her infant who has hyperbilirubinemia. Which instruction regarding the best way to resolve the problem of physiologic jaundice should be included in the teaching?

　　○ A. Stop breastfeeding if the jaundice worsens

　　○ B. Give the infant extra liquids orally

　　○ C. Administer vitamins with iron

　　○ D. Replace formula feedings with water

162. The client is admitted to the emergency room complaining of severe abdominal pain. A diagnosis of pelvic inflammatory disease is made. Which finding is often associated with pelvic inflammatory disease?

    ○ A. Cirrhosis of the liver

    ○ B. Syphilis

    ○ C. Gonorrhea

    ○ D. *Candida albican*

163. The 50-year-old client is seen in the gynecologic office with complaint of hot flashes. Which medication is often prescribed for the control of hot flashes?

    ○ A. Calcitriol (Calcijex)

    ○ B. Alendronate (Fosamax)

    ○ C. Conjugate estrogen (Premarin)

    ○ D. Calcitonin (Miacalcin)

164. The newborn is admitted to the nursery. Which injection should the nurse plan to administer?

    ○ A. AquaMEPHYTON (vitamin K)

    ○ B. Amikacin (Amikin)

    ○ C. Amiodarone (Cordarone)

    ○ D. Amoxicillin (Amoxil)

165. The infant of a drug-addicted mother is admitted to the intensive care unit. The nurse should anticipate the need for:

    ○ A. Intravenous feedings

    ○ B. Increasing stimuli

    ○ C. Administration of acetaminophen (Tylenol)

    ○ D. Preventing seizure activity

166. The nurse caring for the client one hour after delivery should be most concerned with a:

    ○ A. Temperature of 101° Fahrenheit

    ○ B. Moderate amount of lochia rubra

    ○ C. Distended bladder

    ○ D. Clear discharge from the breast

Practice Exam II

This element consists of 166 questions that are representative of what you should expect on the actual exam. This exam should help you determine how prepared you are for the real exam and provide a good basis for what you still need to review. As you take this exam, treat it as you would the real exam: time yourself (about one minute per question is suggested) and answer each question carefully, marking the ones you want to go back and double-check. You will find the answers and their explanations in the "Practice Exam II Answers" element of the book.

The test items have been divided by chapter content. This format makes it easy for you to review content by subject matter. After you take this exam, remember to load the CD-ROM and check out our exclusive ExamGear test engine, which is one of the best on the market.

Care of the Client with Respiratory Disorders

1. The physician has ordered chest physiotherapy for a client with chronic obstructive lung disease. When performing chest physiotherapy the nurse should give priority to:

   ○ A. Covering the client's chest with a towel

   ○ B. Placing the client in a prone position

   ○ C. Beginning percussion in the lower lobes

   ○ D. Making sure that the client's face is visible

2. A client is admitted to the intensive care unit with a diagnosis of acute respiratory distress syndrome (ARDS). Which statement is true regarding acute respiratory distress syndrome?

   ○ A. The disorder is a direct result of left-sided heart failure.

   ○ B. The disorder affects only clients with chronic pulmonary disease.

   ○ C. The disorder is characterized by refractory hypoxemia.

   ○ D. The disorder responds very favorably to the use of surfactant replacement.

3. While assessing a client with a three-chamber chest drainage system, the nurse observes that the fluid level in the second chamber does not fluctuate. What is the appropriate action for the nurse to take at this time?

   ○ A. Determine if the suction is working properly

   ○ B. Empty the fluid from the second chamber

   ○ C. Call the doctor and prepare to change systems

   ○ D. Increase the amount of suction applied

4. The nurse is teaching a 10-year-old client with cystic fibrosis how to do purse-lipped breathing. Which activity would be effective in helping the client learn the technique?

   ○ A. Using an incentive spirometer three times a day

   ○ B. Blowing a ping pong ball across a table

   ○ C. Doing sit-ups to strengthen abdominal muscles

   ○ D. Blowing out a lit candle

5. The nurse is preparing to administer an infusion of Pentam (pentamidine) to a client with PCP pneumonia. Which lab finding indicates an adverse reaction to the medication?

   ○ A. RBC 2,500,000/cu. mm

   ○ B. WBC 7500/cu. mm

   ○ C. Platelets 200,000/cu. mm

   ○ D. Neutrophils 52%

6. The nurse is providing dietary teaching to a client with emphysema. Which statement made by the client indicates that the teaching has been effective?

   ○ A. "I will need to restrict the amount of fluids I drink each day."

   ○ B. "Smaller, more frequent meals with increased protein and fat will be best."

   ○ C. "I should supplement my meals with high-protein milkshakes."

   ○ D. "Consuming hot meals will be best since I will feel less full after eating."

7. Which one of the following clients is at greatest risk for the development of a pulmonary embolus?

   ○ A. 21-year-old male who has a fractured radius

   ○ B. 40-year-old female who had a total hysterectomy

   ○ C. 55-year-old male with type II diabetes mellitus

   ○ D. 65-year-old female with hyperthyroidism

8. When providing care for the client with a new tracheostomy, the nurse should give priority to:

   ○ A. Using aseptic technique when cleaning the tracheostomy

   ○ B. Ensuring a snug fit between the tracheostomy ties and the neck

   ○ C. Oxygenating the client with 100% oxygen before suctioning

   ○ D. Changing the disposable inner cannula every 48 hours

9. A client with sarcoidosis is to be discharged with a prescription for prednisone. Which one of the following instructions should be included in the client's discharge teaching?

   ○ A. Limit the intake of foods high in potassium.

   ○ B. Notify the physician if you have a fever or sore throat.

   ○ C. Increase the intake of foods high in sodium.

   ○ D. Take the medication at bedtime.

10. While assessing a client who sustained blunt chest trauma to the right rib cage, the nurse notes reduced breath sounds on the affected side with tracheal deviation toward the unaffected side. The nurse should prepare to assist with:

  ○ A. Endotracheal intubation

  ○ B. Chest physiotherapy

  ○ C. Venopuncture for ABGs

  ○ D. Chest tube insertion

11. Which one of the following clients is most susceptible to the development of Legionnaire's disease?

  ○ A. 21-year-old college freshman who lives in a dormitory

  ○ B. 35-year-old automobile salesman who works outside

  ○ C. 55-year-old teacher who frequently travels abroad

  ○ D. 60-year-old coal miner who has a 2 PPD smoking history

12. The nurse is caring for a client admitted with pulmonary tuberculosis. Which type of transmission-based precautions should the nurse institute for this client?

  ○ A. Droplet precautions

  ○ B. Airborne precautions

  ○ C. Contact precautions

  ○ D. Standard precautions

13. A client with a closed chest drainage system is preparing to ambulate. To promote drainage and prevent reflux, the nurse should:

  ○ A. Clamp the tubing while the client is out of bed

  ○ B. Keep the drainage system lower than the chest

  ○ C. Empty the drainage system before ambulating

  ○ D. Keep the drainage system level with the insertion site

14. Which one of the following statements made by the client indicates a need for further teaching regarding the use of a dry-powder inhaler?

  ○ A. "I will keep the inhaler stored in the refrigerator."

  ○ B. "I will keep the inhaler level with the mouthpiece end facing down."

  ○ C. "I will inhale deeply through my mouth for 2–3 seconds."

  ○ D. "I will brush my teeth after I finish using the inhaler."

15. The physician has ordered Myambutol (ethambutol) as part of a four-drug regimen for treating a client with tuberculosis. Which side effect is associated with the use of ethambutol?

   ○ A. Red discoloration of the urine

   ○ B. Deficiency of pyridoxine (B6)

   ○ C. Changes in color perception

   ○ D. Swollen, painful joints

16. The CBC of a client with emphysema reveals a red blood cell count of 8,000,000/ cu mm. Based on the client's lab results, the nurse recognizes that the client has an increased risk for:

   ○ A. Hemorrhagic stroke

   ○ B. Thrombus formation

   ○ C. Hospital-acquired pneumonia

   ○ D. Prolonged bleeding

17. The physician has prescribed Cytoxan (cyclophosphamide) for a client with pulmonary fibrosis. The nurse should tell the client to

   ○ A. Drink 10– 12 glasses of water a day while taking the medication

   ○ B. Take the medication with grapefruit juice to make it more palatable

   ○ C. Avoid the use of acetaminophen while taking the medication

   ○ D. Take the medication with meals or with a snack

18. While preparing to administer a PPD skin test, the nurse learns that the client received the BCG vaccine while she was living in a foreign country. What action should the nurse take?

   ○ A. Obtain an order for a chest x-ray

   ○ B. Administer the PPD skin test

   ○ C. Obtain a sputum specimen

   ○ D. Request an order for isoniazid

19. A client with pleural effusion has developed subcutaneous emphysema following a thoracentesis. Which finding is characteristic of subcutaneous emphysema?

   ○ A. Crackling sensation noted in the skin near the puncture site

   ○ B. Auscultation of reduced breath sounds on the affected side

   ○ C. Paradoxical movement of the chest with inhalation and exhalation

   ○ D. Chest asymmetry and distended neck veins on the opposite side

20. The nurse is planning care for a client on a ventilator. Which intervention gives the client the best sense of control over his environment?

   ○ A. Allowing visits with his family and friends

   ○ B. Keeping the call light within reach

   ○ C. Explaining procedures before they are done

   ○ D. Providing pencil and writing paper

21. A client with community-acquired pneumonia has been receiving intravenous Geopen (carbenicillin). Which finding should alert the nurse to an adverse drug reaction?

   ○ A. Burning at the infusion site

   ○ B. Diarrhea containing blood and mucus

   ○ C. Loss of appetite

   ○ D. Headache and myalgia

22. When performing endotracheal suctioning, the suction setting should be set between:

   ○ A. 20 mm Hg and 50 mm Hg

   ○ B. 70 mm Hg and100 mm Hg

   ○ C. 80 mm Hg and120 mm Hg

   ○ D. 130 mm Hg and170 mm Hg

23. Before administering an annual influenza vaccination, the nurse should question the client about past allergic reaction to:

   ○ A. Eggs

   ○ B. Milk

   ○ C. Shellfish

   ○ D. Nuts

24. Pulse oximetry has been ordered for an elderly client with chronic obstructive lung disease. The best location for probe placement is the client's:

   ○ A. Toe

   ○ B. Finger

   ○ C. Earlobe

   ○ D. Chest

25. The nurse is caring for a client with primary pulmonary hypertension who has developed cor pulmonale. Which finding is characteristic of the client with cor pulmonale?

    ○ A. Expectoration of frothy, pink sputum

    ○ B. Decreased daytime voiding

    ○ C. Edema of the legs and sacrum

    ○ D. Hacking nighttime cough

Care of the Client with Genitourinary Disorders

26. An intravenous pyelogram has been ordered for a client with recurrent urinary tract infection. The nurse should tell the client that the procedure commonly causes:

    ○ A. An increased urgency to void

    ○ B. Feelings of nausea and dizziness

    ○ C. Shortness of breath and itching

    ○ D. A metallic taste in the mouth

27. The nurse is obtaining the intake assessment and history of an adolescent admitted for treatment of acute glomerulonephritis. Which finding during the assessment is significant to the client's diagnosis?

    ○ A. Immunization with varicella zoster immune globulin

    ○ B. Experiencing a bout of cystitis within the past month

    ○ C. Having an untreated sore throat and fever one week ago

    ○ D. Sitting next to a classmate diagnosed with mononucleosis

28. Which action(s) should the nurse anticipate if the client undergoing hemodialysis experiences signs of disequilibrium syndrome?

    ○ A. Continuing the dialysis since this is an expected event

    ○ B. Slowing the dialysis rate and administering an infusion of normal saline

    ○ C. Obtaining baseline arterial blood gases

    ○ D. Slowing the dialysis rate and administering an infusion of mannitol

29. A client with chronic renal failure has chosen to use peritoneal dialysis. When teaching the client about peritoneal dialysis, the nurse should tell the client to notify the physician immediately if:

    ○ A. Discomfort occurs during the inflow of the dialysate.

    ○ B. The abdomen feels tender and dialysate returns become cloudy.

    ○ C. There is a feeling of intra-abdominal pressure during dwell time.

    ○ D. The dialysate outflow is slowed but is light amber in appearance.

30. The physician has ordered Neoral (cyclosporine) for a client following a renal transplant. A suitable beverage to increase the palatability of the medication is:

    ○ A. Apple juice

    ○ B. Chocolate milk

    ○ C. Grape juice

    ○ D. Carbonated soda

31. A client with renal calculi has just returned from having extracorporeal shockwave lithotripsy to the right kidney. Following the procedure the nurse should give priority to:

    ○ A. Straining the urine for the presence of stone fragments

    ○ B. Applying anesthetic cream over the client's right flank

    ○ C. Monitoring the vital signs and color of urine output

    ○ D. Administering medication for pain

32. The nurse is caring for a client who has recently undergone an emergency nephrostomy for treatment of hydronephrosis. When caring for the client with a nephrostomy tube, the nurse should:

    ○ A. Irrigate the tube every 4 hours with sterile water

    ○ B. Measure hourly output from the tube for 24 hours

    ○ C. Clamp the tube for 15 minutes every 2 hours

    ○ D. Report any red-tinged urine coming from the tube

33. The physician has ordered Ditropan (oxybutnin) 5 mg. bid for a client with urinary incontinence. Which instruction is important to include in the teaching of the client taking oxybutnin?

    ○ A. Schedule routine eye examinations.

    ○ B. Avoid the use of over-the-counter antacids.

    ○ C. Discontinue the drug if drowsiness occurs.

    ○ D. Take the medication with ascorbic acid.

34. When assessing a client two hours after a transurethral prostatectomy, the nurse notes that the catheter drainage is dark red in color and contains a few clots. Which actions should the nurse take at this time?

○ A. Document the finding and continue to observe the drainage

○ B. Notify the physician immediately and increase the rate of IV fluids

○ C. Place traction on the catheter and tape it to the client's upper thigh

○ D. Request a CBC to determine the amount of blood loss

35. While undergoing hemodialysis, a client tells the nurse that being dependent on a machine is" no way to live". The nurse can best support the client by:

○ A. Providing him with literature on advances in renal transplantation

○ B. Explaining that most clients on hemodialysis get depressed

○ C. Referring him to the nearest chapter of the American Kidney Foundation

○ D. Allowing him to discuss his feelings about being on hemodialysis

36. Kayexalate (sodium polystyrene sulfonate) has been ordered for a client with acute renal failure. To facilitate action of the medication, it is given with:

○ A. Calcium gluconate

○ B. Sorbitol

○ C. Sodium bicarbonate

○ D. Albumin

37. Dietary interventions for the client with nephrotic syndrome are dependent on the glomerular filtration rate (GFR). Which type of diet is most appropriate for the nephrotic client with a glomerular filtration rate of 120 ml/ min?

○ A. Increased protein

○ B. Decreased carbohydrate

○ C. Decreased protein

○ D. Increased carbohydrate

38. The nurse is caring for a client with a history of polycystic kidney disease. Which complaint by the client should alert the nurse to a possible complication of PKD?

○ A. Abdominal tenderness

○ B. Severe headache

○ C. Dull flank pain

○ D. Nighttime voiding

39. The physician has ordered Gantrisin (sulfasoxazole) for a client with cystitis. The client takes several herbal supplements. Which herbal supplement increases the likelihood of the client developing photosensitivity if used concurrently with sulfa-soxazole?

   ○ A. Ginko biloba

   ○ B. Hypericum

   ○ C. Saw palmetto

   ○ D. Flax

40. A client undergoing hemodialyis is to have a diet containing complete proteins. Which one of the following dietary items does not provide a source of complete protein?

   ○ A. Cheese

   ○ B. Poultry

   ○ C. Soy

   ○ D. Legumes

41. The nurse is caring for a client who has undergone a biopsy of the right kidney. Following the biopsy, the nurse can help reduce the risk of bleeding by:

   ○ A. Applying a pressure dressing and placing the client in supine position

   ○ B. Applying an occlusive dressing and placing the client in left Sims position

   ○ C. Applying a moisture proof barrier and placing the client in right Sims position

   ○ D. Applying a pressure dressing and placing the client in prone position

42. The doctor has ordered acid-ash diet for a client with recurrent calcium stones. Which beverage is suitable for the client?

   ○ A. Milk

   ○ B. Prune juice

   ○ C. Tea

   ○ D. Cocoa

43. Intravenous Vancocin (vancomycin) has been ordered for a client with peritonitis. To prevent "*red man*" syndrome, the nurse should:

   ○ A. Protect the medication from light

   ○ B. Flush the line with saline before infusing

   ○ C. Administer the medication slowly

   ○ D. Administer acetaminophen before the infusion

44. A home health nurse has been teaching a client how to carry out peritoneal dialysis. Which observation indicates that the client needs further teaching?

○ A. The client changes position to facilitate the outflow of dialysate.

○ B. The client uses a back-and-forth motion to clean around the catheter.

○ C. The client uses a heating pad to warm the dialysate solution.

○ D. The client applies sterile gloves before instilling the dialysate.

45. A client with recurrent bladder cancer is being treated with intravesical administration of BCG suspension. Prior to the administration of the medication, the nurse should:

○ A. Offer the client additional fluids

○ B. Administer pain medication

○ C. Ask the client to empty her bladder

○ D. Request an x-ray of the bladder

46. A client with chronic glomerulonephritis has been receiving injections of Procrit (epoetin alpha) for the past two months. Which lab finding indicates that the medication is having its intended effect?

○ A. Red cell count of 4,700,000

○ B. White cell count of 8,000

○ C. Neutrophil count of 5,500

○ D. Platelet count of 250,000

47. The nurse in a urology clinic has been asked about herbal supplements that are used in treating the symptoms associated with benign prostatic hypertrophy. Which herbal supplement is used in the treatment of mild to moderate BPH?

○ A. Garlic

○ B. Black cohosh

○ C. Hawthorne

○ D. Saw palmetto

48. The nurse is caring for a client scheduled for a renal transplant. Which information in the client's history raises concern about the possibility of hyperacute graft rejection?

○ A. Allergic reaction to sulfa drugs

○ B. Extensive foreign travel

○ C. Multiple blood transfusions

○ D. Gastric bypass surgery

49. Two days after the creation of an ileal conduit, the nurse notes that the client's urine appears cloudy but is not malodorous. The nurse should:

    ○ A. Document the finding

    ○ B. Obtain an order for an antibiotic

    ○ C. Irrigate the stoma with saline

    ○ D. Limit the protein intake

50. A renal transplant recipient has been maintained on immunosuppressive therapy for three years with Sandimmune (cyclosporine). A primary concern for this client is the development of:

    ○ A. Hepatotoxicity

    ○ B. Hirsutism

    ○ C. Bone loss

    ○ D. Nephrotoxicity

Care of the Client with Integumentary Disorders

51. Eucerin cream has been prescribed for a client with dry skin and pruritis. When moisturizing creams are ordered, they should be applied:

    ○ A. After completely drying the skin

    ○ B. Using vigorous rubbing motions

    ○ C. After bathing while the skin is moist

    ○ D. Using short, back-and-forth strokes

52. The physician has prescribed Folex (methotrexate) for a client with psoriatic arthritis. Which lab finding indicates that the medication is having an adverse effect?

    ○ A. Platelet count of 200,000

    ○ B. Serum ALT of 60 U/L

    ○ C. Neutrophil count of 200 /cu mm

    ○ D. Serum creatinine of 0.6 mg/dL

53. The nurse is formulating a plan of care for a client with thermal burns of the face, neck, and upper chest. Which nursing diagnosis should receive priority?

    ○ A. Fluid volume deficit R/T increased capillary permeability

    ○ B. Risk for impaired gas exchange R/T upper airway swelling

    ○ C. Pain R/T tissue and nerve injury

    ○ D. Anxiety R/T emotional changes caused by burn injury

54. A client with exfoliative psoriasis is being treated with ultraviolet radiation therapy three times a week. Which finding indicates overexposure?

○ A. Lightening of the skin

○ B. Crusting of lesions

○ C. Appearance of blisters

○ D. Desquamation

55. Which snack is suitable for a client recovering from full thickness burns?

○ A. Orange slices

○ B. Raisin oatmeal cookies

○ C. Ice cream

○ D. Stewed prunes

56. A client has partial thickness burns to the legs, anterior trunk, and arms. Using the Rule of Nines, the nurse determines that the client's TBSA is:

○ A. 90%

○ B. 72%

○ C. 54%

○ D. 36%

57. The nurse is changing the dressings of a client with full thickness burns who is being treated with Sulfamylon (mafenide acetate). When changing the dressing, the nurse's actions should include:

○ A. Administering pain medication

○ B. Soaking the site with normal saline

○ C. Checking the white cell count

○ D. Covering the site with a dermal substitute

58. The nurse is teaching a client with HSV regarding transmission of the virus. The nurse should tell the client that she can transmit the virus to others for:

○ A. 3– 5 days

○ B. 10– 14 days

○ C. 4– 6 weeks

○ D. 8– 10 weeks

59. The physician has ordered hyperbaric oxygen therapy for a client with a stage III pressure ulcer. Before instituting the therapy, the nurse should:

   ○ A. Ask the client whether she has a pacemaker

   ○ B. Encourage additional fluid intake

   ○ C. Assess the client's ability to lie still for an hour

   ○ D. Ask the client if she has claustrophobia

60. The nurse is teaching a client about immunization with Zostavax (zoster vaccine live solution). Which statement indicates that the client needs further teaching about the medication?

   ○ A. "I can transmit chickenpox to those who have not had the illness."

   ○ B. "I can't take Zostavax if I am taking immunosuppressive drugs."

   ○ C. "The immunization is used to treat shingles and the pain it causes."

   ○ D. "Reactions to other vaccines may prevent me from taking Zostavax."

61. The client's chart notes the presence of a Stage II pressure ulcer over the sacrum. What is the typical appearance of a Stage II pressure ulcer?

   ○ A. Blistered areas with shallow crater

   ○ B. Reddened areas with intact skin

   ○ C. Areas of eschar-covered crater

   ○ D. Necrotic areas with undermining

62. Gastrointestinal complications associated with major burn injury include paralytic ileus and Curling's ulcers. Which medication is commonly prescribed to prevent Curling's ulcers?

   ○ A. Maalox (aluminum magnesium hydroxide)

   ○ B. Cytotec (misoprostol)

   ○ C. PhosLo (calcium acetate)

   ○ D. Zantac (rantidine hydrochloride)

63. While caring for a client with full thickness burns, the nurse finds that the client's urine output has become burgundy in color. The appearance of burgundy- or brown-colored urinary output is due to:

   ○ A. Metabolic acidosis secondary to burn injury

   ○ B. Underlying muscle damage and RBC destruction

   ○ C. Resuscitative efforts using plasma expanders

   ○ D. Dehydration from rapid fluid shifts

64. A client with a history of HSV II tells the nurse that he uses topical Zovirax (acyclovir) daily to prevent recurrent outbreaks. The nurse should give priority to:

○ A. Determining when the client last had an outbreak of herpes

○ B. Asking how many times a day the medication is applied

○ C. Explaining that the medication will not prevent recurrent outbreaks

○ D. Determining if the client is also taking oral antiviral medication

65. Which behavior increases the risk of infestation with pediculosis capitis in children?

○ A. Not washing hands after toileting

○ B. Sharing combs, brushes, and hats

○ C. Playing in sandboxes and dirt

○ D. Not drying the feet after swimming

66. The physician has prescribed Tazorac (tazaretene) topical for a female client with psoriasis vulgaris. Which lab study should be done before beginning therapy with Tazorac?

○ A. Complete blood count

○ B. Renal profile

○ C. Liver panel

○ D. Pregnancy test

67. Three days after receiving major burns, a client's lab reveals a hematocrit of 30%. The nurse recognizes changes in normal hematocrit levels after burns are related to:

○ A. Hemodilution from fluid resuscitation

○ B. Lack of sufficient oral intake

○ C. Hemoconcentration from fluid loss

○ D. Decreased erythropoietin production

Care of the Client with Sensory Disorders

68. The nurse is teaching a client with glaucoma about activities that can increase intraocular pressure. The nurse should tell the client to avoid activities that require

○ A. Bending from the waist

○ B. Moving the head side-to-side

○ C. Reaching overhead

○ D. Prolonged sitting

69. The physician has prescribed Ocupress (carteolol HCl) ophthalmic drops for an elderly client with primary open-angle glaucoma. To decrease the systemic effects associated with the medication's use, the nurse should:

    ◯ A. Administer the client's oral medication first

    ◯ B. Ask the client to sit upright as the drops are instilled

    ◯ C. Place gentle pressure over the puncta after instilling the drops

    ◯ D. Wash the lids and lashes before instilling new drops

70. Four hours after an extracapsular extraction to remove a cataract, the client complains of seeing flashes of light in the operative eye. Although the client denies pain, the nurse should notify the doctor immediately because the client's complaints suggest the possibility of:

    ◯ A. Ocular hemorrhage

    ◯ B. Uveitis

    ◯ C. Corneal dystrophy

    ◯ D. Retinal tear

71. A home health nurse is making a visit to a client with low vision. Which finding indicates that the client needs further teaching regarding environmental safety?

    ◯ A. Throw rugs have been eliminated from the household.

    ◯ B. Non-breakable dishes are used for meals.

    ◯ C. Hook-and-loop Velcro strips locate light switches.

    ◯ D. Furnishings include a lounge chair and footstool.

72. The nurse is administering medication to four clients. Which client should be most closely monitored for signs of ototoxicity?

    ◯ A. A 20-year-old receiving Cipro (ciprofloxacin) for a urinary tract infection

    ◯ B. A 75-year-old receiving Amikin (amikacin sulfate) for pneumonia

    ◯ C. A 46-year-old receiving Ancef (cefazolin sodium) for sinusitis

    ◯ D. A 6-month-old receiving Augmentin (amoxicillin/clavulanate potassium) for acute otitis media

73. The nurse is formulating a plan of care for a client with an acute episode of Ménière's disease. The nurse should give priority to:

    ○ A. Relieving pain

    ○ B. Offering extra fluids

    ○ C. Reducing noise level

    ○ D. Preventing injury

74. An adolescent client developed hyphema of the left eye after being hit with a baseball. Which position is recommended for the client?

    ○ A. Semi-Fowler's

    ○ B. Supine

    ○ C. Prone

    ○ D. Low Trendelenburg

75. A client with reduced vision is being trained to ambulate with a cane. Which observation indicates that the client is using the cane properly?

    ○ A. The client holds the cane in the non-dominant hand.

    ○ B. The client taps the cane on the floor with each step.

    ○ C. The client moves the cane back and forth above the floor.

    ○ D. The client keeps the cane still as he ambulates.

76. Some improvement in age-related hearing loss might be obtained by supplementing the client's diet with:

    ○ A. Retinol

    ○ B. Folacin

    ○ C. Ascorbic acid

    ○ D. Alpha-tocopherol

77. Ear irrigations have been ordered for a client with impacted cerumen. When performing the irrigation, the nurse should:

    ○ A. Use cool water to reduce edema in the ear canal

    ○ B. Direct the irrigating solution onto the cerumen

    ○ C. Direct the irrigating solution to one side of the ear canal

    ○ D. Irrigate the ear continuously until the cerumen is removed

78. The nurse is caring for a client scheduled for a tympanoplasty. Preop orders usually include irrigations of the ear with a solution of sterile water and:

     ⭘ A. Vinegar

     ⭘ B. Baking soda

     ⭘ C. Hydrogen peroxide

     ⭘ D. Glycerin

79. Which intervention is most helpful in decreasing the social isolation of a hearing-impaired client who resides in a nursing home?

     ⭘ A. Obtaining a closed-captioned television for her room

     ⭘ B. Providing activities that do not require her to hear accurately

     ⭘ C. Seating the client with a friend in a quiet corner of the dining room

     ⭘ D. Providing the client books on tape with a headset

80. The nurse is doing an intake history on a 30-year-old with bilateral progressive hearing loss. Which finding in the client's history is most significant?

     ⭘ A. The client had recurrent acute otitis media as an infant.

     ⭘ B. The client has a history of osteogenesis imperfect.

     ⭘ C. The client had a tonsillectomy as an adult.

     ⭘ D. The client had otitis externa from swimming.

81. Fundoscopic examination of the client's eyes reveals the presence of "copper wiring" and "arteriovenous nicking". These ocular changes are associated with:

     ⭘ A. Peripheral vascular disease

     ⭘ B. Sjogren's syndrome

     ⭘ C. Uncontrolled hypertension

     ⭘ D. Fluctuations in blood glucose

82. The physician has prescribed maintenance therapy with Pred-Forte (prednisolone) 1% ophthalmic drops for a client with chronic iritis. The use of the medication predisposes the client to the development of:

     ⭘ A. Acute glaucoma

     ⭘ B. Retinal detachment

     ⭘ C. Corneal dystrophy

     ⭘ D. Cataract formation

83. A client states that although her eye does not hurt, she is concerned because she has developed a "curtain-like" loss of vision in one eye. The nurse recognizes that the client's loss of vision describes:

   ○ A. Ocular melanoma

   ○ B. Retinitis pigmentosa

   ○ C. Retinal detachment

   ○ D. Macular degeneration

84. A client scheduled for a Type II tympanoplasty asks the nurse to explain what is involved in the surgery. The nurse should tell the client that:

   ○ A. A small surgical incision will be made in the eardrum to relieve pressure.

   ○ B. The three bones in the middle ear will be replaced with muscle or fascia.

   ○ C. The bones in the middle ear will be reconnected to the tympanic membrane to restore hearing.

   ○ D. A polyethylene tube will be surgically placed through the tympanic membrane.

85. Examination with the Snellen chart reveals that a client has a visual acuity of 20/60. The nurse recognizes that the client:

   ○ A. Has better than 20/20 vision

   ○ B. Is by definition legally blind

   ○ C. Has a correctible astigmatism

   ○ D. Sees at 20 feet what others see at 60 feet

86. The nurse is reinforcing concepts of topographic mapping for a client with low vision. Which of the following is an example of topographic mapping?

   ○ A. Using the hands of a clock to help the client located foods on his meal tray

   ○ B. Labeling items used by the client with large tags printed in Braille

   ○ C. Surrounding light switches with brightly colored paper

   ○ D. Offering assistance by providing a sensor-tipped cane

87. The nurse is assessing a client following a stapedectomy. The nurse would suspect damage to the 7th cranial nerve following the procedure if the client complains of:

   ○ A. Changes in taste

   ○ B. Changes in hearing

   ○ C. Changes in voice quality

   ○ D. Changes in oral sensation

Care of the Pediatric Client

88. The physician has ordered chelation therapy for a child admitted with an iron overdose. Which drug should the nurse prepare to administer?

   ○ A. Chemet (succimer)

   ○ B. Desferal (deferoxamine mesylate)

   ○ C. Calcium EDTA (edetate calcium disodium)

   ○ D. British anti-Lewisite (dimercaprol)

89. An 18-month-old with cystic fibrosis has been started on Viokase (pancrelipase). Which finding indicates that the medication is having the desired effect?

   ○ A. Decrease in the number of respiratory infections

   ○ B. Increase in the number of stools

   ○ C. Increase in weight of four pounds in one month

   ○ D. Decrease in the amount mucus production

90. The nurse is preparing a 5-year-old for a tonsillectomy. The nurse should recognize that the preschool-aged child:

   ○ A. Is not interested in explanations about his body

   ○ B. Fears the loss of his body's integrity

   ○ C. Is able to conceptualize his feelings

   ○ D. Pays little attention to environmental changes

91. Children with valvular heart disease are at risk for thrombus formation. The nurse can help reduce the risk by:

   ○ A. Performing passive range-of-motion exercises

   ○ B. Applying elastic wraps to the lower extremities

   ○ C. Providing age-appropriate sedentary activities

   ○ D. Offering additional fluids to prevent dehydration

92. The nurse is taking the history of a 4-year-old admitted with Reye's syndrome. Which one of the following illnesses, if treated with salicylates, has been associated with the development of Reye's syndrome?

    ○ A. Lyme's disease

    ○ B. Hepatitis A

    ○ C. Pertussis

    ○ D. Influenza

93. Parents of a child with varicella ask the nurse how soon their child can return to daycare. The nurse should tell the parents that the child is contagious:

    ○ A. Only when the papular rash is present

    ○ B. When vesicles begin to appear

    ○ C. Until all the lesions have crusted

    ○ D. For one week after the lesions have faded

94. While assessing a newborn, the nurse notes very faint femoral pulses. Further assessment reveals that brachial pulses are strong and bounding. The nurse should notify the physician because these findings raise the possibility of which congenital heart defect?

    ○ A. Ventricular septal defect

    ○ B. Coarctation of the aorta

    ○ C. Truncus arteriosus

    ○ D. Patent ductus arteriosus

95. The nurse is providing postop teaching to the mother of a 15-month-old male scheduled for a cleft palate repair. The nurse should tell the mother that her son:

    ○ A. Must be kept in a supine or side lying position

    ○ B. Will have elbow restraints applied to both his arms

    ○ C. Will need to be cradled instead of being carried upright

    ○ D. May have a bottle or pacifier to make him more comfortable

96. Which toy encourages the development of Piaget's concept of object permanence by the infant?

    ○ A. Jack-in-the-box

    ○ B. Shape sorter

    ○ C. Stuffed bear

    ○ D. Stackable blocks

97. The nurse is caring for a 4-year-old receiving treatment for acute lymphocytic leukemia. Which finding should be reported to the physician immediately?

     ○ A. A temp of 100° F

     ○ B. Presence of perianal ulcerations

     ○ C. Complaints of joint pain

     ○ D. Respiratory rate of 26

98. The nurse is providing dietary teaching to the mother of a child with gluten-induced enteropathy. Which statement indicates that the mother understands the nurse's teaching?

     ○ A. "Many sources of protein will need to be restricted to prevent brain damage."

     ○ B. "Most breads, cereals, and crackers will have to be eliminated from his diet."

     ○ C. "Sources of lactose, including milk, can lead to the development of cataracts."

     ○ D. "Restricting fat in the diet will help to prevent problems with malabsorption."

99. The physician has ordered a 1% hydrocortisone topical preparation for an infant with diaper dermatitis. Which instruction should be given to the mother?

     ○ A. Apply the medication in a thick layer

     ○ B. Remove old applications with cold water

     ○ C. Apply the medication only at bedtime

     ○ D. Use cloth diapers instead of disposable diapers

100. A 2-year-old is admitted with suspected intussusception. Classic signs of intussusception include:

     ○ A. Abdominal distention, dark urine, and growth failure

     ○ B. Projectile vomiting and palpable, olive-shaped abdominal mass

     ○ C. Pain, sausage-shaped abdominal mass and currant jelly stools

     ○ D. Abdominal distention, general malnutrition, and bulky stools

101. Which observation is an example of the expected development in early childhood?

     ○ A. A 2-year-old consistently complies with parental requests.

     ○ B. A 3-year-old gives his favorite toy to another child.

     ○ C. A 4-year-old no longer has imaginary friends.

     ○ D. A 5-year-old enjoys doing simple household chores.

102. The nurse is assessing an infant with Down syndrome. The nurse can expect the infant to have:

    ○ A. micrognathia and a short, upturned nose

    ○ B. Pointed ears and pointed nose

    ○ C. Hypotonia and transpalmar creases

    ○ D. Macrosomia and ruddy skin color

103. A newborn is admitted to the nursery with gastroschisis. The nurse should:

    ○ A. Place the newborn prone in low Trendelenburg position

    ○ B. Place the newborn in a side-lying position with his head elevated

    ○ C. Place the newborn in an isolette and leave the area open

    ○ D. Apply a warm, sterile saline gauze and plastic wrap to the area

104. The physician has prescribed Tofranil (imipramine) for a child with enuresis. What information should the nurse include in parental teaching about the medication?

    ○ A. The medication should be taken on an empty stomach.

    ○ B. The medication takes the place of other forms of treatment.

    ○ C. The medication could take 2–3 weeks to be effective.

    ○ D. The medication can be stopped at any time.

105. Which menu item is least appropriate for an 8-year-old with nephrotic syndrome?

    ○ A. Roast beef and potatoes

    ○ B. Hotdog with ketchup

    ○ C. Baked turkey breast

    ○ D. Hamburger with cheese

106. The nurse is caring for a newborn with a right-sided diaphragmatic hernia. The nurse should give priority to:

    ○ A. Placing the newborn on the affected side with the head elevated

    ○ B. Placing the newborn in supine position with the head lowered

    ○ C. Placing the newborn on the unaffected side with the head lowered

    ○ D. Placing the newborn in supine position with the head elevated

107. Which intervention is important when caring for an infant with osteogenesis imperfecta?

   ○ A. Raising the infant by its hips when changing diapers

   ○ B. Providing additional fluids throughout the day

   ○ C. Observing for the presence of blue-tinged sclera

   ○ D. Using moisturizing baby wash for bathing

108. An infant with respiratory synctial virus is being treated with Virazole (ribavirin) aerosol. The nurse is aware that:

   ○ A. The drug is only effective if given within 24 hours of developing symptoms.

   ○ B. The drug is administered for 30 minutes, three times a day.

   ○ C. The medication can be used with other aerosol therapies.

   ○ D. Goggles and a respirator should be worn when administering the medication.

109. A toddler has been admitted with Kawasaki's disease. The nurse knows that the treatment of Kawasaki's disease includes the use of:

   ○ A. Acetaminophen

   ○ B. Penicillin

   ○ C. Cortisone

   ○ D. Aspirin

110. The nurse is observing a group of preschool children. Which statement is true regarding the language skills of a 3-year-old?

   ○ A. The 3-year-old knows simple songs.

   ○ B. The 3-year-old talks incessantly although no one is listening.

   ○ C. The 3-year-old knows the days of the week.

   ○ D. The 3-year-old tells exaggerated stories.

111. The physician has prescribed Pulmozyme (dornase alpha) for a child with cystic fibrosis. Which finding indicates the effectiveness of the medication?

   ○ A. The stools are brown and formed.

   ○ B. There is a notable decline in sweating.

   ○ C. Clotting time has improved.

   ○ D. Pulmonary secretions are thinner.

112. A 1-year-old is admitted with diarrhea and moderate dehydration. Which of the following is used to treat the infant with moderate dehydration?

    ❍ A. Initiation of intravenous fluids

    ❍ B. Oral rehydration therapy with electrolyte solution

    ❍ C. Replacing regular formula with soy-based formula

    ❍ D. Offering clear liquids every 3–4 hours

113. The nurse is caring for a child with meningitis caused by *Neisseria meningitidis*. Which transmission-based precaution should be used?

    ❍ A. Standard precautions

    ❍ B. Airborne precautions

    ❍ C. Droplet precautions

    ❍ D. Contact precautions

114. The nurse is obtaining a history of a child admitted with influenza and suspected Reye's syndrome. Which medication might have contributed to the development of Reye's syndrome?

    ❍ A. Compazine (prochlorperazine)

    ❍ B. Lomotil (diphenoxylate and atropine)

    ❍ C. Pepto Bismol (bismuth subsalicylate)

    ❍ D. Dramamine (dimenhydrinate)

115. An adolescent with hemophilia wants to participate in one of the school's sports programs. If all the following sports are available, which sport is best suited to the adolescent with hemophilia?

    ❍ A. Wrestling

    ❍ B. Swimming

    ❍ C. Soccer

    ❍ D. Basketball

116. The nurse is caring for a 6-year-old admitted with suspected child abuse. The nurse can expect the abused child to:

    ❍ A. Display little or no emotion during painful procedures

    ❍ B. Readily accept different caregivers

    ❍ C. Socialize with other children in the playroom

    ❍ D. Demonstrate behaviors that reflect the development of industry

117. Which cultural group has been found to have an increased incidence of hip dislocation in newborn infants?

    ◯ A. Mexican

    ◯ B. African-American

    ◯ C. Asian

    ◯ D. Eskimo

118. The nurse is teaching the mother of a child with Hirschsprung's disease regarding the use of enemas. The nurse should tell the mother to use enemas prepared with:

    ◯ A. Tap water

    ◯ B. Normal saline

    ◯ C. Phosphate

    ◯ D. Concentrated salt

119. A newborn is admitted to the nursery with a maternal history of polyhydramnios. The nurse should carefully assess the newborn for:

    ◯ A. Changes in reactivity

    ◯ B. Difficulty with feeding

    ◯ C. Decreased urine output

    ◯ D. Increased bleeding time

120. The physician has ordered Pediazole (sulfisoxazole) for an infant with acute otitis media. Which instruction should be given to the mother?

    ◯ A. All the medication should be given even though the infant appears well.

    ◯ B. The medication will taste better if it is given in the infant's formula.

    ◯ C. The medication can be stopped once the fever is no longer present.

    ◯ D. The medication will be absorbed better if it is given with fruit juice.

121. The nurse is caring for a child with von Willebrand disease. Which complaint is most often associated with von Willebrand disease?

    ◯ A. Slow healing

    ◯ B. Ear aches

    ◯ C. Stiff joints

    ◯ D. Nosebleeds

122. Which playground activity is best suited to the needs of an 8-year-old with cystic fibrosis?

   ○ A. Skateboarding

   ○ B. Monkey bars

   ○ C. Kickball

   ○ D. Soccer

123. The mother of a toddler asks the nurse when she should begin toilet training her child. The nurse knows that most children are ready for toilet training between the ages of:

   ○ A. 12 and 15 months

   ○ B. 15 and 18 months

   ○ C. 18 and 24 months

   ○ D. 30 and 36 months

124. The physician has ordered Mucomyst (acetylcysteine) for a child following an overdose of acetaminophen. What is the proper method for administering the medication?

   ○ A. By aerosol inhalation

   ○ B. Orally after mixing in water

   ○ C. Intramuscular injection

   ○ D. Orally after mixing in juice

125. The nurse is assessing a child with subacute bacterial endocarditis. Which finding suggests the development of thrombi?

   ○ A. Koplik's spots on buccal mucosa

   ○ B. Splinter hemorrhages

   ○ C. Subcutaneous nodules

   ○ D. Strawberry tongue

Care of the Client with Psychiatric Disorders

126. The physician has prescribed sertraline (Zoloft) 50 mg daily for a client with depression. Which finding should be reported to the physician?

   ○ A. The client takes Tagamet (cimetidine) for acid reflux.

   ○ B. The client takes the medication with meals.

   ○ C. The client takes the medication once a day at bedtime.

   ○ D. The client takes Aleve (naproxen) for arthritis.

127. A client with mania is unable to complete her meals because of her elevated level of activity. To help her maintain sufficient nourishment, the nurse should:

   ○ A. Allow her access to the kitchen between meals

   ○ B. Serve high-calorie foods she can carry with her

   ○ C. Provide small, attractively arranged trays

   ○ D. Allow her to order meals outside the hospital

128. A 20-year-old college student is admitted to the eating disorder unit with a diagnosis of bulimia nervosa. Which of the following statements describes the client with bulimia nervosa?

   ○ A. The client negates the feminine role.

   ○ B. The client maintains rigid control.

   ○ C. The client is extroverted and seeks intimacy.

   ○ D. The client is often described as the "model child."

129. A client admitted to the chemical dependency unit states, "My wife is making too much of this. I don't drink any more than the next guy." What defense mechanism is the client using?

   ○ A. Rationalization

   ○ B. Projection

   ○ C. Dissociation

   ○ D. Splitting

130. The nurse is formulating a plan of care for a client with paranoid schizophrenia. Which activity is best for increasing the client's social interaction?

    ◯ A. Participating in a game of volleyball

    ◯ B. Selecting a book from the hospital library

    ◯ C. Participating in a card game

    ◯ D. Watching TV in the unit dayroom

131. A client who developed a conversion reaction after his fiancée cancelled the wedding has developed symptoms of paralysis in his lower extremities. When caring for the client the nurse should:

    ◯ A. Ask the doctor for a physical therapy consult

    ◯ B. Avoid focusing on the client's physical complaints

    ◯ C. Explain that there is no reason for the paralysis

    ◯ D. Encourage the client to walk using a walker

132. Lithobid (lithium carbonate) has been ordered for a client with mania. Which lab finding increases the possibility of lithium toxicity?

    ◯ A. Calcium level of 8.2 mg/dL

    ◯ B. Potassium level of 4.0 mEq/L

    ◯ C. Magnesium level of 1.8 mg/dL

    ◯ D. Sodium level of 120 mEq/L

133. Which of the following is an example of a delusion?

    ◯ A. The client claims that the FBI is following him.

    ◯ B. The client states that voices are telling him to kill his family.

    ◯ C. The client sees a rope and thinks it is a snake.

    ◯ D. The client states that bugs are crawling under his skin.

134. A client with depression is scheduled for electroconvulsive therapy (ECT). Which statement is true regarding the use of ECT?

    ◯ A. Anticonvulsant medication is given prior to ECT to prevent a tonic-clonic seizure.

    ◯ B. Failure to remember events occurring near the time of ECT is common.

    ◯ C. Most clients suffer long-term memory loss after receiving ECT.

    ◯ D. The procedure is brief, so no medication is given prior to ECT.

135. During morning assessments, the nurse finds that a client who has been taking Thorazine (chlorpromazine) has developed muscle rigidity of the face and neck. The nurse should give priority to:

    ○ A. Applying an O_2 saturation monitor to detect hypoxia

    ○ B. Administering prescribed anti-Parkinson medication

    ○ C. Applying a heating pad to the neck and shoulders

    ○ D. Notifying the physician of the client's symptoms

136. Which one of the following clients is most likely to be the victim of elder abuse?

    ○ A. A 78-year-old female with Alzheimer's dementia

    ○ B. A 70-year-old male with Parkinson's disease

    ○ C. A 64-year-old female with diabetes mellitus

    ○ D. A 68-year-old male with cancer of the prostate

137. A client with bulimia nervosa reports that she binges at least two times a week. The nurse recognizes that binge episodes are associated with:

    ○ A. A sense of euphoria

    ○ B. Substantial weight gain

    ○ C. Feelings of self-loathing

    ○ D. Severe weight loss

138. While conducting morning goal-setting activities, the nurse is interrupted by a client hospitalized with severe anxiety. The client states, "I'm so upset. I feel like I am falling apart and nobody seems to care." Which one of the following responses is most therapeutic?

    ○ A. "Why do you think that nobody cares about you?"

    ○ B. "You are not really falling apart; you are just having an anxiety attack."

    ○ C. "You can help regain control of your feelings by thinking of a positive goal for yourself."

    ○ D. "I can see that you are upset. I will talk with you as soon as I finish with goal setting."

139. Which action is best for the nurse to take when he observes a client engaging in ritualistic behavior?

     ○ A. Ask the client to carry out his rituals in his room

     ○ B. Help the client explore the dynamics of his behavior

     ○ C. Allow the client to complete his ritualistic behavior

     ○ D. Administer sedative medication when the client begins his use of rituals

140. The nurse is caring for a client who is receiving Zyprexia (olanzapine). Which observation requires immediate nursing intervention?

     ○ A. The client asks for additional water.

     ○ B. The client's morning temperature was 104° F.

     ○ C. The client complains of dizziness when he stands.

     ○ D. The client's skin is red after sitting in the sunlight.

141. Which symptom distinguishes post-traumatic stress disorder from other anxiety disorders?

     ○ A. Lack of interest in social relationships

     ○ B. Avoidance of stressful situations

     ○ C. Depression and sleep disturbances

     ○ D. Reliving the event in dreams and flashbacks

142. A behavioral program for weight gain is started for a client with anorexia nervosa. Which nursing intervention is most specific to goal attainment?

     ○ A. Providing emotional support and active listening

     ○ B. Giving positive rewards for weight gain

     ○ C. Assisting with identification of maladaptive behaviors

     ○ D. Initiating tube feedings with high-calorie supplements

143. The diagnosis of attention deficit hyperactive disorder (ADHD) and childhood depression are both characterized by signs of hyperactivity, impulsivity, and distractibility. The feature that helps to differentiate the two is:

     ○ A. The age of onset

     ○ B. The sex of the child

     ○ C. Academic difficulties

     ○ D. Rejection by peers

144. The nurse is preparing to discharge a client with a prescription for Parnate (tranyl-cypromine). Which statement indicates that the client needs further teaching?

    ○ A. "I need to avoid eating bananas."

    ○ B. "I should be less depressed in two to three weeks."

    ○ C. "I can continue to use St. John's wort."

    ○ D. "I need to avoid some sandwich meats."

145. An adolescent client diagnosed with depression has been taking Zoloft (sertraline). Which finding should be reported immediately?

    ○ A. The client has gained five pounds in the past two months.

    ○ B. The client recently gave away his favorite collection of baseball cards.

    ○ C. The client sleeps 8–10 hours per day.

    ○ D. The client has asked when he can return to school.

146. A client with bipolar disorder has a morning Depakote (divalproex) level of 75mcg/mL. The nurse should:

    ○ A. Request additional medication

    ○ B. Take no action; the level is therapeutic

    ○ C. Request another level in the evening

    ○ D. Omit the next dose of medication

147. The nurse is formulating a nursing care plan for a client with paranoid schizo-phrenia who is experiencing command hallucinations. Which nursing diagnosis should receive priority?

    ○ A. Altered thought process related to impaired judgment

    ○ B. Social isolation related to mistrust of others

    ○ C. Ineffective individual coping related to inadequate support systems

    ○ D. Risk for violence directed at self or others related to disturbed thinking

148. The physician has changed a client's medication order from a monoamine oxidase inhibitor to a selective serotonin reuptake inhibitor. To decrease the risk of sero-tonin syndrome, the time period between the two medications should be:

    ○ A. 5 days

    ○ B. 10 days

    ○ C. 14 days

    ○ D. 21 days

149. A client who has been taking Thorazine (chlorpromazine) has developed akathisia. Which behavior should the nurse expect the client to exhibit?

    ○ A. Pacing and generalized restlessness

    ○ B. Involuntary repetition of words spoken by others

    ○ C. Use of words by sound rather than meaning

    ○ D. Slow, rhythmic movements of muscle groups

Emergency Care

150. The nurse is caring for a client admitted to the emergency department after taking an overdose of morphine sulfate (MS Contin). The nurse should give priority to monitoring the client for:

    ○ A. Decreased urinary output

    ○ B. Nausea and vomiting

    ○ C. Respiratory depression

    ○ D. Increased blood pressure

151. A 13-month-old is transferred to the emergency department from the physician's office with a tentative diagnosis of "shaken baby" syndrome. Which finding is associated with the diagnosis?

    ○ A. Fractures of the humerus

    ○ B. Retinal hemorrhage

    ○ C. Periorbital bruising

    ○ D. Sacral ecchymosis

152. The nurse is checking the lab results of a client admitted with abdominal trauma. Which lab results indicate damage to the liver?

    ○ A. Increased WBC

    ○ B. Increased amylase, lipase

    ○ C. Increased ALT, AST

    ○ D. Decreased hematocrit

153. Which of the following interventions is contraindicated when treating a client with severe hypothermia?

   ○ A. Placing the client in a horizontal position

   ○ B. Administering warm intravenous fluids

   ○ C. Administering heated oxygen

   ○ D. Applying external heating devices

154. The nurse is rendering first aid at the scene of a motor vehicle accident. Before moving a client with an apparent fracture of lower leg, the nurse should give priority to:

   ○ A. Removing the client's shoes to see whether there is trauma to the foot

   ○ B. Immobilizing the extremity by splinting the joint above and below the fracture

   ○ C. Keeping the client in a semi-sitting position

   ○ D. Checking the neurovascular status of the area distal to the fracture

155. Which nursing diagnosis should receive priority when the nurse is caring for a client with esophageal varices?

   ○ A. Imbalanced nutrition: less than body requirements related to difficulty swallowing

   ○ B. High risk for injury related to altered clotting mechanisms

   ○ C. Fluid volume deficit related to reduced oral intake

   ○ D. Activity intolerance related to fatigue

156. Using the coding system for triaging mass casualties, which of the following clients would receive treatment first?

   ○ A. The client with a black tag

   ○ B. The client with a green tag

   ○ C. The client with a yellow tag

   ○ D. The client with a red tag

157. A client with diabetes is admitted to the emergency department with seizures and loss of consciousness. Stat lab work reveals a blood glucose level of 50 mg/dL. Emergency management of the client includes the administration of:

   ○ A. Humalog

   ○ B. Glucagon

   ○ C. Glucotrol

   ○ D. Byetta

158. The nurse is providing first aid to a client who just received a sting from a yellow jacket. Which action should the nurse take first?

  ○ A. Place the client in a flat supine position

  ○ B. Take the client to the nearest hospital

  ○ C. Administer diphenhydramine (Benadryl)

  ○ D. Remove the stinger and apply ice to the area

159. The nurse is caring for an adolescent who has been shot with a paint gun. The nurse should expect:

  ○ A. Tissue damage only along the path of wound

  ○ B. Limited penetration or dissipation of injury

  ○ C. Complete recovery since the wound is not severe

  ○ D. High-pressure injury characterized by a minor puncture wound

160. A client is admitted to the emergency with a temperature of 96.8° F. Which one of the following findings is characteristic of mild hypothermia?

  ○ A. Absence of shivering

  ○ B. Diminished fine motor skills

  ○ C. Dilated pupils

  ○ D. Atrial fibrillation

161. The nurse is caring for a client with organophosphate poisoning that has produced symptoms of cholinergic crisis. The nurse should prepare to administer:

  ○ A. Adrenalin

  ○ B. Vasopressin

  ○ C. Atropine

  ○ D. Lithium

162. Which one of the following clients is at greatest risk for developing heat exhaustion?

  ○ A. A 17-year-old skateboarder

  ○ B. A 30-year-old electrical worker

  ○ C. A 45-year-old landscaper

  ○ D. A 65-year-old farmer

163. Which one of the following clients falls into the category of emergent care?

   ○ A. A client admitted with a simple fracture of the arm

   ○ B. A client admitted with abdominal pain

   ○ C. A client admitted with chest pain, dyspnea, and diaphoresis

   ○ D. A client admitted with a cough and temp of 101° F

164. A client with a history of myasthenia gravis is admitted with signs of a myasthenic crisis. Emergency interventions for the client with a myasthenic crisis focus on:

   ○ A. Administering diphenhydramine

   ○ B. Maintaining adequate respiratory function

   ○ C. Assessing the degree of muscle weakness

   ○ D. Administering atropine sulfate

165. The nurse is assessing a client admitted to the emergency room with a diagnosis of Legionnaire's disease. Which precautions should be used when caring for the client?

   ○ A. Standard precautions because it is transmitted by blood and body fluids

   ○ B. Airborne precautions because it is transmitted by droplets from the respiratory tract

   ○ C. Contact precautions because it is transmitted by articles used by the client

   ○ D. No special precautions because there is no evidence of human-to-human transmission

166. A client is admitted with protruding abdominal organs after being stabbed. The nurse should give priority to:

   ○ A. Applying a sterile, saline-soaked dressing

   ○ B. Administering pain medication

   ○ C. Determining the type of weapon used

   ○ D. Applying oxygen at 2 liters/ min via nasal cannula

Practice Exam III

This element consists of 166 questions that are representative of what you should expect on the actual exam. This exam should help you determine how prepared you are for the real exam, and provide a good basis for what you still need to review. As you take this exam, treat it as you would the real exam: Time yourself (about one minute per question is suggested), and answer each question carefully, marking the ones you want to go back and double-check. You will find the answers and their explanations in the "Practice Exam III Answers" element of the book.

The test items have been divided by chapter content. This format makes it easy for you to review content by subject matter. After you take this exam, remember to load the CD-ROM and check out our exclusive MeasureUp test engine, which is one of the best on the market. (See Appendix F, "What's on the CD-ROM," for more information.)

Care of the Client with Musculoskeletal and Connective Tissue Disorders

1. A client with a fractured right femur begins to complain of pain and swelling in the left leg. What is the most appropriate initial nursing action?

   ○ A. Notify the healthcare provider of the client's complaints

   ○ B. Perform an assessment of the client's left leg

   ○ C. Elevate the left leg on two pillows to reduce edema

   ○ D. Administer ordered analgesic for pain relief

2. A client has been diagnosed with fibromyalgia. Which of the following exercises would the nurse recommend?

   ○ A. Swimming classes

   ○ B. Biking

   ○ C. Strength training

   ○ D. Walking

3. Which client would the nurse consider most at risk for systemic lupus erythematosus?

   ○ A. A 25-year-old Asian woman taking birth control pills

   ○ B. A 20-year-old African-American female with epilepsy

   ○ C. A 40-year-old male with a history of asthma

   ○ D. A 50-year-old Caucasian female with osteopenia

4. The nurse on the orthopedic floor receives report from the previous shift. Which client should the nurse go see first?

   ○ A. A client 2 hours post total hip replacement who is complaining of pain

   ○ B. A client admitted during the previous shift with a fractured tibia

   ○ C. A client with a fractured femur and a reported rash on the chest

   ○ D. A newly admitted client with a fiberglass cast applied 1 hour ago

5. The nurse is performing discharge teaching on a client with gout. Which meal choice by the client would indicate a need for further teaching?

   ○ A. Grilled pork chop with baked potato

   ○ B. Sliced turkey breast with a green salad

   ○ C. Steamed vegetables with rice pilaf

   ○ D. Vegetable omelet with hash browns

6. The nurse is performing discharge teaching to the parents of a 5-year-old who has recently had a cast applied to the left tibia. Which statement indicates a lack of understanding of proper cast care?

   ○ A. "I can elevate the extremity on a pillow to reduce swelling."

   ○ B. "If it starts to itch, I can use a blow dryer on cool to blow into the cast."

   ○ C. "I should check the toes for movement, color, and awareness of my touch."

   ○ D. "If it starts to swell and hurt, I should apply a heating pad to the cast."

7. The nurse in an industrial plant receives a client with a traumatic amputation of a finger. Which action is most appropriate to preserve the amputated finger?

   ○ A. Place the finger in a plastic bag and place the bag on cold normal saline

   ○ B. Wrap the finger in Vaseline-saturated gauze 4 X 4 sponges

   ○ C. Put the digit on crushed ice in a plastic-covered container

   ○ D. Place the digit on a saline-soaked 4 X 4 and put it in a plastic bag

8. A client postoperative fractured hip repair is prescribed 1 unit of packed cells. Which would the nurse implement in preparation for the transfusion?

   ○ A. Start an IV with a 22-gauge needle

   ○ B. Obtain signature of consent for the transfusion

   ○ C. Hang D5W to transfuse with the blood

   ○ D. Figure the rate of transfusion for 500 mL in 6 hours

9. A client with gout has been treated with prednisone with no improvement. The healthcare provider prescribes colchicine. Which teaching plan will the nurse include for a client prescribed colchicine?

   ○ A. Teach the client to take the pill after meals

   ○ B. Restrict fluids to one liter a day

   ○ C. Avoid the use of aspirin when taking this drug

   ○ D. Explain how the drug prevents uric acid formation

10. The nurse is assessing a client admitted with lupus. Which assessment outcome should receive priority status?

   ○ A. Temperature of 36.7° centigrade

   ○ B. Swelling and pain of the ankle joints

   ○ C. Pericardial friction rub on chest auscultation

   ○ D. Rash on the face and nose area

11. The nurse is caring for a client with a fractured leg. Which assessment result requires immediate attention?

  ○ A. A dime-sized area of blood on the cast

  ○ B. Complaints of itching from within the cast

  ○ C. Pale, cool toes with decreased movement

  ○ D. Pain in the leg relieved by pain medication

12. A client with a fractured leg exhibits the following: pink, frothy sputum; dyspnea; and diaphoresis. Which nursing action is most appropriate?

  ○ A. Lower the head of the bed

  ○ B. Check the client's vital signs

  ○ C. Notify the physician

  ○ D. Turn the client to the left side

13. The nurse on the orthopedic unit is observing a student perform an assessment of a client with a fractured tibia who is in skin traction. Which assessment result indicates adequate function of the peroneal nerve?

  ○ A. Plantar flexion of the foot

  ○ B. Inversion of the foot

  ○ C. Dorsiflexion of the foot

  ○ D. Strong posterior tibial pulses

14. The nurse is caring for a group of clients on an orthopedic unit. Which client should the nurse give priority status?

  ○ A. A client with a fractured hip and 400 mL of blood in the wound suction device within a two-hour period

  ○ B. A client with a cast and slight edema to the toes who is complaining of pain

  ○ C. A client with an external fixator on the right arm with serous drainage from the pin sites

  ○ D. A client with a fractured right femur who has a temperature of 101.5° Fahrenheit

15. The nurse is reviewing the postoperative vital signs of a client after a right total knee replacement. The results are as follows:

Time	Vital Signs
1400	BP-120/60, P-70, R-16 T-97 F
1430	BP-100/50, P-96, R-18
1500	BP-90/48, P-120, R-22 T-97 F

What should the nurse do?

○ A. Notify the physician of the client's vital signs

○ B. Start oxygen at 6 L/min by nasal cannula

○ C. Continue to monitor the client and document

○ D. Administer ordered pain medication of meperidine (Demerol)

16. A 65-year-old male client is scheduled for joint replacement surgery in the a.m. The nurse assesses the laboratory values. Which finding is most important for the nurse to report to the orthopedic surgeon?

○ A. WBC 16,000/mm

○ B. Potassium 3.8 mEq/L

○ C. Sodium 133 mEq/L

○ D. Hgb 12.6 g/dL

17. The nurse is observing a student performing pin care on a client with skeletal traction. Which action by the student nurse requires intervention?

○ A. Using a sterile cotton applicator to cleanse the pin site

○ B. Administering ordered analgesic prior to the procedure

○ C. Instructing the client that weights will be removed prior to pin care being performed

○ D. Pouring hydrogen peroxide into a sterile container for cleansing per hospital protocol

18. Which diet selection should the nurse encourage the client with osteoporosis to initiate for the highest calcium amount?

○ A. Shrimp

○ B. Oysters

○ C. Sardines

○ D. Halibut

19. A client with rheumatoid arthritis is prescribed infliximab (Remicade). Which assessment finding warrants notification to the healthcare provider prior to starting the infusion?

   ○ A. Nasal drainage, temperature of 101.8° F, frontal headache

   ○ B. BP 136/70, joint pain complaints, wrist nodules

   ○ C. Elevated C reactive protein levels on laboratory results

   ○ D. Documented allergies to cephalosporin antibiotics

20. The nurse is caring for a client with rheumatoid arthritis who has been prescribed the drug etanercept (Enbrel). A senior student is preparing to administer the drug. Which observation by the nurse merits intervention?

   ○ A. The student adds liquid to the powder and mixes it by swirling.

   ○ B. The student obtains a 100 mL bag of normal saline to prepare for IV infusion of the drug.

   ○ C. The student tells the instructor she will administer the drug in the client's thigh.

   ○ D. The student makes the statement that the drug should not be shaken.

21. A client with systematic lupus erythematosus has been admitted to a medical unit. Emergency room diagnostic exams are assessed by the nurse. Which exam result indicates the most negative affect?

   ○ A. Heart ejection fraction of 25%

   ○ B. HCT of 38%

   ○ C. Scant proteinuria

   ○ D. Resolving pleural effusion

22. A client is eight hours post right hip replacement. Which should be excluded from the teaching plan?

   ○ A. Keep legs adducted

   ○ B. Do not flex hip more than 90°

   ○ C. Place pillows between the legs when in bed

   ○ D. May use a raised toilet seat

23. The nurse in a clinic is preparing a teaching plan for clients with fibromyalgia who have been prescribed pregabalin (Lyrica). Which would the nurse include in the teaching plan?

   ○ A. The drug can cause extreme hyperactivity.

   ○ B. Constipation can require discontinuation of the drug.

   ○ C. Take as directed and do not stop or skip doses.

   ○ D. Expect weight loss while taking the drug.

24. The nurse is serving as preceptor to a new nurse on the orthopedic unit. Which action by the new nurse requires intervention?

   ○ A. Asking the client with a cast on the leg to move the toes

   ○ B. Checking and documenting the weight amounts on the client's with traction

   ○ C. Assisting with a bed change on a client with traction by removing and replacing the linen top to bottom

   ○ D. Helping a family member get a client with a prosthetic hip into a straight chair

25. The client is admitted to the orthopedic unit diagnosed with a fractured pelvis. Which assessment requires immediate attention?

   ○ A. BP 120/70, heart rate 100

   ○ B. Pain in the suprapubic area, pelvic deformities

   ○ C. Dysuria, anorexia

   ○ D. Boardlike abdomen, temperature 101.4° Fahrenheit

26. A client with gout has been instructed to avoid high-purine foods. Which diet selection indicates to the nurse that further instruction is needed?

   ○ A. Broccoli

   ○ B. Kale

   ○ C. Spinach

   ○ D. Cabbage

27. The nurse is preparing assignments and tasks for the shifts. Which task should be assigned to the nurse's assistant?

   ○ A. Teaching home care to the client with a fractured hip

   ○ B. Counseling a client with a below-the-knee amputation

   ○ C. Feeding a client with a fractured arm

   ○ D. Monitoring a client with newly diagnosed osteomyelitis

28. A client is five hours postoperative total knee replacement. Which assessment result requires the nurse to notify the physician?

   ○ A. Temperature of 100° Fahrenheit

   ○ B. Hematocrit of 24%

   ○ C. Dime-size serous drainage on dressing

   ○ D. 300 mL Foley output in five hours

29. The nurse is caring for a client immediate postoperative hip repair. Assessment reveals a blood saturated pressure dressing, BP 98/50, heart rate 120. Which should the nurse implement first?

   ○ A. Remove the dressing and assess the wound

   ○ B. Reinforce the dressing with 4 X 4s

   ○ C. Notify the surgeon

   ○ D. Reassess the vital signs

30. The nurse has received a client from the emergency room with a fractured right hip. Which task should the nurse assign to the unlicensed assistive personnel (UAP)?

   ○ A. Obtain personal care items and place at bedside

   ○ B. Assess the skin for any signs of breakdown

   ○ C. Administer meperidine (Demerol) 75 mg IM

   ○ D. Apply Buck's traction 5# to right leg

Care of the Client with Gastrointestinal Disorders

31. The nurse is examining the chart of a client with a suspected duodenal ulcer. Which diagnostic exam best indicates a confirmation of the diagnosis?

   ○ A. Elevated WBC count on laboratory results

   ○ B. Gastric irritation indicated on upper GI

   ○ C. A positive H. Pylori on endoscopic biopsy

   ○ D. A positive hemocult stool specimen result

32. A client presents to the emergency room with a sudden onset of abdominal pain. Nursing assessment reveals a bluish discoloration around the umbilicus. What initial action is most appropriate?

   ○ A. Notify the physician

   ○ B. Assess the distal pulses

   ○ C. Elevate the head of the bed

   ○ D. Perform a complete head-to-toe assessment

33. The nurse is preparing dietary teaching for a client with gastroesophageal reflux disease (GERD). Which food would be allowed for a client with a GERD diagnosis?

   ○ A. Oranges

   ○ B. Tomatoes

   ○ C. Bananas

   ○ D. Lemons

34. A client with a suspected duodenal ulcer is tested for H. pylori. Which medication, noted in the client history, could produce a false negative result in the test?

   ○ A. Ampicillin

   ○ B. Digoxin (Lanoxin)

   ○ C. Propoxyphene napsylate (Darvocet)

   ○ D. Ibuprofen (Advil)

35. The nurse has established a goal to limit the amount of blood loss in a client with peptic ulcer disease (PUD) and GI bleeding. Which plan best correlates with the accomplishment of the goal?

   ○ A. Administer blood products as appropriate

   ○ B. Administer appropriate medications (antacids, histamine blockers)

   ○ C. Monitor for fluid loss (bleeding, vomiting, and so on)

   ○ D. Monitor vital signs, as appropriate

36. A client is admitted with acute diverticulitis. Which order would the nurse question?

   ○ A. Initiate preparation for a colonoscopy in the AM

   ○ B. Start IV of normal saline at 100 mL per hour

   ○ C. Meperidine (Demerol) 100 mg IM every 4 hours as needed for pain

   ○ D. Cefazolin (Ancef) 1 gm Intravenous piggyback (IVPB) every 8 hours

37. The nurse is caring for a client in the emergency room who is admitted after an MVA. Which assessment finding best indicates a possible spleen rupture?

   ○ A. Diminished bowel sounds

   ○ B. BP 120/70, pulse rate 100, respiration 18

   ○ C. Ballance's sign

   ○ D. Wheezing on chest auscultation

38. A client with a hiatal hernia has undergone a laparoscopic Nissen fundoplication (LNF). Which should the nurse teach the client to avoid if gas bloat syndrome occurs?

   ○ A. Carbonated beverages

   ○ B. Beef or red meats

   ○ C. Antireflux medications

   ○ D. Exercise

39. The nurse is assigning task for a client with acute pancreatitis. Which would be assigned to the nurse's assistant?

   ○ A. Monitor NG drainage for color, character, and amount

   ○ B. Provide oral hygiene every two hours

   ○ C. Administer pain medication as appropriate

   ○ D. Teach the client to assume the fetal position to help decrease her pain

40. The RN on a surgical unit is serving as preceptor to a newly licensed RN. Which action by the new RN requires preceptor intervention?

   ○ A. Preparation for manipulation of an NG tube on a client 2 hours postoperative bariatric surgery

   ○ B. Instructing a client to splint the surgical site during coughing and deep breathing exercises

   ○ C. Assisting a two-day postoperative client to ambulate in the hallway

   ○ D. Beginning an abdominal assessment by auscultating bowel sounds

41. A client with hepatitis C has just arrived after a liver biopsy. Which action does the nurse perform first?

   ○ A. Assess preprocedure coagulation studies

   ○ B. Provide pressure at the site by positioning the client on the right side

   ○ C. Do a detailed chest and abdominal assessment

   ○ D. Perform discharge teaching of allowed activities

42. The nurse receives information on the following four clients. Which should the nurse see first?

    ○ A. A client diagnosed with peptic ulcer disease who is complaining of epigastric pain

    ○ B. A postoperative cholecystectomy with a temperature of 101.2° F

    ○ C. A client admitted on the previous shift who vomits 275 mL of bright red emesis

    ○ D. A client with GI bleeding who reports a new episode of melena

43. A client is admitted with a possible appendicitis. The nurse recognizes that which diagnostic test result will best assist the physician to confirm the diagnosis?

    ○ A. WBC count of 16,000/mm with a shift to the left

    ○ B. Ultrasound shows enlarged appendix

    ○ C. A normal CT scan

    ○ D. An elevated sedimentation rate

44. The nurse is assisting the physician with a paracentesis procedure on a client with cirrhosis of the liver. Which would the nurse do first?

    ○ A. Instruct the client to empty the bladder

    ○ B. Obtain consent

    ○ C. Place the client in a sitting position

    ○ D. Identify the client

45. The nurse is caring for a client with cholecystitis. Which clinical manifestation would the nurse expect the client to exhibit?

    ○ A. Hiccups

    ○ B. Dysphagia

    ○ C. Fever

    ○ D. Bradycardia

46. A client has an esophageal balloon in place for bleeding esophageal varices. Which item is most essential to keep at the bedside?

    ○ A. Scissors

    ○ B. Emesis basin

    ○ C. Mouth swabs

    ○ D. Tracheostomy

47. The nurse is caring for a client following conventional surgery for a sliding hiatal hernia. Which intervention would be the priority?

   ○ A. Monitoring for abdominal pain and medicating appropriately

   ○ B. Teaching and ensuring incentive spirometry use as appropriate

   ○ C. Assessing the dressing site for bleeding

   ○ D. Monitoring the NG tube for patency and repositioning the tube if it is not working properly

48. A client has completed a gastroscopy procedure. The gastroenterologist informs the client of a GERD diagnosis. Which teaching is included in the discharge plans?

   ○ A. Eat a bedtime snack nightly

   ○ B. Recumbent position after meals

   ○ C. Limit or eliminate alcohol and tobacco

   ○ D. Eat regular meals three times a day

49. A client with an ulcer had a Billroth II procedure performed 2 days ago. Which intervention would the nurse employ to prevent dumping syndrome?

   ○ A. Elevate the head of the bed 45° after meals

   ○ B. Encourage at least 500 mL of fluids with meals

   ○ C. Provide a low-carbohydrate, high-protein, and high-fat diet

   ○ D. Serve high-volume meal contents

50. The nurse is working on a medical surgical unit. A client with pancreatitis is complaining of dyspnea. Which is the appropriate initial nursing action?

   ○ A. Instruct the client to breathe in through the mouth and out via the nostrils

   ○ B. Elevate the head of the bed

   ○ C. Notify the healthcare provider

   ○ D. Assess the vital signs and record them in the client's medical record

51. A client arrives from the emergency room with a diagnosis of end-stage liver disease. Which task can the nurse delegate to the UAP?

   ○ A. Evaluate the degree of ascites

   ○ B. Obtain dressing supplies for the room from a provided list

   ○ C. Assess the skin for signs of breakdown

   ○ D. Administer the requested antacid per physician's order

52. A client with cirrhosis of the liver returns from banding procedure for esophageal varices. Which complaint warrants the nurse's greatest concern?

   ○ A. Chest pain

   ○ B. Eructation

   ○ C. Drowsiness

   ○ D. Nausea

53. A client has just returned from a gastroscopy procedure where he received midazolam HCl (Versed) and propofol (Diprivan). Upon the client's arrival in the recovery area, the nurse notes an O_2 saturation of 75, BP 88/40, and heart rate of 110. The nurse's initial primary focus should be measures to:

   ○ A. Increase the O_2 saturation levels

   ○ B. Increase the blood pressure

   ○ C. Prevent aspiration

   ○ D. Decrease the heart rate

54. A client has cirrhosis of the liver with a new prescription for lactulose (Cephalac). Which indicates the drug is having the desired effect?

   ○ A. The client sleeping more

   ○ B. An increase in bowel movements

   ○ C. Hypoactive bowel sounds

   ○ D. A generalized increase in bruising

55. A client with hepatitis C returned from a liver biopsy with complaints of shortness of breath. Which assessment should the nurse make first?

   ○ A. Auscultation of breath sounds

   ○ B. Liver biopsy site assessment

   ○ C. Mental status

   ○ D. Motor strength and movement of extremities

56. The nurse is preparing to make a home visit to a client with hepatitis A. Which plan would the nurse include to prevent the family from contracting hepatitis A from the client?

   ○ A. Emphasize the need for good hand-washing and personal hygiene

   ○ B. Inform the family to place the client in isolation

   ○ C. Avoid contact with the client's blood

   ○ D. Tell the client to wear a mask at all times

57. The nurse is caring for a client after a gastrectomy. Which of the following vitamins will the nurse expect to be administered throughout the client's lifespan?

   ⭕ A. Phytonadione (vitamin K)

   ⭕ B. Cyanocobalamin (vitamin B 12)

   ⭕ C. Thiamine (vitamin B1)

   ⭕ D. Ascorbic acid (Ascorba-cap)

58. A client is admitted with pancreatitis on the previous shift. The nurse evaluates the laboratory results. Which result requires immediate intervention by the nurse?

   ⭕ A. Potassium 4.0 mEq/L

   ⭕ B. Sodium 120 mEq/L

   ⭕ C. Serum amylase 300 units/dL

   ⭕ D. White blood cell 12,000 cells/mm

59. The nurse is caring for a client three days after a bowel resection and colostomy due to acute diverticulitis. Which postoperative assessment finding necessitates physician notification?

   ⭕ A. Stoma protrudes above the abdominal wall

   ⭕ B. Absence of feces in the colostomy bag

   ⭕ C. Gray dusky color of the stoma

   ⭕ D. Mucus oozing from the stoma opening

60. A client with cirrhosis and bleeding esophageal varices has a Sengstaken-Blakemore tube in place. Which nurse's assessment finding is the priority?

   ⭕ A. Wheezing on chest auscultation.

   ⭕ B. Blood pressure elevation by 20 mm/Hg.

   ⭕ C. Blood noted in the lumen that is in the stomach.

   ⭕ D. The label is missing from one of the three tube lumens.

Care of the Client with Neoplastic Disorders

61. Which of the following nursing interventions would not be implemented in the client with a cervical radiation implant in place?

○ A. Use of a lead apron for shielding when providing client care

○ B. Limit visitors to 30 minutes per day

○ C. Implement strict isolation protocol

○ D. Insert a Foley catheter

62. What task on the oncology unit can be assigned to assistive personnel by the RN?

○ A. Assist a postsurgical client to the bathroom

○ B. Monitor vital signs during blood transfusion

○ C. Irrigate a Foley catheter

○ D. Perform a dressing change

63. An oncology surgical client's pain is being controlled with patient control analgesia (PCA) Morphine Sulfate 30mg/30mL concentration. The healthcare provider has ordered a maximum dose of 20mg/4hours, patient control of 2mL/dose, and lock out of 12 minutes. The client has pushed the device eight times in 4 hours. How many milligrams did the client receive?

○ A. 20 mg

○ B. 16 mg

○ C. 10 mg

○ D. 4 mg

64. The oncology client has ordered two units of blood to be infused. What is the nurse's highest priority?

○ A. Obtain vital signs prior to transfusion

○ B. Use an infusion pump for accuracy

○ C. Infuse the blood slowly for the first 10–15 minutes

○ D. Determine proper type and cross-match it

65. A client with colon cancer is being discharged with a new colostomy. Which response by the client indicates a need for further discharge instructions by the nurse?

   ○ A. "I can eat anything I want as long as I chew the food properly."

   ○ B. "I should change my appliance only when it becomes loose and nonadhering."

   ○ C. "I should drink at least eight glasses of fluid per day."

   ○ D. "I should irrigate my colostomy every day."

66. Which client task is most appropriately delegated to the licensed practical nurse (LPN) on the oncology unit?

   ○ A. Sterile wound care

   ○ B. Administer blood product

   ○ C. Access a vascular access device

   ○ D. Perform discharge teaching

67. Which of the following actions by a cancer client indicates a need for further teaching by the nurse?

   ○ A. Brushing teeth with a soft bristle toothbrush

   ○ B. Lubricating lips with petroleum jelly

   ○ C. Avoiding hard or spicy foods

   ○ D. Rinsing with an alcohol-based mouthwash

68. A client returns to the room post–total laryngectomy and is having difficulty breathing. Secretions are noted in the tracheostomy tube. What is the nurse's first action?

   ○ A. Obtain the vital signs

   ○ B. Notify the physician

   ○ C. Suction the tube

   ○ D. Start oxygen via a tracheostomy collar

69. The nurse determines that the transcribed dose of hydromorphone (Dilaudid) on the medication record of the oncology client is not within a safe range. Which action should the nurse take first?

   ○ A. Verify the order was transcribed correctly

   ○ B. Give the dose anyway because client is terminal

   ○ C. Alter the dose to the recommended amount

   ○ D. Call the pharmacy to approve the dosage

70. In which position should the nurse place the client following a right pneumonectomy for tumor removal?

○ A. Left lateral decubitus

○ B. Right lateral decubitus

○ C. Semi-Fowler's

○ D. High Fowler's

71. Which of the following exercises in the mastectomy client is most appropriate as initial therapy during the immediate postop period?

○ A. Self-feeding and hair combing

○ B. Passive/active flexion and extension on elbow and wrist

○ C. Abduction and external rotation of right shoulder

○ D. Early ambulation and active extension on the elbow

72. A client with terminal cancer has been receiving a fentanyl patch for pain control. The client dies 24 hours after application of the patch. Which action should the nurse take?

○ A. Document the transfer of the patch to the morgue

○ B. Have another nurse witness the disposal of the patch

○ C. Remove the patch and place it with client's belongings

○ D. Remove the patch and return it to the pharmacy

73. A client with neutropenia has been admitted from the emergency department. What is the priority nursing intervention?

○ A. Thorough hand-washing before client contact

○ B. Start two or more large-bore IVs

○ C. Give pain medication as ordered

○ D. Request hypoallergenic sheets from the laundry

74. During chemotherapy administration, a nurse accidentally spills 30 mLs of a chemotherapeutic solution on the floor. What is the appropriate nursing action?

○ A. Call housekeeping

○ B. Exit the room immediately

○ C. Use the spill kit to clean up

○ D. Call infection control

75. Which of the following would it be most important for the nurse to teach a client scheduled for a laryngectomy?

    ○ A. Communication measures for the postoperative period

    ○ B. Demonstration of how to care for the stoma

    ○ C. Explanation of swallowing techniques

    ○ D. Teaching expectoration of sputum per stoma

76. A client with leukemia is neutropenic. Which of the following drugs would the nurse expect the physician to order to treat this condition?

    ○ A. Epoetin (Procrit)

    ○ B. Filgrastim (Neupogen)

    ○ C. Oprelvekin (Neumega)

    ○ D. Porfimer sodium (Photofrin)

77. The nurse recognizes which of the following population groups is at highest risk for melanoma?

    ○ A. Adults older than 35

    ○ B. Senior citizens who have had repeated exposure to the sun

    ○ C. Employees of a chemical plant

    ○ D. 22-year-olds who tan in tanning beds three times a week

78. A client receiving chemotherapy has a white blood cell count of 3500/cu mm and red blood cell count of 4.5 million/ cu mm. Which client instruction is appropriate by the nurse based on these findings?

    ○ A. Omit daily dose of steroids

    ○ B. Avoid crowds and infected persons

    ○ C. Shave with an electric razor

    ○ D. Increase red meat and protein intake

79. The nurse is suctioning a new postop laryngectomy client and notices bright red blood streaks in the sputum. Which action is appropriate?

    ○ A. Immediately stop suctioning and call the physician

    ○ B. Flush saline through the tubing and call the physician

    ○ C. Document the finding as normal

    ○ D. Prepare the client to go back to surgery

80. A post-chemotherapy client is experiencing hypokalemia and has an order for intravenous potassium chloride 10 mEq in 100 mL of normal saline. Which does the nurse select as the most appropriate means to deliver this medication?

   ○ A. The largest antecubital vein

   ○ B. The vein in the back of the dominant hand

   ○ C. The cephalic vein

   ○ D. A vascular access device

81. A chest tube with suction is placed in a client with lung cancer following a lobectomy. Which nursing observation should be reported to the physician?

   ○ A. Clots in the tubing during the first 24 hours

   ○ B. Subcutaneous emphysema on the second postoperative day

   ○ C. Decreased bubbling in the water seal

   ○ D. Bloody fluid in the drainage collection chamber in the first 24 hours

82. A client is scheduled for a bone scan to determine the presence of metastasis. Which information is most important that the nurse obtain prior to the procedure?

   ○ A. Allergies for shellfish and iodine

   ○ B. Blood, urea, and nitrogen (BUN) and creatinine (Cr)

   ○ C. A signed consent form

   ○ D. Venipuncture for intravenous access

83. Which of the following food choices would the nurse select as best for a neutropenic client?

   ○ A. Baked chicken, green beans, potatoes, and bananas

   ○ B. Garden salad, spaghetti, and garlic bread

   ○ C. Chef's salad, crackers, and apple

   ○ D. Meatloaf, green beans, mashed potatoes, and pie

84. A client is scheduled for a pancreatoduodenectomy (Whipple procedure) due to pancreatic cancer. When formulating the plan of care, what would be most important for the nurse to know?

   ○ A. Any history of alcohol or tobacco use

   ○ B. The stage and grade of the cancer

   ○ C. Any previous exposure to carcinogens

   ○ D. Survival rates for pancreatic cancer

85. A nurse is obtaining a health history from a client newly diagnosed with cervical cancer. What would be most important for the nurse to determine?

   ○ A. Sexual history

   ○ B. Support system

   ○ C. Obstetrical history

   ○ D. Elimination patterns

86. A client with advanced cancer of the bladder is scheduled for a cystectomy and ileal conduit. Preparation would include which nursing intervention?

   ○ A. Instillation of urinary antiseptics

   ○ B. Insertion of an indwelling catheter

   ○ C. Initiation of enteral feedings

   ○ D. Administration of neomycin

87. A client has a peripherally inserted central catheter (PICC) line in place for chemotherapy administration. Which nursing action will be performed first when administering the drug?

   ○ A. Ensure patency by aspirating for a blood return

   ○ B. Flush the line with normal saline

   ○ C. Administer a low-dose heparin flush per protocol

   ○ D. Infuse the chemotherapeutic agent

88. A client with lung cancer has an order for cisplatin (Platinol). Which laboratory result would cause the nurse to be concerned about administering this drug?

   ○ A. White blood cells 7000/mm

   ○ B. Platelet count 700,000

   ○ C. Serum creatinine level 3.0mg/dL

   ○ D. Total LDH 250IU/L

89. A client with esophageal cancer returns to the endoscopy recovery area after an esophogastroduodenoscopy (EGD) was performed via conscious sedation with midazolam (Versed). Assessment reveals an O_2 saturation of 85%, respirations 8, and nonresponsiveness. The nurse prepares to administer which of the following drugs?

   ○ A. Flumazenil (Romazicon)

   ○ B. Chlorpromazine (Thorazine)

   ○ C. Methylphenidate (Ritalin)

   ○ D. Epinephrine (Epifrin)

90. A client with an infectious process is receiving IV vancomycin (Vancocin). When will the nurse instruct the laboratory to draw blood for a 30-minute trough level if the Vancomycin IVPB is scheduled to be hung at 2000?

○ A. 1900

○ B. 1930

○ C. 2000

○ D. 2030

91. A client with cancer has been receiving the oprelvekin (Neumega). Which of the following laboratory results best indicates that the drug is not having the desired effect and further evaluation is necessary?

○ A. An increase in WBC to 14,000 cells/mm

○ B. A drop in hematocrit to 29%

○ C. An increase in cretinine level to 4.2 mg/dL

○ D. A drop in platelet count to 50,000 mm

92. The charge nurse is making client assignments for the oncology staff. Which nurse should not care for a client with a vaginal radiation implant?

○ A. The nurse with diabetes

○ B. The pregnant nurse

○ C. The nurse scheduled to administer chemotherapy

○ D. The nurse who has been cured of cancer

93. The oncology staff has been preparing the spouse of a terminally ill client for her death. Which of the following best indicates the nursing interventions have been effective?

○ A. Observing that the spouse controls his emotions when with the client

○ B. The spouse asks a friend to come during visiting hours

○ C. The spouse discusses plans for living as a widower

○ D. The spouse is researching for information on the client's disease

94. A person who has undergone a radical prostatectomy for advanced cancer is receiving diethylstilbestrol (DES). The nurse would expect to see which effect of this drug?

○ A. Increased facial hair

○ B. Testicular atrophy

○ C. Deepening voice

○ D. Weight loss

95. Which of the following nursing interventions should be avoided in a client with acute lymphoblastic leukemia?

   ○ A. Frequent oral care

   ○ B. Rectal temperatures

   ○ C. Assessing skin for petechiae

   ○ D. Limiting visitors with illness

96. The nurse on the cancer unit is performing assessments. Which finding would require prompt further evaluation?

   ○ A. Alopecia

   ○ B. Xerostomia

   ○ C. Anorexia

   ○ D. Hematuria

97. When turning the right-modified mastectomy client to her left side, the nurse notes a moderate amount of serosanguinous drainage on the bed sheets. Which nursing action is appropriate?

   ○ A. Remove the dressing to ascertain the origin of the bleeding

   ○ B. Milk the hemovac tubing using a continuous downward motion

   ○ C. Note vital signs, reinforce the dressing, and notify the surgeon

   ○ D. Recognize this is a frequent occurrence with this type of surgery

98. The nurse has instructed a male group on cancer detection practices. Which statement by a member suggest further instructions are needed?

   ○ A. "I should have a yearly prostate specific antigen (PSA) test beginning at age 50."

   ○ B. "Testicular exams should be done monthly."

   ○ C. "The PSA test normal is less than 4ng/mL."

   ○ D. "When I become 50, I should have a colonoscopy every 20 years."

99. A client has a radium implant in place for cervical cancer. The nurse enters the room and notes that the implant is on the floor. What is the nurse's action?

   ○ A. Don sterile gloves, pick up the implant, and take it to x-ray

   ○ B. Remove the client from the room and call the physician

   ○ C. Use long-handled forceps to pick up the implant and then place it in a lead container

   ○ D. Pick up the implant, place it into a biohazard bag, and put it in a contaminated waste container

100. The nurse is caring for a client with cancer who is exhibiting the following symptomology: back pain, lower extremity weakness, decreased motor abilities, numbness of the legs, and bladder incontinence. What is the most appropriate initial nursing action?

  ○ A. Notify the physician

  ○ B. Administer acetaminophen (Tylenol) for pain

  ○ C. Call supply to obtain incontinent pads

  ○ D. Insert a Foley catheter

101. The nurse is caring for a client with a diagnosis of metastatic breast carcinoma who is receiving tamoxifen citrate(Nolvadex) 10 mg twice a day. Which would cause the nurse the most concern?

  ○ A. Hot flashes

  ○ B. Bone pain

  ○ C. Weight loss

  ○ D. Vaginal bleeding

102. A client with acute lymphocytic leukemia is receiving asparaginase (Elspar) intravenously. Which of the following laboratory values indicates that the client is experiencing an adverse reaction to this drug?

  ○ A. WBC 5,000 mm

  ○ B. BUN 15 mg/dL

  ○ C. Platelet count 200,000 mm

  ○ D. Alkaline phosphatase 25 units/dL

103. A nurse is caring for a 65-year-old client with lung cancer who is receiving the second unit of a packed red blood cells transfusion. Assessment reveals dyspnea, tachycardia, neck vein distention, and rales on chest auscultation. The nurse expects to administer which of the following drugs?

  ○ A. Dexamethasone (Decadron)

  ○ B. Furosemide (Lasix)

  ○ C. Propranolol (Inderal)

  ○ D. Diphenhydramine (Benadryl)

104. A client with cancer has been having severe diarrhea and tested positive for clostridium difficile. Which infection-control measure should the nurse take?

   ○ A. Continue to follow standard precautions

   ○ B. Prepare to place the client on contact precautions

   ○ C. Contact environmental services to mop the floor

   ○ D. Use hand hygiene prior to client contact

105. Which of the following orders should the nurse question for chemotherapy induced nausea and vomiting?

   ○ A. Ondansetron (Zofran) 8 mg every eight hours

   ○ B. Dolasetron (Anzemet) 1.8 mg per kg

   ○ C. Prochlorperazine maleate (Compazine) 50 mg four times daily

   ○ D. Metoclopramide (Reglan) 20 mg four times daily

106. A client with Hodgkin's disease is scheduled for a cyclophosphamide (Cytoxan) infusion. Which of the following manifestations causes the nurse the most concern?

   ○ A. Blood in the urine

   ○ B. Reports of a feeling of nausea

   ○ C. White patches on the tongue

   ○ D. Client weight gain

107. The RN on the oncology unit is serving as preceptor for a senior nursing student. Which action by the student during performance of the tracheostomy care warrants intervention by the RN?

   ○ A. Suctioning the tracheostomy prior to beginning the procedure

   ○ B. Applying sterile gloves to perform the procedure

   ○ C. Removing tracheostomy ties and then applying new ones

   ○ D. Cleansing with H_2O_2 and then normal saline

108. The client with Wilms' tumor is scheduled to receive vincristine (Oncovin). Which would the nurse include in the teaching plan?

   ○ A. Report any kind of colon disturbances such as diarrhea

   ○ B. Report neurological symptoms, such as tingling or numb fingers or hands

   ○ C. Report any urinary symptoms, such as burning on urination

   ○ D. Report any pulmonary symptoms, such as a hacking cough

109. A client with stage III-B Hodgkin's disease is started on chemotherapy. What should the nurse teach the client to report immediately?

   ❍ A. A sore mouth

   ❍ B. A fever of 99° F

   ❍ C. Moderate diarrhea

   ❍ D. Transient nausea

110. The nurse is caring for a client recently diagnosed with myelocytic leukemia who refers to the diagnosis with the use of facts, figures, and statistics. Which defense mechanism is the client utilizing?

   ❍ A. Projection

   ❍ B. Sublimation

   ❍ C. Intellectualization

   ❍ D. Reaction formation

Care of the Client with Neurological Disorders

111. The nurse is caring for a client who complained of a severe headache prior to becoming unconscious. Which ordered diagnostic exam will best confirm the suspected cause of the loss of consciousness?

   ❍ A. CT scan

   ❍ B. Serum electrolytes

   ❍ C. EKG

   ❍ D. Protime

112. A client has been scheduled for a lumbar puncture. Which would the nurse include in the implementation plans?

   ❍ A. Get the consent form signed for the lumbar puncture procedure

   ❍ B. Place the client in the prone position during the procedure

   ❍ C. Instruct the client that there will be no pain or discomfort

   ❍ D. Encourage fluid intake to assure a full bladder

113. A client experiencing migraine headaches has been placed on abortive therapy. Which drug would the nurse expect the client to receive?

   ○ A. Sumatriptan succinate (Imitrex)

   ○ B. Propranolol (Inderal)

   ○ C. Nifedipine (Procardia)

   ○ D. Divalproex (Depakote)

114. A client with myasthenia gravis, who has been taking pyridostigmine (Mestinon), tells the nurse, "This medication's side effects are making me uncomfortable." The nurse would expect the client to complain of the medication causing which of the following effects?

   ○ A. Muscle cramps

   ○ B. Dry mouth

   ○ C. Decreased lacrimation

   ○ D. Hyperactivity episodes

115. A client has a head injury due to a motor vehicle accident. What would be the earliest indicator of increased intracranial pressure that the nurse would observe for?

   ○ A. Seizures

   ○ B. Ipsilateral pupils

   ○ C. Headache

   ○ D. Restlessness

116. The critical care nurse is observing a senior nursing student performing client care to a client after a craniotomy. Which action by the student would require nurse intervention?

   ○ A. The student elevates the head of the bed 30°.

   ○ B. The student instructs the client to cough forcefully.

   ○ C. The student is preparing to perform a cranial dressing change with sterile gloves.

   ○ D. When turning the client, the student keeps the head in a neutral position.

117. A nurse is caring for a client scheduled for a CT scan with contrast. Which action is most appropriate?

  ○ A. Checking the history for and asking the patient about metal or clips in or on the body

  ○ B. Keeping the patient NPO after midnight the night before the procedure

  ○ C. Assessing the client's hemoglobin and hematocrit

  ○ D. Checking the client's creatinine level

118. The nurse is caring for a client with myasthenia gravis who might have swallowing impairment. Which diet selection would require intervention by the nurse?

  ○ A. Boiled potatoes

  ○ B. Soft scrambled eggs

  ○ C. Green peas

  ○ D. Macaroni and cheese

119. The nurse is caring for a client with a spinal cord injury at the C7 level. Which would not be included in the nursing care plan?

  ○ A. Monitor neurological status every two hours

  ○ B. Assess for changes in respiratory function

  ○ C. Telling the client to turn himself every two hours

  ○ D. Administering ordered dextran IV to increase capillary blood flow

120. A client with a stroke has been diagnosed with syndrome of inappropriate antidiuretic hormone (SIADH). Which physician's prescription would the nurse question?

  ○ A. Weigh the client daily

  ○ B. Demeclocycline (Declomycin) 300 mg PO bid

  ○ C. Monitor neurological status every four hours

  ○ D. Force fluids to three to four liters/day

121. A client with a cervical spinal cord injury is experiencing a loss of motor function below the level of injury with sensation, touch, position, and vibration intact. The nurse recognizes that the client has damage in which area of the following areas?

  ○ A. Anterior cord injury

  ○ B. Posterior cord injury

  ○ C. Central cord injury

  ○ D. Brown-Sequard's paralysis

122. The nurse caring for a client with multiple sclerosis would expect which of the following medications to be included in the treatment plan?

　　❍ A. Meperidine (Demerol)

　　❍ B. Interferon, Beta 1a (Avonex)

　　❍ C. Infliximab (Remicade)

　　❍ D. Mannitol (Osmitrol)

123. The nurse is caring for a client in the ER with a spinal cord injury at T4. Assessment reveals a BP of 76/48, heart rate of 52, and no reflex activity below the T4 area. The nurse should further assess the client for which of the following complications?

　　❍ A. Neurogenic shock

　　❍ B. Autonomic dysreflexia

　　❍ C. Meningitis

　　❍ D. Increased intracranial pressure

124. The nurse is called to the room of a client experiencing a tonic-clonic seizure. Which action would the nurse perform first?

　　❍ A. Loosen restrictive clothing

　　❍ B. Turn the client to the side-lying position

　　❍ C. Ensure patency of the client's airway

　　❍ D. Document the sequence of the client's movements

125. The nurse is evaluating cerebrospinal fluid (CSF) results on a client with suspected meningitis. Which would correlate with the suspected diagnosis?

　　❍ A. Increased white blood cell count

　　❍ B. Protein level decreased

　　❍ C. Glucose normal

　　❍ D. Numerous red blood cells

126. The nurse would expect to find which information when reviewing the history of a client diagnosed with multiple sclerosis?

　　❍ A. Visual problems

　　❍ B. Increased sensitivity to pain

　　❍ C. Ascending weakness and numbness

　　❍ D. Confusion and disorientation

127. The nurse is caring for a client with a head injury. Which of the following assessment findings cause the nurse the most concern?

   ◯ A. Sluggish-to-react pupil

   ◯ B. Negative babinski reflex

   ◯ C. Bilateral decreased hand grips

   ◯ D. Decerebrate posturing

128. The nurse is caring for a client with multiple sclerosis who is experiencing diplopia. Which intervention would the nurse implement?

   ◯ A. The use of an eye patch

   ◯ B. Moving the furniture to one side of the room

   ◯ C. Instructing the client to stay in bed

   ◯ D. Administering ordered antibiotic eye ointment

129. The nurse working in the intensive care unit has received a report of decorticate posturing in a client with a head injury. Nursing assessment now reveals the bilateral extension of extremities after stimuli. What does the nurse deduce from this assessment finding?

   ◯ A. The client's ICP is lower.

   ◯ B. The client probably has brain stem dysfunction.

   ◯ C. The client should be evaluated for meningitis.

   ◯ D. This is a normal assessment finding for clients who are comatose.

130. The nurse is performing a detailed neurological assessment on a client with a suspected brain tumor. When performing the Romberg test, the client sways when the eyes are both open and closed. What does this indicate?

   ◯ A. The problem is probably in the cerebellum.

   ◯ B. It is a position sense abnormality.

   ◯ C. This is not an abnormal test result.

   ◯ D. The client has lost proprioception.

131. A client is admitted with low back pain. Which position would the nurse place the client in to provide the most comfort?

   ◯ A. Flat with the head of the bed elevated on 6" blocks

   ◯ B. Semi-Fowler's with the foot of the bed elevated

   ◯ C. Prone with a pillow under the knee

   ◯ D. Semi-Fowler's with the knee gatch raised slightly

132. A client arrives at the emergency room after being hit in the head with a baseball. Which question is most important for the nurse to ask?

   ○ A. "Do you have a headache?"

   ○ B. "Did you lose consciousness?"

   ○ C. "How often do you play baseball?"

   ○ D. "Are you upset with the person who hit you?"

133. A client with a cerebral aneurysm has been prescribed the drug nimodipine (Nimotop). What does the nurse explain as the purpose of this drug?

   ○ A. Treat spasm of the blood vessel

   ○ B. Cause bleeding at the vessel site

   ○ C. Stabilize the clot that has developed at the vessel

   ○ D. Reduce the client's blood pressure

134. The nurse in the critical care unit is caring for a client with an ICP monitor in place. Assessment reveals a consistent ICP reading of 28. Which action is appropriate?

   ○ A. Lower the head of the bed

   ○ B. Notify the physician

   ○ C. Administer an extra dose of Decadron

   ○ D. Document the finding

135. A client is in the intensive care unit following a motor vehicle accident with a sustained head injury. Intracranial pressure monitor (ICP) is in place with a reading of 32. Arterial line shows a mean arterial pressure (MAP) of 80. Which nursing action is appropriate?

   ○ A. Notify the physician that the client has a cerebral perfusion pressure (CPP) of 48

   ○ B. Document these results on the client record in the nurse's notes

   ○ C. Turn the client on her side with her knees bent upward in preparation for a lumbar puncture

   ○ D. Notify the doctor that the client has a CPP of 112

136. The physician is in route to perform a lumbar puncture on a client with encephalitis. The nurse assesses lethargy and sluggish pupil reactions. Which action is most appropriate?

    ○ A. Notify the physician of the assessment findings

    ○ B. Obtain the lumbar puncture tray from supply

    ○ C. Explain the lumbar puncture procedure to the family

    ○ D. Elevate the head of the bed to high Fowler's

137. The nurse is preparing to teach a group of clients who experience migraine headaches. Which would not be included in the teaching plans?

    ○ A. Clients who have migraines should avoid alcoholic beverages.

    ○ B. Some medication, such as birth control pills and Tagamet, can trigger an attack.

    ○ C. Stress, anger, and conflict have no effect on the headaches.

    ○ D. Eating foods made with yeast or preservatives can trigger an attack.

138. A client arrives at the ER exhibiting right-sided weakness and expressive aphasia of one hour duration. Several exams are ordered by the physician. Which exam should the nurse make sure is done first?

    ○ A. CT scan

    ○ B. CBC

    ○ C. Chest X-ray

    ○ D. Carotid Doppler study

139. A nurse is a consultant on interior construction details for a long-term care facility's Alzheimer's unit. Which environmental stimulus would the nurse recognize as being the least helpful to a client with Alzheimer's disease?

    ○ A. Muted colors

    ○ B. Quiet surroundings

    ○ C. Television

    ○ D. A waterfall

140. The nurse is working on a neurological unit. A client with a hemorrhagic stroke develops a fever of 101.8° F. Which drug is best for the nurse to administer?

    ○ A. Naproxen (Naprosyn)

    ○ B. Ibuprofen (Advil)

    ○ C. Acetaminophen (Tylenol)

    ○ D. Salicylates (Aspirin)

141. A client is admitted with Guillain-Barré syndrome. The doctor performs a lumbar puncture. What would the nurse expect the CSF to reveal?

   ○ A. Increased glucose and decreased protein

   ○ B. Increased protein and normal cell count

   ○ C. Increased red blood cells and elevated WBCs

   ○ D. Normal protein with increased WBC count

142. A client with epilepsy who had a vagal nerve stimulator (VNS) inserted two days ago calls the neurological unit complaining of hoarseness. Which is the appropriate nurse response?

   ○ A. "Hoarseness is a side effect of the procedure but generally improves over time."

   ○ B. "Come to the emergency room immediately. The VNS will have to be removed because of the hoarseness."

   ○ C. "Are you having any seizure activity with the hoarseness? This would mean another surgery is required."

   ○ D. "Gargle with warm, salty water every hour, and the hoarseness should soon go away."

143. The nurse is reviewing the orders of a client with a severe head injury due to a fall. Which order would the nurse question?

   ○ A. Prepare for insertion of an ICP monitor

   ○ B. Start D5W IV at 200 mL/hour

   ○ C. Maintain head of bed 25°–30° elevation

   ○ D. Keep the head in neutral alignment

144. The nurse is performing an admission history on a client with Guillain-Barré syndrome. Which would the nurse expect to find in the client's history?

   ○ A. Surgical procedure three months ago

   ○ B. A recent virus

   ○ C. Anticonvulsant medications

   ○ D. Recent seizure activity

145. The nurse is caring for a client with a head injury. When administering mannitol (Osmitrol), which precaution should the nurse take?

 ○ A. Obtain a filter for the IV tubing

 ○ B. Have flumazenil (Romazicon) available at the bedside

 ○ C. Hyperventilate the client before administration

 ○ D. Assess the client's WBC count

146. The nurse is caring for a 23-year-old client with a diagnosis of a thrombotic stroke. Which element in the client's history is a risk factor for strokes?

 ○ A. Seizure disorder

 ○ B. Influenza

 ○ C. Cocaine abuse

 ○ D. Childhood rheumatic fever

147. The client who experienced an ischemic stroke is halfway finished with an altepase(t-PA) infusion when he suddenly complains of an excruciating headache. What is the best nursing action?

 ○ A. Slow the transfusion of TPA and reassess in 10 minutes

 ○ B. Obtain a set of vital signs and ensure TPA IV patency

 ○ C. Stop the TPA and notify the neurologist

 ○ D. Stop the TPA and lower the head of the bed

148. A client with myasthenia gravis is receiving plasmapheresis. Which assessment finding correlates to a complication of the procedure?

 ○ A. Pulse rate of 50

 ○ B. BP of 80/42

 ○ C. Potassium of 5.4 mEq/L

 ○ D. INR of 3.0

149. A client is transferred from the ER to the neurological unit with a diagnosis of ischemic stroke. The nurse is preparing to begin a heparin infusion. Which piece of equipment is essential?

 ○ A. 18-gauge IV catheter

 ○ B. Bag of normal saline

 ○ C. IV regulation device

 ○ D. Extension tubing

150. A client with cancer metastatic to the brain is scheduled for an MRI. The spouse states, "I don't know that she will be able to be still for the procedure." Which medication would the nurse expect to be ordered prior to the procedure?

   ❍ A. Diphenhydramine (Benadryl)

   ❍ B. Lorazepam (Ativan)

   ❍ C. Ciprofloxacin (Cipro)

   ❍ D. Propofol (Diprivan)

Care of the Client with Hematological Disorders

151. The nurse is caring for a child newly diagnosed with hemophilia. Which would the nurse omit when writing a discharge plan?

   ❍ A. The child needs to wear a medic-alert bracelet.

   ❍ B. Avoid drugs containing aspirin and NSAIDs.

   ❍ C. Apply heat if bleeding in the joint occurs.

   ❍ D. Rectal temperatures should not be done.

152. The nurse is assigning staff for clients with hematological disorders. Which staff member would best be assigned to perform primary care to the client with thalassemia major?

   ❍ A. Registered nurse

   ❍ B. Licensed practical nurse

   ❍ C. Nurse's assistant

   ❍ D. Nursing student

153. A client with iron deficiency anemia has been prescribed an oral iron preparation. Which beverage is best to take with this medication?

   ❍ A. Milk

   ❍ B. Orange juice

   ❍ C. Water

   ❍ D. iced tea

154. A client presents to the clinic exhibiting symptoms of pernicious anemia. Which diagnostic test would the nurse expect the physician to order that would most likely confirm the diagnosis?

○ A. Urine analysis

○ B. White blood cell count

○ C. Prothrombin time test

○ D. Schilling test

155. A client is admitted with polycythemia vera. Which would the nurse include in the plan of care for this client?

○ A. Assessing the client for signs of hypokalemia

○ B. Preparing for administration of a blood transfusion

○ C. Monitoring the client for stroke symptoms

○ D. Restricting fluids to prevent excess fluid volume

156. A client with vitamin deficiencies is admitted to the acute care setting due to signs of dehydration. The nurse's assessment of laboratory values reveals a potassium of 2.9 mEq/L. Which dietary selection would be best for this client?

○ A. Banana

○ B. Apricot

○ C. Spinach

○ D. Artichoke

157. The nurse is caring for a client admitted with bleeding tendencies. The physician suspects hemophilia. Which laboratory value supports the diagnosis?

○ A. Prolonged aPTT

○ B. Increased protime

○ C. Abnormal fibrinogen level

○ D. Increased platelet count

158. A child is admitted in sickle cell crisis. Assessment includes a low HCT, reduced BP, and symptoms of shock. The nurse deduces that the child is in which type of crisis?

○ A. Vaso-occlusive

○ B. Sequestration

○ C. Hypoxemia

○ D. Septic

159. A client has been diagnosed with folic acid deficiency. The nurse's discharge teaching will focus on foods high in folic acid. Which of the following foods has the highest folic acid level?

   ○ A. Citrus fruits

   ○ B. Raisins

   ○ C. Brewer's yeast

   ○ D. Eggs

160. A 25-year-old female client with sickle cell disease has been prescribed the drug hydroxurea (Droxia). Which statement by the client indicates a need for clarification by the nurse?

   ○ A. "This drug works by getting me more fetal hemoglobin."

   ○ B. "I will have to obtain regular laboratory test to check my blood levels."

   ○ C. "I am thinking about getting pregnant within the next three months."

   ○ D. "I should notify the doctor if I have any signs of infection or abnormal bleeding."

161. The nurse would teach clients with iron deficiency anemia to add foods high in iron to their diets. Which of the following foods would be included?

   ○ A. Nuts

   ○ B. Egg whites

   ○ C. Carrots

   ○ D. Oranges

162. The nurse is performing a physical assessment on a 20-year-old African-American client with hemolytic anemia. Which area would be the best location for the nurse to assess skin color?

   ○ A. Sclera of the eyes

   ○ B. Soles of the feet

   ○ C. Palms of the hands

   ○ D. Roof of the mouth

163. A client with iron deficiency anemia has been noncompliant with oral medications. The nurse is preparing to administer Imferon. Which technique will the nurse utilize to administer this drug?

  ○ A. Selecting the deltoid muscle

  ○ B. Inserting the needle subcutaneously

  ○ C. Massaging the site after injection

  ○ D. Adding 0.25 mL of air to the syringe

164. A 20-year-old college student who has just finished a tennis tournament is admitted to the medical unit in sickle cell crisis. Which prescription should the nurse perform first?

  ○ A. Administer ketorolac (Toradol) 15 mg for pain

  ○ B. Start IV D51/2NS at 200 mL/hr

  ○ C. Obtain a routine laboratory test

  ○ D. Apply a heating pad to painful joints as needed

165. A client has been receiving a blood transfusion for 5 minutes. The client begins to have chest and low back pain. Which action should the nurse take first?

  ○ A. Stop the blood

  ○ B. Turn on the IV normal saline infusion

  ○ C. Take the client's vital signs

  ○ D. Notify the physician of assessment findings

166. A client has iron deficiency anemia and an order for iron to be administered IV push. Which nursing intervention is most important to safely administer the drug?

  ○ A. Assessing the client's hemoglobin level

  ○ B. Ensuring that the client has a systolic BP of >120

  ○ C. Finding out the date of the client's last bowel movement

  ○ D. Administering a small test dose prior to the full dose

Practice Exam IV
Management and Alternative
Item Exam Questions

This test consists of 102 questions that ask you to manage a number of clients and to delegate nursing care to other members of the health care team. We have also included questions in the alternative format that ask you to respond in a manner other than the typical multiple choice question. For example, you might be asked to place answers in sequence, to fill in the blank, or to check all that apply. Like the other practice exams, this section will help you determine your preparation for the NCLEX RN licensure exam. As you complete this section, remember to read each question and all the answers before selecting your answer. You might want to have a standard calculator on hand for use with dosage calculations.

After you take this exam, remember to load the CD-ROM and check out our exclusive ExamGear test engine, which is one of the best on the market.

Management Questions

1. The nurse is preparing to administer four medications to the client with dysphagia. Which medication should be administered first?

   ○ A. Conjugated estrogen (Premarin)

   ○ B. Furosemide (Lasix)

   ○ C. Ceclor (cephaclor)

   ○ D. Diphenhydramine (Benadryl)

2. The nurse is preparing to make rounds. Which client should be seen first?

   ○ A. A 1-year-old with hand-and-foot syndrome

   ○ B. A 69-year-old with congestive heart failure

   ○ C. A 40-year-old with resolving pancreatitis

   ○ D. A 56-year-old with Cushing's disease

3. A category four tornado has injured 50 people from the community. The nurse is responsible for in field triage. According to triage protocol, which client should be treated last?

   ○ A. The 30-year-old with lacerations to the neck and face

   ○ B. The 70-year-old with chest pain and shortness of breath

   ○ C. The 6-year-old with fixed, dilated pupils who is nonresponsive

   ○ D. The 40-year-old with tachypnea and tachycardia

4. Which nurse should be assigned to care for the client who has recently returned from surgery following a coronary artery bypass graft?

   ○ A. The nurse with 2 years experience in surgery

   ○ B. The nurse with 1 year experience in oncology

   ○ C. The nurse with 10 years experience in neonatal intensive care

   ○ D. The nurse with 5 years experience in the emergency room

5. The charge nurse is responsible for assigning clients to share a semi-private room. Which two clients can be assigned to share the room?

   ○ A. The 15-year-old with pneumonia and a 10-year-old with human immunovirus

   ○ B. The 30-year-old with leukemia receiving chemotherapy and the 25-year-old with bronchitis

   ○ C. The 60-year-old with gastroenteritis and the 65-year-old with Cushing's disease

   ○ D. The 70-year-old with diabetes and the 75-year-old with a fractured hip

6. Four clients arrive in the emergency room. Which client should receive priority?

    ○ A. The client with burns of the chest and neck

    ○ B. The client with gastroenteritis

    ○ C. The client with a migraine headache

    ○ D. The client with a fractured tibia

7. A nursing assistant has reported to work late for the last three days. Which action should be taken first?

    ○ A. Document the lateness in the employee's record

    ○ B. Terminate the employee immediately

    ○ C. Discuss the problem with the employee

    ○ D. Confront the employee during the change of shift

8. Which task must be performed by the registered nurse?

    ○ A. Hanging a bag of total parenteral nutrition solution

    ○ B. Inserting an indwelling urinary catheter

    ○ C. Administering a vaginal suppository

    ○ D. Checking the weights used with skeletal traction

9. Which task is best delegated to the licensed practical nurse?

    ○ A. Beginning an infusion of platelets

    ○ B. Inserting a nasogastric tube

    ○ C. Flushing a central venous catheter

    ○ D. Administering intravenous dexamethasone (Decadron)

10. The nurse observes the nursing assistant speaking harshly to an elderly client. Which action is most appropriate?

    ○ A. Ask the nursing assistant to speak in a lower tone because he is disturbing the other clients

    ○ B. Report the nursing assistant to the charge nurse

    ○ C. Reassign the nursing assistant to a younger client

    ○ D. Call the nursing assistant aside to discuss the observation

11. The nurse realizes that the nursing assistant needs further teaching if she observes the nursing assistant:

   ○ A. Walking the postoperative client with leg pain

   ○ B. Bathing the client using soap and water

   ○ C. Changing the bed of the client in traction from top to bottom

   ○ D. Feeding the client using a disposable spoon and fork

12. During morning report, the nurse is told that the postoperative client has complained of unremitting pain during the night. Although she has been given pain medication several times, there seems to be no change in the client's condition. Which action should the nurse take at this time?

   ○ A. Call the doctor and ask for a change in the client's medication

   ○ B. Perform a head-to-toe assessment

   ○ C. Administer another dose of the client's prescribed analgesic

   ○ D. Ask the client whether she is addicted to pain medications

13. The nurse observes a co-worker putting a contaminated dressing on the client's bedside table. Which action is most appropriate?

   ○ A. Remove the contaminated dressing and clean the surface of the bedside table with a hypochlorite solution

   ○ B. Wait until after the co-worker finishes and then request house-keeping to completely clean the room

   ○ C. Remove the contaminated dressing and place it in the client's waste can

   ○ D. Ask the co-worker why he placed the contaminated dressing on the client's bedside table

14. The nurse observes a co-worker striking a client with Alzheimer's disease. The co-worker can be charged with:

   ○ A. Battery

   ○ B. Assault

   ○ C. Malpractice

   ○ D. Negligence

15. The nurse is making several room assignments. Which client should be placed in the private room near the nurse's station?

     ○ A. The 75-year-old with emphysema and fever

     ○ B. The 70-year-old who is two days post appendectomy

     ○ C. The 65-year-old scheduled for surgery for suspected ovarian cancer

     ○ D. The 60-year-old who is one day post thyroidectomy

16. The charge nurse has noticed that there has been an increase in the number of nosocomial infections on the unit. Which action can help to decrease the spread of infection from the nurse to the client?

     ○ A. Using a mask while emptying the urinary drainage system

     ○ B. Keeping the door closed to each client's room

     ○ C. Asking the client's family to wear gowns and mask while visiting

     ○ D. Washing hands between each client contact

17. The nurse is performing a chart review of a client who fell in the bathroom while trying to shower. Which information must be included in the incident report?

     ○ A. The cause of the incident

     ○ B. The client's status on admission to the unit

     ○ C. The action taken by the nurse as a result of the incident

     ○ D. Those family members present at the time of the incident

18. Four clients have been assigned to the nurse for a home visit. Which client should the nurse visit first?

     ○ A. A 65-year-old with diabetes and venous stasis ulcers

     ○ B. A 10-year-old with spina bifida who performs daily self-catheterization

     ○ C. A 75-year-old with a stroke who receives peg tube feedings

     ○ D. A 35-year-old with systemic lupus who complains of blurred vision and headaches

19. The charge nurse is making assignments for the day. Which client should be cared for by the RN?

     ○ A. A client receiving radiation therapy for Graves' disease

     ○ B. A client with cachexia who is receiving total parenteral nutrition

     ○ C. A client who is three days post-gastrectomy

     ○ D. A client with an above-the-knee amputation

20. The nursing staff consists of two registered nurses, two licensed vocational nurses, and a certified nursing assistant. The skills of the nursing assistant are best suited to:

   ○ A. Feeding a client with Alzheimer's dementia

   ○ B. Bathing a client with a central line

   ○ C. Obtaining vital signs on a client with pneumonia

   ○ D. Collecting the output from a client with preeclampsia

21. A client with a high thoracic spinal cord injury develops an episode of autonomic hyperreflexia. After placing the client in high Fowler's position, the nurse's next action should be to:

   ○ A. Administer an antihypertensive agent

   ○ B. Notify the physician immediately

   ○ C. Make sure that the urinary catheter is patent

   ○ D. Request medication for pain

22. The nurse is making room assignments for four newly admitted clients. Which client should be placed closest to the nurse's station?

   ○ A. A 47-year-old with an esophageal tamponade

   ○ B. A 58-year-old with complaints of abdominal tenderness and fever

   ○ C. A 15-year-old with a fractured tibia and fibula

   ○ D. A 70-year-old with diabetes and intermittent leg pain

23. While making rounds, the nurse smells smoke coming from a client's room. On checking the room, the nurse finds a fire in the trash can. The nurse should give priority to:

   ○ A. Activating the fire alarm

   ○ B. Locating the unit fire extinguisher

   ○ C. Moving the client to a safe location

   ○ D. Evacuating all the clients to another unit

24. The nurse is caring for a client with tuberculosis. Which of the following is not a part of the client's care?

   ○ A. Keeping the client's door closed at all times

   ○ B. Wearing an N95 mask only when providing direct care

   ○ C. Maintaining the client in a room with at least six exchanges of fresh air per hour

   ○ D. Providing phototherapy with a source of ultraviolet light

25. Which of the following nursing duties is within the scope of practice of the licensed practical nurse?

    ○ A. Providing final discharge teaching for a client with a diagnosis of peptic ulcer disease

    ○ B. Instructing a newly diagnosed diabetic on how to administer his insulin injections

    ○ C. Monitoring the vital signs of a client receiving a blood transfusion

    ○ D. Flushing a central line with a heparin solution

26. The nurse is caring for an infant with suspected Munchausen's syndrome. While making rounds, the nurse finds the mother putting something in the infant's bottle. The nurse should:

    ○ A. Remove the bottle and report the incident to the charge nurse

    ○ B. Ask the mother what she added to the infant's bottle

    ○ C. Check to see whether the infant becomes ill after taking the bottle

    ○ D. Request that a dietician visit with the mother

27. The nursing staff of a local clinic is made up of two registered nurses and two licensed practical nurses. Which duty is within the scope of practice of the licensed practical nurse?

    ○ A. Administering a monthly infusion of Remicade to a client with rheumatoid arthritis

    ○ B. Removing sutures from a client following abdominal surgery

    ○ C. Changing a peg tube in a client with a stroke

    ○ D. Flushing a Groshong catheter in a client receiving chemotherapy

28. Four clients have requested medication for pain. Which client should receive pain medication first?

    ○ A. A 35-year-old client with fractures of the right femur

    ○ B. An 18-year-old client who is one day post appendectomy

    ○ C. A 55-year-old client with diverticulitis

    ○ D. A 47-year-old client who is one week post myocardial infarction

29. The nurse on a busy surgical unit has just completed receiving the morning shift report. Which client should the nurse assess first?

    ○ A. A post-gastrectomy client with 75 mL bright red nasogastric drainage in the past hour

    ○ B. A client receiving total parenteral nutrition following a bowel resection

    ○ C. A diabetic client with a morning blood glucose of 210 mg/dL

    ○ D. A client with pneumonia receiving intravenous antibiotics

30. The nurse is assigning duties for the day's staff, which consists of RNs, LPNs, and certified nursing assistants. Which facet of care is within the scope of practice of the certified nursing assistant?

    ○ A. Performing a sterile dressing change

    ○ B. Administering a tube feeding

    ○ C. Applying a nitroglycerin patch

    ○ D. Cleaning an ocular prosthesis

31. The charge nurse is making room assignments for four newly admitted pediatric clients. Which client should be assigned to the room occupied by a 3-year-old with burns of the hand and arm?

    ○ A. A 6-year-old with diabetes

    ○ B. A 10-year-old with pneumonia

    ○ C. A 2-year-old with facial cellulitis

    ○ D. A 4-year-old with gastroenteritis

32. A client diagnosed with acute mania is admitted to the psychiatric unit for stabilization. Which client is the most suitable roommate for a client with mania?

    ○ A. A client with paranoid schizophrenia

    ○ B. A client with antisocial personality disorder

    ○ C. A client with anorexia nervosa

    ○ D. A client with situational depression

33. The nurse is preparing to administer intravenous morphine sulfate to a client recently returned from surgery. Before giving the medication, what is the priority nursing assessment?

     ○ A. Checking the client's respirations

     ○ B. Obtaining the client's temperature

     ○ C. Checking the client's blood pressure

     ○ D. Counting the client's pulse rate

34. During her orientation, a graduate nurse is assigned to work with the staff of a large oncology unit. Which client is best assigned to the new graduate?

     ○ A. A client receiving chemotherapy via central line for breast cancer

     ○ B. A client receiving linear acceleration therapy for lung cancer

     ○ C. A client receiving brachytherapy for cervical cancer

     ○ D. A client receiving experimental therapy for malignant melanoma

35. The nurse is preparing a care plan for a client with a nutritional deficit. Which plan could be implemented by the nursing assistant?

     ○ A. Assess the client's knowledge of a proper diet

     ○ B. Monitor the client's laboratory values

     ○ C. Weigh the client daily

     ○ D. Administer multivitamins as prescribed

36. The charge nurse on the orthopedic unit is giving instructions to a student nurse caring for a client in skeletal traction. Which is most important for the charge nurse to tell the student to report?

     ○ A. Complaints of mild pain

     ○ B. Small amounts of clear drainage from the pin sites

     ○ C. Requests for a position change

     ○ D. Looseness of the pins on the traction device

37. The nurse is preparing to make rounds after shift report. Which client requires further assessment by the nurse?

     ○ A. A 40-year-old 12 hours post-thyroidectomy experiencing numbness in the face

     ○ B. A 34-year-old laparoscopic cholecystectomy with a temperature of 99.8° F

     ○ C. A 22-year-old being discharged after an appendectomy

     ○ D. A 56-year-old diabetic postop colon resection with a blood sugar of 128

38. The nurse is giving a report to a senior nursing student. Which would the nurse instruct the student to report on a client diagnosed with hyperthyroidism?

  ○ A. Tachycardia

  ○ B. Subnormal temperature

  ○ C. Frontal headache

  ○ D. Insomnia

39. A client presents to the emergency room complaining of dyspnea, shortness of breath, and a productive cough. The vital signs are temperature 101.4° F, respiratory rate 30, heart rate 108, and BP 124/80. The client is receiving oxygen, with an oxygen saturation rate of 86%. Which of the following physician's orders should the nurse complete first?

  ○ A. Obtain a chest x-ray

  ○ B. Administer acetaminophen (Tylenol) X grain

  ○ C. Obtain arterial blood gases

  ○ D. Administer chlorpheniramine/hydrocodone (Tussionex)

40. The nurse is caring for several clients on an orthopedic unit. If the following requests were made simultaneously, which should the nurse do first?

  ○ A. A family member calls and requests to speak to the nurse about a patient.

  ○ B. A client with a fractured femur complains of pleuritic pain and reports a rash on the chest and under the arms.

  ○ C. A client with a fractured leg requests pain medications.

  ○ D. A client with a cast reports itching within the cast.

41. A client with a stroke is receiving heparin intravenously. Which action of the nurse's assistant would cause a need for the nurse to intervene?

  ○ A. Assisting the client with tray setup

  ○ B. Writing the client a note to assist with communication

  ○ C. Shaving the client with a straight razor

  ○ D. Repositioning the client in bed

42. The nurse is caring for clients on an oncology unit. The supervisor calls to report a need to place two of the patients in the same room. Which of the following patient pairs is best?

   ○ A. A postoperative laminectomy done to decrease spinal cord compression and a patient with a craniotomy due to lung cancer metastasis

   ○ B. A patient with neutropenia and a patient receiving a blood transfusion

   ○ C. A patient with pancreatic cancer and a patient with a white blood cell count of 200

   ○ D. A patient on high dose chemotherapy and a patient with prostate cancer who is receiving radiation by external beam

43. The nurse has received a report from the emergency room of a direct-admit client with congestive heart failure. Which physician prescription should be the priority?

   ○ A. Low-sodium diet

   ○ B. Identify and continue home medications

   ○ C. Limit fluids to 500 mL per shift

   ○ D. Administer furosemide (Lasix) IV push

44. The nurse discovers a solution of Heparin IV infusing on a client when D5W is ordered. What is the appropriate initial action?

   ○ A. Remove the Heparin and hang D5W

   ○ B. Notify the physician about the incident

   ○ C. Inform the charge nurse of the error

   ○ D. Complete an occurrence report

45. A client is admitted with severe diarrhea. Which laboratory value is it most important to report to the physician?

   ○ A. Hgb 10.8 g/dL

   ○ B. WBC count of 12,500/mm

   ○ C. BUN 30 mg/dL

   ○ D. Potassium 2.0 mEq/L

46. A client has just died from terminal pancreatic cancer. Which task is best delegated to the nurse's assistant?

   ○ A. Talking with the family about aftercare

   ○ B. Assisting with postmortem care

   ○ C. Assessing the chart for funeral arrangements

   ○ D. Calling the doctor about the patient's death

47. The charge nurse is assigning staff on an oncology unit. One of the staff is a nurse that was transferred from the psychiatric unit. Which client should the nurse assign to the psychiatric nurse?

   ○ A. A client from the intensive care unit who is post-thoracotomy for lung cancer

   ○ B. A client requiring extensive chemotherapy administration on this shift

   ○ C. A client who has just been told that her cancer is terminal

   ○ D. A client with metastatic colon cancer, returning from a colon resection this shift

48. A client with an abdominal aortic aneurysm complains of sudden lower back pain. What is the nurse's initial action?

   ○ A. Start an IV with an 18-gauge needle

   ○ B. Measure the client's abdominal girth

   ○ C. Assess the peripheral pulses

   ○ D. Administer morphine sulfate 6 mg

49. A nurse's assessment of a client reveals shortness of breath, anxiety, and asymmetrical chest expansion. After starting the patient on ordered O_2 at 3 L/min, what is the nurse's next action?

   ○ A. Assess the chart for pulmonary function test results

   ○ B. Place the client in a supine position with his head flat

   ○ C. Notify the physician

   ○ D. Order a portable chest x-ray

50. If the following respiratory clients present in the emergency room at the same time, which client should be seen first?

   ○ A. A 2-year-old with cough, congestion, and a temperature of 102° F

   ○ B. A 22-year-old with fractured ribs complaining of pain in the chest area

   ○ C. A 60-year-old with dyspnea, distended neck veins, and 2+ pitting edema of lower extremities

   ○ D. A 35-year-old with a sore throat and temperature of 100.5° F

51. The emergency room nurse is assigned to triage four clients. Which client should be seen first?

 ○ A. The pregnant client with mild abdominal pain

 ○ B. The client with emphysema with an oxygen saturation level of 83%

 ○ C. The client with chronic glomerulonephritis with loss of his AV fistula

 ○ D. The client with diabetes with a blood glucose level of 277 mg/dl

52. Which nurse would be best to assign to the client who is 48 hours bone marrow transplant?

 ○ A. The RN with 4 years experience in the emergency room setting

 ○ B. The RN with 4 years experience on the geriatric unit

 ○ C. The RN with 5 years experience working with clients with AIDS

 ○ D. The RN with 10 years experience working in the labor and delivery unit

53. The nurse is observing the certified nursing assistant caring for a client who is taking Thorazine (chlorpromazine) for psychosis. Which action by the nursing assistant indicates a need for further teaching?

 ○ A. The nursing assistant offers the client a magazine to read.

 ○ B. The nursing assistant stands on the client's dominant side during ambulation.

 ○ C. The nursing assistant asks the client if he wants to take a walk.

 ○ D. The nursing assistant allows the client to have hard candy.

54. After taking the morning report, the nurse should visit which client first?

 ○ A. The client with pheochromocytoma

 ○ B. The client with breast cancer

 ○ C. The client with a urinary tract infection

 ○ D. The client with myxedema

55. The nurse observes the nursing assistant looking through the belongings of the geriatric client. Which action is most appropriate at this time?

 ○ A. Call the social worker so that she can investigate the matter

 ○ B. Question the nursing assistant regarding the matter

 ○ C. Report the matter to the physician

 ○ D. Chart the observation in the client's medical record

56. The nurse is preparing to perform a sterile dressing change. He has collected materials needed for the procedure and opened the sterile tray when he is called away to an emergency. Should a second nurse be asked to continue the procedure, she should:

   ○ A. Go to the sterile utility room and obtain another tray

   ○ B. Continue the procedure utilizing the opened tray

   ○ C. Question the nurse regarding the sterility of the tray

   ○ D. Call the physician to discuss the procedure

57. The charge nurse is instructing several graduate nurses regarding the need to maintain confidentiality. Which action by the graduate constitutes a breech in client confidentiality?

   ○ A. The graduate asks the family member of the client who has had a CVA to sign the permit for surgery.

   ○ B. The graduate examines the chart of a relative of her family who is hospitalized for surgery.

   ○ C. The graduate talks harshly to the elderly client with dementia.

   ○ D. The graduate asks the client's son if she has a living will.

58. The nurse is preparing to administer four medications to the client with dysphagia following a stroke. Because all of the client's medications are to be given by mouth, the nurse should administer which medication first?

   ○ A. Ketoralac (Toradol)

   ○ B. Glypizide (Glucotrol)

   ○ C. Doxazosin mesylate (Cardura)

   ○ D. Spironalactone (Aldactone)

59. The client is scheduled for a positron emission tomography (PETT) scan. Which action indicates the nurse is aware of the needs of the client during the PET scan?

   ○ A. The nurse checks the client's blood glucose level prior to the procedure.

   ○ B. The nurse inserts a nasogastric tube for lavage to monitor gastric pH.

   ○ C. The nurse tells the client that a catheter will be inserted into his brachial artery.

   ○ D. The nurse informs the client that he will be asleep during the procedure.

60. The nurse is caring for a group of clients on a medical surgical unit. Which of the following clients should receive priority status?

    ○ A. A client with chronic renal failure whose Hgb is 10.2 g/dL

    ○ B. A client with pernicious anemia who is complaining of tingling in the right arm

    ○ C. A client with a pleural effusion and an oxygen saturation of 95%

    ○ D. A client with hypertension reporting numbness in the right hand

61. The family member of a client with terminal cancer is concerned about providing adequate home care. Which of the following agencies would be the best for the nurse to consider advocating?

    ○ A. Hospice home health

    ○ B. Meals on Wheels services

    ○ C. Community action agency

    ○ D. Cooperative extension services

62. A client is diagnosed with a suspected pulmonary embolus after hip surgery. Which of the following nursing interventions should the nurse complete first?

    ○ A. Assess the client's hip surgical wound

    ○ B. Connect ordered oxygen at 2L/min by nasal cannula

    ○ C. Administer daily dose of enoxaparin (Lovenox)

    ○ D. Notify the physician of the client's admission

63. The nurse is to obtain surgical consent for a client who is scheduled to be transferred to OR for an appendectomy. The emergency room report indicates meperidine (Demerol) IM and ceftriaxone (Rocephin) IVPB was administered 15 minutes ago. Which action is most appropriate?

    ○ A. Get the patient to sign the operative permit

    ○ B. Obtain consent signature from the client's spouse

    ○ C. Call surgery and inform the staff to cancel the procedure

    ○ D. Waive the signing of the permit because of the emergency

64. Which of the following occurrences qualify as provider of care outside the scope of practice of the LPN?

    ○ A. Performance of tracheostomy care

    ○ B. Administering conscious sedation

    ○ C. Monitoring a blood transfusion

    ○ D. Inserting a Foley catheter

65. A client is in status epilepticus and has the following medications ordered IV. Which does the nurse administer first?

   ○ A. Lorazepam (Ativan)

   ○ B. Phenytoin (Dilantin)

   ○ C. Cefazolin (Ancef)

   ○ D. Dexamethasone (Decadron)

66. The nurse is approached by a friend in a community setting. The friend asks the nurse about the results of another friend's x-ray test. Which of the following responses is most appropriate?

   ○ A. "If you can get me her Social Security number, I will look it up."

   ○ B. "Why don't you just ask her the result of the test yourself?"

   ○ C. "I cannot give out any client information."

   ○ D. "I don't have that information right now."

67. Four clients on a busy medical-surgical unit are requesting medication. Which client should receive medication first?

   ○ A. A 34-year-old client with a fractured femur who requests pain medication

   ○ B. A 48-year-old client with cirrhosis who requests medication for nausea

   ○ C. A 55-year-old client with peptic ulcer disease who requests an antacid

   ○ D. A 36-year-old with ulcerative colitis who requests medication for diarrhea

68. Which client should be cared for using airborne transmission-based precautions?

   ○ A. A 5-year-old with rubella

   ○ B. A 6-month-old with rotovirus

   ○ C. A 2-month-old with pertussis

   ○ D. A 6-year-old with varicella

69. A mass casualty has necessitated the emptying of several hospital beds. Which one of the following clients should be discharged to provide a bed for a trauma victim?

   ○ A. A client who is one day postop thyroidectomy

   ○ B. A client who is two days postop gastrectomy

   ○ C. A client who is two days postop stapedectomy

   ○ D. A client who is one day postop abdominal cholecystectomy

70. The nurse is making assignments for the day. Which client is least appropriate to assign to the novice RN?

   ○ A. A client with a newly created arteriovenous fistula who is undergoing dialysis

   ○ B. A client with Crohn's disease who is receiving intravenous immuno-suppresives

   ○ C. A client with burns who is scheduled for mechanical debridement

   ○ D. A client with an abdominal cholecystectomy with a Jackson Pratt drain

71. The RN is making assignments for the staff, which contains an LPN. Which duty can be assigned to the LPN?

   ○ A. Performing tracheostomy suctioning on a client with a permanent trach

   ○ B. Administering total parenteral nutrition to a client with cancer

   ○ C. Obtaining initial vital signs on a client receiving a blood transfusion

   ○ D. Performing discharge teaching for a client with diabetes mellitus

72. The nursing staff consists of an RN, an LPN, two nursing assistants, and a float RN from the hospital's psychiatric unit. Which client should be assigned to the float RN?

   ○ A. A 25-year-old with traumatic amputation of the right lower leg

   ○ B. A 48-year-old with a pulmonary tuberculosis

   ○ C. A 56-year-old with cirrhosis and portal hypertension

   ○ D. A 72-year-old with end-stage renal disease

Alternative Items

1. While performing a neurological exam on a child with bacterial meningitis, the nurse notes a positive Kernig sign. Place an X on the picture that demonstrates Kernig sign.

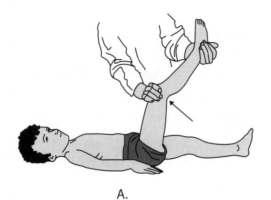

A.

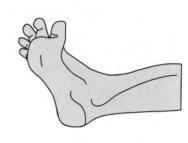

B.

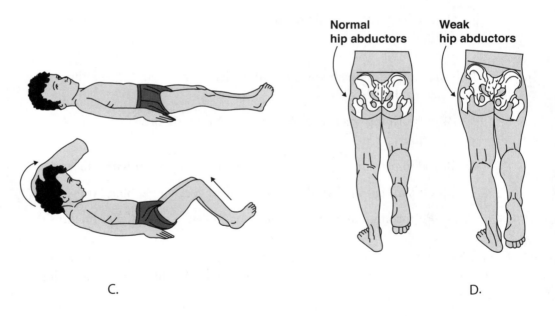

C.

D.

2. The physician has prescribed an MAO inhibitor for a client with depression. Place an X by each food choice that should be avoided by clients receiving MAO inhibitors:

___Chocolate pudding

___Hamburger steak

___Yogurt

___Cheddar cheese

___Banana

___Grilled tuna

___Avocados

3. Viral hepatitis can be either enteric or parenteral in origin. Place an X beside the parenteral forms of viral hepatitis:

    ___Hepatitis A

    ___Hepatitis B

    ___Hepatitis C

    ___Hepatitis D

    ___Hepatitis E

    ___Hepatitis G

4. The physician has ordered Augmentin oral suspension (amoxicillin/clavulanate) 325 mg three times a day for a child with otitis media. After reconstitution, the medication yields Augmentin oral suspension 250 mg per 5 mL. How much medication should the nurse administer each time?

5. The nurse is caring for a client following an abdominal cholecystectomy with insertion of a T-tube. Which aspects of care apply to the client with a T-tube? Check all that apply.

    ___Documenting the amount, color, and consistency of the drainage

    ___Irrigating the T-tube every four hours

    ___Preventing kinking or tangling of the tubing

    ___Clamping the tube for 30 minutes every four hours on the second post-operative day

    ___Observing for the return of brown-colored stools

    ___Maintaining the drainage system below the level of the gallbladder

6. The physician has ordered an IV infusion of dextrose 5% in normal saline 1000 mL to infuse over eight hours. The IV set delivers 15 drops per mL. The IV rate should be set at ___ drops per minute.

7. The nurse is caring for a client in isolation. Place in sequence the correct order for removing isolation garb:

    ___Remove eyewear or goggles

    ___Untie neck strings and back strings of gown

    ___Remove gloves

    ___Without touching outside surface, remove gown

    ___Fold gown inside out and discard

    ___Wash hands for 10–15 seconds

    ___Allow gown to fall from shoulders

    ___Pull mask away from face and discard

8. A client is diagnosed with paraplegia following a motor vehicle accident. Place an X beside the figure that depicts the client with paraplegia.

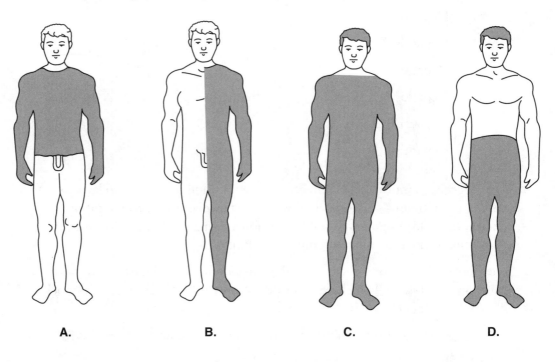

    A.   **B.**   **C.**   **D.**

9. The nurse is assisting the physician with the removal of a closed chest drainage system. Place an X by the item/items that will not be needed for the procedure:

    ___Xylocaine and 5 mL syringe

    ___Petroleum gauze

    ___Silk or paper tape

    ___Suture removal kit

    ___Sterile hemostats

    ___Sterile 4 x 4 pads

10. The nurse is preparing to administer an intramuscular injection of a 14-month-old infant. Place an X on the site to be used for intramuscular injections given to infants and young children.

IM Injection Sites

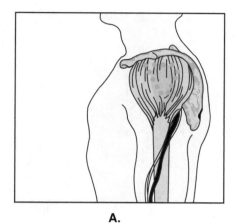

A.

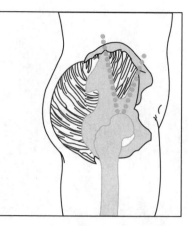

B.

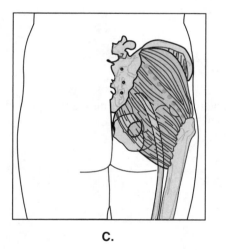

C.

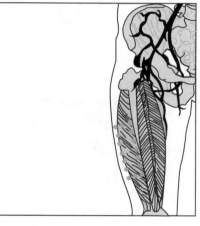

D.

11. Identify the apex of the heart:

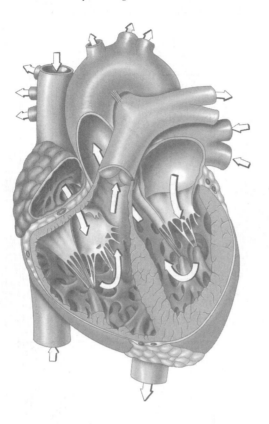

12. The nurse is preparing to perform a dressing change. Place in sequence the correct order for performing a dressing change:

___Wash hands

___Explain the procedure

___Assess the client's pain level

___Gather equipment

___Don sterile gloves

___Remove the old dressing

___Place a clean towel under the wound area

___Apply a pair of nonsterile gloves

13. Check all that apply to the skill of traction application:

___Weights on floor

___No knots in the cords

___Sheets off the traction device

___No frayed cords

___Weights hanging freely

14. Identify the greater trochanter of the femur:

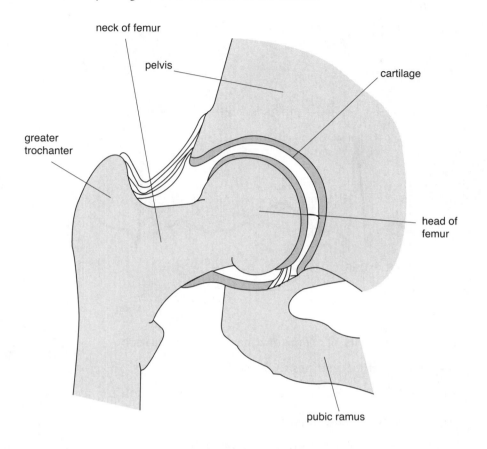

THE HIP JOINT

15. The physician has ordered 50 mg of meperidine (Demerol) and 25 mg of promethazine (Phenergan). How many total milliliters will be administered if the meperidine is supplied in 100 mg equals 1 mL and promethazine 25 mg equals 1 mL?

16. Calculate the intake in milliliters for an eight-hour period for the following:

     ___1 cup of juice

     ___3 ounces of Jell-o

     ___8 ounces of iced tea

     ___800 milliliters of intravenous fluid

17. Identify the p wave on the ECG strip.

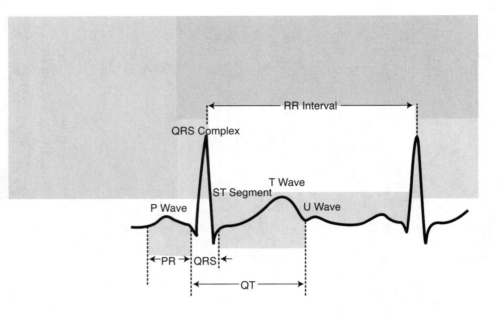

18. Place in sequence the priority of clients in a mass casualty situation:

___40-year-old with lacerations to the scalp

___20-year-old with a fractured femur

___30-year-old with chest trauma

___5-year-old with a head injury who is pulseless

19. The client's first day of her last menstrual period is October 24. Using Naegele's rule, calculate the expected date of delivery.

20. Place a check by the members of the healthcare team who can be assigned to the care of a client 12 hours following a thyroidectomy:

___Resident physician with 1 year experience

___Registered nurse with 2 months experience

___Licensed practical nurse with 1 year experience

___Nursing assistant with 20 years experience

21. The nurse in the following photo is testing for which cranial nerve function?

22. Place an X by the physiological changes associated with the aging process.

___Presbyopia

___Arcus senilis

___Presbycusis

___Brudzinski's sign

___Sundowning syndrome

___Aphasia

23. The nurse is performing an assessment on a comatose client with a severe head injury. The client exhibits the following position. Name this position.

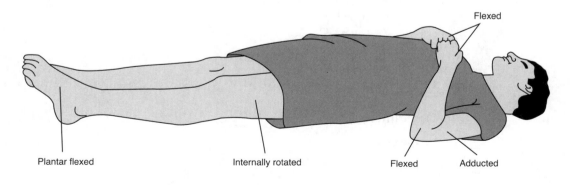

Flexed

Plantar flexed   Internally rotated   Flexed   Adducted

24. The nurse is caring for a client with a fracture. The client develops a deep vein thrombosis in the opposite extremity. Physician orders include a heparin drip of D5W 250 mL with heparin 12,500 units at 16 mL/hr. How many units of heparin is this client receiving per hour?

25. The nurse is observing a student nurse as he checks deep tendon reflexes on a client with myasthenia gravis. The nurse recognizes that the student nurse is assessing the _____ reflex when the following is observed?

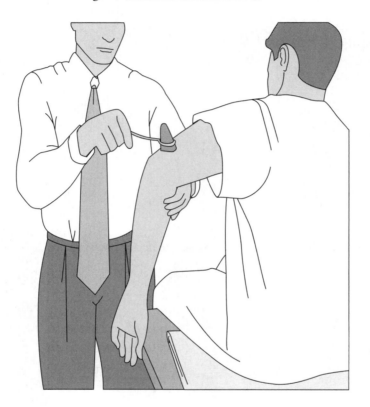

26. The nurse is preparing to insert an indwelling urinary catheter. Place the following steps of an indwelling urinary catheter insertion in the proper sequence:

      ___Gather equipment

      ___Check physician order

      ___Position client

      ___Explain the procedure

      ___Ensure proper lighting

      ___Test the catheter balloon

      ___Insert the catheter

      ___Cleanse the meatus

      ___Apply sterile gloves

      ___Open catheter kit

      ___Lubricate catheter tip

27. The nurse is preparing a care plan for a client on the neurological unit with a nursing diagnosis of alteration in cerebral tissue perfusion. Which plans would be beneficial to maintenance or improvement in cerebral tissue perfusion? Check all that apply.

   ___Elevate the head of the bed 30°

   ___Administer mannitol (Osmitrol) as ordered

   ___Assist the client to turn, cough, and deep breathe every two hours

   ___Monitor neurological status hourly

   ___Keep the client's head turned to the side

28. A client admitted with gastrointestinal bleeding requires insertion of a nasogastric tube. Place the steps for insertion of a nasogastric tube in the proper order:

   ___Assess the client's nostrils

   ___Insert the nasogastric tube

   ___Check the physician's order

   ___Measure the tube for length of insertion

   ___Check the nasogastric tube for proper placement

   ___Seat the client, place pillows behind the shoulders

   ___Inform the client about the procedure

   ___Lubricate the nasogastric tube

29. The nurse is working on a cardiac step-down unit. The following rhythm is assessed. Name the rhythm.

30. Which of the following foods are allowed on a low-sodium diet? Check all that apply.

___An orange

___Broiled chicken

___Potato chips

___Yogurt

___Parmesan cheese

___Tomato ketchup

___Canned soup

___Buttermilk

___Broccoli

Answers to Practice Exam I

Answers at a Glance to Practice Exam I

1. C	30. A	59. B
2. D	31. C	60. B
3. D	32. A	61. C
4. C	33. A	62. A
5. A	34. A	63. B
6. C	35. B	64. D
7. B	36. A	65. B
8. B	37. C	66. A
9. C	38. D	67. D
10. C	39. B	68. D
11. B	40. A	69. B
12. A	41. B	70. A
13. B	42. D	71. B
14. B	43. C	72. D
15. D	44. C	73. D
16. C	45. A	74. C
17. B	46. C	75. A
18. C	47. B	76. A
19. C	48. C	77. C
20. A	49. A	78. B
21. A	50. C	79. B
22. B	51. B	80. B
23. C	52. A	81. B
24. C	53. B	82. A
25. B	54. C	83. B
26. B	55. A	84. C
27. D	56. B	85. A
28. C	57. A	86. B
29. D	58. C	87. D

88. A	**115.** D	**142.** B
89. B	**116.** B	**143.** D
90. D	**117.** A	**144.** B
91. D	**118.** B	**145.** C
92. B	**119.** C	**146.** C
93. D	**120.** B	**147.** B
94. C	**121.** B	**148.** C
95. D	**122.** C	**149.** C
96. B	**123.** C	**150.** B
97. C	**124.** A	**151.** B
98. D	**125.** B	**152.** B
99. A	**126.** B	**153.** D
100. B	**127.** C	**154.** C
101. D	**128.** A	**155.** B
102. B	**129.** B	**156.** B
103. B	**130.** A	**157.** B
104. D	**131.** C	**158.** C
105. B	**132.** C	**159.** A
106. C	**133.** C	**160.** A
107. C	**134.** B	**161.** B
108. C	**135.** B	**162.** C
109. B	**136.** C	**163.** C
110. D	**137.** A	**164.** A
111. C	**138.** B	**165.** D
112. B	**139.** C	**166.** C
113. A	**140.** D	
114. C	**141.** A	

Answers with Explanations

Fluid and Electrolytes and Acid/Base Balance

1. Answer C is correct. To treat isotonic dehydration, the doctor will order fluids containing normal saline. Answers A and D are incorrect because 5% dextrose and water and .45% sodium chloride are hypotonic solutions. Answer B is incorrect because 3% sodium chloride is a hypertonic solution.

2. Answer D is correct. The normal serum carbon-dioxide level is 24–30. This is different from the normal arterial blood gas level of 35–45 mEq/L. A serum carbon-dioxide level of 42 mEq/L is elevated. The client with COPD might require a prescription for a bronchodilator to assist with exhalation of carbon dioxide. Answers A and C are incorrect because his condition does not require NPH insulin or dialysis. Answer B is incorrect because oxygen should be applied by nasal cannula, not a mask.

3. Answer D is correct. Answers A, B, and C are incorrect because these levels are within normal limits.

4. Answer C is correct. The client with a blood glucose of 430 mg/dl is at risk for diabetic coma. Answers A, B, and D are incorrect because the alterations in the oxygen saturation, CO_2 level, and BUN are expected in the alterations mentioned.

5. Answer A is correct. Prior to administering potassium, the nurse should check renal function. This can be done by checking the client's creatinine level. The normal creatinine level is .60–1.60 mg/dL. If the client's creatinine level is elevated, the nurse should contact the physician prior to administering the potassium. There is no need to ask the doctor to order an ECG, so answer B is incorrect. Inserting a nasogastric tube is also not necessary, so answer C is incorrect. D is incorrect because the nurse should acquire fruit juice, not milk, to give the potassium.

6. Answer C is correct. Potassium should be administered in a juice containing ascorbic acid. The liquid with the most ascorbic acid is the tomato juice. Other acceptable juices are orange juice, pineapple juice, and grape juice. Answer A and B are incorrect because cranberry juice and prune juice are less acidic. Answer D is incorrect because chocolate milk does not contain significant amounts of ascorbic acid.

7. Answer B is incorrect. The normal sodium level is 135–145 mEq/L. Answer A is incorrect because simply charting the finding is not the correct action. The client will require a high-sodium diet, not a low-sodium diet, so C is incorrect. Answer D is incorrect because checking the client's deep tendon reflexes will most likely reveal hyporeflexia, not hyperreflexia.

8. Answer B is correct. A positive Trousseau's sign would be indicated by jerking of the wrist when the blood pressure cuff is inflated. This indicates hypocalcemia. Answer A is incorrect because facial grimacing is indicative of Chvostek's sign. This is also indicative of hypocalcemia. Answers C and D are incorrect because they are not associated with Trousseau's sign.

9. Answer C is correct. To facilitate lowering of the client's cholesterol level, the doctor might order that the client supplement his diet with niacin or B3. Answers A, B, and D are incorrect because these vitamins do not help to lower cholesterol levels.

10. Answer C is correct. The client with hypoparathyroidism will require supplementation with parathyroid hormone. Answers A, B, and D are incorrect because these medications are not used to treat hypoparathyroidism.

11. Answer B is correct. The signs of toxicity to magnesium include oliguria, absence of deep tendon reflexes, and decreased respiration (fewer than 12 per minute). Answer A is incorrect because hot flashes are a side effect of magnesium. Answer C is incorrect because a deep tendon reflex of 2+ is normal. Answer D is incorrect because a urinary output of 40 mL per hour is within the lower limits of normal.

12. Answer A is correct. Magnesium can cause renal failure and apnea. The nursing assistant should not be assigned to care for this client. The licensed practical nurse can evaluate the urinary output and report to the registered nurse alterations in renal function, so answer B is incorrect. The graduate registered nurse can evaluate renal function and respiratory status and report abnormalities, so answer C is incorrect. Answer D is incorrect for the same reason. A surgical resident has finished medical school and is furthering her career as a surgeon.

13. Answer B is correct. Calcium gluconate is the antidote for magnesium sulfate. Answer A is incorrect because protamine sulfate is the antidote for heparin. Answer C is incorrect because AquaMEPHYTON (vitamin K) is the antidote for Coumadin (sodium warfarin). Answer D is incorrect because aminocaproic acid (Amicar) is the antidote for streptokinase.

14. Answer B is correct. The pH is elevated, as are the HCO_3 and CO_2 levels. This indicates metabolic alkalosis; therefore, answers A, C, and D are incorrect assessments of the laboratory findings.

15. Answer D is correct. The pH is below normal. The HCO_3 and CO_2 are elevated. This indicates respiratory acidosis; therefore, answers A, B, and C are incorrect.

16. Answer C is correct. A potassium level of 3.0 is low. Answers A, B, and D are within normal limits, so these answers are incorrect.

17. Answer B is correct. Dried fruits contain large amounts of potassium. Answers A, C, and D are incorrect because they contain lesser amounts of potassium than raisins.

18. Answer C is correct. Spironolactone is the only answer that is a potassium-sparing diuretic. Answers A, B, and D are not potassium-sparing diuretics, so they are incorrect.

19. Answer C is correct. Clients with Cushing's disease often retain sodium. Answers A, B, and D are incorrect because there is less likelihood of hypercalcemia, hyperkalemia, or hypermagnesemia in the client with Cushing's disease.

20. Answer A is correct. Diabetes insipidus is a lack of antidiuretic hormone. This results in a large volume of urinary output with an extremely low specific gravity. The specific gravity in answer A is low. The normal is 1.010–1.030. Answers B, C, and D are not directly related to diabetes insipidus and are within normal limits; therefore, they are incorrect.

Care of the Client with Cardiovascular Disorders

21. Answer A is correct. The normal CVP reading is 8–12 mm Hg. A reading of 4 indicates possible bleeding and fluid loss. The nurse should administer IV fluid as ordered. Answers B, C, and D are incorrect actions at this time.

22. Answer B is correct. While taking beta blockers, the client should be taught to check his pulse daily. This category of blood pressure drugs slows the pulse rate. Answer A is incorrect because the client can operate heavy equipment when taking beta blockers. Answer C is incorrect because beta blockers reach their optimal levels within days of beginning the medication. Answer D is incorrect because there is no need to increase potassium-rich foods when taking beta blockers. There is a need to increase potassium-rich foods while taking diuretics that are not potassium-sparing.

23. Answer C is correct. The peel of a baked potato contains large amounts of potassium. Answers A, B, and D contain lesser amounts of potassium and are therefore incorrect.

24. Answer C is correct. Palm oil and coconut oil are extremely high in cholesterol. These oils contribute to coronary artery disease. Answers A and B are incorrect because these oils are recommended for clients with coronary artery disease. Answer D is incorrect because canola oil contains less fat and cholesterol than palm oil.

25. Answer B is correct. Because simvastatin (Zocor) can damage the liver, liver enzymes should be checked every six months. Answer A is incorrect because this medication should not be taken with grapefruit juice. Answer C is incorrect because Zocor should be taken at night for optimal absorption. Answer D is incorrect because weakness or drowsiness is not associated with Zocor. It is true, however, that extreme muscle soreness and weakness while taking Zocar can be related to rhabdomylysis. Rhabdomylysis is a muscle-wasting disorder.

26. Answer B is correct. Lisinopril (Zestril) can cause postural hypotension. The client should be taught to supine for approximately 3–4 hours after the initial dose. The blood pressure should be checked frequently to determine the effects of the medication. Answer A is incorrect because lisinopril is an ACE inhibitor and does not have a direct effect on the pulse rate. Answer C is incorrect because lisinopril does not lower cholesterol levels. Answer D is incorrect because there is no need to increase folic acid while taking lisinopril.

27. Answer D is correct. A hacking cough, often associated with angiotensin-converting agents, is an untoward effect that should be reported to the doctor. The cough might indicate an allergic reaction to the medication. Answer A is incorrect because the client might experience dizziness upon arising. Answer B is incorrect because occasional nausea is not associated with an untoward effect of angiotensin-converting agents. Answer C is incorrect because pedal edema is associated with fluid retention and peripheral vascular disease, not angiotensin-converting agents.

28. Answer C is correct. The medication should be kept in a brown bottle because light deteriorates the medication. Answer A is incorrect because the client can take one pill every five minutes times three doses. If the pain does not subside, he should go to the emergency department immediately. Answer B is incorrect because a burning sensation is expected. Answer D is incorrect because the supply of nitroglycerine should be refilled every six months.

29. Answer D is correct. Clients with a pacemaker or an internal defibrillator should not have a magnetic resonance imaging test. Answers A and B are incorrect because a client with a pacemaker can use a cellular phone or carry a pager if the device is used on the opposite side of the pacemaker. Answer C is incorrect because the client can travel by airplane. Use of a handheld metal detector is contraindicated.

30. Answer A is correct. The client taking digitalis (Lanoxin) can avoid toxicity by increasing the amount of fiber in his diet. The bran muffin and orange juice provide the most fiber and ensure a diet that includes potassium (in the orange juice). Potassium has to be consumed in moderate amounts to avoid toxicity. Answers B, C, and D are incorrect because they are lower in fiber.

31. Answer C is correct. The signs of digitalis toxicity are halos around lights, brachy-cardia, nausea, and vomiting. Answer A is incorrect because the client will experi-ence brachycardia not tachycardia. Hypotension can occur but is not a sign of toxi-city, so answer B is incorrect. Answer D is incorrect because a client with constipa-tion, not a client with diarrhea, is more likely to be toxic.

32. Answer A is correct. The white lead or negative lead is placed on the client's right side at the second intercostal space. Answers B, C, and D are incorrect because the negative lead is not placed at these locations.

33. Answer A is correct. If the pulse rate is less than 100 beats per minute in the infant, the rate should be reported to the physician. Answers B and C are incorrect because the nurse should not administer the medication if the pulse rate is less than 100 beats per minute. Answer D is incorrect because the nurse should report the finding.

34. Answer A is correct. Amiodarone (Cordarone) can be used to treat premature ventricular contractions. This drug, along with lidocaine and magnesium sulfate, will slow the heart rate. Answers B and C are incorrect because both these drugs speed the heart rate. Answer D is incorrect because enoxaparin (Lovenox) is a heparin derivative used as an anticoagulant.

35. Answer B is correct. When defibrillation is performed, three quick successive shocks are delivered with the third at 360 Joules. Answer A is incorrect because the third shock should be at 360 Joules. Answers C and D are incorrect because 400 and 600 Joules are too high.

36. Answer A is correct. The nurse should be ready to apply oxygen when caring for the client experiencing chest pain. Using standard protocol, oxygen can be administered to increase the oxygenation of the myocardium. Morphine can be administered after acquiring an order, so answer B is incorrect. Answer C is incorrect because at this time it is not necessary to defibrillate the client. Answer D is incorrect because a complete history should be taken when the client is stable.

37. Answer C is correct. The primary responsibility of the nurse is to obtain the vital signs. The doctor is primarily responsible for explaining the procedure, checking the laboratory results for a prothrombin time, and obtaining a permit; therefore answers A, B, and D are incorrect.

38. Answer D is correct. Checking the pulse in the procedure extremity is imperative because a clot might be present. A clot will result in decreased pulse rate and strength. Answers A and B are incorrect because checking for allergies and withholding fluids should be done prior to the procedure. The client should be instructed to drink more after the procedure to increase the excretion of the dye by the kidneys. Answer C is incorrect because the client should keep the leg straight.

39. Answer B is correct. Troponin levels can remain elevated for as long as two weeks. If the client had an MI two weeks ago, the creatine kinase (CK-MB) will most likely have returned to normal; therefore, answer A is incorrect. Answers C and D are incorrect because they can be elevated with an MI but are not specific to this condition.

40. Answer A is correct. Muffled heart sounds and a lack of drainage from the mediastinal tube indicate cardiac tamponade or fluid around the heart. This must be reported immediately to the physician. Answer B is incorrect because rechecking the vital signs wastes valuable time. Answer C is incorrect because there is no data to support the need for pain medication and it might lower the blood pressure. Answer D is incorrect because decreasing the intravenous flow rate can further shock.

41. Answer B is correct. Puffed rice, puffed wheat, and shredded wheat have less sodium than any of the other choices. Answers A, C, and D are incorrect for this reason.

42. Answer D is correct. To ensure accuracy of the BNP laboratory test, Primacor should be stopped two hours prior to the test. Answers A, B, and C are incorrect actions.

43. Answer C is correct. Constipation can lead to an elevated level when taking sodium warfarin. Both diarrhea and constipation can affect the absorption of this medication. Answer A is incorrect because the medication can be taken with fruit juice or other liquids. Answer B is incorrect because the client should not exceed one serving of green leafy vegetables per week. Answer D is incorrect because sodium is taken orally, not by injection.

44. Answer C is correct. The client's symptoms, while vague, can indicate a myocardial infarction. Taking the vital signs and contacting the physician will allow the doctor to order laboratory tests and an ECG to rule out an MI. Answers A, B, and D are incorrect because they waste time that could be vital to ensure life and improve the prognosis.

45. Answer A is correct. The other name for vitamin K is AquaMEPHYTON. Answer B is incorrect because physostigmine is Antilirium, an anticholinesterase medication used to reverse the effects of diazepam (Valium). Answer C is incorrect because ropivacaine is Naropin, a drug used as a local anesthetic. Answer D is incorrect because methimazole is Tapazole, a drug used to treat hypothyroidism.

46. Answer C is correct. Symptoms of left-sided congestive heart failure include jugular vein distention; coughing with frothy, pink-tinged sputum; and shortness of breath. Answers A and B are symptoms of right-sided congestive failure. Answer D is incorrect because fatigue is not specific to a diagnosis of left-sided congestive heart failure.

47. Answer B is correct. A common complaint in a client with an abdominal aortic aneurysm is the presence of pulsation in the abdomen. Answer A is incorrect because indigestion when lying down indicates gastroesophageal reflux disorder (GERD). Answer C is incorrect because feeling fatigue and shortness of breath with minimal exertion can indicate many problems, one of which is congestive heart failure. Answer D is incorrect because pain radiating down the left arm indicates a possible myocardial infarction.

48. Answer C is correct. Clients with a metallic valve replacement require lifelong anticoagulant therapy with drugs such as sodium warfarin (Coumadin). Answer A is incorrect because chlorothiazide (Diuril) is a diuretic. Answer B is incorrect because clonidine HCl (Catapres) is an antihypertensive. Answer D is incorrect because propranolol (Inderal) is a beta blocker used for hypertension, for mitral valve prolapse, and to lower the pulse rate in anxiety disorders.

49. Answer A is correct. Intermittent claudication is burning and pain when the client is ambulating. Applying antithrombolytic stockings helps support muscles and blood vessels and decreases the pooling of blood. Answer B is incorrect because a heating pad can cause burning in the client with peripheral vascular disease. Answer C is incorrect because massaging the extremity can lead to a pulmonary embolism. Answer D is incorrect because ambulation increases the client's pain.

50. Answer C is correct. The client with a femoral popliteal bypass graft should be taught to keep the procedural leg as straight as possible because bending the leg or crossing the leg at the knee can impede circulation and close the grafted vessel. Answer A is incorrect because the client should rest in a supine or semi-Fowler's position. Answer B is incorrect because the client can cross the legs at the ankles, but not at the knee. Answer D is incorrect because the radial pulse (pulse in the wrist) need not be checked daily. Checking the pedal and posterior tibial pulses can reveal decreased blood flow.

51. Answer B is correct. A client who has experienced a myocardial infarction should take nitroglycerine at the first sign of chest pain. Three sublingual tablets can be taken to treat angina pain. If the pain persists, the client should go to the hospital. Answer A is incorrect because the client can begin having intercourse when he can climb one flight of stairs without being breathless. Answer C is incorrect because sildenafil (Viagra) should not be taken within 24 hours of taking a nitrite such as nitroglycerine. Answer D is incorrect because the client should begin a "step" program that consists of a progressive exercise plan that does not mandate three miles per day.

52. Answer A is correct. When thrombophlebitis is suspected, the client should remain in bed to decrease the threat of a pulmonary embolus. Answer B is incorrect because Homan's sign is no longer used to assess the client for the presence of thrombophlebitis since this subjective assessment tool can cause the clot to dislodge and travel to the lungs. Answer C is incorrect because the doctor will schedule the client for a Doppler study. Answer D is incorrect because applying a heating pad to the extremity will be ordered by the doctor after the client is fully assessed.

53. Answer B is correct. Raynaud's phenomena is a vascular spasm occurring when the client is exposed to cold. The hands, nose, and chin are commonly affected. Wearing mittens when is exposed to cold will help decrease the symptoms of Raynaud's phenomena. Answer A is incorrect because there is no correlation to keeping the feet elevated and the incidence of Raynaud's. Answer C is incorrect because caffeine intake is not associated with Raynaud's phenomena. Answer D is incorrect because Raynaud's phenomena is not a problem associated with lung disorders.

54. Answer C is correct. Buerger's disease results when spasms of the arteries and veins occur, primarily in the lower extremities. These spasms result in blood clot formation and eventual destruction of the vessels. Answer A is incorrect because thrombophlebitis is a blood clot with an inflammation of the vein. Answer B is incorrect because coronary thrombosis is a clot in the coronary arteries. Answer D is incorrect because arteritis is an inflammation of the arteries.

55. Answer A is correct. To correctly assess the CVP, the nurse should place the client in a supine position. The zero of the manometer should be placed at the fifth intercostals space, mid-axillary line (phlebostatic axis). Answers B, C, and D are incorrect because they will not give a correct reading.

Care of the Client with Endocrine Disorders

56. Answer B is correct. A prolactinoma is a pituitary tumor. This tumor results in anovulation, irregular menses, reduced sex drive, and lactation. Answer A is incorrect because agranulocytosis is a decrease in white cells and is not associated with a prolactinoma. Answer C is incorrect because polyuria is associated with diabetes insipidus, not a prolactinoma. Answer D is incorrect because bone pain is not associated with a prolactinoma.

57. Answer A is correct. Clients with myxedema often have constipation due to a slow metabolic rate. Green, leafy vegetable such as turnip greens help to facilitate bowel mobility. Answers B, C, and D are more constipating foods and are therefore incorrect.

58. Answer C is correct. A transphenoidal approach is done to remove a pituitary tumor. This type of surgery is done by removing the tumor through the nose or upper palate. Because the pituitary gland is adjacent to the brain, checking for the presence of glucose in the nasal discharge is a priority. Its presence can indicate leaking of cerebrospinal fluid. This leakage should be reported to the doctor immediately. Other assessments include checking the airway. Answer A is incorrect because checking the gag reflex can cause damage to the surgical area. Answer B is incorrect because assessing the urinary output is of lesser priority. Answer D is incorrect because checking Homan's sign is no longer recommended for thrombophlebitis.

59. Answer B is correct. Diabetes insipidus is caused by a lack of antidiuretic hormone. This results in polyuria with a low specific gravity. Answers A, C, and D are incorrect because they are not associated with diabetes insipidus.

60. Answer B is correct. Clients with myxedema (hypothyroidism) are often cold. Answer A is incorrect because clients with hypothyroidism do not require a private room. Answer C is incorrect because clients with myxedema do not require high-calorie foods. Answer D is incorrect because clients with myxedema often have hypotension, not hypertension.

61. Answer C is correct. Thyroid medications can cause tachycardia. For this reason, the pulse rate should be checked prior to taking the medication. Answers A, B, and D are false statements and are therefore incorrect.

62. Answer A is correct. Sicca is dry eyes. This problem is often associated with bulging eyeballs and the inability to adequately close the eyelids. This lack of lubrication causes drying of the cornea. Application of artificial tears helps to prevent and treat dry eyes. Answer B is incorrect because sicca is not associated with dry mouth. Answer C is incorrect because the need for mouth care is not associated with sicca. Answer D is incorrect because sicca is not associated with the need to avoid eating uncooked foods.

63. Answer B is correct. A thyroidectomy is the removal of the thyroid. The incision is located at the base of the neck. The airway should be checked frequently because swelling and closure of the trachea can occur following this surgery. For this

reason, a tracheostomy set should be placed at the bedside in case of airway closure. Answer A is incorrect because there is no association between a thyroidectomy and kidney function. Answer C is incorrect because pain medication should be offered as ordered, usually every three to four hours and as needed. Answer D is incorrect because there is no abdominal dressing.

64. Answer D is correct. The parathyroid is responsible for absorption of calcium and phosphorus. When a client has hypoparathyroidism, the serum calcium levels are low (as stated in answer D) and the serum phosphorus levels are high. The normal is 1.5–4.5 mEq/L or 9.3–10.9 mg/L. Answers A, B, and C are incorrect because all these results are within normal range. There is also a lesser correlation between these levels and the parathyroid function.

65. Answer B is correct. Trousseau's sign, which indicates hypocalcemia, is elicited by placing a blood pressure cuff on the arm. If carpopedal spasms are noted when the cuff is inflated, the test is considered positive. Answer A is incorrect because this answer describes Chvostek's sign. Answer C is incorrect because checking the deep tendon reflexes is not part of checking for Trousseau's sign. Answer D is incorrect for the same reason.

66. Answer A is correct. Because the parathyroid is located on the thyroid gland, the client will have an incision in the lower neck. The client should be placed in a dorsal recumbent position when he returns from surgery. Bleeding might not be noted on the dressing because blood can trickle behind the neck. Answers B, C, and D are incorrect because parathyroid incisions are not located behind the ear, on the abdomen, or in the groin area.

67. Answer D is correct. The best indicator of diabetes mellitus is the glucose tolerance test. Answer A is incorrect because, although a two-hour postprandial blood glucose test is good, it is not the best test for diabetes mellitus. Answer B is incorrect because a dextrostix is not the best test for diabetes mellitus. Answer C is incorrect because a glycosylated hemoglobin test indicates compliance to diet and medication regimen used to treat diabetes mellitus. It is not a study used to determine the diagnosis of diabetes mellitus.

68. Answer D is correct. The diabetic with hypoglycemia will present with altered level of consciousness; dilated pupils; and cool, clammy skin. Giving the client juice will facilitate elevating the blood glucose levels. Answers A, B, and C are incorrect because they will not correct hypoglycemia.

69. Answer B is correct. If the client has altered sensorium and the skin is cold and clammy, he is probably suffering from hypoglycemia. The treatment is to provide a rapid source of glucose. Answer A is incorrect because this answer indicates that the nurse believes the blood glucose level is elevated. Answer C is incorrect because normal saline will not help to increase the blood glucose levels. Answer D is incorrect because inserting a Foley catheter will not help to increase the glucose level.

70. Answer A is correct. The Somogyi effect occurs when there is a drop in the blood glucose level during the night with an abrupt rise in blood glucose levels in the early morning. Checking the blood glucose levels and offering a bedtime snack consisting of a protein and glucose source is the treatment. Answer B is incorrect and will further lower the glucose level. Answer C is incorrect because checking the urine for glucose and ketones will not correct the problem. Answer D is incorrect because offering an antiemetic will not correct the hypoglycemia associated with the Somogyi effect.

71. Answer B is correct. Dawn phenomena occurs when there is a decrease in blood glucose levels during the night with elevations in the early morning. Treatment of dawn phenomena includes waking the client to check blood glucose levels and sliding scale insulin administration. Answer A is incorrect because offering peanut butter and crackers will help to prevent the Somogyi effect not dawn phenomena. Answer C is incorrect because administering NPH insulin will not treat or prevent dawn phenomena. Answer D is incorrect because there is no need to check cortisole levels when the client is experiencing dawn phenomena.

72. Answer D is correct. Regular insulin peaks in approximately two hours. A mid-morning snack will help to prevent a hypoglycemic reaction. Answers A, B, and C are incorrect because regular insulin does not peak at these times if it is administered at 7:00 a.m.

73. Answer D is correct. NPH insulin peaks in 6–12 hours. A snack will help to ensure that the client does not experience a hypoglycemic reaction. Answers A, B, and C are incorrect because NPH insulin does not peak at 9:00 a.m., 11:00 a.m., or 1:00 p.m. if administered at 8:00 a.m.

74. Answer C is correct. Metformin (Glucophage) is a medication used to treat diabetes mellitus. If the client is scheduled for a dye procedure such as a cardiac catheterization or pacemaker insertion, he should be instructed to stop the medication at the time of the procedure and resume after renal function has resumed. Metformin is detrimental to the kidneys, as is the dye procedure. These two factors can contribute to renal failure. Giving insulin to control the blood glucose levels is the safest way to treat the client at this time. Answer A is incorrect because the medication should be held the morning of the procedure. Answer B is incorrect because letting the doctor know that the client has burning urinates is important but is not associated with the use of metformin. Answer D is incorrect because the nurse cannot tell the client to halve the dose of medication, and half the dose can still cause problems with renal function.

75. Answer A is correct. A client with pheochromocytoma, an adrenal tumor, can have malignant hypertension resulting in a cerebro-vascular accident or a myocardial infarction. Answers B, C, and D are incorrect because these symptoms are associated with Addison's disease, which is an adrenal insufficiency not pheochromocytoma.

76. Answer A is correct. Addisonian crises occur when there is a lack of cortisole. The lack of cortisole can result in death due to shock. Answer B is incorrect because the

blood pressure will be low not high. Answer C is incorrect because in Addisonian crises, osteoporosis is not the priority action. Answer D is incorrect because teaching can be done later. Cortisole should never be stopped suddenly.

77. Answer C is correct. A client with Cushing's disease will have a pendulous abdomen, a buffalo hump, a moon face, hirsutism, and a ruddy complexion. Osteoporosis is often evident because elevations in cortisole can cause calcium to leave the bones. Pathological fractures often result. Answer A is incorrect because Cushing's disease results in hyperglycemia and weight gain. Answer B is incorrect because Cushing's disease results in decreased lymphocytes and a ruddy complexion. Answer D is incorrect because Cushing's disease results in increased blood pressure and a ruddy complexion.

78. Answer B is correct. Rosiglitazone (Avandia) can lead to renal and liver failure. A creatinine of 3.0 mg/dL is elevated from the normal of 0.6–1.35 mg/dL. Answer A is incorrect because 110 mg/dL is in the upper limits of normal. Answer C is incorrect because a blood urea nitrogen level of 10 mg/dL is within normal limits. Answer D is incorrect because a white blood cell count of 8,000 is within normal limits.

79. Answer B is correct. Lantus insulin should not be mixed with any other insulin because mixing can alter the absorption of the medication and cause clouding of the medication. Answers A and D are incorrect because the Lantus insulin cannot be mixed. Answer C is incorrect because there is no need to give the insulins one hour apart.

80. Answer B is correct. Clients of the Jewish faith often reject the consumption of pork. Answer A, C, and D are incorrect because clients of the Jewish faith usually accept rDNA insulin, beef insulin, and insulin that contains zinc.

81. Answer B is correct. Lugol's solution is bitter to taste. Taking the medication with juice helps to make the drug more palatable. Answer A is incorrect because the drug does not have to be taken in the morning. Answer C is incorrect because there is no need to avoid abrupt change in position. Answer D is incorrect because Lugol's solution is used immediately prior to thyroid surgery to prevent a thyroid storm. The optimal effect is reached quickly.

82. Answer A is correct. The letters *bid* at the end of the medication's name indicate that the medication should be given two times per day. Answer B is incorrect because there is no need to take the medication with milk or meals. The nurse should maintain adequate sodium intake to prevent lithium toxicity. Answer C is incorrect because lithium carbonate (Lithobid) should not be taken with an antiemetic. Answer D is incorrect because lithium carbonate is used in this case to treat the symptoms of increased thyroid function and is not used to treat psychosis.

83. Answer B is correct. Acarbose (Precose) is an antidiabetic medication that can be harmful to the liver. The normal blood urea nitrogen level is 7–22 mg/dL. Answers A, C, and D are incorrect because all of these laboratory findings are within normal limits.

84. Answer C is correct. For best utilization of cortisol, the medication should be given in the early morning. Answer A is incorrect because there is no need to check the pulse prior to giving cortisol. Answer B is incorrect because there is no need to check the specific gravity of the urine prior to giving cortisol. Answer D is incorrect for the same reason.

85. Answer A is correct. Spironolactone (Aldactone) is a potassium diuretic that interferes with cortisol. Answer B is incorrect because nitroprusside (Nitropress) is used for malignant hypertension. Answer C is incorrect because Cushing's disease is hypersecretion of cortisol; dexamethasone (Decadron) is a type of cortisol and will worsen the illness. Answer D is incorrect because demclocycline is an antibiotic.

86. Answer B is correct. Acromegaly is an increase in growth hormone. This problem can be due to pituitary tumors. Answers A, C, and D are signs or symptoms associated with increased cortisol levels and are therefore incorrect.

87. Answer D is correct. Glucagon (GlucaGen) is used to treat extreme hypoglycemia. Answers A, B, and C are incorrect because all these drugs are antidiabetic medications.

88. Answer A is correct. Clients with a carbon dioxide level of 46 mEq/L are experiencing respiratory complications related to acidosis. Kussmaul respirations are rapid respirations with periods of apnea. Answer B is incorrect because the client will increase the respirations in an attempt to blow off carbon dioxide. Answer C is incorrect because eupnea is normal respiration. Answer D is incorrect because the client will have audible respirations.

89. Answer B is correct. The client with hyperosmolar nonketonic coma associated with hyperosmolar nonketonic ketoacidosis (HHNK) requires adequate fluids to treat hypotension. The hypotension is associated with polyuria. Answer A is incorrect because oxygen will not help the hypotension. Oxygen should be administered by mask to provide a higher concentration. Answer C is incorrect because the problem is caused by increased blood glucose levels. Giving carbohydrates will only worsen the problem. Answer D is incorrect because the client should be treated with insulin, not oral antidiabetic medications.

90. Answer D is correct. Clients with Syndrome of Inappropriate Anti-diuretic Hormone have low sodium levels. The nurse should prepare to administer a solution containing sodium. Answers A, B, C are incorrect because they do not increase sodium levels.

Care of the Client with Immunologic Disorders

91. Answer D is correct. The indirect immunofluorescence assay (IFA) test along with the Western Blot test can be used to confirm the diagnosis of HIV. Answer A is incorrect because the RIPA test detects HIV protein rather than showing antibodies. Answer B is incorrect because the p24 count detects the amount of virus core protein (p24 antigen). Answer C is incorrect because the lymphocyte is used to detect progression of the illness.

92. Answer B is correct. A viral load of less than 400 copies per mL indicates the client is relatively free of circulating virus. Answers A, C, and D are incorrect statements.

93. Answer D is correct. Human immunodeficiency virus can be transmitted through blood fluids such as breast milk. Answer A is incorrect because breast milk and colostrum can contain HIV. Answer B is incorrect because heating does not kill the virus in breast milk. Answer C is incorrect because HIV can be transmitted at any stage of the illness.

94. Answer C is correct. Fresh fruits are often contaminated with germs that can cause opportunistic infections in the immune-suppressed client. The best choice for the client with HIV is the banana because it is peeled prior to eating. Answers A, B, and D are incorrect because these fruits are not peeled prior to eating.

95. Answer D is correct. Use of latex condoms helps to decrease the transmission of HIV. Answer A is incorrect because, although oral contraceptives prevent pregnancy, they do not prevent the transmission of sexually transmitted infections. Answer B is incorrect because lamb's skin condoms are more porous than latex and are therefore less effective in preventing the transmission of HIV. Answer C is incorrect because use of an intrauterine device does not prevent the transmission of HIV.

96. Answer B is correct. Turtles carry salmonella that can be transmitted to the immune-suppressed client. Answer A is incorrect because petting his dog does not pose an extreme risk to a client with HIV. Answer C is incorrect because feeding wild birds does not pose a risk to a client with HIV. Clients with HIV should not, however, have birds in the house because histoplasmosis can be carried by birds. Answer D is incorrect because simply feeding his cat does not pose a risk to the client.

97. Answer C is correct. Blood and body fluids should be cleaned using a hypochlorite solution composed of 1 part bleach and 10 parts water. Answers A, B, and D are incorrect because these products are less effective in destroying the virus.

98. Answer D is correct. *Clostridium difficile* is spread by contamination with feces. Healthcare providers who do not wear gloves or wash their hands after caring for a client with *Clostridium difficile* should wash their hands and wear gloves during care to prevent spread of the illness. Other examples of infections treated with contact precautions include respiratory syncytial virus (RSV), scabies, and methicillin-resistant *Staphylococcus aureus* (MRSA). Answers A, B, and C are incorrect because *Clostridium difficile* is an infection of the gastrointestinal tract, and not an infection of the lungs spread by sputum.

99. Answer A is correct. Highly active retroviral therapy (HAART) is a combination of three categories of medications. Answers B, C, and D are incorrect because none of these answers describe HAART.

100. Answer B is incorrect. Taking metronidazole (Flagyl) with alcohol causes extreme nausea. Answer A is incorrect because metronidazole can be taken at other times of the day than in the morning. Answer C is incorrect because metronidazole takes effect very quickly. Answer D is incorrect because there is no need to take the medication with an antacid.

101. Answer D is correct. *Pneumocytis carinii* is commonly treated with sulfa antibiotics such as sulfamethoxazole (Bactrim or Septra). Other drugs used to treat *Pneumocytis carinii* pneumonia are metronidazole (Flagyl) and pentamidine isethionate (Pentim). Answers A, B, and C are incorrect because these drugs are antivirals used to treat illnesses such as cytomegalovirus and herpes.

102. Answer B is correct. The diagnosis of HIV can be traumatic. Allowing the client to express emotions will help him to accept the diagnosis. Answer A is incorrect because including the family might be more psychologically traumatic to the client. Later the family can be included in the teaching if the client chooses. Answer C is incorrect because now is not the time to thoroughly explain the disease and prognosis. Answer D is incorrect because asking the client what he knows about the disease will not help him accept the disease or prepare him psychologically.

103. Answer B is correct. Clients with AIDS have decreased protein absorption. Protein is needed for tissue repair. Answer A is incorrect because the client will have decreased appetite, not increased. Answer C is incorrect because the client does not have increased secretions of digestive juices. Answer D is incorrect because the client does not have decreased gastrointestinal absorption.

104. Answer D is correct. Toxoplasmosis is a protazoa spread by cat feces. Emptying the cat's litter box can lead to contamination, causing the client to contract the disease. Answers A, B, and C are incorrect because toxoplasmosis is not spreads by these routes.

105. Answer B is correct. An elevated temperature is often the first sign of an infection in the immune-suppressed client. Answer A is incorrect because the immune-suppressed client might not have a sore throat with an infection. Answers C and D are incorrect because they are later signs of infection.

106. Answer C is correct. Kaposi's sarcoma is a malignancy of the skin and connective tissue. Painful multifocal lesions often can be seen on the skin and mucous membranes. Placing the client on a floatation mattress and providing skin care can help the client to be more comfortable. Answers A, B, and D are incorrect because these actions will not help the client to be more comfortable.

107. Answer C is correct. The client with a CD4 +T cell count of greater than or equal to 500 cu.mm/liter is most likely asymptomatic. If the client's CD4 +T cell count drops below 200 cu.mm/liter, he will most likely be at risk for opportunistic diseases. Answers A, B, and D are incorrect assessments of this data.

108. Answer C is correct. Zidovudine (AZT) is given to the mother during pregnancy and to the infant after birth to decrease the chances of the infant contracting the illness. Answer A is an incorrect statement. Answer B is incorrect because an

antibiotic will not prevent the infant from contracting the disease. Answer D is incorrect because TMC-114 darunavir (Prezista) is not the drug of choice for maternal transmission of the illness.

109. Answer B is correct. Cytomegalovirus is often exhibited by alterations in vision. Cytomegalovirus retinitis can lead to blindness if not treated. Answers A, C, and D are incorrect because these are not common manifestations of cytomegalovirus.

110. Answer D is correct. Acyclovir (Zovirax) a drug used to treat herpes. Answers A, B, and C are incorrect because the drugs listed in these answers are used to treat tuberculosis.

Care of the Childbearing Client and the Neonatal Client

111. Answer C is correct. Folic acid (B9) is helpful in decreasing the likelihood of neural tube defects in the neonate. Answer A is niacin (B3), Answer B is riboflavin (B2), and Answer D is thiamine (B1). These are all good vitamins, but they do not help to decrease the likelihood of a neural tube defect.

112. Answer B is correct. Around 36 pounds is allowable weight gain during pregnancy. The client should take multivitamins and minerals and drink about one quart of milk per day to ensure adequate nutrition. Answers A and D are incorrect because 15 or 25 pounds weight gain during pregnancy is probably not enough to accommodate for fluid and neonatal weight gain. Answer C is incorrect because 55 pounds is probably too much weight gain during pregnancy.

113. Answer A is correct. If the Alpha Feta protein levels are abnormal, the doctor will probably order an amniocentesis to confirm or eliminate the diagnosis of a neural tube defect. Answer B is incorrect because an Alpha Feta protein level is a screening test and is not diagnostic. Answer C is incorrect because the client will not be asleep for this blood test. Answer D is incorrect because Alpha Feta protein does not indicate lung disorders.

114. Answer C is correct. Tetracycline (Achromycin) is a class X medication that causes staining of the teeth and can lead to a child with short stature. Answer A is incorrect because propranolol (Inderal) is a beta blocker used to treat hypertension, mitral valve prolapse, and anxiety. Answer B is incorrect because penicillin (Amoxicillin) is an antibiotic used to treat bacterial infections. Answer D is incorrect because propafenone (Rythmol) is an antidysrhythmic used to treat a slow conduction system of the heart. The medications in answers A, B, and D are allowable in pregnancy.

115. Answer D is correct. If polyhydramnios is seen on ultrasound, the fetus is most likely experiencing hyperglycemia. Answers A, B, and C are incorrect because they do not indicate hyperglycemia.

116. Answer B is correct. Prior to 20 weeks, the bladder should remain full for an amniocentesis. The full bladder helps to elevate the uterus, making it easier to get a sample of amniotic fluid. Answer A is incorrect because after 20 weeks the bladder should be empty. This client is at 17 weeks gestation. Answer C is incorrect because an amniocentesis can be done immediately after the ultrasound exam. Answer D is incorrect because the amniocentesis can be done after 16 weeks.

117. Answer A is correct. A positive nonstress test indicates that the fetus has periodic fetal movement with periods of rest. A positive nonstress is therefore a reassuring pattern. Answers B and C are incorrect because they indicate that the nonstress test is abnormal. Answer D is incorrect because there is no data to indicate a need to repeat the test in one week.

118. Answer B is correct. The information noted in the question stem is within normal limits and does not require intervention. Answers A, C, and D indicate that the nurse believes that the information is abnormal.

119. Answer C is correct. To ensure that the client is not having hypertonic contractions, the client will be placed on the fetal monitor. The correct amount of intravenous medication must be evaluated to ensure safety. Answer A is incorrect because it is not necessary to insert a Foley catheter. Answer B is incorrect because there is no need to check the urinary output every hour. Answer D is incorrect because there is no need to give an antiemetic prior to beginning the infusion.

120. Answer B is correct. Because there is no information indicating that the nurse has evaluated the contractions and fetal heart tones using the fetal monitor, the next action should be to assess the client using the more objective machine. Answer A is incorrect because simply charting the finding is not enough action. Answer C is incorrect because more data needs to be collected prior to calling the physician. Answer D is incorrect because there is no data to indicate it is time for the delivery.

121. Answer B is correct. Rubella is a live virus and should not be given during pregnancy. Answer A is incorrect because the immunization is contraindicated. Answer C is incorrect because the nurse should not administer the medication. Answer D is incorrect for the same reason.

122. Answer C is correct. Prostaglandin gel should remain in the cervix for at least 30 minutes after insertion for optimal effect. Elevating the hips helps to ensure that the medication stays in place. Answer A is incorrect because Stadol (butorphanol) is not routinely given at the time prostaglandin gel is inserted. Answer B is incorrect because the answer will make the client more anxious. Answer D is incorrect because it is not necessary to insert a Foley catheter when prostaglandin is used. The client should not be allowed out of bed for at least 30 minutes because the gel can be lost due to pressure on the perineum with voiding.

123. Answer C is correct. The answer describes late decelerations caused by uteroplacental insufficiency. Answer A is incorrect because the answer describes a normal finding. Answer B is incorrect because the desire to push can indicate complete

dilation. The nurse should assess for dilation and continue the medication. Answer D is incorrect because nausea and vomiting are not reasons to discontinue the medication.

124. Answer A is correct. The first action that the nurse should take is to place the client in Trendelenburg position. Placing the client in Trendelenburg position will help to relieve pressure on the umbilical cord. Answer B is incorrect because this action should be taken after positioning the client. Answer C is incorrect because an IV of normal saline or lactated Ringer's would be the IV fluids of choice. Dextrose will cause drying of the cord. Answer D is incorrect because the umbilical cord should be covered with moist, sterile, saline gauze.

125. Answer B is correct. If the client had hypertension during pregnancy, the blood pressure should be further assessed prior to starting oral contraceptive. Hypertension and the use of oral contraceptive can lead to cardiac disease and strokes due to blood clots. Answer A is incorrect because the diagnosis of HIV does not affect the client's ability to take oral contraceptives. Condoms should be used to decrease the likelihood of spreading of the virus. Answer C is incorrect because the client's age does not affect her ability to take oral contraceptives. Answer D is incorrect because the client who is a gravida 5 para 4 can take oral contraceptives.

126. Answer B is correct. The safest method of birth control for a client with diabetes is the condom because oral contraceptives can cause elevations in blood glucose levels. Answers A, C, and D are incorrect facts regarding oral contraceptives.

127. Answer C is correct. If the anterior fontanel is toward the rectum, the occipital portion of the skull is anterior to the mother's pelvis. This portion is known as *occipital anterior*. Answer A is incorrect because if the client's fetus is positioned in the occipital posterior position, the anterior fontanel would be directly beneath the pubic bone. Answer B is incorrect because in transverse position, the suture line is directly in line with the mother's right or left side. Answer D is incorrect because breech presentation is when the feet or buttocks present first.

128. Answer A is correct. Zero station is at the level of the ischial spines of the pelvic bone. Plus station is below the ischial spines and minus station is above the ischial spines. The presenting part of this client is at +4 station; therefore, the client is crowning the presenting part. Answer B is incorrect because charting the finding is not enough action. Answer C is incorrect because pain medication should not be given immediately prior to delivery for the reason that it can suppress fetal heart tones and respirations. Answer D is incorrect because increasing the rate of the pitocin (oxytocin) speeds the delivery process.

129. Answer B is correct. The data described in the question stem indicates fetal distress. Applying an oxygen via mask is the most appropriate action. Answers A, C, and D are lower-priority actions.

130. Answer A is correct. After completing the assessment, the nurse should call the physician. The symptoms are consistent with congestive heart failure and require immediate action. Answer B is incorrect because the client's condition can deteriorate quickly. Answer C is incorrect because elevating the head can help, but the nurse is wasting time with continued assessment. Answer D is incorrect because the nurse needs an order for a diuretic.

131. Answer C is correct. A class II cardiac client is symptomatic with moderate activity. Answer A is incorrect because this client does not have to remain on strict bed rest during pregnancy. Answer B is incorrect because clients with class II cardiac disease can probably continue the pregnancy with prenatal care. Answer D is incorrect because there is probably no need for oxygen therapy.

132. Answer C is correct. The Heimlich maneuver can be performed on the pregnant client by performing back blows and chest thrusts. Answer A is incorrect because abdominal thrusts are contraindicated in a pregnant client. Answer B is incorrect because the nurse should not wait until the client loses consciousness to perform the Heimlich maneuver. Answer D is incorrect because a finger sweep can force food farther into the throat.

133. Answer C is correct. Blood glucose levels in the pregnant client should be controlled with insulin. Answer A is incorrect because oral antidiabetic drugs should not be used during pregnancy. Answer B is incorrect because the client should gain approximately 30–36 pounds. Answer D is incorrect because urine checks are a poor indicator of glucose levels.

134. Answer B is correct. The client is experiencing late decelerations caused by cord compression. Turning the client to her left side can relieve pressure on the cord and improve oxygenation to the uterus. Answers A, C, and D are incorrect actions because they will not improve oxygenation.

135. Answer B is correct. Instructions for having a glucose tolerance test should include remaining NPO after midnight the day of the test. A fasting blood glucose sample is collected followed by consumption of a glucose drink. Blood glucose levels are checked at one hour, two hours, and perhaps three hours after the glucose is consumed. Answer A is incorrect because, although a high-carbohydrate diet should be consumed for three days prior to the test, most of us consume enough carbohydrate in our diet to ensure correct readings. This is not the most important instruction. Answer C is incorrect because a glucose drink is consumed after the fasting blood glucose is collected, not prior to the test. Answer D is incorrect because blood, not urine, is collected.

136. Answer C is correct. Urine protein levels above 5 grams in a 24-hour urine sample indicate severe preeclampsia. Answer A is incorrect because a blood pressure of 140/90 is a borderline elevation. Answer B is incorrect because pedal edema is common in pregnancy. Answer D is incorrect because a platelet count of 280,000 is a normal finding.

137. Answer A is correct. Urinary output must be monitored hourly when the client is receiving magnesium sulfate. Signs of toxicity include oliguria, absence of the deep tendon reflexes, and a respiratory rate of less than 12 per minute. Answer B is incorrect because checking the deep tendon reflexes is done during care. Answer C is incorrect because there is no data to indicate the need for pain medication. Answer D is incorrect because darkening the room can help to decrease the potential for seizures in the client with preeclampsia; however, this should be done after beginning the magnesium sulfate.

138. Answer B is correct. 4.8–9.6 mg/dL is a therapeutic level for magnesium sulfate. The nurse should chart the finding and continue the infusion. Answer A is incorrect because there is no need to obtain another sample. Answer C is incorrect because there is no need to call the doctor. Answer D is incorrect because there is no need to administer calcium gluconate.

139. Answer C is correct. An ectopic pregnancy is a pregnancy outside the body of the uterus. The nurse should be aware that treatment of an ectopic pregnancy includes evacuation of the tube by laparoscopic surgery. Answers A, B, and D are incorrect because the nurse should be concerned with all of these problems.

140. Answer D is correct. A hydatidiform is a false pregnancy. The treatment is evacuation of the uterus by dilation and curettage. The client should refrain from becoming pregnant again for at least one year because chorionic carcinoma is associated with the presence of a hydatidiform mole. If the client becomes pregnant while chorionic cancer cells are present, the elevations in human chorionic gonadotropin hormone levels can cause the cancer to grow. Answer A is incorrect because some bleeding is expected after the dilation and curettage. Answer B is incorrect because the client should refrain from having intercourse for approximately six weeks. Answer C is incorrect because there is no fetus to preserve.

141. Answer A is correct. Prostaglandin can lead to nausea and vomiting. Answer B is incorrect because prostaglandin can cause diarrhea, not constipation. Answer C is an incorrect statement. Answer D is incorrect because the client should be instructed to void every two hours. She will not require a treatment with a Foley catheter.

142. Answer B is correct. The client with placenta previa who is in labor is bleeding. This is an emergency situation that requires immediate action to control bleeding. Answers A, C, and D are incorrect because these clients can be seen later.

143. Answer D is correct. If the client has placenta previa, a vaginal exam can lead to further bleeding. Answer A is incorrect because the client can ambulate to the bathroom if there is no bleeding. Answers B and C are incorrect because there is no contraindication to these nursing actions.

144. Answer B is correct. Terbutaline (Brethine) is a tocolytic drug used to treat premature labor. This drug can cause elevations in blood glucose levels. Answers A, C, and D are incorrect because these drugs can be taken by the client with diabetes.

145. Answer C is correct. Terbutaline (Brethine) can be given intravenously, by mouth, or subcutaneously. Answers A, B, and D are incorrect because these needles and syringes are too large to administer the medication subcutaneously.

146. Answer C is correct. A pulse rate of 120 is tachycardia. Answers A, B, and D are within normal limits. A temperature of 37° centigrade is equal to 98° Fahrenheit.

147. Answer B is correct. The antidote for magnesium sulfate is calcium gluconate. Answer A is incorrect because protamine sulfate is the antidote for heparin. Answer C is incorrect because atropine sulfate is an anticholenergic drug. Answer D is incorrect because AquaMEPHYTON (Vitamin K) is the antidote for sodium warfarin (Coumadin).

148. Answer C is correct. Heparin derivatives are the only classification of anticoagulants that can safely be administered in pregnancy. Answers A, B, and D can cross the placental barrier and lead to bleeding in the fetus.

149. Answer C is correct. The treatment for a prolapsed cord is to elevate the client's hips; apply oxygen by mask; and cover the cord with a sterile, moist saline gauze. Preparations for a cesarean section should begin immediately. Answer A is incorrect because the gauze should be moist and sterile. Answer B is incorrect because the cord should not be reinserted. Answer D is incorrect because oxygen should be applied by mask.

150. Answer B is correct. The licensed practical nurse with 10 years experience in the postpartal unit is aware of the bleeding problems that a mother of a baby that is large for gestational weight might encounter. Answers A, C, and D are incorrect because these nurses are less aware of the normal amount of postpartal bleeding.

151. Answer B is correct. The information given in the question describes an early deceleration caused by head compression. The appropriate action is to check the client for cervical dilation. If the client is completely dilated and pushing, a drop in the fetal heart tones can be seen. The fetal heart tones between contractions are normal. Answer A is incorrect because the nurse should assess the client for cervical dilation prior to preparing for delivery. Answer C is incorrect because the nurse should perform a vaginal exam for dilation prior to asking the client to begin pushing. Answer D is incorrect for the same reason.

152. Answer B is correct. A V-shaped deceleration that occurs randomly in relation to the contractions is a variable deceleration. This type of deceleration is caused by cord compression and requires intervention. Answer A is incorrect because there is no data that indicates that the client is in the transition phase of labor. Answer C is incorrect because an early deceleration is caused by head compression. Answer D is incorrect because fetal hypoxia and uteroplacental insufficiency cause late decelerations.

153. Answer D is correct. Clients having spinal or epidural anesthesia often experience hypotension. To decrease the potential for hypotensive crises, the nurse should give the client 2000 mL of intravenous fluid. Answer A is incorrect because offering oral liquids will not prevent hypotension. Answer B is incorrect because

inserting a Foley catheter is not necessary. Answer C is incorrect because offering pain medication is not necessary and can further lead to hypotension.

154. Answer C is correct. A uterus displaced to the left side of the abdomen indicates a full bladder. The nurse should instruct the client to void or empty the bladder by catheterization. Answer A is incorrect because redness and edema of the perineum is expected after delivery of a 9 lb. infant. After the bladder is empty, an ice pack can be applied. Answer B is incorrect because these problems can be addressed after emptying the bladder. Answer D is incorrect because breast tenderness and dripping of colostrum is expected.

155. Answer B is correct. Two identification bands should be applied, one to each ankle. Some hospitals require a code system that is scanned when the infant leaves the nursery to visit the mother. Only one form of identification is not enough to ensure the infant's safety. Answer A is incorrect because an Apgar score of 8 at one minute and 10 at 5 minutes is normal. Answer C is incorrect because slightly blue feet are expected. Answer D is incorrect because a heart rate of 110 beats per minute is normal.

156. Answer B is correct. The correct method for obtaining blood for a dextrose stick is to prick the lateral aspect of the heel. The tip of the heel should not be used to obtain blood because this action can cause damage to the nerve located in this area. Answer A is incorrect because cradling the infant during feeding is allowed. Answer C is incorrect because placing a drape over the scales is recommended. Answer D is incorrect because the best type of tape measure is the paper tape measure.

157. Answer B is correct. Edema that crosses the suture line is known as a *caput succedaneum*. This finding is often seen following a vaginal delivery and requires no action other than to document the finding. Answer A is incorrect because this is not a dangerous finding. Answer C is incorrect because a cephalohematoma does not cross the suture line. Answer D is incorrect because the description given is not consistent with a subdural hematoma.

158. Answer C is correct. Dark spots on the back and buttocks of the African-American infant are Mongolian spots. These spots are normal variations in this population. Answers A, B, and D are incorrect because these answers indicate that the nurse believes that the finding is abnormal.

159. Answer A is correct. When the mother has Rh negative blood and the infant has Rh positive blood, an Rh incompatibility problem exists. This incompatibility can lead to destruction of the infant's red blood cells. The hemolysis of the red blood cells often leads to elevations in unconjugated bilirubin. This is known as *kernicterus*. Answer B is incorrect because there is no direct correlation between hypertension and Rh incompatibility. Answer C is incorrect because the infant might not need a cesarean section. Answer D is incorrect because the infant might need an exchange, not the mother.

160. Answer A is correct. Rh (D) immune globulin is given to the mother to prevent isoimmunization. Answer B is incorrect because Ribavirin is an antiviral medication. Answer C is incorrect because Repaglinide is an antidiabetic medication. Answer D is incorrect because Raloxifene is a selective estrogen receptor modulator used to treat osteoporosis.

161. Answer B is correct. Extra liquids should be given to help speed excretion of conjugated bilirubin though the kidneys. The infant should be placed in the sunshine. Answer A is incorrect because, although breast-fed babies have more jaundice, breast-feeding need not be stopped. Answer C is incorrect because administering vitamins with iron will not help. Answer D is incorrect because formula should not be replaced with water.

162. Answer C is correct. Gonorrhea is often associated with pelvic inflammatory disease. Answers A, B, and D are incorrect because these infections are not associated with pelvic inflammatory disease.

163. Answer C is correct. Conjugate estrogen (Premarin) is often prescribed to treat hot flashes caused by a lack of estrogen. Answers A, B, and D are incorrect because all these medications are used to treat osteoporosis commonly seen after menopause.

164. Answer A is correct. Vitamin K is given to prevent newborn bleeding. Answer B is incorrect because amikacin (Amikin) is an antibiotic. Answer C is incorrect because amiodarone (Cordarone) is a cardiac medication. Answer D is incorrect because amoxicillin (Amoxil) is an antibiotic.

165. Answer D is correct. The infant of a drug-addicted mother often has seizure disorder due to withdrawal. Answer A is incorrect because intravenous feedings might be ordered, but oral feedings can continue. Answer B is incorrect because there is a need for decreased stimulation, not increased stimulation. Answer C is incorrect because there is no correlation between drug addiction and the need for acetaminophen (Tylenol).

166. Answer C is correct. A distended bladder can cause pain and increase vaginal bleeding and bladder spasms. Answer A is incorrect because it is not unusual to see a slight elevation in the temperature after delivery. After asking the client to void or performing a urinary catheterization, the temperature can be further evaluated. Answer B is incorrect because a moderate amount of lochia rubra is a normal finding. Answer D is incorrect because clear discharge from the breast is colostrum, a normal finding.

Answers to Practice Exam II

Answers at a Glance to Practice Exam II

1. D	30. B	59. D
2. C	31. C	60. C
3. A	32. B	61. A
4. B	33. A	62. D
5. A	34. C	63. B
6. B	35. D	64. C
7. B	36. B	65. B
8. C	37. A	66. D
9. B	38. B	67. A
10. D	39. B	68. A
11. D	40. D	69. C
12. B	41. A	70. D
13. B	42. B	71. D
14. A	43. C	72. B
15. C	44. B	73. D
16. B	45. C	74. A
17. A	46. A	75. C
18. A	47. D	76. B
19. A	48. C	77. C
20. B	49. A	78. A
21. B	50. D	79. C
22. C	51. C	80. B
23. A	52. B	81. C
24. C	53. B	82. D
25. C	54. C	83. C
26. D	55. C	84. C
27. C	56. B	85. D
28. D	57. A	86. A
29. B	58. A	87. A

88. B	**115.** B	**142.** B
89. C	**116.** A	**143.** A
90. B	**117.** D	**144.** C
91. D	**118.** B	**145.** B
92. D	**119.** B	**146.** B
93. C	**120.** A	**147.** D
94. B	**121.** D	**148.** C
95. B	**122.** B	**149.** A
96. A	**123.** C	**150.** C
97. A	**124.** D	**151.** B
98. B	**125.** B	**152.** C
99. D	**126.** A	**153.** D
100. C	**127.** B	**154.** B
101. D	**128.** C	**155.** B
102. C	**129.** A	**156.** D
103. D	**130.** C	**157.** B
104. C	**131.** B	**158.** D
105. B	**132.** D	**159.** D
106. A	**133.** A	**160.** B
107. A	**134.** B	**161.** C
108. D	**135.** B	**162.** D
109. D	**136.** A	**163.** C
110. B	**137.** C	**164.** B
111. D	**138.** D	**165.** D
112. B	**139.** C	**166.** A
113. C	**140.** B	
114. C	**141.** D	

Answers with Explanations

Care of the Client with Respiratory Disorders

1. Answer D is correct. The nurse should be able to see the client's face when performing percussion in case a mucus plug obstructs the airway and the client is unable to speak. Answers A, B, and C are a part of performing chest physiotherapy; however, they do not take priority over maintaining patency of the airway therefore they are incorrect choices

2. Answer C is correct. Acute respiratory distress syndrome (ARDS) is characterized by the appearance of "ground glass" infiltrates that minimize gas exchange in the lungs ultimately leading to refractory hypoxemia. Answers A, B, and D are incorrect statements.

3. Answer A is correct. Absence of fluctuation in the second (water seal) chamber may be the result of the suction not working properly so the nurse should first determine if this is the cause. Absence of fluctuation in the water seal chamber can also be caused by an obstruction in the tubing or reinflation of the lung. Answer B is incorrect because fluid should not be removed from the chamber. Answer C is incorrect because there is no indication that the doctor needs to be notified at this time or that the chest tube needs to be reinserted. Answer D is incorrect because the nurse cannot increase the amount of suction without a doctor's order.

4. Answer B is correct. Activities such as blowing a ping pong ball across the table help to encourage purse-lipped breathing. This activity can be made into a game when working with the child with chronic obstructive lung diseases such as cystic fibrosis. Answer A is incorrect because it concentrates on deep breathing, not purse-lipped breathing. Answer C is too strenuous for the child with cystic fibrosis and does not teach purse-lipped breathing. Answer D is incorrect because the candle should be blown enough to bend the flame without extinguishing it.

5. Answer A is correct. The client's RBC indicates anemia. Adverse reactions to pentamidine include anemia, nephrotoxicity, and thrombocytopenia. Answers B, C, and D are within normal range; therefore, they are incorrect choices.

6. Answer B is correct. The nutritional needs of the client with emphysema are best met by eating 5–6 small meals a day. The client's diet should have increased calories, protein, and fat. Answer A is incorrect because the client needs to increase his intake of fluids to liquefy secretions. Answer C is incorrect because the client needs to avoid beverages such as milk that would thicken secretions. Answer D is incorrect because consuming hot foods increases a sense of fullness.

7. Answer B is correct. The most common risk factors in the development of pulmonary embolus are immobilization, surgery within the last three months, stoke, history of DVT, and malignancy. Answers A, C, and D are not associated with an increased risk of pulmonary embolus; therefore, they are incorrect.

8. Answer C is correct. The client should receive 100% oxygen prior to suctioning to prevent hypoxia. Answer A is incorrect because sterile, not aseptic, technique is used when providing care for a new tracheostomy. Answer B is incorrect because the nurse should be able to place two fingers between the tracheostomy ties and the client's neck. Answer D is incorrect because the inner cannula of a new tracheostomy should be changed every 12–24 hours.

9. Answer B is correct. The client receiving glucocortiocoids such as prednisone is at increased risk of infection. Fever and sore throat are early signs of infection that should be reported to the physician. Answer A is incorrect because the client needs to increase the intake of foods rich in potassium. Answer C is incorrect because the client needs to decrease the intake of foods high in sodium to decrease fluid retention. Answer D is incorrect because the medication should be taken before 9 a.m. daily, not at bedtime.

10. Answer D is correct. The client is exhibiting signs of a pneumothorax. The nurse should prepare to assist the physician with chest tube insertion. Answer A is incorrect because there is no indication of the need for endotracheal intubation. Answer B is incorrect because chest physiotherapy is contraindicated in the client with thoracic trauma. Answer C is incorrect because ABGs are obtained on arterial, not venous, blood.

11. Answer D is correct. Smokers, older adults, and people with chronic disease are most susceptible to Legionnaire's disease. The client's age, occupation, and smoking are all factors that place the client at risk for Legionnaire's disease. The clients in Answers A, B, and C are not at increased risk for Legionnaire's disease; therefore, they are incorrect choices.

12. Answer B is correct. The organism that causes tuberculosis is spread by droplets-from the respiratory tract. These droplets remain suspended in the air for several hours; therefore, airborne precautions are used when caring for the client with pulmonary tuberculosis. Healthcare workers should apply a respirator mask (some-times referred to as an N-95 or HEPA mask) before entering the client's room. Answers A, C, and D are not used to prevent the spread of tuberculosis, so they are incorrect choices.

13. Answer B is correct. To promote drainage and prevent reflux, the chest drainage system should be kept lower than the chest. Answers A, C, and D are wrong because they are incorrect ways of managing closed-chest drainage systems.

14. Answer A is correct. The inhaler should be stored in a clean, dry location. It should not be stored in a refrigerator or humid area such as the bathroom. The client's statement that it should be stored in the refrigerator indicates a need for further teaching. Answers B, C, and D indicate a correct understanding of the proper use of a dry powder inhaler; therefore, they are incorrect choices.

15. Answer C is correct. A side effect of ethambutol is a change in vision and color perception. The client should have a baseline visual exam before beginning therapy and periodic eye exams scheduled during the course of treatment. Answer A is

incorrect because red discoloration of urine is a side effect of rifampin. Answer B is incorrect because deficiency of pyridoxine (B6) is a side effect of isoniazid. Answer D is incorrect because swollen, painful joints are a side effect of pyrazinamide.

16. **Answer B is correct.** The client's CBC shows an elevation in red blood cells, which increases the client's risk for thrombus formation. Answers A and D are incorrect because they are associated with a decrease in the number of platelets, not an increase in the number of red blood cells. Although the client with emphysema is at risk for both community-acquired and hospital-acquired pneumonia, it is not related to the increased number of red blood cells; therefore, Answer C is incorrect.

17. **Answer A is correct.** The nurse should tell the client to drink 10–12 glasses of water a day and to void often to reduce the risk of developing hemorrhagic cystitis. Answer B is incorrect because taking the medication with grapefruit juice will not make the medication more palatable. Answer C is incorrect because the client can continue to use acetaminophen. Answer D is incorrect because the medication is taken on an empty stomach.

18. **Answer A is correct.** The nurse should request an order for a chest x-ray because prior vaccination with the BCG vaccine will cause the client to have a have false positive reading on the PPD skin test. Answer B is incorrect because administering the PPD skin test to this client would result in a false positive reading. Answer C is incorrect because the client needs a chest x-ray and follow-up sputum if needed. Answer D is incorrect because the client should first be evaluated with a chest x-ray and sputum specimen before medication is begun.

19. **Answer A is correct.** Subcutaneous emphysema results when air enters the subcutaneous tissue. This produces a crackling sensation when the area is palpated. Answer B is incorrect because it describes a pneumothorax. Answer C is incorrect because it describes a flail chest. Answer D is incorrect because it describes a tension pneumothorax.

20. **Answer B is correct.** Keeping the call light within reach is the best means of allowing the client control over his environment. Answer A is incorrect because it decreases his sense of isolation but does not allow him to control his environment. Answer C is incorrect because the nurse, not the client, is in control. Answer D is incorrect because it provides a means of communication.

21. **Answer B is correct.** Pseudomembraneous colitis, an adverse reaction to antibiotic therapy, is characterized by diarrhea stools that contain blood, mucus, and white blood cells. Burning at the infusion site is not associated with an adverse drug reaction; therefore, Answer A is incorrect. Answers C and D are incorrect because they are symptoms associated with the illness not with the prescribed drug.

22. **Answer C is correct.** When performing endotracheal suctioning, the suction should be set between 80 mm Hg and 120 mm Hg. Answers A and B are incorrect choices because the suction setting is too low. Answer D is incorrect because the suction setting is too high.

848
Answers to Practice Exam II

23. Answer A is correct. The client should be questioned about past allergic reaction to eggs because eggs are used in the production of the influenza vaccine. Answers B, C, and D are not associated with the production of influenza vaccine; therefore, they are incorrect choices.

24. Answer C is correct. The earlobe is the best site for probe placement because it is least affected by decreased blood flow. Decreased blood flow to the fingers and toes interferes with pulse oximetry readings, so Answers A and B are incorrect. Answer D is incorrect because the chest is not a suitable site for placement of the oximetry probe.

25. Answer C is correct. A common finding associated with cor pulmonale (right sided heart failure) is edema of the legs and sacrum. Answer A, B, and D are incorrect because they are symptoms of left-sided heart failure.

Care of the Client with Genitourinary Disorders

26. Answer D is correct. The client undergoing an intravenous pyelogram frequently experiences facial flushing, feeling a warm sensation, and a metallic taste in the mouth. Answers A and B are not associated with the contrast media used for an intravenous pyelogram; therefore, they are incorrect choices. Answer C is incorrect because it is associated with anaphylaxis, which is rare.

27. Answer C is correct. Acute glomerulonephritis can result from a preceding sore throat caused by *a beta hemolytic streptococcus*. Answers A, B, and D are incorrect because they are not associated with acute glomerulonephritis.

28. Answer D is correct. If the client undergoing hemodialysis experiences signs of disequilibrium syndrome, the nurse should slow or discontinue the dialysis. Hypertonic solutions such as mannitol or albumin are administered to draw fluid from the brain cells back into the systemic circulation. Answer A is incorrect because the rate of dialysis should be slowed or discontinued. Answer B is incorrect because a hypertonic solution—not normal saline—should be administered. Answer C is incorrect because it is not a treatment for disequilibrium syndrome.

29. Answer B is correct. Abdominal tenderness and the appearance of cloudy dialysate are indications of peritonitis. Answer A is incorrect because pain and discomfort can occur for a week or two after peritoneal dialysis begins. Answer C is incorrect because feelings of intra-abdominal pressure are common with peritoneal dialysis. Answer D is incorrect because, from time to time, the outflow might be slowed (have the client change positions) and the light amber color of the urine is normal.

30. Answer B is correct. Suitable beverages for increasing the palatability of Neoral (cyclosporine) include plain milk, chocolate milk, and orange juice. Answers A, C, and D are incorrect because they do not increase the palatability of the medication.

31. Answer C is correct. The nurse should give priority to monitoring the vital signs and color of the urine. The kidney is highly vascular; therefore, hemorrhage and resulting shock are potential complications of extracorporeal shock wave lithotripsy. The urine might be bright red initially, but bleeding should diminish within 48– 72 hours. Answers A and D are incorrect because they do not take priority over assessing for signs of hemorrhage. Answer B is incorrect because an ice compress, not anesthetic cream, is usually applied to the site.

32. Answer B is correct. The nurse should measure the hourly output from the tube for 24 hours to make sure that the tube is patent. Answer A is incorrect because the tube is irrigated only with a physician's order and sterile saline, not sterile water, is used. Answer C is incorrect because the tube should not be kinked, compressed, or clamped. Answer D is incorrect because red-tinged urine is expected after the insertion of a nephrostomy tube.

33. Answer A is correct. Oxybutnin can cause an increase in intraocular, so the client should schedule routine eye examinations. Answers B, C, and D do not relate to the use of oxybutnin; therefore, they are incorrect choices.

34. Answer C is correct. The presence of dark red catheter drainage following a TURP indicates venous bleeding. At this time, the nurse should place traction on the catheter and tape it to the client's upper thigh or the lower abdomen. Answer A is incorrect because it does not intervene to stop the bleeding. Answer B is incorrect because there is no need to contact the physician before taking appropriate steps to stop the venous bleeding. Answer D is incorrect because the physician, not the nurse, will request a follow-up CBC.

35. Answer D is correct. Clients undergoing hemodialysis frequently express feelings of depression, anger, sadness, and loss of control. The nurse can best support the client by allowing him to discuss his feelings. Answers A and C do not offer the client the opportunity to discuss his feelings; therefore, they are incorrect. Answer B is incorrect because it minimizes the client's feelings.

36. Answer B is correct. Kayexalate is given to treat the client's hyperkalemia. The medication is mixed in water with sorbitol, a sugar, to produce osmotic diarrhea. Answers A, C, and D are not given with Kayexalate, so they are incorrect choices.

37. Answer A is correct. Clients with nephrotic syndrome who have normal GFR (normal GFR 120 mL /min–125 mL/min) should have a diet with increased amounts of protein. Answers B, C, and D are incorrect because they do not meet the nutritional needs of the client with nephrotic syndrome with a normal GFR.

38. Answer B is correct. Clients with polycystic kidney disease are prone to the development of cerebral aneurysms. Complaints of severe headache, with or without neurological or visual changes, should alert the nurse to the possibility of an aneurysm. Answers A, C, and D are incorrect because they are commonly associated with polycystic kidney disease.

39. Answer B is correct. Concurrent use of sulfasoxazole and hypericum (St. John's wort) increases the likelihood of the client developing photosensitivity. Answers A, C, and D are incorrect because concurrent use with sulfasoxazole is not associated with an increase in the development of photosensitivity.

40. Answer D is correct. Legumes do not provide a source of complete protein because they lack one or more of the essential amino acids or contain inadequate phosphorus. Examples of other incomplete proteins are vegetables, breads, cereals, grains, seeds, and nuts. Answers A, B, and C are incorrect choices because they are examples of complete proteins that supply all the nutrients needed for growth and tissue maintenance. Examples of complete proteins are milk, cheese, eggs, meats, poultry, fish, and soy.

41. Answer A is correct. Following a renal biopsy, the nurse can reduce the risk of bleeding by applying a pressure dressing and placing the client in a supine position. Lying in a supine position helps to maintain pressure on the biopsy site. Answers B, C, and D are incorrect choices because they do not reduce the risk of post-biopsy bleeding.

42. Answer B is correct. Suitable juices on an acid-ash diet include prune, grape, and cranberry. Answers A, C, and D are incorrect because they are not included in an acid-ash diet.

43. Answer C is correct. To prevent "*red man*" syndrome, vancomycin should be infused slowly over 60– 90 minutes. Answers A, B, and D have no bearing on the development of "*red man*" syndrome; therefore, they are incorrect choices.

44. Answer B is correct. The client should use a circular motion, rather than a back-and-forth motion, when cleaning around the catheter, thus the client needs further teaching. Answers A, C, and D indicate that the client understands the proper ways of carrying out peritoneal dialysis at home; therefore, they are incorrect choices.

45. Answer C is correct. The nurse should ask the client to empty her bladder prior to administration of the medication so that more of the medication comes in contact with the bladder lining. Answer A is incorrect because additional fluids are offered after administration of the medication, not before. Answer B is incorrect because administration of the medication is not painful. Answer D is incorrect because an x-ray of the bladder is not needed.

46. Answer A is correct. Procrit (epoetin alpha) is a colony-stimulating factor that increases the production of red blood cells. The red cell count of 4,700,000 is within the normal range. Answers B, C, and D are not associated with the use of Procrit, so they are incorrect choices.

47. Answer D is correct. Saw palmetto has been used to treat symptoms associated with BPH, although no large randomized clinical trials are available on its effectiveness. Saw palmetto can actually falsely lower the PSA, which can delay the time to diagnose and treat prostate cancer. Answers A, B, and C are incorrect because they are not used in the treatment of BPH.

48. Answer C is correct. A history of multiple blood transfusions increases the possibility of hyperacute graft rejection following a renal transplant. Answers A, B, and D are not associated with an increased risk of hyperacute graft rejection; therefore, they are incorrect.

49. Answer A is correct. The urine might be cloudy due to the mucous production by bowel mucosa. This is an expected finding in the new ileal conduit so the nurse should document the finding in the client's chart. Answers B, C, and D do not pertain to the nurse's observation; therefore, they are incorrect.

50. Answer D is correct. A primary concern for the client with renal transplant is the development of nephrotoxicity. Nephrotoxicity is an adverse effect associated with the use of cyclosporine. Answers A and B are incorrect. Hepatotoxicity and hirsutism are adverse effects of the medication; however, they are not the primary concern for the client who received a renal transplant. Answer C is incorrect because bone loss is associated with the use of glucocorticoids, not cyclosporine.

Care of the Client with Integumentary Disorders

51. Answer C is correct. Moisturizing creams and lotions should be applied after bathing while the skin is still moist. Answer A is incorrect because the skin should be moist, not dry. Answers B and D are incorrect because the cream should be applied using long, smooth stokes that follow the direction of hair growth.

52. Answer B is correct. Adverse effects of methotrexate include hepatotoxicity, nephrotoxicity, and myelosuppression. A serum ALT of 60 U/L indicates hepatotoxicity. Answers A, C, and D are incorrect choices because the lab values are all within normal range.

53. Answer B is correct. Burns of the face, neck, and upper chest increase the likelihood of airway obstruction, so the risk for impaired gas exchange takes priority in the client's nursing diagnoses. Answers A, C, and D do not take priority over gas exchange; therefore, they are incorrect choices.

54. Answer C is correct. Signs of overexposure to ultraviolet light radiation therapy include severe redness and edema, tenderness on palpation, and blister formation. Answers A, B, and D are not signs of overexposure; therefore, they are incorrect.

55. Answer C is correct. Ice cream provides the client with a source of protein and minerals for healing. Answers A, B, and D are not suitable snacks for the client because they are high in potassium and the client with burns tends to have elevated potassium levels caused by damage to capillary and cell membranes.

56. Answer B is correct. Using the Rule of Nines, the legs = 36%, the arms = 18%, and the anterior torso = 18%, for a total of 72%. Answers A, C, and D are incorrect answers for the amount of area involved.

57. Answer A is correct. Sulfamylon (mafenide acetate) produces a burning sensation when applied to the burn site. The nurse should administer pain medication before applying the medication. Answer B is incorrect because the medication keeps the eschar soft; therefore, there is no need to soak the site with normal saline. Answer C is incorrect because Silvadene (silver sulfadiazine), not Sulfamylon, reduces the WBC. Answer D is incorrect because a mesh gauze, not a dermal substitute, is used to cover the burn after the medication is applied.

58. Answer A is correct. The client sheds the virus and is contagious for 3–5 days. Answers B, C, and D are incorrect because they are outside the period of contagion.

59. Answer D is correct. The client undergoing hyperbaric oxygen therapy will be enclosed in a chamber for 60–90 minutes, so it is important to ask the client if she has claustrophobia. Answers A, B, and C do not apply to the client undergoing hyperbaric oxygen therapy; therefore, they are incorrect.

60. Answer C is correct. Zostavax is used to prevent shingles in persons age 60 and over. It is not used to treat shingles or pain associated with shingles. Answers A, B, and D indicate that the client understands the nurse's teaching about the medication, so they are incorrect choices.

61. Answer A is correct. Stage II pressure ulcers are characterized by the appearance of an abrasion, blister, or shallow crater. Answer B is incorrect because it describes the appearance of a Stage I pressure ulcer. Answer C is incorrect because it describes the appearance of a Stage III pressure ulcer. Answer D is incorrect because it describes a Stage IV pressure ulcer.

62. Answer D is correct. Zantac (rantidine hydrochloride) is given prophylactically to prevent stress-induced ulcers such as Curling's ulcers. Proton pump inhibitors such as Protonix (pantoprazole) can also be given. Answers A, B, and C are incorrect because they are not effective in preventing Curling's ulcer.

63. Answer B is correct. Myoglobinuria is the result of underlying muscle damage or the release of large amounts of dead or damaged red blood cells after burn injury. Answers A, C, and D do not relate to myoglobinuria; therefore, they are incorrect answers.

64. Answer C is correct. The nurse should explain that topical acyclovir has not shown any clinical benefits in preventing recurrent outbreaks of HSV II. Answers A, B, and D do not take priority over explaining the correct use of the medication; therefore, they are incorrect.

65. Answer B is correct. Sharing combs, brushes, and hats are behaviors that increase the risk of pediculosis capitis (head lice) in children. Answers A, C, and D are not behaviors associated with pediculosis capitis, so they are incorrect choices.

66. Answer D is correct. Tazorac (tazaretene), a retinoid, is a category X medication. Because of this, the client should have a pregnancy test done before beginning therapy with the medication. Answers A, B, and C are incorrect because they are not needed prior to beginning therapy with the medication.

67. Answer A is correct. The decrease in normal hematocrit is related to hemodilution from fluid resuscitation. Answers B, C, and D do not relate to a decrease in normal hematocrit; therefore, they are incorrect.

Care of the Client with Sensory Disorders

68. Answer A is correct. Bending from the waist, blowing the nose, wearing tight shirt collars, and keeping the head in a dependent position are some activities that can increase intraocular pressure. Answers B, C, and D do not increase intraocular pressure; therefore, they are incorrect.

69. Answer C is correct. Gentle pressure should be applied to the puncta (inner canthus) to decrease the systemic effects associated with absorption of the drug. Answers A, B, and D are incorrect because they do not decrease the systemic effects of the medication.

70. Answer D is correct. The nurse should notify the doctor because complaints of seeing flashes of light are associated with possible retinal tear. Other symptoms of retinal tear and detachment include visual floaters and dark spots with absence of pain. Answers A and B are incorrect since they are accompanied by pain and increased intraocular pressure. Corneal dystrophy results in cloudy, blurred vision, not flashes of light; therefore, Answer C is incorrect.

71. Answer D is correct. A client with low vision should avoid the use of footstools because they can result in falls. Chairs with built-in foot rests are a better choice for such clients. Answers A, B, and C are incorrect because they show that the client did understand the nurse's teaching regarding ways to increase environmental safety.

72. Answer B is correct. Amikin (amikacin sulfate) is an aminoglycoside that is capable of producing both ototoxicity and nephrotoxicity. The fact that the client is elderly increases the likelihood of the drug's toxicity. Answers A, C, and D are incorrect because these medications are not generally associated with ototoxicity.

73. Answer D is correct. The nurse should give priority to preventing injury, particularly from falls. Answer A is incorrect because pain is not associated with Ménière's disease. Answer B is incorrect because fluid intake is usually restricted to decrease symptoms. Reducing the noise level might make the client more comfortable, but it does not take priority over preventing injury; therefore, Answer C is incorrect.

74. Answer A is correct. The client with hyphema should be placed in semi-Fowler's position. This position helps to keep blood away from the center of the cornea. Answers B, C, and D are incorrect because they do not keep blood away from the center of the cornea. Additional interventions include keeping the head elevated and applying cold compresses to the eye.

75. Answer C is correct. The cane should be held in the dominant hand several inches above the floor. It should be moved back and forth in a sweeping motion as the client walks to detect objects in his path. Answers A, B, and D indicate that the client is using the cane improperly; therefore, they are incorrect.

76. Answer B is correct. Supplementing the client's diet with folacin (vitamin B9) might result in the improvement of age-related hearing loss. The use of retinol (vitamin A), ascorbic acid (vitamin C), and alpha-tocopherol (vitamin E) do not result in improved hearing; therefore, Answers A, C, and D are incorrect.

77. Answer C is correct. Directing the irrigating solution to one side of the ear canal allows the fluid to get behind the impacted cerumen and helps facilitate its removal. Answer A is incorrect because the solution should be warm, not cold. Answer B is incorrect because directing the irrigation onto the impacted cerumen makes removal more difficult. Answer D is incorrect because intermittent irrigation, not continuous, is used.

78. Answer A is correct. An irrigating solution of equal parts of sterile water and vinegar are often ordered before a tympanoplasty to restore the normal pH of the ear. Baking soda, hydrogen peroxide, and glycerin are not used to restore the normal pH of the ear; therefore, Answers B, C, and D are incorrect.

79. Answer C is correct. Seating the client with a friend in a quiet area eliminates environmental noises that interfere with hearing and allows the client to socialize appropriately with others. Answers A, B, and D are interventions for the hearing-impaired client; however, they do not help prevent social isolation. Therefore, they are incorrect.

80. Answer B is correct. Clients with a history of osteogenesis imperfecta often develop bilateral progressive hearing loss in the second and third decades of life. Answers A, C, and D are not significant to the client's hearing loss; therefore, they are incorrect

81. Answer C is correct. "Copper wiring" and "arteriovenous nicking" are vascular changes associated with uncontrolled hypertension. These changes are not associated with peripheral vascular disease, Sjogren's syndrome, or fluctuations in blood glucose; therefore, Answers A, B, and D are incorrect.

82. Answer D is correct. The early formation of cataracts is more common in those who use steroid preparations. Answers A, B, and C are incorrect because they are not associated with the use of steroid medication.

83. Answer C is correct. "Curtain-like" loss of vision is a symptom of retinal detachment. Answers A, B, and D are incorrect because "curtain-like" loss of vision is not a characteristic of ocular melanoma, retinitis pigmentosa, or macular degeneration.

84. Answer C is correct. A Type II tympanoplasty involves the reconnection of the bones of the middle ear to the ear drum as a means of restoring hearing. Answers A and D are incorrect because they describe a myringotomy and insertion of PE tubes to relieve pressure on the tympanic membrane. Answer B is incorrect because it describes a stapedectomy.

85. Answer D is correct. The client with 20/60 vision can see from a distance of 20 feet what the normal eye sees at 60 feet. Answer A is incorrect because a vision of 20/60 is not better than vision of 20/20. Answer B is incorrect because *legally blind* is defined as a vision of 20/200. Answer C is incorrect because astigmatism is not determined by the Snellen chart.

86. Answer A is correct. Topographic concepts can be reinforced by using the hands of a clock to help the client locate items on her tray. For example, milk is at 3 o'clock, peas are at 5 o'clock, and so on. Answers B, C, and D might assist the client with low vision; however, they do not reinforce topographic concepts. Therefore, they are incorrect.

87. Answer A is correct. Changes in taste are associated with damage to the 7th cranial nerve. Changes in hearing (acoustic or 8th cranial nerve), changes in voice quality (vagus or 10th cranial nerve), and changes in oral sensation (trigeminal or 5th cranial nerve) are incorrect.

Care of the Pediatric Client

88. Answer B is correct. Chelation therapy for the client with iron overdose is deferoxamine (Desferal). Answers A, C, and D are incorrect because they are chelating agents used to treat lead poisoning.

89. Answer C is correct. Viokase (pancrelipase) promotes the absorption of nutrients needed for growth. An increase in weight of 4 lbs. in one month indicates that the medication is having its desired effect. Answers A, B, and D are not associated with the use of Viokase; therefore, they are incorrect.

90. Answer B is correct. Hospitalization and surgery are particularly stressful to the preschool-aged child who fears loss of body integrity. Answer A is incorrect because the preschool-aged child asks many questions about his body. Answer C is incorrect because the preschool-aged child has difficulty conceptualizing and expressing his fears. Answer D is incorrect because the preschool-aged child pays a great deal of attention to environmental changes. For this reason, it is best to provide a consistent caregiver.

91. Answer D is correct. Dehydration increases the viscosity of the blood and raises the likelihood of thrombus formation. Making sure that the child with valvular heart disease is well hydrated decreases the risk of thrombi. There are no indications for the interventions mentioned in Answers A, B, and C; therefore, they are incorrect.

92. Answer D is correct. The use of salicylates to treat fever in the child with influenza or chickenpox has been associated with the development of Reye's syndrome. Therefore, their use is no longer advised. Answers A, B, and C are incorrect because they are not treated with salicylates and are not associated with the development of Reye's syndrome.

93. Answer C is correct. The child with varicella is considered contagious for 24 hours before the eruptions appear and until all the lesions have crusted. Answers A, B, and D are inaccurate statements; therefore, they are incorrect.

94. Answer B is correct. The presence of faint femoral pulses and strong, bounding brachial pulses suggest the possibility of coarctation of the aorta. These findings are not associated with ventricular septal defect, truncus arteriosus, or patent ductus arteriosus; therefore, Answers A, C, and D are incorrect.

95. Answer B is correct. Elbow restraints will be applied to the client's arms to prevent him from placing his fingers in his mouth. Answers A and C are incorrect because they refer to post-op care of the infant with a cleft lip repair. Answer D is incorrect because he cannot suck on a bottle or pacifier since doing so would place pressure on palatal sutures.

96. Answer A is correct. Nesting toys, a Jack-in-the-Box, and hide and seek all help encourage the development of object permanence. Answer B is incorrect because a shape sorter teaches spatial relationships, not object permanence. Stuffed animals and stackable blocks, although appropriate for the infant, do not foster the development of object permanence; therefore, Answers C and D are incorrect.

97. Answer A is correct. Complications associated with acute lymphocytic leukemia include anemia, infection, and hemorrhage. A temp of 100° F is significant and should be reported immediately. Answer B is incorrect because perianal ulcerations are an expected side effect of chemotherapy. Answer C is incorrect because painful joints are a symptom of leukemia. Answer D is incorrect because a respiratory rate of 26 in the four-year-old is not abnormal.

98. Answer B is correct. The child with gluten-induced enteropathy (celiac disease) should have a gluten-free diet. Gluten is found in most grains and grain products, such as breads, cereals, and crackers. These foods will need to be eliminated from the diet. Answer A is incorrect because it refers to dietary management of a child with phenylketonuria. Answer C is incorrect because it refers to dietary management of a child with galactosemia. Answer D is incorrect because it refers to dietary management of a child with cystic fibrosis.

99. Answer D is correct. The mother should use cloth diapers instead of disposable diapers. Occlusive dressings, such as disposable diapers, should not be used over topical preparations containing cortisone because they increase absorption of the medication. Answer A is incorrect because the medication should be applied in a thin layer. Answer B is incorrect because old applications should be gently removed with warm water. The medication is applied with diaper changes, not just at bedtime; therefore, Answer C is incorrect.

100. Answer C is correct. Classic signs of intussusception include colicky abdominal pain, sausage-shaped abdominal mass, and currant jelly stools. Answers A, B, and D are incorrect because Answer A describes signs of biliary atresia, Answer B describes signs of pyloric stenosis, and Answer D describes signs of celiac disease.

101. Answer D is correct. The five-year-old enjoys doing simple household chores such as setting the table for a meal The two- year- old does not consistently comply with parental requests; therefore, Answer A is incorrect. Sharing a favorite toy with another child is not an expected behavior of a three-year-old, so Answer B is incorrect. Having imaginary friends is an expected behavior of a four-year-old; therefore, Answer C is incorrect.

102. Answer C is correct. Infants with Down syndrome have hypotonia, transpalmar creases, and epicanthal folds. Answers A, B, and D are not associated with Down syndrome; therefore, they are incorrect.

103. Answer D is correct. The nurse should cover the area with a warm sterile, saline guaze and plastic wrap to prevent the area from drying until surgical closure of the abdomen can be performed. Answers A and B are incorrect because they do not prevent trauma to the area. Answer C is incorrect because it does not protect the intestinal contents from drying.

104. Answer C is correct. Tofranil (imipramine), a tricyclic, might take 2–3weeks to be effective in treating enuresis. Answer A is incorrect because the medication should be taken with food. Answer B is incorrect because other forms of treatment are employed along with the use of medication. Answer D is incorrect because the medication should not be stopped abruptly.

105. Answer B is correct. The child with nephrotic syndrome is usually placed on a regular diet with moderate amounts of protein and low sodium. A hot dog with ketchup is least appropriate because it contains more sodium and fat and less protein than the other choices. Answers A, C, and D are better choices for the child with nephrotic syndrome; therefore, they are incorrect.

106. Answer A is correct. The newborn with a diaphragmatic hernia should be placed on the affected side with his head slightly elevated to allow maximum expansion of the unaffected lung. Answers B, C, and D are incorrect because they do not allow for maximum expansion of the unaffected lung.

107. Answer A is correct. Lifting the infant by the hips rather than the ankles helps to reduce the risk of fractures associated with osteogenesis imperfecta. Answers B and D are incorrect answers because they are not indicated in the care of the infant with osteogenesis imperfecta. Blue-tinged sclera is a common characteristic of osteogenesis imperfecta. It requires no intervention, so Answer C is incorrect.

108. Answer D is correct. The nurse should wear goggles and a respirator to protect mucus membranes. Answer A is incorrect because the medication is most effective if given within the first three days of infection. Answer B is incorrect because the medication is administered 12– 18 hours a day for 3–7 days. Answer C is incorrect because the medication cannot be used with any other aerosolized medication.

109. Answer D is correct. The treatment of Kawasaki's disease includes the use of intravenous immunoglobulin and high doses of aspirin. Acetaminophen, penicillin, and cortisone are not used in the treatment of Kawasaki's disease; therefore, Answers A, B, and C are incorrect.

110. Answer B is correct. A three-year-old talks incessantly even if no one is listening. Answers A and D refer to the language skills of a four-year-old; therefore, they are incorrect. Answer C is incorrect because it refers to the language skills of a five-year-old.

111. Answer D is correct. Inhalation therapy with Pulmozyme helps to thin and liquefy pulmonary secretions. Answers A, B, and C refer to the effects of other therapies; therefore, they are incorrect.

112. Answer B is correct. Oral rehydration with electrolyte solution is the recommended treatment for an infant with moderate dehydration. Answer A is incorrect because intravenous fluids are the recommended treatment for severe dehydration. Answer C is incorrect because soy-based formulas are not used until symptoms have subsided. Answer D is incorrect because clear liquids include fruit juice, soft drinks, and gelatin, which can make diarrhea worse.

113. Answer C is correct. Droplet precautions should be used when caring for the client with meningitis caused by *Neisseria meningitides*. Answers A, B, and D are not correct ways of caring for the client with *Neiserria meningitidis* meningitis, so they are wrong.

114. Answer C is correct. Salicylates, such as Pepto Bismol and aspirin, have been implicated in the development of Reye's syndrome in children with influenza or varicella. Answers A, B, and D are not associated with the development of Reye's syndrome; therefore, they are incorrect.

115. Answer B is correct. Swimming poses the least risk of injury for an adolescent with hemophilia. Answers A, C, and D are incorrect because wrestling, soccer, and basketball are contact sports that have a high risk of injury; therefore, they are not good choices for an adolescent with hemophilia.

116. Answer A is correct. The abused child typically endures painful procedures with little or no emotion. Answers B, C, and D are not typical behaviors of the abused child; therefore, they are incorrect.

117. Answer D is correct. Eskimo and Navaho practices of swaddling newborns and strapping them to cradle boards increase the incidence of hip dislocation. Answers A, B, and C do not have cultural practices that increase the incidence of hip dislocation, so they are incorrect.

118. Answer B is correct. The nurse should tell the mother to use only isotonic enemas or those prepared with normal saline because these pose no risk of electrolyte imbalances. Answers A, C, and D are incorrect because they can lead to serious electrolyte imbalances.

119. Answer B is correct. A history of maternal polyhydramnios can indicate gastrointestinal obstructions, such as esophageal atresia. Therefore, the nurse should carefully assess the newborn for difficulty with feeding. Answers A, C, and D are not associated with maternal polyhydramnios; therefore, they are incorrect.

120. Answer A is correct. All the medication should be taken, even though the infant no longer has symptoms of infection. The medication should not be mixed with formula or fruit juice; therefore, Answers B and D are incorrect. Answer C is incorrect because the medication should be continued even though the infant no longer has a fever.

121. Answer D is correct. Nosebleeds and gingival bleeding are the most common complaints associated with von Willebrand's disease, an inherited bleeding disorder. Answers A, B, and C do not characterize von Willebrand disease, so they are incorrect.

122. Answer B is correct. Hanging upside down on monkey bars is the best playground activity because it provides for postural drainage. Answers A, C, and D are not the best activities for the child with cystic fibrosis because they overexert the child and increase oxygen demands.

123. Answer C is correct. Most children are ready for toilet training between 18 and 24 months of age. Answers A and B are incorrect because the child is not physically or psychologically mature enough for toilet training. Answer D is incorrect because most children are ready for toilet training by 24 months of age.

124. Answer D is correct. The medication should be given orally after mixing in juice to disguise the taste and smell. Answer A is incorrect because aerosol inhalation methods are not used to treat acetaminophen overdose. Answer B is incorrect because mixing it in water will not help disguise the taste or smell. Answer C is incorrect because the medication is not administered intramuscularly.

125. Answer B is correct. Splinter hemorrhages, black lines beneath the nails, suggest the development of thrombi formation in the client with subacute bacterial endocarditis. Koplik's spots, subcutaneous nodules, and strawberry tongue are not associated with subacute bacterial endocarditis or development of thrombi. Therefore, Answers A, C, and D are incorrect.

Care of the Client with Psychiatric Disorders

126. Answer A is correct. Tagamet (cimetadine) decreases the clearance time of Zoloft, thereby increasing the likelihood of toxicity. The medication can be taken with meals or once a day at bedtime; therefore, Answers B and C are incorrect. The medication can be taken with Aleve (naproxen); therefore, Answer D is incorrect.

127. Answer B is correct. The nurse should provide the client with high-calorie foods that she can eat as she moves about. Answers A, C, and D might not help her maintain sufficient nourishment, so they are incorrect.

128. Answer C is correct. A client with bulimia is often described as an extrovert who seeks intimate relationships. Answers A, B, and D describe the client with anorexia nervosa, not bulimia nervosa; therefore, they are incorrect.

129. Answer A is correct. The client is using the defense mechanism of rationalization to justify his behavior. Answers B, C, and D are not reflected by the client's statement; therefore, they are incorrect.

130. Answer C is correct. Participating in a card game allows the client with paranoid schizophrenia to socially interact with a limited number of others. Participating in a game of volleyball can be overwhelming for a client with paranoid schizophrenia; therefore, Answer A is incorrect. Reading and watching TV do not encourage social interaction, so Answers B and D are incorrect.

131. Answer B is correct. The nurse should avoid focusing on the client's physical complaints because this reinforces his use of conversion as a defense mechanism. Answer A is incorrect because, in conversion reactions, there are no physical reasons for the symptoms. Answers C and D focus on the client's physical complaints by challenging them; therefore, they are incorrect.

132. Answer D is correct. Hyponatremia increases the possibility of lithium toxicity. Answers A, B, and C, which are within normal limits, are not associated with an increased risk for lithium toxicity.

133. Answer A is correct. The client's claim that the FBI is following him is an example of a delusion of persecution. Answers B and D are examples of hallucinations; therefore, they are incorrect. Answer C is an example of an illusion, so it is incorrect.

134. Answer B is correct. The client should be told that there might be a loss of memory for events that happen near the time of ECT. Answers A, C, and D are incorrect statements; therefore, they are incorrect.

135. Answer B is correct. The client's symptoms of dystonia are a life-threatening reaction to Thorazine. The nurse should give priority to administering the prescribed anti-Parkinson medication. Answers A and C do not take priority over administering medication to treat dystonia; therefore, they are incorrect. Answer D should be done after administering the prescribed anti-Parkinson medication, so it is incorrect.

136. Answer A is correct. Clients with chronic or debilitating conditions that require dependence on others are more likely to be the victims of elder abuse. Female clients are more likely to be victims of abuse than male clients. Answers B, C, and D are not as likely to be abused; therefore, they are incorrect.

137. Answer C is correct. Feelings of self-loathing and low self-esteem are associated with binge episodes. Answer A is incorrect because the client is depressed rather than euphoric. Answer B is incorrect because the client's weight is normal or near normal. Answer D is incorrect because it refers to the client with anorexia nervosa, rather than bulimia nervosa.

138. Answer D is correct. The statement shows that the nurse recognizes and respects the client's feelings. Answer A is incorrect because it can cause the client to become defensive. Answer B is incorrect because it intellectualizes the client's feelings. Answer C is incorrect because it does not allow the client to vent feelings of frustration.

139. Answer C is correct. Allowing the client to complete his ritualistic behavior will help reduce the client's anxiety level. Answers A, B, and D do not effective ways of decreasing the client's ritualistic behavior; therefore, they are incorrect.

140. Answer B is correct. An adverse reaction associated with Zyprexa (olanzapine) is neuroleptic malignant hyperthermia, which is reflected by extreme elevations in temperature. Answers A, C, and D are side effects associated with antipsychotic medication that require the nurse's attention; however, they are not as severe as elevations in temperature.

141. Answer D is correct. Post-traumatic stress disorder is distinguished from other anxiety disorders by the client's reliving the event in dreams and flashbacks. Answers A, B, and C are incorrect because they are common to all anxiety disorders.

142. Answer B is correct. Giving positive rewards for weight gain is most specific to the client's behavioral program. Answers A and C are not specific to the client's behavioral program for weight gain; therefore, they are incorrect. Answer D is incorrect because tube feedings are a last resort in the treatment of a client with anorexia nervosa.

143. Answer A is correct. The feature that distinguishes ADHD from childhood depression is the age of onset (that is, symptoms appear before age 7), that they last for a period of at least 6 months, and that behavior is disruptive and inappropriate for the developmental level. Answers B, C, and D are incorrect because they do not distinguish between ADHD and childhood depression.

144. Answer C is correct. The client's belief that he can continue to take St. John's wort indicates a need for further teaching because the medication has properties similar to Parnate. Answers A, B, and D indicate that the client needs no further teaching; therefore, they are incorrect.

145. Answer B is correct. Giving away one's prized possessions is a sign of increased depression and possible suicidal ideation. The use of certain antidepressants, such as Zoloft, raises the risk for suicide in some individuals, especially adolescents; therefore, this behavior needs to be reported immediately. Answers A, C, and D indicate that the client is improving, so they are incorrect.

146. Answer B is correct. The therapeutic level for Depakote is 50µg–100µg; therefore, the nurse need take no action. Answers A, C, and D are incorrect because no further action is needed.

147. Answer D is correct. A client with paranoid schizophrenia who is experiencing command hallucinations represents a risk of violence to himself and others. Answers A, B, and C are incorrect because they do not take priority over the risk of violence.

148. Answer C is correct. To decrease the risk of serotonin syndrome the recommended time between discontinuing a monoamine oxidase inhibitor and beginning a selective serotonin reuptake inhibitor is 14 days. Answers A, B, and D are incorrect times; therefore, they are wrong.

149. Answer A is correct. Akathisia, a side effect of antipsychotic drug therapy, is characterized by motor restlessness such as pacing and rocking. Answer B is incorrect because it refers to echolalia. Answer C is incorrect because it refers to clang association. Answer D is incorrect because it refers to tardive dyskinesia.

Emergency Care

150. Answer C is correct. MS Contin is capable of producing severe or fatal respiratory depression. Answers A and B do not take priority over the client's respiratory status; therefore, they are incorrect. Answer D is incorrect because the blood pressure would be decreased, not increased.

151. Answer B is correct. Signs associated with "shaken baby" syndrome include retinal hemorrhage, cerebral edema, and subdural hematoma. Answers A, C, and D are not specific to "shaken baby" syndrome; therefore, they are incorrect.

152. Answer C is correct. Elevations in the ALT and AST indicate damage to the liver. Answer A is incorrect because an increased WBC indicates damage to the spleen or intestines. Answer B is incorrect because an increased amylase and lipase indicate damage to the pancreas or bowel. Answer D is incorrect because decreased hematocrit indicates bleeding.

153. Answer D is correct. Application of external heating devices to a client being treated for hypothermia is contraindicated since it produces "after drop." "After drop" occurs when cold blood is moved from the periphery to the warmer core. Answers A, B, and C are incorrect choices because they are appropriate interventions for the client being treated for hypothermia.

154. Answer B is correct. The joint above and below a fracture should be immobilized before the client is moved to prevent further damage to the soft tissue, nerves, and blood vessels. Answer A is incorrect because removing the shoe can result in movement and further trauma. Answer C is incorrect because the client should lie down, not sit up. Answer D is incorrect because it is not necessary before moving the client.

155. Answer B is correct. The client with esophageal varices has a high risk of injury and bleeding from dilated esophageal blood vessels and altered clotting mechanisms. Answers A, C, and D are incorrect because they do not take priority over the client's risk for injury and bleeding.

156. Answer D is correct. The client with a red tag is classified as emergent or Class 1. Answer A is incorrect because the client is classified as expectant or Class 4. Answer B is incorrect because the client is classified as non-urgent or Class 3. Answer C is incorrect because the client is classified as urgent or Class 2.

157. Answer B is correct. The client's symptoms and lab results reveal extreme hypoglycemia, which is treated with Glucagon. Answers A, C, and D are incorrect because they are not treatments for hypoglycemia.

158. Answer D is correct. The nurse should carefully remove the stinger and apply ice to the area. Answers A, B, and C are incorrect because they are not the first actions the nurse should take.

159. Answer D is correct. The nurse should expect a high-pressure injury characterized by a small puncture wound. The wound may be life-threatening if tissue damage occurs to highly vascular areas or to hollow organs. Answers A, B, and C are incorrect statements; therefore, they are incorrect.

160. Answer B is correct. Mild hypothermia (91.4 ° F.–96.8° F) is characterized by diminished fine motor skills. Absence of shivering, dilated pupils, and atrial fibrillation are characteristics of moderate to severe hypothermia, so Answers A, C, and D are incorrect choices.

161. Answer C is correct. The nurse should prepare to administer atropine since it is the treatment for cholinergic crisis. Answers A, B, and D are not used in the treatment of cholinergic crisis; therefore, they are incorrect choices.

162. Answer D is correct. Older adults are at greatest risk for developing heat exhaustion. Answers A, B, and C are not as likely to develop heat exhaustion as the older client; therefore, they are incorrect choices.

163. Answer C is correct. The client's symptoms suggest a possible myocardial infarction; therefore, the client is classified as emergent. The client with a simple fracture is classified as non-urgent, so Answer A is incorrect. The client with abdominal pain is classified as urgent; therefore, Answer B is incorrect. The client with a cough and temp of 101° F is classified as urgent; therefore, Answer D is incorrect.

164. Answer B is correct. Priority should be given to maintaining the client's respiratory function. Answers A and D are incorrect because the medications are not used in the treatment of myasthenic crisis. Answer C is incorrect because it does not take priority over assessment of the client's respiratory function.

165. Answer D is correct. There is no evidence of human-to-human transmission with Legionnaire's disease, so no special precautions are needed. Answers A, B, and C are incorrect because they do not apply to the care of the client with Legionnaire's disease

166. Answer A is correct. The nurse should give priority to covering the protruding abdominal organs with a sterile, saline-soaked dressing. Answers B and C do not take priority over protecting the abdominal contents; therefore, they are incorrect. There is no indication that the client requires supplemental oxygen at this time; therefore, Answer D is incorrect.

Answers to Practice Exam III

Answers at a Glance to Practice Exam III

1. B	30. A	59. C
2. D	31. C	60. A
3. B	32. A	61. C
4. C	33. C	62. A
5. B	34. A	63. B
6. D	35. B	64. D
7. A	36. A	65. D
8. B	37. C	66. A
9. A	38. A	67. D
10. C	39. B	68. C
11. C	40. A	69. A
12. B	41. B	70. C
13. C	42. C	71. B
14. A	43. B	72. B
15. A	44. D	73. A
16. A	45. C	74. C
17. C	46. A	75. A
18. C	47. B	76. B
19. A	48. C	77. B
20. B	49. C	78. B
21. A	50. B	79. C
22. A	51. B	80. D
23. C	52. A	81. B
24. D	53. A	82. A
25. D	54. B	83. D
26. C	55. A	84. B
27. C	56. A	85. B
28. B	57. B	86. D
29. C	58. B	87. A

88. C	115. D	142. A
89. A	116. B	143. B
90. B	117. D	144. B
91. D	118. C	145. A
92. B	119. C	146. C
93. C	120. D	147. C
94. B	121. A	148. B
95. B	122. B	149. C
96. D	123. A	150. B
97. C	124. C	151. C
98. D	125. A	152. A
99. C	126. A	153. B
100. A	127. D	154. D
101. D	128. A	155. C
102. D	129. B	156. C
103. B	130. A	157. A
104. B	131. D	158. B
105. C	132. B	159. D
106. A	133. A	160. C
107. C	134. B	161. C
108. B	135. A	162. D
109. A	136. A	163. D
110. C	137. C	164. B
111. A	138. A	165. A
112. A	139. C	166. D
113. A	140. C	
114. A	141. B	

Answers with Explanations

Care of the Client with Musculoskeletal and Connective Tissue Disorders

1. Answer B is correct. The initial action is for the nurse to further investigate the complaint by performing a detailed assessment of the leg. Answers A, D, and C might also be appropriate actions but would not be the initial action to implement, so they are incorrect.

2. Answer D is correct. Weight-bearing exercises such as walking are recommended for clients with fibromyalgia. The answers in A, B, and C require no weight bearing during the activity and would not be beneficial, so they are incorrect.

3. Answer B is correct. Lupus is an autoimmune systemic disease three times more likely to occur in the African-American population than other population groups. It has also been linked to anticonvulsant medications. The people in Answers A, C, and D don't have conditions or characteristics that put them at a greater risk, so they are incorrect.

4. Answer C is correct. The nurse would assess the client with the fractured femur and rash. This could indicate fat embolism. Pain is expected in a client 2 hours postoperative total hip (Answer A), so it is wrong. There is nothing that needs immediate attention in the clients listed in Answers B and D, so they are incorrect.

5. Answer B is correct. Clients with gout should avoid high-purine foods such as poultry, organ meats, and shellfish. Answers C and D are not high-purine foods, so they are incorrect. Answer A is a medium-purine food allowed once a day when gout is under control, so it is incorrect.

6. Answer D is correct. Application of heat to the cast would be contraindicated and increase the swelling. Any complaints of pain should be further investigated for possible compartment syndrome. The answers in A, B, and C are correct practices for cast care and are therefore incorrect.

7. Answer A is correct. The correct action for the severed finger is to place it in a bag and put it on cold saline. The answers in B, C, and D are not the best to utilize to preserve the digit, so they are incorrect.

8. Answer B is correct. Consent must be obtained for the transfusion prior to the procedure. An 18g needle, rather than a 22g as in Answer A, is recommended for blood. Normal saline is the IV solution transfused with the blood, which makes Answer C incorrect. Answer D is incorrect because blood has to infuse in 4 hours. One unit of packed cells is 250 mL instead of 500 mL.

9. Answer A is correct. Colchicine should be taken after meals or with milk to decrease gastric irritation. Fluids should be increased to three to four quarts/day, so Answer B is incorrect. Aspirin is not contraindicated with colchicine, so Answer C is incorrect. Answer D is not the action of colchicine, so it is incorrect.

10. Answer C is correct. This finding indicates cardiovascular involvement of inflammation of the heart muscle or pleural effusion. Answer A is normal (98° Fahrenheit), so it is incorrect. Answers B and D are expected clinical manifestations of lupus, so they are incorrect.

11. Answer C is correct. The symptoms listed might indicate nerve damage and compartment syndrome, so the physician should be notified. Answers A and B need to be addressed but are not a priority, so they are incorrect. Pain is expected in clients with bone fractures, so Answer D is incorrect.

12. Answer B is correct. The nurse should further assess the patient prior to notifying the physician. Lowering the head of the bed would possibly increase the breathing difficulty, making Answer A incorrect. Answer C, notifying the physician, might be appropriate, but not until an assessment has been performed. Answer D has no rationale for being performed, so it is wrong.

13. Answer C is correct. Pressure on the peroneal nerve can cause foot drop. Dorsiflexion of the foot indicates peroneal nerve function. Because inversion of the foot can indicate pressure on the peroneal nerve, Answer B is incorrect. Answer A demonstrates adequate function of the tibial nerve, so it is incorrect. Answer D gives no indication of nerve function, so it is incorrect.

14. Answer A is correct. When deciding priority status, this client is experiencing excessive blood loss, which correlates with the C in airway, breathing, and circulation. The clients in Answers B and C have expected findings, so they are incorrect. The client in Answer D has an elevated temperature, which would require antipyretics and further assessments, but is not the priority, so it is incorrect.

15. Answer A is correct. The nurse should notify the physician of the trend in the client's vital signs. Answer C, continuing to monitor the client and document, is not appropriate because the trend of hypovolemia is already established. Answers B and D have no criteria of relevance in the stem, so they are incorrect.

16. Answer A is correct. This laboratory value indicates leukocytosis and a possible infection. Surgery is contraindicated with infection anywhere in the body; therefore, surgeon notification is required. Answers B and D are normal, so they are incorrect. The sodium level in Answer C is slightly abnormal (normal Na 135–145 mEq/L) and not a priority, so it is incorrect.

17. Answer C is correct. It is contraindicated for weights to be removed from a client's skeletal traction set-up except in life-threatening situations. Answers A, B, and D are all correct for the performance of pin care, so they are incorrect.

18. Answer C is correct. The highest calcium amount is in sardines. Answers A, B, and D do not have as much calcium, so they are incorrect.

19. Answer A is correct. The clinical manifestations listed are indicative of a sinus infection. Clients with infections should not receive infliximab (Remicade). Answer B are expected symptoms of rheumatoid arthritis (RA), and Answer C is also an expected blood value with RA, so they are incorrect. There is no connection between allergies to cephalosporins and Remicade, so Answer D is incorrect.

20. Answer B is correct. The drug is not available for IV administration, so the nurse would need to intervene to prevent patient injury. Answers A, C, and D are correct interventions when administering this drug, so they are incorrect.

21. Answer A is correct. This result indicates a decrease in the function of the heart. Normal ejection fraction (the percentage of blood ejected from the heart during systole) is 50%–70%. Answers B and C are only slightly abnormal, so they are incorrect. Answer D indicates a positive result, so it is incorrect.

22. Answer A is correct. The client should avoid bringing the legs together (adduction) to prevent dislocation of the hip prosthesis. Answers B, C, and D are recommended practices for clients after joint replacement surgery, so they are incorrect.

23. Answer C is correct. Stopping the medication abruptly or skipping a dose could cause a withdrawal reaction (difficulty sleeping, nausea, headache, and diarrhea). The drug can cause drowsiness rather than hyperactivity, which makes Answer A incorrect. The drug causes weight gain, so Answer D is wrong. Answer B is incorrect because this side effect does not signify a serious reaction and discontinuation of the drug.

24. Answer D is correct. Clients with prosthetic hips cannot sit in straight chairs. They are limited to decreased hip flexion but are allowed to sit in recliners. Answers A, B, and C are all appropriate interventions so they require no interventions by the preceptor; therefore, they are incorrect.

25. Answer D is correct. Laceration of the colon can occur with a pelvic fracture resulting in these symptoms. Answer A is normal, so it is incorrect. Answer B contains expected clinical manifestations of pelvic fractures, so it is incorrect. Answer C is not specific to pelvic fractures, so it is wrong.

26. Answer C is correct. Spinach is a high-purine food and should be avoided by clients with gout. Answers A, B, and D are not high-purine foods, so they are incorrect.

27. Answer C is correct. Feeding a client without swallowing difficulty can be done by a nurse's assistant. Answers A, B, and D are beyond the preparation of a nurse's assistant, so they are incorrect.

28. Answer B is correct. The client has an abnormal Hct and might need a blood transfusion. Answers A and C are incorrect because doctor notification is not appropriate at this time. Answer D is normal, so it is incorrect.

29. Answer C is correct. The initial action by the nurse should be to notify the physician. Assessments indicate bleeding with hypovolemia. The action in Answer A is not appropriate for the nurse because releasing the pressure dressing can cause an increase in bleeding. Therefore, Answer A is incorrect. Answers B and D are appropriate actions but would not be the initial actions, so they are incorrect.

30. Answer A is correct. It is within the role of the UAP to perform personal hygiene and put these items at the bedside. The nurse cannot delegate assessments, medication administration, or traction set-up to the UAP, so Answers B, C, and D are incorrect.

Care of the Client with Gastrointestinal Disorders

31. Answer C is correct. The actual biopsy test result is the most accurate and specific for the diagnosis of an ulcer. Although Answers A, B, and D can occur with an ulcer, they are not as specific to an ulcer, so they are incorrect.

32. Answer A is correct. The assessment describes Cullen's sign, which indicates intra-abdominal bleeding and the physician should be notified. The assessments in Answers B and D are not appropriate at this time, so they are incorrect. The change in position in Answer C will not correct the situation and would be contraindicated in a volume deficit, so it is wrong.

33. Answer C is correct. Foods and beverages that should be avoided include citrus fruits, tomatoes, fatty foods, caffeinated beverages, chocolate, tomato products, and peppermint. Answers A and D (citrus fruits), and Answer B can lower the LES pressure, so they are incorrect.

34. Answer A is correct. Other medications that can affect the test results include proton pump inhibitors (for example, Prilosec), bismuth preparations (for example, Pepto-Bismol), and histamine blockers (for example, Tagamet). The drugs in Answers B, C, and D do not affect *H. Pylori* test results, so they are incorrect.

35. Answer B is correct. The nurse would want to administer these medications to avoid extremes in gastric PH and assist with healing of the ulcer. Answers A, C, and D are associated with the management of hypovolemia, so they are incorrect.

36. Answer A is correct. It is contraindicated for clients with acute diverticulitis to have a colonoscopy. It could cause perforation of the colon. The orders in Answers B, C, and D are appropriate prescriptives and would not be questionable, so they are incorrect.

37. Answer C is correct. Ballance's sign is resonance over the right flank when the client is lying on the left side and is assessed. This indicates a ruptured spleen. Answer A is incorrect because, although this can be associated with blood in the abdomen, it is not specific to spleen rupture. Answer B shows normal vital signs. Clients with spleen rupture would exhibit shock symptoms (low BP and elevated heart rate), so Answer B is incorrect. Answer D is not associated with spleen rupture, so it is wrong.

38. Answer A is correct. Gas bloat syndrome occurs when clients are unable to belch. These clients should avoid carbonated beverages, gas-producing foods (for example, cabbage, broccoli, and beans), chewing gum, and use of a straw. Answers B, C, and D do not increase or produce gas, so they are incorrect.

39. Answer B is correct. Assistive personal can provide personal hygiene and comfort measures. The task in Answers A, C, and D must be performed by licensed personnel, so they are incorrect.

40. Answer A is correct. Manipulating the NG tube on this client could lead to disruption of the anastomosis or the suture line. The physician should be notified if patency of the tube is in doubt. Answers B, C, and D are all correct interventions, so they are incorrect.

41. Answer B is correct. The nurse would focus on circulation by application of pressure to the site because the danger is bleeding. Answer A is more of a priority before the procedure, so it is incorrect. Answers C and D are both important but should not be the first action, so they are incorrect.

42. Answer C is correct. Bright red blood indicates an arterial source, which makes this client at risk for hypovolemia and the priority client to assess. Clinical manifestations of peptic ulcer disease (PUD) include epigastric pain, so Answer A is incorrect. Although the clients in Answers B and D would need an assessment by the nurse, they are not a priority, so these options are incorrect.

43. Answer B is correct. This gives the best diagnostic evaluation. Answers A and D could occur with appendicitis but are not as significant as the ultrasound, so they are incorrect. The CT scan would be abnormal with appendicitis, so Answer C is wrong.

44. Answer D is correct. When performing any procedure, identification of the client is one of the initial actions to ensure safety. The other steps would be done in the following order: B, A, and C, so they are incorrect.

45. Answer C is correct. Other clinical manifestations include pain, nausea, and vomiting, rebound tenderness upon palpation, flatulence, and indigestion. Answers A, B, and D are not associated with cholecystitis, so they are incorrect.

46. Answer A is correct. The scissors would be necessary to cut the tube if the balloon were to slip upward and obstruct the client's airway. Answers B and C are used for comfort measures but are not essential, so they are incorrect. Answer D is unnecessary, so it is wrong.

47. Answer B is correct. Interventions associated with the respiratory system would be the priority focus due to the high risk of respiratory complications. Answers A and C are appropriate, but not the primary focus, so they are incorrect. Answer D is incorrect because of the danger of perforating the incision line while attempting to reposition the tube.

48. Answer C is correct. The client is taught to eliminate anything that lowers the LES—alcohol and tobacco. The client should also be taught to eat 4–6 small meals a day, be upright for 1–2 hours after meals, and avoid food 2–3 hours before bedtime. For these reasons, Answers A, B, and D are incorrect.

49. Answer C is correct. Dumping syndrome is thought to be caused by rapid emptying of gastric contents into the small intestine. This diet will serve to decrease the incidence of dumping syndrome, which makes it the correct choice. The client needs to eat small amounts at a meal, which makes Answer D incorrect. The client also cannot drink liquids when eating, which makes Answer B incorrect. The client would need to lie down after meals, so Answer A is incorrect.

50. Answer B is correct. Elevating the head of the bed will relieve pressure from the abdomen and increase the breathing ability. Answers A and D are not effective for helping the dyspnea, so they are incorrect. Answer C is appropriate but is not the initial action, so it is incorrect.

51. Answer B is correct. A UAP can obtain supplies from a list provided but cannot determine the dressing supplies needed. Answers A, C, and D require nursing skills and are beyond the role of the UAP, so they are incorrect.

52. Answer A is correct. Any complaint of chest pain warrants concern. In this case, the bands could cause ulceration of the mucosa and bleeding, so the physician should be notified. Answers B and C are expected and related to the procedure, so they are incorrect. Answer D requires further investigation but is not the priority, so it is wrong.

53. Answer A is correct. The normal O_2 saturation is 95–100 and the client shows severe O_2 deficiency. There is no direct evidence of an increased risk of aspiration, so Answer C is incorrect. Answer B is a priority also, but oxygenation is the main focus, so it is incorrect. The assessment result in Answer D is not an immediate priority, so it is incorrect.

54. Answer B is correct. Lactulose causes ammonia from the blood to pass into the colon. An increase in bowel movements would indicate the drug is serving to eliminate the ammonia. Answer A would indicate a worsening of the condition and build-up of ammonia in the blood, so it is incorrect. Answers C and D do not indicate improvements or relate to lactulose, so they are incorrect.

55. Answer A is correct. The lung could have accidentally been punctured during the procedure, so verifying breath sounds prior to physician notification would be important. Answer B is also an important assessment, but less likely to correlate with the shortness of breath. The assessments in Answers C and D are not a priority for the situation, so they are incorrect.

56. Answer A is correct. Hepatitis A is transmitted by the fecal-oral route; therefore, hand-washing, sanitation, and good personal hygiene are appropriate measures to prevent transmission of the virus. Answers C and D are not directly related to hepatitis A, so they are wrong. Answer B is neither necessary nor required, so it is incorrect.

57. Answer B is correct. The intrinsic factor is reduced with gastrectomy procedures and the client is no longer able to absorb vitamins B9 and B12. Answers A, C, and D are not affected by this surgical procedure, so they are incorrect.

58. Answer B is correct. The sodium level is extremely low (normal sodium is 135–145 mEq/L), resulting in the need for immediate intervention. Answer A is a normal level (potassium normal 3.5–5.0 mEq/L), so it is wrong. Answer C is above normal (60–160 units/L is normal amylase level) but is expected with pancreatitis, so it is incorrect. Answer D is slightly elevated above the normal of 5,000–10,000 cells/mm but is not the priority for this situation, so it is wrong.

59. Answer C is correct. This color indicates necrosis and should be reported to the physician. Answers A and D are normal, so they are incorrect. It can take a colostomy two to four days to function; therefore, Answer B is incorrect.

60. Answer A is correct. Aspiration and airway occlusion are the most dangerous complications of the use of the Sengstaken-Blakemore tube, which this assessment result might indicate. Answers B and D would require further interventions, but are not the priority. Blood would be an expected finding in the gastric contents, so Answer C is incorrect.

Care of the Client with Neoplastic Disorders

61. Answer C is correct. Strict isolation is not required for this client. Answer B is incorrect because visitors and staff need to limit time, distance, and shielding. Answer D is true because a Foley catheter is required due to bedrest and potential dislodgment of the implant. Answer A is recommended to provide maximum shielding for the nurse, so answers A, B, and D are incorrect.

62. Answer A is correct. The assistive personnel may ambulate and transfer clients. Monitoring a client during a blood transfusion is the registered nurse's responsibility, so Answer B is incorrect. Irrigating a Foley catheter and performing a dressing change are considered invasive and require the skills of a nurse, so Answers C and D are incorrect.

63. Answer B is correct. The calculation is 16mg in a 4-hour period (2mg X 8 doses = 16mg). The answers in A, C, and D are not correct calculations of the amount of drug given, so they are wrong.

64. Answer D is correct. The nurse's highest priority is to properly identify the blood products against the client identification with another registered nurse. All the other answer options should be done, but identification takes the highest priority. Therefore, Answers A, B, and C are incorrect.

65. Answer D is correct. The colostomy should be irrigated only when a regular enema is required. The appliance needs to be changed only when it becomes loose. Answer A is incorrect because foods are not restricted unless a specific diet is ordered for another medical condition. Answer B is incorrect because changing the appliance frequently would cause skin irritation. Answer C is incorrect because drinking liquids prevents constipation.

66. Answer A is correct. The LPN can perform sterile dressing changes. The LPN cannot hang blood, access a VAD, or perform discharge teaching, so Answers B, C, and D are incorrect. These are the duties of the registered nurse (RN).

67. Answer D is correct. Rinsing with an alcohol-based mouthwash will dry and break down oral tissue. Answer A is incorrect because a soft toothbrush will prevent oral trauma. Answer B is incorrect because lubricating lips will soften them and prevent cracking. Answer C is incorrect because avoiding hard or spicy foods helps to prevent irritation.

68. Answer C is correct. The airway is occluded by secretions. The client needs to be suctioned. Although all actions are appropriate, Answers A, B, and D are incorrect initial actions.

69. Answer A is correct. Many medication errors are made by human error in transcription. Answer B is incorrect and could be considered a tort. Answer C is incorrect because nurses cannot alter parameters without healthcare provider orders. Answer D is incorrect because the pharmacy can verify dosage, side effects, and help with medication prep but must follow healthcare provider's orders.

70. Answer C is correct. A semi-Fowler's position is recommended. Answer A is incorrect because placement on the unaffected side tends to promote mediastinal shift. Answer B is incorrect because placing the client on the affected side might put pressure on the bronchial stump. Answer D is incorrect because high Fowler's would be too high and would probably fatigue the client.

71. Answer B is correct. The earliest exercises are passive range of motion of the elbow, wrist, and hand, and are started on the first post operative day. The exercises in Answers A, C, and D are done later but not as initial therapy, so they are incorrect.

72. Answer B is correct. Proper disposal of a controlled substance is witnessed destruction. Answer A is incorrect because the patch needs to be destroyed by two nurses. Answer C is incorrect because removal of the patch and giving it to family could promote abuse. Answer D is incorrect because the item is considered contaminated; therefore, it would not be returned to the pharmacy.

73. Answer A is correct. The client with neutropenia is at high risk for infection due to low white blood cell count; therefore, hand-washing is the first-line barrier that will protect them from infection. Answers B, C, and D can be done at another time, but are not priorities, so they are incorrect.

74. Answer C is correct. The spill kit should be used and followed as directions indicate because this is considered hazardous waste. Answer A is incorrect because housekeeping is not responsible for cleaning hazardous waste. Answer B is incorrect because the nurse should never leave the spill unattended on the floor. Answer D is incorrect because this spill would not indicate a need to notify infection control.

75. Answer A is correct. Communication is priority. It facilitates interaction, limits anxiety, and promotes safety. Nursing measures would also be done but are not priority, so Answers B and C are incorrect. Answer D would not be a priority immediately postoperatively because the client will have a tracheostomy and be suctioned by nurses, so it is wrong.

76. Answer B is correct. *Neutropenia* is a decrease in white blood cells. Neupogen is a white cell booster. Answer A is incorrect because Procrit is given to stimulate erythropoietin. Answer C is incorrect because Neumega is given to boost platelets. Answer D is incorrect because photofrin is a photoactivated drug used for other types of cancer.

77. Answer B is correct. The older adult is at greatest risk due to the skin exposure to the sun over an extended period of time. Answer D is incorrect because the 22-year-old client would also be at risk, but not the greatest, so it is wrong. Answers A and C do not give enough information to determine a risk level, so they are incorrect.

78. Answer B is correct. Leukopenia increases the risk of an infection, so crowds should be avoided. Answer C is incorrect because the platelet count is not given, so bleeding precautions are not indicated. Answer D, increasing protein and red meat, would correct anemia, so it is wrong. Answer A is incorrect because it does not relate to the situation and nurses are not allowed to alter medication orders.

79. Answer C is correct. Blood-streaked sputum would be a normal finding in the immediate post operative period, but should last no more than two to three days. Answers A and B are incorrect because the nurse would not notify the physician; these are normal findings. Answer D is incorrect because it is the physician's responsibility to determine whether the client goes back to surgery.

80. Answer D is correct. Potassium chloride is irritating to veins. Using the largest vein possible, via a venous access device (VAD), is best. The antecubital would restrict movement, so Answer A is wrong. Answer B and C are incorrect because these are smaller peripheral veins.

81. Answer B is correct. Subcutaneous emphysema the second postoperative day is abnormal and can indicate incorrect tube placement. Answers A and D are normal, so they are incorrect. Answer C is a positive assessment result, so it is wrong.

82. Answer A is correct. A bone scan maps the uptake of bone-seeking radioactive isotope by injecting dye. Those allergic to shellfish and iodine are not candidates for this exam. Answers B, C, and D would be performed, but Answer A is the most important.

83. Answer D is correct. The neutropenic client is at high risk for infection. Therefore, fresh fruits and vegetables are not allowed due to possible microbial contamination. All foods should be thoroughly cooked before serving to this client. Answers A, B, and C all contain fresh fruits and are incorrect.

84. Answer B is correct. This information would be the best basis for predicting the outcome of therapy. Answer D would be useful but is not specific for this client, so it is wrong. Answers A and C are wrong because they are not useful for predicting outcome in this client.

85. Answer B is correct. During a health crisis, the client will need support from significant others. Answers A, C, and D are part of the complete health history but are not priority, so they are wrong.

86. Answer D is correct. Intestinal antibiotics and a complete cleansing of the bowel with enemas until clear are necessary to prevent fecal contamination. Answer A is incorrect because there is no evidence of infection. Answer B is not required because the bladder will be removed, so it is wrong. Answer C, a clear liquid diet, is usually ordered for several days prior to surgery, which makes it an incorrect answer.

87. Answer A is correct. The nurse would begin the procedure by assessing the site and ensuring patency. Answer B is the next step, so it is incorrect. Answer D would be performed after steps A and B, so it is incorrect. The final steps include flushing the line with more saline after the drug is infused and administering a heparin flush, so Answer C is wrong.

88. Answer C is correct. Cisplatin is toxic to the kidney; therefore, the nurse would be concerned about the elevated creatinine level before administration of the drug. Answer A is normal, so it is wrong. Answer B is a high level but is not related to the drug administration, so it is incorrect. Answer D is abnormally high (normal is 100–190 IU/L) but is associated with liver cells rather than the kidney, so it is wrong.

89. Answer A is correct. This is the reversal agent for Versed and should be given immediately. Answers B, C, and D are drugs not effective for reversal of Versed, so they are incorrect.

90. Answer B is correct. Vancomycin trough levels should be done 30–60 minutes prior to the fourth dose of vancomycin. The question stem directs the examinee that this is a 30-minute trough level, making the 1930 time correct. Answers A, C, and D are not appropriate for the vancomycin 30-minute trough level, so they are incorrect.

91. Answer D is correct. Neumega is given to increase platelets. A continuing abnormal (or dropping) platelet result indicates the drug is not working and further evaluation is needed. Answers A, B, and C are abnormal but do not relate to the drug Neumega, so they are incorrect.

92. Answer B is correct. Acute or chronic exposure to ionizing radiation can cause gene mutation and birth defects. All nurses are at risk if they do not follow time, distance, and shielding precautions. Answer A is incorrect because chronic disease should not be a factor in assignments. Answer C is incorrect because the nurse scheduled to administer chemotherapy could care for this client. Answer D is incorrect because the nurse cured of cancer could care for this client.

93. Answer C is correct. The criterion for evaluation of how well a person is coping with grief is the ability to discuss future plans. Controlling emotions, as in Answer A, is not a healthy behavior, so it is incorrect. Answer B, asking friends to visit, shows an effort to develop network of support, but is not the best indicator, so it is incorrect. Answer D, researching information could indicate that the spouse is in denial, so it is incorrect.

94. Answer B is correct. Testicular atrophy occurs after diethylstilbestrol use because it is a synthetic estrogen given to men. It is used as a palliative treatment of prostate cancer. Answer A is incorrect because the feminizing effect would be a decrease in facial hair. Answer C is incorrect because a high-pitched voice would be a feminizing effect. Answer D is incorrect because weight gain from fluid retention is a feminizing effect.

95. Answer B is correct. Rectal temperatures are avoided when a client has leukemia due to the danger of hemorrhage and perirectal abscesses. Answers A, C, and D are other nursing interventions that are acceptable, so they are incorrect.

96. Answer D is correct. Blood in the urine would require further evaluation due to the high possibility that the oncology client's platelets might be low. Loss of hair, dry mouth, and loss of appetite are expected in the oncology client and do not pose an immediate risk for injury, so Answers A, B, and C are incorrect.

97. Answer C is correct. Pressure dressings are never removed, but if saturated, they should be reinforced with sterile dressings. This is not a normal occurrence. Vital signs should be taken, drain contents noted, and surgeon notified. Answer A is incorrect because the nurse should not remove the dressing. Answer B is incorrect because milking the tubing would not take care of the problem. Answer D is incorrect because this might be a frequent occurrence, but nursing action is needed.

98. Answer D is correct. Colonoscopy exams should be done once every 10 years starting at age 50 instead of once every 20 years. Answers A, B, and C are all correct education for cancer prevention, so they are incorrect.

99. Answer C is correct. The nurse should not directly touch the radium implant at any time. Answers A, B, and D are not recommendations for handling the radiation, so they are incorrect.

100. Answer A is correct. The nurse should notify the physician because the client is exhibiting symptoms of cord compression. Answer B is important but is not the initial action, so it is incorrect. Answers C or D might be appropriate but are not the initial action, so they are incorrect.

101. Answer D is correct. Nolvadex is an antineoplastic drug that competes with estradiol for binding of estrogen in receptors that are found in the breast, uterus, and vagina, and can cause vaginal bleeding. This would necessitate notification of the physician. Answers A and C are side effects of this drug that are expected, so they are incorrect. Answer B is not a side effect but could occur. Weight gain would be a greater concern, so it is incorrect.

102. Answer D is correct. Asparaginase (Elspar) is an antineoplastic medication. Adverse reactions include hepatotoxicity, which usually occurs within two weeks of initial treatment. Normal alkaline phosphatase is 4.5–13 units/dL. The laboratory values in Answers A, B, and C are normal, so they are incorrect.

103. Answer B is correct. The client is exhibiting symptoms of circulatory overload. Lasix is the diuretic the nurse would be prepared to administer to remove the fluid. Answers A, C, and D are not drugs ordered for fluid overload, so they are incorrect.

104. Answer B is correct. The client should be placed on contact precautions to prevent spread of the organism. Answer A is incorrect because more than standard precautions are necessary. Answer C is incorrect because the entire room would need to be cleaned to rid the organism from the surfaces (usually required twice daily). Hand hygiene is required before and after contact, which makes Answer D incorrect.

105. Answer C is correct. The recommended dose of Compazine is 10–20 mg four times daily. Answers A, B, and D—Zofran, Anzemet, and Reglan doses—are all within normal range, so they are incorrect.

106. Answer A is correct. Cytoxan can be toxic to the kidney and bladder. Hemorrhagic cystitis can occur. Fluid intake needs to be 1,000–2,000 mL/day for children and 3,000 mL/day for adults. Answer B is incorrect because nausea is an expected finding with chemotherapy. Answer C is incorrect because candida is not a problem. Answer D is incorrect because the client usually loses weight, instead of gaining, due to side effects of the drug, but this is not priority.

107. Answer C is correct. Someone should hold the tube in place to prevent accidental dislodgment of the tracheostomy tube. Answers A, B, and D are correct techniques for performance of tracheostomy care, so they are incorrect.

108. Answer B is correct. Vincristine is noted for causing neurological side effects such as numbness, tingling, loss of deep tendon reflexes, wrist and foot drop, and cranial palsies. The physician should be notified if any of these occur. Answers A, C, and D are not major side effects of this drug, so they are incorrect.

109. Answer A is correct. Stomatitis is common with chemotherapy and should be brought to the MD's attention. This occurs due to rapidly dividing cells. Answer B is a low-grade fever and does not require immediate attention, so it is wrong. Answer C is expected and not a concern unless dehydration occurs, so it is wrong. Answer D is expected and should be reported if it last more than 24 hours, so it is wrong.

110. Answer C is correct. Intellectualizaion is use of reasoning to avoid emotional aspects of a situation. This is a defense mechanism against anxiety. Projection puts the blame on another person and sublimation redirects it, so Answers A and B are incorrect. Answer D, reaction formation, is opposite of normal behavior, so it is wrong.

Care of the Client with Neurological Disorders

111. Answer A is correct. A severe headache is a hallmark symptom of cerebral aneurysm rupture. A CT scan would confirm the rupture. Answers B, C, and D are all tests that might be ordered but will not best support the suspected diagnosis of cerebral aneurysm rupture, so they are incorrect.

112. Answer A is correct. Client preparation for a lumbar puncture procedure also includes explanation of the procedure with expectations of some pain and discomfort with injection of the local anesthetic, as well as spinal needle insertion, positioning of the client on the side with assistance into a fetal-like position, and asking the client to empty the bladder. For these reasons, Answers B, C, and D are incorrect.

113. Answer A is correct. Imitrex is given PO, subcutaneously, or intranasally to relieve migraine headaches. The drugs listed in Answer B (beta blocker), and Answers C and D (calcium channel blockers) are used to prevent a migraine headache, so they are incorrect.

114. Answer A is correct. This medication can cause muscle cramps and muscle weakness. It can also cause hypersalivation, increase lacrimation, and fatigue, which makes the side effects in Answers B, C, and D incorrect.

115. Answer D is correct. Restlessness or any behavioral change gives an early indication of increased intracranial pressure. Answers A, B, and C are clinical manifestations of increased intracranial pressure, but are not early indicators, so they are incorrect.

116. Answer B is correct. The post-craniotomy client should avoid forceful coughing because it increases the intracranial pressure. Answers A, C, and D are correct nursing measures, requiring no nursing intervention, so they are incorrect.

117. Answer D is correct. Clients with a creatinine level higher than 1.5 mg/dL are at risk for contrast-induced nephropathy. Answer A is important for clients having magnetic resonance imagery (MRI), so it is incorrect. Clients are generally not NPO after midnight for CT scans and can usually have liquids, so answer B is incorrect. Answer C might be assessed, but is not directly related to CT scans or contrast, so it is incorrect.

118. Answer C is correct. Chunky, raw, or stringy vegetables should be excluded from the diet of clients with dysphagia. Answers A, B, and D are soft and warm, which can stimulate the swallowing reflex, so they are incorrect.

119. Answer C is correct. A client with a cervical fracture would require log rolling to keep the spine in alignment and prevent damage and injury to the spinal cord. Answers A, B, and D are usual treatments measures for clients with spinal cord injuries, so they are incorrect.

120. Answer D is correct. Clients with SIADH should have fluids restricted to 500–600 mL/day, so the nurse would question the fluid order. Answers A, B, and C are recommended treatment measures for clients with SIADH, so they are incorrect.

121. Answer A is correct. These are characteristics of injury to the anterior cord. The descriptions in Answers B, C, and D are not characterized in this manner, so they are incorrect.

122. Answer B is correct. Biologic response modifiers (for example, Avonex, Betaseron, and Copaxone) are used for continuous treatment of multiple sclerosis. Other drugs included in the treatment are steroids, immunosuppressants, and muscle relaxers. Answer A (narcotic) and Answer D (osmotic diuretic) are not recommended drugs for MS, so they are incorrect. The drug in Answer C is used for arthritis and Crohn's disease, so it is wrong.

123. Answer A is correct. Spinal-neurogenic shock occurs immediately after the injury and can last for a few days to several months. Answers B, C, and D are not associated with a low BP and bradycardia, so they are incorrect.

124. Answer C is correct. The first action in any nursing situation is airway and breathing. The nurse would next turn the client to the side, as in Answer B. Answer A is important, but not a first action, so it is incorrect. Answer D is done after the seizure is over, so it is an incorrect answer.

125. Answer A is correct. The white blood cell count would be increased and the CSF would appear cloudy in bacterial meningitis. Increased protein and decreased glucose are characteristic features in a client with bacterial meningitis, so Answers B and C are incorrect. Increased red blood cells are not associated with meningitis, so Answer D is incorrect.

126. Answer A is correct. Early clinical manifestations include visual changes, motor skill deficiencies, and paresthesia. There is usually a decrease in sensitivity to pain, so Answer B is incorrect. Answer C correlates with Guillain-Barré, so it is wrong. Emotional liability and depression are common, but confusion and disorientation are not associated with multiple sclerosis, so Answer D is incorrect.

127. Answer D is correct. Decerebrate posturing indicates a poor prognosis and indicates brain stem dysfunction. Answers A and C can also indicate a problem but are not indicative of the brainstem dysfunction, so they are incorrect. Answer B is normal, so it is wrong.

128. Answer A is correct. An eye patch is used for the double vision and the patch is switched every few hours from one eye to the other. Answers B, C, and D are inappropriate for clients with diplopia, so they are incorrect.

129. Answer B is correct. The description is of decerebrate posturing, which usually indicates brain stem dysfunction and a poor prognosis. Answers A and D suggests the posturing is normal or an improvement, so they are incorrect. Decerebrate posturing is not directly related to meningitis, so Answer C is incorrect.

130. Answer A is correct. Being unable to remain erect with eyes open and closed indicates a probable problem with the cerebellum. Answers B and D are the same, so they are incorrect. A client who exhibits swaying when asked to stand is experiencing an abnormality; therefore, Answer C is wrong.

131. Answer D is correct. This position (sometimes called the *William position*) relaxes the lower back and relieves pressure on the spinal nerves. The positions in Answers A, B, and C will not help and might increase the stress on the lower back, so they are incorrect.

132. Answer B is correct. The nurse should find out whether the client has lost consciousness and if so, for how long? A loss of consciousness signifies more extensive damage. The question in Answer A would be appropriate, but is not the priority question, so it is incorrect. The questions in Answers C and D are inappropriate for the situation, so they are wrong.

133. Answer A is correct. The drug is given to clients with aneurysm to treat the vasospasm, which will prevent decreased blood flow to the area. The purpose in Answer B is a negative effect, not an action, of the drug Nimotop, so it is incorrect. Answer C is the purpose of Amicar, also given to patients with aneurysms, so it is incorrect. Answer D is also an effect of the drug, but not the purpose for administration to this client, so it is wrong.

134. Answer B is correct. The normal ICP reading is below 15 mm. The physician should be notified of the abnormal reading. Answers A and D would be detrimental to the client, so they are incorrect. Answer C requires a doctor's order, so it is wrong.

135. Answer A is correct. The correct calculated CPP is 48 (ICP minus MAP = CPP). The client's CPP needs to be at least 70 for adequate brain perfusion to occur. Answer B is inappropriate because action needs to be taken about the low CPP level, so it is wrong. Answer C is an incorrect calculation for the CPP, so it is wrong. A lumbar puncture is contraindicated in increased ICP, which makes answer D incorrect.

136. Answer A is correct. A client with increased ICP should not have a lumbar puncture due to the risk of sudden release of CSF pressure. Lethargy and sluggish pupil reaction are symptoms associated with increased ICP. Answers B and C would not be appropriate because the procedure would likely be canceled. The client's head of the bed should be elevated to 30° for increased ICP, so Answer D is incorrect.

137. Answer C is correct. These emotions and activities can cause a migraine headache to occur. The plans in Answers A, B, and D are elements that should be covered during a teaching session, so they are incorrect.

138. Answer A is correct. The CT scan is a priority to identify the type of stroke—ischemic or hemorrhagic—so that, if indicated, TPA administration can begin before the three-hour window closes. The exams in Answers B, C, and D would need to be completed, but aren't the priority, so they are incorrect.

139. Answer C is correct. A television or radio would cause too much stimuli and not be beneficial for a client with Alzheimer's disease. Answers A, B, and D are recommended for clients with Alzheimer's disease, so they are incorrect.

140. Answer C is correct. Tylenol would be the safest medication to administer to this client for the fever. Aspirin and NSAIDs could cause an increase in bleeding, possibly enlarging the affected area, so Answers A, B, and D are incorrect.

141. Answer B is correct. These levels are the distinguishing characteristics of Guillain-Barré syndrome. The levels in Answers A, C, and D aren't associated with Guillain-Barré, so they are incorrect.

142. Answer A is correct. This is a true statement about the procedure and is appropriate. Answer B is incorrect because this is not required due to the expectation of this side effect with this procedure. Answer C is not related to the VNS, so it is incorrect. Answer D is not related to the procedure and is untrue, so it is wrong.

143. Answer B is correct. D5W should not be given because it increases cerebral edema and the rate of 200 mL/hr is too much fluid volume for the client with a head injury. Answers B, C, and D are appropriate orders for clients with a head injury, so they are incorrect.

144. Answer B is correct. A client with Guillain-Barré usually has a history of illness, trauma, surgery, or immunization 1–3 weeks prior to the onset of symptoms. Answers A, C, and D are not associated with Guillain-Barré risk factors, so they are incorrect.

145. Answer A is correct. Mannitol is an osmotic diuretic. Preparation includes obtaining IV tubing that has a filter. Romazicon is a reversal agent for Versed, so Answer B is incorrect. The actions in Answers C and D are not necessary for mannitol administration, so they are wrong.

146. Answer C is correct. Illicit drug use increases the likelihood of strokes. The risk factors in Answers A, B, and D are not risk factors associated with a stroke, so they are incorrect.

147. Answer C is correct. The altepase (t-PA) administration might have caused a bleed and continuing it would be detrimental. The nurse should stop the altepase (t-PA) and notify the doctor immediately. Answer A allows the transfusion to continue and the client could be much worse in 10 minutes, so it is wrong. Answer B wastes time and is inappropriate, so it is incorrect. Answer D is wrong because lowering the head of the bed would be contraindicated and would increase the intracranial pressure.

148. Answer B is correct. Clinical manifestations of hypovolemia (increased heart rate and low BP) would correlate with the deficient fluid volume associated with plasmapheresis. Answers A and C (elevated potassium), and D (increased INR), are not associated with a complication of plasmapheresis, so they are incorrect.

149. Answer C is correct. Safety is a major concern when administering IV anticoagulants. The nurse would need a device that would ensure that the client is receiving an accurate dose of heparin. The nurse should use small-gauge needles to perform venipunctures in clients receiving anticoagulants; therefore, Answer A is incorrect. The equipment in Answers B and D is not essential for a heparin infusion, so those answers are incorrect.

150. Answer B is correct. The client may receive an antianxiety drug such as Ativan before the procedure. Answers A (antihistamine), C (antibiotic), and D (general anesthesia) would not be appropriate to administer to the client prior to the procedure during this situation, so they are incorrect.

Care of the Client with Hematological Disorders

151. Answer C is correct. Hemarthrosis interventions include rest, ice, compression, and elevation. Heat would be contraindicated due to vasodilation causing increased bleeding. Answers in A, B, and D are recommended plans for clients with hemophilia, so they are incorrect.

152. Answer A is correct. Clients with thalassemia major must have blood transfusions to live, so the person assigned to this patient should be able to administer needed blood transfusions. The staff in Answers B, C, and D could not independently perform the task of blood transfusions, so they are incorrect.

153. Answer B is correct. The orange juice will improve absorption of the iron. Answer A can inhibit absorption of the iron, so it is wrong. The beverages in Answers C and D don't help absorb the drug, so they are incorrect.

154. Answer D is correct. The Schilling test is used to diagnose pernicious anemia. The tests in Answers A, B, and C cannot confirm a B12 deficiency, so they are incorrect.

155. Answer C is correct. Hyperviscosity of the blood occurs with polycythemia vera. Answer A is incorrect because hyperkalemia is most likely to occur. Answer B is not a recommended treatment for polycythemia vera, so it is incorrect. Clients need increase in fluid intake, so Answer D is wrong.

156. Answer C is correct. Normal potassium level is 3.5–5.0 mEq/L; therefore, a diet is needed that is high in potassium. Spinach has the most potassium at 662 mg. The foods in Answers A (420 mg), B (440 mg), and D (430 mg) have less potassium per 100 g, so they are incorrect.

157. Answer A is correct. Supportive data includes a prolonged aPTT, decreased Factor VIII or IX, and normal protime, fibrinogen, and platelets. Answers B, C, and D don't correlate with hemophilia, so they are wrong.

158. Answer B is correct. These symptoms are associated with sequestration crisis. In this crisis, blood pools in the spleen and the client has profound anemia and hypovolemia. The crisis in answer A is not exhibited by the symptoms provided, so it is incorrect. Clinical manifestations of vaso-occlusive crisis include fever, pain, and engorged tissues. Answers C and D are not recognized sickle cell crisis, so they are incorrect.

159. Answer D is correct. Foods high in folic acid include liver, organ meats, eggs, cabbage, broccoli, and Brussels sprouts. The foods listed in Answers A, B, and C aren't high in folic acid, so they are incorrect.

160. Answer C is correct. Hydroxurea can cause birth defects, so at least two methods of birth control are needed while on this drug. The statements made in Answers A, B, and D are correct information associated with the drug hydroxurea, so they are incorrect.

161. Answer C is correct. Foods high in iron include liver, red meat, organ meats, kidney beans, whole wheat bread and cereals, green leafy vegetables, carrots, egg yolks, and raisins. The foods in Answers A, B, and D are not high in iron, so they are incorrect.

162. Answer D is correct. The nurse should inspect the roof of the mouth in dark-skinned individuals. The area in answer A is not an accurate place to assess due to fat deposits that can appear yellow in contrast to dark skin around the eyes. The areas in Answers B and C can appear yellow if callused, so they are incorrect.

163. Answer D is correct. The nurse should add air to the syringe with the medication to prevent tracking of the medication after injection. The medication must be administered in a large muscle (dorsal gluteal), is given IM, and massaging the area after injection is contraindicated. These facts make Answers A, B, and C incorrect.

164. Answer B is correct. Hydration is an important aspect of treatment to provide volume and improve blood vessel circulation. The client is probably dehydrated, and fluids would need to be replenished. Answer C would not be the priority, so it is incorrect. Answer A would be necessary to help the patient's pain, but the fluids could also help in this situation. This would be the next intervention, so it is wrong. Heat is a comfort measure that would be employed with the pain medication, so Answer D is wrong.

165. Answer A is correct. These are symptoms of a hemolytic transfusion reaction and initial action is to prevent further damage by stopping the transfusion. The actions in Answers B, C, and D are appropriate but are not the initial action, so they are incorrect.

166. Answer D is correct. Because of the risk of anaphylaxis with IV administration, it is imperative that the nurse administer a test dose of 25 mg 1 hour before therapy. Checking the client's Hgb level would be important, but not as important as the test dose, so Answer A is wrong. Assessing for constipation would not be important to administer the dose, so Answer C is incorrect. Ensuring that the blood pressure systolic is over 120 is not necessary, although the medication can cause orthostatic hypotension, so Answer B is incorrect.

Answers to Practice Exam IV: Management and Alternative Item Exam Questions

Answers to Management Questions

1. Answer B is correct. Furosemide (Lasix) is a diuretic commonly used to treat congestive heart failure and hypertension. This drug should be given first to ensure that the client receives medication to treat potential life-threatening condition. Answers A, C, and D are incorrect because these drugs can be given after the furosemide (Lasix).

2. Answer B is correct. The nurse should first see the client with congestive heart failure in order to evaluate the client's respirations. This client is in the most immediate danger. Answer A is incorrect because the 1 year old with hand foot syndrome is experiencing swelling and pain in the joints related to sickle cell anemia. This client can be seen after the client in Answer B. Answers C and D are incorrect because the client with resolving pancreatitis and the client with Cushing's disease is more stable than the client with congestive heart failure.

3. Answer C is correct. The six-year-old with fixed, dilated pupils who is unresponsive is unlikely to survive. According to disaster triage protocol, priority is given to those clients who are expected to survive with fewer resource expenditures. Answers A, B, and D are incorrect for this reason.

4. Answer A is correct. The nurse with experience in surgery is most qualified to care for the client recently returned from having a coronary artery bypass graft. Answers B, C, and D are incorrect because these nurses are less experienced in the care of the surgical client.

5. Answer D is correct. The 70-year-old with diabetes and the 75-year-old with a fractured hip can be assigned to the semi-private room because neither one has an infection or is immune compromised. Answer A is incorrect because the client with pneumonia can infect the client with human immunovirus. Answer B is incorrect because the client with bronchitis poses a risk of infection to the client with leukemia. Answer C is incorrect because the client with gastroenteritis poses a risk of infection to the client with Cushing's disease due to immunosuppression.

6. Answer A is correct. The client with burns of burns chest and neck should be seen first because he is at risk for airway obstruction. Answers B, C, and D are incorrect because these clients do not take priority over the client with potential airway obstruction.

7. Answer C is correct. Discussing the problem with the employee will allow the employee to explain the lateness. This action should be taken first. Answer A is incorrect because documentation will be done after the meeting. Answer B is incorrect because the employee should be given the opportunity to explain the lateness. The employee should also be told what action will be taken if the problem is not corrected. Answer D is incorrect because the employee should be confronted privately.

8. Answer A is correct. The registered nurse should be assigned to hang total parenteral nutrition solution. Total parenteral nutrition, administered by central line, contains lipids and other nutrients needed by the client in negative nitrogen balance. Answer B is incorrect because the licensed practical nurse can insert an indwelling urinary catheter. Answer C is incorrect because the licensed practical nurse can administer a vaginal suppository. Answer D is incorrect because the licensed practical nurse can check the weights used with skeletal traction.

9. Answer B is correct. The licensed practical nurse is skilled in the insertion of naso-gastric feeding tubes. Answers A, C, and D are incorrect because these are tasks are best performed by the registered nurse. Some states allow the licensed practical nurse to obtain certification in intravenous administration; however, IV adminis-tration cannot be performed by licensed practical nurses in all states. Nurses should be familiar with the nurse practice act in the state in which they practice.

10. Answer D is correct. The best action is to call the nursing assistant aside and explore the reason for her harsh behavior toward the elderly client. The nurse's priority action should be to protect the client. Answer A is incorrect because this answer does not address the problem. Answer B is incorrect because this answer does not foster a resolution of the problem. Answer C is incorrect because this answer does not ensure that the nursing assistant will behave differently toward a younger client.

11. Answer A is correct. The client with leg pain might be experiencing a deep vein thrombus. Activities that can dislodge the clot can result in pulmonary embolus. The client should be returned to bed immediately and the finding should be reported to the physician. Answer B is incorrect because there is no contraindica-tion to using soap and water to bathe the client. If the client is in traction, it is often easier to change the bed from top to bottom; therefore, Answer C is incor-rect. Answer D is incorrect because disposable utensils are suitable for use when feeding the client.

12. Answer B is correct. Because the client has had no relief from pain, even with administration of pain medication, the nurse should fully assess the cause of the pain. Answer A is incorrect because an assessment should be done prior to changing the medication. Answer C is incorrect because administration of an analgesic has done little to relieve the client's pain during the night; therefore, it is unlikely that another dose will offer relief. Answer D is incorrect because there is no data to suggest that the client is addicted and implies an assumption on the part of the nurse.

13. Answer A is correct. The nurse should remove the contaminated dressing and clean the surface of the bed side table with a hypochlorite solution. A hypochlorite solution is one part bleach and ten parts water. Answer B is incorrect because there is no indication that the entire room needs cleaning. Answer C is incorrect because the dressing should be placed in a red bag before placing in the waste can. Answer D is incorrect because asking why is nontherapeutic. The nurse should discuss the proper disposal of contaminated articles with the co-worker.

14. Answer A is correct. Battery, an intentional tort, refers to physical contact in an offensive manner without the intent to do harm. Striking the client is a form of battery. Answer B is incorrect because assault, also an intentional tort, refers to threatening or attempting violence without physical contact. Answer C is incorrect because malpractice refers to unreasonable lack of skill in performing professional duties that results in injury or death of the client. Answer D is incorrect because negligence refers to acts of omission or commission that results in injury to the client or the client's property. Malpractice and negligence are examples of unintentional torts.

15. Answer A is correct. The client with emphysema with fever requires closer observation than the other four clients because of his chronic respiratory disease; therefore he should be placed nearest the nurse's station. Answer B is incorrect because the client with an appendectomy two days ago is more stable. Answer C is incorrect because there is no data to support a need for the client to be placed in the room near the nurse's station. Answer D is incorrect because the client with a thyroidectomy 24 hours earlier is more stable than the client with emphysema and fever.

16. Answer D is correct. Good hand-washing is the best way to prevent the spread of nosocomial infections as well as infections in the home. Answer A is incorrect because there is usually no need to wear a mask when emptying a urinary drainage system. Answer B is incorrect because there is no need to keep the doors closed to all client rooms. Answer C is incorrect because the focus is on preventing transmission of pathogens from the nurse to the client, not on preventing transmission of pathogens from the family to the client.

17. Answer C is correct. The nurse should include in the incident report the injury to the client and the action taken as a result of the incident. Answer A is incorrect because charting the cause of the incident is speculative on the part of the nurse and can imply liability. Answer B is incorrect because there is no need to chart the client's status on admission. Answer D is incorrect because there is no need to chart which family members were present at the time of the incident.

18. Answer D is correct. Complaints of headache and blurred vision by the client with SLE can indicate increasing hypertension, which accompanies renal failure, stroke, and myocardial infarction. Answers A, B, and C are incorrect because these clients have more stable conditions; therefore they can be visited later.

19. Answer B is correct. TPN is infused via central line; therefore, the client should be cared for by the RN. The RN should assess the client for complications associated with the use of TPN, which include injury during central line placement, sepsis, and metabolic disturbances. Answers A, C, and D are incorrect because the clients can be cared for by the LPN.

20. Answer A is correct. The certified nursing assistant is prepared to provide basic care, such as feeding or bathing, to clients with predictable conditions such as Alzheimer's dementia. Answer B is incorrect because the nursing assistant will not know what to do if problems are encountered with a central line. Answer C is incorrect because the nurse, not the nursing assistant, is best suited to assess the vital signs of a client with a respiratory infection. Answer D is incorrect because the client with preeclampsia will require hourly output measurements; therefore the output should be measured by the nurse.

21. Answer C is correct. Common causes of autonomic hyperreflexia in the client with a spinal cord injury are bladder distention and fecal impaction. After placing the client in high Fowler's position, the nurse should make sure that the urinary catheter is patent. Answer A is incorrect because an antihypertensive is not administered until other measures are taken. Answer B is incorrect because it is not necessary to notify the doctor immediately; autonomic hyperreflexia is a common occurrence in the client with a spinal cord injury. Answer D is incorrect because pain medication is not the treatment for autonomic hyperreflexia.

22. Answer A is correct. The client with an esophageal tamponade is hemorrhaging from esophageal varices; therefore, the client needs to be near the nurse's station for frequent assessment. Answers B, C, and D are incorrect because the clients have conditions which are more stable.

23. Answer C is correct. The nurse should give priority to ensuring the safety of the client who is in harm's way; therefore, the client should be moved to a safe location. Answers A and B are performed after the client is moved; therefore, they are incorrect. Answer D is incorrect because the unit should not be evacuated unless there is a danger to others.

24. Answer B is correct. The N95 mask should be worn when the nurse is in the room of a client with TB, not just when providing direct care. Answers A, C, and D are incorrect choices because they are a part of the care for the client with tuberculosis.

25. Answer C is correct. The LPN can monitor the vital signs of a client receiving a blood transfusion and assess the client for problems related to the transfusion. Answer A is incorrect because the RN, not the LPN, should provide final discharge teaching. The RN provides instruction to the client with a new diagnosis; therefore, Answer B is incorrect. Answer D is incorrect because flushing a central line is not within the scope of practice of the LPN.

26. Answer A is correct. Munchausen's syndrome (abuse by proxy) occurs when illness is caused by the caregiver. Removing the bottle and reporting the incident to the charge nurse can prevent further injury to the infant and provide a means of therapeutic intervention. Answer B is incorrect because of a lack of therapeutic communication between the nurse and mother. Answer C is incorrect because further harm might come to the infant. Answer D is incorrect because the problem is not with the infant's diet.

27. Answer B is correct. Removing sutures is within the scope of practice of the LPN. Answers A, C, and D are incorrect because they involve skills outside the scope of practice of the LPN.

28. Answer D is correct. The nurse should give priority to assessing and medicating the client who is one week post-myocardial infarction. Answers A, B, and C are incorrect because the clients' conditions are more stable; therefore, they can receive medication later.

29. Answer A is correct. The nurse should assess the post-gastrectomy client first because the report of 75 mL bright red bleeding in the past hour indicates excessive bleeding. Answers B, C, and D relate to clients with more stable conditions; therefore, they can be seen after the gastrectomy client.

30. Answer D is correct. Cleaning an ocular prosthesis can be performed by the certified nursing assistant. Performing sterile dressing changes, administering tube feedings, and applying medicated patches are not within the scope of practice of the certified nursing assistant; therefore answers A, B, and C are incorrect.

31. Answer A is correct. A child with burns should not be placed in the room with any child that poses a risk of infection. The children in Answers B, C, and D all pose a risk of infection; therefore, they are incorrect.

32. Answer D is correct. The most suitable roommate for the client with acute mania is the client with situational depression. Answer A is incorrect because the client with paranoid schizophrenia does not cope well with drastic changes in environment, such as those created by a client with mania. Answer B is incorrect because a client with antisocial personality disorder can manipulate the behavior of the client with mania to disrupt the unit. Answer C is incorrect because a client with anorexia nervosa usually has activity restrictions and the client with acute mania usually incites activity in others.

33. Answer A is correct. Morphine sulfate depresses the respiratory center; therefore, the nurse should check the client's respirations before administering the medication. Answer B is incorrect because temperature is not affected by the medication. Answers C and D can be lowered by the medication but are not as much concern as the rate of respiration; therefore, they are incorrect.

34. Answer B is correct. The new graduate who is orienting to an oncology unit is best assigned to the client receiving linear acceleration therapy (radiation therapy) for lung cancer. Answers A, C, and D require higher levels of knowledge and skill than those possessed by a new graduate in orientation; therefore, they are incorrect.

35. Answer C is correct. It is within the role of the nurse's assistant to weigh clients. Answers A, B, and D are beyond the scope of practice of a nurse's assistant, so they are incorrect.

36. Answer D is correct. A client in skeletal traction with a loose pin is in danger of losing the effect of the pull of the traction, which could produce severe damage, so this is the priority. Answers A and B are both expected in a client with a fracture in skeletal traction, so they are incorrect. In Answer C, the nurse might have to assist the student with positioning the client, but it is not the most important consideration, so it is incorrect.

37. Answer A is correct. Complaints of facial numbness in the post-thyroidectomy client suggest hypocalcemia, therefore the client needs further assessment and findings should be reported to the physician. Answers B and D indicate mild abnormalities in temperature and blood sugar, but are not a need for immediate concern, so they are incorrect. Answer C is incorrect because the client is well enough for discharge.

38. Answer A is correct. Clients with hyperthyroidism can have cardiac problems with associated rapid heart rate, increased systolic blood pressure, and increased body temperature. Answers B and C are not associated with hyperthyroidism, so they are incorrect. Answer D might be associated with hyperthyroidism but is not an immediate concern, so it is incorrect.

39. Answer C is correct. The client's O_2 saturation is below normal; therefore, evaluation of the client's arterial blood is important. Answer A is also important, but not as immediate. Answers B and D are both drugs that might be helpful, but they are not indicated at this time, so they are incorrect.

40. Answer B is correct. The client with pleuritic chest pain and a rash in these areas should be assessed first due to clinical manifestations of an embolus. The situation in Answer A could be done later by the nurse calling the family member back, so it is incorrect. The clients in Answers C and D could have their care delegated to others.

41. Answer C is correct. Clients receiving anticoagulants are at risk for bleeding and should be shaved with an electric razor to decrease this risk. Answers A, B, and D are not contraindicated or associated with the use of heparin and a stroke, so they are incorrect.

42. Answer A is correct. The most suitable roommates would be the two similar clients with palliative treatments. The clients in Answers B and C each involve a risk for infection due to their low WBC counts. Answer D also has some similarities in diagnoses, but do not fit as well as the clients in Answer A.

43. Answer D is correct. The priority is to remove the excess fluid. Answers A, B, and C are not a priority at this time, so they are incorrect.

44. Answer A is correct. The initial action by the nurse should be to correct the error, if possible. In this case, the action would be to hang the correct fluid. Answers B, C, and D are all correct interventions but are not the initial action, so they are incorrect.

45. Answer D is correct. The normal potassium is 3.5–5.0 mEq/L. Low potassium can be life-threatening and affect every body system, which makes this answer the priority. Answers A and B are near the normal levels, so they are incorrect. Answer C is expected in dehydration and can easily be corrected, so it is incorrect.

46. Answer B is correct. Assisting with postmortem care is within the role of a nurse's assistant. Answers A, C, and D are beyond the role of a nurse's assistant and are best performed by a licensed nurse, so these answers are incorrect.

47. Answer C is correct. The best client choice for a psychiatric nurse is the client that would benefit from therapeutic communication techniques. The clients in Answers A, B, and D require clinical, surgical or specific cancer skills, so they are incorrect.

48. Answer B is correct. The nurse should measure the girth to determine whether it has increased. The client might have an expanding or rupturing aneurysm. Answers A and D would need a physician's order, so they are incorrect. Answer C is not important initially, so it is incorrect.

49. Answer C is correct. The client has symptoms of a pneumothorax and the physician should be notified. Answer A is not appropriate at this time, so it is incorrect. Answer B is incorrect because lowering the head might increase the client's shortness of breath. Answer D is beyond the scope of the nurse, so it is incorrect.

50. Answer C is correct. The client is exhibiting symptoms of congestive heart failure and is the priority client in this group. The clients in Answers A and D require attention but have no immediate need, so they are incorrect. The client in Answer B exhibits an expected manifestation of rib fractures, so it is an incorrect answer.

51. Answer B is correct. The oxygen saturation is extremely low even for a client with emphysema. Answer A is incorrect because the client's symptom is mild abdominal pain, which is a vague complaint. Answer C is incorrect because the client with chronic glomerulonephritis with loss of AV fistula does not require immediate attention. Answer D is incorrect because a blood glucose level of 277 mg/dL in the client with diabetes is not life-threatening, although it does require intervention. This client should be seen next.

892
Answers to Practice Exam IV

52. Answer C is correct. The nurse with five years of experience working with clients with AIDS is most aware of the needs of the immune-suppressed client. The nurses with experience in the other units as noted in A, B, and D are not as well prepared to care for this client, so these answers are incorrect.

53. Answer A is correct. The client taking Thorazine will probably have blurring of vision, making reading difficult. Answers B, C, and D are appropriate actions by the nursing assistant and do not require further teaching, so they are incorrect.

54. Answer A is correct. The client with pheochromocytoma (a type of adrenal tumor) will have extremely high blood pressure readings that might result in cardiac and neurological symptoms. The clients in Answers B, C, and D are less acute and can be seen later, so those answers are wrong.

55. Answer B is correct. The nurse should first ask the nursing assistant about the incident. The client might have requested that the nursing assistant help her in finding an article. Answers A, C, and D are inappropriate actions at this time, so they are incorrect.

56. Answer A is correct. Because the nurse who is performing the procedure is not fully aware of the sterility of the tray, she should obtain a new, unopened tray. Answers B, C, and D are incorrect actions and are therefore incorrect.

57. Answer B is correct. According to the HIPPA law, it is a violation of client confidentiality to examine a chart of a client who is not in the nurse's immediate care. Answer A is incorrect because it is not unlawful to ask the son to sign the permit when the client is unable to sign for herself. Answers C and D are not a breech in confidentiality, so they are incorrect.

58. Answer C is correct. Doxazosin mesylate (Cardura) is an antihypertensive/cardiac medication and should be given first. The nurse should give glypizide second because it is an antidiabetic drug; therefore, answer B is wrong. Spironalactone should be given third because this is a diuretic, so answer D is incorrect. Ketoralac can be given last because it is an NSAID, so answer A is wrong.

59. Answer A is correct. A positron emission tomography uses glucose tagged contrast medium. For accuracy of the exam the blood glucose levels must be between 60 and 140 mg/dl. Answers B, C, and D are incorrect statements and are therefore incorrect.

60. Answer D is correct. The client with hypertension might be exhibiting stroke symptoms, making this the priority. Answer A is incorrect because a low Hgb level is expected with a client diagnosed with chronic renal failure. Clinical manifestations of pernicious anemia include paresthesia, so Answer B is wrong. Answer C includes a normal oxygen saturation, so this client is low priority, making it incorrect.

61. Answer A is correct. The client with terminal cancer, as well as the caregivers, could be benefited by a hospice home health referral, making this the best option. Answers C and D do not offer the correct assistance for this type of client, so they are wrong. Answer B would assist with only one aspect of service, so it is not the best option and is therefore incorrect.

62. Answer B is correct. The oxygen order takes priority in this situation. Answers A, C, and D would all be interventions that are appropriate but are not the priority intervention, so they are incorrect.

63. Answer B is correct. The closest adult relative can give consent if the patient is not able to do so. This client is under sedation and unable to give surgical consent; therefore, Answer A is wrong. Answer C is wrong because canceling the procedure is beyond the scope of practice of the registered nurse. There is no information in the stem that justifies an emergency, so Answer D is wrong.

64. Answer B is correct. Conscious sedation administration is beyond the scope of the LPN. The answers in A, C, and D are all within the scope of the LPN, so they are incorrect.

65. Answer A is correct. Status epilepticus is a life-threatening condition due to the continual seizures; therefore, stopping the seizure activity is the priority. Ativan is the drug of choice in this situation and is the priority drug to be given. Answers B, C, and D could all be administered after the Ativan, so they are incorrect.

66. Answer C is correct. Giving out information of this type violates HIPPA and is not allowed, so this is the best response for the nurse to make in this situation. Answer A is inappropriate because of HIPPA, so it is wrong. Answer B is non-therapeutic communication, so it is wrong. Answer D implies that the nurse is not giving the information only because she doesn't have it at this time, so it is wrong.

67. Answer B is correct. Complications of cirrhosis include portal hypertension. Increased pressure in portal circulation caused by activities such vomiting, coughing, and straining at stool can result in hemorrhage. Therefore, the client with cirrhosis should receive medication before the client with pain, indigestion, or diarrhea, making Answers A, C, and D incorrect.

68. Answer D is correct. Airborne precautions are used when caring for the child with varicella. Droplet precautions are used when caring for the child with rubella and the child with pertussis. Contact precautions are used when caring for the child with rotovirus. Therefore Answers A, B, and C are incorrect.

69. Answer C is correct. The client who is two days post stapedectomy can be discharged for follow-up at home. Answers A and B are incorrect because bleeding is a complication associated with both thyroidectomy and gastrectomy. Answer D is incorrect because clients with abdominal cholecystectomy have large abdominal incisions and placement of drains that require nursing assessment and interventions.

70. Answer A is correct. The novice RN is least appropriate to assign to the client with a newly created arteriovenous fistula who is undergoing dialysis because the client is less stable than the other clients. Answers B, C, and D are incorrect because the client with Crohn's disease, the client undergoing mechanical debridement for burns, and the client recovering from an abdominal cholecystectomy have more stable conditions and are more appropriate to assign to the novice RN.

71. Answer A is correct. Performing tracheostomy care and suctioning are within the scope of practice of the LPN. Answer B is incorrect because administering TPN is the duty of the RN. Answer C is incorrect because obtaining initial vital signs on the client receiving a blood transfusion is the duty of the RN. Answer D is incorrect because providing discharge teaching is the duty of the RN.

72. Answer A is correct. The skills of the psychiatric nurse are best used for the 25-year-old client with a traumatic amputation of the leg because the client can be expected to have altered body image and depression. Answers B, C, and D are incorrect because these clients are best assigned to the nurse with more extensive experience with medical-surgical nursing.

Alternative Item Answers

1. Answer A is correct. A positive Kernig sign is indicated by extreme stiffness in the hamstrings and inability to straighten the leg when the hip is flexed to 90 degrees. A positive Kernig sign is one of the symptoms of bacterial meningitis. Answer B is incorrect because it depicts a positive Babinski's reflex. Answer C is incorrect because it depicts a positive Brudzinski's reflex. Answer D is incorrect because it depicts a positive Trendelenburg reflex.

2. The client taking MAO inhibitors should avoid chocolate, yogurt, cheddar cheese, bananas, and avocados because they are sources of tyramine.

3. Hepatitis B, Hepatitis C, Hepatitis D, and Hepatitis G are parenteral forms of hepatitis. Hepatitis A and Hepatitis E are enteral forms of hepatitis.

4. The nurse should administer 6.5 mL each time.

5. Nursing care of the client with a T-tube includes documenting the amount, color, and consistency of drainage; preventing kinking or tangling of the tubing; observing for the return of brown-colored stools; and maintaining the drainage system below the level of the gallbladder. The T-tube should not be clamped or irrigated.

6. The IV infusion rate should be set at 31 drops per minute. (The actual rate is 31.25 drops per minute.)

7. Sequence for removing isolation garb:

    7 Remove eyewear or goggles

    2 Untie neck strings and back strings of gown

    1 Remove gloves

    5 Without touching outside surface, remove gown

    6 Fold gown inside out and discard

    8 Wash hands for 10 to 15 seconds

    4 Allow gown to fall from shoulders

    3 Pull mask away from face and discard

8. Figure D depicts a client with paraplegia. Answer A is incorrect because it depicts a situation that cannot exist. Answer B is incorrect because it depicts hemiplegia. Answer C is incorrect because it depicts quadriplegia.

9. Xylocaine and a 5 mL syringe, and sterile hemostats are not need for the removal of a closed chest drainage system. Petroleum gauze, silk or paper tape, a suture removal kit, and sterile 4×4 pads are needed; therefore, they are incorrect choices.

10. Figure D, vastus lateralis, is the correct location for administering intramuscular injections to infants and young children. The sites depicted in Figures A, B, and C are unsuitable for intramuscular injections in infants and young children because the muscles are not yet well developed.

11. The apex of the heart is at the base of the heart as illustrated here:

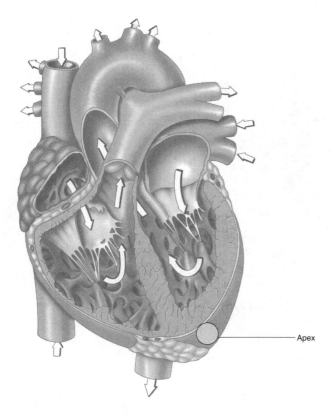

Apex

12. The correct sequence for changing a dressing is

    3 Wash hands

    4 Explain the procedure

    1 Assess the client's pain level

    2 Gather equipment

    8 Don sterile gloves

    6 Remove the old dressing

    7 Place a clean towel under the wound area

    5 Apply a pair of nonsterile gloves

13. The answers that should be checked are

   ____ Weights on floor

     X No knots in the cords

     X Sheets off the traction device

     X No frayed cords

     X Weights hanging freely

14. The greater trochanter of the femur is located at the top of the femur as illustrated here:

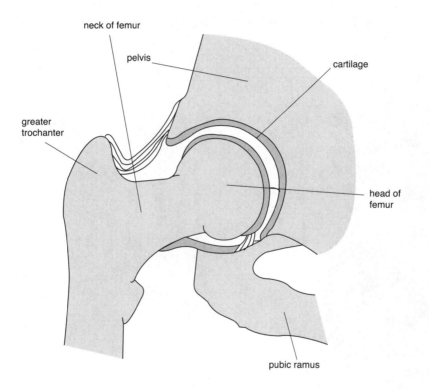

THE HIP JOINT

15. ? mL = 1 mL/100 mg ∞ 50 mg/1 = 0.5 mL ? mL = 25 mg = 1 mL

Total 0.5 mL + 1 mL = 1.5 mL

Answer: .5 mL of Demerol + 1 mL of Phenergan = 1.5 mL

16. 30 mL = 1 ounce

    1 cup = 8 fluid ounces

    Total: 1 cup = 240 mL

    3 ounces = 90 mL

    8 ounces = 240 mL

    IV fluid = 800 mL

    Total: 1370 mL

17. The P wave on an ECG strip is the sinus node firing.

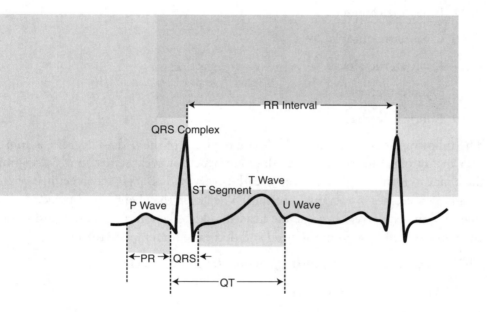

18. The correct sequence of treatment is C, B, A, and D (the five-year-old should be cared for last because he is emergent). In the case of mass casualty triage, clients who can be saved with limited use of resources are cared for first.

19. To calculate the expected date of delivery, the nurse should subtract three months from the first day of the last menstrual period and add seven days. The expected date of delivery is July 31 of the following year.

20. All members of the healthcare team can care for the client.

21. Cranial nerve II—optic. The picture depicts the use of a variation of the Snellen chart for visual acuity. This nerve can also be assessed by visual fields and ophthal-moscopic examination.

22. The following should have an X: presbyopia, presbycusis, arcus senilis. The other choices are abnormal conditions not associated with the aging process, so they are incorrect.

23. It is the decorticate position.

24. 12,500 U/250 * 16 mL/1 = 800 units/hr

25. The triceps reflex is being assessed.

26. The following lists the correct sequence for indwelling catheterization procedure:

    2 Gather equipment

    1 Check physician order

    4 Position the client

    3 Explain the procedure

    5 Ensure proper lighting

    8 Test the catheter balloon

  11 Insert the catheter

  10 Cleanse the meatus

    7 Apply sterile gloves

    6 Open catheter kit

    9 Lubricate catheter tip

27. The following should be checked: elevate the head of the bed 30 degrees; administer mannitol (Osmitrol) as ordered; monitor neurological status hourly. Assisting the client to turn, cough, and deep breathe every two hours is incorrect because coughing increases intracranial pressure. The "keep the client's head turned to the side" action is incorrect because the head should be kept in the neutral position to encourage blood flow from the head and decrease intracranial pressure.

28. The correct sequence for inserting a nasogastric tube is as follows:

    5 Assess the client's nostrils

    7 Insert the nasogastric tube

    1 Check the physician's order

    3 Measure the tube for length of insertion

    8 Check the nasogastric tube for proper placement

    4 Seat the client, place pillows behind the shoulders

    2 Inform the client about the procedure

    6 Lubricate the nasogastric tube

29. The name of the rhythm is ventricular fibrillation. There is no functional cardiac activity in ventricular fibrillation. Death will occur if not corrected. Treatment includes defibrillation followed by anti-arrhythmic drugs (refer to Chapter 3, "Care of the Client with Cardiovascular Disorders," for other interventions associated with heart disease).

30. The following foods should be checked: an orange, broiled chicken, yogurt, and broccoli. The other foods listed are high in sodium and should be avoided by the client on a low-sodium diet, so they are incorrect.

Things You Forgot

Throughout this book, we have tried to help you to simplify preparation for the NCLEX exam. This appendix includes information you have learned during nursing school but might have forgotten.

Therapeutic Drug Levels

Here are some of the therapeutic blood levels that are important for the nurse to be aware of when taking the NCLEX® exam:

▶ **Digoxin:** 0.5–2.0 ng/mL

▶ **Lithium:** 0.6–1.5 mEq/L

▶ **Dilantin:** 10–20 mcg/dL

▶ **Theophylline:** 10–20 mcg/dL

> **NOTE**
>
> Lab values vary by age, and some books might have different reference values.

Vital Signs

Here are some of the normal ranges for vital signs:

▶ **Heart rate:** 80–100 beats per minute

▶ **Newborn heart rate:** 100–180 beats per minute

▶ **Respiratory rate:** 12–20 respirations per minute

▶ **Blood pressure:** systolic = 110–120 mm Hg; diastolic = 60–90 mm Hg

▶ **Newborn blood pressure:** systolic = 65 mm Hg; diastolic = 41 mm Hg

▶ **Temperature:** 98.6 +/-

Anticoagulant Therapy

These are the tests to be done for the client taking anticoagulants and their control levels. Remember that the therapeutic range is 1.5–2 times the control:

▶ **Coumadin (sodium warfarin) PT/Protime:** 12–20 seconds

▶ **International normalizing ratio (INR):** 2–3

▶ **Antidote for sodium warfarin:** Vitamin K

> **NOTE**
>
> Lab values vary by age, and some books might have different reference values.

▶ **Heparin and heparin derivatives partial thromboplastin time (PTT):** 30–60 seconds. If the client is taking Lovenox (enoxaparin), the nurse should check her platelet count because Lovenox can cause thrombocytopenia. Note some texts record PTT values as low as 24-35 seconds.

▶ **Antidote for heparin:** Protamine sulfate.

Intrapartal Normal Values

Here are some of the normal ranges to remember when caring for the client during the intrapartal period:

▶ **Fetal heart rate:** 120–160 beats per minute

▶ **Variability:** 6–10 beats per minute

▶ **Contractions:**

    ▶ **Frequency of contractions:** Every 2–5 minutes

    ▶ **Duration of contractions:** Less than 90 seconds

    ▶ **Intensity of contractions:** Less than 100 mmHg

▶ **Amniotic fluid amount:** 500–1200 ml

Standard Precautions

Standard precautions are a set of guidelines for the nurse to take when caring for the client. These precautions protect the nurse from transmitting the disease to another client or to himself:

▶ Gloves should be worn when there is a chance of contact with blood and body fluids, when handling other potentially infected material, and when performing vascular access procedures.

▶ Gloves should be changed after each client contact and between contact procedures with the same client.

▶ Masks and protective eyewear should be worn when there is a likelihood of splashes or when body fluids might become airborne.

▶ Gloves and aprons should be worn during procedures in which there is the likelihood of splashes of blood or body fluids.

▶ Handwashing should be done immediately after contact with body fluids or other potentially infected material and as soon as gloves are removed.

▶ Needles and sharps should be disposed of in sharps containers. No recapping, bending, or breaking of needles should occur.

▶ Mouth-to-mouth resuscitation should be performed using a mouthpiece or other ventilation device.

CAUTION

Body fluids likely to transmit blood-borne disease include blood, semen, vaginal/cervical secretions, tissues, cerebral spinal fluid, amniotic fluid, synovial fluid, pleural fluid, peritoneal fluid, and breast milk. Body fluids not likely to transmit blood-borne disease unless blood is visible include feces, nasal secretions, sputum, vomitus, sweat, tears, urine, and saliva (the exception is during oral surgery or dentistry).

Airborne Precautions

Examples of infections caused by organisms suspended in the air for prolonged periods of time are tuberculosis, measles (rubella), and chickenpox. Place these clients in a private room. Healthcare workers should wear a HEPA mask or N-95 mask when dealing with such clients. These mask contain fine fibers and filter out particles, preventing them from passing through to the healthcare worker.

Droplet Precautions

Infections caused by organisms suspended in droplets that can travel 3 feet, but are not suspended in the air for long periods of time are influenza, mumps, pertussis, rubella (German measles), diphtheria, pneumonia, scarlet fever, streptococcal pharyngitis, and meningitis. Place the client in a private room or in a room with a client who has the same illness. The clients should be no closer than 3 feet away from one another. Caregivers should wear a mask, and the door can remain open.

Contact Precautions

Infections caused by organisms spread by direct contact include RSV, scabies, colonization with MRSA, and VRE. Place the client in a private room or with a client with the same condition. Caregivers should wear gloves when entering the room and wear gowns to prevent contact with the client. Hands should be washed with an antimicrobial soap before leaving the client's room. Equipment used by the client should remain in the room and should be disinfected before being used by anyone else. The client should be transported only for essential procedures; during transport, precautions should be taken to prevent disease transmission.

Revised Life Support Guidelines (American Heart Association)

Frequently the American Heart Association releases guidelines for the care of the client experiencing dysrrhythmias. Refer to http://www.aafp.org/afp/2006050/practice.html for these guidelines.

Defense Mechanisms

Here is a quick reference to some of the defense mechanisms used by the client to help him cope with stressors:

- **Compensation:** The development of attributes that take the place of more desirable ones
- **Conversion reaction:** The development of physical symptoms in response to emotional distress
- **Denial:** The failure to regard an event or a feeling
- **Displacement:** The transference of emotions to another other than the intended
- **Projection:** The transferring of unacceptable feelings to another person
- **Rationalization:** The dismissal of one's responsibility by placing fault on another
- **Reaction formation:** The expression of feelings opposite to one's true feelings
- **Regression:** The returning to a previous state of development in which one felt secure
- **Repression:** The unconscious forgetting of unpleasant memories
- **Sublimation:** The channeling of unacceptable behaviors into behaviors that are socially acceptable
- **Suppression:** The conscious forgetting of an undesirable memory

Nutrition Notes

It is important for the nurse to be aware of different diets used in the disease processes we have discussed. Table A.1 provides a quick reference to help you remember the diets.

TABLE A.1   Dietary and Nutrition Notes to Remember

Diseases Being Treated	Foods to Include	Foods to Avoid
Bone marrow transplant clients	Cook or peel and wash all foods.	Avoid foods from salad bars, foods grown on or in the ground, and foods that are cultured.
Celiac/gluten-induced diarrhea	Milk, buttermilk, lean meats, eggs, cheese, fish, creamy peanut butter, cooked or canned juice, corn, bread stuffing from corn, cornstarch, rice, soybeans, potatoes, bouillon, and broth.	Malted milk, fat meats, luncheon meats, wheat, salmon, prunes, plums, rye, oats, barley, and soups thickened with gluten containing grains.
Congestive heart failure, hypertension	Meats low in cholesterol and fats, breads, starches, fruits, sweets, vegetables, dairy products.	Foods high in salts, canned products, frozen meats, cheeses, eggs, organ meats, fried foods, and alcohol.
Crohn's/ulcerative colitis	Meats, breads, and starches, fruits, vegetables, dairy products.	Whole grains, legumes, nuts, vegetables with skins, prune juice, and gristly meats.
Full liquid diets for clients who require a decrease in gastric motility	Milk, ice cream, soups, puddings, custards, plain yogurt, strained meats, strained fruits and vegetables, fruit and vegetable juices, cereal gruel, butter, margarine, and any component or combination of clear liquids.	All solid foods.
Lacto-vegetarian	Primary sources of protein, dairy products, peanut butter, legumes, soy analogs.	All meat products.
Peptic ulcer/hiatal hernia	Meats, breads, starches, fruits, vegetables, and dairy products.	Alcohol, coffee, chocolate, black or red pepper, chili powder, carminatives such as oil of peppermint and spearmint, garlic, onions, and cinnamon.
Radium implant clients	Same as for Crohn's and ulcerative colitis.	Same as for Crohn's and ulcerative colitis.
Renal transplant clients	Meats, dairy products, breads and starches, vegetables, and sweets.	Eggs, organ meats, fried or fatty food, foods containing salt, dried foods, salt substitutes, and fruits.

Immunization Schedule

It is important for the nurse to be aware of the recommended immunization schedule for various age groups. Figure A.1 provides a recommended schedule for infants and children through 6 years. Figure A.2 provides a recommended schedule for adolescent immunizations, and Figure A.3 is a recommended schedule for adult immunizations.

Recommended Immunization Schedule for Persons Aged 0 Through 6 Years—United States · 2010
For those who fall behind or start late, see the catch-up schedule

Vaccine ▼ Age ▶	Birth	1 month	2 months	4 months	6 months	12 months	15 months	18 months	19-23 months	2-3 years	4-6 years
Hepatitis B[1]	HepB	HepB				HepB					
Rotavirus[2]			RV	RV	RV[2]						
Diptheria, Tetanus, Pertussis[3]			DTaP	DTaP	DTaP		DTaP				DTaP
Haemophilus influenzae type b[4]			Hib	Hib	Hib[4]	Hib					
Pneumococcal[5]			PCV	PCV	PCV	PCV				PPSV	
Inactivated Poliovirus[6]			IPV	IPV		IPV					IPV
Influenza[7]						Influenza (Yearly)					
Measles, Mumps, Rubella[8]						MMR					MMR
Varicella[9]						Varicella					Varicella
Hepatitis A[10]						HepA (2 doses)				HepA Series	
Meningococcal[11]										MCV	

Range of recommended ages for all children except certain high-risk groups

Range of recommended ages for certain high-risk groups

FIGURE A.1
Recommended immunization schedule for persons aged 0–6 years.

Recommended Immunization Schedule for Persons Aged 7 Through 18 Years—United States · 2010
For those who fall behind or start late, see the catch-up schedule

Vaccine ▼ Age ▶	7-10 years	11-12 years	13-18 years
Tetanus, Diptheria, Pertussis[1]		Tdap	Tdap
Human Papillomavirus[2]		HPV (3 doses)	HPV series
Meningococcal[3]	MCV	MCV	MCV
Influenza[4]		Influenza (Yearly)	
Pneumococcal[5]		PPSV	
Hepatitis A[6]		HepA Series	
Hepatitis B[7]		HepB Series	
Inactivated Poliovirus[8]		IPV Series	
Measles, Mumps, Rubella[9]		MMR Series	
Varicella[10]		Varicella Series	

Range of recommended ages for all children except certain high-risk groups

Range of recommended ages for catch-up Immunization

Range of recommended ages for certain high-risk groups

FIGURE A.2
Recommended immunization schedule for persons aged 7–18 years.

Vaccine ▼ Age Group ▶	19-26 years	27-49 years	50-59 years	60-64 years	65 years
Tetanus, Diptheria, Pertussis (Td/Tdap)[1,*]	Substitute one-time dose for Td booster; then boost with Td every 10 years				Td booster every 10 years
Human Papillomavirus[2,*]	3 doses (females)				
Varicella[3,*]	2 doses				
Zoster[4]				1 dose	
Measles, Mumps, Rubella[5,*]	1 or 2 doses		1 dose		
Influenza[6,*]			1 dose annually		
Pneumococcal (polysaccharide)[7,8]	1 or 2 doses				1 dose
Hepatitis A[9,*]	2 doses				
Hepatitis B[10,*]	3 doses				
Meningococcal[11,*]	1 or more doses				

*Covered by the Vaccine Injury Compensation Program.

For all persons in the category who meet the age requirements and who lack evidence of immunity (e.g., lack documentation of vaccination or have no evidence of prior infection)

Recommended if some other risk factor is present (e.g., based on Medical, occupational, lifestyle, or other indications)

No recommendation

FIGURE A.3
Recommended immunization schedule for adults.

For more detailed information, consult the CDC website at http://www.cdc.gov/vaccines/recs/schedules/default.htm.

Need to Know More?

Pharmacology

http://www.druginfonet.com

http://www.fda.gov/search/databases.html

http://www.globalrph.com

http://www.mosbysdrugconsult.com

http://www.needymeds.com

http://www.nlm.nih.gov/medlineplus

http://www.nursespdr.com

Deglin, Judith H., and April H. Vallerand. *Davis Drug Guide for Nurses.* Philadelphia: F. A. Davis, 2009.

Care of the Client with Respiratory Disorders

http://www.aaaai.org—The website for the American Academy of Allergy, Asthma, and Immunology

http://www.cdc.gov—The website for the Centers for Disease Control and Prevention

http://www.lungusa.org—The website for the American Lung Association

Brunner, L., and D. Suddarth. *Textbook of Medical Surgical Nursing.* 12th ed. Philadelphia: Lippincott, Williams & Wilkins, 2009.

Ignatavicius, D., and S. Workman. *Medical Surgical Nursing: Critical Thinking for Collaborative Care.* 5th ed. Philadelphia: Elsevier, 2007.

Lehne, R. *Pharmacology for Nursing Care.* 7th ed. Philadelphia: Elsevier, 2009.

LeMone, P,. and K. Burke. *Medical Surgical Nursing: Critical Thinking in Client Care.* 4th ed. Upper Saddle River, NJ: Pearson Prentice Hall, 2008.

Lewis, S., M. Heitkemper, S. Dirksen, P. Obrien, and L. Bucher. *Medical Surgical Nursing: Assessment and Management of Clinical Problems.* 7th ed. Philadelphia: Elsevier, 2007.

Care of the Client with Genitourinary Disorders

http://www.kidney.org—The website for the National Kidney Foundation

http://www.pkd.cure.org—The website for the Polycystic Kidney Disease Foundation

Brunner, L., and D. Suddarth. *Textbook of Medical Surgical Nursing.* 12th ed. Philadelphia: Lippincott, Williams & Wilkins, 2009.

Ignatavicius, D., and S. Workman. *Medical Surgical Nursing: Critical Thinking for Collaborative Care.* 5th ed. Philadelphia: Elsevier, 2007.

Lehne, R. *Pharmacology for Nursing Care.* 7th ed. Philadelphia: Elsevier, 2009.

LeMone, P., and K. Burke. *Medical Surgical Nursing: Critical Thinking in Client Care.* 4th ed. Upper Saddle River, NJ: Pearson Prentice Hall, 2008.

Lewis, S., M. Heitkemper, S. Dirksen, P. Obrien, and L. Bucher. *Medical Surgical Nursing: Assessment and Management of Clinical Problems.* 7th ed. Philadelphia: Elsevier, 2007.

Care of the Client with Hematological Disorders

http://www.americanhs.org—The website for the American Hemochromatosis Society

http://www.aplastic.org—The website for the Aplastic Anemia and MDS International Foundation

http://www.emedicine.com/med/topic3387.htm

http://www.hemophilia.org—The website for the National Hemophilia Foundation

http://www.marrow.org

http://www.nci.nih.gov—The website for the National Cancer Institute Information Center

http://www.ons.org—The website for the Oncology Nursing Society

http://www.sicklecelldisease.org—The website for the Sickle Cell Disease Association of America, Inc.

Brunner, L., and D. Suddarth. *Textbook of Medical Surgical Nursing.* 12th ed. Philadelphia: Lippincott, Williams & Wilkins, 2009.

Lewis, S., M. Heitkemper, S. Dirksen, P. Obrien, and L. Bucher. *Medical Surgical Nursing: Assessment and Management of Clinical Problems.* 7th ed. Philadelphia: Elsevier, 2007.

Fluid and Electrolytes and Acid/Base Balance

http://www.enursescribe.com.

http://www.umed.utah.edu/ms2/renal.

Brunner, L., and D. Suddarth. *Textbook of Medical Surgical Nursing.* 12th ed. Philadelphia: Lippincott, Williams & Wilkins, 2009.

Ignatavicius, D., and S. Workman. *Medical Surgical Nursing: Critical Thinking for Collaborative Care*. 5th ed. Philadelphia: Elsevier, 2007.

Care of the Client with Burns

Brunner, L., and D. Suddarth. *Textbook of Medical Surgical Nursing*. 12th ed. Philadelphia: Lippincott, Williams & Wilkins, 2009.

Ignatavicius, D., and S. Workman. *Medical Surgical Nursing: Critical Thinking for Collaborative Care*. 5th ed. Philadelphia: Elsevier, 2007.

Lehne, R. *Pharmacology for Nursing Care*. 7th ed. Philadelphia: Elsevier, 2009.

LeMone, P., and K. Burke. *Medical Surgical Nursing: Critical Thinking in Client Care*. 4th ed. Upper Saddle River, NJ: Pearson Prentice Hall, 2008.

Lewis, S., M. Heitkemper, S. Dirksen, P. Obrien, and L. Bucher. *Medical Surgical Nursing: Assessment and Management of Clinical Problems*. 7th ed. Philadelphia: Elsevier, 2007.

Care of the Client with Sensory Disorders

http://www.afb.org—The website for the American Foundation for the Blind

http://www.loc.gov.nis—The website for the National Library Services for the Blind and Physically Handicapped

Brunner, L., and D. Suddarth. *Textbook of Medical Surgical Nursing*. 12th ed. Philadelphia: Lippincott, Williams & Wilkins, 2009.

Ignatavicius, D., and S. Workman. *Medical Surgical Nursing: Critical Thinking for Collaborative Care*. 5th ed. Philadelphia: Elsevier, 2007.

Lehne, R. *Pharmacology for Nursing Care*. 7th ed. Philadelphia: Elsevier, 2009.

LeMone, P., and K. Burke. in *Medical Surgical Nursing: Critical Thinking in Client Care*. 4th ed. Upper Saddle River, NJ: Pearson Prentice Hall, 2008.

Lewis, S., M. Heitkemper, S. Dirksen, P. Obrien, and L. Bucher. *Medical Surgical Nursing: Assessment and Management of Clinical Problems*. 7th ed. Philadelphia: Elsevier, 2007.

Care of the Client with Neoplastic Disorders

http://www.abta.org—The website for the American Brain Tumor Association

http://www.cancer.gov—The website for the National Cancer Institute

http://www.komen.org—The website for the Susan G. Komen Breast Cancer Foundation

http://www.leukemia.org

http://www.leukemia-research.org

http://www.ons.org—The website for the Oncology Nursing Society

http://www.skincancer.org—The website for the Skin Cancer Foundation

Brunner, L., and D. Suddarth. *Textbook of Medical Surgical Nursing*. 12th ed. Philadelphia: Lippincott, Williams & Wilkins, 2009.

Ignatavicius, D., and S. Workman. *Medical Surgical Nursing: Critical Thinking for Collaborative Care*. 5th ed. Philadelphia: Elsevier, 2007.

Care of the Client with Gastrointestinal Disorders

http://www.asge.org—The website for the American Society for Gastrointestinal Endoscopy

http://www.ccfa.org—The website for the Crohn's and Colitis Foundation

http://www.cdc.gov—The website for the Centers for Disease Control and Prevention

http://www.uoaa.org—The website for the United Ostomy Association

Brunner, L., and D. Suddarth. *Textbook of Medical Surgical Nursing*. 12th ed. Philadelphia: Lippincott, Williams & Wilkins, 2009.

Ignatavicius, D., and S. Workman. *Medical Surgical Nursing: Critical Thinking for Collaborative Care*. 5th ed. Philadelphia: Elsevier, 2007.

LeMone, P., and K. Burke. *Medical Surgical Nursing: Critical Thinking in Client Care*. 4th ed. Upper Saddle River, NJ: Pearson Prentice Hall, 2008.

Lewis, S., M. Heitkemper, S. Dirksen, P. Obrien, and L. Bucher. *Medical Surgical Nursing: Assessment and Management of Clinical Problems*. 7th ed. Philadelphia: Elsevier, 2007.

Care of the Client with Musculoskeletal and Connective Tissue Disorder

http://www.amputee-coalition.org—The website for the Amputee Coalition of America

http://www.niams.nih.gov—The website for the National Institute of Arthritis and Musculoskeletal and Skin Diseases

http://www.nof.org—The website for the National Osteoporosis Foundation

http://www.orthonurse.org—The website for the National Association of Orthopaedic Nurses

Ignatavicius, D., and S. Workman. *Medical Surgical Nursing: Critical Thinking for Collaborative Care*. 5th ed. Philadelphia: Elsevier, 2007.

LeMone, P., and K. Burke. in *Medical Surgical Nursing: Critical Thinking in Client Care*. 4th ed. Upper Saddle River, NJ: Pearson Prentice Hall, 2008.

Lewis, S., M. Heitkemper, S. Dirksen, P. Obrien, and L. Bucher. *Medical Surgical Nursing: Assessment and Management of Clinical Problems*. 7th ed. Philadelphia: Elsevier, 2007.

Care of the Client with Endocrine Disorders

http://www.cdc.gov/diabetes—The website for the Centers for Disease Control and Prevention

http://www.diabetes.org—The website for the American Diabetes Association

http://www.diabetesnet.com—The website for the American Association of Diabetes Educators

http://www.eatright.org—The website for the American Dietetic Association

http://www.endo-society.org—The website for the National Endocrine Society

http://www.medhelp.org/nadf—The website for the National Adrenal Disease Foundation

http://www.niddk.nih.gov—The website for the National Diabetes Clearing House

http://www.pancreasfoundation.org—The website for the National Pancreas Foundation

http://www.thyroid.org—The website for the American Thyroid Association

Brunner, L., and D. Suddarth. *Textbook of Medical Surgical Nursing*. 12th ed. Philadelphia: Lippincott, Williams & Wilkins, 2009.

Ignatavicius, D., and S. Workman. *Medical Surgical Nursing: Critical Thinking for Collaborative Care*. 5th ed. Philadelphia: Elsevier, 2007.

Care of the Client with Cardiac Disorders

http://www.americanheart.org—The website for the American Heart Association

http://www.nursebeat.com—The website for the *Nurse Beat: Cardiac Nursing Electronic Journal*

Brunner, L., and D. Suddarth. *Textbook of Medical Surgical Nursing*. 12th ed. Philadelphia: Lippincott, Williams & Wilkins, 2009.

Ignatavicius, D., and S. Workman. *Medical Surgical Nursing: Critical Thinking for Collaborative Care*. 5th ed. Philadelphia: Elsevier, 2007.

Woods, A. "An ACE Up Your Sleeve and an ARB in Your Back Pocket." *Nursing Made Incredibly Easy*, Sept.–Oct. 2003: 36–42.

Care of the Client with Neurological Disorders

http://www.apdaparkinson.com—The website for the American Parkinson's Disease Association

http://www.biausa.org—The website for the Brain Injury Association

http://www.epilepsyfoundation.org—The website for the Epilepsy Foundation http://www.gbs-cidp.org—The website for the Guillain-Barré Syndrome Foundation

http://www.nmss.org—The website for the National Multiple Sclerosis Society

http://www.apdaparkinson.org—The website for the National Parkinson's Foundation

http://www.stroke.org—The website for the American Stroke Association

Brunner, L., and D. Suddarth. *Textbook of Medical Surgical Nursing*. 12th ed. Philadelphia: Lippincott, Williams & Wilkins, 2009.

Ignatavicius, D., and S. Workman. *Medical Surgical Nursing: Critical Thinking for Collaborative Care*. 5th ed. Philadelphia: Elsevier, 2007.

LeMone, P., and K. Burke. *Medical Surgical Nursing: Critical Thinking in Client Care*. 4th ed. Upper Saddle River, NJ: Pearson Prentice Hall, 2008.

Lewis, S., M. Heitkemper, S. Dirksen, P. Obrien, and L. Bucher. *Medical Surgical Nursing: Assessment and Management of Clinical Problems*. 7th ed. Philadelphia: Elsevier, 2007.

Care of the Client with Psychiatric Disorders

http://www.nami.org—The website for the National Alliance on Mental Illness

Ball, J., and R. Bindler. *Pediatric Nursing: Caring for Children*. 4th ed. Upper Saddle River, NJ: Pearson Prentice Hall, 2008.

Kneisl, C., and E. Trigoboff. *Contemporary Psychiatric Mental Health Nursing*. 2nd ed. Upper Saddle River, NJ: Pearson Prentice Hall, 2009.

Lehne, R. *Pharmacology for Nursing Care*. 7th ed. Philadelphia: Elsevier, 2009.

Townsend, Mary C. *Essentials of Psychiatric Mental Health Nursing*. 4th ed. Philadelphia: F. A. Davis, 2008.

Maternal-Newborn Care

Lowdermilk, Deitra Leonard, et al., eds. *Maternity and Women's Health Care*. 8th ed. St. Louis: C. V. Mosby, 2000.

McKinney, Emily Slone, et al., eds. *Maternal-Child Nursing*. 2nd ed. St. Louis: W. B. Saunders, 2005.

Wong, Donna L., et al., eds. *Maternal-Child Nursing Care*. 3rd ed. St. Louis: C. V. Mosby, 2002.

Care of the Pediatric Client

www.aaai.org—American Academy of Allergy, Asthma, and Immunology

www.aafp.org—The American Academy of Family Practice

www.candlelighters.org—Candlelighters Childhood Cancer Foundation www.cdc.gov—Centers for Disease Control

www.cff.org—Cystic Fibrosis Foundation

www.lungusa.org—The American Lung Association

www.pathguy.com—Dr. Ed Friedlander, pathologist

Ball, J., and R. Bindler. *Pediatric Nursing: Caring for Children*. 4th ed. Upper Saddle River, NJ: Pearson Prentice Hall, 2008.

Hockenberry, M., and D. Wilson. *Wong's Essentials of Pediatric Nursing*. 8th ed. St. Louis: Elsevier, 2009.

Cultural Practices Influencing Nursing Care

Brunner, L., and D. Suddarth. *Textbook of Medical Surgical Nursing*. 12th ed. Philadelphia: Lippincott, Williams & Wilkins, 2009.

Ignatavicius, D., and S. Workman. *Medical Surgical Nursing: Critical Thinking for Collaborative Care*. 5th ed. Philadelphia: Elsevier, 2007.

Potter, Patricia A., and Anne Griffin Perry. *Fundamentals of Nursing*. 6th ed. St. Louis: C. V. Mosby, 2005.

Legal Issues in Nursing Practice

Tappen, Ruth M. *Nursing Leadership and Management: Concepts and Practice*. 5th ed. Philadelphia: F. A. Davis, 2004.

Calculations

Math calculation is an integral part of safe nursing care. This section is a review of the conversion tables and sample problems.

The Apothecary System of Measurement

Equivalents/Conversion Factors

- 1 minim = 1 drop
- 1 fluid dram = 60 minims
- 1 fluid ounce = 8 fluid drams
- 1 dram = 60 grains
- 30 ml = 2 tbs (tablespoons)
- 15 ml = 1 tbs
- 5 ml = 1 tsp (teaspoon)

The Household System of Measurement

Equivalents/Conversion Factors

- 1 teaspoon = 60 drops
- 2 tablespoon = 1 ounce
- 1 cup = 8 ounces
- 2 cups = 1 pint
- 2 pint = 1 quart
- 4 quarts = 1 gallon
- 1 pound = 16 ounces
- 1 teaspoon = 15–16 minims = 1 mL (milliliter)
- 2.2 pounds = 1 kilogram = 1000 gm (gram)

Metric Measurements

Equivalents/Conversion Factors

- ▶ 1 gr (grain) = 60–65 mg (milligram)

- ▶ 1 mg = 1000 mcg (microgram)

- ▶ 1 gm = 1000 mg = 15 gr

- ▶ 1 kg = 2.2 lbs

Test Your Math Skills

1. The doctor has ordered a nitroglycerin infusion to infuse at 15 mcg/minute. Available is 50 mg of nitroglycerin in 250 mL. A microdrop set is utilized to administer this medication. How many mL per hour will you infuse? (In a microdrop set, the number of gtts per minute equals mL per hour.)

2. The doctor has ordered one unit of blood (500 mL) to be given over four hours. After verifying the order, calculate the rate in gtts/minute. (A 20 drop per mL blood set is available.)

3. The doctor has ordered 15 mg of meperidine (Demerol) for pain. Available is Demerol 25 mg per mL. How many mL will you administer?

4. The doctor has ordered 250 mg of methyldopa (Aldomet) for control of the client's primary hypertension. The pharmacy sent the medication labeled 1 tablet contains 125 mg. How many tablets will you administer?

5. The doctor has ordered 35 mg of meperidine (Demerol) IM stat for pain. Available is 1 mL containing 50 mg. How many ml will you administer?

6. The doctor has ordered doxycycline (Vibramycin) 100 mg orally every 12 hours. The pharmacy sent the medication labeled 50 mg/5 mL. How many mL will you administer?

7. The doctor has ordered digoxin (Lanoxin) 0.25 mg orally qd (every day). The tablets are labeled 0.50 mg per tablet. How many tablets will you give?

8. The doctor has ordered a medication labeled gr 1/300 for atrial fibrillation. The cart contains a unidose container labeled 0.1 mg per tablet. How many tablets will you administer?

9. The doctor has ordered acetaminophen (Tylenol) gr 10 orally every four hours for headache. Available is 325 mg in one tablet. How many tablets will you administer?

10. The doctor has ordered glycopyrrolate (Robinul) 0.2 mg intramuscular. Available is 0.6 mg in 1 mL. How many mL will you administer?

11. The doctor has ordered phenytoin (Dilantin) 5 mg/kg of body weight to be given to the client with seizure disorder. Available is Dilantin 50 mg in 1 mL. How many mL will you administer to the client who weighs 110 pounds?

12. The doctor has ordered heparin 7500 units subcutaneously. Available is heparin 5000 units per mL. How many mL will you administer?

Answers

1. $$\frac{? \text{ ml}}{1 \text{ hour}} = \frac{250 \text{ ml}}{50 \text{ mg}} \times \frac{1 \text{ mg}}{1000 \text{ mcg}} \times \frac{15 \text{ mcg}}{1 \text{ minute}} \times \frac{60 \text{ minutes}}{1 \text{ hour}} = 4.5 \text{ or } 5 \text{ ml/hr}$$

   (Note: In a microdrip set, $\frac{\text{ml}}{\text{hour}}$ is equal to gtts per minute.)

2. $$\frac{? \text{ gtt}}{1 \text{ minute}} = \frac{20 \text{ gtt}}{1 \text{ ml}} \times \frac{500 \text{ ml}}{4 \text{ hours}} \times \frac{1 \text{ hour}}{60 \text{ minutes}} = \frac{1000}{24} = 41.66 \text{ or } \frac{42 \text{ gtt}}{1 \text{ minute}}$$

3. $$? \text{ ml} = \frac{1 \text{ ml}}{25 \text{ mg}} \times \frac{15 \text{ mg}}{1} = \frac{15}{25} = .6 \text{ ml}$$

4. $$? \text{ tablet} = \frac{1 \text{ tablet}}{125 \text{ mg}} \times \frac{250 \text{ mg}}{1} = 250 \text{mg} = 2 \text{ tablets}$$

5. $$? \text{ ml} = \frac{1 \text{ ml}}{50 \text{ mg}} \times \frac{35 \text{ mg}}{1} = \frac{35}{50} = .7 \text{ ml}$$

6. $$? \text{ ml} = \frac{5 \text{ ml}}{50 \text{ mg}} \times \frac{100 \text{ mg}}{1} = \frac{500}{50} = 10 \text{ ml}$$

7. $$? \text{ tablet} = \frac{1 \text{ tablet}}{0.50 \text{ mg}} \times \frac{0.25 \text{ mg}}{1} = \frac{0.25}{0.50} = .5 \text{ tablet}$$

8. $$? \text{ tablets} = \frac{1/300 \text{ gr}}{1} \times \frac{1 \text{ tablet}}{0.1 \text{ mg}} = \frac{60 \text{ mg}}{1 \text{ gr}} = \frac{60/300}{1} = 2 \text{ tablets}$$

9. $$? \text{ tablets} = \frac{1 \text{ tablet}}{325 \text{ mg}} \times \frac{60 \text{ mg}}{1 \text{ gr}} = \frac{10 \text{ gr}}{1} = \frac{650}{325} = 2 \text{ tablets}$$

10. $$? \text{ ml} = \frac{1 \text{ ml}}{0.6 \text{ mg}} \times \frac{0.2 \text{ mg}}{1} = \frac{0.2}{0.6} = .3 \text{ ml}$$

11. $$? \text{ ml} = \frac{1 \text{ ml}}{50 \text{ mg}} \times \frac{5 \text{ mg}}{1 \text{ kg}} \times \frac{1 \text{ kg}}{2.2 \text{ lb}} \times \frac{110 \text{ lb}}{1} = \frac{550}{110} = 5 \text{ ml}$$

12. $$? \text{ ml} = \frac{1 \text{ ml}}{5000 \text{ units}} \times \frac{7500 \text{ units}}{1} = \frac{7500}{5000} = \frac{75}{50} = 1.5 \text{ ml}$$

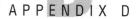

Most-Prescribed Medications in the United States

The NCLEX exam includes pharmacology as a subcategory under the area of physiological integrity. Because nurses are responsible for administering medications, it is extremely important for the nurse to be aware of those drugs that are frequently prescribed. Table D.1 provides a listing of the most prescribed medications in the United States, including the generic and trade names of the medication, as well as primary uses and major concerns associated with the medication. Using this list will help you to prepare for these questions.

Information in this table was adapted from information found at the following sites/sources:

- ▶ http/apps.humana/marketing/documents.asp
- ▶ http://google.com
- ▶ *Davis's Drug Guide for Nurses*

TABLE D.1   Most-Prescribed Medications in the United States

Generic Name	Trade Name	Uses	Major Concerns
Acetaminophen	Tylenol	Analgesic	Watch for liver and kidney problems.
Albuterol	Proventil	Bronchodilator	This drug can cause tachycardia. The doctor needs to check blood levels for toxicity to this drug.
Alendronate	Fosamax	Osteoporosis	Remain upright for at least 30 minutes after taking to prevent gastroesophageal reflux disease (GERD). Take this drug with water.
Allopurinol	Zyloprim	Antigout	This client should drink at least eight glasses of water per day.
Alprazolam	Xanax	Antianxiety	This drug can be addictive.
Amiodipine	Norvasc	Antihypertensive	This drug can lead to hypotension.
Amitriptyline HCl	Elavil	Antidepressant	
Amoxicillin	Augmentin	Antibiotic	Watch for allergic reactions.
Atenolol	Tenormin	Antihypertensive	This drug can cause a drop in pulse rate, so check your pulse daily.

(continues)

918

Appendix D: Most-Prescribed Medications in the United States

TABLE D.1 *Continued*

Generic Name	Trade Name	Uses	Major Concerns
Azithromycin	Zithromax Z-Pak	Antibiotic	Watch for allergies.
Cephalexin	Keflex	Antibiotic	If you are allergic to cephalosporins, you might also be allergic to penicillin.
Cetirizine	Zyrtec	Antihistimine	
Clonazepam	Klonopin	Anticonvulsant	This drug should not be stopped abruptly.
Cyclobenzaprine HCl	Flexeril	Muscle relaxant	This drug can cause sedation.
Diazepam	Valium	Anticonvulsant/ antianxiety	Watch for allergies.
Doxazosin mesylate	Cardura	Antihypertensive	
Doxycycline hyclate	Vibramycin	Antibiotic	Women should not take this drug if pregnant.
Estrogen	Premarin	Hormone	This drug can increase the chances of blood clots.
Fexofenadine	Allegra	Antihistimine	This drug can lead to dry mouth.
Furosemide	Lasix	Diuretic	This drug can lead to hypokalemia.
Glipizide	Glucotrol	Antidiabetic	Watch for hypoglycemia.
Hydrochloro-thiazide	HCTZ	Diuretic	This drug can lead to hypokalemia.
Hydrocodone with acetaminophen	Lortab	Analgesic	This drug can be addictive.
Ibuprofen	Motrin	Analgesic/ anti-inflammatory	This drug can lead to hypertension and kidney disease.
Lansoprazole	Prevacid	Proton pump inhibitor/antiulcer	Take the medication prior to meals.
Levothyroxin	Synthroid	Hormone	Teach the client to check his pulse.
Levothyroxine	Levoxyl	Hormone	This drug can increase the chances of blood clotting.
Lisinopril	Zestril	Antihypertensive	This drug can lead to postural hypotension. Remain supine for at least 30 minutes when beginning the medication.
Lorazepam	Antivan	Anticonvulsant/ antianxiety	This drug can cause sedation.
Metformin	Glucophage	Antidiabetic	This drug should be stopped prior to a dye study such as a cardiac catheterization.
Metoprolol succinate	Toprol XL	Antihypertensive	The nurse needs to teach the client to check his pulse.
Metoprolol tartrate	Lopressor, Toprol	Antihypertensive	The client should be taught to check his pulse rate.
Montelukast	Singulair	Asthmatic medication	

TABLE D.1 *Continued*

Generic Name	Trade Name	Uses	Major Concerns
Naproxen	Aleve	Analgesic	This drug can lead to hypertension and kidney disease.
Necon	Ortho-Novum 7/7/7	Oral contraceptive	This drug can increase the chances of blood clots.
Omeprazole	Prilosec	Proton pump inhibitor/antiulcer	
Penicillin V potassium	Penicillin	Antibiotic	Watch for allergies.
Potassium chloride	K-Lyte	Supplement	The nurse should check renal function prior to giving the medication.
Prednisone	Deltasone	Anti- inflammatory	This drug can cause Cushing's syndrome. This drug can cause gastrointestinal problems.
Promethazine HCl	Phenergan	Antiemetic/antianxiety	
Rantidine HCl	Zantac	Histamine blocker/ antiulcer	Usually it is best to take this drug with meals.
Sertraline	Zoloft	Antidepressant	This drug can cause sedation.
Simvastatin	Zocor	Antilipidemic	This drug can cause liver problems and muscle soreness. Taking the drug at night will increase the drug's effectiveness. Do not take this drug with grapefruit juice.
Sulfamethoxazole	Septra, Bactrim	Antibiotic	This drug can cause gastrointestinal disturbance.
Trazodone HCl	Desyrel	Antidepressant	
Trinessa	Ortho TriClen	Oral contraceptive	This drug can increase chances of blood clotting.
Verapamil HCl	Calan	Antihypertensive/ antianginal	
Warfarin sodium	Coumadin	Anticoagulant	The nurse should teach the client to limit the intake of green leafy vegetables and watch for signs of bleeding.
Zolpidem	Ambien	Sleep aid	Allow at least eight hours of sleep time to prevent daytime drowsiness.

Alphabetical Listing of Nursing Boards in the United States and Protectorates

This appendix contains contact information for nursing boards throughout the United States. The information found here is current as of this writing, but be aware that names, phone numbers, and websites do change. If the information here is not completely current, most likely some of the information will be useful enough for you to still make contact with the organization. If all the information is incorrect, a helpful hint is to use an Internet search engine, such as Yahoo! or Google, and enter the name of the nursing board you are trying to contact. In addition, the following website keeps an up-to-date register of the various boards of nursing in the United States and its territories: https://www.ncsbn.org/515.htm. Most likely, you'll find some contact information there. Also, if you don't have access to the Internet, you can contact your state government because they should be able to help you find the information you need.

Alabama Board of Nursing
770 Washington Avenue
RSA Plaza, Suite 250
Montgomery, AL 36104

Phone: 334-242-4060
Fax: 334-242-4360

Contact person: N. Genell Lee, MSN, JD, RN, Executive Officer
Website: http://www.abn.state.al.us/

Alaska Board of Nursing
550 West Seventh Avenue, Suite 1500
Anchorage, AK 99501-3567

Phone: 907-269-8161
Fax: 907-269-8196

Contact person: Nancy Sanders, PhD, RN, Executive Administrator
Website: http://www.dced.state.ak.us/occ/pnur.htm

American Samoa Health Services
Regulatory Board
LBJ Tropical Medical Center
Pago Pago, AS 96799

Phone: 684-633-1222
Fax: 684-633-1869

Contact person: Toaga Atuatasi Seumalo, MS, RN, Executive Secretary

Arizona State Board of Nursing
4747 North 7th Street, Suite 200
Phoenix, AZ 85014-3655

Phone: 602-771-7800
Fax: 602-771-7888

Contact person: Joey Ridenour, MN, RN, FANN, Executive Director
Website: http://www.azbn.gov/

Arkansas State Board of Nursing
University Tower Building
1123 S. University, Suite 800
Little Rock, AR 72204-1619

Phone: 501-686-2700
Fax: 501-686-2714

Contact person: Faith Fields, MSN, RN, Executive Director
Website: http://www.arsbn.org/

California Board of Registered Nursing
1625 North Market Boulevard, Suite N-217
Sacramento, CA 95834-1924

Phone: 916-322-3350
Fax: 916-574-8637

Contact person: Louise Bailey, MEd, RN, Interim Executive Officer
Website: http://www.rn.ca.gov/

California Board of Vocational Nurses and Psychiatric Technicians
2535 Capitol Oaks Drive, Suite 205
Sacramento, CA 95833

Phone: 916-263-7800
Fax: 916-263-7859

Contact person: Teresa Bello-Jones, JD, MSN, RN, Executive Officer
Website: http://www.bvnpt.ca.gov/

Colorado Board of Nursing
1560 Broadway, Suite 880
Denver, CO 80202

Phone: 303-894-2430
Fax: 303-894-2821

Contact person: Mark Merrill, Program Director
Website: http://www.dora.state.co.us/nursing/

Connecticut Board of Examiners for Nursing
Dept. of Public Health
410 Capitol Avenue, MS# 13PHO
P.O. Box 340308
Hartford, CT 06134-0328

Phone: 860-509-7624
Fax: 860-509-7553

Contact person: Jennifer L. Filippone, Chief, Practitioner Licensing and
Investigations Section
Website: http://www.state.ct.us/dph/

Delaware Board of Nursing
861 Silver Lake Boulevard
Cannon Building, Suite 203
Dover, DE 19904

Phone: 302-744-4500
Fax: 302-739-2711

Contact person: David Mangler, MS, RN, Executive Director
Website: http://dpr.delaware.gov/boards/nursing/

District of Columbia Board of Nursing
Department of Health
Health Professional Licensing Administration
District of Columbia Board of Nursing
717 14th Street, NW
Suite 600
Washington, DC 20005

Phone: 877-672-2174
Fax: 202-727-8471

Contact person: Karen Scipio-Skinner, MSN, RNC, Executive Director
Website: http://hpla.doh.dc.gov/hpla/cwp/
view,A,1195,Q,488526,hplaNav,|30661|,.asp

Florida Board of Nursing
Mailing Address:
4052 Bald Cypress Way, BIN C02
Tallahassee, FL 32399-3252

Street Address:
4042 Bald Cypress Way, Room 120
Tallahassee, FL 32399

Phone: 850-245-4125
Fax: 850-245-4172

Contact person: Joe Baker, Jr., Executive Director
Website: http://www.doh.state.fl.us/mqa/

Georgia Board of Nursing
237 Coliseum Drive
Macon, GA 31217-3858

Phone: 478-207-2440
Fax: 478-207-1354

Contact person: Sylvia Bond, RN, MSN, MBA, Executive Director
Website: http://www.sos.state.ga.us/plb/rn

Georgia State Board of Licensed Practical Nurses
237 Coliseum Drive
Macon, GA 31217-3858

Phone: 478-207-2440
Fax: 478-207-1354

Contact person: Sylvia Bond, RN, MSN, MBA, Executive Director
Website: http://www.sos.state.ga.us/plb/lpn

Guam Board of Nurse Examiners
#123 Chalan Kareta
Mangilao, Guam 96913-6304

Phone: 671-735-7407
Fax: 671-735-7413

Contact person: Margarita Bautista-Gay, RN, BSN, MN, Interim Executive Director
Website: http://www.dphss.guam.gov/

Hawaii Board of Nursing
King Kalakaua Building
335 Merchant Street, 3rd Floor
Honolulu, HI 96813

Phone: 808-586-3000
Fax: 808-586-2689

Contact person: Lee Ann Teshima, Executive Officer
Website: www.hawaii.gov/dcca/areas/pvl/boards/nursing

Idaho Board of Nursing
280 N. 8th Street, Suite 210
P.O. Box 83720
Boise, ID 83720

Phone: 208-334-3110
Fax: 208-334-3262

Contact person: Sandra Evans, MA.Ed, RN, Executive Director
Website: http://ibn.idaho.gov/

Illinois Board of Nursing
James R. Thompson Center
100 West Randolph, Suite 9-300
Chicago, IL 60601

Phone: 312-814-2715
Fax: 312-814-3145

Contact person: Michele Bromberg, MSN, APN, BC, Nursing Act Coordinator
Website: http://www.idfpr.com/dpr/WHO/nurs.asp

Indiana State Board of Nursing
Professional Licensing Agency
402 W. Washington Street, Room W072
Indianapolis, IN 46204

Phone: 317-234-2043
Fax: 317-233-4236

Contact person: Sean Gorman, Board Director
Website: http://www.in.gov/pla/

Iowa Board of Nursing
RiverPoint Business Park
400 S.W. 8th Street, Suite B
Des Moines, IA 50309-4685

Phone: 515-281-3255
Fax: 515-281-4825

Contact person: Lorinda Inman, MSN, RN, Executive Director
Website: http://nursing.iowa.gov/

Kansas State Board of Nursing
Landon State Office Building
900 S.W. Jackson, Suite 1051
Topeka, KS 66612

Phone: 785-296-4929
Fax: 785-296-3929

Contact person: Mary Blubaugh, MSN, RN, Executive Administrator
Website: http://www.ksbn.org/

Kentucky Board of Nursing
312 Whittington Parkway, Suite 300
Louisville, KY 40222

Phone: 502-429-3300
Fax: 502-429-3311

Contact person: Charlotte F. Beason, Ed.D, RN, NEA, Executive Director
Website: http://www.kbn.ky.gov/

Louisiana State Board of Nursing
17373 Perkins Road
Baton Rouge, LA 70810

Phone: 225-755-7500
Fax: 225-755-7585

Contact person: Barbara Morvant, MN, RN, Executive Director
Website: http://www.lsbn.state.la.us/

Louisiana State Board of Practical Nurse Examiners
3421 N. Causeway Boulevard, Suite 505
Metairie, LA 70002

Phone: 504-838-5791
Fax: 504-838-5279

Contact person: Claire Glaviano, BSN, MN, RN, Executive Director
Website: http://www.lsbpne.com/

Maine State Board of Nursing
158 State House Station
Augusta, ME 04333

Street Address (for FedEx & UPS):
161 Capitol Street
Augusta, ME 04333

Phone: 207-287-1133
Fax: 207-287-1149

Contact person: Myra Broadway, JD, MS, RN, Executive Director
Website: http://www.maine.gov/boardofnursing/

Maryland Board of Nursing
4140 Patterson Avenue
Baltimore, MD 21215

Phone: 410-585-1900
Fax: 410-358-3530

Contact person: Patricia Ann Noble, MSN, RN Executive Director
Website: http://www.mbon.org/

Massachusetts Board of Registration in Nursing
Commonwealth of Massachusetts
239 Causeway Street, Second Floor
Boston, MA 02114

Phone: 617-973-0900
Fax: 617-973-0984

Contact person: Rula Faris Harb, MS, RN, Acting Executive Director
Website: http://www.mass.gov/dpl/boards/rn/

Michigan/DCH/Bureau of Health Professions
Ottawa Towers North
611 W. Ottawa, 1st Floor
Lansing, MI 48933

Phone: 517-335-0918
Fax: 517-373-2179

Contact person: Amy Shell, Executive Officer
Website: http://www.michigan.gov/healthlicense

Minnesota Board of Nursing
2829 University Avenue SE , Suite 200
Minneapolis, MN 55414

Phone: 612-617-2270
Fax: 612-617-2190

Contact person: Shirley Brekken, MS, RN, Executive Director
Website: http://www.nursingboard.state.mn.us/

Mississippi Board of Nursing
1080 River Oaks Drive
Flowood, MS 39232

Phone: 601-664-9303
Fax: 601-664-9304

Contact person: Melinda E. Rush, DSN, FNP, Executive Director
Website: http://www.msbn.state.ms.us/

Missouri State Board of Nursing
3605 Missouri Boulevard
P.O. Box 656
Jefferson City, MO 65102-0656

Phone: 573-751-0681
Fax: 573-751-0075

Contact person: Lori Scheidt, BS, Executive Director
Website: http://pr.mo.gov/nursing.asp

Montana State Board of Nursing
301 South Park
P.O. Box 200513
Helena, MT 59620-0513

Phone: 406-841-2345
Fax: 406-841-2305

Contact person: Vacant, Executive Director
Website: http://www.nurse.mt.gov

Nebraska Board of Nursing
301 Centennial Mall South
Lincoln, NE 68509-4986

Phone: 402-471-4376
Fax: 402-471-1066

Contact person: Diana Baker, MSN, RN, Executive Director
Website: http://www.hhs.state.ne.us/crl/nursing/nursingindex.htm

Nevada State Board of Nursing
5011 Meadowood Mall, Suite 300
Reno, NV 89502

Phone: 775-687-7700
Fax: 775-687-7707

Contact person: Debra Scott, MS, RN, FRE, Executive Director
Website: http://www.nursingboard.state.nv.us/

New Hampshire Board of Nursing
21 South Fruit Street, Suite 16
Concord, NH 03301-2341

Phone: 603-271-2323
Fax: 603-271-6605

Contact person: Margaret Walker, MBA, BSN, RN, Executive Director
Website: http://www.state.nh.us/nursing/

New Jersey Board of Nursing
P.O. Box 45010
124 Halsey Street, 6th Floor
Newark, NJ 07101

Phone: 973-504-6430
Fax: 973-648-3481

Contact person: George Hebert, Executive Director
Website: http://www.state.nj.us/lps/ca/medical/nursing.htm

New Mexico Board of Nursing
6301 Indian School Road, NE, Suite 710
Albuquerque, NM 87110

Phone: 505-841-8340
Fax: 505-841-8347

Contact person: Deborah Walker, MSN, RN, Executive Director
Website: http://www.bon.state.nm.us/

New York State Board of Nursing
Education Bldg.
89 Washington Avenue
2nd Floor West Wing
Albany, NY 12234

Phone: 518-474-3817, extension 120
Fax: 518-474-3706

Contact person: Barbara Zittel, PhD, RN, Executive Secretary
Website: http://www.nysed.gov/prof/nurse.htm

North Carolina Board of Nursing
4516 Lake Boone Trail
Raleigh, NC 27607

Phone: 919-782-3211
Fax: 919-781-9461

Contact person: Julia L. George, RN, MSN, FRE, Executive Director
Website: http://www.ncbon.com/

North Dakota Board of Nursing
919 South 7th Street, Suite 504
Bismarck, ND 58504

Phone: 701-328-9777
Fax: 701-328-9785

Contact person: Constance Kalanek, PhD, RN, Executive Director
Website: http://www.ndbon.org/

Northern Mariana Islands
Commonwealth Board of Nurse Examiners
P.O. Box 501458
Saipan, MP 96950

Phone: 670-234-8950, ext. 3587
Fax: 670-664-4813

Contact person: Sinforosa D. Guerrero, Executive Officer Designee

Ohio Board of Nursing
17 South High Street, Suite 400
Columbus, OH 43215-3413

Phone: 614-466-3947
Fax: 614-466-0388

Contact person: Betsy J. Houchen, RN, MS, JD, Executive Director
Website: http://www.nursing.ohio.gov/

Oklahoma Board of Nursing
2915 N. Classen Boulevard, Suite 524
Oklahoma City, OK 73106

Phone: 405-962-1800
Fax: 405-962-1821

Contact person: Kimberly Glazier, M.Ed., RN, Executive Director
Website: http://www.ok.gov/nursing/

Oregon State Board of Nursing
17938 SW Upper Boones Ferry Road
Portland, OR 97224

Phone: 971-673-0865
Fax: 971-673-0684

Contact person: Holly Mercer, JD, RN, Executive Director
Website: http://www.osbn.state.or.us/

Pennsylvania State Board of Nursing
P.O. Box 2649
Harrisburg, PA 17105-2649

Phone: 717-783-7142
Fax: 717-783-0822

Contact person: Laurette D. Keiser, RN, MSN, Executive Secretary/Section Chief
Website: http://www.dos.state.pa.us/bpoa

Commonwealth of Puerto Rico Board of Nurse Examiners
800 Roberto H. Todd Avenue
Room 202, Stop 18
Santurce, PR 00908

Phone: 787-725-7506
Fax: 787-725-7903

Contact person: Roberto Figueroa, RN, MSN, Executive Director of the Office of
Regulations and Certifications of Health Care Professions

Rhode Island Board of Nurse Registration and Nursing Education
105 Cannon Building
Three Capitol Hill
Providence, RI 02908

Phone: 401-222-5700
Fax: 401-222-3352

Contact person: Pamela McCue, MS, RN, Executive Officer
Website: http://www.health.ri.gov/

South Carolina State Board of Nursing
Mailing Address:
P.O. Box 12367
Columbia, SC 29211

Street Address:
Synergy Business Park, Kingstree Building
110 Centerview Drive, Suite 202
Columbia, SC 29210

Phone: 803-896-4550
Fax: 803-896-4525

Contact person: Joan K. Bainer, MN, RN, NE, BC, Administrator
Website: http://www.llr.state.sc.us/pol/nursing

South Dakota Board of Nursing
4305 South Louise Avenue, Suite 201
Sioux Falls, SD 57106-3115

Phone: 605-362-2760
Fax: 605-362-2768

Contact person: Gloria Damgaard, RN, MS, Executive Secretary
Website: http://www.state.sd.us/doh/nursing/

Tennessee State Board of Nursing
227 French Landing, Suite 300
Heritage Place MetroCenter
Nashville, TN 37243

Phone: 615-532-5166
Fax: 615-741-7899

Contact person: Elizabeth Lund, MSN, RN, Executive Director
Website: http://health.state.tn.us/Boards/Nursing/index.htm

Texas Board of Nurse Examiners
333 Guadalupe, Suite 3-460
Austin, TX 78701

Phone: 512-305-7400
Fax: 512-305-7401

Contact person: Katherine Thomas, MN, RN, Executive Director
Website: http://www.bon.state.tx.us/

Utah State Board of Nursing
Heber M. Wells Bldg., 4th Floor
160 East 300 South
Salt Lake City, UT 84111

Phone: 801-530-6628
Fax: 801-530-6511

Contact person: Laura Poe, MS, RN, Executive Administrator
Website: http://www.dopl.utah.gov/licensing/nursing.html

Vermont State Board of Nursing
Office of Professional Regulation
National Life Building North F1.2
Montpelier, VT 05620-3402

Phone: 802-828-2396
Fax: 802-828-2484

Contact person: Mary L. Botter, PhD, RN, Executive Director
Website: http://www.vtprofessionals.org/opr1/nurses/

Virgin Islands Board of Nurse Licensure
Veterans Drive Station
St. Thomas, VI 00803

Phone: 340-776-7397
Fax: 340-777-4003

Contact person: Winifred Garfield, CRNA, RN, Executive Secretary

Virginia Board of Nursing
Mailing Address:
6603 West Broad Street
5th Floor
Richmond, VA 23230-1712

Phone: 804-662-9909

Fax: 804-662-9512

Contact person: jay Douglas, RN, MSN, CSAC, Executive Director
Website: http://www.dhp.state.va.us/

Virgin Islands Board of Nursing

Mailing Address:

P.O. Box 304247, Veterans Drive Station
St. Thomas, Virgin Islands 00803

Physical Address (For FedEx and UPS):
Virgin Island Board of Nurse Licensure
#3 Kongens Gade (Government Hill)
St. Thomas, Virgin Islands 00802 Phone: 340-776-7131
Fax: 340-777-4003

Contact person: Diane Ruan-Viville, MA, BSN, RN, Executive Director
Website: http://www.vibnl.org/

Washington State Nursing Care Quality Assurance Commission
Department of Health
HPQA #6
310 Israel Road SE
Tumwater, WA 98501-7864

Phone: 360-236-4700
Fax: 360-236-4738

Contact person: Paula Meyer, MSN, RN, Executive Director
Website: http://www.doh.wa.gov/hsqa/professions/nursing/default.htm

West Virginia Board of Examiners for Registered Professional Nurses
101 Dee Drive
Charleston, WV 25311

Phone: 304-558-3596
Fax: 304-558-3666

Contact person: Laura Rhodes, MSN, RN, Executive Director
Website: http://www.wvrnboard.com/

West Virginia State Board of Examiners for Licensed Practical Nurses
101 Dee Drive
Charleston, WV 25311

Phone: 304-558-3572
Fax: 304-558-4367

Contact person: Lanette Anderson, RN, BSN, JD, Executive Director
Website: http://www.lpnboard.state.wv.us/

Wisconsin Department of Regulation and Licensing
Mailing Address:
P.O. Box 8935
Madison, WI 53708-8935

Street Address:
1400 E. Washington Avenue
Madison, WI 53703

Phone: 608-266-2112
Fax: 608-261-7083

Contact person: Jeff Scanlan, Bureau Director, Health Services Boards
Website: http://drl..wi.gov/

Wyoming State Board of Nursing
1810 Pioneer Avenue
Cheyenne, WY 82001

Phone: 307-777-7601
Fax: 307-777-3519

Contact person: Mary Kay Goetter, Executive Officer
Website: http://nursing.state.wy.us/

Index

activated charcoal, 547

active transport, 41-42

Activity, Pulse, Grimace, Appearance, Respiration (APGAR) score, 505-506

acute disorders
    acute glomerulonephritis (AGN), 172-173
    acute otitis media (AOM), 531
    acute radiation syndrome (ARS), 635
    acute renal failure (ARF), 179-180
    acute respiratory distress syndrome (ARDS), 148-154
    epiglottitis, 532
    glaucoma, 234
    graft rejection, 185
    laryngotracheobronchitis (LTB), 532-533
    mania (bipolar disorder), 600
    pancreatitis, 285-287
    PTSD (post traumatic stress disorder), 590
    pyelonephritis, 178
    spasmodic laryngitis, 533
    subdural hematomas, 332

acyclovir (Zovirax), 206

adalimumab (Humira), 264

Adams position, 576

addiction (substance abuse), 602
    alcoholism, 602-604
    chemical dependence, 604-606

Addiction Research Foundation Chemical Institute Withdrawal Assessment-Alcohol (CIWA-Ar), 603

Addison's Disease (adrenocortical insufficiency), 119-120

ADDM (adult-onset diabetes mellitus), 114

adenocarcinomas, 409

adenohypophysis, 106

adenoidectomy, 529

ADH (antidiuretic hormone), 106-108, 365

ADHD (attention deficit hyperactive disorder), 608

administration
    iron, 310-311
    medications, 18, 649

adolescence
    emotional/behavioral disorders, 606
        ADHD (attention deficit hyperactive disorder), 608
        autism, 607
        conduct disorder, 607
        eating disorders, 608-609
        oppositional defiant disorder, 608
    growth and development, 527-528
    immunization schedule, 903
    signs of depression, 602

adrenal gland, 118-119
    Addison's Disease, 119-120
    Conn's Syndrome, 119
    Cushing's Disease, 120-121

adrenal medulla, 118

adrenocortical hypersecretion (Cushing's Disease), 120-121

adrenocortical insufficiency (Addison's Disease), 119-120

adrenocorticotropic hormone (ACTH), 106, 118

adult-onset diabetes mellitus (ADDM), 114

adverse effects
    angiotensin-converting enzyme inhibitors, 20
    angiotension receptor blockers, 30
    anti-infectives, 22
    anticoagulants, 32
    antivirals, 27
    benzodiazepines, 23
    beta adrenergic blockers, 21
    cholesterol-lowering agents, 29
    glucocorticoids, 26
    histamine 2 antagonists, 31
    phenothiazines, 25
    proton pump inhibitors, 32

advocacy, 650

AFP (Alpha-fetoprotein) testing, 486

afterload, 86

age related macular degeneration, 237

AGN (acute glomerulonephritis), 172-173

agoraphobia, 591-592

AHA (American Heart Association), life support guidelines, 902

AIDS (acquired immune deficiency syndrome), 380, 385-387, 510

airborne precautions, 901
    HIV prevention, 384
    TB (tuberculosis), 147

airway assessment, emergency care, 624-625

akathisia, 599

akinesia, 599

akinetic seizures, 349

Alaskan natives, 661-662

albumin levels, 116

alcohol, as teratogenic agent, 485

alcoholism, 602-604

Aldactone (Spironolactone), 119, 121

aldosterone, 118

aldosteronism, 119-120

alkalosis, 43
    metabolic, 41, 56-57
    respiratory, 57-58

alkylating agents, 423, 434

all trans-retinoic acid (ATRA), 439

allergenic asthma, 135

allergic reactions, 24, 379

Allis' sign, 574

allogenic transplant, 428

allografts, 220

Allopurinol (Zyloprim), 462

alpha adrenergic receptor blockers, 71

alpha interferon injections, 277

alpha-adrenergic receptor agonists, 71

Alpha-fetoprotein (AFP) testing, 486

alpha-glucosidase inhibitors, 116

alpha-receptor blockers, 98

B

F

G

H

interventions (management)